# Psychological Asse
# and Theory

## CREATING AND USING PSYCHOLOGICAL TESTS

# Psychological Assessment and Theory

## CREATING AND USING PSYCHOLOGICAL TESTS

Eighth Edition

ROBERT M. KAPLAN
*University of California, Los Angeles*

DENNIS P. SACCUZZO
*San Diego State University*

WADSWORTH
CENGAGE Learning·

Australia • Brazil • Japan • Korea • Mexico • Singapore • Spain • United Kingdom • United States

*Psychological Assessment and Theory: Creating and Using Psychological Tests,* **Eighth Edition, International Edition**
Robert M. Kaplan and Dennis P. Saccuzzo

Publisher: Jon-David Hague

Executive Editor: Jaime Perkins

Assistant Editor: Jessica Alderman

Senior Media Editor: Mary Noel

Marketing Program Manager: Janay Pryor

Marketing Communications Manager: Talia Wise

Art and Cover Direction, Production Management, and Composition: PreMediaGlobal

Manufacturing Planner: Karen Hunt

Rights Acquisitions Specialist: Roberta Broyer

Cover Image: Alexander Putyata/2012 Photos.com

International Edition:

ISBN-13: 978-1-133-49255-9

ISBN-10: 1-133-49255-X

**Cengage Learning International Offices**

**Asia**
www.cengageasia.com
tel: (65) 6410 1200

**Australia/New Zealand**
www.cengage.com.au
tel: (61) 3 9685 4111

**Brazil**
www.cengage.com.br
tel: (55) 11 3665 9900

**India**
www.cengage.co.in
tel: (91) 11 4364 1111

**Latin America**
www.cengage.com.mx
tel: (52) 55 1500 6000

**UK/Europe/Middle East/Africa**
www.cengage.co.uk
tel: (44) 0 1264 332 424

**Represented in Canada by Nelson Education, Ltd.**
www.nelson.com
tel: (416) 752 9100 / (800) 668 0671

Cengage Learning is a leading provider of customized learning solutions with office locations around the globe, including Singapore, the United Kingdom, Australia, Mexico, Brazil, and Japan. Locate your local office at: **www.cengage.com/global**.

For product information and free companion resources: **www.cengage.com/international**
Visit your local office: **www.cengage.com/global**
Visit our corporate website: **www.cengage.com**

Printed in Canada
1 2 3 4 5 6 7 16 15 14 13 12

# Brief Contents

# Contents

## 7  Writing and Evaluating Test Items   193

## 8  Interviewing Techniques   221

# List of Sample Test Profiles

# Preface

Psychology is a broad, exciting field. Psychologists work in settings ranging from schools and clinics to basic research laboratories, pharmaceutical firms, and private international companies. Despite this diversity, all psychologists have at least two things in common: They all study behavior, and they all depend to some extent on its measurement. This book concerns a particular type of measurement, psychological tests, which measure characteristics pertaining to all aspects of behavior in human beings.

*Psychological Assessment and Theory: Creating and Using Psychological Tests* is the result of a long-standing partnership between the authors. As active participants in the development and use of psychological tests, we became disheartened because far too many undergraduate college students view psychological testing courses as boring and unrelated to their goals or career interests. In contrast, we view psychological testing as an exciting field. It has a solid place in the history of psychology, yet it is constantly in flux because of challenges, new developments, and controversies. A book on testing should encourage, not dampen, a student's interest. Thus, we provide an overview of the many facets of psychological tests and measurement principles in a style that will appeal to the contemporary college student.

To understand the applications and issues in psychological testing, the student must learn some basic principles, which requires some knowledge of introductory statistics. Therefore, some reviewing and a careful reading of the first few chapters will pave the way for an understanding of the applications of tests discussed later on. Lastly, we examine the issues now shaping the future of testing. Such issues include test anxiety and test bias. The future of applied psychology may depend on the ability of psychologists to face these challenging issues.

Throughout the book, we present a series of focused discussions and focused examples. These sections illustrate the material in the book through examples or provide a more detailed discussion of a particular issue. We also use box features called "Psychological Testing in Everyday Life" to demonstrate material such as statistical calculations.

# Increased Emphasis on Application

Students today often favor informal discussions and personally relevant examples. Consequently, we decided to use models from various fields and to write in an informal style. However, because testing is a serious and complicated field in which major disagreements exist even among scholars and experts, we have treated the controversial aspects of testing with more formal discussion and detailed referencing.

The first edition of *Psychological Assessment and Theory* was published in 1982. In over 30 years since the text was first introduced, the world has changed in many ways. For example, personal computers were new in 1982. Most students and professors had never heard of Internet, nobody communicated by e-mail, and the inventor of Facebook had not been born. The first edition of *Psychological Assessment and Theory* was produced on typewriters before word processors were commonly used. At the time, few professors or students had access to private computers. The early editions of the book offered instruction for preparing the submission of statistical analyses to mainframe computers. There were far fewer applications of psychological testing than there are today. On the other hand, principles of psychological testing have remained relatively constant. Thus, newer editions have included improvements and refinements in the Principles chapters. The later chapters on Applications and Issues have evolved considerably.

Not only has the field of psychological testing changed, but so have the authors. One of us (RMK) spent most of his career as a professor in a school of medicine, eventually moved to a school of public health, and is now working for the federal government. The other (DPS) completed law school and works extensively with attorneys and the legal system on many of the applied issues discussed in this book. While maintaining our central identities as psychologists, we have also had the opportunity to explore cutting-edge practice in medicine, public health, education, and law. The eighth edition goes further than any previous edition in spelling out the applications of psychological testing in a wide variety of applied fields.

In developing the eighth edition, we have organized topics around the application areas. Chapter 12 considers psychological testing in education and special education. Chapter 13 looks at the use of standardized tests in education, civil service, and the military. Chapter 16 considers the use of psychological tests in clinical and counseling settings.

The age of computers has completely revolutionized psychological testing. We deal with some of these issues by discussing computer-adaptive testing and item response theory. In Chapter 9, we discuss applications of psychological science in the computer age. Chapter 15 discusses the use of psychological testing in the field of counseling psychology and focuses primarily on interest inventories. Chapter 17 explores the rapidly developing fields of psychological assessment in health psychology, medicine, and health care. Chapter 18 reviews psychological testing in industry and business settings. Several of these chapters discuss the role of new electronic technologies, such as cell phones and sensors, in the acquisition of information about human behavior.

Following a trend in our recent editions, the final chapters on issues in psychological testing have been extensively updated to reflect new developments in ethics and the future of the field.

# Organization of the Eighth Edition: A Note to Professors for Planning

Producing eight editions of *Psychological Assessment and Theory* over more than 30 years has been challenging and rewarding. We are honored that hundreds of professors have adopted our text and that it is now used in hundreds of colleges and universities all over the world. However, some professors have suggested that we reorganize the book to facilitate their approach to the class. To accommodate the large variety of approaches, we have tried to keep the chapters independent enough for professors to teach them in whatever order they choose.

# Supplements Beyond Compare

Professors have access to an instructor's manual and a bank of electronic test items.

## Instructor's Resource Manual/Test Bank

The Instructor's Resource Manual (IRM) was written by Katherine Nicolai of Rockhurst University. It contains a bevy of resources, including guides on designing your course, the use of psychological tests in the classroom, the use of student test data to teach measurement, suggested use of class time, and demonstrations, activities, and activity-based lectures. The IRM provides integrative assignments and gives the instructors unique mock projectives and much more. The test bank contains more than 750 multiple-choice questions in addition to many "thought" essay questions.

# Acknowledgments

We are highly indebted to the many reviewers and professors who provided feedback that helped shape this textbook. Special thanks go to reviewers of this edition, including: Glen M. Adams, *Harding University*; John Dale Alden III, *Lipscomb University*; Steven Anolik, *St. Francis College*; Michael DeDonno, *Barry University*; John C. Hotz, *St. Cloud State University*; Jacqueline Massa, *Kean University*; Katherine Noll, *University of Illinois at Chicago*; Janet Panter, *Rhodes College*; Joneis Frandele Thomas, *Howard University*.

We would also like to thank reviewers of past editions, including Virginia Allen, *Idaho State University*; David Bush, *Utah State University*; Ira Bernstein, *University of Texas, Arlington*; Jeff Conte, *San Diego State University*; Imogen Hall, *University of Windsor*; Maureen Hannah, *Siena College*; Ronald McLaughlin, *Juniata College*; Michael Mills, *Loyola Marymount University*; Philip Moberg, *University of Akron*; M. J. Monnot, *Central Michigan University*; Jennifer Neemann, *University of Baltimore*; Karen Obremski Brandon, *University of South Florida*;

Frederick Oswald, *Michigan State University*; S. Mark Pancer, *Wilfrid Laurier University*; Christopher Ralston, *Iowa State University*; Sharon Rostosky, *University of Kentucky*; Stefan Schulenberg, *University of Mississippi*; Theresa Sparks, *Clayton State University*; Chockalingam Viswesvaran, *Florida International University*; Mark Wagner, *Wagner College*; and Nancy Zook, *SUNY Purchase*.

The eight editions of this book have been developed under six different editors at Wadsworth. The earlier editions benefited from the patient and inspired supervision of Todd Lueders, C. Deborah Laughton, Phil Curson, Marianne Taflinger, and Jim Brace-Thompson. We are most appreciative of the support we have received from editor Jaime Perkins, who oversaw the seventh and eighth editions. He has been patient, helpful, and very well organized in directing the development of the current edition. Each of our editors has come to the task with a different personality and a different set of insights. We learned immensely from each of them, and the eighth edition represents a collection of what we have gained from advice and consultations over many years. We want to give particular thanks to Kate Nicolai for authoring the much expanded Instructor's Resource Manual.

Special thanks go Wendy Koen. Wendy conducted much of the research for the updating of about half the chapters and attended to numerous details. Without Wendy, publication of this edition would have been much delayed.

*Robert M. Kaplan*
*Dennis P. Saccuzzo*
*January 2012*

ROBERT M. KAPLAN is Associate Director for Behavioral and Social Sciences at the National Institutes of Health[1]. He also serves as Director of the Office of Behavioral and Social Sciences Research (OBSSR). Revisions for the Eighth Edition were completed when Kaplan was Distinguished Professor of Health Services at UCLA and Distinguished Professor of Medicine at the UCLA David Geffen School of Medicine, where he led the UCLA/RAND health services training program and the UCLA/RAND CDC Prevention Research Center. Kaplan was Chair of the Department of Health Services from 2004 to 2009. From 1997 to 2004 he was Professor and Chair of the Department of Family and Preventive Medicine at the University of California, San Diego. He is a past President of several organizations, including the American Psychological Association Division of Health Psychology, Section J of the American Association for the Advancement of Science (Pacific), the International Society for Quality of Life Research, the Society for Behavioral Medicine, and the Academy of Behavioral Medicine Research. He is a Past Chair of the Behavioral Science Council of the American Thoracic Society. Dr. Kaplan is a former Editor-in-Chief of *Health Psychology* and of the *Annals of Behavioral Medicine*. He is the author, co-author or editor of more than 18 books and approximately 470 articles or chapters. The ISI includes him in the listing of the most cited authors in the world (defined as above the 99.5th percentile). In 2005 he was elected to the Institute of Medicine of the National Academies of Sciences.

---

[1] *Psychological Testing: Principles, Applications, and Issues* was completed before Dr. Kaplan became a federal employee. Conclusions and interpretations in the book do not represent the positions of the National Institutes of Health, the Department of Health and Human Services, or the U.S. Government.

DENNIS P. SACCUZZO is a professor Emeritus at San Diego State University, an adjunct professor of law at Thomas Jefferson School of Law, and President and co-founder of Applications of Psychology to Law, Inc., an educational corporation devoted to applying cutting edge psychological concepts to the law. He has been a scholar and practitioner of psychological testing for over 36 years and has numerous peer-reviewed publications and professional presentations in the field. Dr. Saccuzzo's research has been supported by the National Science Foundation, the National Institutes of Mental Health, the National Institutes of Health, the U.S. Department of Education, the Scottish Rite Foundation, and the U.S. armed services. He is also a California-licensed psychologist and a California-licensed attorney. He is board certified in clinical psychology by the American Board of Professional Psychology (ABPP). In addition, he is a Diplomate of the American Board of Assessment Psychology (ABAP). He is a fellow of the American Psychological Association, American Psychological Society, and Western Psychological Association for outstanding and unusual contributions to the field of psychology. Dr. Saccuzzo is the author or co-author of over 300 peer-reviewed papers and publications, including nine textbooks and over 20 law manuals.

CHAPTER

**1**

# Introduction

## LEARNING OBJECTIVES

*When you have completed this chapter, you should be able to:*

▶ Define the basic terms pertaining to psychological and educational tests

▶ Distinguish between an individual test and a group test

▶ Define the terms *achievement, aptitude,* and *intelligence* and identify a concept that can encompass all three terms

▶ Distinguish between ability tests and personality tests

▶ Define the term *structured personality test*

▶ Explain how structured personality tests differ from projective personality tests

▶ Explain what a normative or standardization sample is and why such a sample is important

▶ Identify the major developments in the history of psychological testing

▶ Explain the relevance of psychological tests in contemporary society

You are sitting at a table. You have just been fingerprinted and have shown a picture ID. You look around and see 40 nervous people. A stern-looking test proctor with a stopwatch passes out booklets. You are warned not to open the booklet until told to do so; you face possible disciplinary action if you disobey. This is not a nightmare or some futuristic fantasy—this is real.

Finally, after what seems like an eternity, you are told to open your booklet to page 3 and begin working. Your mouth is dry; your palms are soaking wet. You open to page 3. You have 10 minutes to solve a five-part problem based on the following information.[1]

A car drives into the center ring of a circus and exactly eight clowns—Q, R, S, T, V, W, Y, and Z—get out of the car, one clown at a time. The order in which the clowns get out of the car is consistent with the following conditions:

V gets out at some time before both Y and Q.
Q gets out at some time after Z.
T gets out at some time before V but at some time after R.
S gets out at some time after V.
R gets out at some time before W.

*Question 1.* If Q is the fifth clown to get out of the car, then each of the following could be true *except*:

Z is the first clown to get out of the car.
T is the second clown to get out of the car.
V is the third clown to get out of the car.
W is the fourth clown to get out of the car.
Y is the sixth clown to get out of the car.
Not quite sure how to proceed, you look at the next question.

*Question 2.* If R is the second clown to get out of the car, which of the following must be true?

S gets out of the car at some time before T does.
T gets out of the car at some time before W does.
W gets out of the car at some time before V does.
Y gets out of the car at some time before Q does.
Z gets out of the car at some time before W does.

Your heart beats a little faster and your mind starts to freeze up like an overloaded computer with too little working memory. You glance at your watch and notice that 2 minutes have elapsed and you still don't have your bearings. The person sitting next to you looks a bit faint. Another three rows up, someone storms up to the test proctor and complains frantically that he cannot do this type of problem. While the proctor struggles to calm this person down, another makes a mad dash for the restroom.

Welcome to the world of competitive, "high stakes," standardized psychological tests in the 21st century. The questions you just faced were actual problems from a past version of the LSAT—the Law School Admission Test. Whether or not a

---

[1] Used by permission from the Law School Admission Test, October 2002. Answer to Question 1 is D; answer to Question 2 is E.

student is admitted into law school in the United States is almost entirely determined by that person's score on the LSAT and undergraduate college grade point average. Thus, one's future can depend to a tremendous extent on a single score from a single test given in a tension-packed morning or afternoon. Despite efforts to improve tests like the LSAT to increase diversity (Pashley, Thornton, & Duffy, 2005), standardized tests tend to disadvantage women, test takers whose parents have lower incomes and levels of education, and ethnic minorities (Atkinson & Geiser, 2009).

Partly because of diversity concerns, growing numbers of four-year colleges are not relying on the SAT test (Espenshade & Chung, 2010; Jaschik, 2006). In 2011, the website of the National Center for Fair and Open Testing named close to 850 four-year colleges that do not use the SAT test to admit substantial numbers of freshmen (Fair Test, 2011). However, the percentage of colleges indicating that they attach "considerable importance" to admission test scores rose from 46 percent in 1993 to 60 percent in 2006 (National Association for College Admission Counseling, 2008).

Similar problems have appeared on the GRE—the Graduate Record Exam, a test that plays a major role in determining who gets to study at the graduate level in the United States. (Later in this book we discuss how to prepare for such tests and what their significance, or predictive validity, is.) ETS, creator of the GRE General Test, recently revised the test in several significant ways. The revised GRE General Test was introduced on August 1, 2011 (http://www.ets.org/gre/institutions/about/general).

Tests such as the LSAT and GRE are the most difficult modern psychological tests. The scenes we've described are real, and some careers do ride on a single test. Perhaps you have already taken the GRE or LSAT. Or perhaps you have not graduated yet but are thinking about applying for an advanced degree or professional program and will soon be facing the GRE, LSAT, or MCAT (Medical College Admission Test). Clearly, it will help you have a basic understanding of the multitude of psychological tests people are asked to take throughout their lives.

From birth, tests have a major influence on our lives. When the pediatrician strokes the palms of our hands and the soles of our feet, he or she is performing a test. When we enter school, tests decide whether we pass or fail classes. Testing may determine if we need special education. In the United States and many industrialized countries, competence tests determine if students will graduate from high school (Lamb, 2011; Reardon, 2010). More tests determine which college we may attend. And, of course, we face still more tests once we are in college.

After graduation, those who choose to avoid tests such as the GRE may need to take tests to determine where they will work. In the modern world, a large part of everyone's life and success depends on test results. Indeed, tests even have international significance.

For example, 15-year-old children in 32 nations were given problems such as the following from the Organization for Economic Co-operation and Development (OECD) and the Programme for International Student Assessment (PISA) (Schleicher & Tamassia, 2000):

> A result of global warming is that ice of some glaciers is melting.
>     Twelve years after the ice disappears, tiny plants, called lichen, start to grow on the rocks. Each lichen grows approximately in the shape of a circle.

The relationship between the diameter of the circles and the age of the lichen can be approximated with the formula: $d = 7.0 \times$ the square root of $(t - 12)$ for any $t$ less than or equal to 12, where $d$ represents the diameter of the lichen in millimeters, and $t$ represents the number of years after the ice has disappeared.

Calculate the diameter of the lichen 16 years after the ice disappeared. The complete and correct answer is:

$$d = 7.0 \times \text{the square root of } (16-12 \text{ mm})$$
$$d = 7.0 \times \text{the square root of } 4 \text{ mm}$$
$$d = 14 \text{ mm}$$

Eighteen countries ranked above the United States in the percentage of 15-year-olds who had mastered such concepts (see Figure 1.1).

**FIGURE 1.1**

Approximate average scores of 15-year-old students on the OECD mathematical literacy test.

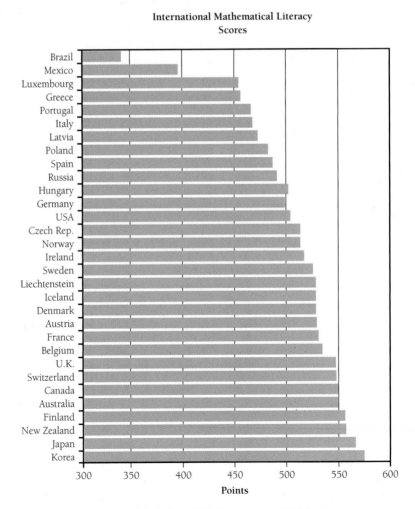

International Mathematical Literacy Scores

(Statistics used by permission of the OECD and PISA. Figure courtesy of W. J. Koen.)

FIGURE 1.2

Approximate average scores of 15-year-old students on the OECD scientific literacy test.

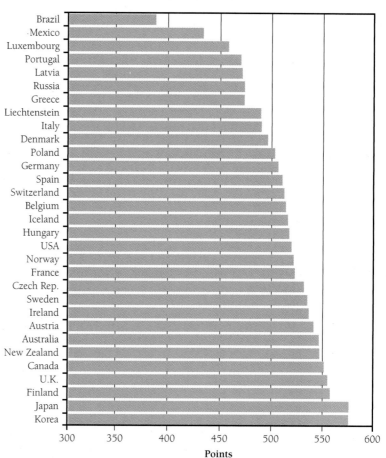

International Scientific Literacy Scores

(Statistics used by permission of the OECD and PISA. Figure courtesy of W. J. Koen.)

The results were similar for an OECD science literacy test (see Figure 1.2), which had questions such as the following:

A bus is moving along a straight stretch of road. The bus driver, named Ray, has a cup of water resting in a holder on the dashboard. Suddenly Ray has to slam on the brakes. What is most likely to happen to the water in the cup immediately after Ray slams on the brakes?

A. The water will stay horizontal.
B. The water will spill over side 1.
C. The water will spill over side 2.
D. The water will spill but you cannot tell if it will spill over side 1 or side 2.

The correct answer is C.

How useful are tests such as these? Do they measure anything meaningful? How accurate are they? Such questions concern not only every U.S. citizen but also all members of the highly competitive international community. To answer them, you must understand the principles of psychological testing that you are about to learn.

To answer questions about tests, you must understand the concepts presented in this book, such as reliability, validity, item analysis, and test construction. A full understanding of these concepts will require careful study and a knowledge of basic statistics, but your efforts will be richly rewarded. When you finish this book, you will be a better consumer of tests.

# Basic Concepts

You are probably already familiar with some of the elementary concepts of psychological testing. For the sake of clarity, however, we shall begin with definitions of the most basic terms so that you will know how they are used in this textbook.

## What a Test Is

Everyone has had experience with tests. A **test** is a measurement device or technique used to quantify behavior or aid in the understanding and prediction of behavior. A spelling test, for example, measures how well someone spells or the extent to which someone has learned to spell a specific list of words. At some time during the next few weeks, your instructor will likely want to measure how well you have learned the material in this book. To accomplish this, your instructor may give you a test.

As you well know, the test your instructor gives may not measure your full understanding of the material. This is because a test measures only a sample of behavior, and error is always associated with a sampling process. Test scores are not perfect measures of a behavior or characteristic, but they do add significantly to the prediction process, as you will see.

An **item** is a specific stimulus to which a person responds overtly; this response can be scored or evaluated (for example, classified, graded on a scale, or counted). Because psychological and educational tests are made up of items, the data they produce are explicit and hence subject to scientific inquiry.

In simple terms, items are the specific questions or problems that make up a test. The problems presented at the beginning of this chapter are examples of test items. The overt response would be to fill in or blacken one of the spaces:

A **psychological test** or educational test is a set of items that are designed to measure characteristics of human beings that pertain to behavior. There are many types of behavior. *Overt* behavior is an individual's observable activity. Some psychological tests attempt to measure the extent to which someone might engage in or "emit" a particular overt behavior. Other tests measure how much a person has previously engaged in some overt behavior. Behavior can also be *covert*—that is, it takes place within an individual and cannot be directly observed. For example, your feelings and thoughts are types of covert behavior. Some tests attempt to measure such behavior. Psychological and educational tests thus measure past or current behavior. Some also attempt to predict future behavior, such as success in college or in an advanced degree program.

What does it mean when someone gets 75 items correct on a 100-item test? One thing it means, of course, is that 75% of the items were answered correctly. In many situations, however, knowing the percentage of correct items a person obtained can be misleading. Consider two extreme examples. In one case, out of 100 students who took the exam, 99 had 90% correct or higher, and 1 had 75% correct. In another case, 99 of the 100 students had scores of 25% or lower, while 1 had 75% correct. The meaning of the scores can change dramatically, depending on how a well-defined sample of individuals scores on a test. In the first case, a score of 75% is poor because it is in the bottom of the distribution; in the second case, 75% is actually a top score. To deal with such problems of interpretation, psychologists make use of **scales**, which relate raw scores on test items to some defined theoretical or empirical distribution. Later in the book you will learn about such distributions.

Scores on tests may be related to traits, which are enduring characteristics or tendencies to respond in a certain manner. "Determination," sometimes seen as "stubbornness," is an example of a trait; "shyness" is another. Test scores may also be related to the state, or the specific condition or status, of an individual. A determined individual after many setbacks may, for instance, be in a weakened state and therefore be less inclined than usual to manifest determination. Tests measure many types of behavior.

## Types of Tests

Just as there are many types of behavior, so there are many types of tests. Those that can be given to only one person at a time are known as **individual tests** (see Figure 1.3). The examiner or **test administrator** (the person giving the test) gives the test to only one person at a time, the same way that psychotherapists see only one person at a time. A **group test**, by contrast, can be administered to more than one person at a time by a single examiner, such as when an instructor gives everyone in the class a test at the same time.

One can also categorize tests according to the type of behavior they measure. Ability tests contain items that can be scored in terms of speed, accuracy, or both. On an ability test, the faster or the more accurate your responses, the better your scores on a particular characteristic. The more algebra problems you can correctly solve in a given amount of time, the higher you score in ability to solve such problems.

Historically, experts have distinguished among achievement, aptitude, and intelligence as different types of ability. **Achievement** refers to previous learning. A test that measures or evaluates how many words you can spell correctly is called a *spelling achievement test*. **Aptitude**, by contrast, refers to the potential for learning or acquiring a specific skill. A spelling aptitude test measures how many words you might be able to spell given a certain amount of training, education, and

**FIGURE 1.3**
An individual test administration.

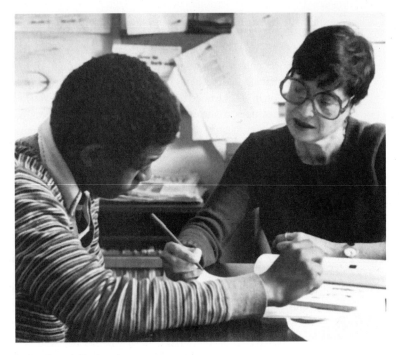

(© Ann Chwatsky/Jeroboam)

experience. Your musical aptitude refers in part to how well you might be able to learn to play a musical instrument given a certain number of lessons. Traditionally distinguished from achievement and aptitude, **intelligence** refers to a person's general potential to solve problems, adapt to changing circumstances, think abstractly, and profit from experience. When we say a person is "smart," we are usually referring to intelligence. When a father scolds his daughter because she has not done as well in school as she can, he most likely believes that she has not used her intelligence (general potential) to achieve (acquire new knowledge).

The distinctions among achievement, aptitude, and intelligence are not always so cut-and-dried because all three are highly interrelated. Attempts to separate prior learning from potential for learning, for example, have not succeeded. In view of the considerable overlap of achievement, aptitude, and intelligence tests, all three concepts are encompassed by the term **human ability**.

There is a clear-cut distinction between ability tests and personality tests. Whereas ability tests are related to capacity or potential, **personality tests** are related to the overt and covert dispositions of the individual—for example, the tendency of a person to show a particular behavior or response in a given situation. Remaining isolated from others, for instance, does not require any special skill or ability, but some people typically prefer or tend to remain thus isolated. Personality tests measure typical behavior.

There are several types of personality tests. In Chapter 16, you will learn about structured, or objective, personality tests. **Structured personality tests** provide a statement, usually of the "self-report" variety, and require the subject to choose between two or more alternative responses such as "True" or "False" (see Figure 1.4).

FIGURE 1.4
Self-report test items.

|  | True | False |
|---|:---:|:---:|
| 1. I like heavy metal music. | ☐ | ☐ |
| 2. I believe that honesty is the best policy. | ☐ | ☐ |
| 3. I am in good health. | ☐ | ☐ |
| 4. I am easily fatigued. | ☐ | ☐ |
| 5. I sleep well at night. | ☐ | ☐ |

**TABLE 1.1** Types of Tests

I. **Ability tests:** Measure skills in terms of speed, accuracy, or both.

　A. **Achievement:** Measures previous learning.

　B. **Aptitude:** Measures potential for acquiring a specific skill.

　C. **Intelligence:** Measures potential to solve problems, adapt to changing circumstances, and profit from experience.

II. **Personality tests:** Measure typical behavior—traits, temperaments, and dispositions.

　A. **Structured (objective):** Provides a self-report statement to which the person responds "True" or "False," "Yes" or "No."

　B. **Projective:** Provides an ambiguous test stimulus; response requirements are unclear.

In contrast to structured personality tests, projective personality tests are unstructured. In a **projective personality test**, either the stimulus (test materials) or the required response—or both—are ambiguous. For example, in the highly controversial Rorschach test, the stimulus is an inkblot. Furthermore, rather than being asked to choose among alternative responses, as in structured personality tests, the individual is asked to provide a spontaneous response. The inkblot is presented to the subject, who is asked, "What might this be?" Projective tests assume that a person's interpretation of an ambiguous stimulus will reflect his or her unique characteristics (see Chapter 14).

See Table 1.1 for a brief overview of ability and personality tests.

**Psychological testing** refers to all the possible uses, applications, and underlying concepts of psychological and educational tests. The main use of these tests, though, is to evaluate individual differences or variations among individuals. Such tests measure individual differences in ability and personality and assume that the differences shown on the test reflect actual differences among individuals. For instance, individuals who score high on an IQ test are assumed to have a higher degree of intelligence than those who obtain low scores. Thus, the most important purpose of testing is to differentiate among those taking the tests. We shall discuss the idea of individual differences later in this chapter.

# Overview of the Book

This book covers psychological testing from the most basic ideas to the most complex. Basic ideas and events are introduced early and stressed throughout to reinforce what you have just learned. As we cover relevant principles, applications, and issues, we intend to provide not only the *who*'s of psychological testing but also the *how*'s and *why*'s of major developments in the field. We also address an important concern of many students—relevance—by examining the diverse uses of tests and the resulting data.

## Principles of Psychological Testing

By *principles of psychological testing*, we mean the basic concepts and fundamental ideas that underlie all psychological and educational tests. Chapters 2 and 3 present statistical concepts that provide the foundation for understanding tests. Chapters 4 and 5 cover two of the most fundamental concepts in testing: reliability and validity. **Reliability** refers to the accuracy, dependability, consistency, or repeatability of test results. In more technical terms, reliability refers to the degree to which test scores are free of measurement errors. As you will learn, there are many ways a test can be reliable. For example, test results may be reliable over time, which means that when the same test is given twice within any given time interval, the results tend to be the same or highly similar. **Validity** refers to the meaning and usefulness of test results. More specifically, validity refers to the degree to which a certain inference or interpretation based on a test is appropriate. When one asks the question, "What does this psychological test measure?" one is essentially asking "For what inference is this test valid?"

## Applications of Psychological Testing

Our focus on applications provides a detailed analysis of many of the most popular tests and how they are used or applied. It begins with an overview of the essential terms and concepts that relate to the application of tests. Chapter 8 discusses interviewing techniques. An **interview** is a method of gathering information through verbal interaction, such as direct questions. Not only has the interview traditionally served as a major technique of gathering psychological information in general, but also data from interviews provide an important complement to test results.

Chapters 10 and 11 cover individual tests of human ability. In these chapters, you will learn not only about tests but also about the theories of intelligence that underlie them. In Chapter 12, we cover testing in education with an emphasis on special education. In Chapter 13, we present group tests of human ability. Chapter 16 covers structured personality tests, and Chapter 14 covers projective personality tests. In Chapter 9, we discuss the important role of computers in the testing field. We also consider the influence of cognitive psychology, which today is the most prominent of the various schools of thought within psychology (Klauer, 2011; Gentner, 2010; Rips, 2011).

These chapters not only provide descriptive information but also delve into the ideas underlying the various tests. Chapter 15 examines interest tests, which measure behavior relevant to such factors as occupational preferences. Chapter 17 reviews the relatively new area of medical testing for brain damage and health status. It also covers important recent advancements in developmental neuropsychology. Finally, Chapter 18 covers tests for industrial and organizational psychology and business.

## Issues of Psychological Testing

Many social and theoretical issues, such as the controversial topic of racial differences in ability, accompany testing. As a compromise between breadth and depth of coverage, we focus on a comprehensive discussion of those issues that have particular importance in the current professional, social, and political environment.

Chapter 6 examines test bias, one of the most volatile issues in the field (Moreno & Wong-Lo, 2011; Cormier, McGrew, & Jeffrey, 2011). Because psychological tests have been accused of being discriminatory or biased against certain groups, this chapter takes a careful look at both sides of the argument. Because of charges of bias and other problems, psychological testing is increasingly coming under the scrutiny of the law (Caffrey, 2009; Saccuzzo, 1999). Chapter 19 presents a general overview of other major issues currently shaping the future of psychological testing in the United States with an emphasis on ethics. From our review of the issues, we also speculate on what the future holds for psychological testing.

# Historical Perspective

We now briefly provide the historical context of psychological testing. This discussion touches on some of the material presented earlier in this chapter.

## Early Antecedents

Most of the major developments in testing have occurred over the last century, many of them in the United States. The origins of testing, however, are neither recent nor American. Evidence suggests that the Chinese had a relatively sophisticated civil service testing program more than 4000 years ago (DuBois, 1970, 1972). Every third year in China, oral examinations were given to help determine work evaluations and promotion decisions.

By the Han Dynasty (206 B.C.E. to 220 C.E.), the use of **test batteries** (two or more tests used in conjunction) was quite common. These early tests related to such diverse topics as civil law, military affairs, agriculture, revenue, and geography. Tests had become quite well developed by the Ming Dynasty (1368–1644 C.E.). During this period, a national multistage testing program involved local and regional testing centers equipped with special testing booths. Those who did well on the tests at the local level went on to provincial capitals for more extensive essay examinations. After this second testing, those with the highest test scores went on to the nation's capital for a final round. Only those who passed this third set of tests were eligible for public office.

The Western world most likely learned about testing programs through the Chinese. Reports by British missionaries and diplomats encouraged the English East India Company in 1832 to copy the Chinese system as a method of selecting employees for overseas duty. Because testing programs worked well for the company, the British government adopted a similar system of testing for its civil service in 1855. After the British endorsement of a civil service testing system, the French and German governments followed suit. In 1883, the U.S. government established the American Civil Service Commission, which developed and administered competitive examinations for certain government jobs. The impetus of the testing movement in the Western world grew rapidly at that time (Wiggins, 1973).

## Charles Darwin and Individual Differences

Perhaps the most basic concept underlying psychological and educational testing pertains to individual differences. No two snowflakes are identical, no two fingerprints the same. Similarly, no two people are exactly alike in ability and typical behavior. As we have noted, tests are specifically designed to measure these individual differences in ability and personality among people.

Although human beings realized long ago that individuals differ, developing tools for measuring such differences was no easy matter. To develop a measuring device, we must understand what we want to measure. An important step toward understanding individual differences came with the publication of Charles Darwin's highly influential book, *The Origin of Species*, in 1859. According to Darwin's theory, higher forms of life evolved partially because of differences among individual forms of life within a species. Given that individual members of a species differ, some possess characteristics that are more adaptive or successful in a given environment than are those of other members. Darwin also believed that those with the best or most adaptive characteristics survive at the expense of those who are less fit and that the survivors pass their characteristics on to the next generation. Through this process, he argued, life has evolved to its currently complex and intelligent levels.

Sir Francis Galton, a relative of Darwin's, soon began applying Darwin's theories to the study of human beings (see Figure 1.5). Given the concepts of survival of the fittest and individual differences, Galton set out to show that some people possessed characteristics that made them more fit than others, a theory he articulated in his book *Hereditary Genius*, published in 1869. Galton (1883) subsequently began a series of experimental studies to document the validity of his position. He concentrated on demonstrating that individual differences exist in human sensory and motor functioning, such as reaction time, visual acuity, and physical strength. In doing so, Galton initiated a search for knowledge concerning human individual differences, which is now one of the most important domains of scientific psychology.

Galton's work was extended by the U.S. psychologist James McKeen Cattell, who coined the term *mental test* (Cattell, 1890). Cattell's doctoral dissertation was based on Galton's work on individual differences in reaction time. As such, Cattell

FIGURE 1.5
Sir Francis Galton.

(From the National Library of Medicine)

perpetuated and stimulated the forces that ultimately led to the development of modern tests.

## Experimental Psychology and Psychophysical Measurement

A second major foundation of testing can be found in experimental psychology and early attempts to unlock the mysteries of human consciousness through the scientific method. Before psychology was practiced as a science, mathematical models of the mind were developed, in particular those of J. E. Herbart. Herbart eventually used these models as the basis for educational theories that strongly influenced 19th-century educational practices. Following Herbart, E. H. Weber attempted to demonstrate the existence of a psychological threshold, the minimum stimulus necessary to activate a sensory system. Then, following Weber, G. T. Fechner devised the law that the strength of a sensation grows as the logarithm of the stimulus intensity.

Wilhelm Wundt, who set up a laboratory at the University of Leipzig in 1879, is credited with founding the science of psychology, following in the tradition of Weber and Fechner (Hearst, 1979). Wundt was succeeded by E. B. Titchner, whose student, G. Whipple, recruited L. L. Thurstone. Whipple provided the basis for immense changes in the field of testing by conducting a seminar at the Carnegie Institute in 1919 attended by Thurstone, E. Strong, and other early prominent U.S. psychologists. From this seminar came the Carnegie Interest Inventory and later the Strong Vocational Interest Blank. Later in this book we discuss in greater detail the work of these pioneers and the tests they helped develop.

Thus, psychological testing developed from at least two lines of inquiry: one based on the work of Darwin, Galton, and Cattell on the measurement of individual differences, and the other (more theoretically relevant and probably stronger) based on the work of the German psychophysicists Herbart, Weber, Fechner, and

Wundt. Experimental psychology developed from the latter. From this work also came the idea that testing, like an experiment, requires rigorous experimental control. Such control, as you will see, comes from administering tests under highly standardized conditions.

The efforts of these researchers, however necessary, did not by themselves lead to the creation of modern psychological tests. Such tests also arose in response to important needs such as classifying and identifying the mentally and emotionally handicapped. One of the earliest tests resembling current procedures, the Seguin Form Board Test (Seguin, 1866/1907), was developed in an effort to educate and evaluate the mentally disabled. Similarly, Kraepelin (1912) devised a series of examinations for evaluating emotionally impaired people.

An important breakthrough in the creation of modern tests came at the turn of the 20th century. The French minister of public instruction appointed a commission to study ways of identifying intellectually subnormal individuals in order to provide them with appropriate educational experiences. One member of that commission was Alfred Binet. Working in conjunction with the French physician T. Simon, Binet developed the first major general intelligence test. Binet's early effort launched the first systematic attempt to evaluate individual differences in human intelligence (see Chapter 10).

## The Evolution of Intelligence and Standardized Achievement Tests

The history and evolution of Binet's intelligence test are instructive. The first version of the test, known as the Binet-Simon Scale, was published in 1905. This instrument contained 30 items of increasing difficulty and was designed to identify intellectually subnormal individuals. Like all well-constructed tests, the Binet-Simon Scale of 1905 was augmented by a comparison or standardization sample. Binet's standardization sample consisted of 50 children who had been given the test under *standard conditions*—that is, with precisely the same instructions and format. In obtaining this standardization sample, the authors of the Binet test had norms with which they could compare the results from any new subject. Without such norms, the meaning of scores would have been difficult, if not impossible, to evaluate. However, by knowing such things as the average number of correct responses found in the standardization sample, one could at least state whether a new subject was below or above it.

It is easy to understand the importance of a standardization sample. However, the importance of obtaining a standardization sample that represents the population for which a test will be used has sometimes been ignored or overlooked by test users. For example, if a standardization sample consists of 50 white men from wealthy families, then one cannot easily or fairly evaluate the score of an African American girl from a poverty-stricken family. Nevertheless, comparisons of this kind are sometimes made. Clearly, it is not appropriate to compare an individual with a group that does not have the same characteristics as the individual.

Binet was aware of the importance of a standardization sample. Further development of the Binet test involved attempts to increase the size and representativeness of the standardization sample. A **representative sample** is one that comprises individuals similar to those for whom the test is to be used. When the test is used for the general population, a representative sample must reflect all segments of the population in proportion to their actual numbers.

By 1908, the Binet-Simon Scale had been substantially improved. It was revised to include nearly twice as many items as the 1905 scale. Even more significantly, the size of the standardization sample was increased to more than 200. The 1908 Binet-Simon Scale also determined a child's **mental age**, thereby introducing a historically significant concept. In simplified terms, you might think of mental age as a measurement of a child's performance on the test relative to other children of that particular age group. If a child's test performance equals that of the average 8-year-old, for example, then his or her mental age is 8. In other words, in terms of the abilities measured by the test, this child can be viewed as having a similar level of ability as the average 8-year-old. The chronological age of the child may be 4 or 12, but in terms of test performance, the child functions at the same level as the average 8-year-old. The mental age concept was one of the most important contributions of the revised 1908 Binet-Simon Scale.

In 1911, the Binet-Simon Scale received a minor revision. By this time, the idea of intelligence testing had swept across the world. By 1916, L. M. Terman of Stanford University had revised the Binet test for use in the United States. Terman's revision, known as the Stanford-Binet Intelligence Scale (Terman, 1916), was the only American version of the Binet test that flourished. It also characterizes one of the most important trends in testing—the drive toward better tests.

Terman's 1916 revision of the Binet-Simon Scale contained many improvements. The standardization sample was increased to include 1000 people, original items were revised, and many new items were added. Terman's 1916 Stanford-Binet Intelligence Scale added respectability and momentum to the newly developing testing movement.

## World War I

The testing movement grew enormously in the United States because of the demand for a quick, efficient way of evaluating the emotional and intellectual functioning of thousands of military recruits in World War I. The war created a demand for large-scale group testing because relatively few trained personnel could evaluate the huge influx of military recruits. However, the Binet test was an individual test.

Shortly after the United States became actively involved in World War I, the army requested the assistance of Robert Yerkes, who was then the president of the American Psychological Association (see Yerkes, 1921). Yerkes headed a committee of distinguished psychologists who soon developed two structured group tests of human abilities: the Army Alpha and the Army Beta. The Army Alpha required reading ability, whereas the Army Beta measured the intelligence of illiterate adults.

World War I fueled the widespread development of group tests. About this time, the scope of testing also broadened to include tests of achievement, aptitude, interest, and personality. Because achievement, aptitude, and intelligence tests overlapped considerably, the distinctions proved to be more illusory than real. Even so, the 1916 Stanford-Binet Intelligence Scale had appeared at a time of strong demand and high optimism for the potential of measuring human behavior through tests.

World War I and the creation of group tests had then added momentum to the testing movement. Shortly after the appearance of the 1916 Stanford-Binet Intelligence Scale and the Army Alpha test, schools, colleges, and industry began using tests. It appeared to many that this new phenomenon, the psychological test, held the key to solving the problems emerging from the rapid growth of population and technology.

## Achievement Tests

Among the most important developments following World War I was the development of standardized achievement tests. In contrast to essay tests, standardized achievement tests provide multiple-choice questions that are standardized on a large sample to produce norms against which the results of new examinees can be compared.

Standardized achievement tests caught on quickly because of the relative ease of administration and scoring and the lack of subjectivity or favoritism that can occur in essay or other written tests. In school settings, standardized achievement tests allowed one to maintain identical testing conditions and scoring standards for a large number of children. Such tests also allowed a broader coverage of content and were less expensive and more efficient than essays. In 1923, the development of standardized achievement tests culminated in the publication of the Stanford Achievement Test by T. L. Kelley, G. M. Ruch, and L. M. Terman.

By the 1930s, it was widely held that the objectivity and reliability of these new standardized tests made them superior to essay tests. Their use proliferated widely. It is interesting, as we shall discuss later in the book, that teachers of today appear to have come full circle. Currently, many people favor written tests and work samples (portfolios) over standardized achievement tests as the best way to evaluate children (McKenna, Walpole, & Conradi, 2010; Chu & Flores, 2011).

## Rising to the Challenge

For every movement there is a countermovement, and the testing movement in the United States in the 1930s was no exception. Critics soon became vocal enough to dampen enthusiasm and to make even the most optimistic advocates of tests defensive. Researchers, who demanded nothing short of the highest standards, noted the limitations and weaknesses of existing tests. Not even the Stanford-Binet, a landmark in the testing field, was safe from criticism. Although tests were used between the two world wars and many new tests were developed, their accuracy and utility remained under heavy fire.

Near the end of the 1930s, developers began to reestablish the respectability of tests. New, improved tests reflected the knowledge and experience of the previous two decades. By 1937, the Stanford-Binet had been revised again. Among the many improvements was the inclusion of a standardization sample of more than 3000 individuals. A mere 2 years after the 1937 revision of the Stanford-Binet test, David Wechsler published the first version of the Wechsler intelligence scales (see Chapter 11), the Wechsler-Bellevue Intelligence Scale (W-B) (Wechsler, 1939). The Wechsler-Bellevue scale contained several interesting innovations in intelligence testing. Unlike the Stanford-Binet test, which produced only a single score (the so-called IQ, or intelligence quotient), Wechsler's test yielded several scores, permitting an analysis of an individual's pattern or combination of abilities.

Among the various scores produced by the Wechsler test was the performance IQ. Performance tests do not require a verbal response; one can use them to evaluate intelligence in people who have few verbal or language skills. The Stanford-Binet test had long been criticized because of its emphasis on language and verbal skills, making it inappropriate for many individuals, such as those who cannot speak or who cannot read. In addition, few people believed that language or verbal skills play an exclusive role in human intelligence. Wechsler's inclusion of a nonverbal scale thus helped overcome some of the practical and theoretical weaknesses of the Binet test. In 1986, the Binet test was drastically revised to include performance subtests. More recently, it was overhauled again in 2003, as we shall see in Chapter 10. (Other important concepts in intelligence testing will be formally defined in Chapter 11, which covers the various forms of the Wechsler intelligence scales.)

## Personality Tests: 1920–1940

Just before and after World War II, personality tests began to blossom. Whereas intelligence tests measured ability or potential, personality tests measured presumably stable characteristics or traits that theoretically underlie behavior. **Traits** are relatively enduring dispositions (tendencies to act, think, or feel in a certain manner in any given circumstance) that distinguish one individual from another. For example, we say that some people are optimistic and some pessimistic. Optimistic people tend to remain so regardless of whether or not things are going well. A pessimist, by contrast, tends to look at the negative side of things. Optimism and pessimism can thus be viewed as traits. One of the basic goals of traditional personality tests is to measure traits. As you will learn, however, the notion of traits has important limitations.

The earliest personality tests were structured paper-and-pencil group tests. These tests provided multiple-choice and true-false questions that could be administered to a large group. Because it provides a high degree of structure—that is, a definite stimulus and specific alternative responses that can be unequivocally scored—this sort of test is a type of structured personality test. The first structured personality test, the Woodworth Personal Data Sheet, was developed during World War I and was published in final form just after the war (see Figure 1.6).

**FIGURE 1.6**

The Woodworth Personal Data Sheet represented an attempt to standardize the psychiatric interview. It contains questions such as those shown here.

|   |   | Yes | No |
|---|---|---|---|
| **1.** | I wet the bed. | ☐ | ☐ |
| **2.** | I drink a quart of whiskey each day. | ☐ | ☐ |
| **3.** | I am afraid of closed spaces. | ☐ | ☐ |
| **4.** | I believe I am being followed. | ☐ | ☐ |
| **5.** | People are out to get me. | ☐ | ☐ |
| **6.** | Sometimes I see or hear things that other people do not hear or see. | ☐ | ☐ |

As indicated earlier, the motivation underlying the development of the first personality test was the need to screen military recruits. History indicates that tests such as the Binet and the Woodworth were created by necessity to meet unique challenges. Like the early ability tests, however, the first structured personality test was simple by today's standards. Interpretation of the Woodworth test depended on the now-discredited assumption that the content of an item could be accepted at face value. If the person marked "False" for the statement "I wet the bed," then it was assumed that he or she did not "wet the bed." As logical as this assumption seems, experience has shown that it is often false. In addition to being dishonest, the person responding to the question may not interpret the meaning of "wet the bed" the same way as the test administrator does. (Other problems with tests such as the Woodworth are discussed in Chapter 16.)

The introduction of the Woodworth test was enthusiastically followed by the creation of a variety of structured personality tests, all of which assumed that a subject's response could be taken at face value. However, researchers scrutinized, analyzed, and criticized the early structured personality tests, just as they had done with the ability tests. Indeed, the criticism of tests that relied on face value alone became so intense that structured personality tests were nearly driven out of existence. The development of new tests based on more modern concepts followed, revitalizing the use of structured personality tests. Thus, after an initial surge of interest and optimism during most of the 1920s, structured personality tests declined by the late 1930s and early 1940s. Following World War II, however, personality tests based on fewer or different assumptions were introduced, thereby rescuing the structured personality test.

During the brief but dramatic rise and fall of the first structured personality tests, interest in projective tests began to grow. In contrast to structured personality tests, which in general provide a relatively unambiguous test stimulus and specific alternative responses, projective personality tests provide an ambiguous stimulus and unclear response requirements. Furthermore, the scoring of projective tests is often subjective.

Unlike the early structured personality tests, interest in the projective Rorschach inkblot test grew slowly (see Figure 1.7). The Rorschach test was first published by

**FIGURE 1.7**
Card 1 of the Rorschach inkblot test, a projective personality test. Such tests provide an ambiguous stimulus to which a subject is asked to make some response.

Herman Rorschach of Switzerland in 1921. However, several years passed before the Rorschach came to the United States, where David Levy introduced it. The first Rorschach doctoral dissertation written in a U.S. university was not completed until 1932, when Sam Beck, Levy's student, decided to investigate the properties of the Rorschach test scientifically. Although initial interest in the Rorschach test was lukewarm at best, its popularity grew rapidly after Beck's work, despite suspicion, doubt, and criticism from the scientific community. Today, however, the Rorschach is under a dark cloud (see Chapter 14).

Adding to the momentum for the acceptance and use of projective tests was the development of the Thematic Apperception Test (TAT) by Henry Murray and Christina Morgan in 1935. Whereas the Rorschach test contained completely ambiguous inkblot stimuli, the TAT was more structured. Its stimuli consisted of ambiguous pictures depicting a variety of scenes and situations, such as a boy sitting in front of a table with a violin on it. Unlike the Rorschach test, which asked the subject to explain what the inkblot might be, the TAT required the subject to make up a story about the ambiguous scene. The TAT purported to measure human needs and thus to ascertain individual differences in motivation.

## The Emergence of New Approaches to Personality Testing

The popularity of the two most important projective personality tests, the Rorschach and TAT, grew rapidly by the late 1930s and early 1940s, perhaps because of disillusionment with structured personality tests (Dahlstrom, 1969a). However, as we shall see in Chapter 14, projective tests, particularly the Rorschach, have not withstood a vigorous examination of their psychometric properties (Wood, Lilienfeld, Nezworski, Garb, Allen, & Wildermuth, 2010).

In 1943, the Minnesota Multiphasic Personality Inventory (MMPI) began a new era for structured personality tests. The idea behind the MMPI—to use empirical methods to determine the meaning of a test response—helped revolutionize structured personality tests. The problem with early structured personality tests such as the Woodworth was that they made far too many assumptions that subsequent scientific investigations failed to substantiate. The authors of the MMPI, by contrast, argued that the meaning of a test response could be determined only by empirical research. The MMPI, along with its updated companion the MMPI-2 (Butcher, 1989, 1990), is currently the most widely used and referenced personality test (Wise, 2010). Its emphasis on the need for empirical data has stimulated the development of tens of thousands of studies.

Just about the time the MMPI appeared, personality tests based on the statistical procedure called *factor analysis* began to emerge. **Factor analysis** is a method of finding the minimum number of dimensions (characteristics, attributes), called *factors*, to account for a large number of variables. We may say a person is outgoing, is gregarious, seeks company, is talkative, and enjoys relating to others. However, these descriptions contain a certain amount of redundancy. A factor analysis can identify how much they overlap and whether they can all be accounted for or subsumed under a single dimension (or factor) such as extroversion.

In the early 1940s, J. R Guilford made the first serious attempt to use factor analytic techniques in the development of a structured personality test. By the end

---

**TABLE 1.2**   Summary of Personality Tests

**Woodworth Personal Data Sheet:** An early structured personality test that assumed that a test response can be taken at face value.

**The Rorschach Inkblot Test:** A highly controversial projective test that provided an ambiguous stimulus (an inkblot) and asked the subject what it might be.

**The Thematic Apperception Test (TAT):** A projective test that provided ambiguous pictures and asked subjects to make up a story.

**The Minnesota Multiphasic Personality Inventory (MMPI):** A structured personality test that made no assumptions about the meaning of a test response. Such meaning was to be determined by empirical research.

**The California Psychological Inventory (CPI):** A structured personality test developed according to the same principles as the MMPI.

**The Sixteen Personality Factor Questionnaire (16PF):** A structured personality test based on the statistical procedure of factor analysis.

---

of that decade, R. B. Cattell had introduced the Sixteen Personality Factor Questionnaire (16PF); despite its declining popularity, it remains one of the most well-constructed structured personality tests and an important example of a test developed with the aid of factor analysis. Today, factor analysis is a tool used in the design or validation of just about all major tests. (Factor analytic personality tests will be discussed in Chapter 16.) See Table 1.2 for a brief overview of personality tests.

## The Period of Rapid Changes in the Status of Testing

The 1940s saw not only the emergence of a whole new technology in psychological testing but also the growth of applied aspects of psychology. The role and significance of tests used in World War I were reaffirmed in World War II. By this time, the U.S. government had begun to encourage the continued development of applied psychological technology. As a result, considerable federal funding provided paid, supervised training for clinically oriented psychologists. By 1949, formal university training standards had been developed and accepted, and clinical psychology was born. Other applied branches of psychology—such as industrial, counseling, educational, and school psychology—soon began to blossom.

One of the major functions of the applied psychologist was providing psychological testing. The Shakow, Hilgard, Kelly, Sanford, and Shaffer (1947) report, which was the foundation of the formal training standards in clinical psychology, specified that psychological testing was a unique function of the clinical psychologist and recommended that testing methods be taught only to doctoral psychology students. A position paper of the American Psychological Association published 7 years later (APA, 1954) affirmed that the domain of the clinical psychologist included testing. It formally declared, however, that the psychologist would conduct psychotherapy only in "true" collaboration with physicians. Thus, psychologists could conduct testing independently, but not psychotherapy. Indeed, as long as psychologists assumed the role of testers, they played a complementary but often secondary role vis-à-vis medical practitioners. Though the medical profession could have hindered the emergence of clinical psychology, it did not, because as tester the psychologist aided the physician. Therefore, in the late 1940s and early 1950s, testing was the major function of the clinical psychologist (Shaffer, 1953).

For better or worse, depending on one's perspective, the government's efforts to stimulate the development of applied aspects of psychology, especially clinical psychology, were extremely successful. Hundreds of highly talented and creative young people were attracted to clinical and other applied areas of psychology. These individuals, who would use tests and other psychological techniques to solve practical human problems, were uniquely trained as practitioners of the principles, empirical foundations, and applications of the science of psychology.

Armed with powerful knowledge from scientific psychology, many of these early clinical practitioners must have felt frustrated by their relationship to physicians (see Saccuzzo & Kaplan, 1984). Unable to engage independently in the practice of psychotherapy, some psychologists felt like technicians serving the medical profession. The highly talented group of post–World War II psychologists quickly began to reject this secondary role. Further, because many psychologists associated tests with this secondary relationship, they rejected testing (Lewandowski & Saccuzzo, 1976). At the same time, the potentially intrusive nature of tests and fears of misuse began to create public suspicion, distrust, and contempt for tests. Attacks on testing came from within and without the profession. These attacks intensified and multiplied so fast that many psychologists jettisoned all ties to the traditional tests developed during the first half of the 20th century. Testing therefore underwent another sharp decline in status in the late 1950s that persisted into the 1970s (see Holt, 1967).

## The Current Environment

During the 1980s, 1990s, and 2000s several major branches of applied psychology emerged and flourished: neuropsychology, health psychology, forensic psychology, and child psychology. Because each of these important areas of psychology makes extensive use of psychological tests, psychological testing again grew in status and use. Neuropsychologists use tests in hospitals and other clinical settings to assess brain injury. Health psychologists use tests and surveys in a variety of medical settings. Forensic psychologists use tests in the legal system to assess mental state as it relates to an insanity defense, competency to stand trial or to be executed, and emotional damages. Child psychologists use tests to assess childhood disorders. Tests are presently in use in developed countries throughout the world (Marsh, Hau, Artelt, Baumet, & Peschar, 2006; Black & William, 2007). As in the past, psychological testing remains one of the most important yet controversial topics in psychology.

As a student, no matter what your occupational or professional goals, you will find the material in this text invaluable. If you are among those who are interested in using psychological techniques in an applied setting, then this information will be particularly significant. From the roots of psychology to the present, psychological tests have remained among the most important instruments of the psychologist in general and of those who apply psychology in particular.

Testing is indeed one of the essential elements of psychology. Though not all psychologists use tests and some psychologists are opposed to them, all areas of psychology depend on knowledge gained in research studies that rely on measurements. The meaning and dependability of these measurements are essential to psychological research. To study any area of human behavior effectively, one must understand the basic principles of measurement.

In today's complex society, the relevance of the principles, applications, and issues of psychological testing extends far beyond the field of psychology. Even if you do not plan to become a psychologist, you will likely encounter psychological tests. Attorneys, physicians, social workers, business managers, educators, and many other professionals must frequently deal with reports based on such tests. Even as a parent, you are likely to encounter tests (taken by your children). To interpret such information adequately, you need the information presented in this book.

The more you know about psychological tests, the more confident you can be in your encounters with them. Given the attacks on tests and threats to prohibit or greatly limit their use, you have a responsibility to yourself and to society to know as much as you can about psychological tests. The future of testing may well depend on you and people like you. A thorough knowledge of testing will allow you to base your decisions on facts and to ensure that tests are used for the most beneficial and constructive purposes.

Tests have probably never been as important as they are today. For example, consider just one type of testing that has become central to educational advancement—academic aptitude (see Russo, 2011). Every year more than 2.5 million students take tests that are designed to measure academic progress or suitability, and the testing process begins early in students' lives. Some presecondary schools require certain tests, and thousands of children take them each year. When these students become adolescents and want to get into college preparatory schools, tens of thousands will take a screening examination. Few students who want to go to a 4-year college can avoid taking a college entrance test. The SAT Reasoning Test alone was administered to 1.59 million high-school seniors, 1.57 million juniors, and 1.57 million sophomores in 2010 (College Board, 2010). More than 1.8 million high school students took advanced placement tests in 2010, some of them taking more than one, resulting in the administration of more than 3.2 million advance placement exams in 2010 (College Board, 2010). In 2010, the GRE General Test was taken by about 675,000 candidates.

These figures do not include the 75,000 people who take a special test for admission to business school, the 148,000 who take a Law School Admission Test (Schnipke, 2011), or the 675,000 who take the GRE (GRE news release)—or other tests for graduate programs such as medical school, dental school, the military, professional licenses, and others. In fact, the Educational Testing Service alone administers more than 50 million tests annually in 181 countries (GRE news release, 2010). Nor do they include the millions of tests given around the world for research and evaluation purposes (Black & William, 2007; Marsh et al., 2006). As sources of information about human characteristics, the results of these tests affect critical life decisions.

# Summary

The history of psychological testing in the United States has been brief but intense. Although these sorts of tests have long been available, psychological testing is very much a product of modern society with its unprecedented technology and population growth and unique problems. Conversely, by helping solve the challenges posed by modern developments, tests have played an important role in recent U.S. and world history. You should realize, however, that despite advances in the theory and technique of psychological testing, many unsolved technical problems and hotly debated social, political, and economic issues remain. Nevertheless, the prevalence of tests despite strong opposition indicates that, although they are far from perfect, psychological tests must fulfill some important need in the decision-making processes permeating all facets of society. Because decisions must be made, such tests will probably flourish until a better or more objective way of making decisions emerges.

Modern history shows that psychological tests have evolved in a complicated environment in which hostile and friendly forces have produced a balance characterized by innovation and a continuous quest for better methods. One interesting thing about tests is that people never seem to remain neutral about them. If you are not in favor of tests, then we ask that you maintain an open mind while studying them. Our goal is to give you enough information to assess psychological tests intelligently throughout your life.

# CHAPTER 2

# Norms and Basic Statistics for Testing

## LEARNING OBJECTIVES

*When you have completed this chapter, you should be able to:*

- ▶ Discuss three properties of scales of measurement

- ▶ Determine why properties of scales are important in the field of measurement

- ▶ Identify methods for displaying distributions of scores

- ▶ Calculate the mean and the standard deviation for a set of scores

- ▶ Define a *Z* score and explain how it is used

- ▶ Relate the concepts of mean, standard deviation, and *Z* score to the concept of a standard normal distribution

- ▶ Define quartiles, deciles, and stanines and explain how they are used

- ▶ Tell how norms are created

- ▶ Relate the notion of tracking to the establishment of norms

We all use numbers as a basic way of communicating: Our money system requires us to understand and manipulate numbers, we estimate how long it will take to do things, we count, we express evaluations on scales, and so on. Think about how many times you use numbers in an average day. There is no way to avoid them.

One advantage of number systems is that they allow us to manipulate information. Through sets of well-defined rules, we can use numbers to learn more about the world. *Tests* are devices used to translate observations into numbers. Because the outcome of a test is almost always represented as a score, much of this book is about what scores mean. This chapter reviews some of the basic rules used to evaluate number systems. These rules and number systems are the psychologist's partners in learning about human behavior.

If you have had a course in basic statistics, then this chapter will reinforce the basic concepts you have already learned. If you need additional review, reread your introductory statistics book. Most such books cover the information in this chapter. If you have not had a course in statistics, then this chapter will provide some of the information needed for understanding other chapters in this book.

# Why We Need Statistics

Through its commitment to the scientific method, modern psychology has advanced beyond centuries of speculation about human nature. Scientific study requires systematic observations and an estimation of the extent to which observations could have been influenced by chance alone (Madsen & SpringerLink (online service), 2011). Statistical methods serve two important purposes in the quest for scientific understanding.

First, statistics are used for purposes of description. Numbers provide convenient summaries and allow us to evaluate some observations relative to others (Dytham, 2011; Madsen & SpringerLink (online service), 2011; Vasishth, Broe, & SpringerLink (online service), 2011). For example, if you get a score of 54 on a psychology examination, you probably want to know what the 54 means. Is it lower than the average score, or is it about the same? Knowing the answer can make the feedback you get from your examination more meaningful. If you discover that the 54 puts you in the top 5% of the class, then you might assume you have a good chance for an A. If it puts you in the bottom 5%, then you will feel differently.

Second, we can use statistics to make **inferences**, which are logical deductions about events that cannot be observed directly. For example, you do not know how many people watched a particular television movie unless you ask everyone. However, by using scientific sample surveys, you can infer the percentage of people who saw the film. Data gathering and analysis might be considered analogous to criminal investigation and prosecution (Cox, 2006; Regenwetter, 2006; Tukey, 1977). First comes the detective work of gathering and displaying clues, or what the statistician John Tukey calls *exploratory data analysis*. Then comes a period of *confirmatory data analysis*, when the clues are evaluated against rigid statistical rules. This latter phase is like the work done by judges and juries.

Some students have an aversion to numbers and anything mathematical. If you find yourself among them, you are not alone. Professional psychologists can also feel uneasy about statistics. However, statistics and the basic principles of measurement lie at the center of the modern science of psychology. Scientific statements are usually based on careful study, and such systematic study requires some numerical analysis.

This chapter reviews both descriptive and inferential statistics. **Descriptive statistics** are methods used to provide a concise description of a collection of quantitative information. **Inferential statistics** are methods used to make inferences from observations of a small group of people known as a *sample* to a larger group of individuals known as a *population*. Typically, the psychologist wants to make statements about the larger group but cannot possibly make all the necessary observations. Instead, he or she observes a relatively small group of subjects (sample) and uses inferential statistics to estimate the characteristics of the larger group (Madsen & SpringerLink (online service), 2011).

# Scales of Measurement

One may define *measurement* as the application of rules for assigning numbers to objects. The rules are the specific procedures used to transform qualities of attributes into numbers (Nunnally & Bernstein, 1994; Rust & Golombok, 2009; Yanai, 2003). For example, to rate the quality of wines, wine tasters must use a specific set of rules. They might rate the wine on a 10-point scale, where 1 means extremely bad and 10 means extremely good. For a taster to assign the numbers, the system of rules must be clearly defined. The basic feature of these types of systems is the scale of measurement. For example, to measure the height of your classmates, you might use the scale of inches; to measure their weight, you might use the scale of pounds.

There are numerous systems by which we assign numbers in psychology. Indeed, the study of measurement systems is what this book is about. Before we consider any specific scale of measurement, however, we should consider the general properties of measurement scales.

## Properties of Scales

Three important properties make scales of measurement different from one another: magnitude, equal intervals, and an absolute 0.

### Magnitude

Magnitude is the property of "moreness." A scale has the property of magnitude if we can say that a particular instance of the attribute represents more, less, or equal amounts of the given quantity than does another instance (Aron & Aron, 2003; Hurlburt, 2003; McCall, 2001; Howell, 2008). On a scale of height, for example, if we can say that John is taller than Fred, then the scale has the property of magnitude. A scale that does not have this property arises, for example, when a gym coach assigns identification numbers to teams in a league (team 1, team 2, and so forth). Because the numbers only label the teams, they do not have the property of magnitude. If the coach were to rank the teams by the number of games they have won, then the new numbering system (games won) would have the property of magnitude.

### Equal Intervals

The concept of equal intervals is a little more complex than that of magnitude. A scale has the property of equal intervals if the difference between two points at any place on the scale has the same meaning as the difference between two other points that differ by the same number of scale units. For example, the difference between inch 2 and inch 4 on a ruler represents the same quantity as the difference between inch 10 and inch 12: exactly 2 inches.

As simple as this concept seems, a psychological test rarely has the property of equal intervals. For example, the difference between intelligence quotients (IQs) of 45 and 50 does not mean the same thing as the difference between IQs of 105 and 110. Although each of these differences is 5 points ($50 - 45 = 5$ and $110 - 105 = 5$), the 5 points at the first level do not mean the same thing as 5 points at the second. We know that IQ predicts classroom performance. However, the difference in classroom performance associated with differences between IQ scores of 45 and 50 is not the same as the differences in classroom performance associated with IQ score differences of 105 and 110. In later chapters we will discuss this problem in more detail.

When a scale has the property of *equal intervals*, the relationship between the measured units and some outcome can be described by a straight line or a linear equation in the form $Y = a + bX$. This equation shows that an increase in equal units on a given scale reflects equal increases in the meaningful correlates of units. For example, Figure 2.1 shows the hypothetical relationship between scores on a test of manual dexterity and ratings of artwork. Notice that the relationship is not a straight line. By examining the points on the figure, you can see that at first the relationship is nearly linear: Increases in manual dexterity are associated with increases in ratings of artwork. Then the relationship becomes nonlinear. The figure shows that after a manual dexterity score of approximately 5, increases in dexterity produce relatively smaller increases in quality of artwork.

### Absolute 0

An absolute 0 is obtained when nothing of the property being measured exists. For example, if you are measuring heart rate and observe that your patient has a rate of 0 and has died, then you would conclude that there is no heart rate at all.

**FIGURE 2.1**

Hypothetical relationship between ratings of artwork and manual dexterity. In some ranges of the scale, the relationship is more direct than it is in others.

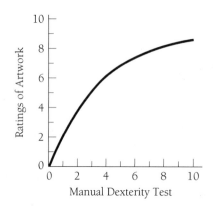

**TABLE 2.1**   Scales of Measurement and Their Properties

| Type of scale | Property | | |
| --- | --- | --- | --- |
| | Magnitude | Equal intervals | Absolute 0 |
| Nominal | No | No | No |
| Ordinal | Yes | No | No |
| Interval | Yes | Yes | No |
| Ratio | Yes | Yes | Yes |

For many psychological qualities, it is extremely difficult, if not impossible, to define an absolute 0 point. For example, if one measures shyness on a scale from 0 through 10, then it is hard to define what it means for a person to have absolutely no shyness (McCall, 2001).

## Types of Scales

Table 2.1 defines four scales of measurement based on the properties we have just discussed. You can see that a nominal scale does not have the property of magnitude, equal intervals, or an absolute 0. **Nominal scales** are really not scales at all; their only purpose is to name objects. For example, the numbers on the backs of football players' uniforms are nominal. Nominal scales are used when the information is qualitative rather than quantitative. Social science researchers commonly label groups in sample surveys with numbers (such as 1 = African American, 2 = white, and 3 = Mexican American). When these numbers have been attached to categories, most statistical procedures are not meaningful. On the scale for ethnic groups, for instance, what would a mean of 1.87 signify? This is not to say that the sophisticated statistical analysis of nominal data is impossible. Indeed, several new and exciting developments in data analysis allow extensive and detailed use of nominal data (Hu, Szapary, Yeilding, & Zhou, 2011; Notelaers, Vermunt, Baillien, Einarsen, & De Witte, 2011; Ruscio & Walters, 2011; Sanderson, Hewlett, Richards, Morris, & Calnan, 2011).

A scale with the property of magnitude but not equal intervals or an absolute 0 is an **ordinal scale**. This scale allows you to rank individuals or objects but not to say anything about the meaning of the differences between the ranks. If you were to rank the members of your class by height, then you would have an ordinal scale. For example, if Fred was the tallest, Susan the second tallest, and George the third tallest, you would assign them the ranks 1, 2, and 3, respectively. You would not give any consideration to the fact that Fred is 8 inches taller than Susan, but Susan is only 2 inches taller than George.

For most problems in psychology, the precision to measure the exact differences between intervals does not exist. So, most often one must use ordinal scales of measurement. For example, IQ tests do not have the property of equal intervals or an absolute 0, but they do have the property of magnitude. If they had the property of equal intervals, then the difference between an IQ of 70 and one of 90 should have the same meaning as the difference between an IQ of 125 and one of 145. Because it does not, the scale can only be considered ordinal. Furthermore, there is no point on the scale that represents no intelligence at all—that is, the scale does not have an absolute 0.

When a scale has the properties of magnitude and equal intervals but not absolute 0, we refer to it as an **interval scale**. The most common example of an interval scale is the measurement of temperature in degrees Fahrenheit. This temperature scale clearly has the property of magnitude, because 35°F is warmer than 32°F, 65°F is warmer than 64°F, and so on. Also, the difference between 90°F and 80°F is equal to a similar difference of 10° at any point on the scale. However, on the Fahrenheit scale, temperature does not have the property of absolute 0. If it did, then the 0 point would be more meaningful. As it is, 0 on the Fahrenheit scale does not have a particular meaning. Water freezes at 32°F and boils at 212°F. Because the scale does not have an absolute 0, we cannot make statements in terms of ratios. A temperature of 22°F is not twice as hot as 11°F, and 70°F is not twice as hot as 35°F.

The Celsius scale of temperature is also an interval rather than a ratio scale. Although 0 represents freezing on the Celsius scale, it is not an absolute 0. Remember that an absolute 0 is a point at which nothing of the property being measured exists. Even on the Celsius scale of temperature, there is still plenty of room on the thermometer below 0. When the temperature goes below freezing, some aspect of heat is still being measured.

A scale that has all three properties (magnitude, equal intervals, and an absolute 0) is called a **ratio scale**. To continue our example, a ratio scale of temperature would have the properties of the Fahrenheit and Celsius scales but also include a meaningful 0 point. There is a point at which all molecular activity ceases, a point of absolute 0 on a temperature scale. Because the Kelvin scale is based on the absolute 0 point, it is a ratio scale: 22°K is twice as cold as 44°K. Examples of ratio scales also appear in the numbers we see on a regular basis. For example, consider the number of yards gained by running backs on football teams. Zero yards actually means that the player has gained no yards at all. If one player has gained 1000 yards and another has gained only 500, then we can say that the first athlete has gained twice as many yards as the second.

Another example is the speed of travel. For instance, 0 miles per hour (mph) is the point at which there is no speed at all. If you are driving onto a highway at 30 mph and increase your speed to 60 when you merge, then you have doubled your speed.

## Permissible Operations

Level of measurement is important because it defines which mathematical operations we can apply to numerical data. For nominal data, each observation can be placed in only one mutually exclusive category. For example, you are a member of only one gender. One can use nominal data to create frequency distributions (see the next section), but no mathematical manipulations of the data are permissible. Ordinal measurements can be manipulated using arithmetic; however, the result is often difficult to interpret because it reflects neither the magnitudes of the manipulated observations nor the true amounts of the property that have been measured. For example, if the heights of 15 children are rank ordered, knowing a given child's rank does not reveal how tall he or she stands. Averages of these ranks are equally uninformative about height.

With interval data, one can apply any arithmetic operation to the differences between scores. The results can be interpreted in relation to the magnitudes of the underlying property. However, interval data cannot be used to make statements about ratios. For example, if IQ is measured on an interval scale, one cannot say that an IQ of 160 is twice as high as an IQ of 80. This mathematical operation is reserved for ratio scales, for which any mathematical operation is permissible.

# Frequency Distributions

A single test score means more if one relates it to other test scores. A *distribution* of scores summarizes the scores for a group of individuals. In testing, there are many ways to record a distribution of scores.

The **frequency distribution** displays scores on a variable or a measure to reflect how frequently each value was obtained. With a frequency distribution, one defines all the possible scores and determines how many people obtained each of those scores. Usually, scores are arranged on the horizontal axis from the lowest to the highest value. The vertical axis reflects how many times each of the values on the horizontal axis was observed. For most distributions of test scores, the frequency distribution is bell-shaped, with the greatest frequency of scores toward the center of the distribution and decreasing scores as the values become greater or less than the value in the center of the distribution.

Figure 2.2 shows a frequency distribution of 1000 observations that takes on values between 61 and 90. Notice that the most frequent observations fall toward the center of the distribution, around 75 and 76. As you look toward the extremes of the distribution, you will find a systematic decline in the frequency with which the scores occur. For example, the score of 71 is observed less frequently than 72,

**FIGURE 2.2**

Frequency distribution approximating a normal distribution of 1000 observations.

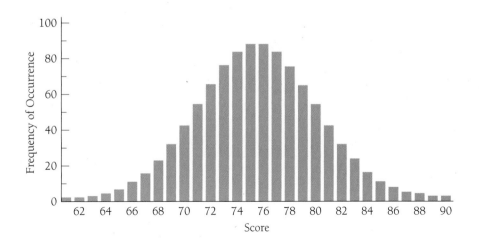

which is observed less frequently than 73, and so on. Similarly, 78 is observed more frequently than 79, which is noted more often than 80, and so forth.

Though this neat symmetric relationship does not characterize all sets of scores, it occurs frequently enough in practice for us to devote special attention to it. We explain this concept in greater detail in the section on the normal distribution.

Table 2.2 lists the rainfall amounts in San Diego, California, between 1964 and 2011. Figure 2.3 is a histogram based on the observations. The distribution is

**TABLE 2.2**  Inches of Rainfall in San Diego, 1964–2011.

| Year | Rainfall (Inches) | Year | Rainfall (Inches) |
|------|------------------|------|------------------|
| 1964 | 5.15 | 1989 | 5.88 |
| 1965 | 8.81 | 1990 | 7.62 |
| 1966 | 14.76 | 1991 | 12.31 |
| 1967 | 10.86 | 1992 | 12.48 |
| 1968 | 7.86 | 1993 | 18.26 |
| 1969 | 11.48 | 1994 | 9.93 |
| 1970 | 6.23 | 1995 | 17.13 |
| 1971 | 8.03 | 1996 | 5.18 |
| 1972 | 6.12 | 1997 | 8.74 |
| 1973 | 10.99 | 1998 | 20.89 |
| 1974 | 6.59 | 1999 | 6.51 |
| 1975 | 10.64 | 2000 | 5.77 |
| 1976 | 10.14 | 2001 | 8.82 |
| 1977 | 9.18 | 2002 | 3.44 |
| 1978 | 17.30 | 2003 | 10.24 |
| 1979 | 14.93 | 2004 | 5.18 |
| 1980 | 15.62 | 2005 | 22.50 |
| 1981 | 8.13 | 2006 | 5.46 |
| 1982 | 11.85 | 2007 | 3.80 |
| 1983 | 18.49 | 2008 | 7.25 |
| 1984 | 5.37 | 2009 | 9.15 |
| 1985 | 9.60 | 2010 | 10.57 |
| 1986 | 14.64 | 2011 | 12.60 |
| 1987 | 9.30 | Mean | 10.30 |
| 1988 | 12.44 | SD | 4.52 |

Data from http://cdec.water.ca.gov/cgi-progs/staMeta?station_id=SDG.

**FIGURE 2.3**

Histogram for San Diego rainfall, 1964–2011.

**FIGURE 2.4**

Frequency polygon for San Diego rainfall, 1964–2011.

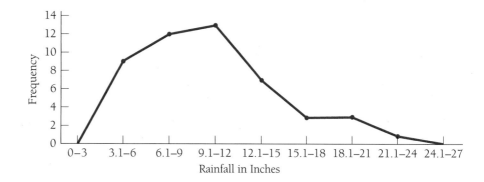

slightly skewed, or asymmetrical. We say that Figure 2.3 has a *positive* skew because the tail goes off toward the higher or positive side of the $X$ axis. There is a slight skew in Figures 2.3 and 2.4, but the asymmetry in these figures is relatively hard to detect. Figure 2.5 gives an example of a distribution that is clearly skewed. The figure summarizes annual household income in the United States in 2010. Very few people make high incomes, while the great bulk of the population is bunched toward the low end of the income distribution. Of particular interest is that this figure only includes household incomes less than $100,000. For household incomes greater than $100,000, the government only reports incomes using class intervals of $50,000. In 2011, about 16% of the U.S. households had incomes greater than $100,000. Because some households have extremely high incomes, you can imagine that the tail of this distribution would go very far to the right. Thus, income is an example of a variable that has positive skew.

One can also present this same set of data as a frequency polygon (see Figure 2.4). Here the amount of rainfall is placed on the graph as a point that represents the frequencies with which each interval occurs. Lines are then drawn to connect these points.

Whenever you draw a frequency distribution or a frequency polygon, you must decide on the width of the class interval. The **class interval** for inches of rainfall is the unit on the horizontal axis. For example, in Figures 2.3 and 2.4, the class interval is 3 inches—that is, the demarcations along the $X$ axis increase in 3-inch

**FIGURE 2.5**

Household income up to $100,000 in the United States for 2010. This is an example of positive skew.

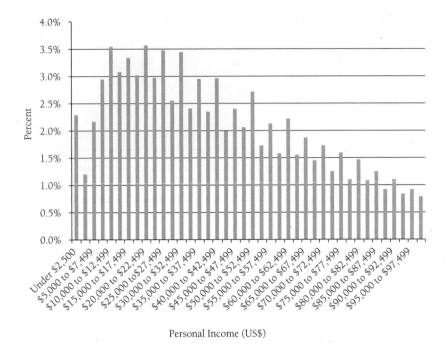

Personal Income (US$)

(Data from the United States Department of Labor Statistics and the Bureau the Census. http://ferret.bls.census.gov/macro/032003/hhinc/new06_000.htm.)

intervals. This interval is used here for convenience; the choice of 3 inches is otherwise arbitrary.

# Percentile Ranks

Percentile ranks replace simple ranks when we want to adjust for the number of scores in a group. A **percentile rank** answers the question, "What percent of the scores fall below a particular score ($X_i$)?" To calculate a percentile rank, you need only follow these simple steps: (1) determine how many cases fall below the score of interest, (2) determine how many cases are in the group, (3) divide the number of cases below the score of interest (Step 1) by the total number of cases in the group (Step 2), and (4) multiply the result of Step 3 by 100.

The formula is

$$P_r = \frac{B}{N} \times 100 = \text{percentile rank of } X_i$$

where

$$P_r = \text{percentile rank}$$
$$X_i = \text{the score of interest}$$
$$B = \text{the number of scores below } X_i$$
$$N = \text{the total number of scores}$$

This means that you form a ratio of the number of cases below the score of interest and the total number of scores. Because there will always be either the same or fewer cases in the numerator (top half) of the equation than there are in the denominator (bottom half), this ratio will always be less than or equal to 1. To get rid of the decimal points, you multiply by 100.

As an example, consider the runner who finishes 62nd out of 63 racers in a gym class. To obtain the percentile rank, divide 1 (the number of people who finish behind the person of interest) by 63 (the number of scores in the group). This gives you 1/63, or .016. Then multiply this result by 100 to obtain the percentile rank, which is 1.6. This rank tells you the runner is below the 2nd percentile.

Now consider the Bay to Breakers race, which attracts 50,000 runners to San Francisco. If you had finished 62nd out of 50,000, then the number of people who were behind you would be 49,938. Dividing this by the number of entrants gives you .9988. When you multiply by 100, you get a percentile rank of 99.88. This tells you that finishing 62nd in the Bay to Breakers race is exceptionally good because it places you in the 99.88th percentile.

Psychological Testing in Everyday Life 2.1 presents the calculation of percentile ranks of the infant mortality rates of selected countries as reported by the Central Intelligence Agency (CIA) in 2011 (based on 2009 data). Infant mortality is defined as the number of babies out of 1000 who are born alive but die before their first birthday. Before proceeding, we should point out that the meaning of this calculation depends on which countries are used in the comparison.

In this example, the calculation of the percentile rank is broken into five steps and uses the raw data in the table. In Step 1, we arrange the data points in ascending order. Singapore has the lowest infant mortality rate (2.31), Japan is next (2.79), and Afghanistan has the highest rate (151.95).

In Step 2, we determine the number of cases with worse rates than that of the case of interest. In this example, the case of interest is the United States. Therefore, we count the number of cases with a worse rate than that of the United States. Ten countries—Saudi Arabia, Colombia, China, Turkey, Morocco, Bolivia, Laos, Ethiopia, Mozambique, and Afghanistan—have infant mortality rates greater than 6.26.

In Step 3, we determine the total number of cases (18).

In Step 4, we divide the number of scores worse than the score of interest by the total number of scores:

$$\frac{10}{18} = .55$$

Technically, the percentile rank is a percentage. Step 4 gives a proportion. Therefore, in Step 5 you transform this into a whole number by multiplying by 100:

$$.55 \times 100 = 55$$

Thus, the United States is in the 55th percentile.

The percentile rank depends absolutely on the cases used for comparison. In this example, you calculated that the United States is in the 55th percentile for

## 2.1 / PSYCHOLOGICAL TESTING IN EVERYDAY LIFE

### Infant Mortality in Selected Countries, 2011

| Country | 1000 Live Births |
| --- | --- |
| Afghanistan | 151.95 |
| Australia | 4.75 |
| Bolivia | 44.96 |
| China | 20.25 |
| Colombia | 18.90 |
| Ethiopia | 80.80 |
| France | 3.33 |
| Israel | 4.22 |
| Italy | 5.51 |
| Japan | 2.79 |
| Laos | 77.82 |
| Morocco | 36.88 |
| Mozambique | 105.80 |
| Saudi Arabia | 11.57 |
| Singapore | 2.31 |
| Spain | 4.21 |
| Turkey | 25.78 |
| United States | 6.26 |
| Mean | 33.78 |
| SD | 42.99 |

To calculate the percentile rank of infant mortality in the United States in comparison to that in selected countries, use the following formula:

$$P_r = \frac{B}{N} \times 100$$

where

$P_r$ = the percentile rank

$B$ = the number of cases with worse rates than the case of interest

$N$ = the total number of cases

| Country | 1000 Live Births |
|---|---|
| Singapore | 2.31 |
| Japan | 2.79 |
| France | 3.33 |
| Spain | 4.21 |
| Israel | 4.22 |
| Australia | 4.75 |
| Italy | 5.51 |
| United States | 6.26 |
| Saudi Arabia | 11.57 |
| Colombia | 18.90 |
| China | 20.25 |
| Turkey | 25.78 |
| Morocco | 36.88 |
| Bolivia | 44.96 |
| Laos | 77.82 |
| Ethiopia | 80.80 |
| Mozambique | 105.80 |
| Afghanistan | 151.95 |

**Steps**

1. Arrange data in ascending order—that is, the lowest score first, the second lowest score second, and so on.

$$N = 18, \text{ mean} = 33.78, \text{ standard deviation} = 42.99$$

2. Determine the number of cases with worse rates than the score of interest. There are 10 countries in this sample with infant mortality rates greater than that in the United States.
3. Determine the number of cases in the sample (18).
4. Divide the number of scores worse than the score of interest (Step 2) by the total number of scores (Step 3):

$$\frac{10}{18} = .55$$

5. Multiply by 100:

$$0.55 \times 100 = 55\text{th percentile rank}$$

infant mortality within this group of countries. If all countries in the world had been included, then the ranking of the United States have been different.[1]

Using this procedure, try to calculate the percentile rank for Bolivia. The calculation is the same, except that there are four countries with worse rates than Bolivia (as opposed to 11 worse than the United States). Thus, the percentile rank for Bolivia is

$$\frac{4}{18} = .22 \times 100 = 22$$

or the 22nd percentile. Now try France. You should get a percentile rank of 83.

# Percentiles

Percentiles are the specific scores or points within a distribution. Percentiles divide the total frequency for a set of observations into hundredths. Instead of indicating what percentage of scores fall below a particular score, as percentile ranks do, percentiles indicate the particular score, below which a defined percentage of scores falls.

Try to calculate the percentile and percentile rank for some of the data in Psychological Testing in Everyday Life 2.1. As an example, look at Italy. The infant mortality rate in Italy is 5.51/1000. When calculating the percentile rank, you exclude the score of interest and count those below (in other words, Italy is

---

[1]We put these numbers together for an example, but it is not representative of all countries in the world. The complete CIA data set includes 224 counties, among them, the United States ranks 46th in infant mortality. So, the United States is in about the 21st percentile among all nations (46/224 = 0.205). Further, the distribution of infant mortality is highly skewed, with many counties having low rates and a few having high rates. The following graph presents a complete and more accurate picture.

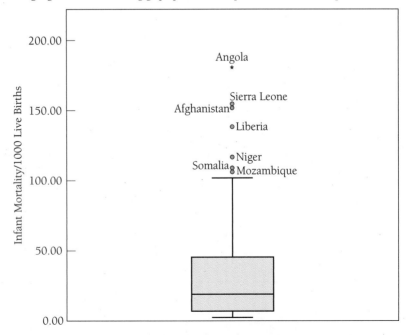

not included in the count). There are 11 countries in this sample with infant mortality rates worse than Italy's. To calculate the percentile rank, divide this number of countries by the total number of cases and multiply by 100:

$$P_r = \frac{B}{N} \times 100 = \frac{11}{18} \times 100 = .61 \times 100 = 61$$

Thus, Italy is in the 61st percentile rank, or the 61st percentile in this example is 5.51/1000 or 5.51 deaths per 1000 live births.

Now take the example of Israel. The calculation of percentile rank requires looking at the number of cases below the case of interest. In this example, 13 countries in this group have infant mortality rates worse than Israel's. Thus, the percentile rank for Israel is 13/18 × 100 = 72. The 72nd percentile corresponds with the point or score of 6.75 (6.75/1000 live births).

In summary, the percentile and the percentile rank are similar. The percentile gives the point in a distribution below which a specified percentage of cases fall (4.22/1000 for Israel). The percentile is in raw score units. The percentile rank gives the percentage of cases below the percentile; in this example, the percentile rank is 56.

When reporting percentiles and percentile ranks, you must carefully specify the population you are working with. Remember that a percentile rank is a measure of relative performance. When interpreting a percentile rank, you should always ask the question, "Relative to what?" Suppose, for instance, that you finished in the 17th percentile in a swimming race (or fifth in a heat of six competitors). Does this mean that you are a slow swimmer? Not necessarily. It may be that this was a heat in the Olympic games, and the participants were the fastest swimmers in the world. An Olympic swimmer competing against a random sample of all people in the world would probably finish in the 99.99th percentile. The example for infant mortality rates depends on which countries in the world were selected for comparison. The United States actually does quite poorly when compared with European countries and the advanced economies in Asia (Singapore and Japan). However, the U.S. infant mortality rate looks much better compared with countries in the developing world.

# Describing Distributions

## Mean

Statistics are used to summarize data. If you consider a set of scores, the mass of information may be too much to interpret all at once. That is why we need numerical conveniences to help summarize the information. An example of a set of scores that can be summarized is shown in Table 2.2 (see page 32): amounts of rainfall in San Diego. We signify the variable as $X$. A *variable* is a score that can have different values. The amount of rain is a variable because different amounts of rain fell in different years.

The arithmetic average score in a distribution is called the **mean**. To calculate the mean, we total the scores and divide the sum by the number of cases, or $N$. The capital Greek letter sigma ($\Sigma$) means summation. Thus, the formula for the mean, which we signify as $\overline{X}$ is

$$\overline{X} = \frac{\Sigma X}{N}$$

In words, this formula says to total the scores and divide the sum by the number of cases. Using the information in Table 2.2, we find the mean by following these steps:

1. Obtain $\Sigma X$, or the sum of the scores: $5.15 + 8.81 + 14.76 + 10.86 + 7.86 + \cdots + 12.60 = 494.22$

2. Find $N$, or the number of scores:

$$N = 48$$

3. Divide $\Sigma X$ by $N$: $494.22/48 = 10.30$

Psychological Testing in Everyday Life 2.2 summarizes common symbols used in basic statistics.

## Standard Deviation

The standard deviation is an approximation of the average deviation around the mean. The standard deviation for the amount of rainfall in San Diego is 4.52. To understand rainfall in San Diego, you need to consider at least two dimensions: first, the amount of rain that falls in a particular year; second, the degree of variation from year to year in the amount of rain that falls. The calculation suggests that, on the average, the variation around the mean is approximately 4.52 inches.

However informative, knowing the mean of a group of scores does not give you that much information. As an illustration, look at the following sets of numbers.

| Set 1 | Set 2 | Set 3 |
|:-----:|:-----:|:-----:|
| 4 | 5 | 8 |
| 4 | 5 | 8 |
| 4 | 4 | 6 |
| 4 | 4 | 2 |
| 4 | 3 | 0 |
| 4 | 3 | 0 |

Calculate the mean of the first set. You should get 4. What is the mean of the second set? If you calculate correctly, you should get 4 again. Next find the mean for Set 3. It is also 4. The three distributions of scores appear quite different but have the same mean, so it is important to consider other characteristics of the distribution of scores besides the mean. The difference between the three sets lies in *variability*. There is no variability in Set 1, a small amount in Set 2, and a lot in Set 3.

### 2.2 PSYCHOLOGICAL TESTING IN EVERYDAY LIFE

**Common Symbols**

You need to understand and recognize the symbols used throughout this book. $\overline{X}$ is the mean; it is pronounced "X bar." $\Sigma$ is the summation sign. It means sum, or add, scores together and is the capital Greek letter sigma. $X$ is a variable that takes on different values. Each value of $X_i$ represents a raw score, also called an *obtained score*.

Measuring this variation is similar to finding the average deviation around the mean. One way to measure variability is to subtract the mean from each score $(X - \overline{X})$ and then total the deviations. Statisticians often signify this with a lowercase $x$, as in $x = (X - \overline{X})$. Try this for the data in Table 2.2. Did you get 0? You should have, and this is not an unusual example. In fact, the sum of the deviations around the mean will always equal 0. However, you do have an alternative: You can square all the deviations around the mean in order to get rid of any negative signs. Then you can obtain the average squared deviation around the mean, known as the **variance**. The formula for the variance is

$$\sigma^2 = \frac{\Sigma(X - \overline{X})^2}{N}$$

where $(X - \overline{X})$ is the deviation of a score from the mean. The symbol $\sigma$ is the lowercase Greek sigma; $\sigma^2$ is used as a standard description of the variance.

Though the variance is a useful statistic commonly used in data analysis, it shows the variable in squared deviations around the mean rather than in deviations around the mean. In other words, the variance is the average squared deviation around the mean. To get it back into the units that will make sense to us, we need to take the square root of the variance. The square root of the variance is the standard deviation $(\sigma)$, and it is represented by the following formula:

$$\sigma = \sqrt{\frac{\Sigma(X - \overline{X})^2}{N}}$$

The **standard deviation** is thus the square root of the average squared deviation around the mean. Although the standard deviation is not an average deviation, it gives a useful approximation of how much a typical score is above or below the average score.

Because of their mathematical properties, the variance and the standard deviation have many advantages. For example, knowing the standard deviation of a normally distributed batch of data allows us to make precise statements about the distribution. The formulas just presented are for computing the variance and the standard deviation of a population. That is why we use the lowercase Greek sigma ($\sigma$ and $\sigma^2$). Psychological Testing in Everyday Life 2.3 summarizes when you should use Greek and Roman letters. Most often we use the standard deviation for a sample to estimate the standard deviation for a population. When we talk about a sample, we replace the Greek $\sigma$ with a Roman letter $S$. Also, we divide by $N - 1$ rather than $N$ to recognize that $S$ of a sample is only an estimate of the variance of the population.

$$S = \sqrt{\frac{\Sigma(X - \overline{X})^2}{N - 1}}$$

In calculating the standard deviation, it is often easier to use the raw score equivalent formula, which is

$$S = \sqrt{\frac{\Sigma X^2 - \dfrac{(\Sigma X)^2}{N}}{N - 1}}$$

This calculation can also be done automatically by some minicalculators, iPhones, or Excel.

**Terms and Symbols Used to Describe Populations and Samples**

|  | Population | Sample |
|---|---|---|
| Definition | All elements with the same definition | A subset of the population, usually drawn to represen it in an unbiased fashion |
| Descriptive characteristics | Parameters | Statistics |
| Symbols used to describe | Greek | Roman |
| Symbol for mean | $\mu$ | $\overline{X}$ |
| Symbol for standard deviation | $\sigma$ | $S$ |

In reading the formula, you may be confused by a few points. In particular, be careful not to confuse $\Sigma X^2$ and $(\Sigma X)^2$. To get $\Sigma X^2$, each individual score is squared and the values are summed. For the scores 3, 5, 7, and 8, $\Sigma X^2$ would be $3^2 + 5^2 + 7^2 + 8^2 = 9 + 25 + 49 + 64 = 147$. To obtain $(\Sigma X)^2$, the scores are first summed and the total is squared. Using the example, $(\Sigma X)^2 = (3 + 5 + 7 + 8)^2 = 23^2 = 529$.

## Z Score

One problem with means and standard deviations is that they do not convey enough information for us to make meaningful assessments or accurate interpretations of data. Other metrics are designed for more exact interpretations. The $Z$ score transforms data into standardized units that are easier to interpret. A $Z$ score is the difference between a score and the mean, divided by the standard deviation:

$$Z = \frac{X_i - \overline{X}}{S}$$

In other words, a $Z$ score is the deviation of a score $X_i$ from the mean in standard deviation units. If a score is equal to the mean, then its $Z$ score is 0. For example, suppose the score and the mean are both 6; then $6 - 6 = 0$. Zero divided by anything is still 0. If the score is greater than the mean, then the $Z$ score is positive; if the score is less than the mean, then the $Z$ score is negative.

Let's try an example. Suppose that $X_i = 6$, the mean $\overline{X} = 3$, and the standard deviation $S = 3$. Plugging these values into the formula, we get

$$Z = \frac{6 - 3}{3} = \frac{3}{3} = 1$$

Let's try another example. Suppose $X_i = 4$, $\overline{X} = 5.75$, and $S = 2.11$. What is the $Z$ score? It is $-.83$:

$$Z = \frac{4 - 5.75}{2.11} = \frac{-1.74}{2.11} = -.83$$

This means that the score we observed (4) is .83 standard deviation below the average score, or that the score is below the mean but its difference from the mean is slightly less than the average deviation.

### Example of Depression in Medical Students: Center for Epidemiologic Studies Depression Scale (CES-D)

The CES-D is a general measure of depression that has been used extensively in epidemiological studies. The scale includes 20 items and taps dimensions of depressed mood, hopelessness, appetite loss, sleep disturbance, and energy level. Each year, students at the University of California, San Diego, School of Medicine are asked to report how often they experienced a particular symptom during the first week of school on a 4-point scale ranging from rarely or none of the time [0 to 1 days (0)] to most or all of the time [5 to 7 days (3)]. Items 4, 8, 12, and 16 on the CES-D are reverse scored. For these items, 0 is scored as 3, 1 is scored as 2, 2 as 1, and 3 as 0. The CES-D score is obtained by summing the circled numbers. Scores on the CES-D range from 0 to 60, with scores greater than 16 indicating clinically significant levels of depressive symptomatology in adults.

Feel free to take the CES-D measure yourself. Calculate your score by summing the numbers you have circled. However, you must first reverse the scores on items 4, 8, 12, and 16. As you will see in Chapter 5, the CES-D does not have high validity for determining clinical depression. If your score is less than 16, the evidence suggests that you are not clinically depressed. If your score is high, it raises suspicions about depression—though this does not mean you have a problem. (Of course, you may want to talk with your college counselor if you are feeling depressed.)

Table 2.3 shows CES-D scores for a selected sample of medical students. You can use these data to practice calculating means, standard deviations, and Z scores.

In creating the frequency distribution for the CES-D scores of medical students, we used an arbitrary class interval of 5.

## Standard Normal Distribution

Now we consider the standard normal distribution because it is central to statistics and psychological testing. However, you should first participate in a short exercise. Take any coin and flip it 10 times. Repeat this exercise of 10 coin flips 25 times. Record the number of heads you observe in each group of 10 flips. When you are done, make a frequency distribution showing how many times you observed 1 head in your 10 flips, 2 heads, 3 heads, and so on.

Your frequency distribution might look like the example shown in Figure 2.6. The most frequently observed events are approximately equal numbers of heads and tails. Toward the extremes of 10 heads and 0 tails or 10 tails and 0 heads, events are observed with decreasing frequency. For example, there were no occasions in which fewer than 2 heads were observed and only one occasion in which more than 8 heads were observed. This is what we would expect from the laws of probability. On the average, we would expect half of the flips to show heads and half to show tails if heads and tails are equally probable events. Although observing a long string of heads or tails is possible,

# Center for Epidemiologic Studies Depression Scale (CES-D)

**Instructions:** *Circle the number for each statement that best describes how often you felt or behaved this way DURING THE PAST WEEK.*

| | Rarely or none of the time (less than 1 day) | Some or a little of the time (1–2 days) | Occasionally or a moderate amount of the time (3–4 days) | Most or all of the time (5–7 days) |
|---|---|---|---|---|
| 1. I was bothered by things that usually don't bother me | 0 | .......1 | .......2 | .......3 |
| 2. I did not feel like eating | 0 | .......1 | .......2 | .......3 |
| 3. I felt that I could not shake off the blues even with help from my family or friends | 0 | .......1 | .......2 | .......3 |
| R 4. I felt that I was just as good as other people | 0 | .......1 | .......2 | .......3 |
| 5. I had trouble keeping my mind on what I was doing | 0 | .......1 | .......2 | .......3 |
| 6. I felt depressed | 0 | .......1 | .......2 | .......3 |
| 7. I felt that everything I did was an effort. | 0 | .......1 | .......2 | .......3 |
| R 8. I felt hopeful about the future | 0 | .......1 | .......2 | .......3 |
| 9. I thought my life had been a failure | 0 | .......1 | .......2 | .......3 |
| 10. I felt fearful | 0 | .......1 | .......2 | .......3 |
| 11. My sleep was restless | 0 | .......1 | .......2 | .......3 |
| R 12. I was happy | 0 | .......1 | .......2 | .......3 |
| 13. I talked less than usual | 0 | .......1 | .......2 | .......3 |
| 14. I felt lonely | 0 | .......1 | .......2 | .......3 |
| 15. People were unfriendly | 0 | .......1 | .......2 | .......3 |
| R 16. I enjoyed life | 0 | .......1 | .......2 | .......3 |
| 17. I had crying spells | 0 | .......1 | .......2 | .......3 |
| 18. I felt sad | 0 | .......1 | .......2 | .......3 |
| 19. I felt that people disliked me | 0 | .......1 | .......2 | .......3 |
| 20. I could not get "going." | 0 | .......1 | .......2 | .......3 |

**TABLE 2.3** The Calculation of Mean, Standard Deviation, and $Z$ Scores for CES-D Scores

| Name | Test score ($X$) | $X^2$ | $Z$ score |
|------|------------------|-------|-----------|
| John | 14 | 196 | .42 |
| Carla | 10 | 100 | −.15 |
| Fred | 8 | 64 | −.44 |
| Monica | 8 | 64 | −.44 |
| Eng | 26 | 676 | −.13 |
| Fritz | 0 | 0 | −1.58 |
| Mary | 14 | 196 | .42 |
| Susan | 3 | 9 | −1.15 |
| Debbie | 9 | 81 | −.29 |
| Elizabeth | 10 | 100 | −.15 |
| Sarah | 7 | 49 | −.58 |
| Marcel | 12 | 144 | .14 |
| Robin | 10 | 100 | −.15 |
| Mike | 25 | 625 | 1.99 |
| Carl | 9 | 81 | .29 |
| Phyllis | 12 | 144 | .14 |
| Jennie | 23 | 529 | 1.70 |
| Richard | 7 | 49 | −.58 |
| Tyler | 13 | 169 | .28 |
| Frank | 1 | 1 | −1.43 |
|  | $\Sigma X = 221$ | $\Sigma X^2 = 3377$ |  |

$$\overline{X} = \frac{\Sigma X}{N} = \frac{221}{20} = 11.05$$

$$S = \sqrt{\frac{\Sigma X^2 - \frac{(\Sigma X)^2}{N}}{N-1}} = \sqrt{\frac{3377 - \frac{(22)^2}{20}}{20-1}} = 7.01$$

$$\text{Monica's } Z \text{ score} = \frac{X - \overline{X}}{S} = \frac{8 - 11.05}{7.01} = -.44$$

$$\text{Marcel's } Z \text{ score} = \frac{X - \overline{X}}{S} = \frac{12 - 11.05}{7.01} = .14$$

$$\text{Jennie's } Z \text{ score} = \frac{X - \overline{X}}{S} = \frac{23 - 11.05}{7.01} = 1.70$$

it is improbable. In other words, we sometimes see the coin come up heads in 9 out of 10 flips. The likelihood that this will happen, however, is quite small.

Figure 2.7 shows the theoretical distribution of heads in an infinite number of flips of the coin. This figure might look a little like the distribution from your coin-flipping exercise or the distribution shown in Figure 2.6. Actually, this is a normal distribution, or what is known as a *symmetrical binomial probability distribution*.

On most occasions, we refer to units on the $X$ (or horizontal) axis of the normal distribution in $Z$ score units. Any variable transformed into $Z$ score units takes on special properties. First, $Z$ scores have a mean of 0 and a standard deviation of 1.0. If you think about this for a minute, you should be able to figure out why this is true. Recall that the sum of the deviations around the mean is always equal to 0. The numerator of the $Z$ score equation is the deviation around the mean, while the denominator is a constant. Thus, the mean of $Z$ scores can be expressed as

$$\frac{\Sigma(X_i - \overline{X})/S}{N} \text{ or } \frac{\Sigma Z}{N}$$

Because $\Sigma(X_i - \overline{X})$ will always equal 0, the mean of $Z$ scores will always be 0. In Figure 2.7, the standardized, or $Z$ score, units are marked on the $X$ axis. The numbers under the curve are the proportions of cases (in decimal form) that we would expect to observe in each area. Multiplying these proportions by 100 yields percentages. For example, we see that 34.13% or .3413 of the cases fall between the mean and one standard deviation above the mean. Do not forget that 50% of

**FIGURE 2.6**

Frequency distribution of the number of heads in 25 sets of 10 flips.

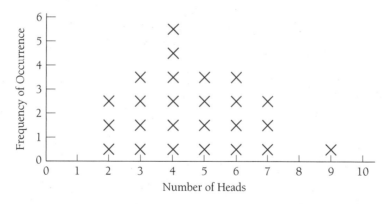

**FIGURE 2.7**

The theoretical distribution of the number of heads in an infinite number of coin flips.

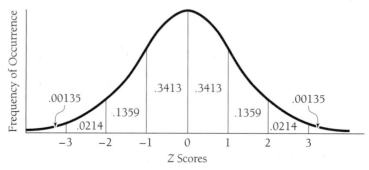

the cases fall below the mean. Putting these two bits of information together, we can conclude that if a score is one standard deviation above the mean, then it is at about the 84th percentile rank (50 + 34.13 = 84.13 to be exact). A score that is one standard deviation below the mean would be about the 16th percentile rank (50 − 34.13 = 15.87). Thus, you can use what you have learned about means, standard deviations, $Z$ scores, and the normal curve to transform raw scores, which have little meaning, into percentile scores, which are easier to interpret. These methods can be used only when the distribution of scores is normal or approximately normal. Methods for nonnormal distributions are discussed in most statistics books under "nonparametric statistics."

### Percentiles and Z Scores

These percentile ranks are the percentage of scores that fall below the observed $Z$ score. For example, the $Z$ score −1.6 is associated with the percentile rank of 5.48. The $Z$ score 1.0 (third column) is associated with the percentile rank of 84.13.

Part I of Appendix 1 is a simplified version of Part II, which you need for more advanced use of $Z$ scores. Part II gives the areas between the mean and various $Z$ scores. Standard scored values are listed in the "$Z$" column. To find the proportion of the distribution between the mean of the distribution and a given $Z$ score, you must locate the entry indicated by a specific $Z$ score. $Z$ scores are carried to a second decimal place in the columns that go across the table. First, consider the second column of the table because it is similar to Part I of Appendix 1. Take the $Z$ score of 1.0. The second column is labeled .00, which means that the second decimal place is also 0. The number listed in the table is .3413. Because this is a positive number, it is above the mean. Because the area below the mean is .5, the total area below a $Z$ score of 1.0 is .5 + .3413 = .8413. To make this into a percentile (as shown in Part I of the appendix), multiply by 100 to get 84.13. Now try the example of a $Z$ score of 1.64. To locate this value, find 1.6 in the first column. Then move your hand across the row until you get to the number below the heading .04. The number is .4495. Again, this is a positive $Z$ score, so you must add the observed proportion to the .5 that falls below the mean. The proportion below 1.64 is .9495. Stated another way, 94.95% of the cases fall below a $Z$ score of 1.64. Now try to find the percentile rank of cases that fall below a $Z$ score of 1.10. If you are using the table correctly, you should obtain 86.43.

Now try −.75. Because this is a negative $Z$ score, the percentage of cases falling below the mean should be less than 50. But there are no negative values in Part II of Appendix 1. For a negative $Z$ score, there are several ways to obtain the appropriate area under the curve. The tables in Appendix 1 give the area from the mean to the $Z$ score. For a $Z$ score of −.75, the area between the mean and the $Z$ score is .2734. You can find this by entering the table in the row labeled .7 and then moving across the row until you get to the figure in that row below the heading .05. There you should find the number .2734. We know that .5 of the cases fall below the mean. Thus, for a negative $Z$ score, we can obtain the proportion of cases falling below the score by subtracting .2734, the tabled value listed in the appendix, from .5. In this case, the result is

$$.5 − .2734 = .2266$$

Because finding the percentile ranks associated with negative $Z$ scores can be tricky, you might want to use Part I of Appendix 1 to see if you are in the right ballpark. This table gives both negative and positive $Z$ scores but does not give the detail associated with the second decimal place. Look up −.7 in Part I. The percentile rank is 24.20. Now consider a $Z$ score of −.8. That percentile rank is 21.19. Thus, you know that a $Z$ score of −.75 should be associated with a percentile rank between 21.19 and 24.20. In fact, we have calculated that the actual percentile rank is 22.66.

Practice with Appendix 1 until you are confident you understand how it works. Do not hesitate to ask your professor or teaching assistant if you are confused. This is an important concept that you will need throughout the rest of the book. After you have mastered using the Tables in Appendix 1, you might try a nifty website (http://davidmlane.com/hyperstat/z_table.html) that can find the probabilities for you.

Look at one more example from Table 2.2 (rainfall in San Diego, page 32). California had a dry year in 1999 and in 2007. In both years, the newscasters frequently commented that this was highly unusual. They described it as the "La Niña" effect; some even claimed that it signaled global warming. The question is whether the amount of rainfall received in 1999 and 2007 was unusual given what we know about rainfall in general. To evaluate this, calculate the $Z$ score for rainfall. According to Table 2.2, there were 6.51 inches of rainfall in 1999 and 3.8 inches in 2007. The mean for rainfall is 10.30 inches and the standard deviation is 4.52. Thus, the $Z$ score for 1999 is

$$\frac{6.51 - 10.30}{4.52} = -0.84$$

Next determine where a $Z$ score of −.84 falls within the $Z$ distribution. According to Appendix 1, a $Z$ score of −.84 is equal to the 20th percentile (.5 − .2995 = .2005). Thus, the low rainfall year in 1999 was unusual—given all years, it was in about the 20th percentile. However, it was not *that* unusual. You can estimate that there would be less rainfall in approximately 20% of all years. 2007 was a different case. The $Z$ score for 2007 was −1.44. This is obtained by subtracting the mean rainfall (10.30) from the 2007 value (3.80) and dividing by the standard deviation of rainfall (4.52).

$$(3.80 - 10.30)/4.52 = -1.44$$

Rainfall in 2007 was in the 7.49th percentile. (Using Appendix 1, you can look up the $Z$ score of −1.44 and find an area below the mean of 0.4236. Then you can estimate the percentile as 50 − 42.51 = 7.49.)

You can also turn the process around. Instead of using $Z$ scores to find the percentile ranks, you can use the percentile ranks to find the corresponding $Z$ scores. To do this, look in Part II of Appendix 1 under percentiles and find the corresponding $Z$ score. For example, suppose you wish to find the $Z$ score associated with the 90th percentile. When you enter Part II of Appendix 1, look for the value closest to the 90th percentile. This can be a little tricky because of the way the table is structured. Because the 90th percentile is associated with a positive $Z$ score, you are actually looking for the area above the 50th percentile. So you should look for the entry closest to .4000 (.5000 + .4000 = .9000). The closest value to .4000 is .3997, which is found in the row labeled 1.2 and the column labeled .08. This tells you that a person who obtains a $Z$ score of 1.28 is at approximately the 90th percentile in the distribution.

Now return to the example of CES-D scores for medical students (Table 2.3). Monica had a $Z$ score on the CES-D of $-.44$. Using Appendix 1, you can see that she was in the 33rd percentile (obtained as $.50 - .1700 = .33 \times 100 = 33$). Marcel, with his $Z$ score of .14, was in the 56th percentile; and Jennie, with a $Z$ score of 1.70, was in the 96th percentile. You might have few worries about Monica and Marcel. However, it appears that Jennie is more depressed than 96% of her classmates and may need to talk to someone.

### An Example Close to Home

One of the difficulties in grading students is that performance is usually rated in terms of raw scores, such as the number of items a person correctly answers on an examination. You are probably familiar with the experience of having a test returned to you with some number that makes little sense to you. For instance, the professor comes into class and hands you your test with a 72 on it. You must then wait patiently while he or she draws the distribution on the board and tries to put your 72 into some category that you understand, such as B+.

An alternative way of doing things would be to give you a $Z$ score as feedback on your performance. To do this, your professor would subtract the average score (mean) from your score and divide by the standard deviation. If your $Z$ score was positive, you would immediately know that your score was above average; if it was negative, you would know your performance was below average.

Suppose your professor tells you in advance that you will be graded on a curve according to the following rigid criteria. If you are in the top 15% of the class, you will get an A (85th percentile or above); between the 60th and the 84th percentiles, a B; between the 20th and the 59th percentiles, a C; between the 6th and the 19th percentiles, a D; and in the 5th percentile or below, an F. Using Appendix 1, you should be able to find the $Z$ scores associated with each of these cutoff points for normal distributions of scores. Try it on your own and then consult Table 2.4 to see if you are correct. Looking at Table 2.4, you should be able to determine what your grade would be in this class on the basis of your $Z$ score. If your $Z$ score is 1.04 or greater, you would receive an A; if it were greater than .25 but less than 1.04, you would get a B; and so on. This system assumes that the scores are distributed normally.

Now try an example that puts a few of these concepts together. Suppose you get a 60 on a social psychology examination. You learned in class that the mean

**TABLE 2.4**  *Z* Score Cutoffs for a Grading System

| Grade | Percentiles | Z score cutoff |
|-------|-------------|----------------|
| A | 85–100 | 1.04 |
| B | 60–84 | .25 |
| C | 20–59 | −.84 |
| D | 6–19 | −1.56 |
| F | 0–5 | <−1.56 |

for the test was 55.70 and that the standard deviation was 6.08. If your professor uses the grading system that was just described, what would your grade be?

To solve this problem, first find your $Z$ score. Recall the formula for a $Z$ score:

$$Z = \frac{X_i - \overline{X}}{S}$$

So your $Z$ score would be

$$Z = \frac{60 - 55.70}{6.08} = \frac{4.30}{6.08} = .707$$

Looking at Table 2.4, you see that .707 is greater than .25 (the cutoff for a B) but less than 1.04 (the cutoff for an A). Now find your exact standing in the class. To do this, look again at Appendix 1. Because the table gives $Z$ scores only to the second decimal, round .707 to .71. You will find that 76.11% of the scores fall below a $Z$ score of .71. This means that you would be in approximately the 76th percentile, or you would have performed better on this examination than approximately 76 out of every 100 students.

## McCall's *T*

There are many other systems by which one can transform raw scores to give them more intuitive meaning. One system was established in 1939 by W. A. McCall, who originally intended to develop a system to derive equal units on mental quantities. He suggested that a random sample of 12-year-olds be tested and that the distribution of their scores be obtained. Then percentile equivalents were to be assigned to each raw score, showing the percentile rank in the group for the people who had obtained that raw score. After this had been accomplished, the mean of the distribution would be set at 50 to correspond with the 50th percentile. In McCall's system, called **McCall's *T***, the standard deviation was set at 10.

In effect, McCall generated a system that is exactly the same as standard scores ($Z$ scores), except that the mean in McCall's system is 50 rather than 0 and the standard deviation is 10 rather than 1. Indeed, a $Z$ score can be transformed to a **T score** by applying the linear transformation

$$T = 10Z + 50$$

You can thus get from a $Z$ score to McCall's $T$ by multiplying the $Z$ score by 10 and adding 50. It should be noted that McCall did not originally intend to create an alternative to the $Z$ score. He wanted to obtain one set of scores that could then be applied to other situations without standardizing the entire set of numbers.

There is nothing magical about the mean of 50 and the standard deviation of 10. It is a simple matter to create systems such as standard scores with any mean and standard deviation you like. If you want to say that you got a score 1000 points higher than a person who was one standard deviation below you, then you could devise a system with a mean of 100,000 and a standard deviation of 1000. If you had calculated $Z$ scores for this distribution, then you would obtain this with the transformation

$$NS \text{ (for new score)} = 1000Z + 100,000$$

In fact, you can create any system you desire. To do so, just multiply the $Z$ score by whatever you would like the standard deviation of your distribution to be and then add the number you would like the mean of your new distribution to be.

An example of a test developed using standardized scores is the SAT Reasoning Test. When this test was created in 1941, the developers decided to make the mean score 500 and the standard deviation 100. Thus, they multiplied the $Z$ scores for those who took the test by 100 and added 500. For a long time, the basic scoring system was used and the 1941 norms were applied. In other words, if the average score of test takers was below the 1941 reference point, the mean for any year could be less than or more than 500. However, in 1995, the test was changed so that the mean each year would be 500 and the standard deviation would be 100. In other words, the test is recalibrated each year. However, drifts continue. For example, in 2011 the average scores on the SAT were 510 for writing, 508 for critical reading and 520 for math (data from www.collegeboard.com).

It is important to make the distinction between standardization and normalization. McCall's $T$ and the other methods described in this section standardize scores by applying a linear transformation. These transformations do not change the characteristics of the distributions. If a distribution of scores is skewed before the transformation is applied, it will also be skewed after the transformation has been used. In other words, transformations standardize but do not normalize.

## Quartiles and Deciles

The terms *quartiles* and *deciles* are frequently used when tests and test results are discussed. The two terms refer to divisions of the percentile scale into groups. The quartile system divides the percentage scale into four groups, whereas the decile system divides the scale into 10 groups.

**Quartiles** are points that divide the frequency distribution into equal fourths. The first quartile is the 25th percentile; the second quartile is the **median**, or 50th, percentile; and the third quartile is the 75th percentile. These are abbreviated Q1, Q2, and Q3, respectively. One fourth of the cases will fall below Q1, one half will fall below Q2, and three fourths will fall below Q3. The interquartile range is the interval of scores bounded by the 25th and 75th percentiles. In other words, the **interquartile range** is bounded by the range of scores that represents the middle 50% of the distribution.

**Deciles** are similar to quartiles except that they use points that mark 10% rather than 25% intervals. Thus, the top decile, or D9, is the point below which 90% of the cases fall. The next decile (D8) marks the 80th percentile, and so forth.

Another system developed in the U.S. Air Force during World War II is known as the **stanine system**. This system converts any set of scores into a transformed scale, which ranges from 1 to 9. Actually the term *stanine* comes from "standard nine." The scale is standardized to have a mean of 5 and a standard deviation of approximately 2. It has been suggested that stanines had computational advantages because they required only one column on a computer card (Anastasi & Urbina, 1997). Because computer cards are no longer used, this advantage is now questionable.

Table 2.5 shows how percentile scores are converted into stanines. As you can see, for every 100 scores, the lowest 4 (or bottom 4% of the cases) fall into the first stanine. The next 7 (or 7% of the cases) fall into the second stanine, and so on.

**TABLE 2.5**   Transformation of Percentile Scores into Stanines

| Percentage of cases | Percentiles | Stanines |
|:---:|:---:|:---|
| 4 | 1–4 | 1 Bottom 4 percent |
| 7 | 5–11 | 2 |
| 12 | 12–23 | 3 |
| 17 | 24–40 | 4 |
| 20 | 41–60 | 5 |
| 17 | 61–77 | 6 |
| 12 | 78–89 | 7 |
| 7 | 90–96 | 8 |
| 4 | 97–100 | 9 Top 4 percent |

Finally, the top 4 cases fall into the top stanine. Using what you have learned about $Z$ scores and the standard normal distribution, you should be able to figure out the stanine for a score if you know the mean and the standard deviation of the distribution that the score comes from. For example, suppose that Igor received a 48 on his normally distributed chemistry midterm. The mean in Igor's class was 42.6, and the standard deviation was 3.6. First you must find Igor's $Z$ score. Do this by using the formula

$$Z = \frac{X_i - \overline{X}}{S} \text{ so } Z = \frac{48 - 42.6}{3.6} = 1.5$$

Now you need to transform Igor's $Z$ score into his percentile rank. To do this, use Appendix 1. Part I shows that a $Z$ score of 1.5 is in approximately the 93rd percentile. Thus, it falls into the 8th stanine.

Actually, you would rarely go through all these steps to find a stanine. There are easier ways of doing this, including computer programs that do it automatically. However, working out stanines the long way will help you become familiar with a variety of concepts covered in this chapter, including standard scores, means, standard deviations, and percentiles. First, review the five steps to go from raw scores to stanines:

1. Find the mean of the raw scores.
2. Find the standard deviation of the raw scores.
3. Change the raw scores to $Z$ scores.
4. Change the $Z$ scores to percentiles (using Appendix 1).
5. Use Table 2.5 to convert percentiles into stanines.

An alternative method is to calculate the percentile rank for each score and use Table 2.5 to obtain the stanines. Remember: In practice, you would probably use a computer program to obtain the stanines. Although stanines are not used much in the modern computer era, you can still find them in popular educational tests such as the Stanford Achievement Test.

# Norms

**Norms** refer to the performances by defined groups on particular tests. There are many ways to express norms, and we have discussed some of these under the headings of $Z$ scores, percentiles, and means. The norms for a test are based on the distribution of scores obtained by some defined sample of individuals. The mean is a norm, and the 50th percentile is a norm. Norms are used to give information about performance relative to what has been observed in a standardization sample.

Much has been written about norms and their inadequacies. In later chapters, we shall discuss this material in relation to particular tests. We cover only the highlights here. Whenever you see a norm for a test, you should ask how it was established. Norms are obtained by administering the test to a sample of people and obtaining the distribution of scores for that group.

For example, say you develop a measure of anxiety associated with taking tests in college. After establishing some psychometric properties for the test, you administer the test to normative groups of college students. The scores of these groups of students might then serve as the norms. Say that, for the normative groups of students, the average score is 19. When your friend Alice comes to take the test and obtains a score of 24, the psychologist using the test might conclude that Alice is above average in test anxiety.

The SAT, as indicated earlier, has norms. The test was administered to millions of high-school seniors from all over the United States. With distributions of scores for this normative group, one could obtain a distribution to provide meaning for particular categories of scores. For example, in the 1941 national sample, a person who scored 650 on the verbal portion of the SAT was at the 93rd percentile of high-school seniors. However, if you took the test before 1995 and scored 650, it did not mean that you were in the 93rd percentile of the people who took the test when you did. Rather, it meant that you would have been at the 93rd percentile if you had been in the group the test had been standardized on. However, if the normative group was a representative sample of the group to which you belonged (and there is every reason to believe it was), then you could reasonably assume that you were in approximately the 93rd percentile of your own group.[2] After 1995, an SAT score of 650 would place you in the 93rd percentile of the people who took the test during the year you completed it. Some controversies surrounding norms are discussed in Psychological Testing in Everyday Life 2.4.

In Chapters 10 and 11, we will review intelligence tests. Most intelligence tests are transformed to have a mean of 100 and a standard deviation of 15. Thus, an IQ score of 115 is one standard deviation above the mean and an IQ score of 130 is two standard deviations above the mean. Using the information we have reviewed, you can determine that an IQ score of 115 is approximately in the 84th percentile, while an IQ score of 85 is approximately in the 16th percentile. Only some 0.13% of the population obtains an IQ score of 145, which is three standard deviations above the mean. Figure 2.8 shows the standard normal distribution with the $Z$ scores, $T$ scores, IQ scores, and stanines. Examining the figure, locate the

---

[2] Based on the *American Testing Program Guide for 1989–1991*, College Board of the Educational Testing Service, Princeton, New Jersey.

FIGURE 2.8

Standard normal
distribution with
cumulative percentages,
percentiles, Z scores,
T scores, IQ scores, and
stanines.

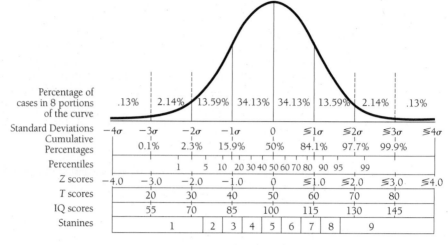

point that is one standard deviation above the mean. That point is associated with a $Z$ score of 1.0, a $T$ score of 60, an IQ score of 115, and the seventh stanine. Using the figure, try to find the score on each scale for an observation that falls two standard deviations below the mean. You should get a $Z$ score of $-2.0$, a $T$ score of 30, an IQ score of 70, and a stanine of 1.

## 2.4  PSYCHOLOGICAL TESTING IN EVERYDAY LIFE

### Within-Group Norming Controversy

One of the most troubling issues in psychological testing is that different racial and ethnic groups do not have the same average level of performance on many tests (see Chapter 6). When tests are used to select employees, a higher percentage of majority applicants are typically selected than their representation in the general population would indicate. For example, employers who use general aptitude tests consistently overselect white applicants and underselect African Americans and Latinos or Latinas. *Overselection* is defined as selecting a higher percentage from a particular group than would be expected on the basis of the representation of that group in the applicant pool. If 60% of the applicants are white and 75% of those hired are white, then overselection has occurred.

The U.S. Department of Labor uses the General Aptitude Test Battery (GATB) to refer job applicants to employers. At one point, however, studies demonstrated that the GATB adversely affected the hiring of African Americans and Latinos and Latinas. To remedy this problem, a few years ago the department created separate norms for different groups. In other words, to obtain a standardized score, each applicant was compared only with members of his or her own racial or ethnic group. As a result, overselection based on test scores was eliminated. However, this provoked other problems. For example, consider two applicants, one white and one African American, who are in the 70th percentile on the GATB. Although they have the same score, they are compared with different normative groups. The raw score for the white applicant would be 327, while that for the African American would be 283 (Brown, 1994).

## Age-Related Norms

Certain tests have different normative groups for particular age groups. Most IQ tests are of this sort. When the Stanford-Binet IQ test was originally created, distributions of the performance of random samples of children were obtained for various age groups. When applying an IQ test, the tester's task is to determine the mental age of the person being tested. This is accomplished through various exercises that help locate the age-level norm at which a child is performing.

## Tracking

One of the most common uses of age-related norms is for growth charts used by pediatricians. Consider the question "Is my son tall or short?" The answer will usually depend on a comparison of your son to other boys of the same age. Your son would be quite tall if he were 5 feet at age 8 but quite short if he were only 5 feet at age 18. Thus, the comparison is usually with people of the same age.

Beyond this rather obvious type of age-related comparison, child experts have discovered that children at the same age level tend to go through different growth patterns. Children who are small as infants often remain small and continue to grow at a slower pace than do others. Pediatricians must therefore know more than a child's age; they must also know the child's percentile within a given age group. For a variety

This was seen as a problem because an African American applicant might be selected for a job even though she had a lower raw score, or got fewer items correct, than did a white applicant.

The problem of within-group norming is highlighted by opposing opinions from different prestigious groups. The National Academy of Sciences, the most elite group of scholars in the United States, reviewed the issue and concluded that separate norms were appropriate. Specifically, they argued that minority workers at a given level of expected job performance are less likely to be hired than are majority group members. The use of separate norms was therefore required in order to avoid adverse impact in hiring decisions (Gottfredson, 1994; Hartigan & Wigdor, 1989).

In contrast to this conclusion, legislation has led to different policies. Section 106 of the Civil Rights Act of 1991 made it illegal to use separate norms. The act states that it is unlawful for employers

> in connection with the selection or referral of applicants or candidates for employment or promotion to adjust the scores of, use different cut-offs for, or otherwise alter the results of employment-related tests on the basis of race, color, religion, sex, or national origin.

Employers may have a variety of different objectives when making employment decisions. One goal may be to enhance the ethnic and racial diversity of their workforce. Another goal may be to hire those with the best individual profiles. Often these goals compete. The law may now prohibit employers from attempting to balance these competing objectives (Sackett & Wilk, 1994).

of physical characteristics, children tend to stay at about their same percentile level, relative to other children in their age group, as they grow older. This tendency to stay at about the same level relative to one's peers is known as **tracking**. Height and weight are good examples of physical characteristics that track. Figures 2.9 and 2.10 show the expected rates of growth in terms of length (height) for boys and girls. The charts are based on national norms from the U.S. Centers

**FIGURE 2.9**
Tracking chart for boys' physical growth from birth to 36 months.

## CDC Growth Charts: United States

Length-for-age percentiles: Boys, birth to 36 months

Published May 30, 2000.
SOURCE: Developed by the National Center for Health Statistics in collaboration with the National Center for Chronic Disease Prevention and Health Promotion (2000).

FIGURE 2.10
Tracking chart for girls'
physical growth from birth
to 36 months.

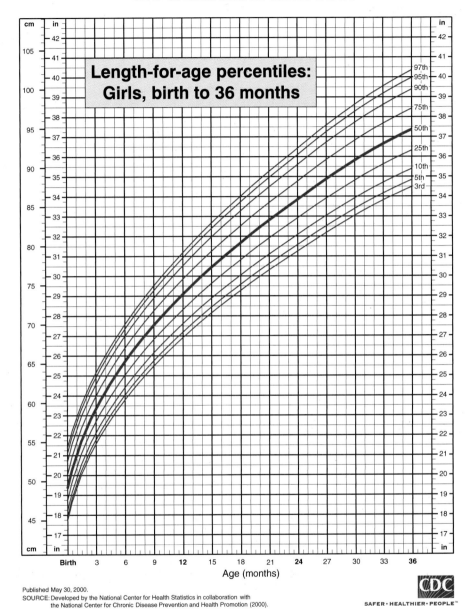

**CDC Growth Charts: United States**

**Length-for-age percentiles: Girls, birth to 36 months**

Age (months)

Published May 30, 2000.
SOURCE: Developed by the National Center for Health Statistics in collaboration with
the National Center for Chronic Disease Prevention and Health Promotion (2000).

for Disease Control and Prevention (CDC). Notice that the children who were the largest as babies are expected to remain the largest as they get older.

Pediatricians use the charts to determine the expected course of growth for a child. For example, if a 3-month-old boy was 24 inches in length (about 61 cm), the doctor would locate the child on the center line on the bottom half of

Figure 2.9. By age 36 months, the child would be expected to be about 37.5 inches (or about 95 cm). The tracking charts are quite useful to doctors because they help determine whether the child is going through an unusual growth pattern. A boy who had a length of 24 inches at age 3 months might come under scrutiny if at age 36 months he had a length of 35 inches. He would have gone from the 50th percentile to about the 3rd percentile in relation to other boys. This might be normal for 3-year-olds if the boy had always been in the 3rd percentile, but unusual for a boy who had been in the middle of the length distribution. The doctor might want to determine why the child did not stay in his track.

Figure 2.11 shows an example of a child going off track. There is some concern that children who are fed a fat-restricted diet experience stunted growth (Kaplan & Toshima, 1992). The consequences of a slightly restricted vegetarian diet are mild if they exist at all. However, highly restricted diets may affect growth. For instance, Pugliese, Lifshitz, Grad, Fort, and Marks-Katz (1983) studied 24 adolescents who had voluntarily undergone severe caloric restrictions because they wanted to lose weight. Though they did not have anorexia nervosa, they consumed only a small percentage of the calories recommended for their age. Figure 2.11 shows the growth pattern for one of these children. As the figure suggests, the child grew normally until age 9. At that point, highly restricted dieting began. Within a few years, growth was interrupted. The arrow in the figure shows the point at which psychotherapy began. After this point, normal feeding resumed,

**FIGURE 2.11**
Growth in the case of severe dietary restriction. The scales represent percentile standards for height and weight, and the plotted values are for the clinical case.

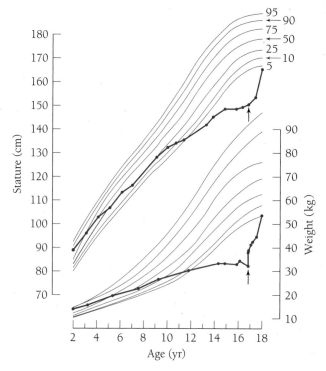

(From Pugliese et al., 1983, p. 514; reprinted by permission of *The New England Journal of Medicine, 309,* 513–518, 1983.)

and growth started once again. However, at age 18, the child was still below the 5th percentile in height and weight. Given normal tracking, this child should have been between the 25th and 50th percentiles.

Although the tracking system has worked well for medicine, it has stirred considerable controversy in education. Some people believe there is an analogy between the rates of physical growth and the rates of intellectual growth: just as there are some slow growers who eventually will be shorter than average adults, there are slow learners who will eventually know less as adults. Furthermore, some suggest that children learn at different rates. Children are therefore separated early in their educational careers and placed in classrooms that correspond with these different tracks. Many educators have attacked the tracking system because it discriminates against some children. Because people use psychological tests to place children in these tracks, some tests have come under severe scrutiny and attack. We shall return to this controversy in Chapter 6.

## Criterion-Referenced Tests

The purpose of establishing norms for a test is to determine how a test taker compares with others. A **norm-referenced test** compares each person with a norm. Many critics

---

### 2.5  PSYCHOLOGICAL TESTING IN EVERYDAY LIFE

#### Within High-School Norms for University Admission

Beginning in 2002, the University of California changed its admissions policy. The university had discovered that its admissions did not reflect the demographic characteristics of the state. In particular, students from underrepresented groups and those from low-income neighborhoods were not gaining admission to the university. When the university was required to give up its affirmative action program, there were serious concerns that the student classes would not reflect the diversity of the state of California.

To address this problem, the university created the Eligibility in Local Context (ELC) program. This program guarantees eligibility for university admission to the top 4% of graduates of California high schools. The plan focuses only on high-school grades and does not require the SAT test.

The purpose of this policy is to provide norming within particular high schools. In other words, students are not competing with all other students in the state but are being compared only with those who have had similar educational exposures. The policy was designed to increase the number of students from underrepresented ethnic and minority groups who were admitted to the university. Unfortunately, the program was not successful. Latino acceptance rates dropped from 68% in 1995 to 45% in 2003. African American acceptance rates were 58% in 1995 and dropped to 35% by 2003. As a result, the program was abandoned.

Details can be obtained from www.ucop.edu/sas/elc.

have objected that this use of tests forces competition among people. Young children exposed to many norm-referenced tests in elementary school can get caught up in a never-ending battle to perform better than average. In addition to ranking people according to performance, however, tests can play an important role in identifying problems and suggesting new directions for individualized programs of instruction. During the last two decades, interest has grown in tests that are applied to determine whether students know specific information. These tests do not compare students with one another; they compare each student's performance with a criterion or an expected level of performance (Hartman & Looney, 2003; Wiberg, 2003).

A **criterion-referenced test** describes the specific types of skills, tasks, or knowledge that the test taker can demonstrate such as mathematical skills. The results of such a test might demonstrate that a particular child can add, subtract, and multiply

## 2.6 PSYCHOLOGICAL TESTING IN EVERYDAY LIFE

### No Child Left Behind

Several contemporary issues in testing are relevant to the No Child Left Behind (NCLB) Act. NCLB was initiated by President George W. Bush with the justification that every child should receive a quality education and that "no child is left behind." In 2002, Congress passed the legislation with significant support from both Democrats and Republicans. The key provisions of the bill require greater accountability for school performance. In particular, performance information about school districts was made public. Schools were required to show how well they were doing by reporting the proportions of students who passed standardized tests. The law required that states test each child for proficiency in reading and math in grades 3 through 8. Further, each child is tested at least once during the high school years.

On the surface, it seemed like there was little to dislike about NCLB. However, by the time the legislation was considered for reauthorization in 2011, numerous concerns had emerged. In particular, critics were very concerned about the application of testing and the effects the test results might have on school funding. NCLB uses standardized achievement tests to evaluate school performance. The tests are "standards based." This means that children must demonstrate specific critical knowledge in order to pass the test, and passing is defined by an arbitrary cut point. Those above the cut point pass the exam, and those below the cut point fail. Because tests became such an important component of school evaluation, many critics believed that teachers and schools were simply "teaching to the test." In other words, schools and teachers focused on subjects that were covered on the test, like reading and math, while disregarding many other important topics, including the arts and some humanities. There were several unintended consequences of these policies. One example was the discovery of a massive cheating scandal in Georgia. Under pressure to meet the criterion, evidence emerged suggesting that some teachers modified student answer sheets in order to increase the pass rates.

## 2.7   PSYCHOLOGICAL TESTING IN EVERYDAY LIFE

### Are 4th Graders Smarter than 3rd Graders?

One of the most important instruments for measuring school performance is the standardized achievement test. California uses a standardized testing and reporting (STAR) system. STAR is very important because it evaluates performance for high stakes programs such as No Child Left Behind. In an average year, nearly 5 million children are tested in the STAR program. The evaluation of information from the STAR program reveals some interesting trends. The test reveals several indicators of school performance, and these measures are taken quite seriously. Figure 2.12 summarizes the percentage of students who perform at an advanced level in different grades. The data are from three separate years: 2005, 2006, and 2007. The graph shows that each year, relatively few 3rd graders perform at the advanced level while many 4th graders perform at the advanced level. Does this mean that 4th grade students are smarter than 3rd grade students? Norm-referenced test results would never lead to this conclusion because students at each level are compared relative to other students in their same grade level. Standards-based testing does not attend to how students are performing in relation to other students. Instead, the tests consider performance relative to a defined standard. One explanation for the data shown in the graph is that there was an exceptional crop of good students in a particular 4th grade. However, this explanation seems unlikely because the effect occurs each year. A more plausible explanation is that the definition of performing at an advanced level is somewhat arbitrary. The test may be too hard for 3rd graders but perhaps too easy for 4th graders.

**FIGURE 2.12**

STAR test performance by grade in three years.

but has difficulty with both long and short division. The results of the test would not be used to make comparisons between the child and other members of his or her class. Instead, they would be employed to design an individualized program of instruction that focuses on division. Thus, the criterion-referenced testing movement emphasizes the diagnostic use of tests—that is, using them to identify problems that can be remedied. Criterion-referenced tests became an important trend in clinical psychology in the 1980s and 1990s. In educational testing, the same ideas formed the basis of the standards-based testing movement. Instead of comparing how well children were performing in relation to other children, schools were evaluated on the basis of how many students exceeded a criterion score. Under the No Child Left Behind legislation, schools could lose funding if the number of students failing to meet the criterion was too high. By 2011, it became apparent that too many districts could meet the criterion, and the Obama administration offered relief from the criterion standard for districts willing to engage in other reform. Thus, the criterion-referenced testing movement, originally thought to be a humanistic trend, became associated with a more conservative approach to public education. Advocates for standards-based testing emphasize that schools must enforce high standards. Critics of the standards movement argue that the cut points for passing high stakes tests are often arbitrary (see Psychological Testing in Everyday Life 2.6).

# Summary

In this chapter, we discussed some basic rules for translating observations of human activities into numbers. The use of number systems is important for precision in all scientific exercises. Measures of psychological processes are represented by one of four types of scales. A *nominal scale* simply assigns numbers to categories. This type of scale has none of the properties of a numbered scale. An *ordinal scale* has the property of magnitude and allows us to rank objects, but it does not have the property of equal intervals or an absolute 0. An *interval scale* can describe the distances between objects because it has the property of equal intervals in addition to the property of magnitude. A *ratio scale* has an absolute 0 in addition to equal intervals and magnitude. Any mathematical operation on a ratio scale is permissible.

To make sense out of test scores, we have to examine the score of an individual relative to the scores of others. To do this requires creating a distribution of test scores. There are several ways to display the distribution of scores, including frequency distributions and frequency polygons. We also need statistics to describe the distribution. The *mean* is the average score, the *variance* is the averaged squared deviation around the mean, and the *standard deviation* is the square root of the variance. Using these statistics, we can tell a lot about a particular score by relating it to characteristics of a well-known probability distribution known as the standard normal distribution.

*Norms* are used to relate a score to a particular distribution for a subgroup of a population. For example, norms are used to describe where a child is on some measure relative to other children of the same age. In contrast, *criterion-referenced tests* are used to document specific skills rather than to compare people. Criterion-referenced tests are the basis for standards-based assessment in public education. Standards-based assessment requires that students pass tests demonstrating that they have critical knowledge and skills in defined areas. Some critics believe the cut points for passing the tests are arbitrary.

In summary, this chapter reviewed basic statistical methods for describing scores on one variable. In Chapter 3, we shall discuss statistical methods for showing the relationship between two or more variables.

CHAPTER

3

# Correlation and Regression

## LEARNING OBJECTIVES

*When you have completed this chapter,[1] you should be able to:*

▶ Express the extent to which two measures are associated

▶ Explain what a scatter diagram is and how it is used

▶ Define a positive correlation and a negative correlation

▶ Discuss some of the differences between correlation and regression

▶ Tell how a regression line describes the relationship between two variables

▶ Discuss under which circumstances you would use the point biserial correlation, the phi coefficient, and the tetrachoric correlation

▶ Outline the procedure you would use to predict one score from the linear combination of several scores

▶ Explain factor analysis and how it is used

---

[1] Portions of this chapter are taken from *Basic Statistics for the Behavioral Sciences* by Robert M. Kaplan (Newton, MA: Allyn & Bacon, 1987).

A banner headline in an issue of the *National Enquirer* read, "Food Causes Most Marriage Problems." The article talked about the "startling results of studies by doctors and marriage counselors." Before we are willing to accept the magazine's conclusion, we must ask many questions. Did the *National Enquirer* report enough data for us to evaluate the hypothesis? Do we feel comfortable concluding that an association between diet and divorce has been established?

There were many problems with the *National Enquirer* report. The observation was based on the clinical experiences of some health practitioners who found that many couples who came in for counseling had poor diets. One major oversight was that there was no control group of people who were not having marriage problems. We do not know from the study whether couples with problems have poor diets more often than do people in general. Another problem is that neither diet nor marital happiness was measured in a systematic way. Thus, we are left with subjective opinions about the levels of these variables. Finally, we do not know the direction of the causation: Does poor diet cause unhappiness, or does unhappiness cause poor diet? Another possibility is that some other problem (such as stress) may cause both poor diet and unhappiness. So it turns out that the article was not based on any systematic study. It merely cited the opinions of some physicians and marriage counselors who felt that high levels of blood sugar are related to low energy levels, which in turn cause marital unhappiness.

This chapter focuses on one of the many issues raised in the report—the level of association between variables. The *Enquirer* tells us that diet and unhappiness are associated, but not to what extent. Is the association greater than we would expect by chance? Is it a strong or is it a weak association?

Lots of things seem to be related. For example, long-term stress is associated with heart disease, training is associated with good performance in athletics, overeating is associated with indigestion. People often observe associations between events. For some events, the association is obvious. For example, the angle of the sun in the sky and the time of day are associated in a predictable way. This is because time was originally defined by the angle of the sun in the sky. Other associations are less obvious, such as the association between performing well on the SAT Reasoning Test and obtaining good grades in college.

Sometimes, we do not know whether events are meaningfully associated with one another. If we do conclude that events are fundamentally associated, then we need to determine a precise index of the degree. This chapter discusses statistical procedures that allow us to make precise estimates of the degree to which variables are associated. These methods are quite important; we shall refer to them frequently in the remainder of this book. The indexes of association used most frequently in testing are *correlation*, *regression*, and *multiple regression*.

# The Scatter Diagram

Before discussing the measures of association, we shall look at visual displays of the relationships between variables. In Chapter 2, we concentrated on univariate distributions of scores, which involve only one variable for each individual under study. This chapter considers statistical methods for studying *bivariate distributions*,

FIGURE 3.1

A scatter diagram. The circled point shows a person who had a score of 21 on *X* and 14 on *Y*.

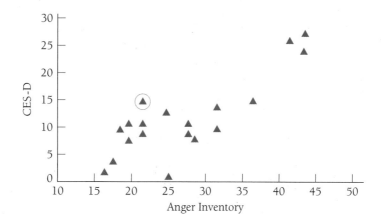

which have two scores for each individual. For example, when we study the relationship between test scores and classroom performance, we are dealing with a bivariate distribution. Each person has a score on the test and a score for classroom performance. We must examine the scores of all the individuals to know whether these two variables are associated.

The American Psychological Association's Task Force on Statistical Inference has suggested that visual inspection of data is an important step in data analysis (Wilkinson, 1999) and there is increasing interest in data visualization (Fox & Hendler, 2011). A **scatter diagram** is a picture of the relationship between two variables. An example of a scatter diagram is shown in Figure 3.1, which relates scores on a measure of anger for medical students to scores on the CES-D. The axes in the figure represent the scales for two variables. Values of *X* for the anger inventory are shown on the horizontal axis, and values of *Y* for the CES-D are on the vertical axis. Each point on the scatter diagram shows where a particular individual scored on both *X* and *Y*. For example, one person had a score of 14 on the CES-D and a score of 21 on the anger inventory. This point is circled in the figure. You can locate it by finding 21 on the *X* axis and then going straight up to the level of 14 on the *Y* axis. Each point indicates the scores for *X* and *Y* for one individual. As you can see, the figure presents a lot of information. Each point represents the performance of one person who has been assessed on two measures.

The next sections present methods for summarizing the information in a scatter diagram by finding the straight line that comes closest to more points than any other line. One important reason for examining the scatter diagram is that the relationships between *X* and *Y* are not always best described by a straight line. For example, Figure 3.2 shows the hypothetical relationship between levels of antidepressant medication in the blood of depressed patients and the number of symptoms they report. However, the relationship is systematic. Patients who have too little or too much medication experience more symptoms than do those who get an intermediate amount. The methods of linear correlation or linear regression to be presented in this chapter are not appropriate for describing nonlinear relationships such as this.

**FIGURE 3.2**
A scatter diagram showing
a nonlinear relationship.

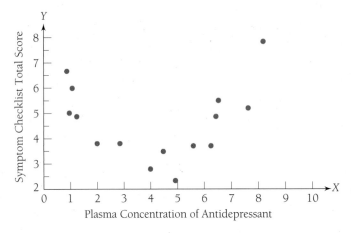

(From R. M. Kaplan & Grant, 2000).

# Correlation

In correlational analysis, we ask whether two variables covary. In other words, does Y get larger as X gets larger? For example, does the patient feel dizzier when the doctor increases the dose of a drug? Do people get more diseases when they are under more stress? Correlational analysis is designed primarily to examine linear relationships between variables. Although one can use correlational techniques to study nonlinear relationships, doing so lies beyond the scope of this book.[2]

A **correlation coefficient** is a mathematical index that describes the direction and magnitude of a relationship. Figure 3.3 shows three different types of relationships between variables. Part (a) of the figure demonstrates a *positive correlation*. This means that high scores on Y are associated with high scores on X, and low scores on Y correspond to low scores on X. Part (b) shows *negative correlation*. When there is a negative correlation, higher scores on Y are associated with lower scores on X, and lower scores on Y are associated with higher scores on X. This might describe the relationship between barbiturate use and amount of activity: the higher the drug dose, the less active the patients are. Part (c) of Figure 3.3 shows no correlation, or a situation in which the variables are not related. Here, scores on X do not give us information about scores on Y. An example of this sort of relationship is the lack of correlation between shoe size and IQ.

There are many ways to calculate a correlation coefficient. All involve pairs of observations: for each observation on one variable, there is an observation on one other variable for the same person.[3] Appendix 3.1 (at the end of this chapter) offers an example of the calculation of a correlation. All methods of calculating a correlation

---

[2] Readers who are interested in studying nonlinear relationships should review Gelman and Hill (2007).

[3] The pairs of scores do not always need to be for a person. They might also be for a group, an institution, a team, and so on.

**FIGURE 3.3**
Three hypothetical
relationships:
(a) positive correlation,
(b) negative correlation,
(c) no correlation.

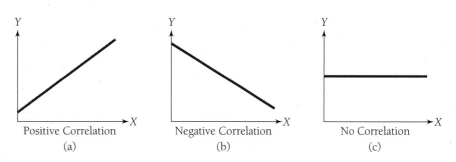

coefficient are mathematically equivalent. Before we present methods for calculating the correlation coefficient, however, we shall discuss regression, the method on which correlation is based.

# Regression

## The Regression Line

We use correlation to assess the magnitude and direction of a relationship. A related technique, known as *regression*, is used to make predictions about scores on one variable from knowledge of scores on another variable. These predictions are obtained from the **regression line**, which is defined as the best-fitting straight line through a set of points in a scatter diagram. It is found by using the *principle of least squares*, which minimizes the squared deviation around the regression line. Let us explain.

The mean is the point of least squares for any single variable. This means that the sum of the squared deviations around the mean will be less than it is around any value other than the mean. For example, consider the scores 5, 4, 3, 2, and 1. The mean is $\Sigma X_i/N = 15/5 = 3$. The squared deviation of each score around the mean can be found. For the score 5, the squared deviation is $(5 - 3)^2 = 4$. For the score 4, it is $(4 - 3)^2 = 1$. The score 3 is equal to the mean, so the squared deviation around the mean will be $(3 - 3)^2 = 0$. By definition, the mean will always be the point of least squares.

The regression line is the running mean or the line of least squares in two dimensions or in the space created by two variables. Consider the situation shown in the scatter diagram in Figure 3.1. For each level of $X$ (or point on the $X$ scale), there is a distribution of scores on $Y$. In other words, we could find a mean of $Y$ when $X$ is 3, another mean of $Y$ when $X$ is 4, and so on. The least squares method in regression finds the straight line that comes as close to as many of these $Y$ means as possible. In other words, it is the line for which the squared deviations around the line are at a minimum.

Before we get to the regression equation, we must define some of the terms it includes. The term on the left of the equation is $Y'$. This is the predicted value of $Y$. When we create the equation, we use observed values of $Y$ and $X$. The equation is the result of the least squares procedure and shows the best linear relationship between $X$ and $Y$. When the equation is available, we can take a score on $X$ and plug it into the formula. What results is a predicted value of $Y$, or $Y'$.

The most important term in the equation is the *regression coefficient*, or $b$, which is the slope of the regression line. The regression coefficient can be expressed as the ratio of the sum of squares for the covariance to the sum of squares for $X$. *Sum of squares* is defined as the sum of the squared deviations around the mean. For $X$, this is the sum of the squared deviations around the $X$ variable. *Covariance* is used to express how much two measures covary, or vary together. To understand covariance, let's look at the extreme case of the relationship between two identical sets of scores. In this case, there will be a perfect association. We know that we can create a new score that exactly repeats the scores on any one variable. If we created this new twin variable, then it would covary perfectly with the original variable. Regression analysis attempts to determine how similar the variance between two variables is by dividing the covariance by the average variance of each variable. The covariance is calculated from the cross products, or products of variations around each mean. Symbolically, this is

$$\Sigma XY = \Sigma(X - \overline{X})(Y - \overline{Y})$$

The regression coefficient or slope is:

$$b = \frac{N(\Sigma XY) - (\Sigma X)(\Sigma Y)}{N\Sigma X^2 - (\Sigma X)^2}$$

The *slope* describes how much change is expected in $Y$ each time $X$ increases by one unit. For example, Figure 3.4 shows a regression line with a slope of .67. In this figure, the difference between 1 and 2 in units of $X$ is associated with an expected difference of .67 in units of $Y$ (for $X = 1$, $Y = 2.67$ and for $X = 2$, $Y = 3.34$; $3.34 - 2.67 = .67$). The regression coefficient is sometimes expressed in different notation. For example, the Greek $\beta$ is often used for a population estimate of the regression coefficient.

The **intercept**, $a$, is the value of $Y$ when $X$ is 0. In other words, it is the point at which the regression line crosses the $Y$ axis. This is shown in Figure 3.4. It is easy to find the intercept when we know the regression coefficient. The intercept is found by using the following formula:

$$a = \overline{Y} - b\overline{X}$$

**FIGURE 3.4**

The regression equation. The slope $a$ is the change in $Y$ per unit change in $X$. The intercept $b$ is value of $Y$ when $X$ is 0.

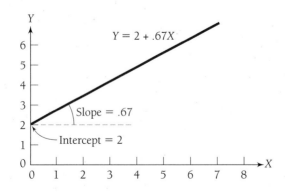

# The Best-Fitting Line

Correlational methods require finding the best-fitting line through a series of data points. In Figure 3.4, a regression line is shown that is based on a series of observations for particular individuals. Each individual had actually obtained a score on $X$ and on $Y$. Take the example of someone who obtained a score of 4 on $X$ and 6 on $Y$. The regression equation gives a predicted value for $Y$, denoted as $Y'$. Using the regression equation, we can calculate $Y'$ for this person. It is

$$Y' = 2 + .67X$$

so

$$Y' = 2 + .67(4)$$
$$= 4.68$$

The actual and predicted scores on $Y$ are rarely exactly the same. Suppose that the person actually received a score of 4 on $Y$ and that the regression equation predicted that he or she would have a score of 4.68 on $Y$. The difference between the observed and predicted score $(Y - Y')$ is called the **residual**. The best-fitting line keeps residuals to a minimum. In other words, it minimizes the deviation between observed and predicted $Y$ scores. Because residuals can be positive or negative and will cancel to 0 if averaged, the best-fitting line is most appropriately found by squaring each residual. Thus, the best-fitting line is obtained by keeping these squared residuals as small as possible. This is known as the *principle of least squares*. Formally, it is stated as

$$\Sigma(Y - Y')^2 \text{ is at a minimum}$$

An example showing how to calculate a regression equation is given in Appendix 3.1. Whether or not you become proficient at calculating regression equations, you should learn to interpret them in order to be a good consumer of research information.

Table 3.1 and Figure 3.5 present an example of a regression problem. The data come from international studies on the relationship between price per pack of cigarettes and the number of cigarettes consumed per capita. There is considerable variability in the price per pack of cigarettes among European countries. The differences between countries is primarily defined by the level of taxation. Some countries, such as Norway, have high taxes on tobacco; therefore, the price per pack for cigarettes is much higher. Figure 3.5 shows the scatter diagram as it relates price to number of cigarettes consumed.

Although the relationship is not strong, there is a negative trend, which is defined by the regression equation. The intercept in this equation is 2764.6. This means the line intersects the $Y$ axis at 2764.6. The intercept provides an estimate of the number of cigarettes that would be consumed if cigarettes were free. The regression coefficient for this model is $b = -243.99$ and tells how much cigarette consumption should decline for each dollar that is added to the price of a pack of cigarettes. In other words, this equation suggests that, on average, people will smoke 244 fewer cigarettes per year for each dollar added to the price of cigarettes. Thus, according to this simple model, adding a $2 tax to

**TABLE 3.1**    Relationship of Cigarette Price and Consumption

|     | Country | Average cigarettes/year | Price per pack ($) |
| --- | --- | --- | --- |
| 1. | Belgium | 1990 | 1.54 |
| 2. | Czechoslovakia | 2520 | 1.90 |
| 3. | Denmark | 2110 | 3.60 |
| 4. | Finland | 1720 | 2.50 |
| 5. | France | 2400 | 0.80 |
| 6. | GFR | 2380 | 2.90 |
| 7. | GDR | 2340 | 1.78 |
| 8. | Greece | 3640 | 0.48 |
| 9. | Hungary | 3260 | 0.36 |
| 10. | Iceland | 3100 | 3.51 |
| 11. | Ireland | 2560 | 2.77 |
| 12. | Italy | 2460 | 1.21 |
| 13. | Netherlands | 1690 | 1.65 |
| 14. | Norway | 710 | 4.17 |
| 15. | Portugal | 1730 | 0.72 |
| 16. | Romania | 2110 | 0.37 |
| 17. | Spain | 2740 | 0.55 |
| 18. | Sweden | 1660 | 2.30 |
| 19. | Switzerland | 2960 | 1.84 |
| 20. | Turkey | 3000 | 0.54 |
| 21. | USSR | 2170 | 0.80 |
| 22. | UK | 2120 | 2.45 |

cigarettes would decrease consumption on average by approximately 488 cigarettes per year (Kaplan et al., 1995).

Correlation is a special case of regression in which the scores for both variables are in standardized, or Z, units. Having the scores in Z units is a nice convenience because it eliminates the need to find the intercept. In correlation, the intercept is always 0. Furthermore, the slope in correlation is easier to interpret because it is in a standardized unit. An example of how to calculate a correlation coefficient is given in Appendix 3.1. In calculating the correlation coefficient, we can bypass the step of changing all the scores into Z units. This gets done as part of the calculation process. You may notice that Steps 1–13 are identical for calculating regression and correlation (Appendix 3.1). Psychological Testing in Everyday Life 3.1 gives a theoretical discussion of correlation and regression.

The **Pearson product moment correlation** coefficient is a ratio used to determine the degree of variation in one variable that can be estimated from knowledge

**FIGURE 3.5**

Scatter diagram relating price to number of cigarettes consumed.

$$Y = 2764.6 - 243.99X \quad R^2 = 0.187$$

*Cigarettes per Person* (y-axis)

*Price per Pack (in U.S. $)* (x-axis)

---

**3.1**    **PSYCHOLOGICAL TESTING IN EVERYDAY LIFE**

## A More Theoretical Discussion of Correlation and Regression

The difference between correlation and regression is analogous to the difference between standardized scores and raw scores. In correlation, we look at the relationship between variables when each one is transformed into standardized scores. In Chapter 2, standardized scores ($Z$ scores) were defined as $(X - \overline{X})/S$. In correlation, both variables are in $Z$ scores, so they both have a mean of 0. In other words, the mean for the two variables will always be the same. As a result of this convenience, the intercept will always be 0 (when $X$ is 0, $Y$ is also 0) and will drop out of the equation. The resulting equation for translating $X$ into $Y$ then becomes $Y = rX$. The correlation coefficient ($r$) is equal to the regression coefficient when both $X$ and $Y$ are measured in standardized units. In other words, the predicted value of $Y$ equals $X$ times the correlation between $X$ and $Y$. If the correlation between $X$ and $Y$ is .80 and the standardized ($Z$) score for the $X$ variable is 1.0, then the predicted value of $Y$ will be .80. Unless there is a perfect correlation (1.0 or $-1.0$), scores on $Y$ will be predicted to be closer to the $Y$ mean than scores on $X$ will be to the $X$ mean. A correlation of .80 means that the prediction for $Y$ is 80% as far from the mean as is the observation for $X$. A correlation of .50 means that the predicted distance between the mean of $Y$ and the predicted $Y$ is half of the distance between the associated $X$ and the mean of $X$. For example, if the $Z$ score for $X$ is 1.0, then $X$ is one unit above the mean of $X$. If the correlation is .50, then we predict that $Y$ will have a $Z$ score of .50.

One benefit of using the correlation coefficient is that it has a reciprocal nature. The correlation between $X$ and $Y$ will always be the same as the

*(continues)*

correlation between $Y$ and $X$. For example, if the correlation between drug dose and activity is .68, the correlation between activity and drug dose is .68.

On the other hand, regression does not have this property. Regression is used to transform scores on one variable into estimated scores on the other. We often use regression to predict raw scores on $Y$ on the basis of raw scores on $X$. For instance, we might seek an equation to predict a student's grade point average (GPA) on the basis of his or her SAT score. Because regression uses the raw units of the variables, the reciprocal property does not hold. The coefficient that describes the regression of $X$ on $Y$ is usually not the same as the coefficient that describes the regression of $Y$ on $X$.

The term *regression* was first used in 1885 by an extraordinary British intellectual named Sir Francis Galton. Fond of describing social and political changes that occur over successive generations, Galton noted that extraordinarily tall men tended to have sons who were a little shorter than they and that unusually small men tended to have sons closer to the average height (but still shorter than average). Over time, individuals with all sorts of unusual characteristics tended to produce offspring who were closer to the average. Galton thought of this as a regression toward mediocrity, an idea that became the basis for a statistical procedure that described how scores tend to regress toward the mean. If a person is extreme on $X$, then regression predicts that he or she will be less extreme on $Y$. Karl Pearson developed the first statistical models of correlation and regression in the late 19th century.

### Statistical Definition of Regression

Regression analysis shows how change in one variable is related to change in another variable. In psychological testing, we often use regression to determine whether changes in test scores are related to changes in performance. Do people who score higher on tests of manual dexterity perform better in dental school? Can IQ scores measured during high school predict monetary income 20 years later? Regression analysis and related correlational methods reveal the degree to which these variables are linearly related. In addition, they offer an equation that estimates scores on a criterion (such as dental-school grades) on the basis of scores on a predictor (such as manual dexterity).

In Chapter 2, we introduced the concept of variance. You might remember that *variance* was defined as the average squared deviation around the mean. We used the term *sum of squares* for the sum of squared deviations around the mean. Symbolically, this is

$$\Sigma(X - \overline{X})^2$$

The variance is the sum of squares divided by $N - 1$. The formula for this is

$$S_X^2 = \frac{\Sigma(X - \overline{X})^2}{N - 1}$$

We also gave some formulas for the variance of raw scores. The variance of $X$ can be calculated from raw scores using the formula

$$S_X^2 = \frac{\Sigma X^2 - \frac{(\Sigma X)^2}{N}}{N - 1}$$

If there is another variable, $Y$, then we can calculate the variance using a similar formula:

$$S_Y^2 = \frac{\Sigma Y^2 - \frac{(\Sigma Y)^2}{N}}{N - 1}$$

To calculate regression, we need a term for the covariance. To calculate the covariance, we need to find the sum of cross products, which is defined as

$$\Sigma XY = \Sigma(X - \overline{X})(Y - \overline{Y})$$

and the raw score formula, which is often used for calculation, is

$$\Sigma XY - \frac{(\Sigma X)(\Sigma Y)}{N}$$

The covariance is the sum of cross products divided by $N - 1$.

Now look at the similarity of the formula for the covariance and the formula for the variance:

$$S_{XY}^2 = \frac{\Sigma XY - \frac{(\Sigma X)(\Sigma Y)}{N}}{N - 1}$$

$$S_X^2 = \frac{\Sigma X^2 - \frac{(\Sigma X)^2}{N}}{N - 1}$$

Try substituting $X$ for $Y$ in the formula for the covariance. You should get

$$\frac{\Sigma XX - \frac{(\Sigma X)(\Sigma X)}{N}}{N - 1}$$

If you replace $\Sigma XX$ with $\Sigma X^2$ and $(\Sigma X)(\Sigma X)$ with $(\Sigma X)^2$, you will see the relationship between variance and covariance:

$$\frac{\Sigma X^2 - \frac{(\Sigma X)^2}{N}}{N - 1}$$

In regression analysis, we examine the ratio of the covariance to the average of the variances for the two separate measures. This gives us an estimate of how much variance in one variable we can determine by knowing about the variation in the other variable.

about variation in the other variable. The correlation coefficient can take on any value from −1.0 to 1.0.

Table 3.2 gives the raw data for CES-D scores ($X$) and anger inventory scores ($Y$) for medical students. Try to find the regression of anger on CES-D and the correlation between these two measures. The correct answer is $r = .82$.

As you will see from Appendix 3.1, calculations of the correlation coefficient and the regression can be long and difficult. You may be able to avoid the many computational steps by using a calculator or one of the many calculation tools on the Internet. Many inexpensive pocket calculators automatically perform correlation and regression.

## Testing the Statistical Significance of a Correlation Coefficient

One of the most important questions in evaluating a correlation is whether it is larger than we would expect by chance. The correlation between two randomly created variables will not always be 0.0. By chance alone, it is possible to observe a correlation higher or lower than 0.0. However, the expected value the correlation averaged over many randomly created data sets is 0.0, and we can estimate the probability that correlations of various magnitudes occurred by chance alone. We begin with the null hypothesis that there is no relationship between variables. The null hypothesis is rejected if there is evidence that the association between two variables is significantly different from 0. Correlation coefficients can be tested for statistical significance using the $t$ distribution. The $t$ distribution is not a single distribution (such as the $Z$ distribution) but a family of distributions, each with its own degrees of freedom. The *degrees of freedom* ($df$) are defined as the sample size minus two, or $N - 2$. The formula for calculating the $t$ value is

$$t = r\sqrt{\frac{N - 2}{1 - r^2}}$$

The significance of the $t$ value—where, $df = N - 2$ and $N$ is the number of pairs—can then be obtained by using Appendix 3.1

Let's take one example of a correlation of .37 based on 50 pairs of observations. Using the formula, we obtain

$$t = .37\sqrt{\frac{48}{.86}}$$
$$= .37(7.47)$$
$$= 2.76$$

Suppose we had stated the null hypothesis that the population association between these two variables is 0. Test statistics are used to estimate whether the observed correlation based on samples is significantly different from 0. This would be tested against the alternative hypothesis that the association between the two measures is significantly different from 0 in a **two-tailed test**. A significance level of .05 is used. Formally, then, the hypothesis and alternative hypothesis are

$$H_0 : \quad r = 0$$
$$H_1 : \quad r \neq 0$$

**TABLE 3.2**  CES-D Correlation Example

| X, anger inventory | Y, CES-D | $X^2$ | $Y^2$ | XY | Predicted | Residual |
|---|---|---|---|---|---|---|
| 21 | 14 | 441 | 196 | 294 | 7.31 | 6.69 |
| 21 | 10 | 441 | 100 | 210 | 7.31 | 2.69 |
| 21 | 8 | 441 | 64 | 168 | 7.31 | .69 |
| 27 | 8 | 729 | 64 | 216 | 11.35 | −3.35 |
| 43 | 26 | 1849 | 676 | 1118 | 22.14 | 3.86 |
| 24 | 0 | 576 | 0 | 0 | 9.33 | −9.33 |
| 36 | 14 | 1296 | 196 | 504 | 17.42 | −3.42 |
| 17 | 3 | 289 | 9 | 51 | 4.61 | 1.61 |
| 31 | 9 | 961 | 81 | 279 | 14.05 | −5.05 |
| 19 | 10 | 361 | 100 | 190 | 5.96 | 4.04 |
| 19 | 7 | 361 | 49 | 133 | 5.96 | 1.04 |
| 24 | 12 | 576 | 144 | 288 | 9.33 | 2.67 |
| 27 | 10 | 729 | 100 | 270 | 11.35 | −1.35 |
| 41 | 25 | 1681 | 625 | 1025 | 20.79 | 4.21 |
| 18 | 9 | 324 | 81 | 162 | 5.29 | 3.71 |
| 24 | 12 | 576 | 144 | 288 | 9.33 | 2.67 |
| 43 | 23 | 1849 | 529 | 989 | 22.14 | .86 |
| 28 | 7 | 784 | 49 | 196 | 12.03 | −5.03 |
| 31 | 13 | 961 | 169 | 403 | 14.05 | −1.05 |
| 16 | 1 | 256 | 1 | 16 | 3.94 | −2.94 |

See Appendix 3.1 for definitions of steps.

Step 1: $N = 20$

Step 2: $\Sigma X = 531$

Step 3: $\Sigma Y = 221$

Step 4: $\Sigma X^2 = 15,481$

Step 5: $\Sigma Y^2 = 3377$

Step 6: $\Sigma XY = 6800$

Step 7: 281,961

Step 8: 48,841

Steps 9, 10, 11: $20(6800) - (531)(221) = 18,649$

Steps 12, 13: $20(15,481) - (531)(531) = 27,659$

Step 14: $b = .67$

Step 15: $\bar{X} = 26.55$

Step 16: $\bar{Y} = 11.05$

Steps 17, 18: $a = 6.85$

Step 19: CES-D $= -6.85 + .67$(anger)

For correlation:

Step 16: 22,741.93

Step 17 correlation: .82

Using the formula, we obtain a $t$ value of 2.76 with 48 degrees of freedom. According to Appendix 3.1, this $t$ value is sufficient to reject the null hypothesis. Thus, we conclude that the association between these two variables was not the result of chance.

There are also statistical tables that give the critical values for $r$. One of these tables is included as Appendix 2. The table lists critical values of $r$ for both the .05 and the .01 alpha levels according to degrees of freedom. For the correlation coefficient, $df = N - 2$. Suppose, for example, that you want to determine whether a correlation coefficient of .45 is statistically significant for a sample of 20 subjects. The degrees of freedom would be 18 ($20 - 2 = 18$). According to Appendix 2, the critical value for the .05 level is .444 with 18 $df$. Because .45 exceeds .444, you would conclude that the chances of finding a correlation as large as the one observed by chance alone would be less than 5 in 100. However, the observed correlation is less than the criterion value for the .01 level (that would require .561 with 18 $df$).

## How to Interpret a Regression Plot

*Regression plots* are pictures that show the relationship between variables. A common use of correlation is to determine the **criterion validity evidence** for a test, or the relationship between a test score and some well-defined criterion. The association between a test of job aptitude and the criterion of actual performance on the job is an example of criterion validity evidence. The problems dealt with in studies of criterion validity evidence require one to predict some criterion score on the basis of a predictor or test score. Suppose that you want to build a test to predict how enjoyable someone will turn out to be as a date. If you selected your dates randomly and with no information about them in advance, then you might be best off just using normative information.

You might expect the distribution of enjoyableness of dates to be normal. In other words, some people are absolutely no fun for you to go out with, others are exceptionally enjoyable, and the great majority are somewhere between these two extremes. Figure 3.6 shows what a frequency distribution of enjoyableness of dates might look like. As you can see, the highest point, which shows where dates are most frequently classified, is the location of the average date.

If you had no other way of predicting how much you would like your dates, the safest prediction would be to pick this middle level of enjoyableness because it is the one observed most frequently. This is called *normative* because it uses information gained from representative groups. Knowing nothing else about an individual, you can make an educated guess that a person will be average in enjoyableness because past experience has demonstrated that the mean, or average, score is also the one observed most frequently. In other words, knowing about the average date gives you some information about what to expect from a particular date. But it is doubtful that you would really want to choose dates this way. You probably would rather use other information such as educational background, attitudes, and hobbies to predict a good date.

Most of us, in fact, use some system to help us make important personal choices. The systems we come up with, however, are never perfect, but they are better than using normative information alone. In regression studies, researchers develop equations that help them describe more precisely where tests fall between being perfect predictors and being no better than just using the normative information. This is

FIGURE 3.6

Hypothetical distribution of the enjoyableness of dates. Few dates are extremely enjoyable or extremely unenjoyable. The greatest number fall near the middle.

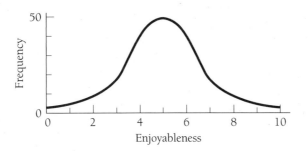

FIGURE 3.7

Hypothetical relationship between dating desirability and the enjoyableness of dates. Each point summarizes the dating desirability score and the enjoyableness rating for a single subject. The line was derived from a mathematical procedure to come as close to as many points as possible.

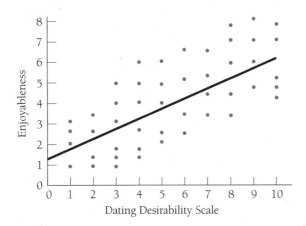

done by graphing the relationship between test scores and the criterion. Then a mathematical procedure is used to find the straight line that comes as close to as many of the points as possible. (You may want to review this chapter's earlier section on the regression line.)

Figure 3.7 shows the points on hypothetical scales of dating desirability and the enjoyableness of dates. The line through the points is the one that minimizes the squared distance between the line and the data points. In other words, the line is the one straight line that summarizes more about the relationship between dating desirability and enjoyableness than does any other straight line.

Figure 3.8 shows the hypothetical relationship between a test score and a criterion. Using this figure, you should be able to find the predicted value on the criterion variable by knowing the score on the test or the predictor. Here is how you read the graph. First, pick a particular score on the test—say, 8. Find 8 on the axis of the graph labeled "Test Score." Now draw a line straight up until you hit the slanted line on the graph. This is the regression line. Now make a 90-degree left turn and draw another line until it hits the other axis, which is labeled "Criterion Score." The dashed line in Figure 3.8 shows the course you should take. Now read the number on the criterion axis where your line has stopped. On the basis of information you gained by using the test, you would thus expect to obtain 7.4 as the criterion variable.

Notice that the line in Figure 3.8 is not at a 45° angle and that the two variables are measured in the same units. If it were at a 45° angle, then the test would be a perfect (or close to perfect) forecaster of the criterion. However, this is almost

**FIGURE 3.8**

Predicted relationship between a test score and a criterion. The dotted line shows how you should have obtained a predicted criterion score of 7.4 from the test score of 8.

never the case in practice. Now do the same exercise you did for the test score of 8 with test scores from the extremes of the distributions. Try the scores 0 and 10. You will find that the score of 10 for the test gives a criterion score of 8.95, and the test score of 0 gives a criterion score of 1.25. Notice how far apart 0 and 10 are on the test. Now look at how far apart 1.25 and 8.95 are on the criterion. You can see that using the test as a predictor is not as good as perfect prediction, but it is still better than using the normative information. If you had used only the normative information, you would have predicted that all scores would be the average score on the criterion. If there were perfect prediction, then the distance between 1.25 and 8.95 on the criterion would be the same as the distance between 0 and 10 on the test.

Figure 3.9 shows a variety of different regression slopes. Notice that the higher the standardized regression coefficient (*b*), the steeper the line. Now look at the regression line with a slope of 0. It is parallel to the "Test Score" axis and perpendicular to the "Criterion Score" axis. A regression line such as this shows that the test score tells us nothing about the criterion beyond the normative information. Whatever test score you choose, the criterion score will be the same—the average score on the criterion. The slope of 0 tells you that the test and the criterion are unrelated and that your best bet under these circumstances is to predict the average score on the criterion.

Now try to find the predicted score on the criterion for test scores of 11 and 3 for several of the different slopes shown in Figure 3.9. Notice that the steeper the slope of the regression line, the farther apart the predicted scores on the criterion. Table 3.3 shows the predicted scores for all of the different slopes. You can use it to check your answers.

When the regression lines have slopes of 0 or nearly 0, it is best not to take any chances in forecasting the criterion. Instead, you should depend on the normative information and guess the mean of *Y*. As the slope becomes steeper, it makes more sense to take some chances and estimate that there will be differences in criterion scores.

Figure 3.9 is also instructive regarding psychological tests. For example, if SAT scores have a slope of .5 for predicting grades in college, this means that the relationship between the SAT and performance is defined by the "*b* = .5" line. Using this sort of

FIGURE 3.9
Regression lines with
different standardized
slopes.

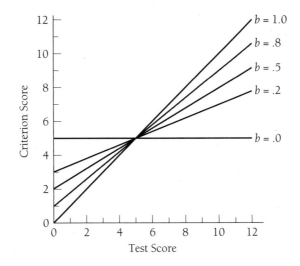

**TABLE 3.3**    Expected Criterion Scores for Two Test Scores When Predicted from Regression Lines with Different Slopes

| Test score | Slope | Predicted criterion score |
|:---:|:---:|:---:|
| 11 | 1.0 | 11.00 |
| 3 | 1.0 | 3.00 |
| 11 | .8 | 9.90 |
| 3 | .8 | 3.50 |
| 11 | .5 | 8.25 |
| 3 | .5 | 4.25 |
| 11 | .2 | 6.60 |
| 3 | .2 | 5.00 |
| 11 | .0 | 5.50 |
| 3 | .0 | 5.50 |

information, college administrators can infer that SAT scores may predict differences in college performance. However, because the slope is not steep, those predictions are not far from what they would get if they used the normative information.

# Other Correlation Coefficients

The Pearson product moment correlation is only one of many types of correlation coefficients. It is the most commonly used because most often we want to find the correlation between two continuous variables. Continuous variables such as height, weight, and intelligence can take on any values over a range of values. But sometimes we want to find the correlations between variables scaled in other ways.

**Spearman's rho** is a method of correlation for finding the association between two sets of ranks. The rho coefficient ($r$) is easy to calculate and is often used when the individuals in a sample can be ranked on two variables but their actual scores are not known or have a normal distribution.

One whole family of correlation coefficients involves dichotomous variables. Dichotomous variables have only two levels. Examples are yes–no, correct–incorrect, and male–female. Some dichotomous variables are called *true dichotomous* because they naturally form two categories. For example, gender is a true dichotomous variable. Other dichotomous variables are called *artificially dichotomous* because they reflect an underlying continuous scale forced into a dichotomy. Passing or failing a bar examination is an example of such an artificial dichotomy; although many scores can be obtained, the examiners consider only pass and fail. The types of correlation coefficients used to find the relationship between dichotomous and continuous variables are shown in Table 3.4.

The **biserial correlation** expresses the relationship between a continuous variable and an artificial dichotomous variable. For example, the biserial correlation might be used to assess the relationship between passing or failing the bar examination (artificial dichotomous variable) and grade point average (GPA) in law school (continuous variable). If the dichotomous variable had been "true" (such as gender), then we would use the *point biserial correlation*. For instance, the point biserial correlation would be used to find the relationship between gender and GPA. When both variables are dichotomous and at least one of the dichotomies is "true," then the association between them can be estimated using the *phi coefficient*. For example, the relationship between passing or failing the bar examination and gender could be estimated using the phi coefficient. If both dichotomous variables are artificial, we might use a special correlation coefficient known as the *tetrachoric correlation*. Among these special correlation coefficients, the point biserial, phi, and Spearman's rho coefficients are probably used most often. The formulas for calculating these correlations are given in Psychological Testing in Everyday Life 3.2.

---

**TABLE 3.4**    Appropriate Correlation Coefficients for Relationships Between Dichotomous and Continuous Variables*

| | Variable *X* | | |
|---|---|---|---|
| **Variable *Y*** | **Continuous** | **Artificial dichotomous** | **True dichotomous** |
| Continuous | Pearson *r* | Biserial *r* | Point biserial *r* |
| Artificial dichotomous | Biserial *r* | Tetrachoric *r* | Phi |
| True dichotomous | Point biserial *r* | Phi | Phi |

*The entries in the table suggest which type of correlation coefficient is appropriate given the characteristics of the two variables. For example, if variable *Y* is continuous and variable *X* is true dichotomous, you would use the point biserial correlation.

## 3.2 / PSYCHOLOGICAL TESTING IN EVERYDAY LIFE

### Formulas for Spearman's Rho, the Point Biserial Correlation, and the Phi Coefficient

$$\text{Spearman's rho formula: } \rho = 1 - \frac{6\Sigma d_i^2}{N^3 - 3}$$

where

$\rho$ = Spearman's rho coefficient

$d_i$ = a subject's rank order on variable 2 minus his or her rank order on variable 1

$N$ = the number of paired ranks

When used: To find the association between pairs of observations, each expressed in ranks.

$$\text{Point biserial correlation formula: } r_{\text{pbis}} = \left[\frac{\overline{Y}_1 - \overline{Y}}{S_y}\right]\sqrt{\frac{P_x}{1 - P_x}}$$

where

$r_{\text{pbis}}$ = the point biserial correlation coefficient

$X$ = a true dichotomous (two-choice) variable

$Y$ = a continuous (multilevel) variable

$Y_1$ = the mean of $Y$ for subjects have a "plus" score on $X$

$P$ = the mean of $Y$ for all subjects

$S_y$ = the standard deviation for scores

$P_x$ = the proportion of subjects giving a "plus" score on $X$

When used: To find the association between a dichotomous (two-choice) variable and a continuous variable. For the true dichotomous variable, one of the two choices is arbitrarily designated as a "plus" response.

$$\text{Phi coefficient formula: } \phi = \frac{P_c - P_x P_y}{P_x(1 - P_x)P_y(1 - P_y)}$$

where

$\phi$ = the phi coefficient

$P_c$ = the proportion in the "plus" category for both variables

$P_x$ = the proportion in the "plus" category for the first variable

$P_y$ = the proportion in the "plus" category for the second variable

When used: To find the association between two dichotomous (two-category) variables. A dichotomous variable might be yes/no or on/off. In each case, one of the two choices is arbitrarily chosen as a "plus" response. When you use phi, one of the variables must be "true" dichotomy (if both were "artificial," the tetrachoric correlation would be more appropriate).

# Terms and Issues in the Use of Correlation

When you use correlation or read studies that report correlational analysis, you will need to know the terminology. Some of the terms and issues you should be familiar with are *residual, standard error of estimate, coefficient of determination, coefficient of alienation, shrinkage, cross validation, correlation–causation problem,* and *third variable.* Brief discussions of these terms and concepts follow.

## Residual

A regression equation gives a predicted value of $Y'$ for each value of $X$. In addition to these predicted values, there are observed values of $Y$. The difference between the predicted and the observed values is called the **residual**. Symbolically, the residual is defined as $Y - Y'$.

Consider the example of the CES-D. Earlier we calculated the regression equation that predicted CES-D scores from scores on the anger inventory. The equation suggested that predicted CES-D $= -6.85 + .67 \times$ anger score. Let's take the example of a person who had an anger score of 19 and an observed CES-D score of 7. The predicted CES-D score is

$$-6.85 + (.67 \times 19) = 5.88$$

In other words, the person had an observed score of 7 and a predicted score of 5.88. The residual is[4]

$$7 - 5.88 = 1.12$$

In regression analysis, the residuals have certain properties. One important property is that the sum of the residuals always equals 0 $[\Sigma(Y - Y') = 0]$. In addition, the sum of the squared residuals is the smallest value according to the principle of least squares $[\Sigma(Y - Y')^2 = \text{smallest value}]$.

## Standard Error of Estimate

Once we have obtained the residuals, we can find their standard deviation. However, in creating the regression equation, we have found two constants ($a$ and $b$). Thus, we must use two degrees of freedom rather than one, as is usually the case in finding the standard deviation. The standard deviation of the residuals is known as the **standard error of estimate**, which is defined as

$$S_{yx} = \sqrt{\frac{\Sigma(Y - Y')^2}{N - 2}}$$

The standard error of estimate is a measure of the accuracy of prediction. Prediction is most accurate when the standard error of estimate is relatively small. As it becomes larger, the prediction becomes less accurate.

---

[4] *Note:* There is a small discrepancy between 1.12 and the 1.04 for the example in Table 3.2, page 77. The difference is the result of rounding error.

## Coefficient of Determination

The correlation coefficient squared is known as the **coefficient of determination**. This value tells us the proportion of the total variation in scores on $Y$ that we know as a function of information about $X$. For example, if the correlation between the SAT score and performance in the first year of college is .40, then the coefficient of determination is .16. The calculation is simply $.40^2 = .16$. This means that we can explain 16% of the variation in first-year college performance by knowing SAT scores. In the CES-D and anger example, the correlation is .82. Therefore, the coefficient of determination is .67 (calculated as $.82^2 = .67$), suggesting that 67% of the variance in CES-D can be accounted for by the anger score.

## Coefficient of Alienation

The **coefficient of alienation** is a measure of nonassociation between two variables. This is calculated as $\sqrt{1 - r^2}$, where $r$ is the coefficient of determination. For the SAT example, the coefficient of alienation is $\sqrt{1 - .16} = \sqrt{.84} = .92$. This means that there is a high degree of nonassociation between SAT scores and college performance. In the CES-D and anger example, the coefficient of alienation is $\sqrt{1 - .67} = .57$. Figure 3.10 shows the coefficient of determination and the coefficient of alienation represented in a pie chart.

## Shrinkage

Many times a regression equation is created on one group of subjects and then used to predict the performance of another group. One problem with regression analysis is that it takes advantage of chance relationships within a particular sample of subjects. Thus, there is a tendency to overestimate the relationship, particularly if the sample of subjects is small. **Shrinkage** is the amount of decrease observed when a regression equation is created for one population and then applied to another. Formulas are available to estimate the amount of shrinkage to expect given the characteristics of variance, covariance, and sample size (Wang & Thompson, 2007).

**FIGURE 3.10**
Proportion of variance in first-year college performance explained by SAT score. Despite a significant relationship between SAT and college performance ($r = .40$), the coefficient of determination shows that only 16% of college performance is explained by SAT scores. The coefficient of alienation is .92, suggesting that most of the variance in college performance is not explained by SAT scores.

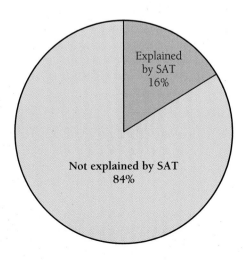

Here is an example of shrinkage. Say a regression equation is developed to predict first-year college GPAs on the basis of SAT scores. Although the proportion of variance in GPA might be fairly high for the original group, we can expect to account for a smaller proportion of the variance when the equation is used to predict GPA in the next year's class. This decrease in the proportion of variance accounted for is the shrinkage.

## Cross Validation

The best way to ensure that proper references are being made is to use the regression equation to predict performance in a group of subjects other than the ones to which the equation was applied. Then a standard error of estimate can be obtained for the relationship between the values predicted by the equation and the values actually observed. This process is known as **cross validation**.

## The Correlation–Causation Problem

Just because two variables are correlated does not necessarily imply that one has caused the other (see Focused Example 3.1). For example, a correlation between aggressive behavior and the number of hours spent viewing television does not mean that excessive viewing of television causes aggression. This relationship could mean that an aggressive child might prefer to watch a lot of television. There are many examples of misinterpretation of correlations. We know, for example, that physically active elderly people live longer than do those who are sedentary. However, we do not know if physical activity causes long life or if healthier people are more likely to be physically active. Usually, experiments are required to determine whether manipulation of one variable causes changes in another variable. A correlation alone does not prove causality, although it might lead to other research that is designed to establish the causal relationships between variables.

## Third Variable Explanation

There are other possible explanations for the observed relationship between television viewing and aggressive behavior. One is that some third variable, such as poor social adjustment, causes both. Thus, the apparent relationship between viewing and aggression actually might be the result of some variable not included in the analysis. In the example of the relationship between physical activity and life expectancy, chronic disease may cause both sedentary lifestyle and shortened life expectancy. We usually refer to this external influence as a **third variable**.

## Restricted Range

Correlation and regression use variability on one variable to explain variability on a second variable. In this chapter, we use many different examples such as the relationship between smoking and the price of a pack of cigarettes, the relationship between anger and depression, and the relationship between dating desirability and satisfaction. In each of these cases, there was meaningful variability on each of the two variables under study. However, there are circumstances in which the ranges of variability are restricted. Imagine, for example, that you were attempting

## 3.1    FOCUSED EXAMPLE

### The Danger of Inferring Causation from Correlation

A newspaper article once rated 130 job categories for stressfulness by examining Tennessee hospital and death records for evidence of stress-related diseases such as heart attacks, ulcers, arthritis, and mental disorders. The 12 highest and the 12 lowest jobs are listed in the table to the right.

    The article advises readers to avoid the "most stressful" job categories. The evidence, however, may not warrant the advice offered in the article. Although certain diseases may be associated with particular occupations, holding these jobs does not necessarily cause the illnesses. Other explanations abound. For example, people with a propensity for heart attacks and ulcers might tend to select jobs as unskilled laborers or secretaries. Thus, the direction of causation might be that a health condition causes job selection rather than the reverse. Another possibility involves a third variable, some other factor that causes the apparent relationship between job and health. For example, a certain income level might cause both stress and illness. Finally, wealthy people tend to have better health than poor people. Impoverished conditions may cause a person to accept certain jobs and also to have more diseases.

    These three possible explanations are diagrammed in the right-hand column. An arrow indicates a causal connection. In this example we are not ruling out the possibility that jobs cause illness. In fact, it is quite plausible. However, because the nature of the evidence is correlational, we cannot say with certainty that job causes illness.

| Most Stressful | Least Stressful |
|---|---|
| 1. Unskilled laborer | 1. Clothing sewer |
| 2. Secretary | 2. Garment checker |
| 3. Assembly-line inspector | 3. Stock clerk |
| 4. Clinical lab technician | 4. Skilled craftsperson |
| 5. Office manager | 5. Housekeeper |
| 6. Foreperson | 6. Farm laborer |
| 7. Manager/administrator | 7. Heavy-equipment operator |
| 8. Waiter | 8. Freight handler |
| 9. Factory machine operator | 9. Child-care worker |
| 10. Farm owner | 10. Factory package wrapper |
| 11. Miner | 11. College professor |
| 12. House painter | 12. Personnel worker |

| Job → Illness | Illness → Job | Economic Status |
|---|---|---|
| | | ↙  ↘ |
| | | Job    Illness |
| Job causes illness | Tendency toward illness causes people to choose certain jobs | Economic status (third variable) causes job selection and illness |

to study the relationship between scores on the GRE quantitative test and performance during the first year of graduate school in the math department of an elite Ivy League university. No students had been admitted to the program with GRE verbal scores less than 700. Further, most grades given in the graduate school were A's. Under these circumstances, it might be extremely difficult to demonstrate a relationship even though a true underlying relationship may exist.

    This is illustrated in Figure 3.11. The squares in the hypothetical example represent the relationship between SAT quantitative and graduate school GPA across all potential students. For all students, the correlation is 0.53. The open circles in the figure show the same relationship for the elite group of students under consideration. Because the elite students (closed circles in Figure 3.11) do not vary much

**FIGURE 3.11**

Hypothetical relationship between GRE-Q and GPA for all students and for students in elite program.

on GRE quantitative, it is difficult to observe significant correlation between GRE quantitative (GRE-Q) and any other variable. In this example, the correlation is 0.08. This is called the **restricted range problem**. Correlation requires variability. If the variability is restricted, then significant correlations are difficult to find.

# Multivariate Analysis (Optional)

**Multivariate analysis** considers the relationship among combinations of three or more variables. For example, the prediction of success in the first year of college from the linear combination of SAT verbal and quantitative scores is a problem for multivariate analysis. However, because the field of multivariate analysis requires an understanding of linear and matrix algebra, a detailed discussion of it lies beyond the scope of this book.

On the other hand, you should have at least a general idea of what the different common testing methods entail. This section will familiarize you with some of the multivariate analysis terminology. It will also help you identify the situations in which some of the different multivariate methods are used. Several references are available in case you would like to learn more about the technical details (Hammond, 2006; Hardle & Simar, 2007; Peck, Olsen, & Devore, 2011; Valero-Mora & Ledesma, 2011).

## General Approach

The correlational techniques presented to this point describe the relationship between only two variables such as stress and illness. To understand more fully the causes of illness, we need to consider many potential factors besides stress. Multivariate analysis allows us to study the relationship between many predictors and one outcome, as well as the relationship among the predictors.

Multivariate methods differ in the number and kind of predictor variables they use. All of these methods transform groups of variables into linear combinations. A *linear combination* of variables is a weighted composite of the original variables. The weighting system combines the variables in order to achieve some goal. Multivariate techniques differ according to the goal they are trying to achieve.

A linear combination of variables looks like this:

$$Y' = a + b_1X_1 + b_2X_2 + b_3X_3 + \cdots + b_kX_k$$

where $Y'$ is the predicted value of $Y$, $a$ is a constant, $X_1$ to $X_k$ are variables and there are $k$ such variables, and the $b$'s are regression coefficients. If you feel anxious about such a complex-looking equation, there is no need to panic. Actually, this equation describes something similar to what was presented in the section on regression. The difference is that instead of relating $Y$ to $X$, we are now dealing with a linear combination of $X$'s. The whole right side of the equation creates a new composite variable by transforming a set of predictor variables.

## An Example Using Multiple Regression

Suppose we want to predict success in law school from three variables: undergraduate GPA, rating by former professors, and age. This type of multivariate analysis is called **multiple regression**, and the goal of the analysis is to find the linear combination of the three variables that provides the best prediction of law school success. We find the correlation between the criterion (law school GPA) and some composite of the predictors (undergraduate GPA plus professor rating plus age). The combination of the three predictors, however, is not just the sum of the three scores. Instead, we program the computer to find a specific way of adding the predictors that will make the correlation between the composite and the criterion as high as possible. A weighted composite might look something like this:

$$\text{law school GPA} = .80 \, (Z \text{ scores of undergraduate GPA})$$
$$+ .54 \, (Z \text{ scores of professor ratings})$$
$$+ .03 \, (Z \text{ scores of age})$$

This example suggests that undergraduate GPA is given more weight in the prediction of law school GPA than are the other variables. The undergraduate GPA is multiplied by .80, whereas the other variables are multiplied by much smaller coefficients. Age is multiplied by only .03, which is almost no contribution. This is because .03 times any $Z$ score for age will give a number that is nearly 0; in effect, we would be adding 0 to the composite.

The reason for using $Z$ scores for the three predictors is that the coefficients in the linear composite are greatly affected by the range of values taken on by the variables. GPA is measured on a scale from 0 to 4.0, whereas the range in age might be 21 to 70. To compare the coefficients to one another, we need to transform all the variables into similar units. This is accomplished by using $Z$ scores (see Chapter 2). When the variables are expressed in $Z$ units, the coefficients, or weights for the variables, are known as *standardized regression coefficients* (sometimes called $B$'s or betas). There are also some cases in which we would want to use the variables' original units. For example, we sometimes want to find an equation we can use to estimate someone's predicted level of success on the basis of personal characteristics, and we do not want to bother changing these characteristics into $Z$ units. When we do this, the weights in the model are called *raw regression coefficients* (sometimes called $b$'s).

Before moving on, we should caution you about interpreting regression coefficients. Besides reflecting the relationship between a particular variable and the criterion, the coefficients are affected by the relationship among the predictor variables. Be careful when the predictor variables are highly correlated with one another. Two predictor variables that are highly correlated with the criterion will not both have large regression coefficients if they are highly correlated with each other as well. For example, suppose that undergraduate GPA and the professors' rating are both highly correlated with law school GPA. However, these two predictors also are highly correlated with each other. In effect, the two measures seem to be of the same thing (which would not be surprising, because the professors assigned the grades). As such, professors' rating may get a lower regression coefficient because some of its predictive power is already taken into consideration through its association with undergraduate GPA. We can only interpret regression coefficients confidently when the predictor variables do not overlap and are uncorrelated. They may do so when the predictors are uncorrelated.

## Discriminant Analysis

Multiple regression is appropriate when the criterion variable is continuous (not nominal). However, there are many cases in testing where the criterion is a set of categories. For example, we often want to know the linear combination of variables that differentiates passing from failing. When the task is to find the linear combination of variables that provides a maximum discrimination between categories, the appropriate multivariate method is **discriminant analysis**. An example of discriminant analysis involves attempts to determine whether a set of measures predicts success or failure on a particular performance evaluation.

Sometimes we want to determine the categorization in more than two categories. To accomplish this we use multiple discriminant analysis.

Discriminant analysis has many advantages in the field of test construction. One approach to test construction is to identify two groups of people who represent two distinct categories of some trait. For example, say that two groups of children are classified as "language disabled" and "normal." After a variety of items are presented, discriminant analysis is used to find the linear combination of items that best accounts for differences between the two groups. With this information, researchers could develop new tests to help diagnose language impairment. This information might also provide insight into the nature of the problem and eventually lead to better treatments.

## Factor Analysis

Discriminant analysis and multiple regression analysis find linear combinations of variables that maximize the prediction of some criterion. Factor analysis is used to study the interrelationships among a set of variables without reference to a criterion. You might think of factor analysis as a data-reduction technique. When we have responses to a large number of items or a large number of tests, we often want to reduce all this information to more manageable chunks. In Figure 3.1, we presented a two-dimensional scatter diagram. The task in correlation is to find the best-fitting line through the space created by these two dimensions. As we add more variables in multivariate analysis, we increase the number of dimensions. For example, a three-dimensional plot is shown in Figure 3.12. You can use your imagination to visualize what a larger set of dimensions would look like. Some people claim they can visualize more than three dimensions, while others feel they cannot. In any case, consider that points are plotted in the domain created by a given dimension.

In factor analysis, we first create a matrix that shows the correlation between every variable and every other variable. Then we find the linear combinations, or *principal components*, of the variables that describe as many of the interrelationships among the variables as possible. We can find as many principal components as there are variables. However, each principal component is extracted according to mathematical rules that make it independent of or uncorrelated with the other principal components. The first component will be the most successful in describing the variation among the variables, with each succeeding component somewhat less successful. Thus, we often decide to examine only a few components that account for larger proportions of the variation. Technically, principal components analysis and true factor analysis differ in how the correlation matrix is created. Even so, principal components are often called *factors*.

Once the linear combinations or principal components have been found, we can find the correlation between the original items and the factors. These

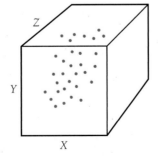

**FIGURE 3.12**

A three-dimensional scatter plot might be represented by this box. In addition to plotting points on the X and Y axes, we must locate them in relation to a third Z axis.

## The Factors of Trust

Rotter (1967) described a scale for the measurement of interpersonal trust. *Trust* was defined as "an expectancy held by an individual or a group that the word, promise, verbal or written statement of another individual or group can be relied upon" (p. 651). However, after the publication of the original trust article, several authors reported that trust seems to be composed of several independent factors (Chun & Campbell, 1974; R. M. Kaplan, 1973; T. L. Wright & Tedeschi, 1975). In each case, the items were given to a large group of people, and the results were subjected to factor analysis. This procedure reduces the many items down to a smaller number of *factors*, or linear combinations of the original items. Then *item loadings*, or the correlations of the original items with the factors, are studied in order to name the factors. The table that follows shows the loadings of the items on three of the factors (R. M. Kaplan, 1973).

Once they have obtained the factor loadings, researchers must attempt to name the factors by examining which items load highly on them. In this case, an item was used to help interpret a factor if its item loading on the factor was greater than .35 or less than −.35. Three factors of trust were found.

*Factor I: Institutional trust.* This represented trust toward major social agents in society. It included items regarding the competence of politicians, such as "This country has a dark future unless we can attract better people into politics" (−.67). Many of the items conveyed the idea of misrepresentation of public events by either the government or the mass media. For example, some items with high loadings were "Most people would be horrified if they knew how much news the public hears and sees is distorted" (−.69) and "Even though we have reports in newspapers, radio, and TV, it is hard to get objective accounts of public events" (−.67).

*Factor II: Sincerity.* Items loading highly on sincerity tended to focus on the perceived sincerity of others. These items included "Most idealists are sincere and usually practice what they preach" (.62) and "Most people answer public opinion polls honestly" (.58). Nearly all the items with high loadings on the second factor began with the word "most." Because of this loose wording, it would be possible for people to agree with the items because they believe in the sincerity of most people in a given group but still feel little trust for the group because of a few "rotten eggs." Thus, a woman could believe most car repairers are sincere but still service her car herself because she fears being overcharged.

*Factor III: Caution.* This contained items that expressed fear that some people will take advantage of others, such as "In dealing with strangers, one is better off being cautious until they have provided evidence that they are trustworthy" (.74) and "In these competitive times you have to be alert or someone is likely to take advantage of you" (.53). Note that caution appears to be independent of perceived sincerity.

The data imply that generalized trust may be composed of several dimensions. It also implies that focusing on specific components of trust rather than the generalized case will likely help researchers the most in using this trust scale.

Focused Example adapted from Rotter (1967); table taken from R. M. Kaplan (1973).

correlations are called *factor loadings*. The expression "item 7 loaded highly on factor I" means there is a high correlation between item 7 and the first principal component. By examining which variables load highly on each factor, we can start interpreting the meanings of the factors. Focused Example 3.2 shows how the meanings of various factors in a scale on interpersonal trust are evaluated.

Factor analysis is a complex and technical method with many options the user must learn about. For example, users frequently use methods that help them get a

| Item number | Item | Loading factor | | |
|---|---|---|---|---|
| | | I | II | III |
| **A. Items with high loadings on institutional factor** | | | | |
| 4. | This country has a dark future unless we can attract better people into politics. | −.67 | −.12 | −.06 |
| 5. | Fear of social disgrace or punishment rather than conscience prevents most people from breaking the law. | −.54 | .02 | −.06 |
| 13. | The United Nations will never be an effective force in keeping world peace. | −.41 | .09 | −.21 |
| 16. | The judiciary is a place where we can all get unbiased treatment. | .37 | .23 | .00 |
| 19. | Most people would be horrified if they knew how much news the public hears and sees is distorted. | −.69 | .18 | .28 |
| 21. | Most elected public officials are really sincere in their campaign promises. | .44 | .17 | −.02 |
| 24. | Even though we have reports in newspapers, radio, and TV, it is hard to get objective accounts of public events. | −.67 | −.08 | .00 |
| 28. | If we really knew what was going on in international politics, the public would have more reason to be more frightened than it now seems to be. | −.49 | .01 | .24 |
| 33. | Many major national sports contests are fixed in one way or another. | −.55 | −.04 | .28 |
| **B. Items with high loadings on sincerity factor** | | | | |
| 1. | Hypocrisy is on the increase in our society. | .09 | −.52 | .08 |
| 12. | Most students in school would not cheat even if they were sure of getting away with it. | .29 | .45 | .07 |
| 27. | Most experts can be relied upon to tell the truth about the limits of their knowledge. | .20 | .66 | .20 |
| 34. | Most idealists are sincere and usually practice what they preach. | .12 | .62 | −.20 |
| 38. | Most repair persons will not overcharge even if they think you are ignorant of their specialty. | .11 | .48 | −.35 |
| 44. | Most people answer public opinion polls honestly. | .04 | .58 | .16 |
| **C. Items with high loadings on caution factor** | | | | |
| 2. | In dealing with strangers, one is better off being cautious until they have provided evidence that they are trustworthy. | −.22 | −.03 | .74 |
| 7. | Using the honor system of not having a teacher present during examinations would probably result in increased cheating. | .13 | .08 | .45 |
| 32. | In these competitive times you have to be alert or someone is likely to take advantage of you. | −.12 | −.01 | .53 |
| 42. | A large share of the accident claims filed against insurance companies are phony. | −.07 | −.14 | .57 |

clearer picture of the meaning of the components by transforming the variables in a way that pushes the factor loadings toward the high or the low extreme. Because these transformational methods involve rotating the axes in the space created by the factors, they are called *methods of rotation*. Researchers have many options for transforming variables. They can choose among several methods of rotation, and they can explore the many characteristics of the matrix originally used in their analyses. If you are interested, several books discuss factor analysis methods in great detail (Child, 2006; Hammond, 2006; Hardle & Simar, 2007).

# Summary

This chapter began with a discussion of a claim made in the *National Enquirer* that poor diet causes marital problems. Actually, there was no specific evidence that diet causes the problems—only that diet and marital difficulties are associated. However, the *Enquirer* failed to specify the exact strength of the association. The rest of the chapter was designed to help you be more specific than the *Enquirer* by learning to specify associations with precise mathematical indexes known as *correlation coefficients*.

First, we presented pictures of the association between two variables; these pictures are called *scatter diagrams*. Second, we presented a method for finding a linear equation to describe the relationship between two variables. This regression method uses the data in raw units. The results of regression analysis are two constants: a *slope* describes the degree of relatedness between the variables, and an *intercept* gives the value of the $Y$ variable when the $X$ variable is 0. When both of the variables are in standardized or $Z$ units, the intercept is always 0 and drops out of the equation. In this unique situation, we solve for only one constant, which is $r$, or the *correlation coefficient*.

When using correlational methods, we must take many things into consideration. For example, correlation does not mean the same thing as causation. In the case of the *National Enquirer* article, the observed correlation between diet and problems in marriage may mean that diet causes the personal difficulties. However, it may also mean that marriage problems cause poor eating habits or that some *third variable* causes both diet habits and marital problems. In addition to the difficulties associated with causation, we must always consider the strength of the correlational relationship. The *coefficient of determination* describes the percentage of variation in one variable that is known on the basis of its association with another variable. The *coefficient of alienation* is an index of what is not known from information about the other variable.

A *regression line* is the best-fitting straight line through a set of points in a scatter diagram. The regression line is described by a mathematical index known as the regression equation. The *regression coefficient* is the ratio of covariance to variance and is also known as the slope of the regression line. The regression coefficient describes how much change is expected in the $Y$ variable each time the $X$ variable increases by one unit. Other concepts discussed were the *intercept*, the *residual* (the difference between the predicted value given by a regression equation and the observed value), and the *standard error of estimate* (the standard deviation of the residuals obtained from the regression equation).

The field of *multivariate analysis* involves a complicated but important set of methods for studying the relationships among many variables. *Multiple regression* is a multivariate method for studying the relationship between one criterion variable and two or more predictor variables. A similar method known as *discriminant analysis* is used to study the relationship between a categorical criterion and two or more predictors. *Factor analysis* is another multivariate method for reducing a large set of variables down to a smaller set of composite variables.

Correlational methods are the most commonly used statistical techniques in the testing field. The concepts presented in this overview will be referred to throughout the rest of this book.

# APPENDIX 3.1:
# Calculation of a Regression Equation and a Correlation Coefficient

In this appendix, we consider the relationship between team performance and payroll for teams in baseball's National League. Data used here are from the 2011 season and available on the Internet at www.espn.com. The 2011 season was of particular interest to baseball fans because the World Series pitted the St Louis Cardinals with a payroll of more than $105 million against the Colorado Rockies with a payroll of a mere $92 million. The Cardinals won the Series, raising the question of whether there is a relationship between expenditure and performance of professional baseball teams.

In this example, payroll for National League teams is measured as median player salary (expressed in millions of dollars) whereas performance is measured by the number of games won. The data are shown in Table 3.5 and summarized in Figure 3.13. Each dot in the figure represents one team. In 2011, there was a positive relationship between payroll and performance. In other words, teams with higher median salaries had better performance. As Figure 3.13 indicates, each

**TABLE 3.5**  Games Won and Median Salaries for Teams in Baseball's National League, 2011

| Team | Median Salary (in millions) (X) | Games won (Y) | XY | $X^2$ | $Y^2$ |
|---|---|---|---|---|---|
| Philadelphia Phillies | 2.63 | 102 | 268.26 | 6.92 | 10404 |
| Chicago Cubs | 1.60 | 71 | 113.60 | 2.56 | 5041 |
| New York Mets | 0.90 | 77 | 69.30 | 0.81 | 5929 |
| San Francisco Giants | 2.20 | 86 | 189.20 | 4.84 | 7396 |
| St. Louis Cardinals | 1.00 | 90 | 90.00 | 1.00 | 8100 |
| Los Angeles Dodgers | 2.14 | 82 | 175.48 | 4.58 | 6724 |
| Colorado Rockies | 2.32 | 73 | 169.36 | 5.38 | 5329 |
| Atlanta Braves | 1.27 | 89 | 113.03 | 1.61 | 7921 |
| Milwaukee Brewers | 1.05 | 96 | 100.80 | 1.10 | 9216 |
| Cincinnati Reds | 0.83 | 79 | 65.57 | 0.69 | 6241 |
| Houston Astros | 0.47 | 56 | 26.32 | 0.22 | 3136 |
| Washington Nationals | 1.05 | 80 | 84.00 | 1.10 | 6400 |
| Florida Marlins | 0.55 | 72 | 39.60 | 0.30 | 5184 |
| Arizona Diamondbacks | 1.00 | 94 | 94.00 | 1.00 | 8836 |
| San Diego Padres | 0.47 | 71 | 33.37 | 0.22 | 5041 |
| Pittsburgh Pirates | 0.45 | 72 | 32.40 | 0.20 | 5184 |
| TOTAL | 19.93 | 1,290.00 | 1664.29 | 32.54 | 106,082.00 |

**FIGURE 3.13**
Payroll (in $ million) versus
performance (games won)
by National League teams
in 2011.

increase in expenditure is associated with an increase in performance. The regression coefficient (7.44) suggests that for each million dollar increase in median salary, the team's performance increases by an average of 7.44 games per season. We also did the same exercise for total payroll. In 2011 the Philadelphia Phillies had the highest payroll in the National League, at $173 million. Across the state of Pennsylvania, the Pittsburgh Pirates has the lowest payroll at $45 million. The correlation between total payroll and games won was 0.45 and the regression equation was:

$$Y = 67.166 + 0.15(X)$$

This tells us that for each investment of $0.15 million, the team's performance is estimated to improve by one game. In other words, an owner must spend about $6,666,667 to win one game. Overall, the relationship is significant, and the best explanation is that there is an association between payroll and performance.

## Calculation of a Regression Equation (Data from Table 3.5)

Formulas:

$$b = \frac{N(\Sigma XY) - (\Sigma Y)(\Sigma Y)}{N\Sigma X^2 - (\Sigma X)^2}$$

$$a = \overline{Y} - b\overline{X}$$

**STEPS**

**1.** Find $N$ by counting the number of pairs of observations. $N = 16$

**2.** Find $\Sigma X$ by summing the $X$ scores.

$$2.63 + 1.60 + 0.90 + 2.20 + 1.00 + 2.14 + 2.32 + 1.27$$
$$+ 1.05 + 0.83 + 0.47 + 1.05 + 0.55 + 1.00 + 0.47 + 0.45 = 19.93$$

**3.** Find $\Sigma Y$ by summing the $Y$ scores.

$$102 + 71 + 77 + 86 + 90 + 82 + 73 + 89 + 96$$
$$+ 79 + 56 + 80 + 72 + 94 + 71 + 72 = 1,290.00$$

**4.** Find $\Sigma X^2$. Square each $X$ score and then sum them.

$$6.92 + 2.56 + 0.81 + 4.84 + 1.00 + 4.58$$
$$+ 5.38 + 1.61 + 1.10 + 0.69 + 0.22 + 1.10$$
$$+ 0.30 + 1.00 + .22 + 0.20 = 32.54$$

**5.** Find $\Sigma Y^2$. Square each $Y$ score and then sum them.

$$10404 + 5041 + 5929 + 7396 + 8100 + 6724$$
$$+ 5329 + 7921 + 9216 + 6241 + 3136$$
$$+ 6400 + 5184 + 8836 + 5041 + 5184 = 106{,}082$$

**6.** Find $\Sigma XY$. For each pair of observations multiply $X$ by $Y$. Then sum the products.

$$(2.63 \times 102) + (1.60 \times 71) + (0.90 \times 77) + (2.20 \times 86) + (1.00 \times 90)$$
$$+ (2.14 \times 82) + (2.32 \times 73) + (1.27 \times 89) + (1.05 \times 96)$$
$$+ (0.83 \times 79) + (0.47 \times 56) + (1.05 \times 80) + (0.55 \times 72)$$
$$+ (1.00 \times 94) + (0.47 \times 71) + (0.45 \times 72)$$

$$= 268.26 + 113.60 + 69.30 + 189.20 + 90.00$$
$$+ 175.48 + 169.36 + 113.03 + 100.80 + 65.57$$
$$+ 26.32 + 84.00 + 39.60 + 94.00 + 33.37 + 32.40$$

$$= 1664.29$$

**7.** Find $(\Sigma X)^2$ by squaring the results of Step 2.

$$(19.93)^2 = 397.20$$

**8.** Find $(\Sigma Y)^2$ by squaring the results of Step 3.

$$(1290)^2 = 1{,}664{,}100$$

**9.** Find $N\Sigma XY$ by multiplying the results of Step 1 by Step 6.

$$16 \times 1664.29 = 26{,}628.64$$

**10.** Find $(\Sigma X)(\Sigma Y)$ by multiplying the results of Steps 2 and 3.

$$19.93 \times 1{,}290.00 = 25{,}709.70$$

**11.** Find $(N\Sigma XY) - (\Sigma X)(\Sigma Y)$ by subtracting the results of Step 10 from the result of Step 9.

$$26{,}628.64 - 25{,}709.70 = 918.94$$

**12.** Find $N\Sigma X^2$ by multiplying the results of Steps 1 and 4.

$$16 \times 32.54 = 520.68$$

**13.** Find $N\Sigma X^2 - (\Sigma X)^2$ by subtracting the result of Step 7 from that of Step 12.

$$520.68 - 397.20 = 123.46$$

**14.** Find $b$ by dividing the result of Step 11 by that of Step 13.

$$918.94/123.46 = 7.44$$

**15.** Find the mean of $X$ by dividing the result of Step 2 by that of Step 1.

$$19.93/16 = 1.24$$

**16.** Find the mean of $Y$ by dividing the result of Step 3 by that of Step 1.

$$= 1290/16 = 80.63$$

**17.** Find $b\overline{X}$ by multiplying the results of Steps 14 and 15.

$$= 7.44 \times 1.24 = 8.69$$

**18.** Find $a$ by subtracting the results of Step 17 from Step 16.

$$= 80.63 - 8.69 = 71.94$$

**19.** The resultant regression equation is

$$Y = a + bX$$
$$Y = 71.94 + 7.44(X)$$

## Calculation of a Correlation Coefficient (Data from Table 3.5)

Formula:

$$r = \frac{N\Sigma XY - (\Sigma X)(\Sigma Y)}{\sqrt{[N\Sigma X^2 - (\Sigma X)^2][N\Sigma Y^2 - (\Sigma Y)^2]}}$$

**1.** Find $N$ by counting the number of pairs of observations. $N = 16$

**2.** Find $\Sigma X$ by summing the $X$ scores.

$$2.63 + 1.60 + 0.90 + 2.20 + 1.00 + 2.14 + 2.32 + 1.27$$
$$+ 1.05 + 0.83 + 0.47 + 1.05 + 0.55 + 1.00 + 0.47 + 0.45 = 19.93$$

**3.** Find $\Sigma Y$ by summing the $Y$ scores.

$$102 + 71 + 77 + 86 + 90 + 82 + 73 + 89 + 96$$
$$+ 79 + 56 + 80 + 72 + 94 + 71 + 72 = 1,290.00$$

**4.** Find $\Sigma X^2$. Square each $X$ score and then sum them.

$$6.92 + 2.56 + 0.81 + 4.84 + 1.00 + 4.58$$
$$+ 5.38 + 1.61 + 1.10 + 0.69 + 0.22 + 1.10$$
$$+ 0.30 + 1.00 + .22 + 0.20 = 32.54$$

**5.** Find $\Sigma Y^2$. Square each $Y$ score and then sum them.

$$10404 + 5041 + 5929 + 7396 + 8100 + 6724$$
$$+ 5329 + 7921 + 9216 + 6241 + 3136 + 6400$$
$$+ 5184 + 8836 + 5041 + 5184 = 106,082$$

6. Find $\Sigma XY$. For each pair of observations multiply $X$ by $Y$. Then sum the products.

$$(2.63 \times 102) + (1.60 \times 71) + (0.90 \times 77) + (2.20 \times 86)$$
$$+ (1.00 \times 90) + (2.14 \times 82) + (2.32 \times 73) + (1.27 \times 89)$$
$$+ (1.05 \times 96) + (0.83 \times 79) + (0.47 \times 56) + (1.05 \times 80)$$
$$+ (0.55 \times 72) + (1.00 \times 94) + (0.47 \times 71) + (0.45 \times 72)$$

$$= 268.26 + 113.60 + 69.30 + 189.20 + 90.00 + 175.48$$
$$+ 169.36 + 113.03 + 100.80 + 65.57 + 26.32$$
$$+ 84.00 + 39.60 + 94.00 + 33.37 + 32.40$$

$$= 1664.29$$

7. Find $(\Sigma X)^2$ by squaring the results of Step 2.

$$(19.93)^2 = 397.20$$

8. Find $(\Sigma Y)^2$ by squaring the results of Step 3.

$$(1290)^2 = 1,664,100$$

9. Find $N\Sigma XY$ by multiplying the results of Step 1 by Step 6.

$$16 \times 1664.29 = 26,628.64$$

10. Find $(\Sigma X)(\Sigma Y)$ by multiplying the results of Steps 2 and 3.

$$19.93 \times 1,290.00 = 25,709.70$$

11. Find $(N\Sigma XY) - (\Sigma X)(\Sigma Y)$ by subtracting the results of Step 10 from the result of Step 9.

$$26,628.64 - 25,709.70 = 918.94$$

12. Find $N\Sigma X^2$ by multiplying the results of Steps 1 and 4.

$$16 \times 32.54 = 520.68$$

13. Find $N\Sigma X^2 - (\Sigma X)^2$ by subtracting the result of Step 7 from that of Step 12.

$$520.68 - 397.20 = 123.46$$

14. Find $N\Sigma Y^2$ by multiplying the results of Steps 1 and 5.

$$16 \times 106,082 = 1,697,312$$

15. Find $N\Sigma Y^2 - (\Sigma Y)^2$ by subtracting the result of Step 8 from that of Step 14.

$$1,697,312 - 1,664,100 = 33,212$$

16. Find $\sqrt{[N\Sigma X^2 - (\Sigma X)^2][N\Sigma Y^2 - (\Sigma Y)^2]}$ by multiplying the results of Steps 13 and 15 and taking the square root of the product.

$$\sqrt{123.48 \times 33,212.00} = 2025.07$$

**17.** Find $r = \dfrac{N\Sigma XY - (\Sigma X)(\Sigma Y)}{\sqrt{[N\Sigma X^2 - (\Sigma X)^2][N\Sigma Y^2 - (\Sigma Y)^2]}}$, dividing the result of Step 11 by that of Step 16.

$$918.94/2025.06$$
$$r = 0.45$$

# 4 CHAPTER

# Reliability

## LEARNING OBJECTIVES

*When you have completed this chapter, you should be able to:*

▶ Describe the role of measurement error in scientific studies of behavior

▶ Know that reliability is the ratio of true variability to observed variability and explain what this tells us about a test with a reliability of .30, .60, or .90

▶ Describe how test–retest reliability is assessed

▶ Explain the difference between test–retest reliability estimates and split-half reliability estimates

▶ Discuss how the split-half method underestimates the reliability of a short test and what can be done to correct this problem

▶ Know the easiest way to find average reliability

▶ Define *coefficient alpha* and tell how it differs from other methods of estimating reliability

▶ Discuss how high a reliability coefficient must be before you would be willing to say the test is "reliable enough"

▶ Explain what can be done to increase the reliability of a test

▶ Tell how the reliability of behavioral observations is assessed n the gymnastics competition at an international meet, a young Romanian woman received an 8.9 for the first portion of her routine. As she reappeared for the second portion, the television commentator said, "The 8.9 rating for her first routine does not accurately represent her ability. This young woman is clearly a 9.5 performer." With this remark, the commentator indicated a discrepancy between the gymnast's score for the first routine and her true ability, a common occurrence in the measurement of human abilities. For example, after an examination, students sometimes feel that the questions on the test did not allow them to display their real knowledge. And actors sometimes complain that a 5-minute audition is not an adequate measure of their talents.

Discrepancies between true ability and measurement of ability constitute errors of measurement. In psychological testing, the word *error* does not imply that a mistake has been made. Rather than having a negative connotation, *error* implies that there will always be some inaccuracy in our measurements. Our task is to find the magnitude of such errors and to develop ways to minimize them. This chapter discusses the conceptualization and assessment of measurement error. Tests that are relatively free of measurement error are deemed to be *reliable*, hence the name of this chapter. Tests that have "too much" measurement error are considered unreliable. We shall see the ways we can determine "how much is too much" in these cases.

# History and Theory of Reliability

## Conceptualization of Error

Students who major in physical science have chosen to study phenomena that are relatively easy to measure with precision. If you want to measure the width of this book, for example, you need only apply a ruler and record the number of inches or centimeters.

In psychology, the measurement task is more difficult. First, researchers are rarely interested in measuring simple qualities such as width. Instead, they usually pursue complex traits such as intelligence or aggressiveness, which one can neither see nor touch. Further, with no rigid yardsticks available to measure such characteristics, testers must use "rubber yardsticks"; these may stretch to overestimate some measurements and shrink to underestimate others (Mislevy, 2002; Bootzin & McKnight, 2006; Hand, 2011; Thomas, 2012). Psychologists must assess their measuring instruments to determine how much "rubber" is in them. A psychologist who is attempting to understand human behavior on the basis of unreliable tests is like a carpenter trying to build a house with a rubber measuring tape that never records the same length for the same piece of board.

As you will learn from this chapter, the theory of measurement error is well developed within psychology. This is not to say that measurement error is unique to psychology. In fact, serious measurement error occurs in most physical, social, and biological sciences. For example, measures of the gross national product (economics) and blood pressure (medicine) are known to be less reliable than well-constructed psychological tests. However, the concern with reliability has been a particular obsession for psychologists and provides evidence of the advanced scientific status of the field (Shavelson & Ruiz-Primo, 2000; Raykov & Marcoulides, 2010).

## Spearman's Early Studies

Psychology owes the advanced development of reliability assessment to the early work of the British psychologist Charles Spearman. In 1733, Abraham De Moivre introduced the basic notion of sampling error (Stanley, 1971); and in 1896, Karl Pearson developed the product moment correlation (see Chapter 3 and Pearson, 1901). Reliability theory puts these two concepts together in the context of measurement. A contemporary of Pearson, Spearman actually worked out most of the basics of contemporary reliability theory and published his work in a 1904 article entitled "The Proof and Measurement of Association between Two Things." Because the *British Journal of Psychology* did not begin until 1907, Spearman published his work in the *American Journal of Psychology*. Spearman's work quickly became known in the United States. The article came to the attention of measurement pioneer Edward L. Thorndike, who was then writing the first edition of *An Introduction to the Theory of Mental and Social Measurements* (1904).

Thorndike's book is remarkably sophisticated, even by contemporary standards. Since 1904, many developments on both sides of the Atlantic Ocean have led to further refinements in the assessment of reliability. Most important among these is a 1937 article by Kuder and Richardson, in which several new reliability coefficients were introduced. Later, Cronbach and his colleagues (Cronbach, 1989, 1995) made a major advance by developing methods for evaluating many sources of error in behavioral research. Reliability theory continues to evolve. In recent years, sophisticated mathematical models have been developed to quantify "latent" variables based on multiple measures (Bartholomew & Knott, 1999; Bentler, 1990, 1991, 1994). More recently, item response theory (IRT) has taken advantage of computer technology to advance psychological measurement significantly (DeMars, 2010; Raykov & Marcoulides, 2010). However, IRT is built on many of the ideas Spearman introduced a century ago (Thomas, 2012).

## Basics of Test Score Theory

Classical test score theory assumes that each person has a true score that would be obtained if there were no errors in measurement. However, because measuring instruments are imperfect, the score observed for each person almost always differs from the person's true ability or characteristic. The difference between the true score and the observed score results from measurement error. In symbolic representation, the observed score ($X$) has two components; a true score ($T$) and an error component ($E$):

$$X \quad = \quad T \quad + \quad E$$

| | | |
|---|---|---|
| ↓ | ↓ | ↓ |
| Observed score | True score | Error |

**FIGURE 4.1**

Distribution of observed scores for repeated testing of the same person. The mean of the distribution is the estimated true score, and the dispersion represents the distribution of random errors.

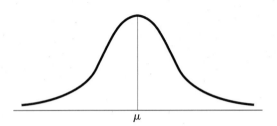

$\mu$

Or we can say that the difference between the score we obtain and the score we are really interested in equals the error of measurement:

$$X - T = E$$

A major assumption in classical test theory is that errors of measurement are random. Although systematic errors are acknowledged in most measurement problems, they are less likely than other errors to force an investigator to make the wrong conclusions. A carpenter who always misreads a tape measure by 2 inches (or makes a systematic error of 2 inches) would still be able to cut boards the same length. Using the rubber-yardstick analogy, we would say that this carpenter works with a ruler that is always 2 inches too long. Classical test theory, however, deals with rubber-yardstick problems in which the ruler stretches and contracts at random.

Using a rubber yardstick, we would not get the same score on each measurement. Instead, we would get a distribution of scores like that shown in Figure 4.1. Basic sampling theory tells us that the distribution of random errors is bell-shaped. Thus, the center of the distribution should represent the true score, and the dispersion around the mean of the distribution should display the distribution of sampling errors. Though any one application of the rubber yardstick may or may not tell us the true score, we can estimate the true score by finding the mean of the observations from repeated applications.

Figure 4.2 shows three different distributions. In the far left distribution, there is a great dispersion around the true score. In this case, you might not want to depend on a single observation because it might fall far from the true score. The far-right distribution displays a tiny dispersion around the true score. In this case, most of the observations are extremely close to the true score so that drawing conclusions on the basis of fewer observations will likely produce fewer errors than it will for the far-left curve.

The dispersions around the true score in Figures 4.1 and 4.2 tell us how much error there is in the measure. Classical test theory assumes that the true score for an individual will not change with repeated applications of the same test. Because of random error, however, repeated applications of the same test can produce different scores. Random error is responsible for the distribution of scores shown in Figures 4.1 and 4.2. Theoretically, the standard deviation of the distribution of errors for each person tells us about the magnitude of measurement error. Because we usually assume that the distribution of random errors will be the same for all

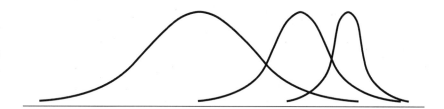

people, classical test theory uses the standard deviation of errors as the basic measure of error. Usually this is called the **standard error of measurement**:

$$\sigma_{meas}$$

The rubber-yardstick analogy may help you understand this concept. Suppose you have a table that is 30 inches high. You measure the height of the table several times using a steel yardstick and keep coming up with the same height: 30 inches. Next you try to measure the table with the rubber yardstick. The first time you try, the stick has stretched, and you record 28 inches. The next time, you discover the stick has shrunk, and it gives you 32 inches. Now you are in trouble, because repeated applications of the yardstick do not always give you the same information about the height of the table.

There is one way out of this situation. Assuming that the yardstick stretches and shrinks randomly, you can say that the distribution of scores given by the yardstick will be normal. Most scores will be close to the actual or true score. Scores that greatly differ from the true score will occur less frequently—that is, you will rarely observe a score as low as 5 inches or as high as 53 inches. The mean of the distribution of scores from repeated applications of the rubber yardstick will be an estimate of the table's true height. The standard deviation will be the standard error of measurement. Remember from Chapter 3 that the standard deviation tells us something about the average deviation around the mean. The standard error of measurement tells us, on the average, how much a score varies from the true score. In practice, the standard deviation of the observed score and the reliability of the test are used to estimate the standard error of measurement.

# The Domain Sampling Model

The domain sampling model is another central concept in classical test theory. This model considers the problems created by using a limited number of items to represent a larger and more complicated construct. For example, suppose we want to evaluate your spelling ability. The best technique would be to go systematically through a dictionary, have you spell each word, and then determine the percentage you spelled correctly. However, it is unlikely that we would have time for this. Instead, we need to find a way to evaluate your spelling without having you spell every word. To accomplish this evaluation, we decide to use a *sample* of words. Remember that what we are really attempting to evaluate is how well you can spell, which would be determined by your percentage correct if you had been given all the words in the English language. This percentage would be your "true score." Our task in reliability analysis is to estimate how much error we would make by using the score from the shorter test as an estimate of your true ability.

This model conceptualizes reliability as the ratio of the variance of the observed score on the shorter test and the variance of the long-run true score. The measurement considered in the domain sampling model is the error introduced by using a sample of items (or words in this case) rather than the entire domain.[1] As the sample gets larger, it represents the domain more and more accurately. As a result, the greater the number of items, the higher the reliability. A later section of this chapter shows how a larger number of items increases test reliability.

When tests are constructed, each item is a sample of the ability or behavior to be measured. Long tests have many such samples, and short tests have few. However, each item should equally represent the studied ability. When testing your spelling ability, for example, we could use 5 words, 100 words, or 5000 words.

Reliability can be estimated from the correlation of the observed test score with the true score.[2] This would be easy to find if we knew the true score. However, finding the true scores is not practical and is rarely possible. In the spelling example, finding the true score would involve testing people on all of the words in the English language.

Because true scores are not available, our only alternative is to estimate what they would be. Given that items are randomly drawn from a given domain, each test or group of items should yield an unbiased estimate of the true score. Because of sampling error, however, different random samples of items might give different estimates of the true score. The distribution of these estimates should be random and normally distributed. If we create many tests by sampling from the same domain, then we should get a normal distribution of unbiased estimates of the true score. To estimate reliability, we can create many randomly parallel tests by drawing repeated random samples of items from the same domain. In the spelling example, we would draw several different lists of words randomly from the dictionary and consider each of these samples to be an unbiased test of spelling ability. Then we would find the correlation between each of these tests and each of the other tests. The correlations then would be averaged.[3] Psychological Testing in Everyday Life 4.1 considers one of the technical issues in estimating true reliability.

# Item Response Theory

Perhaps the most important new development relevant to psychometrics is item response theory. Most of the methods for assessing reliability depend on classical test theory (DeVellis, 2006; Thomas, 2012). Classical test theory has been around

---

[1] The term *domain* is used to describe an extremely large collection of items. Some authors prefer the term *universe* or *population* to describe the same concept (Nunnally & Bernstein, 1994).

[2] As M. J. Allen and Yen (1979) point out, there are at least six alternative interpretations of the reliability coefficient. The interpretation we offer here is the one most commonly used.

[3] Technically, it is inappropriate to average correlation coefficients. The appropriate method is to use Fisher's *r* to *Z* transformation to convert the correlations into approximate *Z* scores. Then the *Z* scores are averaged, and the mean *Z* is transformed back into a correlation (Silver & Dunlap, 1987).

## 4.1  PSYCHOLOGICAL TESTING IN EVERYDAY LIFE

### The Unbiased Estimate of Reliability

Theorists have demonstrated mathematically that an unbiased estimate of a test's reliability is given by the square root of the average correlation between all other randomly parallel tests from the domain. Symbolically,

$$r_{1t} = \sqrt{\bar{r}_{1j}}$$

where

$1$ = scores on test 1

$t$ = the true score for the ability of interest

$\bar{r}_{1j}$ = the average correlation between test 1 and all other randomly parallel tests

As you learned in Chapter 3, product moment correlation coefficients always take on values between $-1$ and 1. When we estimate reliability, the correlation will always be positive. When a number is less than 1.0, its square root will always be larger than itself. Thus, the correlation between two randomly parallel tests will be smaller than the estimated correlation between one of the tests and the true score according to the formula. For example, if the correlation between two randomly parallel tests is .64, the estimated reliability of the test will be $\sqrt{.64} = .80$. This is built into the estimation of reliability because it would be impossible for a test to correlate more highly with any other test than it would correlate with its own true score. Thus, the correlation between two randomly parallel tests would be expected to be less than the correlation of either test with the true score.

for over 100 years and it has served the field well. However, a growing movement is turning away from classical test theory for a variety of different reasons. First, classical test theory requires that exactly the same test items be administered to each person. For a trait such as intelligence, a relatively small number of items concentrate on an individual's particular level of ability. For example, many of the items are too easy and some of them may be too hard. Because so few of the items concentrate on a person's exact ability level, the reliability of the intelligence score may not inspire confidence.

A newer approach, known as item response theory (IRT), has been the subject of intense development over the last decade (DeMars, 2010). Using IRT, the computer is used to focus on the range of item difficulty that helps assess an individual's ability level. For example, if the person gets several easy items correct, the computer might quickly move to more difficult items. If the person gets several difficult items wrong, the computer moves back to the area of item difficulty where the person gets some items right and some wrong. Then, this level of ability is intensely sampled. The overall result is that a more reliable estimate of ability is obtained using a shorter test with fewer items. Of course, there are many difficulties with applications of IRT. For instance, the method requires a bank of items that have been systematically evaluated for level of difficulty (Hays et al., 2006; Hays et al., 2007; Teresi et al., 2009). Considerable effort must go into test development, and complex computer software is required. Because of the importance of IRT in current testing, we will return to discuss this issue in more detail in Chapter 7.

# Models of Reliability

Federal government guidelines require that a test be reliable before one can use it to make employment or educational placement decisions (Larson, 2011). In this section, we hope to justify the need for high standards of reliability. Most reliability coefficients are correlations; however, it is sometimes more useful to define reliability as its mathematically equivalent ratio. The reliability coefficient is the ratio of the variance of the true scores on a test to the variance of the observed scores:

$$r = \frac{\sigma_T^2}{\sigma_X^2}$$

where

$r$ = the theoretical reliability of the test

$\sigma_T^2$ = the variance of the true scores

$\sigma_X^2$ = the variance of the observed scores

We have used the Greek $\sigma^2$ instead of $S^2$ to symbolize the variance because the equation describes theoretical values in a population rather than those actually obtained from a sample. The ratio of true score variance to observed score variance can be thought of as a percentage. In this case, it is the percentage of the observed variation $(\sigma_X^2)$ that is attributable to variation in the true score. If we subtract this ratio from 1.0, then we will have the percentage of variation attributable to random error. $\sigma_T^2 + \sigma_E^2$ could also be used as the denominator because

$$(\sigma_X^2) = \sigma_T^2 + \sigma_E^2$$

Suppose you are given a test that will be used to select people for a particular job, and the reliability of the test is .40. When the employer gets the test back and begins comparing applicants, 40% of the variation or difference among the people will be explained by real differences among people, and 60% must be ascribed to random or chance factors. Now you can see why the government needs to insist on high standards of reliability.

## Sources of Error

An observed score may differ from a true score for many reasons. There may be situational factors such as loud noises in the room while the test is being administered. The room may be too hot or too cold. Some of the test takers may have a cold or be feeling depressed. Also, the items on the test might not be representative of the domain. For example, suppose you could spell 96% of the words in the English language correctly but the 20-item spelling test you took included 5 items (20%) that you could not spell.

Test reliability is usually estimated in one of three ways. In the *test–retest method*, we consider the consistency of the test results when the test is administered on different occasions. Using the method of *parallel forms*, we evaluate the test across different forms of the test. With the method of *internal consistency*, we examine how people perform on similar subsets of items selected from the same form of the measure. Each approach is based on a different source of variability. We shall consider each method separately.

## Time Sampling: The Test–Retest Method

Test–retest reliability estimates are used to evaluate the error associated with administering a test at two different times. This type of analysis is of value only when we measure "traits" or characteristics that do not change over time. For instance, we usually assume that an intelligence test measures a consistent general ability. As such, if an IQ test administered at two points in time produces different scores, then we might conclude that the lack of correspondence is the result of random measurement error. Usually we do not assume that a person got more or less intelligent in the time between tests.

Tests that measure some constantly changing characteristic are not appropriate for test–retest evaluation. For example, the value of the Rorschach inkblot test seems to be to tell the clinician how the client is functioning at a particular time. Thus, differences between Rorschach scores at two times could reflect one of two things: (1) a change in the true score being measured or (2) measurement error. Clearly the test–retest method applies only to measures of stable traits.

Test–retest reliability is relatively easy to evaluate: Just administer the same test on two well-specified occasions and then find the correlation between scores from the two administrations using the methods presented in Chapter 3.

However, you need to consider many other details besides the methods for calculating the test–retest reliability coefficient. Understanding and using the information gained from these mechanical exercises requires careful thought. One thing you should always consider is the possibility of a *carryover effect*. This effect occurs when the first testing session influences scores from the second session. For example, test takers sometimes remember their answers from the first time they took the test. Suppose we ask someone the trivia question "Who was the half sister of Dr. Grey on the television program *Grey's Anatomy?*" Then we ask the same question 2 days later. Some of the test takers might have watched the show in the meantime and found out they were wrong the first time. When there are carryover effects, the test–retest correlation usually overestimates the true reliability.

Carryover problems are of concern only when the changes over time are random. In cases where the changes are systematic, carryover effects do not harm the reliability. An example of a systematic carryover is when everyone's score improves exactly 5 points. In this case, no new variability occurs. Random carryover effects occur when the changes are not predictable from earlier scores or when something affects some but not all test takers. If something affects all the test takers equally, then the results are uniformly affected and no net error occurs.

Practice effects are one important type of carryover effect. Some skills improve with practice. When a test is given a second time, test takers score better because they have sharpened their skills by having taken the test the first time. Asking people trivia questions about old movies might stimulate them to think more about the movies or may actually give them some of the information. Practice can also affect tests of manual dexterity: Experience taking the test can improve dexterity skills. As a result, scores on the second administration are usually higher than they were on the first. Practice may affect test takers in different ways, so the changes are not constant across a group.

Because of these problems, the time interval between testing sessions must be selected and evaluated carefully. If the two administrations of the test are close in time, there is a relatively great risk of carryover and practice effects. However, as the time between testing sessions increases, many other factors can intervene to affect scores. For example, if a test is given to children at ages 4 and 5, and the scores from the two administrations of the test correlate at .43, then we must deal with many possible explanations. The low correlation might mean that (1) the test has poor reliability, (2) children change on this characteristic between ages 4 and 5, or (3) some combination of low reliability and change in the children is responsible for the .43 correlation. Further, most test–retest evaluations do not indicate a most likely choice among alternative explanations.

When you find a test–retest correlation in a test manual, you should pay careful attention to the interval between the two testing sessions. A well-evaluated test will have many retest correlations associated with different time intervals between testing sessions. Most often you want to be assured that the test is reliable over the time interval of your own study. You also should consider what events occurred between the original testing and the retest. For example, activities such as reading a book, participating in a course of study, or watching a TV documentary can alter the test–retest reliability estimate.

Of course, sometimes poor test–retest correlations do not mean that a test is unreliable. Instead, they suggest that the characteristic under study has changed. One of the problems with classical test theory is that it assumes that behavioral dispositions are constant over time. For example, if you are an aggressive person, it is assumed that you will be aggressive all the time. However, some authors have suggested that important behavioral characteristics, such as motivation, fluctuate over time. In fact, important variables such as health status are expected to vary (Jones & Kaplan, 2003; Kaplan & Ries, 2007; Patrick, Bushnell, & Rothman, 2004). In classical test theory, these variations are assumed to be errors. Because advanced theories of motivation actually predict these variations, test theorists have been challenged to develop models to account for systematic variations (Atkinson, 1981; Langenbucher et al., 2004; McClelland, 1994; Pattishall, 1992; Yanai, 2003; Caspi et al., 2005; Roberts et al., 2007; Hand, 2011; Thomas, 2012).

## Item Sampling: Parallel Forms Method

Building a reliable test also involves making sure that the test scores do not represent any one particular set of items or a subset of items from the entire domain. For example, if you are developing a test of spelling ability, then you would include a particular subset of words from the dictionary in the test. But, as we saw earlier, a test taker may get a score different from the ideal precisely because of the items you have chosen. One form of reliability analysis is to determine the error variance that is attributable to the selection of one particular set of items.

**Parallel forms reliability** compares two equivalent forms of a test that measure the same attribute. The two forms use different items; however, the rules used to select items of a particular difficulty level are the same.

When two forms of the test are available, one can compare performance on one form versus the other. Some textbooks refer to this process as *equivalent forms reliability*, whereas others call it simply *parallel forms*. Sometimes the two forms are administered to the same group of people on the same day. The Pearson product moment correlation coefficient (see Chapter 3) is used as an estimate of the reliability. When both forms of the test are given on the same day, the only sources of variation are random error and the difference between the forms of the test. (The order of administration is usually counterbalanced to avoid practice effects.) Sometimes the two forms of the test are given at different times. In these cases, error associated with time sampling is also included in the estimate of reliability.

The method of parallel forms provides one of the most rigorous assessments of reliability commonly in use. Unfortunately, the use of parallel forms occurs in practice less often than is desirable. Often test developers find it burdensome to develop two forms of the same test, and practical constraints make it difficult to retest the same group of individuals. Instead, many test developers prefer to base their estimate of reliability on a single form of a test.

In practice, psychologists do not always have two forms of a test. More often they have only one test form and must estimate the reliability for this single group of items. You can assess the different sources of variation within a single test in many ways. One method is to evaluate the internal consistency of the test by dividing it into subcomponents.

## Split-Half Method

In split-half reliability, a test is given and divided into halves that are scored separately. The results of one half of the test are then compared with the results of the other. The two halves of the test can be created in a variety of ways. If the test is long, the best method is to divide the items randomly into two halves. For ease in computing scores for the different halves, however, some people prefer to calculate a score for the first half of the items and another score for the second half. Although convenient, this method can cause problems when items on the second half of the test are more difficult than items on the first half. If the items get progressively more difficult, then you might be better advised to use the *odd-even system*, whereby one subscore is obtained for the odd-numbered items in the test and another for the even-numbered items.

To estimate the reliability of the test, you could find the correlation between the two halves. However, this would be an underestimate because each subtest is only half as long as the full test. As we discussed earlier, test scores gain reliability as the number of items increases. An estimate of reliability based on two half-tests would be deflated because each half would be less reliable than the whole test.

---

**TABLE 4.1**    Estimates of Split-Half Reliability Before and After Correction for Half-Length Using the Spearman-Brown Formula

| Before correction | After correction | Amount of change |
|:---:|:---:|:---:|
| .05 | .09 | .04 |
| .15 | .26 | .11 |
| .25 | .40 | .15 |
| .35 | .52 | .17 |
| .45 | .62 | .17 |
| .55 | .71 | .16 |
| .65 | .79 | .14 |
| .75 | .86 | .11 |
| .85 | .92 | .07 |
| .95 | .97 | .02 |

The correlation between the two halves of the test would be a reasonable estimate of the reliability of half the test. To correct for half-length, you can apply the *Spearman-Brown formula*, which allows you to estimate what the correlation between the two halves would have been if each half had been the length of the whole test:

$$\text{corrected } r = \frac{2r}{1+r}$$

where $r$ is the estimated correlation between the two halves of the test if each had had the total number of items, and $r$ is the correlation between the two halves of the test. (There are different forms of the estimation formula, as you will see later in the chapter.) For example, when the CES-D (which was described in Chapter 3) is divided into two equal parts, the correlation between the two halves of the test (for medical students) is .78. According to the formula, the estimated reliability would be

$$\text{corrected } r = \frac{2(.78)}{1+.78} = \frac{1.56}{1.78} = .876$$

Using the Spearman-Brown formula increases the estimate of reliability. The left-hand column in Table 4.1 shows several estimates of reliability that are not corrected using the Spearman-Brown procedure. The middle column shows the same values after they have been corrected. The right-hand column shows the amount of change the correction introduces. As you can see, the Spearman-Brown procedure has a substantial effect, particularly in the middle ranges.

Using the Spearman-Brown correction is not always advisable. For instance, when the two halves of a test have unequal variances, Cronbach's (1951) coefficient alpha (*a*) can be used. This general reliability coefficient provides the lowest estimate of reliability that one can expect. If alpha is high, then you might assume that the reliability of the test is acceptable because the lowest boundary of reliability is still high; the reliability will not drop below alpha. A low alpha level, on the other hand, gives you less information. Because the alpha coefficient marks only the lower bound for the reliability, the actual reliability may still be high. Thus, if the variances for the two halves of the test are unequal, coefficient alpha can confirm that a test has substantial reliability; however, it cannot tell you that a test is unreliable. (Appendix 4.1 provides an example.) The formula for coefficient alpha is

$$\alpha = \frac{2\left[\sigma_x^2 - \left(\sigma_{y1}^2 \sigma_{y2}^2\right)\right]}{\sigma_x^2}$$

where

$\alpha =$ the coefficient alpha for estimating split-half reliability

$\sigma_x^2 =$ the variance for scores on the whole test

$\sigma_{y1}^2 \sigma_{y2}^2 =$ the variance for the two separate halves of the test

When the variances for the two halves of the test are equal, the Spearman-Brown coefficient and coefficient alpha give the same results. Although the use of Cronbach's alpha is nearly universal, some questions about the procedure have been raised (Falk & Savalei, 2011). One of the problems is that skewness can affect the average correlation among the items. In theory, the average correlation between items is zero when the items are measuring different traits. However, when responses to the items are not normally distributed, the alpha coefficient can be greater than zero even though the items are not assessing the same trait. To address this problem, a newer method known as coefficient omega is applied. Omega estimates the extent to which all items measure the same underlying trait (Revelle, 2009). Although there have been conceptual advances in reliability assessment, Cronbach's alpha remains the most commonly used reliability index.

## $KR_{20}$ Formula

In addition to the split-half technique, there are many other methods for estimating the internal consistency of a test. Many years ago, Kuder and Richardson (1937) greatly advanced reliability assessment by developing methods for evaluating reliability within a single test administration.

Their approach does not depend on some arbitrary splitting of the test into halves. Decisions about how to split tests into halves cause many potential problems for split-half reliability. The two halves may have different variances. The split-half method also requires that each half be scored separately, possibly creating additional work. The Kuder-Richardson technique avoids these problems because it simultaneously considers all possible ways of splitting the items.

The formula for calculating the reliability of a test in which the items are dichotomous, scored 0 or 1 (usually for right or wrong), is known as the **Kuder-Richardson 20**, or $KR_{20}$ or KR20. The formula came to be labeled this way because it was the 20th formula presented in the famous article by Kuder and Richardson.

The formula is

$$KR_{20} = r = \frac{N}{N-1}\left(\frac{S^2 - \Sigma pq}{S^2}\right)$$

where

$KR_{20}$ = the reliability estimate ($r$)

$N$ = the number of items on the test

$S^2$ = the variance of the total test score

$p$ = the proportion of the people getting each item correct (this is found separately for each item)

$q$ = the proportion of people getting each item incorrect. For each item, $q$ equals $1 - p$.

$\Sigma pq$ = sum of the products of $p$ times $q$ for each item on the test

Studying the components of the formula may give you a better understanding of how it works. First, you will recognize the term $S^2$ from Chapter 2. This is the variance of the test scores. The variance appears twice in the formula: once on the top of the right portion in the equation and once on the bottom of the right portion. The other term in the right portion is $\Sigma pq$. This is the sum of the product of the proportion of people passing each item times the proportion of people failing each item. The product $pq$ is the variance for an individual item. Thus, $\Sigma pq$ is the sum of the individual item variances.

Think about conditions that would make the term on the right side of the equation either large or small. First, consider the situation in which the variance ($S^2$) is equal to the sum of the variances of the individual items. Symbolically, this would be $S^2 = \Sigma pq$. In this case, the right-hand term in the formula would be 0 and, as a result, the estimate of reliability would be 0. This tells us that to have nonzero reliability, the variance for the total test score must be greater than the sum of the variances for the individual items. This will happen only when the items are measuring the same trait. The total test score variance is the sum of the item variances and the covariances between items (Crocker & Algina, 1986).

The only situation that will make the sum of the item variance less than the total test score variance is when there is covariance between the items. Covariance occurs when the items are correlated with each other. The greater the covariance, the smaller the $\Sigma pq$ term will be. When the items covary, they can be assumed to measure the same general trait, and the reliability for the test will be high. As $\Sigma pq$ approaches 0, the right side of the equation approaches 1.0. The other factor in the formula is an adjustment for the number of items in the test. This will allow an adjustment for the greater error associated with shorter tests. (Appendix 4.2 provides an example.)

In addition to the $KR_{20}$, Kuder and Richardson presented Formula 21, or $KR_{21}$, a special case of the reliability formula that does not require the calculation of the $p$'s and $q$'s for every item. Instead, the $KR_{21}$ uses an approximation of the sum of the $pq$ products—the mean test score. The $KR_{21}$ procedure rests on several important assumptions. The most important is that all the items are of equal difficulty, or that the average difficulty level is 50%. *Difficulty* is defined as the percentage of test takers who pass the item. In practice, these assumptions are rarely met, and it is usually found that the $KR_{21}$ formula underestimates the split-half reliability:

$$KR_{21} = \frac{N}{N-1}\left[1 - \frac{\overline{X}(1 - \overline{X}/N)}{S^2}\right]$$

where all terms are as previously defined.

Mathematical proofs have demonstrated that the $KR_{20}$ formula gives the same estimate of reliability that you would get if you took the mean of the split-half reliability estimates obtained by dividing the test in all possible ways (Cronbach, 1951). You can see that because the Kuder-Richardson procedure is general, it is usually more valuable than a split-half estimate of internal consistency.

## Coefficient Alpha

The $KR_{20}$ formula is not appropriate for evaluating internal consistency in some cases. The $KR_{20}$ formula requires that you find the proportion of people who got each item "correct." There are many types of tests, though, for which there are no right or wrong answers, such as many personality and attitude scales. For example, on an attitude questionnaire, you might be presented with a statement such as, "I believe extramarital sexual intercourse is immoral." You must indicate whether you *strongly disagree, disagree, are neutral, agree,* or *strongly agree.* None of these choices is incorrect, and none is correct. Rather, your response indicates where you stand on the continuum between agreement and disagreement. To use the Kuder-Richardson method with this sort of item, Cronbach developed a formula that estimates the internal consistency of tests in which the items are not scored as 0 or 1 (right or wrong). In doing so, Cronbach developed a more general reliability estimate, which he called **coefficient alpha**, or $\alpha$. The formula for coefficient alpha is[4]

$$r = \alpha = \left(\frac{N}{N-1}\right)\left(\frac{S^2 - \Sigma S_i^2}{S^2}\right)$$

As you may notice, this looks quite similar to the $KR_{20}$ formula. The only difference is that $\Sigma pq$ has been replaced by $\Sigma S_i^2$. This new term, $S_i^2$, is for the variance of the individual items ($i$). The summation sign informs us that we are to sum the individual item variances. $S^2$ is for the variance of the total test score. The only real difference is the way the variance of the items is expressed. Actually, coefficient alpha is a more general reliability coefficient than $KR_{20}$ because $S_i^2$ can describe the variance of items whether or not they are in a right-wrong format. Thus, coefficient alpha is the most general method of finding estimates of reliability through internal consistency.

All of the measures of internal consistency evaluate the extent to which the different items on a test measure the same ability or trait. They will all give low estimates of reliability if the test is designed to measure several traits. Using the domain sampling model, we define a domain that represents a single trait or characteristic, and each item is an individual sample of this general characteristic. When the items do not measure the same characteristic, the test will not be internally consistent.

---

[4] Although this formula appears different from the formula for coefficient alpha from the section "Split-Half Method," the equations are mathematically equivalent.

Factor analysis is one popular method for dealing with the situation in which a test apparently measures several different characteristics (see Chapter 3). This can be used to divide the items into subgroups, each internally consistent; however, the subgroups of items will not be related to one another (Raykov & Zinbarg, 2011). Factor analysis can help a test constructor build a test that has submeasures for several different traits. When factor analysis is used correctly, these subtests will be internally consistent (highly reliable) and independent of one another. For example, you might use factor analysis to divide a group of items on interpersonal communication into two subgroups, perhaps assertiveness items and self-esteem items. The reliability of the self-esteem and the assertiveness subscales might be quite high; however, the correlation between assertiveness and self-esteem scores could be quite low. The nature of the factor analysis method ensures these characteristics. Thus, factor analysis is of great value in the process of test construction.

## Reliability of a Difference Score

Some applications of psychological testing require a *difference score*, which is created by subtracting one test score from another. This might be the difference between performances at two points in time—for example, when you test a group of children before and after they have experienced a special training program. Or it may be the difference between measures of two different abilities, such as whether a child is doing better in reading than in math. Whenever comparisons between two different attributes are being made, one must make the comparison in Z, or standardized, units (see Chapter 2).

Difference scores create a host of problems that make them more difficult to work with than single scores. To understand the problems, you must refer back to the definition of an observed score as composed of both true score ($T$) and error ($E$). In a difference score, $E$ is expected to be larger than either the observed score or $T$ because $E$ absorbs error from both of the scores used to create the difference score. Furthermore, $T$ might be expected to be smaller than $E$ because whatever is common to both measures is canceled out when the difference score is created. As a result of these two factors, the reliability of a difference score is expected to be lower than the reliability of either score on which it is based. If two tests measure exactly the same trait, then the score representing the difference between them is expected to have a reliability of 0.

As we have previously mentioned, it is most convenient to find difference scores by first creating Z scores for each measure and then finding the difference between them (score 2 − score 1). The reliability of scores that represent the difference between two standard scores (or Z scores) is given by the formula

$$r = \frac{\frac{1}{2}(r_{11} + r_{22}) - r_{12}}{1 - r_{12}}$$

where

$r_{11}$ = the reliability of the first measure

$r_{22}$ = the reliability of the second measure

$r_{12}$ = the correlation between the first and the second measures

Using this formula, you can calculate the reliability of a difference score for any two tests for which the reliabilities and the correlation between them are known. For example, suppose that the correlation between two measures is .70 and the reliabilities of the two measures are .90 and .70, respectively. The reliability of the difference between these two measures is

$$r = \frac{\frac{1}{2}(.90 + .70) - .70}{1 - .70}$$

$$= \frac{.10}{.30}$$

$$= .33$$

As this example demonstrates, the reliability of the difference score between tests with reliabilities as high as .90 and .70 is only .33. The situation in which the reliability of the difference score is lower than the average reliabilities of the two initial measures is not unusual. In fact, it occurs in all cases except when the correlation between the two tests is 0.

The low reliability of a difference score should concern the practicing psychologist and education researcher. Because of their poor reliabilities, difference scores cannot be depended on for interpreting patterns.

For example, it may be difficult to draw the conclusion that a patient is more depressed than schizophrenic on the basis of an MMPI profile that shows a lower depression than schizophrenia score. Any differences between these two scales must be interpreted cautiously because the reliability of the score that represents the difference between the two scales can be expected to be low. The difficulties associated with using difference scores have been well studied. In a widely cited article, Cronbach and Furby (1970) demonstrated that there are many pitfalls associated with using difference scores to measure change. For example, it appears impossible to make a meaningful interpretation of the difference between scores on the same children that are taken at the beginning and at the end of a school year. Measuring the "change" that occurred during that school year requires the use of sophisticated experimental designs in which children are randomly assigned to experimental and control conditions.

Although reliability estimates are often interpreted for individuals, estimates of reliability are usually based on observations of populations, not observations of the same individual. One distinction is between reliability and information. Low reliability implies that comparing gain scores in a population may be problematic. For example, average improvements by schools on a statewide achievement test may be untrustworthy if the test has low reliability. Low information suggests that we cannot trust *gain-score* information about a particular person. This might occur if the test taker was sick on one of the days a test was administered, but not the other. However, low reliability of a change score for a population does not necessarily mean that gains for individual people are not meaningful (Mellenbergh, 1999). An improvement for an individual student might offer important information even though the test may have low reliability for the population.

Although reliability is often difficult to calculate, computer programs that do much of the work are now available.

# Reliability in Behavioral Observation Studies

Psychologists with behavioral orientations usually prefer not to use psychological tests. Instead, they favor the direct observation of behavior. To measure aggression, for example, they would record the number of times a child hits or kicks another child. Observers would tabulate the number of observable responses in each category. Thus, there would be one score for "hits," another for "kicks," and so on.

Some people feel that behavioral observation systems are so simple that they have no psychometric problems, but they have many sources of error. Because psychologists cannot always monitor behavior continuously, they often take samples of behavior at certain time intervals. Under these circumstances, sampling error must be considered (C. Kaplan, 1993).

Sources of error introduced by time sampling are similar to those with sampling items from a large domain. When each time sample is thought of as an "item," these problems can be handled using sampling theory and methods such as alpha reliability.

In practice, behavioral observation systems are frequently unreliable because of discrepancies between true scores and the scores recorded by the observer. For example, an observer might miss one or two times a child hits or kicks; another observer might catch them all. The problem of error associated with different observers presents unique difficulties. To assess these problems, one needs to estimate the reliability of the observers (Cordes, 1994). These reliability estimates have various names, including *interrrater, interscorer, interobserver*, or *interjudge reliability*. All of the terms consider the consistency among different judges who are evaluating the same behavior. There are at least three different ways to do this. The most common method is to record the percentage of times that two or more observers agree. Unfortunately, this method is not the best one, for at least two reasons. First, this percentage does not consider the level of agreement that would be expected by chance alone. For instance, if two observers are recording whether a particular behavior either occurred or did not occur, then they would have a 50% likelihood of agreeing by chance alone. A method for assessing such reliability should include an adjustment for chance agreement. Second, percentages should not be mathematically manipulated. For example, it is not technically appropriate to average percentages. Indexes such as $Z$ scores are manipulable and thus better suited to the task of reliability assessment.

The *kappa statistic* is the best method for assessing the level of agreement among several observers. The kappa statistic was introduced by J. Cohen (1960) as a measure of agreement between two judges who each rate a set of objects using nominal scales. Fleiss (1971) extended the method to consider the agreement between any number of observers. *Kappa* indicates the actual agreement as a proportion of the potential agreement following correction for chance agreement. Values of kappa may vary between 1 (perfect agreement) and $-1$ (less agreement than can be expected on the basis of chance alone). A value greater than .75 generally indicates "excellent" agreement, a value between .40 and .75 indicates "fair to good" ("satisfactory") agreement, and a value less than .40 indicates "poor" agreement (Fleiss, 1981). The calculation of kappa is beyond the scope of this presentation, but interested readers can find the procedures in Fleiss (1971) and Shrout,

## 4.2 ▼ PSYCHOLOGICAL TESTING IN EVERYDAY LIFE

### Behavioral Observation and Physical Activity in Children

Determining levels of physical activity has become one of the most crucial goals of research in child development. Physical activity is an important determinant of weight management and the risk for obesity. To address these measurement needs, researchers developed the System for Observing Children's Activity and Relationships during Play (SOCARP). This system is used to keep track of a variety of behaviors, including physical activity levels, type of activity, the size of social groups, and the amount of social behavior that occurs during play. The reliability of the system was evaluated over 24 days in eight elementary schools using a total sample of 48 boys and 66 girls. Among the children, 42% were overweight. On half of the days, the activity was videotaped. To get an objective measure of activity a uniaxial accelerometer was attached to 99 during the period recess observation. The study showed that activity could be reliably assessed by trained observers. Interobserver reliabilities (i.e., percentage agreement) were 89% for activity level, 88% for group size, 90% for activity type, and 88% for interactions. Further, the level of energy expenditure estimated by the SOCARP system correlated r = 0.67 with objective measurement using the accelerometer (Ridgers, Stratton, & McKenzie, 2011).

Spitzer, and Fleiss (1987) and Sim and Wright (Sim & Wright, 2005; Viera & Garrett, 2005). An approximation of the coefficient for the agreement between two observers is also given by the phi coefficient, which was discussed in Chapter 3. An example of a study using behavioral assessment is discussed in Psychological Testing in Everyday Life 4.2.

# Connecting Sources of Error with Reliability Assessment Method

Table 4.2 relates sources of measurement error to the methods used to assess reliability. Remember that *reliability* is a generic term. Psychologists use different methods of reliability assessment to describe different sources of measurement error, and each has a different meaning. As Table 4.2 suggests, one source of measurement error is *time sampling*. The same test given at different points in time may produce different scores, even if given to the same test takers. This source of error is typically assessed using the test–retest method. Another source of error is *item sampling*. The same construct or attribute may be assessed using a wide pool of items. For example, no one item is used to assess human intelligence, yet different items used to measure this general construct may not always give the same reflection of the true ability. This sort of error is assessed using alternate forms, or parallel forms reliability. Typically, the correlation between two forms of a test is created by randomly sampling a large pool of items believed to assess a particular construct. This correlation is used as an estimate of this type of reliability.

**TABLE 4.2**    Sources of Measurement Error and Methods of Reliability Assessment

| Source of error | Example | Method | How assessed |
| --- | --- | --- | --- |
| Time sampling | Same test given at two points in time | Test–retest | Correlation between scores obtained on the two occasions |
| Item sampling | Different items used to assess the same attribute | Alternate forms or parallel forms | Correlation between equivalent forms of the test that have different items |
| Internal consistency | Consistency of items within the same test | 1. Split-half | 1. Corrected correlation between two halves of the test |
| | | 2. $KR_{20}$ | 2. See Appendix 4.2 |
| | | 3. Alpha | 3. See Appendix 4.1 |
| Observer differences | Different observers recording | Kappa statistic | See Fleiss (1981) |

The *internal consistency* of a test refers to the intercorrelations among items within the same test. If the test is designed to measure a single construct and all items are equally good candidates to measure that attribute, then there should be a high correspondence among the items. This internal consistency is evaluated using split-half reliability, the $KR_{20}$ method, or coefficient alpha. Another source of measurement error occurs when different observers record the same behavior. Even though they have the same instructions, different judges observing the same event may record different numbers. To determine the extent of this type of error, researchers can use an adjusted index of agreement such as the kappa statistic.

As you can see, the term *reliability* refers to several methods that are used to assess different sources of error. Sometimes different sources of error occur in the same situation—for example, error associated with item sampling and additional error linked to time sampling. When evaluating reliability information, you should take into consideration all potential sources of error. Interrater agreement can be a problem in basic medical as well as behavioral studies (see Focused Example 4.1). A summary of the standards for reporting information about reliability is presented in Focused Example 4.2.

# Using Reliability Information

Now that you have learned about reliability theory and methods, you will benefit from reviewing some practical aspects of reliability assessment. Different situations call for different levels of reliability.

## Standard Errors of Measurement and the Rubber Yardstick

Earlier in this chapter, we used the rubber yardstick to introduce the concept of the standard error of measurement. Remember that psychologists working with

▼ **4.1**    **FOCUSED EXAMPLE** °

## Interrater Agreement in Pathology

Psychologists have always been self-critical about the less-than-perfect reliability rates in behavioral studies. They assume that agreement must be higher in other fields, particularly when there is an opportunity for more careful study. For example, we would expect high interrater agreement among pathologists who study tissue under a microscope. However, many studies suggest that agreement among pathologists who study the same specimens is often no better than among behavioral scientists who observe the activities of the same individuals. For example, one study evaluated the reliability of pathologist-assessed ductal carcinoma in situ (DCIS). Six pathologist subjects were given written guidelines and examples of each of the problems they were looking for. Following this training, these experienced pathologists were given 24 high-quality slides of breast tissue.

There was considerable variability in the propensity to see DCIS: one pathologist saw cancer in 12% of the slides, while another saw DCIS in 33% of the same slides.

Figure 4.3 summarizes the results for 10 slides where at least one pathologist saw DCIS. The columns represent women, and the rows represent pathologists. Hatched squares indicate that the pathologist saw DCIS; open squares indicate that DCIS was not seen. No two pathologists had the same pattern of identification. One pathologist saw cancer in eight of the ten cases, while another saw DCIS in only three. One case was diagnosed by only one pathologist, and only two cases were seen by all six. These variations in diagnostic patterns imply that patients with the same problem, going to different doctors, may get different diagnoses (Welch, 2004).

**FIGURE 4.3**

Interobserver agreement among six pathologists on DCIS for 10 cases.

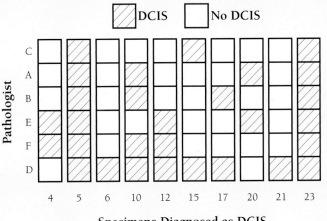

**Specimens Diagnosed as DCIS**

From Welch H. G., and Black W. C. (2007, December 1). Using autopsy series to estimate the disease "reservoir" for ductal carcinoma in situ of the breast: "How much more breast cancer can we find?" *Ann Intern Med.*, 127(11): 1023–1028. Copyright © 1997 American College of Physicians. Reprinted by permission.

unreliable tests are like carpenters working with rubber yardsticks that stretch or contract and misrepresent the true length of a board. However, as all rubber yardsticks are not equally inaccurate, all psychological tests are not equally inaccurate. The standard error of measurement allows us to estimate the degree to which a test provides inaccurate readings; that is, it tells us how much "rubber" there is in a measurement. The larger the standard error of measurement, the less certain we can be about the accuracy with which an attribute is measured. Conversely, a

---

### 4.2 FOCUSED EXAMPLE

## Summary of Guidelines for Reliability

The American Psychological Association, American Educational Research Association, and National Council on Measurement in Education (1999) suggest 20 standards for reliability.* Here is a summary of these standards:

1. Estimates of reliabilities and standard errors of measurement should be provided for each total score, subscore, or combination of scores.

2. The standard error of measurement should be reported in both raw score units and derived score units.

3. Sometimes test interpretation involves comparison between two observed scores for an individual or average scores for two groups. In these situations, reliability data, including standard errors, should be reported for differences.

4. When reporting reliability, information on the method of subject selection, sample size, and characteristics of the groups under study should be reported.

5. Reliability coefficients and standard errors, typically derived using a particular technique, should

not be used interchangeably with estimates obtained using other methods.

6. If reliability coefficients are adjusted for a restricted range, these adjustments must be reported.

7. If a test has multiple factors or measures multiple traits simultaneously, this multifactorial structure must be recognized in the reports of reliability.

8. Those who take the test must be told if the rate of work may affect their performance.

9. For tests that are timed, reliability estimates should be obtained using alternate form or test–retest methods that adjust for the amount of time subjects have to complete the test.

10. Judges can make subjective errors in rating behavior. When subjective errors are possible, an interrater consistency evaluation should consider within-examinee comparisons as well as between rater reliability.

11. Whenever feasible, test publishers should provide reliability evidence for major subpopulations. For example, they should provide separate reliability

---

small standard error of measurement tells us that an individual score is probably close to the measured value. Some textbooks refer to the standard error of measurement as the standard error of a score. To calculate the standard error of measurement, we need to use the standard deviation and the reliability coefficient. The formula for this calculation is

$$S_m = S\sqrt{1 - r}$$

where

$$S_m = \text{the standard error for the measurement}$$
$$S = \text{the standard deviation of the scores}$$
$$r = \text{the reliability coefficient}$$

For example, suppose that an IQ test has a mean of 100 for a particular sample, with a standard deviation of 14. You are particularly interested in a person with a score of 106. The reliability of the test is .89. Plugging these values into the formula, you find

$$S_m = 14\sqrt{1 - .89} = 4.64$$

estimates for white, African American, Asian American, and Hispanic groups.

12. If a test is applied to different grade levels or different age groups and separate norms are provided for each group, reliability data should be provided for each age or population group separately.

13. Sometimes national tests are applied in local areas. Whenever possible, reliability data should be evaluated and reported at the local level.

14. Conditional standard errors of measurement should be reported. This means that if the test divides examinees into specific subgroups, the standard error of measurement for each of these subgroups should be considered.

15. If a test is used to divide examinees into categories, estimates should be reported for the percentage of people who would be placed in the same category if the test were administered on two separate occasions.

16. Sometimes different examinees complete tests with different items. The items might be randomly selected from some larger pool of items (as is often the case using item response theory). Under these circumstances, reliability should be estimated on the basis of successive administrations of the test under conditions similar to those under which the test is typically administered.

17. Some tests are available in both long and short versions. Under these circumstances, reliability should be reported for each version of the test.

18. If variations are allowed in the procedures for test administration, separate reliability estimates should be provided under each of the major variations.

19. When average scores for groups are used to evaluate programs, the groups tested should be considered samples from a larger population. The standard error of the group mean should be reported.

20. Sometimes, program evaluation administrators give small subsets of items to many subsamples of examinees. Then the data are aggregated to estimate performance for the group. When these procedures are used, the reliability analysis must take the sampling scheme into consideration.

*Standards not applicable to basic psychometrics are not listed here. Adapted from American Educational Research Association et al. (1999, pp. 31–36).

Researchers use standard errors of measurement to create confidence intervals around specific observed scores. You may want to review the concept of a confidence interval in your introductory statistics textbook. Briefly, we never know whether an observed score is the "true" score. However, we can form intervals around an observed score and use statistical procedures to estimate the probability that the true score falls within a certain interval. Common intervals used in testing are the 68% interval, the 95% interval, and the 99% interval. These intervals are created using $Z$ scores (see Chapter 2).

Let's suppose we wish to create the 95% confidence interval for this specific IQ test. The 95% confidence interval is associated with the $Z$ score of 1.96. The upper bound of the confidence interval is equal to the mean plus $1.96(S_m)$, or, in this example,

$$106 + 1.96(4.64) = 115.09$$

The lower bound of the interval is equal to the mean minus

$$1.96 \times S_m$$

So, in this example, the lower bound would be

$$106 - 1.96(4.64) = 96.91$$

---

### 4.3 / PSYCHOLOGICAL TESTING IN EVERYDAY LIFE

### Are Scores Really Getting Worse?

In September 2011, newspapers across the nation reported that declining SAT scores mean that the U.S. educational system is losing ground. According to the College Board, SAT reading scores have dropped 3 points, while math scores have dropped 1 point and writing scores 2 points.

What do we make of these declines? Education journalists are quick to cite declining investments in public education. Further, they attribute some of the decline to more poorly prepared teachers, to student apathy, and to a general decline in the academic preparation of American students.

There are other explanations for the decline and, before we even go there, it is worth considering whether there has been, indeed, a measureable decline. First, we must consider the reliability of the SAT components. The ETS reports that the reliability of the SAT is quite high. For critical reading, mathematics, and writing, it suggests that reliabilities tend to be about 0.90. However, there may be some problems with the reliability of the scoring of essays. For example, different readers who evaluate the same essay do not always agree. For a group of 2006 college-bound seniors, the interrater reliability of the evaluation of essays ranged from 0.77 to 0.81. When students were asked to write more than one essay, the reliability of the estimates was only 0.67 (Ridgers et al., 2011).

Using the formula for the standard error of measurement, we can calculate the 95% confidence interval around the mean of 489 for the writing component of the SAT. For simplicity, we will use the SD of 100, which is the standard for the SAT.

The standard error of measurement is:

$$S_m = 100\sqrt{1 - .67} = 57.45$$

---

Although we do not know the true score for a person who received the score of 106, we can be 95% confident that the true score falls between 96.9 and 115.1. As you can see, however, the scores of 96 and 115 on an IQ test (see Chapters 12 and 13) are quite different. Tests with more measurement error include more "rubber." In other words, the larger the standard error of measurement, the larger the confidence interval. When confidence intervals are especially wide, our ability to make precise statements is greatly diminished. Psychological Testing in Everyday Life 4.3 applies these principles to the interpretation of changes in the average SAT score.

## How Reliable Is Reliable?

People often ask how high a reliability coefficient must be before it is "high enough." The answer depends on the use of the test. It has been suggested that reliability estimates in the range of .70 and .80 are good enough for most purposes in basic research. In many studies, researchers attempt to gain only approximate estimates of how two variables are related. For research, it may be appropriate to estimate what the correlation between two variables would have been if the measures had been

Many thousands of college-bound students take the SAT, so there is a lot of precision for estimating mean scores. However, we can use the formula to estimate the usual range to be expected around different scores. For example, we can estimate the 68% confidence interval, which would be equivalent to one standard deviation above or below the mean score of 489 for the writing component of the SAT. This would result in a range from 432 to about 546. The observed difference of 2 points is well within the range defined by one adjusted standard deviation from the mean.

Sampling is another explanation for the changes in scores between 2010 and 2011. We would expect the average performance on the test to be the same if the population of test takers was also the same. Increasing the number of less-prepared test takers is another alternative explanation for the decline in the average score. In 2011, more people than ever before took the SAT. Historically, the SAT had been taken by students most directed toward obtaining an education at a 4-year college. When the population of test takers expands, it is most likely that the population becomes more inclusive of students who have not had exposure to college preparation, including coaching for standardized tests. In 2011, not all test takers had completed the college preparative curriculum, which includes 4 years of English, 3 years of math, 3 years of natural science, and 3 years of social science and history. Those who did not complete the college prep core scored an average of 143 points lower than those who had finished the traditional preparation. This might be regarded as a positive sign because it represents increasing access to collage and greater interest in more people obtaining a college education.

more reliable. Promising results can justify spending extra time and money to make the research instruments more reliable. Some people have argued that it would be a waste of time and effort to refine research instruments beyond a reliability of .90. In fact, it has even been suggested that reliabilities greater than .95 are not very useful because they suggest that all of the items are testing essentially the same thing and that the measure could easily be shortened. Although the higher reliability is usually desirable, it may not be worth the added burden and costs (Nunnally & Bernstein, 1994). A report from the National Academy of Sciences notes that extremely high reliability might be expected for tests that are highly focused. For example, a test of skill at using the multiplication tables for one-digit numbers would be expected to have an especially high reliability. Tests of complex constructs, such as creativity, might be expected to be less reliable (Hammond, 2006).

In clinical settings, high reliability is extremely important. When tests are used to make important decisions about someone's future, evaluators must be certain to minimize any error in classification. Thus, a test with a reliability of .90 might not be good enough. For a test used to make a decision that affects some person's future, evaluators should attempt to find a test with a reliability greater than .95.

Perhaps the most useful index of reliability for the interpretation of individual scores is the standard error of measurement. This index is used to create an interval around an observed score. The wider the interval, the lower the reliability of the score. Using the standard error of measurement, we can say that we are 95% confident that a person's true score falls between two values.

## What to Do About Low Reliability

Often, test constructors want their tests to be used in applied settings, but analysis reveals inadequate test reliability. Fortunately, psychometric theory offers some options. Two common approaches are to increase the length of the test and to throw out items that run down the reliability. Another procedure is to estimate what the true correlation would have been if the test did not have measurement error.

### Increase the Number of Items

According to the domain sampling model, each item in a test is an independent sample of the trait or ability being measured. The larger the sample, the more likely that the test will represent the true characteristic. In the domain sampling model, the reliability of a test increases as the number of items increases.

A medical example will clarify why longer tests are more reliable. Suppose that you go to the doctor with indigestion. You want the doctor to make a reliable judgment about what is causing it. How comfortable would you feel if the doctor asked only one question before making a diagnosis? You would probably feel more comfortable if the doctor asked many questions. In general, people feel that the more information a doctor obtains by asking questions and performing tests, the more reliable the diagnosis will be. This same principle applies to psychological tests.

A decision to increase the number of items in a test might engender a long and costly process. With new items added, the test must be reevaluated; it may turn out to fall below an acceptable level of reliability. In addition, adding new items can be costly and can make a test so long that few people would be able to sit through it. Fortunately, by applying the Spearman-Brown prophecy formula, one can estimate how many items will have to be added in order to bring a test to an acceptable level of reliability.

The prophecy formula for estimating how long a test must be to achieve a desired level of reliability is another case of the general Spearman-Brown method for estimating reliability. Algebraic manipulations of the general formula allow one to solve it for the length needed for any desired level of reliability:

$$N = \frac{r_d(1 - r_o)}{r_o(1 - r_d)}$$

where

$N =$ the number of tests of the current version's length that would be needed

$r_d =$ the desired level of reliability

$r_0 =$ the observed level of reliability based on the current version of the test

Consider the example of the 20-item CES-D test that had a reliability for medical students of .87. We would like to raise the reliability to .95. Putting these numbers into the prophecy formula, we get

$$N = \frac{.95(1 - .87)}{.87(1 - .95)} = \frac{.124}{.044} = 2.82$$

These calculations tell us that we would need 2.82 tests of the same length as the current 20-item test to bring the reliability up to the desired level. To find the number of items required, we must multiply the number of items on the current test by $N$ from the preceding formula. In the example, this would give $20 \times 2.82 = 56.4$. So the test would have to be expanded from 20 to approximately 56 items to achieve the desired reliability, assuming that the added items come from the same pool as the original items and that they have the same psychometric properties.

The decision to expand a test from 20 to 56 items must depend on economic and practical considerations. The test developer must first ask whether the increase in reliability is worth the extra time, effort, and expense required to achieve this goal. If the test is to be used for personnel decisions, then it may be dangerous to ignore any enhancement of the test's reliability. On the other hand, if the test is to be used only to see if two variables are associated, the expense of extending it may not be worth the effort and cost.

When the prophecy formula is used, certain assumptions are made that may or may not be valid. One of these assumptions is that the probability of error in items added to the test is the same as the probability of error for the original items in the test. However, adding many items may bring about new sources of error, such as the fatigue associated with taking an extremely long test.

As an example of a situation in which increasing the reliability of a test may not be worthwhile, consider a 40-item test with a reliability of .50. We would like to bring the reliability up to .90. Using the prophecy formula, we get

$$N = \frac{.90(1 - .50)}{.50(1 - .90)} = \frac{.90(.50)}{.50(.10)} = \frac{.45}{.05} = 9$$

These figures tell us that the test would have to be nine times its present length to have a projected reliability of .90. This is calculated as $9 \times 40 = 360$ items long. Creating a test that long would be prohibitively expensive, and validating it would require a considerable investment of time for both test constructors and test takers. Also, new sources of error might arise that were not present in the shorter measure. For example, many errors may occur on the longer test simply because people get tired and bored during the long process of answering 360 questions. There is no way to take these factors into account by using the prophecy formula.

### Factor and Item Analysis

The reliability of a test depends on the extent to which all of the items measure one common characteristic. Although psychologists set out to design test items that are consistent, often some items do not measure the given construct. Leaving these items in the test reduces its reliability. To ensure that the items measure the same thing, two approaches are suggested. One is to perform factor analysis (see Chapter 3 and Hand, 2011; Raykov & Marcoulides, 2010; Raykov & Zinbarg, 2011). Tests are most reliable if they are *unidimensional*. This means that one factor should account for considerably more of the variance than any other factor. Items that do not load on this factor might be best omitted.

Another approach is to examine the correlation between each item and the total score for the test. This form of item analysis (see Chapter 7) is often called **discriminability analysis**. When the correlation between the performance on a single item and the total test score is low, the item is probably measuring something different from the other items on the test. It also might mean that the item is so easy or so hard that people do not differ in their response to it. In either case, the low correlation indicates that the item drags down the estimate of reliability and should be excluded.

## Correction for Attenuation

Low reliability is a real problem in psychological research and practice because it reduces the chances of finding significant correlations between measures. If a test is unreliable, information obtained with it is of little or no value. Thus, we say that potential correlations are attenuated, or diminished, by measurement error.

Fortunately, measurement theory does allow one to estimate what the correlation between two measures would have been if they had not been measured with error. These methods "correct" for the attenuation in the correlations caused by the measurement error. To use the methods, one needs to know only the reliabilities of two tests and the correlation between them. The **correction for attenuation** is

$$\hat{r}_{12} = \frac{r_{12}}{\sqrt{r_{11}r_{22}}}$$

where

$\hat{r}_{12}$ = the estimated true correlation between tests 1 and 2

$r_{12}$ = the observed correlation between tests 1 and 2

$r_{11}$ = the reliability of test 1

$r_{22}$ = the reliability of test 2

Suppose, for example, that the correlation between the CES-D and ratings of clinical skill was .34; the reliabilities of the tests were .87 and .70 for the CES-D and the clinical skill tests, respectively. The estimated true correlation between depression and clinical skill would be

$$\frac{.34}{\sqrt{(.87)(.70)}} = \frac{.34}{\sqrt{.609}} = \frac{.34}{.78} = .44$$

As the example shows, the estimated correlation increases from .34 to .44 when the correction is used.

Sometimes one measure meets an acceptable standard of reliability but the other one does not. In this case, we would want to correct for the attenuation caused only by the one unreliable test. To do this, we use the formula

$$\hat{r}_{12} = \frac{r_{12}}{\sqrt{r_{11}}}$$

where

$\hat{r}_{12}$ = the estimated true correlation

$r_{12}$ = the observed correlation

$r_{11}$ = the reliability of the variable that does not meet our standard of reliability

For example, suppose we want to estimate the correlation between the CES-D score and GPA in medical school. The reliability of the CES-D test is .75, which is not quite as good as we would like, but medical school GPA is assumed to be measured without error. Using the fallible CES-D depression test, we observe the correlation to be .53. Plugging these numbers into the formula, we get

$$\frac{.53}{\sqrt{.75}} = \frac{.53}{.87} = .61$$

This informs us that correcting for the attenuation caused by the CES-D test would increase our observed correlation from .53 to .61.

## Summary

*Measurement error* is common in all fields of science. Psychological and educational specialists, however, have devoted a great deal of time and study to measurement error and its effects. Tests that are relatively free of measurement error are considered to be reliable, and tests that contain relatively large measurement error are considered unreliable. In the early part of the 20th century, Charles Spearman worked out the basics of contemporary theories and methods of reliability. Test score and reliability theories have gone through continual refinements.

When we evaluate *reliability*, we must first specify the source of measurement error we are trying to evaluate. If we are concerned about errors that result from tests being given at different times, then we might consider the *test–retest method* in which test scores obtained at two different points in time are correlated. On other occasions, we may be concerned about errors that arise because we have selected a small sample of items to represent a larger conceptual domain. To evaluate this type of measurement error, we could use a method that assesses the internal consistency of the test such as the *split-half method*. The $KR_{20}$ method and *alpha coefficient* are other methods for estimating the internal consistency of a test.

The standard of reliability for a test depends on the situation in which the test will be used. In some research settings, bringing a test up to an exceptionally high level of reliability may not be worth the extra time and money. On the other hand, strict standards for reliability are required for a test used to make decisions that will affect people's lives. When a test has unacceptably low reliability, the test constructor might wish to boost the reliability by increasing the test length or by using factor analysis to divide the test into homogeneous subgroups of items. In research settings, we can sometimes deal with the problem of low reliability by estimating what the correlation between tests would have been if there had been no measurement error. This procedure is called *correction for attenuation*.

Evaluating the reliability of behavioral observations is also an important challenge. The percentage of items on which observers agree is not the best index of reliability for these studies because it does not take into consideration how much agreement is to be expected by chance alone. Correlation-like indexes such as kappa or phi are better suited to estimate reliability in these behavioral studies.

Reliability is one of the basic foundations of behavioral research. If a test is not reliable, then one cannot demonstrate that it has any meaning. In the next chapter, we focus on how the meaning of tests is defined.

# APPENDIX 4.1:
# Using Coefficient Alpha to Estimate Split-Half Reliability When the Variances for the Two Halves of the Test Are Unequal

Formula:

$$\alpha = \frac{2[S_x^2 - (S_{y1}^2 + S_{y2}^2)]}{S_x^2}$$

Data:

$$S_x^2 = 11.5$$
$$S_{y1}^2 = 4.5$$
$$S_{y2}^2 = 3.2$$

**STEPS**

1.  Find the variance for the whole test.

$$S_x^2 = 11.5$$

2.  Add the variances for the two halves of the test.

$$S_{y1}^2 = 4.5 \qquad S_{y2}^2 = 3.2 \qquad 4.5 + 3.2 = 7.7$$

3.  Find $S_x^2 - (S_{y1}^2 + S_{y2}^2)$ by subtracting the result of Step 2 from that of Step 1.

$$11.5 - 7.7 = 3.8$$

4.  Find $2[S_x^2 - (S_{y1}^2 + S_{y2}^2)]$ by multiplying the result of Step 3 times 2.

$$2(3.8) = 7.6$$

5.  Find alpha by dividing the result of Step 4 by that of Step 1.

$$\frac{7.6}{11.5} = .66$$

# APPENDIX 4.2:
# The Calculation of Reliability Using $KR_{20}$

Formula:

$$KR_{20} = \frac{N}{N-1}\left(\frac{S^2 - \Sigma pq}{S^2}\right)$$

Data:

$$NS \ = \text{number of test takers} = 50$$
$$N \ = \text{number of items} = 6$$
$$S^2 \ = \text{variance (Step 6)} = 2.8$$

| Item | Number of Test Takers Responding Correctly | $p$ (from Step 2) | $q$ (from Step 3) | $pq$ (from Step 4) |
|------|------|------|------|------|
| 1 | 12 | .24 | .76 | .18 |
| 2 | 41 | .82 | .18 | .15 |
| 3 | 18 | .36 | .64 | .23 |
| 4 | 29 | .58 | .42 | .24 |
| 5 | 30 | .60 | .40 | .24 |
| 6 | 47 | .94 | .06 | .06 |

$$\Sigma pq = 1.10$$
(from Step 5)

**STEPS**

1. Determine the number of test takers $NS$.

$$NS = 50$$

2. Find $p$ by dividing the number of people responding correctly to each item by the number of people taking the test (Step 1). This is the level of difficulty.

$$\frac{12}{50} = .24 \qquad \frac{41}{50} = .48 \cdots$$

3. Find $q$ for each item by subtracting $p$ (the result of Step 2) from 1.0. This gives the proportion responding incorrectly to each item.

$$1.0 - 2.4 = .76 \qquad 1.0 - .82 = .18 \cdots$$

4. Find $pq$ for each item by multiplying the results of Steps 2 and 3.

$$(.24)(.76) = .18 \qquad (.82)(.18) = .15 \cdots$$

5. Find $\Sigma pq$ by summing the results of Step 4 over the $N$ items.

$$.18 + .15 + .23 + .24 + .24 + .06 = 1.1$$

6. Find $S^2$, which is the variance for the test sources. To do this, you need the scores for each individual in the group. The formula for the variance is

$$S^2 = \frac{\Sigma X^2 - \left[\frac{(\Sigma X)^2}{NS}\right]}{NS - 1}$$

In this example $S^2 = 2.8$.

7. Find $S^2 - \Sigma pq$ by subtracting the result of Step 5 from that of Step 6.

$$2.8 - 1.1 = 1.7$$

8. Find $(S^2 - \Sigma pq)/S^2$ by dividing the result of Step 7 by that of Step 6.

$$\frac{1.7}{2.8} = .607$$

9. Find $N$ or the number of items.

$$N = 6$$

10. Find $N/(N - 1)$ by dividing the result of Step 9 by Step 9 minus 1.

$$\frac{6}{5} = 1.2$$

11. Find $KR_{20}$ by multiplying the results of Steps 8 and 10.

$$(1.2)(.607) = .73$$

# Validity

## LEARNING OBJECTIVES

*When you have completed this chapter, you should be able to:*

▶ Determine the relationship between establishing test validity and using the scientific method

▶ Explain why it is inappropriate to refer to so-called face validity as real evidence of validity

▶ List the categories of validity evidence recognized in the booklet *Standards for Educational and Psychological Testing*

▶ Tell how the strategy for establishing content validity evidence differs from the strategy used to obtain other types of validity evidence

▶ Discuss the difference between predictive and concurrent criterion validity evidence

▶ Relate the concept of the coefficient of determination (from Chapter 3) to the interpretation of the validity coefficient in criterion validity evidence

▶ Tell how to interpret the results of a test that, for example, had a validity coefficient of .35 for predicting success on a particular job

▶ List some of the issues to consider when you interpret a validity coefficient

▶ Know how to evaluate evidence for construct validity

▶ Select a hypothetical construct and describe how you would go about developing a measure for it

**133**

The case of Willie Griggs was argued before the U.S. Supreme Court in October 1970. Griggs and 12 other black laborers were employees of the Dan River Steam Station of the Duke Power Company in Draper, North Carolina. The company classified Griggs and the other complainants as laborers whose primary work assignment was sweeping and cleaning. The men would have preferred promotion to the next higher classification level of coal handler. However, the company required a passing score on a general intelligence test for that promotion. Of the 95 employees at the power station, 14 were black. Among the 14 black workers, 13 were assigned to sweeping and cleaning duties. The main obstacle for the men who wanted to move up in the company was their performance on the test.

Because the test appeared to render ineligible a much higher proportion of black employees than white ones, the power company was sued for engaging in discriminatory employment practice. The lawsuit centered on the meaning of the test scores. The power company managers argued that using the test "would improve the overall quality of the work force." They suggested that they did not intend to discriminate on the basis of race and that the test only helped them find the most capable employees (*Griggs v. Duke Power*, 1971).

In court, the power company was required to show why the test had meaning for the particular jobs within its establishment. In other words, the company had to prove that the test had a specific meaning for particular jobs such as laborer or coal handler. On hearing the arguments, the Supreme Court ruled that the tests served as "built-in head winds" for minority groups and had no meaning for the purpose of hiring or promoting workers to the classification of coal handler. In other words, the test did not measure specific job capabilities. The decision has been reaffirmed and eventually became the basis of the Civil Rights Bill of 1991.

As a result of the *Griggs v. Duke Power* decision, employers must provide evidence that a test used for the selection or promotion of employees has a specific meaning (Larson, 2011). In the field of testing, we refer to this meaning as *validity*. The meaning of a test is defined by specific evidence acquired by specific methods. Not only must there be evidence that a test has meaning in general, but also there must be evidence that it has validity for the particular situation in which it is applied. This evidence—not the word of a psychologist—is what establishes the meaning of a test. As in a legal court proceeding, a psychologist must obey specific rules of evidence in establishing that a test has a particular meaning for a specific purpose. This chapter reviews the rules of evidence that people use the most.

Obtaining data in validity studies is like gathering evidence for a court trial. For instance, psychologists always begin by assuming that there is no reason to believe a measure is valid. Evidence for validity comes from showing the association between the test and other variables. The rules strictly forbid saying there is a relationship without showing some proof, which is similar to the legal notion of innocent until proven guilty. Proof of guilt must be persuasive. In a similar manner, one must have convincing proof that there is a relationship between two variables before one justifiably touts the connection.

Psychologists and other professionals continually attempt to convince the public that their discipline is meaningful. Regarding psychological tests, certain segments of the public may have become too trusting. After you read this chapter, we hope that you can determine when test results are meaningful and when they are questionable.

# Defining Validity

*Validity* can be defined as the agreement between a test score or measure and the quality it is believed to measure. Validity is sometimes defined as the answer to the question, "Does the test measure what it is supposed to measure?" To address this question, we use systematic studies to determine whether the conclusions from test results are justified by evidence. Throughout the 20th century, psychologists created many subcategories of validity. Definitions of validity blossomed, making it hard to determine whether psychologists who referred to different types of validity were really talking about different things. Though validity defined the meaning of tests and measures, the term itself was beginning to lose its meaning. In 1985, a joint committee of the American Educational Research Association (AERA), the American Psychological Association (APA), and the National Council on Measurement in Education (NCME) published a booklet entitled *Standards for Educational and Psychological Testing*. These standards were revised in 1999 and again in 2012. The latest version of *Standards* is organized into three sections: foundations, operations, and applications. In many ways, this organization follows the way we have organized the eight editions of this book, into principles, applications, and issues. In *Standards*, foundations is similar to our principles and focuses on basic psychometric concepts such as validity and reliability. Operations in the *Standards* considers how tests are designed and built and how they are administered, scored and reported. It also reviews standards for test manuals and other documentation. The applications section of *Standards* takes on a wide range of issues, ranging from training required to administer and interpret tests. We shall refer to the standards frequently because they provide a sensible set of psychological test guidelines that have won approval by major professional groups.

In their original work, the joint committee set aside numerous possible definitions of validity by suggesting the following: Validity is the evidence for inferences made about a test score. There are three types of evidence: (1) construct-related, (2) criterion-related, and (3) content-related. People have many other names for different aspects of validity, but most aspects can be seen in terms of these categories.

The most recent standards emphasize that validity is a unitary concept that represents all of the evidence that supports the intended interpretation of a measure. The consensus document cautions against separating validity into subcategories such as content validity, predictive validity, and criterion validity. Though categories for grouping different types of validity are convenient, the use of categories does not imply that there are distinct forms of validity. Sometimes psychologists have been overly rigorous about making distinctions among categories when, indeed, the categories overlap (Anastasi, 1995; Hammond, 2006; Chen, Donaldson, et al., 2011).

# Aspects of Validity

In this section, we discuss the three aspects of validity suggested by the joint committee. First, however, we address what some call *face validity*. The joint committee refused to recognize face validity as a legitimate category because it is not technically a form of validity. The term needs to be mentioned because it is commonly used in the testing literature.

## Face Validity

**Face validity** is the mere appearance that a measure has validity. We often say a test has face validity if the items seem to be reasonably related to the perceived purpose of the test. For example, a scale to measure anxiety might include items such as "My stomach gets upset when I think about taking tests" and "My heart starts pounding fast whenever I think about all of the things I need to get done." On the basis of positive responses to these items, can we conclude that the person is anxious? Remember that validity requires evidence in order to justify conclusions. In this case, we can only conclude that the person answers these two items in a particular way. If we want to conclude that the person has a problem with anxiety, then we need systematic evidence that shows how responses to these items relate to the psychological condition of anxiety. Face validity is really not validity at all because it does not offer evidence to support conclusions drawn from test scores.

We are not suggesting that face validity is unimportant. In many settings, it is crucial to have a test that "looks like" it is valid. These appearances can help motivate test takers because they can see that the test is relevant. For example, suppose you developed a test to screen applicants for a training program in accounting. Items that ask about balance sheets and ledgers might make applicants more motivated than items about fuel consumption. However, both types of items might be testing the same arithmetic reasoning skill.

## Content-Related Evidence for Validity

How many times have you studied for an examination and known almost everything only to find that the professor has come up with some strange items that do not represent the content of the course? If this has happened, you may have encountered a test with poor content-related evidence for validity. Content-related evidence for validity of a test or measure considers the adequacy of representation of the conceptual domain the test is designed to cover. For example, if you are being tested on the first five chapters of this book, then content-related evidence of validity is provided by the correspondence between the items on the test and the information in the chapters.

Traditionally, **content validity evidence** has been of greatest concern in educational testing. The score on your history test should represent your comprehension of the history you are expected to know. Many factors can limit performance on history tests, however, making the professor's inferences about your knowledge less valid. These factors could include characteristics of the items (such as vocabulary words that some students do not understand) and the sampling of items (such as items on World War I in a test on ancient Chinese culture).

Because the boundaries between content and other types of evidence for validity are not clearly defined, we no longer think of content validity evidence as something separate from other types of validity evidence (Cook & Beckman, 2006;

### Challenging the Professor

Most professors have had the content validity evidence of their tests challenged at some time or other. A student may complain, "Your test did not give me an opportunity to demonstrate what I know" or "You assigned Chapters 1 through 5, but nearly all of the items came from Chapters 1 and 2—how can you evaluate whether we know anything about the other material we were supposed to read?" In the process of creating good and fair tests, professors should continually face this sort of questioning and attempt to create tests that will not evoke legitimate criticism. Good judgment is always required in test development: We can never get around the need for careful planning (Cureton, Cronbach, Meehl, Ebel, et al., 1996).

Messick, 1998a, 1998b; Chen, Donaldson, et al., 2011). However, content validity evidence offers some unique features. For example, it is the only type of evidence besides face validity that is logical rather than statistical.

In looking for content validity evidence, we attempt to determine whether a test has been constructed adequately. (See Focused Example 5.1.) For example, we ask whether the items are a fair sample of the total potential content. Establishing content validity evidence for a test requires good logic, intuitive skills, and perseverance. The content of the items must be carefully evaluated. For example, test developers must consider the wording of the items and the appropriateness of the reading level (Messick, 1998a, 1998b). Determination of content validity evidence is often made by expert judgment. There are several methods for aggregating judgments into an index of content representation. Typically, multiple judges rate each item in terms of its match or relevance to the content (Rubio, Berg-Weger, Tebb, Lee, & Rauch, 2003). Statistical methods such as factor analysis have also been used to determine whether items fit into conceptual domains (Child, 2006).

Two new concepts that are relevant to content validity evidence were emphasized in the latest version of the standards for educational and psychological tests (AERA, APA, & NCME, 2012): construct underrepresentation and construct-irrelevant variance. *Construct underrepresentation* describes the failure to capture important components of a construct. For example, if a test of mathematical knowledge included algebra but not geometry, the validity of the test would be threatened by construct underrepresentation. *Construct-irrelevant variance* occurs when scores are influenced by factors irrelevant to the construct. For example, a test of intelligence might be influenced by reading comprehension, test anxiety, or illness.

Often, test scores reflect many factors besides what the test supposedly measures. For example, many students do poorly on tests because of anxiety or reading problems. A slow reader may get a low score on an examination because he or she did not have adequate time to read through all of the questions. Only by taking such factors into account can we make accurate generalizations about what the test score really means.

# Criterion-Related Evidence for Validity

Folklore includes stories about fortune tellers who can look into crystal balls and see the future. Most people in our society do not believe that anyone can actually do this. When we want to know how well someone will do on a job, which students we should select for our graduate program, or who is most likely to get a serious disease, we often depend on psychological testing to forecast behavior and inclinations.

*Criterion validity evidence* tells us just how well a test corresponds with a particular criterion. Such evidence is provided by high correlations between a test and a well-defined criterion measure. A criterion is the standard against which the test is compared. For example, a test might be used to predict which engaged couples will have successful marriages and which ones will get divorced. Marital success is the criterion, but it cannot be known at the time the couples take the premarital test. The reason for gathering criterion validity evidence is that the test or measure is to serve as a "stand-in" for the measure we are really interested in. In the marital example, the premarital test serves as a stand-in for estimating future marital happiness.

## Predictive and Concurrent Evidence

The forecasting function of tests is actually a type or form of criterion validity evidence known as **predictive validity evidence**. For example, the SAT Critical Reading Test serves as predictive validity evidence as a college admissions test if it accurately forecasts how well high-school students will do in their college studies. The SAT, including its quantitative and verbal subtests, is the *predictor variable*, and the college grade point average (GPA) is the *criterion*. The purpose of the test is to predict the likelihood of succeeding on the criterion—that is, achieving a high GPA in college. A valid test for this purpose would greatly help college admissions committees because they would have some idea about which students would most likely succeed. Unfortunately, many tests do not have exceptional prediction records, and we must search continually for better ways to predict outcomes.

Data from an analysis of scores from students at 110 colleges and universities that participated in the College Board's National SAT Validity Study (Korbin, 2008) suggest that high-school GPA remains the best predictor of first year college GPA. The study had data on SAT scores obtained in 2006 and first-year grade point averages obtained during the spring term of 2007. There were 195,099 participants in the study. Among these, 150,377 had data available on all of the elements needed to complete the analysis. However, the correlation is quite modest ($r = 0.36$). Among the SAT components, the SAT Writing score correlates with first-year grade point average at 0.33. SAT-Critical reading is slightly less correlated ($r = 0.29$), followed by SAT-Math ($r = 0.26$).

Correcting for restricted range boosts the correlations significantly. Restricted range occurs when colleges do not have the full range of GPA scores or SAT scores because they select only the best students. This problem may reduce the level of observed correlation. When corrections for restricted range are made, correlations between the SAT components and first year college GPA typically approach about $r = 0.50$ (Korbin, Sinharay, et al., 2011). However, there is some debate about whether correction for a restricted range is appropriate.

Another type of evidence for criterion validity is concurrent. Concurrent-related evidence for validity comes from assessments of the simultaneous relationship between the test and the criterion—such as between a learning disability test and school performance. Here the measures and criterion measures are taken at the same time because the test is designed to explain why the person is now having difficulty in school. The test may give diagnostic information that can help guide the development of individualized learning programs. Concurrent evidence for validity applies when the test and the criterion can be measured at the same time.

Job samples provide a good example of the use of **concurrent validity evidence** (Landy & Conte, 2006). Industrial psychologists often have to select employees on the basis of limited information. One method is to test potential employees on a sample of behaviors that represent the tasks to be required of them. For example, Campion (1972) found that the most effective ways to select maintenance mechanics was to obtain samples of their mechanical work. Because these samples were shown to correlate well with performance on the job, the samples alone could be used for the selection and screening of applicants. Impressive results support the use of work samples for selecting employees in a variety of areas, including motor skills (Asher & Sciarrino, 1974) and work in the petroleum industry (Dunnette, 1972). However, samples seem to be more meaningful for blue-collar trades or jobs that require the manipulation of objects. They may not be equally meaningful for all jobs (Callinan & Robertson, 2000).

According to current standards for equal employment opportunity, employers must demonstrate that tasks used to test potential new employees relate to actual job performance (Larson, 2011). Thompson and Thompson (1982) reviewed 26 federal court decisions in which the validity of tests used to screen employees was challenged. The judgments in the various cases show that the job-related test must focus on tasks, should be in a written form, and must include several data sources with large samples. In other words, the courts require good scientific evidence that a test used to screen employees is valid in terms of how job candidates will perform if employed (Zedeck & Cascio, 1984). Focused Example 5.2 describes the process of validating a measure of depression.

Another use of concurrent validity evidence occurs when a person does not know how he or she will respond to the criterion measure. For example, suppose you do not know what occupation you want to enter. In each occupation, some people are happy and others are less satisfied. The Strong Interest Inventory (SII) uses as criteria patterns of interest among people who are satisfied with their careers (See Chapter 15). Then the patterns of interest for people taking the tests before they have chosen an occupation are matched to patterns of interest among people who are happy in various occupations. Vocational interests are better predictors of perceived job fit than are personality characteristics (Ehrhart & Makransky, 2007).

## Validity Coefficient

The relationship between a test and a criterion is usually expressed as a correlation called a *validity coefficient*. This coefficient tells the extent to which the test is valid for making statements about the criterion.

There are no hard-and-fast rules about how large a validity coefficient must be to be meaningful. In practice, one rarely sees a validity coefficient larger than .60,

## 5.2 FOCUSED EXAMPLE

## Validation of a Self-Report Measure of Depression

In Chapters 2, 3, and 4, we offered some data on depression based on the Center for Epidemiologic Studies Depression Scale (CES-D). The CES-D is a general measure of depressive symptoms that has been used extensively in epidemiologic studies (M. M. Weissman et al., 1977). Recall that the scale includes 20 items and taps dimensions of depressed mood, feelings of guilt and worthlessness, appetite loss, sleep disturbance, and energy level. These items are assumed to represent all the major components of depressive symptomatology. Sixteen of the items are worded negatively, whereas the other four are worded positively to avoid the possibility of patterned responses. The respondents are asked to report how often they experienced a particular "symptom" during the past week on a 4-point scale: 0 (rarely or none of the time—less than 1 day), 1 (some or a little of the time—1 to 2 days), 2 (occasionally or a moderate amount of the time—3 or 4 days), and 3 (most or all of the time—5 to 7 days). The responses to the four positive items are reverse scored. Scores on the CES-D scale can range from 0 to 60, with scores greater than 18 suggesting clinically significant levels of depression.

Validity studies have demonstrated that the CES-D is highly correlated with other measures of depression. For example, one validity study demonstrated significant correlations with the more complete Beck Depression Inventory. The CES-D, however, was designed for studies of nonpsychiatric populations (Gottlib & Cine, 1989). A series of studies have demonstrated that the CES-D is associated with

clinical diagnoses of depression; however, the CES-D is a better screening instrument than diagnostic tool. Lewinsohn and Teri (1982) demonstrated that scores of less than 16 on the CES-D were highly associated with clinical judgments of nondepression. Conversely, scores of 17 or greater had only a moderate association with psychiatric diagnoses of depression.

Because the CES-D has only moderate evidence of validity for the evaluation of clinical depression, one needs more complex methods for such evaluations. It has been suggested that as much as 3% of the population experiences major depressive problems at any given time. The American Psychiatric Association, in the fourth edition of its *Diagnostic and Statistical Manual of Mental Disorders* (DSM-IV) (1995), suggests that the diagnosis of major depressive disorder involves three components:

1. A clinician identifies a series of specific symptoms.

2. The symptoms persist for at least 2 weeks.

3. The diagnosis is not ruled out for another reason.

A diagnosis of depression thus requires the active involvement of a trained psychiatrist or psychologist. Most measures of depression do not provide enough information for anyone to make such a complex judgment.

M. Zimmerman and Coryell (1987) have offered a 22-item self-report scale that can be used to diagnose major depressive disorder. They suggest that the scale may give an accurate estimate of the prevalence of these problems in the general population. Thus,

and validity coefficients in the range of .30 to .40 are commonly considered high. A coefficient is statistically significant if the chances of obtaining its value by chance alone are quite small: usually less than 5 in 100. For example, suppose that the SAT had a validity coefficient of .40 for predicting GPA at a particular university. Because this coefficient is likely to be statistically significant, we can say that the SAT score tells us more about how well people will do in college than we would know by chance.

College students differ in their academic performance for many reasons. You probably could easily list a dozen. Because there are so many factors that contribute to college performance, it would be too much to expect the SAT to explain all of researchers can estimate the proportion of the general population that suffers from depression but not incur the expense of having a psychiatrist or psychologist interview large samples. Zimmerman and Coryell call their measure the Inventory to Diagnose Depression (IDD). The IDD includes 22 items. For each item, the person records a score of 0 (which represents no disturbance) through 4 (which indicates that the symptom is present). The numbers 1, 2, and 3 suggest different gradations of the symptom. For example, the IDD item about insomnia includes the following choices:

0 = I am not sleeping less than usual.

1 = I occasionally have slight difficulty sleeping.

2 = I clearly don't sleep as well as usual.

3 = I sleep about half my normal amount of time.

4 = I sleep less than 2 hours per night.

The IDD also considers whether the symptoms have been present for less than or more than 2 weeks. Some of the depressive symptoms considered by the IDD are decreased energy, decreased interest in sex, guilt, weight gain, anxiety, irritability, and weight loss.

Although the IDD seems to measure the concept of depression (face validity), systematic evidence obtained in validity studies is required. In other words, we need to ask, "What is the evidence that self-reports on this scale actually measure depression?"

The first step in establishing the validity of the IDD is to demonstrate that it is related to other measures designed to assess depression. For example, studies have shown it to be significantly correlated with the Hamilton Rating Scale for Depression in 234 adults ($r = .80$), the Beck Depression Inventory in 234 adults ($r = .87$), and the Carroll Depression Scale in 105 adults ($r = .81$). In addition, reports of the experience of specific symptoms on the IDD were systematically related to clinicians' judgments of individual symptoms for the same patients.

In another study, first-degree relatives of patients with psychiatric disorders were interviewed using a highly structured system known as the *diagnostic interview schedule*. The system uses a computer program to generate diagnoses for specific disorders. In 97.2% of the 394 cases, the IDD gave the same diagnostic classification of depression as did the more complex interview. Though the detailed interview identified some cases not detected by the IDD, the estimates of the rates of major depression assessed with the IDD came quite close to those found in major studies of the general population. In other studies, the IDD has helped gain an understanding of some of the determinants of depression. For example, 4332 women who had recently given birth completed the IDD. The study demonstrated that postpartum depression was significantly more common among low-income women in comparison to those with more financial resources. Postpartum depression was also associated with lower occupational prestige and having more children at home (Segre, O'Hara, Arndt, & Stuart, 2007).

There are many other measures of depression besides the IDD. However, most of these are not designed to make the specific diagnosis of major depressive disorder. Discriminant evidence for validity demonstrates the advantage of the IDD over other approaches. In particular, other measures do not feed directly into the DSM-IV classification system.

the variation. The question we must ask is "How *much* of the variation in college performance will we be able to predict on the basis of SAT scores?"

The validity coefficient squared is the percentage of variation in the criterion that we can expect to know in advance because of our knowledge of the test scores. Thus, we will know .40 squared, or 16%, of the variation in college performance because of the information we have from the SAT test. This is the coefficient of determination that was discussed in Chapter 3. The remainder of the variation in college performance is actually the greater proportion: 84% of the total variation is still unexplained. In other words, when students arrive at college, most of the reasons they perform differently will be a mystery to college administrators and professors. (See Focused Examples 5.3 and 5.4.) In many circumstances, using a test is

## 5.3 FOCUSED EXAMPLE

### The Testing Industry and the Public

Aptitude testing has become a major industry. All college-bound high-school students must take the SAT or the American College Test (ACT). Often these tests are taken several times. In addition, students often take subject area tests (SAT-II) and enroll in preparation courses, such as the Princeton Review or the Stanley Kaplan preparation class.

Concern about the power of the testing industry is not new. Ralph Nader, an aggressive attorney and consumer advocate, earned a solid reputation over the years for his attacks on giant corporations, including automobile manufacturers and food producers. Nader "exposed" the misdeeds of corporations to the public. Early in 1980, Nader released the results of his 6-year investigation of the Educational Testing Service (ETS)—the largest test producer in the United States. At a press conference he exclaimed, "What this report makes clear is that ETS's claims to measure aptitude and predict success are false and unsubstantiated and can be described as a specialized kind of fraud" (R. M. Kaplan, 1982).

What Nader disputed was the use of ETS tests such as the SAT and Graduate Record Examination

(GRE) as evidence for predictive validity. The data used by Nader and his team of researchers were no different from those used by ETS officials; however, the way Nader chose to interpret the data was markedly different. ETS has consistently reported that the SAT, for example, accounts for a small but significant percentage of the variance in first-year college grade point averages. Nader did not interpret the results in the typical terms of percentage of variance. Instead, he reported the percentage of cases the test successfully predicted according to his own criteria. On the basis of this approach, he concluded that the test predicted successfully in only 12% of the cases; however, Nader's calculations were not based on an appropriate statistical model (Kaplan, 1982, 1985). On the basis of his interpretation, Nader suggested that there should be more regulation of the testing industry. Referring to ETS, he explained, "They have assumed a rare kind of corporate power, the power to change the way people think about their own potential, and through the passive acceptance of their test scores by admissions officers, to decide who will be granted and who will be denied access

not worth the effort because it contributes only a few percentage points to the understanding of variation in a criterion. However, low validity coefficients (.30 to .40) can sometimes be especially useful even though they may explain only 10% of the variation in the criterion. For example, Dunnette (1967) demonstrated how a simple questionnaire used for military screening could save taxpayers millions of dollars every month even though the validity was not remarkably high. Landy, Farr, and Jacobs (1982) found that a performance evaluation and feedback system for computer programmers with a validity of .30 could translate into increased earnings of $5.3 million in 1 year. In some circumstances, though, a validity coefficient of .30 or .40 means almost nothing. In Chapter 18, we show how validity coefficients are translated into specific decision models and how industrial psychologists use information about test validity to save money (Landy, 2003; Landy & Shankster, 1994). Focused Example 5.5 discusses the validity of tests used in the medical field.

### Evaluating Validity Coefficients

To be an informed consumer of testing information, you should learn to review carefully any information offered by a test developer. Because not all validity to education and career opportunities" [from *APA Monitor*, 1980, *11*(2), 1–7].

Though Nader uncovered an important problem, it is not certain that the ETS deserves all of the blame. ETS puts out its own guidelines for the use of the SAT and other tests. Designed to be read by college admissions officers, these booklets clearly acknowledge the limitations of the tests. For example, college administrators are told that the test accounts for a small but significant percentage of the variation in college performance, and they are advised to look at other criteria in addition to test scores. Thus, much of the problem lies with admissions committees and with college administrators who passively accept SAT scores as the ultimate predictor of college performance. However, the Nader report started the process of questioning the value of testing. Personnel testing is now more closely regulated (Tenopyr, 1998), and some people have seriously questioned aptitude testing.

In 1997, President Bill Clinton proposed to create voluntary national tests in reading and mathematics. The Clinton proposal aroused considerable debate about the value of tests. As a result, the administration and Congress asked the National Research Council of the prestigious National Academy of Sciences to study test use. In 1999, the committee released a report entitled *High Stakes: Testing for Tracking, Promotion, and Graduation*. Although generally supportive of testing, the report raised some of the same issues originally surfaced by Nader. In particular, the National Academy expressed concern that test results are commonly misinterpreted and that misunderstanding of test results can damage individuals (Heubert & Hauser, 1999).

In response to these criticisms, a new SAT was released in 2005 for the entering college classes of 2006. The SAT verbal section was replaced by a new test called *Critical Reading*. The SAT no longer uses analogies and instead focuses on reading short passages. A new writing section was also added to the test. It includes both multiple-choice questions on grammar and a written essay. Further, the SAT math section was completely revised. Previously, the SAT math section covered only geometry and algebra I. Because so many more high-school students take advanced math, the new math section covers 3 years of high-school math and includes material covered in Algebra II.

coefficients of .40 have the same meaning, you should watch for several things in evaluating such information.

In its booklet *Standards for Educational and Psychological Testing*, the joint committee of the AERA, the APA, and the NCME (2012) lists several issues of concern when interpreting validity coefficients. Here are some of its recommendations.

**Look for Changes in the Cause of Relationships**   Be aware that the conditions of a validity study are never exactly reproduced. For example, if you take the GRE to gain admission to graduate school, the conditions under which you take the test may not be exactly the same as those in the studies that established the validity of the GRE. Many things may differ, including the way grades are assigned in graduate school and the population taking the test.

The logic of criterion validation presumes that the causes of the relationship between the test and the criterion will still exist when the test is in use. Though this presumption is true for the most part, there may be circumstances under which the relationship changes. For example, a test might be used and shown to be valid for selecting supervisors in industry; however, the validity study may have been done at a time when all the employees were men, making the test valid for selecting supervisors for male employees. If the company hires female employees,

**5.4**   FOCUSED EXAMPLE

## Why the University of California Rejected the SAT-I

In 2001, Richard Atkinson, a psychologist and president of the University of California (UC) system, proposed that the statewide university no longer require the SAT Reasoning Test (SAT-I) for freshman admission. This made the University of California the first major university system to reject the use of the SAT-I. The decision was based on a major study of 78,000 first-time UC freshmen. The study compared the SAT-I with the SAT-II. The SAT-I is the traditional test that evaluates reasoning ability, while the SAT-II is an achievement test that evaluates student knowledge in particular areas.

The study found that the SAT-II achievement tests were consistently better predictors of grades during the freshman year than was the SAT-I. In fact, controlling for SAT-II and high-school grades, the SAT-I contributes little or nothing to the prediction of first-year grades in the university. Furthermore, the study found that SAT-I scores were more sensitive to the socioeconomic background of students than were SAT-II scores. When compared against students with similar socioeconomic backgrounds, the SAT-I was unable to predict college performance. However, even after statistically controlling for socioeconomic background, the SAT-II remained a good predictor.

To learn more about this issue, see http://www.ucop.edu/pathways/ucnotes/march05/news1.html.

then the test may no longer be valid for selecting supervisors because it may not consider the abilities necessary to supervise a sexually mixed group of employees.

**What Does the Criterion Mean?**   Criterion-related validity studies mean nothing at all unless the criterion is valid and reliable. Some test constructors attempt to correlate their tests with other tests that have unknown validity. A meaningless group of items that correlates well with another meaningless group remains meaningless.

For applied research, the criterion should relate specifically to the use of the test. Because the SAT attempts to predict performance in college, the appropriate criterion is GPA, a measure of college performance. Any other inferences made on the basis of the SAT require additional evidence. For example, if you want to say that the SAT tells you something about adaptability, then you must obtain evidence on the relationship between the SAT and a separate measure of adaptability.

**Review the Subject Population in the Validity Study**   Another reason to be cautious of validity coefficients is that the validity study might have been done on a population that does not represent the group to which inferences will be made. For example, some researchers have debated whether validity coefficients for intelligence and personnel tests that are based primarily on white samples are accurate when used to test African American students (Daley & Onwuegbuzie, 2011; Murphy, 2003b; Sackett, 2003). We review this problem in detail in Chapter 6.

In industrial settings, attrition can seriously jeopardize validity studies. Those who do poorly on the job either drop out or get fired and thus cannot be studied when it comes time to do the job assessment. If there was a group that did well on the test but failed on the job, then it might not be represented and could be systematically eliminated from the study because the workers were already off the job by the time the assessment came around.

## 5.5 FOCUSED EXAMPLE

### The Cholesterol Test: Predictive Validity Evidence

The concept of predictive validity evidence applies to medical tests as well as to psychological measures. A major issue in contemporary public health is the relationship between cholesterol levels and death from heart disease. Systematic studies have demonstrated that high levels of cholesterol in the blood can help predict early death from heart disease and stroke. To learn more about these problems, physicians take blood samples to examine cholesterol levels. To evaluate this information, they must consider the relationship between the test (blood cholesterol level) and the criterion (premature death). Although this relationship has been established in many studies, the level of association is actually quite low. Some studies show the relationship to fall near .1, or to account for about 1% of the variance in mortality.

Furthermore, those with high levels of blood cholesterol are advised to eat foods low in saturated fats and cholesterol. However, some systematic studies have failed to find strong, statistically significant relationships between these dietary habits and mortality rates (Stallones, 1983). These low validity coefficients suggest that these measures tell us little about what can be predicted for a particular individual. However, heart disease is a profoundly serious problem for the general population. Each year, more than 600,000 Americans die of these problems. Thus, even weak associations help explain a significant number of cases. As a society, if we reduce blood cholesterol levels, there will be a significant reduction in the number of deaths associated with cholesterol. The low correlation between cholesterol tests and heart disease suggests that we cannot say precisely which specific individuals will benefit. However, the small but significant statistical relationship tells us that there is some important predictive value in cholesterol tests (Golomb, Stattin, & Mednick, 2000; R. M. Kaplan & Golomb, 2001; Clarke et al., 2007).

**Be Sure the Sample Size Was Adequate**  Another problem to look for is a validity coefficient that is based on a small number of cases. Sometimes a proper validity study cannot be done because there are too few people to study. A common practice is to do a small validity study with the people available. Unfortunately, such a study can be quite misleading. You cannot depend on a correlation obtained from a small sample, particularly for multiple correlation and multiple regression. The smaller the sample, the more likely chance variation in the data will affect the correlation. Thus, a validity coefficient based on a small sample tends to be artificially inflated.

A good validity study will present some evidence for cross validation. A cross validation study assesses how well the test actually forecasts performance for an independent group of subjects.[1] In other words, the initial validity study assesses the relationship between the test and the criterion, whereas the cross validation study checks how well this relationship holds for an independent group of subjects. The larger the sample size in the initial study, the better the likelihood that the relationship will cross validate.

**Never Confuse the Criterion with the Predictor**  In at least one university, students are required to meet a certain cutoff score on the GRE before they can

---

[1] Correct cross validation methodology requires that the raw score weights from the original sample be applied to the validation sample (Raykov & Marcoulides, 2010; Hand 2011).

be admitted to a graduate program. Occasionally, the department admits a student who did not get the cutoff score and these students go on to complete all of the requirements for graduation. But it still requires the student to meet the minimum GRE score before it confers a degree. The logic behind this policy represents a clear misunderstanding of the test and its purpose.

In this case, the GRE is the predictor, and success in graduate school is the criterion. The only reason for using the test in the first place is to help select students who have the highest probability of success in the program. By completing the program, the students have already succeeded on the criterion (success in the program). Before the university would acknowledge that the students indeed had succeeded, the students had to go back and demonstrate that they would have been predicted to do well on the criterion. This reflects a clear confusion between predictor and criterion. Further, most of the students provisionally admitted because of low GRE scores succeeded by completing the program.

**Check for Restricted Range on Both Predictor and Criterion**    A variable has a "restricted range" if all scores for that variable fall very close together. For example, the GPAs of graduate students in Ph.D. programs tend to fall within a limited range of the scale—usually above 3.5 on a 4-point scale. The problem this creates is that correlation depends on variability. If all the people in your class have a GPA of 4.0, then you cannot predict variability in graduate-school GPA. Correlation requires that there be variability in both the predictor and the criterion.

One major problem with the GRE is that it does not correlate well with graduate-school GPAs. Sternberg and Williams (1997) did a detailed study of predictors of success among Yale psychology graduate students. They found that GRE verbal scores were weakly correlated with GPA at Yale ($r = 0.17$) but that GRE quantitative scores were not significant predictors of graduate-school performance. Further GRE scores were not significantly related to faculty ratings of analytical skills, creativity, practicality, research skills, teaching skills, or the quality of doctoral dissertations. Some studies make a strong argument in favor of the GRE, but the results are actually quite similar. For example, Kuncel and colleagues aggregated results from 100 studies involving more than 10,000 students. When predicting first year graduate grade point average in doctoral programs, the predictive validity of the GRE Verbal and GRE Quantitative was statistically significant, but quite modest (GRE-Verbal $r = .22$, GRE-Quantitative $r = .24$). Of course, GPA is not the best criterion for graduate school success. Yet ratings of student performance by faculty were in the same range (GRE-Verbal $r = .23$, GRE-Quantitative $r = .20$) (Kuncel, Wee, et al., 2010). Other measures, such as career success, are rarely available.

There are at least three explanations for the modest performance of the GRE for predicting graduate-school performance. First, the GRE may not be a valid test for selecting graduate students. Second, those students who are admitted to graduate school represent such a restricted range of ability that it is not possible to find significant correlations. Students with low GRE scores are usually not admitted to graduate school and, therefore, are not considered in validity studies. Third, grades in graduate school often represent a restricted range. Once admitted, students in graduate programs usually receive A's and B's. A grade of C is usually considered a failing grade. Although the restricted-range problem cannot be ruled out, many studies do show substantial variability in GRE scores and in graduate-school grades. Even in the study of the prestigious Yale program, GRE verbal scores ranged from 250 to 800 (mean = 653), and GRE quantitative scores ranged from 320 to 840 (mean = 672). Ratings by professors had substantial variability (Sternberg & Williams, 1997).

In addition to graduate schools, most schools of veterinary medicine use the GRE. Because veterinary schools are larger than most graduate programs, estimating veterinary school success from the GRE provides a good opportunity for study. There are 27 schools of veterinary medicine in the United States. One study obtained data from approximately 1400 students who had applied to 16 schools. The study suggested that undergraduate GPA is the best predictor of grades in veterinary school ($r$ = .53). The correlation for the GRE-V verbal was 0.41; the correlation for the quantitative portion of the GRE (GRE-Q) was 0.47; and the correlation for the analytic section (GRE-A) was 0.45. The authors of the study corrected for the restricted range and measurement error in the GRE. As would be expected, these validity coefficients increase with these corrections (Powers, 2001). However, not all reviewers believe that correction is appropriate. In summary, even the best evidence suggests that GRE accounts for only one-fifth of the variation in veterinary school success ($0.47^2$ = 0.22).

**Review Evidence for Validity Generalization**    Criterion-related validity evidence obtained in one situation may not be generalized to other similar situations. *Generalizability* refers to the evidence that the findings obtained in one situation can be generalized—that is, applied to other situations. This is an issue of empirical study rather than judgment. In other words, we must prove that the results obtained in a validity study are not specific to the original situation. There are many reasons why results may not be generalized. For example, there may be differences in the way the predictor construct is measured or in the type of job or curriculum involved—in the actual criterion measure—between the groups of people who take the test; there may also be differences in the time period—year or month—when the test is administered. Because of these problems, we cannot always be certain that the validity coefficient reported by a test developer will be the same for our particular situation. An employer, for example, might use a work-sample test based on information reported in the manual, yet the situation in which he or she uses the test may differ from the situations of the original validation studies. When using the test, the employer might be using different demographic groups or different criterion measures or else predicting performance on a similar but different task. Generalizations from the original validity studies to these other situations should be made only on the basis of new evidence.

**Consider Differential Prediction**    Predictive relationships may not be the same for all demographic groups. The validity for men could differ in some circumstances from the validity for women. Or the validity of the test may be questionable because it is used for a group whose native language is not English, even though the test was validated for those who spoke only English. Under these circumstances, separate validity studies for different groups may be necessary. This issue will be discussed in more detail in Chapter 6.

Although criterion-related validity evidence is common in psychological and educational research, it simply does not apply in some instances. By definition, the criterion must be the most accurate measure of the phenomenon if it is to serve as the "gold standard." If a criterion exists, then only greater practicality or less expense justifies the use of concurrent measures as proxies or substitutes for the criterion. If the criterion is not a superior measure, then failure of correspondence by any new measure may reveal a defect in the criterion itself. For example, studies on the validity of measures of general health have been hindered because a clear criterion of health has never been defined (Kaplan, 2002). The development of a health index helped define the meaning of the term *health*. Often work on a psychological test involves the simultaneous development of a concept and the instrumentation to measure the concept. This cannot be accomplished by criterion-related validity studies. Instead, we need a more involved approach that involves construct-related evidence for validity.

## Construct-Related Evidence for Validity

Before 1950, most social scientists considered only criterion and content evidence for validity. By the mid-1950s, investigators concluded that no clear criteria existed for most of the social and psychological characteristics they wanted to measure. Developing a measure of intelligence, for example, was difficult because no one could say for certain what intelligence was. Studies of criterion validity evidence would require that a specific criterion of intelligence be established against which tests could be compared. However, there was no criterion for intelligence because it is a hypothetical construct. A *construct* is defined as something built by mental synthesis. As a construct, intelligence does not exist as a separate thing we can touch or feel, so it cannot be used as an objective criterion.

Contemporary psychologists often want to measure intelligence, love, curiosity, or mental health. None of these constructs are clearly defined, and there is no established criterion against which psychologists can compare the accuracy of their tests. These are the truly challenging problems in measurement.

**Construct validity evidence** is established through a series of activities in which a researcher simultaneously defines some construct and develops the instrumentation to measure it. This process is required when "no criterion or universe of content is accepted as entirely adequate to define the quality to be measured" (Cronbach & Meehl, 1955, p. 282; Sackett, 2003). Construct validation involves assembling evidence about what a test means. This is done by showing the relationship between a test and other tests and measures. Each time a relationship is demonstrated, one additional bit of meaning can be attached to the test. Over a series of studies, the meaning of the test gradually begins to take shape. The gathering of construct validity evidence is an ongoing process that is similar to amassing support for a complex scientific theory. Although no single set of observations provides crucial or critical evidence, many observations over time gradually clarify what the test means. An example of construct validity evidence is given in Focused Example 5.6.

Years ago, D. T. Campbell and Fiske (1959) introduced an important set of logical considerations for establishing evidence of construct validity. They distinguished between two types of evidence essential for a meaningful test: convergent and discriminant. To argue that a test has meaning, a test constructor must be armed with as much of these two types of evidence as possible.

## Convergent Evidence

When a measure correlates well with other tests believed to measure the same construct, **convergent evidence** for validity is obtained. This sort of evidence shows that measures of the same construct *converge*, or narrow in, on the same thing. In many ways, convergent evidence that is also construct validity evidence is like criterion validity evidence. In each case, scores on the test are related to scores on some other measure. In the case of convergent evidence for construct-related validity, however, there is no criterion to define what we are attempting to measure. Criterion-related evidence for validity is fine for situations in which we are attempting to predict performance on a particular variable, such as success in graduate school. Here the task is well defined, and all we need to do is find the items that are good predictors of this graduate-school criterion. Because there is no well-defined criterion in construct-related validity, the meaning of the test comes to be defined by the variables it can be shown to be associated with.

An example of the need to obtain construct validation evidence comes from studies that attempt to define and measure the construct "health," a complex concept. Because of this complexity, no single measure can serve as the criterion against which a measure of health can be assessed. This situation requires establishment of evidence for construct validity. Some of the construct validation studies were used to demonstrate the convergent validity evidence for the measure of health that the authors called a *health index*.

Convergent evidence is obtained in one of two ways. In the first, we show that a test measures the same things as other tests used for the same purpose. In the second, we demonstrate specific relationships that we can expect if the test is really doing its job. The studies on the health index included both types of evidence. In demonstrating the meaning of the health index, the authors continually asked themselves, "If we were really measuring health, which relationships would we expect to observe between the health index and other measures?" The simplest relationship, between health index scores and the way people rate their own health status, was strong and clearly showed that the index captured some of the same information that individuals used to evaluate their own health. However, a good measure must go beyond this simple bit of validity evidence because self-ratings are unreliable. If they were not, then we would use self-perceived health status itself as the index of health and not bother to develop another health index.

In construct validity evidence, no single variable can serve as the criterion. In the case of the health index, other studies were used to show a variety of other relationships. For example, people who scored as less healthy on the health index also tended to report more symptoms and chronic medical conditions. The authors also hypothesized that health status would be related to age, and they observed that these two variables were indeed systematically related: older people in the sample tended to have a lower health status than did younger people.

The researchers also evaluated specific hypotheses based on certain theoretical notions about the construct. In the health index studies, the authors reasoned that "if the index really measures health, then we would expect that people who score low on the measure will visit doctors more often." A study confirming that those scoring lower on health status visited doctors more often provided evidence for one more inference. Also, certain groups (such as disabled people) should have

## 5.6 FOCUSED EXAMPLE

### The Meaning of Love

An interesting example of construct validity evidence comes from the work of Zick Rubin (1970, 1973), who noted that love has been one of the most discussed issues of all time. Throughout history, men and women have written and sung about love more than any other topic. The index to Bartlett's *Familiar Quotations* shows that references to love are second only to citations to "man" (with "love" cited 769 times and "man" cited 843 times). All this preoccupation with love, however, has not led to a better understanding of its true meaning. Perhaps it is something we can feel but not necessarily understand well enough to describe in a definite way.

In the mid-1970s, there was a famous trial in Los Angeles in which singer Michelle Triola Marvin sued actor Lee Marvin for half the earnings he gained while the couple lived together. A major issue in the trial was the couple's unmarried status during the period in which the earnings occurred. During the trial, Lee's attorney questioned the actor about the extent to which he loved Michelle while they lived together. If he had been asked his height, he could have used the scale of inches. But love? How could he put that into a number? The actor instead resorted to a gas-tank analogy. He said his love for the singer was like when you are driving your car and you look over at your gas gauge and find it "about half full." That is about how much he loved Michelle—about half a tank. If there had been a measure of love, he would not have needed to use such a vague analogy (Rubin, 1979).

In developing his love scale, Rubin first had to create a list of items that represented all the different things people might call love. This was not an easy task because we all have different ideals. To create a measure of love, Rubin had to condense conventional wisdom about loving and liking into sets of statements to which people could respond on a scale. He eventually developed statements that subjects could agree or disagree with on a 5-point scale (where 1 is for strong disagreement and 5 is for strong agreement).

Collecting a set of items for construct validation is not easy because we never know which items eventually will be relevant to the construct we are attempting to measure. Building the love scale was particularly difficult in this regard. To prepare his measure, Rubin read extensively about love. Elizabeth Barrett Browning wrote, "How do I love thee? Let me count the ways." Indeed, after reading the many diverse views of love, Rubin hardly knew where to begin counting. However, because this was a study in construct validity evidence, it was important that Rubin consider counting. Construct validity evidence requires that there be content validity evidence. Content validity evidence in turn requires that the items fully represent the domain of inference (in this case, love). All the ways that love is defined by different people must be included in this collection.

Rubin began his study with his sets of statements that people could respond to on a scale ranging from disagreement to agreement. Some of the items were intended to measure love, whereas others were supposed to tap liking. Next he gave the pool of items to 198 students from the University of Michigan. Each item had a blank in which a name could be

lower average scores on the index than do other groups (such as nondisabled people). Again, a study confirmed this hypothesis (Kaplan, Ganiats, Sieber, & Anderson, 1998; Fryback et al., 2007).

In another series of studies, investigators argued that a health index should correlate with specific physiological measures representing disease states. In one study, for example, patients with chronic lung diseases took measures of lung function. These measures were more strongly correlated with the general health index than they were with a variety of other physiological and social variables (Kaplan & Ries, 2007). Other studies demonstrated that the measures were related to clinical indicators of arthritis, Alzheimer's disease, depression, schizophrenia, and other conditions. If a health index really measures health, then treatments designed to filled in. The students responded to the questions twice, one time filling in the name of their lover and another time filling in the name of a friend. Then the items were subjected to factor analysis. Recall from Chapter 3 that this is a method for reducing a large number of items or variables into smaller and more manageable composites of items called *factors*.

In the love scale, three factors were obtained: attachment, caring, and intimacy. The items on the attachment scale emphasized desire to be with the loved person or to seek him or her out if lonely. The caring scale included items about empathy and concern for the loved person's welfare. The intimacy scale considered exclusive aspects of the relationship—for example, the willingness to confide in him or her about intimate personal problems. The items on the liking scale focused on favorable aspects of the other person along such dimensions as adjustment, maturity, good judgment, and intelligence.

The data from these scales were subjected to several statistical procedures that helped discriminate between the responses of lovers and friends and eventually led to the establishment of two measures: a love scale and a liking scale. With these measures of liking and loving in hand, Rubin next had to determine whether they were really measuring what they were supposed to measure. One study using the test with dating couples suggested that loving and liking were not necessarily related. There was a modest relationship between scores on the two scales, which was weaker for women than for men. This suggested, especially for women, that we can love someone we do not particularly like.

Several things indicated that the love scale really was measuring "love." For example, men and women scored higher on the love scale when they filled in the names of their lovers than when they filled in the name of a same-sex friend (all were assumed to be heterosexual). There also was a substantial correlation between love-scale scores and estimates of the likelihood of marriage. The greater the love score, the more probable marriage was considered to be.

Finally, some of the dating couples were separated into groups of "strong love" (high love scores) and "weak love" (low love scores). From behind a one-way mirror, the researchers noted how much eye contact the lovers had with each other. Strong lovers spent more time simply gazing into each other's eyes than did weak lovers. When paired with a strong opposite-sex lover from another couple, strong lovers made no more mutual eye contact than did weak lovers.

In summary, Rubin began his study of love with neither a clear definition of love nor a method of measuring it. Through a series of structured exercises, he gradually came to have a better grasp of the construct. For example, he discovered that lovers mark some items differently than do couples who are just friends. He also discovered that "love" may have at least three independent components. Once the basic scale was developed, each new application defined a new meaning. For instance, one study showed that the scale predicts how much time lovers will spend gazing into each other's eyes. Thus, in future applications of the love scale, we would expect couples who score as strong lovers (for one another) to spend much time in mutual gazing.

improve health should be reflected by changes in the measure. In one study, patients with arthritis underwent a new treatment believed to remedy their condition. The general health index demonstrated the significant improvements caused by the treatment (Bombardier, Ware, Russell, et al., 1986). Other studies showed the measure was related to improvements in conditions such as Alzheimer's disease (Kerner, Patterson, Grant, & Kaplan, 1998), schizophrenia (T. Patterson et al., 1996), arthritis (Groessl, Kaplan, & Cronan, 2003), diseases of the veins (Kaplan, Criqui, Denenberg, Bergan, & Fronek, 2003), depression (Pyne et al., 2003), aging (Groessl et al., 2007), and several other conditions (Kaplan & Ries, 2007).

A series of studies thus expanded the number of meanings that could be given to the health index. Yet, convergent validity evidence does not constitute all of the

## 5.7 FOCUSED EXAMPLE

### Construct Validity of the Women's Health Initiative Insomnia Rating Scale

A brief measure known as the Women's Health Initiative Insomnia Rating Scale (WHIIRS) was administered to 67,999 postmenopausal women. The study also measured a wide variety of other variables.

Validity of the WHIIRS is defined by its associations with other measures. Some of the validity coefficients are shown in Figure 5.1. In the figure, three of these validity coefficients are negative. For example, higher scores on insomnia that represents poor sleep are associated with low levels of emotional well-being, energy, and general health. The researchers did not expect emotional expression to be associated with sleep. Indeed, they observed little correlation between emotional expression and the WHIIRS. The WHIIRS was positively correlated with hot flashes and sleep duration. This suggests that women with high scores on insomnia experienced more hot flashes at night and slept fewer hours. Overall, these findings support the validity of the WHIIRS (Levine et al., 2003).

**FIGURE 5.1**
Validity correlations for WHIIRS.

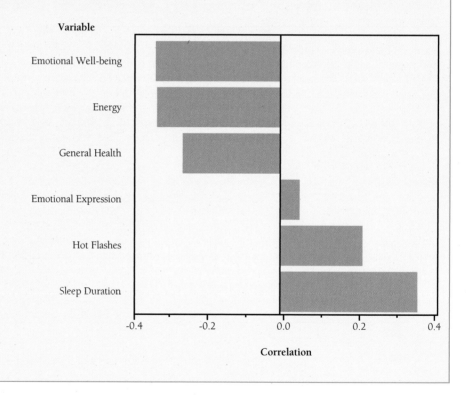

evidence necessary to argue for the meaning of a psychological test or measure. In this case, we also must have discriminant evidence (see Focused Example 5.7).

### Discriminant Evidence

Scientists often confront other scientists with difficult questions such as, "Why should we believe your theory if we already have a theory that seems to say the same thing?" An eager scientist may answer this question by arguing that his or her theory is distinctive and better. In testing, psychologists face a similar challenge. Why should they create a new test if there is already one available to do the job? Thus, one type of evidence a person needs in test validation is proof that the test measures something unique. For example, if a health index measures the same thing that self-ratings of health, symptoms, and chronic medical conditions measure, then why do we need it in addition to all these other measures? The answer is that the index taps something other than the tests used in the convergent evidence studies. This demonstration of uniqueness is called **discriminant evidence**, or what some call *divergent validation*. To demonstrate discriminant evidence for validity, a test should have low correlations with measures of unrelated constructs, or evidence for what the test does not measure.

By providing evidence that a test measures something different from other tests, we also provide evidence that we are measuring a unique construct. Discriminant evidence indicates that the measure does not represent a construct other than the one for which it was devised.

As this discussion implies, construct-related validity evidence actually subsumes all the activities used in other types of validity evidence studies. In construct-related validation, for example, content-related validation is an essential step. Furthermore, convergent and discriminant studies actually correlate the tests with many different criteria. For example, a measure of health status might be validated by showing correlations with symptoms, doctor visits, or physiological variables. Assembling construct-related evidence for validity requires validation against many criteria. Until quite recently, textbooks divided validity into different types. However, this was often confusing because there is a similarity between what was called *construct-* and *criterion-related validity*. Many psychologists now believe that construct-related evidence for validity actually is the only major type of validity that need concern us. Validity is defined by evidence and other categories (such as criterion-related and convergent) that might be thought of as subcategories of validity evidence (Anastasi & Urbina, 1997; Heubert & Hauser, 1999; Landy, 2003; Messick, 1998a, 1998b, 1999; Murphy, 2003a, 2003b; Rothstein, 2003; Sackett, 2003; Schmidt & Hunter, 2003; Raykov & Marcoulides, 2010; Ridgers, Stratton, et al., 2011; Thomas, 2012). According to the testing pioneer Lee Cronbach, it may not be appropriate to continue to divide validity into three parts: "All validation is one, and in a sense all is construct validation" (1980, p. 99). Recall that the 2012 edition of *Standards for Educational and Psychological Testing* no longer recognizes different categories of validity. Instead, it recognizes different categories of evidence for validity.

## Criterion-Referenced Tests

The procedures for establishing the validity of a criterion-referenced test resemble those for studying the validity of any other test. As you may recall from Chapter 2, criterion-referenced tests have items that are designed to match certain specific instructional objectives. For example, if the objective of some educational program is for children to be able to list 75% of the countries in Europe, then the criterion-referenced test could ask that the countries be listed. Children who listed 75% of the countries would pass the test. They would be evaluated against this specific criterion rather than on the basis of how they perform relative to other students. Validity studies for the criterion-referenced tests would compare scores on the test to scores on other measures that are believed to be related to the test. Specific procedures for evaluating the validity of a criterion-referenced test have been discussed in more technical articles (see Forsyth, 1991; Hambleton, 1994; Popham, 1994). The idea of comparing an individual with himself or herself rather than to the norms of a group remains appealing (Freeman & Miller, 2001).

## Relationship Between Reliability and Validity

Attempting to define the validity of a test will be futile if the test is not reliable. Theoretically, a test should not correlate more highly with any other variable than it correlates with itself. The maximum validity coefficient ($r_{12max}$) between two variables is equal to the square root of the product of their reliabilities, or $r_{12max} = \sqrt{r_{11}r_{22}}$, where $r_{11}$ and $r_{22}$ are the reliabilities for the two variables.

Because validity coefficients are not usually expected to be exceptionally high, a modest correlation between the true scores on two traits may be missed if the test for each of the traits is not highly reliable. Table 5.1 shows the maximum validity you can expect to find given various levels of reliability for two tests. Sometimes we cannot demonstrate that a reliable test has meaning. In other words, we can have

**TABLE 5.1**  How Reliability Affects Validity*

| Reliability of test | Reliability of criterion | Maximum validity (correlation) |
|:---:|:---:|:---:|
| 1.0 | 1.0 | 1.00 |
| .8 | 1.0 | .89 |
| .6 | 1.0 | .77 |
| .4 | 1.0 | .63 |
| .2 | 1.0 | .45 |
| .0 | 1.0 | .00 |
| 1.0 | .5 | .71 |
| .8 | .5 | .63 |
| .6 | .5 | .55 |
| .4 | .5 | .45 |
| .2 | .5 | .32 |
| .0 | .5 | .00 |
| 1.0 | .0 | .00 |
| .8 | .0 | .00 |
| .6 | .0 | .00 |
| .4 | .0 | .00 |
| .2 | .0 | .00 |
| .0 | .0 | .00 |

*The first column shows the reliability of the test. The second column displays the reliability of the validity criterion. The numbers in the third column are the maximum theoretical correlations between tests, given the reliability of the measures.

**FIGURE 5.2**
Division of total variation
on a performance measure
as a function of validity
and reliability. Many
sources of variation are
reflected in a test score.
Most of the variance in
scores remains unexplained
(60%). Internal error (14%)
and timesampling error
(10%) are two types of
reliability that reduce the
validity of the test. Validity
accounts for approximately
16% of the total variance
in this example.

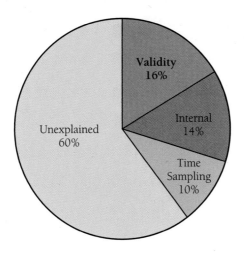

reliability without validity. However, it is logically impossible to demonstrate that an unreliable test is valid.

Reliability and validity are related concepts. Figure 5.2 divides the total variation of a test score into different parts. The example used is a test with a validity coefficient of .40. If we consider the total variability on some measure, such as college performance, approximately 16% of the variation might be explained by performance on a predictor test. There is also variation in the score, part of which is explained by measurement error. As noted in Chapter 4, this error might be related to time sampling, internal consistency, item sampling, and so forth. The figure hypothetically shows these relationships. Finally, some of the variability is "un-explained" or explained by factors of which we are unaware.

# Summary

*Validity* is a basic idea in measurement and in the science of psychology. Although we have emphasized the validity of psychological tests, the ideas we discussed apply equally to all measures. To make any inference, a good scientist must have substantiating data.

Once a test is "validated," many psychologists mistakenly think it can be used to support many different inferences. Actually, there should be as many validity studies as there are inferences about the scores (Cronbach, 1995). Validity really refers to evidence supporting what can be said on the basis of the test scores and not to the tests themselves (Landy, 2003). Any time we claim that a test score means something different from before, we need a new validity study.

Acquiring evidence about the meaning of tests should be an ongoing process. The more a test or a measure is used, the more we learn about what it means. According to two well-known applied psychologists, "Test users should never feel that they know enough about the behavioral meaning of their selection methods" (Dunnette & Borman, 1979, p. 484).

To establish the validity of a test, we need to gather several types of evidence. It is usually valuable to have *face validity*, or the appearance that a measure has meaning, even though this is not a formally recognized type of validity. *Content validity evidence* is based on the correspondence between the item content and the domain the items represent. Sometimes tests are evaluated against a well-defined criterion. *Predictive validity evidence* comes from studies that use a test to forecast performance on a criterion that is measured at some point in the future. *Concurrent validity evidence* is obtained from correlations between the test and a criterion when both are measured at the same point in time. *Construct validity evidence* is used when a specific criterion is not well defined. *Convergent evidence* comes from correlations between the test and other variables that are hypothetically related to the construct. *Discriminant evidence* shows that the measure does not include superfluous items and that the test measures something distinct from other tests. Reliability and validity are related because it is difficult to obtain evidence for validity unless a measure has reasonable validity. On the other hand, a measure can have high reliability without supporting evidence for its validity. Validity is central to the understanding of psychological tests and measures. We shall refer to validity in all of the remaining chapters.

# 6

## CHAPTER

# Test Bias

## LEARNING OBJECTIVES

*When you have completed this chapter, you should be able to:*

▶ Discuss some of the current controversies surrounding the use of intelligence tests

▶ Give arguments for and against the belief that the content of standardized tests is biased in favor of white, middle-class children

▶ Explain how criterion-related validity studies, which review the slopes and intercepts of regression lines, are used in the study of test bias

▶ Discuss some of the problems with tests such as the Chitling Test and the BITCH

▶ List the components of the SOMPA and some of its advantages and disadvantages

▶ Describe how different social, political, and ethical viewpoints are represented by different definitions of test fairness

▶ Discuss some of the opportunities for developing improved predictors for minority group members

▶ Describe some of the problems with the criteria commonly used to evaluate standardized tests

▶ Describe how one can use differences in test scores to justify efforts to change the social environment

▶ Using the information from this chapter and from other sources, write an essay for or against the use of standardized tests for minority children

For the last 50 years, serious emotional debates have flourished about the meaning of tests for the placement and classification of individuals. This chapter reviews test bias, an issue so controversial that it has inspired court evaluations of the meaning of tests for minority group members.

Although test bias is an unmistakably important issue (Reynolds & Livingston, 2012; Kuncel & Hezlett, 2007), it was not the first controversy surrounding mental testing. Mental testing has faced serious questions since test reports began in 1905, and psychologists and others have debated the issues since the 1920s (Cronbach, 1975; Haney, 1981).

We feel that it is important to offer some context for this chapter. Differences in educational attainment not only predict wealth, but are also associated with health, well-being and life expectancy. Inequality is perhaps the most challenging social problem we face. Some people believe that differences in educational achievement are a reflection of basic traits, such as intelligence. Many textbooks avoid the topic because it is controversial and emotionally loaded. It is repugnant when someone suggests that some ethnic and racial groups do not have the same potential. Yet, over the course of the last 40 years, this discussion has appeared in the scholarly literature and we felt it was our responsibility to attempt to summarize what has been said. We do our best to explain the differing points of view without taking a position on whether we agree or disagree with each position. In this chapter, we also try to offer some historical context by discussing points of view that have evolved over the last 40 years. The goal is to help you understand how scholars have dealt with this topic without taking a position about which point of view is correct or incorrect.

# Why Is Test Bias Controversial?

That all persons are created equal is the cornerstone of political and social thought in U.S. society, yet all individuals are not treated equally. The history of social action is replete with attempts to remedy this situation. However, psychological tests are designed to measure differences among people, often in terms of desirable personal characteristics such as intelligence and aptitude. Test scores that demonstrate differences among people may suggest to some that people are not created with the same basic abilities.

The most difficult problem is that some ethnic groups obtain lower average scores on some psychological tests. The most controversial case concerns intelligence tests. On average, African Americans score about 15 points lower than white Americans on standardized IQ tests. (See Chapter 12 for the meaning of IQ scores.) This difference equates to approximately one standard deviation. Nobody disagrees that the two distributions overlap greatly and that some African Americans score as high as the highest whites. Similarly, some whites score as low as the lowest African Americans. Yet only some 15% to 20% of the African American population score above the average white score, and only approximately 15% to 20% of the white population score below the average African American score. Figure 6.1 shows the overlap between African American, white, and Asian American college-bound seniors on the SAT Reasoning Test (SAT-I) math section. All distributions significantly overlap, but Asian American students obtained the highest average scores, followed by white and African American students.

This finding has appeared in many different studies. If you were to administer the Stanford-Binet or the Wechsler scale (see Chapter 12) to large random samples

**FIGURE 6.1**

SAT-I Math score distributions for African American, white, and Asian American college-bound seniors, 1999.

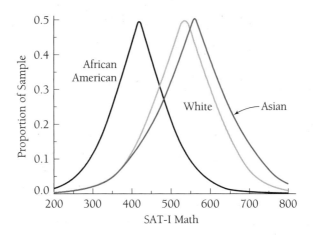

(Data provided by the College Board.)

of African Americans and white Americans, it is likely you would get the same results. The dispute has not been over *whether* these differences exist but over *why* they do. Many have argued that the differences result from environmental factors (Kamin, 1974; Nisbett, 2005; Rosenthal & Jacobson, 1968; Turkheimer, 1991; Wiggan, 2007; Zuckerman, 1990; Tong, Baghurst, Vimpani, & McMichael, 2007; Walker, Spohn, & DeLone, 2011; Shenk, 2011b), while others have suggested that the differences are biological (Hoekstra, Bartels, Hudziak, Van Beijsterveldt, & Boomsma, 2007; van Leeuwen, van den Berg, & Boomsma, 2008; Eysenck, 1991; Jensen, 1969, 1972; Munsinger, 1975; Rushton, 1991) and related to the general (*g*) factor measured by IQ tests (Nyborg & Jensen, 2000). This debate lies beyond our concerns here, which center on the problems inherent in tests apart from environmental and biological factors (Fancher, 2011). See Focused Example 19.1 for a brief look at the issue of genes and IQ. Then see Focused Example 19.2 offers for a possible environmental source of differences in test results. Finally, Focused Example 19.3 examines the very idea of race.

Beyond the other issues relevant to race and ethnicity, an increasing number of people no longer report their race when asked. Each year the College Board releases a report that summarizes SAT scores. In 2011, the report showed that overall SAT scores had had gone down very slightly, but were very close to performance in previous years. However, the gap between African American and Hispanic students and Asian and non-Hispanic white peers was not closing. One of the difficulties in evaluating the report is that one in four test takers did not disclose their ethnicity. As a result, it is difficult to determine why the performance gap is not narrowing. Previous studies have shown that students who did not report ethnicity tended to get lower scores on the SAT. More recent studies indicate that the test performance of the nonresponder group is comparable to the rest of the SAT takers. It is not clear why so many students failed to report their racial identity. Steele believes that African American students perform more poorly on tests when they reveal their race (Steele & Aronson, 2004). Whittington (2004) reports that many white students decline to report their race because they feel there is discrimination in favor of ethnic minorities and that their majority status puts them at a disadvantage. Other studies suggest that reporting multiple race identity can be a source of tension or anxiety (Kaplan et al., 2011). The College Board believes that the reason for the increase in nonreporting ethnicity results from a poorly designed online questionnaire. The questionnaire has been redesigned to force respondents to click a box that reads, "I choose not to respond." It is still too early to determine whether the change on the online questionnaire will affect the rate of ethnic nonreporting.

# Test Fairness and the Law

The U.S. government has attempted to establish clear standards for the use of psychological tests. Regulation of tests comes in many forms, including executive orders, laws, and court actions. The most important legal development was the passage of the 1964 Civil Rights Act. Title VII of this act created the Equal

## 6.1    FOCUSED EXAMPLE

### Genes and Improving IQ

If intelligence were really determined genetically, then we would expect average IQ scores for different groups to be relatively constant over time. However, performance on intelligence tests has improved rather dramatically for some groups over the last 60 years. Figure 6.2 shows gains in IQ as estimated from the progressive matrix tests. These changes have been observed in a variety of Western countries, including Great Britain, the Netherlands, and Israel. Jensen has argued that environment may affect IQ, suggesting that equalizing environments would reduce the 15-point gap between African Americans and their white counterparts by approximately 10 points. Indeed, in recent years African Americans have gained more in IQ than have whites. Since 1945, it appears that African Americans have increased average IQ by 16 points. By 1995, African Americans were performing on IQ tests at about the same level as whites in 1945 (Flynn, 1999).

There have also been slow improvements in achievement tests. School performance differences between black and white children persist, despite a

**FIGURE 6.2**

Gains in average IQ over time in five countries.

Note: Every nation is normed on its own samples. Therefore, although nations can be roughly compared in terms of different rates of IQ gain, they cannot be compared in terms of IQ scores. That is, the fact that the mean IQ of one nation appears higher than another at a given time is purely an artifact.

Employment Opportunity Commission (EEOC). In 1970, **EEOC guidelines** were published for employee-selection procedures. In 1978, the EEOC released *Uniform Guidelines on Employee Selection Procedures*, which are the major guidelines for the use of psychological tests in education and in industry.

Regarding allowable uses of psychological test scores, the 1978 guidelines are stricter, more condensed, and less ambiguous than the 1970 guidelines. The original act clearly prohibited discrimination in employment on the basis of race, color, religion, gender, or national origin. However, the 1978 guidelines made clear that the government will view any screening procedure, including the use of psychological tests, as having an **adverse impact** if it systematically rejects substantially higher

variety of efforts. The National Assessment of Educational Programs (NAEP). The good news is that mathematics scores for both African American and white public schools students in the 4th and 8th grade have been improving since the early 1990s. Similarly, performance on reading has also been improving. For all of the years of the assessment, there has been a gap in performance between black and white students. However, that gap is beginning to narrow. But, progress has been slow in 2007. For example, there were significant gaps between black and white students for scores in 4th grade mathematics in 46 of the 50 states. In 15 of these states, the gaps were narrower than they were in 1992. For reading, there were significant gaps in 44 of the 50 states. In three states (Delaware, Florida, and New Jersey) the gaps narrowed between 1992 and 2007, largely due to

improved performance among African American students. Figure 6.3 shows the trends of improving mathematics scores for 13 year olds between 1978 and 2004. As the figure shows, all students are generally performing better, but there is a gap between black and white students. That gap narrows over the course of time, but still persists.

Because genetic change takes several generations, only an environmental hypothesis can explain these results. Many features of contemporary society have been used to explain these gains. One interesting suggestion is that heavy use of interactive video games may contribute to the IQ gains (Greenfield, 1998). Others have suggested that the core components of intelligence represented by the *g* factor have not changed, but that other factors in the IQ tests are responsible for the trends in IQ improvement (Nijenhuis & van der Flier, 2007).

**FIGURE 6.3**

Gradual closing of black–white achievement differences in 8th grade mathematics.

\* Significantly different (p<.05) from 2004.
Note: Detail may not sum to totals due to rounding.
Source: U.S. Department of Education, Institute of Education Sciences, National Center for Education Statistics, National Assessment of Educational Progress (NAEP), various years, 1978–2004 Long-Term Trend Mathematics Assessments.

## Can Stereotyping Affect Test Performance?

Some research suggests that being a member of a group that is negatively stereotyped may adversely affect performance on standardized tests (Mayer & Hanges, 2003). As noted in this chapter, large studies consistently show that standardized tests (such as the SAT-I) overpredict college performance for African American, Latino, Latina, and Native American students. The overprediction occurs because many students from underrepresented groups do not get high grades in college. Steele argues that stereotyping adversely affects the victims' college grades, performance on standardized tests, and employment testing (Steele & Davies, 2003). In particular, he argues that doing well requires identification with one's school and other features of the school environment. Through a series of experiments, Steele and Aronson demonstrated how victimization by stereotyping could affect test performance. In one experiment, they subjected African American and white students to a test that included the hardest verbal items from the GRE. Half of the students were told that the test was measuring their intellectual ability, while the others were told that the test was about problem solving unrelated to ability. They hypothesized that informing subjects that they are going to take an ability test makes people who have been victims of stereotyping worry about their performance. This threatening experience, in turn, interferes with actual test performance (Aronson, Lustina, Good, Keough, Steele, & Brown, 1999; Steele & Aronson, 1998).

When told they were taking a test of intellectual abilities, white students scored significantly higher than African American students. However, some subjects were randomly assigned to take the same test but under conditions where there was no threat. Without a threat present, white and African American students performed equivalently. The results are summarized in Figure 6.4 (Steele, 1997). A related experiment showed that simply having African American students complete a demographic questionnaire that asks about their race also suppresses performance. These clever experiments suggest that stereotyping can create self-doubts that, in turn, explain some of the difference in test performance (Aronson et al., 1999; McGlone & Pfiester, 2007).

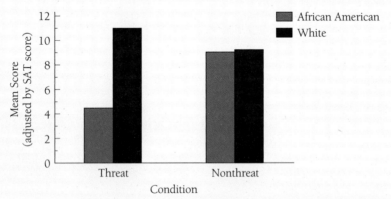

**FIGURE 6.4** Effects of stereotyping upon test performance. When told they were taking a test of intellectual abilities, white students scored significantly higher than African American students. However, some students were randomly assigned to take the same test but under conditions where there was no threat. Without a threat present, white and African American students performed equivalently.
(Adapted from Steele, 1997, p. 621.)

proportions of minority than nonminority applicants. When any selection procedure does so, the employer must demonstrate that the procedure has validity for the inferences the employer wants to make. These criteria for the validity of a selection procedure are similar to those discussed in Chapter 5. In particular, the guidelines detail the acceptable criteria for using a test.

These guidelines have been adopted by several federal agencies, including the Civil Service Commission, the Department of Justice, the Department of Labor, and the Department of the Treasury. The Office of Federal Contract Compliance has the direct power to cancel government contracts held by employers who do not comply with these guidelines.

The guidelines became the focus of several political controversies in 1991. For example, when Clarence Thomas was nominated for a position on the U.S. Supreme Court, he was challenged because of his enforcement of the guidelines while he was the head of the EEOC. Also, former president George H. W. Bush had planned to relax these guidelines in the 1991 Civil Rights Bill, but last-minute political pressure caused Bush to leave them unchanged. The standards have remained in place since then.

# The Traditional Defense of Testing

This chapter focuses on a central issue: Are standardized tests as valid for African Americans and other minority groups as they are for whites? All of the types of evidence for validity we discussed in Chapter 5 come into play when the issue of test bias is considered (Cole, 1981). Some psychologists argue that the tests are differentially valid for African Americans and whites. Because **differential validity** is so controversial and emotional, it has forced psychologists to think carefully about many issues in test validation. Differences among ethnic groups on test performance do not necessarily indicate test bias. The question is whether the test has different meanings for different groups. In psychometrics, validity defines the meaning of a test. Some researchers still argue that there are important differences in performance across racial groups. For example, Roth and colleagues summarized studies on differences in job performance. They compared differences between black and white employees on subjective measures such as supervisor ratings versus objective measures based on more formal evaluations. Their analysis suggested that the objective measures showed even larger differences between African American and white employees than the subjective evaluations for measures of work quality, quantity, and absenteeism. Differences between Hispanic and white employees were not as large as those between African American and white employees (Roth, Huffcutt, & Bobko, 2003).

## Content-Related Evidence for Validity

Articles have been published in the popular media on cultural fairness in testing. A *Newsweek* article listed several items from the general information portion of the Stanford-Binet scale that people with disadvantaged backgrounds might find problematic. Test constructors and users were accused of being biased because some children never have the opportunity to learn about some of the items; furthermore, members of ethnic groups might answer some items differently but still correctly.

**6.3** **FOCUSED EXAMPLE**

## Is Race a Meaningful Concept?

Race is one of the most commonly reported variables in social science. However, there has been considerable debate about the genetic basis for racial differences. One side argues that human races are highly similar to one another and that the construct of race has no biological meaning (Swallen, 2003). The evidence comes from studies in population genetics, the human genome, and physical anthropology (Freeman & Payne, 2000). Significant investigation has shown that the populations of the world are significantly intermingled—that is, humans have common genetic roots and the races of the world are not independent. The biological similarities among peoples of the world greatly outnumber the few differences.

There are many reasons to believe that classifying people as simply black or white is extremely misleading. For example, variations in human skin tone evolved to represent different adaptations to the amount of sunlight people were exposed to. There is a wide continuum of skin tones among human populations (see Figure 6.5). Assigning people to groups based on the color of their skin or other physical features, ignores the massive amount of information that defines people as individuals (Jablonski & Chaplin, 2010).

Because very strong sun exposure can damage the body, there is a biological adaptation favoring darker skin for people living closer to the equator.

Those with darker skin tones were more likely to survive to the age of reproduction. Variations in skin color had little to do with race, but instead were an adaptation to different levels of sunlight exposure (Singer, Erickson, Leatherman, & Goodman, 2011).

The other side of the argument suggests that there are, indeed, important genetic differences between the populations in the world. Advocates for this position acknowledge that at least 85% of a person's genetic makeup is shared by all human groups. But, they suggest that the genetic information that differentiates human populations is hidden in the interactions between genes. Newer methods are able to identify racial background on the basis of genetic information (Edwards, 2003; Witherspoon et al., 2007).

Nevertheless, race has remained an important variable in demography. Brawley and Freeman (1999) point out that "race medicine" dominated the last few centuries. Race medicine was based on the belief that diseases behave differently in different races and was promoted by prominent 18th-century scientists whose opinions were used as the justification for slavery. However, medical research consistently shows that diseases function equivalently in people of different racial backgrounds (Freeman & Payne, 2000). Furthermore, equivalent treatment typically produces equivalent benefit for those of different racial backgrounds (Ellis, 2008). Nevertheless,

Many researchers also argued that scores on intelligence tests are affected by language skills inculcated as part of a white, middle-class upbringing but foreign to inner-city children (Castenell & Castenell, 1988; Kagan, Moss, & Siegel, 1963; Lesser, Fifer, & Clark, 1965; Mercer, 1971; Pettigrew, 1964; Waldman, Weinberg, & Scarr, 1994). Children who are unfamiliar with the language have no chance of doing well on standardized IQ tests. For example, an American child does not usually know what a *shilling* is, but a British child probably does. Similarly, the American child would not know where one puts the *petrol*; a British child would. Some psychologists argue that asking an inner-city child about *opera* is just as unfair as asking an American child about *petrol*. In each case, the term is not familiar to the child (Hardy, Welcher, Mellits, & Kagan, 1976).

In response to this focus on the language and content of individual test items, Flaugher (1978) concluded that many perceived test bias problems are

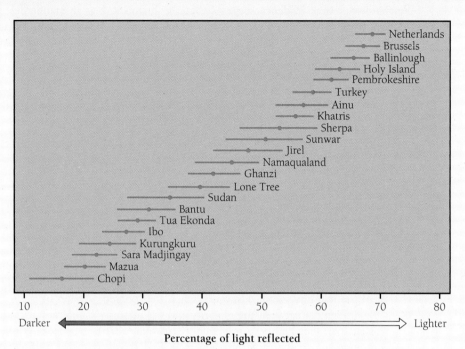

**FIGURE 6.5** Range of skin colors in human populations. This wide variation suggests that classifying humans as "black" or "white" ignores most of the information on skin tone.

there are substantial disparities in the amount and quality of care that is available to those of different racial groups. This discrimination in access to health care may be the best explanation for the disparity in health outcomes among people of different races (Flores & Tomany-Korman, 2008).

based on misunderstandings about the way tests are usually interpreted. Many people feel that a fair test asks questions they can answer. By contrast, a biased test does not ask about things a test taker knows. Flaugher argued that the purpose of aptitude and achievement tests is to measure performance on items sampled from a wide range of information. Not particularly concerned about individual items, test developers focus on test performance, making judgments about it based on correlations between the tests and external criteria. Many test critics, though, focus attention on specific items. For example, D. Owen (1985) reported that several intelligent and well-educated people had difficulty with specific items on the SAT and Law School Admission Test (LSAT) examinations. He also asserted that some items on standardized tests are familiar only to those with a middle-class background. Test developers are indifferent to the opportunities people have to learn the information on the tests. Again, the meaning they eventually assign to the tests comes from correlations of test scores with other variables.

Furthermore, some evidence suggests that the linguistic bias in standardized tests does not cause the observed differences (Scheuneman, 1987). Quay (1971) administered the Stanford-Binet test to 100 children in an inner-city Head Start program. Half of the children took a version of the test that used African American dialect, while the others took the standard version. The results demonstrated that the advantage produced by having the test in African American dialect translates into less than a 1-point increase in test scores. This finding is consistent with other research findings demonstrating that African American children can comprehend standard English about as well as they can comprehend African American dialect (Clarizio, 1979a; Copple & Succi, 1974). This finding does not hold for white children, who seem to comprehend only the standard dialect.

Systematic studies have failed to demonstrate that biased items in well-known standardized tests account for the differences in scores among ethnic groups (Flaugher, 1978). In one approach, developers ask experts to judge the unfairness of particular items. Without these unfair items, the test should be less biased. Unexpectedly, the many attempts to "purify" tests using this approach have not yielded positive results. In one study, 16% of the items in an elementary reading test were eliminated after experts reviewed them and labeled them as potentially biased toward the majority group. However, when the "purged" version of the test was used, the differences between the majority and the minority school populations were no smaller than they had been originally (Bianchini, 1976).

Another approach to the same problem is to find those classes of items that are most likely to be missed by members of a particular minority group. If a test is biased against that group, then significant differences between minority and nonminority groups should appear in certain categories of items. These studies are particularly important; if they identify certain *types* of items that discriminate among groups, then these types of items can be avoided on future tests. Again, the results have not been encouraging; studies have not clearly identified such categories of items (Wild, McPeek, Koffler, Braun, & Cowell, 1989). The studies show that groups differ for certain items but not whether these are real or chance differences.

## Differential Item Functioning (DIF) Analysis

Another approach to the analysis of test bias has been developed by the Educational Testing Service (ETS) (Elder, McNamara, & Congdon, 2003; Educational Testing Service, 1991). The ETS creates and administers a variety of aptitude tests, including the Graduate Record Examination (GRE), the SAT-I, and the LSAT. In each of these programs, the performance of white test takers differs significantly from the performances of other racial and ethnic groups on verbal and analysis measures. On quantitative measures, Asian Americans tend to have the highest scores. On the GRE, men and women score equivalently on verbal and analytic measures. Men, however, obtain higher scores on the quantitative measures.

DIF analysis attempts to identify items that are specifically biased against any ethnic, racial, or gender group (Borsboom, Mellenbergh, & van Heerden, 2002). The analysis first equates groups on the basis of overall score. For example, it would find subgroups of test takers who obtain equivalent scores. These might be groups of men and women who obtain scores of approximately 500 on the verbal portion of the GRE. Using these groups, it evaluates differences in performance between men and women on particular items. Items that differ significantly between the groups are thrown out and the entire test is rescored.

Similarly, items that show differences among racial and ethnic groups can be eliminated and the test rescored. In one study, 27 items from the original SAT were eliminated because ethnic groups consistently answered them differently. Then the test was rescored for everyone. Although it seems this procedure should have eliminated the differences between the two groups, it actually had only slight effects because the items that differentiated the groups tended to be the easiest items in the set. When these items were eliminated, the test was harder for everyone (Flaugher & Schrader, 1978).

There is at least some evidence that test items that depict people do not accurately portray the distribution of genders and races in the population. Zores and Williams (1980) reviewed the Wechsler Adult Intelligence Scale (WAIS), Wechsler Intelligence Scale for Children–Revised (WISC-R), Stanford-Binet, and Slosson Intelligence test items for race and gender characterization and found that white male characterization occurred with disproportionate frequency. Nevertheless, no one has yet established that the frequency of different groups appearing in items affects the outcome of tests. Studies have failed to demonstrate serious bias in item content. Most critics argue that the verbal content of test items is most objectionable because it is unfamiliar to minority groups. However, Scheuneman (1981) reviewed the problem and concluded that the verbal material reflected the life experiences of African Americans more closely than did the nonverbal material. In a related example, studies that manipulate gender bias by creating neutral, male, and female items demonstrate little effect on the performance differences between male and female test takers (McCarty, Noble, & Huntley, 1989). Other studies have used DIF to help understand the experiences of discrimination in the community (Cunningham et al., 2011).

Other statistical models have been used to evaluate item fairness. In these studies, which use a variety of populations and methods of analysis, little evidence has been produced of bias in test items (Gotkin & Reynolds, 1981). However, different models may identify different items in the same test as biased. In one comparison, Ironson and Sebkovial (1979) applied four different methods to analyze item bias in the National Longitudinal Study test battery. Three differential statistical methods identified many of the same items as biased in evaluating 1691 African American high-school seniors in contrast to 1794 white 12th graders. However, there was little agreement among these item evaluations and the bias items selected by a method proposed by D. R. Green and Draper (1972).

How do biased test items affect the differential validity of a test? In one theoretical example, 25% of the items on a test were presumed to be so biased that minority test takers would be expected to perform at chance level. Despite random performance, there would be only slight and perhaps undetectable differences in validity coefficients for minority and majority group members (Drasgow, 1982). However, this result may be artificial and depend on an unusual use of the phrase *test bias* (Dobko & Kehoe, 1983). Using a relatively general definition of test bias and biased items, they suggested that failure to find differences in validity co-efficients is consistent with the belief that the tests are equally valid for members of different ethnic and racial groups (Kuncel & Hezlett, 2007).

In spite of the many studies about item bias, its role remains poorly understood. For example, those students who have taken the most tests may be best able to answer questions that are irrelevant to the knowledge base being assessed. Because such test-wise students tend to get these items correct, item analysis may incorrectly identify the irrelevant items as useful. These problems magnify the differences between high-achieving and low-achieving students (Masters, 1988).

In summary, studies have not supported the popular belief that items have different meanings for different groups; however, people must continue to scrutinize the content of tests. On some occasions, careful reviews of tests have turned up questionable items. Many tests are carelessly constructed, and every effort should be taken to purge items that have the potential for being biased.

## Criterion-Related Sources of Bias

Each night on the evening news, the weatherperson forecasts the conditions for the next day. If such forecasts are consistently accurate, we come to depend on them. In evaluating the weather report, we make a subjective assessment of validity. Similarly, we evaluate tests by asking whether they forecast future performance accurately. Standardized tests such as the SAT-I have been found to satisfactorily predict performance during the first year of college. These tests clearly do not give us all of the information needed for perfect prediction, but they give enough information to make us pay attention to them.

College administrators who use the test scores face difficult problems. On the average, minority applicants have lower test scores than do nonminority applicants. At the same time, most universities and colleges are attempting to increase their minority enrollments. Because minority applicants are considered as a separate category, we should ask whether the tests have differential predictive power for the two groups of applicants.

As we mentioned in Chapter 5, we assess the criterion-related evidence for validity of a test by the coefficient of correlation between the test and some criterion. The higher the correlation, the more confident we can feel about making predictions. If college grades are the criterion (the variable we are trying to forecast), then the validity of a test such as the SAT-I is represented by the correlation between the SAT-I score and first-year college grades. If students who score well on the SAT-I do well in college and students who score poorly on it get lower grades, then the test might be considered valid for helping administrators decide which college students to admit.

In Chapter 3, we reviewed the interpretation of regression plots as they relate to the validity of psychological tests. Showing plots like the one in Figure 6.6, we explained how to obtain a predicted criterion score from a test score. First, you find

**FIGURE 6.6**

A sample regression plot. The slope of the line shows the relationship between a test and a criterion. The steeper the slope of the line, the better the prediction of the criterion score.

the test score on the horizontal axis of the graph and draw a line directly upward until it hits the regression line. Then you draw a line directly left until it comes to the vertical axis. This gives the predicted criterion score. The only difference between Figure 6.6 and Figure 3.8 is that we have added an ellipse, called an **isodensity curve**, around the regression line. This ellipse is used to encircle a specified portion of the cases that constitute a particular group.

Figure 6.7 shows a regression line that represents two groups equally well. Group A appears to be performing less well than Group B on both the test (predictor) and the criterion scores. You can demonstrate this for yourself by selecting some points from the test scores for Group A and finding the expected scores on the criterion. By repeating this exercise for a few points in Group B, you will find that Group A is expected to do poorly on the criterion because it did more poorly on the test. However, for both Group A and Group B, the relationship between the test score and performance on the criterion is the same. Thus, Figure 6.7 shows there is little evidence for test bias.

Figure 6.8 represents a different situation—a separate regression line for each group. Because their slopes are the same, the lines are parallel. However, the intercepts, or the points where the regression lines cross the vertical axis, differ. If you pick a particular test score, you get one expected criterion score if you use regression line A and another if you use B. For a test score of 8, the expected criterion score from regression line A is 6, whereas the expected criterion score from regression line B is 10. The broken line in Figure 6.8 is based on a combination of regression lines A and B. Now try finding the predicted score for a test score of 8 from this combined (broken) regression line. You should get 8. The combined

**FIGURE 6.7**

A single regression slope predicts performance equally well for two groups. However, the means of the groups differ.

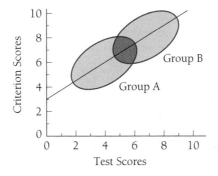

**FIGURE 6.8**

Regression lines with equal slopes but different intercepts.

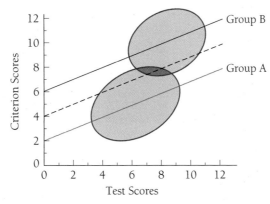

regression line actually overpredicts performance on the criterion for Group A and underpredicts it for Group B. According to this example, the use of a single regression line produces discrimination in favor of Group A and against Group B.

This situation seems to fit the use of the SAT (Cleary, 1968; Jensen, 1984; Kallingal, 1971; Pfeifer & Sedlacek, 1971; Reynolds, 1986; Schneider & Briel, 1990; Temp, 1971). Each of these studies showed that the relationship between college performance and SAT scores was best described by two separate regression equations. The commonly used combined regression equation overpredicts how well minority students will do in college and underpredicts the performance of majority group students. In other words, it appears that the SAT used with a single regression line yields biased predictions in favor of minority groups and against majority groups.

The equal slopes of the lines in Figure 6.6 suggest equal predictive evidence for validity. Most standardized intelligence, aptitude, and achievement tests in fact do confirm the relationships shown in the figure (Reschly & Sabers, 1979; Reynolds, 1980; Reynolds & Nigl, 1981). Thus, there is little evidence that tests such as the SAT-I predict college performance differently for different groups or that IQ tests have different correlations with achievement tests for African American, white, or Latino and Latina children. This finding has been reported for the original SAT (Temp, 1971), preschool tests (Reynolds, 1980), and IQ tests such as the WISC-R (Reschly & Sabers, 1979). Whether separate or combined regression lines are used depends on different definitions of bias. (We shall return to this issue later in the chapter. As you will see, the interpretation of tests for assessing different groups can be strongly influenced by personal and moral convictions.) The situation shown in Figure 6.6 is independent of differences in mean scores, which are equal to the differences between the two regression lines.

Some studies have shown that these problems are not specific to U.S. culture. Psychometric aptitude tests are currently used by all Israeli universities. A wide variety of cultural and ethnic groups makes up Israeli society. As in the United States, there is interest in determining whether or not aptitude tests include biases against specific ethnic or cultural groups. In a study of 1538 Israeli college candidates of varying ethnic backgrounds, the predictive test–criterion relationship was the same across groups in spite of mean differences among the groups (Zeidner, 1987).

A third situation outlined by Cleary and coworkers (1975) is shown in Figure 6.9. The two regression lines are not parallel; the coefficient of one group differs from that of the other. In the situation presented in Figure 6.6, each group was best represented by its own regression line. Using a common regression line causes error in predicting the scores for each group. However, the situation depicted in Figure 6.6 is not hopeless, and indeed some psychologists feel that this situation is useful because it may

**FIGURE 6.9**
Regression lines with different slopes suggest that a test has different meanings for different groups. This is the most clear-cut example of test bias.

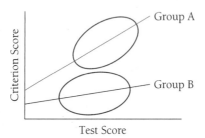

help increase the accuracy of predictions (Cleary, 1968). In Figure 6.7, however, the test is differentially valid for the two groups, meaning that the test has an entirely different meaning for each group. Although empirical studies have rarely turned up such a case, there are some known examples of differential slopes (Mercer, 1979). For example, a test that is designed to predict performance in a mechanical training program would show differential validity if it predicted performance much better for men than for women. Women who have traditionally had less previous experience with mechanical concepts than men may score more poorly. However, when taking the course, many women would easily acquire this information and perform well. Thus, the test would provide relatively little information about how these women would perform in the program, but it would tend to predict how men would perform. An extensive discussion of differential validity is presented by Bartlett and O'Leary (1989). Focused Example 19.4 illustrates the application of both content- and criterion-related evidence of validity.

# Other Approaches to Testing Minority Group Members

To many U.S. psychologists, the defense of psychological tests has not been totally satisfactory. Although some consider the defense of the tests strong enough, others emphasize that developers must try to find selection procedures that will end all discriminatory practices and protect the interests of minority group members. Those who do not think that the tests are fair suggest one of two alternatives: outlaw the use of psychological tests for minority students (Williams, 1974) or develop psychological assessment strategies that suit minority children. Advocates of the first alternative have launched a legal battle to restrict the use of tests. In this section, we review various approaches to the second alternative. In particular, we look at three different assessment approaches: the Chitling Test, the Black Intelligence Test of Cultural Homogeneity (BITCH), and the System of Multicultural Pluralistic Assessment (SOMPA). Though each approach differs, they are all based on one common assumption: Minority children have not had the opportunity to learn how to answer items on tests that reflect traditional, white, middle-class values.

## Ignorance Versus Stupidity

In a California trial about the use of testing in public schools, *Larry P. v. Wilson Riles*, the judge made an abrasive but insightful comment. Both sides in the case agreed that minority children perform more poorly than white children on standardized tests. The main issue debated was the meaning of the scores. One side argued that the scores reflect the underlying trait of intelligence. In other words, the tests allegedly measure how smart a child is. Witnesses for the other side suggested that the tests measure only whether the child has learned the appropriate responses needed to perform well on the test. This position claims that the tests do not measure how smart the child is but only whether the child has been exposed to the information on the test. Studies do show that it is possible to teach people to perform better on IQ tests (Perkins & Grotzer, 1997). After hearing the testimony for the different points of view, the judge commented that the issue was really one of ignorance versus stupidity. Although this comment appears insensitive and racist, it deserves reflection. There are two potential explanations for why some children do more poorly on standardized tests than do other children. One explanation is that they are less intelligent—the "stupidity" explanation. The other is that some children do more poorly because they are ignorant of the right responses for a particular test. If ignorance is the explanation, then differences in IQ scores are of less concern because they can be changed. The stupidity explanation is more damning because it implies that the lower test scores obtained by African American students are a product of some deficit that cannot be changed.

## 6.4 FOCUSED EXAMPLE

### Scoring the WISC-R for Inner-City Children: The Evolution of Strict Scoring Rules

The WISC-R requires that a test administrator follow a rigid protocol in allowing credit for certain types of responses. Over the years, many people have questioned whether these scoring procedures should be so stringent. In particular, they have suggested that some children may be giving an appropriate response for the subculture they are familiar with but it may not be given credit. The Johns Hopkins Child Development Study favors this conclusion (Hardy et al., 1976).

As part of the Johns Hopkins study, 200 children from the inner city of Baltimore received selected questions from the WISC-R. For this study, however, the standard WISC-R scoring instructions were abandoned, and an attempt was made to understand the reasoning behind the children's answers. For example, this WISC-R question was given: "What would you do if you were sent to buy a loaf of bread, and the grocer said he did not have any more?" The WISC-R scoring instructions state that the correct answer is "Go to another store." Among the 200 children in the study, 61 gave an incorrect response. However, when the examiners probed the children about their responses, they discovered that many of the children had given replies that were reasonable considering their circumstances. For instance, the rigid WISC-R scoring procedures do not allow credit for the response "Go home." Yet many of the inner-city children explained that there were no other stores near their homes and they were not allowed to go away from home without permission. Others reported that they used family credit to shop and would need to go home to get money if they had to go to another store. In each of these cases, the researchers suggested that the children had given correct and reasonable responses to the question (Hardy et al., 1976).

Standardization implies that all children take the test with the same set of rules. Beyond this objection,

Sattler (1979b) carefully reviewed the study and found a variety of methodological problems. In particular, there was no control group of children not from the inner city. Thus, one cannot determine whether children in general would have benefited from a more liberal interpretation of the criteria for a correct answer. Abundant evidence suggests that permitting a tester to exercise judgment about the reasonableness of a response results in higher scores for children from many different walks of life.

Another of Sattler's objections is that the study may have had serious rater bias. Quite likely, the psychologists who tested the inner-city children knew that the study was on test bias, and their interpretations of a reasonable response were thus influenced by a subjective predisposition.

Ultimately, a test is evaluated using criterion-related evidence for validity. How well does it do its job in predicting performance on some criterion of interest? Some researchers have argued that any scoring procedure is valid if it enhances the relationship between a test and a criterion (McDowell, 2006). In the Johns Hopkins study, there was no evidence that the liberal scoring system enhanced the criterion-related validity of the test (Hardy et al., 1976). Thus, different scoring procedures may make the scores of inner-city children higher, but whether the revised procedures would make the tests more meaningful remains to be seen (Sattler, 1979b). Most studies on the validity of IQ tests identify few meaningful differences between the test and outcome criteria for different groups of children.

Problems such as these led to the development of strict scoring procedures for the WISC-R and other tests. In the current versions, trained test administrators must follow strict rules and are not allowed to exercise their own judgment (Fiscella et al., 2011).

Ignorance implies that differences can be abolished. It also implies that IQ test performance is relative to content for whites as well as for minorities. Just as some minority children have not learned how to answer items that might predict success in white, middle-class culture, so many white, middle-class children have not learned how to succeed in the inner city. This proposition is illustrated by the Chitling Test.

## The Chitling Test

Many years ago, animal psychologists talked about higher and lower animals. The higher animals were considered to be intelligent because they could do some of the same things humans could do, and the lower animals were considered to be unintelligent because they could not perform like humans. However, in 1969 Hodos and Campbell argued that all animals are equally intelligent for the environments in which they live. We cannot compare the intelligence of a rat with that of a cat, because a rat is adapted to a rat's environment and a cat to a cat's environment.

This insight seems not to have permeated the world of human affairs. Because of poverty and discrimination, minority and nonminority children grow up in different environments. To succeed in each requires different skills and knowledge. A psychological test may consider survival in only one of these environments, usually the white, middle-class one. Thus, using one of these tests for impoverished children is analogous to testing a cat on a task designed to determine how well a rat is adapted to a rat's environment.

Originally named the Dove Counterbalance General Intelligence Test, the Chitling Test was developed to demonstrate that there is a body of information about which the white middle class is ignorant (Dove, 1968). A major aim in developing this was to show that African Americans and whites are just not talking the same language.

Some of the items from the Chitling Test are listed in Table 6.1. If you do not know many of the answers, it may be because you have not been exposed to African American culture of the mid-1960s. People who have grown up in a ghetto in this era should clearly outperform you. On this test, a white, middle-class student would probably score as culturally deprived.

The Chitling Test may be a valid test for inferring how streetwise someone is, but this has not been demonstrated in studies. Currently, no more than face validity has been established for this test. No body of evidence demonstrates that the test successfully predicts performance on any important criterion. If we want to predict which students will do well in college, the Chitling Test will not help us. In fact, standardized tests predict performance for both minority and nonminority students, but the Chitling Test predicts performance for neither group. We must await validity evidence before we can make any generalizations. Dove described his efforts to develop an intelligence test as "half serious." But we have seen that the test does identify an area of content in which the races differ and African Americans outperform whites.

**TABLE 6.1**    Selected Items from the Dove Counterbalance General Intelligence Test (the Chitling Test)

1. A "handkerchief head" is: (a) a cool cat, (b) a porter, (c) an Uncle Tom, (d) a hoddi, (e) a preacher.

2. Which word is most out of place here? (a) splib, (b) blood, (c) gray, (d) spook, (e) African-American.

3. A "gas head" is a person who has a: (a) fast-moving car, (b) stable of "lace," (c) "process," (d) habit of stealing cars, (e) long jail record for arson.

4. "Bo Diddley" is a: (a) game for children, (b) down-home cheap wine, (c) down-home singer, (d) new dance, (e) Moejoe call.

5. If a pimp is uptight with a woman who gets state aid, what does he mean when he talks about "Mother's Day"? (a) second Sunday in May, (b) third Sunday in June, (c) first of every month, (d) none of these, (e) first and fifteenth of every month.

6. If a man is called a "blood," then he is a: (a) fighter, (b) Mexican-American, (c) Negro, (d) hungry hemophile, (e) Redman or Indian.

7. What are the "Dixie Hummingbirds"? (a) part of the KKK, (b) a swamp disease, (c) a modern gospel group, (d) a Mississippi Negro paramilitary group, (e) deacons.

8. T'Bone Walker got famous for playing what? (a) trombone, (b) piano, (c) "T-flute," (d) guitar, (e) "hambone."

*Note:* The correct answers are: 1) c, 2) c, 3) c, 4) c, 5) e, 6) c, 7) c, and 8) d. (From "Taking the Chitling Test," by A. Dove. In *Newsweek*, 1968. 72, 51–52. Copyright 1968 by Newsweek, Inc. All rights reserved. Reprinted by permission.).

## The Black Intelligence Test of Cultural Homogeneity

Some psychologists regard most achievement and intelligence tests as instruments of racism. Most racist actions are felt to be illogical and emotional. However, the use of intelligence tests is seen as a subtle and thus more dangerous racist move because the tests are supported by scientific validity studies (Garcia, 1981). R. L. Williams (1974) has labeled this phenomenon *scientific racism*. He views IQ and standardized achievement tests as "nothing but updated versions of the old signs down South that read 'For Whites Only'" (1974, p. 34).

Of particular interest to Williams and his colleagues is the assessment of the ability to survive in the African American community. Indeed, they feel that assessment of survival potential with a survival quotient (SQ) is more important than assessment of IQ, which indicates only the likelihood of succeeding in the white community. As a beginning, Williams developed the BITCH, which asks respondents to define 100 vocabulary words relevant to African American culture. The words came from the *Afro-American Slang Dictionary* and from Williams's personal experience interacting with African Americans. African American people obtain higher scores than do their white counterparts on the BITCH. When Williams administered the BITCH to 100 16- to 18-year-olds from each group, the average score for African American subjects was 87.07 (out of 100). The mean score for the whites was significantly lower (51.07). Williams argues that traditional IQ and achievement tests are nothing more than culture-specific tests that assess how much white children know about white culture. The BITCH is also a culture-specific test, but one on which African American subjects outperform whites.

Although the BITCH does tell us a lot about the cultural loading in intelligence and achievement tests, it has received mixed reviews. The reliability data reported by Williams show that the BITCH is quite reliable for African American test takers (standard error less than 3 points on the 100-point scale) and acceptably reliable for white test takers (standard error approximately 6). Conventional tests have similar reliabilities for both groups (Oakland & Feigenbaum, 1979). However, little convincing validity data on the BITCH are available. Although the test manual does report some studies, the samples are small and do not represent any clearly defined population (Cronbach, 1978). The difficulty is that one cannot determine whether the BITCH predicts how well a person will survive on the streets or how well he or she will do in school, in life, or in anything else. To support the conclusion that the BITCH is an intelligence test, one must have some evidence. Though the test does assess word association, it gives no information on reasoning abilities.

More studies are needed to determine whether the BITCH does what it is supposed to do. One of the rationales for the test is that it will identify children who have been unfairly assigned to classes for the educable mentally retarded (EMR)[1] on the basis of IQ scores. In one study, Long and Anthony (1974) attempted to determine how many African American EMR children would be reclassified if they were retested with the BITCH. Among a small and limited sample of 30 African American EMR high-school students from Gainesville, Florida, all the students who performed poorly on the Wechsler Intelligence Scale for Children (WISC) also performed below the first percentile on the BITCH. Using the BITCH served to reclassify none of the students. However, this was just one small and nonrepresentative study. In its present state, the BITCH can be a valuable tool for measuring white familiarity with the African American community. When white teachers or administrators are sent to schools that have predominantly African American enrollments, the BITCH can help determine how much they know about the culture. Furthermore, the BITCH can help assess the extent to which an African American is in touch with his or her own community. As Cronbach (1978) has noted, people with good abstract reasoning skills may function poorly if they are unfamiliar with the community in which they live. Similarly, people with poor reasoning skills may get along just fine in a familiar community.

## The System of Multicultural Pluralistic Assessment

No assessment technique covered in this book challenges traditional beliefs about testing as much as the SOMPA (Mercer, 1979). This system was adopted by several states in the 1980s.

Like many tests, the SOMPA is based on the values of its developers. Mercer asserted that people's beliefs about what is fair and what knowledge exists are related to the social structure. She agreed with Mannheim (1936) that members of

---

[1] We use the term "EMR" because it is part of the International Classification of Disease and Disability. However, we prefer the more modern terms "intellectual disability" or "cognitive disability."

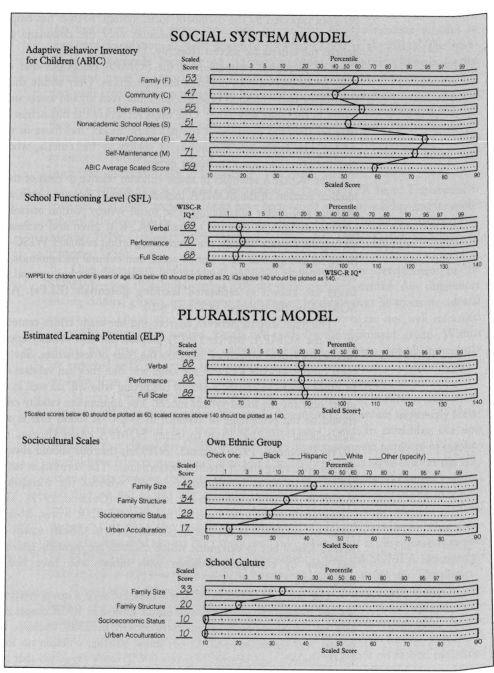

**FIGURE 6.10** Sample SOMPA profile.
(From the System of Multicultural Pluralistic Assessment by June Lewis and Jane Mercer. Copyright © 1978 by The Psychological Corporation. Reproduced by permission of the authors. All rights reserved.)

# Suggestions for Solutions

Focusing on problems associated with ethnic differences in test scores, we have presented many different arguments from various perspectives. In the following pages, we offer some solutions; however, we must warn you that these solutions depend on different social and political beliefs about the definition of bias.

## Ethical Concerns and the Definition of Test Bias

It is difficult to define *test bias*; different authors present various views (Barrett & Dupinet, 1991; Cole, 1981; Darlington, 1978; Flaugher, 1978; Hunter & Schmidt, 1976; Fancher, 2011; Groth-Marnat, 2009). These definitions represent commitments to ethical viewpoints about the way one should treat certain groups. Many years ago, Hunter and Schmidt (1976) identified three ethical positions that set the tone for much of the debate: unqualified individualism, the use of quotas, and qualified individualism. These positions focus on the use of tests to select people either for jobs or for training programs (including college).

Supporters of *unqualified individualism* would use tests to select the most qualified individuals they could find (Kuncel & Hezlett, 2007). In this case, users of tests would remain indifferent to the race or gender of applicants. The goal would be to predict those who would perform best on the job or in school. According to this viewpoint, a test is fair if it finds the best candidates for the job or for admission to school. If race or gender was a valid predictor of performance over and above the information in the test, then the unqualified individualist would see nothing wrong with considering this information in the selection process.

In a quite different ethical approach to selection, one uses *quotas*, which explicitly recognize race and gender differences. If the population of a state is 20% African American, then supporters of a quota system might argue that 20% of the new medical students in the state-supported medical school should also be African American. Selection procedures are regarded as biased if the actual percentage of applicants admitted differs from the percentage in the population; each group should demonstrate a fair share of the representation (Gordon & Terrell, 1981). This fair-share process places less emphasis than does testing on how well people in the different groups will do once selected (Markham, 2011).

The final moral position considered by Hunter and Schmidt might be viewed as a compromise between unqualified individualism and a quota system. Like unqualified individualism, *qualified individualism* embraces the notion that one should select the best-qualified people. But unqualified individualists also take information about race, gender, and religion into consideration if it helps to predict performance on the criterion—that is, if not to do so results in underprediction of performance for one group and overprediction for another. Qualified individualists, however, recognize that although failing to include group characteristics (race, gender, and religion) may lead to differential accuracy in prediction, this differential prediction may counteract known effects of discrimination. It may, for example, lead to underprediction of performance for the majority group and overprediction for the minority group. The qualified individualist may choose not to include information about personal characteristics in selection because ignoring this information may serve the interests of minority group members. Many people have argued that increased minority hiring will result in lower average job performance because some applicants with lower test scores will be hired. However, systematic study of this issue has not always supported these arguments. In fact, universities and business typically benefit from increasing the diversity of their workforce. Further, the broader goals of organizations are likely to benefit from greater diversity (Hamdani & Buckley, 2011).

One can relate each of these ethical positions to a particular statistical definition of test bias. Table 6.2 shows several different models of test bias, based on different definitions of fairness. All these models are based on regression lines. These models also apply to tests used for selection purposes, such as job placement and college, or for advanced degree programs.

The regression model described in this table (see also Cleary, 1968) represents unqualified individualism. The result of this approach is that a large number of majority group members may be selected. This approach maintains that an employer or a school should be absolutely color- and gender-blind. The reason for considering ethnicity or gender is to improve the prediction of future performance. This approach has been favored by business because it ensures the highest employee productivity.

At the other extreme is the quota system. To achieve fair-share representation, separate selection procedures are developed. One procedure, for example, is used to select the best available African American applicants, and another to select the best available non-African American applicants. If a community has 42% African American residents, then the first procedure would be used to select 42% of the employees, the other procedure to select the other 58%.

The quota system may lead to greater rates of failure among some groups. Suppose that a test devised to select telephone operators did indeed predict who would succeed on the job, but it selected 70% women and 30% men. The quota system would encourage the use of separate cutoff scores so that the proportion of men selected would approach 50%. But because the women scored higher on the average, they would perform better on the job, resulting in a higher rate of failure among the men. Thus, although quota systems often increase the selection of underrepresented groups, they also make it likely that the underrepresented groups will experience failure.

Table 6.2 shows two other models (Cole, 1973; Darlington, 1971; Thorndike, 1971), which represent compromises between the quota and the unqualified individualism points of view. Each of these cases reflects an attempt to select the most qualified people, yet there is some adjustment for minority-group members. When people from two different groups have the same test score, these procedures give a slight edge to those from the lower group and put those from the higher group at a slight disadvantage.

Although these approaches have been attacked for faulty logic (Hunter & Schmidt, 1976, 1978), plausible defenses have been offered. These procedures increase the number of people selected from underrepresented groups. However, these procedures also reduce the average performance score on the criterion. More recently, some methods have been proposed to address the quandary between maximizing performance on the criterion and increasing opportunity of

**TABLE 6.2**    Different Models of Test Fairness

| Model | Reference | Use of regression | Rationale | Effect on minority selection | Effect on average criterion performance |
|---|---|---|---|---|---|
| Regression | Cleary (1968) | Separate regression lines are used for different groups. Those with predicted criterion scores are selected. | This is fair because those with the highest estimated level of success are selected. | Few minority group members selected | Good performance on criteria |
| Constant ratio | Thorndike (1971) | Points equal to approximately half of the average difference between the groups are added to the test scores of the group with the lower score. Then a single regression line is used, and those with the highest predicted scores are selected. | This is fair because it best reflects the potential of the lower-scoring group. | Some increase in the number of minority group members selected | Somewhat lower |
| Cole/ Darlington | Cole (1973), Darlington (1971, 1978) | Separate regression equations are used for each group, and points are added to the scores of those from the lower group to ensure that those with the same criterion score have the same predictor score. | This is fair because it selects more potentially successful people from the lower group. | Larger increase in the number of minority group members selected | Lower |
| Quota | Dunnette and Borman (1979) | The proportion of people to be selected from each group is predetermined. Separate regression equations are used to select those from each group who are expected to perform highest on the criterion. | This is fair because members of different subgroups are selected based on their proportions in the community. | Best representation of minority groups | About the same as for the Cole/ Darlington model |

Based on Dunnette & Borman (1979).

underrepresented groups. As noted above, emphasizing performance on the criterion may result in adverse selection for some groups (unqualified individualism). However, there may be reasonable tradeoffs between the philosophical positions. One method attempts to find the best decision when there are competing goals, such as criterion performance and diversity in the workforce. A decision is considered *Pareto optimal* when it balances competing goals, in this case between criterion performance and ethnic or racial balance. The term *Pareto* derives from the work of the 19th-century Italian economist and philosopher Vilfredo Pareto. In the ideal "Pareto improvement, at least one person is made better off, without making anybody worse off." Using mathematical decision-modeling methods originally developed for engineering science, Pareto optimization methods attempt to balance these competing goals. The methods systematically balance selection and expected performance (De Corte, Lievens, & Sackett, 2007).

We cannot tell you which of these approaches is right and which is wrong. That decision depends on your own values and judgment about what is fair.

Despite the many problems and controversies surrounding psychological testing, surveys show that psychologists and educational specialists generally have positive attitudes about intelligence and aptitude tests. In one survey, 1020 experts agreed that there were some sociocultural biases in the tests (Snyderman & Rothman, 1987). However, these experts also generally agreed that the tests were valid for predictive purposes. Their main concerns involved the interpretation and application of test results by elementary and secondary schools. In general, industrial and organizational psychologists tend to feel that ability testing does not discriminate by race. In one study of 703 members of the Society of Industrial and Organizational Psychology, there appeared to be consensus that cognitive ability tests are valid and fair. However, the I/O psychologists also felt that tests provide an incomplete picture of human abilities and that job selection should consider tests as only one component.

Perhaps the most controversial defense of testing was presented in a 1994 book entitled *The Bell Curve*. This book is reviewed in Focused Example 19.5.

## Thinking Differently: Finding New Interpretations of Data

Clearly, the observed differences between minority and nonminority groups on standardized tests pose a problem. Sometimes a problem stimulates us to think differently; in the words of the famous entrepreneur Henry Kaiser, "A problem is an opportunity in work clothes." The opportunity for test developers and users is to see test results in new ways.

For example, instead of indicating genetic variations or social handicaps, differences in test scores may reflect patterns of problem solving that characterize different subcultures. Knowing how groups differ in their approaches to problem solving can be helpful for two reasons. First, it can teach us important things about the relationship between socialization and problem-solving approaches. This information can guide the development of pluralistic educational programs (Pitts, 2012). Second, knowing more about the ways different groups approach problems can lead to the development of improved predictors of success for minority groups (Jeltova et al., 2011).

Along these lines, R. D. Goldman (1973) proposed the *differential process theory,* which maintains that different strategies may lead to effective solutions for many types of tasks. According to this theory, strategies—ways people go about solving problems—mediate abilities and performance (Sternberg & Kaufman, 2011).

For example, African American college students tend to score higher on the verbal subtest of the SAT-I on average than they do on the quantitative subtest. White students on average score about the same on both subtests. As the result of their socialization, African American students possibly structure the task of getting through school differently: they develop their verbal skills rather than their quantitative abilities. This result may also reflect differences in the opportunity to learn proper quantitative skills. In any case, African American students tend to choose college majors that emphasize their verbal abilities. It may thus be appropriate to build specific tests that predict how well these students will do in the majors they choose. These tests could deemphasize quantitative skills if the skills are shown to be unrelated to success for these particular majors. In other words, the test would be validated for the specific majors chosen by African American students.

A variety of studies have shown differences in information processing for different groups. For example, Native American and Hispanic groups tend to do better on visual-reasoning than verbal-reasoning subtasks (Suzuki & Valencia, 1997). In one quantitative review of the literature, Native American groups obtained average performance IQ scores of 100 while their average scores on verbal IQ tests were just 83 (Vraniak, 1997). One study used high-school grade point average to predict performance for 22,105 freshmen in the University of California system. For white students, grade point average (GPA) and SAT-V (Verbal) scores were the best predictors of freshman success. SAT-M (Math) added little, once GPA and SAT-V were in the prediction equation. However, for Asian American students, GPA and SAT-M predicted success, with SAT-V adding minimal information (Sue, 1999).

In a related argument, H. Gardner (1993; Gardner, Krechevsky, Sternberg, & Okagaki, 1994) suggested that there are seven distinct types of intelligence: linguistic, musical, logical-mathematical, spatial, bodily-kinesthetic, and two different forms of personal intelligence. Gardner sees no reason to call logical thinking "intelligence" and musical ability a "talent." Instead, he believes that these abilities are equal. Groups that perform best on tests of general intelligence do not necessarily excel in all of Gardner's talent domains.

## Developing Different Criteria

Criterion-related evidence for validity is the correlation between the test and the criterion. But what are the criteria used to validate the tests for assessing the potential of children? Most of these tests are simply valid predictors of how well children will do on other standardized tests. In other words, most standardized tests are evaluated against other standardized tests. However, the criterion simply may be the test dressed in different clothes. For example, one may evaluate an intelligence test to determine how well it predicts performance on a standardized achievement test. This means that the intelligence test really measures achievement, not native ability. Differences in scores on this test between minority and nonminority groups are therefore the result of the opportunity to learn rather than the ability to learn.

## 6.5 FOCUSED EXAMPLE

### The Bell Curve: 20 Years Later

In 1994 Richard Herrnstein, a noted Harvard psychologist, and Charles Murray, a professional writer, published a controversial book titled *The Bell Curve: Intelligence and Class Structure in American Life*. The controversial book provoked an immediate reaction from the mass media and serious scholars alike. Some praised the book as important scholarship, but many regarded it as "scientific racism." In contrast to the many testing professionals who question the value of intelligence tests, Herrnstein and Murray argued that, indeed, intelligence tests are the primary correlates of success in American life. Consistent with Spearman, they argued that the *g* factor is essential to a variety of different skills and abilities.

*The Bell Curve* used data from the National Longitudinal Study of Youth, which had begun in 1979. The study has involved a representative sample of 12,686 youths who were between 14 and 21 years old in 1979 and who have been restudied each year. The book used data collected through 1990. For the analysis, testers used the Armed Services Vocational Aptitude Battery (ASVAB). Various analyses showed that IQ scores are related to a wide variety of indexes of success in life ranging from completion of a college degree through the attainment of substantial income. Some researchers argued that IQ tests predict who will fill the important leadership roles in society. According to the book, those with low IQs are likely to become involved in crime and delinquency, to end up on welfare, and to have illegitimate children.

Herrnstein and Murray were unusually optimistic about the relationship between job performance and IQ. From their data, they suggested that the correlation is .53 between IQ and job-performance rating, .22 between education and job performance, and .11 between college grades and performance. They even argued that the Supreme Court case of *Griggs v. Duke Power Company*, which restricted the use of IQ testing for job selection, has cost U.S. companies billions of dollars because it prevented the most-qualified individuals from being selected for various jobs. They attributed most social problems—such as school dropout rates, unemployment, and work-related injury and crime—to low intelligence. Furthermore, they suggested that the differences in economic attainment for various ethnic groups probably reflect differences in IQ. They concluded by arguing that the United States must face up to differences in intelligence. Finally, they suggested that we must recognize that not all people are created equal and that traditional approaches to these problems will simply not work.

Upon publication, *The Bell Curve* was robustly attacked for a variety of reasons. First, many complained about its arrogant writing style. For example, Herrnstein and Murray described themselves as classicists who favor the traditional view of *g* intelligence. They discussed alternative views of intelligence proposed by "revisionists" and "radicals." They then wrote off these theories as approaches that scholars do not take seriously, even though scholars do seriously consider them. Critics of the book's statistical methods focused on the simplified analyses. For example, many of the correlations between IQ and outcome depend highly on those in the lowest decimal of intelligence. Indeed, it may be that those with low IQs under 80 may have difficulty in various aspects of their lives. However, removing the bottom decile from the analyses would

This is recognized by the ETS, which requests special care in interpreting SAT-I and GRE scores for students who have had "an educational and cultural experience somewhat different from that of the traditional majority" (*GRE Guide*, 2012). These concerns forced the ETS to change their tests. Beginning in 2005, the test will focus more on writing skills and less on analogies and traditional work problems.

If we do not accept standardized tests as a validity criterion for other tests, then how can we determine the meaning of the tests? A considerable debate concerns whether classroom grades should serve as this criterion. Supporters of the use of classroom grades claim that these grades are the only independent measure significantly reduce the relationship between IQ and several of the outcome variables.

Others have attacked *The Bell Curve* for not using measures of intelligence but measures of developed ability as captured by the ASVAB. Leman (1995) claimed that people from higher social classes would be expected to do better on the ASVAB because the test better reflects their culture. Finally, there is concern that comparisons on the basis of race have little meaning because race is not clearly defined. Gould (1996) argued persuasively that it is inappropriate to compare racial groups in countries such as the United States. In the biological sciences, races are considered to be biological subspecies defined by well-identified genetic markers. Today, there are few individuals who represent biologically distinct subgroups. To some extent, all human races are intermingled; we are all genetically linked. We tend to use racial terms in a social rather than a biological sense (Suzuki & Valencia, 1997).

Now, nearly 20 years after the publication of the *Bell Curve*, new evidence is forcing us to rethink many of the basic foundations of the genetic determinism argument. We now know that genes are affected by environment and that the structure of the brain itself is a function of early experiences.

The science of early childhood development has progressed rapidly in the last few decades (J. P. Shonkoff, 2011; J. P. Shonkoff et al., 2012). In particular, there has been an explosion of research on the development of the brain and the nervous system. Evidence now suggests that from the time of conception through the earliest stages of life, the brain is highly "plastic," suggesting that it is very adaptable to environmental stimulation (J. P. Shonkoff & Levitt, 2010). Children are born with many more synapses or connections

between neurons than they will ever use. We are all born with the neurological capacity to learn virtually any language in the world. However, exposure to particular languages shapes the neurological pathways that will be developed. Many of these experiences occur early in life. Pathways that are not used eventually are pruned, suggesting that the unused neural pathways may go away. Early life experiences shape the development of the functioning brain. Abusive or neglectful care might provide a dangerous environment for the developing brain (Garner et al., 2012). However, brains develop to the environments they are exposed to. Children exposed to language and music early in life may develop brains that have highly developed processing pathways for these fields. Children who grow up in environments that require physical adaptation to survive might develop neural pathways that are best able to cope with these threatening experiences. Each brain becomes highly adapted to the situations it faces, but not all brains develop in the same way.

These insights on human brain development, which were first described in a National Academy of Sciences report titled "From Neurons to Neighborhoods: A Science of Early Child Development" (Shonkoff & Phillips, National Research Council (U.S.), Board on Children Youth and Families, and Institute of Medicine (U.S.), 2000). The report became one of the most important challenges to the idea that nature and nurture are independent forces in human development. Biology, to a large extent, can be determined by environmental influences.

In the era when *The Bell Curve* was written, there was a clear distinction between biological and environmental determinants of behavior. Now, there is strong evidence that environment influences biology.

of how well the child is doing. It is no surprise, they maintain, that a correlation exists between IQ tests and scores on standardized achievement tests because both measure similar content. However, they argue that because they do not predict classroom grades for minority children, IQ tests are not valid for such youngsters. The support for this position comes from studies like one by R. D. Goldman and Hartig (1976). This study found scores on the WISC to be unrelated to teacher ratings of classroom performance for minority children. For the nonminority children, it found a significant relationship between IQ and teacher ratings. If the criterion becomes classroom grades rather than another standardized test, the IQ test appears valid for nonminority but not for minority children.

Supporters of the use of the tests give three reasons not to use grades as the criterion. First, teacher-assigned grades are unstandardized and open to subjective bias (Sattler, 1979a). For example, teachers sometimes reward effort more than ability (Weiner, 2011). Second, few available studies have used grades as the criterion. Third, the most frequently cited study (Goldman & Hartig, 1976) is open to other explanations. In this study, the teachers rated the classroom performance of nearly all of the minority children as poor. These low ratings resulted in little variance on the criterion measure. As we saw in Chapter 3, any variable for which there is no variability cannot correlate well with other variables.

The problem with criterion measures becomes even more apparent in relation to measures used with adults. For example, the Medical College Admissions Test (MCAT) predicts success in medical school. Yet, it does not predict who will be a successful doctor. Similarly, the LSAT predicts performance in law school, yet there is little evidence that it predicts who will be a good attorney. The professional school admission tests may thus be eliminating people who are potentially better doctors and lawyers than those who are admitted. Imagine, for example, that an Anglo and a Latina doctor, trained equally well in the science of medical care, both practice in a public hospital in a Latino neighborhood. The Latina doctor will more likely be effective because she understands the culture and the language of the patients and thus can better understand specific complaints and symptoms. The Anglo doctor may do a poorer job at diagnosing the problems. The MCAT would have done its job poorly by focusing on the short-term criterion of medical school grades. More work is needed to develop measures that are good predictors of the long-range goal of clinical success (Altmaier, Smith, O'Halloran, &

## 6.6 FOCUSED EXAMPLE

### Does Affirmative Action Cause African American Students to Fail the Bar Exam?

In addition to the psychology and education fields, the issue of test bias can also be found in the legal literature. One controversy was spearheaded by Richard Sander, a professor at the UCLA School of Law. Sander contends that affirmative action at U.S. law schools has been responsible for the high rate of failure of the California Bar Exam. Passing the bar exam is required for the practice of law. Sander published "A Systematic Analysis of Affirmative Action in American Law Schools" (2004). In this analysis, he reported that African American students are more than two and a half times more likely than white students not to graduate from law school and four times more likely to fail the bar exam on their first attempt. Further, they are six times more likely to fail the bar exam after multiple attempts. He argued that this gap in performance is explained by overall lower average scores on the LSAT and lower undergraduate grade point averages for African American students who are admitted to law school. Sander's position was not well received by other legal scholars. They contend that his analysis did not offer a fair comparison. In particular, they produced evidence showing that African Americans and white law students do not enter law school with equal backgrounds. For the data in Sander's analysis, African American students did not have the same exposure to the highest quality undergraduate education. When African American and white students are matched by quality of their undergraduate training experience, differences in passing the bar exam go away (Ho, 2005). Other research has also challenged the idea that minority students who are given a boost through affirmative action programs fail to compete academically. One large study found that students who entered the university through special admissions programs did not earn lower grades or leave school earlier than other students admitted to the same campuses (Massey & Mooney, 2007).

Franken, 1992). See Focused Example 6.6, which discusses controversies relevant to law school admission.

A related problem is that many tests are not normed for different cultural groups. For example, cross-cultural norms are not available for most neuropsychological tests (Nell, 2000).

# Changing the Social Environment

It is not hard to determine that majority and minority children grow up in different social environments. You can learn this by reading any sociology textbook or by getting in your car and driving around awhile. Given this disparity in environment, it is not surprising that tests favor the majority (Walker et al., 2011). Many critics of tests, though, seem to hold the tests responsible for inequality of opportunity (Flaugher, 1978).

Another view claims that test scores accurately reflect the effects of social and economic inequality (Green, 1978). We know, for instance, that family income is one of the best predictors of performance on standardized tests. Figure 6.11 shows the relationship between family income and performance on the SAT-V and SAT-M components. The graph summarizes performance for all students who completed the test in 1999.

To understand these arguments, one must consider the purpose of testing. In educational settings, tests such as the SAT-I and the GRE or even IQ tests are usually considered to be tests of aptitude: they measure some inborn trait that is unlikely to change with environment. But most experts now agree that tests measure not just inborn potential but also the effects of cumulative experience. The University of California decided in 2001 to drop the aptitude-focused SAT-I in favor of the SAT-II, which is more clearly an achievement test. The impact of this decision is discussed in Focused Example 6.7. Verbal and numerical abilities are acquired through experience, so with proper nurturing, a student can change his or her score. Thus, low test scores should not be viewed as insurmountable problems; they can improve.

This chapter summarizes some studies identifying differences between minority and nonminority students in test performance. Although tests may have contributed to this problem, we think the problem is much deeper. Many minority students do well on the tests, which accurately predict that these students will do well on the criterion. An African American student and a white student who both achieve a score of 1100 on the SAT-I are predicted to do equally well in college, and studies show that indeed they do perform at about the same level. However, the test is a relatively weak predictor for both white and African American studies because the tests have limitations in predicting who will be successful.

There is little question that wealthy students have greater access to programs that might enhance their test scores. Although the value of special test preparation courses has been debated, it appears that coaching does provide some benefit and that less access to test preparation may explain some of the difference between groups in test performance (Aaronson et al., 2011). However, blaming the tests for observed differences between groups may be a convenient way to avoid a much larger problem. No one has suggested that the tuberculin test is unfair because it

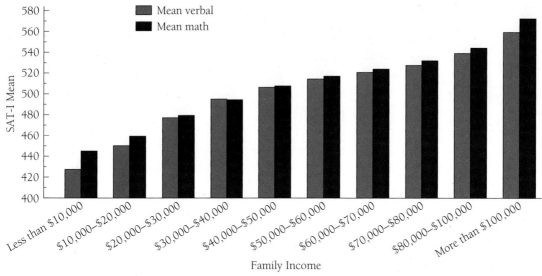

**FIGURE 6.11** Relation between family income and performance on SAT-Verbal and SAT-Math for college-bound seniors in 1999. (Data from College Board, 1999.)

6.7 **FOCUSED EXAMPLE**

## Consequences of the University of California Decision to Drop the SAT-I

In Chapter 5 (Focused Example 5.4, page 144), we discussed the University of California's decision to reject the SAT-I. The University of California decision underscores many of the issues that challenge testing today. For example, the decision raised the important distinction between aptitude and achievement tests. When Carl Brigham from Princeton University stimulated the earliest work on the SAT, his intention was to develop an IQ-like test. Brigham and other early leaders eventually turned against the idea that aptitude tests were precise enough to select college students. Later in his life, Alfred Binet rejected the idea that IQ tests could be used to provide reliable distinctions between individuals at the higher end of the IQ continuum. The SAT-I has always been considered an aptitude test, whereas the SAT-II was designed as an achievement test. As we reported in Chapter 5, a large study of 78,000 University of California freshmen demonstrated that the SAT-II was a better predictor of college grades than the SAT-I. In addition, statistically controlling for socioeconomic background did not affect the predicted value of the SAT-II but had a significant effect on the predictive value of the SAT-I. Once the SAT-II and high-school grades are in a statistical equation,

adding the SAT-I contributes essentially no new information. Thus, the achievement-oriented SAT-II was less influenced by social background than the aptitude-focused SAT-I.

The decision by the University of California to drop the SAT-I was interpreted by many people as a rejection of college admissions testing. In fact, the University of California has retained its policy of requiring the SAT-II. Furthermore, the decision stimulated the College Board to rethink the content of the SAT-I. In particular, the University of California decision emphasized the need for tests to include both a writing sample and higher levels of mathematics.

It took little time for the decision to have a significant impact. The University of California decision was announced in 2001. One year later, the College Board acknowledged that it would create a new SAT that included writing samples and higher-level mathematics. Use of the new test began in 2006. In response to the new SAT, high schools began revising their curricula to include more math and more essay writing experiences for college-bound students. Framers of the test can help improve curricula and the quality of public education (Atkinson, 2004).

demonstrates that poor people have the disease more often than wealthy people. Public health officials have correctly concluded that some people live in environments that predispose them to the disease. Along the same lines, getting rid of scales that identify underweight children will not cure malnutrition (Flaugher, 1978). Although measuring intelligence may not be the same as testing for tuberculosis or measuring weight, the analogy may be worth considering.

If unequal access to adequate education and to stimulating experiences results in differences in test scores, it would be more useful to change the social environment than to bicker continuously about the tests. The tests may merely be the bearers of bad news. By documenting the problem's severity, the tests may be telling us that overcoming this problem will be expensive, difficult, and time-consuming. Blaming the tests for a problem that they did not cause seems to be shortsighted and nonproductive (Shenk, 2011a). Focused Example 6.8 describes how early environmental intervention can make an important difference.

## 6.8 FOCUSED EXAMPLE

### The Value of Prekindergarten Intervention

One of the most compelling arguments for investment in early childhood education has been advanced by James Heckman, a Nobel Prize–winning economist from the University of Chicago. Heckman argues that poor literacy skills are responsible for many major social problems, including crime, teenage pregnancy, and poor health (Heckman, 2012). He also posits that the measurement of cognitive abilities through IQ tests misses some of the most important contributors to success, including socioemotional skills, physical and mental health, motivation, and self-confidence (Conti & Heckman, 2010).

Heckman believes that early intervention to improve socioemotional abilities is valuable and that it is cost-effective. His work suggests that early stimulation, which may be crucial for emotional and cognitive development, is more difficult for nontraditional families, where parents have less time to spend with their children. However, very early intervention may be an appropriate remedy for some of these problems. One well-known study is the Perry Preschool Program, which was designed to enrich the lives of low-income African American children whose IQs were estimated to be below 85 at age 3. The program provided 2.5 hours a day of interaction 5 days a week for a period of approximately 2 years during the academic school year (October to May). It also involved home visits. When the children were followed, those in the treatment group improved IQ scores by nearly 15 points in comparison to only about 4 points in a control group. However, by age 10 the scores had come back together. When the children were followed into early adulthood, an economic analysis showed that those who had participated in the preschool program were more likely to be gainfully employed and to have avoided other legal difficulties. The economists estimated that the rate of return for investment in the preschool program was about 7% to 10% per year, which was better rate of return on investment than investing in the stock market (Heckman, Moon, Pinto, Savelyev, & Yavitz, 2010). Other programs, such as the Abecedarian program, have shown improvements in IQ that last over an extended period of time (Heckman & Lafontaine, 2010).

Overall, the Heckman study suggests that early significant investments in skill development pay dividends in terms of long-term changes in IQ, job skill, and participation in society. Further, Heckman and his associates argue that the return on investment for these early interventions avoids later costs associated with public assistance programs and criminal corrections. The investment in early education produces dividends at a rate that exceeds other conservative investments. Linking to the work on brain development, the argument suggests that intervention should occur early in life, prior to entrance into preschool.

# Summary

In this chapter, we examined two sides of the issue of test bias. Table 6.3 offers a summary of some of the arguments for and against the use of tests. As the table shows, there are strong differences of opinion about the value of intelligence and aptitude tests for minority group members. As a result of the challenge to traditional tests, approaches such as the Chitling Test, the BITCH, and the SOMPA have been developed. Among these, the SOMPA is clearly the most sophisticated. All of these approaches are based on the assumption that social groups do not differ in their average potential. These approaches have been

**TABLE 6.3**   For and Against the Use of Tests

| Against | For |
| --- | --- |
| The Stanford-Binet was standardized on only 1000 children and 400 adults. None of these people were African American (Guthrie, 1976). | Although not originally standardized on minority group members, modern tests are validated using representative samples from most major ethnic and minority groups. The tests appear to have the same validity for minority students as they do for majority students. Therefore, neglecting to include minorities in the original validation studies was not relevant (Fiscella et al., 2011; McDowell, 2006). |
| The use of intelligence tests can have a damaging social impact. For example, the IQ scores of ethnic groups were used to limit immigration of certain groups into the United States during the early years of the 20th century (Kamin, 1974). | Examination of the *Congressional Record* covering the debates about the 1924 Immigration Act failed to uncover discussion of intelligence test data or claims that the mean IQ of Americans would decline if the immigration of certain groups was allowed (DuBois, 1972). |
| If a teacher just thinks some children have higher IQs, the actual test scores of those children will improve (Rosenthal & Jacobson, 1968). | Studies that document the effects of self-fulfilling prophecies and teacher expectations overinterpreted their original data, contained some results that are statistically impossible, and cannot be depended on (Elashoff & Snow, 1971; Snow, 1969; Thorndike, 1968). |
| Minority children can only be damaged by the continued use of psychological tests. | Psychological tests can be used to identify the most capable members of each group. Without the tests, people will be selected on the basis of personal judgment, which might be more racist than the tests (Ones, Chockalingam, & Schmidt, 1995). |
| The validity of IQ tests was documented using other standardized tests as the criterion rather than measures of classroom performance (Mercer, 1988). | The objective tests are better validity criteria than classroom performance, which is more subjective. Teachers may grade on the basis of effort rather than ability (Weiner, 2011). |
| Most test administrators are white; the scores of African American children would improve if they were tested by African American examiners (Forrester & Klaus, 1964; Pasamanick & Knobloch, 1955). | Some studies do indeed show that the race of the examiner is an important factor. However, most studies do not. Among 28 different studies on the effects of the examiner's race, 24 fail to show that the race of the examiner significantly affects scores (McDowell, 2006). |

challenged because they do not have the same sort of validity evidence that traditional tests have.

Part of the debate about test bias results from different moral views about what is fair. Some have argued that a testing and selection program is fair if it selects the best-suited people, regardless of their social group. This approach is called *unqualified individualism*. It may lead to overrepresentation of one group. Another moral position supports *quotas*, or the selection of members from different racial and ethnic groups according to their proportions in the general population. A third moral position, *qualified individualism*, is a compromise between the other two. New methods have been introduced to balance the objectives of these competing belief systems. For example, the methods attempt to address the goals of criterion performance and racial and ethnic diversity.

Although test bias will surely remain an area of considerable controversy, some positive potential solutions have come to light. For example, differences in test scores may reflect patterns of problem solving that characterize different subcultures. Also, one might evaluate tests against outcome criteria relevant to minority groups.

A current controversy rages on about the nature of differences in test performance (Dewey et al., 2011). One group believes the differences are biological in origin (Herrnstein, 1982; Rushton, 1991; Vandenburg & Vogler, 1985), while another believes the differences result from the influence of social environment (Zuckerman, 1990; Checa & Rueda, 2011). Some people believe is the best evidence for supports and interaction between genetic and environmental explanations (Ansari, 2011; Simos, Breznitz, & Berninger, 2011). Further, we now have evidence that gene expression is affected by environments. The social environment explanation (Gould, 1981) seems to be the most popular. If people accept this view, then differences in test performance might suggest that people need to escalate their efforts to wipe out inequality. If one endorses the genetic position, then one acknowledges that little can be done to equalize performance among different groups.

# CHAPTER 7

# Writing and Evaluating Test Items

## LEARNING OBJECTIVES

*When you have completed this chapter, you should be able to:*

▶ Describe two types of item formats commonly used in objective classroom examinations

▶ Know whether or not you should guess on a multiple-choice examination when you are not sure of the correct answer

▶ Explain the types of measurement problems the Likert format is used for

▶ Discuss what sorts of problems you might encounter if you used a 10-point category scale to rate the abilities of a group of similar individuals

▶ Set the level of item difficulty needed for a test that discriminates well among individuals

▶ Describe the process of assessing item discriminability

▶ Define an item characteristic curve and tell how it is used

▶ Draw an item characteristic curve for an item that discriminates well at high but not low levels of performance

▶ Explain how item response theory can lead to more accurate tests and also require fewer responses

▶ Discuss some of the limitations of item analysis for tests that are designed to find specific learning problems

At this point in your studies, you are almost certainly an experienced test taker. Most of these have been classroom exercises; however, you have also been exposed to standardized tests such as the SAT Reasoning Test or the Iowa Test of Basic Skills.

As a seasoned test taker, you also may have become an experienced test critic. After taking a test, most students are willing to judge whether it was a fair or good test. When you feel that you have taken a bad test, you might ask yourself how it could have been better. As an exercise, you might consider creating a fair test of the material covered in the first five chapters of this book. In this chapter, we offer the basics of creating test items.

# Item Writing

When a professor announces that there will be a test, one of the first questions is "What kind of test?" Will it be a true-false, multiple-choice, essay, or fill-in-the-blank test? As you will learn later in this book, personality and intelligence tests require different sorts of responses. The test constructor must determine the best format for getting these responses. In part, this choice stems from the objectives and purpose of the test. For example, if the test requires right or wrong answers, then it will usually be a true-false, multiple-choice, matching, or essay task.

Writing test items can be difficult. DeVellis (2012) provided several simple guidelines for item writing. Here are six of them:

1. *Define clearly what you want to measure.* To do this, use substantive theory as a guide and try to make items as specific as possible.

2. *Generate an item pool.* Theoretically, all items are randomly chosen from a universe of item content. In practice, however, care in selecting and developing items is valuable. Avoid redundant items. In the initial phases, you may want to write three or four items for each one that will eventually be used on the test or scale.

3. *Avoid exceptionally long items.* Long items are often confusing or misleading.

4. *Keep the level of reading difficulty appropriate for those who will complete the scale.*

5. *Avoid "double-barreled" items that convey two or more ideas at the same time.* For example, consider an item that asks the respondent to agree or disagree with the statement, "I vote Democratic because I support social programs." There are two different statements with which the person could agree: "I vote Democratic" and "I support social programs."

6. *Consider mixing positively and negatively worded items.* Sometimes, respondents develop the "acquiescence response set." This means that the respondents will tend to agree with most items. To avoid this bias, you can include items that are worded in the opposite direction. For example, in asking about depression, the CES-D (see Chapter 2) uses mostly negatively worded items (such as "I felt depressed"). However, the CES-D also includes items worded in the opposite direction ("I felt hopeful about the future").

Times change, and tests can get outdated (Chan, Drasgow, & Sawin, 1999). When writing items, you need to be sensitive to ethnic and cultural differences. For example, items on the CES-D concerning appetite, hopefulness, and social interactions may have a different meaning for African American respondents than for white respondents (Foley, Reed, Mutran, & DeVellis, 2002, DeVellis, 2012). Sometimes, the factor structure, or the way items aggregate, may be different from African American respondents in comparison to white respondents (Allen, DeVellis, Renner, Kraus, & Jordan, 2007). It is also important to recognize that tests may become obsolete. In one study, the reliability of items in the Armed Services Vocational Aptitude Battery was studied over a 16-year period. Approximately 12% of the items became less reliable over this time. Items that retained their reliability were more likely to focus on skills, while those that lost reliability focused on more abstract concepts.

## Item Formats

The type of test you have probably experienced most in the classroom is one in which you receive credit for a specific response, or selection of the single "correct" alternative for each test item. True-false and multiple-choice examinations use this system. Similar formats are used for many other purposes such as evaluating attitudes, determining knowledge about traffic laws, or deciding whether someone has characteristics that are associated with a particular health condition. The simplest test of this type uses a dichotomous format.

### The Dichotomous Format

The **dichotomous format** offers two alternatives for each item. Usually a point is given for the selection of one of the alternatives. The most common example of this format is the true-false examination. This test presents students with a series of statements. The student's task is to determine which statements are true and which are false. There are many virtues of the true-false test, including ease of construction and ease of scoring, but the method has also become popular because a teacher can easily construct a test by copying lines out of a textbook. The lines that are copied verbatim are designated as "true." Other statements are altered so that they are no longer true.

The advantages of true-false items include their obvious simplicity, ease of administration, and quick scoring. Another attractive feature is that the true-false items require absolute judgment. The test taker must declare one of the two alternatives. However, there are also disadvantages. For example, true-false items encourage students to memorize material, making it possible for students to perform well on a test that covers materials they do not really understand. Furthermore, "truth" often comes in shades of gray, and true-false tests do not allow test takers the opportunity to show they understand this complexity. Also, the mere chance of getting any item correct is 50%. Thus, to be reliable, a true-false test must include many items. Overall, dichotomous items tend to be less reliable, and therefore less precise than some of the other item formats.

The dichotomous format does not appear only as true-false on educational tests. Many personality tests require responses in a true-false or some other two-choice format, such as yes-no. Personality test constructors often prefer this type of format because it requires absolute judgment. For example, in response to an item such as "I often worry about my sexual performance," people cannot be ambivalent—they must respond "True" or "False." Dichotomous items have many advantages for personality tests with many subscales. One is that they make the scoring of the subscales easy. All that a tester needs to do is count the number of items a person endorses from each subscale.

Although the true-false format is popular in educational tests, it is not used as frequently as the multiple-choice test, which represents the polytomous format.

## The Polytomous Format

The **polytomous format** (sometimes called *polychotomous*) resembles the dichotomous format except that each item has more than two alternatives. Typically, a point is given for the selection of one of the alternatives, and no point is given for selecting any other choice. Because it is a popular method of measuring academic performance in large classes, the multiple-choice examination is the polytomous format you have likely encountered most often. Multiple-choice tests are easy to score, and the probability of obtaining a correct response by chance is lower than it is for true-false items. A major advantage of this format is that it takes little time for test takers to respond to a particular item because they do not have to write. Thus, the test can cover a large amount of information in a relatively short time.

When taking a multiple-choice examination, you must determine which of several alternatives is "correct." Incorrect choices are called **distractors**. As we shall demonstrate in the section on item analysis, the choice of distractors is critically important.

Because most students are familiar with multiple-choice tests and related formats such as matching, there is no need to elaborate on their description. However, it is worthwhile to consider some of the issues in the construction and scoring of multiple-choice tests.

First, how many distractors should a test have? Psychometric theory suggests that adding more distractors should increase the reliability of the items. However, in practice, adding distractors may not actually increase the reliability because it is difficult to find good ones. The reliability of an item is not enhanced by distractors that no one would ever select. Studies have shown that it is rare to find items for which more than three or four distractors operate efficiently. Ineffective distractors actually may hurt the reliability of the test because they are time-consuming to read and can limit the number of good items that can be included in a test. A review of the problems associated with selecting distractors suggests that it is usually best to develop three or four good distractors for each item (Anastasi & Urbina, 1997). Well-chosen distractors are an essential ingredient of good items.

Sometimes psychometric analysis can pave the way for simpler tests. For example, most multiple-choice tests have followed the suggestion of four or five alternatives. However, this traditional practice may not be the best use of resources. In one evaluation of tests for entry-level police officers, applicants completed a test battery with either five alternative multiple-choice items or three alternative items. Psychometric analysis showed that the validity and reliability were about equal for the two types of tests. This result suggests that three alternative multiple-choice items may be better than five alternative items because they retain the psychometric value but take less time to develop and administer (Sidick, Barrett, & Doverspike, 1994). A review of more than 80 years of psychometric research confirms that three-option multiple-choice items are as good as, if not better than, items that have more than three alternatives (Rodriguez, 2005).

Poorly written distractors can adversely affect the quality of the test. Sometimes a test maker will throw in "cute" distractors that are extremely unlikely to be chosen. If distractors are too easy, then a poorly prepared test taker has a high chance of guessing the correct answer. As a result, the test will have lower reliability and validity.

Another issue concerns the scoring of multiple-choice examinations. Suppose you bring your roommate to your sociology test, and he or she fills out an answer sheet without reading the items. Will your roommate get any items correct? The answer is yes—by chance alone. If each test item has four choices, the test taker would be expected to get 25% of the total number of items correct. If the test items had three choices, then a 33.33% rate of success would be expected. Because test takers get some "correct" answers simply by guessing, a correction for guessing is sometimes used. The formula to correct for guessing on a test is

$$\text{corrected score} = R - \frac{W}{n-1}$$

where

$R =$ the number of right responses
$W =$ the number of wrong responses
$n =$ the number of choices for each item

Omitted responses are not included; they provide neither credit nor penalty. The expression $W/(n-1)$ is an estimate of how many items the test taker is expected to get right by chance. For example, suppose that your roommate randomly filled out the answer sheet to your sociology test. The test had 100 items, each with four choices. By chance, her expected score would be 25 correct. Let's assume that she got exactly that, though in practice this may not occur, because 25 is the *average* random score. The expected score corrected for guessing would be

$$R - \frac{W}{n-1}$$
$$= 25 - \frac{75}{4-1}$$
$$= 25 - \frac{75}{3}$$
$$= 25 - 25 = 0$$

In other words, when the correction for guessing is applied, the expected score is 0.

A question that students frequently ask is "Should I guess on multiple-choice items when I don't know the answer?" The answer depends on how the test will be scored. If a correction for guessing is not used, then the best advice is "guess away." By guessing, you have a chance of getting the item correct. You do not have this chance if you do not guess. However, if a correction for guessing is used, then random guessing will do you no good. Some speeded tests are scored so that the correction for the guessing formula includes only the items that were attempted—that is, those that were not attempted are not counted either right or wrong. In this case, random guessing and leaving the items blank have the same expected effect.

How about cases where you do not know the right answer but can eliminate one or two of the alternatives? How many times have you narrowed your answer down to two alternatives but could not figure out which of the two was correct? In this case, we advise you to guess. The correction formula assumes that you are equally likely to respond to each of the four categories. For a four-choice item, it would estimate your chance of getting the item correct by chance alone to be 1 in 4. However, if you can eliminate two alternatives, then the chances are actually 1 in 2. This gives you a slight advantage over the correction formula.

Research has shown that students are more likely to guess when they anticipate a low grade on a test than when they are more confident (Bereby-Meyer, Meyer, & Flascher, 2002). Mathematical methods have been introduced to summarize information in multiple-choice tests and dichotomous-item tests (Huibregtse, Admiraal, & Meara, 2002). These methods summarize the mean, the reliability as calculated from the binomial distribution, and a guessing threshold. The *guessing threshold* describes the chances that a low-ability test taker will obtain each score. These newer methods are highly technical and are beyond the scope of this book. In summary, the techniques are derived from the first three moments of the test score distribution. Mathematically inclined readers who are interested in the methods should consult Carlin and Rubin (1991).

As you have seen, true-false and multiple-choice formats are common to educational and achievement tests. Similar formats are found on personality tests. For example, frequently used personality inventories such as the Minnesota Multiphasic Personality Inventory (MMPI) or the California Psychological Inventory (CPI) present subjects with a long list of statements to which one responds either "True" or "False" (see Chapter 9).

Other personality and attitude measures do not judge any response as "right" or "wrong." Rather, they attempt to quantify characteristics of the response. These formats include the Likert format, the category scale, and the Q-sort. Some of these formats will be discussed in more detail in Chapter 9.

Another format, the essay, is commonly used in classroom evaluation, and the Educational Testing Service now uses a writing sample as a component of its testing programs. Essay exams can be evaluated using the same principles used for structured tests. For example, the validity of the test can be established through correlations with other tests. The reliability of the scoring procedure should be assessed by determining the association between two scores provided by independent scorers. In practice, however, the psychometric properties of essay exams are rarely evaluated.

### The Likert Format

One popular format for attitude and personality scales requires that a respondent indicate the degree of agreement with a particular attitudinal question. This technique is called the **Likert format** because it was used as part of Likert's (1932) method of attitude scale construction. A scale using the Likert format consists of items such as "I am afraid of heights." Instead of asking for a yes-no reply, five alternatives are offered: *strongly disagree, disagree, neutral, agree,* and *strongly agree*. Examples of Likert scale items are given in Table 7.1. In some applications, six options are used to avoid

**TABLE 7.1**    Examples of Likert Scale Items

Following is a list of statements. Please indicate how strongly you agree or disagree by circling your answer to the right of the statement.

Five-choice format with neutral point

| Some politicians can be trusted | Strongly disagree | Somewhat disagree | Neither agree nor disagree | Somewhat agree | Strongly agree |
|---|---|---|---|---|---|
| I am confident that I will achieve my life goals | Strongly disagree | Somewhat disagree | Neither agree nor disagree | Somewhat agree | Strongly agree |
| I am comfortable talking to my parents about personal problems | Strongly disagree | Somewhat disagree | Neither agree nor disagree | Somewhat agree | Strongly agree |

Alternative set of choices: strongly disagree, disagree, undecided, agree, strongly agree

Six-choice format without neutral point

| Some politicians can be trusted | Strongly disagree | Moderately disagree | Mildly disagree | Mildly agree | Moderately agree | Strongly agree |
|---|---|---|---|---|---|---|
| I am confident that I will achieve my life goals | Strongly disagree | Moderately disagree | Mildly disagree | Mildly agree | Moderately agree | Strongly agree |
| I am comfortable talking to my parents about personal problems | Strongly disagree | Moderately disagree | Mildly disagree | Mildly agree | Moderately agree | Strongly agree |

Alternative set of choices: strongly disagree, disagree, lean toward disagree, lean toward agree, agree, strongly agree

allowing the respondent to be neutral. The six responses might be *strongly disagree, moderately disagree, mildly disagree, mildly agree, moderately agree,* and *strongly agree.* Scoring requires that any negatively worded items be reverse scored and the responses are then summed. This format is especially popular in measurements of attitude. For example, it allows researchers to determine how much people endorse statements such as "The government should not regulate private business."

Because responses in a Likert format can be subjected to factor analysis, test developers can find groups of items that go together. The Likert format is often used to create Likert scales (Clark & Watson, 1998). The scales require assessment of item discriminability, a concept that we address later in the chapter. A variety of technical approaches to Likert scale development are available (Ferrando, 1999). Some research favors the validity of forced-choice formats over the traditional Likert format (Roberts, Laughlin, & Wendel, 1999). Some studies have

## 7.1 FOCUSED EXAMPLE

### The Effect of Context on Value Ratings

The numbers we assign when using rating scales are sometimes influenced by the context or the background against which objects are rated. In one experiment, college students were asked to rate how immoral they believed certain acts to be. The students were divided into two groups. One group rated the items that typically represented "mild" actions (List 1) with items ranging from keeping a dime found in a phone booth to avoiding criticism by contributing money to a cause you don't believe in. The other group rated items that typically represented more severe actions (List 2). These ranged from failure to repay money borrowed from friends to murdering your mother. The numbers on the right represent average ratings by a large number of college students. The six items included on both lists are marked with asterisks. These items are judged more leniently when included in List 2 than when in List 1. This experiment shows that the numbers we assign when using rating scales are affected by context (Parducci, 1968).

**List 1**

| | |
|---|---|
| Registering in a hotel under a false name. | 1.68 |
| Bawling out servants publicly.* | 2.64 |
| Contributing money to a cause in which you do not believe in order to escape criticism. | 3.03 |
| Keeping a dime you find in a telephone booth. | 1.08 |
| Publishing under your own name an investigation originated and carried out without remuneration by a graduate student working under you.* | 3.95 |
| Failing to pay your bus fare when the conductor overlooks you. | 2.36 |
| Playing poker on Sunday. | 1.17 |
| Failing to put back in the water lobsters shorter than the legal limit.* | 2.22 |
| Cheating at solitaire. | 1.53 |
| Fishing without a license. | 2.27 |
| Habitually borrowing small sums of money from friends and failing to return them.* | 2.93 |
| Stealing towels from a hotel. | 2.58 |
| Stealing a loaf of bread from a store when you are starving. | 1.79 |

demonstrated that the Likert format is superior to methods such as the visual analogue scale for measuring complex coping responses (Flynn, Schaik, & van Wersch, 2004). Others have challenged the appropriateness of using traditional parametric statistics to analyze Likert responses because the data are at the ordinal rather than at an interval level (Jamieson, 2004). Nevertheless, the Likert format is familiar and easy to use. It is likely to remain popular in personality and attitude tests.

### The Category Format

A technique that is similar to the Likert format but that uses an even greater number of choices is the **category format**. Most people are familiar with 10-point rating systems because we are regularly asked questions such as, "On a scale from 1 to 10, with 1 as the lowest and 10 as the highest, how would you rate your new boyfriend in terms of attractiveness?" Doctors often ask their patients to rate their pain on a scale from 1 to 10, where 1 is little or no pain and 10 is intolerable pain. A category scale need not have exactly 10 points; it can have either more or fewer categories.

Although the 10-point scale is common in psychological research and everyday conversation, controversy exists regarding when and how it should be used. We recently encountered a college basketball coach who rates the quality of high-school prospects on a 10-point rating scale. It is assumed that this rating provides

| | |
|---|---|
| Poisoning a neighbor's dog whose barking bothers you.* | 4.19 |
| Lying about your whereabouts to protect a friend's reputation. | 1.60 |
| Wearing shorts on the street where it is illegal. | 1.59 |
| Pocketing the tip the previous customer left for the waitress.* | 3.32 |
| Getting your own way by playing on people's sympathies. | 2.90 |

**List 2**

| | |
|---|---|
| Using guns on striking workers. | 3.82 |
| Bawling out servants publicly.* | 2.39 |
| Stealing ten dollars from an impecunious acquaintance. | 3.79 |
| Selling to a hospital milk from diseased cattle. | 4.51 |
| Publishing under your own name an investigation originated and carried out without remuneration by a graduate student working under you.* | 3.47 |
| Spreading rumors that an acquaintance is a sexual pervert. | 3.91 |

| | |
|---|---|
| Having a sane person committed to a mental hospital in order to get rid of him. | 4.46 |
| Failing to put back in the water lobsters that are shorter than the legal limit.* | 1.82 |
| Having sexual relations with a sibling (brother or sister). | 3.72 |
| Putting your deformed child in the circus. | 3.81 |
| Habitually borrowing small sums of money from friends and failing to return them.* | 2.37 |
| Having incestuous relations with your parent. | 3.88 |
| Murdering your mother without justification or provocation. | 4.79 |
| Poisoning a neighbor's dog whose barking bothers you.* | 3.65 |
| Testifying falsely against someone for pay. | 4.07 |
| Teaching adolescents to become dope addicts. | 4.51 |
| Pocketing the tip the previous customer left for the waitress.* | 2.46 |
| Sending another person to take a civil service exam for you. | 3.39 |

*Items followed by an asterisk appear on both lists. From Parducci (1968).

a reliable estimate of the players' abilities. However, experiments have shown that responses to items on 10-point scales are affected by the groupings of the people or things being rated. For example, if coaches are asked to rate the abilities of a group of 20 talented players, they may tend to make fine distinctions among them so as to use most or all of the categories on the 10-point scale. A particular player rated as a 6 when he was on a team with many outstanding players might be rated as a 9 if he were judged with a group of poorly coordinated players (Parducci, 1968, 1995). We know from a variety of studies that people will change ratings depending on context (Norman, 2003). When given a group of objects to rate, subjects have a tendency to spread their responses evenly across the 10 categories (Stevens, 1966). See Focused Example 7.1 for more on the effect of context on value ratings. Other advice on creating category items involves making the response options clearer for the respondent. For example, reliability and validity may be higher if all response options are clearly labeled, as opposed to just labeling the categories at the extremes (Green and Yang, 2009).

Experiments have shown that this problem can be avoided if the endpoints of the scale are clearly defined and the subjects are frequently reminded of the definitions of the endpoints. For example, instead of asking coaches to rate the ability of basketball players on a 10-point scale, testers might show them films that depict the performance of a player rated as 10 and other films showing what the rating of 1 means. Under these circumstances, the subjects are less likely to offer a response that is affected by other stimuli in the group (Kaplan & Ernst, 1983).

People often ask, "Why use a 10-point scale instead of a 13-point or a 43-point scale?" This question has generated considerable study. More than 80 years ago, researchers argued that the optimal number of points is 7 (Symonds, 1924), whereas others have suggested that the optimal number of categories should be three times this number (Champney & Marshall, 1939). As is often the case, the number of categories required depends on the fineness of the discrimination that subjects are willing to make. If the subjects are unconcerned about a given topic, then they will not make fine discriminations about it, and a scale with a few categories will do about as well as a scale with many. However, when people are highly involved with some issue, they will tend to respond best to a greater number of categories. For most rating tasks, however, a 10-point scale seems to provide enough discrimination. N. H. Anderson (1991) has found that a 10-point scale provides substantial discrimination among objects for a wide variety of stimuli. Some evidence suggests that increasing the number of response categories may not increase reliability and validity. In fact, increasing the number of choices beyond nine or so can reduce reliability because responses may be more likely to include an element of randomness when there are so many alternatives that respondents cannot clearly discriminate between the fine-grained choices (Clark & Watson, 1998). One analysis showed that the optimum number of categories is between four and seven. Reliability suffers when fewer than four categories are used, but the increase in reliability does not increase much when form than seven categories are available (Lozano, García-Cueto, et al., 2008). An approach related to category scales is the *visual analogue* scale. Using this method, the respondent is given a 100-millimeter line and asked to place a mark between two well-defined endpoints. The scales are scored according to the measured distance from the first endpoint to the mark (see Figure 7.1). Visual analogue scales are popular for measuring self-rated health. However, they are not used often for multi-item scales, because scoring is time-consuming (Clark & Watson 1998). Methods are available for creating confidence intervals around item means for rating scales (Penfield, 2003b).

### Checklists and Q-Sorts

One format common in personality measurement is the adjective checklist (Gough, 1960). With this method, a subject receives a long list of adjectives and indicates whether each one is characteristic of himself or herself. Adjective checklists can be used for describing either oneself or someone else. For example, in one study at the University of California at Berkeley, raters checked the traits they thought charac-

**FIGURE 7.1**
The 100-mm visual analogue scale. The subject has rated her pain 63 mm from the base of no pain at all. On a scale ranging from 0 to 100, this level of pain is scored as 63.

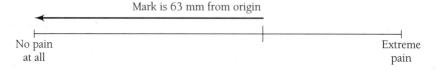

terized a group of 40 graduate students. Half of these students had been designated by their instructors as exceptional in originality, and the other half low in originality. The results demonstrated that the adjectives chosen to describe members of these two groups differed. The highly original students were described most often by the traits *adventurous, alert, curious, quiet, imaginative,* and *fair-minded.* In contrast, the low-originality students were seen as *confused, conventional, defensive, polished, prejudiced,* and *suggestible.*

The adjective checklist requires subjects either to endorse such adjectives or not, thus allowing only two choices for each item. A similar technique known as the *Q-sort* increases the number of categories. The Q-sort can be used to describe oneself or to provide ratings of others (Stephenson, 1953). With this technique, a subject is given statements and asked to sort them into nine piles. For example, Block (1961) gave observers 100 statements about personal characteristics. The statements were sorted into piles that indicated the degree to which they appeared to describe a given person accurately. If you were using this method, you might be asked to rate your roommate. You would receive a set of 100 cards, each with a statement on it such as the following:

Has a wide range of interests.

Is productive; gets things done.

Is self-dramatizing; is histrionic.

Is overreactive to minor frustrations; is irritable.

Seeks reassurance from others.

Appears to have a high degree of intellectual capacity.

Is basically anxious.

If a statement really hit home, you would place it in pile 9. Those that were not at all descriptive would be placed in pile 1. Most of the cards are usually placed in piles 4, 5, and 6. The frequency of items placed in each of the categories usually looks like a bell-shaped curve (see Figure 7.2). The items that end up in the extreme categories usually say something interesting about the person.

## Other Possibilities

We have discussed only a few of many item formats. The forced-choice (such as multiple-choice and Q-sort) and Likert formats are clearly the most popular in contemporary tests and measures. Other formats have become less popular in

**FIGURE 7.2**

The California Q-sort. The numbers of items distributed in the nine piles of the California Q-sort approach a normal distribution.

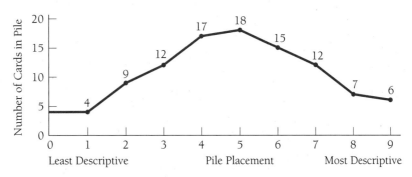

**TABLE 7.2** Summary of Advice About Item Writing from 20 Textbooks

| | Frequency | % | Research support | Multiple-choice | Matching | True-false | Completion |
|---|---|---|---|---|---|---|---|
| 1. "All of the Above" should not be an answer option | 16 | 80.0 | X | X | | | |
| 2. "None of the Above" should not be an answer option | 15 | 75.0 | | X | | | |
| 3. All answer options should be plausible | 14 | 70.0 | | X | X | | |
| 4. Order of answer options should be logical or vary | 13 | 65.0 | X | X | | | |
| 5. Items should cover important concepts and objectives | 12 | 60.0 | | X | X | X | X |
| 6. Negative wording should not be used | 11 | 55.0 | | X | | | |
| 7. Answer options should include only one correct answer | 11 | 55.0 | | X | X | | |
| 8. Answer options should all be grammatically consistent with stem | 10 | 50.0 | | X | X | | |
| 9. Specific determiners (e.g., *always, never*) should not be used | 10 | 50.0 | | X | | | |
| 10. Answer options should be homogenous | 10 | 50.0 | | X | X | | |
| 11. Stems must be unambiguous and clearly state the problem | 10 | 50.0 | | X | | | |
| 12. Correct answer options should not be the longest answer option | 9 | 45.0 | | X | | | |
| 13. Answer options should not be longer than the stem | 8 | 40.0 | X | | | | |
| 14. Items should use appropriate vocabulary | 8 | 40.0 | X | X | X | X | |
| 15. In fill-in-the-blank items, a single blank should be used, at the end | 8 | 40.0 | | | | X | |
| 16. Items should be independent of each other | 8 | 40.0 | X | | | | |
| 17. In matching, there should be more answer options than stems | 8 | 40.0 | | X | | | |
| 18. All parts of an item or exercise should appear on the same page | 8 | 40.0 | X | X | X | X | |
| 19. True-false items should have simple structure | 6 | 30.0 | | | X | | |

| | Frequency | % | Research support | Multiple-choice | Matching | True-false | Completion |
|---|---|---|---|---|---|---|---|
| 20. True-false items should be entirely true or entirely false | 6 | 30.0 | | | X | | |
| 21. There should be 3–5 answer options | 6 | 30.0 | X | X | | | |
| 22. Answer options should not have repetitive wording | 6 | 30.0 | X | X | | | |
| 23. Point value of items should be presented | 6 | 30.0 | X | X | X | X | |
| 24. Stems and examples should not come directly from textbook | 5 | 25.0 | X | X | X | X | |
| 25. Matching item directions should include basis for match | 5 | 25.0 | | X | | | |
| 26. Answer options should be logically independent of one another | 5 | 25.0 | X | X | | | |
| 27. Directions should be included | 5 | 25.0 | X | X | X | X | |
| 28. Questions using the same format should be together | 5 | 25.0 | X | X | X | X | |
| 29. Vague frequency terms (e.g., *often, usually*) should not be used | 4 | 20.0 | X | | X | | |
| 30. Multiple-choice stems should be complete sentences | 4 | 20.0 | X | | | | |
| 31. There should be an equal number of true and false statements | 4 | 20.0 | | | X | | |
| 32. True-false statements should be of equal length | 4 | 20.0 | | | X | | |
| 33. Individual items should be short | 4 | 20.0 | X | X | X | | |
| 34. Answer options should be available more than once | 4 | 20.0 | | X | | | |
| 35. Number of answer options should be <7 for elementary age tests | 4 | 20.0 | | X | | | |
| 36. Number of answer options should be <17 for secondary age tests | 4 | 20.0 | | X | | | |
| 37. Complex item formats ("a and b, but not c") should not be used | 3 | 15.0 | X | X | | | |
| 38. All items should be numbered | 3 | 15.0 | X | X | X | X | |
| 39. Test copies should be clear, readable and not handwritten | 2 | 10.0 | X | X | X | X | |
| 40. Stems should be on the left, and answer options on the right | 2 | 10.0 | | X | | | |

Source: From *Teaching and Teacher Education* 21(2005), 360–361.

recent years. For example, checklists have fallen out of favor because they are more prone to error than are formats that require responses to every item. If you are interested in learning more about item writing and item formats, then you might check some general references (Clark & Watson, 1998).

Unfortunately, there is no simple recipe for item writing. One group analyzed 20 different textbooks that offered rules on item writing. The textbooks reviewed offered 40 different bits of advice. These are summarized in Table 7.2. The table also summarizes whether there is research support for each suggestion in relation to multiple-choice, matching, true-false, or completion items. The most frequent advice (given in 80% of the textbooks) was not to use "all of the above" as a response option. As a student, you may have noticed that this frequent advice is commonly ignored (Frey, Petersen, Edwards, Pedrotti, & Peyton, 2005). However, writing good items remains an art rather than a science. There is no substitute for using precise language, knowing the subject matter, being familiar with the level of examinees, and using your imagination. Once the items are written and have been administered, you can use item-analysis techniques to evaluate them.

# Item Analysis

A good test has good items. But what are good items? How many times have you been in a class in which students launched a full-scale battle over particular items in a multiple-choice test? Tests with good items are hard to create. Good test making requires careful attention to the principles of test construction. **Item analysis**, a general term for a set of methods used to evaluate test items, is one of the most important aspects of test construction. The basic methods involve assessment of item difficulty and item discriminability.

## Item Difficulty

For a test that measures achievement or ability, **item difficulty** is defined by the number of people who get a particular item correct. For example, if 84% of the people taking a particular test get item 24 correct, then the difficulty level for that item is .84. Some people have suggested that these proportions do not really indicate item "difficulty" but item "easiness." The higher the proportion of people who get the item correct, the easier the item.

How hard should items be in a good test? This depends on the uses of the test and the types of items. The first thing a test constructor needs to determine is the probability that an item could be answered correctly by chance alone. A true-false item could be answered correctly half the time if people just guessed randomly. Thus, a true-false item with a difficulty level of .50 would not be a good item. A multiple-choice item with four alternatives could be answered correctly 25% of the time. Therefore, we would require difficulty greater than 25% for an item to be reasonable in this context. Other obvious limits are the extremes of the scale. An item that is answered correctly by 100% of the respondents offers little value because it does not discriminate among individuals.

The optimal difficulty level for items is usually about halfway between 100% of the respondents getting the item correct and the level of success expected by chance alone. Thus, the optimum difficulty level for a four-choice item is approximately .625. To arrive at this value, we take the 100% success level (1.00) and subtract from it the chance performance level (.25). Then we divide the result by 2 to find the halfway point and add this value to the expected chance level. The steps are outlined here.

*Step 1.* Find half of the difference between 100% (or 1.00) success and chance performance.

$$\frac{1.0 - .25}{2} = \frac{.75}{2} = .375$$

*Step 2.* Add this value to the probability of performing correctly by chance.

A simpler method for obtaining the same result is to add 1.00 to chance performance and divide by 2.0. For this example, the result would be

$$\frac{.25 + 1.0}{2.00} = .625$$

In most tests, the items should have a variety of difficulty levels because a good test discriminates at many levels. For example, a professor who wants to determine how much his or her students have studied might like to discriminate between students who have not studied at all and those who have studied just a little, or between those who have studied just a little and those who have studied a fair amount, or perhaps between those students who have studied more than average and those who have worked and studied exceptionally hard. In other words, the professor needs to make many discriminations. To accomplish this, he or she requires items at many different levels of difficulty.

For most tests, items in the difficulty range of .30 to .70 tend to maximize information about the differences among individuals. However, some tests require a concentration of more-difficult items. For example, if a test is to be used to select medical students and only a small number of qualified applicants can be accepted, then a test with especially difficult items will make fine discriminations in a way that a test with a broader range of difficulty would not. Conversely, a test used to select students for educable mentally challenged classes should have a greater concentration of easier items to make fine discriminations among individuals who ordinarily do not perform well on tests (Allen & Yen, 1979). In constructing a good test, one must also consider human factors. For example, though items answered correctly by all students will have poor psychometric qualities, they may help the morale of the students who take the test. A few easier items may help keep test anxiety in check, which in turn adds to the reliability of the test. Although we have discussed item analysis in relation to achievement tests, the same methods can be used to evaluate other measures. For example, instead of considering an item as right or wrong, one could set it up to indicate whether it is or is not associated with a particular diagnosis, group membership, and so forth.

Item difficulty is only one way to evaluate test items. Another way is to examine the relationship between performance on particular items and performance on the whole test. This is known as discriminability.

## Discriminability

In the previous section, we discussed the analysis of item difficulty, which determines the proportion of people who succeed on a particular item. Another way to examine the value of items is to ask, "Who gets this item correct?" Assessment of **item discriminability** determines whether the people who have done well on particular items have also done well on the whole test. One can evaluate the discriminability of test items in many ways.

### The Extreme Group Method

This method compares people who have done well with those who have done poorly on a test. For example, you might find the students with test scores in the top third and those in the bottom third of the class. Then you would find the proportions of people in each group who got each item correct. The difference between these proportions is called the *discrimination index*. Psychological Testing in Everyday Life 7.1 demonstrates this method.

### The Point Biserial Method

Another way to examine the discriminability of items is to find the correlation between performance on the item and performance on the total test. You might remember from Chapter 3 that the correlation between a dichotomous (two-category) variable and a continuous variable is called a *point biserial correlation*. The point biserial correlation between an item and a total test score is

$$r_{\text{pbis}} = \left[ \frac{\overline{Y}_1 - \overline{Y}}{S_y} \right] \sqrt{\frac{P_x}{1 - P_x}}$$

where

$r_{\text{pbis}}$ = the point biserial correlation or index of discriminability
$\overline{Y}_1$ = the mean score on the test for those who got item 1 correct
$\overline{Y}$ = the mean score on the test for all persons
$S_y$ = the standard deviation of the exam scores for all persons
$P_x$ = the proportion of persons getting the item correct (Allen & Yen, 1979)

For example, suppose that 58% of the students in a psychology class gave the correct response to item 15 on their midterm exam. The mean score on the whole test for these students who got item 15 correct was 57.6, and the mean score for the entire class was 54.3. The standard deviation on the test was 9.7. To calculate

**7.1 / PSYCHOLOGICAL TESTING IN EVERYDAY LIFE**

## Finding the Item Discrimination Index by Using the Extreme Group Method

Step 1.    Identify a group of students who have done well on the test—or example, those in the 67th percentile and above. Also identify a group that has done poorly—for example, those in the 33rd percentile and below.

Step 2.    Find the proportion of students in the high group and the proportion of students in the low group who got each item correct.

Step 3.    For each item, subtract the proportion of correct responses for the low group from the proportion of correct responses for the high group. This gives the item discrimination index ($d_i$).

**Example**

| Item Number | Proportion Correct for Students in the Top Third of Class ($P_t$) | Proportion Correct for Students in the Bottom Third of Class ($P_b$) | Discriminability Index ($d_i = P_t - P_b$) |
|:---:|:---:|:---:|:---:|
| 1 | .89 | .34 | .55 |
| 2 | .76 | .36 | .40 |
| 3 | .97 | .45 | .52 |
| 4 | .98 | .95 | .03 |
| 5 | .56 | .74 | −.18 |

In this example, items 1, 2, and 3 appear to discriminate reasonably well. Item 4 does not discriminate well because the level of success is high for both groups; it must be too easy. Item 5 appears to be a bad item because it is a "negative discriminator." This sometimes happens on multiple-choice examinations when overprepared students find some reason to disqualify the response keyed as "correct."

the discriminability of item 15 by the point biserial method, you would enter this information into the formula:

$$\left[\frac{57.6 - 54.3}{9.7}\right]\sqrt{\frac{.58}{.42}} = .34 \times \sqrt{1.38} = (.34)(1.17) = .40$$

In other words, the correlation between succeeding on item 15 and total test performance is .40.

On tests with only a few items, using the point biserial correlation is problematic because performance on the item contributes to the total test score.

For example, if a test has six items, there is bound to be a positive correlation between getting a particular item correct and the total test score because one sixth of the total score is performance on that item. To compensate for this problem, it is sometimes advisable to exclude the item from the total test score. For the six-item test, we might look at the point biserial correlation between passing item 1 and the test score derived from items 2 through 6.

The point biserial correlation ($r_{\text{pbis}}$) between an item and the total test score is evaluated in much the same way as the extreme group discriminability index. If this value is negative or low, then the item should be eliminated from the test. The closer the value of the index is to 1.0, the better the item. Note that the easiest items, such as those answered correctly by 90% or more, usually do not appear to be good items on the discriminability index. If 90% of test takers get an item correct, then there is too little variability in performance for there to be a substantial correlation with the total test score. Similarly, if items are so hard that they are answered correctly by 10% or fewer of the test takers, then there is too little room to show a correlation between the items and the total test score.

## Pictures of Item Characteristics

A valuable way to learn about items is to graph their characteristics, which you can do with the **item characteristic curve**. For particular items, one can prepare a graph for each individual test item. On these individual item graphs, the total test score is plotted on the horizontal ($X$) axis and the proportion of examinees who get the item correct is plotted on the vertical ($Y$) axis. The total test score is used as an estimate of the amount of a "trait" possessed by individuals. Because we can never measure traits directly, the total test score is the best approximation we have. Thus, the relationship between performance on the item and performance on the test gives some information about how well the item is tapping the information we want.

### Drawing the Item Characteristic Curve

To draw the item characteristic curve, we need to define discrete categories of test performance. If the test has been given to many people, we might choose to make each test score a single category (65, 66, 67, and so on). However, if the test has been given to a smaller group, then we might use a smaller number of class intervals (such as 66–68, 69–71). When only a small number of people took the test, some scores would not be observed and would appear as gaps on the graph. Using fewer class intervals allows the curve to take on a smoother appearance. Once you have arrived at these categories, you need to determine what proportion of the people within each category got each item correct. For example, you must determine what proportion of the people with a total test score of 65 got item 34 correct, what proportion of the people with a total test score of 66 got item 34 correct, and so on. Once you have this series of breakdowns, you can create a plot of the proportions of correct responses to an item by total test scores. Examples of these graphs are shown in Figures 7.3 through 7.7.

Figure 7.3 shows the item characteristic curve for a "good" test item. The gradual positive slope of the line demonstrates that the proportion of people who pass the item gradually increases as test scores increase. This means that the item successfully discriminates at all levels of test performance. The curve shown in

**FIGURE 7.3**

Item characteristic curve for a "good" test item. The proportion of test takers who get the item correct increases as a function of the total test score.

**FIGURE 7.4**

Item characteristic curve for a test item that discriminates well at low levels of performance but not at higher levels.

Figure 7.4 illustrates an item that discriminates especially well among people at the lower level of performance. However, because all of the people who scored above average on the test got this item correct, it did not provide much discrimination in the higher ranges of performance.

Figure 7.5 shows a variety of item characteristic curves. Ranges in which the curve changes suggest that the item is sensitive, while flat ranges suggest areas of low sensitivity. The items are each sensitive in a particular range. Figures 7.6 and 7.7 show item characteristic curves for poor items. The flat curve in Figure 7.6 indicates that test takers at all levels of ability were equally likely to get the item correct. Figure 7.7 demonstrates a particularly troublesome problem. The item characteristic curve gradually rises, showing that the item is sensitive to most levels of performance. Then it turns down for people at the highest levels of performance, suggesting that those with the best overall performance on the test did not have the best chances of getting the item correct. This can happen on multiple-choice examinations when one of the alternatives is "none of the above." Students who are exceptionally knowledgeable in the subject area can sometimes rule out all the choices even though one of the alternatives has actually been designated as correct.

Another convenient picture of item characteristics is shown in Figure 7.8. This graph plots the item numbers within the space created by difficulty on one axis and

**FIGURE 7.5**

Item characteristic curves for several items.

**FIGURE 7.6**

Item characteristic curve for a poor item. People with different test scores were equally likely to get the item correct.

**FIGURE 7.7**

Another example of a problem item. Sometimes test takers who "know too much" will rule out the alternative designated as correct.

discriminability (in this case, point biserial correlation between item passage and test score) on the other axis. Item 12 has been circled on the graph so that you can identify it. Of all respondents, 46% got this item correct, and its discriminability level is .60. Thus, item 12 on the graph is aligned with 46 on the difficulty axis

Items from a 30-item test are plotted on a graph with discriminability on one axis and difficulty on the other. Each number on the graph represents a test item: 1 is for item 1 and so on. The shaded area represents items above a discriminability level of .30 and between 30% and 70% in difficulty level. These items would be the best candidates to include in the final version of the test. Item 12 (circled) was passed by 46% of the respondents and was correlated .60 with total test score, so it should be retained.

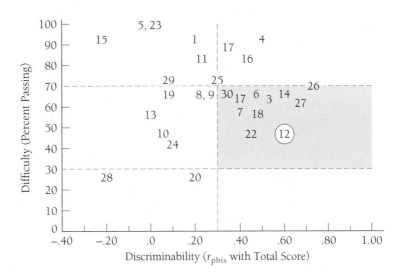

and .60 on the discriminability axis. Earlier in the discussion we noted that "good" items usually fall within a difficulty range of 30% and 70%. In Figure 7.8, the shaded region bound by the dotted lines represents the region in which acceptable levels of difficulty and discriminability are achieved. Thus, items for the final version of the test should be selected from this area.

In summary, item analysis breaks the general rule that increasing the number of items makes a test more reliable. When bad items are eliminated, the effects of chance responding can be eliminated and the test can become more efficient, reliable, and valid. In the next section, we will consider item response theory, which is a modern method to improve test efficiency even further.

## Item Response Theory

New approaches to item analysis have generated a new model of psychological testing (Yanai, 2003). According to classical test theory, a score is derived from the sum of an individual's responses to various items, which are sampled from a larger domain that represents a specific trait or ability. Newer approaches to testing based on item analysis consider the chances of getting particular items right or wrong. These approaches, now known as *item response theory* (IRT), make extensive use of item analysis (DeMars, 2010; DeVellis, 2012). According to these approaches, each item on a test has its own item characteristic curve that describes the probability of getting each particular item right or wrong given the ability level of each test taker. With the computer, items can be sampled, and the specific range of items where the test taker begins to have difficulty can be identified (Bolt, 2003; Schmidt & Embretson, 2003). In this way, testers can make an ability judgment without subjecting the test taker to all of the test items. Computer programs are now available to teach the complex theory underlying IRT (DeMars, 2010; DeVellis, 2012).

This theory has many technical advantages. It builds on traditional models of item analysis and can provide information on item functioning, the value of specific items, and the reliability of a scale (DeMars, 2010; DeVellis, 2012). Perhaps the most important message for the test taker is that his or her score is no longer defined by the total number of items correct, but instead by the level of difficulty of items that he or she can answer correctly. The implications of IRT are profound. In fact, some people believe that IRT was the most important development in psychological testing in the second half of the 20th century. However, many psychology training programs have not yet added these methods to their curriculum (Aiken, 2008).

There are various approaches to the construction of tests using IRT. Some of the approaches use the two dimensions shown in Figure 7.8: difficulty and discriminability. Other approaches add a third dimension for the probability that test takers with the lowest levels of ability will get a correct response. Still other approaches use only the difficulty parameter. All of the approaches grade items in relation to the probability that those who do well or poorly on the exam will have different levels of performance. One can average item characteristic curves to create a test characteristic curve that gives the proportion of responses expected to be correct for each level of ability (Guion & Ironson, 1983).

Perhaps the most attractive advantage of tests based on IRT is that one can easily adapt them for computer administration. The computer can rapidly identify the specific items that are required to assess a particular ability level. With this approach, test takers do not have to suffer the embarrassment of attempting multiple items beyond their ability. Conversely, they do not need to waste their time and effort on items far below their capability. In addition, each test taker may get different items to answer, greatly reducing the chances of cheating. It has been suggested that computer-adaptive testing will increase efficiency by 50% or more by reducing the amount of time each test taker spends responding to items (Schmidt & Embretson, 2003).

Figure 7.9 shows the measurement precision associated with conventional and computer-adaptive tests. Most conventional tests have the majority of their items at or near an average level of difficulty; this is represented by the "peaked conventional" portion of the figure. Though the precision of the test is best for those at average ability levels, those with the lowest or highest ability levels are not well assessed by this type of test. An alternative approach, labeled "rectangular conventional" in Figure 7.9, requires that test items be selected to create a wide range in level of difficulty. These items are pretested and selected to cover evenly the span from easiest to most difficult. The problem with this approach is that only a few items of the test

**FIGURE 7.9**

Measurement precision as a function of trail level for adaptive, peaked, and rectangular conventional tests. Adaptive tests based on item response theory (IRT) have higher precision across the range of ability levels.

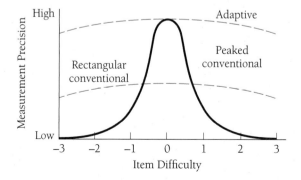

are appropriate for individuals at each ability level; that is, many test takers spend much of their time responding to items either considerably below their ability level or too difficult to solve. As a result, measurement precision is constant across the range of test-taker abilities but relatively low for all people, as shown in Figure 7.9.

The supporters of IRT believe that the solution to this problem lies in computer-adaptive testing. The computer samples items and determines the range of ability that best represents each test taker. Then testing time is spent focusing on the specific range that challenges the respondent—specifically, items that have a 50% probability of a correct response (assuming no guessing) for each individual. This results in a measurement instrument of equally high precision for all test takers.

IRT is now widely used in many areas of applied research, and there are specialized applications for specific problems such as the measurement of self-efficacy (Smith, Wakely, De Kruif, & Swartz, 2003), psychopathology (Nugent, 2003; Reise & Waller, 2003), industrial psychology (Schneider, Goff, Anderson, & Borman, 2003), and health (Meijer, 2003). Along with the many technical developments in IRT, new technical problems have sprung up. For example, difficulties arise when tests measure multiple dimensions. However, IRT addresses traditional problems in test construction well. For example, IRT can handle items that are written in different formats (Hayes, 2000). In addition, IRT can identify respondents with unusual response patterns and offer insights into cognitive processes of the test taker (Sijtsma & Verweij, 1999). Use of IRT may also reduce the biases against people who are slow in completing test problems. In other words, by presenting questions at the test-taker's ability level, IRT and computer adaptive testing allow the defined time spent on taking the test to be used most efficiently by test takers (van der Linden, Scrams, & Schnipke, 1999). Psychological Testing in Everyday Life 7.2 describes how IRT is now being used in medical care.

### External Criteria

Item analysis has been persistently plagued by researchers' continued dependence on *internal criteria*, or total test score, for evaluating items. The examples we have just given demonstrate how to compare performance on an item with performance on the total test. You can use similar procedures to compare performance on an item with performance on an external criterion. For example, if you were building a test to select airplane pilots, you might want to evaluate how well the individual items predict success in pilot training or flying performance. The advantages of using external rather than internal criteria against which to validate items were outlined by Guttman (1950) more than 60 years ago. Nevertheless, external criteria are rarely used in practice (Linn, 1994a, 1994b).

## Linking Uncommon Measures

One challenge in test applications is how to determine linkages between two different measures. There are many cases in which linkages are needed. For example, the SAT uses different items each time it is administered. Interpretation of the test results for students who took the test at different times requires that scores on each administration have the same meaning, even though the tests include different items—that is, we assume that a score of 600 means the same thing for two students even though the two students completed different tests. Attempts to link

## IRT Meets Medicine

### PROMIS Initiative

One of the major users of IRT and computer-adaptive testing is being evaluated by the National Institutes of Health (NIH). Many people feel that diagnoses in medicine can be done exclusively from biological tests, and for many years, doctors simply ignored most of the information that was told to them by their patients. However, it has become increasingly clear that patient-reported outcomes provide the key to understanding many important chronic illnesses. People come to doctors because they experience symptoms and problems, and it is important to have these issues addressed. Further, many problems are embarrassing to talk about. For example, many people are uncomfortable talking about bowel habits or sexual functioning. Yet they may feel more comfortable responding to questions about these common problems using a standardized questionnaire.

In response to these concerns, the National Institutes of Health funded the Patient Reported Outcomes Measurement Information System or PROMIS. The purpose of this exercise was to develop highly reliable and precise measures that described how patients report their health status, including physical, mental, and social well-being. The PROMIS initiative is designed to provide practicing clinicians with highly valid and reliable measures that can be used in clinical practice and in research. PROMIS operates through a series of centers throughout the United States, including Boston University, Children's Hospital of Philadelphia, Cincinnati's Children's Hospital, Duke University, Georgetown University, Stanford University, Stony Brook University, University of North Carolina at Chapel Hill, University of Maryland, University of Pittsburgh, UCLA, University of Washington, and several related sites.

The PROMIS study is evaluating measures in a variety of different areas, including HIV infection, drug safety, sexual function, GI distress, mental health, and self-efficacy. Some specialized centers focus on problems associated with children. In all of these areas, a large item bank is created. Using IRT and computer-adaptive testing, patients are able to communicate information about their health problems through questioning that gets the most information using the fewest number of questions.

scores on a test such as the SAT with those of an equivalent test, such as the American College Test (ACT), pose a more difficult problem. Often these linkages are achieved through statistical formulas. This is analogous to converting a temperature from Celsius to Fahrenheit. Between tests, however, such conversions are not so straightforward. For instance, public schools often give reading and mathematics tests. Although researchers can create a formula that will link mathematics scores to reading scores, it makes little sense to try to interpret mathematical ability in terms of reading skill.

Problems in test linkages became important in the late 1990s when the National Assessment of Educational Progress (NAEP) program was proposed. As part of the program, different students took different tests and were compared on these "uncommon measures." The National Research Council of the National Academy of Sciences was asked if it was feasible to develop equivalency measures that would allow commercial and state test developers to link their measures together. After a detailed study, the committee concluded that it was not feasible to compare the wide array of commercial and state achievement tests to one another. Further, they concluded that developing transformation methods for individual scores should not be done (Feuer et al., 1999).

## Items for Criterion-Referenced Tests

In Chapter 2, we briefly mentioned criterion-referenced testing. The traditional use of tests requires that we determine how well someone has done on a test by comparing the person's performance to that of others. For example, the meaning of Jeff's 67 on a geography test is interpreted by his percentile rank in the geography class. Another way of evaluating Jeff's performance is to ask how much he learned in comparison to how much he "should have" learned. Jeff is no longer in competition with everyone else. Instead, we have defined what Jeff must do to be considered knowledgeable about a certain unit. How much Jeff knows rather than whether or not he knows more than someone else determines his grade.

A *criterion-referenced test* compares performance with some clearly defined criterion for learning. This approach is popular in individualized instruction programs. For each student, a set of objectives is defined that state exactly what the student should be able to do after an educational experience. For example, an objective for a middle-school algebra student might be to solve linear equations with two unknowns. The criterion-referenced test would be used to determine whether this objective had been achieved. After demonstrating this knowledge, the student could move ahead to another objective. Many educators regard criterion-referenced tests as diagnostic instruments. When a student does poorly on some items, the teacher knows that the individualized education program needs more focus in a particular area.

The first step in developing criterion-referenced tests involves clearly specifying the objectives by writing clear and precise statements about what the learning program is attempting to achieve. These statements are usually stated in terms of something the student will be able to do. For example, a unit in high-school civics might aim at getting students to understand the operation of municipal government. Test items that assess the attainment of this objective might ask about the taxation powers of local governments, the relation of municipal to state government, and so on.

To evaluate the items in the criterion-referenced test, one should give the test to two groups of students—one that has been exposed to the learning unit and one that has not. Figure 7.10 shows what the distribution of scores would look like. The frequency polygon looks like a V. The scores on the left side of the V are probably those from students who have not experienced the unit. Scores on the right represent those who have been exposed to the unit. The bottom of the V is the *antimode*, or the least frequent score. This point divides those who have been exposed to the unit from those who have not been exposed and is usually taken as the *cutting score* or *point*, or what marks the point of decision. When people get

**FIGURE 7.10**

Frequency polygon used to evaluate a criterion-referenced test.

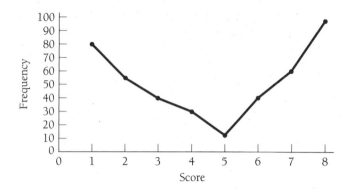

scores higher than the antimode, we assume that they have met the objective of the test. When they get lower scores, we assume they have not. In Figure 7.10, the cutting score is 5.

Criterion-referenced tests offer many advantages to newer educational approaches. For example, in computer-assisted instruction, each student works at his or her own pace on an individualized program of instruction, after which a criterion-referenced test is used to evaluate progress. Students who pass the test can move on to the next unit. Students who do not pass can repeat some of the instruction until they pass.

Similarly, the Internet has provided abundant opportunities for "distance learning" (Black, 2003). Using the Internet, students can gain educational experiences interactively. As more college courses come online, there will be a variety of challenges for evaluation and student assessment.

## Limitations of Item Analysis

The growing interest in criterion-referenced tests has posed new questions about the adequacy of item-analysis procedures. The main problem is this: though statistical methods for item analysis tell the test constructor which items do a good job of separating students, they do not help the students learn. Young children do not care as much about how many items they missed as they do about what they are doing wrong. Many times children make specific errors and will continue to make them until they discover why they are making them.

For example, an achievement test might ask a fourth-grade student to add .40 and .30. One of the multiple-choice alternatives would be .07 because item analysis had demonstrated that this was a good distractor. The child who selected .07 would not receive a point on the item and also might continue to make similar errors. Although the data are available to give the child feedback on the "bug" in his or her thinking, nothing in the testing procedure initiates this guidance (Linn, 1994a). One study that involved 1300 fourth, fifth, and sixth graders found that 40% of the children made the same type of error when given problems of a particular kind (Brown & Burton, 1978). Some researchers in educational measurement now appear to be moving toward testing programs that diagnose as well as assess (Linn, 1994a, 1994b; Linn & Burton, 1994). Tests can have different purposes. In the past, many have placed too much emphasis on ranking students and not enough on discovering specific weaknesses or gaps in knowledge. There are other disadvantages of criterion-referenced tests. One that has caused considerable concern is that teachers "teach to the test." For example, they may concentrate on skills that are easy to test while ignoring more important skills such as critical thinking, judgment, reading comprehension, and self-expression.

# Summary

There is an art and a science to test construction. Writing good items is a complex and demanding task. In the first step, developers decide what sort of information they are trying to obtain. If they want to know whether or not test takers know "the right information," developers may use true-false items—that is, a *dichotomous format*. They may also use for the same purpose multiple-choice items, a *polytomous format*, in which a correct choice must be selected among several alternatives. With these types of formats, the test constructor must always consider the probability that someone will get an answer correct by chance.

Many formats are available for tests that do not have right or wrong answers. The *Likert format* is popular for attitude scales. In this format, respondents check on a 5-point scale the degree to which they agree or disagree with the given statements. Similarly, in the category-scaling method, ratings are obtained on a scale with defined endpoints. The familiar 10-point scale is an example of a category scale. Unfortunately, category scales are subject to some bias when the endpoints are not clearly defined. Checklists and Q-sorts are among the many item formats used in personality research. These methods require people to make judgments about whether or not certain items describe themselves or others.

Once developers have created test items, they can administer them to groups of individuals and systematically assess the values of the items. One method of item analysis requires evaluation of item difficulty, which is usually assessed by examining the number of people who get each item correct. In addition to difficulty analysis, test constructors usually examine the correlation between getting any item correct and the total test score. This correlation is used as an index of *discriminability*.

Another way to learn about the value of items is to draw a picture of the *item characteristic curve*. For example, the proportion of people who get an item correct can be plotted as a function of the total test score. The best items are those for which the probability of getting the item correct is highest among those with the highest test scores.

The most important contemporary development in psychological testing is *item response theory* (IRT). In this method, a computer identifies the specific items that characterize the skill level of a particular test taker. The test is tailored to that individual. This method allows more precision and less burden on the test taker. Although all test takers may be scored on the same dimensions, the actual items they complete are likely to differ.

*Criterion-referenced* tests require a different approach to test construction. With such tests, a person's knowledge is evaluated against what he or she is expected to know rather than against what others know. To evaluate items in criterion-referenced tests, one compares the performance of those who would be expected to know the material with the performance of others who would not be expected to have learned the information.

CHAPTER

8

# Interviewing Techniques

## LEARNING OBJECTIVES

*When you have completed this chapter, you should be able to:*

▶ Explain the difference between a structured and an unstructured interview

▶ Discuss the importance of setting the proper tone for an interview

▶ Describe the role of the interviewer's attitude in the interviewing process

▶ Identify some of the characteristics of effective interviewing

▶ List which types of statements tend to keep the interaction flowing or to elicit self-exploration in the interviewee

▶ Explain the effects of empathy statements on interviewee responses

▶ Identify the various sources of error in the interview

▶ Appreciate the role of cultural, ethnic, and socioeconomic factors in the interview process

▶ Explain how interview skills are acquired and developed

Maria was being considered for a high-level public relations position with the computer firm for which she worked. The job duties would require her to interact with a wide variety of people, ranging from heads of state and corporation presidents to rank-and-file employees and union officials. In addition, the position would involve making formal policy statements for news media. Any poorly phrased statement or inappropriate reaction on her part could result in adverse publicity, which could cost the firm millions of dollars. The application process therefore involved an elaborate testing procedure, including two lengthy interviews. The first was with the firm's personnel selection officer, the second with the firm's clinical psychologist (see Figure 8.1).

Knowing the importance of first impressions (Dougherty, Turban, & Callender, 1994; Roeckelein, 2002), Maria took care to appear neat and well groomed. In her first interview, the personnel officer read from a form as she conducted the interview, which went something like this:

**OFFICER:**   I've read your application form and have gone over your qualifications. Would you now please outline your educational experiences, beginning with high school?

**MARIA:**   I graduated from high school in June 1995 with an emphasis in history and social studies. I began attending college in September 1995. I graduated in June 1995 with a major in psychology and minor in business management. I then entered the university's graduate program in business. I earned my master's degree in business administration in 2001.

**OFFICER:**   What is your work history? Begin with your first full-time employment.

**FIGURE 8.1**
An interview.

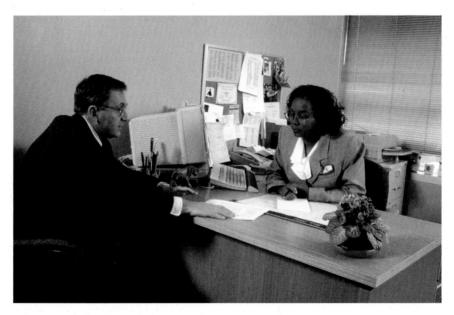

(© Steven Lunetta/PhotoEdit)

Maria described her work history. The personnel officer then continued a series of questions, which Maria systematically answered. The questions went something like this:

How do your education and experience relate to the job for which you are applying?

What educational experiences have you had that might help you function in the job for which you are applying?

What employment experiences have you had that might help you function in the job for which you are applying?

Identify any deficiencies in your educational and work experiences.

What educational and work experiences have you had that might impair your ability to function in the job for which you are applying?

The interview continued in a similar manner. With each question, the personnel officer attempted to relate Maria's educational and work experiences to the particular job duties she hoped to assume. For her final question, the personnel officer asked, "Why do you believe you are a good candidate for this position?"

Maria felt good about her interview with the personnel officer. She thought the questions were clear and straightforward, and she was pleased by her answers. The next day she appeared for her interview with the clinical psychologist. Unlike the personnel officer, the psychologist conducted the interview without using written interview questions. This second interview, quite different from the first, went something like this:

**PSYCHOLOGIST:** Maria, why don't you tell me a little bit about yourself?

**MARIA:** Where do you want me to begin?

**PSYCHOLOGIST:** Oh, it doesn't matter. Just tell me about yourself.

**MARIA:** I graduated from high school in June of 1995. I majored in history and social studies.

**PSYCHOLOGIST:** Yes, I see.

**MARIA:** I then attended college and finally finished graduate school in 2001. My master's degree should help me assume the duties of the new position.

**PSYCHOLOGIST:** You feel that your master's degree is a useful asset in your application.

**MARIA:** Yes, my graduate experiences taught me how to work with others.

**PSYCHOLOGIST:** With these graduate experiences, you learned the art of working with other people.

**MARIA:** Well, I guess I didn't learn it all in graduate school. I've always managed to get along well with others.

**PSYCHOLOGIST:** As far as you can tell, you work pretty well with people.

**MARIA:** That's right. As the oldest of four children, I've always had the responsibility for supervising others. You know what I mean?

**PSYCHOLOGIST:** Being the oldest, you were given extra responsibilities as a child.

MARIA: Not that I resented it. Well, maybe sometimes. It's just that I never had much time for myself.

PSYCHOLOGIST: And having time for yourself is important to you.

MARIA: Yes, of course it is. I guess everybody needs some time alone.

PSYCHOLOGIST: As a person who deals with others all day long, you must treasure those few moments you have to yourself.

MARIA: I really do. Whenever I get a chance I like to drive up to the lake all by myself and just think.

PSYCHOLOGIST: Those moments are precious to you.

The interview continued like this for about an hour. After it was over, Maria wasn't sure how she had done. Think about the two interviews. In what ways were they alike? How did they differ? As you contemplate your answers, you will soon realize that there is more than one type of interview, and that interviews can differ considerably.

The first interview with the personnel officer was highly structured. The interviewer read from a printed set of questions, using a standardized interview. Thus, all applicants for the position were asked the same questions in the same sequence. By contrast, the second was an unstructured interview and therefore unstandardized. The clinical psychologist didn't appear to have any specific or particular questions in mind, and the sequence of questions followed from Maria's statements. Each applicant, no doubt, would be asked different questions, depending on his or her responses.

Can you identify other differences between the two interviews? The first was narrow and restricted. It focused on two specific areas: Maria's education and her work experiences. The second was broad and unrestricted. Although the interview clearly focused on Maria herself, it touched on a variety of areas. The first interview was *directive*. The personnel officer directed, guided, and controlled the course of the interview. The second interview was *nondirective*. The clinical psychologist let Maria determine the direction of the interview. When Maria talked about her master's degree, the psychologist discussed it. When Maria talked about being the oldest of four children, this became the focus of the psychologist's response. Further, unlike the personnel officer, the psychologist rarely asked questions. Instead, the psychologist tended to comment or reflect on Maria's previous statement. Last, but perhaps most important, Maria's interview with the personnel officer can best be described as an employment interview, also called a *selection interview*; it was designed to elicit information pertaining to Maria's qualifications and capabilities for particular employment duties (employment interviews are discussed in greater detail in Chapter 18). The second interview, on the other hand, was a diagnostic interview, centered on Maria's emotional functioning rather than her qualifications—that is, the clinical psychologist was interested in uncovering those feelings, thoughts, and attitudes that might impede or facilitate Maria's competence.

# The Interview as a Test

In many respects, an interview resembles a test (see Table 8.1). Like any psychological or educational test, an interview is a method for gathering data or information about an individual. This information is then used to describe the individual, make

**TABLE 8.1**   Similarities Between an Interview and a Test

Method for gathering data
Used to make predictions
Evaluated in terms of reliability
Evaluated in terms of validity
Group or individual
Structured or unstructured

future predictions, or both. Like tests, interviews can be evaluated in terms of standard psychometric qualities such as reliability and validity. Furthermore, there are several types of interview procedures; each is chosen according to the type of information sought and the interviewer's goals.

Like any test, the interview involves the interaction of two or more people. Some interviews proceed like individually administered tests, with the interviewer interacting with a single individual at a time. In others, such as the family interview, a single interviewer works with two or more individuals at the same time, as in a group test. Like all tests, an interview has a defined purpose. Furthermore, just as the person who gives a test must take responsibility for the test-administration process, so the interviewer must assume responsibility for the conduct of the interview.

Many tests, such as the Thematic Apperception Test (TAT), cannot be properly used without adequate interview data. The interview, on the other hand, is often the only or most important source of data. The interview remains one of the most prevalent selection devices for employment (Macan, 2009). Good interviewing skills may be one of the most important tools for functioning in today's society. Furthermore, interviewing is the chief method of collecting data in clinical psychiatry (Machado et al., 2011; Groth-Marnat, 2003). It is also used in all health-related professions, including general medicine and nursing (Eggly, 2002). Interviewing is an essential testing tool in subspecialties such as clinical, industrial, counseling, school, and correctional psychology.

A wide variety of other professions depend on interviewing. Indeed, interview skills are important in most professions that involve people: social workers, vocational and guidance counselors, and marriage and family counselors; parole boards; researchers; businesspeople (to evaluate employees as well as potential clients); courtroom attorneys; contractors or architects (to determine exactly what their customers want them to do)—the list goes on and on. Interviewing also plays a role in our nonprofessional lives, such as when a parent questions a group of children to find out whose soccer ball broke the window. To begin new relationships on a positive note, one must possess a degree of interviewing skill. Given such a broad application, no introductory text on psychological tests could be complete without reference to the interview.

# Reciprocal Nature of Interviewing

Although there are many types and purposes of interviews, all share certain factors. First, all interviews involve mutual interaction whereby the participants are interdependent—that is, they influence each other (Breggin, 2002; Ridge, Campbell, & Martin, 2002). A study by Akehurst and Vrij (1999) illustrates the transactional or reciprocal nature of the interview process. Criminal suspects were observed while being interrogated. The researchers found that if one of the participants in the interview increased his or her activity level, then the activity of the other participant also increased. Similarly, a reduction in activity by one triggered a reduction in the other. The researchers concluded that the participants in an interview profoundly affect each other. Unfortunately for the suspects, a second experiment demonstrated that increased activity on the part of the suspect was related to increased suspiciousness on the part of the interrogator. Results revealed that highly active interrogators increased activity in the suspects, which, in turn, increased the interrogators' suspiciousness (Akehurst & Vrij, 1999).

Interview participants also affect each other's mood. In a classic study, Heller (1971) found that when professional actors responded with anger to highly trained, experienced interviewers, the interviewers became angry themselves and showed anger toward the actors. In this phenomenon, called *social facilitation*, we tend to act like the models around us (see Augustine, 2011). If the interviewer is tense, anxious, defensive, and aloof, then the interviewee tends to respond in kind. Thus, if the interviewer wishes to create conditions of openness, warmth, acceptance, comfort, calmness, and support, then he or she must exhibit these qualities.

Because the participants in an interview influence each other, the good interviewer knows how to provide a relaxed and safe atmosphere through social facilitation. However, although both parties influence each other, the good interviewer remains in control and sets the tone. If he or she reacts to the interviewee's tension and anxiety with more tension and anxiety, then these feelings will mount. By remaining relaxed, confident, and self-assured, the interviewer has a calming effect on the interviewee. Even potentially violent prison inmates or disturbed psychotic people can become manageable when the interviewer sets the proper tone. Clearly, social facilitation is one of the most important concepts underlying the interview process.

# Principles of Effective Interviewing

Naturally, specific interviewing techniques and approaches vary, depending on such factors as the type of interview (e.g., employment versus diagnostic) and the goals of the interviewer (e.g., description versus prediction). Thus, there are no set rules that apply to all interviewing situations. However, some principles facilitate the conduct of almost any interview. Knowing these principles will not only increase your understanding of the factors and processes that underlie the interview but also help you acquire interview skills of your own.

## The Proper Attitudes

Good interviewing is actually more a matter of attitude than skill (Duan & Kivlighan, 2002). Experiments in social psychology have shown that *interpersonal influence* (the degree to which one person can influence another) is related to *interpersonal attraction* (the degree to which people share a feeling of understanding, mutual respect, similarity, and the like) (Dillard & Marshall, 2003). Attitudes related to good interviewing skills include warmth, genuineness, acceptance, understanding, openness, honesty, and fairness. For example, Saccuzzo (1975) studied the initial psychotherapeutic interviews of first-year clinical psychology graduate students. Patients and therapists both responded to a questionnaire. Their task was to rate the quality of the interview and indicate the topics, concerns, problems, and feelings of the patient as well as the feelings of the therapist.

The most important factor in the patients' evaluation was their perception of the interviewer's feelings. The session received a good evaluation by both participants when the patient saw the interviewer as warm, open, concerned, involved, committed, and interested, regardless of subject matter or the type or severity of the problem. On the other hand, independent of all other factors, when the interviewer was seen as cold, defensive, uninterested, uninvolved, aloof, and bored, the session was rated poorly. To appear effective and establish rapport, the interviewer must display the proper attitudes.

## Responses to Avoid

In a "stress interview," the interviewer may deliberately induce discomfort or anxiety in the interviewee. As a rule, however, making interviewees feel uncomfortable tends to place them on guard, and guarded or anxious interviewees tend to reveal little information about themselves. However, one purpose of the stress interview is to determine how well an individual functions in adversity and the types of responses that interviewers should avoid. If the goal is to elicit as much information as possible or to receive a good rating from the interviewee, then interviewers should avoid certain responses, including judgmental or evaluative statements, probing statements, hostility, and false reassurance.

Judgmental or evaluative statements are particularly likely to inhibit the interviewee. Being *judgmental* means evaluating the thoughts, feelings, or actions of another. When we use such terms as *good, bad, excellent, terrible, disgusting, disgraceful*, and *stupid*, we make evaluative statements. By judging others, we put them on guard because we communicate the message, "I don't approve of this aspect of you." Such judgments also inhibit others' ease in revealing important information. Thus, unless the goal of the interview is to determine how a person responds to being evaluated, evaluative or judgmental statements should usually be avoided.

Most interviewers should also avoid probing statements. These demand more information than the interviewee wishes to provide voluntarily. The most common way to phrase a probing statement is to ask a question that begins with "Why?" Asking "Why?" tends to place others on the defensive. When we ask "Why?," as in "Why did you stay out so late?," we are demanding that the person explain his or her behavior. Such a demand has an obvious judgmental quality. Furthermore, in probing we may induce the interviewee to reveal something that he or she is not yet ready to reveal. If this happens, the interviewee will probably feel anxious and thus not well disposed to revealing additional information.

In some circumstances, probes are appropriate and necessary. With children or individuals with mental retardation, for instance, one often needs to ask questions to elicit meaningful information (Devoe & Faller, 2002). Highly anxious or withdrawn individuals may also need a probe to get beyond a superficial interchange. In such circumstances, one must use the probe wisely, avoiding "Why?" statements and replacing them with "Tell me" or "How?" statements, as illustrated in Table 8.2.

The hostile statement directs anger toward the interviewee. Clearly, one should avoid such responses unless one has a specific purpose, such as determining how an interviewee responds to anger.

The reassuring statement attempts to comfort or support the interviewee: "Don't worry. Everything will be all right." Though reassurance is sometimes appropriate, you should almost always avoid false reassurance. For example, imagine a friend of yours flunks out of college, loses her job, and gets kicked out of her home by her parents. You are lying to this person when you say, "Don't worry; no problem; it's okay." This false reassurance does nothing to help your friend except perhaps make her realize that you are not going to help her. What has happened to your friend is terrible and will require specific action on her part to prevent even more disastrous developments. Naturally, you should not overwhelm your friend with all the facts at once, but she needs to come to grips with the situation in manageable doses before taking the necessary steps to constructively solve the problem. The person who gives false reassurance usually knows he or she is doing it, as does the person who receives it (see Figure 8.2).

**TABLE 8.2**    Effective Probing Statements

| Poor | Better |
|------|--------|
| Why did you yell at him? | 1. Tell me more about what happened. |
| | 2. How did you happen to yell at him? |
| | 3. What led up to the situation? |
| Why did you say that? | 1. Can you tell me what you mean? |
| | 2. I'm not sure I understand. |
| | 3. How did you happen to say that? |
| Why can't you sleep? | 1. Tell me more about your sleeping problem. |
| | 2. Can you identify what prevents you from sleeping? |
| | 3. How is it that you are unable to sleep? |

**FIGURE 8.2**

Responses to avoid in an unstructured interview.

Avoid — Judgmental or evaluative statements
— Probing statements
— Hostile responses
— False reassurance

# Effective Responses

Knowing what types of responses to avoid, how does one go about conducting an effective interview? One major principle of effective interviewing is keeping the interaction flowing. The interview is a two-way process; one person speaks first, then the other, and so on. Furthermore, the interviewer usually exerts a minimum amount of effort to keep the interaction flowing. As long as the interviewee's verbalizations relate to the purpose of the interview, the interviewer listens with interest by maintaining face-to-face contact.

Except in structured interviews or for a particular purpose, one can effectively initiate the interview process by using an open-ended question. This is one that usually cannot be answered specifically, as opposed to a closed-ended question, which can. Examples of open-ended questions include, "Tell me a little bit about yourself," "Tell me about what interests you," and "What is it that brings you here to see me?" Examples of closed-ended questions include, "Do you like sports?," "Are you married?," and "How old are you?"

A closed-ended question brings the interview to a dead halt, thus violating the principle of keeping the interaction flowing. In the example at the beginning of this chapter, even the personnel officer's opening question—"Would you now please outline your educational experiences, beginning with high school?"—was sufficiently open-ended to permit a variety of responses, depending on the interviewee. Where one individual might provide every minute detail of his or her education, a second might simply include major events. The clinical psychologist's opening statement—"Maria, why don't you tell me a little bit about yourself?"—was even more open-ended. Maria could have replied with just about anything.

Open-ended questions give the interviewee wide latitude in choosing the topics that he or she feels are important. Except for highly specific structured interviews, we usually can learn a lot more about people when they tell us what they think is important than when we try to guess by asking a series of closed-ended questions. The open-ended question requires the interviewee to produce something spontaneously; the closed-ended question to recall something. Table 8.3 presents some closed-ended questions along with corresponding open-ended ones.

**TABLE 8.3**    Closed- and Open-Ended Questions

| Closed-ended | Open-ended |
|---|---|
| Do you like sports cars? | What kinds of cars do you like? |
| Do you like baseball? | What kinds of recreational activities do you prefer? |
| Are you having a problem? | Can you tell me about your problems? |
| Is your father strict? | What is your father like? |
| Would you like to vacation in Hawaii? | What are your favorite vacation spots? |

Conducting an interview requires flexibility. If not structured, most interviews cannot be conducted in precisely the same way. In therapeutic or diagnostic interviews, interviewers usually follow only general guidelines in conducting the interview. Their goal is to get to know the interviewees as well as possible to understand them and predict their behavior.

## Responses to Keep the Interaction Flowing

After asking the open-ended question, the interviewer as a rule lets the interviewee respond without interruption; that is, the interviewer remains quiet and listens. Unless the interview is structured, once the interviewee's response dies down, the interviewer usually responds in a way that will keep the interaction flowing. (See Table 8.4 for a summary of responses that do this.) He or she should use minimum effort to maintain the flow, such as using a transitional phrase such as "Yes," "And," or "I see." These phrases imply that the interviewee should continue on the same topic. In Maria's interview with the clinical psychologist, for example, Maria stated, "I graduated from high school in June 1995. I majored in history and social studies." The clinical psychologist simply responded with the transition, "Yes, I see." Maria then elaborated.

Sometimes the transitional phrase fails to have the desired effect. When this occurs, the interviewer should make a response relevant to what has just been communicated. In other words, the interview is thematic; it does not jump from one unrelated topic to another as it might if the interviewer asked a series of set questions. The theme in Maria's interview with the clinical psychologist was Maria. Although the topics changed from Maria's education to her feelings about being the oldest of four, Maria herself remained the central focus. The psychologist accomplished this by making statements relevant to what Maria was saying.

To make such a response, the interviewer may use any of the following types of statements: verbatim playback, paraphrasing, restatement, summarizing, clarifying, and understanding. You can view these statements on a continuum ranging from being totally interchangeable with the interviewee's response to adding to or going beyond it.

In a *verbatim playback*, the interviewer simply repeats the interviewee's last response. For example, in her interview with the clinical psychologist, Maria stated,

**TABLE 8.4**  Responses to Keep the Interaction Flowing

| Response | Definition or example |
|---|---|
| Transitional phrase | "Yes," "I see," "Go on" |
| Verbatim playback | Repeats interviewee's exact words |
| Paraphrasing and restatement | Repeats interviewee's response using different words |
| Summarizing | Pulls together the meaning of several responses |
| Clarification response | Clarifies the interviewee's response |
| Empathy and understanding | Communicates understanding |

"I majored in history and social studies." The psychologist replied with the transitional phrase "Yes, I see." A verbatim playback, "You majored in history and social studies," would have been equally effective. In either case, Maria most likely would continue to elaborate on her previous response. Thus, like the transitional phrase, the verbatim playback generally leads to an elaboration of the interviewee's previous response.

*Paraphrasing* and *restatement* responses are also interchangeable with the interviewee's response. A paraphrase tends to be more similar to the interviewee's response than a restatement, but both capture the meaning of the interviewee's response. When Maria said, "My master's degree should help me assume the duties of the new position," the psychologist replied, "You feel that your master's degree is a useful asset in your application"—a restatement. A paraphrase might have taken the form, "You feel that your master's degree will be an important aid in taking on the responsibilities of the new position." In his restatement, the psychologist introduced "useful asset" to restate Maria's attitude toward her master's degree. The paraphrase, on the other hand, simply substituted "important aid" for "help" and "taking on the responsibilities" for "assuming the duties." Neither statement added anything to Maria's. Both, however, communicated to Maria that the interviewer was listening, and made it easy for Maria to elaborate.

*Summarizing* and *clarification* statements go just beyond the interviewee's response. In summarizing, the interviewer pulls together the meaning of several interviewee responses. To Maria's last statement in the example, the psychologist could have replied with the summarizing statement, "As a youth, you never had much time to yourself because you were responsible for taking care of your three younger siblings. Today you enjoy those few moments you have to be alone. Whenever you get a chance to be alone, you drive to the lake all by yourself and just think." Notice that this summarizing statement involves verbatim playback, paraphrasing, and restating. With these three types of statements, the psychologist summarizes an entire sequence of responses.

The clarification statement, as its name implies, serves to clarify the interviewee's response. When Maria stated, "Not that I resented it. Well, maybe sometimes. It's just that I never had much time for myself," the psychologist attempted to clarify what Maria was trying to say. It was not that Maria resented the extra responsibilities; rather, she simply wanted some time to be alone. Thus, the psychologist clarified Maria's statement by saying, "And having time for yourself is important to you."

Like summarizing, paraphrasing, restatement, and verbatim playback, the clarification statement remains close to the meaning of the interviewee's response. Each of these interviewer responses communicates a degree of understanding. At the lowest level, the verbatim playback communicates that the interviewer at least heard the communication. The restatement, paraphrase, and summarizing responses go a bit further by communicating that the interviewer has a good idea of what the interviewee is trying to communicate. And clarification shows yet further comprehension.

Even more powerful is the empathy or understanding response. This response communicates that the interviewer understands how the interviewee *feels*. When the psychologist stated, "These moments are precious to you," he did not simply paraphrase or restate. Instead, he communicated that he understood how Maria felt about having time to herself.

Many students find it difficult to see the value of statements that stay close to the interviewee's response. Some students consider such statements artificial and weak because of their noncommittal quality. However, the rationale for such responses is based on the well-known and well-documented finding that when we show people we understand, they will talk about or explore themselves at ever deeper levels (Maj, Gaebel, Lopez-Ibor, & Sartorius, 2002; Rogers, 1980; Walker, 2001). Accurate empathy elicits self-exploration. Consider the following example:

PSYCHOLOGIST:  What's been happening today, Kerry? (*open-ended question*)

KERRY:  My physics teacher yelled at me in front of the whole class.

PSYCHOLOGIST:  That's embarrassing. (*understanding*)

KERRY:  Not only that, she seems to pick on me all the time.

PSYCHOLOGIST:  That must make you angry. (*understanding*)

KERRY:  Yeah, I guess so. It seems like she's always finding fault with my work. No matter what I do, she just doesn't like it.

PSYCHOLOGIST:  That is really frustrating, Kerry. You just can't seem to please her. (*understanding*)

KERRY:  The other day we had an exam, and I got an F. I checked my answers with Hector, and mine were the same as his. Yet I got an F and Hector got a B.

PSYCHOLOGIST:  Hey, that doesn't seem fair. (*clarification and understanding*)

KERRY:  You bet it isn't fair. But when I tried to talk to her about it, she refused to listen.

PSYCHOLOGIST:  That's scary. (*understanding*)

KERRY:  It sure is. If I get one more F, I'll be kicked out of school.

PSYCHOLOGIST:  This is really serious. (*clarification*)

KERRY:  Yeah. If I got kicked out of school, I couldn't face my parents or friends.

PSYCHOLOGIST:  This whole thing has got you really upset. (*understanding*)

Certainly, the psychologist's responses are not the only ones that would work. However, note how the psychologist, in providing a series of understanding responses, "uncovered" the real source of Kerry's anguish. The feelings Kerry expressed moved from embarrassment to anger to fear of being kicked out of school and finally to fear of how his friends and family would view his failure.

Let's consider four other responses that the psychologist could have made to Kerry's initial statement, "My physics teacher yelled at me in front of the whole class."

1. "Why did she do that?" With this probing statement, Kerry has to defend himself or explain why it happened. He has to go over the circumstances that preceded the incident, actually leading away from Kerry's real feelings and concerns.

2. "Why did you let her do that to you? That wasn't very smart of you." This evaluative statement places Kerry on the defensive, criticizes him, and possibly hurts his feelings. Given this type of reaction from the psychologist, Kerry will not feel safe exploring his real feelings.

3. "That woman is always yelling at somebody. You should report her to the dean." With this off-the-cuff advice, the psychologist again removes himself from Kerry's real concerns. The two might spend the rest of their time together weighing the pros and cons of reporting Kerry's physics teacher. Still worse, Kerry might impulsively follow the advice and get into real trouble if he cannot substantiate his claims.

4. "Don't worry. That physics teacher yells at everyone. It doesn't mean a thing." With this false reassurance, Kerry is no longer free to express his real concern. The psychologist has already dismissed the whole matter as insignificant.

In short, understanding responses that stay close to the content and underlying feeling provided by interviewees permit them to explore their situations more and more fully. Effective unstructured interviewing serves to uncover information from the interviewee. One good way to accomplish this involves what we call *understanding statements*. To establish a positive atmosphere, interviewers begin with an open-ended question followed by understanding statements that capture the meaning and feeling of the interviewee's communication. See Figure 8.3 for an exercise in keeping the interaction flowing.

## Measuring Understanding

We can further appreciate understanding statements by analyzing measures of understanding. Attempts to measure understanding or empathy originated with Carl Rogers's seminal research into the effects of client-centered therapy (Rogers, 1959a, 1959b; Walker, Rablen, & Rogers, 1960). It culminated in a 5-point scoring system (Truax & Carkhuff, 1967, pp. 46–58). Each level in this system represents a degree of empathy. The levels range from a response that bears little or no relationship to the previous statement to a response that captures the precise meaning and feeling of the statement. The highest degrees of empathy, levels four and five, are relevant primarily for therapeutic interviews. Level three represents various degrees of true empathy or understanding and may be used in all types of unstructured or semistructured (i.e., partially structured) interviews. The lowest levels, one and two, have no place in a professional interview and should be avoided. Low-level responses, however, occur frequently in everyday conversations. We discuss these levels to illustrate one way to measure understanding.

### Level-One Responses

Level-one responses bear little or no relationship to the interviewee's response. A level-one conversation might proceed as follows:

**SARAH:**  Victor, look at my new dress.

**VICTOR:**  I sure hope it doesn't rain today.

**SARAH:**  See, it's red with blue stripes.

**VICTOR:**  If it rains, my baseball game might get canceled.

**SARAH:**  I really love this dress, it's my favorite.

**VICTOR:**  It's sure going to tick me off if that game gets canceled.

The two people are really talking only to themselves.

**Directions:** Below is a list of statements, each followed by two possible replies. Select the one that would tend to keep the interaction flowing.

**1.** I hate school.
☐  a. It sounds like you're fed up with school.
☐  b. What's wrong with school?

**2.** My dad is a jerk.
☐  a. Why don't you just tell him to "chill out"?
☐  b. You're angry with your dad.

**3.** Most people are liars.
☐  a. Don't be so negative.
☐  b. You feel that most people can't be trusted.

**4.** We were ahead until the last minute of the game.
☐  a. That's disappointing.
☐  b. Why didn't you win?

**5.** She stood me up again.
☐  a. If I were you, I wouldn't ask her out again.
☐  b. It hurts to be treated like that.

**6.** I hope I passed the test.
☐  a. You're worried about how you did on the test.
☐  b. Don't worry. I'm sure you passed.

**Answers:** 1. a; 2. b; 3. b; 4. a; 5. b; 6. a

**Notes:**
1b is a probing statement.
2a is advice.
3a is advice.
4b is a probing statement.
5a is advice.
6b is false reassurance.

## Level-Two Responses

The level-two response communicates a superficial awareness of the meaning of a statement. The individual who makes a level-two response never quite goes beyond his or her own limited perspective. Level-two responses impede the flow of communication. For example:

**SARAH:** Boy, I feel good. I just got a beautiful new dress.

**VICTOR:** I feel bad. It's probably going to rain.

**SARAH:** I'll wear this dress to your baseball game.

**VICTOR:** If it rains, there won't be a game.

Here the conversation is related, but only superficially. Neither person really responds to what is going on with the other.

### Level-Three Responses

A level-three response is interchangeable with the interviewee's statement. According to Carkhuff and Berenson (1967), level three is the minimum level of responding that can help the interviewee. Paraphrasing, verbatim playback, clarification statements, and restatements are all examples of level-three responses.

### Level-Four and Level-Five Responses

Level-four and level-five responses not only provide accurate empathy but also go beyond the statement given. In a level-four response, the interviewer adds "noticeably" to the interviewee's response.

In a level-five response, the interviewer adds "significantly" to it (Carkhuff & Berenson, 1967). We recommend that beginning interviewers learn to respond at level three before going on to the more advanced levels. In the example with Sarah and Victor, a level-four interchange might proceed as follows:

SARAH:  I just got a new dress.

VICTOR:  You feel happy because you like new clothes.

SARAH:  This one is beautiful; it has red and blue stripes.

VICTOR:  You really love that new dress. It is a nice addition to your wardrobe.

### Active Listening

An impressive array of research has accumulated to document the power of the understanding response (Fitzgerald & Leudar, 2010; Laub, 2002; Münte & Klump; Georg, 2008; Rogers, 1980; Truax & Mitchell, 1971). This type of responding, sometimes called *active listening*, is the foundation of good interviewing skills for many different types of interviews.

# Types of Interviews

The previously discussed guides provide a general format for conducting an interview. The specifics vary, however, depending on the interviewer's goal, purpose, and theoretical orientation. We shall distinguish here among four types of interviews: the evaluation interview, the structured clinical interview, the case history interview, and the mental status examination. (For information on the employment or selection interview, see Chapter 18.)

## Evaluation Interview

A confrontation is a statement that points out a discrepancy or inconsistency. Though confrontation is usually most appropriate in therapeutic interviews, all experienced interviewers should have this technique at their disposal. Carkhuff (1969) distinguished among three types: (1) a discrepancy between what the person is and what he or she wants to become, (2) a discrepancy between what the person says about himself or herself and what he or she does, and (3) a discrepancy between the person's perception of himself or herself and the interviewer's experience of the person.

Confrontation may induce anxiety by bringing conflicts or inconsistencies into a person's awareness when he or she is not ready to handle them. We therefore strongly recommend that the beginning student leave confrontation for the more experienced practitioner.

Direct questions can be used toward the end of the interview to fill in any needed details or gaps in the interviewer's knowledge. For unstructured or semistructured interviews, we advocate the use of direct questions whenever (1) the data can be obtained in no other way, (2) time is limited and the interviewer needs specific information, or (3) the interviewee cannot or will not cooperate with the interviewer. The open-ended, facilitative technique does not work well for nonverbal, intellectually limited, and uncooperative subjects (Othmer & Othmer, 2002). It also doesn't work well with children, who require direct questioning and careful observation (Devoe & Faller, 2002; Hershkowitz, 2002). With these subjects, it is exceedingly difficult to get the interview off the ground. Thus, direct questioning becomes necessary.

## Structured Clinical Interviews

Over the past 25 years, structured clinical interviews have proliferated (see Horowitz, Murphy, Gregory, & Wojcik, 2009) a structured clinical interview is the best practice for postpartum depression screening; Jackson et al., 2011, determined that structured or semistructured diagnostic interviews are usually the most appropriate for interviews with children (See also Frick, Barry, & Kamphaus, 2010; Knafl & colleagues, 2007). Recall that structured interviews provide a specific set of questions presented in a particular order. In addition, there is usually a carefully specified set of rules for probing so that, as in a standardized test, all interviewees are handled in the same manner. Structured interviews lend themselves to scoring procedures from which norms can be developed and applied. Typically, cutoff scores are used so that a particular score indicates the presence or absence of a given condition.

The development of structured clinical interviews followed the evolution of the *Diagnostic and Statistical Manual of Mental Disorders* (DSM). First published in 1952 and revised numerous times, the DSM attempts to classify mental disorders into specific, definable categories. Before the 1980 DSM-III, however, mental disorders were poorly defined. The result was a markedly low reliability in psychiatric diagnosis.

The DSM-III and subsequent editions (DSM-IV and DSM-V—to be published May 2013) attempted to overcome this lack of reliability by providing a specific set of criteria for each category of mental disorder. As an example, Table 8.5 shows the main diagnostic criteria for an obsessive–compulsive disorder from the DSM-IV (American Psychiatric Association, 1994).

With specifiable criteria for mental disorders, one could develop a specific set of questions to determine whether or not a person met the criteria. For example, Spitzer and colleagues developed a comprehensive interview specifically for making diagnoses from the DSM-III-R called the Structured Clinical Interview for the

**TABLE 8.5**   Diagnostic Criteria for an Obsessive–Compulsive Disorder

A. Either obsessions or compulsions

**Obsessions**

1. Recurrent and persistent thoughts, impulses, or images that are experienced as intrusive and inappropriate and that cause marked anxiety or distress.
2. The thoughts, impulses, or images are not simply excessive worries about real-life problems.
3. The person attempts to ignore or suppress such thoughts, impulses, or images or to neutralize them with some other thought or action.
4. The person recognizes that the obsessions, impulses, or images are the product of his or her own mind.

**Compulsions**

1. Repetitive behaviors (e.g., hand washing, ordering, checking) or mental acts (e.g., praying, counting, repeating words silently) that the person feels driven to perform in response to an obsession, or according to rules that must be applied rigidly.
2. The behavior or mental acts are aimed at preventing or reducing distress or preventing some dreaded event or situation; however, these behaviors or mental acts either are not connected in a realistic way with what they are designed to neutralize or prevent or are clearly excessive.

From *Diagnostic and Statistical Manual of Mental Disorders*, Fourth Edition, Revised (DSM-IV). Washington, DC: American Psychiatric Association, 1994.

DSM-III-R, or the SCID (Spitzer, Williams, Gibbon, & First, 1990a). Table 8.6 provides an example of the SCID used to diagnose obsessive–compulsive disorder. Notice that the interview formula is quite specific, allows for a specific scoring system, and makes clear-cut provisions for unclear responses.

There are countless structured interviews for just about every imaginable problem. Interviews are available to:

▶ assess the degree to which individuals exhibit core symptoms of borderline personality disorder with the Diagnostic Interview for Borderlines–Revised (DIB-R). This semistructured interview yields four subscales: affect regulation, cognitive disturbance, interpersonal relationships, and action impulse patterns (Zanarini, Frankenburg, & Vujanovic, 2002);

▶ assess various components of self-injurious thoughts and behaviors, including frequency, severity, and age of onset with the Self-Injurious Thoughts & Behaviors Interview (SITBI) (Nock, Holmberg, Photos, & Michel, 2007);

▶ assess disorders in children such as the Diagnostic Interview Schedule for Children (DISC) and various revisions (DISC-R, DISC-2; Hodges, 1994; Shaffer, 1994), DISCO-9 (Leekham, Libby, Wing, Gould, & Taylor, 2002), and the Child Assessment Schedule (CAS; Allen, 1994);

▶ asses impulsive behavior with the UPPS-R Interview (UPPS-R), a semistructured interview format for UPPS-P Impulsive Behavior Scale that divides traditional conceptualization of impulsivity into five subscales: negative urgency, positive urgency, sensation seeking, (lack of) perseverance, and (lack of) premeditation (Fischer, Smith, Spillane, & Cyders, 2005);

▶ assess personality disorders such as the Structured Clinical Interview for DSM-III-R-Personality Disorders, or SCID-II (Lobbestael, Leurgans, & Arntz, 2010); and

**TABLE 8.6** SCID 9/1/89 Version Obsessive–Compulsive Disorder Anxiety Disorders

| *Obsessive–compulsive disorder* | Obsessive–compulsive disorder criteria | | | | |
|---|---|---|---|---|---|
| | A. Either obsessions or compulsions: | | | | |
| Now I would like to ask you if you have ever been bothered by thoughts that didn't make any sense and kept coming back to you even when you tried not to have them? (What were they?) | Obsessions: (1), (2), (3), and (4): | ? | 1 | 2 | 3 |
| | (1) Recurrent and persistent ideas, thoughts, impulses, or images that are experienced, at least initially, as intrusive and senseless, e.g., a parent's having repeated impulses to hurt a loved child, a religious person's having recurrent blasphemous thoughts | | | | |
| (What about awful thoughts, like actually hurting someone even though you didn't want to, or being contaminated by germs or dirt?) | NOTE: DO NOT INCLUDE BROODING ABOUT PROBLEMS (SUCH AS HAVING A PANIC ATTACK) OR ANXIOUS RUMINATIONS ABOUT REALISTIC DANGERS. | | | | |
| When you had these thoughts, did you try hard to get them out of your head? (What would you try to do?) | (2) The person attempts to ignore or suppress such thoughts or to neutralize them with some other thoughts or action | ? | 1 | 2 | 3 |
| IF UNCLEAR: Where did you think these thoughts were coming from? | (3) The person recognizes that the obsessions are the product of his or her own mind, not imposed from without (as in thought insertion) | ? | 1 | 2 | 3 |
| | (4) If another Axis I disorder is present, the content of the obsession is unrelated to it, i.e., the ideas, thoughts, impulses, or images are not about food in the presence of an Eating Disorder, about drugs in the presence of a Psychoactive Substance Use Disorder, or guilty thoughts in the presence of a Major Depression | ? | 1 | 2 | 3 |
| | | | | | OBSES-SIONS |
| | DESCRIBE: | | | | |
| Was there ever anything that you had to do over and over again and couldn't resist doing, like washing your hands again and again, or checking something several times to make sure you'd done it right? | Compulsions: (1), (2), and (3): | ? | 1 | 2 | 3 |
| | (1) Repetitive, purposeful, and intentional behaviors that are performed in response to an obsession, or according to certain rules, or in a stereotyped fashion | | | | |
| IF YES: What did you have to do? (What were you afraid would happen if you didn't do it?) (How many times did you have to_____? How much time did you spend each day_____?) | (2) The behavior is designed to neutralize or prevent discomfort or some dreaded event or situation; however, either the activity is not connected in a realistic way with what it is designed to neutralize or prevent, or it is clearly excessive | ? | 1 | 2 | 3 |
| IF UNCLEAR: Do you think that you (DO COMPULSIVE BEHAVIOR) more than you should? (Do you think [COMPULSION] makes sense?) | (3) The person recognizes that the behavior is excessive or unreasonable (this may no longer be true for people whose obsessions have evolved into overvalued ideas) | ? | 1 | 2 | 3 |

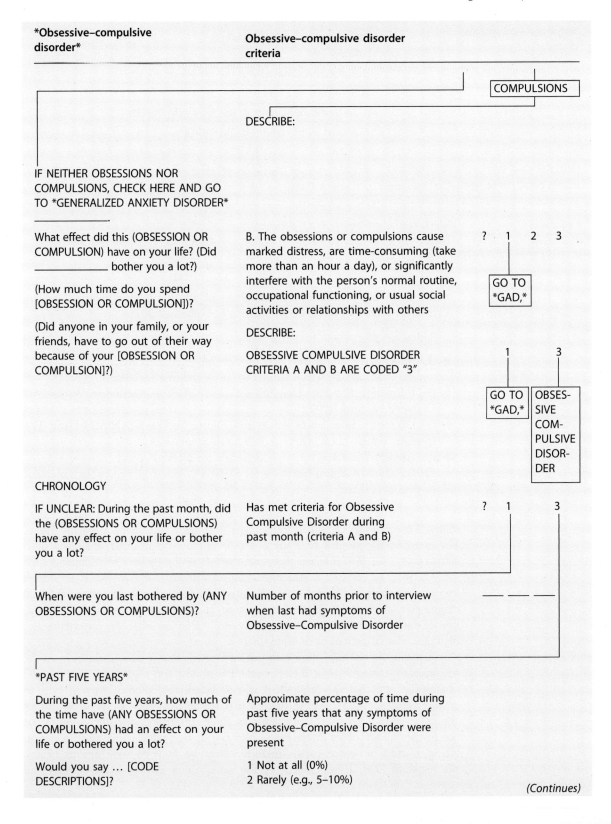

**\*Obsessive–compulsive disorder\***

**Obsessive–compulsive disorder criteria**

COMPULSIONS

DESCRIBE:

IF NEITHER OBSESSIONS NOR COMPULSIONS, CHECK HERE AND GO TO \*GENERALIZED ANXIETY DISORDER\*

_____

What effect did this (OBSESSION OR COMPULSION) have on your life? (Did _____ bother you a lot?)

(How much time do you spend [OBSESSION OR COMPULSION])?

(Did anyone in your family, or your friends, have to go out of their way because of your [OBSESSION OR COMPULSION]?)

B. The obsessions or compulsions cause marked distress, are time-consuming (take more than an hour a day), or significantly interfere with the person's normal routine, occupational functioning, or usual social activities or relationships with others

?    1    2    3

GO TO \*GAD,\*

DESCRIBE:

OBSESSIVE COMPULSIVE DISORDER CRITERIA A AND B ARE CODED "3"

1              3

GO TO \*GAD,\*    OBSES-SIVE COM-PULSIVE DISOR-DER

CHRONOLOGY

IF UNCLEAR: During the past month, did the (OBSESSIONS OR COMPULSIONS) have any effect on your life or bother you a lot?

Has met criteria for Obsessive Compulsive Disorder during past month (criteria A and B)

?    1         3

When were you last bothered by (ANY OBSESSIONS OR COMPULSIONS)?

Number of months prior to interview when last had symptoms of Obsessive–Compulsive Disorder

___  ___  ___

\*PAST FIVE YEARS\*

During the past five years, how much of the time have (ANY OBSESSIONS OR COMPULSIONS) had an effect on your life or bothered you a lot?

Would you say … [CODE DESCRIPTIONS]?

Approximate percentage of time during past five years that any symptoms of Obsessive–Compulsive Disorder were present

1 Not at all (0%)
2 Rarely (e.g., 5–10%)

*(Continues)*

| *Obsessive–compulsive disorder* | Obsessive–compulsive disorder criteria | |
|---|---|---|
| | 3 A significant minority of the time (e.g., 20–30%) | |
| | 4 About half the time | |
| | 5 A significant majority of the time (e.g., 70–80%) | |
| | 6 Almost all the time (e.g., 90–100%) | |
| | 7 Unknown | |
| How old were you when the (OBSESSIONS OR COMPULSIONS) first had any effect on your life or bothered you a lot? | Age at onset of Obsessive–Compulsive Disorder (criteria A and B) (CODE 99 IF UNKNOWN) | —— —— |

? = inadequate information   1 = absent or false   2 = subthreshold   3 = threshold or true

From R. Spitzer, J. B. W. Williams, M. Gibbon et al., *Structured Clinical Interview for DSM-III-R*, 1990. Copyright © 1990 American Psychiatric Press. Reprinted by permission of Michael First.

▶ do preliminary screening of mental illness in jails through the Referral Decision Scale or RDS (Hewitta, Perry, Adams, & Gilbodyd, 2011).

There are also:

▶ the Structured Clinical Interview for Separation Anxiety Symptoms (Cyranowski et al., 2002), which is used for both children and adults;
▶ the Edinburgh Postnatal Depression Scale (EPDS; Garcia-Esteve, Ascaso, Ojuel, & Navarro, 2003);
▶ the Diagnostic Interview Schedule for Children Version IV (NIMH DISC-IV) (Shaffer, Fisher, Lucas, Dulcan, & Schwab-Stone, 2000);
▶ the Anxiety Disorders Interview Schedule for DSM-IV; and
▶ the Structured Clinical Interview for DSM-IV Axis-I Disorders (Summerfeldt & Antony, 2002).

As we have emphasized, structured interviews offer reliability but sacrifice flexibility. They can especially help researchers document and define a specific group. For example, if you plan to study obsessive–compulsive disorder, then you need subjects who fall into this category, and there is no better way to document such subjects than to conduct a structured clinical interview. Of course, if you don't know what you're looking for, a structured interview that covers more than 20 diagnoses could become quite a lengthy task. Such interviews require the cooperation of the interviewee, which is not always easy to obtain when the interviewee is a disturbed mental patient or in acute distress.

A major limitation of the structured interview is that it relies exclusively on the respondent. It assumes that the respondent is honest and capable of accurate self-observation and that the respondent will provide frank, candid answers, even to embarrassing questions. As we discuss in Chapter 16, such assumptions cannot always be considered valid. Particularly in forensic settings, one often should not accept the validity of an interviewee's response at face value. After all, if a person facing a death sentence pleads insanity, then we may be wise not to believe the response "Yes, I hear voices all the time." In a less dramatic situation, an interviewee may simply be trying to impress the interviewer or dramatize his or her plight by endorsing symptoms that are not really present. Thus, although structured interviews may be a valuable source of information, you should interpret the results from such procedures cautiously. The same is true for some of the most recent innovations, such as computer administered interviews (Garb, 2007) and online surveys (Chang, 2005).

## Case History Interview

An interview that begins with an open-ended question followed by level-three and perhaps level-four responses can yield a wealth of data about an individual. The interviewer obtains an in-depth description of those factors most important to the interviewee. However, case history data may or may not be revealed, depending on their relevance to central issues in the interviewee's life. To obtain a complete case history—that is, a biographical sketch—one often needs to ask specific questions. Case history data may include a chronology of major events in the person's life, a work history, a medical history, and a family history. A family history should include a complete listing of the ages and genders of each member of the immediate family. One should also note whether any family members—including parents, grandparents, uncles, aunts, and siblings—have had difficulties similar to those of the interviewee. Many conditions occur more frequently in families than in the general population (Stein, Woolley, Cooper, & Winterbottom, 2006; Foster et al., 2008).

In obtaining a case history, the interviewer often takes a developmental approach, examining an individual's entire life, beginning with infancy or the point at which the given type of history is first relevant. For example, the interviewer may say, "Tell me about your work record, beginning with your first paid job." After the work history is clarified, another category such as medical history can be explored.

The purpose of obtaining a case history is to understand individuals' backgrounds so that one can accurately interpret individual test scores. Toward this end, one should attempt to uncover information pertaining to religious preference, premarital and marital experiences, hobbies, education, accomplishments, and habits. Lifestyle information such as smoking behavior, use of alcohol, exercise patterns, and current stressors can also be useful. If a child is the focus of the interview, then information about the parent as well as the child should be obtained (Kefyalew, 1996).

Case history interviews are relatively easy to present on a computer rather than in person (Harlow, Boulmetis, Clark, & Willis, 2003; Rogers, Lerner, & Adler, 2010). Naturally, such interviews are highly structured. They do, however, possess some flexibility through structured branching in which algorithms make questions contingent on an examinee's responses. For example, the interviewee may be asked, "Do you smoke?" If the answer is "no," then the program goes to the next main question. If the answer is "yes," however, the questioning branches into other questions about smoking, such as "How many cigarettes do you smoke per day?" "How long have you been smoking?" and "Have you ever tried to quit?" Still another branch may relate to previous efforts to quit, such as "How many times

**TABLE 8.7**    Part of a Branching Algorithm for a Computerized Interview

1. Have you ever used tobacco?
   If No, go to 2.
   If Yes, answer *a–d.*

   a. At what age did you first start smoking?
   b. About how many cigarettes did you smoke on the average?
   c. Have you ever tried to quit?
      If No, go to *d.*
      If Yes, answer *i–iii.*

      i. When was the first time you tried to quit?
      ii. To what extent were you able to reduce the number of cigarettes you smoked each day?
      iii. How many times have you tried to quit?

   d. Identify any stressors that seem to cause you to smoke more.
2. Have you ever used alcohol?
   If No, go to 3.
   If Yes, answer *a–e.*

have you tried to quit?" See Table 8.7 for an example of part of a branching algorithm.

Computerized interviews have the advantage of nearly perfect interviewer reliability. However, unlike a human interviewer, the computer cannot respond to facial expressions and similar nonverbal cues, so in some situations valuable information is lost.

## Mental Status Examination

An important tool in psychiatric and neurological examinations, the mental status examination is used primarily to diagnose psychosis, brain damage, and other major mental health problems. Its purpose is to evaluate a person suspected of having neurological or emotional problems in terms of variables known to be related to these problems.

The areas covered in the mental status examination include the person's appearance, attitudes, and general behavior. The interviewer is also alert to the interviewee's emotions. For example, is there one dominant emotion that fluctuates little? Is there an absence of emotion (i.e., a flat affect)? Are the emotions appropriate? Do the emotions fluctuate widely? The person's thought processes are also evaluated. Intelligence can be evaluated by such factors as speed and accuracy of thinking, richness of thought content, memory, judgment, and ability to interpret proverbs. Especially important in the assessment of schizophrenia, a major form of psychosis that involves loss of contact with reality, is the quality of the person's thought processes. This can be assessed through an analysis of thought content. For example, is there anything unusual or peculiar about the person's thoughts? Is the person preoccupied with any particular idea? Are the person's ideas realistic?

Other important areas evaluated in the mental status examination include the person's ability to direct and deploy attention. Is the person distracted? Can he or she stick to a task as long as needed to complete it? Sensory factors also are considered. Is the person seeing things that are not there? What is the accuracy of the person's perceptions? Several guides for conducting mental status exams are available (see, for example, Groth-Marnat, 2009; Levitas, Hurley, & Pary, 2002).

Keep in mind that to make proper use of the mental status examination, you must have a broad understanding of the major mental disorders and the various forms of brain damage. There is no room for amateurs or self-appointed practitioners when a mental status examination is needed. However, knowledge of those areas covered in the mental status examination can be useful to interviewers who are interested in knowing the important variables in observing and evaluating another human being.

## Developing Interviewing Skills

A continuing controversy in the field of interviewing concerns whether interviewing skills can be learned. The general consensus is that people can acquire them (Boegels, van der Vleuten, Blok, & Kreutzkamp, 1996; Levinson, Lesser, & Epstein, 2010; Posthuma, Morgeson, & Campion, 2002; Prinstein, 2004). The first step in doing so is to become familiar with research and theory on the interview in order to understand the principles and underlying variables in the interview.

A second step in learning such skills is supervised practice. Experience truly is the best teacher. No amount of book learning can compare with having one's taped interview analyzed by an expert. Maurer, Solamon, and Troxtel (2001) found that applicants who received coaching performed better in an interview than applicants who did not.

As a third step, one must make a conscious effort to apply the principles involved in good interviewing, such as guidelines for keeping the interaction flowing. This application includes constant self-evaluation—for example, continually asking oneself questions such as, "What does this person mean? Am I communicating that I understand? Is the person exploring at deeper levels? What is being communicated nonverbally?"

The initial phase of learning any new skill seems to involve attending to a hundred things at once—an impossible task. However, with persistent effort, people eventually respond appropriately by habit. Thus, experienced interviewers automatically attend to the person's appearance, nonverbal communications, emotional tone, and so on. They do so not because they are endowed with special abilities, but because they have trained themselves to do so. To facilitate this process, cognitive interviews, a relatively recent innovation, are used to assess a respondent's understanding of information (Knafl & colleagues, 2007).

# Sources of Error in the Interview

To make appropriate use of the interview, people must develop an awareness of the various sources of error or potential bias in data from interviews. Then they can try to compensate for these negative effects. Furthermore, this knowledge allows one to develop a better awareness of the limitations inherent in judging human beings on the basis of the interview.

## Interview Validity

Many sources of interview error come from the extreme difficulty we have in making accurate, logical observations and judgments (Cesare, 1996). Suppose, for example, in the first day of teaching a 5th grade class, a teacher observes that one child follows all of the rules and directions, but a second child just cannot seem to stay out of trouble. If that teacher is not careful, then he or she might develop a bias. The teacher might see the first child as good even if she breaks the rules for several weeks in a row. On the other hand, the teacher might see the second child as bad even if she follows the rules for the rest of the school term. Similarly, a child may turn in a paper replete with grammatical and spelling errors. This child may have just had a bad day. However, even if his or her next paper is relatively free of errors, the teacher will have a tendency to look for them and to view the child as weak in grammar. Furthermore, the teacher may see the child as weak in other areas just on the basis of his or her early impression of the child's grammatical skills.

It has been demonstrated that interviewers form an impression of the interviewee within the first minute or so and spend the rest of the interview trying to confirm that impression (Metzger, 2005). Long ago, E. L. Thorndike (1920) labeled this tendency to judge specific traits on the basis of a general impression the *halo effect*. Thorndike became aware of this effect when he noticed that ratings of behavioral tendencies (traits) based on interview data tended to correlate more highly than reasonably expected.

People apparently tend to generalize judgments from a single limited experience (Li, Wang, & Zhang, 2002). In the interview, halo effects occur when the interviewer forms a favorable or unfavorable early impression. The early impression then biases the remainder of the judgment process (Howard & Ferris, 1996). Thus, with an early favorable impression or positive halo, the interviewer will have difficulty seeing the negatives. Similarly, with an early negative halo, the interviewer will have difficulty seeing the positives. In short, halo effects impair objectivity and must be consciously avoided.

Similarly, people tend to judge on the basis of one outstanding characteristic. Hollingworth (1922) first called this error *general standoutishness*. One prominent characteristic can bias the interviewer's judgments and prevent an objective evaluation. In an early classic paper, Burtt (1926) noted the tendency of interviewers to make unwarranted inferences from personal appearance. A well-groomed, attractive individual might be rated higher in intelligence than would a poorly groomed, unattractive individual, even if the latter was actually more intelligent than the former. Results from a 2001 study (Strauss, Miles, & Levesque) showed that less attractive applicants were more favorably rated when interviewed by telephone than in person. This supports the widely recognized concept that physical appearance can play a major role in how a job applicant is perceived and rated (Huffcutt, Roth, & McDaniel, 1996; Reed, 2000). It is important to note, however, that appearance factors that contribute most to the decision-making process are factors that are controllable by the applicant, such as grooming and weight. When it appears that applicants have attempted to manage the controllable factors, they are viewed more favorably, even if they are viewed as unattractive (Posthuma, Morgeson, & Campion, 2002). Another potential source of error in the interview can be found in cross-ethnic, cross-cultural, and cross-class interviewing (Fish, 2001; Miyamoto, 2005; Vatrapu & Pérez-Quiñones, 2006). In the international business community, ignorance of cultural differences is becoming increasingly apparent. Japanese and Arabs consider direct eye contact a sign of aggression. The Japanese person avoids eye contact as a sign of deference and respect. The Japanese also tend to pay more attention to the entire social surrounding, as indicated by eye-tracking data (Takahiko, Ellsworth, Mesquita, Leu, Tanida, & Van de Veerdonk, 2008). In the middle-class United States, by contrast, direct eye contact is expected as a sign of honesty and sincerity. Unless we understand and take cultural differences into account, we can easily send the wrong message or misinterpret others' intentions.

The misunderstanding of cultural differences within the United States also leads to interviewer bias (McCarthy, Lee, Itakura, & Muir, 2008; Schouten & Meeuwesen, 2006). Researchers are making some progress however, in attempts to reduce interviewer bias. For example, organizations that adopt carefully administered interviews that conform to the key components of structure can minimize concerns of applicant discrimination on the basis of gender and race (McCarthy, Van Iddekinge, & Campion, 2010).

Although reviews of the literature (Nevo & Jager, 1993; Ralston, 1988) have failed to provide a framework from which to understand bias in the interview process, virtually every review has concluded that carefully structuring and administering the selection interview improves its psychometric properties (Campion, Palmer, & Campion, 1997). That does not mean error such as cultural distortions do not still reduce the validity of interview data. Even in a highly structured interview, initial impressions formed during rapport building appear to influence the evaluation, whether they are clearly relevant or not (Barrick, Dustin, Giluk, Stewart, Shaffer, & Swider, 2011).

Given the choice between alternative selection processes, such as relying on intelligence test alone, the highly structured interview continues to be the most effective means of eliminating, or at least reducing bias (Ployhart & Holtz, 2008). Research suggests that highly structured interviews draw individuating information, from the interviewee and this, in turn, overrides initial perceptions, providing resistance against bias (McCarthy, Van Iddekinge, & Campion, 2010, p. 336). Thus, to override initial perceptions, interviews must be structured to accomplish three goals. First, the interviewers must be motivated to form an accurate impression of the interviewee. Second, the interviewer must focus more attention on the interviewee in order to notice, remember, and use individuating information that is *not* consistent with initial perceptions. Finally, interviewers must focus on information that is predictive of job performance. Table 8.8 details the process of accomplishing these three goals.

Mean score differences between racioethnic minority (Black, Hispanic, Asian) or female subgroups, and racioethnic majority (white) or male subgroups, contribute to adverse impact (Pyburn, Ployhart, & Kravitz, 2008). Sources of error such as cultural distortions can reduce the validity of interview data. Recall that validity

---

**TABLE 8.8** Suggestions for Structuring Cross-Ethnic, Cross-Cultural, and Cross-Class Interviews

**Increase interviewers' motivation to form an accurate impression**

- When interviewers expect that their judgments will be made known or compared to the judgments of other interviewers, they are more motivated to present an accurate impression. Thus, in structured interviews, the use of panels increases the interviewer motivation to attend to individuating information.

**Provide structure that innately moves interviewers past initial judgments**

- Interviewers move past their initial judgment when the interview is structured so that the interviewers ask a series of predetermined, job-relevant questions and then rate each of the interviewees' responses.

**Focus attention on the interviewee**

- Interviewers who are forced to focus on the interviewee by being required to retrieve and record specific information about the interviewee are less able to remember the interviewee's stereotyped traits. Thus, simply taking notes reduces the impact of preexisting bias.

- Highly structured interviews tend to take longer than less structured interviews, allowing more opportunity for interviewers to obtain individuating information.

**Focus attention on information predictive of job performance**

- The questions in high-structure interviews are designed to measure the interviewees' knowledge, skills, abilities, and characteristics as well as compatibility with behaviors required for a specific job.

- The interviewer rates each interviewee as low, moderate, or high for each category. This focuses attention on the information vital for making a valid judgment about each interviewee.

- Highly structured interviews minimize the extent to which applicants can express irrelevant information by limiting opportunity for the interviewee to ask questions.

(Information used in Table 8.8 is from: McCarthy, J. M., Van Iddekinge, C. H., & Campion, M. A. (2010). Are highly structured job interviews resistant to demographic similarity effects? *Personnel Psychology, 63*(2), 325–359, 336–338.)

---

tells us about the meaning of test scores. Errors that reduce the objectivity of the interviewer produce inaccurate judgments, thus biasing the validity of the evaluation. These tendencies perhaps explain why the predictive validity of interview data varies so widely. R. Wagner (1949), for example, earlier reported studies that attempted to correlate judgments from interview data with such factors as grades, intelligence, and performance on standardized tests. The correlations ranged from .09 to .94, with a median of .19. Studies reviewed by Ulrich and Trumbo (1965) revealed a similar range of predictive validity coefficients, with correlations as low as −.05 and as high as .72 when ratings based on interview data were correlated with a variety of indexes such as job performance. Later research reported similar findings (Arvey & Campion, 1982; Carlson, Thayer, Mayfield, & Peterson,

1971). Other reviews have suggested higher and more consistent coefficients especially when specific characteristics such as cognitive ability are being assessed. In a meta-analytic review of 49 studies, for example, Huffcutt, Roth, and McDaniel (1996) found that .4 provided a good estimate of the relationship between test scores and interview ratings of cognitive abilities.

When examining the relationship between structured interviews and subsequent supervisor ratings, researchers found correlations from 0.30–0.60, however, unstructured interviews typically correlate less than 0.20 with the same outcome measures (Ebmeier, Dillon, & Ng, 2007).

Although one can question the validity of interview data, the interview does provide a wealth of unique data. The safest approach is to consider interview data as tentative: a hypothesis or a set of hypotheses to be confirmed by other sources of data. Interview data may have dubious value without the support of more standardized procedures. Results from standardized tests, on the other hand, are often meaningless if not placed in the context of case history or other interview data. The two go together, each complementing the other, each essential in the process of evaluating human beings.

## Interview Reliability

Recall that reliability refers to the stability, dependability, or consistency of test results. For interview data, the critical questions about reliability have centered on inter-interviewer agreement (agreement between two or more interviewers). As with the validity studies, reliability coefficients for inter-interviewer agreement vary widely. For example, in R. Wagner's (1949) classic study, reliability coefficients ranged from .23 to .97 (median .57) for ratings of traits. The range of coefficients for ratings of overall ability was even wider (−.20 to .85; median .53). Ulrich and Trumbo's (1965) widely cited review reported similar findings.

Research consistently indicates unstructured interviews have low levels of reliability (U.S. Office of Personnel Management, 2008). Research also shows that in terms of adverse impact, interviews give fairer outcomes than many other widely used selection tools, including psychometric tests of ability and intelligence (Moscoso, 2000).

McCarthy, Van Iddekinge, and Campion (2010) argued that one reason for fluctuations in interview reliability is, in part, because interview procedures vary considerably in their degree of standardization in terms of interview development, administration, and/or scoring. Simply, different interviewers look for different things, an argument echoed by others (Harasym, Woloschuk, Mandin, & Brundin-Mather, 1996; Zedeck, Tziner, & Middlestadt, 1983). Thus, whereas one interviewer might focus on strengths, another might focus on weaknesses. The two interviewers would disagree because their judgments are based on different aspects of the individual.

As we have noted, agreement among interviewers varies for different types of interviews. The research suggests that a highly structured interview in which specific questions are asked in a specific order can produce highly stable results (Huffcutt, Conway, Roth, & Stone, 2001). For example, if we ask a person his or her name, date of birth, and parents' names as well as the addresses of all residences within a particular time span, and then ask the same questions a year later, results should be nearly identical. Reliability would be limited only by the memory and honesty of the interviewee and the clerical capabilities of the interviewer. Although extreme, this example should make it clear that highly structured interviews should produce fairly dependable results. In fact, the internal consistency reliability for scores on highly structured interviews was .79 where the interviewer was gathering information about the interviewee's experience, .90 where interviewees responded to hypothetical dilemmas they may experience on the job, and .86 where the interviewer was gathering information about the interviewees' past behavior (McCarthy et. al., 2010). The problem is that such structure can limit the content of the interview, thus defeating the purpose of providing a broad range of data.

Unstructured or semistructured interviews frequently provide data that other sources cannot provide. However, the dependability of such results is clearly limited. The same question may not be asked twice, or it may be asked in different ways. Thus, interviewers readily acknowledge the limited reliability of interview data.

# Summary

In a *structured interview*, the interviewer asks a specific set of questions. In the structured *standardized* interview, these questions are printed. The interviewer reads the questions in a specific order or sequence. In the *unstructured interview*, there are no specific questions or guidelines for the interviewer to follow. Thus, each unstructured interview is unique. Such interviews provide considerable flexibility at the expense of data stability.

An interview is an *interactive* process. The participants (interviewer and interviewee) influence each other. The tendency for people to behave like the models around them is called *social facilitation*. Good interviewers thus can set a good tone in an interview by maintaining a warm, open, confident atmosphere.

Good interviewing involves developing the proper *attitudes* and displaying them during the interview. Interviewees give positive evaluations to interviewers when the interviewer is seen as warm, genuine, accepting, understanding, open, committed, and involved. Poor evaluations result when interviewers exhibit the opposite attitudes and feelings.

The process of interviewing involves facilitating the flow of communication. An interviewer should avoid statements that are *judgmental* or *evaluative, probing, hostile,* or *reassuring*. An unstructured interview should begin with an *open-ended question*—that is, one that cannot be answered briefly. The process of interviewing then involves facilitating the flow of communication. *Closed-ended questions*, which can be answered with a "yes" or "no" or a specific response, usually bring the interview to a halt and typically should be reserved for instances where less directive procedures fail to produce the desired information. Further, transitional phrases such as "I see" help keep the interview flowing. Statements that communicate understanding or are interchangeable with the interviewee's responses tend to elicit self-exploration at increasingly deeper levels. These interviewer responses include *verbatim playback, paraphrasing, restatement, summarizing, clarification,* and *understanding. Confrontation* is another response that experienced interviewers use for specific purposes, but it is not recommended as a general strategy.

Efforts to assess the quality of understanding or empathetic statements have led to a 5-point scale system developed by Rogers, Truax, Carkhuff, and coworkers. Understanding statements are extremely powerful in helping the interviewee uncover and explore underlying feelings. Types of interviews include the *evaluation or assessment interview*, the *structured clinical interview*, the *case history interview*, the *mental status examination*, and the *employment interview*.

There are two primary sources of error in the interview: those pertaining to the *validity* or meaning of data and those pertaining to its dependability or *reliability*. Tendencies to draw general conclusions about an individual that are based on just the data of a first impression limit the meaning and accuracy of interview data. Such tendencies have been labeled *the halo effect* and *standoutishness*. Cultural misunderstandings can also bias interview data and lead to inaccurate conclusions. Furthermore, predictive validity coefficients for interview data vary widely. The reliability of interview data has been measured primarily in terms of agreement among interviewers on variables, such as intelligence and traits. The more structured the interview, the more the interviewers agree. Thus, like predictive validity coefficients, reliability coefficients for interview data vary widely. Training tends to enhance reliability.

One develops interviewing skills through knowledge about good interviewing behavior and principles, supervised practice, and a conscious effort to form the right habits. However, the interview is fallible. Interview data can best be seen as the complement of other data sources.

CHAPTER

9

# Computers and Basic Psychological Science in Testing

## LEARNING OBJECTIVES

*When you have completed this chapter, you should be able to:*

▶ Identify the differences between cognitive-behavioral assessment and traditional assessment procedures

▶ Identify the difference between the *beliefs* underlying traditional tests and the beliefs underlying behavioral tests

▶ Briefly describe cognitive-behavioral assessment based on operant conditioning

▶ Identify the main difference between cognitive-behavioral self-report techniques and traditional self-report techniques

▶ List four types of behavioral self-report techniques

▶ Briefly describe the functional, or behavior-analytic, approach to behavioral assessment

▶ Describe a cognitive-functional analysis

▶ Briefly describe psychophysical assessment

▶ Discuss the role of computers in modern psychological testing

A high-school teacher once contacted us regarding her 7-year-old son. At the age of 4, the boy had suffered from an illness in which he could not eat solid food for 25 days because it made him gag. If he managed to swallow, he became extremely nauseous. Ever since he had recovered from the illness, he was reluctant to eat all but a few select foods. His usual menu was cold cereal for breakfast, a peanut butter sandwich for lunch, and plain spaghetti for dinner. He refused to eat meat or vegetables of any kind. His parents tried everything, but nothing worked. The mother was concerned that the boy was not developing properly. She had taken him to a pediatrician who told her that unless something could be done to get the boy to eat, he would have to be hospitalized. The physician suggested psychiatric intervention and gave the boy 1 month to improve.

After explaining this problem, the mother asked us whether we could administer a test that might explain why the child wasn't eating. A school psychologist had suggested to her that psychological tests might help facilitate the treatment process. If we could understand why the boy wasn't eating, perhaps this information would help us treat him. During our interview, we discovered that the boy had been in psychiatric treatment when he was 5. The treatment had lasted approximately 1 year, with little improvement. Partly because of this previous failure and partly because of her desperation, the mother insisted we do some testing. As we thought about the various tests we might use, we could see little value in using any of the traditional tests for this problem.

We did administer the Wechsler Intelligence Scale for Children, Third Edition (WISC-III) and found that the boy had above-average intelligence (full-scale IQ = 115). In achievement, the boy was functioning about half a grade level above his current grade placement in both reading and arithmetic. Thus, intellectual and achievement factors could not account for the problem. Unfortunately, personality tests were not much more useful than the ability tests had been. After administering the Children's Apperception Test and conducting extensive interviewing and observation (see Chapter 14), our interpretation confirmed our suspicion that the boy's eating problem originated with the trauma he had suffered when he could not eat solid foods. In simple terms, the boy had a fear of eating.

Knowing why the boy wasn't eating certainly wasn't much help. One of the weaknesses of the original model of testing as reflected in traditional tests is that they provide little information concerning possible treatment approaches. When we explained the situation to the mother, she pleaded, "Isn't there any other type of test you can give him? Isn't there a test that might also indicate what type of treatment would be most effective?" Thanks to advances within scientific psychology, we could answer, "Yes."

We told the mother that numerous alternatives to traditional tests had been developed by psychologists in the specialty based on learning principles known as *behavior modification*, or *behavior therapy*. Collectively, these testing techniques are known as *cognitive-behavioral assessment*. "Please try these procedures," she said. "If they might help, by all means use them."

In the hands of highly trained experts, traditional psychological tests may be extremely valuable, but they still fall short on several grounds. The traditional tests discussed thus far in this book offer little information concerning treatment approaches. As a rule, these traditional procedures also provide little information

**TABLE 9.1**  Varieties of Alternatives to Traditional Testing Procedures

Operant conditioning techniques

Self-report techniques

Kanfer and Saslow's behavior-analytic approach

Cognitive techniques

Psychophysiological techniques

Psychophysiological and signal detection procedures

about how a person might behave in a particular situation. Even if these traditional procedures do explain the reason behind a particular symptom, this information usually offers little to the overall treatment process. The result of such shortcomings in traditional tests has been an explosion of alternative approaches based on principles of human learning and cognition, and more recently the advent of personal computers.

Behavioral assessment can be divided into several categories. These include procedures based on operant conditioning techniques, self-report techniques, Kanfer and Saslow's behavior-analytic approach, a variety of cognitive techniques, psychophysiological techniques, and signal-detection procedures. Each of these is discussed in turn (see Table 9.1).

# Cognitive-Behavioral Assessment Procedures

## The Rationale for Cognitive-Behavioral Assessment

Traditional testing procedures are based on a medical model. According to this model, the overt manifestations of a disordered psychological condition (e.g., overeating or undereating) are only symptoms—surface expressions of an underlying cause. Disordered behavior is believed to be caused by some underlying characteristic such as an early traumatic experience. In the example at the beginning of this chapter, the boy's avoidance of food was, in a sense, caused by the trauma of an illness in which solid food made him nauseous. Treatment in the medical model is based on the idea that unless the cause of a symptom is removed, a new symptom may develop. Thus, one major function of traditional psychological tests is to ascertain the possible underlying causes of disordered behaviors.

In cognitive-behavioral assessment, by contrast, the behaviors, thought processes, or physiological responses that define a disordered condition are considered the real problem. If the person eats too much, then the problem is simply overeating and not some underlying cause. The overeating may, in fact, have been caused by some early experience, just as in the 7-year-old boy. However, in cognitive-behavioral assessment, the eating behavior becomes the direct target of treatment. Therefore, the testing procedure in this case would evaluate eating behavior.

This is not to say that cognitive-behavioral assessment denies, ignores, or negates the causes of psychological disorders. On the contrary, certain techniques of

**TABLE 9.2**   Traditional Versus Cognitive-Behavioral Assessment

|  | Traditional assessment | Cognitive-behavioral assessment |
|---|---|---|
| Target | Underlying cause | Disordered behavior |
| Symptoms | Superficial | Focus of treatment |
| Assessment | Indirect; not related to treatment | Direct; related to treatment |
| Theory | Medical model | Behavioral model |
| Goal | Determine cause of symptoms | Analyze disordered behavior |

cognitive-behavioral assessment include an evaluation of the factors that precede, coexist with, and follow (maintain) disordered behavior (DiCaccavo, 2010; Kounti, Tsolaki, & Kiosseoglou, 2006). These may be environmental factors (such as working conditions, home situation), thought processes (such as internal dialogue), or both. Thus, cognitive-behavioral assessment often includes an evaluation of the internal and external factors that lead to and maintain disordered behavior as well as an evaluation of the behavior itself (Mack & Rybarczyk, 2011, p. 89; Sheldon, 2011, pp. 3–4).

Cognitive-behavioral assessment is more direct than traditional psychological tests. It is characterized by fewer inferential assumptions and remains closer to observable phenomena (Sheldon, 2011). Through cognitive-behavioral assessment, one might find that, just before eating, the 7-year-old boy in our example says to himself, "I don't want to eat; it will make me sick." Subsequently, the boy refuses to eat. As he leaves the dinner table, his mother says, "That's okay, honey, you don't have to eat." The boy's statement, "I don't want to eat," precedes the disordered behavior. His avoidance of food is the core of the disorder. His mother's comment, plus the boy's relief that he doesn't have to eat, reinforces or maintains the disorder. In cognitive-behavioral assessment, psychologists analyze preceding and subsequent factors and focus on a direct change in overt behavior, thoughts, or physiological processes. The treatment process thus involves an attempt to alter the disordered behavior (e.g., increasing the frequency of eating). Treatment may also involve modifying the internal dialogue before and after the boy eats and modifying the mother's behavior so that she no longer reinforces avoidance of food but instead reinforces eating.

In traditional procedures, the boy's failure to eat would be viewed as only a symptom. Testing would be aimed at determining the cause of this symptom (the early trauma of the illness he had when he was 4), and treatment would be directed at the cause rather than at the behavior itself. Presumably, by giving the boy insight into the causes of his behavior, a psychologist could get the boy to understand why he wasn't eating. When he achieved this understanding, he would no longer need to avoid eating. Table 9.2 compares traditional and cognitive-behavioral assessment.

It is beyond the scope of this text to debate the pros and cons of the cognitive-behavioral and medical models. Our goal is to help you understand the differences between the two. Suffice it to say that cognitive-behavioral testing procedures, based on psychology's scientific base, have added a whole new dimension to the field of psychological testing.

# Procedures Based on Operant Conditioning

In operant conditioning, psychologists observe the behaviors of an individual. After the individual has made a response, they can do something to the individual to alter the probability of the recurrence of the response. They may present something positive or remove something negative following the response, which should increase the rate of recurrence, or else they may present something aversive or remove something positive preceding the response, which should reduce the rate of recurrence.

In cognitive-behavioral assessment based on operant conditioning, one must first identify the critical response or responses involved in the disorder. One can then evaluate these critical responses for frequency, intensity, or duration. This evaluation establishes the baseline (usual rate of occurrence) for the particular behavior. According to an early system developed by Kanfer and Saslow (1969), if the behaviors occur too frequently, then they are called *behavioral excesses*. If they occur too infrequently, they are called *behavioral deficits*. Obviously, with a behavioral excess, treatment centers on reducing the frequency, intensity, or duration of the behavior in question. With a behavioral deficit, treatment focuses on increasing the behavior. Table 9.3 outlines the steps in cognitive-behavioral assessment based on operant conditioning.

After attempting to increase or decrease the behavior (treatment intervention), psychologists observe the effect of the intervention on the behavior in question relative to the baseline. If the goal was to decrease the behavior, then there should be a decrease relative to the baseline. If the critical behavior remains at or above baseline levels, then the intervention has failed.

In the example at the beginning of this chapter, we decided to use cognitive-behavioral assessment based on operant conditioning. The critical behavior was obvious: frequency of eating. Furthermore, the critical behavior was a deficit; that is, the boy wasn't eating enough. To evaluate the critical behavior (Step 3), we asked the boy's mother to record the amount and kind of food that the boy ate each day. Using standard calorie references, we converted the amount of food the boy ate into calories. The baseline looked something like the graph in Figure 9.1. The boy was eating an average of approximately 800 calories a day, with a range of 600 to 1000 calories on any given day. This number of calories is too few to prevent a small, gradual weight loss.

Because the behavior was a deficit, we tried to increase the boy's frequency of eating. For our intervention, we used a reward system based on points. The boy

---

**TABLE 9.3** Steps in a Cognitive-Behavioral Assessment

| | |
|---|---|
| Step 1: | Identify critical behaviors. |
| Step 2: | Determine whether critical behaviors are excesses or deficits. |
| Step 3: | Evaluate critical behaviors for frequency, duration, or intensity (that is, obtain a baseline). |
| Step 4: | If excesses, attempt to decrease frequency, duration, or intensity of behaviors; if deficits, attempt to increase behaviors. |

**FIGURE 9.1**

Baseline in eating difficulty example.

received points for everything he ate. The more he ate, the more points he got. Following each meal, his mother recorded the number of points that he received as well as the cumulative total. She posted this record on a bulletin board in the boy's room so he could observe his own progress. She also posted a chart that we had worked out with the two of them. The chart listed toys and other rewards that he could trade for points. For example, he could exchange 10 points for a package of baseball cards any time he wanted. He could also save his points for bigger prizes. For 350 points, he could get a computer game he had been wanting, and so on. In the treatment procedure, his mother recorded exactly what he ate each day just as she had during the pretreatment assessment in which the baseline was obtained. This record was then converted into calories, and each week we made a graph of his day-to-day calorie intake.

The intervention proved highly effective. Within 1 week, the boy had earned some 200 points and was well on the way to securing his computer game. The graph for this first week of treatment is shown in Figure 9.2. As the graph indicates, the boy doubled his average intake of calories to some 1600 (range 1400 to 1800). Thus, his intake of calories was far above baseline following the intervention. Assessment continued throughout the treatment and also provided feedback about the effects of the treatment. In the second week, the boy's consumption of calories fell below the dramatic increases of the first week, but it never fell below baseline levels. In 6 weeks, the boy gained approximately eight pounds. He had earned just about every toy he had ever wanted. At this point, his mother became concerned that he might gain too much weight or that she might go broke paying for rewards. After consultation with us, she terminated the point system. Following termination, there was a substantial drop in his eating behavior for 3 or 4 days, but then it increased to about a normal level for his age.

Over the course of treatment, the boy's parents had developed a different attitude about his eating behavior. So had the boy. Everybody concerned now knew that the boy could eat without negative consequences. The parents refused to permit the boy to get away without eating, and the boy no longer had an excuse not to eat. Although the therapy never attempted to get at an original or hypothetical underlying cause of the behavior, the boy was in every sense cured. He wasn't hospitalized, and his eating behavior was adequate 6 months following treatment. His mother complained that he was still a finicky eater, but his weight was within normal limits.

FIGURE 9.2
Eating behavior during the
first week of intervention.

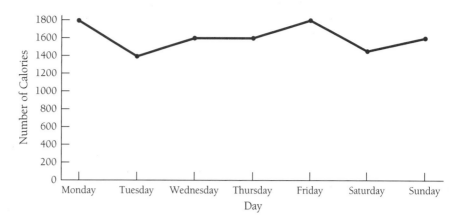

Practitioners can use the operant approach to solve a variety of problems, including smoking (Hogarth, Dickinson, & Duka, 2005; Hogarth, Dickinson, Wright, Kouvaraki, & Duka, 2007; Winkler, Weyers, Mucha, Stippekohl, Stark, & Pauli, 2011), poor study habits (Gallo & Rinaldo, 2010), coping with chronic pain (Hölzl, Kleinböhl, & Huse, 2005; Vlaeyen, de Jong, Onghena, Kerckhoffs-Hanssen, & Kole-Snijders, 2002), addiction (Treisman & Clark, 2011), and poor diet (Douglas, 2002; Tazaki & Landlaw, 2006). In each case, one first calculates a baseline. Then one implements an intervention. Finally, one observes the effects of this intervention on the baseline. If you feel you don't study enough, for instance, you can try the approach yourself. To assess your study behavior, record the number of minutes you study each day for 1 week. This is your baseline. Then decide on a reward for yourself. Every day record how long you study. Give yourself the reward whenever you study longer than 25% above the average time for your baseline. See whether this procedure doesn't increase the time you spend studying.

## Self-Report Techniques

In our example, the frequency of the 7-year-old boy's disordered eating behavior was recorded by his mother because the assessment process required that someone observe the boy. Not all problems, however, can be so easily and readily observed. Further, when a parent or other relative of the subject does the observing and recording, the practitioner must depend on the skill, accuracy, and honesty of the well-meaning but untrained relative. Thus, in the ideal situation, the practitioner or a trained assistant observes the individual to be assessed. The practitioner directly observes and records specific problem behaviors in a variety of situations and notes the factors that precede and maintain these behaviors. Like any observer, the practitioner must make him- or herself as inconspicuous and as unobtrusive as possible to avoid interfering with or influencing the subject. Unfortunately, following a subject around to record behaviors is difficult, time-consuming, and often unrealistic. In most cases, the observer can hardly avoid influencing the subject. Indeed, psychologists have long known that the mere presence of an observer may alter the behavior of an individual (Polansky et al., 1949).

One attempt to deal with the problems inherent in observation is the *self-report technique* (Muris & Field, 2011, p. 77). The typical self-report is a list of

**TABLE 9.4** Examples of a Behavioral Self-Report

Circle    1 if the item elicits no fear

          2 if the item elicits some fear

          3 if the item elicits a little fear

          4 if the item elicits a lot of fear

          5 if the item elicits extreme fear

| | | | | | |
|---|---|---|---|---|---|
| Worms | 1 | 2 | 3 | 4 | 5 |
| Bats | 1 | 2 | 3 | 4 | 5 |
| Psychological tests | 1 | 2 | 3 | 4 | 5 |
| Dogs | 1 | 2 | 3 | 4 | 5 |
| Snakes | 1 | 2 | 3 | 4 | 5 |
| Highways | 1 | 2 | 3 | 4 | 5 |
| Men | 1 | 2 | 3 | 4 | 5 |

*Circle true or false as the item applies to you.*

| | | |
|---|---|---|
| I like to talk when in a group. | True | False |
| I relate easily to persons of the opposite sex. | True | False |
| I like to walk in dark places. | True | False |
| I like to give speeches to large groups. | True | False |
| I feel most comfortable with strangers. | True | False |
| I feel most comfortable with family. | True | False |
| I feel most comfortable with friends. | True | False |
| I like to be the leader in a group. | True | False |
| I would rather follow than lead in a group. | True | False |

statements about particular situations. The subject's task may be either to respond "True" or "False" to each statement or to circle a number (1 to 5, for example) to indicate the importance or relevance of the statement. Table 9.4 gives examples of the types of statements used. Self-report techniques assume that the person's responses reflect individual differences and measure some other observable behavior. If, for example, one person circles 5 for fear of snakes and another person circles 1, then psychologists assume that direct observation of these two individuals in the presence of snakes would reveal different, measurable responses. The person who circled 5 might scream and run. The person who circled 1 might simply ignore the snakes. In place of direct observation, the practitioner accepts the face validity of the subject's responses.

That cognitive-behavioral assessment has concentrated on phenomena such as fear illustrates the major distinction between cognitive-behavioral and traditional self-report procedures. Cognitive-behavioral procedures focus on situations that lead to particular response patterns; that is, situations are the primary determinant of behavior. Traditional self-report procedures focus on relatively enduring internal characteristics of the individual (personality traits) that lead to particular response patterns. In the cognitive-behavioral approach, one sees situations as the primary determinant of behavior. In the traditional approach, one sees characteristics that the person brings to a situation (e.g., traits) as the primary determinant of behavior. Thus, in the cognitive-behavioral approach, a person is not simply fearful and therefore fearful no matter what the situation; a person is fearful only in certain circumstances or situations because these circumstances elicit fear in that person (Ramirez & Andreu, 2006).

### The Fear Survey Schedule (FSS)

The FSS is the oldest and most researched of the cognitive-behavioral self-report procedures. In clinical and experimental use since the 1950s, it continues to be used for a variety of purposes (Beck, Carmin, & Henninger, 1998; Harris, Robinson, & Menzies, 2001; Westenberg, Gullone, Bokhorst, Heyne, & King, 2007). Since the FSS was introduced into the literature by Akutagawa (1956) as a 50-item test, it has undergone a variety of changes, and various versions have from 50 to 122 items, with ratings of fear on either 5-point or 7-point scales (Burnham, 2005). It has been adapted for use with children (Burnham & Giesen, 2005; Murisa, Huijdinga, Mayera, & de Vriesa, 2011) and adolescents (Muris & Field, 2011) as well as adults with intellectual disabilities (Hermans, van der Pas & Evenhuis, 2011). One adaptation of the FSS was created for measuring specific phobias (Antony, 2001; Ten Berge & Veerkamp, 2005). From its world-wide use (Bajrić, Kobašlija & Hrvoje, 2011; Diercke, Ollinger, Bermejo et al., 2012; Du, Lee, & Christinam, 2011), numerous cross-cultural studies are available (e.g., Hawkins-Gilligan, Dygdon & Conger, 2011; Lahikainen, Kraav, Kirmanen, & Taimalu, 2006).

Items are typically related to situations that involve fear and avoidance behaviors, such as fear of open places, fear of snakes, fear of dead animals. Subjects rate each item according to the degree to which they experience that particular fear. Developers have derived items on the FSS from clinical observation of actual cases (Wolpe & Lang, 1964) and from experimental investigations in laboratory settings (Geer, 1965). The FSS attempts to identify those situations that elicit fear and thus avoidance. Once psychologists have identified these situations, they can aim treatment at helping people deal with these situations, thus reducing fear.

### Assertiveness

Some individuals have difficulty speaking up for themselves. When they finally do speak up, they are often aggressive. Suppose someone cuts in front of you in a long line to see a popular movie. Assertiveness experts might suggest that you calmly and firmly inform this person of the location of the end of the line. If you encounter resistance, you calmly explain that everyone has been waiting in line and that the only polite and appropriate thing for the intruder to do is to go to the end of the line. Many people have difficulty acting appropriately in this type of situation. They may stew inside or go to the other extreme and display aggression, such as striking the intruder or throwing a temper tantrum.

---

**TABLE 9.5**    Sample Questions from a Behavioral Assertiveness Questionnaire

I. Suppose you were in the following situations. How would you respond? Indicate by circling number 1, 2, or 3.

   A. You have ordered filet mignon for you and your date at an expensive restaurant. You wanted yours cooked rare. The waiter brings it well done. What would you do?

     1. Tell the waiter to bring you another, cooked the way you wanted it.

     2. Complain to the waiter, but eat what he had brought for you anyway.

     3. Say nothing.

   B. You are at a bank. You've been waiting in line for nearly 10 minutes. Finally, you reach the head of the line. A man with a large briefcase comes from the outside and steps right in front of you. What would you do?

     1. Tell him to go to the end of the line.

     2. Tell him there is a long line, but let him go in front of you anyway.

     3. Say nothing.

II. In those situations in which you say nothing, what are you afraid of? (Check the best answer.)

   A. Being yelled at ( )

   B. Being beat up ( )

   C. Being embarrassed ( )

   D. Being rejected ( )

   E. Violating a personal or religious belief ( )

   F. Expending excessive energy ( )

Adapted from Cautela and Upper (1976, pp. 97–98).

Clinical practitioners have constructed various measures of assertiveness. Table 9.5 illustrates the type of item found in a self-report questionnaire for assertiveness, such as the Assertive Behavior Survey Schedule (ABSS). If you were taking the ABSS, you would indicate the responses you would make in specific situations that call for assertiveness. You would also be asked to speculate on the consequences of assertiveness for you. Thus, the ABSS can help determine whether you can be assertive if necessary, situations in which you might have difficulty being assertive, and your personal attitude toward assertiveness.

### Self-Report Battery

Cautela and Upper (1976) have proposed the use of a self-report battery that incorporates many of the commonly used self-report techniques, such as a variety of behavioral self-rating checklists and the FSS. The battery contains three types of scales. Primary scales request general information, such as historical data, and assess general needs. Secondary scales yield information about the need for specific techniques such as relaxation or assertiveness training. Requiring a highly specific response, tertiary scales yield information about specific problems such as alcohol and drug abuse, overeating, and inappropriate sexual behavior (Delinsky, Thomas, Germain, et al., 2011).

### Evaluation of Self-Report Procedures

Obviously, any practitioner with a problem to assess can simply devise and publish a self-report device. Indeed, there appears to be no shortage of such practitioners. Unfortunately, psychometric data has rarely been presented to help evaluate these devices, although this trend seems to be shifting (see Dubowitz, Villodas, Litrownik, et al., 2011; Vorstenboscha, Antonya, Koernera, & Boivinb, 2012; Wuyek, Antony, & McCabe, 2011).

In their use of self-report techniques, some psychologists "reinvent the wheel." For example, Cautela and Upper (1976) do not hesitate to admit that the prototypes of current self-report techniques are tests such as the Woodworth Personal Data Sheet. Early paper-and-pencil structured personality tests, finally abandoned in the 1930s, are indeed difficult to distinguish from many modern self-report procedures. Both implicitly assume that test responses have face validity. Thus, all of the problems associated with face validity—subject capacity and willingness to be truthful, response bias, poor reliability, poor validity, lack of norms—usually plague cognitive-behavioral self-report techniques. Unfortunately, only one of these self-report techniques, the FSS, has been subjected to anything close to an adequate psychometric analysis, with over 1000 published research articles through 2012.

Practitioners have a long way to go before they can offer cognitive-behavioral self-report procedures as established clinical tools. However, when used in conjunction with other sources of data, such as psychophysiological recordings and direct observation, self-report data can provide useful information in clinical as well as research settings. Indeed, this is the modern trend (Carlbring, Björnstjerna, Bergström, Waara, & Andersson, 2007; Chan, 2009; Grana-Gomez, Andreu, Rogers, & Arango-Lasprilla, 2003; Lewis & Drewett, 2006; Steinberg, Krejci, Collett, Brandon, Ziedonis, & Chen, 2007; Tucker, Slifer, & Dahlquist, 2001; Wilson, Smith, Chattington, Ford, & Marple-Horvat, 2006).

## Kanfer and Saslow's Functional Approach

In the discussion of operant conditioning, we mentioned Kanfer and Saslow's (1969) original concepts of behavioral deficits and excesses. Now we shall discuss this approach in detail, particularly as it goes beyond the principles of operant conditioning.

Kanfer and Saslow (1969) are among the most important pioneers in the field of cognitive-behavioral assessment. Their method of cognitive-behavioral assessment provides an alternative to the traditional diagnostic labeling of the medical model (neurotic, psychotic, and so forth). These authors propose what they call a *functional (behavior-analytic) approach* to assessment. Rather than labeling people as schizophrenic or neurotic, the psychologist would focus on behavioral excesses and deficits. As previously indicated, a *behavioral excess* is any behavior or class of behaviors described as problematic by an individual because of its inappropriateness or because of excesses in its frequency, intensity, or duration. The functional approach adheres to the assumptions of the learning approach (to the study of disordered behavior); that is, the functional approach assumes that both normal and disordered behaviors develop according to the same laws and differ only in extremes. Taking a shower, for example, is a normal behavior. What about taking two showers a day? Clearly, the laws that govern the acquisition of the behaviors involved in taking one shower are the same as those for taking two showers. What about eight showers a day? Consider three hour-long showers a day, or a 2-hour-long shower taken within minutes after company arrives for an unexpected visit. This sort of behavior is abnormal only because it is excessive. Similarly, most of us blow off steam by yelling every now and then. However, if a person yells intensely every half an hour for 30 seconds at a time every time she goes to the library, then yelling behavior is clearly extreme and maladaptive.

*Behavioral deficits* are classes of behaviors described as problematic because they fail to occur with sufficient frequency, with adequate intensity, in appropriate form, or under socially expected conditions (Kanfer & Saslow, 1969; Ferro & Madureira, 2002). For example, one may view lack of assertiveness as a behavioral deficit.

Again, the behavior, or lack of it, is not by itself a disorder. If, for example, a gang of high-school dropouts drive their motorcycles into the parking spot you were prepared to pull into, then it may not be too wise to say, "That's my spot; there's another around the block." Finding another parking spot yourself is proba-bly a far more adaptive behavior.

Besides isolating behavioral excesses and deficits, a functional analysis involves other procedures, including clarifying the problem and making suggestions for treatment. In the traditional approaches, knowing a person has a particular disorder or conflict does little to suggest treatment strategies. However, when behavioral excesses are identified, the psychologist can make efforts to reduce the behaviors' intensity, frequency, and so forth. When behavioral deficits are identified, the psy-chologist can make efforts to provide new behaviors or increase the frequency of existing behaviors.

## The Dysfunctional Attitude Scale

A major pillar of cognitive-behavioral assessment that focuses primarily on thinking patterns rather than overt behavior is A. T. Beck's (1967, 1976, 2002) Cognitive Model of Psychopathology. The model is based on *schemas*, which are cognitive frameworks or organizing principles of thought. For example, in your first impres-sion of an individual, you create a schema of that person. In your subsequent inter-actions with that person, you add to or subtract from that original schema. Moreover, the original schema influences your subsequent perceptions. For instance, if you originally pegged the person as a nerd, then you will likely label subsequent behavior accordingly. According to Beck, schemas serve to organize prior experience, guide the interpretations of new experiences, and shape expectan-cies and predictions. Beck's theory holds that dysfunctional schemas predispose an individual to develop pathological behaviors (Lomax & Lam, 2011; Newman, Leahy, Beck, Reilly-Harrington, & Gyulia, 2003).

To evaluate negative schemas, Beck and colleagues have developed the Dys-functional Attitude Scale (DAS) (Weissman, 1979; Weissman & Beck, 1978). The DAS has two parallel forms (Power, Katz, McGuffin, & Duggan, 1994). It identifies beliefs that might interact with a stressor to produce psychopathology (Whisman, Johnson, & Smolen, 2011). For instance, a person may believe that he cannot find happiness without being loved by another or that turning to someone else for advice or help is an admission of weakness. The subject is provided with a list of statements such as "Others can care for me even if they know all my weaknesses" and is asked to respond on a 7-point Likert scale ranging from "totally agree" to "totally disagree." The validity of the scale is supported by a variety of factor analytic data (Beck et al., 1991; also see D'Alessandro, 2005; Lomax, & Lam, 2011; Thomas & Altareb, 2011; Whisman, Johnson, & Smolen, 2011).

## Irrational Beliefs Test

According to the cognitive viewpoint, human behavior is often determined by beliefs and expectations rather than reality. If, for example, your instructor announces that there will be an exam in the third week of classes, you will do most of your studying for it the day or two before it if you are like most students. Suppose, however, you miss the class just before the announced exam. And suppose that a "friend" of yours plays a trick on you: he tells you the exam has been canceled. If you believe him and therefore expect that there will be no exam, will you study as hard as you would have before (if at all)? It's unlikely. The exam will still be given (reality), but your behavior will have changed because of your belief that the exam has been canceled. In view of the influence of beliefs and expectations, several cognitive-behavioral tests have been developed to measure them. R. A. Jones (1968), for example, developed a 100-item Irrational Beliefs Test (IBT) to measure irrational beliefs (e.g., the belief that you must always succeed to be worthwhile).

The IBT requires subjects to indicate their level of agreement or disagreement with each of the 100 items on a 5-point scale (e.g., "I frequently worry about things over which I have no control"). Half of the items indicate the presence of a particular irrational belief; the other half, its absence.

The IBT found widespread use in clinical as well as research settings and has received considerable attention (Bridges & Sanderman, 2002; Taghavi, Goodarzi, Kazemi, & Ghorbani, 2006; Warren, 2011). Although the IBT was initially one of the most popular measures of irrational beliefs, its use has gradually diminished due to criticisms that these beliefs were not measured independently of the emotional consequences they were hypothesized to cause (Bridges & Harnish, 2010, p. 871). The reliability of the IBT appears to be similar to that of structured personality tests, with test–retest coefficients for short intervals (2 weeks or less) ranging from .48 to .90 for individual scales and .88 for the full scale. The validity documentation of the IBT is weak (Smith & Zurawski, 1983), although the IBT does appear to be related to both anxiety and depression (Cook & Peterson, 1986; Deffenbacher et al., 1986).

## Irrational Beliefs Inventory (IBI)

The IBI was developed to improve upon some of the weaknesses of the IBT. This 50-item scale, developed in the Netherlands by Koopmans, Sanderman, Timmerman, and Emmelkamp, is based in part on the item pool of the IBT. Because it measures cognitions rather than negative affect, the IBI avoids the criticisms leveled at the IBT—that beliefs were not measured separately from the negative consequences of those beliefs. The IBI uses a 5-point scale and consists of five subscales (worrying, rigidity, need for approval, problem avoidance, and emotional irresponsibility) plus a total score.

The IBI has consistent psychometric properties across several cultures (Bridges & Sanderman, 2002). Its internal consistency is acceptable, and the five subscales were found to be independent of each other. It has been useful in clinical and research settings when exploring the role of irrational beliefs in obsessive-compulsive disorder, social phobias, and therapy for depression (Bridges & Sanderman, 2002).

## Cognitive Functional Analysis

What people say to themselves also influences behavior. If you tell yourself that you can't learn statistics, then you will likely avoid statistics. Furthermore, when confronted with a difficult statistics problem, you will tend to give up quickly. If you tell yourself you like statistics, you will probably confront difficult statistics problems by taking your time and systematically figuring out the answers. Self-statements have been shown to influence behaviors as diverse as coping behavior in patients with fear of public speaking (Gallego, Emmelkamp, van der Kooij, & Mees, 2011), pain during pregnancy (Chang, Yang, Jensen, Lee, & Lai, 2011), treatment of schizophrenia (Bennouna-Greene, Berna, Conway, Rathbone et al., 2011), and athletic performance (Perkos, Theodorakis, & Chroni, 2002). Interestingly, positive and negative self-statements do not function in the same way. Apparently, negative self-statements do far more harm than positive self-statements do good. Thus, treatment generally involves identifying and then eliminating negative self-statements rather than increasing positive self-statements. Try to become aware of your own self-statements for a moment. What do you say to yourself as you go about your daily activities? Odds are, if you make a lot of negative self-statements, you are hindering your personal efficiency and ability to cope.

One of the most important examples of cognitive-behavioral assessment is called *cognitive-functional analysis* (Meichenbaum, 1976, 2003). The premise underlying a cognitive-functional analysis is that what a person says to him- or herself plays a critical role in behavior. The cognitive-functional analyst is thus interested in internal dialogue such as self-appraisals and expectations. Again, what do you say to yourself about yourself as you go about your daily activities? Do you constantly criticize or belittle yourself? Or do you always reassure yourself of your capabilities? Research clearly indicates these self-statements influence your behavior and even your feelings (Longe, Maratos, & Gilbert, 2010; Martin & Swinson, 2000; Masuda, Twohig, Stormo et al., 2010).

Cognitive-functional analysis is concerned with ascertaining the environmental factors that precede behavior (environmental antecedents) as well as those that maintain behavior (environmental consequences). In addition, however, a cognitive-functional analysis attempts to ascertain the internal or cognitive antecedents and consequences for the behavioral sequence (the internal dialogue). What does the person say to him- or herself before, during, and following the behavior? What is said before the behavior may influence what is done. What is said during the behavior may influence the way the behavior manifests itself. What is said following the behavior may influence its probability of recurrence.

If thoughts influence overt behavior, then modifying one's thoughts can lead to modifications in one's actions. In other words, to the extent that thoughts play a role in eliciting or maintaining one's actions, modification of the thoughts underlying the actions should lead to behavioral changes. For example, if the thought "I must have a cigarette" is consistently associated with the behavioral sequence involved in smoking, then changing that thought to "My lungs are clean, I feel healthy, and I have no desire to smoke" could help to modify the person's pattern of smoking behavior.

Parallel to Meichenbaum's technique of cognitive-functional analysis are procedures and devices that allow a person to test him- or herself, or *self-monitoring devices*. Because cognitive-behavioral practitioners value the role and responsibility of the individual in the therapeutic process, they have developed a wide variety of these devices. In the simplest case, an individual must record the frequency of a particular behavior—that is, to monitor it so that he or she becomes aware of the behavior. To monitor your smoking behavior, simply count the number of cigarettes you smoke each day. To monitor your weight, weigh yourself each morning and record the number of pounds.

Some self-monitoring procedures are quite sophisticated. For example, a mechanical counter, marketed to the general public, can be attached to the jaw to count the number of bites a person takes when eating. The idea is to take fewer bites each day, even if only one less than the day before. Presumably, this procedure will ultimately result in a lower intake of food and eventually weight loss. Similarly, timing devices and procedures allow people to assess how long they engage in an activity. In one method, the subject plugs in a clock every time she studies, thus recording total study time. The goal is to increase this length of time, either by increasing the length of individual study sessions or by increasing the total study time within a specific period. These self-monitoring assessment tools are limited only by the imagination of the practitioner. Azrin and Powell (1968) developed an electronic device that counts the number of times a cigarette case is opened. Treatment is aimed at opening the case fewer times each day. Naturally, one can easily cheat with these devices, but to think of this possibility is to miss the point of these procedures. These devices help people help themselves by increasing awareness through feedback. You test yourself. If you cheat, you cheat yourself. Later in this chapter in our section about computerized psychological tests and measurement, we discuss the latest computer equipment used to analyze thoughts and behaviors regarding everything from social regulation of emotion (Perrez, Wilhelm, Schoebi, & Horner, 2001) to fear responses (South, Larson, White, Dana, & Crowley, 2011).

# Psychophysiological Procedures

Seen as a variant of cognitive-behavioral assessment by some and as an independent category by others, psychophysiological methods of assessment use such indicators as heart rate, blood pressure, galvanic skin response (GSR), and skin temperature to assess psychological problems (Hsieh, Ferrer, Chen, Mauss, John, & Gross, 2011). In essence, psychophysiological assessment procedures attempt to quantify physiological responses (Humphreys, Foley, Feinstein, et al., 2011). This quantification is then translated into psychological factors (Steptoe & Johnston, 1991). Thus, physiological data are used to draw inferences about the psychological state of the individual (Fredrikson, 1991). As Haynes (1991) stated,

"A fundamental tenet of [psychophysiological assessment] is that social, behavioral, cognitive, and emotional phenomena are often a function of, and are often reflected in, physiological processes" (p. 307).

## Physiological Variables with Treatment Implications

The feasibility of psychophysiological assessment received support in an early study conducted by Ax (1953). Ax demonstrated that the fear response was related to specific physiological changes such as increases in blood pressure and skin conductance levels. He found that he could distinguish fear and anger based on physiological data. Ax's early work, which has subsequently been supported (see Ekman, Levenson, & Friesen, 1983; Turpin, 1991), had interesting implications. For instance, it suggested the possibility of assessing abnormally chronic and intense anger or fear through strictly physiological methods.

This type of assessment represents a quantum leap from traditional procedures, which depend on voluntary responses from subjects. In addition, as with other methods of behavioral assessment, psychophysiological assessment has direct implications for treatment (Wichers, Lothmann, Simons, Nicolson, & Peeters, 2011).

The polygraph and related devices that measure blood pressure, heart rate, and GSR have been the primary tools of the psychophysiological assessment specialist. However, imaginative researchers continue to develop tools for special purposes. For example, psychophysiologists have been particularly interested in measuring adult sexual responses (Janssen, Everaerd, Vanlunsen, & Oerlemans, 1994; Morales, 1994). Measures of sexual arousal make use of the fact that it is directly related to the flow of blood into the penis in men and into the vagina in women (Masters & Johnson, 1966; Janssen, 2002). Using this knowledge, researchers have developed measures of human sexual arousal. For example, penile erection can be measured by the penile transducer, a device that encircles the penis (Baxter, Barbaree, & Marshall, 1986; Zuckerman, 1971). As erection occurs, an electrical signal is generated, and this signal can then be recorded. The procedure can be used to determine the type of stimuli (pictures, fantasies, men, women, and so forth) that lead to arousal in men as well as the strength of the male sexual response. The penile transducer and related devices are much more objective than traditional tools.

## Evaluation of Psychophysiological Techniques

Support for psychophysiological assessment has come from investigations that have revealed a systematic covariation between measurable physiological processes and cognitive processes (Jacobson, Bondi, & Salmon, 2002; Kossowsky, Wilhelm, Roth, & Schneider, 2011). For example, Ahern and Beatty (1979) found that more-intelligent subjects show smaller task-evoked pupillary dilations than do less-intelligent subjects (as evaluated by their scores on the SAT Reasoning Test). These results reveal physiological differences in individuals with differing mental abilities. Later research supports these findings (Langer, Pedroni, Gianotti, Hänggi, Knoch, & Jäncke, 2011). In other studies, Beatty and colleagues (e.g., Geiselman, Woodward, & Beatty, 1982) used measures of heart-rate variability and skin conductance to evaluate *processing intensity*, the amount of effort or energy devoted to a cognitive task. Presumably, brighter individuals expend less of their total available processing resources in solving a difficult problem, either because they have greater resources or because they make more efficient use of them.

Psychophysiological hardware seems to hold considerable promise for raising the scientific respectability of psychological testing. Problems still remain, however, and considerably more research and development are needed. One of the most serious problems in psychophysiological assessment concerns artifacts. For instance, movement by a subject may result in the recording of a physiological response that did not occur. In many cases, furthermore, direct measurement is difficult if not impossible. To measure brain-wave patterns, for example, one places electrodes on the head, whereas the electrical current measured actually comes from the brain. Thus, the skull distorts the electrical impulse measured by the recording device. There are other problems as well, including the long-known effect of initial values (Wilder, 1950), by which the strength of a response is influenced by the absolute prestimulus strength. Which is the stronger response: an increase in heart rate from 60 to 85 beats per minute or an increase from 110 to 125 beats per minute? Obviously, one must take initial values into account in evaluating the strength, intensity, and significance of a physiological response. Another problem, which you have seen throughout this book, is that demographic factors such as age, gender, and ethnicity influence psychophysiological responses (Anderson & McNeilly, 1991). Thus, one must always consider cultural, ethnic, economic, gender, and other variables in making any kind of assessment. In spite of these problems, psychophysiological procedures appear to hold great promise for the future of psychological testing.

# Computers and Psychological Testing

The application and use of computers in testing have been a major development in the field (Florell, 2011; Mills, 2002; Clauser, 2002; Wainer, 2000). For testing, one can use computers in two basic ways: (1) to administer, score, and even interpret traditional tests and (2) to create new tasks and perhaps measure abilities that traditional procedures cannot tap. We will briefly look at the history and development of computers and psychological testing and recent applications of computers to the testing field, particularly to cognitive-behavioral assessment. In the last section, we briefly discuss signal-detection procedures.

In 1966, a Rogerian therapist named Eliza marked the beginning of a new phase in psychological testing and assessment (Epstein & Klinkenberg, 2001). With a great amount of empathy, Eliza encouraged her clients to talk about their experiences and how these experiences made them feel. Clients responded warmly and enjoyed the sense of empathy resulting from their interaction. The warmth and connection between Eliza and her clients came as a big surprise to researcher Dr. Joseph Weizenbaum. Eliza was his creation, a computer program developed to emulate the behavior of a psychotherapist. Weizenbaum had produced the program in an attempt to show that human-computer interaction was superficial and ineffective for therapy. Dr. Weizenbaum discovered that sessions with Eliza engendered positive emotions in the clients who had actually enjoyed the interaction and attributed human characteristics to the program. The research by Weizenbaum gave credence to the theory that human–computer interaction may be beneficial and opened the door for further study.

As Fowler (1985) has noted, computers began to be applied to psychological testing almost as soon as they were available. Early on, progress in the use of computer–human interaction in the field of psychology took a decided turn away from psychotherapy and to the area of interview and assessment. Currently, there are numerous programs for administering, scoring, and even interpreting a host of tests.

## Computer-Assisted Interview

As it became apparent that the computer could be an effective means of gathering information from individuals, psychological computer testing began to encompass the presentation of interviews and assessments traditionally completed in paper-and-pencil form. The computer-assisted interview has been used for everything from comprehensive behavioral psychological assessment and diagnostics (Coid et al., 2006) to special topic evaluations such as screenings for suicide (Kohli, Salyakina, Pfennig, et al., 2010), human immunodeficiency virus (HIV) risk (Fenton et al., 2005; Millett, Ding, Marks, et al., 2011; Morin et al., 2005;), depression (Leventhal, Gelernter, Oslin, et al., 2011), sexual behaviors (Dolezal, Marhefka, Santamaria, et al., 2011), drug abuse (Chan, Gelernter, Oslin, Farrer, & Kranzler, 2011), and phobias (Crome, Baillie, Slade, Ruscio, et al., 2010).

Although there has been some controversy as to the equivalence of computer-based interviewing and paper-and-pencil forms, much of the research has indicated that the validity of computer-administered interviews is equal to or better than that of paper-and-pencil forms (Dolezal, Marhefka, Santamaria, et al., 2011; Porter, Forbes, Manzi, & Kalish, 2010). In part, this equivalence can be attributed to the fact that in creating computer-administered versions, it has been the goal to make these tests as similar to the original versions as possible (Epstein & Klinkenberg, 2001).

The explanation for computer versions that produce more accurate assessment is slightly more complicated and often debated. Computer interview success may exceed the interview accomplishments of some clinicians because the computer programs ask more standardized questions, covering areas that a clinician may neglect (Hugh, 1981). It has also been noted by Hugh that computer administration ensures that crucial facts are recorded more systematically.

More important, computer-administered interviews appear to reduce the likelihood of clients skewing their responses in an attempt to appear socially acceptable to the clinician. When gathering information about more sensitive topics, such as sexual behaviors, the popularity of computer-assisted interviews is steadily increasing (Dolezal, Marhefka, Santamaria, et al., 2011). It has been shown that participants are more likely to share sensitive information about other personal subjects when computer-assisted interviewing is used. This has been the case for the evaluation of potentially embarrassing conditions such as incontinence (Parnell, Dunivan, Connolly, et al., 2011). Research consistently shows that the computer-based versions of psychological interviews make individuals more at ease and willing to disclose information concerning issues that might otherwise not be discussed (see Cooley, Rogers, Turner, Al-Tayyib, Willis, & Ganapathii, 2001; Hewitt, 2002; Lessler, Caspar, Penne, & Barker, 2000). Although some studies show the effects of social desirability may be reducing over time (Dwight & Feigelson, 2000), studies of distortion caused by social desirability supports the idea that social desirability has less of an impact with computer-assisted interviewing than with traditional administration (Dolezal, Marhefka, Santamaria, et al., 2011; Lowndes, Jayachandran, Banandur, et al., 2011).

It is interesting to note that as computers become more sophisticated and begin to more closely emulate human characteristics, prompting clients to respond as if they are responding to a human, the likelihood of responding to sensitive personal questions in socially desirable ways does not increase (Tourangeau, Couper, & Steiger, 2003). In fact, people are sometimes more frank and candid in response to a computer than to a skilled therapist.

## Computer-Administered Tests

Traditional assessments other than computer-assisted interviews have also been made available as computer-based tests and the use of computerized testing in assessment has steadily increased in recent years (Blazek & Forbey, 2011). As with computer-assisted interviews, there has been much discussion about the equivalence of the paper-and-pencil forms and the computer-administered versions. A preponderance of the research suggests that, in general, tests such as the Minnesota Multiphasic Personality Inventory (MMPI-2) (Blazek & Forbey, 2011), Big Five Personality tests (Vecchione, Alessandri, & Barbaranelli, 2011), and the Ansell-Casey Life Skills Assessment (Bressani & Downs, 2001) result in similar evaluations when administered by computer or by paper and pencil.

A small number of psychological tests that measure negative affect tend to produce different results than their paper-and-pencil forms (Clay, Lankford, & Wilson, 1992). Some have found that negative affect scores are particularly elevated when testing computer-anxious individuals and using the Beck Depression Inventory. However, more recent analyses have validated the computer administration of the BDI-II against paper-and-pencil administration (Satre, Chi, Eisendrath, & Weisner, 2011).Computer anxiety also has an effect on educational testing and appears to be most pronounced when evaluating math skills (Kröhne & Martens, 2011; Stone & Davey, 2011, p. 20).

Although questions remain about the impact of computer anxiety on test takers (Shermis, Mzumara, & Bublitz, 2001), research suggests the benefits of computer administration outweigh the benefits of paper-and-pencil administration in several ways (Norris, Pauli, & Bray, 2007). Computer administration is generally less time-consuming for both the individual being tested and the test administrator, more cost-effective, better accepted by test takers who are adults or children and often more accurate (Konradt, Syperek, & Hertel, 2011; Kröhne & Martens, 2011).

Computer-administered psychological testing is not without drawbacks. The finer subtleties of human communication cannot be read by a computer program. Body language that may suggest hesitation or distortion of the truth to a human would not be captured by computer (Space, 1981). The use of subtle techniques by the clinician also cannot be emulated by a computer. To gather sensitive information, a clinician's line of questioning must be flexible and selective based on the client's responses (Erdman et al., 1985). Although some programs are becoming sophisticated to the extent that they can sense emotion and adjust responses accordingly (Lopatovska & Arapakis, 2011; Picard & Klein, 2002), they have yet to match the clinician's ability to detect subtle emotional cues.

## Computer Diagnosis, Scoring, and Reporting of Results

From educational testing to tests that evaluate personality and psychopathology, computers are taking a prominent role in the scoring of tests, reporting of results, and diagnosis of clients (Frase et al., 2003; Greenea, 2011).

The effectiveness of computer scoring, computer-generated diagnosis, and narrative reports has been the issue of controversy since their inception (Tallent, 1987). From neuropsychological assessments such as the Halstead-Reitan Battery (Russell, 2000), to personnel screening tests, the scoring and report generation of certain tests seem to be straightforward, efficient, and accurate (Vale, Keller, & Bentz, 1986). Since early in the history of computers in psychological testing, there has been evidence suggesting computer diagnosis provides reliability comparable to that of psychiatrists (Sletten, Ulett, Altman, & Sundland, 1970).

Computer software that has been developed using criteria for diagnosis taken from the *Diagnostic and Statistical Manual of Mental Disorders, Fourth Edition* (DSM-IV) is being developed to screen for psychopathology (Krol, DeBruyn, van Aarle, & van der Bercken, 2001; Leung, French, & Chui, 2007; Simmsa, Goldberg, Roberts, et al., 2011). When the usefulness of this program was examined, it appeared to serve as a supportive function in the process of diagnosis. Others have shown that severity of depression (Mitchell, Smith, Al-salihy, et al., 2011), suicidal ideation (Miranda, Gallagher, Bauchner, et al., 2011), and certain phobias (Grenier, Schuurmans, Goldfarb, et al., 2011) can be effectively diagnosed by computer (Aharonson, Halperin, & Korczyn, 2007).

Projective tests have also been successfully scored by computer for decades. When examining the computer-scoring version of the Holtzman Inkblot Test, validity was confirmed by acceptable correlations between the computer-scoring methods and traditional methods of scoring (Gorham, Moseley, & Holtzman, 1968). Evaluation of the online version of the Rorschach determined that the computer can provide a report similar to that of a clinician (Harris, Robinson, & Menzies, 1981). Similarly, the Rotter Incomplete Sentence Blank showed only small differences between administration types that were not significant once attitudes toward computers were adjusted for (Rasulis, Schuldberg, & Murtagh, 1996).

In the field of educational testing, sophisticated computer programs have been designed to score essays. The oldest system of computerized writing analysis, Project Essay Grade (PEG), was developed in 1966 by E. Page (Rudner & Gagne, 2001). This system analyses the quality of a writing sample by measuring writing traits such as average word length, use of rare words, and the number of semicolons used. For more than 30 years, this system of analysis has consistently shown correlations with human scores as high as .87. A modern version of a PEG is the Expository Text Analysis Tool (ETAT). The ETAT is software designed to analyze text rapidly and objectively (Vidal-Abarca, Reyes, Gilabert, Calpe, Soria, & Graesser, 2002). ETAT accomplishes this task by a symbolic representation system that segments text into nodes, classifies the unidentified nodes, and links them with relational arcs.

The next generation of computerized essay scoring is the Intelligent Essay Assessor (IEA), which was introduced by T. Landauer and P. Foltz (Rudner & Gagne, 2001). The IEA was created in 1989 to index information from documents to allow for simple retrieval of facts. The IEA is used to evaluate essays according to content. This is done by listing every relevant content term used by the writer. Relevant terms are weighted, and a score is derived by a tally of the terms included. As with PEG, IEA scores are highly correlated with human scores.

A newer instrument dubbed "E-rater" (the Educational Testing Services Essay Rater) is a hybrid of PEG and IEA. E-rater analyzes the structure of the essay in the same fashion as PEG and measures the content of the essay as does the IEA. In addition, E-rater measures syntactic variety by counting the number of modal verbs and subordinate, infinitive, complimentary, and relative clauses. Analysis of assessment scores generated by E-rater revealed significant correlations between automated essay scoring and nontest indicators of proficiency such as academic success with writing (Powers, Burstein, Chodorow, Fowles, & Kukich, 2000) and returns grades that are highly correlated with grades given by human scorers (Rudner & Gagne, 2001).

E-rater is currently used in conjunction with human scoring to evaluate the writing tasks on the Test of English as a Foreign Language (TOEFL) Internet-based writing test (Haberman, 2011). TOEFL measures the ability to use and understand English at the university level. In analyzing scoring data from human graders and E-rater, it is clear that E-rater scores are more reliable than are human scores (Haberman, 2011, p. 10).

Caution is still in order, however, and researchers are striving to improve systems such as the E-rater (Lee, Choi, & Kim, 2011). The fact that computer scoring of essays correlates well with human scoring may not be that impressive. The use of essays as components of tests has sometimes been rejected, in part because human scoring of written work tends to be highly subjective, and correlations between human scorers are generally between .70 and .75 (Rudner & Gagne, 2001). In other words, the proficiency of computers to score essays consistently has barely risen to a standard that is rather low and especially problematic when considering the importance of some high-stakes tests.

For every study that confirms the reliability of computer-generated scores, diagnoses, and reports, there is one that suggests caution is in order. Even the most popular tests such as the MMPI have been criticized for including scoring errors (Pope, Butcher, & Seelen, 2000) and generating reports that are markedly less accurate than those of clinicians (Epstein & Rotunda, 2000). Allard and Faust (2000) also detected scoring errors when evaluating the MMPI, the Beck Depression Inventory, and the Spielberger State-Trait Anxiety inventory. The overall message gathered from decades of research concludes that computers are a tool, and interpretations of the scores, reports, and diagnoses they produce are appendages to clinical judgment (Butcher, Perry, & Atlis, 2000) that require the assessment and expertise of clinicians (Russell, 2000).

## Internet Usage for Psychological Testing

The advent of computers and the Internet has revolutionized testing and played a major role in the proliferation of modern techniques. In the early 1990s, the

Internet began to thrive, and its growth, development, and diversity of use have exploded since 1995 (Crespin & Austin, 2002). Today the Internet is inundated with a wide variety of psychological tests: from personality tests that are neither reliable nor valid and meant only for entertainment to tests used in the selection of qualified employees and massive scientifically complex research projects that use the Internet as a source of large numbers of participants and data collection. The Internet has already shown itself to be useful to the science of psychological testing and measurement.

Any interested person can easily find free psychological tests on the World Wide Web. Humanmetrics.com offers an online test based on Jung and Briggs Myers' personality approaches, the results of which provide personality type and guidance on career choices. Teamtechnology.co.uk offers an online test that analyzes styles of leadership, while free-iqtest.net will tell you how intelligent you are. These tests are touted as statistically sound Instruments based on decades of research. Because individuals are often interested in evaluations about themselves, by offering free psychological tests, sites can gather massive amounts of useful data for research purposes.

Although some researchers doubt the quality of data gathered online, the use of the Web to gather data has generally been shown to be adequate (McGraw, Tew, & Williams, 2000; Sethuraman, Kerin, & Cron, 2005). Problems concerning the inability to standardize testing conditions when participants are testing at different locations, using different types of computers, and with different amounts of distraction in their environments may be compensated for by the massive sample sizes available to Web-based laboratories. Davis (1999) has shown that results gathered from Web-based participants in different environments did not covary. A study that compared Web-based assessment, traditional paper-and-pencil assessment, and Web-based assessment in a disruptive environment found no significant differences between assessment techniques and resulted in significantly high test–retest reliability coefficients for all three types of administration (Miller et al., 2002). Traditional tests conducted via the Internet are found to have similar results to their paper-and-pencil versions (Cronk & West, 2002) and to include less error in data collection (Pettit, 2002; Miller et al., 2002). It is also becoming evident that Web-based samples can more closely match the intended sample (McCabe, Boyd, Couper, Crawford, & D'Arcy, 2002), especially when methods that are used to publicize the project target specific interests (Epstein & Klinkenberg, 2002). And, once again, some evidence suggests that, as with the use of the computer alone, Web-based testing facilitates more thorough self-disclosure from participants (Davis, 1999).

The ease at which participants can be recruited to participate in online testing, the ease of data collection, and the reduction of error make Web-based data collection appealing to researchers (Pettit, 2002) and ensure its use in the future.

## The Computerization of Cognitive-Behavioral Assessment

Farrell (1992) has identified seven major applications of computers to cognitive-behavioral assessment: (1) collecting self-report data, (2) coding observational data, (3) directly recording behavior, (4) training, (5) organizing and synthesizing behavioral assessment data, (6) analyzing behavioral assessment data, and (7) supporting decision making. As Farrell notes, the computerization of cognitive-behavioral self-report tests, such as those discussed earlier in the chapter, would be a relatively simple endeavor. Once computerized, such questionnaires could be easily administered and immediately scored by the computer, thus saving valuable professional time.

According to Farrell (1991), several factors have impeded the widespread use of computers in cognitive-behavioral assessment. Perhaps first among these is lack of acceptance by some practitioners. Another obstacle to this use of computers involves evaluation of software (Farrell, 1992). Apparently, vendors are reluctant to make their products available for review; consequently, potential users do not have sufficient information to evaluate the quality of the software. Despite such obstacles, it seems inevitable that the future will see a greater use of computers in all areas of assessment.

As with other computer-based psychological assessments, computer-based cognitive-behavioral evaluations appear to have equivalent results as their paper-and-pencil counterparts (Franceschina, Dorz, & Bari, 2001). In addition to success in computer-based evaluation, computer-based cognitive-behavioral treatments have been found effective for the motivation, engagement, and treatment of drug-dependent individuals (Bickel, Christensen, & Marsch, 2011) and for treating anxiety disorders (Khanna, Aschenbrand, & Kendall, 2007), including generalized anxiety disorder (Lorian, Titov, & Grisham, 2011), panic disorder (Carper, McHugh, & Barlow, 2011), and social phobia (Heimberg, 2001). They have also been found useful for evaluating body image disturbance in individuals with eating disorders (Shibata, 2002), levels of conflict and cooperation in individuals' social interactions (Aidman & Shmelyov, 2002), and different aspects of individuals' natural social, linguistic, and psychological lives (Mehl, Pennebaker, Crow, Dabbs, & Price, 2001).

Newman, Szkodny, Llera, and Przeworski (2011) conducted a review of research on the efficacy of computer-assisted self-help in conjunction with minimal contact therapies for drug and alcohol abuse and smoking addiction. They found that, in the treatment of substance use and abuse, self-administered and predominantly self-help computer-based cognitive and behavioral interventions are efficacious, but some therapist contact is important for greater and more sustained reductions in addictive behavior. Similarly, evaluations of a palmtop computer-based treatment for panic disorder has been shown to be effective (Newman et al., 1997). Comparisons were made between panic disorder symptom improvement by a group using 12 sessions of cognitive-behavioral treatment without the aid of a computer, and a group using only four sessions of cognitive-behavioral treatment with the aid of a computer. The computer-based treatment group carried palmtop computers with a cognitive-behavioral treatment program that they were told to use whenever they felt anxious or wanted to practice techniques. Although the computer-based treatment group did not show any greater improvement than the traditionally treated group at the time of follow-up, it is noteworthy that the computer-based group only required four sessions for an equivalent level of improvement.

The use of computers in cognitive-behavioral therapy substantially improves the quality and effectiveness of traditional techniques. The ability for a client to instantly record a target behavior and to access a tool to help deal with the behavior as it occurs is efficient and reduces the length of time needed to alter a pattern of behavior.

Computer programs can also generate schedules of reinforcement including fixed ratio, variable ratio, fixed interval, and variable interval schedules (Wolach & McHale, 2002). A cumulative recording of subjects' responses can then be documented, simplifying the evaluation concerning the effectiveness of the type of schedule used.

## Tests Possible Only by Computer

In addition to tests that are merely computer-friendly versions of their traditional paper-and-pencil forms and tests conducted over the Internet, there are developments in psychological testing made possible only with the use of computers.

The use of computer-generated virtual reality programs for psychological testing and treatment of phobias has grown rapidly in the past decade (Bohil, Alicea, & Biocca, 2011). Virtual reality technology is ideal for safely and efficiently exposing clients to the objects of their phobias while evaluating physiological responses (Wiederhold, Jang, Kim, & Wiederhold, 2002), systematically recording those responses, and evaluating patient improvement (Bohil, Alicea, & Biocca, 2011). Equipment that measures heart rate, skin resistance, and skin temperature informs clinicians of the level of distress caused by a phobia and levels of improvement as treatment continues.

Virtual reality environments that mimic an airplane ride, an encounter with a spider, social situations, and being in front of an audience have all been found to engender the same reactions as the actual environment, only to a lesser degree and with the added confidence of the client being in control of the program. Studies that have measured physiological responses have found that controlled exposure to virtual environments can desensitize individuals to the object of their fear (Wiederhold et al., 2002). When using virtual reality to treat and measure fear responses associated with spider phobia, Garcia-Palacios and colleagues (2002) found that 83% of those being treated showed clinical signs of improvement. There have also been studies boasting success rates of 65 to 80% when treating fear of flying (Maltby, Kirsch, Mayers, & Allen, 2002; Mühlberger, Weik, Pauli, & Wiedemann, 2006; Rothbaum, Anderson, Zimand, Hodges, Lang, & Wilson, 2006; Wiederhold, Gervirtz, & Spira, 2001), and great improvements have been seen when treating clients with claustrophobia (Safir & Wallach, 2011), fear of public speaking (Lee et al., 2002), fear of driving (Mühlberger, Bülthoff, & Wiedemann, 2007; Wald & Taylor, 2000), and fear of heights (Cottraux, 2005; Pull, 2005).

Because of the relative safety of facing one's fear in a virtual environment, because virtual reality reduces the possibility of embarrassment to clients (Bohil, Alicea, & Biocca, 2011), and because virtual reality requires less time and money to conduct than does in vivo desensitization, it is seen as ideal for the treatment and measurement of phobic responses. These positive attributes of virtual reality also make individuals with phobias more likely to seek and complete treatment (Garcia-Palacios, Hoffman, See, Tsai, & Botella, 2001). The success of virtual reality in the treatment of phobias has spawned interest in those who are looking for improved ways to evaluate and treat those with schizophrenia, attention deficit and hyperactivity disorder, autism (Costa, De Carvalho, Drummond, Wauke, & De Sa Guimaraes, 2002), posttraumatic stress disorder (Wood, Murphy, Center, et al., 2007), obsessive compulsive disorder, body image disorders (North,

North, & Coble, 2002), and sexual dysfunction (Vincelli & Riva, 2000). Interesting concepts, including the use of interactive computer games with embedded recording and assessment facilities that measure responses to virtual situations, are beginning to be used in the assessment of personality and psychopathology (Aidman & Shmelyov, 2002). Interactive virtual reality programs are also being appraised as a tool for educational assessment (Byers, 2001). As computer technology advances, computer-generated virtual reality will play a major role in several areas of psychological testing and measurement in the coming decades.

## Computer-Adaptive Testing

Although to a smaller extent traditional tests allow for some adaptation according to the test taker's responses, advancements in computer technology have allowed for the construction of tests that adapt and metamorphize according to each response given. After each response, the computer updates the estimation of the test taker's ability. That estimation is then used to select the next item on the test. The selection of only items necessary for the evaluation of the test taker limits the number of items needed for an exact evaluation. Computer-adaptive tests have been found to be more precise and efficient than fixed-item tests (Kantrowitz, Dawson & Fetzer, 2011). Over the past two decades, computer-adaptive tests have been used for classroom testing (Wang, Chang, & Huebner, 2011), for evaluating general intelligence (Murphy, 2010), in the selection process for remedial instruction (Saine, Lerkkanen, Ahonen, Tolvanen, & Lyytinen, 2011), to assess military personnel (PACE 2011) and employees (Kantrowitz, Dawson, & Fetzer, 2011), for college and graduate student placement, and in nursing licensure (Economides, & Roupas, 2007; Schmidt, 2000).

There are several practical benefits of computer-adaptive testing (Rudner, 1998). One benefit that is enjoyed by test takers is the decrease in time needed for test taking. In addition, efficiency is increased as scores are immediately recorded and made available. Expenses are reduced because no highly trained test administrators are needed because the computer acts as administrator. Finally, computer-adaptive tests are self-paced and provide accurate scores for test takers whose abilities range from gifted to impaired.

However, there are limitations to computer-adaptive tests. There may be some difficulty in presenting long reading passages, intricate graphs, or artwork. Computer-adaptive tests may not be suitable for all test subjects or skills. They may not calibrate with paper-and-pencil versions. Administrator facility with a large number of computers is required for group testing. The computer literacy levels of test takers may significantly affect performance. Finally, examinees often question the equity of computer-adaptive tests as each test taker answers a different set of questions.

One of the most frequently debated drawbacks of computer-adaptive testing is the inability of test takers to go back and change previously answered questions (Wise, Finney, Enders, Freeman, & Severance, 1999). If allowed to do so, a test taker could purposefully answer the initial items incorrectly. The computer would then generate a simpler test for which the examinee is overqualified. After answering the simpler questions correctly, the examinee could then go back to the initial questions and change them to the right answer. Although some feel that this strategy would not be attractive to test takers (Wise et al., 1999), caution is still in order when considering item review.

In addition, there is concern that a test taker who is reviewing a completed test may be able to distinguish easier items from difficult items. The examinee would then be aware of which items were answered incorrectly and change the incorrect answers according to that feedback. Although this argument against item review in computer-adaptive testing appears to be sound, Wise and colleagues (1999) and others (Green, 1983) have found that test takers do not discriminate well between easy and difficult questions and therefore would not be informed of which items were answered incorrectly.

Regardless of the drawbacks, computer-adaptive testing is highly effective and frequently used. Of the Educational Testing Service's 11 million test administrations worldwide each year, some of its most frequently used tests [Graduate Record Examination (GRE), GMAT, and Test of English as a Foreign Language (TOEFL)] are computer-adaptive.

## Psychophysical and Signal-Detection Procedures

An early impetus for using computers to generate tasks that one cannot present through traditional methods came from the application of psychophysical and signal-detection procedures. In these procedures, a signal is presented and the subject is required to report whether he or she saw it. Many variations in presenting a signal are possible. The examiner can vary the strength of the signal, use more than one signal and require the subject to guess which one has been presented, or follow the signal with noise or another signal to determine the effects of one signal on another.

Saccuzzo and colleagues suggest that one can use psychophysical methods to evaluate psychological disorders and perhaps detect them in their early stages (Saccuzzo, 1977, 1981; Saccuzzo & Braff, 1981, 1986; Saccuzzo, Kerr, Marcus, & Brown, 1979; Saccuzzo & Miller, 1977; Saccuzzo & Schubert, 1981). In a series of studies, beginning with Saccuzzo, Hirt, and Spencer (1974), Saccuzzo provided considerable evidence that schizophrenia may be related to the speed with which information is transferred throughout the nervous system (Saccuzzo, 1993). If schizophrenia does in fact develop because of slow processing by the individual, then it seems sensible to use a direct measure of processing speed to assess schizophrenia rather than indirect procedures such as the Rorschach.

Indeed, one can assess information-processing speed by flashing two stimuli in brief succession on a microcomputer screen or a tachistoscope. If a stimulus, such as the letter *T*, is presented and then terminated, the information is first registered by the nervous system. After the information is registered, it theoretically enters a brief perceptual memory system, which Neisser (1967) calls *iconic storage*. The person does not become consciously aware of the stimulus until it is transferred to the higher brain centers, where it is compared with previous learning. The rate of this transfer of information is the speed of information processing (Saccuzzo et al., 1974).

If a stimulus that has been presented and terminated is then followed by a second, noninformational stimulus such as a random pattern, the second and first stimuli may become integrated together in the visual system. Only this unidentifiable composite will then be transferred to the higher brain centers. Obviously, if this

Target:          T    or    A

                              X
Mask:                  X  X
                              X

**FIGURE 9.3**

Target and mask in signal detection. In signal-detection experiments, the target and mask are presented to the same visual area in close temporal succession. The minimum interval between presentation of the target and presentation of the mask at which the mask no longer interferes with processing of the target is used to evaluate the information-processing speed.

occurs, the individual will not be able to identify the originally presented *T*. However, if the *T* is transferred to the higher centers before the noninformational stimulus is presented, then the person can identify the letter. By finding the minimum interval between presentation of the letter and presentation of the noninformational stimulus at which the noninformational stimulus no longer interferes with processing of the letter, one can estimate how long it took the letter to reach the higher centers (Saccuzzo & Miller, 1977). Thus, the speed of information processing can be determined by finding this minimum interval (see Figure 9.3). Furthermore, one can often use this information for diagnostic purposes. For example, Saccuzzo and colleagues have shown that schizophrenic people can be distinguished from normal people and others (e.g., neurotic people) on the basis of information-processing speed (see Alain, Bernstein, He, Cortese, & Zipursky, 2002; Li, 2002; Saccuzzo, Cadenhead, & Braff, 1996). Normal people require a much shorter interval (150 milliseconds) to avoid the effects of the noninformational stimulus than do schizophrenics (300 milliseconds) (Saccuzzo et al., 1974).

Psychophysical and signal-detection procedures have also been applied to ability testing (Ruberto, Vassos, Lewis, et al., 2011). Reaction time and backward masking tasks (in which a briefly presented informational target stimulus is followed by a noninformational noise stimulus known as a *mask*) are used to measure the speed, capacity, or efficiency of information processing (Saccuzzo, Larson, & Rimland, 1986). The general idea is that variations among individuals who differ in psychometric intelligence reflect different information-processing capabilities (Mervis & Robinson, 2003).

Support for a relationship between information-processing capabilities and individual differences in intelligence has come from studies in which the individual must make a rapid response to two or more choices (Jensen, 1979; Jensen & Munro, 1979; Lunneborg, 1978; Smith & Stanley, 1983). When one uses parameters such as median reaction time, slope of reaction time as a function of the number of choices, and intraindividual standard deviations of reaction-time performance, large differences emerge between groups with mental retardation and those with normal IQs as well as between groups of vocational college students and university students (Jensen, 1980, 1982). However, results differ across samples (Lunneborg, 1978). Although the correlations vary widely, with estimates ranging from the high .60's to the low .20's, the correlations are almost always in the expected direction (Jensen, 1982).

The visual paradigm for studying the relationship between information processing and intelligence, in which the subject must respond to a visual stimulus,

Stimulus: ————————— ● —————————

Mask: ————————————————————

FIGURE 9.4

Stimuli used in signal-detection studies of intelligence. The stimulus and mask are presented in close temporal succession. The subject must estimate which line is longer.

parallels the backward masking approach used by Saccuzzo and colleagues to study schizophrenia. The subject is required to discriminate between two briefly exposed target stimuli, such as identifying which of two lines presented to the right and left of central fixation is longer (see Figure 9.4). The targets are then followed by a spatially overlapping, noninformational mask (e.g., two uniform lines that completely superimpose the lines of the target stimulus). Extensive literature indicates that the mask limits the time the informational impulse is available for processing in the nervous system (Felsten & Wasserman, 1980). Speed of processing, or inspection time (Vickers, Nettelbeck, & Wilson, 1972), can be evaluated by systematically varying the exposure duration of the target and estimating the minimum duration needed for accuracy (Brand, 1981; Lally & Nettelbeck, 1977; Nettelbeck & Lally, 1976) or by keeping the stimulus duration constant and varying the interval between target and mask (Saccuzzo et al., 1979; Saccuzzo & Marcus, 1983).

Numerous studies have reported a statistically significant (nonchance) difference between mentally retarded and nonretarded (average IQ) individuals in their speed of visual information processing as evaluated in a backward masking paradigm (Saccuzzo et al., 1979; Saccuzzo & Michael, 1984). Such differences occur in spite of wide variations in the nature of the stimuli, method of stimulus presentation, and technique used to estimate visual processing speed (Saccuzzo & Michael, 1984). In addition, there are clear-cut developmental differences, with a direct relationship between chronological or mental age and performance (Blake, 1974; Liss & Haith, 1970; Saccuzzo et al., 1979). Gifted children have a greater speed of processing than do nongifted children (Saccuzzo, Johnson, & Guertin, 1994). Finally, the evidence supports a significant relationship between degrees of normal intelligence and visual information processing. As in reaction-time studies, however, correlations vary widely, and the magnitude of the relationship remains highly controversial (Mackintosh, 1981; Nettelbeck, 1982).

The signal-detection approach offers many advantages over other procedures. Scoring can be simplified, administration can be easily standardized, and the effects of the examiner can be minimized. Developers have adapted the reaction time and backward masking tasks for presentation by personal computers (see Brand, 1981; Saccuzzo & Larson, 1987; Saccuzzo et al., 1986; Mallinckrodt, Tamura, & Tanaka, 2011). With standard software, independent investigators can readily verify results from psychophysical and signal-detection procedures. Thus far, the findings seem to indicate a clear but modest relationship between information-processing capabilities and intelligence (Saccuzzo et al., 1994). In addition, there appears to be an interesting relationship between perceptual sensitivity and response bias and "Big Five" personality factors (Rose, Murphy, Byard, & Nikzad, 2002).

In their current state of development, however, information-processing tests cannot replace more standard procedures, but are used as a check for accuracy because the objectivity of assessment is markedly enhanced.

Because of the objectivity of signal detection assessment, this approach is used as a baseline measure of the effects of medications. Mallinckrodt, Tamura, & Tanaka, (2011) analyzed available data from 2007–2010. They found that signal detection assessment of the effects of intervention shows better control of false positive and false negative results which are due to the placebo effect. In addition, signal detection is used to detect *overclaiming* (Swami, Papanicolaou & Furnham, 2011). Akin to faking good, overclaiming is a concrete operationalization of self-enhancement based on respondents' ratings of their knowledge. Using signal detection analysis, Swami et al. (2011), used responses on the overclaiming measure to compute an accuracy index.

## Summary

Cognitive-behavioral procedures differ from traditional tests in that they are more direct, have fewer inferential assumptions, and remain closer to observable phenomena. Traditional tests are based on the medical model, which views the overt manifestations of psychological disorders merely as symptoms of some underlying cause. This underlying cause is the target of the traditional procedures. Cognitive-behavioral tests are based on the belief that the overt manifestations of psychological disorders are more than mere symptoms. Although possibly caused by some other factor, the behaviors themselves—including actions, thoughts, and physiological processes—are the targets of behavioral tests.

In cognitive-behavioral assessment based on *operant conditioning*, one must first identify the critical response or responses involved in a disorder. These critical responses are then evaluated for frequency, intensity, or duration. The resulting data provide the baseline for the particular behaviors. Once a baseline is obtained, an intervention is introduced. The effect of this intervention on the baseline is then observed.

*Self-report techniques* focus on situations that lead to particular response patterns, whereas traditional procedures focus on determining the internal characteristics of the individual that lead to particular response patterns. Furthermore, the cognitive-behavioral procedures purport to be more related to observable phenomena than are traditional procedures.

Kanfer and Saslow developed the *functional*, or *behavior-analytic, approach* to cognitive-behavioral assessment. Rather than labeling people as schizophrenic or neurotic, this approach focuses on behavioral deficits and excesses. A behavioral excess is any behavior described as problematic because of excesses in its frequency, intensity, duration, or because of its inappropriateness; a behavioral deficit is the opposite (occurs too infrequently, etc.).

One of the most important examples of the cognitive-behavioral assessment approach is Meichenbaum's technique, *cognitive-functional analysis*. The premise underlying cognitive-functional analysis is that what a person says to him- or herself plays a critical role in determining behavior. A cognitive-functional analysis ascertains the environmental factors that precede behavior as well as those that maintain it. In addition, this kind of analysis attempts to ascertain the internal or cognitive antecedents and consequences of a behavioral sequence.

An important development is the application of computers to testing. In the psychophysical and signal-detection approaches, computers present tasks that cannot be given by traditional means. For example, the subject is required to make a visual discrimination or to respond rapidly to a stimulus in an effort to measure information-processing capabilities. Computers are also used more and more frequently for testing in all its phases, from administration to analysis; however, care must be taken in using computers wisely. Farrel (1992) has identified seven applications of computers in the field of cognitive-behavioral assessment: (1) collecting self-report data, (2) coding observational data, (3) directly recording behavior, (4) training, (5) organizing and synthesizing behavioral assessment data, (6) analyzing behavioral assessment data, and (7) supporting decision making.

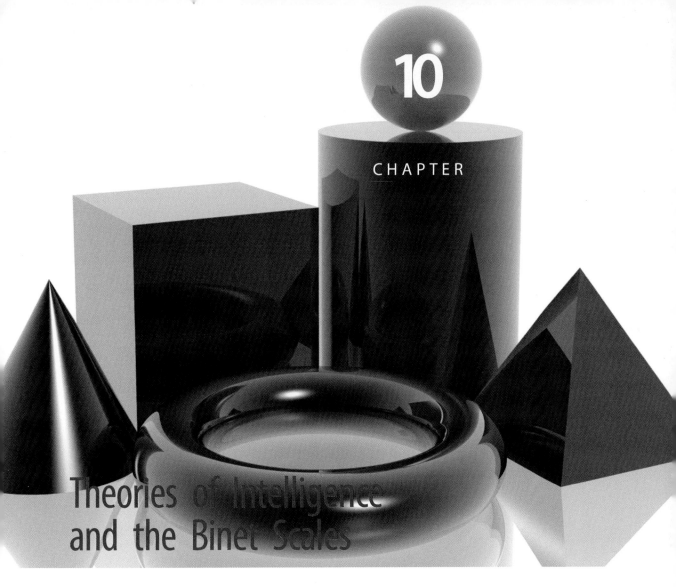

CHAPTER

**10**

# Theories of Intelligence and the Binet Scales

## LEARNING OBJECTIVES

*When you have completed this chapter, you should be able to:*

► Explain how Binet and other psychologists have defined intelligence

► Compare Spearman's g with contemporary *gf-gc* theory

► Identify Binet's two guiding principles of test construction

► Describe the concept of age differentiation

► Describe the concept of mental age (MA)

► Describe the intelligence quotient (IQ) concept

► Define deviation IQ

► Discuss the various editions of the Stanford-Binet Intelligence Scale

Three 8-year-old children, Fred, Maria, and Roberto, were being evaluated for a special program for the gifted in a magnet school. Those who qualified would be placed in a special accelerated program in which the student–teacher ratio was 15 to 1 rather than the usual 25 to 1. The gifted program also had special funds for enrichment programs such as field trips and hands-on exposure to computers. To qualify, a child had to score three standard deviations above the mean on the Stanford-Binet Intelligence Scale (fifth edition; Roid, 2003a, 2003b, 2003c).

Because the Stanford-Binet is standardized, all three children were exposed to the same conditions. The test began with a set of vocabulary items.

Only Maria scored high enough on the test to be placed in the gifted program. Given that all children were exposed to the same test conditions, can we rest assured that the procedure was fair and that Maria was indeed the most intelligent of the three? As critical thinkers, we of course cannot give an unqualified "Yes" to the question. We need much more information.

# The Problem of Defining Intelligence

To say that one person is more intelligent than a second, we must be prepared to define *intelligence*. Unfortunately, of all the major concepts in the field of testing, intelligence is among the most elusive (see Fletcher & Hattie, 2011).

Alfred Binet, one of the original authors of the test that bears his name, defined intelligence as "the tendency to take and maintain a definite direction; the capacity to make adaptations for the purpose of attaining a desired end, and the power of autocriticism" (cited in Terman, 1916, p. 45). Spearman (1923), by contrast, defined intelligence as the ability to educe either relations or correlates. According to Freeman (1955), intelligence is "adjustment or adaptation of the individual to his total environment," "the ability to learn," and "the ability to carry on abstract thinking" (pp. 60–61). And Das (1973) defined intelligence as "the ability to plan and structure one's behavior with an end in view" (p. 27). H. Gardner (1983) defined intelligence in terms of the ability "to resolve genuine problems or difficulties as they are encountered" (p. 60), while Sternberg (1986, 1988) defined intelligence in terms of "mental activities involved in purposive adaptation to, shaping of, and selection of real-world environments relevant to one's life" (1986, p. 33). For Anderson (2001), intelligence is two-dimensional and based on individual differences in information-processing speed and executive functioning influenced largely by inhibitory processes. More recent views depict intelligence as a blend of abilities including personality and various aspects of memory (Deary, Penke, & Johnson, 2010).

Such definitions reflect the more general trends and theories that researchers follow. T. R. Taylor (1994) identified three independent research traditions that have been employed to study the nature of human intelligence: the psychometric, the information-processing, and the cognitive approaches. The *psychometric approach* examines the elemental structure of a test (DiStefano & Dombrowski, 2006; Taylor, 1994). Following the psychometric approach, we examine the properties of a test through an evaluation of its correlates and underlying dimensions (Helmbold & Rammsayer, 2006). In the *information-processing* approach, we examine the processes that underlie how we learn and solve problems (Gary, 2010). Finally, the cognitive tradition focuses on how humans adapt to real-world demands (Sternberg, Mio, & Mio, 2009). Of the three approaches, the psychometric is the oldest and is the focus of this chapter. (The information-processing and cognitive approaches will be discussed more thoroughly in Chapter 9.) As you will see, Binet's approach is based heavily on the psychometric tradition.

Returning to our example, how can we begin to judge whether the Binet test allowed testers to judge the three children fairly? A test such as the Binet that examines one's ability to define words and identify numerical sequences certainly does not meet the standards of all or even most definitions of intelligence. Even if we assume that the Stanford-Binet scale is a valid measure of intelligence, can we safely say that the evaluation procedure for Fred, Maria, and Roberto was fair?

Again, we cannot answer unequivocally. Roberto, a Mexican American, had Spanish-speaking parents, neither of whom finished high school. His father spent most of his life working as a farmer. Fred, an African American, came from a family of five children. As with Roberto, neither of Fred's parents completed high school. Although Fred's father worked long hard hours as a machine operator on an assembly line, the family was poor. Maria's parents, by contrast, had a combined income of $300,000 per year and were well educated. Her mother was a clinical psychologist, her father an attorney.

There is a correlation between socioeconomic background and scores on all standardized intelligence tests (Bornstein, Hahn, Suwalsky, & Haynes, 2003; Hart, Petrill, Deckard, & Thompson, 2007), including Stanford-Binet (Sangwan, 2001). Thus, many people have charged that intelligence tests are biased, especially against ethnic minorities and the poor (Hays, 2001; Miele, 2002). Ironically, intelligence tests were initially developed to eliminate subjectivity in the evaluation of children's ability. And it should be noted that among standardized tests, the Stanford-Binet fifth edition is among the best in providing appropriate cautions for test users.

For many people, the topic of intelligence testing arouses strong feelings and sometimes strong personal biases, even among experts (Naglieri & Goldstein, 2009; Reynolds & Ramsay, 2003). Proponents hold that properly used intelligence tests provide an objective standard of competence and potential (Greisinger, 2003). Critics charge that intelligence tests are not only biased against certain racial and economic groups (Jones, 2003) but also used by those in power to maintain the status quo (Gould, 1981). In fact, intelligence tests have been under attack almost from their inception.

Formal intelligence testing began with a decision of a French minister of public instruction around the turn of the 20th century. Some people today might criticize the minister's decision to create a procedure for identifying intellectually limited individuals so they could be removed from the regular classroom and receive special educational experiences. This decision provided the force behind the development of modern intelligence tests and the heated controversy now associated with them.

In 1904, the French minister officially appointed a commission, to which he gave a definite assignment: to recommend a procedure for identifying so-called subnormal (intellectually limited) children. One member of this commission, Alfred Binet, had demonstrated his qualifications for the job by his earlier research on human abilities (Binet, 1890a, 1890b). The task of the commission was indeed formidable. No one doubted that human beings were capable of incredible accomplishments, which obviously reflected intelligence. Nor was there much doubt that differences existed among individuals in their level of intelligence. But how was one to define intelligence?

Binet and his colleagues had few guideposts. A study by Wissler (1901) indicated that simple functions such as reaction time and sensory acuity failed to discriminate well among individuals of high and low scholastic ability. Therefore, Binet looked for complex processes in his struggle to understand human intelligence. However, unlike today, there were few available definitions of intelligence. Binet's first problem was to decide what he wanted to measure—that is, to define intelligence. Beginning with this definition, Binet and his colleagues developed the world's first intelligence test.

# Binet's Principles of Test Construction

As you have seen, Binet defined intelligence as the capacity (1) to find and maintain a definite direction or purpose, (2) to make necessary adaptations—that is, strategy adjustments—to achieve that purpose, and (3) to engage in self-criticism so that necessary adjustments in strategy can be made. In choosing a definition, Binet took the necessary first step in developing a measure of intelligence.

However, he still faced the problem of deciding exactly what he wanted to measure. Because Binet believed that intelligence expressed itself through the judgmental, attentional, and reasoning facilities of the individual (Binet & Simon, 1905), he decided to concentrate on finding tasks related to these three facilities.

In developing tasks to measure judgment, attention, and reasoning, Binet used trial and error as well as experimentation and hypothesis-testing procedures. He was guided by two major concepts that to this day underlie not only the Binet scale but also major modern theories of intelligence: age differentiation and general mental ability. These principles, which perhaps represent Binet's most profound contribution to the study of human intelligence, provided the foundation for subsequent generations of human ability tests.

## Principle 1: Age Differentiation

**Age differentiation** refers to the simple fact that one can differentiate older children from younger children by the former's greater capabilities. For example, whereas most 9-year-olds can tell that a quarter is worth more than a dime, a dime is worth more than a nickel, and so on, most 4-year-olds cannot. In employing the principle of age differentiation, Binet searched for tasks that could be completed by between 66.67% and 75% of the children of a particular age group and also by a smaller proportion of younger children but a larger proportion of older ones. Thus, Binet eventually assembled a set of tasks that an increasing proportion of children could complete as a function of increases in age.

Using these tasks, he could estimate the mental ability of a child in terms of his or her completion of the tasks designed for the average child of a particular age, regardless of the child's actual or chronological age. A particular 5-year-old child might be able to complete tasks that the average 8-year-old could complete. On the other hand, another 5-year-old might not be capable of completing even those tasks that the average 3-year-old could complete. With the principle of age differentiation, one could determine the equivalent age capabilities of a child independent of his or her chronological age. This equivalent age capability was eventually called *mental age*. If a 6-year-old completed tasks that were appropriate for the average 9-year-old, then the 6-year-old had demonstrated that he or she had capabilities equivalent to those of the average 9-year-old, or a mental age of 9. Today, psychologists use the more sophisticated technique of item response theory (see Chapter 7) and other techniques to accomplish the goal of evaluating age equivalent capabilities (Bolt, 2003; Horn, 2005; Roid, 2003a).

## Principle 2: General Mental Ability

Binet was also guided in his selection of tasks by his decision to measure only the total product of the various separate and distinct elements of intelligence, that is, *general mental ability*. With this concept, Binet freed himself from the burden of identifying each element or independent aspect of intelligence. He also was freed from finding the relation of each element to the whole. Binet's decision to measure general mental ability was based, in part, on practical considerations. He could restrict the search for tasks to anything related to the total or the final product of intelligence. He could judge the value of any particular task in terms of its correlation with the combined result (total score) of all other tasks. Tasks with low correlations could be eliminated, and tasks with high correlations retained. The notion of general mental ability is critical to understanding modern conceptions of human intelligence as well as the various editions of the Binet from the first through the present modern fifth edition.

# Spearman's Model of General Mental Ability

Binet was not alone in his conception of general mental ability. Before Binet, this notion was propounded by F. Galton (1869) in his classic work, *Hereditary Genius: An Inquiry into Its Laws and Consequences* (see Chapter 1). Independently of Binet, in Great Britain, Charles Spearman (1904, 1927) advanced the notion of a general mental ability factor underlying all intelligent behavior (see Thorndike, 1990a, 1990b). According to Spearman's theory, intelligence consists of one general factor ($g$) plus a large number of specific factors (see Figure 10.1). Spearman's notion of general mental ability, which he referred to as *psychometric g* (or simply $g$), was based on the well-documented phenomenon that when a set of diverse ability tests are administered to large unbiased samples of the population, almost all of the correlations are positive. This phenomenon is called *positive manifold*, which,

**FIGURE 10.1**

Spearman's model of intelligence. According to the model, intelligence can be viewed in terms of one general underlying factor ($g$) and a large number of specific factors ($S_1$, $S_2$, ... $S_n$). Thus, intelligence can be viewed in terms of $g$ (general mental ability) and $S$ (specific factors). Spearman's theory was consistent with Binet's approach to constructing the first intelligence test.

according to Spearman, resulted from the fact that all tests, no matter how diverse, are influenced by $g$. For Spearman, $g$ could best be conceptualized in terms of mental energy.

To understand how a single general factor can underlie all intelligent behavior, consider the analogy of a central power station for a large metropolitan city. The same station provides the power for lights of all sizes and types. Although some lights may be brighter or better than others, all depend on power from the central power source. Reducing the output from the central source affects all of the lights.

To support the notion of $g$, Spearman developed a statistical technique called *factor analysis* (Willis, Dumont, & Kaufman, 2011). Factor analysis is a method for reducing a set of variables or scores to a smaller number of hypothetical variables called *factors*. Through factor analysis, one can determine how much variance a set of tests or scores has in common (Abbott, Amtmann, & Munson, 2003; Lorenzo-Seva, 2003; Timmerman & Kiers, 2003). This common variance represents the $g$ factor. The $g$ in a factor analysis of any set of mental ability tasks can be represented in the first unrotated factor in a principal components analysis (Saccuzzo, Johnson, & Guertin, 1994). Spearman found that, as a general rule, approximately half of the variance in a set of diverse mental-ability tests is represented in the $g$ factor. Today, Spearman's $g$ "is the most established and ubiquitous predictor of occupational and educational performance" (Willis, Dumont, & Kaufman, 2011).

## Implications of General Mental Intelligence (*g*)

The concept of general intelligence implies that a person's intelligence can best be represented by a single score, $g$, that presumably reflects the shared variance underlying performance on a diverse set of tests. True, performance on any given individual task can be attributed to $g$ as well as to some specific or unique variance (just as the luminance of a light depends on the central power source as well as the individual qualities of the light). However, if the set of tasks is large and broad enough, the role of any given task can be reduced to a minimum. Differences in unique ability stemming from the specific task tend to cancel each other, and overall performance comes to depend most heavily on the general factor. Such reasoning guided the development of the Binet scale as well as all its subsequent revisions through the most current fifth edition (Roid, 2003a).

## The *gf-gc* Theory of Intelligence

Recent theories of intelligence have suggested that human intelligence can best be conceptualized in terms of multiple intelligences rather than a single score (Furnham & Petrides, 2003; Mulhollen, 2007; Riggio, Murphy, & Pirozzolo, 2002). One such theory is called the *gf-gc* theory (Horn & Noll, 1997; Horn & Blankson, 2005).

According to *gf-gc* theory, there are two basic types of intelligence: fluid (*f*) and crystallized (*c*). Fluid intelligence can best be thought of as those abilities that allow us to reason, think, and acquire new knowledge (Kane & Engle, 2002; Primi, 2002; Stankov, 2003). Crystallized intelligence, by contrast, represents the knowledge and understanding that we have acquired (Bates & Shieles, 2003; Horn & Masunaga, 2006). You might think of this distinction in terms of the abilities that allow us to learn and acquire information (fluid) and the actual learning that has occurred (crystallized).

The Binet began with the notion of a single intelligence, *g*. As the test progressed to its modern form, it has implicitly adopted a model of intelligence that acknowledges these two forms of intelligence. Thus, the evolution of the Binet has in many ways reflected and paralleled the evolution of modern psychometric theory and approaches to intelligence.

# The Early Binet Scales

Using the principles of age differentiation and general mental ability, Binet and another appointee of the French minister of public instruction, T. Simon, collaborated to develop the first version of what would eventually be called the Stanford-Binet Intelligence Scale. The first version, the 1905 Binet-Simon scale, was quite limited compared with current applications of intelligence tests. Its purpose was restricted to identifying mentally disabled children in the Paris school system.

## The 1905 Binet-Simon Scale

The 1905 Binet-Simon scale was an individual intelligence test consisting of 30 items presented in an increasing order of difficulty. Item 4, for example, tested the subject's ability to recognize food (e.g., to discriminate between chocolate and wood). Item 14 required subjects to define familiar objects such as a fork. The most difficult item, 30, required subjects to define and distinguish between paired abstract terms (e.g., *sad* and *bored*).

In Binet's time, three levels of intellectual deficiency were designated by terms no longer in use today because of the derogatory connotations they have acquired. *Idiot* described the most severe form of intellectual impairment, *imbecile* moderate levels of impairment, and *moron* the mildest level of impairment. Binet believed that the ability to follow simple directions and imitate simple gestures (item 6 on the 1905 scale) was the upper limit of adult idiots. The ability to identify parts of the body or simple objects (item 8) would rule out the most severe intellectual impairment in an adult. The upper limit for adult imbeciles was item 16, which required the subject to state the differences between two common objects such as wood and glass.

**FIGURE 10.2**
Schematic summary of the
evolution of the 1905 Binet
scale.

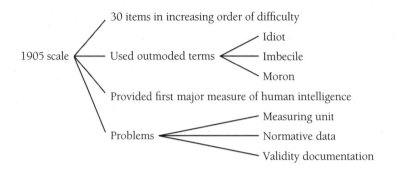

The collection of 30 tasks of increasing difficulty in the Binet-Simon scale provided the first major measure of human intelligence. Binet had solved two major problems of test construction: He determined exactly what he wanted to measure, and he developed items for this purpose. He fell short, however, in several other areas. The 1905 Binet-Simon scale lacked an adequate measuring unit to express results; it also lacked adequate normative data and evidence to support its validity. The classifications Binet used (idiot, imbecile, and moron) can hardly be considered sufficient for expressing results and, as Binet himself knew, little had been done to document the scale's validity. Furthermore, norms for the 1905 scale were based on only 50 children who had been considered normal based on average school performance (see Figure 10.2).

## The 1908 Scale

In the 1908 scale, Binet and Simon retained the principle of age differentiation. Indeed, the 1908 scale was an **age scale**, which means items were grouped according to age level rather than simply one set of items of increasing difficulty, as in the 1905 scale (see Table 10.1). The age scale provided a model for innumerable tests still used in educational and clinical settings. However, the age scale format also presented several challenges and, as we will see, is used in only a modified or "hybrid" fashion in the most recent, fifth edition. When items are grouped according to age level, comparing a child's performance on different kinds of tasks is difficult, if not impossible, unless items are exquisitely balanced as in the fifth edition. For example, does the child perform exceptionally well on one type of item? The current edition has a procedure that allows test users to combine all verbal items into a single scale and all nonverbal items into a single scale to overcome such problems with the age scale format.

Despite its limitations, the 1908 Binet scale clearly reflected improvement over the 1905 scale. However, Binet had done little to meet one persistent criticism: The scale produced only one score, almost exclusively related to verbal, language, and reading ability. Binet claimed that a single score was consistent with the notion of general mental ability and therefore appropriate. Unfortunately, Binet made little effort to diversify the range of abilities tapped. As a result, the scale remained heavily weighted on language, reading, and verbal skills at the expense of other factors such as the integration of visual and motor functioning (e.g., eye–hand coordination). Not until the 1986 revision were these problems seriously addressed, and in the fifth revision major efforts were made to provide a wide diversity of scores as well as a balance of verbal and nonverbal items.

**TABLE 10.1**    Sample Items from the 1908 Binet-Simon Scale

**Age level 3 (five items)**

1. Point to various parts of face.

2. Repeat two digits forward.

**Age level 5 (five items)**

1. Copy a square.

2. Repeat a sentence containing 10 syllables.

**Age level 7 (eight items)**

1. Copy a diamond.

2. Repeat five digits forward.

**Age level 9 (six items)**

1. Recall six items from a passage.

2. Recite the days of the week.

**Age level 11 (five items)**

1. Define abstract words (for example, *justice*).

2. Determine what is wrong with absurd statements.

**Age level 13 (three items)**

1. State the differences between pairs of abstract terms.

**Age level 4 (four items)**

1. Name familiar objects.

2. Repeat three digits forward.

**Age level 6 (seven items)**

1. State age.

2. Repeat a sentence containing 16 syllables.

**Age level 8 (six items)**

1. Recall two items from a passage.

2. State the differences between two objects.

**Age level 10 (five items)**

1. Given three common words, construct a sentence.

2. Recite the months of the year in order.

**Age level 12 (five items)**

1. Repeat seven digits forward.

2. Provide the meaning of pictures.

Perhaps the main improvement in the 1908 scale was the introduction of the concept of mental age. Here Binet attempted to solve the problem of expressing the results in adequate units. A subject's mental age was based on his or her performance compared with the average performance of individuals in a specific chronological age group. In simple terms, if a 6-year-old can perform the tasks that can be done by two-thirds to three-fourths of the representative group of 8-year-old children, then this child has a mental age of 8. A 10-year-old who can do no more than pass items that two-thirds to three-fourths of the representative group of 5-year-olds can pass is said to have a mental age of 5.

To summarize, the 1908 Binet-Simon scale introduced two major concepts: the age scale format and the concept of mental age. However, even though the mental age concept was eventually abandoned and the age scale format modified, these two concepts found widespread use and application in a host of new tests that are still in use today (see Figure 10.3).

**FIGURE 10.3**

Schematic summary of the evolution of the 1908 Binet scale.

1908 scale
— Retained principle of age differentiation
— Used age scale format
— Introduced concept of mental age

# Terman's Stanford-Binet Intelligence Scale

Though Binet and Simon again revised their intelligence scale in 1911, this third version contained only minor improvements. By this time, the potential utility of the Binet-Simon scale had been recognized throughout Europe and in the United States. For example, in the United States, H. H. Goddard published a translation of the 1905 Binet-Simon scale in 1908, and the 1908 scale in 1911 (Herrnstein, 1981). Other U.S. developers subsequently published many versions of the scale. However, it was the 1916 Stanford-Binet version, developed under the direction of L. M. Terman, that flourished and served for quite some time as the dominant intelligence scale for the world.

In this section, we continue our look at the evolution of the Binet scale and its relation to theories of intelligence. First, we examine Terman's 1916 version of the scale and see how he related the concepts of mental age and intelligence quotient (IQ). Then we look at the 1937 and 1960 revisions before we move on to the modern versions of the Binet. Each version illustrates important test concepts as well as the evolution of intelligence tests throughout the world.

## The 1916 Stanford-Binet Intelligence Scale

In developing the 1916 Stanford-Binet version, Terman relied heavily on Binet's earlier work. The principles of age differentiation, general mental ability, and the age scale were retained. The mental age concept also was retained (see Figure 10.4).

Terman's 1916 revision increased the size of the standardization sample. Unfortunately, the entire standardization sample of the 1916 revision consisted exclusively of white, native-Californian children. Thus, although the standardization sample was markedly increased, it was far from representative. In fact, given that even geographic location may affect test performance, this sample cannot even be considered to represent white, native-born Americans. Nevertheless, the increased sample size clearly marked an improvement over the meager 50 and 203 individuals of the 1905 and 1908 Binet-Simon versions.

## The Intelligence Quotient (IQ)

The 1916 scale provided the first significant application of the now outdated **intelligence quotient (IQ)** concept. This particular IQ concept, recommended by Stern

**FIGURE 10.4**

Schematic summary of the evolution of the 1916 Binet scale.

(1912), used a subject's mental age in conjunction with his or her chronological age to obtain a ratio score. This ratio score presumably reflected the subject's rate of mental development. Table 10.2 illustrates how IQ is determined.

In calculating IQ, the first step is to determine the subject's chronological age. To obtain this, we need only know his or her birthday. In the second step, the subject's mental age is determined by his or her score on the scale. Finally, to obtain the IQ, the chronological age (CA) is divided into the mental age (MA) and the result multiplied by 100 to eliminate fractions: $IQ = MA/CA \times 100$.

As you can see in Table 10.2, when MA is less than CA, the IQ is below 100. In this case, the subject was said to have slower-than-average mental development. When MA exceeded CA, the subject was said to have faster-than-average mental development.

The IQ score altered the nature of the measuring unit used to express the results. However, the method may have actually been a step backward; the MA/CA method of calculating IQ scores was ultimately abandoned in all major tests. The 1916 scale had a maximum possible mental age of 19.5 years; that is, if every group of items was passed, this score would result. Given this limitation, anyone older than 19.5 would have an IQ of less than 100 even if all items were passed. Therefore, a maximum limit on the chronological age had to be set. Because back in 1916 people believed that mental age ceased to improve after 16 years of age, 16 was used as the maximum chronological age.

---

**TABLE 10.2**  The Intelligence Quotient Concept

**Child 1:**

Chronological age (CA): 6 years

Mental age (MA): 6 years

$$IQ = \frac{MA}{CA} \times 100 = \frac{6}{6} \times 100 = 100$$

**Child 2:**

Chronological age (CA): 6 years

Mental age (MA): 3 years

$$IQ = \frac{MA}{CA} \times 100 = \frac{3}{6} \times 100 = 50$$

**Child 3:**

$CA = 6; MA = 12; IQ = 200$

**Adult 1:**

$CA = 50; MA = 16$

$$IQ = \frac{16^*}{16} \times 100 = 100$$

*(the maximum CA)

## The 1937 Scale

The 1937 scale extended the age range down to the 2-year-old level. Also, by adding new tasks, developers increased the maximum possible mental age to 22 years, 10 months. Scoring standards and instructions were improved to reduce ambiguities, enhance the standardization of administration, and increase interscorer reliability. Furthermore, several performance items, which required the subject to do things such as copy designs, were added to decrease the scale's emphasis on verbal skills. However, only some 25% of the items were nonverbal, so the test was not balanced between the two types of items (Becker, 2003).

The standardization sample was markedly improved. Whereas the 1916 norms were restricted to Californians, the new subjects for the 1937 Stanford-Binet standardization sample came from 11 U.S. states representing a variety of regions. Subjects were selected according to their fathers' occupations. In addition, the standardization sample was substantially increased. Unfortunately, the sample included only whites and more urban subjects than rural ones. Nevertheless, this improved sample represented a desirable trend. The 3184 individuals included in the 1937 standardization sample represented more than a threefold increase from the 1916 scale and was more than 63 times larger than the original sample of the 1905 scale.

Perhaps the most important improvement in the 1937 version was the inclusion of an alternate equivalent form. Forms L and M were designed to be equivalent in terms of both difficulty and content. With two such forms, the psychometric properties of the scale could be readily examined (see Figure 10.5).

**FIGURE 10.5**
Schematic summary of the evolution of the 1937 Binet scale.

*Problems with the 1937 Scale*

A major problem with the 1937 scale was that its reliability coefficients were higher for older subjects than for younger ones. Thus, results for the latter were not as stable as those for the former. Reliability figures also varied as a function of IQ level, with higher reliabilities in the lower IQ ranges (i.e., less than 70) and poorer ones in the higher ranges. The lowest reliabilities occurred in the youngest age groups in the highest IQ ranges. These findings apply generally to all modern intelligence tests: Scores are most unstable for young children in high IQ ranges.

Along with the differing reliabilities, each age group in the standardization sample produced a unique standard deviation of IQ scores. This differential variability in IQ scores as a function of age created the single most important problem in the 1937 scale. More specifically, despite the great care taken in selecting the standardization sample, different age groups showed significant differences in the standard deviation of IQ scores. For example, the standard deviation in the IQ scores at age 6 was approximately 12.5. The standard deviations at ages 2.5 and 12, on the other hand, were 20.6 and 20.0, respectively. Because of these discrepancies, IQs at one age level were not equivalent to IQs at another (see Focused Example 10.1).

## The 1960 Stanford-Binet Revision and Deviation IQ (SB-LM)

The developers of the 1960 revision (SB-LM) tried to create a single instrument by selecting the best from the two forms of the 1937 scale. Tasks that showed an increase in the percentage passing with an increase in age—a main criterion and guiding principle for the construction of the Binet scale—received the highest priority, as did tasks that correlated highly with scores as a whole—a second guiding principle of the Binet scale. In addition, instructions for scoring and test administration were improved, and IQ tables were extended from age 16 to 18. Perhaps most important, the problem of differential variation in IQs was solved by the deviation IQ concept.

As used in the Stanford-Binet scale, the *deviation IQ* was simply a standard score with a mean of 100 and a standard deviation of 16 (today the standard deviation is set at 15). With the mean set at 100 and assigned to scores at the

---

## 10.1    FOCUSED EXAMPLE

### Differential Variability in IQ Scores

Recall our discussion of standard deviations and percentiles in Chapter 2. A score that is two standard deviations above the mean is approximately at the 98th percentile. Therefore, if the mean IQ is 100, a 6-year-old, where the standard deviation is 12.5, would need an IQ of 125 to be two standard deviations above the mean, or the 98th percentile. However, at 12 years of age, where the standard deviation is 20, the same child would need an IQ of 140 to be two standard deviations above the mean and in the 98th percentile. Say a child at age 6 with an IQ of 125 also obtained an IQ of 125 at age 12. He or she would then be only 1.25 standard deviations above the mean (because the standard deviation at age 12 is 20) and thus at only about the 89th percentile. You can see that in the 1937 scale, an IQ at one age range was not comparable to an IQ at another age range in terms of percentiles.

**FIGURE 10.6**

Schematic summary of the
evolution of the 1960 Binet
scale.

50th percentile, the deviation IQ was ascertained by evaluating the standard deviation of mental age for a representative sample at each age level. New IQ tables were then constructed that corrected for differences in variability at the various age levels. By correcting for these differences in variability, one could compare the IQs of one age level with those of another. Thus, scores could be interpreted in terms of standard deviations and percentiles with the assurance that IQ scores for every age group corresponded to the same percentile. Today, the deviation IQ method is considered the most precise way of expressing the results of an intelligence test (see Figure 10.6).

The 1960s revision did not include a new normative sample or restandardization. However, by 1972, a new standardization group consisting of a representative sample of 2100 children (approximately 100 at each Stanford-Binet age level) had been obtained for use with the 1960 revision (Thorndike, 1973). Unlike all previous norms, the 1972 norms included nonwhites. For many, however, the general improvements in the 1960 revision, even with the new 1972 norms, did not suffice. In 1986, a new and drastically revised version of the Binet scale was published (Thorndike, Hagen, & Sattler, 1986). Then, in 2003, there was another major revision in which many of the concepts added to the 1986 edition were abandoned in favor of concepts used in the 1960 (SB-LM) version. The changes in 1986 and the possible reasons for the return to the older 1960 model are instructive.

## The Modern Binet Scale

Our discussion of the evolution of the Binet scale has illustrated many of the concepts that have dominated intelligence testing from its inception to the present. The fourth and fifth editions of the Stanford-Binet scale continue this tradition of innovation and incorporation of central psychometric and theoretical concepts. In this section, we examine the fourth and fifth editions of the scale, which its authors developed in response to cultural and social changes and new research in cognitive psychology. First, we consider the basic model that guided this development and briefly discuss the features common to both editions. Next, we compare these latest editions to their predecessors. We begin with a brief look at how the fourth edition was changed. Then we consider the 2003 edition in greater detail—the various subtests, summary scores, and procedures. We also examine the scale's psychometric properties. Finally, we examine the modern 2003 edition of the Binet in light of a relatively new theory of intelligence.

# Model for the Fourth and Fifth Editions of the Binet Scale

The model for the latest editions of the Binet (Figure 10.7) is far more elaborate than the Spearman model that best characterized the original versions of the scale. These versions incorporate the *gf-gc* theory of intelligence. They are based on a hierarchical model. At the top of the hierarchy is *g* (general intelligence), which reflects the common variability of all tasks. At the next level are three group factors. *Crystallized abilities* reflect learning—the realization of original potential through experience. *Fluid-analytic abilities* represent original potential, or the basic capabilities that a person uses to acquire crystallized abilities (Horn, 1994; Horn & Cattell, 1966; Horn & Noll, 1997). *Short-term memory* refers to one's memory during short intervals—the amount of information one can retain briefly after a single, short presentation (Colom, Flores-Mendoza, Quiroga, & Privado, 2005). In addition, crystallized ability has two subcategories: verbal reasoning and nonverbal reasoning (Pomplun & Custer, 2005).

## The Role of Thurstone's Multidimensional Model

The model of the modern Binet represents an attempt to place an evaluation of *g* in the context of a multidimensional model of intelligence from which one can evaluate specific abilities. The impetus for a multidimensional model stemmed from the work of Thurstone (1938). He argued that, contrary to Spearman's notion of intelligence as a single process, intelligence could best be conceptualized as comprising independent factors, or "primary mental abilities." Years of painstaking work ultimately revealed evidence for group abilities factors that were relatively, but not totally, independent. The group factors were correlated, and from them a *g* factor could be extracted, as in the hierarchical model of the fourth and fifth editions of the Binet.

# Characteristics of the 1986 Revision

The 1986 revision attempted to retain all of the strengths of the earlier revisions while eliminating the weaknesses. This was no easy task; nor was it a complete success as indicated by the backtracking that occurred in the fifth edition. To continue to provide a measure of general mental ability, the authors of the 1986 revision decided to retain the wide variety of content and task characteristics of earlier versions. However, to avoid having this wide content unevenly distributed across age groups, the age scale format was entirely eliminated. In place of the age scale, items with the same content were placed together into any one of 15 separate tests to create point scales. For example, all vocabulary items were placed together in one test; all matrix items placed together in a second.

The more modern 2003 fifth edition provided a more standardized hierarchical model with five factors, as illustrated in Figure 10.8. At the top of the hierarchy is general intelligence, just as in the 1986 edition. However, there are now five rather than four main factors. Each factor, in turn, has an equally weighted nonverbal and verbal measure. Figure 10.9 indicates the types of activities used to measure the various factors.

9-74534

**STANFORD-BINET INTELLIGENCE SCALE**

**RECORD BOOKLET**

# Stanford-Binet Intelligence Scale: Fourth Edition

Name _____

_____ Sex _____

Ethnicity   NA   H   B   W/NH   O/AA   PI   Other _____

|  | YEAR | MONTH | DAY |
|---|---|---|---|
| Date of Testing | _____ | _____ | _____ |
| Birth Date | _____ | _____ | _____ |
| Age | _____ | _____ | _____ |

School _____

Grade _____

Examiner _____

Father's Occupation: _____

Mother's Occupation: _____

**FACTORS AFFECTING TEST PERFORMANCE**
Overall Rating of Conditions

| Optimal | Good | Average | Detrimental | Seriously detrimental |
|---|---|---|---|---|

|  | RAW SCORE | STANDARD AGE SCORE |
|---|---|---|
| **Verbal Reasoning** | | |
| 1  Vocabulary | _____ | _____ |
| 6  Comprehension | _____ | _____ |
| 7  Absurdities | _____ | _____ |
| 14  Verbal Relations | _____ | _____ |
| Sum of Subtest SAS's | | |
| Verbal Reasoning SAS | | |
| **Abstract/Visual Reasoning** | | |
| 5  Pattern Analysis | _____ | _____ |
| 9  Copying | _____ | _____ |
| 11  Matrices | _____ | _____ |
| 13  Paper Folding & Cutting | _____ | _____ |
| Sum of Subtest SAS's | | |
| Abstract/Visual Reasoning SAS | | |
| **Quantitative Reasoning** | | |
| 3  Quantitative | _____ | _____ |
| 12  Number Series | _____ | _____ |
| 15  Equation Building | _____ | _____ |
| Sum of Subtest SAS's | | |
| Quantitative Reasoning SAS | | |
| **Short-Term Memory** | | |
| 2  Bead Memory | _____ | _____ |
| 4  Memory For Sentences | _____ | _____ |
| 8  Memory For Digits | _____ | _____ |
| 10  Memory For Objects | _____ | _____ |
| Sum of Subtest SAS's | | |
| Short-Term Memory SAS | | |
| Sum of Area SAS's | | |

COMPOSITE SCORE

Test Composite ............................... _____
Partial Composite ........................... _____
Partial Composite based on _____

|  | 1 | 2 | 3 | 4 | 5 |  |
|---|---|---|---|---|---|---|
| **Attention** | | | | | | |
| a) Absorbed by task | | | | | | Easily distracted |
| **Reactions During Test Performance** | | | | | | |
| a) Normal activity level | | | | | | Abnormal activity level |
| b) Initiates activity | | | | | | Waits to be told |
| c) Quick to respond | | | | | | Urging needed |
| **Emotional Independence** | | | | | | |
| a) Socially confident | | | | | | Insecure |
| b) Realistically self-confident | | | | | | Distrusts own ability |
| c) Comfortable in adult company | | | | | | Ill-at-ease |
| d) Assured | | | | | | Anxious |
| **Problem-Solving Behavior** | | | | | | |
| a) Persistent | | | | | | Gives up easily |
| b) Reacts to failure realistically | | | | | | Reacts to failure unrealistically |
| c) Eager to continue | | | | | | Seeks to terminate |
| d) Challenged by hard tasks | | | | | | Prefers only easy tasks |
| **Independence of Examiner Support** | | | | | | |
| a) Needs minimum of commendation | | | | | | Needs constant praise and encouragement |
| **Expressive Language** | | | | | | |
| a) Excellent articulation | | | | | | Very poor articulation |
| **Receptive Language** | | | | | | |
| a) Excellent sound discrimination | | | | | | Very poor sound discrimination |

Was it difficult to establish rapport with this person?
Easy |____|____|____|____|____| Difficult

**The Riverside Publishing Company**

Robert L. Thorndike
Elizabeth P. Hagen
Jerome M. Sattler

**FIGURE 10.7**
Cover page of Stanford-Binet Intelligence Scale.
(Stanford-Binet Intelligence Scales, Fifth Edition (SB-5). © 2003 by PRO-ED. Reproduced with permission.)

FIGURE 10.8
Three-level hierarchical
model of the 2003 fifth
edition.

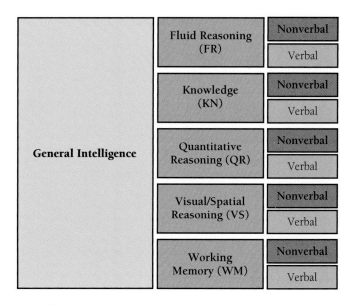

FIGURE 10.8
Three-level hierarchical
model of the 2003 fifth
edition.

(Adapted from Figure 2.1, p. 24 in G. H. Roid, 2003b.)

FIGURE 10.9
Verbal and nonverbal tasks
on 2003 fifth edition.

(Adapted from Figure 2.1, p. 24 in G. H. Roid, 2003b.)

Placing together items of similar content in a point scale permits the calculation of specific scores for each of the 15 tests. Thus, in addition to an overall score that presumably reflects *g*, one can obtain scores related to each specific content area. The drawback is less variety to the items. In addition, each of the specific 15 tests were grouped into one of four content areas or factors. Figure 10.10 summarizes the characteristics of the 1986 fourth edition.

**FIGURE 10.10**
Characteristics of the
modern (1986) Binet.

## Characteristics of the 2003 Fifth Edition

The fifth edition represents an elegant integration of the age-scale and point-scale formats. First, the nonverbal and verbal scales are equally weighted. The examination begins with one of two routing measures (subtests): one nonverbal, one verbal. The routing tests are organized in a point scale, which means that each contains similar content of increasing difficulty. For example, the verbal routing test consists of a set of vocabulary items of increasing difficulty.

The purpose of the routing tests is to estimate the examinee's level of ability. The nonverbal routing test is used to estimate nonverbal ability; the verbal routing test to estimate verbal ability. The remaining eight subtests are arranged in an age-scale format. This means that tasks of differing content are grouped together on the basis of difficulty. For example, an age scale–based subtest might have a mixture of different types of verbal and nonverbal tasks, with the tasks grouped according to the typical age at which individuals are able to correctly complete the task. This mixing of tasks was the procedure used in all prior versions of the Binet except the fourth edition. The difference with the 2003 fifth edition is that because of the equal weighting of verbal and nonverbal items, it is possible to summarize an examinee's score on all items of similar content. As a result, the fifth edition retains the advantage of the point scale by allowing examiners to summarize scores within any given content area while also using a mixture of tasks to maintain an examinee's interest.

Using the routing tests to estimate ability, the examiner then goes to an age scale–based subtest at the appropriate level for the examinee. In that way, items that are too easy are skipped to save time and provide for a more efficient examination.

The estimated level of ability is called the *start point*. However, if a certain number of early items are missed, then the examiner moves to a lower (and therefore easier) level. The level at which a minimum criterion number of correct responses is obtained is known as the **basal**. Testing continues until examinees reach the **ceiling**, which is a certain number of incorrect responses that indicate the items are too difficult.

**FIGURE 10.11**
Characteristics of the 2003
fifth edition.

Examiners can complete scaled scores for each of the five nonverbal subtests and each of the five corresponding verbal subtests. These scaled scores have a mean of 10 and a standard deviation of 3. In addition, a standard score with a mean of 100 and a standard deviation of 15 is computed for nonverbal IQ, verbal IQ, full-scale IQ, and each of the five factors: fluid reasoning, knowledge, quantitative reasoning, visual-spatial processing, and working memory. Nonverbal and verbal IQ scores are based on summing the five nonverbal and five verbal subtests. The full-scale IQ is based on all 10. The standard scores for each of the five factors are based on summing the nonverbal and corresponding verbal subtest for each respective factor. Figure 10.11 summarizes the characteristics of the 2003 fifth edition.

## Psychometric Properties of the 2003 Fifth Edition

The 2003 fifth edition was constructed with exceptional diligence. It continues the tradition of its predecessors in providing a state-of-the-art model for intelligence tests in terms of its psychometric standards and construction.

The awkward standard deviation of 16 for major indexes was finally abandoned in favor of the more common standard deviation of 15. Several new subtests were added, while those that were retained were updated with new artwork, toys, and better items. A major goal of the fifth edition is to tap the extremes in intelligence—the major historical strength of the Binet that had been essentially lost in the fourth edition. The age range touted by the fifth edition spans from 2 to 85+ years of age.

Norms were based on a representative sample of 4800 individuals from age 2 through 85+, stratified by gender, ethnicity, region, and education according to the 2001 census. To augment the standardization sample, 3000 additional individuals were included, encompassing various subpopulations such as gifted, mentally retarded, attention-deficit/hyperactivity disorder (ADHD), and those with speech, language, and hearing problems. The range of possible scores runs from a low of 40 to a high of 160, reestablishing the Binet as one of the most appropriate tests for evaluating extremes in intelligence (see Canivez, 2008).

Overall, the reliability of the fifth edition is quite good. Coefficients for the full-scale IQ are either .97 or .98 for each of the 23 age ranges reported in the manual. Average reliabilities for the three IQ scores are .98 (full-scale IQ), .95 (nonverbal IQ), and .96 (verbal IQ). Coefficients for the five-factor index scores range from .90 to .92. Coefficients for verbal and nonverbal subtests are comparable and consistently in the high .8's. Test–retest coefficients are likewise excellent, with a range from the high .7's to the low .9's, depending on age and testing interval. Interscorer agreement was made high by eliminating items where such agreement was low, with an overall median of .9 reported in the technical manual (Roid, 2003c).

However, Canivez reports that results from more recent independent studies have seriously challenged the claim that the fifth edition measures five factors (Canivez, 2008, citing DiStefano & Dombrowski, 2006). DiStefano and Dombrowski concluded that the fifth edition was probably best explained as a unidimensional test of intelligence. Canivez opines that failure to find support for Roid's (2003c) five factors and limited support for even two factors may be the result of Roid extracting too many factors due to not considering exploratory factor analyses and multiple factor extraction criteria (Canivez, citing Frazier & Youngstrom, 2007). As a result, clinical interpretation of the fifth edition should primarily reside at the global, general intelligence level until research adequately supports interpretation of lower-order (Stratum II) dimensions.

## Median Validity

The technical manual reports four types of evidence that support the validity of the test: (1) content validity, (2) construct validity, (3) empirical item analysis, and (4) considerable criterion-related evidence of validity. Full-scale IQs for the fifth edition correlate in the low to mid .8's, with established measures including the Wechsler scales, which are discussed in the next chapter.

# Summary

Binet defined *intelligence* as the capacity (1) to find and maintain a definite direction or purpose; (2) to make necessary adaptations—that is, strategy adjustments—to achieve that purpose; and (3) to engage in self-criticism so that necessary adjustments in strategy can be made.

Binet's two principles of test construction were age differentiation and general mental ability. *Age differentiation* refers to the fact that with increasing age, children develop their abilities. Thus, older children have greater abilities than do younger ones. Spearman developed his own theory of general mental ability, or *g*, based on the idea that a single general factor underlies all intelligence. Modern theorists have taken this concept further in *gf-gc* theory, in which there are two basic types of intelligence: fluid (*gf*) and crystallized (*gc*).

*Mental age* is a unit of measurement for expressing the results of intelligence tests. The concept was introduced in the second revision of the Binet scale in 1908. A subject's mental age is based on his or her performance compared with the average performance of individuals in a specific chronological age group. For example, if a 6-year-old child can perform tasks that the average 8-year-old can do, then the 6-year-old child is said to have a mental age of 8.

Like mental age, the *intelligence quotient* (IQ) is a unit of measure for expressing the results of intelligence tests. Introduced in the Terman 1916 Stanford-Binet revision of the Binet scale, the IQ is a ratio score. Specifically, the IQ is the ratio of a subject's mental age (as determined by his or her performance on the intelligence scale) and chronological age. This ratio is then multiplied by 100 to eliminate fractions.

The *deviation IQ*, as it is now used in the Stanford-Binet Scale (fifth edition), is a standard score with a mean of 100 and a standard deviation of 15. Older versions had a standard deviation of 16.

The most recent revision of the Binet scale, the fifth edition, was released in 2003. This edition combines the age and point scale methods of test construction.

# 11 CHAPTER

# The Wechsler Intelligence Scales: WAIS-IV, WISC-IV, and WPPSI-III

## LEARNING OBJECTIVES

*When you have completed this chapter, you should be able to:*

- ▶ Identify the major motivation for the development of the Wechsler scales

- ▶ Briefly describe the point and performance scale concepts

- ▶ Distinguish between verbal and performance tasks

- ▶ Explain how IQ scores are determined on the Wechsler scales

- ▶ Describe the reliability of the Wechsler scales

- ▶ Describe the validity of the Wechsler scales

- ▶ Identify some of the major advantages and disadvantages of the Wechsler scales

- ▶ Describe the advances in testing reflected in the WISC-IV and WPPSI-III

S usan's family has just moved from a small rural town to a large city on the East Coast. At age 9, she remains shy around strangers and lacks confidence. Her attempt to adjust to a new school has been disastrous. Because she started in the middle of the school term, all of the other children seem way ahead of her; she feels hopelessly behind. To make matters worse, she has an unusually strong fear of failure. Rather than make an error, she remains silent even if she knows an answer. With all of her negative experiences in the new school, she begins to develop a poor attitude toward school tasks and therefore avoids them. Eventually, her teacher refers her to the school psychologist for testing. To Susan, this referral is the school's way of punishing her for not doing her homework. Fearful, upset, and angry, she makes up her mind not to cooperate with the psychologist.

When the time finally comes for her appointment, Susan begins to cry. The principal is called in to accompany her to the psychologist's office. Although she appears to calm down, Susan remains fearful and anxious. Finally, the psychologist decides to begin the testing. He starts with a relatively simple task that requires Susan to repeat digits. The psychologist states, "I want you to repeat some numbers that I'm going to say to you. Please say them as I do." He begins the first set of digits and states in a soft, clear voice, "Six, one, three." Susan does not even respond. She has been staring blankly at the walls and has not heard what the psychologist has said. The psychologist attracts her attention and says, "Now say what I say: four, two, seven." This time Susan hears him but again remains silent.

Now think for a moment. How many different factors are involved in the psychologist's ostensibly simple request to repeat three digits forward? To comply with this request, Susan has to direct her attention to the words of the psychologist, possess adequate hearing, and understand the instructions. She also has to cooperate, make an effort, and be capable of repeating what she has heard. Certainly her familiarity with numerals—that is, her previous learning and experience—can influence her performance. If the children in her new school have had more exposure to numerals than she has, then they might have an advantage over her in this regard. Furthermore, her lack of confidence, negative attitude toward school, fear of failure, and shyness have all played a role in her performance. A more confident, less fearful child with positive attitudes toward school would have a clear advantage over Susan. Thus, in addition to memory and other indicators of intelligence, many nonintellective factors (e.g., attitude, experience, and emotional functioning) play an extremely important role in a person's ability to perform a task even as "simple" as repeating three digits forward.

Though both Binet and Terman considered the influence of nonintellective factors on results from intelligence tests, David Wechsler, author of the Wechsler scales, has been perhaps one of the most influential advocates of the role of nonintellective factors in these tests. Throughout his career, Wechsler emphasized that factors other than intellectual ability are involved in intelligent behavior. Today, there are three Wechsler intelligence tests, the Wechsler Adult Intelligence Scale, Fourth Edition (WAIS-IV), the Wechsler Intelligence Scale for Children, Fourth Edition (WISC-IV), and the Wechsler Preschool and Primary Scale of Intelligence, Third Edition (WPPSI-III).

# The Wechsler Intelligence Scales

The role of nonintellective factors is apparent in the Wechsler intelligence scales. Just 2 years after the Binet scale's monumental 1937 revision, the Wechsler–Bellevue Intelligence Scale challenged its supremacy as a measure of human intelligence. With so many different and varied abilities associated with intelligence, Wechsler objected to the single score offered by the 1937 Binet scale. In addition, although Wechsler's test did not directly measure nonintellective factors, it took these factors into careful account in its underlying theory. In constructing his own intelligence test, Wechsler deviated considerably from many of the Binet scale's central concepts.

Wechsler (1939) capitalized on the inappropriateness of the 1937 Binet scale as a measure of the intelligence of adults. Because the Binet scale items were selected for use with children, Wechsler concluded that these items lacked validity when answered by adults. Further, examiner–subject rapport was often impaired when adults were tested with the Binet scale. Wechsler (1939) also correctly noted that the Binet scale's emphasis on speed, with timed tasks scattered throughout the scale, tended to unduly handicap older adults. Furthermore, mental age norms clearly did not apply to adults. Finally, Wechsler criticized the then existing Binet scale because it did not consider that intellectual performance could deteriorate as a person grew older. (As noted in Chapter 10, the modern Binet scale has addressed these and many other criticisms of its earlier predecessors.)

## Point and Performance Scale Concepts

Many of the differences between the Wechsler and the original Binet scales were profound. Two of the most critical differences were (1) Wechsler's use of the point scale concept rather than an age scale and (2) Wechsler's inclusion of a non-verbal performance scale.

### The Point Scale Concept

Recall that from 1908 to 1972, the Binet scale grouped items by age level. Each age level included a group of tasks that could be passed by two-thirds to three-fourths of the individuals at that age level. In an age-scale format, the arrangement of items has nothing to do with their content. At a particular year level, there might be one task related to memory, a second to reasoning, and a third to skill in using numerical data. Another level might also include a task related to memory but then include other tasks related to concentration or language skills. Thus, various types of content are scattered throughout the scale. Furthermore, on the earlier Binet scale, subjects did not receive a specific amount of points or credit for each task completed. For example, if a Binet scale subject is required to pass three out of four tasks in order to receive credit for a particular test, then passing only two tasks would produce no credit at all for that test.

In a point scale, credits or points are assigned to each item. An individual receives a specific amount of credit for each item passed. The point scale offers an inherent advantage. This scale makes it easy to group items of a particular content together, which is exactly what Wechsler did. The effect of such groupings appeared so powerful that a similar concept was used in the 1986 Binet scale.

FIGURE 11.1
Advantages of Wechsler's
scale.

By arranging items according to content and assigning a specific number of points to each item, Wechsler constructed an intelligence test that yielded not only a total overall score but also scores for each content area. Thus, the point scale concept allowed Wechsler to devise a test that permitted an analysis of the individual's ability in a variety of content areas (e.g., judgment, vocabulary, and range of general knowledge). Today, Wechsler's concept is the standard.

### The Performance Scale Concept

The early Binet scale had been persistently and consistently criticized for its emphasis on language and verbal skills. To deal with this problem, Wechsler included an entire scale that provided a measure of nonverbal intelligence: a performance scale. Thus, in addition to measuring intelligence in adults and yielding separate scores, Wechsler's approach offered a third major advantage over the early Binet scales. The performance scale consisted of tasks that require a subject to do something (e.g., copy symbols or point to a missing detail) rather than merely answer questions (see Figure 11.1).

Although the early Binet scales contained some performance tasks, these tended to be concentrated at the younger age levels. Furthermore, the results of a subject's response to a performance task on the Binet scale were extremely difficult to separate from the results for verbal tasks, as can be done today. Thus, one could not determine the precise extent to which a subject's response to a nonverbal performance task increased or decreased the total score. The original Wechsler scale, however, included two separate scales. The verbal scale provided a measure of verbal intelligence, and the performance scale a measure of nonverbal intelligence. As we will see, the most recent editions of the Wechsler scales, the WAIS-IV, the WISC-IV, and the WPPSI-III, now have four major scales instead of the original two.

The concept of a performance scale was far from new. Before the Wechsler scale, several performance tests served as supplements or alternatives to the then verbally weighted Binet scale (such as the Leiter International Performance Scale, discussed in Chapter 12). However, Wechsler's new scale was the first to offer the possibility of directly comparing an individual's verbal and nonverbal intelligence—that is, both the verbal and performance scales were standardized on the same sample, and the results of both scales were expressed in comparable units. Again, this procedure of standardizing multiple scales on the same sample represents the current standard in modern psychological testing.

A performance scale attempts to overcome biases caused by language, culture, and education. Furthermore, if verbal tasks provide a useful context in which to observe problem solving, then tasks that require the subject to do something physical, such as pointing, can offer an even richer and more varied context. Indeed, performance tasks tend to require a longer interval of sustained effort, concentration, and attention than most verbal tasks. Therefore, they not only measure intelligence but also provide the clinician with a rich opportunity to observe behavior in a standard setting.

# From the Wechsler-Bellevue Intelligence Scale to the WAIS-IV

Despite his conceptual improvements, Wechsler's first effort to measure adult intelligence, the Wechsler–Bellevue scale (Wechsler, 1939), was poorly standardized. Its normative sample consisted of a nonrepresentative sample of 1081 whites from the eastern United States (primarily New York residents). By 1955, however, Wechsler had revised the Wechsler–Bellevue scale into its modern form, the Wechsler Adult Intelligence Scale (WAIS), which was revised in 1981 (the WAIS-R), again in 1997 (the WAIS-III), and yet again in 2008 (WAIS-IV). To better understand the modern Wechsler scales, it is important to reflect on the concepts underlying the original distinction between the verbal and performance IQs.

# Scales, Subtests, and Indexes

Like Binet, Wechsler defined intelligence as the capacity to act purposefully and to adapt to the environment. In his words, intelligence is "the aggregate or global capacity of the individual to act purposefully, to think rationally and to deal effectively with his environment" (1958, p. 7). Wechsler believed that intelligence comprised specific elements that one could individually define and measure; however, these elements were interrelated—that is, not entirely independent. This is why he used the terms *global* and *aggregate*. Wechsler's definition implies that intelligence comprises several specific interrelated functions or elements and that general intelligence results from the interplay of these elements. Modern research overwhelmingly supports this view (Corballis, 2011; Goldstein & Beers, 2003; Sternberg, 2000; Weiss, Saklofske, Coalson, & Engi Raiford, 2010). Theoretically, by measuring each of the elements, one can measure general intelligence by summing the individual's capacities on each element. Thus, Wechsler tried to measure separate abilities, which Binet had avoided in adopting the concept of general mental ability.

In the WAIS-IV, Wechsler's basic approach is maintained. First, there are individual subtests, each of which is related to a basic underlying skill or ability (see Table 11.1). For example, the information subtest measures one's range of knowledge. Each of the various subtests is also part of a broader "index." On the WAIS-IV, the subtests are sorted into four indexes: verbal comprehension,

**TABLE 11.1**    Core Wechsler Subtests

| Subtest | Major function measured by various subtests |
|---|---|
| Vocabulary | Vocabulary level |
| Similarities | Abstract thinking |
| Arithmetic | Concentration |
| Digit span | Immediate memory, anxiety |
| Information | Range of knowledge |
| Coding | Visual–motor functioning |
| Block design | Nonverbal reasoning |
| Matrix reasoning | Inductive reasoning |
| Visual puzzles | Perceptual reasoning |
| Symbol search | Information-processing speed |

perceptual reasoning, working memory, and processing speed. The full-scale IQ (FSIQ) is then based on the summed scores of these four indexes.

An *index* is created where two or more subtests are related to a basic underlying skill (see Dehn, 2008; Lange, Schoenberg, Chelune, Scott, & Adams, 2005). Figure 11.2 shows the WAIS-IV's four indexes and their corresponding subtests.

## A Closer Look at Subtests

To get a better understanding of subtests, let's look at some of these in greater detail. In describing these and all other tests in this book, our examples are not those actually used in the test itself unless express permission has been obtained. Our goal is merely to illustrate the type of content to give readers a better understanding of how the actual subtest works.

### The Vocabulary Subtest

The ability to define words is not only one of the best single measures of intelligence but also the most stable. Vocabulary tests appear on nearly every individual test that involves verbal intelligence. The relative stability of the vocabulary subtest and verbal comprehension index of which it is a part, is one of its most important features. If an individual has shown *deterioration* (i.e., lowered performance compared with a previously higher level) because of emotional factors or brain damage, for example, vocabulary is one of the last functions to be affected. It is more stable and less vulnerable than other aspects of intelligence. For example, the poor concentration of schizophrenic people lowers their performance on arithmetic or digit span tasks (respecting numbers spoken out loud) long before vocabulary is affected (Behrwind et al., 2011; Bryson, Greig, Lysaker, & Bell, 2002; Schwarz, Gfeller, & Oliveri, 2006). Also, whereas mild concentration difficulties lower optimal performance on arithmetic and digit span tasks, such difficulties generally do not affect vocabulary until they become quite severe (Almkvist, Adveen, Henning, &

FIGURE 11.2

Schematic overview of WAIS-IV index scores.

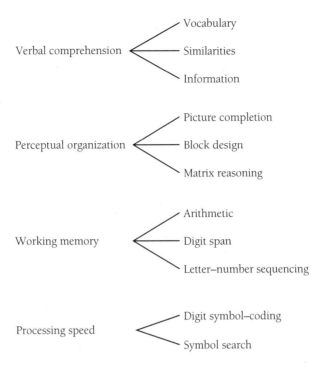

Verbal comprehension
- Vocabulary
- Similarities
- Information

Perceptual organization
- Picture completion
- Block design
- Matrix reasoning

Working memory
- Arithmetic
- Digit span
- Letter–number sequencing

Processing speed
- Digit symbol–coding
- Symbol search

Tallberg, 2007; Weiss, Saklofske, Coalson, & Engi Raiford, 2010). Because the vocabulary subtest provides a relatively stable estimate of general verbal intelligence, one can use it to evaluate baseline or premorbid intelligence (i.e., what a person's intellectual capacity probably was prior to an emotional illness, brain injury, or trauma) (Carlozzia, 2011; Seidman, Buka, Goldstein, & Tsuang, 2006).

### The Similarities Subtest

The similarities subtest consists of paired items of increasing difficulty. The subject must identify the similarity between the items in each pair. The examiner asks, for example, "In what way are bread and water alike?" Many of the early, easier items are so well known that responses simply reflect previously learned associations (Kaufman, 1990). However, the more difficult items might be something like, "In what way are an ant and a rose alike?" Some items definitely require the subject to think abstractly. This subtest measures the subject's ability to see the similarity between apparently dissimilar objects or things.

The character of a person's thought processes can be seen in many cases. For example, individuals with schizophrenia tend to give *idiosyncratic* concepts, or concepts that have meaning only to them. Such a response to the bread and water item might be "Both are used for torture." Such a response has meaning only to the schizophrenic person.

### The Arithmetic Subtest

The arithmetic subtest contains approximately 15 relatively simple problems in increasing order of difficulty. The ninth most difficult item is as easy as this:

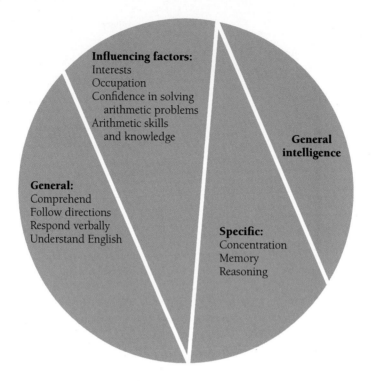

"A person with $28.00 spends $.50. How much does he have left?" Obviously, you need not be a mathematician to figure this one out; however, you must be able to retain the figures in memory while manipulating them. In a few cases, such as in mentally handicapped or educationally deprived subjects, arithmetic skills can play a significant role. Generally, however, concentration, motivation, and memory are the main factors underlying performance. Figure 11.3 illustrates some of the intellective and nonintellective components of the arithmetic subtest as revealed by factor analytic and logical analyses.

### The Digit Span Subtest

The digit span subtest requires the subject to repeat digits, given at the rate of one per second, forward and backward. In terms of intellective factors, the digit span subtest measures short-term auditory memory, and is one of the core subtests in the working memory index. As with other Wechsler subtests, however, nonintellective factors (e.g., attention) often influence the results (Davidson & Kemp, 2011; Hale, Hoeppner, & Fiorello, 2002; Hopko, Hunt, & Armento, 2005). For example, anxiety in the test situation may impair performance on the digit span subtest (Gass & Curiel, 2011; Hopko et al., 2005; Marchand, Lefebvre, & Connolly, 2006).

### The Information Subtest

College students typically find the information subtest relatively easy and fun. As in all Wechsler subtests, items appear in order of increasing difficulty. Item 6 asks something like, "Name two people who have been generals in the U.S. Army" or "How many members are there in the U.S. Congress?" Like all Wechsler subtests,

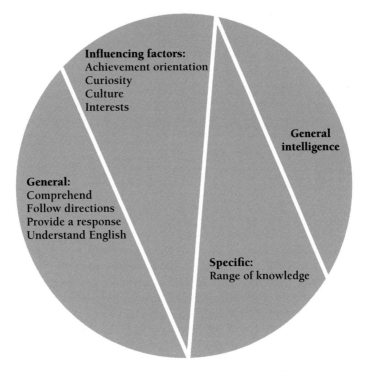

(Based on factor analytic and logical analyses of intellective and nonintellective components in the information subtest.)

the information subtest involves both intellective and nonintellective components, including several abilities to comprehend instructions, follow directions, and provide a response. Although purportedly a measure of the subject's range of knowledge, nonintellective factors such as curiosity and interest in the acquisition of knowledge tend to influence test scores. The subtest is also linked to alertness to the environment and alertness to cultural opportunities (Gregory, 1999). Figure 11.4 illustrates how one can parcel a score on the information subtest.

### The Comprehension Subtest

The comprehension subtest has three types of questions. The first asks the subject what should be done in a given situation, as in, "What should you do if you find an injured person lying in the street?" The second type of question asks the subject to provide a logical explanation for some rule or phenomenon, as in, "Why do we bury the dead?" The third type asks the subject to define proverbs such as, "A journey of 1000 miles begins with the first step." Generally, the comprehension subtest measures judgment in everyday practical situations, or common sense. Emotional difficulties frequently reveal themselves on this subtest and lower the person's score (Goldstein, Minshew, Allen, & Seaton, 2002). For example, to the question concerning what to do if you find an injured person, a psychopathic individual might respond, "Tell them I didn't do it." A phobic neurotic might respond, "Make sure I don't get any blood on myself." A schizophrenic might say, "Run!" In each case, the person's emotional disturbance interferes with his or her judgment and results in an inappropriate response.

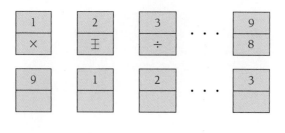

### The Letter–Number Sequencing Subtest

The letter–number sequencing task is supplementary on the working memory index; it is not required to obtain an index score, but it may be used as a supplement for additional information about the person's intellectual functioning (Phares & Trull, 2000; Wechsler, Coalson, & Engi Raiford, 2008). It is made up of items in which the individual is asked to reorder lists of numbers and letters. For example, Z, 3, B, 1, 2, A, would be reordered as 1, 2, 3, A, B, Z. This subtest is related to working memory and attention (Phares & Trull, 2000; Wechsler, Coalson, & Engi Raiford, 2008.).

### The Digit Symbol–Coding Subtest

The coding subtest (formerly called digit symbol) requires the subject to copy symbols. In the standard WAIS-IV response form, the numbers 1 through 9 are each paired with a symbol (see Figure 11.5). After completing a short practice sample, the subject has 120 seconds to copy as many symbols as possible. The subtest measures such factors as ability to learn an unfamiliar task, visual-motor dexterity, degree of persistence, and speed of performance (Gregory, 1999; Kaufman, 1990; Weschler, Coalson, & Engi Raiford, 2008). Naturally, the subject must have adequate visual acuity and appropriate motor capabilities to complete this subtest successfully, and factors that affect these capabilities, such as age, may affect test results (Kreiner & Ryan, 2001).

### The Block Design Subtest

Block design tasks have long been included in nonverbal measures of intelligence (Arthur, 1930; Kohs, 1923). Materials for the block design subtest include nine variously colored blocks. The materials also include a booklet with pictures of the blocks arranged according to a specific geometric design or configuration. The subject must arrange the blocks to reproduce increasingly difficult designs. This subtest requires the subject to reason, analyze spatial relationships, and integrate visual and motor functions. The input information (i.e., pictures of designs) is visual, but the response (output) is motor. The subtest provides an excellent measure of nonverbal concept formation, abstract thinking, and neurocognitive impairment (Lysaker,

Clements, Wright, Evans, & Marks, 2001; Paul, Cohen, Moser, Ott, Zawacki, & Gordon, 2001). It is one of the core measures of the perceptual reasoning index scale in the WAIS-IV.

### The Matrix Reasoning Subtest

As indicated in the previous chapter, modern theories of intelligence emphasize its multidimensional quality (Flanagan, McGrew, & Ortiz, 2000; McGrew & Flanagan, 1998). The matrix reasoning subtest was included in the WAIS-IV as a core subtest in the perceptual reasoning index scale in an effort to enhance the assessment of fluid intelligence, which involves our ability to reason. In the matrix reasoning subtest, the subject is presented with nonverbal, figural stimuli. The task is to identify a pattern or relationship between the stimuli. In addition to its role in measuring fluid intelligence, this subtest is a good measure of information-processing and abstract-reasoning skills (Phares & Trull, 2000; Wechsler, Coalson, & Engi Raiford, 2008).

### The Symbol Search Subtest

Symbol search is a relatively new subtest. It was optional in WAIS-III, but now is a core measure in the processing speed index scale. It was added in recognition of the role of speed of information processing in intelligence (Joy, Kaplan, & Fein, 2004; Kaufman, DeYoung, Reis, & Gray, 2011; Saccuzzo, Johnson, & Guertin, 1994). In this subtest, the subject is shown two target geometric figures. The task is then to search from among a set of five additional search figures and determine whether the target appears in the search group. Presumably, the faster a subject performs this task, the faster his or her information-processing speed will be. Chapter 9 discusses other measures of information-processing speed.

## From Raw Scores to Scaled and Index Scale Scores

Together each subtest produces a raw score—that is, a total number of points—and has a different maximum total.

To allow testers to compare scores on individual subtests, raw scores can be converted to standard or scaled scores with a mean of 10 and a standard deviation of 3. In deriving a subtest scaled score for the WAIS-IV, the test developers used a statistical method called inferential norming (Wilkins, Rolfhus, Weiss, & Zhu, 2005). A variety of statistical indexes or "moments," such as means and standard deviations, were calculated for each of the 13 age groups of the stratified normative sample (Weschler, Coalson, & Engi Raiford, 2008, p. 39). These were plotted across age groups to derive estimates of age group midpoint population moments. In the end, the test developers were able to derive reference-group norms, which allow the test user to compare subjects at the subtest level. As will be seen later, such reference group norms can be extremely valuable in interpreting scores.

The four composite index scales are then derived by summing the core subtest scores (see Figure 11.2). For example, the verbal comprehension index is determined from scaled scores on the vocabulary, similarities, and information subtests. Each of the four index scores were normalized to have a mean of 100 and a standard deviation of 15. Let's look more closely at these index scores.

## Index Scores

As indicated in Figure 11.2, there are four such scores: verbal comprehension, perceptual organization, working memory, and processing speed.

As a measure of acquired knowledge and verbal reasoning, the verbal comprehension index might best be thought of as a measure of crystallized intelligence. According to the test developers, this index is a "more refined," "purer" measure of verbal comprehension than is the VIQ because it excludes the arithmetic and digit span subtests, which have attentional or working memory components (Tulsky et al., 1997, p. 186; Weschler, Coalson, & Engi Raiford, 2008).

The perceptual reasoning index, consisting of visual puzzles, block design, and matrix reasoning (see Figure 11.2), is believed to be a measure of fluid intelligence. Other factors that influence one's performance on this group of tests are attentiveness to details and visual motor integration (Tulsky et al., 1997; Weschler, Coalson, & Engi Raiford, 2008).

The notion of working memory is perhaps one of the most important innovations on the modern WAIS. *Working memory* refers to the information that we actively hold in our minds, in contrast to our stored knowledge, or long-term memory (Pascanu & Jaeger, 2011). Consider the following question: "If you have $10.00 and give $4.50 to your brother and spend 75¢ on candy, how much do you have left?" To answer this question, you must mentally hold $10.00 in your head, subtract $4.50, and then hold that result while you subtract 75¢. It is your working memory that allows you to do this.

Finally, the processing speed index attempts to measure how quickly your mind works. For example, while one person may require 20 seconds to solve the given problem, another may require only 5 seconds.

**FIGURE 11.6**

Hierarchical Structure of the WAIS-IV

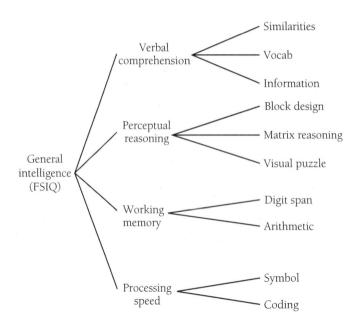

## FSIQs

The FSIQ follows the same principles of index scores. It is obtained by summing the age-corrected scaled scores all four index composites. Again, a deviation IQ with a mean of 100 and a standard deviation of 15 is obtained. The FSIQ represents a measure of general intelligence.

The WAIS-IV follows a hierarchical model with general intelligence (FSIQ) at the top. The index scores form the next level, with the subtests providing the base (see Figure 11.6).

# Interpretive Features of the Wechsler Tests

The WAIS-IV provides a rich source of data that often furnishes significant cues for diagnosing various conditions. The comparison of index scores and analysis of the pattern of subtest scores may be helpful, for example, in evaluating brain damage and disordered states. (The original Wechsler scale, through the WAIS-III, was based on just two indexes, called verbal and performance IQs.) As with modern index scores, these had a mean of 100 and standard deviations of 15. As the vast bulk of assessment is based on comparing the old verbal and performance IQs, these will be used to illustrate the process of index comparisons.

## Index Comparisons

In providing measures of nonverbal intelligence in conjunction with a nonverbal IQ measure, the Wechsler offers an extremely useful opportunity not offered by the early Binet scales. First, the nonverbal measures aid in the interpretation of the verbal measures (now called the verbal comprehension subtest). Assume, for example, that a subject obtains a VIQ in the low ranges (such as VIQ = 60). If the PIQ is also approximately 60, then the VIQ has been confirmed, and we have a good indication that the individual is, in fact, intellectually retarded. Remember, however, that a diagnosis of mental retardation should not be made on the basis of IQ alone. The individual must show significant deficits in adaptive functioning as well as an FSIQ below 70. What if the PIQ exceeds 100, but the VIQ is 55? In this case, the individual is at least average in his or her nonverbal skills but three standard deviations below the mean in the verbal area. Even though the FSIQ might still fall within the retarded range, it is quite unlikely that such a person is mentally retarded. Instead, language, cultural, or educational factors might account for the differences in the two measures of intellectual performance. However, there are limits to index comparisons as well.

In one study of verbal versus performance IQs, Saccuzzo, Johnson, and Russell (1992) examined approximately 5000 gifted children from four ethnic backgrounds: African American, Caucasian, Filipino, and Hispanic. Results showed that even though all children had IQs of 125 or greater, the nature of the verbal-performance discrepancy, if any, depended on ethnic background. The African American and Caucasian groups had higher verbal than performance IQs. The reverse was found for the Filipinos, who had significantly higher PIQs. No differences were found between the verbal and performance IQs for the Hispanics.

Results such as these indicate that it is not appropriate to make sweeping generalizations about the meaning of index discrepancies, and should provide a warning as new research begins to look at comparisons among the four index scores of the modern WAIS-IV.

## Pattern Analysis

The separate subtest scores of the WAIS-IV and other Wechsler tests offer an opportunity for *pattern analysis*. In such analysis, one evaluates relatively large differences between subtest scaled scores. Wechsler (1958) reasoned that different types of emotional problems might have differential effects on the subtests and cause unique score patterns. For example, people with conversion disorders often use denial and repression—that is, they put things out of awareness as a defense mechanism. Therefore, they should show lapses in their long-term store of knowledge, which might produce a relatively low score on the information subtest. Schizophrenia involves poor concentration and impaired judgment, which might turn up as relatively low scores on arithmetic and comprehension. Wechsler (1958) provided a host of patterns tentatively proposed as diagnostically significant.

Following Wechsler's (1958) proposed patterns, many investigators empirically studied the potential validity of pattern analysis. As is the case in many fields of psychology, results were inconclusive and contradictory.

Years of investigation have revealed that analysis of patterns must be done cautiously. At best, such analysis should be used to generate hypotheses. Such hypotheses must then be either corroborated or refuted by other sources of data, such as historical information, medical records, family interviews, and direct observation (Tulsky et al., 1997; Weschler, Coalson, & Engi Raiford, 2008). The next section presents two hypothetical case studies to illustrate how hypotheses might be generated from an administration of the older WAIS-III, which, as you will recall, used only two indexes—a verbal (VIQ) and a performance (PIQ) IQ score.

## Hypothetical Case Studies

### A Drop in Grades

Consider the following example of a 16-year-old high-school junior who has a D average, although he previously had a stable B average. Standard achievement tests found his reading and arithmetic grades appropriate. Table 11.2 shows his age-corrected scaled scores on the WAIS-III (remember, the mean is 10 and the standard deviation is 3).

The previously stable B average indicates that this individual is probably of at least average intelligence. The rapid decline in his grades, however, suggests some dramatic change or shift in functioning. His scaled score of 11 on vocabulary is above the mean. Because vocabulary is a relatively stable measure of IQ, the scaled score of 11 also indicates this individual's IQ of 93 is most likely an underestimate of his intelligence. Assuming that this individual's typical scaled score performance would be approximately 11, as reflected in his scaled score on vocabulary and confirmed by his scaled scores on information and similarities, we find evidence for deterioration in his judgment (comprehension), concentration (arithmetic), and

**TABLE 11.2**  Hypothetical Scaled Scores for a High-School Junior

| Verbal scales | Performance scales |
|---|---|
| Vocabulary: 11 | Picture completion: 10 |
| Similarities: 11 | Digit symbol–coding: 4 |
| Arithmetic: 7 | Block design: 5 |
| Digit span: 5 | Matrix reasoning: 6 |
| Information: 11 | Picture arrangement: 1 |
| Comprehension: 9 | |
| Scaled score sum: 54 | Scaled score sum: 36 |
| Verbal IQ: 104 | Performance IQ: 83 |
| Full-scale IQ: 93 | |

immediate memory (digit span) in the verbal areas. We also find deterioration in his visual-motor speed and integration (digit symbol–coding), nonverbal reasoning (block design), and fluid intelligence (matrix reasoning) in the performance areas.

With no evidence to the contrary, the clinician would strongly suspect that the subject's shift in grades may be the result of a brain injury or tumor, because these impair performance on all the subtests in which the subject has shown evidence of deterioration (e.g., Lincoln, Crosson, Bauer, & Cooper, 1994; Ryan, Paolo, & Van Fleet, 1994). However, the clinician would consider other possibilities as well. Environmental or situational factors could lead to impairment on the various subtests. For example, because the subject may have become involved with drugs, this possibility must be examined. Furthermore, schizophrenia may cause similar decrements in performance. Therefore, signs of peculiar behavior or other symptoms of schizophrenia should be ruled out by an interview and other tests. Ruling out situational, environmental, and schizophrenic factors, the examiner might interview to determine whether the subject has suffered a recent blow to the head. If these possibilities prove to be negative, then the subject should be immediately referred for a neurological examination. As you no doubt have observed, this analysis resulted in several speculations, and the clinician exercised the usual caution in using the results.

### A Slow Learner

Table 11.3 shows the hypothetical age-corrected scaled scores of a 16-year-old girl with chronic school problems. Identified as a slow learner in the earlier grades, she reads far below her grade level.

The subject is nearly one standard deviation above the mean in her PIQ; all her subtests in the performance area are at or greater than the mean. Clearly, she does not lack intellectual potential. Thus, her VIQ of 89 most likely underestimates her intellectual capacity. Furthermore, she obtains an above-average score on similarities, a noneducationally related measure of abstract thinking skills. Her major weaknesses arise in the subtests related to academic achievement, information, and arithmetic. In addition, she shows some impairment in her judgment. Her VIQ thus appears to be lowered because of her lack of motivation for

**TABLE 11.3** Hypothetical Scaled Scores for a Slow Learner

| Verbal scales | Performance scales |
|---|---|
| Vocabulary: 8 | Picture completion: 11 |
| Similarities: 11 | Digit symbol–coding: 12 |
| Arithmetic: 4 | Block design: 13 |
| Digit span: 10 | Matrix reasoning: 12 |
| Information: 3 | Picture arrangement: 10 |
| Comprehension: 7 | |
| Scaled score sum: 43 | Scaled score sum: 58 |
| Verbal IQ: 89 | Performance IQ: 112 |
| Full-scale IQ: 99 | |

academic achievement and her poor judgment. Her pattern of subtest scores is one typically found in poor readers and delinquents.

In considering these illustrations, remember that the validity of pattern analysis is still questionable. Saccuzzo and Lewandowski (1976) found a pattern for acting-out behavior that Wickham later substantiated (1978). However, evidence supporting the validity of most patterns, for reasons we shall discuss more fully, is still questionable (Alexander, Prohovnik, Stem, & Mayeux, 1994; Fitzgerald et al., 2007). Our illustrations are designed to give you a flavor of the approach taken by many practicing psychologists. Most real-life examples are nowhere nearly as clear-cut as our hypothetical ones.

# Psychometric Properties of the Wechsler Adult Scale

## Standardization

The WAIS-III standardization sample consisted of a stratified sample 2200 adults divided into 13 age groups from 16:00 through 90:11 as well as 13 specialty groups (Tulsky et al., 1997, p. 19; Weschler, Coalson, & Engi Raiford, 2008). The sample was stratified according to gender, race, education, and geographic region based on 2005 census data.

## Reliability

The impressive reliability coefficients for the WAIS-IV attest to the internal and temporal reliability of the four index scores, and full-scale IQ. When the split-half method is used for all subtests except speeded tests (digit symbol–coding and symbol search), the typical average coefficients across age levels are .98 for the FSIQ, .96 for the verbal comprehension index VIQ, and .95 for the perceptual reasoning index, .94 for the working memory index, and .90 for the processing speed index (Weschler, Coalson, & Engi Raiford, 2008, p. 42). Test–retest coefficients reported in the manual are only slightly lower.

The technical manual reports an overall standard error of measurement of 2.16 for the FSIQ, and 2.85 for the verbal comprehension index. The error is a bit higher for the other indexes (Weschler, Coalson, & Engi Raiford, 2008, p. 45). As you may recall from our discussion of correlation and reliability (see Chapter 4), all tests possess a certain degree of measurement error. The standard error of measurement (SEM) is the standard deviation of the distribution of error scores. According to classical test theory, an error score is the difference between the score actually obtained by giving the test and the score that would be obtained if the measuring instrument were perfect. In practice, the SEM is based on the reliability coefficient, given by the formula

$$SEM = SD\sqrt{1 - r_{xx}}$$

where SD is the standard deviation of the test scores and $r_{xx}$ is the reliability coefficient. In practice, the SEM can be used to form a confidence interval within which an individual's true score is likely to fall. More specifically, we can determine the probability that an individual's true score will fall within a certain range a given percentage of the time. To be roughly at the 68% level, an obtained score must fall within the range of one SEM. The 95% confidence interval is approximately two SEMs.

Using this information, we can see that the smaller SEM for the verbal comprehension index and full-scale IQs means that we can have considerably more confidence that an obtained score represents an individual's true score than we can have for the other indexes. Thus, given an FSIQ of 110, we can assume that 95% of the time the subject's true score would fall at $(+/-)4.32$ (two SEMs) of the true score. In other words, 95% of subjects with a score of 110 have a true score between 105.68 and 114.32, and only 5% do not.

## Validity

The validity of the WAIS-IV rests heavily on its correlation with earlier versions of the test. However, the Wechsler tests are considered among the most valid.

# Evaluation of the Wechsler Adult Scales

The Wechsler adult scale is extensively used as a measure of adult intelligence. This scale is well constructed and its primary measures—the four index components and full-scale IQ—are highly reliable. As with all modern tests, including the modern Binet, the reliability of the individual subtests is lower and therefore makes analysis of subtest patterns dubious for the purpose of making decisions about individuals. Yet making such conclusions is commonplace. As we have noted, though such analysis may be useful for generating hypotheses, it calls for extreme caution.

# Downward Extensions of the WAIS-III: The WISC-IV and the WPPSI-III

Many of the basic ideas of the WAIS-IV apply to its downward extension, the WISC-IV, first published in 1949, revised in 1974 and 1991, and most recently revised in 2003. The WISC-IV measures intelligence from ages 6 through

16 years, 11 months. Many basic ideas of the WAIS-IV also apply to the Wechsler Preschool and Primary Scale of Intelligence, Third Edition (WPPSI-III). The WPPSI-III, first published in 1967, revised in 1989 and again in 2003, measures intelligence in children from 2.5 to 7 years, 3 months. Because you already know the basic ideas that apply to all Wechsler scales, we present here only the major distinguishing features of the WISC-IV and the WPPSI-III.

## The WISC-IV

The WISC-IV is the latest version of this scale to measure global intelligence and, in an attempt to mirror advances in the understanding of intellectual properties, the WISC-IV also provides composite index (Wechsler, 2003). The original form of the WISC was based on Form 11 of the Wechsler–Bellevue scale, which provided a point scale measure of intelligence for children between the ages of 6 years and 16 years, 11 months. The WISC-IV contains 15 subtests, 10 of which were retained from the earlier WISC-III and 5 entirely new ones. Three subtests used in earlier versions—picture arrangement, object assembly, and mazes—were entirely deleted. As indicated, like the WAIS-IV, the WISC-IV abandoned the VIQ-PIQ dichotomy. In place of these scales are the four major indexes, which can be summed to arrive at an FSIQ.

Within the WISC-IV verbal comprehension index are comprehension, similarities, and vocabulary subtests. Information and word reasoning are supplementary subtests. Within the WISC-IV perceptual reasoning index are the subtests block design, picture concepts, and matrix reasoning. The supplementary test is a picture completion task.

The processing speed index comprises a coding subtest and a symbol search subtest that consists of paired groups of symbols. In this latter subtest, each pair contains a target group and a search group, just as in the comparable WAIS-IV subtest. The child scans the two groups and indicates whether a target symbol appears in the search group. A cancellation subtest is supplementary to the processing speed index.

Finally, the working memory index consists of digit span, letter–number sequencing, and a supplemental arithmetic subtest. These subtests, with the exception of symbol search and the deleted mazes, parallel the corresponding WAIS-IV subtests in content and functions measured. Items are arranged in order of difficulty and are grouped by content.

The WISC-IV is a major improvement from the earlier WISC-III and, as indicated, has introduced important innovations from earlier versions of the Wechsler scales. As with the modern Binet, the modern WISC-IV has updated its theoretical underpinnings. In addition to the important concept of fluid reasoning, there is an emphasis on the modern cognitive psychology concepts of working memory and processing speed. To add to its clinical utility, the test manual provides numerous studies of special groups, and the WISC-IV is linked to an achievement test (the Wechsler Individual Achievement Test, or WIAT-II), which is also published by the Psychological Corporation (2001).

Through the use of teaching items that are not scored, it is possible to reduce errors attributed to a child's lack of understanding. The administration procedures also include many queries and prompts that examiners can use to elicit a maximum performance. Although the use of prompts dates back to early versions of the

Binet, the WISC-IV appears to provide examiners with more latitude to encourage a child to perform as well as possible.

### Item Bias

One of the most important innovations in the WISC-IV is the use of empirical data to identify item biases. Heretofore the primary, and in our opinion inadequate and insufficient, method of examining for item bias was to use trained judges to examine item content. Although the WISC-IV retains this approach, the use of item analysis and other statistical procedures to determine which items may be biased adds an important and necessary dimension in the elimination of bias. The major reason that empirical approaches are needed is that expert judgments simply do not eliminate differential performance as a function of gender, race, ethnicity, and socioeconomic status. Even if a test has been thoroughly and extensively screened by experts to eliminate content that might be biased, bias nevertheless remains in terms of the number of items passed as a function of gender, race, ethnicity, and socioeconomic status. The WISC-IV has not eliminated item bias, but the use of empirical techniques is a major step in the right direction.

Publishers of other tests discussed throughout this book would do well to follow this lead, which hopefully will soon become the standard. For example, it is widely known that men do better than women on multiple-choice tests, which are widely used in high-stakes testing. This bias is not eliminated by making the content gender-neutral or by using as many references to women as men. The use of empirical methods and sophisticated statistical procedures, as has been done with the WISC-IV, offers the best hope of someday devising a test that accurately measures ability without gender, ethnic, racial, or socioeconomic bias.

### Standardization of the WISC-IV

The WISC-IV standardization sample consisted of 2200 children selected to represent the March 2000 U.S. census. The sample was stratified using age, gender, race (African American, Hispanic, white, other), geographic region, parental occupation, and geographic location as variables. As with its predecessor, the WISC-III, the sample contained 100 boys and 100 girls at each age from 6 through 16 years (see Figure 11.7).

### Raw Scores and Scaled Scores

In the WISC-IV, scaled scores are calculated from raw scores on the basis of norms at each age level, just as in the WAIS-IV. The mean scaled score is also set at 10 and the standard deviation at 3. Scaled scores are summed for the four indexes and FSIQs. These totals are then compared against a single table of standard scores with a mean of 100 and a standard deviation of 15 for each of the indexes and FSIQ.

### Interpretation

Interpretation of the WISC-IV also parallels that of the WAIS-III. The basic approach involves evaluating each of the four major indexes to examine for deficits in any given area and evaluate the validity of the FSIQ. To the extent that large discrepancies exist in the indexes, the validity of the FSIQ falls into question. The next step would be to consider the underlying functions measured by each of the subtests and again determine whether large discrepancies exist between one subtest

FIGURE 11.7

Characteristics of the WISC-III standardization sample.

(From Wechsler Intelligence Scale for Children, 1989, Copyright © 1989 The Psychological Corporation. Reprinted by permission.)

and another, or between one subtest and the overall mean of the subtests. As a simple example, if all subtests are roughly average except for an extremely low score on working memory, the clinician would hypothesize a specific deficit in working memory.

### Reliability of the WISC-IV

When the WISC-IV was revised, developers intended to maintain the strong psychometric properties of its predecessors, which they largely did. The procedure for calculating reliability coefficients for the WISC-IV was analogous to that used for the WISC-III and WAIS-IV. Split-half reliabilities for the WISC-IV's composites range from .88 for processing speed to .97 for the FSIQ (Wechsler, 2003, p. 35). Naturally, reliabilities for individual subtests run lower, as in all forms of tests.

As usual, test–retest reliability coefficients run a bit below those obtained using the split-half method. As with the Binet scales and other tests, reliability coefficients are poorest for the youngest groups at the highest levels of ability.

### WISC-IV Validity

In providing evidence of its validity, the WISC-IV manual relies on the modern trend that rejects the distinction between various types of validity and instead examines all of the relevant evidence that indicates whether a test score measures what it purports to (Wechsler, 2003, p. 47). The manual presents several lines of evidence of the test's validity, involving theoretical considerations, the test's internal structure, a variety of intercorrelational studies, factor analytic studies, and evidence based on WISC-IV's relationship with a host of other measures. As with its main competitor, the Binet, the WISC-IV manual presents extensive and comprehensive support for its validity.

A cross-cultural analysis of the factor structure underlying the earlier WISC-III, based on standardized data from 16 countries, suggested substantial cross-cultural similarities. Similar problems have been confirmed by more recent analyses (Keith, Fine, Taub, Reynolds, & Kranzler, 2006; Watkins, Glutting, & Lei, 2007). Also observed were no significant mean score differences across the cultures on the WISC-III subtests, FSIQ, VIQ, PIQ, or index scores, although mean scores were affected by affluence and education (Cohen, Fiorello, & Farley, 2006; Georgas, Weiss, Vijver, & Saklofske, 2003). In addition, a confirmatory factor analysis of the WISC-III supported a five-factor model of intelligence including verbal comprehension, constructional praxis, visual reasoning, freedom from distractibility, and processing speed (Burton, Sepehri, Hecht, VandenBroek, Ryan, & Drabman, 2001). Subsequent research have added to the validity of these findings by showing the value of comparing general intellectual ability and memory (Lange & Chelune, 2006) or achievement (Watkins et al., 2007).

In a study published in 2012, using a population of 1100 children aged 6 through 16, using the WISC-IV core subtests, researchers investigated measurement invariance of the WISC-IV second-order factorial structure between normative and clinical samples. One fundamental aspect of validity is that of measurement invariance, i.e., that the assessment measures the same thing in different populations. In this study, results supported measurement invariance across normative and clinical samples (Chen & Zhu, 2012). Only coding and comprehension subtest intercepts varied slightly between groups. The hypothesized WISC-IV factor model described the data well. Factor patterns, first- and second-order factor loadings, intercepts, residual variances of measured subtests, and disturbances of first-order factors of the WISC-IV were generally invariant. Results suggested that WISC-IV index scores and subtests have the same meaning for children in both normative and clinical groups (Chen & Zhu, 2012).

Another study asked whether the WISC-IV measured the same thing in a normative sample and in a sample of individuals with intellectual disabilities (Bowden, Saklofske, & Weiss, 2011). The model satisfied the assumption of invariance across samples with subtest scores reflecting similar construct measurement in both samples. The results demonstrate the generality of construct validity in measurement of cognitive abilities. Thus, there is much evidence of the validity of the WISC-IV.

## The WPPSI-III

In 1967, Wechsler published a scale for children 4 to 6 years of age, the WPPSI. In its revised (1989) version, the WPPSI-R paralleled the WAIS-IV and WISC-III in format, method of determining reliabilities, and subtests. Only two unique subtests are included: (1) animal pegs, an optional test that is timed and requires the child to place a colored cylinder into an appropriate hole in front of the picture of an animal; and (2) sentences, an optional test of immediate recall in which the child is asked to repeat sentences presented orally by the examiner.

The WPPSI-III was substantially revised. It contains most of the new features of the WISC-IV, including five composites, but did not delete the VIQ or PIQ. The WPPSI-III was also restructured to lower the age range. It can now be used for children as young as 2 years, 6 months, and has a special set of subtests specifically for the age range of 2 to 3 years, 11 months. To support legislation that recommends multiple assessments for identification of children in need of special educational services, WPPSI-III was made compatible with the Adaptive Behavior Assessment System, the WIAT-II, and the Differential Abilities Scale. Seven new subtests were added to enhance the measurement of fluid reasoning, processing speed, and receptive, expressive vocabulary. Clinical studies were conducted with children with mental retardation, developmental delay, giftedness, autism, attention deficit hyperactivity disorder, and language disorder. These validity studies foster a better understanding of the relative performance of clinical and nonclinical groups.

In addition to the extended age range and a special set of core tests for the youngest children, the WPPSI-III includes updated norms stratified as in the WISC-IV and based on the October 2000 census. New subtests were added along with the two additional composites [processing speed quotient (PSQ) and general language composite (GLC)]. These new composites provide a new dimension to evaluate young children.

Reminiscent of the most recent Binet, with its routing procedure, the WPPSI-III has age-specific starting points for each of the various subtests. It also has reversal rules in case a child misses an item at the starting point, as well as discontinuation rules to prevent frustration and reduce total testing time. As with the WISC-IV, there are practice items that are not scored as well as wide scope for an examinee to make use of prompts and queries. In addition, an examiner may repeat an item as often as requested.

The WPPSI-III also uses empirical methods to evaluate test bias, which, as indicated, is a welcome and long-needed development in the testing field. As with the Binet, instructions were modified to make them easier for young children, and materials were revised to make them more interesting. Reliability coefficients are comparable to those of the WISC-IV, and the test manual provides impressive evidence of validity.

There have been numerous research studies since our last edition that have supported the validity and use of the WPPSI, and reviews of the test have been very favorable (Gordon, 2004). Price, Raju, Lurie, Wilkins, and Zhu (2006) supported the validity of WPPSI-III composites using item response theory. Moreover, empirical research supports the proposition that the WPPSI-III has even fewer language demands than its predecessor, the WPPSI-R (Cazassus, 2005). Thus, the WPPSI-III may be a more sensitive measure of ability for younger children with less developed language skills than their older counterparts.

In addition, the criterion validity properties of the WPPSI-III have been demonstrated by examining its convergent validity with measures of general intelligence from other Wechsler scales. The convergent validity between the WISC-IV and WPPSI-III has been previously established (see Engel, Wetmur, Chen, Zhu, Barr, et al., 2011, p. 1184). In psychometric analyses, the correlation between

WPPSI-III and WISC-IV FSIQ scores was 0.89; WPPSI-III verbal IQ and WISC-IV verbal comprehension, 0.83; and WPPSI-III performance IQ and WISC-IV perceptual reasoning, 0.79. In a 2011 study by Engel et al. (at p. 1184) among children who were administered both the WPPSI-III and the WISC-IV (n = 103), the correlations between the composite scores on the WPPSI-III and WISC-IV were likewise very strong: FSIQ = 0.83, verbal IQ/verbal comprehension = 0.84, and performance IQ/perceptual reasoning = 0.78.

# Summary

Motivation for the development of the Wechsler scales began with the search for a more appropriate measure of adult intelligence than that provided by the 1937 Binet scale. The first product of this effort was the Wechsler–Bellevue scale.

In a *point scale*, a specific number of credits or points is assigned to each item. A *performance scale* measures nonverbal intelligence, as opposed to a *verbal scale*, which measures verbal intelligence. On a performance scale, the subject is required to do something other than merely answer questions.

The seven standard verbal subtests of the WAIS-III and the functions they purportedly measure are as follows:

The WAIS-IV contains four index composites in addition to a measure of general intelligence. The indexes are obtained by (1) converting the raw score of each subtest to a *scaled score*, or an age-corrected standard score of 10 with a standard deviation of 3; (2) adding the corresponding core scores to obtain a separate summary or composite score for each index; and (3) converting these two standardized scores with a mean of 100 and a standard deviation of 15. The FSIQ is then base on the index scores and also has a mean of 100 and a standard deviation of 15.

The reliability coefficients of the WAIS-IV are excellent for the four index scores and full-scale IQ. Reliabilities for the individual subtests, however, vary. Evidence for the validity of the WAIS-IV comes from its high correlation with its earlier predecessors. The WISC-IV is a downward extension of the WAIS-IV for measuring children's intelligence. First published in 1949, the WISC was revised in 1974, 1991, and most recently in 2003. It contains many significant changes from earlier versions as well as several important innovations, including empirical testing of item bias.

The WPPSI-III is a downward extension of the WISC-IV for measuring intelligence in the youngest children (2.5 years to 7 years, 3 months). It was first published in 1967 and revised in 1989 and again in 2002. Its changes and innovations parallel those found in the WISC-IV.

# CHAPTER 12

# Other Individual Tests of Ability in Education and Special Education

## LEARNING OBJECTIVES

*When you have completed this chapter, you should be able to:*

▶ Identify the advantages and disadvantages of the alternative individual ability tests compared with the Binet and Wechsler scales

▶ List six differences among the alternative individual ability tests

▶ Discuss the strengths and weaknesses of the Bayley Scales of Infant Development compared with other measures of infant intelligence

▶ Identify some of the purposes of the Columbia Mental Maturity Scale

▶ Explain the main theory behind tests of learning disability

▶ Explain the main idea behind testing for brain damage

▶ List three possible reasons for errors on the Bender Visual Motor Gestalt Test

▶ Describe the general reaction among reviewers to the Torrance Tests of Creative Thinking

▶ Identify problems of the Wide Range Achievement Test

n Long Beach, California, a student was being evaluated for a learning disability. At issue was whether the student qualified for special education. The evaluation used a variety of tests but did not use the Binet or Wechsler test. The student was found not eligible. The parents challenged the evaluation, claiming the district was required to use a standardized IQ test like the Binet or Wechsler in its evaluation. Siding with the school district, the 9th U.S. Circuit Court of Appeals held that the district was not required to use a traditional standardized test such as the Binet or Wechsler in its evaluation of the student (*Ford and Ford v. Long Beach Unified School District*, 37 IDELR I, 9th Circuit 2002). As noted in the *Special Educator 2003 Desk Book* (Norlin, 2003), an important reference book in special education that summarizes recent court decisions in the field, tests must be considered valid for a particular student or they cannot be used. In this case, the Binet and Wechsler apparently did not meet this standard in the court's view.

For assessing general intelligence in relatively normal individuals or to obtain baseline information, the Binet and Wechsler scales are exceptionally good instruments. However, both scales have their limitations and are not valid for all individuals.

How, then, can one fairly evaluate the performance on the Binet scale of someone who has been blind for life? What about individuals who cannot speak?

Clearly, numerous circumstances arise where a score on the major scales would be either impossible to obtain or seriously biased against the individual. Thus, several individual tests have been created to meet special problems, measure specific abilities, or address the limitations of the Binet and Wechsler scales. Such tests are widely used in education and, in particular, in the important field of special education.

There is quite an array of individual ability tests. Because many were designed to supplement or provide an alternative to the Binet and Wechsler scales, we begin this chapter by comparing the general features of these tests with those of the Binet and Wechsler scales. We move on to compare the alternative tests to each other, and then we discuss them one at a time.

# Alternative Individual Ability Tests Compared with the Binet and Wechsler Scales

The tests discussed in this section were developed more recently and are newer and less well established than the Binet and Wechsler scales; however, this does not sufficiently explain why no other individual test is used as much as these two major scales. Despite the limitations of the Binet and Wechsler scales, none of the alternatives is clearly superior from a psychometric standpoint. Although a few of the most recently revised tests are quite good, some of the alternative tests are weaker in terms of the representativeness or quality of the standardization sample. Some are less stable, and most are more limited in their documented validity. Some have inadequacies in the test manual, such as unclear or poorly standardized administration instructions, and others provide insufficient information about psychometric adequacy, appropriate uses, and limitations. Indeed, a few of the alternatives compare poorly on all counts. Except for some specific advantages, perhaps none of the alternatives can be considered better than the two major scales when one considers all relevant factors, except for individuals with special needs.

Though usually weaker in psychometric properties, many of the alternatives to the major scales do not rely on a verbal response as much as the Binet and Wechsler verbal scales do. Many require the individual only to point or to make any response indicating "Yes" or "No," and thus do not depend as much on the complex integration of visual and motor functioning. Like the Wechsler scales, most of the alternatives contain a performance scale or subscale. Indeed, the dearth of performance tasks in the early Binet scales helped to stimulate the development of many alternative individual tests of ability.

In providing a performance component (many alternatives are exclusively performance scales), alternatives to the Binet and Wechsler have particular relevance for special populations. Some were designed for special populations, such as individuals with sensory limitations (e.g., deaf people) or physical limitations (e.g., people who are paralyzed or partially paralyzed). Others were designed to evaluate those with language limitations, such as culturally deprived people, certain brain-damaged individuals, and foreign-born or non-English-speaking individuals. Still others were designed to assess learning disabilities.

Because the tests were designed for special populations or purposes, the existence of alternatives is justifiable. However, their specificity often limits the range of functions or abilities that they can measure. Thus, one may consider the greater specificity of some alternatives as a weakness as well as a strength. Although the alternatives may be much more suitable for special populations than the major scales would be, an IQ score based on one of the alternatives, with rare exception, cannot be compared directly with a score from one of the major scales. However, the alternatives are often useful as a supplement for results obtained with one of the major scales, such as for screening purposes, for follow-up or reevaluations, or when insufficient time is available to administer one of the major scales. In addition, when several such tests are used in conjunction, limitations in one can be reduced or overcome by a particular strength in another. For example, in the case cited at the beginning of this chapter, the evaluation used six alternative measures, and this was considered acceptable (Norlin, 2003).

Because they are designed for special populations, some alternatives can be administered totally without verbal instructions (e.g., through pantomime or chalkboard instructions) (Parissea & Maillartb, 2009; Naglieri & Ford, 2003). Furthermore, most are less related than the Binet and Wechsler scales to reading ability, and a few are almost totally independent of reading ability. As a consequence, the scores from many alternatives contain less variability because of scholastic achievement than either the Binet or the Wechsler scale, both of which correlate strongly with scholastic achievement.

See Table 12.1 for a summary of alternative tests versus the major scales.

TABLE 12.1    Comparison of General Features of Alternatives with the Wechsler and Binet Scales

**Disadvantages of alternatives**

Weaker standardization sample

Less stable

Less documentation on validity

Limitations in test manual

Not as psychometrically sound

IQ scores not interchangeable with Binet or Wechsler

**Advantages of alternatives**

Can be used for specific populations and special purposes:

Sensory limitations

Physical limitations

Language limitations

Culturally deprived people

Foreign-born individuals

Non-English-speaking people

Not as reliant on verbal responses

Not as dependent on complex visual–motor integration

Useful for screening, supplement, and reevaluations

Can be administered nonverbally

Less variability because of scholastic achievement

# Alternatives Compared with One Another

To construct and publish a useful test, we must develop a better method than is currently available. We may develop a test to measure some factor not tapped by any existing measure or provide a test for a particular group for whom existing procedures have not worked. If a new test offers no specific advantages, most examiners will probably stay with a more established test. Therefore, most alternatives tend to differ from one another in some important way. Alternatives to the major scales that do no more than attempt to measure abilities in the same way, only better, have met with little success.

In comparing tests used in education and special education other than the Binet and Wechsler scales, we find that some apply to only the youngest children, others to older children and adolescents, and still others to both children and adults. Thus, some of the alternatives to the major scales differ in their targeted age ranges. A second important difference concerns what is measured. Some of the alternatives attempt to measure language or vocabulary skills through nonverbal techniques, some to measure nonverbal or nonlanguage intelligence, and others to measure perceptual or motor skills. Alternatives also differ in the type of score they produce. Some give only a single score, as in the early Binet scales, whereas others produce several scores, as in the modern Binet and the Wechsler scales. The alternatives differ also in the type of response required of subjects. Some present the items in a multiple-choice format, requiring that the subject choose or point to a correct alternative; others simply require the subject to indicate "Yes" or "No" by whatever means possible.

Other important differences mark the alternative individual tests of human ability. Some require simple motor skills, whereas others demand relatively complex motor behavior. A few sample a wide range of abilities, but most focus on a narrow range. Still another difference concerns the target population, which may include deaf, blind, physically handicapped, learning disabled, language-impaired, or foreign-born people. Furthermore, some provide timed tasks; others do not. Some claim to have significance for personality and clinical diagnoses; others are exclusively related to an ability.

Another difference is the amount of examiner skill and experience necessary for administration. Whereas some tests require as much skill and experience as the Binet or Wechsler scales do, others require only minimal examiner skill and could probably be administered by a trained paraprofessional under supervision. To avoid confusing the various tests in this chapter, you should compare the various alternatives with the Binet and Wechsler scales; you should also compare them with each other in terms of their main distinguishing features, as summarized in Table 12.2.

**TABLE 12.2**   Summary of Differences Among Individual Ability Tests Other Than the Binet and Wechsler Scales

| Difference | Definition or example |
|---|---|
| Age range | Different tests are designed for specific age groups |
| What is measured | Verbal intelligence, nonverbal intelligence, and so on |
| Type of score | Single score versus multiple scores |
| Type of skill required | Simple motor, complex motor, and so on |
| Range of abilities sampled | Single specific ability versus a wide range of abilities |
| Target population | Deaf, blind, learning disabled, and so on |
| Timing | Some are timed; others are not |
| Personality versus ability | Some are relevant for personality and clinical diagnoses, others for ability |
| Examiner skill and experience | Some require far less examiner skill and experience to administer and interpret than others |

# Specific Individual Ability Tests

The earliest individual ability tests were typically designed for specific purposes or populations. One of the first, the Seguin Form Board Test (Seguin, 1907) first published in the 1800s, actually preceded the Binet. This test, of the performance variety, produced only a single score. It consisted of a simple form board with objects of various shapes placed in appropriately shaped holes (such as squares or circles). The Seguin Form Board Test was used primarily to evaluate mentally retarded adults and emphasized speed of performance. A version of this test is still available. Quite a while after the development of the Seguin test, the Healy–Fernald Test (1911) was developed as an exclusively nonverbal test for adolescent delinquents. Although it produced only a single score, the Healy–Fernald Test provided several types of tasks, rather than just one, as in the Seguin Form Board Test, and there was less emphasis on speed. Then Knox (1914) developed a battery of performance tests for non-English-speaking adult immigrants to the United States. The test was one of the first that could be administered without language. Speed was not emphasized.

In sum, early individual ability tests other than the Binet scale were designed for specific populations, produced a single score, and had nonverbal performance scales. The emphasis on speed gradually decreased from the earliest to the more recent tests. These early procedures demonstrated the feasibility of constructing individual nonverbal performance tests that could provide an alternative to the then verbally dependent Binet scale. They could be administered without visual instructions and used with children as well as adults.

## Infant Scales

An important category of individual tests of ability attempts to measure intelligence in infants and young children. Generally, there is not much point to estimating the IQ of an infant or preschool toddler. However, where mental retardation or developmental delays are suspected, these tests can supplement observation, genetic testing, and other medical procedures. Thus, our discussion of educational tests begins with tests that can be used well before the child enters the school system.

### Brazelton Neonatal Assessment Scale (BNAS)

The BNAS is an individual test for infants between 3 days and 4 weeks of age (Botet & Rosales, 1996; Brazelton, 1973, 1984). It purportedly provides an index of a newborn's competence. Developed by a Harvard pediatrician, the Brazelton scale produces 47 scores: 27 behavioral items and 20 elicited responses. These scores are obtained in a variety of areas, including the neurological, social, and behavioral aspects of a newborn's functioning. Factors such as reflexes, responses to stress, startle reactions, cuddliness, motor maturity, ability to habituate to sensory stimuli, and hand–mouth coordination are all assessed. Reviews of the Brazelton scale have been favorable (Aylward, 2011; Guzzetta, 2009). As Sostek (1978) stated, the Brazelton has "the greatest breadth of the available neonatal examinations" (p. 208). The Brazelton also has a considerable research base (e.g., Gauvain, 1994; see also Costa Figueiredo, Tendais, Conde, Pacheco, & Teixeira, 2010; Hays, 2004; Johnson, 2003).

The Brazelton scale has found wide use as a research tool and as a diagnostic tool for special purposes (Lundqvist-Persson, Lau, Nordin, Bona, & Sabel, 2011; Majnemer & Mazer, 1998). For example, the scale has been used to evaluate the effects of low birth weight on premature infants (Lundqvist-Persson, Lau, Nordin, Bona, & Sabel, 2011; Medoff-Cooper, McGrath, & Bilker, 2000). Researchers have used it to study the effects of cocaine use in pregnancy (Morrow et al., 2001), prenatal alcohol exposure (Oberlander, Jacobson, Weinberg, Grunau, Molteno, & Jacobson, 2010), prenatal iron deficiency (Hernández-Martínez, Canals, Aranda, Ribot, Escribano, & Arija, 2011), prenatal maternal mood (Field, Diego, & Hernandez-Reif, 2010; Field, Diego, Hernandez-Reif, Schanberg, & Kuhn, 2002), prenatal maternal dopamine levels (Marcus, Lopez, McDonough, MacKenzie, Flynn, Neal, Gahagan, Volling, Kaciroti, & Vazquez, 2011), and environmental agents (Tronick, 1987). Others have used the scale to study parent–infant attachment (Beal, 1991), gender differences in newborns (Lundqvist & Sabel, 2000), and high-risk neonates (Emory, Tynan, & Dave, 1989). Reviews of the relevant literature have been highly enthusiastic (El-Dib, Massaro, Glass, & Aly, 2011; Gauvain, 1994; Majnemer & Mazer, 1998).

The BNAS remains one of the most commonly used scales for the assessment of neonates (Berger, Hopkins, Bae, Hella, & Strickland, 2010). Despite the enthusiasm for the scale, it has several significant drawbacks. No norms are available (McGregor, 2001). Thus, although examiners and researchers can state that one infant scored higher than another in a particular area, there is no standard sample against which to compare test results. In addition, more research is needed concerning the meaning and implication of scores. The scale purportedly helps one assess the infant's role in the mother–infant social relationship (Guzzetta, 2009; Stern, 2010), and high scores presumably imply high levels of intelligence (Canals, Hernández-Martínez, Esparó, & Fernández-Ballart, 2011; Brazelton, 1993). Like most infant intelligence measures, however, the Brazelton scale has poorly documented predictive and construct validity. The scale has not been shown to be of value in predicting later intelligence (McGregor, 2001; Tronick & Brazelton, 1975). Furthermore, despite relatively good interrater reliability for trained examiners, with coefficients ranging from .85 to .90 (McGregor, 2001), the test–retest reliability (i.e., reliability over time) leaves much to be desired. As for all measures of intelligence when development is rapid and uneven, test–retest reliability coefficients for the Brazelton scale are typically poor and unstable for subjects younger than 8 years (see Figure 12.1).

**FIGURE 12.1**

Schematic summary of the Brazelton Neonatal Assessment Scale.

In conclusion, although the Brazelton scale may offer much as a research tool and a supplement to medical testing procedures, as an individual test of infant intelligence it is unsatisfactory. Its lack of norms is a serious shortcoming, and its failure to predict future intelligence leaves us wondering what the scale is really measuring. In fairness to the Brazelton, the scale is extremely well constructed. Moreover, as you will see, *all* infant ability tests based on sensorimotor functioning have proven ineffective in predicting later intelligence except in the lowest ranges.

### Gesell Developmental Schedules (GDS)

The GDS (also known as the Gesell Maturity Scale, the Gesell Developmental Observation, and the Yale Tests of Child Development) is one of the oldest and most established infant intelligence measures. First published in 1925 (Gesell, 1925), the Gesell scale has been subjected to extensive research and refinement and was updated in 1940, 1965, 1979, and most recently in 2011 (Gesell Institute, 2011). To gather supportive data for the GDS, the Gesell Institute completed a nationwide study in March 2010 which included 1,300 assessments of children aged 2.3 through 6.3 years (Gesell Institute, 2010).

One of the leading infant intelligence measures from the 1930s through the 1960s, the Gesell scale continues to be used as a research tool by those interested in assessing infant intellectual development after exposure to mercury (Marques, Dórea, Bernardi, José, Bastos, & Malm, 2009), diagnoses of abnormal brain formation (Dror, Malinger, Ben-Sira, Lev, Pick, & Lerman-Sagie, 2009) in utero diagnoses of hyperthyroidism (Sun, Chen, Han, Dong, Qiu, Sha, & Guo 2011) and assessing infants with autism (Abel, & Russell, 2005; Yurong, Dun, & Xiurong, 2001). However, because the Gesell scale suffers from several psychometric weaknesses, interest in and use of the scale has fallen despite revisions and improvements.

The Gesell Developmental Schedules claim to provide an appraisal of the developmental status of children from 2.3 months to 6.3 years of age. The original scale is based on normative data from a carefully conducted longitudinal study of early human development (Gesell et al., 1940). The idea behind procedures based on developmental data is that human development unfolds in stages or in sequences over time. Gesell and colleagues obtained normative data concerning these various stages in maturation. With data on when specific developmental milestones manifest themselves (e.g., when the infant first rolls from back to stomach unassisted, when the child first utters words, or when the child learns to walk), one can compare the rate of development of any infant or young child with established norms. If the child shows behavior or responses that are associated with a more mature level of development than is typically found for his or her chronological age, then one can assume that the child is ahead in development compared with others of the same age. Accelerated development can be related to high intelligence.

In the Gesell scale, an individual's **developmental quotient (DQ)** is determined according to a test score, which is evaluated by assessing the presence or absence of behavior associated with maturation. The DQ concept parallels the mental age (MA) concept. Thus, the Gesell produces an intelligence quotient

(IQ) score similar to that of the Binet scale. The formula for IQ in the Gesell scale is as follows:

$$IQ = \frac{Development\ Quotient}{Chronological\ Age} \times 100$$

or more simply,

$$IQ = \frac{DQ}{CA} \times 100$$

Despite years of extensive use and updating, the Gesell scale has fallen short of acceptable psychometric standards. The standardization sample has not been representative of the population. The data gathered in the 2010 national study may serve to improve the standardization sample. In addition, although the test directions have been sometimes vague, and the scoring procedures questionable (Naglieri, 1985), the newest revised schedule includes an updated and improved screening instrument. However, as with most infant tests, evidence of reliability or validity is poorly documented. As with all sensorimotor infant tests, the Gesell does not predict later intelligence except at the low end of scores (see Figure 12.2). Thus, its main value is in obtaining an early estimate of possible mental retardation.

In conclusion, Gesell's concept of empirically determining developmental sequence norms in evaluating infants and young children is logical and promising. When first constructed, the Gesell scale was nothing short of a breakthrough in infant ability testing. The use of a nonrepresentative sample in its initial development, furthermore, was not at all unusual. The Gesell scale has recently undergone revisions that should help it meet today's more rigorous standards for standardization samples. By providing a standard format for observing behavior, the Gesell scale may be of value to the highly trained and experienced examiner. Even so, the available empirical data indicate that it is not highly accurate for predictive

**FIGURE 12.2**
Schematic summary of the Gesell Developmental Schedules.

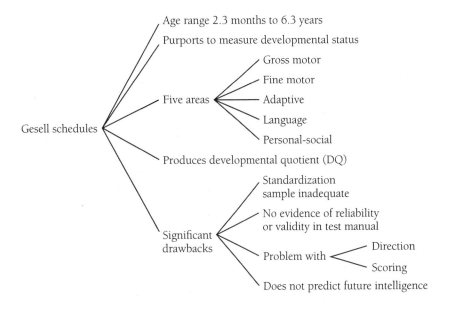

purposes except at the low ranges. The scale does appear to help uncover subtle deficits in infants (Williamson et al., 1990).

### Bayley Scales of Infant and Toddler Development–Third Edition (BSID-III)

Like the Gesell scale, the Bayley Scales of Infant Development base assessments on normative maturational developmental data. Originally published only 4 years before the Brazelton scale, the Bayley scales were the product of 40 years of study (Bayley, 1969; Kimble & Wertheimer, 2003). Revised in 1994, and then again in 2006, the BSID-III, or Bayley-III, was designed for infants between 1 and 42 months of age (Geisinger, Spies, Carlson, & Plake, 2007) and assesses development across five domains: cognitive, language, motor, socioemotional, and adaptive (Aylward, 2011). A more focused measure of test observations has also been incorporated into the Bayley-III with the express goal of better informing intervention planning (Geisinger et al., 2007). To assess mental functions, the Bayley-III uses measures such as the infant's response to a bell, the ability to follow an object with the eyes, and, in older infants, the ability to follow oral instructions. The heart of the Bayley-III is the motor scale because it assumes that later mental functions depend on motor development (Flanagan & Alfonso, 1995) (see Figure 12.3).

Unlike the Gesell and Brazelton scales, the Bayley-III scales have an excellent standardization. With a large normative sample of infants between 1 and 42 months of age divided into subgroups by gender, race, socioeconomic status, rural versus urban area, and geographic region, the Bayley-III is currently the best standardized test of its kind available (Geisinger et al., 2007).

**FIGURE 12.3**
Bayley Scales of Infant Development.

Bayley Scales of Infant Development. ©1969 by NCS Pearson, Inc. Reproduced with permission. All rights reserved. "Pearson" and "Bayley Scales of Infant Development" are trademarks, in the US and/or other countries, of Pearson Education, Inc. or its affiliates (s).

Bayley-III scores include scaled scores, composite scores, and percentile ranks for all five scales. Confidence intervals are available for the scores from the five scales. Growth scores and developmental age scores are available for the cognitive, language, and motor scales. The growth scores are used to create a chart of progress over time for each subtest. The growth scores range from 200 to 800 with a mean of 500 and a standard deviation of 100. Given the care and effort put into its development, the generally positive reviews of the Bayley-III come as no surprise (Geisinger et al., 2007). In addition to its exemplary standardization, the overall reliability coefficients (coefficient alpha for individual scales), as calculated with Fisher's z transformation, ranged from .86 (fine motor) to .91 (cognitive, expressive communication, and gross motor) (Geisinger et al., 2007). The reliabilities of the social-emotional and adaptive behavior scales were similarly strong (.83 to .94; .79 to .98, respectively). Taken together, these results suggest strong internal consistency for the measurement of functioning within these five domains (Geisinger, Spies, Carlson, & Plake, 2007).

Research interest in the Bayley scales continues to grow (see, Weiss, Oakland, & Aylward, 2010). Evidence to support the construct validity of the instrument included a factor analysis of the subtests. This study used the overall sample of 1700 children. The results supported a three-factor model and confirmed that the instrument measures motor, language, and cognitive development (Geisinger, Spies, Carlson, & Plake, 2007). Nevertheless, more validity studies are needed. In terms of construct validity, scores on the performance scale increase with increasing chronological age. However, the bulk of available research casts considerable doubt on the assumption of a relationship between motor behavior and later mental functions (Janssen, Akkermans, Steiner, de Haes, Oostendorp, Kollée, & Nijhuis-van der Sanden, 2011). In its favor, even the earlier editions of the Bayley predict mental retardation (Chung, Liu, Chang, Chen, Tang, & Wong, 2010; Patrianakos-Hoobler, Msall, Huo, Marks, Plesha-Troyke, & Schreiber, 2010). Infants who score two standard deviations below the mean have a high probability of testing in the retarded ranges later in life (DeWitt, Schreck, & Mulick, 1998; Goldstein, Fogle, Wieber, & O'Shea, 1995). However, for infants who score within the normal ranges, there is no more than low correlation between Bayley scores and those obtained from standard intelligence tests such as the WISC-III and Binet scale (Flanagan & Alfonso, 1995).

Like the Brazelton, the Bayley-III is widely used in research. It has been used to assess children with Down syndrome, with pervasive developmental disorders, with cerebral palsy, with language impairment, who are at risk for developmental delay, who suffered asphyxiation at birth, with prenatal alcohol exposure, who are small for gestational age, and with premature or low birth weight (Geisinger, Spies, Carlson, & Plake, 2007). A major research use is to assess infants of drug-using mothers (e.g., Miller-Loncar et al., 2005; Moe, 2002), infants whose mothers suffer from postpartum depression (Righetti-Veltema, Bousquet, & Manzano, 2003), human immunodeficiency virus (HIV)-positive infants (Llorente et al., 2003), and other at-risk infants (Lai, Guo, Guo, & Hsu, 2001; Leslie, Gordon, Ganger, & Gist, 2002; Misri, Corral, Wardrop, & Kendrick, 2006) (see Figure 12.4).

In conclusion, the Bayley-III is probably the most psychometrically sound test of its kind (Geisinger, Spies, Carlson, & Plake, 2007). The question remains as to whether tests of this type can predict future intelligence. Available research

Description of ITPA-3 Subtests from the Illinois Test of Psycholinguistic Abilities–Third Edition ITPA-3 Manual 9476 by Hammill, Mather, and Roberts. Copyright © 2001 PRO-ED, Inc. Reprinted with permission.

indicates that although the Bayley-III may be a good predictor for disabled populations, it does not predict well within the normal ranges.

### Cattell Infant Intelligence Scale (CIIS)

Another noteworthy infant ability test is the CIIS, which is also based on normative developmental data. Designed as a downward extension of the Stanford-Binet scale for infants and preschoolers between 2 and 30 months of age, the Cattell scale purports to measure intelligence in infants and young children. Patterned after the 1937 Binet in an age scale format, the Cattell scale contains five test items for each month between 2 and 12 months of age and five items for each 2-month interval between 12 and 36 months of age. The items are similar to those on other infant tests, such as the Gesell scale. Tasks for infants include attending to a voice and following objects with his or her eyes. Tasks for young children involve using a form board and manipulating common objects. The ability to follow oral instructions becomes more and more important as age increases.

Today, the Cattell is rarely used. It was copyrighted nearly 3 decades before the original Bayley scale and has not been revised. Normative data for the Cattell scale compare unfavorably with those for the original Bayley scales, and even worse with the Bayley-II in several respects. In addition to being outdated and more than four times smaller, the Cattell scale sample is based primarily on children of parents from the lower and middle classes and therefore does not represent the general population.

In one of the few recently published studies comparing the Cattell scale with the Bayley, scores derived from the Bayley predicted Stanford-Binet IQs better than the Cattell scores did (Atkinson, 1990) (see Figure 12.5).

**TABLE 12.3** Summary of Infant Scales

| Scale | Age range | Standardization Sample | Psychometric properties |
|---|---|---|---|
| Brazelton | 3 days–4 weeks | None | Good interrater reliability, poor test–retest reliability |
| Gesell | 2.3 months–6.3 years | 1300 infants | Little evidence, some support for construct validity |
| Bayley | 2–30 months | 1262 infants | Very good split-half reliability |
| Cattell | 2–30 months | 285 infants | Little evidence, some support for construct validity |

**General:** For children younger than 18 months, these measures do not correlate significantly with IQ later in life. After 18 months, there are significant but small and clinically unhelpful correlations. Correlations tend to increase with the age of the infant at the time of testing.

**Major alternative:** Tests of memory, particularly visual memory and abstraction. Such tests do correlate with IQs in later life, even for infants tested in the first few days after birth.

In sum, the Cattell scale has remained relatively unchanged for more than 60 years. It is psychometrically unsatisfactory. Reliability coefficients vary widely, with many being less than acceptable (see Hooper, Conner, & Umansky, 1986). Moreover, what the scale measures is unclear; it does not predict future intelligence for infants in the normal ranges. Its use in clinical settings is highly suspect, and it is presented here only for historical value.

See Table 12.3 for a summary of the properties of infant scales.

## Major Tests for Young Children

In this section, we discuss two major individual tests specifically developed to evaluate intelligence in young children: the McCarthy Scales of Children's Abilities (MSCA) and the Kaufman Assessment Battery for Children (KABC).

### McCarthy Scales of Children's Abilities (MSCA)

A product of the early 1970s, the MSCA measure ability in children between 2 and 8 years old. Overall, the McCarthy scales present a carefully constructed individual test of human ability. In fact, were it not for its relatively meager validity data, the McCarthy might well have reached the status of the Wechsler scale, which overlaps with the McCarthy's age range. Indeed, the McCarthy scales seem to offer some advantages over the WPPSI-III and even the Binet for the 2- to 8-year age range. Unfortunately, because McCarthy died before the test was published, the task of strengthening the McCarthy scales falls to interested researchers (see Figure 12.6).

On the positive side, the McCarthy produces a pattern of scores as well as a variety of composite scores. Its battery of 18 tests samples a wide variety of functions long held to be related to human intelligence. Of the 18 scales, 15 are combined into a composite score known as the **general cognitive index (GCI)**, a standard score with a mean of 100 and a standard deviation of 16. Presumably, the index reflects how well the child has integrated prior learning experiences and adapted them to the demands of the scales. The concept of combining various subtests to form composite scores is an important idea in testing, and it is one of the main features of the 2003 fifth edition of the Stanford-Binet scale (see Figure 12.7).

The psychometric properties of the McCarthy scales are relatively good. Picone, Regine, and Ribaudo (2001) have shown evidence of factorial validity, and a 2002 longitudinal study (Stannard, Wolfgang, Jones, & Phelps, 2001) shows evidence of predictive validity.

Reliability coefficients for the general cognitive index tend to run in the low .90's. Validity data are also encouraging. Although concurrent validity data are limited, correlations with the Stanford-Binet scale (Form L-M) and the WPPSI are quite good. The general cognitive index correlates at .81 with the Binet IQ and at .71 with the WPPSI full-scale IQ. The manual and T. V. Hunt (1978) provide additional validity coefficients based on small samples.

The McCarthy scales have been used in a variety of research studies (Hansen, Dinesen, Hoff, & Greisen, 2002; Smith, 2005). The McCarthy was used to evaluate the effects of nutritional supplements given to nursing mothers on the development of the nursing infants (Jensen et al., 2010), the effects of air-pollution on children's cognitive development (Freire et. al., 2010), and the effects of early intervention on the cognitive development of preterm infants (Nordhov, Rønning,

**FIGURE 12.7**
Schematic overview of the general cognitive index of the McCarthy scales.

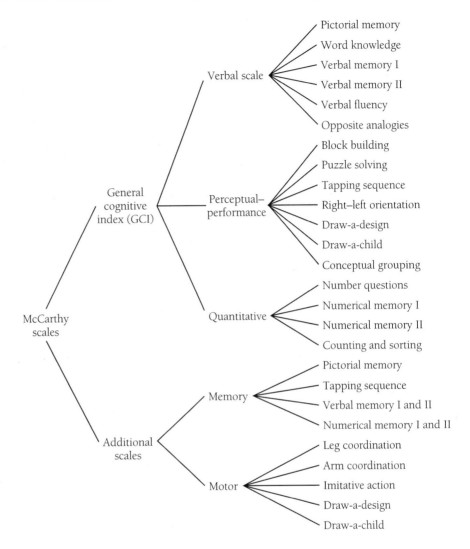

Dahl, Ulvund, Tunby, & Kaaresen, 2010). Hoekstra et al. used the McCarthy to evaluate the relationship between autism and intelligence in a longitudinal study of over 8000 twin pairs (Hoekstra, Happé, Baron-Cohen, & Ronald, 2010). Genetic model fitting showed that autistic traits and IQ were influenced by a common set of genes and a common set of environmental influences that continuously affect these traits throughout childhood. The genetic correlation between autistic traits and IQ was only modest. These findings suggest that individual differences in autistic traits are substantially genetically independent of intellectual functioning. Another longitudinal study evaluated the effects of early intervention on the development of children worldwide (Nores & Barnett, 2010). The study found that children from different contexts and countries receive substantial cognitive, behavioral, health, and schooling benefits from early childhood interventions. The benefits are sustained over time. Interventions that have an educational or stimulation component evidenced the largest cognitive effects. The McCarthy scales were used to show positive effects of parental cognitive stimulation and emotional support on children's cognitive abilities (Hubbs-Tait, Culp, Culp, & Miller, 2002). A study by McGill-Evans and Harrison (2001) used the McCarthy scales to show that preterm birth, parental age, and infant gender accounted for more than 30% of the variance in cognitive–motor skills. Finally, a 2011 study used the McCarthy scales to assess the effect of the mode of delivery (vaginal or caesarean section) on the long-term psychomotor development of extremely low–birth weight infants (Minguez-Milio, Alcázar, Aubá, Ruiz-Zambrana, & Minguez, 2011). Results suggested that a caesarean section provides lower morbidity and better prognosis for neurodevelopment long-term outcome in extremely low–birth weight infants.

In sum, the McCarthy scale is psychometrically sound. The available studies support its validity and its promise as an assessment tool is encouraging.

## Kaufman Assessment Battery for Children– Second Edition (KABC-II)

Originally a product of the early 1980s, the modern 2004 version of the KABC-II is an individual ability test for children between 3 and 18 years of age. The KABC-II consists of 18 subtests combined into five global scales called sequential processing, simultaneous processing, learning, planning, and knowledge.

According to the stated purposes and intentions in its test manuals, the KABC-II is quite ambitious (Kaufman & Kaufman, 1983a, 1983b, 2004a). It is intended for psychological, clinical, minority-group, preschool, and neuropsychological assessment as well as research. The test also purports to enable the psychoeducational evaluation of learning disabled and other exceptional children and educational planning and placement. Before we examine the extent to which the KABC succeeds in meeting such lofty goals, we shall look at some of its underlying concepts.

Theoretically, the KABC is based on several approaches (see Kaufman, 1984; Kaufman & Kaufman, 2004a), including the neuropsychological model of brain functioning of renowned Russian neuroscientist Aleksander Luria (1966); the theory of split brain functioning of U.S. Nobelist Roger Sperry (1968); and the theories of information processing, most notably that of cognitive scientist Ulric Neisser (1967). In the work of these and other scientists, the Kaufmans noted a major distinction between two types of higher brain processes, which they referred to as the *sequential-simultaneous distinction* (Kaufman, 1984). *Sequential processing* refers to a child's ability "to solve problems by mentally arranging input in sequential or serial order." Examples of sequential processing are number and word-order recall. Presented one at a time, items must be dealt with sequentially, rather than all at once. In contrast, simultaneous processing takes place in parallel. It refers to a child's ability to "synthesize information (from mental wholes) in order to solve a problem" (Kaufman, & Kaufman, 1985, p. 250).

The sequential–simultaneous distinction of the KABC is one of the test's most distinguishing characteristics (Reynolds & Kamphaus, 1997). The KABC-II does not claim to provide a pure measure of either sequential or simultaneous processing. Instead, the test developers selected tasks that, from a rational analysis, appeared to distinguish one type of processing from the other. A major intent of providing separate measures of simultaneous and sequential processing is to identify the child's unique strengths and problem-solving strategies. Such information can presumably help others develop educational and remedial intervention strategies for a child.

The KABC-II was conformed with the Kaufman Test of Educational Achievement, Second Edition (KTEA-II), which provides an achievement score. Offering independent and comparable scores for both intelligence and achievement in the same test is a major advantage. In addition, the KABC-II has a nonverbal measure of ability that is specifically designed to be as fair as possible to children who are linguistically different or handicapped.

The KABC-II and its counterpart the KTEA-II are well constructed and psychometrically sound. Raw scores for each of the 18 subtests can be converted to standard scores with a mean of 10 (SD = 3). The global scales can be converted to standard scores (mean = 100, SD = 15), percentiles, and age-equivalent norms.

Validity data reported in the original KABC test manual has received considerable attention. Factor analytic studies support its sequential–simultaneous and mental processing achievement distinctions (Meesters, van Gastel, Ghys, & Merckelbach, 1998). The KABC intelligence estimates also tend to show smaller (approximately 8 points) differences between African Americans and whites than either the Wechsler or Binet scales, in which whites typically score some 15 points higher than African Americans (see Jensen, 1985). Thus, the KABC tends to be less biased against African Americans (Fan, Willson, & Reynolds, 1995; Lamp & Krohn, 2001). However, the KABC also tends to underestimate the scores of gifted children (compared with the Binet Form L-M and the WISC-R), so its validity for evaluating giftedness is questionable (McCallum, Karnes, & Oehler-Stinnett, 1985). Moreover, at least one group of researchers has found KABC items biased against Mexican Americans (Valencia, Rankin, & Livingston, 1995). As of this writing, no data are available on the KABC-II's validity beyond that reported in the manual, so much work needs to be done.

Since its original publication in April 1983, the KABC has generated considerable interest. Reactions have varied widely. On the positive side, Kaufman and Kaufman (1985, p. 268) point to its strong theoretical orientation, separate intelligence and achievement scales, separate nonverbal scale, limited oral instructions, limited verbal responding, colorful and interesting items, inclusion of sociocultural norms, and empirical documentation of smaller differences between groups (Kaufman, 2009). For instance, their studies have established smaller differences between African Americans and whites (Dale, McIntosh, Rothlisberg, Ward, & Bradley, 2011), Latinos or Latinas and whites (Tomes, 2011), and Indians and whites on the KABC compared with other tests (Malda, van de Vijver, Srinivasan, Transler, & Sukumaar, 2010). These strengths are acknowledged by independent reviewers (Aiken, 1987; Anastasi, 1984), and the KABC-II has smoothed many of the edges of the original KABC (Kaufman, Lichtenberger, Fletcher-Janzen, & Kaufman, 2005).

Despite these strengths, criticism has been harsh (Williams, Voelker, & Ricciardi, 1995). According to Jensen (1984), one can attribute the smaller differences between whites and minorities on the KABC to its poorer predictive validity for school achievement and its less effective measurement of general intelligence compared with the Binet and Wechsler scales. Other critics point to the KABC's imperfect match with its theoretical foundation and disproportionate contribution of the simultaneous and mental processing composites (Bracken, 1985). Moreover, the neuropsychological model that underlies the sequential–simultaneous distinction is at best poorly supported and at worst inaccurate and outmoded (Herbert, 1982). None of these criticisms appear to have been clearly addressed by the newer KABC-II.

Perhaps the most severe criticism of the KABC has come from Sternberg (1984), who charged that the KABC manual misrepresents the support for the theory underlying the KABC. He also maintained that the test suffers from a noncorrespondence between its definition and its measurement of intelligence. This criticism continues to be voiced and empirically supported by Cahan and Noyman (2001). Furthermore, Sternberg found that empirical support for the theory underlying the KABC is questionable. And, like Jensen (1984), he noted an overemphasis on rote learning at the expense of ability to learn. Indeed, test scores do show a decrease in $g$ saturation as ability levels increases (Reynolds & Keith, 2007).

Although the criticisms of the KABC are largely valid and generally apply to the newer KABC-II, it is important to see them in context. First, many of these criticisms, such as lack of correspondence between definition and measurement of intelligence, also apply to the test's major competitors. Even the best available instruments have shortcomings and limitations. Although the underlying theory of the test has yet to be fully established, the test at least *has* a theoretical structure. Indeed, the KABC-II is perhaps the best alternative or supplement for specific questions and educational assessment to date and no doubt will continue to be an important assessment tool for some time to come.

## General Individual Ability Tests for Handicapped and Special Populations

Many alternative tests are specifically designed to provide a more valid measure of intellectual functioning for cases in which the Binet and Wechsler may be biased or inappropriate. Each of these general individual ability tests for handicapped and special populations contains unique strengths and limitations.

### Columbia Mental Maturity Scale–Third Edition (CMMS)

A variety of sensory and physical limitations often make a valid administration of the Binet, Wechsler, or even many of the major alternative scales (such as the McCarthy) quite impossible. Therefore, for children who experience physical limitations (such as cerebral palsy), speech impairments, language limitations, or hearing loss, instruments are needed that do not create negative bias. One attempt at such an instrument is the CMMS, which purports to evaluate ability in normal and variously handicapped children from 3 through 12 years of age. When used for individuals with special needs, the test often provides a more suitable measure of intelligence than do the more established scales (Kroese, 2003).

The Columbia scale requires neither a verbal response nor fine motor skills. Presented as a measure of general reasoning ability, the scale requires the subject to discriminate similarities and differences by indicating which drawing does not belong on a 6-by-9-inch card containing three to five drawings, depending on the level of difficulty. The task, then, is multiple-choice.

The Columbia scale contains 92 different cards grouped into eight overlapping levels, or scales, according to chronological age. Testing begins at a scale appropriate for the child's age. Advantages of the Columbia scale include its relative independence of reading skills, the ease of its administration and scoring, and the clarity of its test manual. Because subjects are not timed, pressure is minimal.

Though somewhat outdated, the standardization sample is impressive. It consists of 2600 children divided into 13 levels from 3 years, 6 months to 9 years, 11 months. Each level contains 200 children. The sample is stratified according to the U.S. population in terms of variables that include gender, race, geographic region, and parental occupation.

The scale's manual contains data on both split-half and test–retest reliability for some age groups in the standardization sample. The scale is consistent internally as well as over short intervals of time. Coefficients range between .85 and .90 for both split-half and test–retest reliabilities.

The Columbia scale is highly vulnerable to random error. A young child can obtain a score of 82 simply on chance alone, and a score in the average ranges can be obtained with just a few lucky guesses (Kaufman, 1978). Theoretically, if 100 apes were administered the lower levels of the Columbia scale, an alarming number might obtain scores in the average ranges for human beings.

In conclusion, the Columbia scale is a reliable instrument that is useful in assessing ability in many people with sensory, physical, or language handicaps. Because of its multiple-choice nature, however, and consequent vulnerability to chance variance, one should use results with caution. When used with individuals for whom the major scales would be appropriate, the Columbia scale might best be seen as a screening device. Although its standardization sample is somewhat outdated, the Columbia scale can be used to test a variety of special populations for whom the Wechsler, Binet, and other scales are inappropriate. Even for these populations, however, the Columbia scale might be best used in conjunction with whatever Wechsler or KABC subtests can be given. If the child can point, for example, then Wechsler's picture completion subtest can be given in conjunction with the Columbia scale as an additional check on the accuracy of the results. If the child is physically handicapped but can speak, then some of the Wechsler verbal subtests can be used to support results.

### Peabody Picture Vocabulary Test–Fourth Edition (PPVT-IV)

Similar to the Columbia scale in several respects, the PPVT-IV was originally developed by L. M. Dunn and I. M. Dunn (1981). The most recent revision was published in 2007. Although the age range of 2 through 90 years is considerably wider than the range of the Columbia scale, both are multiple-choice tests that require a subject to indicate only "Yes" or "No" in some manner. Primarily for the physically or language handicapped, the PPVT-IV is not usually used with the deaf, because the instructions are administered aloud. Nonetheless, the test has been used in research with the deaf to evaluate their ability to define words (Beal-Alvarez, Lederberg, & Easterbrooks, 2011).

The test purports to measure hearing or receptive (hearing) vocabulary, presumably providing a nonverbal estimate of verbal intelligence (Dunn & Dunn, 1997). One can use it as a screening instrument or as a supplement to other measures in evaluating learning problems (Camaioni, Ercolani, Penge, Riccio,

& Bernabei, 2001), linguistic problems (Bayles, 1990), and many other special problems (Fielding-Barnsley & Purdie, 2003; Marchman, Saccuman, & Wulfeck, 2004; Ment et al., 2003; Wagner, 1994). Though untimed, the PPVT-IV can be administered in 15 minutes or less, and it requires no reading ability. Two forms (IIIA and IIIB) are available. Each form has 204 plates, with each plate presenting four numbered pictures. The subject must indicate which of the four pictures best relates to a word read aloud by the examiner. Items are arranged in increasing order of difficulty, and the administrator must determine a basal and ceiling performance, as in the modern Binet scale. The number of incorrect responses is subtracted from the ceiling to produce a total score. This score can then be converted to a standard score (mean = 100, SD = 15), percentile rank, stanine, or age-equivalent score.

The PPVT-IV purports a split-half internal consistency of .86 to .97, alternate form reliability from .88 to .94, and retest reliability of .91 to .94. Its validity has been reported as good, with respectable correlations with the WISC-III VIQ at .91.

The Peabody may underestimate Wechsler or Binet IQs for retarded children (Prout & Sheldon, 1984), gifted children (Hayes & Martin, 1986), and adults (Bell, Lassiter, Matthews, & Hutchinson, 2001; Campbell, Bell, & Keith, 2001; Washington & Craig, 1999). Research has supported its use for certain adults, such as those with neurocognitive deficits (Edelstein, D'Agostino, Bernstein, Nathan, Greenberg, Hodgson, Millar, Laperriere, & Spiegler, 2011) or language impairment (Fidler, Plante, & Vance, 2001). Because it evaluates only receptive vocabulary and not problem solving, abstract thinking, and other functions tapped by the major IQ tests, the Peabody test should never be used as a substitute for a Wechsler or Binet IQ. Indeed, researchers have repeatedly noted that the Peabody test cannot be used as a substitute for a major intelligence test (Castellino, Tooze, Flowers, & Parsons, 2011; Ingram, Caroselli, Robinson, Hetzel, Reed, & Masel, 1998). Nevertheless, much care went into the latest revision, and the test meets today's rigorous psychometric standards. According to the test developers, the PPVT-IV test was standardized on a national sample of individuals aged 2 years 6 months to over 90 years. More than 5500 individuals were tested; data from approximately 3500 subjects were used for the normative scores. The sample matches the U.S. Census for gender, race, ethnicity, region, socioeconomic status (SES), and clinical diagnosis or special education placement (Dunn & Dunn, 2007).

The authors were careful to indicate the limitations of the test as well as its appropriate uses. These include "establishing and restoring rapport," "testing preschool children," "screening for verbal ability," "screening for giftedness and mental retardation," and "measuring English language proficiency" (see Dunn & Dunn, 1997) and testing language performance of low-income African American preschool children (Oi, Kaiser, Milan, & Hancock, 2006).

In conclusion, the modern Peabody test can be an important component in a test battery or used as a screening devise. It is easy to administer and is useful for a variety of groups. However, its tendency to underestimate IQ scores, in conjunction with the problems inherent in the multiple-choice format, indicate that the Peabody test cannot be used in place of the Binet and Wechsler scales. One should use it for general screening purposes and to evaluate receptive vocabulary, and heed the careful instructions specified in the test manual.

FIGURE 12.8
Leiter International
Performance Scale.

(Courtesy of Stoelting Company.)

## Leiter International Performance Scale–Revised (LIPS-R)

Whereas the Columbia and Peabody tests measure verbal aspects of intelligence, the LIPS-R (Leiter scale) is strictly a performance scale. It aims at providing a nonverbal alternative to the Stanford-Binet scale for the age range of 2 to 18 years (see Figure 12.8). First developed in the 1930s, and revised most recently in 1997, the Leiter scale is still used by researchers (see Vicario, Martino, Spata, Defazio, Giacchè, Martino, Rappo, Pepi, Silvestri, & Cardona, 2010), although one finds it more frequently used in clinical settings, where it is still widely utilized to assess the intellectual function of children with pervasive developmental disorders, especially those who cannot be tested with standard intelligence tests (Portoghese, Buttiglione, De Giacomo, Lafortezza, Lecce, Martinelli, Lozito, & Margari, 2010 ). The Leiter scale purports to provide a nonverbal measure of general intelligence by sampling a wide variety of functions from memory to nonverbal reasoning. One can administer it without using language, and it requires no verbal response from subjects. For this reason, it is often used when assessing children with autism (see Makkonen, Riikonen, Kuikka. Kokki, Bressler, Marshall, & Kaufmann, 2011).

Presumably, one can apply it to a large range of disabled individuals, particularly the deaf and language-disabled. Like the Peabody test and the Columbia scale, the revised Leiter scale is untimed. Patterned after the old Binet scale, the various tasks of the Leiter scale are arranged in an age scale format at yearly intervals from 2 through 18. The revised Leiter has considerable utility for subjects who cannot or will not provide a verbal response (Bay, 1998; Bos, 1996; Makkonen et al., 2011). The Leiter scale's validity documentation is extremely good, with a range of criterion validity coefficients from .52 to .92 (median = .83). However, there is some evidence that Leiter IQ scores for Latinos and Latinas are significantly higher than corresponding IQs from the Wechsler scales (Cathers-Schiffman & Thompson, 2007).

The Leiter scale merits consideration as an aid to clinical diagnosis in disabled children (Bradley-Johnson, 2001; Tsatsanis, Dartnall, Cicchetti, Sparrow,

Klin, & Volkmar, 2003). However, the test user must exercise caution in interpreting Leiter test results because the meaning of test scores requires more research (Hooper & Mee Bell, 2006). With further revisions of the test, researchers in the next decade may more thoroughly investigate the Leiter's properties and potential.

### Porteus Maze Test (PMT)

The PMT is a popular but poorly standardized nonverbal performance measure of intelligence. Since it was first published at about the time of World War I, it has served as an important individual ability test (Krikorian & Bartok, 1998). As its name implies, the PMT consists of maze problems. Specifically, it includes 12 mazes that increase in complexity across age levels. The participant is required to trace the maze from the starting point to the goal while following certain rules (Kar, Rao, Chandramouli, Thennarasu, & Satishchandra, 2011). Like the Leiter scale, the Porteus test can be administered without verbal instruction and thus can be used for a variety of special populations (Kar, Rao, Chandramouli, Thennarasu, & Satishchandra, 2010; Kugler, 2007; Kulkarni, Sushil, Amin, Pathak, & Sharma, 2010; Leshem & Glicksohn, 2007; Levin, Song, Ewing-Cobbs, & Roberson, 2001; Stevens, Kaplan, & Hesselbrock, 2003).

The Porteus test's standardization sample is quite old (Doctor, 1972). Despite its problems, the Porteus test meets an important need in providing a measure of ability for many groups to whom the Binet and Wechsler scales do not apply. Like many similar tests, a restandardization would greatly improve the quality of the Porteus.

In sum, the widespread use and interest in tests such as the Peabody, Leiter, and Porteus clearly indicate the need for strictly nonverbal or performance measures of intelligence, especially for the disabled.

# Testing Learning Disabilities

One of the most important areas in education involves the study of specific learning disabilities. A major concept in this field is that a child average in intelligence may fail in school because of a specific deficit or disability that prevents learning.

A learning disability is just one of the many types of disabilities that may entitle a child to receive special education services under the Individuals with Disabilities Education Act (IDEA) (20 U.S.C. 1400 et seq.) and its state law counterparts. Federal law entitles every eligible child with a disability to a free appropriate public education that emphasizes special education and related services designed to meet his or her unique needs and prepare him or her for further education, employment, and independent living. To qualify for special education services under IDEA and its state law counterparts, a child must not only have a disability but also have his or her educational performance adversely affected by the disability. Thus, the beginning point for evaluating a learning disability is a problem in how a child is performing in school.

Prior to the 2004 amendment of IDEA, schools were required to wait until a child fell considerably behind grade level before the child became eligible for special education services. That is, it was only when there was a severe discrepancy between a child's potential to achieve and actual school achievement that a child became eligible for special education services on the basis of a "specific learning disability" under federal and most state law counterparts.

Today, school districts are no longer required to follow this discrepancy model. Educators can now find other ways to determine when a child needs extra help (Coleman, Buysse, & Neitzel, 2006). This new way of intervention is being implemented throughout the country through a process called response to intervention, or RTI. The major premise of RTI is that early intervening services can prevent academic failure for many students with learning difficulties. It can also determine which students actually have learning disabilities, and whose underachievement cannot be attributed to other factors such as inadequate instruction.

School problems may be the result of any one or a combination of many factors including very low potential (intelligence) and emotional upset resulting from such factors as divorce, parental separation, bereavement, drug intoxication, and a host of others. However, a child will not be found to have a learning disability if problems in school are the result of a lack of basic instruction in math or reading, or based on limited English proficiency.

Identifying a learning disability is a complex process, and parents are advised to seek professional help. A good resource for parents and teachers is Barbara Z. Novick and Maureen M. Arnold's book *Why is My Child Having Trouble at School?* (Tarcher, 1995). These authors identify several "signs of a learning problem," including:

> *disorganization*—for example, sloppy homework or papers crumpled or out of place;
>
> *careless effort*—for example, misreads instructions or mishears directions;
>
> *forgetfulness*—for example, the child's best excuse is "I forgot";
>
> *refusal to do schoolwork or homework*—for example, turns in work half finished or needs somebody closely supervising in order to complete assignments;
>
> *slow performance*—for example, takes far more than the expected time to complete an assignment;
>
> *poor attention*—for example, mind seems to wander or frequently does not know what she or he is supposed to be doing; and
>
> *moodiness*—for example, child shows anger, sadness, or irritability when asked to complete a school or home assignment.

## Illinois Test of Psycholinguistic Abilities (ITPA-3)

Of the major tests designed specifically to assess learning disabilities, none better illustrates the theory of learning disabilities and has generated more interest than the controversial ITPA-3. Based on modern concepts of human information processing, the ITPA assumes that failure to respond correctly to a stimulus can result not only from a defective output (response) system but also from a defective input or information-processing system. This test assumes that a human response to an outside stimulus can be viewed in terms of discrete stages or processes. In stage 1, the senses receive input, or incoming environmental information. Thus, the information must first be received by the senses before it can be analyzed. During stage 2, this information is analyzed or processed. Finally, having processed the information, the individual must make a response—stage 3 (see Figure 12.9).

Assuming that a learning disability can occur at any level of processing, the Illinois test theorizes that the child may be impaired in one or more specific sensory modalities. Input may be visual, auditory, or tactile. The Illinois test provides 12 subtests that measure the individual's ability to receive visual, auditory, or tactile input independently of processing and output factors. The 12 subtests also have been designed and selected to represent three "global" composites: general language, spoken language, and written language.

The general language composite is formed by combining the results of all 12 subtests; this serves as the test's best single estimate of linguistic ability because it reflects the broadest array of spoken and written language abilities. Other composites are assessed by combinations of two or more subtests. For instance, the spoken language composite is formed by combining the results of the six subtests that measure aspects of oral language. The subtests assess oral language's semantical, grammatical, and phonological aspects. The remainder of the composites that may be formed include the written language composite, semantics composite, grammar composite, phonology composite, comprehension composite, spelling composite, sight–symbol processing composite, and sound–symbol processing composite.

By providing relatively independent measures for each of these areas, the Illinois test purports to help isolate the specific site of a learning disability. For example, a child may receive age-appropriate scores for the written language composite, while receiving unusually low scores on the spoken language composite. This result would indicate that although the child can receive and process information as well as others do when tasks are based on written language, he or she has trouble with tasks based on spoken language. The treatment can therefore focus on enhancing the child's specific area of weakness. Similarly, if the problem involves auditory processing, then this area becomes the focus.

Designed for use with children ages 2 through 10, the Illinois test has found widespread use and interest among educators, psychologists, learning disability specialists, and researchers (Andersson, 1996; Garayzábal Heinze, Lens Villaverde, Moruno López, Conde Magro, Moura, Fernández, & Sampaio, 2011; Klausen, Moller, Holmefjord, Reiseaeter, & Asbjornsen, 2000; Kohnen, & Nickels, 2010; Ottem, 2002a, 2002b; Tong & Zhu, 2006). Original claims of the test's ability to isolate information processing deficiencies proved to be overly optimistic and led to severe criticism (Bell, 1990). The most recent version of the test makes much more modest claims. According to the test manual, the test is useful in determining "specific strengths and weaknesses among linguistic abilities" and "can be used to assess linguistic delays."

The first two versions of the test were criticized because it was difficult to administer and presented no reliability or validity data. Efforts were made to improve the properties of the ITPA-3. According to the test developers, internal consistency,

**TABLE 12.4**   Description of Illinois Test of Psycholinguistic Abilities (ITPA-3) Subtests

| Subtest | Description |
|---|---|
| Spoken Analogies: | The examiner says a four-part analogy, of which the last part is missing. The child then tells the examiner the missing part. For example, in response to "Birds fly, fish _____," the child might say, "swim." |
| Spoken Vocabulary: | The examiner says a word that is actually an attribute of some noun. For example, the examiner may say, "I am thinking of something with a roof," to which the child might respond, "house." |
| Morphological Closure: | The examiner says an oral prompt with the last part missing. For example, the examiner says, "big, bigger, _____," and the child completes the phrase by saying the missing part, "biggest." |
| Syntactic Sentences: | The examiner says a sentence that is syntactically correct but semantically non-sensical (e.g., "Red flowers are smart"). The child repeats the sentence. |
| Sound Deletion: | The examiner asks the child to delete words, syllables, and their phonemes from spoken words. For example, the examiner might ask the student to say "weekend" without the "end." |
| Rhyming Sequences: | The examiner says strings of rhyming words that increase in length, and the child repeats them (e.g., "noon," "soon," "moon"). |
| Sentence Sequencing: | The child reads a series of sentences silently and then orders them into a sequence to form a plausible paragraph. For example, if the following three sentences were rearranged in B, C, A order they would make sense: A. I go to school. B. I get up. C. I get dressed. |
| Written Vocabulary: | After reading an adjective (e.g., "A broken _____"), the child responds by writing a noun that is closely associated with the stimulus word (e.g., "vase" or "mirror"). |
| Sight Decoding: | The child pronounces a list of printed words that contain irregular parts (e.g., "would," "laugh," "height," "recipe"). |
| Sound Decoding: | The child reads aloud phonically regular names of make-believe animal creatures (e.g., Flant, Yang). |
| Sight Spelling: | The examiner reads aloud irregular words one by one in a list. The child is given a printed list of these words, in which the irregular part of the words and one or more phonemes are missing. He or she writes in the omitted part of the words. For example, the examiner says, "said," the child sees s_____d, and he or she writes in the missing letters, "ai." |
| Sound Spelling: | The examiner reads aloud phonically regular nonsense words, and the child writes the word or the missing part. |

ITPA-3: Illinois Test of Psycholinguistic Abilities–Third Edition, online pamphlet, retrieved from http://www.proedinc.com/customer/productView.aspx?ID=788.

stability, and interscorer reliability for all subtests and composites are high enough to allow ITPA-3 scores to be used as the basis for making clinical judgments (i.e., *rs* greater than .90) (see ProEd, 2011; Towne, 2003). Validity evidence shows that all ITPA-3 subtests are useful for measuring both spoken and written language.

Studies showing the absence of gender, ethnic, and racial bias have been included in the manual and normative data are now provided (Towne, 2003). The

ITPA-3 was normed using a sample of 1522 children aged 5 to 12 years from 27 states. This new normative information was collected during the years 1999 and 2000. The normative sample reflects the population characteristics of the United States relative to ethnicity, race, gender, disability status, geographic region, parental education, rural/urban residence, and family income.

The substantial changes made to the ITPA-3 represent a major improvement over previous versions (Towne, 2003). However, although the ITPA-3 can be considered a comprehensive assessment tool, it should be remembered that specific constructs are evaluated with only two subtests (i.e., the spelling and comprehension composites). Clinicians should conduct further assessment with children who demonstrate potential problems in these two areas (Towne, 2003). Overall, the ITPA-3 now appears to be a psychometrically sound measure of children's psycholinguistic abilities.

## Woodcock-Johnson III

One of the better tests for evaluating learning disabilities is the Woodcock-Johnson III (Woodcock, McGrew, & Mather, 2001). The Woodcock-Johnson III was designed as a broad-range individually administered test to be used in educational settings. It assesses general intellectual ability (*g*), specific cognitive abilities, scholastic aptitude, oral language, and achievement (Schrank, McGrew, & Woodcock, 2001). The 2001 version of the Woodcock-Johnson was created based on the Cattell-Horn-Carroll (CHC) three-stratum theory of intelligence, comprising 69 narrow abilities (stratum 1) and grouped into broad categories of cognitive ability (stratum 2). Stratum 3 of the CHC model is the factor of *g* (general intelligence) (Locke, McGrew, & Ford, 2011; Schrank et al., 2001). Basically, the CHC theory was used as a blueprint in the creation of Woodcock-Johnson III, and in turn, the test is a measurement model of CHC theory (Locke, McGrew, & Ford, 2011, pp. 1–3; also see Schrank et al., 2001, p. 3).

By comparing a child's score on cognitive ability with his or her score on achievement, one can evaluate possible learning problems (Mather & Schrank, 2001; Ofiesh, Mather, & Russell, 2005; Schrank, Flanagan, Woodcock, & Mascolo, 2002). Because both the cognitive abilities battery and the achievement battery of the Woodcock-Johnson III were normed together, they provide for evaluating the presence of discrepancies without the errors associated with comparing results based on separately normed tests (Mather & Schrank, 2001). Co-normed batteries have also enabled the creators of the Woodcock-Johnson III to incorporate specific regression coefficients between all predictor and criterion variables for each age and population group. This allows evaluators to calculate the presence and significance of both intra-ability discrepancies (such as a discrepancy between an individual test taker's scores on processing speed and fluid reasoning) and ability–achievement discrepancies (such as a high score on the cognitive abilities battery and a low score on the achievement battery). Such discrepancies are defined in terms of a major discrepancy (usually 1.5 to 2 standard deviations) between cognitive ability (intelligence) and achievement. If a child is at the mean for cognitive ability (i.e., 50th percentile) and is two standard deviations below the mean in achievement (i.e., 2.2 percentile rank), evaluators would suspect a learning disability and call for further evaluation. The Woodcock-Johnson III also allows an evaluator to pinpoint specific deficits in cognitive ability. For instance, in evaluating a child who is struggling to keep up with the class in reading and has scored one standard deviation above the mean on the cognitive ability battery, it would be beneficial to discover that the child's results on the processing speed subtest were slightly below average. In this way, diagnosis of learning disabilities using the Woodcock-Johnson III can help to isolate specific areas of concern, provide accurate diagnoses, and even suggest avenues of intervention.

The Woodcock-Johnson III's cognitive ability standard battery includes 10 tests such as verbal comprehension, visual-auditory learning, spatial relations, and visual matching. The extended battery for cognitive abilities, also made up of 10 subtests, includes tests such as picture recognition, decision speed, and memory for words. The 12 tests of the achievement standard battery cover letter and word identification, reading fluency and comprehension, math fluency, and language development. The remaining 10 tests make up the extended battery of achievement and cover items such as punctuation, reading vocabulary, and quantitative concepts. Scores can be converted to percentile ranks. These ranks, in turn, can be converted to a standard score with a mean of 100 and a standard deviation of 15.

The Woodcock-Johnson III has relatively good psychometric properties. The standardization sample included more than 8818 people representative of the U.S. population in terms of gender, race, occupational status, geographic region, and urban versus rural status. Thirty-eight of the 42 median test reliabilities reported by Schrank et al. (2001) have split-half reliabilities in the .80's and .90's.

In addition, construct validity for the test was evidenced by confirmatory factor analysis (Schrank et al., 2001, p. 17), and clinical research (Floyd, McCormack, Ingram, Davis, Bergeron, & Hamilton, 2006). Virtually every test from the cognitive abilities battery individually loaded solely on a single factor, indicating that the cognitive subtests minimize the influence of variance resulting from construct irrelevance. This is contrasted with the factorial complexity of the achievement battery, suggesting the influence of factors other than $g$ (Krasa, 2007), including African American children (Edwards & Oakland, 2006).

The field of learning disability assessment is relatively new, and so are tests in this area. As a result, with the possible exception of the KABC, new tests of learning disability are in the same stage as early intelligence instruments. When judged by modern standards for individual ability tests, especially those that purportedly measure intelligence, these tests compare unfavorably in many respects.

For learning disability tests, three conclusions seem warranted. First, test constructors appear to be responding to the same criticisms that led to changes in the Binet and Wechsler scales and ultimately to the development of the KABC. Second, much more empirical and theoretical research is needed (Miller, McCardle, & Hernandez, 2010). Finally, users of learning disabilities tests should take great pains to understand the weaknesses of these procedures and not overinterpret results (Shull-Senn, Weatherly, Morgan, & Bradley-Johnson, 1995).

## Visiographic Tests

Visiographic tests require a subject to copy various designs. Such tests are used in education and have achieved a central position in neuropsychological testing because of their sensitivity to many different kinds of brain damage (Jacobson, Delis, & Bondi, 2002). In this section, we briefly describe three such tests and then, in Chapter 18, discuss neuropsychological testing in greater detail.

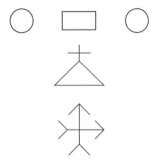

### Benton Visual Retention Test–Fifth Edition (BVRT-V)

Tests for brain damage are based on the concept of *psychological deficit*, in which a poor performance on a specific task is related to or caused by some underlying deficit. By knowing the underlying function or ability measured by a specific psychological test, the test examiner can relate a poor performance on that test to this underlying function (Dige & Wik, 2005). Such is the idea behind the BVRT-V, which assumes that brain damage easily impairs visual memory ability. Thus, a deficit on a visual memory task is consistent with possible brain damage or brain diseases such as Alzheimer's (Yan, Yang, & Wang, 2001).

Designed for individuals ages 8 and older, the Benton test consists of geometric designs briefly presented and then removed (see Figure 12.10). The subject must then reproduce the designs from memory. The responses are scored according to criteria in the manual. The subject loses points for mistakes and omissions and gains points for correct or partially correct responses. Norms are then available to evaluate scores. As the number of errors increases, the subject approaches the organic (brain-damaged) range (Lockwood, Mansoor, Homer-Smith, & Moses, 2011). Errors are also associated with normal aging (Resnick, Trotman, Kawas, & Zonderman, 1995), learning disabilities (Snow, 1998), and schizophrenia (Rollnick et al., 2002; Karageorgiou, Schulz, Gollub, Andreasen, Ho, Lauriello, Calhoun, Bockholt, Sponheim, & Georgopoulos, 2011). More recently, a computerized version has been developed (Thompson, & Chinnery, 2011; Thompson, Ennis, Coffin, & Farman, 2007).

### Bender Visual Motor Gestalt Test (BVMGT)

Also used in the assessment of brain damage, the BVMGT has a variety of uses and is one of the most popular individual tests. It consists of nine geometric figures (such as a circle and a diamond) that the subject is simply asked to copy (see Figure 12.11). With specific errors identified for each design, the Bender test is scored according to the number of errors the subject makes (Bolen, Hewett, Hall, & Mitchell, 1992; Xu, Fu, & Zhang, 1996). Developmental norms are available that describe the number of errors associated with children ages 5 through 8 (see Koppitz, 1964). By age 9, any child of normal intelligence can copy the figures with only one or two errors. Therefore, anyone older than 9 who cannot copy the figures may suffer from some type of deficit.

Research on the Bender test has shown that errors can occur for people whose mental age is less than 9 (e.g., because of low intelligence), those with brain dam-

FIGURE 12.11

The figures of the Bender Visual Motor Gestalt Test.

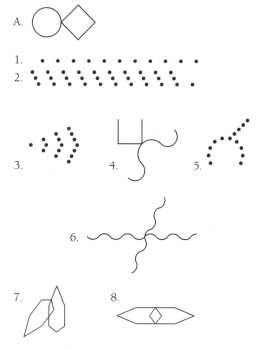

(From the Bender Visual Motor Gestalt Test by L. Bender, 1962.)

age (Bobic, Pavicevic, & Gomzi, 2000), those with nonverbal learning disabilities (Jing, Deqing, & Longhui, 2001), and those with emotional problems (Biswas, Malhotra, Malhotra, & Gupta, 2006; Uber, 2005). Errors associated with brain damage have been identified, and a variety of scoring systems for brain damage are available. However, the reliability of such systems has been questioned (Fuller & Vance, 1995; Lubin & Sands, 1992; Wagner & Flamos, 1988). Nevertheless, the Bender ranks among the top 10 most widely used assessment instruments (Piotrowski, 1995; also see Blasi, Elia, Buono, Ramakers, & di Nuovo, 2007).

### Memory-for-Designs (MFD) Test

Another simple drawing test that involves perceptual–motor coordination is the MFD test. Requiring only a 10-minute administration, the MFD test can be used for individuals 8 to 60 years of age. Empirical data have tended to support its use as an indicator of brain injury and brain disease (Strauss & Brandt, 1990; Teng et al., 1989). As in the Benton test, the subject attempts to draw a briefly presented design from memory. Drawings are scored from 0 to 3, depending on how they compare with representative drawings from normal controls and people with varying degrees of brain injury. A raw score total based on all 15 drawings can then be corrected for age and intelligence by reference to a table. This corrected score can then be evaluated against a relatively large (825) normative sample.

Reported split-half reliability indexes are quite good (.92), and test–retest indexes range from .81 to .90 (Graham & Kendall, 1960). Like so many psychological tests, the MFD needs additional validity documentation. Available studies have been quite supportive (Goldstein, Canavan, & Polkey, 1988; Mandes & Gessner, 1988).

To summarize, like all visiographic psychological tests used in isolation, the Benton, Bender, and MFD have been criticized because of their limitations in reliability and validity documentation. However, all three can be used as screening devices. An excessive number of errors on any of these procedures provide a signal for the examiner that in-depth testing or a medical evaluation may be necessary, and further results may help explain why a student is not performing well in school.

## Creativity: Torrance Tests of Creative Thinking (TTCT)

The measurement of creativity is one of the most underdeveloped areas in the field of psychological testing. One can define *creativity* as the ability to be original, to combine known facts in new ways, or to find new relationships between known facts. Evaluating creativity may provide a possible alternative to IQ testing. Creativity tests may also be useful in a battery to help explain the nature of a student's difficulty in the classroom. However, like learning disability tests, most creativity tests are still in the early stages of development. One of the best, most established, and most popular of these creativity tests is the TTCT.

The Torrance tests separately measure aspects of creative thinking such as fluency, originality, and flexibility (Palaniappan & Torrance, 2001). In measuring fluency, administrators ask an individual to think of as many different solutions to a problem as possible. The more distinct solutions a person can find, the greater his or her fluency. To evaluate originality, a test maker attempts to evaluate how new or unusual a person's solutions to problems are. Finally, flexibility is measured in terms of an individual's ability to shift directions or try a new approach to problem solving. For example, if the way you study for exams has not met your goals, then you would show flexibility if you tried a new approach. Instead of spending all your time passively rereading, you might try the recall method in which you spend half your study time trying to recall and synthesize what you have learned.

Like individual ability tests for the handicapped and tests of learning disability, the TTCT does not meet the Binet and Wechsler scales in terms of standardization, reliability, and validity. Reliability studies have varied widely (e.g., correlations of .35 to .73 for a 3-year period), and validity studies have tended to be varied as well as inconclusive (Kim, Cramond, & Bandalos, 2006). Unlike some creativity tests, the TTCT was conservatively presented as a research tool, but little has been done to prevent it from being applied in educational settings. Caution is indicated. On the positive side, several research studies have supported the utility of the Torrance tests as an unbiased indicator of giftedness (Santosa, 2007; Kim, 2006).

Factor analytic studies have suggested that the various types of creative thinking (fluency, flexibility, originality) tend to load on a single, general factor (Clapham, 1998). A 2006 study indicated that the two-factor model had a much better fit than the one general factor model (Kim, 2006, p. 257). The TTCT consists of two factors, innovative and adaptive, rather than a single factor, contrary to the majority of earlier research. The findings of this study are consistent with several researchers' (e.g., Isaksen & Puccio, 1988; Puccio et al., 1995; Torrance & Horng, 1980) interpretation of Kirton's (1976, 1978, 1987, 1989) model. Clearly, far more work is needed; today, human creativity surprisingly remains a largely unexplained field.

In sum, the Torrance tests are typical of creativity tests. Applied practitioners demand such a tool for their work. Though inconsistent, available data reflect the tests' merit and fine potential. As with so many other tests, however, more work is needed. One should view results from creativity tests as tentative, and to be used only in conjunction with other tests.

## Individual Achievement Tests: Wide Range Achievement Test-3 (WRAT-4)

We have discussed the widely made distinction between intelligence and achievement. As you know, intelligence tests measure potential ability, whereas achievement tests measure what the person has actually acquired or done with that potential. Although scores from intelligence tests and achievement tests often overlap, discrepancies sometimes arise between the two, for instance, when a person of average potential has not made full use of that potential. Such a person would tend to score higher on a general ability test than on a specific achievement test, especially if the general ability test minimizes the effects of learning and the achievement test is highly specific. Similarly, a person may score average on a general intelligence test but, because of a high level of interest, motivation, or special training, score above average on achievement. Thus, despite the overlap of intelligence and ability tests, comparing their data can sometimes be extremely revealing. Indeed, as we indicated, discrepancies between IQ and achievement have traditionally been the main defining feature of a learning disability.

Most achievement tests are group tests, which will be discussed in the next chapter. Among the most widely used individual achievement tests is the WRAT-4, which purportedly permits an estimate of grade-level functioning in word reading, spelling, math computation, and sentence comprehension (Kareken, Gur, & Saykin, 1995; Snelbaker, Wilkinson, Robertson, & Glutting, 2001; Wilkinson & Robertson, 2006). It can be used for children ages 5 and older and has two levels for each of the three achievement areas.

The WRAT-4 is easy to administer and is highly popular. Despite its research and clinical uses, however, it has some problems (Johnstone, Holland, & Larimore, 2000).

The earlier WRAT-R had been severely criticized for its inaccuracy in evaluating grade-level reading ability. The test merely required participants to pronounce words from a list. The 1993 version retained this format, which led one reviewer to conclude that "on no grounds can this be considered a test of reading" (Mabry, 1995, p. 1108). Because the basic concept of the test has not changed for nearly 60 years, it is "already outdated" (Mabry, 1995, p. 1109). The test authors believe that the WRAT-4 provides a quick, simple, and psychometrically measures of fundamental academic skills. Quick and simple, yes, but the jury is still out on psychometrically sound. From a purely technical standpoint, the reliability and validity evidence provided in the manual surpasses that of many small tests (Hoff, 2010). Internal consistency and alternate-form reliability estimates are high, and the inclusion of validity evidence is an improvement over previous editions. Unfortunately, many of the validity studies have sample sizes too small to demonstrate convergent and discriminant validity sufficiently (Hoff, 2010).

# Summary

The number of individual ability tests is almost overwhelming. Most of these tests serve highly specific purposes, and their strength lies in their specificity. Table 12.2 summarizes the major differences among the various individual tests of ability. Of the infant and preschool scales, the Bayley Scales of Infant Development are the most psychometrically sound. The McCarthy Scales of Children's Abilities appear to be promising tests for measuring intelligence in young children, but more work is needed. The KABC-II is a relatively new test of considerable value, but it has been strongly criticized. Overall, general ability tests for handicapped and special populations should be used cautiously. Among ability tests for the handicapped, the Columbia Mental Maturity Scale–Third Edition is one of the most promising.

Learning disability tests are based on information-processing theory. Because these tests are relatively new, one should view their results with caution. As with creativity tests, these tests still have a long way to go to reach the standards of the Binet and Wechsler scales. Drawing tests such as the Bender, the Benton, and the Memory-for-Designs are all excellent and economical screening devices for brain damage. These tests attempt to measure an ability related to brain functioning. In addition to being a screening device for brain damage, the Bender Visual Motor Gestalt Test can be used to measure intellectual and emotional functioning.

Although achievement and intelligence tests often overlap, a comparison of the two can be useful. A major individual achievement test, the Wide Range Achievement Test-4 is a quick and relatively simple way to evaluate certain achievement scores, but its psychometric adequacy remains an issue.

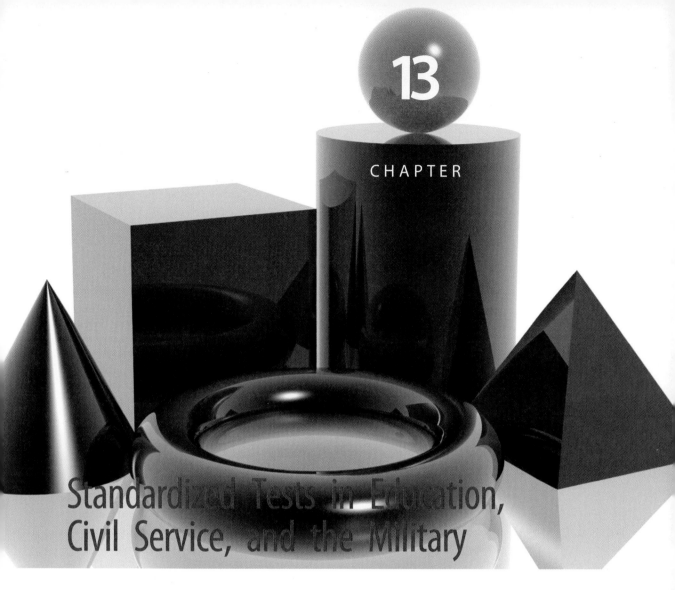

13

CHAPTER

# Standardized Tests in Education, Civil Service, and the Military

## LEARNING OBJECTIVES

*When you have completed this chapter, you should be able to:*

▶ Compare group and individual ability tests

▶ Identify the major characteristics of group tests

▶ List four general rules for using results from group ability tests

▶ Evaluate the adequacy of the group ability tests used in kindergarten through 12th grade

▶ Identify and evaluate two major group ability tests for college entrance

▶ Identify and evaluate two major group ability tests for graduate-school entrance

▶ Identify some of the advantages of the Goodenough-Harris Drawing Test

▶ Identify some group ability tests widely used in business and industry

You no doubt have experienced taking a standardized group test. Such tests are given in kindergarten through 12th grade. Most colleges require standardized group entrance exams.

One test that has been the bane of many psychology and education majors is the GRE Revised General Test (GRE). In 2012, 675,000 GREs were administered in more than 160 countries at more than 700 test centers worldwide (Educational Testing Service, 2011). The GRE is one of the most widely used tests for admission into postgraduate programs. If you plan to go on to graduate school, you will probably face the GRE. The extent to which graduate programs rely on the GRE can best be summed up by Sternberg and Williams (1997). Applications for admission into the Ph.D. program of one major research university are sorted on arrival into one of four boxes: below 1200, 1200–1300, 1301–1400, and above 1400, where the mean is 1000 and the standard deviation is 200. The first applications to be read are from the box above 1400, or two standard deviations above the mean. Applicants who score below 1301 are "rarely admitted" (Sternberg & Williams, 1997). The question is, how do we tell if this approach to admissions is justified?

When justifying the use of group standardized tests, test users often have problems defining what exactly they are trying to predict, or what the test *criterion* is (Thayer, 1992; Thayer & Kalat, 1998). With the GRE, the best criterion appears to be first-year grades in graduate school (Leavitt, Lombard, & Morris, 2011, p. 448). However, historically, the GRE has typically correlated only in the high teens to low twenties with first-year grades (Fairtest, 2007; Schneider & Briel, 1990). According to the National Center for Fair and Open Testing (Fairtest, 2007), the ability of the GRE to predict first-year graduate grades is incredibly weak. Fairtest reports that in one ETS study of 12,000 test takers, the exam accounted for a mere 9% of the variation among students' first-year grades. Undergraduate grades proved to be a stronger predictor of academic success, explaining 14% of the variation in graduate school grades. Considering that a correlation of .2 accounts for only 4% of the variance, it is clear that a lot of weight is placed on a test that contributes relatively little to the criterion. Moreover, tests such as the GRE predict neither clinical skill nor even the ability to solve real-world problems (see Neisser et al., 1996).

To investigate the criterion problem, Saccuzzo and Johnson (2000) examined scores on the Law School Admission Test (LSAT) as they related to first-time bar pass rates. The LSAT was found to correlate from .063 to .146 with bar pass rates, depending on the sample. Strikingly, a student's cumulative law school grade point average (GPA) correlated between .587 and .591 with bar pass rates. Using multiple regression analysis, the researchers found that cumulative law school GPA accounted for 35.2% of the variation in bar pass rate, but the LSAT accounted for only an additional 2.3% of the variance. The implication was clear: although the test did contribute to prediction, its weight was miniscule compared to actual performance as measured by a student's law school GPA.

In this chapter, we continue our discussion of testing in education, evaluating many of the group tests used on a daily basis in schools, colleges, and graduate and professional schools. We also examine standardized tests used in the U.S. civil service and military. Tests used in business and industry are discussed in Chapter 18. As you encounter these tests, keep in mind that even though they do add accuracy in the selection process, the amount of variability they account for is relatively small. If the test correlates with a criterion at the .4 level, then it accounts for 16% of the variability in that criterion, with the other 84% resulting from unknown factors and errors. Before discussing specific tests, we compare group and individual tests and also reexamine the distinctions among achievement, aptitude, and intelligence.

# Comparison of Group and Individual Ability Tests

Individual tests (as discussed in Chapters 10, 11, and 12) require a single examiner for a single subject. The examiner provides the instructions according to a standardized procedure stated in the test manual. The subject responds, and the examiner records the response verbatim. The examiner then evaluates and scores the subject's responses. This scoring process usually involves considerable skill. In contrast, a single examiner can administer group tests to more than one person at the same time. The examiner may read the instructions and impose time limits. Subjects record their own responses, which are usually choices between two or more alternatives. Scoring is usually objective and requires no skill on the part of the examiner, who simply adds the number of correct responses and in some cases subtracts a certain percentage for incorrect responses.

Further, in most individual tests, the examiner takes responsibility for eliciting a maximum performance. If a problem exists that might inhibit a maximum performance—for example, if a subject is frightened, nervous, uncooperative, or unmotivated—the examiner takes action to address this problem. For example, the examiner may encourage guessing by saying in a warm, friendly, and supportive tone, "Sure you know that; just guess." On the other hand, those who use the results of group tests must *assume* that the subject was cooperative and motivated. Subjects are not praised for responding, as they may be on individual tests, and there are no safeguards to prevent a person from receiving a low score for reasons other than low ability—such as lack of motivation, lack of cooperation, or emotional upset. As a result, low scores on group tests are often difficult to interpret. With high scores, and especially high scores, one can logically assume that the subject was motivated and has mental abilities commensurate with the obtained score. Low scores, however, may have resulted from low ability, lack of interest, inadequate motivation, clerical errors in recording responses, or a host of other factors. Table 13.1 compares individual and group tests.

**TABLE 13.1**   Individual Versus Group Tests

| Individual tests | Group tests |
|---|---|
| One subject is tested at a time. | Many subjects are tested at a time. |
| Examiner records responses. | Subjects record own responses. |
| Scoring requires considerable skill. | Scoring is straightforward and objective. |
| Examiner flexibility can elicit maximum performance if permitted by standardization. | There are no safeguards. |

## Advantages of Individual Tests

Individual tests can provide a wealth of information about a subject beyond the test score. In these tests, the instructions and methods of administration are as identical as possible, so subjects take an individual test in typically the same circumstances. Therefore, differences observed in behavior and attitudes most likely reflect differences in the individuals taking the test. One person may respond quickly and enthusiastically when correct but become hesitant or withdrawn following failure. Another person may react to failure by trying harder and may actually do better in the face of frustration and failure.

After examiners have gained experience with an individual test and know how to use it properly, they can observe different reactions from individuals placed in the same situation. Experienced examiners eventually develop internal norms. They have an idea of how most subjects react to a certain task or situation and can easily identify unusual reactions. The opportunity to observe behavior in a standard situation can be invaluable to an examiner who is trying to understand the unique attributes of a person and interpret the meaning of a test score.

By providing the opportunity to observe behavior under standardized conditions, individual tests add a whole new dimension to the information that one can obtain from an interview. Some subjects will not talk; some cannot talk. How can the examiner gain an understanding of such individuals? Information provided by friends or relatives cannot be relied on because they are rarely objective and not usually trained in observing human behavior. Simply observing the person in a natural setting may provide some useful information, but then the examiner has nothing with which to compare these observations. Thus, by allowing observations of behavior under standard conditions, individual tests provide an invaluable opportunity for the examiner to get information beyond what he or she can obtain in an interview.

## Advantages of Group Tests

Group tests also offer unique advantages. Group tests are cost-efficient because they minimize the time needed for administration and scoring; they also involve less expensive materials and usually require less examiner skill and training than do individual tests. Scoring for group tests is more objective and hence typically more reliable than the subjective scoring of many individual tests. Group tests can be used with large numbers of individuals. When combined with data from other sources, group test results can yield information that is as useful and meaningful as that obtained from individual tests.

Whereas individual tests find their greatest application in the assessment and diagnosis of psychological or medical problems, the application of group tests is far broader. Group tests are used in schools at every level. The military, industry, and researchers also use them extensively. Group test results can be used for screening and selection purposes; to assess mental, vocational, or special abilities; to assess learning in a particular discipline or subject area; and to assess interests and aptitudes for specific occupations or job duties.

If the examiner's purpose does not require the benefits of individual tests, or if many individuals must be tested in a limited time with limited personnel, then carefully administered and interpreted group tests can be extremely valuable tools. Table 13.2 summarizes the advantages of individual and group tests.

**TABLE 13.2**  Unique Advantages of Individual and Group Tests

| Individual tests | Group tests |
| --- | --- |
| Provide information beyond the test score | Are cost-efficient |
| Allow the examiner to observe behavior in a standard setting | Minimize professional time for administration and scoring |
| Allow individualized interpretation of test scores | Require less examiner skill and training |
| | Have more objective and more reliable scoring procedures |
| | Have especially broad application |

# Overview of Group Tests

## Characteristics of Group Tests

In general, group tests can be characterized as paper-and-pencil or booklet-and-pencil tests because the only materials required are a printed booklet of test items, a test manual, a scoring key, an answer sheet, and a pencil. However, computerized group testing is becoming more popular (Bennett, 2003; Goldberg & Pedulla, 2002), and the clear trend is toward more computerized testing and less paper and pencil (see Mattson, 2011). Most group tests are multiple choice, but some require a free response such as completing a sentence or design, or writing an essay (Educational Testing Service, 2011), as in the modern GRE (Educational Testing Service, 2011).

Group tests by far outnumber individual tests. Like the latter, group tests vary among themselves in many respects. One major difference is whether the test is primarily verbal (thus requiring reading or language skills), primarily nonverbal, or a combination.

Some group tests group items by type (e.g., all verbal analogy problems are in the same section, with items arranged in order of increasing difficulty). A test of this kind is ideally suited for producing a variety of scores such as those obtained from the Wechsler scales. Other group tests present different tasks arranged in no particular or systematic order. A test of this kind typically produces a single score related to general ability.

Group test scores can be converted to a variety of units. Most produce percentiles or some type of standard score, but a few produce ratio or deviation IQs.

## Selecting Group Tests

Because there are a sufficient number of psychometrically adequate group tests for most purposes, the test user need never settle for anything but well-documented and psychometrically sound tests. This is especially true for ability tests used in the schools.

In view of the large number of psychometrically sound instruments, this chapter will not discuss poorly standardized or marginally reliable tests. However, tests excluded from this discussion are not necessarily psychometrically unsound. We gave highest priority to established, highly used tests that continue to generate interest among researchers and practitioners. We also include tests that illustrate concepts or meet specific needs. Finally, we include a few recent tests as well as tests of historical value.

## Using Group Tests

Overall, the tests included in our discussion are about as reliable and well standardized as the best individual tests. However, as for some individual tests, validity data for some group tests are weak, meager, or contradictory—or all three. Therefore, all users of group tests must carefully interpret and make use of test scores. These tests should not be seen as a simple way of making decisions but as a tool to be used in conjunction with other data.

Test use is an especially important issue for group tests because the results from these procedures are used by more people than are the results from individual tests. All routine users of these tests—thousands of teachers, educators, school administrators, personnel staff, counselors, and so forth—as well as the many consumers of group test information can benefit from the following suggestions.

### Use Results with Caution

Never consider scores in isolation or as absolutes. Try to include the test score as only one bit of data, tentatively accepted unless not confirmed by other data. Be especially careful in using these tests for prediction, except for predicting relatively limited factors over a brief time. Avoid overinterpreting test scores or attributing more to test scores than their limitations warrant.

### Be Especially Suspicious of Low Scores

Users of group tests must assume that subjects understand the purpose of testing, want to do well, and are equally rested and free of emotional problems. Many group tests also require reading ability as well as an interest in solving test problems. Failing to fulfill any of these assumptions and requirements can produce an artificially low score.

### Consider Wide Discrepancies a Warning Signal

When an individual exhibits wide discrepancies either among test scores or between a test score and other data, all may not be well with the individual (assuming no clerical errors). The discrepancy may reflect emotional problems or severe stress. For example, a child with high test scores may obtain poor grades because of emotional upset. Or a child with good grades may obtain a poor test score because of a crisis, such as a death in the family.

### When in Doubt, Refer

With low scores, wide discrepancies, or sufficient reason to doubt the validity or fairness of a test result, the safest course is to refer the subject for individual testing. Given the reasons for the referral, a professional who is trained in individual test use can generally ascertain the cause of the problem and provide the unique interpretation called for in such cases. It is often dangerous as well as reckless to take on a responsibility meant only for a trained specialist.

# Group Tests in the Schools: Kindergarten Through 12th Grade

The purpose of these tests is to measure educational achievement in schoolchildren. Before proceeding to a discussion of the specific tests, this section reviews the nature of achievement tests and how they differ from aptitude tests.

## Achievement Tests Versus Aptitude Tests

Achievement tests attempt to assess what a person has learned following a specific course of instruction. As you saw in Chapter 1, the first achievement tests used in the schools were essay tests. These were rapidly replaced in the 1930s by standardized achievement tests such as the Stanford Achievement Test, which is still in use today. These tests were more cost-effective than their essay counterparts, and scoring was far more objective and reliable. However, like their predecessors, standardized achievement tests had as their goal the endpoint evaluation of a student's knowledge after a standard course of training. In such tests, validity is determined primarily by content-related evidence. In other words, these tests are considered valid if they adequately sample the domain of the construct (e.g., math, science, or history) being assessed.

On the other hand, aptitude tests attempt to evaluate a student's potential for learning rather than how much a student has already learned. Unlike achievement tests, aptitude tests evaluate a wide range of experiences obtained in a variety of ways. They evaluate the effects of unknown and uncontrolled experiences. The validity of an aptitude test is judged primarily on its ability to predict future performance. Thus, such tests rely heavily on criterion-oriented evidence for validity. Table 13.3 summarizes the differences between achievement and aptitude tests.

As you know, the intelligence test measures general ability. Like aptitude tests, intelligence tests attempt to predict future performance. However, such tests predict generally and broadly, as opposed to aptitude tests, which typically predict potential in a specific area such as math, science, or music.

Clearly, achievement, aptitude, and intelligence are highly interrelated. For example, an algebra achievement test might be used to predict success (aptitude) in a geometry course. The following discussion examines all three types, beginning

**TABLE 13.3**  Achievement Tests Versus Aptitude Tests

| Achievement tests | Aptitude tests |
|---|---|
| 1. Evaluate the effects of a known or controlled set of experiences | 1. Evaluate the effects of an unknown, uncontrolled set of experiences |
| 2. Evaluate the product of a course of training | 2. Evaluate the potential to profit from a course of training |
| 3. Rely heavily on content validation procedures | 3. Rely heavily on predictive criterion validation procedures |

with achievement tests. Then we consider group intelligence tests used in the school system. Finally, we examine tests used to measure scholastic aptitude, one of which, the SAT Reasoning Test, has recently been renamed (formerly the Scholastic Aptitude Test), and underscores the points made herein.

## Group Achievement Tests

As previously indicated, the Stanford Achievement Test is one of the oldest of the standardized achievement tests widely used in the school system (Gardner, Rudman, Karlsen, & Merwin, 1982). Now in its 10th edition, this test is well normed and criterion-referenced, with exemplary psychometric documentation. It evaluates achievement in kindergarten through 12th grades in the following areas: spelling, reading comprehension, word study and skills, language arts, social studies, science, mathematics, and listening comprehension. Figure 13.1 shows an example of the scoring output for the Stanford Achievement Test.

Another well-standardized and psychometrically sound group measure of achievement is the Metropolitan Achievement Test (MAT), which measures achievement in reading by evaluating vocabulary, word recognition, and reading comprehension. Now in its eighth edition, the MAT-8 was renormed in 2000, and alternate versions of the test including Braille, large print, and audio formats were made available for use with children having visual limitations (Harcourt Educational Measurement, 2000). An example of a reading item follows:

> Jennifer_____to play house.
>
> Pick the word that best completes the sentence.
>
> **A.** wood   **B.** book   **C.** likes   **D.** hopes

The MAT-8 also measures mathematics by evaluating number concepts (e.g., measurement, decimals, factors, time, money), problem solving (e.g., word problems), and computation (addition, subtraction, multiplication, division). For example, a child might be presented with this item:

> Jason had four candy bars. He gave one to Mary and one to Bill. Which number sentence below shows how many candy bars he had left?
>
> **A.** $4 - 2 =$   **B.** $4 - 1 =$   **C.** $2 - 2 =$   **D.** $2 - 1 =$

Spelling is evaluated on the MAT-8 in a normal spelling test format in which the student is asked to spell an orally dictated word presented in a sentence. Language skills are evaluated with a grammar test as well as a measure of alphabetizing skills. Science knowledge is evaluated in items such as the following:

> A thermometer is used to measure_____.
>
> (Mark the best answer.)
>
> **A.** light   **B.** dark   **C.** temperature   **D.** planets

Finally, the MAT-8 has several social studies items. Students are tested on their knowledge of geography, economics, history, political science, anthropology, sociology, and psychology, as in the following:

Paris is in_____.

(Mark the best answer.)

**A.** England    **B.** Spain    **C.** Canada    **D.** France

The MAT-8 standardization sample reflects a diverse nationwide student population. The sample was stratified by school size, public versus nonpublic school affiliation, geographic region, socioeconomic status, and ethnic background. Reliabilities of the total scores run in the high .90's, while those for the five major content areas range from .90 to .96.

The SAT and the MAT are state-of-the-art achievement tests. Their psychometric documentation is outstanding. The tests are reliable and normed on exceptionally large samples. They sample a variety of school subjects and cover all grade levels.

## Group Tests of Mental Abilities (Intelligence)

This section discusses four group tests of mental abilities: the Kuhlmann-Anderson, the Henmon-Nelson, the Cognitive Abilities Test, and the Developing Cognitive Abilities Test.

### *Kuhlmann-Anderson Test (KAT)–Eighth Edition*

The KAT is a group intelligence test with eight separate levels covering kindergarten through 12th grade. Each level of the KAT contains several tests with a variety of items on each. As in most multilevel batteries that cover many age or grade ranges, KAT items are primarily nonverbal at lower levels, requiring minimal reading and language ability. However, whereas most multilevel batteries become increasingly verbal with increasing age or grade level, the KAT remains primarily nonverbal throughout. Thus, the KAT is suited not only to young children but also to those who might be handicapped in following verbal procedures. It might even be suitable for adaptation for non-English-speaking populations, assuming proper norming.

The results of the most recent (eighth) edition of the KAT can be expressed in verbal, quantitative, and total scores. At some levels, total scores can be expressed as deviation IQs. Scores at other levels can be expressed as percentile bands. A **percentile band** is like a confidence interval. It provides the range of percentiles that most likely represent a subject's true score. One creates it by forming an interval one standard error of measurement above and below the obtained score and then converting the resulting values to percentiles.

An overwhelming majority of reviews have praised the KAT for its construction, standardization, and other excellent psychometric qualities. Normative data have been continually improved and are based on more than 10,000 subjects. Reliability coefficients are quite good, with split-half coefficients running in the low .90's and test–retest coefficients ranging from the low .80's to the low .90's. Validity is also well documented. The KAT correlates highly with a variety of ability and IQ tests. In sum, the KAT is an extremely sound, sophisticated group test. Its nonverbal items make it particularly useful for special purposes. Its impressive validity and reliability also make it one of the most popular group ability tests for all grade levels. Its potential for use and adaptation for non-English-speaking individuals or even non-English-speaking countries needs to be explored.

## Henmon-Nelson Test (H-NT)

A second well-standardized, highly used, and carefully constructed test for all grade levels is the H-NT of mental abilities. Although it produces only a single score that is believed to reflect general intelligence, two sets of norms are available. One set is based on raw score distributions by age, the other on raw score distributions by grade. Raw scores can be converted into deviation IQs as well as percentiles. The availability of only a single score has continued to spur controversy. However, a single score is consistent with the purpose of the test, which is to obtain a relatively quick measure of general intelligence (it takes approximately 30 minutes to complete the 90 items).

As in the other tests for school-aged individuals, most of the reported reliability coefficients, both split-half and test–retest, run in the .90's. Furthermore, the H-NT correlates well with a variety of intelligence tests (median .76, range .50–.84) and achievement test scores (median .79, range .64–.85). Correlations with grades, though not as high, are impressive, with a median coefficient of .60, which would account for 36% of the variability.

In sum, the H-NT is an extremely sound instrument. It can help predict future academic success quickly. However, the H-NT has some important limitations when used as the sole screening instrument for selecting giftedness or identifying learning disabilities in minority, culturally diverse, and economically disadvantaged children.

By providing only a single score related to Spearman's *g* factor, the H-NT does not consider multiple intelligences. When the test was being developed, no special effort was made to check for content bias, either by judges or by statistical analysis. The manual presents no data pertaining to the norms for special racial, ethnic, or socioeconomic groups, nor was the test designed to be used for culturally diverse children. Indeed, the manual pointedly calls for caution when using the H-NT for individuals from an educationally disadvantaged subculture. It also advises caution when extreme scores (below 80 or above 130) are obtained. Consistent with these cautions, research suggests that the H-NT tends to underestimate Wechsler full-scale IQ scores by 10 to 15 points for certain populations (Watson & Klett, 1975). A major problem with the H-NT is its relatively low ceiling. For example, to achieve an IQ of 130, a ninth-grade child would have to answer approximately 85 of the items correctly. This leaves only five items to discriminate all those above 130.

## Cognitive Abilities Test (COGAT)

In terms of its reliability and validity, the COGAT is comparable to the H-NT. Unlike the H-NT, however, the COGAT provides three separate scores: verbal, quantitative, and nonverbal. Reliabilities ($KR_{20}$) for the verbal score are in the high .90's; for the quantitative, the low .90's; and for the nonverbal, the high .90's.

The COGAT's item selection is superior to that of the H-NT in terms of selecting minority, culturally diverse, and economically disadvantaged children. Unlike the H-NT, the COGAT was specifically designed for poor readers, poorly educated people, and people for whom English is a second language. As with the KAT, it can potentially be adopted for use outside of the United States.

The test authors of the COGAT took special steps to eliminate irrelevant sources of test difficulty, especially those pertaining to cultural bias. All items were scrutinized for content that might be biased for or against any particular group. Statistical tests were then performed to eliminate items that might predict differentially for white and minority students. To eliminate the effect of test-taking skills, the test administration includes extensive practice exercises.

The COGAT offers advantages over the H-NT in evaluating minority, culturally diverse, and economically disadvantaged children. In provides reliable assessment of the academic abilities of both English language learners and those whose primary language is English (Lakin, & Lai, 2011). Moreover, research has revealed that the COGAT is a sensitive discriminator for giftedness (Chong, 2000; Harty, Adkins, & Sherwood, 1984) and a good predictor of future performance (Henry & Bardo, 1990; Luo, Thompson, & Detterman, 2003). It also is a good measure of verbal underachievement (Langdon, Rosenblatt, & Mellanby, 1998).

On the negative side, each of the three subtests of the COGAT requires 32 to 34 minutes of actual working time, which the manual recommends be spread out over 2 or 3 days. The manual claims that the tests are primarily "power tests" but provides no data to support this claim. Despite the apparent strength of the norms, uncertainty remains as to whether they are, in fact, representative. For example, when a selected community declined to participate in the norming process, a second, third, fourth, or, in some cases, fifth choice was needed to find a replacement. No data are provided regarding the frequency and magnitude of this type of sampling bias. A more serious potential drawback can be found in the information presented in the manual regarding ethnic group means. The standard age scores (SAS; normalized standard scores with a mean of 100 and standard deviation of 16) averaged some 15 or more points lower for African American students (versus whites) on the verbal battery and quantitative batteries. This negative aspect of the COGAT has been confirmed by independent research (McKay & Doverspike, 2001). Latino and Latina students also tended to score lower than white students across the test batteries and grade levels. Therefore, great care should be taken when scores on the COGAT are used for minority populations.

### Summary of K–12 Group Tests

The Stanford Achievement Test, MAT, KAT, H-NT, and COGAT are all sound, viable instruments. The Stanford Achievement Test and MAT provide outstanding measures of achievement. A particular strength of the KAT in evaluating intelligence is its set of nonverbal items. The H-NT provides a quick estimate of $g$ (general intelligence) for most children but is not as valid as the COGAT for assessing minority or culturally diverse children. Each test should be used only by those who know its particular properties, strengths, and limitations.

# College Entrance Tests

Three of the most widely used and well-known entrance tests are the SAT Reasoning Test (formerly known as the Scholastic Aptitude Test), the Cooperative School and College Ability Tests (SCAT), and the American College Test (ACT).

# The SAT Reasoning Test

Up until March 1995, the SAT Reasoning Test (SAT-I) was known as the Scholastic Aptitude Test. The SAT-I remains the most widely used of the college entrance tests. In the 2000–2001 test year, more than 2.1 million students took the SAT-I: Reasoning Test as part of the admissions process for more than 1000 private and public institutions of higher education (Lawrence, Rigol, Van Essen, & Jackson, 2002).

In continuous use since 1926, the SAT Reasoning Test was given on an annual basis to some 1.5 million students at 5000 test centers around the country. From 1941 through April 1995, norms for the SAT Reasoning Test were based on a sample of 10,000 students who took the test in 1941. When compared with these original norms, modern users tended to score approximately 20 to 80 points lower for each of the two main sections of the test, the SAT-V (Verbal) and the SAT-M (Math). With the original mean at 500 for each of the two sections, national averages in the 1980s and early 1990s tended to run 420 for the SAT-V and 480 for the SAT-M. Numerous explanations were advanced to explain the decline, which became somewhat of a national embarrassment (Hanford, 1986).

In June 1994, the test developers announced that they would restore the national average to the 500-point level of 1941. They accomplished this by renorming the test on 1.8 million students and converting raw scores to standard scores with a mean of 500 and a standard deviation of 100. The new norms pushed up national SAT averages approximately 75 points for the verbal section and 20 points for the math. In 2002, the average scores on the SAT were 504 for the verbal section and 516 for the math section.

The renorming of the SAT did not alter the standing of test takers relative to one another in terms of percentile rank. However, some confusion exists in comparing scores from individuals who took the SAT before April 1995 and those who have since taken the SAT.

More recently, even more changes were made, and the current version of the test now has three scored sections, each scored between 200 and 800 points. The theoretical maximum is now 2400 instead of the original 1600. The new scoring is actually likely to reduce interpretation errors, as interpreters can no longer rely on comparisons with older versions (Liu, Cahn, & Dorans, 2006; Liu & Walker, 2007).

The modern test is 45 minutes longer, requiring 3 hours and 45 minutes to administer. This longer time span would appear to reward stamina, determination, persistence, and sustained attention, and may particularly disadvantage students with disabilities such as attention-deficit/hyperactivity disorder (Lighthouse, 2006; Lindstrom & Gregg, 2007).

The verbal section is now called "critical reading," presumably because of an increased focus on reading comprehension. Indeed, reading comprehension questions dominate this section, with 48 questions devoted to reading comprehension and 19 to sentence completion. The analogies section has been completely eliminated.

The writing section is extremely similar to the older SAT Reasoning Test Subject Test: Writing. Candidates write an essay and answer 49 multiple-choice questions on grammar.

The math section has eliminated much of the basic grammar school math questions, which used to predominate this section. The modern math section includes algebra II, data analysis, and statistics. A major weakness of the original SAT as well as other major college entrance tests is relatively poor predictive power regarding the grades of students who score in the middle ranges. It is not uncommon for a student at the mean on the SAT Reasoning Test to have a higher college GPA than a student who scores a standard deviation above the mean on both sections, perhaps because factors such as motivation, determination, personality, emotional stability, and home and social life also influence first-year grades. In other words, test scores and high-school performance records do not alone determine college success.

There is little doubt that the SAT predicts first-year college GPA (Bridges, 2001; Kelemen, Winningham, & Weaver, 2007). Validity coefficients vary depending on the sample, with a median of approximately .4, which means that SAT scores account for some 16% of the variation in first-year GPA. The predictive validity of the SAT is about as good for Latino and Latina (Fuertes & Sedlacek, 1994) and African American (Lawlor et al., 1997) students as it is for whites. However, studies with the old SAT have shown that African American and Latino and Latina students tend to obtain lower scores on the average, sometimes by as much as 80 points lower on the average (Lawlor et al., 1997). In addition, although women tend to achieve higher grades in college, they tend to score lower than men on the SAT (Mau & Lynn, 2001). Results with the SAT are entirely consistent with those from all modern standardized tests: African Americans and Latinos and Latinas score significantly lower on average compared to whites, and women score lower than men. Critics have asked whether the modern SAT will show similar selection biases (Zwick & Green, 2007).

There is little doubt that the SAT will play a role in college entrance decisions in the years ahead, but the need to study and understand selection bias in standardized tests persists. Moreover, with the numerous and rapid changes that have occurred, it is difficult to make definitive statements. It is time for the test developers to stop and evaluate the modern SAT.

## Cooperative School and College Ability Tests

Second to the SAT in terms of use but falling out of favor is the SCAT. It was developed in 1955 and has not been updated. In addition to the college level, the SCAT covers three precollege levels beginning at the fourth grade. The SCAT purports to measure school-learned abilities as well as an individual's potential to undertake additional schooling.

Although the SCAT is well designed and constructed based on 1950s standards, H. L. Butcher (1972) questioned the representativeness of its standardization sample. Psychometric documentation of the SCAT, furthermore, is neither as strong nor as extensive as that of the SAT. Another problem is that little empirical data support its major assumption—that previous success in acquiring school-learned abilities can predict future success in acquiring such abilities. Even if this assumption were accurate—and it probably is—grades provide about as much information about future performance as does the SCAT, especially at the college level. In view of these considerations, we concur with Butcher that additional evidence on the SCAT would be highly desirable. We would also encourage updates and revisions despite its reasonably good correlation with the SAT; we see no advantage of the SCAT over the SAT for predicting college success.

## The American College Test

The ACT is another popular and widely used college entrance (aptitude) test. It was updated in 2005, and is particularly useful for non-native speakers of English. The ACT produces specific content scores and a composite. The content scores are in English, mathematical usage, social studies reading, and natural science reading. In expressing results, the ACT makes use of the Iowa Test of Educational Development (ITED) scale. Scores on this scale can vary between 1 and 36, with a standard deviation of 5 and a mean of 16 for high-school students and a mean of 19 for college aspirants. Figure 13.2 shows a sample profile report from the ACT.

The ACT compares with the SAT in terms of predicting college GPA alone or in conjunction with high-school GPA (Stumpf & Stanley, 2002). In fact, the

*1991-92 ACT ASSESSMENT COLLEGE REPORT*

**FIGURE 13.2**

A sample student profile from the ACT.

correlation between the two tests is quite high—in the high .80's (Pugh, 1968). However, internal consistency coefficients are not as strong in the ACT, with coefficients in the mid .90's for the composite and in the high .70's to high .80's for the four content scores.

# Graduate and Professional School Entrance Tests

If you plan to go to graduate school, then you will probably have to take a graduate-school entrance test. The two most widely used are the GRE and the Miller Analogies Test. Tens of thousands of potential applicants also take entrance tests for professional-degree programs such as medical and law school. The LSAT serves to illustrate such tests.

## Graduate Record Examination Aptitude Test

The GRE is one of the most commonly used tests for graduate-school entrance. Offered throughout the year at designated examination centers located mostly at universities and colleges in the United States and numerous other countries worldwide, the GRE purports to measure general scholastic ability. It is most frequently used in conjunction with GPA, letters of recommendation, and other academic factors in the highly competitive graduate-school selection process. The GRE contains a general section that produces verbal (GRE-V) and quantitative (GRE-Q) scores. In 2002, the third section of the GRE, which evaluates analytical reasoning (GRE-A), was changed from a multiple-choice format to an essay format. It consists of two essays that require the test taker to analyze an argument based on the evidence presented and to articulate and support an argument (Educational Testing Service, 2002). In addition to this general test for all college majors, the GRE contains an advanced section that measures achievement in at least 20 majors, such as psychology, history, and chemistry (see Figures 13.3 and 13.4).

For a number of years, plans had been underway to launch a major revision of the GRE. On April 2, 2007, the Educational Testing Service (ETS) canceled the plans; instead, two new question types were added gradually from 2007 through 2009. In December 2009, ETS announced plans to move forward with major revisions to the GRE in 2011 (Lewin, 2009). Changes include a new 130–170 scoring scale, the elimination of certain question types such as antonyms and analogies, the addition of an online calculator, and the elimination of the CAT format of question-by-question adjustment, in favor of a section-by-section adjustment (Lewin, 2009). In August 2011, the GRE revised General Test replaced the GRE® General Test (ETS, 2011). According to ETS, the GRE features a new test taker–friendly design and new questions and more closely reflects the kind of thinking required in graduate school.

With a standard mean score of 500 and a standard deviation of 100, the verbal section covers reasoning, identification of opposites, use of analogies, and paragraph comprehension. The quantitative section covers arithmetic reasoning, algebra, and geometry. However, the normative sample for the GRE is relatively small. The psychometric adequacy of the GRE is also less spectacular than that of the SAT, both in the reported coefficients of validity and reliability and in

FIGURE 13.3

GRE verbal ability sample items.

**Directions***

In each of the following questions, a related pair of words or phrases is followed by five lettered pairs of words or phrases. Select the lettered pair that best expresses a relationship similar to that expressed in the original pair.

**Sample Question**

COLOR : SPECTRUM :
(A) tone : scale
(B) sound : waves
(C) verse : poem
(D) dimension : space
(E) cell : organism

**Strategies for Answering**

- Establish a relationship between the given pair before reading the answer choices.
- Consider relationships of kind, size, spatial contiguity, or degree.
- Read all of the options. If more than one seems correct, try to state the relationship more precisely.
- Check to see that you haven't overlooked a possible second meaning for one of the words.
- *Never* decide on the best answer without reading all of the answer choices.

**Answer**

The relationship between *color* and *spectrum* is not merely that of part to whole, in which case (E) or even (C) might be defended as correct. A *spectrum* is made up of a progressive, graduated series of *colors*, as a *scale* is of a progressive, graduated sequence of *tones*. Thus, (A) is the correct answer choice. In this instance, the best answer must be selected from a group of fairly close choices.

## Sentence Completions

Sentence completions measure your ability to recognize words or phrases that both logically and stylistically complete the meaning of a sentence.

**Directions***

Each sentence below has one or two blanks, each blank indicating that something has been omitted. Beneath the sentence are five lettered words or sets of words. Choose the word or set of words for each blank that *best* fits the meaning of the sentence as a whole.

_____
* The directions are presented as they appear on the actual test.

**Sample Question**

Early _____ of hearing loss is _____ by the fact that the other senses are able to compensate for moderate amounts of loss, so that people frequently do not know that their hearing is imperfect.
(A) discovery . . indicated
(B) development . . prevented
(C) detection . . complicated
(D) treatment . . facilitated
(E) incidence . . corrected

**Strategies for Answering**

- Read the incomplete sentence carefully.
- Look for key words or phrases.
- Complete the blank(s) with your own words; see if any options are like yours.
- Pay attention to grammatical cues.
- If there are two blanks, be sure that both parts of your answer choice fit logically and stylistically into the sentence.
- After choosing an answer, read the sentence through again to see if it makes sense.

**Answer**

The statement that the other senses compensate for partial loss of hearing indicates that the hearing loss is not *prevented* or *corrected*; therefore, choices (B) and (E) can be eliminated. Furthermore, the ability to compensate for hearing loss certainly does not facilitate the early *treatment* (D) or the early *discovery* (A) of hearing loss. It is reasonable, however, that early *detection* of hearing loss is *complicated* by the ability to compensate for it. The best answer is (C).

## Reading Comprehension Questions

Reading comprehension questions measure your ability to
- read with understanding, insight, and discrimination
- analyze a written passage from several perspectives

Passages are taken from the humanities, social sciences, and natural sciences.

**Directions***

The passage is followed by questions based on its content. After reading the passage, choose the best answer to each question. Answer all questions following the passage on the basis of what is *stated* or *implied* in the passage.

the extensiveness of documentation. Nevertheless, the GRE is a relatively sound instrument.

The stability of the GRE based on Kuder-Richardson and odd-even reliability is adequate, with coefficients only slightly lower than those of the SAT. However, the predictive validity of the GRE is far from convincing.

Independent studies of the GRE vary from those that find moderate correlations between the GRE and GPA to those that find no or even a negative relationship between the two. House and Johnson (1998), for example, reported

**FIGURE 13.4**
GRE quantitative ability
sample items.

the answer choices given.

**Sample Question**

When walking, a certain person takes 16 complete steps in 10 seconds. At this rate, how many complete steps does the person take in 72 seconds?
(A)  45
(B)  78
(C)  86
(D)  90
(E) 115

**Strategies for Answering**

- Determine what is given and what is being asked.
- Scan all answer choices before answering a question.
- When approximation is required, scan answer choices to determine the degree of approximation.
- Avoid long computations. Use reasoning instead, when possible.

**Answer**

72 seconds represents 7 ten-second intervals plus 2/10 of such an interval. Therefore, the person who takes 16 steps in 10 seconds will take (7.2)(16) steps in 72 seconds.

$$(7.2)(16) = (7)(16) + (0.2)(16)$$
$$= 112 + 3.2$$
$$= 115.2$$

Since the question asks for the number of complete steps, the best answer choice is (E).

## Problem Solving – Data Interpretation Questions

Data interpretation questions measure your ability
- to synthesize information and select appropriate data for answering a question
- to determine that sufficient information for answering a question is not provided

The data interpretation questions usually appear in sets and are based on data presented in tables, graphs, or other diagrams.

**Directions\***

Each of the following questions has five answer

choices. For each of these questions, select the best of the answer choices given.

**Sample Question**

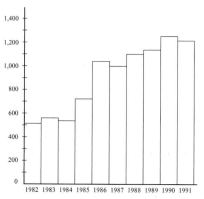

**Number of Graduate Student Applicants at University X, 1982–1991**

In which of the following years did the number of graduate student applicants increase the most from that of the previous year?
(A)  1985
(B)  1986
(C)  1988
(D)  1990
(E)  1991

**Strategies for Answering**

- Scan the set of data to see what it is about.
- Try to make visual comparisons and estimate products and quotients rather than perform computations.
- Answer questions only on the basis of data given.

**Answer**

This question can be answered directly by visually comparing the heights of the bars in the graph. The greatest increase in height between two adjacent bars occurs for the years 1985 and 1986. The best answer

---

\* The directions are presented as they appear on the actual test.

correlations ranging from .22 to .33 between GRE scores and various graduate-school courses, which would account for 4.84% to 10.89% of the variance. In 1999, House found that higher GRE scores were significantly correlated with higher grades in specific courses. Using regression analysis, Ji (1998) reported that GRE scores account for 16% to 6% of the variance in graduate GPA, indicating a correlation from .4 to approximately .25. In another study, House (1997) found that even though GRE scores were significantly correlated with students' degree completion, they were not significant predictors of grades for a group of

Native American students. Another independent study found an even weaker correlation with the GRE and grad school GPA—just 6% of the variation in grades could be predicted by GRE scores (Fairtest, 2007). Moreover, false-negative rates are high, which means that students whose GRE scores would not predict success in graduate school succeed at high rates (Holmes & Beishline, 1996). In addition, the GRE overpredicts the achievement of younger students while underpredicting the performance of older students (House, 1998). It is noteworthy that in one program that offers a GRE waiver to students who are typically older and more experienced, a study found that students who requested and received GRE test waivers tended to perform at a higher level in an MPA program, as measured by grade point average (Leavitt, Lombard, & Morris, 2011, pp. 447–448).

At this point, those who aspire to enter graduate school might be asking, "With its limitations, why is it that the GRE has such a critical effect on my chances for going to graduate school and on my future career?" One answer is that many schools have developed their own norms and psychometric documentation and can use the GRE, either independently or with other sources of data, to predict success in their programs. Furthermore, many graduate selection committees use the GRE broadly, as in requiring a minimum cutoff score to apply. Because more qualified students apply for graduate school than the available resources can train and job markets can absorb, the difficult job of selection must begin somewhere.

Finally, by looking at a GRE score in conjunction with GPA, graduate success can be predicted with greater accuracy than without the GRE (Morrison & Morrison, 1995). A 2001 meta-analysis of the GRE's predictive validity indicated that the GRE and undergraduate GPA can be valid predictors of graduate GPA, comprehensive examination scores, number of publications authored, and ratings by faculty (Kuncel, Hezlett, & Ones, 2001). That same year, a regression analysis conducted by Fenster, Markus, Wiedemann, Brackett, and Fernandez (2001) indicated that a linear combination of the verbal and quantitative sections of the GRE and undergraduate GPA correlated .63 with the GPA achieved in graduate school. As Melchert (1998) has noted, high achievement in any profession relies on a "confluence" of factors. Therefore, any single predictor such as the GRE will necessarily correlate only modestly with success in a profession.

Graduate schools also frequently complain that grades no longer predict scholastic ability well because of *grade inflation*—the phenomenon of rising average college grades despite declines in average SAT scores (Kuh & Hu, 1999). Thus, many people claim that a B today is equivalent to a C 15 or 20 years ago, and that an A today is equivalent to a B then. This grade inflation has led to a corresponding restriction in the range of grades. Thus, the median GPA for applicants to clinical psychology Ph.D. programs can exceed 3.5. Another reason for reliance on GRE scores is that the Freedom of Information Act grants students the right to examine their files, including letters of recommendation. Schools argue that professors and others cannot be candid while knowing the student may someday read the letter. Thus, as the validity of grades and letters of recommendation becomes more questionable, reliance on test scores increases, fair or not. However, students with relatively poor GRE scores can take heart in the knowledge that their score does not necessarily predict performance in graduate school.

In any case, there is a definite overall decline in verbal scores while quantitative and analytical scores are gradually rising. The mean of verbal scores in 1965 was 530. In the decades to follow, the mean continued to decline until reaching a low of 468 in 1999 and 456 in 2009—a drop of 64 points. Conversely, quantitative mean scores rose from 533 in 1965 to 565 in 1999 and 590 in 2009, an increase of 57 points (National Center for Education Statistics, 2011). This increase is mirrored in the mean analytical scores. This decrease in verbal scores has partially been explained by an increase in non-U.S. test takers that started in 1976 (National Center for Education Statistics, 1995). Because non-U.S. students tend to score higher on the quantitative portion of the GREs and lower on the verbal section, the increase from 7.5% non-U.S. examinees in 1976 to 20.5% non-U.S. examinees in 1988 is a plausible explanation for the overall pattern. However, the fact that American high-school students taking the older SATs experienced a similar pattern leads one to question if the number of non-U.S. examinees taking the GREs is the only explanation for the pattern of GRE scores. As any student knows, correlation does not imply causation.

## Miller Analogies Test

A second major graduate-school entrance test is the Miller Analogies Test. Like the GRE, the Miller Analogies Test is designed to measure scholastic aptitudes for graduate studies. However, unlike the GRE, the Miller Analogies Test is strictly verbal. In 60 minutes, the student must discern logical relationships for 120 varied analogy problems, including the most difficult items found on any test (see Figure 13.5).

**FIGURE 13.5**
MAT sample items.

> Look at the first sample analogy below. **Pain** is the right answer because **pain** is related to PLEASURE as DARK is related to LIGHT. On the **Answer Sheet** mark **c** for the first sample to show that choice **c. pain** is the right answer. The diagram at the right shows you how to mark on your **Answer Sheet**.
>
> **How to Mark on Answer Sheet**
>
> **SAMPLES**
> 1. LIGHT : DARK :: PLEASURE : (*a.* picnic, *b.* day, *c.* pain, *d.* night)
> 2. LEAVE : DEPART :: (*a.* stay, *b.* go, *c.* home, *d.* come) : REMAIN
> 3. STAPLE : (*a.* clamp, *b.* paper, *c.* glue, *d.* food) :: NAIL : WOOD
> 4. (*a.* 4, *b.* 5, *c.* 7, *d.* 6) : 12 :: 12 : 24
>
> 1  ⓐ ⓑ ⦿c ⓓ
> 2  ⦿a ⓑ ⓒ ⓓ
>
> Choose the proper word in the **parentheses** in Sample 2 and mark the corresponding letter in the proper place on **your Answer Sheet**. Do the same thing in the third and fourth samples.

Knowledge of specific content and a wide vocabulary are extremely useful in this endeavor. However, the most important factors appear to be the ability to see relationships and a knowledge of the various ways analogies can be formed (by sound, number, similarities, differences, and so forth). Used in a variety of specializations, the Miller Analogies Test offers special norms for various fields.

Odd–even reliability data for the Miller Analogies Test are adequate, with coefficients in the high .80's reported in the manual. Unfortunately, as with the GRE, the Miller Analogies Test lacks predictive validity support. Despite a substantial correlation with the GRE (coefficients run in the low .80's), validity coefficients reported in the manual for grades vary considerably from sample to sample and are only modest (median in the high .30's).

Like the GRE, the Miller Analogies Test has an age bias. Miller Analogies Test scores overpredicted the GPAs of a 25- to 34-year-old group and underpredicted the GPAs of a 35- to 44-year-old group. However, it also overpredicted achievement for a 45-year-old group (House & Keeley, 1996). According to House and Keeley (1996), motivation for academic achievement may be highest in the middle adult years, causing these students to obtain grades that were higher than predicted by their test scores. These same investigators have found that the Miller Analogies Test underpredicts the GPAs of women and overpredicts those of men (House & Keeley, 1995).

Generally, the psychometric adequacy of the Miller Analogies Test is reasonable when compared with ability tests in general, but GRE scores and GPA remain its primary correlates. Furthermore, the Miller Analogies Test does not predict research ability, creativity, and other factors important to graduate-school and professional performance. However, as an aid in discriminating among graduate-school applications and adults at the highest level of verbal ability, the Miller Analogies Test is an excellent device as long as one keeps in mind its possible biases.

## The Law School Admission Test

The LSAT provides a good example of tests for professional-degree programs. LSAT problems require almost no specific knowledge. Students of any major can take it without facing bias. As with the Miller Analogies Test, some of the problems on the LSAT are among the most difficult that one can encounter on a standardization test. The LSAT is taken under extreme time pressure.

The LSAT contains three types of problems: reading comprehension, logical reasoning, and analytical reasoning. Reading comprehension problems are similar to those found on the GRE. The student is given four 450-word passages followed by approximately seven questions per passage. The content of the passages may be drawn from just about any subject—history, the humanities, the women's movement, African American literature, science, and so forth. Each passage is purposefully chosen to be complicated and densely packed with information. The questions that follow may be long and complicated. Students may be asked what was not covered as well as to draw inferences about what was covered. All of this must be done in 35 minutes.

Approximately half of the problems on the LSAT are logical-reasoning problems. These provide a test stimulus as short as four lines or as long as half a page and ask for some type of logical deduction. Here is an example of a logical-reasoning question, as provided by law services:

---

"Electrons orbit around the nucleus of an atom the way the earth orbits around the sun. It is well known that gravity is a major force that determines the orbit of the earth. We may therefore, expect that gravity is the main force that determines the orbit of an electron."

The argument attempts to prove its case by:

(A) applying well-known general laws to a specific case

(B) appealing to well-known specific cases to prove a general law about them

(C) testing the conclusion by a definite experiment

(D) appealing to an apparently similar case

(E) stating its conclusions without giving any kind of reason to think that it might be true

---

Source: *LSAT/LSDAS Registration and Information Handbook*, 1994–1995, p. 42. Copyright 1994 Law School Admission Council. Reprinted by permission.

According to Law Services, this question is a "middle difficulty" item. Approximately 60% of test takers answered correctly (D). Approximately 25% chose A. A student has some 35 minutes to complete 25 problems such as this.

Applying for law school is a little less mystical than applying to graduate school. Unlike graduate schools, the weight given to the LSAT score is openly published for each school approved by the American Bar Association. Although many law schools consider special factors such as overcoming hardship, entrance into most approved schools is based heavily on a weighted sum of GPA and LSAT scores.

The publishers of the LSAT have made available every single previously administered test since the format changed in 1991. With little variation from year to year, one can know what to expect by examining old tests. For each administration, scores are adjusted according to test difficulty; one can then compare scores from one test to the next. Law Services also provides booklets that analyze questions from past tests and explain various test-taking strategies.

The LSAT is psychometrically sound, with reliability coefficients in the .90's. It predicts first-year GPA in law school. Its content validity is exceptional in that the skills tested on the LSAT resemble the ones needed for success in the first year of law school. Although women tend to obtain lower scores than do men, this does not prevent women from applying to prestigious schools. Moreover, a large-scale study found no evidence of bias in the law-school admission process (Wrightsman, 1998). The Law School Admissions Council maintains that the LSAT items go through a rigorous screening and pretesting process to eliminate bias, and that the primary reason that minorities perform less well on the LSAT is lack of preparation (Law School Admissions Council, 2011). The Council also advises that minority group members, particularly African Americans, are more vulnerable to test anxiety than other test takers and that the best way to avoid test anxiety is to prepare thoroughly for the LSAT.

Controversy over the bias issue continues, however (Shultz & Zedeck, 2011). Jay Rosner, executive director of the Princeton Review Foundation, concludes that every question chosen to appear on every LSAT and SAT in the past 10 years has favored whites over blacks (Rosner, 2003). In his view, if a test item is more likely to be answered correctly by nonminorities than by minorities, then it is a biased item. He found this to be true for every question on the LSAT. In addition, it is clear that women and minorities tend to score slightly lower on the LSAT; by some standards, this differential result also defines test bias (Black Issues in Higher Education, 2001), and has led the Law School Admissions Council to create a $ 10-million initiative to increase diversity in American law schools. Thus far, the Council has established a diversity committee, which has spent in excess of $5 million on projects designed to increase the number of minority men and women who attend law schools. The money has been spent, in part, on grants provided to projects that increase the enrollment of minorities in law schools (Law School Admissions Council, 2011).

However, there is evidence that may tend to nullify the arguments based on differential test results. If bias is defined not on the basis of differential item or test results but by how well these test results predict actual success in law school for each group, then the conclusions are much different. Using this second definition, if there is bias, it is in favor of minorities and women (Klein, 2002). Specifically, Klein found that even though females and minorities tend to score lower on the LSAT, the LSAT and undergraduate GPA index scores tend to overpredict their success in the first year of law school. Conversely, nonminority males tend to earn a slightly higher first-year GPA than would be predicted by their index scores. The same is generally true of the GRE and other standardized tests. It is a puzzling paradox in testing that has yet to be solved.

# Nonverbal Group Ability Tests

As we have noted, nonverbal tests are needed for evaluating certain individuals. Like their individual-test counterparts, nonverbal group tests may be performance tests that require the subject to do something (draw, solve maze problems), or they may be paper-and-pencil tests that provide printed nonverbal items and instruct the subject to select the best of two or more multiple-choice responses. Some nonverbal group tests can be administered without the use of language.

## Raven Progressive Matrices

The Raven Progressive Matrices (RPM) test is one of the best known and most popular nonverbal group tests. Although used primarily in educational settings, the Raven is a suitable test anytime one needs an estimate of an individual's general intelligence. Only the SAT Reasoning Test, Wechsler, and Binet tests are referenced more in the *Mental Measurements Yearbook*. One may administer the RPM to groups or individuals, from 5-year-olds to elderly adults. Instructions are simple and, if necessary, the RPM can be administered without the use of language. In fact, the test is used throughout the modern world. The RPM consists exclusively of one of the most common types of stimuli in nonverbal tests of any kind—matrices (see Figures 13.6 and 13.7). The 60 matrices of the Raven Plus are graded in difficulty (Raven, Raven, & Court, 1998). Each contains a logical pattern or design with a missing part. The subject must select the appropriate design from as many as eight choices. The test can be used with or without a time limit.

The original RPM also has 60 items, which were believed to be of increasing difficulty. However, item response and other analyses demonstrated that there were three items in the middle that were of roughly comparable difficulty. This resulted in an overestimation of the IQs of those individuals who were at the level

**FIGURE 13.6**
Sample Progressive Matrices items.

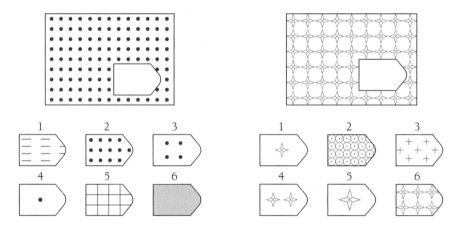

**FIGURE 13.7**
An advanced problem from the alternate Raven by N. E. Johnson et al., 1993.

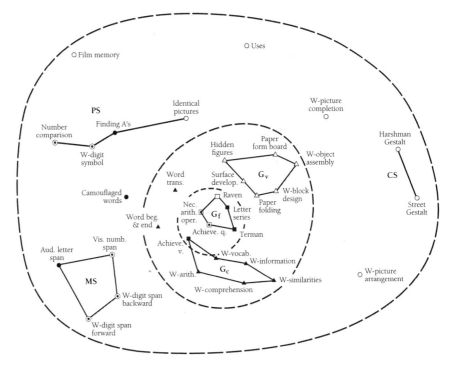

(Courtesy of Richard Snow.)

of these items, because if they got one, they tended to get the other two. The newer 1998 Raven Plus corrects this problem (Raven et al., 1998).

Research supports the RPM as a measure of general intelligence, or Spearman's *g* (see Raven et al., 1998, for an extensive review; see also Colom, Flores-Mendoza, & Rebello, 2003). In fact, the Raven may be the best single measure of *g* available, as shown by a multidimensional scaling by Marshalek, Lohman, and Snow (1983) (see Figure 13.8). Because of the Raven's ability to measure general fluid intelligence, it was used in a recent brain-imaging study that evaluated how the differences in ability to reason and solve problems translate into differences in the firing of neurons in the brain (Gray, 2003). By conducting magnetic resonance imaging (MRI) while participants completed the matrices, brain activity involved with the task was observed. The study revealed that variations in test performances were reflected in brain activity in the lateral prefrontal cortex. In addition, participants who scored highly on the Raven showed an increased amount of brain activity in the anterior cingulated cortex and the cerebellum. As well as providing insight concerning the function of different areas of the brain, the study confirmed that standard intelligence tests such as RPM are measuring the workings of essential and specific brain activities.

Figure 13.6 is the only illustration of an RPM problem that the test publisher allows to be reproduced. Recently, Johnson, Saccuzzo, Larson, Guertin, Christianson, and Longley (1993) developed a parallel research form for the RPM. Initial studies with the parallel form have revealed an alternate form reliability coefficient of .90 with comparable internal reliability coefficients between the two versions of the test (.94). Figure 13.7 illustrates one of the more difficult items from the parallel form. More recently, the publishers of the RPM have released their own parallel version (Raven et al., 1998).

A product of England, the RPM was originally designed to assess military recruits independently of educational factors. For years, the lack of adequate norms for the RPM and weaknesses in the manual received criticism. In spite of these limitations, the RPM and other tests like it flourished. One can see the versatility of matrices in their wide application for such groups as young children, the culturally deprived, the language-handicapped (Saccuzzo, Johnson, & Guertin, 1994), and those suffering traumatic brain injury (Hiscock, Inch, & Gleason, 2002). Analysis of available reliability studies shows a rather respectable range of coefficients, from the high .70's to low .90's (see Raven et al., 1998).

The manual for the Raven has been updated, and an impressive set of norms have been published (Raven, 1986, 1990; Raven et al., 1998). With these new norms, one can compare the performance of children from major cities around the world. Thus, a major criticism of the Raven has finally been addressed in an extremely useful and far-reaching way.

The Raven appears to minimize the effects of language and culture (Raven, 2000). For example, whereas Latinos, Latinas, and African Americans typically score some 15 points lower on the Wechsler and Binet scales than do Caucasians, there is less difference—only 7 or 8 points—with the Raven. Thus, the Raven tends to cut in half the selection bias that occurs with the Binet or Wechsler. Consequently, it has great utility for use in selecting disadvantaged African American and Latino and Latina children for giftedness (Saccuzzo & Johnson, 1995). Moreover, unlike the Kaufman (see Chapter 12), which also has a lower discrepancy between white and other racial groups, the Raven is actually a better measure of general intelligence than the Wechsler scales (Colom et al., 2003). With its new worldwide norms and updated test manual, as well as its successful computer administered version, the Raven holds promise as one of the major players in the testing field.

## Goodenough-Harris Drawing Test (G-HDT)

A remarkable nonverbal intelligence test that can be either group or individually administered is the G-HDT. Although not a standardized test in the strictest sense, the G-HDT is one of the quickest, easiest, and least expensive to administer of all ability tests. Therefore, it is widely used in educational and other settings, including clinical. A pencil and white unlined paper are the only materials needed. The subject is instructed to draw a picture of a whole man and to do the best job possible. The G-HDT was standardized by determining those characteristics of human-figure drawings that differentiated subjects in various age groups. Subjects get credit for each item included in their drawings. As a rule, each detail is given one point, with 70 points possible. For example, if only a head is included with no facial features, then the subject receives only 1 point. Points are added for additional details such as facial features and clothing.

The G-HDT was originally standardized in 1926 and restandardized in 1963 (Harris, 1963). Scoring of the G-HDT follows the principle of age differentiation—older children tend to get more points because of the greater accuracy and detail of their drawings. Thus, one can determine mental ages by comparing scores with those of the normative sample. Raw scores can be converted to standard scores with a mean of 100 and a standard deviation of 15. Split-half, test–retest, and inter-scorer reliability coefficients are good, with ranges in the high .60's to the low .90's for both old and revised forms (Dunn, 1972). Scores begin leveling off at age 14 or 15, so the use of the G-HDT is restricted primarily to children and works best with younger children (Scott, 1981). Despite the relatively outdated norms, scores on the G-HDT remain significantly related to Wechsler IQ scores (Abell, Horkheimer, & Nguyen, 1998; Alexopoulos, Haritos-Fatouros, Sakkas, Skaltsas, & Vlachos, 2000).

Because of their ease of administration and short administration time, the G-HDT and other human-figure drawing tests are used extensively in test batteries. The test allows an examiner to obtain a quick but rough estimate of a child's intelligence. The G-HDT is most appropriately used in conjunction with other sources of information in a battery of tests; results based on G-HDT data alone can be quite misleading (Abell et al., 1998).

## The Culture Fair Intelligence Test

All cultures tend to reinforce certain skills and activities at the expense of others. One purpose of nonverbal and performance tests is to remove factors related to cultural influences so that one can measure pure intelligence independently of learning, culture, and the like. Experience and empirical research have shown that such a test has yet to be developed. Indeed, many doubt whether such an accomplishment is even possible, although the Raven probably comes close to this goal.

The IPAT Culture Fair Intelligence Test was designed to provide an estimate of intelligence relatively free of cultural and language influences. Although this test succeeds no more in this regard than any other such attempt, the popularity of the Culture Fair Intelligence Test reflects the strong desire among users for a test that reduces cultural factors as much as possible (Tan & Tan, 1998).

Constructed under the direction of R. B. Cattell, the Culture Fair Intelligence Test is a paper-and-pencil procedure that covers three levels (ages 4–8 and mentally disabled adults, ages 8–12 and randomly selected adults, and high-school age and above-average adults). Two parallel forms are available.

Standardization varies according to age level. Kuder-Richardson reliabilities are only in the .70's, with substantially lower test–retest coefficients. The test has been correlated with a wide variety of other tests with mixed results. Correlations with the Wechsler and Binet tests are quite good, with a range of .56 to .85. Also, normative data from Western European countries, the United States, and Australia are comparable. Thus, if one wishes to estimate intelligence in a Western European or Australian individual, the Culture Fair Intelligence Test is probably the instrument of choice. The Culture Fair Test is viewed as an acceptable measure of fluid intelligence (Colom & Garcia-Lopez, 2002; Rammsayer & Brandler, 2002), although the norms are becoming outdated, and more work is needed if the Culture Fair Test is to compete with the Raven.

## Standardized Tests Used in the U.S. Civil Service System

The number and variety of group ability tests for measuring aptitude for various occupations are staggering. The General Aptitude Test Battery (GATB), for example, is a reading ability test that purportedly measures aptitude for a variety of occupations.

The U.S. Employment Service developed the GATB for use in making employment decisions in government agencies. It attempts to measure a wide range of aptitudes from general intelligence (*g*) to manual dexterity. The GATB also produces scores for motor coordination, form perception (awareness of relevant details and ability to compare and discriminate various shapes), and clerical perception (e.g., the ability to proofread). Scores are also available for verbal, numerical, and spatial aptitudes.

The GATB was originally standardized in 1952 on a sample of 4000 people believed to represent the working population of the United States in 1940. Stratified according to gender, education, occupation, and geographic location, the sample ranged in age from 18 to 54. The mean educational level of the sample, 11.0 years, reveals that the GATB is most appropriate for those who have not graduated from college. Moreover, with rapidly changing times and the advent of high technology, the GATB may be out of date (see, for example, Avolio & Waidman, 1990; Vandevijer & Harsveld, 1994).

The GATB has engendered considerable controversy because it used within-group norming prior to the passage of the Civil Rights Act of 1991. In within-group norming, individuals are compared with others within a specific subgroup. For example, women may be compared only with other women; African Americans only with other African Americans. Such norming practices were justified on the basis of fairness. If men consistently outperform women on a particular test, then, given an equal number of men and women applying for a job, more men will be selected. However, the Civil Rights Act of 1991 outlawed within-group norming, arguing that such norming was reverse discrimination (see Brown, 1994). Today, any kind of score adjustments through within-group norming in employment practices is strictly forbidden by law (see Kittaeff, 2011, p. 83). (For more on these issues, see Chapter 19.)

## Standardized Tests in the U.S. Military: The Armed Services Vocational Aptitude Battery

Designed for the Department of Defense, the Armed Services Vocational Aptitude Battery (ASVAB) is administered to more than 1.3 million individuals each year. A multiple aptitude battery, the ASVAB was designed for students in grades 11 and 12 and in postsecondary schools. The test yields scores used in both educational and military settings. In the latter, ASVAB results can help identify students who potentially qualify for entry into the military and can recommend assignment to various military occupational training programs.

The ASVAB consists of 10 subtests: general science, arithmetic reasoning, word knowledge, paragraph comprehension, numeral operations, coding speed, auto and shop information, mathematics knowledge, mechanical comprehension, and electronics information. These subtests are grouped into various composites, including three academic composites—academic ability, verbal, and math; four occupational composites—mechanical and crafts, business and clerical, electronics and electrical, and health and social; and an overall composite that reflects general ability.

The psychometric characteristics of the ASVAB are excellent (Ree & Carretta, 1994, 1995). The most recent form of the test was normed on a nationally representative group of nearly 12,000 men and women between the ages of 16 and 23 who took the ASVAB-8a between July and October 1980.

African Americans, Latinos and Latinas, and economically disadvantaged whites were oversampled and then weighted to represent the national population distribution for all groups. Reliability coefficients for composite scores based on the Kuder-Richardson formula are excellent, ranging from .84 to .92 for women and .88 to .95 for men. The test manual and supporting documents strongly support the ASVAB as a valid predictor of performance during training for a variety of military and civilian occupations.

Since the late 1990's, the military has presented the ASVAB via computer rather than in the traditional paper-and-pencil format (see Moreno, Segall, & Hetter, 1997; Hambrick, Rench, Poposki, Darowski, Roland, Bearden, Oswald, & Brou, 2011). Through this computerized format, subjects can be tested *adaptively*, meaning that the questions given each person can be based on his or her unique ability. Briefly, adaptive testing of ability involves presenting an item of a known level of difficulty and then presenting either a more difficult or a less difficult item, depending on whether the subject is correct. The procedure cuts testing time almost in half and is far less fatiguing than the complete test. (We discuss computer adaptive testing in depth in Chapter 9.) After many political battles, the adaptive version of the ASVAB was finally put into use in the late 1990s (Sands, Waters, & McBride, 1997).

# Summary

Standardized ability tests are available for just about any purpose. There appears to be no end to the construction of this type of test. Relative ease in scoring and administration gives group ability tests a major advantage over individual tests. In many cases, the results from group tests are as stable and valid as those from individual tests. However, low scores, wide discrepancies between two group test results, or wide discrepancies between a group test result and some other indicator such as grades are reasons for exercising caution in interpreting results. When in doubt, users of group ability tests should refer the problem to a competent professional who can administer an individual ability test. The public school system makes the most extensive use of group ability tests. Indeed, many sound tests exist for all levels from kindergarten through 12th grade. Achievement tests for this age include the Stanford Achievement Test and the Metropolitan Achievement Test (MAT).

College and graduate-school entrance tests also account for a large proportion of the group ability tests used in the United States. The most popular college entrance tests include the SAT Reasoning Test, the Cooperative School and College Ability Tests (SCAT), and the American College Test (ACT). Students looking toward postgraduate work may have to take the GRE, the Miller Analogies Test, or a more specialized test such as the Law School Admission Test (LSAT).

Several nonverbal group ability tests have proven helpful for determining intelligence in certain populations. The Raven Progressive Matrices (RPM) and the

Goodenough-Harris Drawing Test (G-HDT) can provide helpful data on intelligence; the latest edition of the former has norms that allow worldwide comparisons. The IPAT Culture Fair Intelligence Test also provides good data on intelligence; however, it may soon be obsolete without further revisions.

Other group ability tests can help vocational counselors assess ability for certain occupations; the General Aptitude Test Battery (GATB) is one. Still other group ability tests measure aptitude for advanced or professional training. Developed for the military, the Armed Services Vocational Aptitude Battery (ASVAB) provides helpful data for both military and civilian applications.

In viewing group ability tests, one gets the impression that there is almost no limit to the scope and applicability of psychological tests.

14

CHAPTER

Projective Personality Tests

## LEARNING OBJECTIVES

*When you have completed this chapter, you should be able to:*

▶ Define the projective hypothesis

▶ Identify five individuals who played a dominant role in the development of the Rorschach

▶ Describe the Rorschach stimuli

▶ Briefly describe Rorschach administration and scoring

▶ List the pros and cons of the Rorschach

▶ Describe the Holtzman Inkblot Test

▶ Describe the TAT stimuli

▶ Briefly describe TAT administration

▶ Identify the factors that should be considered in evaluating the TAT

▶ List some of the major similarities and differences between the Rorschach and the TAT few years ago, the wife of an army sergeant sued him for divorce after 14 years of marriage. She claimed that her husband was "mentally unstable and deranged." She accused him of beating her for no apparent reason. The sergeant went to a psychologist to "prove" his sanity. In addition to an interview, an ability test [the Wechsler Adult Intelligence Scale, Third Edition (WAIS-III)], and an objective personality test [the Minnesota Multiphasic Personality Inventory-2 (MMPI-2)], the psychologist administered the Rorschach Inkblot Test. The Rorschach is one of the best known as well as the most controversial of the projective personality tests. According to the psychologist's evaluation, the Rorschach indicated that the sergeant was free of unusual or bizarre thought processes. The psychologist concluded that, based on the Rorschach and other test results, the sergeant was mentally stable, contrary to his wife's claims.

When the matter went to court, the psychologist was called to the witness stand. The cross-examination by the wife's attorney proceeded as follows:

ATTORNEY:  Based on the Rorschach and other tests, you concluded that this man is mentally stable.

PSYCHOLOGIST:  I did.

ATTORNEY:  What is the Rorschach?

PSYCHOLOGIST:  The Rorschach is a projective psychological test that contains 10 cards with inkblots on them. Five of the inkblots are black and gray; two are black, gray, and red; and the remaining three are composed of a variety of pastel colors of various shades.

ATTORNEY:  How do you administer a Rorschach?

PSYCHOLOGIST:  The subject—that is, the person taking the test—is shown each of the cards, one at a time. The subject is required to state what the inkblot might be.

ATTORNEY:  You mean to say that you can tell whether a person is sane or insane by the way he or she interprets 10 black, gray, and variously colored inkblots?

In fact, a competent psychologist would never assert that a single test, or even several tests used in combination, can be used to prove or disprove one's sanity. In practice, psychologists conduct *assessments*, in which tests are used in conjunction with historical data, face-to-face contact, interview procedures, and experience to test hypotheses about individuals. Nevertheless, the ability of psychologists to draw accurate inferences has always been questioned, and nowhere is this more true than where the Rorschach is concerned (see Blasczyk-Schiepa, Kazénb, Kuhlb, & Grygielskic, 2011, for a discussion on criticism of the Rorschach, also see Garb, Wood, Lilienfeld, & Nezworski, 2005; Mattlar, 2004; Meyer, Mihura, & Smith, 2005).

Projective personality tests such as the Rorschach are perhaps the most controversial and most misunderstood psychological tests (Aronow, Reznikoff, & Moreland, 1995; Blatt, 1990; Lilienfeld, Wood, & Garb, 2000). The Rorschach has been vigorously attacked on a variety of scientific and statistical grounds (Krishnamurthy, Archer, & Groth-Marnat, 2011, p. 283; Wood, Nezworski, & Stejskal, 1996; Wood, Lilienfeld, Nezworski, & Garb, 2003), yet surveys of psychological test usage in the United States consistently find that the Rorschach continues to be one of the most widely used tests in clinical settings (see Musewicz, Marczyk, Knauss, & York, 2009; Wood et al., 2003). In addition, it was found that five projective techniques (two of which were the Rorschach and the TAT) were among the 10 testing instruments most frequently used in clinical settings (Watkins, Campbell, Nieberding, & Hallmark, 1995). The Rorschach is used extensively by psychologists and widely taught in doctoral training programs for clinical psychologists (Meloy & Singer, 1991; Piotrowski, 1984; Piotrowski, Sherry, & Keller, 1985; Ritzler & Alter, 1986; Hunsley & DiGiulio, 2001; Weiner, 2003). Moreover, our survey of the testing literature revealed that between 1999 and 2011 the Rorschach was by far the most-referenced projective personality test and continued to rank third only to the MMPI/MMPI-2 and the NEO in number of research citations (also see *Journal of Personality Assessment*, 2005, volume 85, pp. 219–237.)

Feelings against the Rorschach run so high that reviewers of this book have threatened that they would not use it if it includes a discussion of the Rorschach! Proponents of the Rorschach frequently email or send copies of favorable articles to keep us up-to-date with their side of the argument. Why is there such a widespread acceptance of projective tests such as the Rorschach in spite of severe attacks from prominent researchers and psychometricians? And what among clinicians is the true story? To answer these questions, we need to begin with a look at the rationale for and the nature of projective tests.

# The Projective Hypothesis

Numerous definitions have been advanced for the primary rationale underlying projective tests, known as the **projective hypothesis**, with credit for the most complete analysis usually given to L. K. Frank (1939). Simply stated, this hypothesis proposes that when people attempt to understand an ambiguous or vague stimulus, their interpretation of that stimulus reflects their needs, feelings, experiences, prior conditioning, thought processes, and so forth. When a frightened little boy looks into a dark room and sees a huge shadow that he interprets as a monster, he is projecting his fear onto the shadow. The shadow itself is neutral—neither good nor bad, neither fearsome nor pretty. What the child really sees is a reflection of the inner workings of his mind.

The concept of projection is not new. Exner (1993) notes, for example, that Leonardo da Vinci used ambiguous figures to evaluate young art students. The artist presented potential students with an ambiguous figure and presumably evaluated their imaginations according to the quality of the artistic forms the students created from it. The concept of projection is also reflected in Shakespeare's "Nothing is either good or bad, but thinking makes it so."

Although what the subject finally sees in a stimulus is assumed to be a reflection of personal qualities or characteristics, some responses may be more revealing than others. If, for example, you say that a round figure is a ball, you provide a relatively straightforward interpretation of the stimulus. The stimulus itself has little ambiguity; it is round and shaped like a ball. In viewing this stimulus, a high percentage of people probably see, though not necessarily report, a ball. Theoretically, however, even this simple response can reveal a lot about you. For example, your response may indicate that you accurately perceive simple objects in the external environment and are willing to provide a conventional response. Although suppose you said that this same stimulus looked like a square peg in a round hole. Assuming the stimulus is actually round and contains no lines or shapes resembling a square peg, your perception of the stimulus does not conform to its actual property (roundness). Thus, your perceptions in general may not be accurate. Your response may also indicate that you are unwilling to provide the obvious, conventional response. Or it may indicate that you feel out of place, like a square peg in a round hole.

Of course, examiners can never draw absolute, definite conclusions from any single response to an ambiguous stimulus. They can only hypothesize what a test response means. Even the same response to the same stimulus may have several possible meanings, depending on the characteristics of the people who make the response. A problem with all projective tests is that many factors can influence one's response to them. For example, a response may reflect a recent experience or an early experience one has forgotten. It may reflect something one has witnessed (a bloody murder) or something one imagines (flunking out of college) rather than something one has actually experienced directly. It may reflect day-to-day problems, such as an argument with a boyfriend or girlfriend. With all of these possible factors influencing a response, it is no wonder that the validity of projective tests has been questioned. Arguably, the interpretation of projective tests requires highly trained, experienced practitioners, but as in any field, even an expert can draw the wrong conclusions. Further, even the most experienced experts often disagree among themselves (Exner, 1995; Nezworski & Wood, 1995). As in the example at the beginning of the chapter, Rorschach users believe that they can use projective tests to draw valid conclusions. Many researchers, however, remain firmly unconvinced (Erickson, Lilienfeld, & Vitacco, 2007; Sechrest, Stickle, & Stewart, 1998; Wood et al., 1996; Wood et al., 2003).

# The Rorschach Inkblot Test

As an example of a psychological test based on the projective hypothesis, the Rorschach has few peers. Indeed, no general discussion of psychological tests is complete without reference to the Rorschach, despite heated scientific controversies. The Rorschach has been called everything from a psychological X-ray (Piotrowski, 1980) and "perhaps the most powerful psychometric instrument ever envisioned" (Board of Professional Affairs, 1998, p. 392) to an instrument that "bears a charming resemblance to a party game" (Wood et al., 2003, p. 1) and should be "banned in clinical and forensic settings" (Garb, 1999, p. 316). Strangely, the Rorschach is both revered and reviled (compare, for example, Erickson et al., 2007 and Mattlar, 2004).

## Historical Antecedents

Like most concepts, the notion of using inkblots to study human functioning did not simply appear out of thin air. More than 25 years before the birth of Herman Rorschach, the originator of the test that bears his name, J. Kerner (1857) noted that individuals frequently report idiosyncratic or unique personal meanings when viewing inkblot stimuli. The wide variety of possible responses to inkblots does provide a rationale for using them to study individuals. Indeed, Binet proposed the idea of using inkblots to assess personality functioning (Binet & Henri, 1896) when Rorschach was only 10 years old. Several historic investigators then supported Binet's position concerning the potential value of inkblots for investigating human personality (Dearborn, 1897; Kirkpatrick, 1900). Their support led to the publication of the first set of standardized inkblots by Whipple (1910). Rorschach, however, receives credit for finding an original and important use for inkblots: identifying psychological disorders. His investigation of inkblots began in 1911 and culminated in 1921 with the publication of his famous book *Psychodiagnostik*. A year later, he suddenly and unexpectedly died of a serious illness at age 37.

Rorschach's work was viewed with suspicion and even disdain right from the outset. Not even the sole psychiatric journal of Switzerland, Rorschach's homeland, reviewed *Psychodiagnostik* (Allison, Blatt, & Zimet, 1968). In fact, only a few foreign reviews of the book appeared, and these tended to be critical. When David Levy first brought Rorschach's test to the United States from Europe, he found a cold, unenthusiastic response. U.S. psychologists judged the test to be scientifically unsound, and psychiatrists found little use for it. Nevertheless, the use of the test gradually increased, and eventually it became quite popular.

Five individuals have played dominant roles in the use and investigation of the Rorschach. One of these, Samuel J. Beck, was a student of Levy's. Beck was especially interested in studying certain patterns or, as he called them, "configurational tendencies" in Rorschach responses (Beck, 1933). Beck, who died in 1980, eventually wrote several books on the Rorschach and influenced generations of Rorschach practitioners (Beck, 1944, 1945, 1952). Like Beck, Marguerite Hertz stimulated considerable research on the Rorschach during the years when the test first established its foothold in the United States (Hertz, 1937, 1938). Bruno Klopfer, who immigrated to the United States from Germany, published several key Rorschach books and articles and played an important role in the early development of the test (Klopfer & Davidson, 1944; Klopfer & Kelley, 1942). Zygmunt Piotrowski (1947, 1964) and David Rapaport (Rapaport, Gill, & Schafer, 1945–1946) came somewhat later than Beck, Hertz, and Klopfer, but like them continues to exert an influence on clinical practitioners who use the Rorschach. The development of the Rorschach can be attributed primarily to the efforts of these five individuals. Like most experts, however, the five often disagreed. Their disagreements are the source of many of the current problems with the Rorschach (Hunsley & Bailey, 1999). Each expert developed a unique system of administration, scoring, and interpretation; they all found disciples who were willing to accept their biases and use their systems.

## Stimuli, Administration, and Interpretation

Rorschach constructed each stimulus card by dropping ink onto a piece of paper and folding it. The result was a unique, bilaterally symmetrical form on a white background. After experimenting with thousands of such blots, Rorschach selected 20. However, the test publisher would only pay for 10. Of the 10 finally selected, five were black and gray; two contained black, gray, and red; and three contained pastel colors of various shades. An example of a Rorschach card is shown in Figure 14.1.

The Rorschach is an individual test. In the administration procedure, each of the 10 cards is presented to the subject with minimum structure. After preliminary

**FIGURE 14.1**

A Rorschach-type image is created by dropping ink onto a piece of paper and folding it. This is a reproduction of an actual card from the Rorschach.

remarks concerning the purpose of testing, the examiner hands the first card to the subject and asks something like, "What might this be?" No restriction is placed on the type of response permitted, and no clues are given concerning what is expected. If the subject asks for guidance or clarification, the examiner gives little information. If, for example, the subject asks, "Do I use the whole thing or just part of it?" the examiner replies, "As you like" or "Whatever you choose." Anxious subjects or individuals who are made uncomfortable by unstructured situations frequently ask questions, attempting to find out as much as possible before committing themselves. The examiner, however, must not give any cues that might reveal the nature of the expected response. Furthermore, in view of the finding that the examiner may inadvertently reveal information or reinforce certain types of responses through facial expressions and other forms of nonverbal communication (E. Lord, 1950; Wood, Lilienfeld, Garb, & Nezworski, 2000a), Exner (1993) advocated an administration procedure in which the examiner sits next to the subject rather than face-to-face as in Rapaport's system (Blais, Norman, Quintar, & Herzog, 1995).

Notice that the examiner is nonspecific and largely vague. This lack of clear structure or direction with regard to demands and expectations is a primary feature of all projective tests. The idea is to provide as much ambiguity as possible so that the subject's response reflects only the subject. If the examiner inadvertently provides too many guidelines, the response may simply reflect the subject's tendency to perform as expected or to provide a socially desirable response, as discussed in Chapter 16. Therefore, an administration that provides too much structure is antithetical to the main idea behind projective tests.

Each card is administered twice. During the *free-association* phase of the test, the examiner presents the cards one at a time. If the subject gives only one response to the first card, then the examiner may say, "Some people see more than one thing here." The examiner usually makes this remark only once. If the subject rejects the card—that is, states that he or she sees nothing—then the examiner may reply, "Most people do see something here, just take your time." The examiner records every word and even every sound made by the subject verbatim. In addition, the examiner records how long it takes a subject to respond to a card (reaction time) and the position of the card when the response is made (upside down, sideways).

In the second phase, the *inquiry*, the examiner shows the cards again and scores the subject's responses. Responses are scored according to at least five dimensions, including location (where the perception was seen), determinant (what determined the response), form quality (to what extent the response matched the stimulus properties of the inkblot), content (what the perception was), and frequency of occurrence (to what extent the response was popular or original; popular responses occur once in every three protocols on average). A complete discussion of these special scoring categories is beyond the scope of this text. For more information on scoring and interpretation, see Exner's (1993) Rorschach textbooks.

In scoring for location, the examiner must determine where the subject's perception is located on the inkblot. To facilitate determining this location, a small picture of each card, known as the *location chart*, is provided. If necessary, on rare occasions, an examiner may give a subject a pencil and ask the subject to outline the perception on the location chart. In scoring for location, the examiner notes whether the subject used the whole blot (W), a common detail (D), or an unusual detail (Dd). Location may be scored for other factors as well, such as the *confabulatory response* (DW). In this response, the subject overgeneralizes from a part to the whole.

According to such Rorschach proponents as Exner, a summary of a subject's location choices can be extremely valuable. The examiner may, for example, determine the number and percentage of W, D, and Dd responses. This type of information, in which scoring categories are summarized as a frequency or percentage, is known as the quantitative, structural, or statistical aspect of the Rorschach as opposed to the qualitative aspects, which pertain to the content and sequence of responses. Normal subjects typically produce a balance of W, D, and Dd responses. When a subject's pattern deviates from the typical balance, the examiner begins to suspect problems (Tarafder, Mukhopadhyay, & Basu, 2004). However, no one has been able to demonstrate that a particular deviation is linked to a specific problem (e.g., see Acklin, 1995; Bartell & Solanto, 1995; Frank, 1995). A substantial deviation from what is typical or average may suggest several possibilities. The protocol may be invalid. The subject may be original or unconventional and thus fail to respond according to the typical pattern. Or the subject may have a perceptual problem associated with certain types of brain damage or severe emotional problems. The relative proportion of W, D, and Dd location choices varies with maturational development. Ames, Metraux, and Walker (1971), for example, noted that W responses occur most frequently in the 3- to 4-year-old group. As the child grows older, the frequency of W responses gradually decreases until young adulthood. Theoretically, adult protocols with a preponderance of W responses suggest immaturity or low mental age.

Like other quantitative aspects of the Rorschach, location patterns and frequencies have been studied in experimental investigations. Presumably, these investigations provide information about the meaning of various response patterns and thus contribute to the construct validity of the Rorschach. Unfortunately, many of the results of the studies conflict with the opinions of experts. Furthermore, many studies that support the validity of the Rorschach have been denounced as unreplicated, methodologically unsound, and inconsistent (Wood et al., 2003). There appears to be no room for compromise in this area of psychological testing.

Having ascertained the location of a response, the examiner must then determine what it was about the inkblot that led the subject to see that particular percept. This factor is known as the *determinant*. One or more of at least four properties of an inkblot may determine or lead to a response: its form or shape, its perceived movement, its color, and its shading. If the subject uses only the form of the blot to determine a response, then the response is scored F and is called a *pure form response*. Responses are scored for form when the subject justifies or elaborates a response by statements such as "It looks like one," "It is shaped like one," or "Here are the head, legs, feet, ears, and wings." In all of these examples, the response is determined exclusively on the basis of shape. In addition to form, a perception may be based on movement, color, shading, or some combination of these factors. These other determinants can be further subdivided. Movement may be human (M), such as two people hugging; animal (FM), such as two elephants playing; or inanimate (m), such as sparks flying. As you can see, the scoring can become quite complex.

As with location, several attempts have been made to link the presence (or absence) of each determinant as well as the relative proportion of the various determinants to various hypotheses and empirical findings (Daini & Bernardini, 2007; Exner, 1999; Perry, Sprock, Schaible, & McDougall, 1995). Consider the movement response. Most Rorschach practitioners agree that whether and how a subject uses movement can be revealing. Like most Rorschach indicators, however, the meaning of movement is unclear because of disagreements among experts and contradictory or unclear experimental findings. Many experts believe that the movement response is related to motor activity and impulses. Numerous movement responses, for example, may suggest high motor activity or strong impulses. The ratio of M (human movement) to FM (animal movement) responses has been linked by some experts to a person's control and expression of internal impulses.

A special type of movement response is called *cooperative movement*. Such responses involve positive interaction between two or more humans or animals (Exner, 1999). Exner and colleagues believe that such responses provide information about a subject's attitude concerning how people interact. One study, for example, reported that individuals who give more than two such responses tended to be rated by others as fun to be with, easy to be around, and trustworthy (Exner & Farber, 1983). The conclusion seemed to be that such responses were positive. Subsequent research, however, could not confirm the initial findings (Shaffer & Erdberg, 1996). In a study of 20 individuals who had committed sexual homicide, 14 gave cooperative-movement responses. Clearly, there is no simple or clear-cut approach to Rorschach interpretation (Gacano & Meloy, 1994).

As you think about the inferences that can be drawn from the Rorschach, keep in mind that they are at best hypotheses. Competent psychologists never blindly accept one interpretation of a particular quantitative aspect of the Rorschach. Certainly, one who blindly accepts a particular interpretation of a Rorschach pattern is ignoring the available literature. Focused Example 14.1 explains some of the ways that highly trained experts use the Rorschach to make clinically useful inferences.

Identifying the determinant is the most difficult aspect of Rorschach administration. Because of the difficulties of conducting an adequate inquiry and the current lack of standardized administration procedures, examiners vary widely in the conduct of their inquiries (Blais et al., 1995). It has been known for years that examiner differences influence the subject's response (Gibby, Miller, & Walker,

1953; Hartman, 2001; Lis, Parolin, Calvo, Zennaro, & Meyer, 2007). As a result of this problem, much of the Rorschach literature is confounded by differences in administration and scoring alone, let alone interpretation. This is one reason why reliable experimental investigations of the Rorschach are rare (Lewandowski & Saccuzzo, 1976).

On the other hand, scoring content is relatively simple. Most authorities list content categories such as human (H), animal (A), and nature (N). An inquiry is generally not necessary to determine content.

Similarly, most experts generally agree on the so-called populars, those responses frequently given for each card. Exner's (1993, 2003) Comprehensive System, which includes as populars only those responses that occur once in three protocols on the average, provides a standardized method for scoring populars.

*Form quality* is the extent to which the percept (what the subject says the inkblot is) matches the stimulus properties of the inkblot. Scoring form quality is difficult. Some experts argue that if the examiner can also see the percept, then the response has adequate form quality, but if the examiner cannot see it, then the

---

## 14.1 FOCUSED EXAMPLE

### Expert Interpretation of the Rorschach

Rorschach experts resolutely maintain that, if properly used, the Rorschach can be an invaluable tool. Modern scientists are completely unconvinced. At best, Rorschach interpretations should be viewed only as tentative hypotheses. Hypotheses that are confirmed by other sources of data usually have more validity than do those that cannot be confirmed. When the Rorschach is rigidly or blindly interpreted, scientific skepticism is justified. When the Rorschach is interpreted cautiously and in conjunction with other sources of data, however, a highly trained expert may surprise even the most critical scientist.

When Dennis Saccuzzo had a predoctoral internship at a Veterans Administration hospital, Marguerite Hertz, one of the five original Rorschach experts, was a consultant there. Every second Thursday of the month, Hertz would interpret an actual Rorschach protocol presented by interns or staff members. Her interpretations were so detailed and exact that Saccuzzo, who was inexperienced with the Rorschach, doubted their validity. When other interns or staff agreed with everything Hertz said, he became even more skeptical. He thought they were merely awed by Hertz's reputation and were afraid to challenge this spirited woman.

When Saccuzzo's turn came to present a Rorschach, he used the protocol of a patient he had been seeing in psychotherapy for several months. He knew this patient well and fully expected Hertz to make errors in her interpretation. He was surprised, however, when Hertz was able to describe this patient after reading only the first four or five responses and examining the quantitative summary of the various scoring categories and ratios. Within 25 minutes, Hertz told him not only what he already knew but also things he had not seen but were obviously true once pointed out. This experience was most unsettling. Having started with a strong bias against the Rorschach, and still doubting its scientific underpinnings, he could not dismiss what Hertz had done.

Later, he came to believe that Hertz's secret was her experience. She had given or studied so many Rorschachs that she had great insight into the meaning of each pattern. After having seen the Rorschach patterns of dozens, if not hundreds, of disturbed individuals, she could identify a problem. Indeed, her knowledge and experience were so broad that she could even distinguish specific types of disturbances based on the Rorschach.

However, until the experts can specify the exact processes underlying correct interpretations from the Rorschach, the criticism from scientists will continue, as Hertz herself (1986), who has repeatedly called for innovation and rigorous research, has acknowledged.

response has poor form quality and is scored F–. Obviously, such a subjective system is grossly inadequate because scoring depends on the intelligence, imagination, skill, and psychological state of the examiner. Exner's (1993) comprehensive system, which uses the usual frequency of the occurrence of various responses in evaluating form quality, is more objective and thus more scientifically acceptable than the subjective method.

Table 14.1 summarizes our discussion of Rorschach scoring. Though the discussion has been incomplete, we hope it has shown how a projective test can be scored to yield quantitative data. These quantitative data, in turn, permit the

**TABLE 14.1**   Summary of Rorschach Scoring

### I. Location

| | |
|---|---|
| Definition: | Where on the blot was the percept seen (located)? |
| *Types:** | 1. Whole (W). The whole inkblot was used. |
| | 2. Common detail (D). A common or well-defined part of the inkblot was used. |
| | 3. Unusual detail (Dd). An unusual or poorly defined part of the inkblot was used. |

### II. Determinant

| | |
|---|---|
| Definition: | What feature of the inkblot determined the response? |
| *Types:** | 1. Form (F). The shape or outline of the blot determined the response ("because the inkblot looked like one"). |
| | 2. Movement (M, FM, m). Movement was seen ("two animals walking up a hill"). |
| | 3. Color (C). Color played a role in determining the response ("a brown bear," "pink clouds"). |
| | 4. Shading (T). Texture or shading features played a role in determining the response ("a furry bear because of the shading"). |

### III. Form quality

| | |
|---|---|
| Definition: | To what extent did the percept match the stimulus properties of the inkblot? |
| *Types:** | 1. F+ or +. Percept matched stimulus properties of the inkblot in an exceptionally good way. |
| | 2. F. Percept matched stimulus properties of the inkblot. |
| | 3. F– or –. Percept matched the stimulus properties of the inkblot poorly. |

### IV. Content

| | |
|---|---|
| Definition: | What was the percept? |
| *Types:** | 1. Human (H). |
| | 2. Animal (A). |
| | 3. Nature (N). |

### V. Popular-original

| | |
|---|---|
| Definition: | How frequently is the percept seen in normative samples? (Popular responses are seen in about one of every three protocols.) |

*This list is incomplete and does not cover the entire range of possibilities. The information given is designed to illustrate quantitative scoring of a projective test.

accumulation of norms for particular groups. If subjects deviate from the typical or expected performance, then the examiner must determine the reason underlying the deviation. Proponents argue that this process can lead to valuable information about individuals (Acklin, 1995; Groth-Marnat, 1999; Hilsenroth, Fowler, & Padawer, 1998).

Rorschach scoring is obviously difficult and complex. Use of the Rorschach requires advanced graduate training. You should not attempt to score or use a Rorschach without formal and didactic graduate instruction and supervised experience. Without this detailed training, you might make serious errors because the procedure is so complex.

Rorschach protocols may be evaluated not only for its quantitative data but also for qualitative features, including specific content (Moreland, Reznikoff, & Aronow, 1995) and sequence of responses (Exner, 1999). One important aspect of a qualitative interpretation is an evaluation of content reported frequently by emotionally disturbed, mentally retarded, or brain-damaged individuals but infrequently by the normal population. Such responses have been used to discriminate normal from disordered conditions (Moreland et al., 1995).

*Confabulatory responses* also illustrate the idea behind qualitative interpretations. In this type of response, the subject overgeneralizes from a part to a whole: "It looked like my mother because of the eyes. My mother has large piercing eyes just like these." Here the subject sees a detail—"large piercing eyes"—and overgeneralizes so that the entire inkblot looks like his or her mother. Although one such response has no clear or specific meaning, experts believe that the more confabulatory responses a subject makes, the more likely that she or he is in a disordered state.

## Psychometric Properties
### Clinical Validation
The mystique and popularity of the Rorschach became widespread in the 1940s and 1950s. This popularity was widely based on clinical evidence gathered from a select group of Rorschach virtuosos who had the ability to dazzle with blind analysis, a process by which a clinician conducts a Rorschach analysis of a patient with no former knowledge of the patient's history or diagnosis and then validates the results of the Rorschach evaluation by checking other sources (Klopfer & Davidson, 1962). For those who were interested in forming an opinion about the validity of the Rorschach, the impact of one stunning display of insightful blind analysis was far greater than the impact of vast collections of empirical evidence that disproved the Rorschach's scientific validity, and these displays were responsible for much of the wide and unquestioning acceptance of the Rorschach as a sound diagnostic tool (Zubin, 1954).

However, in the early 1960s, research began a long trend that has lasted to the present and has revealed that the Rorschach was less than miraculous. With the application of scientific methods of evaluation, there continue to be clear indications that even the Rorschach elite did not possess the ability to divine true diagnoses (Holtzman & Sells, 1954; Little & Schneidman, 1959). The astounding successes in clinical validation became an enigma that has been explained in several ways. First, it has been suggested that the great successes in blind analysis were the product of a few simple tricks (Wood et al., 2003). One of these tricks, labeled the

Barnum effect by Bertram Forer, is illustrated by a demonstration he used with his introductory psychology class (Forer, 1949). Forer prepared a personality profile for each of his new students based on a questionnaire he had administered. He then requested that each of his students rate their personal profile for accuracy, 0 being inaccurate and 5 being perfect. Forer's students gave an average rating of 4.2 (highly accurate), and more than 40% of the students said their profiles were a perfect description of their personality. The catch is that Forer had given each of the students the exact same profile, which he had compiled from a book of horoscopes. Forer had selected statements that seemed precise but that actually fit most people. He demonstrated the degree to which people overestimate the uniqueness and precision of general statements concerning their personality. Wood et al. (2003) suggest that much of the overwhelming acceptance of diagnosis based on blind analysis resulted from the Barnum effect and not from stunning accuracy.

It has also been suggested that the extraordinary early success of blind analysis could be attributed to the evaluator giving several different, or even contradictory, analyses for an individual client. When the information from other psychological tests and interviews was then revealed, the accuracy of many results of the blind reading could be supported by some of the statements, and the reading only appeared to be a success (Wittenborn & Sarason, 1949).

Others have explained the early successes not by trickery, but by the level of genius of the Rorschach virtuosos and by their ability to succeed in blind analysis because of their vast experience with the Rorschach (Klopfer & Kelly, 1946). But these explanations fall short when considering that the same virtuosos who stunned others with their success in clinical settings were able to perform no better than chance when tested in controlled studies (Holtzman & Sells, 1954). In addition, it has also been shown that experience with the Rorschach does not lend itself to a greater degree of accuracy in diagnosis (Turner, 1966).

Regardless of the means by which early success of blind analysis and clinical proof of the validity of the Rorschach were obtained, scientists contend that clinical evaluation is unreliable, subject to self-deception (Meehl, 1997), and unscientific (Zubin, 1954). Confirmation bias, the tendency to seek out and focus on information that confirms ardent beliefs and to disregard information that tends to contradict those beliefs, can mislead even the most honest and well-meaning clinicians. Consider a clinician who hopes to prove the validity of the Rorschach. The clinician makes an evaluation based on the patient's responses to the inkblots and is then presented with a myriad of details about the patient gleaned from different psychological tests, interviews, and the client's background. From that myriad of information, the data that support the diagnosis based on the Rorschach would tend to be automatically focused on and retained; information not supporting the Rorschach's findings could easily be passed over.

In response to several studies in the late 1950s and early 1960s that served to debunk the greatness of Rorschach, Exner, as indicated, began to develop a system to remedy many of the problems with which the Rorschach was plagued. Exner attempted to address these problems with his creation of the Comprehensive System for scoring. Because the Comprehensive System for scoring the Rorschach is widely taught and the most largely accepted method in use today (Guarnaccia, Dill, Sabatino, & Southwick, 2001; Mattlar, 2004), research concerning the reliability of this system is valuable when discussing the Rorschach (Lis, Parolin,

Calvo, Zennaro, & Meyer, 2007; Mattlar, 2004; Palm, 2005). Lis et al. (2007) investigated the impact of administration and inquiry skills on Rorschach Comprehensive System. The results indicate that administration skills can have a dramatic impact and may contribute to variations in samples collected by different investigators (Lis, Parolin, Calvo, Zennaro, & Meyer, 2007).

Many scientifically minded evaluators of the Rorschach are in agreement that the Comprehensive System has failed to remedy the inadequacies of the Rorschach. In their 2003 book entitled *What's Wrong with the Rorschach?* Wood and colleagues outlined several facets of the Rorschach that raise doubt about its use in situations, such as forensic and clinical settings, which require a high degree of diagnostic accuracy. The following summarizes their contentions.

## Norms

As we have emphasized throughout the book, unless the scores of a client can be compared to the scores of a reference group, they are of no use. Although it has been estimated that the Rorschach is administered yearly to more than 6 million people worldwide (Sutherland, 1992), it has never been adequately normed (Wood et al., 2003). Attempts to create representative national norms have failed on several levels. Today, most clinicians who use the Rorschach depend on the norming carried out by Exner. By 1986, Exner had established norms for average adult Americans; by 1990, Exner's books were filled with normative tables that included norms for practically every Rorschach variable. Although Exner was given credit for establishing the Rorschach's first reliable, nationally representative norms, Wood and colleagues (2003) contend that his attempt was significantly flawed because of a computational error created by using the same 221 cases twice in his sample. In other words, his sample of what was reported to be 700 individuals consisted of 479 individuals, 221 of whom were entered twice. Many clinicians now use Exner's revised norms. Exner (2007) conducted a normative project and released new nonpatient norms. The norms were based on a population of 450 adults recruited from 22 states and assessed by 22 examiners (Krishnamurthy, Archer, & Groth-Marnat, 2011). Although this revision is a positive step, it cannot undo the decade of inaccurate diagnoses that may have resulted because of faulty norms. Also, the revised norms have been criticized as being seriously flawed and differing significantly from those of other researchers. Furthermore, a review of the results from 32 separate studies concluded that the norms used in the Comprehensive System are inaccurate and tend to overidentify psychological disorders in nonpatient populations (Wood, Lilienfeld, Nezworski, Garb, Allen, & Wildermuth, 2010; Wood, Nezworski, Garb, & Lilienfeld, 2001b), a problem discussed in depth in the next section (Sakuragi, 2006).

## Overpathologizing

Research has suggested that diagnoses from the Rorschach, whether using the older system for scoring or Exner's Comprehensive System, wrongly identify more than half of normal individuals as emotionally disturbed. The problem of overpathologizing has been seen not only in the diagnosis of healthy adults (Drogin, Dattilio, Sadoff, & Gutheil, 2011; Shaffer, Erdberg, & Haroian, 1999) but also in children (Erard, 2005; Hamel, 2000). Hamel found that slightly above-average children were labeled as suffering from significant social and cognitive impairments when evaluated with the Rorschach. The possible harm from mislabeling individuals as sick when they are not is immeasurable. Consider the consequences of wrongly diagnosing an individual in the family court setting, where a faulty finding could lead to a parent losing custody of a child. Equally devastating repercussions could result from mislabeling in clinical and forensic settings. Although the Rorschach is not advised in the child-custody evaluation (Drogin et al., 2011), according to clinician surveys, it is used in more than 50% of parent assessments in the child custody determination process (Ackerman & Pritzl, 2011, Table 3). Also, consider the life-altering consequences of mislabeling a child as psychologically unwell, such as the stigma and differential treatment associated with mental or emotional illness and the implementation of costly and time-consuming treatment plans.

### Unreliable Scoring

The traditional belief, especially among opponents of the Rorschach, is that the Rorschach is unreliable. Indeed, when one views individual studies in isolation, especially those published before 1985, the results appear confusing.

For every study that has reported internal consistency coefficients in the .80's and .90's, one can find another with coefficients of .10 or even .01. Psychologists who hope to shed light on this picture through meta-analysis, however, have found themselves in the midst of controversy.

Meta-analysis is a statistical procedure in which the results of numerous studies are averaged in a single, overall investigation. In an early meta-analysis of Rorschach reliability and validity, K. Parker (1983) reported an overall internal reliability coefficient of .83 based on 530 statistics from 39 papers published between 1971 and 1980 in the *Journal of Personality Assessment*, the main outlet for research on projective techniques.

Meta-analyses conducted by Parker and others were subsequently criticized as flawed on the grounds that results on validity were not analyzed separately from results on reliability (Garb, Florio, & Grove, 1998, p. 402). Exner (1999) has countered, finding it "reasonable" to argue for test–retest coefficients in the .70's. Moreover, the lack of separate results on reliability and validity should affect only the assessment of the validity of the Rorschach, not its reliability.

Furthermore, when one uses the Kuder-Richardson formula (which examines all possible ways of splitting the test in two) to calculate internal consistency coefficients rather than the more traditionally used odd–even procedure, Rorschach reliability coefficients are markedly increased. In one study, E. E. Wagner and coworkers (1986) compared the split-half coefficients using the odd–even and the Kuder-Richardson techniques for 12 scoring categories.

With the odd–even technique, coefficients ranged between −.075 and +.785, which reflects the general findings in the literature through the 1990s (see Exner, 1999; Groth-Marnat, 1999; Meyer, 1999; Viglione, 1999). However, with the Kuder-Richardson, the coefficients ranged from .55 to .88, with a mean of .77. Thus, results from both meta-analysis and application of Kuder-Richardson techniques reveal a higher level of Rorschach reliability than has generally been attributed to the test.

### Lack of Relationship to Psychological Diagnosis

Although a few Rorschach scores accurately evaluate some conditions characterized by thought disorder and anxiety, there is a notable absence of proven relationships between the Rorschach and psychological disorders and symptoms. Several classic studies examined the Rorschach's ability as a psychodiagnostic test and were disappointing to those who hoped to prove its accuracy (Holtzman & Sells, 1954; Newton, 1954; Little & Schneidman, 1959). More recently, Nezworski and Garb (2001) contend that Comprehensive System scores do not demonstrate a relationship to psychopathy, conduct disorder, or antisocial personality disorder, and the original and revised versions of the Depression Index have little relationship to depression diagnosis. Wood, Lilienfeld, Garb, and Nezworski (2000) reviewed hundreds of studies examining the diagnostic abilities of the Rorschach and found these studies did not support it as a diagnostic tool for such disorders as major depressive disorder, posttraumatic stress disorder, dissociative identity disorder, conduct disorder, psychopathy, anxiety disorders, or dependent, narcissistic, or antisocial personality disorders. Although even proponents of the Rorschach often agree that it is not a valid diagnostic tool, the Rorschach continues to be used in both clinical and forensic settings for the purpose of diagnosis hundreds of thousands of times each year in the United States alone (Wood et al., 2003).

### Lack of Incremental Validity

Not only has it been shown that adding results obtained with the Rorschach to biographical information and MMPI results does not improve diagnoses or evaluation, but also some studies have determined that the addition of the Rorschach results in *less* accurate findings (Sines, 1959). Although a few studies support the incremental validity of the Rorschach when used with the MMPI (Meehl, 1956), the amount of incremental validity contributed by the Rorschach has been trivial (Lilienfeld et al., 2000).

### The Problem of "R"

Those who are being evaluated with the Rorschach are free to give as many responses ("R") to each inkblot as they wish. As early as 1950, it was determined that this aspect unduly influenced scores (Fiske & Baughman, 1953). As the number of responses goes up, so do other scores on the test. This causes several problems. If a person is generally more cooperative or intellectual, then they are more likely to give more responses. Those who are more likely to give more responses are also more likely to give what are labeled *space responses* (responding to the white space within or around the inkblot instead of responding to the inkblot). More space responses are interpreted by clinicians as indicating oppositional and stubborn characteristics in the test taker. Thus, those who are most cooperative with the test are more likely to be falsely labeled as oppositional. This is just one example of how "R" can negatively affect Rorschach scores (see also Focused Example 14.2). Although the problem with "R" was determined in the early 1950s and continues to be demonstrated (Meyer, 1992), clinicians who use the Rorschach generally ignore the problem.

In sum, evaluating the Rorschach on classical psychometric properties (standardization, norms, reliability, validity) has proven exceptionally difficult. Indeed, this attempt to document or refute the adequacy of the Rorschach has produced one of the greatest divisions of opinion within psychology. Time and again, psychologists heatedly disagreed about the scientific validity of the Rorschach. Despite numerous negative evaluations, the Rorschach has flourished in clinical settings.

In evaluating the Rorschach, keep in mind that there is no universally accepted method of administration. Some examiners provide lengthy introductions and

## 14.2 FOCUSED EXAMPLE

### The Danger of Basing Rorschach Interpretations on Insufficient Evidence

We had the opportunity to become involved in a forensic case in which an individual claimed that the negligence of a large company in sealing pipes together caused a gas leak that resulted in brain damage. This individual consulted an attorney, who sent him to a psychologist. The psychologist administered a Rorschach test. Based on her findings, the psychologist concluded that the person was brain damaged and thus had a legitimate case. The company called us and asked whether the Rorschach could be used to diagnose or identify brain damage. We replied that there is absolutely no support for the idea that one can prove a person is brain damaged simply on the basis of Rorschach results.

Lawyers for the company brought in the psychologist's report and a copy of the Rorschach protocol. The person suspected of brain damage provided only six responses, far fewer than the 22 to 32 responses typically found for the 10 Rorschach cards. The protocol was as follows:

|  | Free Association | Inquiry | Scoring |
|---|---|---|---|
| Card 1 | A bat. | Here are the wings; there is the head. | W F A P |

**Discussion**

The W indicates the whole inkblot was used in the percept. The F indicates that only the form or shape (not color, movement, or shading) determined the response. The A stands for animal content. The P indicates this response is a popular (that is, one that is commonly given).

| Card 2 | I don't know. | No, I still don't. | Rejection |
|---|---|---|---|

**Discussion**

When the subject fails to provide a response, this is known as a *rejection*. Some examiners present the card again in the inquiry and ask, "Now do you see anything?" A rejection could have several meanings. The typical or classical interpretation of a rejection is guardedness or defensiveness.

| Card 3 | I don't know. (Q)<br>No, I don't see anything. | I said I don't know. | Rejection |
|---|---|---|---|

**Discussion**

The (Q) indicates the examiner questioned the subject further, thus attempting to elicit a response. Notice the defensive quality in the subject's response during the inquiry.

| Card 4 | A gorilla. | All of it; big feet, head, body. | W F A |
|---|---|---|---|
| Card 5 | A moth. | Whole thing; wings, feelers, head. | W F A P |
| Card 6 | I don't know. | No, nothing. | Rejection |
| Card 7 | A bird without a head. | Wings, but no head. (Q) All of it. | W F–A |

explanations; others provide almost none. Most of the experts state that the length, content, and flavor of administrative instructions should depend on the subject. Empirical evidence, however, indicates that the method of providing instructions and the content of the instructions influence a subject's response to the Rorschach (Blais et al., 1995; Hartman, 2001). Given the lack of standardized instructions, which has no scientifically legitimate excuse, comparisons of the protocols of two different examiners are tenuous at best (see Wood et al., 1996).

## Discussion

The F− indicates a poor correspondence between the response, bird, and the stimulus properties of the inkblot. *Bird* is an unusual response to this inkblot.

|  | *Free Association* | *Inquiry* | *Scoring* |
|---|---|---|---|
| Card 8 | Animals, maybe rats trying to steal something | Just two animals on the sides. | D F A P |

## Discussion

The two animals were formed from two common details (D). It was scored P because this response is popular (that is, frequently occurring).

|  | | | |
|---|---|---|---|
| Card 9 | I don't know. | No, it doesn't look like anything to me. | Rejection |
| Card 10 | Nothing, wait, looks like a bug here. | Just a bug, legs, pinchers, head. | D F Insect |

In our judgment, the psychologist who conducted this Rorschach administration more than stretched the interpretation when she claimed this person was brain damaged. In fact, her conduct may be viewed as unethical. The argument presented was that a small number of responses, a preponderance of W responses, a lack of determinants other than form, and misperception (the poor form quality response to Card 7) were all consistent with brain damage. Because the protocol contained qualities commonly found in the protocols of brain-damaged individuals, the psychologist argued that she had found evidence for brain damage.

We looked at this Rorschach protocol and concluded that its information alone could in no way be considered sufficient evidence for brain damage. First, a small number of responses in itself cannot be attributed to any single factor (Exner, 1999). A small number of responses can be found in retarded, depressed, and extremely defensive individuals as well as in those who are brain damaged. Second, the small number of responses led to an imbalance in the proportion of W to D responses. Data on the typical ratio of W to D responses are based on protocols with 20 to 30 responses. With only six responses, all bets are off. No one can say anything about the balance with so few responses. In any case, there is no clear evidence that brain-damaged people give a preponderance of W responses. Third, the one F−response proves nothing. Furthermore, the subject gave three popular responses, indicating he was capable of accurate perceptions. Fourth, the lack of determinants other than form can have several possible interpretations. The significance of the exclusive use of form in this protocol is dubious, however, in view of the small number of responses. A protocol with 30 responses, all determined exclusively by form, would have quite a different meaning. Notice how the total number of responses can influence or alter the meaning of Rorschach data. As indicated, the Rorschach places no limit on the number of possible responses.

We suggested that other tests be used to evaluate brain damage in this individual. Taking a conservative approach, we did not deny that this person was brain damaged. We simply stated that the Rorschach in no way documented the presence of brain damage. The person in question, however, dropped his suit after our analysis was communicated to his attorney and psychologist.

Suppose, for example, one hypothesizes that the total number of responses to a Rorschach is related to the level of defensiveness. Even with an adequate criterion measure of defensiveness, if examiner instructions influence the number of responses, then one examiner might obtain an average of 32 responses whereas a second might obtain 22, independent of defensiveness. If protocols from both examiners are averaged in a group, then any direct relationship between number of responses and defensiveness can easily be masked or distorted.

Like administration, Rorschach scoring procedures are not adequately standardized. One system scores for human movement whenever a human is seen, whereas another has elaborate and stringent rules for scoring human movement. The former system obviously finds much more human movement than does the latter, even when the same test protocols are evaluated. Without standardized scoring, determining the frequency, consistency, and meaning of a particular Rorschach response is extremely difficult.

One result of unstandardized Rorschach administration and scoring procedures is that reliability investigations have produced varied and inconsistent results. Even when reliability is shown, validity is questionable. Moreover, scoring as well as interpretation procedures do not show criterion-related evidence for validity and are not linked to any theory, which limits construct-related evidence for validity. Researchers must also share in the responsibility for the contradictory and inconclusive findings that permeate the Rorschach literature. Many research investigations of tests such as the Rorschach have failed to control important variables, including race, sex, age, socioeconomic status, and intelligence. If race, for example, influences test results as research indicates (see Saccuzzo, Johnson, & Guertin, 1995; Wood, 1999; Garb, Wood, Nezworski, Grove, & Stejskal, 2001; Velox, 2005), then studies that fail to control for race may lead to false conclusions. Other problems that are attributable to the research rather than to psychometric properties include lack of relevant training experience in those who score the protocols, poor statistical models, and poor validating criteria (Frank, 1995; Meloy & Singer, 1991).

Whether the problem is lack of standardization, poorly controlled experiments, or both, there continues to be disagreement regarding the scientific status of the Rorschach (Exner, 1995; Nezworski & Wood, 1995; Wood et al., 1996; Garfield, 2000; Wood et al., 2003; Hunsley, 2001; Viglione & Hilsenroth, 2001; Garb, Wood, Lilienfeld, & Nezworski, 2004). As Buros (1970) noted some time ago, "This vast amount of writing and research has produced astonishingly little, if any, agreement among psychologists regarding the specific validities of the Rorschach" (p. xxvi). In brief, the meaning of the thousands of published Rorschach studies is still debatable. For every supportive study, there appears to be a negative or damaging one (see Table 14.2). These words are as true today as they were in 1970.

**TABLE 14.2**  Summary of Arguments Against and in Favor of the Rorschach

| Against | In favor |
|---|---|
| 1. Lacks a universally accepted standard of administration, scoring, and interpretation. | 1. Lack of standardized procedures is a historical accident that can be corrected. |
| 2. Evaluations of data are subjective. | 2. Test interpretation is an art, not a science; all test interpretation involves a subjective component. |
| 3. Results are unstable over time. | 3. A new look at the data reveals that the Rorschach is much more stable than is widely believed. |
| 4. Is unscientific. | 4. Has a large empirical base. |
| 5. Is inadequate by all traditional standards. | 5. Available evidence is biased and poorly controlled and has therefore failed to provide a fair evaluation. |

Clearly, the final word on the Rorschach has yet to be spoken. Far more research is needed, but unless practitioners can agree on a standard method of administration and scoring, the researchers' hands will be tied.

In the first edition of this book, published in 1982, we predicted that the 21st century would see the Rorschach elevated to a position of scientific respectability because of the advent of Exner's Comprehensive System. Over the years, we backed away from this position. Now, nearly 30 years later, we must acknowledge that we do not know the answer. However, it would appear as though the ethical burden rests with the test's users. Any user must be conversant with the literature, and ready against attack.

# An Alternative Inkblot Test: The Holtzman

Among the prime problems of the Rorschach, from a psychometric viewpoint, are its variable number of responses from one subject to another, lack of standard procedures, and lack of an alternative form. The Holtzman Inkblot Test was created to meet these difficulties while maintaining the advantages of the inkblot methodology (Holtzman, Thorpe, Swartz, & Herron, 1961; also see Wong & Jamadi, 2010). In this test, the subject is permitted to give only one response per card. Administration and scoring procedures are standardized and carefully described. An alternate form is available that correlates well with the original test stimuli. Interscorer as well as split-half reliabilities are comparable to those found for objective personality tests.

Both forms, A and B, of the Holtzman contain 45 cards. Each response may be scored on 22 dimensions. Many of these dimensions resemble those found in the Rorschach and include location, determinant, and content. Responses may also be scored for such factors as anxiety and hostility. For each scoring category or variable, well-established norms are presented for several samples ranging from 5-year-olds through adults (Hill, 1972). Given the psychometric advantages of the Holtzman, it is interesting that the test hasn't even begun to challenge the Rorschach's popularity (Reisman, 1976).

There are several factors that contributed to the relative unpopularity of the Holtzman, the most significant of which may have been Holtzman's refusal to exaggerate claims of the test's greatness and his strict adherence to scientifically founded evidence of its utility (Wood et al., 2003). The main difficulty with the Holtzman as a psychometric instrument is its validity (Gamble, 1972; Zubin, 1972). Modern studies are rare and unimpressive. Those studies that show a positive relationship between the Holtzman and various criterion measures are based on qualitative rather than quantitative features. Thus, the available supportive evidence is highly subjective, depending on examiner skill rather than formal interpretive standards. In short, one cannot currently consider the Holtzman any more useful than the Rorschach, despite the former's superior psychometric features. Perhaps the best that can be said is that it is still too early to judge its clinical utility compared with the Rorschach (Darolia & Joshi, 2004; Leichsenring, 1990, 1991).

# The Thematic Apperception Test

The Thematic Apperception Test (TAT) was introduced in 1935 by Christina Morgan and Henry Murray of Harvard University. It is comparable to the Rorschach in many ways, including its importance and psychometric problems. As with the Rorschach, use of the TAT grew rapidly after its introduction; with the exception of the Rorschach, the TAT is used more than any other projective test (Wood et al., 2003). Though its psychometric adequacy was (and still is) vigorously debated (Alvarado, 1994; Keiser & Prather, 1990; Lilienfeld et al., 2000; Weiner & Craighead, 2010), unlike the Rorschach, the TAT has been relatively well received by the scientific community. Also, the TAT is based on Murray's (1938) theory of needs (see Chapter 16), whereas the Rorschach is basically atheoretical. The TAT and the Rorschach differ in other respects as well. The TAT authors were conservative in their evaluation of the TAT and scientific in their outlook. The TAT was not oversold as was the Rorschach, and no extravagant claims were made. Unlike the Rorschach, the TAT was not billed as a diagnostic instrument— that is, a test of disordered emotional states. Instead, the TAT was presented as an instrument for evaluating human personality characteristics (see Table 14.3). This test also differs from the Rorschach because the TAT's nonclinical uses are just as important as its clinical ones. Indeed, the TAT is one of the most important techniques used in personality research (Abrams, 1999; Bellak, 1999; Cramer & Blatt, 1990; McClelland, 1999).

As stated, the TAT is based on Murray's (1938) theory, which distinguishes 28 human needs, including the needs for sex, affiliation, and dominance. Many of these needs have been extensively researched through use of the TAT (McClelland, 1999; Sun, Pan, & Tong, 2004). The theoretical need for achievement—"the desire or tendency to do things as rapidly and/or as well as possible" (Murray, 1938, p. 164)—alone has generated a very large number of studies involving the TAT (Hofer & Chasiotis, 2011; McClelland, 1999; Spangler, 1992). The TAT measure of the achievement need has been related to factors such as parental perceptions, parental expectations, and parental attitudes toward offspring. Need achievement is also related to the standards that you as a student set for yourself (e.g., academic standards). The higher your need for achievement, the more likely you are to study and ultimately achieve a high economic and social position in society (Hofer & Holger, 2011). Studies such as those on the achievement motive have

**TABLE 14.3**    A Comparison of the Rorschach and the TAT

| Rorschach | TAT |
| --- | --- |
| Rejected by scientific community | Well received by scientific community |
| Atheoretical | Based on Murray's (1938) theory of needs |
| Oversold by extravagant claims | Conservative claims |
| Purported diagnostic instrument | Not purported as diagnostic |
| Primarily clinical use | Clinical and nonclinical uses |

provided construct-related evidence for validity and have increased the scientific respectability of the TAT (Annalakshmi, 2006).

## Stimuli, Administration, and Interpretation

The TAT is more structured and less ambiguous than the Rorschach. TAT stimuli consist of pictures that depict a variety of scenes. There are 30 pictures and one blank card. Specific cards are designed for male subjects, others for female. Some of the cards are appropriate for older people, others for young ones. A few of the cards are appropriate for all subjects, such as Card 1. This card shows a boy, neatly dressed and groomed, sitting at a table on which lies a violin. In his description of Card 1, Murray stated that the boy is "contemplating" the violin. According to experts such as Bellak (1986), Card 1 of the TAT tends to reveal a person's relationship toward parental figures.

Other TAT cards tend to elicit other kinds of information. Card 4 is a picture of a woman "clutching the shoulders of a man whose face and body are averted as if he were trying to pull away from her" (Bellak, 1975, p. 51). This card elicits information concerning male–female relationships. Bellak (1986, 1996) and others provide a description of the TAT cards along with the information that each card tends to elicit. This knowledge is essential in TAT interpretation. Figure 14.2 shows Card 12F, which sometimes elicits conflicting emotions about the self. Other feelings may also be elicited.

Standardization of the administration, especially the scoring procedures of the TAT, is about as poor as, if not worse than, those of the Rorschach. Most examiners typically state something like, "I am going to show you some pictures. I want you to tell me a story about each picture. Tell me what led up to the story, what is

**FIGURE 14.2**
Card 12F from the Thematic Apperception Test. This card often gives the subject a chance to express attitudes toward a mother or daughter figure. Sometimes attitudes toward marriage and aging also emerge.

(Reprinted by permission of the publishers from Henry A. Murray, Thematic Apperception Test, Cambridge, Mass.: Harvard University Press, Copyright © 1943 by the President and Fellows of Harvard College, © 1971 by Henry A. Murray.)

happening, what the characters are thinking and feeling, and what the outcome will be." In the original design of the test, 20 cards were to be administered to each subject, 10 cards in each of two separate 1-hour sessions. In actual practice, however, only 10 or 12 cards are typically used (Bellak, 1996) and administration of the entire test typically takes place during one session (Lilienfeld et al., 2000). As with the Rorschach and almost all other individually administered tests, the examiner records the subject's responses verbatim. The examiner also records the *reaction time*—the time interval between the initial presentation of a card and the subject's first response. By recording reaction time, the examiner can determine whether the subject has difficulty with a particular card. Because each card is designed to elicit its own themes, needs, and conflicts, an abnormally long reaction time may indicate a specific problem. If, for example, the reaction time substantially increases for all cards involving heterosexual relationships, then the examiner may hypothesize that the subject is experiencing difficulty in this area.

There are by far more interpretive and scoring systems for the TAT than for the Rorschach. In his comprehensive review of the TAT literature, Murstein (1963, p. 23) states, "There would seem to be as many thematic scoring systems as there were hairs in the beard of Rasputin." Murstein summarizes most of the major methods of interpretation for the TAT, grouping them into quantitative and nonquantitative methods. Unlike the quantitative aspects of the Rorschach, which most examiners consider extremely important, the quantitative methods of TAT interpretation are unpopular (Alvarado, 1994; Groth-Marnat, 1999). Most TAT examiners find the available scoring systems to be overly elaborate, complex, and time-consuming. They therefore tend to use only nonquantitative methods of interpretation. In a survey of more than 100 psychologists who practiced in juvenile and family courts in North America, most clinicians (97%) reported that they did not use any scoring system at all, but relied on their clinical judgment and intuition to interpret and score the TAT (Lilienfeld et al., 2000; Seewaldt, 2006).

Almost all methods of TAT interpretation take into account the *hero, needs, press, themes,* and *outcomes.* The *hero* is the character in each picture with whom the subject seems to identify (Bellak, 1996). In most cases, the story revolves around one easily recognizable character. If more than one character seems to be important, then the character most like the storyteller is selected as the hero. Of particular importance are the motives and *needs* of the hero. Most systems, including Murray's original, consider the intensity, duration, and frequency of each need to indicate the importance and relevance of that need. In TAT interpretation, *press* refers to the environmental forces that interfere with or facilitate satisfaction of the various needs. Again, factors such as frequency, intensity, and duration are used to judge the relative importance of these factors. The frequency of various *themes* (e.g., depression) and *outcomes* (e.g., failures) also indicates their importance.

To understand the potential value of the TAT in evaluating personality characteristics, you should realize that different individuals offer quite different responses to the same card. For example, given Card 1, in which a boy is contemplating a violin, one subject may say, "This boy's mother has just reminded him to practice the violin. The boy hates the violin and is wondering what he can do to make his practice session less boring. As he daydreams, his mother scolds him, so he picks up the violin and plays, resenting every minute." Another subject may respond, "The boy has just come home from school and is getting ready to practice the violin. He hopes to become a great violin player someday but realizes he's just an average, ordinary person. He picks up the violin and plays, dreaming about success." A third story may go as follows: "It's violin practice again and the boy is fed up. Do this, do that; his parents are always trying to live his life. This time he fixes them. He picks up the violin, smashes it, and goes out to play baseball."

Think about these three stories. Because the stimulus was the same in each case, differences in the stories must in some way reflect differences in the storytellers. The primary issue is exactly what is revealed in these stories. Many years ago, Lindzey (1952) analyzed several assumptions underlying the TAT. Table 14.4 lists these major assumptions. Although there were problems with many of the studies cited by Lindzey, positive evidence was found to support these assumptions, the validity of which holds to this day (Johnson, 1994; Bellak, 1996). By understanding these assumptions, you can get an idea of the complexity of TAT interpretation.

Although Lindzey's analysis was conducted some time ago, many TAT practitioners are guided by the assumptions listed in Table 14.4. The primary assumption—in completing an incomplete or unstructured situation, the individual may reveal his or her own strivings, dispositions, and conflicts—provides a rationale and support for projective tests in general. Most of the other assumptions, however,

---

**TABLE 14.4**   Lindzey's Assumptions for TAT Interpretation

**Primary assumption**

In completing an incomplete or unstructured situation, the individual may reveal his or her own characteristics (strivings, dispositions, conflicts).

**Other assumptions**

1. The storyteller ordinarily identifies with one person in the drama. The characteristics (wishes, strivings, conflicts) of this imaginary person may reflect those of the storyteller.

2. The storyteller's characteristics may be represented indirectly or symbolically.

3. All stories are not of equal importance.

4. Themes directly related to stimulus material are less likely to be significant than those unrelated to stimulus material.

5. Recurrent themes (those that show up in three or four different stories) are particularly likely to mirror the characteristics of the storyteller.

6. The stories may reflect momentary characteristics of the storyteller (those aroused by temporary environmental factors) as well as enduring characteristics.

7. Stories may reflect events from the past that the storyteller has only observed or witnessed. However, the selection of these stories suggests that the events may still reflect the storyteller's own characteristics.

8. The stories may also reflect group membership or sociocultural factors.

9. Dispositions and conflicts inferred from the storyteller's creations may be unconscious and thus may not always be reflected directly in overt behavior or consciousness.

Adapted from Lindzey (1952).

pertain specifically to the TAT. As these assumptions indicate, although a story reflects the storyteller, many other factors may influence the story. Therefore, all TAT experts agree that a complete interview and a case history must accompany any attempt to interpret the TAT. No matter how careful and thorough such an interview is, however, final conclusions and interpretations are still based on many factors, including the skill and experience of the examiner.

## Psychometric Properties

Many experts consider the TAT to be psychometrically unsound (see Karp, 1999; Lilienfeld et al., 2000). Given the TAT's unstandardized procedures for administration, scoring, and interpretation, one can easily understand why psychometric evaluations have produced inconsistent, unclear, and conflicting findings. As with the Rorschach, divisions of opinion run deep. Subjectivity affects not only the interpretation of the TAT, but also analysis of the TAT literature. In other words, as with the Rorschach, two experts can look at the same research data and draw different or even opposite conclusions. It should be no surprise, then, that for almost every positive empirical finding there is a negative counterpart.

Even so, an analysis of existing results reveals that the study of specific variables, such as the achievement need, produces respectably high reliability figures (Exner, 1976; Murstein, 1963). Test–retest reliabilities appear to fluctuate, however, and to diminish as the interval between the two testing sessions increases. The median test–retest correlation across studies is only approximately .30 (Kraiger, Hakel, & Cornelius, 1984; Winter & Stewart, 1977). However, J. W. Atkinson (1981) has argued that the validity of the TAT does not depend on test–retest reliability. Splithalf reliabilities have been consistently poor. Many TAT proponents, though, do not consider the split-half method appropriate because each card is designed to produce its own theme and content (Cramer, 1999). What is needed is a study using Kuder-Richardson reliabilities, as has recently been done with the Rorschach.

Validity studies of the TAT have produced even murkier findings. Most experts agree that there is content-related validity evidence for using the TAT to evaluate human personality; however, criterion-related evidence for validity has been difficult to document. In an early but often cited study, Harrison (1940a, 1940b) found that his own inferences based on TAT stories correlated at .78 with hospital records for specific variables. He reported that he was 75% correct in diagnosing patients into major categories, such as psychotic versus neurotic, using TAT data. Little and Shneidman (1959) found, however, that when 12 specialists for each of four tests (TAT, Make-a-Picture Story, Rorschach, MMPI) were asked to match the judgments of a group of criterion judges who had conducted extensive interviews with each of the subjects, not only was there little agreement between the test judges and the criterion judges, but also the TAT had the lowest reliability and the poorest predictive validity of the four tests. Newer studies also report discouraging reliability coefficients (Singh, 1986). A more recent meta-analysis by Spangler (1992) found average correlations between the TAT and various criteria to run between .19 and .22, which is hardly impressive.

In short, like the Rorschach, the TAT has several significant problems. In spite of these problems, however, the TAT continues to find widespread application in clinical as well as research settings (see Ackerman & Pritzl, 2011, Tables 2 & 3; Pirelli, Gottdiener, & Zapf, 2011). As with the Rorschach, the most pressing need appears to be establishing standardized administration and scoring procedures. Until such standardization is achieved, the TAT will continue to fare poorly according to traditional psychometric standards.

# Alternative Apperception Procedures

An alternative thematic apperception test (Ritzler, Sharkey, & Chudy, 1980; Sharkey & Ritzler, 1985) has been constructed with pictures from the *Family of Man* photo-essay collection (Museum of Modern Art, 1955). According to these authors, the relatively new procedure can be scored quantitatively. It provides a balance of positive and negative stories and a variety of action and energy levels for the main character. In comparison, the TAT elicits predominantly negative and low-energy stories (Ritzler et al., 1980). Preliminary results with this new procedure, known as the Southern Mississippi TAT (or SM-TAT), have been encouraging. These results indicate that the SM-TAT preserves many of the advantages of the TAT while providing a more rigorous and modern methodology. Naturally, more research is needed, but this attempt to modernize the TAT is to be applauded.

The versatility and usefulness of the TAT approach are illustrated not only by attempts such as those of Ritzler et al. (1980) to update the test but also by the availability of special forms of the TAT for children and others for the elderly. The Children's Apperception Test (CAT) was created to meet the special needs of children ages 3 through 10 (Bellak, 1975; also see Meersand, P., 2011). The CAT stimuli contain animal rather than human figures as in the TAT.

A special children's apperception test has been developed specifically for Latino and Latina children (Malgady, Constantino, & Rogler, 1984). The Tell Me a Story Test (TEMAS) is a TAT technique that consists of 23 chromatic pictures depicting minority and nonminority characters in urban and familial settings (Constantino, Malgady, Colon-Malgady, & Bailey, 1992; Goodyear-Brown, 2011). Initial research has shown the promise of the TEMAS as a multicultural projective test for use with minority children (Constantino & Malgady, 1999; Costantino, Dana, & Malgady, 2007).

The Gerontological Apperception Test uses stimuli in which one or more elderly individuals are involved in a scene with a theme relevant to the concerns of the elderly, such as loneliness and family conflicts (Verdon, 2011; Wolk & Wolk, 1971). The Senior Apperception Technique is an alternative to the Gerontological Apperception Test and is parallel in content (Bellak, 1975; Bellak & Bellak, 1973).

All of these alternative perception tests hold promise as clinical tools (Verdon, 2011; Mark, 1993).

# Nonpictorial Projective Procedures

Projective tests need not involve the use of a pictorial stimulus. Words or phrases sometimes provide the stimulus, as in the Word Association Test and incomplete sentence tasks. Or a subject can be asked to create or draw something, as in the Draw-a-Man Test. This final section briefly describes each of these procedures.

## Word Association Test

Imagine yourself comfortably seated in a psychologist's examining office. Your task is simple, or at least it seems so. The psychologist says a word and you say the first word that comes to mind. The test begins. The first word is *hat*. You reply *coat*, the most common response of college students according to Rapaport, Gill, and Schafer (1968). The test goes on as follows:

Lamp

Love

Father

Paper

Masturbation

Chair

Breast

Car

Penis

Suicide

Do some of these words arouse any feelings in you? Words such as *love, father, breast*, and *masturbation* do in many people. The purpose of word association tests is to infer possible disturbances and areas of conflict from an individual's response to specific words.

The use of word association tests dates back to Galton (1879) and was first used on a clinical basis by Jung (1910) and G. H. Kent and Rosanoff (1910). In the first to attempt to standardize word association procedures, Kent and Rosanoff developed a list of 100 standard words and presented them to a sample of 1000 normal adults who were partially stratified by geographic location, education, occupation, age, and intelligence. An objective scoring system was developed, and the Kent-Rosanoff word association test enjoyed moderate popularity in the 1920s and 1930s.

Rapaport et al. (1968) subsequently developed a 60-item word association test. The range of words covered familial, household, oral, anal, aggressive, and phobic content. Responses were quantified by collecting norms on college students and schizophrenics, although interpretations were clearly psychoanalytic in nature.

Interest in word association techniques dropped considerably after Rapaport et al. (1968) concluded that the procedures did not live up to their clinical promise. Although the techniques are still in use (Mao, 2011; Oral, Güleç, Aydin, Ozan, & Kırpınar, 2011), they play only a limited role in clinical and counseling settings.

## Sentence Completion Tasks

Another family of projective techniques involving words is incomplete sentence tasks. These tasks provide a stem that the subject is asked to complete.

For example:

1. I am _____
2. I enjoy _____
3. What annoys me _____
4. It pains me to _____
5. Men _____
6. Dancing _____
7. Sports _____

As with all projective techniques, the individual's response is believed to reflect that person's needs, conflicts, values, and thought processes. In clinical use, these tasks also give a person the opportunity to provide information that may have been too embarrassing to present in a face-to-face verbal interview. Clinicians look for recurring themes of conflict and pathological content.

Many incomplete sentence tasks have scoring procedures. Among the most widely used of these tasks is the Rotter Incomplete Sentence Blank (Rotter & Rafferty, 1950). The Rotter provides 40 stems, each of which is scored on a 7-point system. In general, short sentences with some humor and positive content get the highest scores—for example, "Men have their advantages and disadvantages." Long, complex sentences with negative or depressed content receive the lowest scores—for example, "Men who I can't stand and would like to sometimes kill and do away with really know how to make a person feel crazy all the time."

Sentence completion procedures are used widely in clinical as well as in research settings. A relatively recent addition to this family is the Incomplete Sentences Task of Lanyon and Lanyon (1980). Sentences are scored on a 3-point scale (0, 1, 2), and norms are available as a function of age and gender. The reviews of Lanyon and Lanyon's incomplete sentence task have been positive and encouraging (Cundick, 1985; Dush, 1985; also see Yu, 2011).

Quite possibly the most psychometrically impressive projective test (Manners & Derkin, 2001), the Washington University Sentence Completion Test (WUSCT), measures ego development, or degrees of autonomy, acceptance of self, and awareness of personal faults (Pfaffenberger & Marko, 2011, pp. 3–4; Loevinger, 1998). The test consists of 36 incomplete sentences asking individuals to complete sentences similar to "I most regret that … … …" and "When people don't get along … … …" (Wood et al., 2003). Although there is evidence substantiating the validity of the WUSCT (Manners & Derkin, 2001), it is rarely used in clinical settings (Holaday, Smith, & Sherry, 2000). This is disappointing, considering the plethora of popular, psychometrically challenged projective tests that are commonly used by clinicians.

## Figure Drawing Tests

Another set of projective tests uses expressive techniques, in which the subject is asked to create something, usually a drawing. In the Draw-a-Person Test

(Machover, 1949), the subject, most often a child, is asked to draw the picture of a person. Later the child is asked to tell a story about the person. A similar technique is the House-Tree-Person Test (Buck, 1948), in which the subject draws a picture of a house, tree, and person and then makes up a story about it. In the Kinetic Family Drawing Test (Burns & Kaufman, 1970, 1972), the subject draws a picture of his or her family.

Projective drawing tests are scored on several dimensions, including absolute size, relative size, omissions, and disproportions. For example, in drawing her family, a young child may omit herself. Interpreters might then assume that the child feels alienated from her family. In drawing a house-tree-person, the child might draw himself in the house looking out, perhaps reflecting a feeling of being isolated or trapped.

If there is a tendency to overinterpret projective test data without sufficient empirical foundation, then projective drawing tests are among the worst offenders. Although one can draw interpretative hypotheses from such data (see Groth-Marnat, 1999), people tend to go too far. For instance, in the Draw-a-Person Test, a clinician is advised to interpret a large head as indicating an overconcern with matters of intellectual functioning; one system even suggests that it means brain damage (Machover, 1949). One projective drawing test that has been proven valid and useful in clinical settings is the Goodenough Draw-a-Man Test (Wood et al., 2003), which we first discussed in Chapter 13. The Goodenough-Harris Drawing Test (G-HDT) has acceptable correlations (.50 and higher) with intelligence tests such as the Stanford-Binet (Anastasi, 1988). Its benefits include its simplicity and practicality, especially in the evaluation of children who may struggle with the tedious task of completing less child-friendly tests and is useful, especially when used in conjunction with other tests. (See Chapter 13 for a more detailed description of the G-HDT.) Although figure drawing tests have a place in a test battery, great caution is called for in their use until rigorous research can document the valid inferences one can make from them (see Basgul, Uneri, Akkaya, Etiler, & Coskun, 2011).

# Summary

According to the *projective hypothesis*, interpretations of an ambiguous or vague stimulus reflect the subject's own needs, feelings, experiences, prior conditioning, thought processes, and so forth.

The Rorschach is the preeminent projective test. Five individuals played a dominant role in its development: Beck, Hertz, Klopfer, Piotrowski, and Rapaport. Rorschach stimuli consist of 10 inkblots with the colors black, gray, red, and various pastels. These stimuli were formed by dropping ink onto a piece of paper and folding the paper.

Rorschach administration involves two phases: free-association and inquiry. During the first phase, the examiner presents each card with a minimum of structure. During the second phase, the examiner presents each card again to obtain sufficient information for scoring purposes. The five major Rorschach scoring categories are *location* (where), *determinant* (why), *content* (what), *frequency of occurrence* (popular-original), and *form quality* (correspondence of percept to stimulus properties of the inkblot).

The Rorschach is extremely controversial. On the negative side, it has been attacked for its lack of standardized methods for administration, scoring, and interpretation. It has also been criticized because interpretations are subjective and results are unstable over time. With the exception of recent reliability studies, scientific support is weak and ambiguous.

The Holtzman is an alternative to the Rorschach. Though it overcomes much of the scientific criticism of the Rorschach, the value and importance of this procedure have not yet been determined.

Another projective test, the TAT, enjoys wide research as well as clinical use. The TAT stimuli consist of 30 pictures, of various scenes, and one blank card. Card 1, for example, shows a scene in which a boy, neatly dressed and groomed, sits at a table on which rests a violin. Specific cards are suited for adults, children, men, and women. In administering the TAT, the examiner asks the subject to make up a story; he or she looks for the events that led up to the scene, what the characters are thinking and feeling, and the outcome. Almost all methods of TAT interpretation take into account the *hero, needs, press, themes,* and *outcomes.*

Like the Rorschach, the TAT has strong supporters but has also been attacked on a variety of scientific grounds. Though not psychometrically sound by traditional standards, the TAT is in widespread use. Like the Rorschach, it can provide a wealth of information about an individual.

Some of the similarities between the TAT and Rorschach are as follows: They are both individual projective tests for measuring human functioning and personality characteristics. Both are poorly standardized for administration, scoring, and interpretation. Reliability coefficients for both tests vary widely. Both are highly criticized, yet both are used extensively and adopted enthusiastically by practitioners. Both provide a rich source of information about a single individual. Some of the differences between the TAT and Rorschach are as follows: The Rorschach stimuli are inkblots; the TAT stimuli depict scenes. Thus, TAT stimuli are more meaningful than Rorschach stimuli. The TAT is based on Murray's (1938) theory of needs; the Rorschach is atheoretical. Formal scoring and quantitative features, important in the Rorschach, are of little significance in the TAT. The TAT finds extensive use in research as well as in clinical settings; the Rorschach is primarily a clinical tool. TAT interpretation is guided by a variety of assumptions, which were listed and explored by Lindzey (1952). Rorschach interpretation still depends on the opinion of experts and on research surveys such as those described in Exner's (1993) Rorschach textbook.

Several nonpictorial projective tests are available, including word association tests and incomplete sentence tests. Expressive techniques require a person to make something, such as draw a picture of a person or of his or her family.

15

CHAPTER

# Testing in Counseling Psychology

## LEARNING OBJECTIVES

*When you have completed this chapter, you should be able to:*

► Describe the use of the criterion-keying method in the development of the SVIB

► List some of the criticisms of the SVIB

► Describe how the SCII, CISS, and SII improved on the SVIB

► Describe how the KOIS differs from the SVIB, the SCII, the CISS, and the SII

► Outline some of the controversial issues in interest measurement

► Evaluate the proposition that personality traits are stable over time

At age 35, Harry found himself faced with a dilemma. He had studied hard for many years to become a dentist, but what he had suspected for many years was becoming obvious: he did not like dentistry. Although Harry had chosen this occupation, he had not considered dentistry in detail before making a commitment to the field.

Harry could trace his interest in becoming a dentist to an experience he had during his childhood. As a young boy, he liked to play golf. While on the course one day, Harry met a dentist who explained that the practice of dentistry was lucrative but still allowed practitioners enough time to play golf and engage in other activities. Harry was a good student, and the encounter with the golfer-dentist made him think that dentistry would afford him the ideal lifestyle. Harry liked his science classes when he entered college, and he continued to be an outstanding student. After 4 years at a state university, he was accepted by a good dental school.

In dental school, Harry began to question his career choice. Two things were apparent by the end of his third year. First, he did not really enjoy doing dental work. He found himself uneasy when his patients fussed in the chair, and he disliked subjecting people to the discomfort associated with some dental procedures. Second, Harry discovered that he did not share many interests with other people in the field of dentistry.

After completing dental school, Harry did a brief tour of duty as a dentist in the U.S. Air Force. When he left the service, he decided he wanted to get away from dentistry for a while and enrolled in art school. However, despite his dislike for dentistry, he returned to the practice because of the large personal and financial investment he had already made in the profession. Dentistry paid well, and retraining in a field of more interest to him would be difficult and costly. In the 35 years that had passed since he had graduated from dental school, Harry quit and reentered his dental practice on five separate occasions. Throughout the entire experience, he remained unhappy with his choice of profession.

This true story recounts the lives of many people who feel they have made the wrong career choice. Some of the misery that talented people like Harry experience could be avoided with proper career counseling and guidance (Zunker, 2011). In this chapter, we examine the contribution of psychological tests to the selection of and preparation for a career.

The term *career* connotes "adventure" to many people. As a noun, it means "swift course"; as a verb it means "to go swiftly or wildly." The Latin root is *carrus*, "chariot." Thus, the term for today's rat race has its roots in the exciting Roman races (Super & Hall, 1978). Careers can indeed be exciting and the essence of life if they are properly selected. They can also lead to misery if not carefully chosen. Psychological tests can help people select the right career. The first step in the identification of an appropriate career path is the evaluation of interests.

# Measuring Interests

If you want to enter an appropriate career, you must identify your interests. Some people need little help finding work that interests them; others can benefit from the guidance given by a psychological test. In the nearly 90 years since the introduction of interest inventories, millions of people have received feedback about their own interests to help them make wise career choices.

The first interest inventory, introduced in 1921, was called the Carnegie Interest Inventory. When the *Mental Measurements Yearbook* was first published in 1939, it discussed 15 different interest measures (Datta, 1975). The two most widely used interest tests were introduced relatively early: the Strong Vocational Interest Blank in 1927 and the Kuder Preference Survey in 1939.

Today there are more than 80 interest inventories in use; however, the Strong remains one of the most widely used tests in research and practice. Because the Strong is so important, we will take some time to review the various iterations of the test that have evolved over the years.

## The Strong Vocational Interest Blank

Shortly after World War I, E. K. Strong, Jr. and some of his colleagues began to examine the activities that members of different professions liked and disliked. They came to realize that people in different professional groups had different patterns of interests. To some extent, one might expect this, because people tend to choose lines of work that interest them. One might expect carpenters to like woodworking, and painting might interest an artist more than a salesperson. However, Strong and his colleagues also found that people in the same line of work had similar hobbies, liked the same types of entertainment, and read the same sorts of books and magazines.

With this research as a base, Strong set out to develop a test that would match the interests of a subject to the interests and values of a criterion group of people who were happy in the careers they had chosen. This procedure is called criterion keying, or the *criterion-group approach* (see Chapter 9). The test they created with this method was the Strong Vocational Interest Blank (SVIB).

In preliminary studies of the test, groups of individuals from many professions and occupations responded to approximately 400 items dealing with likes and dislikes related to these occupations and to leisure activities. The criterion keying then determined how the interests of new subjects resembled those of the criterion groups.

In the revised 1966 version of the SVIB, the 399 items were related to 54 occupations for men. A separate form presented 32 different occupations for women. Items in the SVIB were weighted according to how frequently an interest occurred in a particular occupational group as opposed to how frequently it occurred in the general population. Raw scores were converted to standard scores, with a mean of 50 and a standard deviation of 10. Each criterion group used in the construction of the SVIB contained approximately 300 people, a good normative sample. Numerous reliability studies produced impressive results, with odd–even and short-term test–retest figures generally running between the low .80's and the low .90's. Long-term (20-year) test–retest coefficients ran in the respectable .60's. Validity data indicated that the SVIB predicted job satisfaction well (e.g., Strong & Campbell, 1966).

One of the most interesting findings to emerge from the hundreds of published studies using the SVIB is that patterns of interest remain relatively stable over time. Strong made a practice of asking a group of Stanford University students who took the test in the 1930s to take the test again as they grew older. These studies showed that interests remain relatively stable for as long as 22 years. Of course, most people did modify their interests slightly over this period, and a few people made complete turnabouts; nevertheless, the great majority remained consistent.

Studies also showed that interest patterns are fairly well established by age 17. For example, Stanford premed students who eventually became physicians scored high on the physician scale of the SVIB. When recontacted throughout life, they tended to remain high on that scale (Tyler & Walsh, 1979). Other studies showed some instability of interests during adolescence, with the patterns becoming stable by the senior year of high school (Hansen & Campbell, 1985).

Despite the widespread acceptance and use of the SVIB, disenchantment with the test began to mount in the late 1960s and early 1970s. Critics cited a gender bias in the scales because different tests were used for men and women. Others complained about the lack of theory associated with the test.

## The Strong-Campbell Interest Inventory

In 1974, D. P. Campbell published a new version of the SVIB, which he called the Strong-Campbell Interest Inventory (SCII). The SCII was Campbell's (1974) response to the shortcomings of the SVIB. Items from both the men's and women's forms of the SVIB were merged into a single form that included scales devoid of gender bias. For example, the scales for waiter and waitress were merged, and items that referred to gender (e.g., salesman) were appropriately modified.

In developing the SVIB, Strong had shied away from providing a theoretical explanation for why certain types of individuals liked some fields and disliked others. However, Campbell became interested in J. L. Holland's (1975) theory of vocational choice. After many years of study, Holland had postulated that interests express personality and that people can be classified into one or more of six categories according to their interests (see Table 15.1). These factors were quite similar to the patterns of interest that emerged from many years of research with the SVIB. In addition, the factors postulated by Holland could be used for either men or women. When Campbell incorporated Holland's theory and his six personality factors into the SCII (Tyler & Walsh, 1979), he provided a theoretical basis for a new test that the SVIB had lacked.

Over the years, research has generally supported Holland's ideas (Carless, 1999). For example, one detailed study that used all 437 occupational titles from the Bureau of the Census demonstrated that Holland's system can better describe work activities, general training requirements, and occupational rewards than can a variety of competing vocational classification systems (Gottfredson, 1980). Holland (1999) has summarized 50 years of research supporting the claim that occupational interests reflect personality.

The SCII in its current form is divided into seven parts. The test, which still retains the core of the SVIB, now has 325 items, to which a person responds "like," "dislike," or "indifferent" (Hansen, 2000).

Various agencies provide automated scoring services for the SCII, and most of them summarize several scores for each profile. The first score is a summary of general themes based on Holland's six personality types (see Table 15.1).

**TABLE 15.1**   Holland's Six Personality Factors

| Factor | Interest Pattern |
|---|---|
| Realistic | Enjoys technical material and outdoor activities |
| Investigative | Is interested in science and the process of investigation |
| Artistic | Enjoys self-expression and being dramatic |
| Social | Is interested in helping others and in activities involving other people |
| Enterprising | Is interested in power and political strength |
| Conventional | Likes to be well organized and has clerical interests |

Adapted from J. L. Holland (1985).

For example, the profile might provide information about the general types of activities the person enjoys, the kinds of people the person might work well with, and the most suitable general occupational environment.

The second score summary given in a report is for the administrative indexes. Of less personal importance to the test taker, these are needed to ensure that errors were not made in the administration, scoring, or processing of the test.

The third set of scores provides a summary of a person's basic interests. For example, they suggest whether a person scored high, low, or about average in preference for science, mechanical activities, and athletics. This information is reported in standardized $T$ scores (see Chapter 2). Remember that $T$ scores have a mean of 50 and a standard deviation of 10. Thus, a $T$ score of 60 would be one standard deviation above the mean or in approximately the 84th percentile (Hansen, 2000).

The final set of summary scores given in the SCII profile is for the occupational scales. These scales occupy most of the space on the SCII profile. The profile shows the person's score for each of 124 occupations, which are broken into six general occupational themes. The scoring for the occupational scales differs from that for the general theme and basic interest scales because the occupational scale compares the test taker's score with the scores of people working in the various professions. The general theme and basic interest scales compare the test taker's score with those of people in general. If you took the SCII, for each scale you would be assigned a score indicating the degree of similarity—very dissimilar, dissimilar, average, similar, or very similar—between your interests and the interests of people happy in their chosen occupations. Many of the occupations are divided so that different criterion groups are provided for men and women. For example, if you scored in the "very similar" category for the occupation social worker (for a female), then this finding would suggest that your interests were close to those of women who had been employed as social workers and enjoyed the profession (Hansen, 2000).

The SCII is no longer used very much because it has been replaced by newer tests (see following sections). The last version of the SCII was released in spring 1985. Although the test booklets and answer sheets did not change, the SCII profile was expanded to include 207 occupational scales, 144 of which have been developed since 1977. The 1985 revision has a national sample that represents every occupational criterion group. In addition, special precautions were taken to rule out potential difficulties in interpretation. For example, one criticism of the SCII has been that members of the criterion groups were older than those who would be just entering the workforce. In the final SCII, younger and older members of each criterion group were compared to determine whether the interests and values of the recent entrants into the workforce differed from those of workers who had been on the job for many years (Hansen & Campbell, 1985).

## The Campbell Interest and Skill Survey

The Strong scales have had an interesting and turbulent recent history. David Campbell began working on the Strong Vocational Interest Blank in 1960 when he was a graduate student at the University of Minnesota (Campbell, 2002). When Strong died in 1963, Campbell, then an assistant professor at the University of Minnesota, became the primary representative of the SVIB. Later versions were published under the authorship of Strong and Campbell. The first version of the Strong-Campbell Interest Inventory was published in 1974. Because Strong had been a professor at Stanford University, Stanford and the University of Minnesota became engaged in a legal dispute over ownership. In an out-of-court settlement in 1988, Stanford received the rights to publish the Strong Interest Inventory while Campbell received the rights to most of the cumulative work. In 1992, Campbell published the Campbell Interest and Skill Survey (CISS) (Campbell, 2002; Campbell, Hyne, & Nilsen, 1992).

The CISS asks respondents to assess their degree of interest in 200 academic and occupational topics. Further, it assesses the degree of skill in 120 specific occupations. The system produces an 11-page profile and a 2-page report summary (Campbell, 1995). The CISS ultimately yields a variety of different types of scales. These are summarized in Table 15.2. For each of these scales, an interest level and a skill score are offered.

---

**TABLE 15.2** Summary of the Components of the Campbell Interest and Skill Survey

**Orientation scales**
Seven scales describe the test taker's occupational orientation: influencing, organizing, helping, creating, analyzing, producing, and adventuring.

**Basic scales**
The basic scales provide an overview for categories of occupations. Examples of basic scales include law/politics, counseling, and mathematics.

**Occupational scales**
Sixty occupational scales describe matches with particular occupations, including attorney, engineer, guidance counselor, and math teacher.

From the Campbell Interest and Skills Survey. Paper presented at the annual meeting of the American Psychological Association, New York, August 1995. Reprinted by permission of David P. Campbell.

In addition to these specific scales, the CISS offers an academic focus scale that helps test takers understand how comfortable or successful they may be in an academic setting, and an extroversion scale that helps guide them to occupations with the appropriate amount and intensity of interpersonal relations. Recently, Campbell teamed up with *US News & World Report* to offer the CISS online (see https://www.profiler.com). For $18 plus tax, you can gain access to the 320-question survey. The fee includes a personalized report that compares your results to the responses of people who are successfully employed in 60 occupations, along with a comprehensive career planner and a guide to help you interpret the results.

To a large extent, the CISS is a continuation of the research on the SVIB and the SCII. The CISS is now shorter and more efficient than the older SCII. The scales are standardized with means of 50 and standard deviations of 10. As with the earlier versions, the CISS uses the theoretical structure of John Holland. The manual provides extensive evidence for validity and reliability (Campbell, 1995). New evidence continues to support the validity of the CISS and its subscales (Hansen & Leuty, 2007).

## The Reemergence of the Strong Interest Inventory

As noted in the previous paragraph, supporters of the Strong and the Campbell inventories engaged in a legal dispute resulting in a "divorce" between Stanford University and the University of Minnesota. In 2007, Stanford released the new Strong, known as the Strong Interest Inventory (SII). The Strong SII represents a substantial revision of the previous measure and features a different item format. Previous editions had used a three-choice format, while the revised version offers a five-choice, Likert-type format with icons for "Strongly Like," "Like," "Indifferent," "Dislike," and "Strongly Dislike." A core component of the SII is the Basic Interest Scales (BIS). Since the original development of the SVIB, there had been substantial changes in work life and workplaces, and the new SII includes 41 content scales to represent these areas. The new Strong includes 244 occupational scales. In comparison to earlier versions, there is more focus on careers in business and technology for both men and women. For example, 122 of the scales include different pairs for men and women. Examples of the new normative groups include greater diversity in terms of ethnic groups, race, and diversity in the workforce.

Over more than 30 years that we have worked on this book, we have had the opportunity to test the same person using Strong tests at different life phases. A summary of this exercise is given in Focused Example 15.1. Psychological Testing in Everyday Life 15.1 shows components of the computerized interpretation of the SII.

The first published evaluation of the SII considered 31 college majors in a national college sample of 1403 women and 469 men to evaluate the relationships between content scales and choice of college major. The study showed substantial concurrent validity for a wide variety of college major choices (Gasser, Larson, & Borgen, 2007). The basic interest scales were the best predictors of selection of major.

In summary, the Strong has reemerged as a major competitor among interest inventories. We expect continuing research to evaluate its validity. If you are

## Stability of Vocational Interests—a 28-Year Case Study

One of the challenges in interest testing is in determining if career preferences are stable. We all change over time, and we would not want to advise someone to follow a particular career path only to discover that his or her interests had changed just a few years later. Most studies do suggest that career-related interests are stable over time (Ehrhart & Makransky, 2007). As an example, we offer a case study. When we wrote the first edition of this book in 1980, we tested Jean A, a 28-year-old psychology graduate student who had not yet started her professional career. Jean was married, but did not have children and was uncertain what career path she would follow. Using the SCII, we retested Jean 11 years later. During this 11-year interval, Jean completed her Ph.D., held three different jobs, and had given birth to two children. She was now a 39-year-old university professor engaged in research and teaching. In 2008, we retested Jean a third time using the new version of

the Strong Interest Inventory. A tremendous amount had changed for both Jean and the test. Jean's career had flourished, and she had risen through the ranks as a senior university administrator in the sciences. Although she remained at the university, the demands on her had changed considerably. Instead of teaching students, she had become responsible for solving problems across many different university departments and programs. Further, her personal life had changed. She had separated from her husband and her children had left home, graduated from college, and started their own lives. Her circle of friends had evolved and she had lost her father, who had instilled in her a strong work ethic. In many ways, Jean had reinvented herself, but had her basic interests changed?

In addition to the changes Jean had experienced, the tests had also changed. The initial test and 11-year follow-up were completed using the SCII.

**TABLE 15.3**   Scores on Occupational Themes for Jean A at Ages 28, 39, and 56

| Theme | 1980, Age 28 | 1991, Age 39 | 2008, Age 56 |
|---|---|---|---|
| Investigative | 58 | 58 | 69 |
| Artistic | 51 | 51 | 56 |
| Social | 45 | 46 | 60 |
| Enterprising | 42 | 37 | 43 |
| Conventional | 37 | 44 | 54 |
| Realistic | 36 | 36 | 50 |

interested in taking the SII, you can complete the measure for a fee of between $39 and $59 at http://www.personalityreports.com

## The Kuder Occupational Interest Survey

Although the SCII is probably the most widely used interest inventory today, it competes with many other interest inventories. The Kuder Occupational Interest Survey (KOIS) ranks second in popularity. It is one of several interest scales that grew out of the original Kuder Preference Survey published in 1939. Throughout the years, the Kuder has offered a unique alternative to the SVIB, SCII, and CISS.

The 28-year follow-up was done using the new SII. The SII is much improved over the earlier tests and has much more advanced scoring templates, particularly for professional women. From the few occupations scales available to women in the 1970s, the SII now has 122 validated occupational scales for women.

Table 15.3 compares Jean A's SCII profiles at ages 28, 39, and 56. As the table shows, her interests remained remarkably stable. Despite the passage of 28 years, not to mention the use of a different testing instrument, the picture we get of Jean is very similar. Her highest theme remained investigative, suggesting interests in science, math, and research. The investigative cluster usually comes with skills in analysis, research, and writing. Jean had always scored high on the investigative theme, and this became stronger as she aged. Although the rank orders changed some, Jean tended to score low on the enterprising theme, a cluster associated with interests in business, politics, and entrepreneurship. People scoring high on entrepreneurship enjoy selling, persuading, and marketing. Clearly this was not Jean as a younger woman nor as a more mature adult.

In 1980, the SCII steered Jean toward four professions: physician, optometrist, psychologist, and university professor. At ages 28 and 39, physician was identified as the best career match for Jean, but university professor had emerged as her second-best match by age 39. By age 56, psychologist was noted as the best match, but university professor was very close. In fact, most of the professions identified at the top of the list in 1980 remained in the top 10 among 122 different occupations when Jean was evaluated in 2008. Given the changes that both Jean and the test experienced, the stability of the picture is quite remarkable (see Table 15.4). In 1980, the SCII suggested that Jean avoid certain professions such as librarian, beautician, flight attendant, and army officer. The 2008 test suggested that her worst matches were art teacher, interior designer, florist, and cosmetologist. At both times, Jean's interests did not match those of women who had chosen more traditionally female roles.

In 2012, as Jean A approached her 60th birthday, she remained happy in her career. It is likely that guidance given by interest inventories early in her adulthood would have directed her toward career fields that would remain good matches throughout her working life.

**TABLE 15.4**    Scores on Occupational Scales for Jean A at Ages 28, 39, and 56

| Profession | 1980, Age 28 | 1991, Age 39 | 2008, Age 56 |
|---|---|---|---|
| Physician | 58 | 53 | 48 |
| Optometrist | 52 | 47 | 51 |
| Psychologist | 50 | 47 | 57 |
| University professor | 49 | 50 | 56 |

The KOIS presents the test taker with 100 triads (sets of three) of alternative activities. For each triad, the test taker selects the most preferred and the least preferred alternatives. Scoring of the KOIS scales gives the same information yielded by the earlier Kuder Preference Surveys—data on 10 general occupational interests (e.g., outdoor interests versus social service interests). However, in its current form (Kuder, 1979), the KOIS examines the similarity between a test taker's interests and those of people employed in various occupations in a manner much like that of the SCII and CISS. Furthermore, the KOIS has developed separate norms for men and women. The KOIS also has a separate set of scales for college majors. Thus, in addition to suggesting which occupational group might work best with a test taker's interests, the KOIS may also help students choose a major (Diamond & Zytowski, 2000).

## 15.1  PSYCHOLOGICAL TESTING IN EVERYDAY LIFE

### Interpreting the SII

In the example of Jean A, the thematic interests ranked by the SII report are as follows:

| THEME | CODE | STANDARD SCORE & INTEREST LEVEL | | | | | STD SCORE |
|---|---|---|---|---|---|---|---|
| | | < 30 | 40 | 50 | 60 | 70 > | |
| Investigative | I | | | | | VERY HIGH | 69 |
| Social | S | | | | HIGH | | 60 |
| Artistic | A | | | MODERATE | | | 55 |
| Conventional | C | | | MODERATE | | | 54 |
| Realistic | R | | MODERATE | | | | 50 |
| Enterprising | E | MODERATE | | | | | 43 |

The charts above display your GOT results in descending order, from your highest to least level of interest. Referring to the Theme Descriptions provided, determine how well your results fit for you. Do your highest Themes ring true? Look at your next highest level of interest and ask yourself the same question. You may wish to highlight the Theme descriptions on this page that seem to fit you best.

(From National Career Assessment Sciences, Inc.™, Report of Scores, Kuder Occupational Survey, Form DD, copyright © 1965, 1968, 1970, 1979. National Career Assessment Services, Inc. Reprinted by permission.)

The report then goes on to suggest specific professions that may be a good or a poor match:

**YOUR TOP TEN STRONG OCCUPATIONS**

1. Psychologist (IA)
2. Geographer (IA)
3. Biologist (IRA)
4. Software Developer (IR)
5. University Professor (IAR)
6. Rehabilitation Counselor (SAI)
7. Computer Systems Analyst (C)
8. Sociologist (IAR)
9. Science Teacher (IRS)
10. Optometrist (IR)

Occupations of
Dissimilar Interest

Art Teacher (ASE)

Interior Designer (EA)

Medical Illustrator (AIR)

Florist (EAC)

Cosmetologist (EC)

SII reports are very detailed and offer lots of specific guidance. For example, they identify next steps, what training should be undertaken, and what skills need to be developed. The end of the report provides a "snapshot summary." Here is the summary for Jean A:

## SNAPSHOT OF RESULTS

**YOUR HIGHEST THEMES**

· Investigative
· Social
· Artistic

**PERSONAL AND WORK ENVIRONMENT DESCRIPTORS**

· Analytical, independent, research oriented
· Helpful, collaborative, cooperative
· Creative, flexible, self-expressive

**SPECIFIC INTERESTS FOR WORK, LEISURE, AND LEARNING**

· Conducting experiments
· Operating scientific equipment
· Studying scientific theory
· Performing statistical analyses
· Using math to solve problems

· Teaching math
· Analyzing research results
· Conducting scientific experiments
· Writing reports

**CAREERS THAT MIGHT BE MOST APPEALING TO YOU**

· Psychologist
· Geographer
· Biologist
· Software Developer
· University Professor

· Rehabilitation Counselor
· Computer Systems Analyst
· Sociologist
· Science Teacher
· Optometrist

**HOW YOU LIKE TO WORK AND LEARN**

· Balance between working with colleagues and
  working alone
· Learning new ideas to apply to abstract problems
· Taking charge of some projects but not others

· Playing it safe and making decisions carefully
· With others, sharing responsibility and achievement

To emphasize nontraditional occupations for men and women, a series of new scales has been added to the KOIS. Examples of these new scales are architect (female norms), journalist (female norms), and film and television producer or director (male norms) (Zytowski, 1985).

Although each test taker is evaluated with regard to the norms for many occupational and college major groups, the KOIS provides a summary of an individual's highest scores by marking them with an asterisk.

In 1999, the National Career Assessment Service became the international distributor for the KOIS. The report is divided into four sections. The first summarizes the dependability of the results. An analysis of answer patterns considers consistency. The report shown in the table suggests that the results appear to be dependable for this particular test taker. The second section rank orders interest patterns in comparison to the normative sample of men and women. In this example, the person taking the test has exceptionally high interests in literary and outdoor areas in comparison to both men and women. The female test taker had low interests in comparison to other women in the mechanical, social service, and persuasive areas.

The core of the KOIS report is shown in the third section. This section ranks the test taker in relation to men and women who are employed in different occupations and are satisfied with their career choices. The report shows that the woman who completed the measure has a pattern of interests that best matches those of journalists who are satisfied with their work. The pattern also shows good correspondence with interests of lawyers, personnel managers, and physicians. The pattern matches most poorly with bank clerk, beautician, and department store sales. The fourth section of the report matches patterns of interests to those of students who have selected different college majors. The woman whose results are shown in this example matches interest patterns most closely with women who are majoring in history, English, or political science. Her interests match most poorly with women majoring in physical education, nursing, and art.

Studies show that the psychometric properties of the KOIS are very good. Short-term reliabilities tend to be high (between .80 and .95), and increasing evidence indicates that scores remain stable for as long as 30 years (Zytowski, 1996). One study on the predictive validity of the KOIS showed that half of one group of adults who had taken an early version of the KOIS while they were high-school students were working in fields that the high-school KOIS suggested they enter. Predictive validity for the college major scales was even better. There was closer correspondence between interests and the occupation a person was working in for those who had completed college than for those who had not. A college degree thus provides more freedom than a high-school diploma does in finding personally desirable work (Zytowski, 1976).

In other studies, high-school students reported greater confidence in their knowledge of themselves when they received KOIS results than when they did not. But knowing the results of the KOIS did not make the high-school students more confident or more satisfied with their career plans, except when the students expressed a special interest in learning about the test results (Zytowski, 1977). Other studies have considered self-efficacy for the specific occupational tasks in the KOIS. *Self-efficacy* represents a person's expectation that he or she could perform the tasks in the occupational groups. The research suggests that, in comparison to women, men have higher expectations that they will succeed in mechanical and physical work, and women have greater expectations that they will succeed when working with people than do men (Lucas, Wanberg, & Zytowski, 1997). Even though the KOIS has been less thoroughly studied than the SVIB-SCII, a growing amount of evidence indicates that it may be quite useful for guidance decisions for high-school and college students. The KOIS, although still in common use, has not undergone a major revision since 1991 (Zytowski, 1992). However, research using the KOIS continues. Studies using the KOIS have shown that career preferences are quite stable over the course of time. For example, one study tested 107 high-school juniors and seniors in 1975 and then retested them 30 years later in 2005. In general, occupational interests remained very stable, but some of the particular interest scales were associated with instability in occupational interests (Rottinghaus, Coon, Gaffey, & Zytowski, 2007).

The Jackson Vocational Interest Survey (JVIS), revised in 1995 and copyrighted in 1999, is used for the career education and counseling of high-school and college students. It can also be used to plan careers for adults, including those who want to make midlife career changes. Douglas Jackson, the developer of the measure, was strongly influenced by the psychometric pioneers from the Educational Testing Service (Jackson, 2002). The JVIS consists of 289 statements describing job-related activities. It takes 45 minutes to complete, and the scoring yields 34 basic interest scales. The test construction carefully avoided gender bias. The scale employs forced-choice formats in which the respondent must indicate a preference between two equally popular interests.

Studies suggest that the reliability for 10 general occupational themes is approximately .89 and that the test–retest stability of the 44 basic interest scales ranges from .84 to .88. Validity studies suggest that the JVIS predicts university and academic majors more accurately than do most other interest inventories. Available in both hand-scored and machine-scored forms, the JVIS offers computer software to administer and score the measure (Jackson & Livesley, 1995).

## The Career Assessment Inventory

Developed by Charles B. Johansson, the Career Assessment Inventory (CAI) is designed for people not oriented toward careers requiring college or professional training. The CAI is written at the sixth-grade reading level and is designed for the 80% of U.S. citizens who have fewer than four years of postsecondary education. The CAI provides information similar to that yielded by the SII and CISS. Each test taker is evaluated on Holland's six occupational theme scales: realistic, investigative, artistic, social, enterprising, and conventional. The second portion of the CAI report describes basic interests. Each test taker is evaluated in 22 specific areas, including carpentry, business, and food service. The third section of the report is a series of occupational scales. Scores for the 89 occupational scales on the CAI were obtained by using a criterion-keying method. The interests of the test takers are matched to the interests of truck drivers, secretaries, waitpersons, and so forth.

Validity and reliability studies reported in the test manual suggest that the CAI has desirable psychometric properties. Scores tend to be quite stable, and people who find employment in occupations for which they have expressed strong interest tend to remain at their jobs and find more satisfaction with work than do those with low scores for those occupations. The test developer also took special pains to make the CAI culturally fair and eliminate gender bias. In many ways, the CAI has become the working person's CISS (Johannson, 1976; Johannson & Johansson, 1978).

## The Self-Directed Search

Most interest inventories require professional or computer-automated scoring. In addition, they typically require interpretation by a trained counselor. J. L. Holland developed the Self-Directed Search (SDS) to be a self-administered, self-scored, and self-interpreted vocational interest inventory (Spokane & Catalano, 2000). The SDS attempts to simulate the counseling process by allowing respondents to list occupational aspirations, indicate occupational preferences in six areas, and rate abilities and skills in these areas (Srsic, Stimac, & Walsh, 2001). Then the test takers can score their own inventory and calculate six summary scores, which they can use to obtain codes that reflect the highest areas of interest. Using the SDS, test takers can develop a meaningful personal career theory. The personal theory goes beyond interests and includes readiness for career decision making and readiness to obtain guidance (Reardon & Lenz, 1999). The SDS is linked to an occupational finder. In the 1994 edition of the system, the individual can locate more than 1300 occupations and match his or her own interest codes to corresponding occupational choices.

The SDS includes 228 items. Six scales with 11 items each describe activities. Another 66 items assess competencies, with six scales of 11 items each. Occupations are evaluated in six scales of 14 items each. Self-estimates are obtained in two sets of six ratings. Studies have demonstrated that respondents accurately score their own tests. Validity studies reflect a moderate, but not high, association between SDS categories and stated vocational aspirations (Holland, 1985).

Another approach similar to the self-directed search is to allow subjects to interact with a computer-assisted guidance system (Spokane & Catalano, 2000). One study analyzed "dialogue" used in interactions with the computer. The SDS is now available online, and users appear to be more satisfied than those who respond to the paper-and-pencil version (Barak & Cohen, 2002). The analysis suggests that most people do not perform comprehensive searches but instead seek information on only some alternatives. The larger the number of choices, the smaller the number explored. This is not unexpected, because most people need to simplify information and gather it selectively (Gati & Tikotzki, 1989).

Despite the common and enthusiastic use of interest inventories, several problems have repeatedly surfaced, including faking, sex bias, and mismatches between abilities and interests.

## Eliminating Gender Bias in Interest Measurement

Not all members of society have found the use and development of interest inventories acceptable. In particular, advocates of women's rights justifiably pointed out that the early interest inventories discriminated against women (Birk, 1974; Campbell, 1995; Diamond, 1979; Peoples, 1975; Tittle, 1983). The Association for Evaluation in Guidance appointed the Commission on Sex Bias in Measurement, which concluded that interest inventories contributed to the policy of guiding young men and women into gender-typed careers. The interest inventories tended to direct women into their traditional work roles, such as nursing, clerical service, and elementary-school teaching. The SVIB, the main interest inventory at the time of the commission report, had separate forms for men and for women. Careers on the women's form, it was noted, tended to be lower in status and to command lower salaries (Harmon, Cole, Wysong, & Zytowski, 1973).

In response to these criticisms, the test developers began using the same forms for both men and women. However, in the 1977 SCII manual, Campbell noted that if Strong were alive, he may have felt that using the same norming tables for both men and women would have harmed the validity of the test. A unisex interest inventory, according to Strong, ignores the social and statistical reality that men and women have different interests. In other words, knowing the sex of the test taker tells us a lot about his or her interests. Nevertheless, the measure developers began to make major efforts to reduce gender bias, and newer measures, such as the CISS (Campbell, 1995), have gone even further. In the most recent versions, normative samples have been expanded to ensure larger and more representative samples. The 2007 SII has separate normative scales for men and women.

Most measures have reduced but not eliminated gender bias. Contemporary studies show that many items in the Strong Interest Inventory function differently for men and for women. Furthermore, these differences have been observed in cultures as different as the United States and Iceland (Einarsdottir, 2002). Interest inventory developers have worked hard to address these concerns. Although the basic interest and general theme portions of the SII and CISS compare a respondent's responses with those from a combined male and female reference group, the occupational scales are normed separately for men and women. Furthermore, the interpretive comments that are provided by most scoring services are geared toward the test taker's gender (Minton & Schneider, 1980). We expect that using the same or different norms for men and women will continue to engender controversy and debate. The current versions of the CISS, KOIS, and SII reflect the growing concern about gender bias (Campbell, 1995; Hansen & Campbell, 1987). Because career choices for many women are complex, interest inventories alone may be inadequate and more comprehensive approaches are needed (McLennan & Arthur, 1999).

Interest inventories have been around for several generations, making it possible to compare interests of groups born at different points in time. In the 1940s and 1950s, when career interest inventories got their start, the world was a very different place. Only a small percentage of women completed college and there was little ethnic and racial variability on most campuses (see Figure 15.1). By 1971, about 42% of college graduates were female and 58% were male. By 2012, that trend had reversed, with women earning nearly 60% of bachelor's degrees.

**FIGURE 15.1**
A crowd of Notre Dame
University students

© Bradley Smith/CORBIS

Budany and Hansen (2011) studied changes in vocational interests across birth cohorts of college students by integrating samples collected between 1976 and 2004. They identified doctoral dissertations and journal articles that had used the Strong Interest Inventory and the Strong-Campbell Interest Inventory and had information on the Holland's RIASEC typology. Across all studies included in the analysis, there were 12,039 females and 9550 subjects. They combined results across studies using meta-analysis and broke down the results by the year the data were collected. Between 1976 and 2004, college women showed an increase in enterprising interests, while college men demonstrated a decrease in the realistic and investigative interests. Back in the 1970s, there were significant differences between college men and women in investigative, enterprising, and conventional interests. As time went on, these differences diminished, suggesting that a greater emphasis on egalitarianism was helping change the basic career interests of young men and women.

## Aptitudes and Interests

Extensive research on interest inventories reinforces an important but often over-looked point: interest inventories measure interests, not the odds that people will succeed in the jobs that they find interesting.

The norm groups for the Strong inventories consist of people successful enough in various fields to remain working in them for defined periods. However, *degree* of success is not defined. If you obtain a high score for a particular occupation, then it means that you have interests similar to those of the people in that field. Self-rated satisfaction with chosen careers does appear to be higher for people whose interests match those of others working in the field, but repeated studies have emphasized that the chances of succeeding in that job depend on aptitudes and abilities.

# Measuring Personal Characteristics for Job Placement

Interests are just one of the many factors to be considered in career planning and placement. Career choices also depend on matches between skills and jobs. Employers want to find the right person for the job, and job hunters continually seek that one position that perfectly suits their personal skills and interests. Thus, psychologists and vocational guidance specialists look at job placement from many different perspectives. Some focus on the person and his or her characteristics, others attend the work environment, while still others concentrate on unique combinations of people and situations. To begin, let's look at some of the theories and measurement methods that focus on the person.

## Trait Factor Approach: Osipow's Vocational Dimensions

Samuel Osipow has been a leading figure in the field of counseling psychology for many years. Like Holland's method of trait assessment, Osipow's (1983) approach to career guidance is to give extensive tests covering personality, abilities, interests, and personal values to learn as much about a person's traits as possible. Osipow's work is consistent with Holland's theory of personality and occupation interest (Osipow, 1999). This approach involves the administration of an extensive battery of tests, including many we have already covered, such as the SCII and the KOIS. Other tests given include the Purdue pegboard (Fleishman & Quaintance, 1984) and the Seashore Measure of Musical Talents (Lezak, 1983). The results of this large battery of tests were factor analyzed (see Chapter 3) to find common factors or traits that characterize different occupational groups. People who require guidance take the battery of tests to learn about their traits. Then the counselor matches their traits to those that characterize the different occupations.

Used extensively in research and practice, Osipow's approach has undoubtedly helped many people find their occupational niches. However, the approach has also come under fire for overemphasizing the person and paying too little attention to the work environment. Furthermore, some critics suggest that Osipow's system focuses too much on a single point in time and does not attend sufficiently to the process of reaching a career decision (Tyler & Walsh, 1979).

## Are There Stable Personality Traits?

Imagine that you are responsible for hiring employees for a large business, and you want to do everything you can to convince your supervisors that you are doing a good job. You need to make decisions about the personalities of the people you interview, and you need to communicate this information to the people who will supervise them. For example, you might ask whether interviewees have the traits of kindness, honesty, trustworthiness, reliability, and dedication. People often believe that knowledge of such personality traits provides them with a convenient way of organizing information about others—for describing how they have behaved in the past and for predicting how they will act in the future (Carver and Schier 2012).

Indeed, all of the approaches to occupational interest assessment that we have presented in this chapter assume that interests are relatively stable personality characteristics. Much of the study of personality has been devoted to creating categories of traits, developing methods for measuring them, and finding out how groups of traits cluster. Indeed, the very concept of personality assumes that the characteristics of a person are stable over time. If Richard is "hardworking," then we expect him to work hard in many different situations. Although we commonly use trait names in this way to describe other people, the evidence that personality characteristics are stable is a little shaky. For example, Mischel (1984) showed that personality traits are simply not good predictors of how people will behave in particular situations. In a classic, well-argued attack on trait theorists, Mischel (1968) demonstrated that knowing how someone scores on measures of psychological traits sometimes gives little better than chance insight into how the person will act in a given situation. Career assessments may be a good exception to Mischel's criticism. The career inventories do not assess personality traits. Instead, they evaluate how people will respond to some well-defined situations. In fact, most studies do suggest that career interests are quite stable over long periods of time (Ehrhart & Makransky, 2007). Further, Mischel and his colleagues eventually softened on their belief about consistency of behaviors over time. For example, they had tested children's ability to delay gratification over 40 years ago. When some of the same people performed similar tasks 40 years later, they found that impulsiveness tended to be relatively stable. Children who were unable to delay gratification were more likely to be impulsive as adults (Casey, Somerville, et al., 2011).

### Attribution Theory

Another problem for traditional trait theories arises from research on *attribution theory*. Originally, attribution theory considered only how people make judgments about others; however, research in this area now covers all aspects of how people attempt to understand the causes of events in their lives.

First presented by Heider (1944, 1958), the ideas behind attribution theory became popular in the late 1960s. Attribution theorists suggested that events in a person's environment can be caused by one of three sources: persons, entities (things or some aspect of the environment), and times (situations) (Kelly, 1967). To determine which of these (or which combination) has caused an event, an observer uses three criteria: distinctiveness, consensus, and consistency. For example, if we want to explain why John is unhappy with his job today, we need to ask whether it has to do with something that happened on the job this particular day (distinctiveness), whether others in the same situation also dislike the job (consensus), or whether John is unhappy on all workdays (consistency).

Attribution theory is thus less concerned with predicting behavior than with studying how individuals make judgments about the causes of behavior. Some researchers have suggested that selecting an explanation for behavior depends on the role played by the person offering the judgment. The person making the judgment acts like a scientist in using all data to come to the best conclusion (Weiner, 1991). When we observe others and make judgments about them, we tend to use dispositional, or trait, explanations; however, we do not use trait explanations for our own behavior (Forsterling, 1988). When we are the actors in a situation, we see our own behavior in terms of the situation. In other words, we describe others in terms of traits, but we explain our own behavior in terms of situations. Why is there a difference between the attributions of actors and observers? E. E. Jones and Nisbett (1971) suggested that we know more about ourselves than about others. By searching our memory, we can remember behaving in many different situations. However, when we make judgments about others, we do not have as much information about how situations caused them to act differently. Yet we may be able to identify with others when they tell us that situations have influenced their behavior (Weiner, 2011). For example, juries may be forgiving of a criminal defendant who claims to have been influenced by a situation and makes a confession (Weiner, Graham, Peter, & Zmuidinas, 1991). Our beliefs about what people are feeling are also important. In judging the motivation of others, we tend to rely more on their perceived emotions than on established personality traits (Weiner, 2011).

To summarize, Mischel and the attribution theorists feel that psychologists have devoted too much attention to personality traits and not enough attention to situations. Thus, they recommend attention to the effect of situations on behavior.

# Summary

The beginning of this chapter presented the real-life case of Harry, a dentist who felt he had made the wrong career choice. Harry's problem might have been avoided through proper interest testing and career counseling. Several methods for assessing vocational interests are available. The best known of these is the Strong (now called the SII), an empirically keyed test that matches the interests of male and female test takers with those of people satisfied with their career choices. Although one of the most widely used tests in the history of psychology, the early version of the Strong (SVIB) was harshly criticized for its sexist and atheoretical orientation. Newer versions, such as the SII and the CISS, respond to these criticisms by including male and female keys in the same form and by embracing Holland's theory of occupational themes.

The KOIS is the next most frequently used interest test. In contrast to earlier versions, the present KOIS provides occupational scores similar to those given by the SII. A unique feature of the KOIS is that it provides scores for college majors. Other occupational interest measures are also available, including the CAI, designed for use with non-college-oriented individuals.

In 1968, Mischel demonstrated that personality measures do not always accurately predict behavior in particular situations. At about the same time, many attribution theorists began demonstrating that people explain the behavior of others by using personality traits; however, when asked about their own behavior, they tend to attribute cause to the situation. These ideas gave rise to the development of measures to assess the characteristics of social environments and work settings. Studies of the stability of occupational interests suggest that some aspects of personal preference are fairly stable over long periods of time.

# 16

## CHAPTER

# Applications in Clinical Psychology

## LEARNING OBJECTIVES

*When you have completed this chapter, you should be able to:*

▶ Identify the major characteristics of a structured personality test

▶ Identify the underlying assumption of the first structured personality test (the Woodworth Personal Data Sheet)

▶ Identify the assumptions of early structured personality tests based on the logical-content strategy

▶ Briefly discuss the strategy used in construction of the MMPI and MMPI-2

▶ Describe the K and F scales on the MMPI and MMPI-2

▶ Identify strengths and weaknesses of the MMPI and MMPI-2

▶ Explain how one uses factor analysis to build structured personality tests

▶ Explain the approach to test construction used in the NEO Personality Inventory

▶ Briefly describe the EPPS and explain the meaning of an ipsative score n his junior year in college, Mike went to the university counseling center for help in finding a direction in life. To aid him in his quest, a psychologist suggested that he respond to a long list of items known as the California Psychological Inventory (CPI). The CPI is a structured personality test used in counseling settings that provides a list of statements and asks the subject to respond "True" or "False" to each. It is widely used as a tool in career assessment (Gasser, Larson, & Borgen, 2004, p. 349; Gough, 1995). The statements included such ideas as these: "I like to read mystery stories." "I am usually alert to my environment." "I would rather follow others than be the leader." "I like to solve difficult problems." "My father is a good man." It took Mike approximately an hour to respond to the 462 items.

A week later, Mike returned for an interpretation of his test scores. The psychologist told him that the test indicated he was highly effective in dealing with other people; his response pattern resembled the pattern of individuals who make effective leaders. The CPI also indicated that Mike could control his desires and impulses and express them effectively and appropriately.

How did the counseling psychologist decide that Mike's responses reflected specific traits and characteristics such as leadership ability and impulse control? Did the interpretations really reflect Mike's characteristics? How stable were the results? Will the CPI indicate after 10 years that Mike still has leadership qualities? This chapter explores these and related questions.

Recall that people have developed tests in part to help solve the problems that face modern societies. Tests of mental ability were created to distinguish those with subnormal mental abilities from those with normal abilities in order to enhance the education of both groups. However, there is far more to being human than having normal or subnormal mental capabilities. It is not enough to know that a person is high or low in such factors as speed of calculation, memory, range of knowledge, and abstract thinking. To make full use of information about a person's mental abilities, one must also know how that person uses those abilities. All the mental abilities in the world remain inert in someone who sits in the corner of a room all day. But even modest mental abilities can go far in a high-energy individual who relates well to others and is organized, persistent, determined, and motivated. These nonintellective aspects of human behavior, typically distinguished from mental abilities, are called *personality characteristics*. Such characteristics are of vital concern in clinical and counseling settings.

One can define *personality* as the relatively stable and distinctive patterns of behavior that characterize an individual and his or her reactions to the environment. Structured personality tests attempt to evaluate personality traits, personality types, personality states, and other aspects of personality, such as self-concept. *Personality traits* refer to relatively enduring dispositions—tendencies to act, think, or feel in a certain manner in any given circumstance and that distinguish one person from another. *Personality types* refer to general descriptions of people; for example, avoiding types have low social interest and low activity and cope by avoiding social situations. *Personality states* refer to emotional reactions that vary from one situation to another. Finally, *self-concept* refers to a person's self-definition or, according to C. R. Rogers (1959a), an organized and relatively consistent set of assumptions that a person has about himself or herself. This chapter focuses on the measurement of personality traits, with some discussion of personality types and self-concept.

Before the first Binet scale was developed, Alfred Binet hypothesized that a person's pattern of intellectual functioning might reveal information about personality factors (Binet & Henri, 1895, 1896). Subsequent investigators agreed with Binet's hypothesis (Hart & Spearman, 1912; Terman, 1916; Thorndike, 1921), and this hypothesis continues to find support (Groth-Marnat, 1999; Kossowska, 2002; von Stumm, Chamorro-Premuzic, & Ackerman, 2011). However, specific tests of human personality were not developed until World War I. This created a need to distinguish people on the basis of emotional well-being.

Like pioneers in the measurement of mental ability, the early developers of personality tests traveled in uncharted territory. Imagine yourself faced with the task of measuring some aspect of human behavior. How would you begin? You could observe and record a person's behavior. However, this approach did not work for early investigators because their task was to identify emotionally unstable military recruits; the volume of applicants for military service in the United States during World War I was so great that it became impossible to use the one available method of the time—the psychiatric interview. Psychologists needed a measure of emotional functioning so they could evaluate large numbers of people and screen out those who were unfit for military service. To meet this need, psychologists used **self-report questionnaires** that provided a list of statements and required subjects to respond in some way to each, such as marking "True" or "False" to indicate whether the statement applied to them.

The general procedure in which the subject is asked to respond to a written statement is known as the *structured*, or objective, method of personality assessment, as distinguished from the *projective* method (see Chapter 14). As their name implies, structured measures of personality, also known as "objective" measures, are characterized by structure and lack of ambiguity. A clear and definite stimulus is provided, and the requirements of the subject are evident and specific. An example of a structured personality-test item is "Respond 'yes' or 'no' to the statement 'I am happy.'" In contrast, a projective test item may provide a picture of an inkblot and ask, "What might this be?" In a projective personality test, the stimulus is ambiguous and the subject has few guidelines about what type of response is required.

# Strategies of Structured Personality-Test Construction

Like measures of mental ability, personality measures evolved through several phases. New features appeared as problems with older approaches became evident. In the realm of structured personality testing, many approaches or strategies have been tried. Psychologists disagree on how these strategies should be classified, what they should be called, and even how many distinctly different strategies exist (Rayner, Roodenburg, & Roodenburg, 2012, p. 47; see also Ben-Porath & Butcher, 1991; Butcher, 2000; Waller, 1999). At the broadest level, the strategies are deductive and empirical. One can in turn divide each of these strategies as follows. Deductive strategies comprise the logical-content and the theoretical approach. Empirical strategies comprise the criterion-group and the factor analysis method. (See Figure 16.1.) Some procedures combine two or more of these strategies.

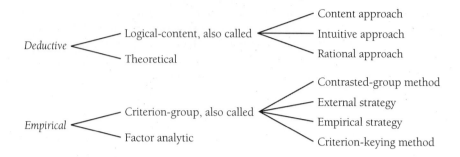

## Deductive Strategies

Deductive strategies use reason and deductive logic to determine the meaning of a test response. The logical-content method has test designers select items on the basis of simple face validity; in the theoretical approach, test construction is guided by a particular psychological theory.

### Logical-Content Strategy

The logical-content strategy, as its name implies, uses reason and deductive logic in the development of personality measures. In the most general use of this strategy, the test designer tries to logically deduce the type of content that should measure the characteristic to be assessed. For example, if one wants to measure eating behavior, it makes sense to include statements such as "I frequently eat between meals." Statements that have no direct logical relevance to eating behavior, such as "I enjoy solving complex puzzles," would not be included in tests that use the logical-content strategy. The principal distinguishing characteristic of this strategy is that it assumes that the test item describes the subject's personality and behavior. If a person marks "True" for the statement "I am outgoing," then testers assume that he or she *is* outgoing. Initial efforts to measure personality used the logical-content approach as the primary strategy.

### Theoretical Strategy

As its name implies, the theoretical strategy begins with a theory about the nature of the particular characteristic to be measured. As in the logical-content approach, an attempt is then made to deduce items. In the theoretical approach, however, items must be consistent with the theory. If the theory hypothesizes that personality can be broken down into six major areas, then developers strive to create items that tap each of these six areas. In addition, theoretical strategies demand that every item in a scale be related to the characteristic being measured. Thus, the theoretical approach attempts to create a homogeneous scale and, toward this end, may use statistical procedures such as item analysis.

## Empirical Strategies

Empirical strategies rely on data collection and statistical analyses to determine the meaning of a test response or the nature of personality and psychopathology. These strategies retain the self-report features of the deductive strategies in that subjects are asked to respond to items that describe their own views, opinions, and feelings.

However, empirical strategies attempt to use experimental research to determine empirically the meaning of a test response, the major dimensions of personality, or both. In the criterion-group approach, test designers choose items to distinguish a group of individuals with certain characteristics, the *criterion group*, from a control group; the factor analytic approach uses the statistical technique of factor analysis to determine the meaning of test items.

## Criterion-Group Strategy

The criterion-group strategy begins with a criterion group, or a collection of individuals who share a characteristic such as leadership or schizophrenia. Test constructors select and administer a group of items to all the people in this criterion group as well as to a control group that represents the general population. Constructors then attempt to locate items that distinguish the criterion and control groups, or how the two groups *contrast.*

Suppose that a group of aggressive individuals mark "True" to items such as "I am not aggressive," "I like to attend concerts," and "I would rather read than write" significantly more often than did individuals in a control group. These items could then be included on an aggression scale. When new subjects endorse a large proportion of items on the aggression scale, one may hypothesize that they are aggressive because they endorsed the same items that distinguished aggressive individuals from control individuals. The content of the items is of little consequence. What matters is that aggressive individuals marked "True" to these items, thereby discriminating the aggressive individuals from the control group. As J. S. Wiggins (1973, p. 394) noted, depressed individuals respond "False" significantly more than controls do to the statement "I sometimes tease animals." There is no logical or rational reason for this response. The actual content or face validity of an item in the criterion-group strategy is of little importance. Instead, the approach attempts to determine which items discriminate the criterion and control groups.

Once distinguishing items have been determined for one sample of subjects to represent the criterion group, the next step is to *cross-validate* the scale by checking how well it distinguishes an independent criterion sample—individuals also known to possess the characteristics to be measured—from a control group. If the scale significantly distinguishes the two groups, then it is said to have been cross-validated. Once a scale has been developed, data from the normal controls can be used to obtain standard scores. One can then determine how far above or below the mean of the normal group each new subject scores in standardized units. Thus, a subject's score on each scale can be converted to percentiles (see Chapter 2).

After a scale has been constructed and cross-validated, the third step in the criterion approach is to conduct additional research to ascertain empirically what it means when subjects endorse a large number of items on a particular scale. An independent group of people who score two standard deviations above the mean on an aggression scale, for example, may be studied intensely to determine how they describe themselves, how others describe them, the characteristics of their family backgrounds, and so on.

## Factor Analytic Strategy

The factor analytic strategy uses factor analysis to derive empirically the basic dimensions of personality. Recall from Chapter 3 that factor analysis boils down or reduces data to a small number of descriptive units or dimensions. A test, for example, may have two scales that correlate highly, such as hostility and aggression. This correlation means that the two overlap in what they measure; that is, they share common variance. Both, for example, may be related to paranoid personality, a problem characterized in part by aggression and hostility. The same test may also have two other scales, suspicion and defensiveness, variables also associated with the paranoid personality. These two scales may correlate not only with each other but also with the hostility and aggression scales. Thus, all four scales may share common variance. If one can show that a substantial proportion of the variability in all four scales is related to some common factor, then a factor analyst could argue that the test actually has only one scale that is related to the paranoid personality.

Factor analysts begin with an empirical database consisting of the intercorrelation of a large number of items or tests. They then factor analyze these intercorrelations, typically to find the minimum number of factors that account for as much of the variability in the data as possible. They then attempt to label these factors by ascertaining what the items related to a particular factor have in common.

## Criteria Used in Selecting Tests for Discussion

There are far too many structured personality tests to discuss them all adequately in a book devoted exclusively to the subject, let alone in a single chapter. (We prefer the term *tests* for general purposes, although for specific procedures other terms such as *inventories, techniques, scales*, and *assessment procedures* are often preferred.) However, all available structured personality tests can be classified according to whether they use one or some combination of the four strategies just discussed: logical-content, theoretical, criterion-group, and factor analytic. The tests in the discussion that follows have been chosen because (1) they illustrate each of the major strategies; (2) they are widely used, as indicated by surveys of psychological test usage in the United States (Lubin, Larson, & Matarazzo, 1984; Watkins, Campbell, Nieberding, & Hallmark, 1995); (3) they interest the research community, as determined by publication in major journals; and (4) they show historical value, as determined by the introduction of new concepts in structured personality testing.

# The Logical-Content Strategy

We begin our discussion with the first personality test ever developed—the Woodworth Personal Data Sheet. We then present other examples of tests based on the logical-content approach.

## Woodworth Personal Data Sheet

The first personality inventory ever, the Woodworth Personal Data Sheet, was developed during World War I and published in its final form after the war (Woodworth, 1920). Its purpose was to identify military recruits who would be likely to break down in combat. The final form of the Woodworth contained 116 questions to which the individual responded "Yes" or "No." The items were selected from lists of known symptoms of emotional disorders and from the questions asked by psychiatrists in their screening interviews. In effect, the scale was a paper-and-pencil psychiatric interview. The Woodworth consisted of questions similar to these: "Do you drink a fifth of whiskey a day?" "Do you wet the bed at night?" "Do you frequently daydream?" "Do you usually feel in good health?" "Do you usually sleep soundly at night?" The Woodworth yielded a single score, providing a global measure of functioning. Only those recruits who reported many symptoms received an interview. In this way, the military could concentrate its efforts on the most likely candidates for rejection.

Although its items were selected through the logical-content approach, the Woodworth had two additional features. First, items endorsed by 25% or more of a normal sample in the scored direction were excluded from the test. This technique tended to reduce the number of *false positives*—that is, subjects identified by the test as risks but who would most likely be cleared in an actual interview. Second, only those symptoms that occurred twice as often in a previously diagnosed neurotic group as in normals were included in the first version of the test.

The success of the Woodworth in solving the problem of mass screening stimulated the development of a host of structured tests aimed at measuring personality characteristics. These tests borrowed items from each other, particularly the Woodworth, and used a variety of methods for clustering and scoring items. However, all of them assumed that test responses had items that could be taken at face value; that is, they assumed the face validity of a test response. If someone marked "No" to "I wet the bed," for example, it was assumed that he or she had not wet the bed.

## Early Multidimensional Logical-Content Scales

Two of the best-known early tests developed with the logical-content strategy were the Bell Adjustment Inventory and the Bernreuter Personality Inventory. The Bell attempted to evaluate the subject's adjustment in a variety of areas such as home life, social life, and emotional functioning. The Bernreuter could be used for subjects as young as age 13 and included items related to six personality traits such as introversion, confidence, and sociability. Each was first published in the 1930s and, in contrast to the Woodworth, produced more than one score. These multidimensional procedures laid a foundation for the many modern tests that yield multiple scores rather than a single overall index.

## Mooney Problem Checklist

Few modern tests rely extensively on the logical-content method of test construction. One of the few such tests still in use is the Mooney Problem Checklist (see Steverink, Veenstra, Oldehinkel, Gans, & Rosmalen, 2011; Woolfson, Taylor, & Mooney, 2011), published in 1950. The Mooney contains a list of problems that recurred in clinical case history data and in the written statements of problems submitted by approximately 4000 high-school students. It resembles the Woodworth in that subjects who check an excessive number of items are considered to have difficulties. The main interpretive procedure is to assume the face validity of a test response. Thus, if a subject checks an item related to finances, then testers assume that the person is having financial difficulties.

## Criticisms of the Logical-Content Approach

Psychologists involved in the development of the Woodworth and the plethora of subsequent tests satisfied an important need. These tests proved extremely useful as screening devices and methods of obtaining information about a person without an extensive interview. Before long, however, the weaknesses of the logical-content strategy became evident.

In assuming that one can interpret test items at face value, the logical content strategy also assumes that the subject takes a normal approach to the test, complies with the instructions, reads each item, and answers as honestly as possible. Even if this were all so, subjects might not be able to evaluate their own behavior objectively in the area covered by the test item (e.g., "I never drink too much alcohol"). And even if subjects can provide accurate self-evaluation, they still may not interpret the test item in the same way as the test constructor or test user, which is also an implicit assumption of the logical content strategy. For example, what does "wet the bed" really mean?

None of these assumptions is necessarily true, and assuming that they are true is certain to produce errors. Indeed, structured personality tests based on the logic of face validity were so sharply criticized that the entire structured approach to personality was all but discarded (Ellis, 1946; Landis, 1936; Landis, Zubin, & Katz, 1935; McNemar & Landis, 1935). It was finally rescued by the introduction of a new conceptualization in personality testing, the empirical criterion-group strategy.

# The Criterion-Group Strategy

Just when the development of an adequate structured personality test seemed nothing more than a pipe dream, the Minnesota Multiphasic Personality Inventory (MMPI) introduced several innovations in the construction of structured personality tests. Though not entirely new, the main idea—assume nothing about the meaning of a subject's response to a test item—was the only way of meeting objections to face validity. Because making assumptions had been the downfall of the logical-content approach, developers of the MMPI argued that the meaning of a test response could be determined only through empirical research. This section discusses the MMPI as well as its most recent offspring, the MMPI-2.

## Minnesota Multiphasic Personality Inventory

The Minnesota Multiphasic Personality Inventory (MMPI and MMPI-2) is a true–false self-report questionnaire. Statements are typically of the self-reference type such as "I like good food" and "I never have trouble falling asleep." Subjects mark "True" or "False" for each statement as it applies to themselves. The heart of the test consists of its validity, clinical, and content scales. The validity scales provide information about the person's approach to testing, such as whether an attempt was made either to "fake bad" by endorsing more items of pathological content than any person's actual problems could justify or to "fake good" by avoiding pathological items. The clinical scales were designed to identify psychological disorders such as depression and schizophrenia. Today, clinicians use formulas, the pattern of scores, codebooks that provide extensive research summaries on the

**FIGURE 16.2** An MMPI profile sheet.
(Reproduced by permission of University of Minnesota Press.)

meaning of test scores, and clinical judgment to assess the meaning of the clinical scales. The content scales consist of groups of items that are empirically related to a specific content area. For example, the anger scale contains references to irritability, hotheadedness, and other symptoms of anger or control problems. Subjects obtain a raw score on each scale based on the number of items they have marked in the scored direction. Raw scores are then converted to $T$ scores, with a mean of 50 and a standard deviation of 10 (see Figure 16.2).

### Purpose

Like the Woodworth, the purpose of the MMPI and MMPI-2 is to assist in distinguishing normal from abnormal groups. Specifically, the test was designed to aid in the diagnosis or assessment of the major psychiatric or psychological disorders. For the most part, it is still used for this purpose. The MMPI requires at least a sixth-grade reading ability; the MMPI-2 requires an eighth-grade reading ability. Administrators must take great care to make sure the individual can read at the appropriate level and has an IQ within normal limits (see Focused Example 16.1).

## Original Development of the Scales

Beginning with a pool of 1000 items selected from a wide variety of sources, including case histories, psychological reports, textbooks, and existing tests, the original authors of the MMPI, S. R. Hathaway, a psychologist, and J. C. McKinley, a physician, selected 504 items judged to be relatively independent of one another. The scales were then determined empirically by presenting the items to criterion and control groups.

The criterion groups used to develop the original MMPI consisted of psychiatric inpatients at the University of Minnesota Hospital. These psychiatric patients were divided into eight groups according to their psychiatric diagnoses. Though the original pool of patients had 800 people, this number was substantially reduced in order to find homogeneous groupings with sufficient agreement on diagnoses. The final eight criterion groups each consisted of approximately 50 patients:

- ▶ *hypochondriacs*—individuals preoccupied with the body and fears of illness;
- ▶ *depressed patients*;
- ▶ *hysterics*—primarily individuals who showed a physical problem with no physi-

---

## 16.1   FOCUSED EXAMPLE

### Reading the MMPI

In one interesting case, a 16-year-old girl was detained by the juvenile court. Her mother had reported her to the police, stating she could not be controlled. A few hours before the girl's preliminary hearing, the judge requested psychological testing to aid in the assessment process. A psychology intern was the only professional staff member available. Though relatively inexperienced with the MMPI, he tried to carry out the judge's orders by administering the test. The intern warned the girl of the validity scales, stating that he could tell if she tried to fake. When presented with the test booklet, the girl groaned and stated, "This test is too hard." The intern assured her not to worry, that there were no right or wrong answers. "Oh, I hope I pass," the girl said. "I'm not good at tests."

Rather than the usual 1 to 2 hours, she took more than 3 hours to complete the MMPI, finishing moments before her court hearing began. The intern immediately scored it and found that she had marked nearly half of the 64 items in the scored direction on the F scale, one of the validity scales containing highly pathological content. Because the average for the general population on this scale is 4 items in the scored direction, with an average of 8 items in the scored direction for adolescents, the girl's endorse-

ment of 30 items indicated she had not taken a normal approach to testing and suggested to the intern that she had "faked bad" by deliberately endorsing pathological items.

In court, the judge asked the intern what the results showed. "I can't tell," said the intern, "because she tried to fake." "Did you fake?" asked the judge. "No sir," said the girl, "I swear I didn't." The judge told her to go back and take the test again.

Irate, the intern again warned the girl not to fake. "Oh, I hope I pass," she moaned. "Just answer truthfully and you'll pass," said the intern. She completed the test, and the intern immediately scored it. The results were almost identical to those for the previous testing. The intern rushed into the testing room and scolded the girl for faking again. "I knew I'd flunk that test," she said. "It was too hard for me." Finally, it dawned on the intern to ask whether she could read the test. A reading test revealed that she could read at only the fourth-grade level. Most of the items were therefore incomprehensible to her. The embarrassed intern was forced to go back into court and explain what had happened. No doubt he never again administered the MMPI without checking the subject's reading level.

cal cause, such as physical pain without cause;

▶ *psychopathic deviates*—delinquent, criminal, or antisocial individuals;

▶ *paranoids*—individuals who showed symptoms such as poor reality testing (e.g., delusions in which they falsely believed that people were plotting against them);

▶ *psychasthenics*—individuals with a disorder characterized by excessive doubts and unreasonable fears;

▶ *schizophrenics*—individuals with a psychotic disorder involving dramatic symptoms (such as hallucinations) and thinking problems (such as illogical reasoning); and

▶ *hypomanics*—individuals with a disorder characterized by hyperactivity and irritability (see Table 16.1).

Those in the criterion groups were then compared with some 700 controls consisting primarily of relatives and visitors of the patients, excluding mental patients, in the University of Minnesota Hospital. The use of this control group was perhaps the original MMPI's greatest source of criticism. There is little basis for saying that the relatives of patients in a large city university hospital are representative of the general population, although the control group was augmented by other subjects such as a group of recent high-school graduates. The MMPI-2, by contrast, has a large and relatively good representative control sample.

Despite its weakness, the original control group did provide a reference sample. After an item analysis was conducted, items that separated the criterion from the control group were included on one or more of the eight scales.

To cross-validate the scales, independent samples of the criterion and control groups were administered the items. To qualify as cross-validated, a scale had to

**TABLE 16.1**  Original Criterion Groups for the MMPI

| | |
|---|---|
| Hypochondriacs | Patients who suffer from overconcern of bodily symptoms and express conflicts through bodily (somatic) symptoms |
| Depressives | Patients with depressed mood, loss of appetite, loss of interest, suicidal thoughts, and other depressive symptoms |
| Hysterics | Immature individuals who overdramatize their plight and may exhibit physical symptoms for which no physical cause exists |
| Psychopathic deviates | Individuals who are antisocial and rebellious and exploit others without remorse or anxiety |
| Paranoids | Individuals who show extreme suspicions, hypersensitivity, and delusions |
| Psychasthenics | Individuals plagued by excessive self-doubts, obsessive thoughts, anxiety, and low energy |
| Schizophrenics | Disorganized, highly disturbed individuals out of contact with reality and having difficulties with communication, interpersonal relations, sensory abnormalities (e.g., hallucinations), or motor abnormalities (e.g., catatonia) |
| Hypomanics | Individuals in a high-energy, agitated state with poor impulse control, inability to sleep, and poor judgment |

distinguish the criterion group from the control group at the .05 level of significance (i.e., the probability of obtaining differences by chance is less than 5 out of 100).

In addition to the eight scales just described, two content scales were added: the masculinity-femininity (MF) scale, which contained items differentially endorsed by men and women, and the social-introversion (Si) scale, which measures introversion and extroversion (L. C. Ward & Perry, 1998). These two scales plus the eight scales already described constitute the original 10 clinical scales of the MMPI.

Because the logical-content approach had been criticized for its many assumptions, Hathaway and McKinley developed special scales called *validity scales* to measure test-taking attitude and to assess whether the subject took a normal, honest approach to the test (see Table 16.2). The L, or lie, scale was designed to detect individuals who attempted to present themselves in an overly favorable way.

The K scale served the same purpose but was empirically constructed. In deriving the K scale, Hathaway and McKinley compared the MMPI scores of nondisturbed individuals showing normal patterns with the MMPI scores of disturbed individuals who produced normal MMPI patterns—that is, they showed no scales that deviated significantly from the mean. The K scale thus attempts to locate those items that distinguished normal from abnormal groups when both groups produced a normal test pattern. It was assumed that pathological groups would produce normal patterns because of defensiveness, a tendency to hide or deny psychological problems, and that this defensiveness could be determined by comparing these individuals to nondisturbed normals.

The F or infrequency scale, which is designed to detect individuals who attempt to fake bad, consists of those items endorsed by less than 10% of the control group. Of the 64 items on the F scale, most of which contain pathological content such as "Odd odors come to me at times," the average number of items endorsed in the scored direction is four. Anyone who marks a lot of these items is taking an unusual approach to the test. Thus, high F scores bring the validity of the whole profile into question (Shores & Carstairs, 1998).

---

**TABLE 16.2**  Original Validity Scales of the MMPI

| | |
|---|---|
| **Lie scale (L)** | Fifteen rationally derived items included in both the MMPI and MMPI-2 designed to evaluate a naive attempt to present oneself in a favorable light. The items reflect personal weaknesses, such as "I never lose control of myself when I drive." Most people are willing to admit to these weaknesses. People who score high on this scale are unwilling to acknowledge minor flaws. |
| **Infrequency scale (F)** | Of the original 64 items from the MMPI developed to detect deviant response patterns, 60 were retained for the MMPI-2. These are items that are scored infrequently (less than 10%) by the normal population. The F scale contains items such as "I am aware of a special presence that others cannot perceive." High scores on the F scale invalidate the profile. |
| **K scale** | Thirty items included on both the MMPI and MMPI-2 that detect attempts to deny problems and present oneself in a favorable light. People who score high on this scale are attempting to project an image of self-control and personal effectiveness. Extremely high scores on this scale invalidate the profile. |

Finally, although it is referred to as a validity scale, the "cannot say" scale consists simply of the items to which the subject failed to respond either "True" or "False." If as few as 10% of the items are omitted, then the entire profile is invalid.

## Initial Interpretations

For all of the scales, the control group provided the reference for which standard scores were determined. McCall's *T*, with a mean of 50 and a standard deviation of 10, was used to compute standard scores. Subjects with *T* scores of 50 were thus at the mean of the control sample for any given scale. *T* scores of 70, two standard deviations above the mean, were considered significantly elevated for the MMPI. With the new norms for the MMPI-2, *T* scores of 65 are now considered significant.

The original approach taken to interpret the MMPI was simple and straightforward. Because the scales significantly discriminated the criterion groups from control groups and withstood the test of cross-validation, most users assumed that individuals with characteristics similar to those of a criterion group would have significant elevation on the appropriate scale. Schizophrenics, for example, would show significant elevation on the schizophrenia scale, hysterics would show elevation on the hysteria scale, and so on. Unfortunately, this assumption turned out to be false. Experience with the MMPI rapidly revealed that only a relatively small number of disturbed subjects showed elevation on only a single scale. More often, elevation was found in two, three, four, or even all of the scales. Thus, a problem had arisen: What did the test mean when someone showed elevation on the hysteria, psychopathic deviate, schizophrenia, and hypomania scales? There is no such thing as a hysterical psychopathic hypomanic schizophrenic!

To deal with multiple-scale elevations, clinicians made use of pattern (configural) analysis, which the test authors had originally suggested (Hathaway & McKinley, 1943). This change led to an avalanche of studies and proposals for identifying clinical groups on the basis of patterns of MMPI scores (e.g., Meehl & Dahlstrom, 1960). However, early investigations soon revealed the futility of this approach (Garfield & Sineps, 1959; Loy, 1959; Meikle & Gerritse, 1970). Either the rules were so complex that only an extremely small portion of the profiles met the criteria, such as the Gilberstadt and Duker (1965) rules, or the rules led to diagnoses that were no more accurate than those made by untrained nonprofessionals (Meehl, 1954, 1956, 1957; Meehl & Rosen, 1955). Led by Meehl, clinicians began to look at the two highest scales.

## Meehl's Extension of the Empirical Approach

Pointing to the possible advantages of analyzing the two highest scales, or *two-point code*, Meehl (1951) emphasized the importance of conducting research on individuals who showed specific two-point codes and other configural patterns. This way, developers could empirically determine the meaning of MMPI elevations. Thus, the validity of the MMPI was extended by finding homogeneous profile patterns and determining the characteristics of individuals who show these patterns. In other words, new criterion groups were established of individuals grouped on the basis of similarities in their MMPI profiles. In this approach, the characteristics of a criterion group, consisting of subjects who showed elevation on two scales (e.g., the psychopathic deviate and hypomania scales), could be empirically determined. The difference in approach meant that MMPI configural patterns, rather than psychiatric diagnosis, became the criterion for the selection of homogeneous criterion groups.

Because the original idea of the contrasted-group method was extended by the use of criterion groups, we use the term *criterion-group strategy* rather than *contrasted-group strategy* to describe the MMPI and related tests. The most recent approach does not attempt to distinguish the criterion group from a control group. Instead, the characteristics of the criterion groups are evaluated through empirical means such as peer ratings, physician ratings, and demographic characteristics. The upshot has been numerous studies that describe the characteristics of individuals who show specific MMPI patterns (Archer, Hagan, Mason, Handel, & Archer, 2011; Demir, Batur, Mercan, & Ulug, 2002; Heinze & Purisch, 2001; McGrath, Sweeney, O'Malley, & Carlton, 1998; Pintor & Bailles, 2005; Wolf, 2007).

Along with an empirical approach, Meehl and others began to advocate a change in the names of the clinical scales. Because elevation on the schizophrenia scale did not necessarily mean the person was schizophrenic, the use of such a name was awkward as well as confusing. Meehl and others therefore suggested that the scales be identified by number rather than by name. Table 16.3 lists the scales by their number. The validity scales retained their original names.

**TABLE 16.3**   Original MMPI Scales

| Symbol currently in use | Old name | Number of items in scale* | Common interpretation of elevation |
|---|---|---|---|
| Validity Scales | | | |
| L | Lie scale | 13 | Naive attempt to fake good |
| K | K scale | 30 | Defensiveness |
| F | F scale | 64 | Attempt to fake bad |
| Clinical Scales | | | |
| 1 | Hypochondriasis | 33 | Physical complaints |
| 2 | Depression | 60 | Depression |
| 3 | Hysteria | 60 | Immaturity |
| 4 | Psychopathic deviate | 50 | Authority conflict |
| 5 | Masculinity–femininity | 60 | Masculine or feminine interests |
| 6 | Paranoia | 40 | Suspicion, hostility |
| 7 | Psychasthenia | 48 | Anxiety |
| 8 | Schizophrenia | 78 | Alienation, withdrawal |
| 9 | Hypomania | 46 | Elated mood, high energy |
| 0 | Social introversion | 70 | Introversion, shyness |

*Because of item overlap, the total number of items here is 654.
*Note:* The validity scales (L, K, and F) determine the individual's approach to testing (normal or honest, fake bad, or fake good). Of the 10 clinical scales, two were developed rationally (5 and 0). The remaining eight scales were developed through the criterion-group method. Numerous interpretive hypotheses can be associated with each MMPI scale; however, the meaning of any MMPI scale depends on the characteristics of the subject (age, race, sex, socioeconomic status, education, IQ, and so forth).

At this point, MMPI patterns could have a numerical code. For each of the two most commonly used coding systems, the clinical scales are listed in rank order from highest $T$ score to lowest. A symbol indicates the level of elevation. In Welsh's (1948) well-established system, for example, $T$ scores of 90 (four standard deviations above the mean) and greater are designated by *; $T$ scores between 80 and 89 are designated by "; $T$ scores between 70 and 79, by '; $T$ scores between 60 and 69, by −; and so on for each 10-point interval down to # placed to the right of $T$ scores below 29. For example, the code 13* 2" 7' 456890− means that Scales 1 and 3 have $T$ scores above 90, Scale 2 above 80, Scale 7 above 70, and the remaining scales between 60 and 69. This pattern is referred to as a one-three two-point pattern or, more simply, a *13 code*, based on the two highest scales.

## The Restandardization: MMPI-2

Beginning in 1982, a major effort was made to update and restandardize the MMPI. The result was the MMPI-2 (Butcher, Graham, Dahlstrom, Tellegen, & Kaernmer, 1989). The purpose of the revision was to update and expand the norms; revise items that were out of date, awkward, sexist, or problematic; and broaden the item pool to extend the range of constructs that one could evaluate. At the same time, developers strove to retain all the features of the original MMPI, including the original validity and clinical scales (Rogers, Sewell, Harrison, & Jordan, 2006). Finally, they wanted to develop a separate form for adolescents. Each of these goals was well accomplished (see Figure 16.3).

The original MMPI contained 550 items, with 16 items repeated on the back of the scoring sheets for convenience of scoring, for a total of 566 items. The MMPI-2 has 567 items. Changes included dropping the 16 repeated items, dropping 13 items from the clinical scales, and dropping 77 items from the range 399 and 550, leaving 460 items from the original test. Then 81 items were added for the new content scales, two items were added to pick up severe pathology (critical items), and 24 unscored items were added for experimental purposes, for a total of 567. An additional 68 items were rewritten with no change in meaning (Ben-Porath & Butcher, 1989). Reasons for rewriting items included outdated language (24), sexist language (11), awkward language (6), and minor changes or simplifications (33).

Interpretation of the clinical scales remained the same because not more than four items were dropped from any scale, and the scales were renormed and scores transformed to uniform $T$ scores. On the original MMPI, more people were scoring above a $T$ score of 70 than a normal distribution would predict, and the scales were not uniform. To maintain consistency with previous research and interpretation, the cutting score was lowered to 65. With uniform $T$ scores, the distribution is the same on all scores, with 8% scoring above 65, and 4% above 70.

In developing new norms, the MMPI project committee (James Butcher of the University of Minnesota, Grant Dahlstrom of the University of North Carolina, Jack Graham of Kent State University, and Auke Tellegen of the University of Minnesota) selected 2900 subjects from seven geographic areas of the United States: California, Minnesota, North Carolina, Ohio, Pennsylvania, Virginia, and Washington. Of these, 300 were eliminated because of incomplete or invalid profiles, resulting in a final sample of 2600 men and women. Potential subjects for the restandardization were initially identified by telephone and then contacted by letter. Testing centers were set up in major cities to make personal contact and

**FIGURE 16.3** An MMPI-2 profile sheet.
(Reproduced by permission of University of Minnesota Press.)

arrange for the testing. The goal was to obtain a sample that reflected the demographics of the 1980 census. However, because participation was completely voluntary, the final sample was more educated and had greater economic means than the general population.

A major feature of the MMPI-2 is the inclusion of additional validity scales. On the original MMPI, all of the F items are in the first 370 items and appear on the front of the answer sheet. The MMPI-2 expanded the F scale to the back of the scoring sheet as well. The FB (Back F) score provides a check on validity and cooperation throughout the test and permits a confirmation of F scores obtained in the first half of the test. Two additional validity scales, the Variable Response Inconsistency Scale (VRIN) and the True Response Inconsistency Scale (TRIN), are included to evaluate response styles (see Baer & Sekirnjak, 1997). The VRIN attempts to evaluate random responding. The scale consists of matched pairs of items that have similar content. Each time the pairs are marked in opposite directions, a point is scored on the scale. The TRIN attempts to measure **acquiescence**—the tendency to agree or mark "True" regardless of content (Handel, Arnau, Archer, & Dandy, 2006). This scale consists of matched pairs of items with opposite content. For example, to receive a point on the TRIN Scale, the person might mark "True" to both "I feel good" and "I feel bad."

There are 154 items on the MMPI-2 that permit the evaluation of various content areas (Arita & Baer, 1998; Strassberg, 1997). The MMPI-2 contains 15 content scales, including HEA (health concerns) and TPA, which evaluates for the hard-driving, irritable, impatient Type A personality. Other MMPI-2 content scales include FAM (family problems), which evaluates family disorders and possible child abuse, and WRK (work interference), which examines behaviors or attitudes likely to interfere with work performance.

## Psychometric Properties

The psychometric properties of the MMPI and MMPI-2 are comparable (Gaston, Nelson, Hart, Quatman, et al., 1994); the newer version maintains strong continuity with the original. For example, the factor structures of the new and original versions are quite similar.

Median split-half reliability coefficients for both the original MMPI and the MMPI-2 run in the .70's, with some coefficients as high as .96 but others much lower. Median test–retest coefficients range from the low .50's to the low .90's (median .80's). Although these coefficients are not as solid as those for the major ability tests such as the Binet and Wechsler, they are as high as or better than those reported in comparable tests. Moreover, when one looks at the basic higher-order factor structure, the MMPI and MMPI-2 are extremely reliable, with coefficients running in the high .90's.

Although the reliability of the MMPI is generally adequate, developers have not yet dealt with some notable problems. For example, because of the way scales were originally constructed, many items are on more than one scale, with some items on as many as six. Scale 8, which has more items than any other scale, contains only 16 unique items. This problem of item overlap was not confronted in the MMPI-2 revision because the goal was to retain all the original scales.

Perhaps as a result of item overlap, intercorrelations among the clinical scales are extremely high. For example, Scales 7 and 8 correlate between .64 and .87, depending on the sample studied (Butcher et al., 1989; Dahlstrom & Welsh, 1960). This high intercorrelation among the scales has led to several factor analytic studies (Johnson, Null, Butcher, & Johnson, 1984), which consistently show that two factors account for most of the variance in the original MMPI scales. These factors have been variously labeled throughout the literature (for instance, as negative or positive affectivity). Because of the high intercorrelations among the scales and the results of factor analytic studies, the validity of pattern analysis has often been questioned (Nichols & Greene, 1997).

Another problem with the MMPI and MMPI-2 is the imbalance in the way items are keyed. Many individuals approach structured tests with a **response style**, or bias, which is a tendency to mark an item in a certain way regardless of content. One of these tendencies, as you have seen, is acquiescence. Given the possibility of response tendencies, one would expect an equal number of items keyed true and keyed false. Not so: all of the items on the L scale and 29 of the 30 items on the K scale are keyed false. Scales 7, 8, and 9 are keyed on a 3:1 true–false ratio. The VRIN and TRIN scales of the MMPI-2 allow the examiner to evaluate response tendencies and represent a clear positive step toward overcoming this imbalance.

Major works devoted to the MMPI and MMPI-2 strongly emphasize the importance of taking into account the subject's demographic characteristics when interpreting profiles (Butcher, 1990; Butcher, Graham, Williams, & Ben-Porath, 1990; Nelson, Novy, Averill, & Berry, 1996). This advice is indeed warranted in that most of the studies have shown that age (Butcher, Aidwin, Levenson, & Ben-Porath, 1991; Osberg & Poland, 2002), gender (Butcher et al., 1989), race (Butcher, 1990), place of residence (Erdberg, 1969), and other demographic factors such as intelligence, education, and socioeconomic status (Butcher, 1990) are all related to the MMPI and MMPI-2 scales (Slatkoff, 2007). This overwhelming evidence supporting the covariation between demographic factors and the meaning of MMPI and MMPI-2 scores clearly shows that two exact profile patterns can have quite different meanings, depending on the demographic characteristics of each subject. Despite these differences in interpretation, some evidence suggests that the MMPI-2 predicts equally well for at least whites and African Americans (Arbisi, Ben-Porath, & McNulty, 2002; Stewart, 2007; Timbrook & Graham, 1994).

The major source of validity for the MMPI and MMPI-2 comes from the many research studies that describe the characteristics of particular profile patterns. Tens of thousands of studies have been conducted, with the number of new studies increasing every year (Groth-Marnat, 1999). In fact, our survey of the relevant literature between 1999 and 2004 revealed more citations for the MMPI and MMPI-2 than for any other personality test. This trend continues; in the year 2011, it was the subject of 12% of all cited research on personality tests. In comparison, the Woodworth Personal Data Sheet was the subject of less than 1%, and the Mooney Problem Checklist was 2% of cited research. This body of research provides ample evidence for the construct validity of the MMPI and MMPI-2. Many studies, for example, have related MMPI response patterns to alcoholism and substance abuse (Egger et al., 2007; Gallucci, 1997; Galli, Pozzi, & Frustaci, et al., 2011; Guan, Tang, Xue, & Zhou, 2002; McMahon, Davidson, Gersh, & Flynn, 1991). For instance, evidence indicates that the MMPI and MMPI-2 might help detect individuals who might later become alcoholics (Hoffman, Loper, & Kammeier, 1974; Kammeier, Hoffman, & Loper, 1973; Malinchoc, Oxford, Colligan, & Morse, 1994). The items of the original MMPI were administered to a group of men while they were still in college. The response patterns of those individuals who later became alcoholics were compared with those of a control group who did not become alcoholics. Results showed that the subjects who eventually became alcoholics had significantly higher scores on one validity scale (F) and two clinical scales (4 and 9). Thus, these scales may be related to characteristics that contribute to alcoholism in men. Interestingly, the response pattern of those in the alcoholic group was the same as their retest pattern after they had become alcoholics.

Indeed, the range of problems that the MMPI and MMPI-2 can help with spans everything from eating disorders (Berg, Peterson, Frazier, & Crow, 2011; Exterkate, Bakker-Brehm, & de-Jong, 2007; Gleaves, May, & Eberenz, 1996; Strassberg, Ross, & Todt, 1995), soldiers' reaction in battle (Leach, 2002), posttraumatic stress syndrome (Gaston, Brunet, Koszychi, & Bradwejn, 1996; Glenn, Beckham, Sampson, Feldman, Hertzberg, & Moore, 2002; Pupo, Jorge, & Schoedl, et al., 2011), the detection of sexual abuse in children (Holifield, Nelson, & Hart, 2002), the characteristics of child sexual abusers (Sullivan, Beech, Leam, & Gannon, 2011), risk factors of female criminals (Lui et al., 2002), the effects of acculturation

(Kwon, 2002), differentiating criminal types (Glaser, Calhoun, & Petrocelli, 2002), and prediction of delinquent behavior (Cumella & O'Connor, 2009) to prediction of probability of dropout from cognitive behavioral therapy for PTSD (Garcia, Kelley, Rentz, & Lee, 2011) and prediction of psychosis (Miettunen, Veijola, & Isohanni, et al., 2011). Of course, not all MMPI studies report positive results (Levenson, Olkin, Herzoff, & DeLancy, 1986), but the vast majority attest to its utility and versatility (Harkness, McNulty, & Ben-Porath, 1995; Iverson, Franzen, & Hammond, 1995). This large database and sound construction explain in part why the MMPI is accepted as evidence in the judicial system (Saccuzzo, 1999).

The effectiveness of the MMPI as a tool in treatment has also been established. Using the MMPI, psychologists can now conduct integrated assessments that take the complexities of an individual's personality into account, serve as the basis for developing an effective treatment plan, and facilitate meaningful reporting and client feedback (Harwood, Beutler, & Groth-Marnat, 2011). Another study provided further insight into the value of the MMPI-2 in assessing clients with chronic personality disorders in long-term psychotherapy and using the results for providing feedback to patients (Finn, 2011). Results in therapy were improved with the repeated use of the MMPI-2 in incorporating feedback in treatment.

### Current Status

The restandardization of the MMPI has eliminated the most serious drawback of the original version: the inadequate control group. With its already widespread use and acceptance, the future of the MMPI appears extremely bright. A new set of clinical scales (MMPI-2 Restructured Clinical Scales) was introduced in 2003 and includes contemporary norms, additional content domains, and a revision of items that eliminates sexist content and dated references (Tellegen, 2003). The addition of new items is sure to generate many new applications. Furthermore, the newer items can be added to the original scales when appropriate to increase their reliability as well as their predictive validity. Indeed, the MMPI and MMPI-2 are without question the leading personality test of the 21st century.

## California Psychological Inventory (CPI)–Third Edition

The CPI (Gough, 1987) is a second example of a structured personality test constructed primarily by the criterion-group strategy. For three of the 36 CPI scales in the most recent revision, criterion groups (e.g., men versus women; homosexual men versus heterosexual men) were contrasted to produce measures of personality categorized as (1) introversion–extroversion, (2) conventional versus unconventional in following norms, and (3) self-realization and sense of integration.

In contrast to the MMPI and MMPI-2, the CPI attempts to evaluate personality in normally adjusted individuals and thus finds more use in counseling settings. The test contains 20 scales, each of which is grouped into one of four classes. Class I scales measure poise, self-assurance, and interpersonal effectiveness. Individuals who score high on these scales tend to be active, resourceful, competitive, outgoing, spontaneous, and self-confident. They are also at ease in interpersonal situations. Individuals who score high on Class II scales, which evaluate socialization, maturity, and responsibility, tend to be conscientious, honest, dependable, calm, practical, cooperative, and alert to ethical and moral issues. Class III scales measure achievement potential and intellectual efficiency. High scores in this class tend to indicate organized, efficient, sincere, mature, forceful, capable, and well-informed people. Class IV scales examine interest modes. High scorers tend to respond well to the inner needs of others and adapt well socially.

In addition, the CPI also includes 13 scales that are designed for special purposes such as managerial potential, tough-mindedness, and creativity as well as several experimental scales evaluating dimensions of operating style (Gough, 1996).

More than a third of the 434 items are almost identical to items in the original MMPI, and many others resemble them. However, the test does more than share items with the MMPI. Like the MMPI, the CPI shows considerable intercorrelation among its scales. Factor analytic studies have shown that only two factors in the CPI, associated with internal controls (Class II scales) and interpersonal effectiveness (Class I scales), account for a large part of the variance (Megargee, 1972). Also like the MMPI, true–false scale keying is often extremely unbalanced. Reliability coefficients are similar to those reported for the MMPI. Short-term test–retest coefficients range from .49 to .90, depending on the sample; long-term coefficients range from .38 to .77. However, the method used to establish some of the criterion groups for the CPI has been questioned. For example, for some of the scales, subjects were placed in criterion groups on the basis of ratings by friends. Nevertheless, one must consider the psychometric properties of the CPI adequate by today's standards because they are comparable to those of most widely used personality tests.

The CPI is commonly used in research settings to examine everything from typologies of sexual offenders (Burtona, Dutyb, & Leibowitzc, 2011; Worling, 2001) to personnel choices (Doherty & Nugent, 2011; Dantzker, 2011). The advantage of the CPI is that it can be used with normal subjects. The MMPI and MMPI-2 generally do not apply to normal subjects, and the meaning of nonelevated profiles is not well established. Therefore, if one intends to assess normal individuals for interpersonal effectiveness and internal controls, then the CPI is a good candidate for the measure. Furthermore, as with the MMPI and MMPI-2, a considerable body of literature has focused on the CPI. Each new piece of literature extends the utility of the test and adds to its construct validity. Therefore, the future of the CPI as a measure of normal personalities has good potential despite its limitations (Bolton, 1992; Groth-Marnat, 1999).

# The Factor Analytic Strategy

Structured personality tests, as they exist today, share one common set of assumptions. These assumptions, simply stated, are that humans possess characteristics or traits that are stable, vary from individual to individual, and can be measured. Nowhere are these assumptions better illustrated than in the factor analytic strategy of test construction.

Recall that factor analysis is a statistical procedure for reducing the redundancy in a set of intercorrelated scores. For example, one major technique of factor analysis, the principal-components method (Bentler & de Leeuw, 2011), finds the minimum number of common factors that can account for an interrelated set of scores. As noted in the previous section, two factors can account for most of the variance in both the CPI and the MMPI, which suggests that these tests are actually measuring only two unique components and that all scales are related to these two components.

The advantages of factor analysis are quite evident. However, before computers, even simple factor analyses required several weeks or even months of tedious arithmetic operations on a hand calculator. Therefore, the development of the factor analytic strategy awaited computer technology. R. B. Cattell has particularly distinguished himself in using the factor analytic strategy of structured personality assessment; this section focuses largely on his work.

## Guilford's Pioneer Efforts

One usual strategy in validating a new test is to correlate the scores on the new test with the scores on other tests that purport to measure the same entity. J. R. Guilford's approach was related to this procedure. However, instead of comparing one test at a time to a series of other tests, Guilford and his associates determined the interrelationship (intercorrelation) of a wide variety of tests and then factor analyzed the results in an effort to find the main dimensions underlying all personality tests. If the results from existing personality tests could be reduced to a few factors, then items that correlated highly with these factors could be used in a new test, which would therefore capture the major dimensions of personality.

The result of the initial attempt to apply this strategy was a series of inventories that Guilford and his associates published in the 1940s and which were ultimately collapsed into a single scale—the Guilford-Zimmerman Temperament Survey (Guilford & Zimmerman, 1956).

This survey reduces personality to 10 dimensions, each of which is measured by 30 different items. The 10 dimensions are general activity, restraint, ascendance (leadership), sociability, emotional stability, objectivity, friendliness, thoughtfulness, personal relations, and masculinity. The test presents a list of statements, most of which are self-statements as in the MMPI and MMPI-2. The subject must indicate "Yes" or "No" for each statement. Three verification keys are included to detect falsification and to evaluate the validity of the profile. However, this first major factor analytic structured personality test failed to catch on, perhaps because it was overshadowed by the MMPI and because of its arbitrary, subjective way of naming factors. Today, the Guilford-Zimmerman Temperament Survey primarily serves only historical interests.

## Cattell's Contribution

Rather than attempting to uncover the major dimensions of personality by intercorrelating personality tests, R. B. Cattell began with all the adjectives applicable to human beings so he could empirically determine and measure the essence of personality. Beginning with a monumental catalog of all the adjectives (trait names) in an unabridged dictionary that apply to humans, Allport and Odbert (1936) reduced their list to 4504 "real" traits. Adding to the list traits found in the psychological and psychiatric literature, Cattell then reduced the list to 171 items that he believed accounted for the meaning of all items on the original list. College students then rated their friends on these 171 terms, and the results were intercorrelated and factor analyzed. The 171 terms were reduced to 36 dimensions, called *surface traits*. Subsequent investigation by factor analysis finally produced 16 distinct factors that accounted for all the variables. Thus, Cattell had reduced personality to 16 basic dimensions, which he called *source traits* (see Table 16.4).

**TABLE 16.4**  The Primary Source Traits Covered by the 16PF Test

| Factor | Low Sten score description (1–3) | High Sten score description (8–10) |
|---|---|---|
| A | *Cool,* reserved, impersonal, detached, formal, aloof<br>Sizothymia* | *Warm,* outgoing, kindly, easygoing, participating, likes people<br>Affectothymia |
| B | *Concrete-thinking,* less intelligent<br>Lower scholastic mental capacity | *Abstract-thinking,* more intelligent, bright<br>Higher scholastic mental capacity |
| C | *Affected by feelings,* emotionally less stable, easily annoyed<br>Lower ego strength | *Emotionally stable,* mature, faces reality, calm<br>Higher ego strength |
| E | *Submissive,* humble, mild, easily led, accommodating<br>Submissiveness | *Dominant,* assertive, aggressive, stubborn, competitive, bossy<br>Dominance |
| F | *Sober,* restrained, prudent, taciturn, serious<br>Desurgency | *Enthusiastic,* spontaneous, heedless, expressive, cheerful<br>Surgency |
| G | *Expedient,* disregards rules, self-indulgent<br><br>Weaker superego strength | *Conscientious,* conforming, moralistic, staid, rule-bound<br>Stronger superego strength |
| H | *Shy,* threat-sensitive, timid, hesitant, intimidated<br>Threctia | *Bold,* venturesome, uninhibited, can take stress<br>Parmia |
| I | *Tough-minded,* self-reliant, no-nonsense, rough, realistic<br>Harria | *Tender-minded,* sensitive, overprotected, intuitive, refined<br>Premsia |
| L | *Trusting,* accepting conditions, easy to get on with<br>Alaxia | *Suspicious,* hard to fool, distrustful, skeptical<br>Protension |
| M | *Practical,* concerned with "down-to-earth" issues, steady<br>Praxernia | *Imaginative,* absent-minded, absorbed in thought, impractical<br>Autia |
| N | *Forthright,* unpretentious, open, genuine, artless<br><br>Artlessness | *Shrewd,* polished, socially aware, diplomatic, calculating<br>Shrewdness |
| O | *Self-assured,* secure, feels free of guilt, untroubled, self-satisfied<br>Untroubled adequacy | *Apprehensive,* self-blaming, guilt-prone, insecure, worrying<br>Guilt proneness |
| Q1 | *Conservative,* respecting traditional ideas<br>Conservatism of temperament | *Experimenting,* liberal, critical, open to change<br>Radicalism |
| Q2 | *Group-oriented,* a "joiner" and sound follower, listens to others<br>Group adherence | *Self-sufficient,* resourceful, prefers own decisions<br>Self-sufficiency |
| Q3 | *Undisciplined self-conflict,* lax, careless of social rules<br>Low integration | *Following self-image,* socially precise, compulsive<br>High self-concept control |
| Q4 | *Relaxed,* tranquil, composed, has low drive, unfrustrated<br>Low ergic tension | *Tense,* frustrated, overwrought, has high drive<br>High ergic tension |

*Titles in roman type are the technical names for the factors and are explained more fully in the *Handbook.*

(From the *Administrator's Manual for the Sixteen Personality Factor Questionnaire.* Copyright © 1972, 1979, 1986 by the Institute for Personality and Ability Testing, Inc. Reproduced by permission.)

The product of Cattell's marathon task was the Sixteen Personality Factor Questionnaire, better known as the 16PF (Schuerger, 1995), which was subsequently revised following continued factor analysis. Consistent with the factor analytic strategy, items that correlated highly with each of the 16 major factors, or source traits, were included, and those with relatively low correlations were excluded.

Developers took great care in standardizing the 16PF. Separate norms were provided for men alone, women alone, and men and women combined for each of three U.S. groups: adults, college students, and high-school seniors. Thus, nine sets of norms are available. To deal further with the covariation of structured personality-test data and demographic variables that plagues the MMPI, the 16PF provides age corrections for those scales that change significantly with age. Six forms of the test are available: two parallel forms for each of three levels of vocabulary proficiency, ranging from newspaper-literate adults through the educationally disadvantaged. For the latter, a tape-recorded (oral) form is also available. Norms for the various forms are based on more than 15,000 subjects representative of geographic area, population density, age, family income, and race according to figures provided by the U.S. census. Unlike the MMPI and CPI, the 16PF contains no item overlap, and keying is balanced among the various alternative responses. Short-term test–retest correlation coefficients for the 16 source traits are impressive, with a range of .65 to .93 and a median coefficient of .83. Long-term test–retest coefficients, however, are not so impressive (.21 to .64), and most such coefficients reported in the literature are lower than those reported for the MMPI and MMPI-2 (Schuerger, Tait, & Tavernelli, 1982). Also a bit disappointing are the correlations between the various forms, which range from a low of .16 to a high of .79, with median coefficients in the .50's and .60's, depending on which forms are correlated. Moreover, despite the method used for deriving the factors, the 16 source traits of the 16PF do intercorrelate, with some correlations as high as .75 (R. B. Cattell, Eber, & Tatsuoka, 1970). To deal with this overlap, the 16 factors themselves were factor analyzed, resulting in four second-order factors, for which one can obtain scores.

Other important features of the test are its provision of a parallel inventory for ages 12 to 18, the Junior Senior High School Personality Questionnaire, and still another parallel extension for use with ages 8 to 12, the Children's Personality Questionnaire. Cross-cultural studies have been conducted in Western Europe, Eastern Europe, the Middle East, Australia, Canada (Schuerger, 1995), and Korea (Sohn, 2002). To extend the test to the assessment of clinical populations, items related to psychological disorders have been factor analyzed, resulting in 12 new factors in addition to the 16 needed to measure normal personalities. These new factors were then used to construct a clinical instrument, the Clinical Analysis Questionnaire (CAQ) (Delhees & Cattell, 1971).

Despite the care that has gone into the 16PF, its research base and use pale when compared with those of the MMPI and MMPI-2. The fact is, neither clinicians nor researchers have found the 16PF to be as useful as the MMPI. Moreover, the claims of the 16PF to have identified the basic source traits of the personality are simply not true. However, various research investigations have supported the validity of Cattell's personality test (see Meyer, 1993).

Factor analysis is one of many ways of constructing tests. It will identify only those traits about which questions are asked, however, and it has no more claim to uniqueness than any other method. Even so, the 16PF remains an exemplary illustration of the factor analytic approach to structured personality testing.

## Problems with the Factor Analytic Strategy

One major criticism of factor analytic approaches centers on the subjective nature of naming factors. To understand this problem, one must understand that each score on any given set of tests or variables can be broken down into three components: common variance, unique variance, and error variance. *Common variance* is the amount of variance a particular variable holds in common with other variables. It results from the overlap of what two or more variables are measuring. *Unique variance* refers to factors uniquely measured by the variable. In other words, it refers to some construct measured *only* by the variable in question. *Error variance* is variance attributable to error.

Factor analytic procedures generally identify sources of common variance at the expense of unique variance. Thus, important factors may be overlooked when the data are categorized solely on the basis of blind groupings by computers. Furthermore, all the computer can do is identify the groupings. The factor analyst must determine which factors these groupings measure, but no definite criteria or rules exist for naming factors. If five items such as *daring, outgoing, determined, excitable,* and *fearless* load high on a factor, then what should one call this factor? In factor analysis, one name for this factor has about as much validity as any other.

# The Theoretical Strategy

To avoid the potential disagreement and biases that stem from factor analytic approaches, developers have proposed using theory as a way to guide the construction of structured personality tests. In this approach, items are selected to measure the variables or constructs specified by a major theory of personality. After the items have been selected and grouped into scales, construct-related evidence for validity is sought. In other words, predictions are made about the nature of the scale; if the predictions hold up, then the scale is supported.

## Edwards Personal Preference Schedule (EPPS)

One of the best-known and earliest examples of a theoretically derived structured personality test is the EPPS (Edwards, 1954, 1959). According to Edwards, the EPPS is not actually a test in the strictest sense of the word because there are no right or wrong answers. At one time, the EPPS was used widely in counseling centers (Lubin, Wallis, & Paine, 1971). It has also been widely researched (Nittono, 1997; Thorson & Powell, 1996). Today, the test is not used extensively. However, in addition to illustrating the theoretical strategy, the EPPS elucidates some interesting concepts in personality-test construction, such as the concept of ipsative scores, which we shall discuss later.

The theoretical basis for the EPPS is the need system proposed by Murray (1938), probably the most influential theory in personality-test construction to date. The human needs proposed by Murray include the need to accomplish (achievement), the need to conform (deference), and the need for attention (exhibition). In developing the EPPS, Edwards selected 15 needs from Murray's list and constructed items with content validity for each.

Having selected items based on theory, Edwards could avoid the blind, subjective, and atheoretical approaches of other strategies. However, he still faced the perpetual problems of response styles and biases, which the MMPI had dealt with by including special scales to detect faking or unusual test-taking approaches. Edwards was especially concerned about faking and social desirability, the tendency to say good things about yourself or to mark items that you believe will be approved by the examiner, regardless of accuracy.

To deal with these sources of bias, Edwards attempted to rate each of his items on social desirability. He then formed pairs of items roughly comparable in social desirability and required subjects to select the item in the pair that was more characteristic of their likes or feelings. Subjects cannot simply provide the socially desirable or expected response because both items in the pair are presumably equal on social desirability. There is also not much point in faking—that is, selecting the less characteristic item. In addition, no problem of balancing scored items arises, as it does from the true-false imbalance of the MMPI.

As a further check on the validity of EPPS results, Edwards included a consistency scale with 15 pairs of statements repeated in identical form. In other words, of the 210 pairs of statements, only 195 are unique. The 15 that occur twice are presented more or less randomly throughout the test. With this format, the number of times a subject makes the identical choice can be converted to a percentile based on normative data. The approach provided the precursor to the VRIN and TRIN scales of the MMPI-2. The EPPS also permits an analysis of within-subject consistency, which consists of the correlation of odd and even scores in the 15 scales.

Norms for the EPPS were based on more than 1500 college men and women and approximately 9000 adults from the general population selected from urban and rural areas in 48 states. Separate normative data are available for each of these two groups and high-school students as well. For a given raw score on each of the 15 scales, a percentile can be obtained immediately from the profile sheet.

In constructing the EPPS, Edwards listed items for each of the scales and then paired them with items from the other 14 scales. When subjects make a choice, they select between one of two needs. In other words, in each choice, a subject selects one need at the expense of another. With this procedure, one can express the selection of items on one scale relative to the selection of items on another, thereby producing an **ipsative score**. Ipsative scores present results in relative terms rather than as absolute totals. Thus, two individuals with identical relative, or ipsative, scores may differ markedly in the absolute strength of a particular need. Ipsative scores compare the individual against himself or herself and produce data that reflect the relative strength of each need for that person; each person thus provides his or her own frame of reference (Popper, 1997).

Although the manual presents only short-term (1-week) test–retest reliability figures, the coefficients, which range from .74 to .88, are quite respectable for personality-test data. Though not as impressive, split-half reliabilities, which range from .60 to .87 as reported in the manual, are generally satisfactory. Furthermore, intercorrelations among the scales are lower than those for either the MMPI or 16PF, ranging between −.34 and .46. The lower intercorrelation is good because it supports the possibility of pattern analysis.

The EPPS has several interesting features. Its forced-choice method, which requires subjects to select one of two items rather than to respond "True" or "False" ("yes" or "no") to a single item, is an interesting solution to the problem of faking and other sources of bias. Because each subject provides his or her own frame of reference, testers can determine the relative strength of needs as well as the internal consistency of each individual subject. Item content follows established theoretical lines. The 15 identical pairs help researchers evaluate the profile's validity. Norms are based on large samples and are available for adults from the general population as well as for high-school and college students. Ipsative scores based on these norms can be converted to percentiles. Reliability data generally are adequate for the short term, and the 15 scales of the EPPS have lower intercorrelations than do the scales of the major tests developed by using factor analytic and criterion-group strategies. Last, but not least, the test is among the most researched of the personality inventories and is used widely in applied settings.

Despite its impressive features and the widespread interest and use it has engendered, the EPPS has not been well received by reviewers (e.g., Heilbrun 1972). Studies have shown that, like other structured personality tests, the EPPS can be faked in spite of its forced-choice procedure (Burnsa & Christiansen, 2011). Other data raise questions about the test's ability to control social-desirability effects (Kim, 2011). The appropriateness of converting ipsative scores, which are relative, to normative percentiles is also questionable.

Since the first attempts at test construction, tests have followed a trend of gradual improvement following criticism and the identification of problems. The EPPS seems to have originated in this spirit, but efforts are not being made to improve it. Many more validity studies are needed (Baburajan, 1998), and new norms are long overdue (Cooper, 1990).

## Personality Research Form, Third Edition (PRF-III) and Jackson Personality Inventory Revised (JPI-R)

Other attempts to use the theoretical strategy in constructing a structured personality test are the PRF-III (Jackson, 1967) and the JPI-R (Jackson, 1976a, 1976b, 1997). Like the EPPS, the original PRF and JPI were based on Murray's (1938) theory of needs. However, unlike Edwards, the constructors of these tests developed specific definitions of each need. In this way, items for each scale could be as independent as possible, an important consideration in creating homogeneous scales. To further increase the homogeneity of scales, more than 100 items were tentatively written for each scale and administered to more than 1000 college students. Biserial correlational analysis then located the items that correlated highest with the proposed scale while showing relatively low correlations with other scales, particularly social desirability. In other words, strict definitional standards and statistical procedures were used in conjunction with the theoretical approach. This use of a combination of procedures is the latest trend in personality-test construction.

To help assess validity, a scale analogous to the F scale of the MMPI was constructed. Like the F scale, the PRF and JPI infrequency scales consist of items with low endorsement rates in a standard sample. Thus, high rates of endorsement on this scale throw doubt on the validity of the results. A social-desirability scale similar to the K scale of the MMPI is also included in the PRF. Two sets of parallel forms (four forms in all) as well as a form based on the best items from other forms were developed for the PRF. The latest revision of the JPI (JPI-R) has one form consisting of 300 true-false items and 15 scales for use with high-school students through college students and adults. These 15 scales have been organized in terms of five higher-order dimensions termed analytical, extroverted, emotional, opportunistic, and dependable. College norms have been updated and new norms for blue- and white-collar workers are now included. The PRF, as its name implies, is intended primarily for research purposes (Paunonen & Ashton, 1998; Randolph, Smart, & Nelson, 1997). The JPI is intended for use on normal individuals to assess various aspects of personality including interpersonal, cognitive, and value orientations (Ashton, 1998; Mikulay & Goffin, 1998). Figure 16.4 shows a profile sheet from the JPI.

# Jackson Personality Inventory

**PROFILE SHEET: MALE**

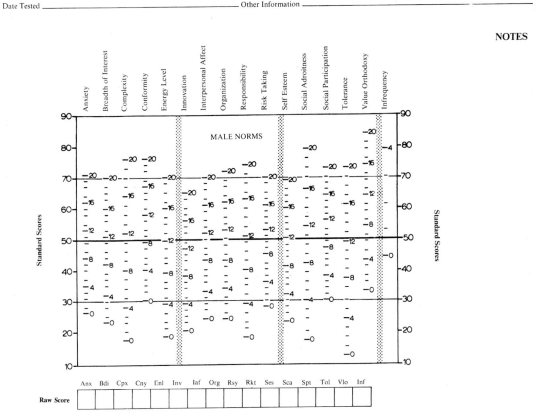

**FIGURE 16.4** Jackson Personality Inventory profile sheet.
(Reprinted with permission of Sigma Assessment Systems, Inc., P.O. Box 610984, Port Huron, MI 48061-0984, copyright 1976.)

**TABLE 16.5** Trait Descriptions for the Jackson Personality Inventory

| Scale trait | |
| --- | --- |
| Anxiety | Tendency to worry over minor matters |
| Breadth of interest | Curiosity; inquisitiveness |
| Complexity | Preference for abstract versus concrete thought |
| Conformity | Compliance; cooperativeness |
| Energy level | Energy; enthusiasm |
| Innovation | Originality; imagination |
| Interpersonal affect | Ability to identify with others |
| Organization | Planfulness; systematic versus disorganized |
| Responsibility | Responsibility; dependability |
| Risk taking | Reckless and bold versus cautious and hesitant |
| Self-esteem | Self-assured versus self-conscious |
| Social adroitness | Skill in persuading others |
| Social participation | Sociable and gregarious versus withdrawn and a loner |
| Tolerance | Broad minded and open versus Intolerant and uncompromising |
| Value orthodoxy | Moralistic and conventional versus modern and liberal |
| Infrequency | Validity of profile |

Items for the PRF and JPI are balanced in true-false keying. Unlike the scales of the MMPI, the PRF and JPI scales have no item overlap. Furthermore, the scales are relatively independent (see Table 16.5).

By combining theory with rigorous statistical procedures, these tests appear to have established a new trend in the construction of structured personality tests. As with other structured personality tests, however, the PRF has yet to challenge the MMPI and MMPI-2 in terms of use (both clinical and research) and status.

## Self-Concept

Many personality tests have evolved from a theoretical strategy to evaluate *self-concept*—the set of assumptions a person has about himself or herself. Presumably, what you believe to be true about yourself will strongly affect your behavior. If you believe you are honest, then you will tend to act in conformity with this belief. If you believe you are effective with others, then you will more likely assume a leadership role than you would if you believed you were ineffective. The extent to which you use your leadership skills or other abilities is influenced by your self-concept.

Several adjective checklists have been developed to evaluate self-concept. In these, a list of adjectives is presented and subjects are asked to indicate which apply to them. Gough's Adjective Checklist, for instance, contains 300 adjectives in alphabetical order (Gough & Heilbrun, 1980). The Piers-Harris Children's Self-Concept

Scale–Second Edition contains 80 self-statements (e.g., "I like my looks") and requires a "Yes" or "No" response (Piers, Harris, & Herzberg, 1999). Beyond checklists, the Tennessee Self-Concept Scale–Second Edition is a formal paper-and-pencil test that is designed to measure self-concept data (Fitts & Warren, 1996).

A novel approach to the assessment of self-concept is based on Carl Rogers's theory of the self. According to Rogers, the self is organized to remain consistent. New experiences that are consistent with a person's self-concept are easily integrated; experiences that are inconsistent with the self-concept tend to be denied or distorted. For example, if you view yourself as honest and moral and find yourself looking at another student's exam during the pressure of a difficult test, then you might try to distort the experience by thinking your classmate purposefully flashed her paper in front of your eyes.

To evaluate self-concept, Rogers uses a *Q-sort technique*, in which a person receives a set of cards with appropriate self-statements such as "I am a good person." The individual then sorts the cards in piles from least to most personally descriptive. The person is asked to make two sorts of the cards. The first describes who the person really is (real self). The second describes what the person believes he or she should be (ideal self). Rogers's theory predicts that large discrepancies between the real and ideal selves reflect poor adjustment and low self-esteem (Rogers, 1961).

# Combination Strategies

Clearly, the modern trend is to use a mix of strategies for developing structured personality tests. Indeed, almost all of the tests we have examined use factor analytic methods regardless of their main strategy. In this section, we briefly discuss a test of positive personality characteristics that relies on a combination of strategies in scale development: the NEO Personality Inventories.

## Positive Personality Measurement and the NEO Personality Inventory–Three (NEO-PI-3)

The early history of personality measurement focused on negative characteristics such as anxiety, depression, and other manifestations of psychopathology. Although the reasons to assess negative affect and psychopathology are numerous and compelling, research suggests that it may be advantageous to evaluate individuals' positive characteristics in an attempt to understand the resources that an individual is endowed with and how this endowment affects behavior and well-being. Early research (Kobasa, 1979) suggested that stressful situations can be better endured by people high on the trait of "hardiness," defined as a way of characterizing stressful situations as meaningful, changeable, and challenging. Similarly, Bandura (1986) has espoused the view that individuals with a strong sense of "self-efficacy" or strong belief in their ability to organize resources and manage situations, are better able to persevere in the face of hardships. Assuming these authors are correct, the ability to live a satisfying life even in the midst of stress and hardship depends on positive personal characteristics rather than only on the *absence* of psychopathology or negative affect.

Although relatively little is known about the structure of positive human characteristics, their measurement, or their effects in mitigating adversity, there has been a recent surge of interest in positive personality (Bermant, Talwar, & Rozin, 2011; Diener, Sapyta, & Suh, 1998; Fredrickson & Joiner, 2002; Gaudreau, Blondin, & Lapierre, 2002; La Guardia, 2002; Pettit, Kline, Gencoz, Gencoz, & Joiner, 2002; Stoeber & Kersting, 2007). Currently, several such measures of positive characteristics exist that evaluate traits such as conscientiousness, hope, optimism, and self-efficacy (Jerusalem & Schwarzer, 1992; McRae, 2011; Scheier, Carver, & Bridges, 1994; Viet & Ware 1989).

## The NEO Personality Inventory–Three (NEO PI-R™)

Forefront in the evaluation of positive personality characteristics has been the NEO-PI-III (Costa & McCrae, 1985, 1995; Costa, McCrae, & Jonsson, 2002; Costa, McCrae, & Kay, 1995; McCrae & Costa, 2003; Sutin & Costa, 2011). The developers of this test used both factor analysis and theory in item development and scale construction. Quite ambitious, the NEO-PI-3 attempts to provide a multipurpose inventory for predicting interests, health and illness behavior, psychological well-being, and characteristic coping styles. Of the personality tests, the NEO-PI-3 has been among the most heavily researched during the last decade (e.g., Caprara, Barbaranelli, & Comrey, 1995; Huprich, 2003; Piedmont, 1998; Sherry, Henson, & Lewis, 2003; Sutin & Costa, 2011).

Based on their review of extensive factor analytic studies and personality theory, the authors of the NEO-PI-3 identified three broad domains: neuroticism (N), extroversion (E), and openness (O)—thus the name NEO. Each domain has six specific facets. Neuroticism (N) is defined primarily by anxiety and depression. The six facets of this domain are anxiety, hostility, depression, self-consciousness, impulsiveness, and vulnerability (describing people who do not feel safe). Extraversion (E) refers to the degree of sociability or withdrawal a person tends to exhibit. Its six facets are warmth, gregariousness, assertiveness, activity, excitement seeking, and positive emotions. Finally, openness (O) refers to the breadth of experience to which a person is amenable. Its six facets are fantasy, aesthetics, feelings (openness to feelings of self and others), actions (willingness to try new activities), ideas (intellectual curiosity), and values. Figure 16.5 is a profile from the original NEO Personality Inventory.

Guided by personality theory and factor analytic findings, the authors of the NEO-PI-R took a rational approach in constructing items. For each of the 18 facets, 14 items were written. Seven were positively worded and seven negatively worded to create a balance. Subjects respond on a 5-point Likert format ranging from "strongly disagree" to "strongly agree." Initial items were then refined using a variety of statistical procedures.

Data in the manual and from a variety of research reports support the NEO-PI-R and its earlier version, the NEO. Factor analytic studies support the grouping of three major areas and associated facets. Reliabilities for the three domains are in the high .80's to the low .90's for both internal consistency and test–retest reliability. As is true of all major personality tests, reliabilities of the individual facets are lower. Predictive and concurrent validity studies are encouraging, with coefficients ranging into the .80's.

The NEO-PI-R has supported what is perhaps becoming one of the most accepted notions in personality and personality assessment—the *five-factor model*

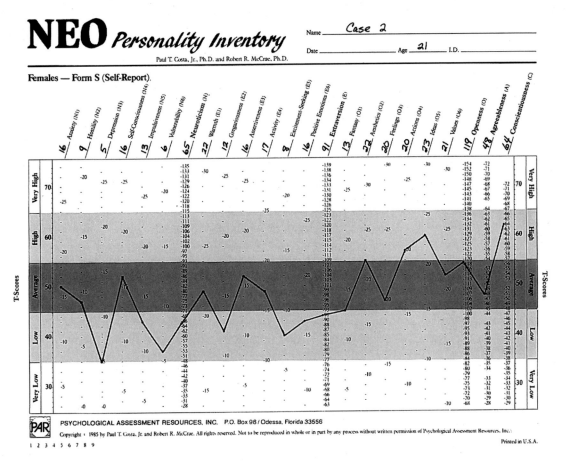

**FIGURE 16.5** NEO Personality Inventory profile sheet.
(Reprinted by permission of Psychological Assessment Resources, Inc.)

of personality (Costa et al., 2002; Sutin & Costa, 2011). Recall that through factor analysis, researchers have repeatedly attempted to find the minimum number of independent personality dimensions to describe the human personality. Research with the NEO has supported the notion of the following five dimensions (after Wiggins, 1994):

1. *Extroversion* is the degree to which a person is sociable, leader-like, and assertive as opposed to withdrawn, quiet, and reserved.

2. *Neuroticism* is the degree to which a person is anxious and insecure as opposed to calm and self-confident.

3. *Conscientiousness* is the degree to which a person is persevering, responsible, and organized as opposed to lazy, irresponsible, and impulsive.

4. *Agreeableness* is the degree to which a person is warm and cooperative as opposed to unpleasant and disagreeable.

5. *Openness to experience* is the degree to which a person is imaginative and curious as opposed to concrete-minded and narrow in thinking.

Among positive characteristics, conscientiousness as identified on the NEO has been of particular interest. Conscientiousness is constructed of two major facets: achievement and dependability (Judge & Bono, 2000). Conscientiousness has been found to be valid as a positive predictor of performance in all occupations studied (Bakker, Demerouti, & ten Brummelhuis, 2011; Barrick et al., 2001; Di Fabio & Busoni, 2007) and to be positively correlated with effective styles of coping with stressful situations (Bartley & Roesch, 2011; Haren & Mitchell, 2003; Hu et al., 2002) and with the Satisfaction with Life Scale (Baudin, Aluja, Rolland, & Blanch, 2011; Hayes & Joseph, 2003), which is discussed later. Barrick, Mount, and Judge (2001) also suggested that results from meta-analysis underscore the importance of the dimension of conscientiousness as a "fundamental individual difference variable that has numerous applications" (p. 21), setting it apart as central in theories seeking to explain positive personality traits.

Other NEO factors have been evaluated by Barrick et al. (2001), who found that an absence of the factor neuroticism could be predictive of performance, though to a lesser degree than was conscientiousness, and with a less consistent relationship to specific performance criteria. Neuroticism was also negatively correlated with effective styles of coping with stressful situations (Hu et al., 2002). In addition, high neuroticism predicted lower scores on the Satisfaction with Life Scale (Hayes & Joseph, 2003).

The trait openness correlated significantly with crystallized intelligence (Bates & Sheiles, 2003), and the traits of openness, agreeableness, and extraversion were found to be beneficial in predicting success in specific job settings. In addition, Judge and Bono (2000) found that extraversion and agreeableness were effective in predicting transformational leadership.

Two converging areas of research with the NEO and NEO-PI-3 discuss whether the five-factor model is actually the best way to categorize the minimum dimensions of human personality, and, if so, whether these dimensions hold up across cultures. Some researchers, including the authors of the JPI, have found support for an alternative model with a six-factor solution (Jackson, Paunonen, Fraboni, & Goffin, 1996; Maltby, Wood, Day, & Pinto, 2011; Rolland, Parker, & Stumpf, 1998). When six factors are found, five tend to parallel the "big five" of NEO-PI-R (Detwiler & Ramanaiah, 1996). As of 2004, evidence for the six-factor model is weak and inconclusive (Heuchert, Parker, Stumpf, & Heinrich, 2000; Piedmont, 1998; Thalmayer, Saucier, & Eigenhuis, 2011). While the amount of research attempting to confirm this alternative model has been subsiding, researchers have turned to the question of whether there is one general factor of personality (GFP) that occupies the apex of the hierarchies of both personality and personality disorders (Rushton & Irwing, 2011). Rushton and Irwing cross-validated data that indicated a two-factor solution. The alpha was labeled stability and the beta was labeled plasticity. Using meta-analysis, research points to the correctness of a single model, which was then tested and confirmed in a representative sample (Rushton & Irwing, 2011). A subsequent meta-analysis of 212 published sets of big-five scores further corroborated this model (van der Linden, te Nijenhuis, & Bakker, 2010). Although the existence of a GFP does not mean that other personality factor lower on the hierarchy are meaningless, knowledge of the GFP is useful where a compound measure of personality is needed (van der

Linden, te Nijenhuis, & Bakker, 2010). An understanding of the GFP has contributed to both theoretical and practical usage of personality tests. In a related line of research, investigators have attempted to determine whether the five factors can be applied across cultures. Testing of this hypothesis is possible because the NEO-PI-R has been translated into numerous languages. The taxonomic structure of the NEO has become widely accepted because its five factors of personality have remained robust across cultures and measures (Egger, DeMay, Derksen, & van der Staak, 2003).

Finding that data from Filipino (Katigbak, Church, Guanzon-Lapena, Carlota, & del Pilar, 2002) and French translations tend to parallel U.S. data in support of the five-factor solution, some researchers have made the bold claim that the five-factor model is a "biologically based human universal" (McCrae, Costa, Del Pilar, Rolland, & Parker, 1998). This work is further supported by research on a Korean version of the NEO-PI-R (Spirrison & Choi, 1998; Yoon, Schmidt, & Ilies, 2002). However, Huang, Church, and Katigbak (1997) reported that even though the factor structure may be similar for Filipino populations, the mean scores tended to differ across populations. Klimstra, Crocetti, Hale, Fermani, and Meeus (2011) also advised caution when interpreting test results from Dutch and Italian adolescence. The translated testing materials had slightly different meanings to the Dutch and Italian adolescent respondents, resulting in subtle cross-national differences in personality. And in a study of approximately 3500 university students and employees in Kuwait, El-Ansarey (1997) reported that the NEO is not a valid or reliable inventory to assess personality in Kuwait society. Finally, a study of father–offspring and mother–offspring correlations indicated significant but "weak" family resemblances for the five personality dimensions (Bratko & Marusic, 1997).

Given its general amenability to cross-cultural and international studies, along with the potential significance of biologically based universal human traits, the NEO-PI-R is likely to engender considerable research for some time. Moreover, the NEO-PI-R reflects modern trends in personality-test construction by its reliance on theory, logic, and the liberal use of factor analysis and statistical approaches in test construction. It appears to be exceptionally promising for measuring a wide range of characteristics in the world community.

# Frequently Used Measures of Positive Personality Traits

## Rosenberg Self-Esteem Scale

The Rosenberg Self-Esteem Scale (Rosenberg, 1965) is widely used today in the United States (Heatherton & Wyland, 2003) and in various countries worldwide such as Hungary (Bödecs, Horváth, & Szilágyi, 2011), Germany (Gudjonsson & Sigurdsson, 2003), the United Kingdom (Huang & Dong, 2011; Schaefer, Koeter, Wouters, Emmelkamp, & Schene, 2003), and Turkey (Kugu, Akyuez, Dogan, Ersan, & Izgic, 2002). This scale measures global feelings of self-worth using 10 simple and straightforward statements that examinees rate on a 4-point Likert scale. The Rosenberg scale was created for use with adult populations. The scale has strong psychometric properties, with considerable evidence of concurrent, known-groups, predictive, and construct validity. Internal reliability is .92, and test–retest reliability shows correlations of .85 and .88 over a 2-week period. One of the measure's greatest strengths is the amount of research conducted using a wide range of populations such as adolescents (Whiteside-Mansell & Corwyn, 2003; Yarcheski, Mahon, & Yarcheski, 2003) and individuals with eating disorders (Chen et al., 2003; Beato, Cano, & Belmonte, 2003) and hearing loss (Crowe, 2003).

## General Self-Efficacy Scale (GSE)

The GSE (Jerusalem & Schwarzer, 1992) was developed to measure an individual's belief in his or her ability to organize resources and manage situations, to persist in the face of barriers, and to recover from setbacks. The scale consists of 10 items and takes only 4 minutes to complete. Internal reliabilities for the GSE range from .76 to .90. Research from 25 countries indicates that the GSE is configurally equivalent across cultures and that the underlying construct of self-efficacy is global (Scholz, Dona, Sud, & Schwarzer, 2002; also see Löve, Moore, & Hensing, 2011). The GSE has been found to be positively correlated with favorable emotions, dispositional optimism, self-esteem, and work satisfaction. Negative correlations have been found with depression, anxiety, stress, burnout and health complaints.

## Ego Resiliency Scale Revised

This measure of ego resiliency or emotional intelligence was developed by Block and Kremen in 1996 (see Alessandri, Vecchione, Caprara1, & Letzring, 2011). The Ego Resiliency Scale (ER89-R) consists of 14 items, each answered using a 4-point Likert scale to rate statements such as "I am regarded as a very energetic person," "I get over my anger at someone reasonably quickly," and "Most of the people I meet are likeable." ER89-R scores correlated highly with ratings for being sympathetic, considerate, dependable, responsible, cheerful, warm, assertive, socially adaptive, and not hostile. Fredrickson (2001) provided evidence of the scale's validity. The scales have been translated into several languages, including French (Callahan et al., 2001), Italian (Alessandri, Vecchione, Caprara1, & Letzring, 2011) and Korean (Min, Kim, Hwang, & Jahng, 1998), and are widely used in psychological research.

## Dispositional Resilience Scale (DRS)

The DRS was developed by Bartone, Wright, Ingraham, and Ursano (1989) to measure "hardiness," which is defined as the ability to view stressful situations as meaningful, changeable, and challenging. The coefficient alpha for the short version of the DRS, referred to as the Short Hardiness Scale, is .70, and the 3-week test–retest reliability coefficient is .78 (Bartone, 2007). In an earlier study by Bartone (1995) using the Short Hardiness Scale, hardiness emerged as a significant predictor of grades among West Point cadets. Furthermore, research has indicated that those who measure high in hardiness have lower levels of worry (Hanton, Evans, & Neil, 2003); others have suggested that hardiness, as measured by the DRS, can function as an index of mental health (Taylor, Pietrobon, Taverniers, Leon, & Fern, 2011).

## Hope Scale

Snyder et al. (1991) proposed a cognitive model that characterizes hope as goal-driven energy (agency) in combination with the capacity to construct systems to meet goals (pathways) (Tennen, Affleck, & Tennen, 2002). The Hope Scale, also referred to as the Dispositional Hope Scale, was developed by Snyder et al. (1991) and measures the components of this cognitive model. The scale consists of 12 items that are rated on an 8-point Likert scale ranging from "definitely false" to "definitely true." Of the 12 items, four measure pathways, four measure agency, and four are distracters that are not scored. Snyder et al. (1991) have reported adequate internal reliability (alphas ranging from .74 to .84) and test–retest reliability (ranging from .76 to .82 over 10 weeks), and it appears that the Hope Scale is particularly invulnerable to faking (Terrill, Friedman, Gottschalk, & Haaga, 2002). High scores on the scale have been shown to be predictive of college graduation (Snyder, Shorey, Cheavens, Pulvers, Adams, & Wiklund, 2002), healthy psychological adjustment, high achievement, good problem-solving skills, and positive health-related outcomes (Snyder, Sympson, Michael, & Cheavens, 2001). It has also been found to be a good measure of hope in traumatized population (Creamer et al., 2009). The Hope Scale takes 2 to 5 minutes to complete and is useful for examinees who read at the seventh-grade level or higher. Snyder and colleagues (1991) report that scores on the Hope Scale are positively correlated with measures of dispositional optimism and positive affect and negatively correlated with hopelessness and depression. Magalette and Oliver (1999) indicate that the Hope Scale predicts variance independent of measures of self-efficacy and optimism, suggesting it measures a related, but not identical, construct.

## Life Orientation Test–Revised (LOT-R)

The LOT-R is the most widely used self-report measure of dispositional optimism, which is defined as an individual's tendency to view the world and the future in positive ways. The LOT-R consists of 10 items developed to assess individual differences in generalized optimism versus pessimism. Items are answered on a 5-point response scale ranging from "strongly disagree" to "strongly agree." Cronbach's alpha is estimated at .82. Test–retest reliability for the LOT-R appears adequate ($r=.79$ over 4 weeks, as reported by Smith, Pope, Rhodewalt, & Poulton, 1989). The LOT-R and its predecessor, the LOT, have been used extensively in studies of stress and coping (Chico-Libran, 2002; Vassend, Quale, Røise, & Schanke, 2011). Dispositional optimism scores correlate highly with self-esteem (.54), neuroticism ($-.50$), and trait anxiety ($-.59$) (Scheier, Carver, & Bridges, 1994). Scheier and Carver (1985) found that the LOT correlates negatively with depression ($-.49$), perceived stress ($-.55$), and hopelessness ($-.47$). A 2002 study by Creed, Patton, and Bartrum replicate these findings. In addition, the LOT-R is strongly positively correlated with active coping strategies (Chico-Libran, 2002; Horney, Smith, & McGurk et al., 2011) and with emotional regulation strategies (Scheier, Weintraub, & Carver, 1986). Although the LOT-R is widely used and has been shown to be a psychometrically sound instrument, it is notable that studies have suggested the LOT-R is more susceptible to faking good than are other tests of optimism (Terrill, Friedman, Gottschalk, & Haaga, 2002).

## Satisfaction with Life Scale (SWLS)

The five-item SWLS (Diener, Emmons, Larsen, & Griffin, 1985) was developed as a multi-item scale for the overall assessment of life satisfaction as a cognitive-judgmental process, rather than for the measurement of specific satisfaction domains. This simple and flexible instrument is one of the most widely used measures of life-satisfaction or global well-being (Lucas, Deiner, & Larson, 2003). As an extremely popular research tool, the SWLS has been used to assess life satisfaction in many groups such as minorities (Constantine & Watt, 2002), cancer patients (Ferrario, Zotti, Massara, & Nuvolone, 2003), the elderly (Richeson & Thorson, 2002), immigrants (Neto, 2002), university students (Matheny et al., 2002; Paolini, Yanez, & Kelly, 2006), those suffering from traumatic injury (Corrigan, Bogner, Mysiw, Clinchot, & Fugate, 2001), and psychiatric patients (Arrindell, van Nieuwenhuizen, & Lutejin, 2001). It has also been translated and validated for use in several countries, including China (Bai, Wu, Zheng, & Ren, 2011) and Germany (Glaesmer, Grande, Braehler, & Roth, 2011). Pons, Atienza, Balaguer, and Garcia-Merita (2002) report adequate internal reliability, and Diener et al. (1985) report satisfactory test–retest stability for a 2-month period ($r=.82$). Others have shown that life satisfaction as measured by the SWLS can be relatively stable between years (Corrigan et al., 2001). Deiner et al. (1985) note that the inventory is designed to assess both fluctuations in life satisfaction and global ratings of this construct. A 6th- to 10th-grade reading level is necessary in order to complete the inventory accurately, and it takes only a minute or two to complete. The SWLS has been found to be positively correlated with healthy psychological and social functioning and negatively associated with measures of psychological distress (Arrindell et al., 2001). The SWLS has been adapted for use with children, and is an appropriate measure for life satisfaction in children (Gadermann, Guhn, & Zumbo, 2011).

## Positive and Negative Affect Schedule (PANAS)

The PANAS was developed by Watson, Clark, and Tellegen (1988) to measure two orthogonal dimensions of affect. One of the most widely used measures of affect (Schmukle, Egloff, & Burns, 2002), the instrument has two scales—one for positive affect (PA) and one for negative affect (NA). Each scale consists of 10 adjectives such as *distressed, interested, guilty, afraid,* and *nervous.* The respondents are asked to rate the extent to which their moods have mirrored the feelings described by each adjective during a specified period of time. Watson et al. (1988) have presented extensive evidence demonstrating that the PANAS scales are internally consistent with coefficient alphas ranging from .84 to .90, and that they are largely uncorrelated with each other and stable over a 2-month period. Watson et al. (1988) have also presented evidence showing that the PANAS scales are valid measures of the underlying NA and PA constructs, with moderately high correlations between the NA scale of the PANAS and other measures of psychological distress. In addition, there is some evidence that the PANAS can be successfully translated into other languages and used across cultures and ethnic groups (Karim, Weisz, & Ur Rehman, 2011; Terraciano, McCrae, & Costa, 2003).

## Coping Intervention for Stressful Situations (CISS)

Active behavioral and cognitive coping strategies have been shown to be associated with measures of positive affect, and the strategy of coping by avoidance has been shown to be associated with high levels of negative affect (Pernas et al., 2001). Understanding individuals' styles of coping is key to understanding components of their personality. Endler and Parker (1990) created the CISS as a 48-item questionnaire that measures coping styles by asking subjects how they would respond to a variety of stressful situations. Using a 5-point Likert scale with choices ranging from "not at all" to "very much," this inventory assesses individuals according to three basic coping styles: task-oriented coping, emotion-oriented coping, and avoidance-oriented coping.

## Core Self-Evaluations

The widespread use of the NEO and other popular tests of positive characteristics has led to a deeper understanding of the fundamentals of personality. It has been suggested that measures of personality, to some extent, are all tapping into a single core construct (Judge, Erez, Bono, & Thoresen, 2002). Core Self-Evaluations is a framework for understanding and evaluating this core (Judge & Larsen, 2001). This broad-based personality construct is composed of four specific traits: self-esteem, generalized self-efficacy, neuroticism, and locus of control. The construct is not simply a descriptive system but explanatory of the dispositional source of life satisfaction and performance. In other words, the system not only describes the positive traits of individuals but also suggests ways in which these positive traits affect emotions and behaviors. Judge, Locke, Durham, and Kluger (1998) showed consistent effects of core evaluations on job satisfaction, with self-esteem and self-efficacy contributing most to the core self-evaluation conception. Heller, Judge, and Watson (2002) suggest that life satisfaction is largely the result of dispositional factors explained through core self-evaluations. Moreover, factor analytic evaluations of the core self-evaluation construct, though limited, have resulted in evidence of its validity for motivation, life satisfaction, and performance (Erez & Judge, 2001).

In 2011, Chang et al conducted a review spanning 15 years of CSE theory and research. The study focused in particular on the outcomes, mediators, and moderators of CSE via both and quantitative literature reviews (Chang, Ferris, Johnson, Rosen, & Tan, 2011). Meta-analytic results support the relation of CSE with various outcomes, including job and life satisfaction, in-role and extra-role job performance, and perceptions of the work environment such as job characteristics and fairness.

In light of all evidence to date, the core self-evaluation construct remains a better predictor of job performance than do individual traits and should give direction to further evaluation (Erez & Judge, 2001). When focusing on life or job satisfaction, a combination of the personality characteristics neuroticism and extroversion as well as measures of positive and negative affect appear to be best suited for prediction. Nevertheless, the interrelatedness among the various measures of positive characteristics remains largely unexplored and has provoked many questions.

# Future of Positive Personality Research

Among the questions raised in the area of positive personality research is whether the various measures are capturing a series of unique and independent traits or are more generally related to a single underlying construct. There also is debate about whether positive characteristics are independent constructs or merely represent the absence of negative traits. The question also has been raised whether the presence of positive characteristics mitigates detrimental effects of negative characteristics, and, if so, to what extent.

In an attempt to answer these questions, Saccuzzo, Kewley, Johnson, Larson and colleagues (2003) analyzed the results of 15 separate tests of positive personality completed by 313 college-aged students. The findings were clear in demonstrating that the various measures of positive affect, from hope through resiliency, are best conceptualized as a single construct or dimension. These measures shared considerable common variance, with no evidence at all for independence. Thus, regardless of what they are called, measures of positive affect measure just that and at varying levels of success. It appears to be feasible to create a robust single measure by locating those items with the highest correlation with the general factor. Furthermore, given the consistency among the measures, it would appear as though positive affect can be reliably and validly measured with relative economy in terms of number of items.

The data likewise indicated that measures of negative affect constitute a single dimension. Although there may be some utility from a clinical perspective in distinguishing among constructs such as anxiety and depression, negative affect can best be thought of as tapping into a broader, more general construct. This negative affect construct, however, has a strong and negative relationship with its positive affect counterpart.

There was strong empirical support to indicate that measures of positive and negative affect fall along a continuum ranging from the highest measures of positive affect through the highest measures of negative affect. In general, individuals who are high on positive are low on negative. Conversely, individuals who are high on negative are not high on positive. Thus, when measures of both positive and negative affect were evaluated in a single factor analysis, positive measures consistently loaded positively, while negative measures loaded negatively.

In effect, scoring high on measures of positive affect has the same meaning as scoring low on measures of negative affect. Conversely, scoring high on negative affect has the same meaning as scoring low on measures of positive affect. However, there are notable exceptions.

Despite the clear relationship between measures of positive and negative affect, there was also strong support for the existence of subgroups that do not conform to the general pattern. In particular, there is a subgroup that, although high on negative affect, also scores high on measures of positive affect. Such individuals are clearly distinguishable from individuals who fit the general pattern.

Differences between participants high on negative affect who either score high or low on positive affect suggest that the presence of positive affect might mitigate or negate the deleterious effects of negative affect. For example, individuals in the mixed group who scored high on negative and relatively high on positive affect scores showed more effective coping strategies, less neuroticism, and greater degrees of conscientiousness.

These findings confirm other research that suggests the understanding of personal characteristics is improved by considering both the positive and negative affect dimensions. At the simplest level, individuals who score high on positive and low on negative represent those best able to function. Conversely, those high on negative affect and low on positive will tend to have a diminished capacity to deal with stressful situations. However, within the negative affect group there may be a significant number of individuals whose scores in the positive dimension have a counterbalancing effect. Obviously, individuals in the mixed category should be further studied in order to confirm the findings of this study. Clearly, positive personality characteristics and their measurement are only beginning to be understood, and the decades ahead should prove interesting to those following the progress of this research.

# Summary

Structured personality tests are self-report procedures that provide statements to which the subject must either respond "True" or "False" ("Yes" or "No") or choose the most characteristic of two or more alternatives. These tests are highly structured and provide a definite, unambiguous stimulus for the subject. Scoring is straightforward and usually involves summing the number of items marked in a scored direction.

The original pressure to develop personality tests came from the demands created by the military in World War I for a screening instrument to identify emotionally unstable recruits who might break down under the pressures of combat. The first structured personality instrument, the Woodworth Personal Data Sheet, was based on a logical-content strategy in which items were interpreted in terms of face validity.

Not long after, tests based on the logical-content strategy fell into disrepute. The problem with these tests was the numerous assumptions underlying them, including the following: the subject complies with the instructions and provides an honest response; the subject understands the items and is an accurate observer capable of evaluating his or her own behavior and responding in a nondefensive manner; and the subject, test constructor, and test interpreter all define the questions in the same way. A wide body of research seriously questioned all of these assumptions.

The first major advance in structured personality assessment came with the MMPI, which used a strategy involving criterion groups. In this criterion-group strategy, groups with known characteristics were contrasted with a control population. Items that distinguished the criterion group were included in a scale that was then cross-validated on an independent sample of criterion and control subjects. The MMPI revitalized structured personality tests. Rather than making assumptions about the meaning of a subject's response to a test item, it attempted to discern empirically the response's meaning. In the criterion-group strategy, the content of the item is irrelevant. If a subject marks "True" to the statement "I hear loud voices when I'm alone," testers do not assume that he or she really does hear loud voices when alone.

In addition to its advantages over logical-content tests in avoiding assumptions, the MMPI featured validity scales. The two most important MMPI validity scales are the K scale, which measures social desirability, and the F scale, which consists of 64 infrequently endorsed items to pick out subjects who take an unusual or unconventional approach to testing. Theoretically, excessively high scores on the validity scales can identify biased results, thus avoiding the problems of faking and social desirability inherent in the logical-content approach.

Despite its extensive use, researchers' widespread interest in it, and its recent restandardization (the MMPI-2), the MMPI has its problems, including item overlap among the scales, an imbalance in true-false keying, high intercorrelation among the scales, and a lack of generalizability across demographic variables.

The factor analytic strategy of test construction attempts to overcome some of the problems inherent in the criterion strategy. Factor analytic strategies try to find areas of common variance in order to locate the minimum number of variables or factors that account for a set of intercorrelated data. R. B. Cattell has been the most important representative of this approach.

Using the factor analytic approach to find the common variance of all trait-descriptive terms in the dictionary, Cattell reduced an original pool of more than 4000 items to 16 and created the 16PF. Great care was taken to provide adequate norms. Nine separate normative samples based on demographic variables, plus an age-correction scale, are available. Also available are three sets of parallel forms that accommodate different levels of subjects' vocabulary proficiency.

The EPPS has found its primary use in counseling centers. It employs a forced-choice strategy that requires subjects to choose the more applicable of two statements. Ipsative scores, which use the subject as his or her own frame of reference, express results in terms of the relative strength of a need.

Several tests have been developed with the theoretical strategy. Among these is the Q-sort technique, which measures self-concept.

The modern trend is to use a combination of strategies in scale construction. This approach is used in the NEO Personality Inventory–Revised (NEO-PI-R), which is the most commonly used measure of positive personality characteristics. Of the structured personality tests, the NEO, along with the MMPI-2, promise to be the dominant tests of the 21st century.

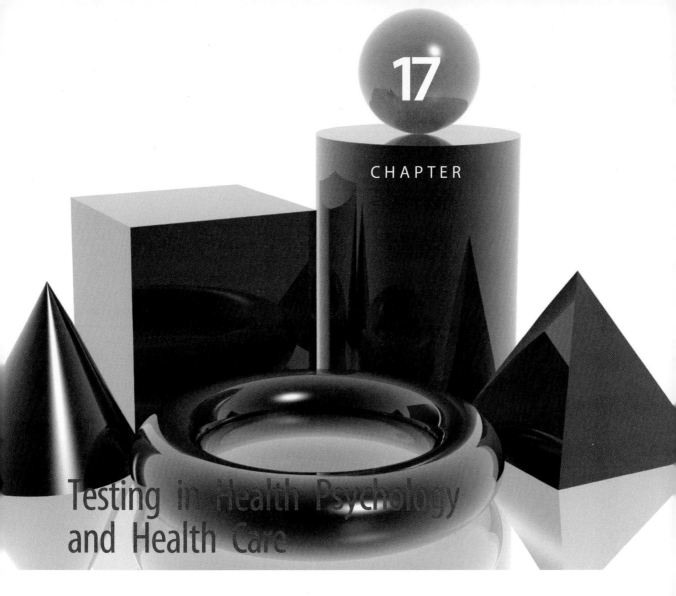

CHAPTER

17

# Testing in Health Psychology and Health Care

## LEARNING OBJECTIVES

*When you have completed this chapter, you should be able to:*

▶ Describe at least three important health-care situations in which psychological tests are used

▶ Define *clinical neuropsychology*

▶ Discuss the use of neuropsychological instruments in both childhood and adulthood

▶ Describe the Halstead-Reitan test battery

▶ Describe the Luria-Nebraska test battery

▶ Discuss the advantages of the California Verbal Learning Test

▶ Describe the strengths and weaknesses of two different approaches for the assessment of life stress

▶ Discuss the relationship among measures of coping, measures of life stress, and measures of social support

▶ Differentiate psychometric and decision theory approaches to quality-of-life measurement

▶ Discuss the concept of a quality-adjusted life-year

▶ Discuss the reasons for adding more behavioral science to the 2015 MCAT

Today, more than 5% of all psychologists are directly employed by hospitals, medical centers, and clinics, and this figure is increasing. One of the main functions of psychologists in these settings is to use and interpret measurement instruments (Kreutzer, DeLuca, Caplan, & SpringerLink (online service), 2011). Although this chapter cannot discuss all of the measures used in medical settings, it focuses on three areas that have experienced rapid development in the last few years: neuropsychological assessment, anxiety and stress assessment, and quality-of-life assessment. Unlike other chapters, this chapter covers three separate topics—that is, the topics are not directly related to one another, except that each describes a common approach to assessment in contemporary health care.

# Neuropsychological Assessment

## Clinical Neuropsychology

Linda had been an intelligent, extremely cooperative 7-year-old when she was hit by a car. Unconscious for only a short time, she appeared to show a rapid physical recovery from the accident. However, by the time 1 year had passed, her parents had become concerned about the behavioral changes they had observed since the accident. Linda was now introverted, did not interact well with others, and seemed anxious, prone to temper tantrums, frustrated, and unable to take criticism. The doctor who had originally examined Linda referred her to a neurologist, who could not find anything abnormal in her computed tomography (CT) scans and electroencephalogram (EEG) tests. Unable to determine the source of her difficulties, the neurologist referred Linda to a specialized psychologist trained in neuropsychological assessment. The psychologist discovered that Linda's visual functioning and her ability to talk were superior; however, she had difficulties in hearing and in writing down phonemes she had heard. Furthermore, tests showed that she did quite well on things she had learned before the accident but that she had lost the ability to discriminate among the sounds of letters closely related to one another. This in turn generated a great deal of strain and caused her to believe that she was stupid and unable to keep up with other children. The test that helped identify Linda's specific problem is called the Luria-Nebraska Neuropsychological Battery. After discovering that Linda's problem was highly specific, her teachers designed a special education program that used a visual approach and avoided auditory presentations. Her parents could also adapt to their child's problem once they realized its nature. Given this support and the reduced pressure, Linda's introversion, sensitivity to criticism, and frustration decreased. As her injuries healed, she returned to normal (Golden, 1981).

Linda's case shows the importance of a rapidly expanding new field known as *clinical neuropsychology*. This field is a scientific discipline that focuses on psychological impairments of the central nervous system and their remediation (Broks, 2003; Kreutzer et al., 2011). *Clinical neuropsychology* is defined as the scientific discipline that studies the relationship between behavior and brain functioning in the realms of cognitive, motor, sensory, and emotional functioning (Schoenberg, Scott, & SpringerLink (online service), 2011). The activities of neuropsychologists include the identification, description, multivariate quantification, and treatment of diseases of the brain and spinal cord.

A multidisciplinary endeavor, clinical neuropsychology overlaps neurology, psychiatry, and psychometric testing in the following ways: Neuropsychology and neurology both focus on sensations and perceptions and on motor movements. Neuropsychology and psychiatry both study mood and adaptations to psychosocial situations (Schoenberg et al., 2011). Finally, neuropsychology and psychometrics both use psychological tests. Neuropsychology differs from these other clinical disciplines because it is finely specialized, focusing on attention, memory, learning, language and communication, spatial integration, and cognitive flexibility. In summary, neuropsychology is a field of study that actively attempts to relate brain dysfunction and damage to observable and measurable behavioral functioning (Cubelli & Sala, 2007; Schoenberg et al., 2011).

The practice of clinical neuropsychology has benefited from remarkable advances in neuroimaging. New methods have made it possible to see diseases in the brain among living people. A few short years ago, the only way to learn about these problems was to study the brains of people who had already died. The rapid advances in neuroimaging produced some surprises for the evolving field of clinical neuropsychology. For example, many people assumed that improvements in brain scanning would eliminate the need for clinical neuropsychology. If tumors can be easily detected with CT or magnetic resonance imaging (MRI), why would we need functional tasks to determine if there was a lesion in the brain? As the field of neuroimaging advanced, it became increasingly clear that behavior and functional assessments were important. One of the problems was that there is remarkable variability among people in the structure of their brains. The early neuroanatomists of the 19th century mapped the brain on the basis of one or two people. Now that thousands of people have had their brains imaged, it has become apparent that there is remarkable variability from person to person in how their brains are structured and organized (Shattuck et al., 2008). In clinical situations, identification of a lesion or tumor does not necessarily relate to functioning. Similarly, people may have important functioning problems that are not clearly traced to specific regions of the brain. Neurologists now believe that performance on neuropsychological tests gives them clues about which part of the brain to examine (Iacoboni & Mazziotta, 2007). In addition to identifying tumors, neuropsychological tests have proven valuable in characterizing the effects of serious medical conditions, such as human immunodeficiency virus (HIV), that might influence the brain and behavior (Woods et al., 2008; Letendre et al., 2008). The latest advances include functional magnetic resonance imaging, or functional MRI (fMRI), which allows estimates to be made of the change in blood flow to various areas of the brain. (Blood flow changes indicate changes in the activity of different brain regions.) One of the most recently developed forms of neuroimaging, fMRI has only been in use for about 20 years. It is an attractive method because it does not require surgery or injections and does not involve exposure to radiation exposure. fMRI is not the most common method used for brain mapping, but fMRI scanners have become more common and are now used for a wide variety of research projects. Figure 17.1 shows an image from an fMRI study.

Despite these major advances in imaging of the brain, neuropsychology is able to detect problems that are often missed even with the latest neuroimaging devices. Furthermore, neuropsychological testing can detect Alzheimer's disease and other clinical problems in their earliest stages and tests are now used to detect a wide range of clinical problems (Benton & Sivan, 2007; Brandt, 2007; Crespo-Facorro et al., 2007). It remains the primary method to diagnose the effects of minor traumatic injury

**FIGURE 17.1**
Image from fMRI.

Philippe Psaila/Photo Researchers, Inc

(Bigler, 2003; Ewing-Cobbs, Barnes, et al., 2004; Hanten, Dennis, et al., 2004). It is unclear how much we will ever be able to understand about human memory and thought on the basis of physiology alone. Beyond physiologic findings, motivation or desire to perform well can profoundly affect performance (Green, 2003).

The roots of clinical neuropsychology can be traced to studies by Pierre Broca and Carl Wernicke in the 19th century. These early investigators recognized that functions such as the recognition of speech were localized in the left hemisphere of the brain. By the first decade of the 20th century, Brodmann had developed the first functional map of the cerebral cortex. A variety of investigators including Benton, Tuber, and Geschwind developed methods for associating function with different areas of the brain. Early neuropsychologists, including Luria and Reitan, used psychological tests to estimate areas of brain damage. However, major advances in brain imaging reduced the need for these types of services. MRI and CT scanning now allow clinicians to examine the brains of living people.

Clinical neuropsychology has developed rapidly over the last few decades (Benton & Sivan, 2007; Kreutzer et al., 2011). In 1970, neuropsychology was viewed as a new field characterized by rapid growth (Parsons, 1970). During the 1970s and early 1980s, research in neuropsychology exploded, and a practice specialty rapidly developed. Currently, neuropsychology has formally joined the ranks of other neurosciences. Using powerful measurement techniques, neuropsychologists have developed many procedures for identifying the relationship between brain problems and behavioral problems (Butters, Delis, & Lucas, 1995). The activities of neuropsychologists are extremely varied and require complex technology. An exploration of this important new discipline in any depth would require a review of neuroanatomy and other topics in neuroscience that we cannot discuss here. Instead, we describe some current activities of active neuropsychological research and practice. The interested reader should consult Baddeley, Wilson, and Watts (1995), Grant and Adams (1996), Hooper and March (1995), Lezak (1995), and Mapou and Spector (1986).

Neuropsychologists are quite specialized. Some focus on brain dysfunction in children (Ansari, 2011; Checa & Rueda, 2011; Dewey et al., 2011; Frampton & Warner-Rogers, 2011; Simos, Breznitz, & Berninger, 2011; Zhou et al., 2011) whereas others work with adults (Gupta et al., 2011; Harvey et al., 2011; Scott et al., 2011) or older adults (Kaszniak & Christenson, 1994; Welsh, Butters, Hughes, Mobs, & Hayman, 1991). Neuropsychologists focus mainly on brain dysfunction, but some are actively developing interventions for those who suffer brain injuries or related problems (Brenner, 2011; Lin et al., 2011). Neuropsychologists also study how cognitive processes are affected by mental illness (McKenna, Clare, & Baddeley, 1995) as well as alcohol abuse (Byrd et al., 2011) or serious diseases such as AIDS (Heaton et al., 2011; Moore et al., 2011). Some specialize in the evaluation of older adults (Coffey, Cummings, & George, 2011). Some neuropsychologists prefer to use batteries of psychological tests, whereas others prefer specific tasks derived from experimental psychology (Atkinson & Adolphs, 2011; Gazzaniga, 2011; McDaniel & Einstein, 2011).

Neuropsychological assessment has been used to evaluate specific problems in memory. Clearly, memory is a heterogeneous phenomenon; scientists make distinctions among memory systems such as short- and long-term memory. Short-term memory occurs when one recollects or produces material immediately after it has been presented. The capacity for short-term memory is probably limited; without repetition one can hold information only a few minutes. Conversely, long-term memory may be stored for a long time (more than a few days), and the capacity for long-term memory is quite large.

Examiners use a variety of clinical techniques to measure memory dysfunction, including the Wechsler Memory Scale–Revised (WMS-R), the Memory Assessment Scales (MAS), the RANDT Memory Test (RMT), and the Luria-Nebraska battery. Short-term memory is best assessed using verbal tests. These include the immediate recall span, the digit span, and several word tests (Butters et al., 1995). The techniques used to assess short-term memory include tests that evaluate memory for specific stories or memory for lists of unrelated words.

Significant progress has been made in linking performance on neuropsychological tests to specific clinical problems (Bilder, 2011). For example, alcoholic dementia, which is caused by long-term chronic alcoholism, is characterized by dysfunction in visuospatial skills. Patients with Huntington's disease perform much better on recognition than do patients with Alzheimer's disease; however, the former may have retrograde amnesia with equally deficient recall of events from all decades, while the latter have more severe difficulties with recall for recent events and less for long-term memories (Butters et al., 1995).

Another example of a study that used neuropsychological evaluations compared recently detoxified alcoholics with nonalcoholic controls who were the same age and with recovering alcoholics who had been abstinent for at least

FIGURE 17.2

Learning and memory
performance by recently
detoxified alcoholics
(abstinent 2 weeks),
long-term abstinent
alcoholics (abstinent
18 months), and
nonalcoholic controls.

(Adapted from data in Dawson & Grant, 2000.)

18 months. The groups were comparable in education, age, and IQ. However, comparisons on learning and retention of new information differed. Figure 17.2 shows some of these differences. Recently detoxified alcoholics scored lower on measures of immediate recall, 20-minute delayed recall, and recognition than did comparable subjects who had been off alcohol for 18 months. Both groups of former alcoholics performed more poorly that did the nonalcoholic controls. These findings suggest that there may be some recovery of learning and memory when alcoholics are abstinent for 18 months or more. However, chronic alcohol use may permanently affect some neuropsychological functioning (Dawson & Grant, 2000).

Research also challenges the idea that functional problems are related to specific locations within the brain. New evidence suggests that complex cognitive, perceptual, and motor functioning are determined by neural systems rather than specific single structures. There are complicated circuits and dense interconnections between different locations in the brain. Neuropsychological evaluation estimates localized problems as well as problems with the brain's complex interconnections.

One of the most studied areas of neuropsychology is the identification of deficits in the left or right hemisphere of the brain. Evidence for left hemisphere control of language in right-handed individuals comes from studies on brain damage, studies of brain stimulation during surgery for patients with epilepsy, and from evaluation of people who have suffered a stroke on one side of the brain. However, approximately two thirds of left-handed people have language organized on the left side of the brain, approximately 20% have language organized in the right hemisphere, and the remainder appear to have language represented on both sides. Table 17.1 summarizes some of the problems associated with left or right hemisphere damage (Swanda et al., 2000).

Trained neuropsychologists can identify specific problems. For example, Wernicke's aphasia is characterized by impaired verbal comprehension and ability to repeat information. People with this pattern of impairment have damage to Wernicke's area of the brain (the superior temporal gyrus), problems monitoring their language output, and often have difficulty with the syntax of their spoken sentences. Sometimes people affected by Wernicke's aphasia utter unintelligible strings of words that can be confused with schizophrenic symptoms.

**TABLE 17.1**  Selected Neuropsychological Deficits Associated with Left or Right Hemisphere Damage

| Left hemisphere | Right hemisphere |
| --- | --- |
| Word memory problems | Visual–spatial deficits |
| Right–left disorientation | Impaired visual perception |
| Finger agnosia | Neglect |
| Problems recognizing written words | Difficulty writing |
| Problems performing calculations | Problems with spatial calculations |
| Problems with detailed voluntary motor activities, not explained by paralysis | Problems with gross coordinated voluntary motor not explained by paralysis activities |
| Problems dressing | Inability to recognize a physical deficit (e.g., denial of a paralyzed limb) |

Adapted from Swanda, Haaland, and LaRue (2000).

Neuropsychological tests can also be used to diagnose motor problems. For example, right-handed people who have damage to their right hemisphere often develop spatial disorders such as the inability to copy or draw objects or difficulties assembling certain objects. Some individuals may develop specific problems associated with right hemisphere damage, such as dressing apraxia. People with this condition have difficulty identifying the top or the bottom of a garment, and sometimes the left or the right side as well. Although these individuals may function well in other aspects of their lives, they have a great deal of difficulty dressing.

Neuropsychologists are also skilled at identifying which aspects of the information-processing systems may be damaged. For example, information retrieval and storage are related but different functions. Some people have problems in recall or retrieval of information. Tests can be used to determine whether the problem is in recognition or actual retrieval of information. Recognition might be evaluated using multiple-choice format items. Patients who have difficulty recognizing information may have deficiencies in storage, which is associated with the medial temporal lobes or the diencephalic system. Impaired retrieval of information may be associated with problems in the frontal lobes, for example. (See Focused Example 17.1.)

## Developmental Neuropsychology

Testing is typically done as part of a complex evaluation. When children are not performing well in school, a medical, educational, and psychological evaluation might be ordered. Sometimes, neuropsychological testing is done to provide a baseline. For example, a child who is undergoing intense medical therapy or a child with a serious medical illness such as epilepsy may face neurological changes over time. Repeated neuropsychological evaluations can help identify such changes (Baron & Fennell, 2000; McDonald et al., 2011).

## 17.1 FOCUSED EXAMPLE

### Case Study: Neuropsychological Consequences of Long-Term Alcohol Abuse

Neuropsychological evaluation uses a variety of approaches to identify problems with brain functioning. One task that is often informative is to have the patient draw a clock. Damage to the right hemisphere of the brain is sometimes reflected in inaccurate global features of the drawing. Left hemisphere damage is associated with the reproduction of small features and details.

A case study helps illustrate the value of the clock drawing task. The patient in this study had been admitted to the hospital after he had called 911 and stated he was suicidal. He was intoxicated at the time of admission and had a significant history of alcohol abuse. The same patient had received neurological evaluations on several previous occasions. The patient was well educated and had completed college. He had good verbal skills, with a Wechsler Adult Intelli-

gence Scale (WAIS) verbal IQ of 103. However, some of his WAIS subscores were lower. For example, the digit span subtest was in the 25th percentile, and his performance on the memory domain was in the first percentile.

Figure 17.3 shows the subject's performance on the Draw-a-Clock task from the Boston Diagnostic Aphasia Examination. The task asks the patient, "Draw a clock, put in all of the numbers, and set the hands for ten after 11." The left-hand portion of the figure shows the clock drawn in 1996. The center section shows the clock drawn in 1998, while the third panel shows the clock drawn during the hospital admission in 1999.

The pattern of performance suggests a deterioration in parietal lobe functioning indicated by poor visuospatial functioning. It is likely that long-term alcohol abuse contributed to these problems.

**FIGURE 17.3**
Results from the
Draw-a-Clock task.

1996          1998          1999

(Dean Delis, Ph.D., provided this example.)

Neuropsychological assessment of children presents unique challenges. For example, a young child with a brain injury may adapt well to most situations, but she may later have problems with, say, her geometry class, which would require more complex visual–perceptual functioning than she had encountered before. Earlier brain injury may be missed until children reach the age where they are challenged with new types of problems.

Another challenge in evaluating children is brain plasticity. The human brain is remarkable in its potential to reorganize in response to injury. Although recovery is often impressive, it usually is not complete, and these problems are often hard to evaluate using neuropsychological tests.

Neuropsychological tests for children differ widely. One category of measures tests general development and adaptive functioning. Examples include the Child Development Inventory, Child Behavior Checklist, Reynolds Depression Scale, and Children's State-Trait Anxiety Scale.

A second group of measures estimates attention and executive function. These tests typically evaluate functioning related to several different aspects of information processing. The Trail Making Tests, for example, scatter sequential numbers (e.g., 1, 2, 3, 4) around different locations on a sheet of paper. The child is asked to draw lines to connect the numbers in sequence. Part B of the test adds scattered sequential letters, and the child must, for example, start at 1, go to *A*, then go to 2, then *B*, and so on. The test evaluates several cognitive skills including attention, sequencing, and thought processing.

Attention and executive function are believed to be separate. Executive function includes volition, such as forming and executing a goal, planning, and taking action to complete a task. It also includes the self-control and self-monitoring to complete the task. Mirsky and colleagues (Mirsky, 1989, 1996; Mirsky, Kugelmass, Ingraham, & Frenkel, 1995) have identified four different factors of mental processing and related them to specific anatomical regions in the brain. One factor is *focus execute*. This refers to the child's ability to scan information and respond in a meaningful way. A second factor is *sustain*, which describes the child's capacity to pay close attention for a defined interval of time. The third factor is *encode* and is related to information storage, recall, and mental manipulation. The final factor, called *shift*, refers to the ability to be flexible. Different neuropsychological tests are used to assess each of these four factors (Baron & Fennell, 2000).

The study of childhood brain dysfunction is extremely important. Neuropsychological problems appear in speech and reading disorders known generally as *learning disabilities*, which account for problems in significant numbers of young children. **Dyslexia** is a specific reading disorder characterized by difficulties in decoding single words. The problem may have a genetic base and may result from difficulties in processing phonemes. Unfortunately, it is difficult to estimate the exact number of children who are affected by dyslexia because different studies apply different definitions. The problem likely affects approximately 4% of school-aged children and approximately 80% of children identified as having a learning disability.

Federal law now requires that children with specific disabilities receive individualized instructional programs and special attention. Thus, the identification of a disability means that considerable attention will be devoted to the child at enormous public expense. In other words, learning disabilities represent major public health problems. As such, considerable effort has been devoted to defining subcategories of learning disabilities, developing procedures to identify them, and instituting methods for helping children overcome these problems (Cleary & Scott, 2011; Frampton & Warner-Rogers, 2011).

In addition to identification of brain injury, neuropsychological evaluations have been used for a variety of other purposes. For example, neuropsychological testing has been used to determine if people are faking illness. One application is the detection of malingering for adults who have traumatic brain injury. In one study, 65 patients who had previous brain injury were referred for a neuropsychological evaluation. Twenty-eight of these patients had been identified as having exaggerated their cognitive dysfunction in order to gain greater benefits or to escape reassignment

## Neuropsychological Consequences of Football Head Injuries

Head injuries and concussions are very common among football players (Guskiewicz & Broglio, 2011). Concussions occur when the head accelerates rapidly and then is stopped, or when the head is spun rapidly. Concussions are not bruises to the brain caused by hitting something hard, and there is usually no physical evidence that the brain is swollen or bleeding. However, violent shaking of the brain may cause some cells to become depolarized and fire their neurotransmitters all at one time. This might result in a flood of neurotransmitters in the brain resulting in a down regulation of receptors that are related to learning and memory. The experience can also result in blurred vision, nausea, and memory loss. In some cases, rapid release of neurotransmitters might result in loss of consciousness. Sequential concussions can cause serious problems because it takes some time for the brain to recover (Ocwieja et al., 2012).

Concussions are particularly common among players in the National Football League (NFL). One study of retired athletes suggested that 61% had had at least one concussion and about a quarter had had three or more concussions (Guskiewicz et al., 2005). Among retired NFL players who reported sustaining one or more concussions while playing football, at least one in five also reported experiencing depression. That rate is about three times higher than the rate of depression among football players who had not experienced multiple concussions. Players who had experienced three or more concussions had a fivefold risk of mild cognitive impairment(Guskiewicz et al., 2007).

As a result of these problems, in early 2012, the NFL was bracing for a series of lawsuits from former players. More than a dozen lawsuits were filed in the later part of 2011, and about 120 former players were considering legal action. Several studies of the long-term neuropsychological consequences of football head injuries are underway, although we still await definitive neuropsychological evidence on the effects of football head trauma. (Based on K. Belson, NFL Concussion Suits May Be Tests for Sport Itself. *New York Times*, December 29, 2011.)

to work. All subjects completed the WAIS (see Chapter 11). Using discriminate function analysis, which is a specialized method for identifying the linear combination of variables that separate groups, the researchers developed an equation that successfully separated malingerers from those who were not exaggerating their brain injury (Greve, Bianchini, Mathias, & Houston, 2003).

Another application of neuropsychological testing is to determine the seriousness of concussions among athletes (Erlanger, Kaushik, Cantu, Barth, Broshek, Freeman, et al., 2003). Head injury for athletes is common, particularly in sports such as boxing and football (See Focused Example 17.2). An injured athlete often wants to return to play promptly. Returning the athlete to the playing field too soon might put him or her at serious risk. One application of clinical neuropsychology is the development of a concussion resolution index (CRI) to track the recovery following a sports-related concussion. CRI is made up of six subtests including reaction time, visual recognition, and speed of information processing. Validity studies show that the CRI is associated with other neuropsychological tests. For example, it correlates with the grooved pegboard test. Studies using athletes who have been injured demonstrated that this computer-based test can identify ongoing neuropsychological difficulties in cases where symptom reports and clinical examinations are normal. Ongoing problems in psychomotor speed and speed of information processing may put athletes at risk for future injury. Use of these new methods could be exceptionally helpful for determining when it is safe for athletes to return to the playing field (Erlanger, Feldman, Kutner, Kaushik, Kroger, et al., 2003).

Other clinical neuropsychologists have been busy identifying the cognitive consequences of early brain lesions. For example, studies have shown that high-risk infants have persistent poor performance on tests of verbal ability, coordination, visual–spatial ability, and the like by the time they are 5-years-old (Caravale, Mirante, Vagnoni, & Vicari, 2011). Other studies focus on recovery from accidents and trauma. For example, a few years after children have been in accidents involving head injuries, neurological tests often show no remaining problems. Nevertheless, neuropsychological tests of intellectual abilities often show that these functions remain somewhat impaired (Butters et al., 1995). In summary, developmental neuropsychologists actively work toward understanding brain-behavior relationships in children. They have created extensive diagnostic procedures for identifying learning disabilities such as articulation disorders, speech disorders, and dyslexia. Furthermore, they have attempted to link specific medical problems such as birth complications and prematurity to later intellectual function. Finally, they have attempted to identify the cognitive consequences of early brain disease and injury.

Developmental neuropsychology is a difficult field because it requires several levels of assessment. Figure 17.4 shows a seven-step model that is used by neuropsychologists in the development of rehabilitation plans. The first step requires the application of formal tests to determine the nature of the problem. The second step calls for an assessment of the environment, such as the demands of the school environment and other academic expectations. The third and fourth steps require the formulation of treatment plans, which involve a prediction of the short- and long-term consequences of the brain problem and the chances that intervention will make a difference. The fifth step concerns the availability of resources. For example, is there a family member who can assist in treatment? Are there facilities and therapists in the community? The sixth step calls for the development of a realistic treatment plan that considers the information gained in Steps 1–5. Even if the neuropsychologist does not deliver the treatment, he or she may remain involved in the seventh step, evaluating progress made in the course of clinical care. When treatment is not achieving its objectives, modifications may be suggested (Fletcher et al., 1995).

As suggested by Figure 17.4, the neuropsychologist has many complex and important tasks that require the administration and interpretation of assessment devices. Developmental neuropsychologists are often called upon for testimony in courts of law. Focused Example 17.3 describes the challenges of deciding whether adolescents can be tried as adults in serious criminal cases.

## Adult Neuropsychology

There are many different approaches to identifying the consequences of brain injury in adults. Perhaps the two best-known approaches involve administration of the Halstead-Reitan and Luria-Nebraska test batteries.

### Halstead-Reitan Neuropsychological Battery

In 1935, Ward Halstead opened a laboratory to study the impact of impairments of brain function on a wide range of human abilities. Some of Halstead's observations were formal, while others involved observations in work and social settings. The formal observations were obtained through modifications of existing psychological tests. Over time, Halstead realized that determining inadequacy in brain function required

FIGURE 17.4

The process of rehabilitation requires at least seven steps: (1) assessment of the child, (2) assessment of the environment, (3) predictions about short- and long-term outcomes, (4) development of an ideal plan, (5) assessment of resources, (6) development of a realistic intervention plan, and (7) ongoing assessment.

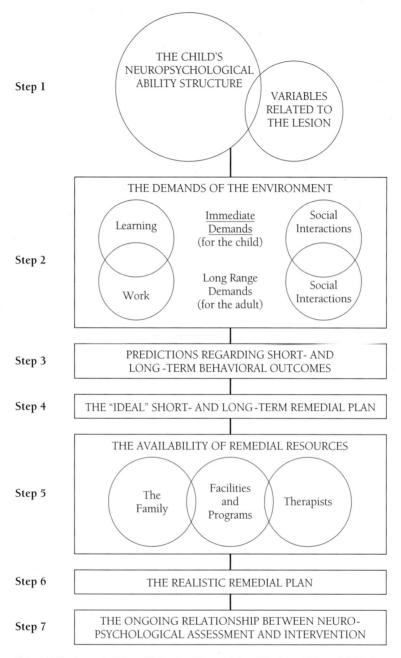

(From J. M. Fletcher et al., 1995, p. 585. Reprinted by permission of Lippincott, Williams, & Wilkins.)

a wide range of tests that measured characteristics and abilities beyond those targeted by existing psychological tests. In 1944, Halstead was joined in his neuropsychological laboratory by his first graduate student, Ralph M. Reitan. Halstead and Reitan worked together until 1950, when Reitan received his Ph.D. Reitan contributed by adding several tests to the assessment procedures. The full battery includes many psychological tests and sometimes requires 8 to 12 hours to administer. In addition,

## 17.3 FOCUSED EXAMPLE

### Should Adolescents Be Tried as Adults? The Developing Adolescent Brain

Our criminal justice system usually has separate processes for trying children and adults. But some terrible crimes have been committed by children and adolescents. When crimes are very serious, many states allow children to be tried as adults. One compelling case was *United States vs. Omar Khadr*. Mr. Khadr was imprisoned at Guantánamo Bay for building improvised explosive devices (IEDs). Khadr was only 15 years old when he allegedly committed these crimes. The prosecution argued that building a bomb requires adult-like cognitive maturity. But is the brain of a 15-year-old the same as an adult brain?

Although adolescents may be similar in size to adults, there is increasing evidence that their brains continue to mature well into their 20s (Albert, 2012). For example, late in adolescence the gray matter in the prefrontal regions decreases in volume. This probably happens because there is a pruning of synapses

that had not been used. In addition, there is a proliferation and then a reduction of dopamine receptors in the paralimbic and prefrontal cortical regions of the brain. These components of the brain are active in reward systems, including the sensitivity to drugs. There is also an increase of white matter in the prefrontal regions and an extension of the white matter tracks to different areas of the brain. In short, the brain of an adolescent is not the same as the brain of an adult (Albert, 2012). The differences affect a wide variety of behaviors ranging from sleep to attention to the ability to operate complex machinery, such as an automobile (Steinberg, 2010). Evidence on the developing brain has only emerged in the last 10 to 15 years, and it has been slow to affect public policy (Midson, 2011). Nevertheless, the role of the developing brain is now gaining greater consideration in public policy discussions.

patients assessed by the Halstead-Reitan battery often receive the full Minnesota Multiphasic Personality Inventory (MMPI) to evaluate their emotional state in response to a medical situation. The battery also includes a full WAIS.

The full Halstead-Reitan Neuropsychological Battery is available in different versions for children and adults. See Table 17.2 for a summary of the components in the adult battery.

A large number of studies validate the Halstead and Reitan procedures (Reitan, 1968). Most of the studies show that performance on specific subtasks of the Halstead-Reitan battery is associated with dysfunction in one of the two hemispheres of the brain. For example, tactile, visual, and auditory problems on one side of the body reflect damage in the opposite hemisphere of the brain. Difficulty on the right side of the body indicates a problem in the left side of the brain (Wheeler & Reitan, 1962). Later studies by Reitan (1968) demonstrated that the battery can locate tumors or lesions in the right or left hemisphere of the brain and in the front or back portion of the brain in a significant number of cases. By studying performance in a systematic way, neuropsychologists have been able to provide important information about the location and the impact of brain problems (Reitan & Wolfson, 1997, 1999).

Critics of the Halstead-Reitan battery point out that the major advantage of the test may not be worth the effort in applying the measures. The battery can assist in localizing injury in either the left or right hemisphere of the brain. However, this advantage may be meager in relation to the many hours it takes to complete the test. New methods of brain imaging (MRI and CT scan) may be more efficient for locating injury (Swanda et al., 2000).

**TABLE 17.2** Components of the Halstead-Reitan Neuropsychological Battery for Adults

| Test | Description |
| --- | --- |
| Halstead category test | This test is a learning experiment for current learning skills, mental efficiency, and abstract concept formation. |
| Tactual test (time, memory, localization) | The patient must put variously shaped blocks into holes of the same shape. The test assesses several abilities, including motor speed and tactual and kinesthetic psychomotor performance, as well as memory. |
| Rhythm test | Thirty pairs of rhythm beats are presented, and the patient is to identify which pairs are the same and which are different. |
| | The task measures auditory perception, concentration, and attention. |
| Speech-sounds perception test | Sixty nonsense words are presented on a tape recorder. |
| | After hearing each word, the patient must choose the word from among four alternatives presented visually. |
| | The test measures auditory–verbal perception, auditory–visual coordination, and some aspects of language and concentration. |
| Finger oscillation test | The patient taps the index finger as rapidly as possible, alternating hands on consecutive trials. The test is used to analyze motor speed and right–left hand preference. |
| Related Procedures | The following tests are often given in conjunction with the Halstead-Reitan battery. |
| Trail-making test | This test requires patients to connect numbers and letters as rapidly as possible. The test measures speed, visual scanning, and ability to process information in sequence. |
| Strength-of-grip test | A mechanical device (the hand dynamometer) is used to measure the strength of grip in each hand. |
| Sensory–perceptual examination | In a variety of sensory modalities, such as touch, hearing, and vision, the patient receives information on one side of the body and then on the other side. The test is used to determine whether stimuli presented on one side of the body are perceived when presented alone and also to determine whether competition with other stimulation reduces the perception of the stimulus. |

From Saccuzzo & Kaplan (1984, pp. 226–227).

## Luria-Nebraska Neuropsychological Battery

A different approach to neuropsychological assessment is found in the work of Luria, who was recognized for many years as an expert on the functions of the human brain (Luria, 1966, 1973). While other researchers such as Halstead and Reitan attempted to find specific areas within the brain that correspond to particular behaviors, Luria did not acknowledge that any single area was solely responsible for any particular behavior. Instead, Luria saw the brain as a functional system, with a limited number of brain areas involved in each behavior. Each area in the functional system might be considered a necessary link in a chain. If any link is injured, the total system will break down.

Luria also introduced the concept of *pluripotentiality*—that any one center in the brain can be involved in several different functional systems (Golden, 1981). For example, one center in the brain may be involved in both visual and tactile senses. Luria also felt that multiple systems might be responsible for the same behavior. Thus, if a child's injury affects one system, another system may take over. Many clinical examples show the value of Luria's methods, particularly for severely disabled patients who may have multiple health problems and cannot complete traditional psychological tests (Guedalia, Finkelstein, Drukker, & Frishberg, 2000).

In practice, Luria applied his theory clinically to make intuitive judgments about deficits in functional systems. Because he did not use a standardized procedure, the amount of time he spent testing individuals varied greatly. In addition, it was difficult for others to repeat the exact steps Luria had used to reach conclusions about particular patients. Reitan (1976) criticized him on the grounds that Luria's opinion was the only known evidence for the validity of the tests.

Although Luria's procedures were widely regarded as important, they did not meet the psychometric standards of many U.S. psychologists. To face these criticisms, Golden (1981) developed a standardized version of Luria's procedures. Because Golden worked at the University of Nebraska, the test has become known as the Luria-Nebraska Neuropsychological Battery. The battery includes 269 items that can be administered in approximately 24 hours. The items are divided into 10 subsections; these are listed in Table 17.3. A similar test for children has also been developed (Plaisted, Gustavson, Wilkening, & Golden, 1983).

The inventory is scored by finding a standardized performance level for each of the 11 subtests. In addition, three more scores are reported. First, a pathognomonic scale consists of 32 items found in previous studies to be highly sensitive to brain dysfunction. The other two scores indicate whether dysfunction is in the right or the left hemisphere of the brain. They are taken from the sections of the battery that independently test the function of the right or left side of the body.

A variety of studies (summarized by Golden, 1981) have demonstrated that the Luria-Nebraska battery can make fine distinctions in neuropsychological functions. Many of these studies used the battery to estimate the area of the brain damaged by a tumor or lesion. In many of these studies, confirmation of localization is made by surgery, angiogram, or CT scan. In one study, the Luria-Nebraska battery localized problems in 22 of 24 right hemisphere and 29 of 36 left hemisphere cases (Golden, 1981). Some evaluations of the Luria-Nebraska battery are highly encouraging, whereas others show that these tests give little more information than do IQ tests (Carr, Sweet, & Rossini, 1986). Statistical methods for interpreting results are continually improving (Moses, Pritchard, & Faustman, 1994; Reynolds, 1982; Webster & Dostrow, 1982); nevertheless, the approach still has serious critics (Spiers, 1982).

An example of a profile from a patient tested with the Luria-Nebraska battery is shown in Figure 17.5. The two dark horizontal lines in the figure represent the normal ranges for performance on the various subtests. Scores above the top dark line indicate significant problem areas. As the figure shows, the patient demonstrates significant impairment in both expressive and receptive language, as well as problems in arithmetic and writing. Neuropsychologists have learned that memory

**TABLE 17.3** Subsections of Luria-Nebraska Neuropsychological Battery

| Test | Description |
|---|---|
| Motor functions | Examines basic and complex motor skills. Some items ask patients to perform fine tasks with the right and left hand and with the eyes open or closed. Other items involve mouth, tongue, and speech movements. |
| Rhythm | Evaluates rhythm and pitch skills. Patients must reproduce melodic sounds such as those from the song "Home on the Range." They are also to identify soft and loud sounds and musical patterns. |
| Tactile | Evaluates a variety of kinesthetic (movement) and tactile (touch) abilities. Patients are blindfolded and asked to identify where they have been touched. Then they must identify a variety of shapes and letters written on the back of the patients' hands. In addition, patients must identify common objects such as quarters, keys, paper clips, and so on. |
| Visual | Investigates visual and spatial skills. Patients are asked to identify objects through pictures and through progressively more difficult items. They are asked to put pieces together or identify objects in overlapping sketches. |
| Receptive speech | Tests ability to understand the spoken language. Items range from simple phonemes to comprehension of complex sentences. |
| Expressive speech | Estimates ability to express speech orally. The word sounds range from "see" to "Massachusetts" to "episcopal." Writing identifies basic writing skills including simple spelling, copying letters and words, and writing names. |
| Reading | Similar to writing section. It tests whether patients can identify individual letters and read symbols, words, sentences, and stories. |
| Arithmetic skills | Tests a variety of simple numeric and algebraic abilities. |
| Memory | Assesses verbal and nonverbal memory skills. Items range from simple recall to complex memorization tasks. |
| Intellectual processes | Evaluates intellectual level using items similar to those on traditional intelligence tests. |

From Saccuzzo & Kaplan (1984, p. 230).

problems are often associated with damage in the temporal lobe of the brain. Thus, the good performance on memory rules out a temporal lobe problem. Receptive and expressive language abilities seem to be localized more in the left than the right side of the brain. Comparing the profile with information acquired in other studies, the neuropsychologists estimated that there was damage in the left side of the brain in the parietal-occipital area (toward the back of the left side). A neurological report confirmed that a stroke had damaged this very area.

Using information from neuropsychological test batteries, clinicians can evaluate damage and suggest programs for rehabilitation. Despite important improvements in the Luria-Nebraska battery, several methodological questions still remain. After a detailed review of the test and the standardization procedures, Lezak (1995) argued that it is important to interpret results of these tests with great caution. Some neuropsychologists prefer to use specific experimental tasks in addition to test batteries. One of the ongoing debates among neuropsychologists concerns

FIGURE 17.5
Profile of a patient tested with the Luria-Nebraska battery.

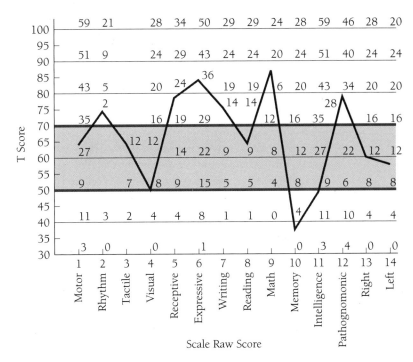

(From Golden, 1981. Copyright © 1981 by John Wiley & Sons, Inc. Reprinted by permission of John Wiley & Sons, Inc.)

the value of qualitative versus quantitative approaches. The Halstead-Reitan is an example of a fixed quantitative battery. Psychologists using this approach simply follow a set of standardized procedures. Qualitative approaches allow greater flexibility in the assessment process. Often the measures are designed to identify a specific information-processing problem and the psychologist can choose the components that may address specific clinical problems (Baron & Fennell, 2000). The California Verbal Learning Test is an example of this more recent approach.

## California Verbal Learning Test (CVLT)

For decades, psychologists have known that people can get a wrong response for different reasons. For example, Werner (1937) objected to the use of global scores based only on the number of right or wrong items. Instead, Werner favored tests that assess how problems are solved in addition to assessing overall level of achievement.

Modern cognitive psychology has identified many levels of human information processing (Squire & Butters, 1984). Contemporary cognitive psychology suggests that many factors determine performance on any given task (Delis & Wetter, 2007). It is not enough to know that there is an impairment in cognitive functioning. Instead, one needs to know which aspects of the human information-processing system are defective and which aspects are functioning well. This information is essential in designing rehabilitation strategies for patients who have selective problems.

The CVLT is a relatively new approach to clinical neuropsychology that builds on research in psychological testing, cognitive psychology, and computer science (Delis, Kramer, Kaplan, & Ober, 1987). The test determines how errors are made in learning tasks. In other words, the intent is to identify different strategies, processes, and errors that are associated with specific deficits. The test attempts to link memory deficits with impaired performance on specific tasks for people who have known neurological problems. The CVLT assesses various variables, including levels of recall and recognition, semantic and serial strategies, serial position effects, learning rates across trials, consistency of item recall across trials, degree of vulnerability to proactive and retroactive interference, retention of information over short and long delays, and learning errors in recall and recognition.

In one component of the CVLT, the subject is asked to imagine that he or she is going to go shopping. Then the subject receives a list of items to buy. The examiner lists 16 items orally at a pace of approximately one word per second. The respondent is asked to repeat the list. This process is repeated through a series of five trials.

Performance on these tasks is analyzed in many ways. For example, learning across trials gives the test taker considerable information. Those who are highly anxious may perform poorly on the first trial but improve as the task is repeated (Lezak, 1995). However, adults with limited learning capacity may do relatively well on early trials but reach a plateau where repeated trials do not reflect improved performance. Adults with limited learning capacity may also have inconsistent recall across trials. This can happen when they abandon one strategy and adopt another. Studies have demonstrated that inconsistent recall across trials characterizes patients with amnesia caused by frontal lobe pathology.

The CVLT also includes other features derived from experimental cognitive psychology. For example, after five trials of exposure to the 16-word lists, a second interference list of 16 words is given. Subjects are tested immediately, and again after 20 minutes, for free recall, cued recall, and recognition of the first list.

Another unique feature of the CVLT is that one can administer it either in a paper-and-pencil form or with a microcomputer. Versions for both the PC and the Macintosh are available. The computer does not replace test administrators but instead assists them. In the computer-assisted form of the test, the examiner can enter responses directly into the computer using a single key or a light pen to touch the words on a monitor screen. This greatly facilitates and speeds up the scoring process.

Several studies have evaluated the CVLT's validity. For example, the test correlates with other measures such as the Wechsler memory scale (Delis et al., 1987). In addition, factor analysis studies of the CVLT suggest independent factors for learning strategy, acquisition rate, serial position, discriminability, and learning performance. These constructs correspond to empirical findings from modern cognitive psychology. The diversity of deficits identified by the CVLT could not be identified using more-traditional psychometric tests (Delis et al., 1987).

The CVLT has been used to compare patients with Alzheimer's disease, Korsakoff's syndrome, and Huntington's disease. Alzheimer's disease is a serious neurological disorder that causes the inability to form short-term memories. Korsakoff's syndrome is an organic brain disorder often associated with long-term alcohol use that also results in the loss of short-term memory. Finally, Huntington's disease is an inherited disorder emerging in adulthood and associated with memory loss. Although all three organic brain problems are associated with memory loss, the nature of the deficit may be different. For example, patients with Alzheimer's and Huntington's may score about the same on measures of recall and memory tests but may differ in measures of forgetting (Bondi, Houston, Salmon, Corey-Bloom, Katzman, Thal, et al., 2003). Studies of brain pathology show that these two diseases affect different parts of the brain. An advantage of the CVLT is that it allows a more precise evaluation of the nature of the problems than do other tests.

When representative groups of patients from these three diagnostic groups are compared on the CVLT, those with Alzheimer's disease and with Korsakoff's syndrome appear quite similar, with comparable scores for recall, learning and forgetting, semantic clustering, and several other cognitive factors. However, each of these groups performed at a lower level than did patients with Huntington's disease on measures of retention, intrusion errors, and recognition (Delis, Magsman, Butters, Salmon, Cermak, & Kramer, 1991).

Studies of patients with Huntington's disease, Alzheimer's disease, and other neuropsychological impairments can help us understand properties of the tests. In one experiment, for example, normal patients, those with Huntington's disease, and those with Alzheimer's disease completed the CVLT. The patients were tested on immediate recall and long-delay free recall. As expected, the controls did significantly better than those with either Alzheimer's disease or Huntington's disease (see Figure 17.6). However, the correlations between the two tests were not the same for the different groups. Immediate recall and long-delayed recall were highly correlated (above $r = .80$) for normal patients and for patients with Huntington's disease. However, the two variables were correlated only .36 for patients with Alzheimer's disease. These findings are critically important because we often assume that the correlations between variables are the same for all patient groups. These findings suggest that the very nature of the association between variables is different for different patient populations. This challenges the idea that measures have the same validity for different patient groups (Delis, Jacobson, et al., 2003). Another study demonstrated that tests of executive functioning can discriminate between conditions that have different anatomical underpinnings. MRI was used to locate sections of the brain that had reduced volumes. Adults with dementia associated with the frontal lobes made more rule violation errors in comparison to

**FIGURE 17.6**
Long-delay recall on CVLT in three patient groups.

(Adapted from Delis et al., 1991.)

those with Alzheimer's disease or healthy adults who were about the same age (Carey et al., 2007).

Figure 17.6 compares CVLT scores for immediate and for long-delay savings for the two patient groups in comparison to a control group. *Long-delay savings* require that subjects learn a list of words. Then, after a long delay, they are given a free-recall test. The results are reported as the average number of correct responses. The figure shows that Huntington's patients have significantly higher recall than do those with Alzheimer's disease but fewer correct responses than controls. These results are consistent with the neuroanatomy of the illnesses. Huntington's disease is a subcortical dementia, whereas Alzheimer's disease is associated with cortical lesions. The CVLT may be helpful in identifying the location of the organic problem.

In 1994, Delis and colleagues released a children's version of the CVLT, the CVLT-C. Appropriate for children aged 5–16, this individually administered test can be used to evaluate mild to severe learning disabilities, attention deficit disorder (ADD), mental retardation, and other neurological disorders. In addition, the CVLT-C provides information for the diagnosis of psychiatric disorders. Like the adult version, the CVLT-C assesses both recall and recognition of words. In a typical testing session, the child may receive a list of 15 words on Monday and an interference list of 15 words on Tuesday. After the interference list, the child is tested on the Monday list. After a 20-minute delay, a nonverbal test is administered, followed by tests of long-delay free recall and long-delay cued recall, then a test designed to assess recognition of the words that were administered the day before. These procedures produce several different scores including total recall, learning strategy, serial position effect, learning rate, consistency of item recall, proactive and retroactive interference, and retention over long and short delays.

The test was standardized on a large national sample. Internal consistency and alpha reliabilities for the test are generally high (usually above .80 for all age levels). Validity studies consistently show that the test is moderately correlated (between .32 and .40) with the Revised Wechsler Intelligence Scale for Children (WISC-R) vocabulary subtest (Delis, Kramer, et al., 2004). In contrast to other tests, however, the CVLT-C provides substantially more diagnostic information (Delis et al., 1994). It is beginning to find a variety of clinical uses. For example, recent studies suggest that the CVLT can be used to detect whether patients are faking head injury in order to gain benefits (Sweet et al., 2000).

## Automated Neuropsychological Testing

One of the most important new developments in clinical neuropsychology is automated neuropsychological assessment. New methods have been developed to provide quick computerized interpretation of neuropsychological tests. The Automated Neuropsychological Metrics (ANAM) test system is one such development. The ANAM was developed by the U.S. Department of Defense, in order to evaluate changes in human performance when people were exposed to difficult environmental circumstances. The measure has now been used in a variety of clinical populations including studies of patients with multiple sclerosis, lupus, Parkinson's disease, Alzheimer's disease, brain injury, and migraine headache. In each of these patient populations, the ANAM was responsive to cognitive changes that result from neurological disorders. A variety of studies suggested that the ANAM can efficiently screen people with cognitive changes and that it may be a valuable tool for monitoring cognitive changes as diseases progress (Kane et al., 2007).

The ANAM includes a variety of different tasks including code substitution, code substitution recognition, matching two samples, mathematics, running memory, and logical reasoning. The reliability of performance on these tasks tends to be in the moderate range with few coefficients above .8. Studies have suggested that the math and running memory tasks are associated with measures that would be expected to correlate with cognitive functioning. These include performances on time limited attention tasks and working memory tasks. Overall, there is reasonably good evidence for the validity of the ANAM (Short et al., 2007).

In summary, clinical neuropsychology is an emerging and important area in psychological testing. It is linked closely to basic research in both neuroscience and cognitive psychology. We expect this field to continue its rapid development over the next few decades.

## Anxiety and Stress Assessment

It is the day of your final exam. You have studied hard and have every reason to expect an A. As you enter the classroom, the back of your neck feels stiff. Your hands sweat as you get out your pencil. Instead of concentrating on the task of test taking, you worry about not doing well, or you think about running out of time. When it is all over, you feel cheated. You knew the material well, but your grade on the exam did not reflect your knowledge.

If this story describes a situation you have experienced, then you have company. Test anxiety is a common problem among college students and a major factor in diminishing the validity of tests.

Test anxiety is also an important and active area in psychological research. Many theories about the relationship of anxiety to performance have led to the development of specific test-anxiety scales and measures (Endler, Kantor, & Parker, 1994; Flett & Blankstein, 1994; Sapp, 1999; Sarason & Sarason, 2011; Williams, 1994). In this section, we review the general concepts of anxiety and stress, and then we review in some detail the theory and measurement of the same.

## Stress and Anxiety

*Stress* is a response to situations that involve demands, constraints, or opportunities (Sarason & Sarason, 2011). We all experience psychological stress at some point in our lives. For some people, stress is a debilitating problem that interferes with virtually every aspect of their lives. For others, stress causes problems in particular situations. Stress helps still others to accomplish important goals. The study of psychological stress has gained an increasingly central position within the psychological and biomedical sciences (Wainwright & Calnan, 2002). Psychological stress can interfere with performance on mental and academic tests (Oostdam & Meijer, 2003; Sapp, 1999), and some medical investigators now believe that stress is involved in 50% to 80% of all illnesses.

Psychological stress has three components: frustration, conflict, and pressure. *Frustration* occurs when the attainment of a goal is blocked. Though frustration takes different forms, the principle remains the same. A fourth-year premed student will likely become frustrated if she is rejected by every major medical school. Or if someone wants to get into a concert and is refused entrance, he may become frustrated. In each case, something or someone has blocked the attainment of a goal. *Conflict* is a type of stress that occurs when we must make a choice between two or more important goals, such as deciding between going to law school and going to graduate school in psychology. The final type of stress is *pressure* to speed up activities. External pressure occurs when your professor assigns a lot of extra reading right before the midterm exam; internal pressure occurs when no such reading is assigned but you take it on yourself because it fits your style and aspirations. Test anxiety does respond to treatment, particularly interventions that combine skills for test taking with cognitive and behavioral modification (Ergene, 2003).

Exposure to stressful situations can cause an observable reaction known as **anxiety**, an emotional state marked by worry, apprehension, and tension. When you are anxious, your autonomic nervous system becomes activated: Your heart beats fast, your pulse rate goes up, your hands tend to sweat. The amount of anxiety you experience depends in part on the intensity of the stress-producing stimulus as you perceive it, or your evaluation of a situation (Potvin et al., 2011). How potentially harmful is the situation for you?

## The State-Trait Anxiety Inventory

Actually, there are two types of anxiety. *State anxiety* is an emotional reaction that varies from one situation to another. *Trait anxiety* is a personality characteristic. Interest in these two types of anxiety led Charles D. Spielberger to develop the state-trait anxiety theory, which in turn led to the development of the State-Trait Anxiety Inventory (STAI). The STAI provides two separate scores: one for state anxiety (A-State) and another for trait anxiety (A-Trait). The STAI A-Trait scale consists of 20 items. On a 4-point scale, subjects indicate how they generally feel about each item. A similar set of items is used to evaluate the A-State.

Good evidence exists for the validity and the reliability of the STAI. Test–retest reliabilities range from .73 to .86 for the trait scale. The state scale, which is supposed to be inconsistent over time, indeed has low test–retest reliability (.16 to .54). Validity studies show that the STAI can be used to make several important and useful generalizations. For example, concurrent validity studies have shown that the STAI trait scale correlates well with other measures of trait anxiety. The STAI trait scale has been correlated with the Taylor Manifest Anxiety Scale (see Spielberger & Sydeman, 1994); it was also associated with another trait-anxiety scale known as the Institute for Personality and Ability Testing (IPAT) Anxiety Scale (Cattell & Scheier, 1961) for the same groups of college students and psychiatric patients. The correlations with the Taylor and the IPAT ranged from .75 to .85, which are quite impressive and suggest that these three scales measure much of the same psychological dimension. Other scales that attempt to measure trait anxiety do not do so well. One example is the Affect Adjective Checklist developed by Zuckerman (1960), which correlated only moderately with other tests designed to measure trait anxiety. In this case, the concurrent validity correlations ranged from .41 to .57 (Spielberger, Gorsuch, & Lushene, 1970). Overall, the STAI seems to measure the same thing as other scales that purport to assess trait anxiety.

To give a test a positive recommendation, we must also find discriminant evidence for construct validity (see Chapter 5). In one validity study for the STAI (Spielberger, Auerbach, Wadsworth, Dun, & Taulbee, 1975), patients scheduled to undergo surgery took the STAI before and after the medical procedure. Patients who had undergone major surgery showed less state anxiety after they had been told they were recovering well than they had before the operation. This finding demonstrates that state anxiety fluctuates with the situation—just as the test constructors said it would. Trait anxiety was not affected by the situation; it remained the same before and after surgery. People high in trait anxiety continued to respond in an anxious way, even in situations that evoked little or no anxiety among people low in trait anxiety (Trotter & Endler, 1999). Each component of the STAI thus appears to measure what it is supposed to measure, and the two components clearly assess different aspects of anxiety. The STAI is useful because behavior is influenced by both situations and personality traits. Studies using the STAI to evaluate tobacco use showed that smoking is influenced by situations, such as enjoyment and stimulation, and that it managed emotions among those with high levels of trait anxiety (Spielberger, Foreyt, Reheiser, & Poston, 1998).

Over the course of several decades, studies have continually supported the value of the STAI. Evidence suggests that the STAI is reliable and that most items perform well, even when the test takers are in extremely stressful situations (Roy & Deb, 1999). Recent factor analysis studies have continued to show the two-factor structure. For example, a study that involved 205 patients with panic disorder confirmed that state and trait anxiety are two different dimensions, even among people with fairly serious emotional problems (Oei, Evans, & Crook, 1990). The factor structure also seems to hold in studies of Japanese workers (Iwata et al., 1998). The STAI has been translated into many different languages and is available in both adult and children's versions. There are good psychometric evaluations of many of these forms. For example, the psychometric properties of the French-Canadian STAI for children have been reported (Turgeon & Chartrand, 2003). There are also comparisons showing modest evidence for the validity of parent reports of their children's anxiety (Turgeon & Chartrand, 2003). The STAI has been validated for older adults (Potvin et al., 2011) and has been shorted for use in special populations, such as critically ill adults (Abed, Hall, & Moser, 2011).

## Measures of Coping

People confronted with the same stressful situation may respond quite differently. For instance, one group of investigators evaluated coping styles among adults suffering from heart failure. Patients with better coping skills were able to see more meaning in life, which in turn led to better outcomes in both physical and mental health status (Park et al., 2008).

Several measures have been developed to assess the ways in which people cope with stress (Lazarus et al., 2006). One of these measures, the Ways of Coping Scale (Folkman, 2010; Lazarus & Folkman, 1984), is a 68-item checklist. Individuals choose those thoughts and actions that they use to deal with stressful situations. The scale includes seven subscales for problem solving, growth, wishful thinking, advice seeking, minimizing threat, seeking support, and self-blame.

Studies have suggested that the seven subscales can be divided into problem-focused and emotion-focused strategies for dealing with stressful situations. Problem-focused strategies involve cognitive and behavioral attempts to change the course of the stress; these are active methods of coping. Emotion-focused strategies do not attempt to alter the stressor but instead focus on ways of dealing with the emotional responses to stress (Folkman, 2010). The Ways of Coping questionnaire is one of the most widely used measures in health psychology. However, some researchers have offered criticism. For example, some studies have failed to replicate the basic factor structure (Parker, Endler, & Bagby, 1993).

A related measure is the Coping Inventory (Horowitz & Wilner, 1980), a 33-item measure derived from clinical interview data. Of three categories of items, the first describes activities and attitudes that people use to avoid stress. The second involves items that characterize strategies for working through stressful events. The third category considers socialization responses, or how each strategy would help the respondent cope with a specific stressful event. These measures and related tests, such as the Coping Resources Inventory (Hammer & Marting, 1985), have been useful in research on both adults and adolescents. For example, one study demonstrated that having good coping capabilities is important whether or not you are under stress (Zeidner & Hammer, 1990).

## Ecological Momentary Assessment

Most psychological tests are designed to evaluate traits, which are constant over the course of time. Even measures of state anxiety are presumed to be reliable. However, levels of stress vary over the course of time. Measuring today's stress may tell us little about stress experienced next week. If we ask today about experiences last week, then the measurements may be inaccurate because memory fades over time. Recall affects virtually all autobiographical information.

New technical developments have made it possible to obtain information on an ongoing basis (Garcia et al., 2007; Litcher-Kelly et al., 2007; Stone & Broderick, 2007; Schneider, Stone, Schwartz, & Broderick, 2011). One can obtain information repeatedly and average the results to get an overall impression of stress. Or information can be assessed with reference to a particular event. For example, suppose that you wanted to determine if levels of perceived stress coincide with particular stressors. Using computer technology, Ecological Momentary Assessment (EMA) would allow you to collect information on a continuing basis. The equipment might measure blood pressure or hormonal state at specific points in time. Furthermore, a subject might be prompted to record information about mood, symptoms, or fatigue. This avoids the biases associated with asking people to remember their moods and symptoms, or experiences with pain (Schneider et al., 2011).

Most information in clinical studies is collected in clinics, offices, or laboratories—not necessarily the situations in which people ordinarily experience life events. One of the advantages of EMA is that the information is collected in the subject's natural environment. The EMA method usually involves a substantial number of repeated observations and shows variability within the subject over time (Stone & Shiffman, 2012).

Studies of the co-use of alcohol and tobacco illustrate the use of EMA. Traditional studies of alcohol consumption might actually miss much of the information about drinking because the assessment is typically done during the day, whereas alcohol consumption often occurs in the evening. EMA allows the continual assessment of these behaviors in the subject's own environment. In one study, 57 subjects were given minicomputers that randomly prompted them to record their behaviors. The study showed that drinking was likely to occur between 8 P.M. and midnight. Smoking was more than twice as likely when subjects had been drinking as when they had not. In other words, smoking and drinking were linked (Shiffman, Fischer, Paty, Gnys, et al., 1995). Some investigators use the latest technologies, including cell phones, to collect information in natural environments (Collins, Kashdan, & Gollnisch, 2003; Ferguson et al., 2011).

Other studies have used daily assessments to evaluate life stress (Todd, 2004). In one study, 74 patients with arthritis rated stress, mood, and pain for 75 days. Those who had experienced major stresses were more likely to experience pain on the day after a stressful event than on other days. This suggests that life stress may amplify the relationship between life events and pain (Affleck et al., 1994). Further technical developments such as the EMA should significantly improve the assessment of variable behaviors, pain, and emotions (Schneider et al., 2011; Stone, Broderick, & Schwartz, 2010).

# Quality-of-Life Assessment

Have you ever thought about what you value most in life? Most people say that their health is more important than anything else. In fact, studies on the preference for different states of being sometimes exclude ratings of health because people show so little variability in their attitudes toward it. The actual definition of health status, however, has remained ambiguous.

Among the many definitions of health, we find two common themes. First, everyone agrees that premature mortality is undesirable, so one aspect of health is the avoidance of death. The health status of nations is often evaluated in terms of mortality rates or infant mortality rates (the number of children who die before 1 year of age per 1000 live births). Second, quality of life is important. In other words, disease and disability are of concern because they affect either life expectancy or life quality. For example, cancer and heart disease are the two major causes of premature death in the United States. A person with heart disease may face restrictions on daily living activities and may be unable to work or participate in social activities. Even relatively minor diseases and disabilities affect quality of life. Think about how a common cold interferes with your ability to attend school or to concentrate. Then think about how a serious problem, such as traumatic brain injury, affects quality of life (Tulsky, Carlozzi, & Cella, 2011).

Within the last few years, medical scientists have come to realize the importance of quality-of-life measurement (Kaplan et al., 2011; Khanna et al., 2011; Palta et al., 2011). Many major as well as minor diseases are evaluated in terms of the degree to which they affect life quality and life expectancy (Kaplan & Ries, 2007). One can also evaluate treatments by the amount of improvement they produce in quality of life. The Food and Drug Administration now considers quality-of-life data in its evaluations of new products, and nearly all major clinical trials in medicine use quality-of-life assessment measures (Fiscella et al., 2011). In the remainder of this chapter, we review several approaches to quality-of-life measurement.

## What Is Health-Related Quality of Life?

Numerous quality-of-life measurement systems have evolved during the last 30 years and represent various traditions in measurement. Recent articles have presented at least two different conceptual approaches. One grows out of the tradition of health status measurement. In the late 1960s and early 1970s, the National Center for Health Services Research funded several major projects to develop general measures of health status. All of the projects were guided by the World Health Organization's (WHO) definition of health status: "Health is a complete state of physical, mental, and social well-being and not merely absence of disease" (WHO, 1948). The projects resulted in a variety of assessment tools, including the Sickness Impact Profile (Bergner, Babbitt, Carter, & Gilson, 1981), the Quality of Well-Being Scale (Kaplan & Anderson, 1990), the McMaster Health Index Questionnaire (Chambers, 1996), the SF-36 (Ware, Kosinski, Bayliss, McHorney, Rogers, & Raczek, 1995), and the Nottingham Health Profile (McEwen, 1992). Many of the measures examine the effect of disease or disability on performance of social role, ability to interact in the community, and physical functioning. Some of the systems have separate components for the measurement of social and mental health. The measures also differ in the extent to which they consider subjective aspects of life quality (Naughton & Shumaker, 2003).

There are two major approaches to quality-of-life assessment: psychometric and decision theory (Kaplan & Ries, 2007). The psychometric approach attempts to provide separate measures for the many different dimensions of quality of life. Perhaps the best-known example of the psychometric tradition is the Sickness Impact Profile (SIP). The SIP is a 136-item measure that yields 12 different scores displayed in a format similar to an MMPI profile.

The decision theory approach attempts to weight the different dimensions of health in order to provide a single expression of health status. Supporters of this approach argue that psychometric methods fail to consider that different health problems are not of equal concern. One hundred runny noses are not the same as 100 missing legs (Bush, 1984). In an experimental trial using the psychometric approach, one will often find that some aspects of quality of life improve while others get worse. For example, a medication might reduce high blood pressure but also produce headaches and impotence. Many argue that the quality-of-life notion is the subjective evaluation of observable or objective health states. The decision theory approach attempts to provide an overall measure of quality of life that integrates subjective function states, preferences for these states, morbidity, and mortality.

## Common Methods for Measuring Quality of Life

This chapter presents some of the most widely used methods for measuring quality of life. Readers who are interested in more detailed reviews should consult the guidelines published by the International Society for Quality of Life Research (Aaronson et al., 2011) or McDowell (McDowell, 2006).

### SF-36

Perhaps the most commonly used outcome measure in the world today is the Medical Outcome Study Short Form-36 (SF-36). The SF-36 grew out of work by the RAND Corporation and the Medical Outcomes Study (MOS) (Ware & Gandek, 1998). The MOS attempted to develop a short, 20-item instrument known as the Short Form-20 or SF-20. However, the SF-20 did not have appropriate reliability for some dimensions. The SF-36 includes eight health concepts: physical functioning, role-physical, bodily pain, general health perceptions, vitality, social functioning, role-emotional, and mental health (Kosinski, Keller, Ware, Hatoum, & Kong, 1999). The SF-36 can be either administered by a trained interviewer or self-administered.

It has many advantages. For example, it is brief, and there is substantial evidence for its reliability and validity. The SF-36 can be machine-scored and has been evaluated in large population studies. The reliability and validity of the SF-36 are well documented (Keller, Ware, Hatoum, & Kong, 1999; Ware, 2000; Ware & Kosinski, 2001).

The SF-36 also presents some disadvantages. For example, it does not have age-specific questions, and one cannot clearly determine whether it is equally appropriate across age levels (Stewart & Ware, 1992). Nevertheless, the SF-36 has become the most commonly used behavioral measure in contemporary medicine (Ware, 2003).

### Nottingham Health Profile (NHP)

Another major approach, the NHP, has particularly influenced the European community (Hagell, Whalley, McKenna, & Lindvall, 2003; Hinz, Klaiberg, Schumacher, & Brahler, 2003; Sivas, Ercin, Tanyolac, Barca, Aydog, & Ozoran, 2003; Uutela, Hakala, & Kautiainen, 2003). The NHP has two parts. The first includes 38 items divided into six categories: sleep, physical mobility, energy, pain, emotional reactions, and social isolation. Items within each section are rated in terms of relative importance. Items are rescaled in order to allow them to vary between 0 and 100 within each section.

The second part of the NHP includes seven statements related to the areas of life most affected by health: employment, household activities, social life, home life, sex life, hobbies and interests, and holidays. The respondent indicates whether or not a health condition has affected his or her life in these areas. Used in a substantial number of studies, the NHP has considerable evidence for its reliability and validity.

The NHP is consumer-based and arises from definitions of health offered by individuals in the community. Furthermore, this scale uses language that is easily interpreted by people in the community and conforms to minimum reading requirements. Substantial testing has been performed on the NHP; however, the NHP does not provide relative-importance weightings across dimensions. As a result, it is difficult to compare the dimensions directly with one another (Bureau-Chalot, Novella, Jolly, Ankri, Guillemin, & Blanchard, 2002). In comparison to the SF-36, there is some evidence that the NHP is more reliable for studies of elderly adults living in the community (Faria et al., 2011).

### Decision Theory Approaches

Within the last few years, interest has grown in using quality-of-life data to help evaluate the cost/utility or cost-effectiveness of health-care programs. Cost studies have gained in popularity because health-care costs have rapidly grown in recent years. All health-care interventions do not return equal benefit for the expended dollar. Cost studies might guide policymakers toward an optimal and equitable distribution of scarce resources. A cost-effectiveness analysis typically quantifies the benefits of a health-care intervention in terms of years of life, or quality-adjusted life-years (QALYs). Cost/utility is a special use of cost-effectiveness that weights observable health states by preferences or utility judgments of quality (Kaplan et al., 2011; Khanna et al., 2011). In cost/utility analysis, the benefits of medical care, behavioral interventions, or preventive programs are expressed in terms of well-years (Kaplan & Ries, 2007).

If a man dies of heart disease at age 50 and we expected him to live to age 75, then we might conclude that the disease precipitated 25 lost life-years. If 100 men died at age 50 (and also had a life expectancy of 75 years), then we might conclude that 2500 life-years (100 men x 25 years) had been lost. Death is not the only relevant outcome of heart disease. Many adults suffer myocardial infarctions that leave them disabled for a long time and suffering diminished quality of life. QALYs take into consideration such consequences. For example, a disease that reduces quality of life by one half will take away .5 QALY over the course of each year. If the disease affects two people, then it will take away 1 year (2 x .5) over each year. A medical treatment that improves quality of life by .2 for each of five individuals will result in the equivalent of 1 QALY if the benefit persists for 1 year. This system has the advantage of considering both benefits and side effects of programs in terms of the common QALY units.

The need to integrate mortality and quality-of-life information is clear in studies of heart disease. Consider hypertension. People with high blood pressure may live shorter lives if untreated, longer if treated. Thus, one benefit of treatment is to add years to life. However, for most patients, high blood pressure does not produce symptoms for many years. Conversely, the treatment for high blood pressure may cause negative side effects. If one evaluates a treatment only in terms of changes in life expectancy, then the benefits of the program will be overestimated because one has not taken side effects into consideration. On the other hand, considering only current quality of life will underestimate the treatment benefits because information on mortality is excluded. In fact, considering only current function might make the treatment look harmful because the side effects of the treatment might be worse than the symptoms of hypertension. A comprehensive measurement system takes into consideration side effects and benefits and provides an overall estimate of the benefit of treatment (Russell, 1986).

Most approaches for obtaining quality-adjusted life-years are similar (Groessl et al., 2007). The approach that we prefer involves several steps. First, patients are classified according to objective levels of functioning. These levels are represented by the scales of mobility, physical activity, and social activity. Next, once observable behavioral levels of functioning have been classified, each individual is placed on the 0 to 1.0 scale of wellness, which describes where a person lies on the continuum between optimum function and death.

Most traditional measures used in medicine and public health consider only whether a person is dead or alive. In other words, all living people get the same score. Yet we know that there are different levels of wellness, and a need to score these levels exists. To accomplish this, the observable health states are weighted by quality ratings for the desirability of these conditions. Human value studies have been conducted to place the observable states onto a preference continuum, with an anchor of 0 for death and 1.0 for completely well (Kaplan, Feeny, & Revicki, 1999). Studies have shown that the weights are highly stable over a 1-year period and consistent across diverse groups of raters (Kaplan, 1994b). Finally, one must consider the duration of stay in various health states. Having a cough or a headache for 1 day is not the same as having the problem for 1 year.

This system has been used to evaluate many different health-care programs (Kaplan, 2003; Kaplan & Groessl, 2002). For example, it was used to demonstrate that a new medication for patients with arthritis produced an average of .023 QALY per year, whereas a new medication for acquired immunodeficiency syndrome (AIDS) produced nearly .46 of these units per year. However, the benefit of the arthritis medication may last as long as 20 years, ultimately producing $.023 \times 20$ years $= .46$ year. The AIDS treatment produced a benefit for only 1 year, so its total effect was $.46 \times 1$ year $= .46$ year. In other words, the general system allows the full potential benefits of these two completely different treatments to be compared (Kaplan et al., 1995).

## mHealth and New Mobile Technologies

One of the most important new developments in health research and practice is "mHealth." mHealth is defined as diverse applications of wireless and mobile technologies designed to improve health research, health-care services, and health outcomes. This includes any wireless device carried by or on the person that can be used to transmit health data/information. The major categories include sensors (e.g., implantable miniature sensors and "nanosensors"), monitors (e.g., wireless accelerometers, blood pressure, and glucose monitors), and mobile phones (see Figure 17.7).

mHealth should not be confused with telehealth. The main difference is that mHealth is fundamentally a revolution in measurement. Devices used for mHealth are portable, real-time systems that provide a rich, potentially continuous data stream and capture information in the context of real, everyday life experiences. These new technologies give the concept of personalized health care a whole new meaning. Importantly, in these fiscally challenging times, mobile technologists are also scalable because they move away from the researcher and clinician working with a patient, to a model where data is collected and often processed automatically (Istepanian, Philip, Wang, & Laxminarayan, 2011).

It is possible that mHealth technologies will revolutionize measurement, change diagnostics and treatment, and ultimately impact health at a global level (Chang et al., 2011).

One of the greatest challenges in improving human health is accounting for and addressing all of the possible exposures a human being encounters during his or her life. mHealth technologies are likely to play a major role in advancing our approach to measuring behavioral and environmental exposures in everyday life (Dobkin & Dorsch, 2011). For example, we now have smartphone applications that help improve dietary choices through digital imaging. The phone captures a picture of a potential meal, identifies the food, and calculates portion size and recommended intake.

FIGURE 17.7
Examples of mHealth
technologies.

Mobisante/Rex Features via AP Images          Roberto Pfeil/dapd via AP Images

Medical diagnosis might also undergo major changes. For example, high-resolution fiber-optic microendoscopes are small portable devices that can be used to make cancer detection in the field. In some locations in the developing world, health workers can take images of skin problems and use cell phone technologies to beam images back to major medical centers around the globe. There they can get quick diagnosis and treatment directions.

Finally, mHealth can help with treatment, such as chronic disease management. Smartphone applications are being developed for disease self-management for asthma, alcohol dependence, and lung cancer.

The promise of mHealth deserves serious scrutiny (Dobkin & Dorsch, 2011). The Affordable Care Act of 2010 allows providers to bill for remote monitoring beginning in 2014. Mobile technologies are likely to have a profound impact on health care and biomedical research, and we will soon be surrounded by more data than we can store, analyze, and interpret. New analysis methods may be necessary. In addition, there will be serious challenges in protecting securing of data and the privacy of people being monitored by the devices.

## NIH Toolbox

One of the biggest challenges in science is the coordination or "harmonization" of measures. In some fields, many different alternative measures are available and, as a result, it is often difficult to compare results across different studies or across different patient groups. In recognition of this problem, the National Institutes of Health is creating an NIH "Toolbox" that can be used for the standardized assessment of neurological and behavioral function. The purpose of this effort is to coordinate research efforts across at least 13 different institutes, to reduce duplication of effort, and to achieve greater efficiencies in measurement.

The NIH Toolbox is developing standardized measures of neural and behavioral health functioning that can be used both in large cohort studies and in clinical trials. So far, the group has created measures of cognitive, emotional, motor, and sensory functioning that might serve as common metrics that can be applied across a wide range of studies and study populations. The goal is to develop measures that can be completed in a relatively brief period of time. For example, an individual should be able to complete all measures in the Toolbox in no more than 2 hours.

Although the Toolbox is designed to capture a very wide range of mental and behavioral function, the core elements are summarized in Table 17.4.

As of this writing, the Toolbox is under active evaluation. However, we expect that national norms for the measures will be available in the not-too-distant future. Ultimately, the Toolbox should provide state-of-the-art measurement that is well validated and psychometrically sound. The measures should be appropriate for individuals ranging in age from 3 to 85 years. Ultimately, standardized assessment will offer many advantages both for the researcher and clinical practitioner.

**TABLE 17.4**    Domains, Subdomains, and Instruments Under Consideration for the NIH Toolbox.

| | Subdomain | Instrument |
|---|---|---|
| **Cognition** | Episodic Memory-Visual | Picture Sequence Memory |
| | Executive Function-Cognitive Flexibility | Dimensional Change Card Sort |
| | Executive Function-Inhibitory Control and Attention | Flanker Inhibitory Control and Attention |
| | Language-Vocabulary Comprehension | Picture Vocabulary Computer Adaptive Test |
| | Processing Speed | Pattern Comparison Processing Speed |
| | Working Memory | List Sorting |
| | Language-Reading Decoding | Oral Reading Recognition |
| **Emotion** | Negative Affect | Age specific measures of Sadness, Fear, Anger |
| | Psychological Well-Being | Age specific measures of Positive Affect, Life Satisfaction, Meaning and Purpose |
| | Social Relationships | Age specific measures of Social Support, Companionship, Social Distress, Positive Social Development |
| | Stress and Self-Efficacy | Age specific measures of Perceived Stress, Self-Efficacy |
| | Negative Affect | Age specific measure of Apathy |
| | Positive Affect | Age specific measure of domain-specific life satisfaction |
| | Social Relationships | Age specific measures of Social Network Integration |
| | Stress and Self-Efficacy | Age specific measures of coping strategies |
| **Motor** | Dexterity | 9-hole Pegboard |
| | Endurance | 2-minute Walk Test |
| | Locomotion | 4-meter Walk Test |
| | Strength-Lower Extremity | Knee Extension Dynamometry |
| | Strength-Upper Extremity | Grip Strength Dynamometry |
| | Vestibular Balance-Vestibulo Spinal Function | Balance Accelerometry Measure-BAM |
| | Dexterity | 25-hole Grooved Pegboard |

*(continued)*

| | Subdomain | Instrument |
|---|---|---|
| | Audition-Hearing Threshold | Hearing Thresholds |
| | Olfaction-Identification | Odor Identification Test |
| | Somatosensation-Texture Discrimination | Tactile Discrimination Test |
| | Taste-Ability to PerceiveTaste in Different Regions of Oral Cavity | Regional Taste Test |
| | Taste-Sweet Preference | Sucrose Preference Test |
| | Vestibular Balance-Vestibular Ocular Reflex | Dynamic Visual Acuity |
| | Vision-Acuity | Visual Acuity |
| Sensory | Audition-Hearing Loss | Hearing Handicap Inventory for Adults— Short Form |
| | Audition-Speech Processing | Words-in-Noise |
| | Audition-Middle Ear Function | Tympanometry |
| | Somatosensation - Pain | Self-Reported Pain |
| | Proprioception | Brief Kinesthesia Test |
| | Taste-Perceived Strength of the Four Basic Tastes | Taste Intensity Test |
| | PROP Taste Blindness | PROP Taste Test |
| | Vision-Visual Function HRQOL | Vision Health-Related Quality of Life Survey. |

(From NIH Toolbox for the Assessment of Neurological and Behavioral Function, July 2011. Accessed December 27, 2011 from http://www.nihtoolbox.org/RFP/Toolbox%20overview%20and%20instrument%20list%207-27-2011.pdf.)

## The 2015 Medical College Admissions Test (MCAT)

The Medical College Admission Test (MCAT) has become a rite of passage for entrance into medical school. The MCAT has evolved over the course of years to identify students who are most likely to succeed with a difficult medical school curriculum. The MCAT is administered by computer, and the current version tests physical and biological sciences, verbal reasoning, and writing skills. The test is quite demanding and it takes 5.5 hours to complete.

Starting in 2015, the MCAT will undergo a significant change. The most important series of changes will involve a new section focusing on several conceptual areas from the behavioral and social sciences. The change in the MCAT follows a comprehensive review by a series of prestigious groups including the Institute of Medicine of the National Academy of Sciences and the American Association of Medical Colleges.

The new psychological, social, and biological foundations of behavior section of the test assesses a wide range of knowledge and draws upon concepts from psychology, sociology, biology, research methods, and statistics. These sections go into detail about the understanding of the social cultural determinants of health. Increasingly, medical scientists have come to recognize that health outcomes, to a large extent, are determined by the circumstances in which people live. In

FIGURE 17.8

Difference in the expected length of life from birth for Black and Asian men and women in Los Angeles, California. On average, Asian men live 11 years longer and Asian women live nearly 10 years longer than Black men and women.

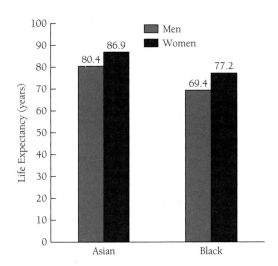

Data adapted from the Los Angeles Department of Public Health, Office of Health Assessment and Epidemiology, July 2010.

Los Angeles, for example, we can consider how long people live as a function of their racial sex, in social circumstances. The discrepancies can be substantial. Asian women, for example, live on average to be about 87 years in Los Angeles. Black men on the other hand, live an average of 69 years. The discrepancy of 18 years is difficult to explain without taking into consideration the social circumstances in which people live (see Figure 17.8).

A related issue is the relationship between economic hardship and how long people live. Within the 88 cities that make up Los Angeles County, life expectancies and economic hardships vary dramatically. For example, life expectancy in wealthy Beverly Hills is 85.6 years, while in tony La Canada-Flintridge, it is 87.8 years. In tough neighborhoods like Compton, people live, on average, 75.7 years; in Willowbrook, life expectancy is only 75.6 years. Figure 17.9 is a scatter diagram showing the relationship between life expectancy and an index of hardship for cities and communities in Los Angeles County in 2010. There is a negative relationship, suggesting that the greater the economic hardship, the shorter the life expectancies of community residents.

The MCAT section on psychological, social, and behavioral foundations of behavior covers a wide range of topics. It considers perceptions and reactions to the world, behavior and behavior change, what people think about themselves and others, and the cultural and social differences that influence well-being. The section also considers how differences in social and economic status affect health, the effects of different resources and access to health care, and the broad social determinants of health.

The new subtest, "Psychological, Social, and Biological Foundations of Behavior," will measure Behavioral and Social Science (BSS) foundational knowledge. Test takers will have 95 minutes to complete the new section primarily composed of brief stimulus paragraphs illustrating behavioral and social science constructs followed by a total of approximately 55 multiple-choice questions. Based on preliminary

**FIGURE 17.9**

Scatter diagram showing the negative relationship between community hardship and life expectancy for cities and communities in Los Angeles County.

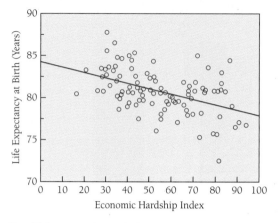

From *Life Expectancy in Los Angeles County. How Long Do We Live and Why?* Office of Health Assessment and Epidemiology: Los Angeles County Department of Public Health, 2010.

drafts, components of the section include five core content areas: 1) ways that individuals perceive, think about, and react to the world; 2) factors that influence behavior and behavior change; 3) factors that influence how we think about ourselves and others; 4) ways in which culture and social differences influence well-being; and 5) ways in which social stratification affects access to resources and well-being. Each of these content areas emphasizes established theory and concepts as well as experimental and observational science. For example, the section on the perception considers sensory processes (vision, hearing, chemosensory senses), and the integration of these senses through attention, cognition, memory, and language. It also considers the role of stress and emotions in the sensory processes. Clinical applications of BSS foundational knowledge are reserved for medical school instruction; however, as with the basic sciences, students will be expected to enter medical school with a sufficient scientific foundation upon which to build medical knowledge.

Medical sciences focus on biological processes, so what value would be obtained from adding yet another MCAT component? Many lines of evidence converge to suggest that behavioral and social factors have profound effects on health—both as determinants and as key factors for preventive or treatment interventions. In November 2011, the Association of American Medical Colleges (AAMC) released a report on behavioral and social science foundations for future physicians—an important companion piece to the influential Scientific Foundations for Future Physicians report on the basic sciences in medical education. The AAMC BSS report emphasized that health is influenced by a wide variety of factors, including biological, genetic, behavioral, interpersonal relationships, cultures, and physical environments. Furthermore, several models have been developed to estimate factors that explain increases in the U.S. life expectancy since 1970. Most of the increase in life expectancy is attributable to declines in premature deaths from heart disease and stroke. These models suggest that between 23% and 46% of the decline in deaths from coronary heart disease are attributable to medical care. On the other hand, between 44% and 72% of the increased life expectancy is attributable to modification of coronary risk factors including tobacco use, lipids, and blood pressure. In fact, reductions in tobacco use and increases in physical activity appear to be the largest contributors to improved life expectancy in the United States. Primary prevention, including the modification of health behaviors, contributes about four times as much to health outcome as medically based secondary prevention efforts.

In addition to the importance of behavioral approaches to disease prevention, there has been significant progress in biobehavioral approaches to the management of illness. Systematic studies emphasize the value of cognitive and behavioral interventions to treat mental illness and substance abuse and to aid in the management in chronic illnesses such as diabetes and heart failure. The behavioral and social sciences form the core of evaluations of cognitive impairment, many neurological diseases, and the gene-environment interaction. Moreover, disparities in health outcomes among racial and ethnic groups persist. In Los Angeles, for example, the difference in life expectancy between African American men and Asian American women is a full 19 years. Disparities in life expectancy between income, race, sex, or age subgroups are usually traceable to differences in tobacco use, obesity, physical activity, alcohol use, and risky sexual behavioral. Tomorrow's physician will need to understand changes in demographic patterns, the impact of culture on adherence to medications, and the rapidly changing economic incentives associated with emerging health care environments.

Although nearly all medical schools include some BSS instruction, students arrive with widely varied levels of BSS preparation, and no minimally sufficient level of training has been established. Just as for biology or chemistry, students are unlikely to comprehend complex research studies without some basic background. The behavioral and social sciences are built upon complex methodologies, theories, and a mature database. Teaching cognitive behavioral intervention to students with no background in learning theory is analogous to teaching pathophysiology to students who have not been exposed to basic biological principles. For all of these reasons, the MCAT committee and the AAMC recognized that future physicians need better, standardized training in the behavioral and social sciences both before and during medical school.

The new MCAT also includes a section on critical analysis and reasoning. This section was added to replace the writing samples sections. Analysis of data from older MCATs had suggested that the writing samples were not valid predictors of medical school success. The new critical analysis and reasoning skills section uses traditional test formats and presents passages that need to be read. Test items then assess the test takers ability to comprehend the topics in the passages. These topics include ethics and philosophy, cross-cultural studies, and population health.

Creating a new MCAT is a significant undertaking. In response, undergraduate curricula may need to be revised to prepare students for this important hurdle on their way to medical school. The plan for the new MCAT was released in 2011, but the new test will not be used until 2015. Focused Example 17.4 shows a sample item from the new MCAT.

## 17.4 FOCUSED EXAMPLE

## Sample Items from the 2015 MCAT

### Sample Passage

Psychologists have identified two distinct forms of bias: explicit and implicit bias. An explicit bias is a conscious preference, whereas an implicit bias is an unconscious preference. Research investigating racial disparities in treatments for heart attacks has found that Blacks are significantly less likely than Whites to receive thrombolytic therapy (i.e., the administration of drugs to break up or dissolve blood clots).

A recent study investigated the relationship between physicians' implicit and explicit biases and their decisions to provide thrombolytic therapy to Black and White patients. Residents were recruited to participate in an online study. Participants received a vignette describing a 50-year-old male who displayed heart attack symptoms. Half the sample's vignettes included a photo of a Black patient, while the other half were provided with a photo of a White patient.

After indicating whether or not they would refer the patient for thrombolysis therapy, participants' explicit preferences for Blacks and Whites were measured using a 5-point Likert scale. Next, participants completed an implicit association task (IAT). The IAT assessed participants' implicit bias by measuring their response time to valenced words (e.g., words with good or bad connotations) presented with images of Black and White individuals. No effect was found for levels of explicit bias and the likelihood of providing thrombolysis therapy. Figure 17.10 summarizes the study's findings related to implicit bias.

1) Which concept is the focus of this study?
   A. Fundamental attribution error
   B. Elaboration likelihood model
   C. Modern prejudice
   D. Self-serving bias

Answer: C

Foundational Concept: 8

Content Category: 8B

Skill: 1

2) Which of the following explanations describes why the amygdala would most likely be activated by the use of the IAT in this study? The amygdala is important for:
   A. Learning
   B. Fear
   C. Anxiety
   D. Value judgments

Answer: B

Foundational Concept: 7

Content Category: 7A

Skill: 1

From: MCAT 2015: Better Best for Tomorrow's Doctors. Association of American Medical Colleges (AAMC). Available at www.aamc.org/mcat2015. **(permission Required)**

**FIGURE 17.10**

Percent of participants referring patients for thrombolytic therapy as a function of participants' levels of implicit bias and patient race.

Adapted from R. A. Green et al. (2007). "Implicit Bias Among Physicians and Its Prediction of Thrombolysis Decisions for Black and White Patients." *Journal of General Internal Medicine*, 22, 1231–1238. The Preview Guide for MCAT 2015 © 2011 AAMC. May not be reproduced without permission. 123

# Summary

In this chapter, we considered three broad areas relevant to testing in health-care settings. First, we reviewed clinical neuropsychology. This remarkable new area of investigation has generated new research and clinical opportunities for psychologists. Neuropsychology involves the application of tests to evaluate the status of the central nervous system. Some of the more common approaches are the Halstead-Reitan and the Luria-Nebraska batteries. Each of these approaches is based on different principles of cognitive psychology. A newer approach, the California Verbal Learning Test, attempts to evaluate brain function by considering not only errors but also how people make errors.

Second, we reviewed some of the existing research on the theory and measurement of anxiety and stress. Research on test anxiety grew from general theories of learning. Early studies by J. Taylor identified anxiety as a motivational state that one could measure with a short scale. Using the scale, she could relate anxiety to a general theory that had previously depended primarily on evidence from animal studies. Later developments divided anxiety into state and trait components. The State-Trait Anxiety Inventory (STAI) provides two separate scores: one for state anxiety (A-State) and another for trait anxiety (A-Trait).

A variety of measures quantify adaptation to stressful situations. These include measures of coping and measures of social support. Not all individuals faced with the same stresses have the same reactions.

The third area for the application of tests in health-care settings involves health status and quality of life assessment. Health-care practitioners try to help people live longer and to live higher-quality lives than they might without health care. The quantification of life quality, however, is difficult. Two approaches to this type of assessment are psychometric methods and decision theory methods. Psychometric methods include the MOS Short Form-36 and the Nottingham Health Profile. Decision theory approaches include methods for estimating the value of the equivalent of a life-year, or a quality-adjusted life year (QALY). We expect the fields of psychological measurement and health-outcome measurement to continue to merge over the next few decades.

One of the biggest challenges in health care practice and research is the harmonization of measures. In clinical practice there are many alternative ways to measure constructs like quality of life, executive functioning, anxiety, and functional capacity. In order to address this problem, the National Institutes of Health is developing the NIH "Toolbox." The goal of this project is to stimulate the use of a common set of measures in research and in clinical care. In recognition of the importance of behavioral and social sciences in health are, the Medical College Admissions Test (MCAT) will devote about 20% of its content to these sciences beginning in 2015.

18

CHAPTER

# Testing in Industrial and Business Settings

## LEARNING OBJECTIVES

*When you have completed this chapter, you should be able to:*

▶ Discuss the application of tests in employee selection

▶ Identify the first consideration in determining whether it is worthwhile to administer a test

▶ Explain the meaning of base rates in personnel selection

▶ Identify three methods for estimating the amount of information a test gives beyond what is known by chance

▶ Define incremental validity

▶ Discuss the significance of utility and decision theory

▶ Explain some problems with utility theory equations

▶ Describe the characteristics of the MBTI and the WPI

▶ List the components of job analysis

▶ Explain the person–situation interaction

▶ Describe the advantages and disadvantages of employment interview

One of the fastest-growing fields of psychology involves the application of psychological principles to the workplace. This specialized field of psychology is known as *industrial/organizational* (I/O) *psychology*. This field is quite similar to the human resource management that is often taught in schools of business. However, I/O psychologists establish themselves by the methods they apply. One of the most important differences is I/O's emphasis on structured psychological testing (Berry, 2003; Conklin & Desselle, 2007). I/O psychologists rely extensively on research, quantitative methods, and testing procedures (Whetzel & Wheaton, 2007). Two major areas of I/O psychology are personnel psychology and organizational psychology. *Personnel psychology* is the study and practice of job analysis, job recruitment, employee selection, and the evaluation of employee performance (Schmitt, 2012). *Organizational psychology* considers leadership, job satisfaction, employee motivation, and a variety of factors surrounding the functioning of organizations (Aamodt, 2004). In this chapter, we focus on some of the interfaces between I/O psychology and psychological testing. We begin by reviewing the oldest approach to employee selection—the employment interview.

# Personnel Psychology—The Selection of Employees

## Employment Interview

The employment interview helps people make selection and promotion decisions in business and industry. These interviews are complicated because the applicant and the employer are motivated to slant their presentation in order to make an impression, not necessarily to be completely honest (Bangerter, Roulin, & König, 2011).

Studies of the validity of the employment interview have revealed extremely valuable information about interviews in general and the employment interview in particular (Huffcutt & Youngcourt, 2007). Most research supports a structured format for the employment interview. Several studies clearly pointed to the superiority of structured interviews for enabling interviewers to reach agreement on their employment decisions. Thus, the loss of flexibility in structured interviews can be balanced by increases in reliability. Meta-analytic investigations of the literature have found that structured interviews produced mean validity coefficients twice as high as did unstructured interviews (Wiesner & Cronshaw, 1988; Williamson, Campion, Malos, Roehling, & Campion, 1997). On the other hand, interviewee performance may play a very important role, even in structured interviews. For example, candidates who work hard at impression management are given higher ratings (Huffcutt, 2011).

Later we shall discuss sources of error in the interview, which studies have found to affect many employment interviews (Cesare, 1996; Schuler, 1993). For now, we briefly touch on what interviewers look for in employment interviews and on methods of presenting oneself in an interview.

It has long been known that the employment interview often involves a search for negative or unfavorable rather than favorable evidence about a person (Schmitt, 2012). If negative evidence is found, the person will probably not be hired unless there is a high demand for workers and few individuals are available to fill open positions. A classic study by E. C. Webster (1964) noted that as few as one unfavorable impression was followed by final rejection in 90% of the cases. This rejection rate, however, dropped to 25% when early impressions were favorable. Webster and others caution employment interviewers against forming an early bias that might result in rejecting a competent individual. Despite widespread knowledge of Webster's cautions, interviewers continue to make basic errors when formulating personnel decisions (Huffcutt, 2011).

Negative factors that commonly lead to the rejection of candidates include poor communication skills, lack of confidence or poise, low enthusiasm, nervousness, and failure to make eye contact (Kager, 2000; Nykodym & Ruud, 1985; Nykodym & Simonetti, 1981; Posthuma et al., 2002). Positive factors include the ability to express oneself, self-confidence and poise, enthusiasm, the ability to sell oneself, and aggressiveness (Baehr, 1987; Huffcutt, 2011).

Can you increase your chances of presenting yourself favorably in a job interview? As Heimberg, Keller, and Peca-Baker (1986) noted, competent performance in job interviews is widely regarded as one of the most important factors in obtaining employment. As such, several prospective employees who wish to tip the balance in their favor can choose any of several recommendations (Huffcutt, 2011).

A good first impression is one of the most important factors in a successful job interview (Dougherty, Turban, & Callender, 1994; Howard & Ferris, 1996). To make a good first impression, one needs to wear professional attire and show good grooming (Cash, 1985; Kennedy, 1994), project an aura of competence and expertise (Baron, 1986; Price & Garland, 1983), and give an impression of friendliness or personal warmth through nonverbal cues (Higgins, 2001; Imada & Hakel, 1977). But going too far with these tactics can sometimes backfire.

R. A. Baron (1986) had female confederates pose as applicants for an entry-level management position. Some wore perfume, others did not. In addition, some attempted to convey friendliness through nonverbal behaviors including a high level of eye contact with the interviewer, an informal friendly posture (such as leaning forward at predetermined points), and frequent smiling.

Interviewees in the neutral-cue condition refrained from these nonverbal behaviors. The results revealed that when used alone, either perfume or positive nonverbal behaviors produced enhanced ratings for the applicants. When used together, however, these tactics produced negative reactions among interviewers, probably because they caused the applicant to be perceived as manipulative (Baron, 1986). Thus, while putting one's best foot forward in an interview is important, one must be careful not to overdo it.

Interviews remain the primary tool for selecting employees. However, personnel psychology places a strong emphasis on formal quantitative models and the use of tests for employee selection.

For many industrial applications, other factors also must be considered, such as the amount of information a selection strategy gives beyond what would be known without it (Sackett & Lievens, 2008). This can be derived from an analysis of base rates and hit rates.

# Base Rates and Hit Rates

Tests must be evaluated in terms of how much they contribute beyond what would be known without them. Often, tests are used to place individuals into one of two categories. For example, on the basis of an employment test, a candidate can be deemed acceptable or unacceptable. In a medical setting, a test may determine whether or not a person has a tumor in a certain area of the brain. Because tests vary in their accuracy, test administrators must examine the possibility of erroneously assigning someone to a category.

If a test is used to make a dichotomous (two-choice) decision, then a cutoff score usually is used. Values above this score might go into the plus category, and values below it into the minus category. The plus category might indicate that the person is suitable for the job (or, in medical testing, that he or she has the tumor). The score marking the point of decision is called the *cutting score.* Those at or above the cutting score might be selected for employment, while those below the score might be turned away. Establishing a cutting score does not ensure correct decisions. For example, suppose that a person scores above the cutting score for an employment test but later fails on the job. This suggests that the test has not done its job.

Tests can be evaluated by how well they sort people into the right categories. For example, in a test that determines which people to hire for a particular job, those who score above the cutting score might be labeled "acceptable" and those below it "unacceptable." In addition to the scores on the test, the employer must have some data on how people really do on the job. To do this, he or she must define some criterion for deciding whether job performance has been acceptable or unacceptable. Using these two sets of categories, the employer can construct a chart such as the one shown in Table 18.1. There are four cells in this table. Two of the four cells are labeled "Hit" because the test has made the correct prediction. Hits occur when (1) the test predicts that the person will be unacceptable and he or she does fail, or (2) the test indicates that the person is acceptable and he or she does succeed. Misses occur when the test makes an inaccurate prediction. The **hit rate** is the percentage of cases in which a test accurately predicts success or failure.

Often, a test does not need a good hit rate, because the rate of predicting success on the job is high without the test. For example, admissions officers might predict who will do well in law school on the basis of information other than scores on the Law School Admission Test (LSAT). They might use college grades. Success on the criterion in this case might be passing the bar examination on the first attempt. The pass rate without using the LSAT would be called the **base rate**. The real value of a test comes from a comparison of the hit rate with the base rate. In other words, the hit rate must tell us how much information a test contributes to the prediction of success beyond what we would know by just examining the proportion of people who succeed.

**TABLE 18.1**  Hits and Misses for Predicting a Dichotomous Outcome Using a Cutting Score

| Performance on the job | Decision on the basis of cutting score | |
|---|---|---|
| | Acceptable | Unacceptable |
| Success | Hit | Miss |
| Failure | Miss | Hit |

For example, suppose the LSAT has a hit rate of 76% for predicting who will pass the bar examination in a certain state. However, 85% of the people who take the test for the first time in that state pass. The LSAT in this case tells us less than we would have known without it. In other cases, you could imagine a low hit rate and an even lower base rate. For example, suppose you need to select people for a position that will involve world-class competition. Under the circumstances, very few people could be expected to do well—say only 3% would be expected to succeed. If a test could be developed that had a 10% hit rate, it might be considered valuable.

Another problem to consider with regard to hit and miss rates is relative cost. Medical situations provide good examples of costly misses. Consider the cost of concluding on the basis of a test that a tumor is benign (not cancerous) when it is really malignant (cancerous). The cost of this sort of miss is that the life of the patient is seriously endangered. In a psychological application, concluding that someone is not suicidal because he or she is below the cutoff score when, in fact, he or she is suicidal may allow a preventable suicide. These cases are examples of **false negatives**. If the cost of a false negative is high, then a test developer might lower the cutting score. With a lower cutting score, the test will make more but safer errors.

The other type of miss is the **false positive**. For example, say someone is selected for a job on the basis of a test. Once on the job, the person does poorly and gets fired. High costs sometimes accompany this type of error. For instance, time and money might be invested to train a person who cannot really do the job. In addition, job failure can hurt the person's self-esteem and self-confidence. If the costs of a false positive are high, then you may want to raise the cutting score.

A few examples may help clarify the concepts of hits and misses for different base rates. Although this chapter is about employment testing, our students often find medical examples best illustrate these concepts. Table 18.2 presents a medical example in which a test indicates whether or not a patient has brain damage. In a validation study, an expensive radiological procedure is used to confirm whether the patient actually has brain damage. The radiological test suggests that 23 of 100 patients have brain damage, while the other 77 are normal. The table also shows the actual number of patients who have brain damage or are normal. In reality, 10 of the 100 have damage, while 90 are normal.

There are two types of hits in Table 18.2. For the 10 patients who actually have brain damage, 8 are detected by the tests. In other words, the test has a detection rate of 80%. In addition, the test says that 75 individuals are normal who, it is confirmed, are actually normal. Both of these cases are hits because the test produces the correct result. There are 83 cases in 100 when the test produces an accurate conclusion; that is, the test has 83% accuracy.

There are also two types of misses. In two cases, the test suggests that a person is normal when he or she actually has brain damage. Those are false negatives. In addition, there are 15 false positives, or cases in which the test suggests that a person has a problem when in fact he or she is normal.

The cells in Table 18.2 are labeled A, B, C, and D. Cells A and D are hit cells. The sum of these cells divided by the sum of all cells (A + B + C + D) is the accuracy rate. Cell B is a false negative, Cell C a false positive. Cell A divided by the sum of A and B is the *detection rate*.

**TABLE 18.2**   Hypothetical Example of Hits and Misses, with 83% Accuracy and 80% Detection*

| | | Test result | | |
|---|---|---|---|---|
| | | **Brain damage** | **Normal** | **Total** |
| | Brain damage | A | B | A + B |
| | | 8 | 2 | 10 |
| Actual | Normal | C | D | C + D |
| | | 15 | 75 | 90 |
| | Total | 23 | 77 | 100 |

A = hit        A + B = base rate

B = false negative

C = false positive

D = hit

A/(A + B) = detection rate (sensitivity)

D/(C + D) = specificity base rate

(A + D)/(A + B + C + D) = accuracy rate

*We are grateful to Dr. Frank M. Rosekrans, Eastern Washington University, for suggesting this example.

The example in Table 18.2 suggests that the test is relatively good at detecting brain damage. One of the reasons the test works well in this situation is that the base rate for brain damage is relatively low. In actuality, only 10% of the patients have this problem, and the test detects 80% of the cases.

Now consider the example in Table 18.3. In this case, a test is used on a population with a quite high base rate for brain damage (90%). The test suggests that 50 of 100 people have brain damage when, in fact, 90 of 100 people have the problem. The test is accurate in 44% (40/90 = .44) of the cases. In this example, there are only 10 false positives. The test, however, has a high false negative rate. Finally, the table suggests that the test never concludes that someone is normal when he or she does not have a problem.

False negatives and false positives may have different meanings, depending on their context. For example, a variety of methods have been developed to predict anti-social behavior in children. Childhood aggression is a good predictor of later aggressive behavior (Dishion, Andrews, & Crosby, 1995). However, measures of childhood aggression identify some children as potentially dangerous who turn out not to be aggressive when they are older (O'Donnell, Hawkins, & Abbott, 1995). Similarly, measures used to predict sexual misconduct also indentify many people who will not commit sexual offenses (Studer, Aylwin, Sribney, & Reddon, 2011).These are false positives. In fact, as many as half the cases may be false positives (Lochman, 1995). A program that identifies and treats high-risk youth may subject many to unnecessary treatment. On one extreme, some people believe high-risk youth should be under police surveillance. Among adults, many people can be identified as potentially

**TABLE 18.3**  Hypothetical Example of Hits and Misses, with 40% Accuracy and 44% Detection*

|  |  | Test result | | |
|---|---|---|---|---|
|  |  | **Brain damage** | **Normal** | **Total** |
| **Actual** | Brain damage | A | B | A + B |
|  |  | 40 | 50 | 90 |
|  | Normal | C | D | C + D |
|  |  | 10 | 0 | 10 |
|  | Total | 50 | 50 | 100 |

A = hit        A + B = base rate

B = false negative

C = false positive

D = hit

$A/(A + B)$ = detection rate (sensitivity)

$D/(C + D)$ = specificity base rate

$(A + D)/(A + B + C + D)$ = accuracy rate

*We are grateful to Dr. Frank M. Rosekrans, Eastern Washington University, for suggesting this example.

dangerous, but the number of people who commit serious violent crimes remains low (Steadman et al., 1998). Because of false positives, these programs would unjustly deprive some youth of their rights. Many controversies in health care are affected by the hit and miss rates of testing (see Focused Example 18.1).

Using cutting scores to find hits and misses involves criterion validity (see Chapter 5). Many years ago, H. C. Taylor and J. T. Russell (1939) demonstrated how to relate validity coefficients to accuracy rates in selection.

## Taylor-Russell Tables

The decision to use a test must depend on what the test offers. In Chapter 5, we showed that tests with significant predictive or concurrent validity coefficients did better than chance in forecasting performance on a criterion. However, knowing that a test is better than chance is not good enough for some applications. In other words, a worthwhile test must provide more information than do the base rates alone.

In 1939, Taylor and Russell developed a method for evaluating the validity of a test in relation to the amount of information it contributes beyond the base rates. This method is neatly summarized in a series of tables known as the **Taylor-Russell tables**. To use them, you must have the following information:

1. *Definition of success.* For each situation in which the test is to be used, success on the outcome must be defined. This could be that the patient lived, that the

person succeeded on the job, or that the student did well in college. One must define success clearly by dichotomizing some outcome variable. For example, first-year grade point averages above 2.3 might be defined as success in college, and those below 2.3 might be defined as failures. Or salespeople who achieve average monthly sales of more than $20,000 might be deemed successful, and those who sell less than $20,000 might be thought of as unsuccessful.

2. *Determination of base rate.* The percentage of people who would succeed if there were no testing or screening procedure must be determined.

3. *Definition of selection ratio.* The **selection ratio** must be defined. This is the percentage of applicants who are selected or admitted.

4. *Determination of validity coefficient.* Finally, a validity coefficient for the test, usually the correlation of the test with the criterion, is required.

---

## 18.1 FOCUSED EXAMPLE

### The Mammography Controversy

Medical tests resemble psychological tests in that they both have validity and reliability and can be assessed in relation to their hit rates and miss rates. One interesting controversy involves the use of mammography to screen women for breast cancer. Mammography has been shown to be a valuable medical test for women age 50 and older. Some controversy, however, surrounds its use for younger women. The reason for this controversy is related to the base rates and the rates of false positives and false negatives.

Breast cancer is strongly related to age. Although the American Cancer Society (ACS) argues that 1 in 9 women will develop breast cancer, these tumors are much more common among older women than among younger ones (see Figure 18.1). For women

in their 20s, breast cancer is an extremely rare disease. In fact, 100,000 mammograms would have to be performed to find one such woman with breast cancer. This suggests that for younger women, the base rate for breast cancer is extremely low (1 in 100,000). This has become somewhat of a controversy because the popular media have launched a campaign to increase the use of mammography for all women. If we pay for mammography from public funds and the cost of a mammogram is $100, then it would cost about $10 million to detect one case. Of course, any investment would be valuable if it saved lives. However, analyses of studies of breast cancer suggest that the rare case of breast cancer detected in young women results in no better chance of survival than does a

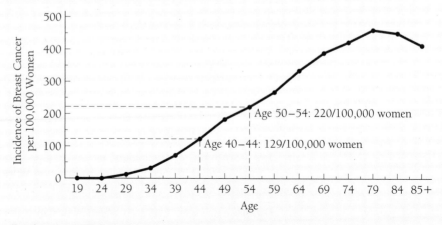

**FIGURE 18.1**

Relationship of age to breast cancer.

Age 50–54: 220/100,000 women
Age 40–44: 129/100,000 women

(Data from National Cancer Institute, Cancer Statistics Review 1973–1988. Bethesda, MD: July 1991, Table II-40.)

The Taylor-Russell tables give the likelihood that a person selected on the basis of the test score will actually succeed. There is a different table for each base rate. Table 18.4 is a Taylor-Russell table for a base rate of .60.

To use the table, find the row that represents the validity of the test that would be used for selection. Then find the column that is associated with the proportion of people who can be selected. The number in the body of the table that is associated with a particular row and a particular column gives an estimate of the percentage of people who could be expected to succeed when selected on the basis of the test.

For example, suppose that you are put in charge of deciding who will be admitted to a program to train secondary-education teachers. The first thing you must do is decide on a definition of success. After meeting with a committee, you

case left undetected. Even so, this remains a matter of considerable debate in the medical community (Kaplan, 2009; Bewley, 2011).

The related concern for performing mammography in younger women is that breast tissue in young women is denser than it is in older women. As a result, there are a significant number of false positives in younger women. One younger woman in three who gets repeated mammograms will have a false positive that requires further medical tests or biopsies (Welch, 2004).

Despite all of the research and discussion, uncertainty about the value of mammography persists. Early in the Clinton administration, the age initiating mammography was set at 50. As a result of this decision, Clinton was attacked for being against preventive medicine (Kaplan, 2000; Kaplan et al., 1996). However, the public health benefit from promoting screening mammography for women 40 to 50 years old may be somewhat limited. All clinical trials and meta-analyses have failed to show a population benefit from screening (Black, Haggstrom, & Welch, 2002).

In January 1997, a panel convened by the National Institutes of Health recommended that women aged 40 to 50 years old need not have routine screening mammograms unless the women are in a high-risk group or have felt a lump. The panel review shocked the ACS, an organization that had worked hard to promote screening of younger women. The headline of *USA Today* (January 24, 1997) read "Mammogram Panel Only Adds to Furor." Commentators on morning talk shows were outraged by the committee's decision. Richard Klausner, the director of the National Cancer Institute, decided to disregard the report of his own expert panel. Shortly thereafter, the ACS appointed a panel of experts chosen because

each already believed that screening was valuable for women aged 40 to 50. To no one's surprise, this ACS panel recommended that 40- to 50-year-old women should be screened (Fletcher, 1997). Following the ACS panel recommendation, the use of mammography increased substantially. In 1999, the Centers for Disease Control studied mammography use in more than 50,000 women living in 38 states. The data were obtained from large cross-sectional surveys in 1989 and again in 1997. By 2007, mammography rates for women over the age of 50 had dropped off about 4% over the peak rate that was observed in 2000 (Breen et al., 2007). But the debate continues. In 2009, the United States Preventive Services Task Force (USPSTF) examined all of the evidence. The USPSTF is an authoritative group of impartial experts that reviews evidence about the value of preventive services and makes recommendations about their uses. Their recommendations are important because they influence what services will be paid for by Medicare and Medicaid. Upon review, the task force concluded that annual mammography for women under age 50 was not justified. Other counties also face debates about the value of mammography. In the United Kingdom, the debate is even more intense, with some groups suggesting that the government has given women misleading information about the value of mammography (Godlee, 2011).

What does this tell us? Clearly, mammography has been shown to be a valuable medical test for older women. For women in their 20s and early 30s, routine screening does not seem to help. For women aged 40–50, the jury is still out. Of course, women with risk factors for breast cancer, such as a strong family history of the condition, may still benefit from routine screening.

**TABLE 18.4** Taylor-Russell Table for a Base Rate of .60

| Validity ($\rho_{xy}$) | Selection Ratio | | | | | | | | | | |
|---|---|---|---|---|---|---|---|---|---|---|---|
| | .05 | .10 | .20 | .30 | .40 | .50 | .60 | .70 | .80 | .90 | .95 |
| .00 | .60 | .60 | .60 | .60 | .60 | .60 | .60 | .60 | .60 | .60 | .60 |
| .05 | .64 | .63 | .63 | .62 | .62 | .62 | .61 | .61 | .61 | .60 | .60 |
| .10 | .68 | .67 | .65 | .64 | .64 | .63 | .63 | .62 | .61 | .61 | .60 |
| .15 | .71 | .70 | .68 | .67 | .66 | .65 | .64 | .63 | .62 | .61 | .61 |
| .20 | .75 | .73 | .71 | .69 | .67 | .66 | .65 | .64 | .63 | .62 | .61 |
| .25 | .78 | .76 | .73 | .71 | .69 | .68 | .66 | .65 | .63 | .62 | .61 |
| .30 | .82 | .79 | .76 | .73 | .71 | .69 | .68 | .66 | .64 | .62 | .61 |
| .35 | .85 | .82 | .78 | .75 | .73 | .71 | .69 | .67 | .65 | .63 | .62 |
| .40 | .88 | .85 | .81 | .78 | .75 | .73 | .70 | .68 | .66 | .63 | .62 |
| .45 | .90 | .87 | .83 | .80 | .77 | .74 | .72 | .69 | .66 | .64 | .62 |
| .50 | .93 | .90 | .86 | .82 | .79 | .76 | .73 | .70 | .67 | .64 | .62 |
| .55 | .95 | .92 | .88 | .84 | .81 | .78 | .75 | .71 | .68 | .64 | .62 |
| .60 | .96 | .94 | .90 | .87 | .83 | .80 | .76 | .73 | .69 | .65 | .63 |
| .65 | .98 | .96 | .92 | .89 | .85 | .82 | .78 | .74 | .70 | .65 | .63 |
| .70 | .99 | .97 | .94 | .91 | .87 | .84 | .80 | .75 | .71 | .66 | .63 |
| .75 | .99 | .99 | .96 | .93 | .90 | .86 | .81 | .77 | .71 | .66 | .63 |
| .80 | 1.00 | .99 | .98 | .95 | .92 | .88 | .83 | .78 | .72 | .66 | .63 |
| .85 | 1.00 | 1.00 | .99 | .97 | .95 | .91 | .86 | .80 | .73 | .66 | .63 |
| .90 | 1.00 | 1.00 | 1.00 | .99 | .97 | .94 | .88 | .82 | .74 | .67 | .63 |
| .95 | 1.00 | 1.00 | 1.00 | 1.00 | .99 | .97 | .92 | .84 | .75 | .67 | .63 |
| 1.00 | 1.00 | 1.00 | 1.00 | 1.00 | 1.00 | 1.00 | 1.00 | .86 | .75 | .67 | .63 |

From Taylor, H.C., and Russell, J. T. The relationship of validity coefficients to the practical effectiveness of tests in selection: Discussion and tables. *Journal of Applied Psychology*, 23, 565–578. Copyright © 1939 American Psychological Association. Reprinted by permission.

may decide that success will be defined as completing the program and obtaining a satisfactory performance evaluation in student teaching. By studying records, you determine that when no selection procedure was used, 60% of the applicants to the program succeeded on this task. Thus, the base rate would be 60%, and the Taylor-Russell table for a base rate of .60 would be used. You then consider using the Graduate Record Examination (GRE) to select people for your program because you can accept only 70% of the applicants. A study is done and determines that the correlation between GRE scores and success (completing the program and obtaining a satisfactory evaluation in student teaching) is .30. This is the validity of the test for predicting the criterion.

Now you must estimate how many people would be expected to succeed if they were selected on the basis of GRE scores. Using the Taylor-Russell table

(Table 18.4) for a base rate of .60, find the row associated with the .30 validity and move across the table until you are in the column for a selection ratio of .70 (the percentage of applicants you can admit to your program). You should arrive at the number .66, which is the proportion of applicants you would expect to be successful if the selection was based on the GRE. This analysis tells you that 66% of those selected on the basis of GRE scores can be expected to be successful, compared with a success rate of 60% for those selected at random. Should the GRE be required for admittance to your program? To answer this question, you must decide whether the increment of 6% associated with the use of the test is worth the extra effort and expense of requiring it.

Try to work through a real-life example using the data from the Yale Ph.D. program in psychology.[1] The correlation between the GRE quantitative score and grade point average (GPA) was approximately 0.10, rounded up (Sternberg & Williams, 1997). Assume that Yale is selective and admits only some 10% of its applicants and that the base rate for success is 60%. Using the Taylor-Russell table, you should find that 67% of the applicants would be successful if selected on the basis of the Graduate Record Exam's quantitative component (GRE-Q), while 60% would be successful if selected by chance. This 67% figure comes from the third row (validity = .10) and second column (selection ratio = .10) of Table 18.4.

Looking at Table 18.4, you can see that tests will be more valuable in some situations than in others. For example, a test is most useful when the validity of the test is high and the selection ratio is low, as the lower left-hand portion of Table 18.4 shows. Conversely, when the validity is low and the selection ratio is high (the upper right-hand portion of the table), the test will be of little value. When the test has no validity (the first row of the table), using the test will be no better than selecting applicants by chance. Similarly, when nearly everyone is selected (last column), there is little reason to use a test.

Whenever a selection procedure is used, always remember that some qualified applicants will be turned away. The use of rational selection procedures should help make the system more fair by decreasing the number of qualified applicants not selected (Sackett & Lievens, 2008). One way to evaluate the selection procedure is to show the ratio of people selected by the test who then succeed and the ratio of those who would have succeeded but were not selected.

Suppose that you are the personnel manager for a company and that you can choose 30 of 100 applicants for a job. To make this decision, you have the results of a test with a validity of .70. You also know that the base rate for success on the job is .60. Using the Taylor-Russell table for a base rate of .60, you find that 91% of those selected on the basis of the test would be expected to succeed on the job. Because you can select 30 people, the table implies that approximately 27 of them will succeed and three will fail (91% of 30 = 27.3).

When you decide to hire 30 of the applicants, you also are deciding not to hire 70 people. It is important to realize that not all of the 70 people would fail if they were selected. In fact, many of them are capable people whom the testing

---

[1] One problem with the Yale study is that it is based on students admitted to the program, not all who apply. If data on all applicants were available, it is possible that the validity of the GRE may have been higher because there would have been a greater range of scores.

---

**TABLE 18.5** What Would Happen to 100 Applicants if 30 People Were Selected on the Basis of a Test with a Validity of .70 for a Job with a 60% Base Success Rate?

| | Decision | | |
| --- | --- | --- | --- |
| Performance | Select | Reject | Total |
| Success* | 27 | 33 | 60 |
| Failure | 3 | 37 | 40 |
| Total | 30 | 70 | 100 |

*Success ratio given selection = 27/30 = .90 (actually .91 without rounding; see Table 7.6). Success ratio given rejection = 33/70 = .47.

---

procedure has "misdiagnosed." To justify your use of the test, it would be your responsibility to explain why your selection procedure is worthwhile even though it turns down some people who would succeed and selects some who fail.

Table 18.5 shows what would happen to all of the applicants. Of 100, 30 would be accepted and 70 rejected (the selection ratio equals .30). However, because the base rate for success is .60, 60 of the 100 applicants would have succeeded on the job and 40 would have failed. As you have seen, the Taylor-Russell table shows that 91% of those selected on the basis of the test will succeed, or 27 of the 30 selected (.9 × 30 = 27.3), while only 3 of the 30 will likely fail.

Among the 60 people who would have succeeded, only 27 could be selected. This means that 33 people who would have been good choices were rejected. However, among the 40 people who would have failed, an estimated 37 would be in the rejected group. Using Table 18.5, we also can calculate the proportion of those rejected on the basis of the test who would be expected to succeed: 33/70 = .47. Although the procedure leads to the rejection of many capable applicants, it can be defended as rational because the proportion of those who succeed is much higher among those who are selected by the procedure than among those who are rejected.

A common argument is that increased minority hiring will result in lower average job performance because some applicants with lower test scores will be hired. However, systematic study of this issue has not always supported these arguments. For example, increased minority hiring in some industries has resulted in only a small loss in job performance. There may be circumstances in which average job performance declines with an overselection of low-scoring job applicants, but the data from these studies are typically complex (Silva & Jacobs, 1993).

The Taylor-Russell tables also help reveal the futility of certain types of assessment procedures. For example, McDaniel (1989) suggested that routine background information may be useful in predicting employee success. In his study, McDaniel used information on school suspension, drug use, quitting school, participation in social clubs, school grades, contacts with the legal system, and socioeconomic status to predict success in the military service. The criterion for success was keeping from being discharged for being unsuitable. The study demonstrated that though most of the background variables predicted unsuitability discharges, the validity coefficients were extremely low, with the highest being approximately .15. Let us assume that the selection ratio for the armed services is .9. In other words, 9 out of every 10 applicants are admitted to the military service. Let us also assume the base rate of success of 60%. (In the McDaniel study, the base rate was approximately 85%, but assuming 60% allows us to do this exercise with Table 18.4.) When we use the Taylor-Russell table for a validity of .15 and a selection ratio of .90, we find that the proportion who succeed in military service goes to .61. Using only base-rate information, we would have predicted that 60% succeed. The information on dropping out of school improves this prediction by only 1%! The low validity for the background information is the reason for this negligible improvement. Although background information may be useful, it may provide only a minimum of information about future success.

## Utility Theory and Decision Analysis

The use of Taylor-Russell tables requires that the criterion be a dichotomous variable. However, success usually is measured on a more refined numerical scale. By considering success only in terms of a dichotomous variable, one ignores much of the information available to the analyst. For example, it seems more reasonable to use a continuum of job performance as the criterion than to consider merely whether or not someone failed on a job. Since the publication of the Taylor-Russell tables, researchers have attempted to define levels besides success and failure. These formulations are based on utility theory (Boudreau & Ramstad, 2003; Brennan, 1994; Broaden, 1946, 1949; Cronbach & Gleser, 1965; Schmidt & Rothstein, 1994; Smith & George, 1994).

Although the use of decision and utility theory serves the industrial psychologist, the equations used to calculate the value of test data are quite complex (Boudreau & Ramstad, 2003). Furthermore, the equations require some information that is hard to estimate. For example, to use the equations, you must estimate the dollar value that is associated with different levels of performance on the job, an estimation that is difficult for most jobs (Dunnette & Borman, 1979). Schmidt and Hunter (1983) presented mathematical arguments showing that 40% of the average salary produces a reasonable estimate of the standard deviation of the output.

Several other approaches have been suggested to solve the problems of utility analysis, although progress has been slow (Cascio, 1998; Cascio & Ramos, 1986; Eaton, Wing, & Mitchell, 1985). For example, Raju and coworkers (1993) developed a new approach to utility assessment that does not require an estimate of the dollar value for performance. They proposed that the value of each individual can be estimated from the total value of his or her compensation package. This approach simplifies the calculations and produces results similar to those of other methods; however, the Raju method may shift the subjective judgment of the standard deviation of the criterion to estimating the coefficient of variation of the criterion. In other words, the estimation problem has not been solved (Judiesch, Schmidt, & Hunter, 1993). Other industrial psychologists believe that utility analysis may actually make managers less likely to use data in personnel selection. They suggest that there is a "futility of utility" (Latham & Whyte, 1994; Whyte & Latham, 1997). Some have argued that managers perceive the use of utility information as an attempt to manipulate them to invest in a personnel intervention (Latham & Whyte 1994; Kataoka, Latham, & Whyte, 1997; Whyte & Latham, 1997).

Clearly, the utility methods hold great promise for making rational personnel decisions, yet the difficulty in applying utility formulations has prevented their widespread use. Even so, studies do demonstrate financial advantages for companies that select employees on the basis of these formal models (Burke & Doran, 1989; Cascio, 1998). Furthermore, the methodology for utility analysis continues to improve (Schmidt, Law, Hunter, Rothstein, et al., 1993). See Focused Example 18.2 for an example of utility calculation.

Although utility theory is used only occasionally in personnel selection, it is beginning to find applications in other fields, including education (Sackett, 1998) and medicine (Newman, Grobman, & Greenland, 2008; Ridenour, Treloar, & Dean, 2003). In education, the placement decisions may have serious consequences. With tests being considered for tracking, promotion, and graduation, any decisions based on poor information may cause personal and financial harm (Heubert & Hauser, 1999). Medical researchers have long been aware that tests have false positive and false negative results. For some problems, such as the screening test for prostate cancer in younger men, there are many false positives for each true positive. Each false positive has financial and personal ramifications: in addition to costing money, a false positive may lead to other painful and unnecessary medical procedures. Analysts often consider such consequences when they interpret test data. The growing interest in utility analysis for medical decisions has led to the formation of the Society for Medical Decision Making and publication of a specialized journal entitled *Medical Decision Making*.

## 18.2 FOCUSED EXAMPLE

### How Much Money Can Be Saved Through Valid Selection?

A major issue in business and industrial psychology is how to get the most productivity out of employees. Employers often use tests to select employees who have the greatest chance of being productive. Some industrial psychologists, however, may have failed to realize just how much economic value can be gained from effective selection procedures. Although Cronbach and Gleser (1965) developed methods for evaluating the cost-effectiveness of testing many years ago, their technique was not frequently used because it required estimating the standard deviation of the dollar value of employee performance. However, newer methods developed to estimate this quantity allow one to determine how much money one saves by using a valid selection procedure.

In one study, a group of personnel psychologists evaluated measures for the selection of bus drivers.

They reasoned that some bus drivers who demonstrated safer driving behaviors should be selected to work more hours. This selection procedure should make the transit companies more efficient. To select the bus drivers, researchers developed several different measures that were administered to 864 bus drivers at nine locations. After a detailed analysis of the skills required for bus drivers, it was concluded that being a good bus operator required the three "Be's": "Be there, be safe, and be courteous." Analysis also showed that supervisor's ratings could be successfully predicted, as could the absence of accidents. Furthermore, a utility analysis of the composite predictor variable demonstrated that use of the selection procedure could reduce overall operating expenses for the bus agencies by more than $500,000 per year (Jacobs, Conte, Day, Silva, et al., 1996).

# Value-Added Employee Assessments

Personnel psychologists typically offer advice on which employees to hire. However, there are also significant challenges in determining which employees should be retained and which should be promoted. These decisions are usually made on the basis of a supervisor's appraisal. However, it might be argued that we should judge work performance on the basis of achieving long-term goals. For example, we should judge doctors on the basis of whether their patients recover from illness and judge teachers on the basis of their students' performance. When evaluating teachers, for example, studies have shown that it is very difficult to identify teaching quality (Strong, Gargani, & Hacifazlioglu, 2011) and that retention decisions are often made of the basis of other factors, such as days of work missed (Jacob, 2011). Why not judge teachers on the basis of the achievement of the people they have taught?

Recently, a controversy has erupted over the appraisal of teachers on the basis of student performance. With the advent of "high-stakes testing," it is even more apparent that some schools are not performing well and that students enrolled in these schools are not getting good educational experiences. Not all teachers are the same: some do an outstanding job of advancing the learning of their students, while others provide less value for the students they teach. What if we could evaluate teachers on the basis of the value they add?

The value-added approach to teacher assessment proposes to promote teachers when their students perform better than expected and deny reappointment for teachers whose students perform poorly. The big challenge is that, in addition to differences in teaching ability, students come to the classroom with different levels of ability. Thus, it would be unfair to punish a teacher whose students come to the classroom with lower performance capabilities. To address this problem, quantitative methods known as the value-added approach can be applied. Statistical modeling can be used to estimate the growth trajectories of students. Then, using a common technique known as multiple regression, an analyst can estimate the value added by a particular teacher. In other words, a statistical model uses a variety of variables to estimate expected student growth over the course of a school year. So it is possible to estimate whether, on average, a class of students outperformed or underperformed the expectation (Mangiante, 2011). A teacher whose class overperforms might be rewarded, while the contract of the teacher whose class underperformed might not be renewed. (Figure 18.2 provides a summary of this model.)

The value-added approach to teacher assessment has gone beyond theory and well into application. It has been endorsed by Arne Duncan, the secretary of education in the Obama Administration, and supported by the Bill and Melinda Gates Foundation. Some policymakers have argued that traditional credentials, such as having a degree in education or holding a master's degree, were unrelated to the value teachers provide to their students (Chingos & Peterson, 2011). On the other hand, value-added scores, at least among math teachers, are correlated with independent estimates of the quality of a teacher's instruction (Hill, Kapitula, & Umland, 2011). But there are significant problems. First, measuring growth has always been challenging. Over 40 years ago, Cronbach and Furby (1970) published their classic article, "How Should We Measure "Change"—or Should We?" The article outlined

**FIGURE 18.2**

Expected student growth based on standardized tests as a function of teacher for 5th grade. Teacher 1 outperformed expectations while teacher 2 underperformed. Under these circumstances, teacher 2 might face challenges in being reappointed.

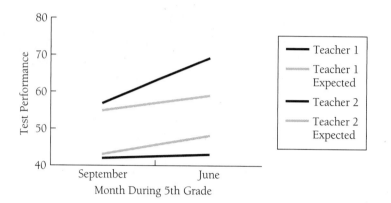

some of the mathematical and statistical problems in estimating rates of intellectual growth. The major statistical problems discussed in this classical article remain unresolved. Simply subtracting beginning-of-the-year from end-of-the-year performance is problematic, particularly because different schools start at different levels and the level of expected growth may be related to the point at which children start. The relationships are not linear. A child who knows basic arithmetic may be ready to grow into algebra while children at a lower level of understanding of arithmetic might be expected to grow more slowly. Perhaps more challenging, creating a growth score by subtracting beginning-of-the-year from end-of-the-year performance violates statistical assumptions because the errors are correlated, while the measurement model assumes they are independent.

One way to attend this problem is to compare students who are in similar schools. However, there are nearly an infinite number of combinations of children's background and school characteristics, and some combinations are too rare to allow reliable modeling. Many factors affect the likelihood of school success, including class size, funding, preparedness of teachers, availability of high-quality teaching materials, and so on. So having enough children in each unique combination can be problematic, even for large school districts.

Many other factors bias the assessment. For example, during summer breaks, some students lose a significant amount of what they learned during the school year. This is much more likely to happen among disadvantaged children whose parents cannot afford summer camps and enrichment programs. Children from more advantaged homes may be more likely to engage in academic-related experiences during the summer months. As a result, teachers assigned to classrooms with more disadvantaged students may start the school year with the cards stacked against them. The value-added approach attempts to take a student's demographic background into consideration, but these unknown or unappreciated variables have been difficult to model. Not all of the value-added approaches disadvantage teachers assigned to low-income schools—in some cases teachers in high-performing schools face biases. These might result from ceiling effects on standardized tests. For example, suppose that a teacher is assigned to teach math for a group of highly gifted students. At the beginning of the school year, the students, on average, get 95% of the test items correct. Because they are already near the ceiling performance for that test, the students have little room to grow, and the teacher has little opportunity to demonstrate overperformance.

There are a variety of unintended consequences for the value-added approach to teacher performance. One is known as assortative selection. In general, it takes a few years for a teacher to learn how to teach. So, most teachers perform poorly the first few years (Koedel & Betts, 2011). However, those teachers who perform very poorly are likely to exit the system while those who perform well tend to be promoted to a school of their choice. Rarely do highly performing teachers move to the inner city. Instead, they end up teaching in highly performing schools while novice and less well-performing teachers drift toward more poorly performing schools. If the school districts seek to dismiss teachers who underperform, they are much more likely to dismiss teachers who are working with the most challenging students. Those teachers are then replaced with novice teachers, who are known to have the greatest difficulty in managing students.

Another major criticism of the value-added approach is that it forces "teaching to the test" or "bubble children." There is more to an education than the ability to perform well on standardized tests. Yet the value-added approach evaluates teachers almost exclusively on the basis of student test performance. The consequences may be decreased classroom time devoted to psychosocial development, recreation, and the development of peer relationships. Further, cheating scandals have broken out in several school districts (see Psychological Testing in Everyday Life 18.1). When teachers and principals know that they may lose their jobs if their students perform poorly on tests, the temptation to fudge results may be almost irresistible.

As attractive as it sounds to fire teachers who are underperforming, value-added assessment does not address a major concern facing public school systems. Public school teaching does not pay well, the hours are long, and the emotional and physical challenges are substantial. In the past, the most attractive feature of public school teaching was job security. Now, with the threat of easy dismissal combined with low pay and stressful circumstances, there is a significant decline in the number of people entering the teaching profession. At the same time, many teachers are preparing to exit the profession. For example, there are about 300,000 teachers in the state of California. Among those, about 1/3 are on the verge of retirement.

Finally, there are consequences to transparency. Not only are some school districts eager to discipline poorly performing teachers, but in some cases, reporters are willing to shame teachers publicly. The *Los Angeles Times*, for example, acquired a list of value-added scores for all the teachers in the Los Angeles unified school district and made it public, including the teachers' names. This led to the suicide of a competent but underperforming teacher. Colleagues reported that the teacher was depressed about the value-added score that the *LA Times* had posted on its website. Although the teacher scored as "average" for boosting his students' English scores, scores on the math section showed him to be "less effective." Although his overall rating suggested that he was slightly "less effective" than other teachers, he was also known as a teacher who went the extra mile for children, even though this contributions would never show on a standardized test. He sought out the kids facing the greatest personal difficulties and tutored them on weekends and after school. He visited their homes, encouraging them to stay in school and to go on to college (Zavis & Barboza, 2010). Many people think the *LA Times* went too far. This doesn't mean we should ignore evidence about underperforming teachers. But we

## 18.1 PSYCHOLOGICAL TESTING IN EVERYDAY LIFE

### Teacher Cheating Scandals

Value-added assessment puts pressure on teachers to ensure that their students perform well on standardized tests. In June 2011, a major scandal broke out in Atlanta when it was learned that teachers and administrators had made changes on student test answer sheets. The following section from the *Los Angeles Times* describes a similar set of problems among Los Angeles teachers.

#### Focus on standardized tests may be pushing some teachers to cheat

*The number of California teachers who have been accused of cheating, lesser misconduct or mistakes on standardized achievement tests has raised alarms about the pressure to improve scores.*

**November 07, 2011**|By Howard Blume, *Los Angeles Times*

The stress was overwhelming.

For years, this veteran teacher had received exemplary evaluations but now was feeling pressured to raise her students' test scores. Her principal criticized her teaching and would show up to take notes on her class. She knew the material would be used against her one day.

"My principal told me right to my face that she—she was feeling sorry for me because I don't know how to teach," the instructor said.

The Los Angeles educator, who did not want to be identified, is one of about three dozen in the state accused this year of cheating, lesser misconduct or mistakes on standardized achievement tests.

The teachers came from 23 schools and 21 districts—an unprecedented number that has raised alarms about the pressure California educators are under to improve test scores. In the worst alleged cases, teachers are accused of changing incorrect responses or filling in missing ones after students returned answer booklets.

Many accused teachers have denied doing anything wrong. But documents and interviews suggest that an increasing focus on test scores has created an atmosphere of such intimidation that the idea teachers would cheat has become plausible.

"One teacher has personally confided in me that if her job was on the line, she indeed would cheat to get the higher test scores," one Los Angeles–area instructor said. "The testing procedures haven't been secure over the past 10-plus years. Some of the 'most effective' teachers could be simply the 'most cunning.'"

must recognize that among all the factors that determine student performance, the value added by a teacher is a relatively small part. For example, the effects of the location of the school on persistent student outcomes are stronger than the effects of teachers (Briggs & Weeks, 2011). As an alternative to firing teachers, we can help them improve by giving feedback, offering additional training, and providing better mentoring (Stronge, Ward, & Grant, 2011). If all of this does not work, teaching might not be the best professional match for those individuals. But there may be many alternatives short of dismissal.

# Incremental Validity

Validity defines the inferences that one can make on the basis of a score or measure (see Chapter 5). Evidence that a test is valid for particular inferences does not necessarily mean that the test is valuable. Though a test may be reliable and valid, the decision to use it depends on additional considerations. For example, does the test give you more information than you could find if it were not used? If so, how much more information does it give? The unique information gained through using the test is known as *incremental validity.*

In the discussions of base and hit rates and Taylor-Russell tables, we presented methods for evaluating what a test contributed beyond what was known from base rates. This kind of evaluation provides evidence for incremental validity. However, the assessment of incremental validity is not necessarily limited to comparisons with base rates. A particularly important form of evidence for incremental validity is the determination of how much information a test contributes beyond some simpler method for making the same prediction.

Most of the examples given in the preceding sections concerned tests used for selection purposes. However, the same rules and methods apply to tests used for the evaluation of personality or in the practice of clinical psychology. One concern is that assessments of personality by trained observers do not correspond well with self-assessments. One analysis aggregated data over thousands of people and found that self and observer ratings of personality have significant overlap. However, self and observer ratings offer unique and different information (Connolly, Kavanagh, & Viswesvaran, 2007). Until recently we have tended to disregard self-ratings. Growing evidence now suggests that self-ratings offer important and valid information.

Recent research on the prediction of behavior in particular situations has yielded some simple but startling results. Although it is difficult to predict behavior on the basis of reports by trained clinical psychologists (Meehl, 1995), people are remarkably good at predicting their own behavior (Bandura, 1994; Funder, Parke, Tomhnson-Keasey, & Widaman, 1993). We can learn a lot simply by asking someone whether he or she will be able to perform a particular behavior.

Frequently, expensive and time-consuming psychological tests are given in order to predict future behavior. Before exerting this effort, one should ask what the tests might reveal beyond information obtained in some simpler manner. For example, for predicting functioning and life expectancy for lung patients, a simple self-rating of health serves about as well as a complex set of medical tests. Detailed interviews and tests give little information beyond the simple patient self-report (Kaplan, Ries, Prewitt, & Eakin, 1994). Through a variety of tests and self-ratings, other studies have attempted to determine how a person will be rated by peers. The results often demonstrate that, in predicting peer ratings, simple self-ratings are as good as complex personality tests that make inferences about underlying traits (Hase & Goldberg, 1967).

Alternatively, work supervisors are known to be inaccurate raters. One variable that may affect ratings is the supervisor's own level of security. For example, studies have demonstrated that supervisors who have conflict over their own roles give relatively higher ratings of the performance of their subordinates (Fried & Tiegs, 1995). Self-predictions are also not always accurate. Even so, they no less accurately predict, for instance, who will go under a hypnotic trance than do complex hypnotizability scales (Melei & Hilgard, 1964). Further, they are at times more accurate than expensive tests. For example, personality tests have been of little value in predicting whether snake phobics will learn to approach a snake after therapy; however, self-predictions have been found to be highly accurate (Bandura, 1994).

A variety of investigations have considered the validity of employment interviews. The most comprehensive summary of these studies, reported by McDaniel and associates (1994), combined results from a variety of other investigations involving a combined total of 86,331 individuals. The analysis suggested that the validity of interview information depends on many variables. Situational interviews had higher validity than did job-related interviews. Psychologically based interviews had the lowest validity of all the categories studied. Structured interviews had higher validity than did unstructured ones. Other studies have demonstrated that biographical information used for employment decisions is often unreliable (Schmidt & Rothstein, 1994). There is some hope for improving ratings. Studies have shown that rating accuracy can improve with specific cognitive training (Day & Sulsky, 1995).

Often, the predictive validity of selection tests is modest. For example, one investigation attempted to predict who would be the best support people for insurance agencies. A battery of tests involving cognitive ability, personality, and biographical data was administered to 357 subjects. Among these, 337 were eventually hired and rated by their immediate supervisor for job performance. The range of the validity coefficients was .17 to .28. In other words, the extensive testing battery explains only about 4% to 9% of the variance in job performance (Bosshardt, Carter, Gialluca, Dunnette, et al., 1992). Another study evaluated applicants for eight telecommunications companies. Using structural behavioral interviews to estimate job performance yielded criterion validity estimates of approximately .22 (Motowidlo, Carter, Dunnette, Tippins, et al., 1992). After decades of research on the value of personality tests for employee selection, we still have very little evidence that personality measures are meaningful predictors of job performance (Murphy & Dzieweczynski, 2005).

We do not offer these examples to convince you that personality tests are meaningless. As you see in Chapters 14 and 16, personality measures make many important contributions. However, test users always should ask themselves whether they can gain the same information with a simpler or less expensive method or with one that will cause the subject less strain. Tests should be used when they provide significantly more information than simpler methods would obtain. To ensure that testing is a worthwhile use of time and resources, one must carefully select the testing materials to be used.

# Personnel Psychology from the Employee's Perspective: Fitting People to Jobs

One challenge in personnel psychology is to find the best matches between characteristics of people and characteristics of jobs. Temperament may be a critical component of job satisfaction. In this section, we review the Myers-Briggs Type Indicator (MBTI), which is perhaps the most widely used measure of temperament in I/O psychology.

## The Myers-Briggs Type Indicator

The MBTI, developed by I. B. Myers and K. C. Briggs, is a theoretically constructed test based on Carl Jung's theory of psychology types (Quenk, 2000). Jung theorized that there are four main ways in which we experience or come to know the world:

- ▶ *sensing*, or knowing through sight, hearing, touch, and so on;
- ▶ *intuition*, inferring what underlies sensory inputs;
- ▶ *feeling*, focusing on the emotional aspect of experience; and
- ▶ *thinking*, reasoning or thinking abstractly.

Jung argued that although we must strive for balance in the four modes, each person tends to emphasize one way of experiencing the world over the others. In addition, Jung believed that one could distinguish all individuals in terms of introversion versus extroversion.

The purpose of the Myers-Briggs test is to determine where people fall on the introversion–extroversion dimension and on which of the four modes they most rely (Quenk, 2000). In line with Jung's theory, the underlying assumption of the MBTI is that we all have specific preferences in the way we construe our experiences, and these preferences underlie our interests, needs, values, and motivation.

The MBTI is widely used and has been extensively researched (Wyman, 1998). It has been used to study such issues as communication styles (Loffredo & Opt, 1998), career choices (McCaulley & Martin, 1995), emotional perception (Martin, Berry, Dobranski, Horne, et al., 1996), leadership (Fitzgerald, 1997), and self-efficacy (Tuel & Betz, 1998). The MBTI has even been used to study the relationship between personality and financial success (Mabon, 1998) and sensitivity and purpose in life (Doerries & Ridley, 1998). In fact, our review of studies published between 1996 and 2000 revealed literally hundreds of studies that have used the MBTI in creative ways to study human personality and its correlates (see Quenk, 2000).

## Tests for Use in Industry: Wonderlic Personnel Test (WPT)

Business and industry make extensive use of tests, especially as an aid in making decisions about employment, placement, and promotion. One such test widely used is the WPT (Bell, 2002). Based on another popular instrument, the Otis Self-Administering Tests of Mental Ability, the WPT is a quick (12-minute) test of mental ability in adults. Normative data are available on more than 50,000 adults 20 to 65 years old. Five forms, whose intercorrelations range from .82 to .94, are available. Odd–even reliability coefficients are also excellent, with a range of .88 to .94 reported in the manual. The main drawback of the WPT is its validity documentation, although available studies tend to support it (Dodrill & Warner, 1988; Rosenstein & Glickman, 1994).

In short, the WPT is a quick and stable paper-and-pencil intelligence test with extensive norms. Widely used for employee-related decisions in industry, it has its greatest value when local validity data are available (Saltzman, Strauss, Hunter, & Spellacy, 1998). In the absence of local data, test scores must be interpreted with some caution. Figure 18.3 shows some sample questions from the Wonderlic.

## Sample Questions

Look at the row of numbers below. What number should come next?

| 8 | 4 | 2 | 1 | 1/2 | 1/4 | ? |

Assume the first 2 statements are true. Is the final one: (1) true, (2) false, (3) not certain?
The boy plays baseball. All baseball players wear hats. The boy wears a hat.

One of the numbered figures in the following drawing is most different from the others. What is the number in that figure?

A train travels 20 feet in 1/5 second. At this same speed, how many feet will it travel in three seconds?

How many of the six pairs of items listed below are exact duplicates?

| 3421 | 1243 |
| 21212 | 21212 |
| 558956 | 558956 |
| 10120210 | 10120210 |
| 612986896 | 612986896 |
| 356471201 | 356571201 |

The hours of daylight and darkness in SEPTEMBER are nearest equal to the hours of daylight and darkness in
(1) June    (2) March    (3) May    (4) November

In 2007, a new version of the Wonderlic, known as the Wonderlic Personnel Test–Revised (WRT-R) was released. The newer version updates the traditional Wonderlic and uses newer technologies for test administration and scoring. For most test takers, the new version can be completed in about 12 minutes.

# Measuring Characteristics of the Work Setting

To study the influence of situations, we need methods to describe and measure them. This section describes these methods.

# The Social-Ecology Approach

*Ecology* is the branch of biology that studies the relationship between living organisms and their environments. Organisms must adapt to the physical environment to survive. Similarly, environments can affect the social lives of their inhabitants. Thus, psychologists have come to recognize the importance of studying people in their natural environments and of analyzing the effects of physical environments on social behavior (Wicker, 1979). As Stokols states, "At a time when environmentalists and economists are proclaiming that 'small is beautiful,' the research literature on human behavior in relation to its environmental settings continues to expand at a staggering rate" (1978, p. 253). This field of study is called *environmental psychology*. A similar area, *ecological psychology*, focuses on events that occur in a behavioral setting. We refer to these topics of study together as **social ecology** (Stokols, 2000). One of the most important areas in social ecology is the study of behavioral settings.

Each day, you participate in a variety of behavioral settings, such as your psychological-testing class. Let's say you and your classmates are talking while you wait for the lecturer to arrive. When she enters the room, everyone grows quiet. As the presentation begins, you and your classmates focus your attention on the speaker. Why does this chain of events occur? It does, in part, because the room is set up to facilitate this kind of social interaction. For example, the chairs face the front of the room, where a chalkboard hangs. What would happen if the chairs were facing the other way? What if there were no chairs?

Barker made the study of behavioral settings his life's work. For many years, he and his colleagues described the publicly available behavioral settings in two small towns: Oskaloosa, Kansas, and Leyburn, England. Both towns included many behavioral settings, such as card games, court sessions, and special businesses. Barker's work involved documenting each setting by describing how long the observed interactions lasted, who participated, the gender of the people in the setting, and so on (Barker, 1979; Barker & Schoggen, 1973; Schoggen, 1979; Wicker, 1979).

The study of behavioral settings reveals a great deal about the social rules of the environment. For example, in both Oskaloosa and Leyburn, women spent less time in public behavioral settings than did men. The studies also confirmed what many feminists have been saying all along—that women are limited to certain settings. For example, women in both towns were observed most often in such settings as churches and schools. In other words, they were more often found in settings that favored social talking than in business and government settings.

Behavioral settings are truly self-regulating ecologies. When a component of the system is missing, the activities in the program are changed to correct the imbalance. For example, if there were no chairs in your psychological testing class, then students would probably go out looking for them in order to bring the situation into balance. If someone in the class made too much noise, then social forces would attempt to eliminate the disruption (Wicker, 1979). Thus, to avoid social condemnation, people must act according to the rules for a given behavioral setting. A catcall during psychology class might bring you strange and rejecting looks. In a rock concert, it is perfectly appropriate. Social adjustment requires that one know and follow the rules of many social behavioral settings.

The study of behavioral settings also involves examining the relationship between work satisfaction and the requirements of the job. Wicker and Kirmeyer (1976) used this approach in a study of coping behavior among park rangers in Yosemite National Park. During the summer, as the workload for the rangers increased, they felt more challenged on the job and used more coping strategies. By the end of the summer, when the workload peaked, the challenge of heavy crowds was no longer associated with job satisfaction. Instead, the rangers were less able to cope and felt physically and emotionally drained. To understand the relationship between work setting and satisfaction, one must consider many aspects of the ecology, including the workload, coping strategies, and the duration of work overload. One must also make a precise description of the work environment. When employees perceive that there is support for creativity at work, they report greater job satisfaction, better social climate, and less stress (Stokols, Clitheroe, & Zmuidzinas, 2002).

There are many applications of the social-ecology approach in clinical and health psychology. For example, restructuring the environment may modify health-damaging behaviors such as smoking and lack of exercise (Johansson, Johnson, & Hall, 1991). Considerable work has gone into characterizing family environments and the interaction between spouses. Like the workplace, the social environment may affect cigarette smoking, diet, and other health behaviors (Cohen & Lichtenstein, 1990; Ewart, 1991).

## Classifying Environments

How do different environments affect our behavior? Can we work better when the sun is out? Or do we get more tired and irritable on hot days? Most of social psychology is based on the premise that situations influence behavior (Moos, 2003). Some of the earliest work in the field of environmental psychology involved building elaborate systems to classify the characteristics of environments that had been shown to affect individual or group behavior (Holahan, 1986). (This was similar to the work done by many early personality psychologists who built elaborate systems to classify personality types.)

Table 18.6 shows a classification system created by Moos (1973). It includes six characteristics of environments and gives examples. Many studies demonstrate that the characteristics of the people in one's environment affect one's behavior. The likelihood that a high-school girl will begin to smoke, for example, can be greatly influenced by how many girls she knows who already smoke or who approve of smoking (Gilpin & Pierce, 2003). Over the years, Moos and his colleagues have developed many different measures to evaluate the characteristics of environments (Moos, 2003). A summary of these scales is shown in Table 18.7.

Moos's work on measuring the characteristics of environments demonstrates the ways in which personal characteristics of the work environment affect job choice and worker satisfaction (Schaefer & Moos, 1996). For example, workers are more satisfied with work environments that promote quality interactions between workers and supervisors than they are with environments that keep these relationships more distant. The quality of the relationship between workers and supervisors also enhances productivity (Moos, 1987c). Some evidence indicates that workers in supportive work environments are less likely to develop disabilities caused by stress

**TABLE 18.6**  Six Characteristics of Environments

| Characteristics | Examples |
|---|---|
| Ecological dimensions | Architectural design, geographic location, weather conditions |
| Behavioral settings | Office, home, store |
| Organizational structure | Percentage of women in the student body, number of people per household, average age of group |
| Characteristics of inhabitants | Proportion of students who date, drink, or vote |
| Psychosocial and organizational climate | Work pressure, encouragement of participation, orientation toward helping with personal problems |
| Functional or reinforcing properties | Is aggression reinforced on the football field? Is it reinforced at home? |

Adapted from Moos (1973).

**TABLE 18.7**  Summary of Scales Used to Evaluate Different Environments

| Type of environment | Scale | Reference |
|---|---|---|
| Treatment | Ward Atmosphere Scale | Moos (1987e) |
| | Community-Oriented Programs | |
| | Environment Scale | Moos (1987a) |
| Institutional | Correctional Institutions | |
| | Environment Scale | Moos (1987b) |
| Educational | University Residence | |
| | Environment Scale | Moos (1987d) |
| | Classroom Environment Scale | Moos and Truckett (1986) |
| Community | Work Environment Scale | Moos (1986b) |
| | Group Environment Scale | Moos (1986a) |
| | Family Environment Scale | Moos and Moos (1986) |

on the job than are workers in nonsupportive environments (Holahan & Moos, 1986). A pleasant work environment is also good for business. Bank customers who perceive employees as friendly and supportive tend to stay at their bank more than do customers who dislike the bank's social environment (Moos, 1986b).

Lemke and Moos (1986) have expanded this work by creating a *multiphasic environmental assessment procedure* (MEAP). There are many ways to apply this

**FIGURE 18.4**

Physical and architectural resources profile for two nursing homes.

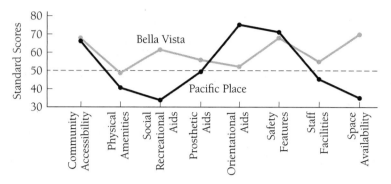

(Moos & Lemke, 1984, p. 22.)

procedure. For example, we can use it to describe sheltered-care settings, including nursing homes and other housing situations for older adults. This complex approach includes evaluating the settings according to physical and architectural features, policy and program information, resident and staff information, attractiveness and other physical characteristics, and a general environment scale. Each feature has many subscales. For example, policy and program information includes how selective the home is in admitting new patients, how clearly its policies are specified, how much control residents have over policies, and so on. The resident and staff information includes the ratio of staff members to residents, the resident activity level, and the functional abilities of the residents. Figure 18.4 describes the physical and architectural resources of two nursing homes: Pacific Place and Bella Vista. As the figure shows, the homes are quite similar on some variables such as community accessibility and safety features. However, Bella Vista receives a much better score for social recreational activities, whereas Pacific Place receives a better score for orientational aids. Using this sort of information, one can quantitatively measure the characteristics of a work or home environment (Moos & Lemke, 1984).

In Chapter 17, we discussed the potential of electronic devices to capture information. These devices have enormous potential for assessing the environment. One of the most important problems in contemporary research is determining how much of our behavior is influenced by genetics and how much is determined by our environments. Most behaviors are the result of complex interactions between genes and environments. Recent advances in molecular biology have made measurement of genetic exposures feasible. In contrast, measurement of environment remains very challenging. Unlike our genomes, which are relatively constant throughout life, environmental exposures are dynamic and constantly changing throughout life. But, the game is changing because new electronic technologies are capable of capturing many of our exposures and behaviors. For example, environmental scientists have developed a sensor system that measures dangerous chemicals in the environment with a sensitivity at the level that we need for the most detailed studies of exposure. The goal is to be able to move beyond assigning everyone in a given geographical region an "average" exposure level to assessing individual exposures as people go about their daily routine.

In sum, behavioral settings and social environments are coming to be recognized as important factors in job and personal satisfaction. The study of work environments is a relatively new area that we expect to blossom in the coming decade.

# Job Analysis

In addition to classifying work environments, the industrial psychologist must describe and measure characteristics of the job. Employers often want to detail the activities of their workplace to determine what type of personnel is needed or why some employees are unhappy working in the setting. Zedeck and Blood (1974) summarize five basic methods for doing so: checklists, critical incidents, observations, interviews, and questionnaires.

*Checklists* are used by job analysts to describe the activities and working conditions usually associated with a job title. An example of a checklist for a research assistant in behavioral research is shown in Table 18.8. The first column of the checklist shows the activities associated with the job title, while the other columns list the frequency of occurrence of these activities. The job analyst must simply record how frequently each activity occurs for people in this job classification.

One of the concerns about job analysis is whether ratings are reliable. Dierdorff and Wilson (2003) reviewed 46 studies involving more than 299 estimates of reliability of job analysis. Ratings of tasks produced higher estimates of interrater reliability than did generalized ratings of jobs. The goals of a rater can also affect the ratings. One study had evaluators rate group projects. Their ratings were higher when they were told that the goal of their ratings was to produce harmony. Harmony goals also reduced the variability between projects. Emphasizing fairness also increased the mean ratings, but did not affect the variability of completed projects (Wong & Kwong, 2007).

In addition to evaluating jobs, employers must evaluate job performance. This is a complex field that is beyond the scope of this text. However, there are excellent summaries of performance evaluation. Although there is some evidence for the validity of job ratings (O'Connell, Hartman, McDaniel, Grubb, & Lawrence, 2007), suffice it to say that problems in performance evaluation are challenging. For example, there is controversy over whether there is racial bias in the evaluation of job performance. Some researchers still argue that there are important differences in performance across racial groups. For example, Roth and colleagues

**TABLE 18.8**  Job Checklist for Research Assistant*

| Activity | Frequency of occurrence Per hour | Per day | Per week | Per month | Per year |
|---|---|---|---|---|---|
| Photocopying | | 1 | | | |
| Typing | | | 2 | | |
| Attending meetings | | | | 1 | |
| Meeting with subjects | | | 3 | | |
| Ordering supplies | | | | 1 | |
| Writing reports | | | | | 1 |

*The assistant would be expected to photocopy materials once per day, type twice per week, meet with subjects three times per week, and so on.

summarized studies on differences in job performance (Roth, Huffcutt, & Bobko, 2003). They compared differences between African American and white employees on subjective measures such as supervisor ratings versus objective measures based on more formal evaluations. Their analysis suggested that the objective measures showed even larger differences between African American and white employees than the subjective measures for work quality, quantity, and absenteeism. Differences between Hispanic and white employees were not as large as those between African American and white employees.

Some researchers criticize checklists for providing neither an integrated picture of the job situation nor information about specific behaviors. There are methodological problems with checklists because it is sometimes difficult to determine if unchecked items were intentionally omitted or if the form was left incomplete (Clark & Watson, 1998). In contrast to Moos's environment scales, checklists do not predict well whether someone will like a particular job environment.

*Critical incidents* are observable behaviors that differentiate successful from unsuccessful employees. The critical-incident method was developed by J. C. Flanagan (1954). By acquiring specific descriptions of the behaviors of successful employees and their unsuccessful counterparts, one can learn something about the differences between the two groups. For example, a critical incident that might describe a successful employee is "always arrives at meetings on time." A critical incident that describes an unsuccessful employee might be "leaves work area disorganized."

*Observation* is another method for learning about the nature of the job. As we discussed in Chapter 8, information gathered through observational methods can sometimes be biased because people change their behavior when they know they are being watched. To avoid this problem, the participant-observation method is sometimes used. A participant-observer is someone who participates in the job and functions as though he or she were one of the workers.

*Interviews* can also be used to find out about a job. However, some workers may give an interviewer information that differs from what they would give another employee because they are uncomfortable or fear that what they say will be held against them. Another problem is that an interviewer unfamiliar with the job may not ask the right questions.

*Questionnaires* are commonly used to find out about job situations, but their use calls for special precautions. Many employers favor questionnaires because they are inexpensive. However, the employer may never know whether the respondent understood the questions. Furthermore, the type of information gained is limited to the specific questions. A more serious problem concerns the selective return rate in questionnaire studies. Those employees who feel highly favorable or highly unfavorable toward the company are the most likely to complete the questionnaire and return it.

Another approach to job description is the Occupational Information Network (O*NET) (Peterson, Mumford, Levin, Green, & Waksberg, 1999). The network was developed because traditional job descriptions in the U.S. Department of Labor's *Dictionary of Occupational Titles* did not provide enough information about how tasks and skills generalized across occupations. Job content can be described by both job-oriented and work-oriented tasks. The system includes three categories: (1) worker requirements, such as skills, knowledge, and abilities; (2) experience requirements, including training and licensure; and (3) job requirements, such as work activities, work context, and characteristics of the organization (Hanson, Borman, Kubisiak, & Sager, 1999). Using O*NET, one can understand divergent occupations in relation to tasks and skills that generalize across occupational categories (Jeanneret, Borman, Kubisiak, & Hanson, 1999). O*NET continues to evolve. The entire database is available to the public at no cost (see ONETCENTER.ORG). The 2012 data base includes thousands of occupational definitions and the system is continually updated.

# Measuring the Person–Situation Interaction

In this chapter, we have presented two different perspectives. First, we reviewed research and methods from counseling psychology that emphasized the importance of people's characteristics or traits in their career satisfaction (Campbell, 2000). Then we discussed how the characteristics of work environments and job requirements affect people.

To a growing number of psychologists, whether traits or situations are more important in determining behavior is a "pseudoquestion" (Anastasi & Urbina, 1997; McFall & McDonell, 1986; Sarason, Sarason, & Pierce, 1990; Trotter & Endler, 1999). Established leaders, for example, change their behavior to fit different situations (Michel & LeBreton, 2011). It is meaningless to ask whether traits or situations are more important in explaining behavior, because behavior is clearly a joint function of both, or *person–situation interaction* (Funder, 2010).

The interactionists support their position by reporting the proportion of variance in behavior explained by person, by situation, and by the interaction between person and situation. You might think of this as a pie divided to represent all the different influences on human behavior, including unknown causes (see Figure 18.5). Unique combinations of traits and situations cause this interaction. The beginning of Chapter 15 featured the case of Harry, a man who suffered throughout his life

**FIGURE 18.5**

Factors influencing behavior. A pie is divided according to the proportion of variation in behavior accounted for by person, situation, and the interaction between person and situation. The interaction is greater than either of the other two sources of influence. However, unexplained or error variance is much greater than any other factor.

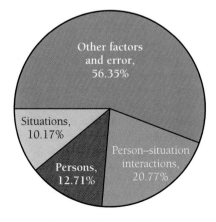

(Adapted from data in Bowers, 1973.)

because he had made a bad career choice to become a dentist. For example, an interaction might describe how Harry reacts to being a dentist. This cause is different from the characteristics of Harry (in all situations) or the effects of anyone performing the role of a dentist. Careful studies that apply a statistical method known as *analysis of variance* have separated the proportion of variance attributable to each of these factors. As shown in Figure 18.5, the interaction accounts for a larger portion of the variance in behavior than does either the person or the situation (Endler, Parker, Bagby, & Cox, 1991).

As you can see, the interaction position explains only some of the people some of the time (Bem & Allen, 1974). As Figure 18.5 shows, the largest slice of the pie represents *error variance*, the proportion of the total not explained by the three sources of influence. After reviewing many studies on the influences of person and situation, I. G. Sarason, Smith, and Diener (1975) concluded that none of the three sources account for an impressive share of the variation when compared with the amount of variation left unexplained. Although the interaction is a better predictor than either trait or situation, it is only slightly better.

To help predict more of the people more of the time, Bem and Funder (1978) introduced the *template-matching technique*, a system that takes advantage of people's ability to predict their own behavior in particular situations. The system attempts to match personality to a specific template of behavior. For example, consider how to answer the question "Should Tom become an insurance salesperson?" Assuming you know nothing about Tom, perhaps the best way to guide him would be to describe how several hypothetical people might react to working in this job. You might say that shy people may have difficulty approaching new customers or that people with families may not like insurance sales because of the irregular work hours. Tom could then predict his own reaction to the job by matching his characteristics with the set of templates you have provided for him.

Along the same lines, Bem and Funder proposed that "situations be characterized as sets of template-behavior pairs, each template being a personality description of an idealized type of person expected to behave in a specified way in that setting" (1978, p. 486). The probability that a particular person will behave in a particular way in a situation is a function of the match between his or her characteristics and a template. For example, if Tom's personality characteristics matched the template for those who hated being insurance salespeople, then he might be best advised to avoid that career.

Because the template-matching idea arose from research in personality and social psychology, it is not often discussed in other areas of psychology. However, the person–situation interaction resembles what educational psychologists call the *aptitude–treatment interaction* (Rodger, 2002; Snow, 1991). The template-matching idea also resembles a popular theory of career choice that J. L. Holland (1997) proposed. Holland suggested that there are six clusters of personality and interest traits; these are the same clusters represented as the six general themes on the Strong-Campbell Interest Inventory (SCII) (realistic, investigative, artistic, social, enterprising, and conventional). Holland contended that six vocational environments correspond to these traits and that people will be happiest if they can match their traits to the characteristics of the work environment (Holland, 1975; Holland & Gottfredson, 1976). For example, an investigative individual will be most content if he or she can work in an investigative field such as science.

The idea of matching traits to situations is intuitively appealing. The concept of "different strokes for different folks" seems like a good way to structure one's search for the right job, the right apartment, or the right psychotherapist. However, this approach has some problems. First, there are an enormous number of combinations of persons and situations. For example, predicting how 10 personality types will perform in 20 different work environments produces $10 \times 20 = 200$ unique combinations. Most real-life decisions require many more factors. Second, research has not yet supported specific examples of matching traits and situations. Psychotherapists, for example, often account for lack of effectiveness by arguing that weak results should be expected because therapies must be tailored to the specific personalities of clients. In other words, some people will do well in behavior therapy, whereas others will have better success with a more cognitive approach. However, research has typically failed to correlate personalities with treatments. When these interactions are found, other studies tend not to replicate them (Smith & Sechrest, 1991). As a result, researchers must go back to the theoretical drawing board for new insights into the selection of treatment.

The fit between persons and situations may depend on how we ask the questions. In one study, university students worked intensively with teams over an extended period of time. Their ratings of their fit with the team remained stable over time, but their ratings of their personal fit with their individual role on the team were less stable. Individuals who receive positive feedback for their contributions tend to feel they have a closer fit with their roles on the team (DeRue & Morgeson, 2007).

One finding that has been supported by research is that people often predict their own behavior better than do experts. However, some people tend to be overly positive in self-evaluations. This enhancement can be evaluated by comparing self-ratings with those provided by friends and professionals (Funder, 2010; Funder & West, 1993). Longitudinal studies show that self-enhancers tend to have poor social skills and poor psychological adjustment. Positive mental health may be associated with accurate self-appraisal (Funder, 2010). Cognitive ability may also play a role in how well people are able to assess their own test performance. For example, people with higher cognitive ability more accurately assess their own performance on a situational test of consumer services skills than people with lower cognitive ability do (Truxillo, Seitz, & Bauer, 2008).

In general, career satisfaction depends on an appropriate match between person and job. The developing technology for finding job–person matches holds great promise for the field of career counseling and guidance testing (Nystul, 1999). Counseling interventions must be tailored to individual needs (Savickas, 2000). Trying to use the same approach with every client might be like a shoe store attempting to sell the same size of shoe to each customer (Weigel, 1999).

# Summary

Making a selection among the many published tests has become a technical skill. One of your first considerations should always be whether it is worthwhile to administer a given test. How much information does the test promise beyond what can be learned without the test? Interviews remain the most common method for employee selection. However, the traditional interview has significant limitations. Modern personnel psychology makes extensive use of systematic selection procedures, often based on tests, performance samples, and job analysis. In personnel selection, the *base rate* is the probability of succeeding without any selection procedure. A variety of methods have been developed to estimate the amount of information a test gives beyond what is known by chance. This estimate depends on the validity of the test, the percentage of people being selected, and the proportion of people who can be expected to succeed if no selection test is used. *Taylor-Russell tables* can be used for outcomes defined in terms of success and failure. You can use utility and decision theories for some outcomes involving more than these two levels. However, the application of the utility theory equations is fairly difficult in most circumstances. To enhance productivity in business and industry, personnel psychologists study characteristics of people, work environments, and the interactions between people and the places they may work. Learning about the interface between people and work environments may hold the key to finding the best methods for employee selection.

# 19

## CHAPTER

# Ethics and the Future of Psychological Testing

## LEARNING OBJECTIVES

*When you have completed this chapter, you should be able to:*

▶ Explain why the question of whether people possess stable traits is an issue in the testing field

▶ Explain the issue of actuarial versus clinical prediction

▶ Identify human rights as they pertain to testing

▶ Explain the problem of labeling

▶ Explain the issue of divided loyalties

▶ Identify some important responsibilities of test users and constructors

▶ Identify four important current trends in the testing field

▶ Describe the future prospects of testing

n a special issue of *Psychological Assessment*, specialists in psychological testing received a glimpse of the field's future (Haynes, 1995). More recently, psychology's future was explored in a provoking analysis by Bray (2009). This future involves the assimilation of new concepts such as chaos theory (Campbell, 2011, p. 51), nonlinear dynamical models (Gorman, 2011), and mathematical models (Peluso, Liebovitch, Gottman, Norman, & Su, 2011), which have been recently applied to fields such as economics, ecology, biology, and physics. Indeed, the future of testing depends on the application of ultramodern theoretical notions and technologies (Eby, Chin, Rollock, Schwartz, & Worrell, 2011), especially computers and the Internet (Florell, 2011). To discuss the future of testing, we must not only look ahead but also remain aware of the many interacting, and sometimes conflicting, issues that currently shape the field. By doing so, we can deepen our understanding of testing and venture a few educated guesses about its future. Keep in mind that the forces influencing this future do not operate in isolation but rather interact with one another in highly complicated ways (Sackett, Borneman, & Connelly, 2008; Spear, 2007), even though we treat each separately here.

# Issues Shaping the Field of Testing

The concerns that currently shape testing include professional, moral, and social issues. Ethical issues underlie each of these concerns.

## Professional Issues

Three major professional issues continually play an especially important role in the current status and the future of psychological testing: theoretical concerns, the adequacy of tests, and actuarial versus clinical prediction (see Figure 19.1).

### Theoretical Concerns

One of the most important considerations underlying tests is the dependability (reliability) of test results (Thomas & Selthon, 2003; Tryon & Bernstein, 2003). Reliability places an upper limit on validity. According to the *Standards for Educational and Psychological Testing* of the American Education Research Association (AERA), the American Psychological Association (APA), and the National Council on Measurement in Education (NCME), a test that is totally unreliable (unstable) has no meaning. There may be exceptions to this rule, but current practice generally demands that tests possess some form of stability. As a corollary, whatever is being measured must itself have stability. Saying that a test has reliability implies that test results are attributable to a systematic source of variance, which is stable itself. In other words, the test is presumed to measure a stable entity. There are various

**FIGURE 19.1**
Schematic summary
of professional issues.

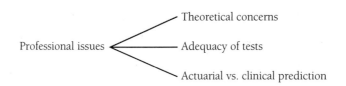

Professional issues ⟨ Theoretical concerns

Adequacy of tests

Actuarial vs. clinical prediction

types of reliability, depending on the different purposes of the tests. Each test must possess the type of reliability that is appropriate to the test's uses (AERA, APA, & NCME, 1999; APA, 2002; Slaney, Storey, & Barnes, 2011; Wyse & Reckase, 2011).

Most existing tests measure a presumably stable entity—either the individual as he or she currently functions or some temporally stable characteristic of the individual. In describing current functioning, psychologists imply that the person functions this way in a fairly stable, though perhaps short-term, manner that is independent of the situation or environment. In other words, they assume that they can describe the person in absolute terms, as if in a vacuum. They may say something like, "The person is emotionally unstable" or "The person is out of contact with reality" or else provide a diagnostic label such as "schizophrenic" or "neurotic." Similarly, and even more strikingly, psychologists purport to measure enduring qualities that will manifest themselves over time regardless of immediate or long-term external (situational, environmental, and so forth) factors. Again, they assume that what they are measuring exists in absolute terms.

Whether measuring current functioning or a temporally stable characteristic, testers always assume that the systematic source of variance measured by the test results entirely from the person rather than some other factor. When we try to measure a stable characteristic of an individual and find less than perfect temporal reliability, we assume that the imperfections proceed from test-related inadequacies, such as measurement error, or from minor fluctuating subject variables, such as fatigue. Presumably, then, the characteristic or variable being measured is stable, it exists, and only the test instrument limits one's ability to measure it. Therefore, the more accurate a test, the more stable the results should be.

In simple terms, testers assume that people possess stable characteristics (e.g., intelligence) and stable response tendencies (e.g., traits) that hold up across situations and exist independently of the environment. However, many empirical investigations (Samuel, Hopwood, & Ansell, et al., 2011) show that even the best tests have yet to achieve such temporal stability. In other words, testers cannot readily attribute differences over time solely to measurement error or fluctuating subject variables. Hence, this primary assumption underlying tests is not entirely correct. Moreover, the social environment affects behavior (Hawkley, Lavelle, Berntson, & Cacioppo, 2011; Kendler, Eaves, & Loken, et al., 2011), as illustrated in a model by Cacioppo and colleagues (1991), which shows the relationship between the psychological and the physiological domain (see Figure 19.2).

The trait question applies to psychology as a whole and to personality psychology in particular (Spear, 2007). Early formulations of human personality tended to view personality as comprising stable and lasting traits (behavioral dispositions). Freud and many of his followers, for example, believed that early experiences, memories, traumas, and anxieties often resulted in behavioral dispositions that persisted throughout life. Views such as Freud's, however, were challenged by those who saw human personality as changing rather than fixed and stationary, as well as by those who saw that situations and external factors influence behavior.

Most of the tests discussed in this text are based on the assumption that one can measure human characteristics independently of the context in which these characteristics occur, a theory not only disputable but also without significant support (Bandura, 1986; Mischel, 1968; Ziskin, 1995). Psychological tests can be

**FIGURE 19.2**

Dimensions of psychophysiological response space. One dimension represents the antecedent of the physiological event (event-related/spontaneous), a second dimension represents the nature of the stimulus (discrete/contextual), and a third represents the time course of the physiological event (tonic/phasic). Each of the pairs of terms in this figure represents endpoints on a continuum rather than narrowly and absolutely defined categories of activity.

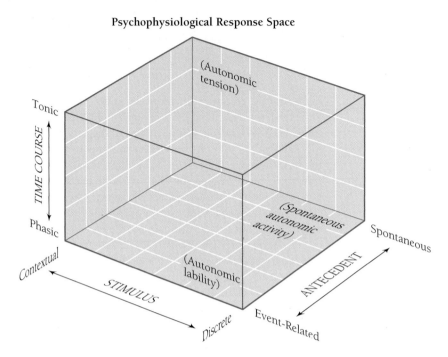

**Psychophysiological Response Space**

(From Cacioppo, Berntson, and Anderson, 1991. Copyright 1991 by the American Psychological Association. Reprinted by permission of the author.)

no better than the science of psychology that underlies them. As the science clarifies basic theoretical issues, testing conforms to the available knowledge. In the meantime, perhaps the single most important theoretical assumption of tests—that human characteristics are stable and can be measured independently of the environment—is debatable.

Human behavior may be the result of long-term stable behavioral tendencies (traits); the external or internal environments that precede, coexist with, and follow behavior; or some other factor such as the interaction between traits and environments. Either tests have a long way to go before they will be able to measure the precise determinants of human behavior or current conceptualizations and underlying assumptions of tests are not precise enough to make accurate predictions.

After reviewing the psychometric qualities and the limits of mental ability and personality tests, we have concluded that, although people exhibit a core of stability, they continually change. Certainly, one explanation for the relatively poor long-term reliability of personality tests is that as the individual adjusts to the environment, he or she changes. Indeed, most definitions of intelligence include the ability to adapt or change according to circumstances. The fact is, people change all the time.

The point here is that all psychological tests are based on theories of human functioning. Unfortunately, the validity of these theories and their underlying assumptions is far from proven. Furthermore, there is no consensus concerning either a definition of human intelligence or the essence of human personality, normal or abnormal. A revolution in psychological theory, therefore, could revolutionize psychological tests. The bottom line is that today's tests are no better than the theories and assumptions that underlie them.

## The Adequacy of Tests

A second professional issue in testing with strong overtones concerns the adequacy of existing tests. This entire book has been aimed at providing you with the knowledge you need to evaluate tests. To this end, the book is filled with statements about standardization, norms, scoring, interpretation, test design, reliability, and validity. Thus far, however, we have evaluated tests relative to traditionally accepted psychometric standards rather than absolute external criteria. David Shakow, who is to many the father of modern clinical psychology, posited that we have not quite reached our goal of providing objective and psychometrically sound assessment of personality and psychological function (Barlow, 2011, pp. 10–11). This was his conclusion after practicing clinical psychology in a career that spanned nearly 50 years. In fact, many psychologists and others have questioned whether even the best existing tests possess sufficiently sound psychometric qualities to warrant their use (Greene, 2000; Wood, Nezworski, Lilienfeld, & Garb, 2003; Ziskin, 1995).

As we have noted, the real issue in testing is how tests are used. One could argue that no test at all is better than a test that often leads to an incorrect conclusion. No doubt there are situations in which all concerned would be better off without test results than with them.

We do not think all tests should be eliminated until better ones are developed, but we do believe that people should view the adequacy of tests from all possible perspectives. Some tests, such as certain ability tests, are generally adequate in reliability. However, just about any test could benefit from greater validity documentation. Clearly, people should consider absolute standards, not just relative ones, when evaluating current and future trends in testing.

In the end, how tests are used may be determined by law or by the threat of litigation. Tests that lead to selection biases are suspect. If the SAT Reasoning Test or LSAT consistently underselects African Americans, Latinos, and Latinas for college, then we have to ask how accurate these tests are, how much they add to prediction, and whether loss of diversity is justified by increased prediction (Geiser & Studley, 2001; Moore & Bell, 2011; Rosner, 2003; Shultz & Zedeck, 2011). In the end, it may be the U.S. Supreme Court or Congress that tells us whether the use of a test is justified.

## Actuarial versus Clinical Prediction

A third issue concerns the accuracy of predictions made by test users. Throughout this book we have argued that tests provide a standard setting in which practitioners can observe behavior. Further, they can use this situation in conjunction with experience and local norms to gain accuracy in their observations and decisions. Certainly, users of psychological tests must feel this way or they simply would not waste their time with tests. However, test users rarely, if ever, receive feedback on the accuracy of their predictions and decisions based on tests. Do tests, then, truly enhance assessment, or are practitioners fooling themselves, repeating their errors, and teaching them to students?

One can examine this question from all sides (see Campbell, 2003; Monahan, 2003; Ogloff & Douglas, 2003). The early work of Meehl (Meehl, 1954; Meehl & Rosen, 1955) and Little and Shneidman (1959) drew attention to the limits of test data even in the hands of trained practitioners. In subsequent analyses, Sawyer (1966) and Sines (1970) reviewed studies that compared an actuarial approach, in which test results were interpreted by using a set of rules, with a clinical approach, in which trained professionals interpreted test results (Quinsey, Harris, Rice, & Cormier, 2006). These reviews indicated that the set of rules was more accurate than the trained professional practitioners, even when the practitioners knew the rules. This research confirmed Meehl's (1954) earlier finding that trained practitioners could not surpass predictions based on statistical formulas. Ziskin (1995) and Dawes (1999) have argued that simple tables of actuarial data, such as number of prior arrests and severity of crime, predict recidivism better than do tests or clinical judgments. Do we really need trained clinicians and sophisticated tests to make decisions? Other studies and analyses indicate that the trained practitioner is a better predictor than actuarial formulas are, especially when practitioners use data from a variety of sources such as a test battery, an interview, and a case history (e.g., Deogun & Spaulding, 2010; see also Scurich & John, 2011; Wood et al., 2003). In this argument, we again find professional disagreement at the most basic levels (ÆgisdÓttir, Spengler, & White, 2006; ÆgisdÓttir et al., 2006; Salzinger, 2005).

The issue of actuarial versus clinical prediction has more recently reemerged with the proliferation of computerized test interpretations (Brooks & Barlow, 2011). As discussed in Chapter 9, computers are taking a prominent role in the scoring of tests, reporting of results, and diagnosis of clients (Frase et al., 2003). Can a computer accurately interpret a psychological test? The many problems inherent in such interpretations have fostered much debate about the computer's potential as a diagnostician (Drigas, Koukianakis, & Papagerasimou, 2011; Ponniah, Weissman, & Bledsoe, et al., 2011; Saccuzzo, 1994). As Hartman (1986) noted, several potential abuses accompany the use of computer software to interpret psychological tests, including trivialization of assessment, use of software inappropriate to the client, and inadequate contribution of the clinician to the assessment process. Further, the question remains as to whether the computer's interpretations can ever be as good as, let alone better than, those of the clinician. Regardless of whether clinicians rely on a computer-generated diagnosis, a testing service, or on their own interpretation of results, the APA guidelines entitled *Ethical Principles of Psychologists and Code of Conduct* specify that it is the clinician who retains responsibility for the appropriateness of the analysis (APA, 2002). Interestingly, with all the available technology, a 2011 survey of the practices of independent practitioners, very few relied on technology in their practices, and most were unsure about what uses of computer technology in practice was and was not ethical (McMinn, Bearse, Heyne, Smithberger, & Erb, 2011).

## Moral Issues

Professional issues alone will not determine the future of testing. The field is also being shaped by moral issues—human rights, labeling, and invasion of privacy (see Figure 19.3). Two other important ethical issues are divided loyalties and the responsibilities of test users and test constructors.

**FIGURE 19.3**
Schematic summary of moral issues.

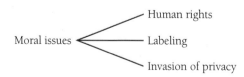

Moral issues — Human rights
Moral issues — Labeling
Moral issues — Invasion of privacy

## Human Rights

Several different kinds of human rights are relevant to psychological testing, including the right not to be tested. Individuals who do not want to subject themselves to testing should not, and ethically cannot, be forced to do so. Nevertheless, exceptions to this directive are noted in the 2010 APA guidelines. Specifically, informed consent to testing is not required when "testing is mandated by law or government," when "informed consent is implied because testing is conducted as a routine educational, institutional, or organizational activity," or when "the purpose of the testing is to evaluate decisional capacity" (p. 13). Clearly, these exceptions negate the right not to be tested in an inestimable number of situations. Swindell et al., 2010, provide a review of the literature regarding the right to refuse testing, covering such issues as autonomy, decision-making capacity, capacity for voluntariness, beneficence, and right to confidentiality (Swindell, Coverdale, Crisp-Han, & McCullough, 2010); what they found parallels the guidelines propagated by the APA.

Another right due test takers is their right to know their test scores and interpretations as well as the bases of any decisions that affect their lives. In the past, guarding the security of tests was of paramount importance. Today, one must still take all precautions to protect test security, but not at the expense of an individual's right to know the basis of detrimental or adverse decisions. Test publishers who hide behind the veil of U.S. copyright laws and special rules protecting secure tests have a responsibility to make public sufficient information to allow users to make a truly informed decision of their adequacy. If the test has a selection bias, then this bias should be openly identified and not hidden by deceptive or misleading advertising. This is especially true of professional licensing exams such as those for physicians and attorneys, as these exams are the last barrier into a profession and would be suspect of bias if they underselected a disproportionate number of women and minorities.

Other human rights, some of which are only now being widely accepted, are the right to know who will have access to test data and the right to confidentiality of test results. The current frequent use of Internet and computer-based services has induced the APA to add a requirement for clinicians to warn clients of the risk to privacy and limits of confidentiality resulting from electronic transmission of information (APA, 2010).

Test interpreters have an ethical obligation to protect human rights. Potential test takers are responsible for knowing and demanding their rights. The increasing awareness among test users and the public of human rights is an important influence on the testing field.

## Labeling

In standard medical practice, a person's disease or disorder is first identified (diagnosed). Once diagnosed, the disease can be labeled and standard medical intervention procedures implemented. It is no embarrassment to be diagnosed as having gall bladder or kidney disease. However, labeling people with certain medical diseases, such as acquired immunodeficiency syndrome (AIDS), and psychiatric disorders can be extremely damaging. The public has little understanding of the label schizophrenia, for example. Therefore, those who receive this label are often stigmatized, perhaps for life (Thoits, 2011). Labels may also affect one's access to help. Chronic schizophrenia, for example, has no cure. Labeling someone a chronic schizophrenic may be a self-fulfilling prophecy (McReynolds, Ward, & Singer, 2002). Because the disorder is incurable, nothing can be done. Because nothing can be done, why should one bother to help? Because no help is given, the person is a chronic case (Corrigan, 2007).

Still another problem with labels, which people unfortunately often justify with psychological tests, is theoretical. As Szasz (1961) originally noted, a medical label such as schizophrenia implies that a person is ill or diseased. Because no one can be blamed for becoming ill, a medical or psychiatric label implies that the person is not responsible for the condition. However, it may well be that those who are labeled as psychiatrically disturbed must take responsibility for their lives if they are to get better.

When we take responsibility for our lives, we believe that we can exercise some degree of control over our fates (after all, what is intelligence?) rather than simply being the victims of uncontrollable external forces. Individuals who feel a sense of control or responsibility for themselves should be able to tolerate more stress, frustration, and pain than do those who feel like passive victims (Sherrer, 2011). Certainly, a person who feels responsible or in control has more incentive to alter negative conditions than one who does not.

Labels that imply a person is not responsible may increase the risk that the person so labeled will feel passive. Thus, the labeling process may not only stigmatize the person but also lower tolerance for stress and make treatment more difficult. In view of the potentially negative effects of labels, a person should have the right not to be labeled. When testing is necessary, a test such as the Rorschach, which has been shown to overpathologize test takers (Carstairs, 2011; Drogin, Dattilio, Sadoff, & Gutheil, 2011; Finn, 2011), should not be relied on to determine pathology (Erard, 2005).

## Invasion of Privacy

When people respond to psychological tests, they have little idea what is being revealed, but they often feel that their privacy has been invaded in a way not justified by the test's benefits. Public concern over this issue once became so strong that tests were investigated by the Senate Subcommittee on Constitutional Rights and the House Subcommittee on invasion of privacy. Neither found evidence of deliberate and widespread misuse of tests (see Brayfield, 1965).

There are two sides to the issue. Dahlstrom (1969b) argued that the issue of invasion of privacy is based on serious misunderstandings. He states that because tests have been oversold, the public doesn't realize their limitations. Psychological tests are so limited that they *cannot* invade one's privacy. Another issue, according to Dahlstrom (1969b), is the ambiguity of the notion of invasion of privacy. It isn't necessarily wrong, evil, or detrimental to find out about a person. The person's privacy is invaded when such information is used inappropriately. Psychologists are ethically and often legally bound to maintain confidentiality and do not have to reveal any more information about a person than is necessary to accomplish the purpose for which testing was initiated. Furthermore, psychologists must inform subjects of the limits of confidentiality. As Dahlstrom (1969b) noted, subjects must cooperate in order to be tested. If the subjects do not like what they hear, they can simply refuse to be tested.

The ethical code of the APA (1992, 2002) includes confidentiality. Guaranteed by law in most states that have laws governing the practice of psychology, this principle means that, as a general rule, personal information obtained by the psychologist from any source is communicated only with the person's consent. Exceptions include circumstances in which withholding information causes danger to the person or society, as well as cases that require subpoenaed records. Therefore, people have the right to know the limits of confidentiality and to know that test data can be subpoenaed and used as evidence in court (Benjamin & Gollan, 2003; Kocsis, 2011) or in employment decisions (Ones et al., 1995).

### Divided Loyalties

Jackson and Messick (1967, Chapter 69) argued long ago that no one has formulated a coherent set of ethical principles that govern all legitimate uses of testing. Today, this is still true. The core of the problem lies in divided loyalties—the often conflicting commitments of the psychologist who uses tests. Despite the more than 45 years that have elapsed since Jackson and Messick first articulated the problem, the issue of divided loyalties remains a central dilemma to all psychologists who use tests in clinics, schools, business, industry, government, the military, and so forth. The question is, who is the client—the individual or the institution that ordered the test?

A conflict arises when the individual's welfare is at odds with that of the institution that employs the psychologist. For example, a psychologist working for an industrial firm to identify individuals who might break down under stress has a responsibility to the institution to identify such individuals as well as a responsibility to protect the rights and welfare of clients who are seeking employment with the firm. Thus, the psychologist's loyalty is divided. Similarly, the psychologist must not only maintain test security but also not violate the client's right to know the basis for an adverse decision. However, if the basis for an adverse decision is explained to one client, this information may leak out, and others with the same problem might then outsmart the test. Again, the test user is trapped between two opposing forces and principles.

The conflict is currently being resolved as follows. Ethically, psychologists must inform all concerned where their loyalty lies. They must tell clients or subjects in advance how tests are to be used and describe the limits of confidentiality. To the institution, they provide only the minimum information needed, such as "This subject has a low probability of breaking down under stress, and the probability that this conclusion is accurate is 68/100." Unnecessary or irrelevant personal information remains confidential.

In addition, the person's right to know the basis of an adverse decision may override issues of test security. Either the results are explained to the client or they are given to a representative of the client who is qualified to explain them (AERA, APA, & NCME, 1999; APA, 2010).

### Responsibilities of Test Users and Test Constructors

A second ethical issue in testing concerns the responsibilities of test users. Because even the best test can be misused, the testing profession has become increasingly stringent and precise in outlining the ethics of responsible test use. According to the APA (2010), almost any test can be useful in the right circumstances, but even the best test, when used inappropriately, can hurt the subject. Of particular concern is the use of tests with different populations. A test that is valid and reliable for one group may not be valid and reliable for another. In light of this issue, the 2002 version of the APA Code of Ethics added two subsections that direct psychologists who administer tests to "use assessment instruments whose validity and reliability have been established for use with members of the population being tested" and to "use assessment methods that are appropriate to an individual's language preference and competence." In addition, when interpreting test results, psychologists are instructed to take into account "characteristics of the person being assessed, such as situational, personal, linguistic, and cultural differences that might affect psychologists' judgments or reduce the accuracy of their interpretations" (p. 13). To aid clinicians in the process of choosing the correct type of test for individuals who are members of different populations, several guidebooks are available (Dana, 2000; Merrell, 2003; Naar-King, Ellis, & Frey, 2003). To reduce potential damage, the APA (1974, 2002) makes users of tests responsible for knowing the reason for using the test, the consequences of using the test, and the procedures necessary to maximize the test's effectiveness and to minimize unfairness. Test users must thus possess sufficient knowledge to understand the principles underlying the construction and supporting research of any test they administer.

They must also know the psychometric qualities of the test being used as well as the literature relevant to the test. In addition, they are to ensure that interpretations based on the test are justified and that the test is properly used. A test user cannot claim ignorance: "I didn't realize normative data were not representative." The test user is responsible for finding out all pertinent information before using any test (APA, 1992, 2002, 2010).

The test developer is responsible for providing the necessary information (Franklin, 2003). Current standards for test use state that test constructors must provide a test manual with sufficient data to permit appropriate use of the test, including adequate validity and reliability data, clearly specified scoring and administration standards, and a clear description of the normative sample (AERA, APA, & NCME, 1999; APA, 2010). It is not unusual for a researcher to receive requests from test designers to investigate a newly developed test. These designers hope that others will conduct the necessary research to provide adequate psychometric documentation. The standards also state that the test manual should warn against possible misinterpretation and identify necessary qualifications for responsible test use. Despite these guidelines, tests that do not meet specified standards continue to be published (Wood et al., 2003).

A test user has no excuse for employing an inadequately documented instrument that has damaging consequences (Embretson & Hershberger, 1999). The test user must know enough to tell the difference between a test that meets present standards and one that does not. Jackson and Messick (1967, Chapter 69) wisely suggested that the test user ask two questions whenever a test is proposed for a particular use. First, "Is the test any good as a measure of the characteristics it purports to measure?" The answer lies in the psychometric qualities of the test, such as reliability and validity documentation. Second, "Should the test be used for this purpose?" The answer to this question rests on the ethical and social values of the test user, who must think about the test's effect on the person and his or her

**FIGURE 19.4**
Schematic summary
of social issues.

human rights. Thus, though test constructors bear some responsibility for a poorly designed test or an inadequate manual, the responsibility for the ethical use of tests ultimately rests on the test user.

## Social Issues

In addition to professional and moral issues, social issues play an important role in the testing field. We discuss three of these issues: dehumanization, the usefulness of tests, and access to psychological testing sources (see Figure 19.4).

### Dehumanization

One social issue in the testing field concerns the dehumanizing tendencies that lurk in the testing process. For example, some corporations provide computerized analyses of the Minnesota Multiphasic Personality Inventory-2 (MMPI-2) and other test results. Such technology tends to minimize individual freedom and uniqueness. With high-speed computers and centralized data banks, the risk that machines will someday make important decisions about our lives is always increasing. Thus, society must weigh the risks against the benefits of the growing application of modern technology to the testing field. People must make this evaluation now before an undesirable but unalterable situation develops. As psychologists and the public allow test results to be stored and analyzed by computers, it may become extremely difficult to reverse this trend. U.S. society is founded on principles of individual rights and freedom. Anything that might threaten these principles—such as computerized test interpretations—must be evaluated. Only when the benefits far outweigh the risks and the risks are minimized can the decision be socially acceptable.

### Usefulness of Tests

Tests need not be perfect in all ways. Society often finds uses for initially crude tools that become precise with research and development. One can discriminate between the useful and the true or correct. For example, when Western society believed the sun revolved around the earth, the available formulas and principles were useful in that they led to some accurate predictions, even though the underlying theories were incorrect. Similarly, the assumptions underlying today's tests may be fundamentally incorrect and the resulting test instruments far from perfect. However, the tests may still be useful as long as they provide information that leads to better predictions and understanding than can otherwise be obtained. A test may be useful to society even if all of the principles that underlie it are totally incorrect.

Thus, the crucial social issue in testing is not whether tests are perfect but whether they are useful to society. Obviously, the answer to this question to date has been a strong but disputed and controversial "Yes" (see McKown, 2007;

Meyer et al., 2003; Sawyer, 2007). However, as new knowledge is gained, society must continually weigh the risks of tests against the benefits. The risks, of course, include the possible misuse of tests, which in turn may adversely affect the life of an individual or may discriminate systematically against a specific cultural group (see Fish, 2002; Henry, Bryson, & Henry, 1990). The benefits include the potential for increased precision and fairness in the decision-making process. Obviously, the resolution of this recurring issue will profoundly affect the field of testing.

Society has used modern tests on a wide scale. First the military, then the schools and psychiatric facilities, and finally business and industry have found important uses for psychological tests. Indeed, there appears to be no end to the proliferation of tests, despite criticism and heated debate. If the pervasiveness of tests indicates society's opinion of their usefulness, then certainly society has found them useful. As long as tests continue to serve a function, they will most likely be used.

## Access to Psychological Testing Services

Who will have access to psychological testing services? Being tested can be expensive. A practitioner in a large metropolitan area often commands a fee of several thousand dollars or more to administer a full battery of individual tests, score and interpret the findings, and produce a written report. In fact, the average cost of a custody evaluation in Southern California is $15,000, and can run as high as more than $25,000. Fees for extensive neurological testing, particularly in a legal battle, can be even higher. Moreover, the cost of test materials continues to skyrocket. A Wechsler Adult Intelligence Scale–Revised (WAIS-R) kit cost $98 in 1983. In 2012, the Wechsler Adult Intelligence Scale, fourth edition (WAIS-IV) cost more than $1,100 with further price increases no doubt in the works. As with many other commodities, this price tag places testing beyond the reach of many. However, if a person's well-being depends on information from a psychological test battery, then how will the decision be made about who will have access to testing and who will not?

As it stands now, the expensive test batteries for neurological and psychiatric assessment are available to those who can afford them and to those who have enough insurance. For example, anyone with a developmental disability in California may be eligible to receive Medi-Cal, which provides free medical care, including the services of a psychologist. The individual may also be eligible for federal assistance such as Medicare and SSI, which provide cash benefits. Further, in California, developmentally disabled people (e.g., persons with mentally retardation) or those with suspected developmental disabilities have access to psychological testing services at regional centers throughout the state. Unless California laws are changed, anyone suspected of having a handicap that originated during the developmental years can request (or have someone request on his or her behalf) an evaluation that may include a medical examination and psychological testing. The service is free, and if a team of specialists finds the person developmentally disabled, then additional services are available. Thus, current California and federal laws and policies help ensure that certain disabled people will have access to psychological testing services. However, such guarantees are not available in all states, and only certain people are covered.

Some in our society have offered national health insurance as a way to provide adequate medical care to everyone. One of the controversies in proposals for such programs concerns the extent of mental health coverage and whether psychological testing services will be included. If they are, then anyone who needs such services will have access to them. If not, then the availability of testing services may become substantially limited. In a sense, society will be judging the value of tests in deciding whether or not to include them in health insurance programs. Because resources are limited, testing services may preclude some other needed service, or vice versa.

# Current Trends

Professional, moral, social, and even legal issues have interacted to produce today's trends in testing. These trends can be placed into four main categories: the proliferation of new tests; higher standards, improved technology, and increased objectivity; greater public awareness and influence; and computer and Internet applications.

## The Proliferation of New Tests

New tests keep coming out all the time, with no end in sight. If we count revised and updated tests, we find hundreds of new tests being published each year. The impetus for developing these new tests comes from professional disagreement over the best strategies for measuring human characteristics, over the nature of these characteristics, and over theories about the causes of human behavior. (For an example, see the discussion of the K-ABC in Chapter 12.) The impetus also stems from public and professional pressure to use only fair, accurate, and unbiased instruments. Finally, if tests are used, then the authors and publishers of tests stand to profit financially. As long as someone can make a profit publishing tests, then new tests will be developed and marketed.

An examination of major reference books on tests indicates that the majority of new tests are based on the same principles and underlying theories as the more established tests. Indeed, most newly developed tests are justified on the grounds that they are either psychometrically superior to the existing tests or more specific and thus more appropriate for particular problems. However, as you saw in Chapter 9, some of the newer tests are based on models, theories, and concepts that fundamentally differ from those that underlie traditional tests. These nontraditional tests stem from modern concepts and theories from learning, social, physiological, and experimental psychology. Most of these newer tests are rooted in empirically derived data.

The proliferation of nontraditional tests is related to two other trends in testing. First, it reflects the increasing role of the science of psychology in testing (Haynes, 1991, 1995; Wertz, Charmaz, McMullen, Josselson, Anderson, & McSpadden, 2011; Wood et al., 2003). Even critics of testing must admit that a responsiveness to criticism and an honest and persistent effort to improve the quality of tests have characterized testing. The application of insights and empirical findings from psychological laboratories currently reflects this responsiveness.

Second, efforts are being made to integrate tests with other aspects of applied psychology (Aidman & Shmelyov, 2002; Wiederhold, Jang, Kim, & Wiederhold, 2002). Many psychologists, especially the cognitive–behaviorally oriented, have long regretted the poor relationship among clinical assessment, traditional tests, and subsequent treatment interventions. They prefer test results that not only have a direct relationship to treatment but also can be used to assess the effectiveness of treatment. Because psychologists continually try to devise such procedures, their products add to the list of the many new tests published each year (Chabanne, Peruch, & Thinus-Blanc, 2003; Cohen, Wolf, Panter, & Insko, 2011; Garcia-Palacios, Hoffman, Carlin, Furness, & Botella, 2002; Mehl, Pennebaker, Crow, Dabbs, & Price, 2001).

## Higher Standards, Improved Technology, and Increasing Objectivity

Various pressures and issues have led to another current trend. The minimum acceptable standards for tests are becoming higher. Before the APA (1974) clearly and specifically defined their responsibilities, test constructors had neither a uniform nor a widely accepted set of guidelines. As a result, the quality of newly published tests varied greatly. With published standards, test constructors no longer have to work in the dark. An increasing percentage of new tests provides the information necessary for test users to make a fully informed choice in test selection, thus maximizing the chance of proper test use.

Higher standards of test construction have encouraged better use of tests (Clauser, 2002). The 1999 and 2010 standards have helped considerably by reemphasizing the critical importance of proper test use and by articulating the responsibilities of test users (AERA, APA, & NCME, 1999; APA 2002, 2010). In addition, a working group of the Joint Committee on Testing Practices sponsored by the American Association for Counseling and Development, the AERA, the APA, the American Speech-Language-Hearing Association, and the NCME has published a thorough document that delineates the qualifications of test users (Eyde, Moreland, & Robertson, 1988). This comprehensive guide clearly specifies the competencies needed to use various types of tests and will provide a beacon for some time to come. Moreover, as we indicated earlier, the ethics of testing have been modified to encourage the proper use of tests and to avoid misuse (APA, 1992, 2002, 2010). Now that test users have a published set of standards, they have no excuse for misusing a test. Naturally, misuse and even abuse will never be entirely eliminated, but the trend toward better use of existing tests is most desirable.

Related to higher standards, improved technology has greatly benefited the testing field (Breithaupt, Mills, & Melican, 2006; Farrell, 1991, 1992; Haynes, 1992; Lowman, 1991; Matarazzo, 1990; Wilson, De Boeck, Moss, & Draney, 2003). Primarily because of advances in computer technology, statistical procedures such as factor analysis and item analysis can be performed with great ease. This technology thus contributes to the current trend toward better tests.

Also related to high standards is the trend toward increasing objectivity in test interpretation. As of this writing, attacks on the Rorschach have become continuous and merciless (see Bornstein & Masling, 2005; Masling, 2006; Masling & Bornstein, 2005; Wood et al., 2003; Carstairs, 2011; Drogin, Dattilio, Sadoff, & Gutheil, 2011; Finn, 2011). As a result, practitioners tend to rely heavily on objective data such as that provided by the MMPI-2. One can readily see this trend in how the relative proportion of references devoted to the Rorschach and the MMPI in the *Mental Measurements Yearbook* and other sources has changed (e.g., Archer, Maruish, Imhof, & Piotrowski, 1991).

The continuing research interest in testing also reflects the trend toward objectivity in the field. In view of the tens of thousands, if not hundreds of thousands, of published studies directly or indirectly related to psychological tests, a casual observer might conclude that little remains to be done. This conclusion is far from correct. Despite more than 10,000 articles already devoted to the MMPI and MMPI-2, for example, hundreds more creative and scientifically rigorous articles are published each year on these tests, not to mention the hundreds of other tests listed in the *Mental Measurements Yearbook* and other resource books. As long as tests are anything but perfect, and in this regard they have a long way to go, psychological researchers will no doubt keep conducting investigations to facilitate the objective use of tests.

## Greater Public Awareness and Influence

Greater public awareness of the nature and use of psychological tests has led to increasing external influence on testing. At one time, the public knew little about psychological tests; psychologists played an almost exclusive role in governing how tests were used. With the public's greater assertiveness during the 1990s, the days when psychologists alone called the shots are gone forever (Saccuzzo, 1994). Today, one can simply perform a Google or other Internet search and find considerable information on just about any test. We believe this trend has affected the field positively.

Public awareness has led to an increased demand for psychological services, including testing services. This demand is balanced by the tendency toward restrictive legislative and judicial regulations and policies such as the judicial decision that restricts the use of standard intelligence tests in diagnosing mental retardation. These restrictions originate in real and imagined public fears. In short, the public seems to be ambivalent about psychological testing, simultaneously desiring the benefits yet fearing the power they attribute to tests.

Perhaps the greatest benefit of increased public awareness of tests has been the extra focus on safeguarding human rights. As more individuals share the responsibility of encouraging the proper use of tests by becoming informed of their rights and insisting on receiving them, the probability of misuse and abuse of tests will be reduced. The commitment of the field of psychology to high ethical standards can be easily seen in the published guidelines, position papers, and debates that have evolved during the relatively short period beginning in 1947 with the development of formal standards for training in clinical psychology (Shakow, Hilgard, Kelly, Sanford, & Shaffer, 1947). Practitioners of psychology, their instructors, and their supervisors show a deep concern for social values and the dignity of the individual human being. However, the pressure of public interest in psychological tests has led practitioners to an even greater awareness about safeguarding the rights and dignity of the individual.

Interrelated with all of these issues is the trend toward greater protection for the public. Nearly every state has laws that govern the use of psychological tests. Several factors give the public significant protection against the inherent risks of testing: limiting testing to reduce the chance that unqualified people will use psychological tests, sensitivity among practitioners to the rights of the individual, relevant court decisions, and a clearly articulated set of ethical guidelines and published standards for proper test use.

## The Computerization of Tests

Throughout this book we have discussed how computers are being applied to testing on a rapid and widespread basis. The computerization of tests is a major trend, and computers, as you saw in Chapter 9, are being used in many different ways.

In adaptive computerized testing, different sets of test questions are administered via computer to different individuals, depending on each individual's status on the trait being measured (Mills, Potenza, Fremer, & Ward, 2002; Weiss, 1983, 1985). In ability testing, for example, the computer adjusts the level of item difficulty according to the subject's response. If the subject's answer is incorrect, then an easier item is given; if correct, then a more difficult item appears next. Such an approach individualizes a test and reduces total testing time. By the year 2020, most students will probably be taking tests such as the SAT, Graduate Record Examination (GRE), and Law School Admission Test (LSAT) through adaptive computer programs. There are currently adaptive versions of several important knowledge and aptitude tests, such as the Armed Services Vocational Aptitude Test, GRE, SAT and TOEFL (Díaz, Abad, Ponsoda Gil, Aguado, & Díaz, 2011).

Computers are also being used to administer, score, and even interpret psychological tests. In addition, computers are being used to generate tasks that cannot be presented by traditional methods (see Chapter 9) (Costa, De Carvalho, Drummond, Wauke, & De Sa Guimaraes, 2002). Through computer technology, one might be able to tap a whole new range of abilities heretofore beyond the scope of traditional tests (Saccuzzo, Johnson, & Guertin, 1994). Objective personality tests such as the MMPI-2 can be processed by a computer that generates a typed report. Each year, developers create more programs that score tests and produce written reports (Frase et al., 2003; Prince & Guastello, 1990). The use of the computer extends to all types of tests, including behavioral assessment (Farrell, 1991, 1992).

## Testing on the Internet

According to Crespin and Austin (2002), one of the most important future applications of psychological testing is through its use on the Internet. Imagine the possibility of taking a test from a Web site and having the results immediately sent to your doctor.

# Future Trends

Having analyzed the major relevant issues and forces in testing and identified current trends, we are now ready to venture a few guesses about what the future holds for the field. Certainly, we are reasonably safe in stating that the current trends will continue and become established in the field. However, our predictions for the future are educated guesses based on limited knowledge.

# Future Prospects for Testing Are Promising

We believe that testing has a promising future. We base our optimism on the integral role that testing has played in the development and recognition of psychology. On a less lofty note, testing is a multibillion-dollar industry, and even relatively small testing companies can gross millions of dollars per year. With so much at stake, testing is probably here to stay. The field gained its first real status from its role in the development of screening tests for the military in World War I. Later, psychologists' creativity and skill in the testing field during World War II no doubt numbered among the factors that ultimately led to government funding through the Veterans Administration to encourage the development of professional psychology. Indeed, this federal funding, first earmarked for psychology in 1945, played an important role in the birth of clinical psychology and formal training standards.

As indicated, the central role played by testing in the development and recognition of psychology does not alone ensure an important future role for testing. Despite division within psychology about the role and value of testing, it remains one of the few unique functions of the professional psychologist. When one sees psychological testing as encompassing not only traditional but also new and innovative uses—as in cognitive-behavioral assessment, psychophysiology, evaluation research, organizational assessment, community assessment, and investigations into the nature of human functioning—one can understand just how important tests are to psychologists.

Thus, with this fundamental tie to testing, psychologists remain the undisputed leaders in the field. It is unlikely that attacks on and dissatisfaction with traditional psychological tests will suddenly compel psychologists to abandon tests. Instead, psychologists will likely continue to take the lead in this field to produce better and better tests, and such a direction will benefit psychologists, the field, and society. Even if this doesn't happen, testing corporations that publish and sell widely used high-stakes standardized tests will no doubt continue to market their products aggressively.

Moreover, tests are used in most institutions—schools, colleges, hospitals, industry, business, the government, and so forth—and new applications and creative uses continue to emerge in response to their demands. Tests will not suddenly disappear with nothing to replace them. If anything, current tests will continue to be used until they are replaced by still better tests, which of course may be based on totally new ideas. Though current tests may gradually fade from the scene, we believe psychological testing will not simply survive but will flourish through the 21st century.

# The Proliferation of New and Improved Tests Will Continue

The future will likely see the development of many more tests. Chapters 10, 11, and 12 presented our belief that currently available intelligence tests are far from perfect and have a long way to go. Further, we believe that the dominant role of the Stanford-Binet and Wechsler tests is far from secure. These two major intelligence scales are probably about as technically adequate as they will ever be. They can, of course, be improved through minor revisions to update test stimuli and to provide larger and even more representative normative samples with special norms for particular groups and through additional research to extend and support validity documentation. However, despite the changes in the modern Binet and the

WAIS-IV, the fundamental characteristics and underlying concepts resemble those of the original scales.

During the next few decades, we shall be surprised if these two major intelligence scales are not challenged at least once or twice by similar tests with superior standardization and normative data or with less bias against certain minorities. However, if history indicates what is to be, then a true challenge can come only from a test based on original concepts and a more comprehensive theoretical rationale than that of the present scales. The Kaufman Assessment Battery for Children may be one such contender in its age range. We believe that the development of such a test is only a question of time. Should a compelling need for such an instrument arise, then we shall see it sooner rather than later.

In structured personality testing, the MMPI-2 appears destined to be the premier test for many years to come. This favorable prediction for the MMPI-2 is a turnabout from the 1982 prediction made in the first edition of this book. We had not anticipated the innovative approach of Butcher and colleagues in dealing with the original MMPI's inadequate normative sample. Thus, future prospects for the MMPI-2 are indeed bright.

As indicated in our discussion of projective tests, the future of the Rorschach is uncertain. The Rorschach is based on the early theories of Freud. Its psychometric properties are under continual attack (Lilienfeld, Garb, & Wood, 2011; Wood et al., 2003). There is serious doubt whether the Rorschach provides clinically useful information (Wood, Nezworski, Lilienfeld, & Garb, 2011). Some say the Rorschach is no better than reading tea leaves. Although we would not go this far, it is clear that proponents of the Rorschach are fighting an uphill battle (Krishnamurthy, Archer, & Groth-Marnat, 2011, p. 283). Again, this prediction is a turnabout from earlier versions of this book. We had thought that Exner's comprehensive system would provide the scoring reliability and standardized administration needed to support the Rorschach. As of 2012, this promise has not been fulfilled (Golden & Simmons, 2008; Lindgren, Carlsson, & Lundbäck, 2007; Masling, 2006). Adding to the concerns associated with the Rorschach, the inkblots have been published on Wikipedia, and other sites offer critical information about the interpretation of the test. Obviously, if this information is accessed by potential test takers, it defeats the purpose of the test (Schultz & Loving, 2012).

The future of the Thematic Apperception Test (TAT) is more difficult to predict. Affixed to some of the main arteries of psychological theory, the TAT has an incredibly extensive research base and is a prominent clinical tool. Unfortunately, the TAT stimuli are outdated. In a projective test, outdated stimuli are not a devastating weakness because projective stimuli are by nature ambiguous. Nevertheless, because the TAT stimuli have been revised (Ritzler, Sharkey, & Chudy, 1980) the TAT may enjoy increased respectability as more data are acquired on the more recent versions.

## Controversy, Disagreement, and Change Will Continue

It doesn't matter whether the topic is testing or animal learning—disagreement and controversy are second nature to psychologists. Disagreement brings with it new data that may ultimately produce some clarification along with brand new contradictions and battle lines. Psychologists will probably never agree that any one test is perfect, and change will be a constant characteristic of the field. We continue to be optimistic because we see the change as ultimately resulting in more empirical data, better theories, continuing innovations and advances, and higher standards.

## The Integration of Cognitive Science and Computer Science Will Lead to Several Innovations in Testing

As you saw in Chapter 9, concepts from basic psychological sciences have worked their way into the field: learning theory in the 1970s and 1980s, and psychophysiological and psychophysical concepts in the 1980s and 1990s. Today, the integration of concepts from experimental cognitive psychology, computer science, neuroscience, and psychometrics are rapidly shaping the field (Miller & Kinsbourne, 2011; Spear, 2007; Wetherell, 2011).

Multimedia computerized tests form the most recent cutting edge in the new generation of assessment instruments. The test taker sits in front of a computer that presents realistically animated situations with full color and sound. The program is both interactive and adaptive. The computer screen freezes and asks the test taker to provide a response. If the response is good, then a more difficult item is presented. For example, in research programs recently developed at companies such as IBM, the computer may show a scene involving sexual harassment. The screen freezes just after an employee has made an inappropriate joke. The test taker, who is applying for a manager's job, is given four choices to deal with the situation. If an effective choice is made, the computer moves on to an even more difficult situation, such as a threat from the offensive employee.

The computer offers test developers unlimited scope in developing new technologies: from interactive virtual reality games that measure and record minute responses to social conflict within a digital world to virtual environments that are suitable for measuring physiological responses while offering safe and effective systematic desensitization experiences to individuals with phobias. As we noted at the outset, the computer holds one of the major keys to the future of psychological testing.

## Summary

The future of psychological testing depends on many issues and developments. Professional issues include theoretical concerns, such as the usefulness of the trait concept as opposed to index of adjustment; the adequacy of tests; and actuarial versus clinical prediction. Moral issues include human rights such as the right to refuse testing, the right not to be labeled, and the right to privacy. Another ethical issue that concerns test users and developers is the divided loyalty that can result from administering a test to an individual for an institution: Whose rights come first? Also, professionals have an ethical duty to provide and understand the information needed to use a test properly. Finally, social issues such as dehumanization, the usefulness of tests, and access to testing services also inform the field of testing today.

Current trends include the proliferation of new tests, higher standards, improved technology, increasing objectivity, greater public awareness and influence, the computerization of tests, and testing on the Internet.

As for the future, anything is possible, especially in a field as controversial as testing. Psychology is now better equipped in technique, methodology, empirical data, and experience than ever before, and the members of this new and expanding field, as a group, are relatively young. Therefore, it does not seem unrealistic or overly optimistic to expect that the next 50 years will see advances equal to those of the last 50. On the other hand, psychology has come so far in the last 50 years that a comparable advance in the next 50 could easily produce results unimaginable today. What happens to testing in the future will depend on the goals and objectives chosen by those in the field and by their persistence and creativity in accomplishing their goals.

# Areas of a Standard Normal Distribution

**PART I** Percentiles Associated with Various $Z$ Scores

| $Z$ | % Rank | $Z$ | % Rank |
|---|---|---|---|
| −3.0 | .13 | 0 | 50.00 |
| −2.9 | .19 | .1 | 53.98 |
| −2.8 | .26 | .2 | 57.93 |
| −2.7 | .35 | .3 | 61.79 |
| −2.6 | .47 | .4 | 66.54 |
| −2.5 | .62 | .5 | 69.15 |
| −2.4 | .82 | .6 | 72.57 |
| −2.3 | 1.07 | .7 | 75.80 |
| −2.2 | 1.39 | .8 | 78.81 |
| −2.1 | 1.79 | .9 | 81.59 |
| −2.0 | 2.28 | 1.0 | 84.13 |
| −1.9 | 2.87 | 1.1 | 86.43 |
| −1.8 | 3.59 | 1.2 | 88.49 |
| −1.7 | 4.46 | 1.3 | 90.32 |
| −1.6 | 5.48 | 1.4 | 91.92 |
| −1.5 | 6.68 | 1.5 | 93.32 |
| −1.4 | 8.08 | 1.6 | 94.52 |
| −1.3 | 9.68 | 1.7 | 95.54 |
| −1.2 | 11.51 | 1.8 | 96.41 |
| −1.1 | 13.57 | 1.9 | 97.13 |
| −1.0 | 15.87 | 2.0 | 97.72 |
| −.9 | 18.41 | 2.1 | 98.21 |
| −.8 | 21.19 | 2.2 | 98.61 |
| −.7 | 24.20 | 2.3 | 98.93 |
| −.6 | 27.43 | 2.4 | 99.18 |
| −.5 | 30.58 | 2.5 | 99.38 |
| −.4 | 34.46 | 2.6 | 99.53 |
| −.3 | 38.21 | 2.7 | 99.65 |
| −.2 | 42.07 | 2.8 | 99.74 |
| −.1 | 46.02 | 2.9 | 99.81 |
| 0 | 50.00 | 3.0 | 99.87 |

**PART II** Areas Between Mean and Various Z Scores

| Z | .00 | .01 | .02 | .03 | .04 | .05 | .06 | .07 | .08 | .09 |
|---|-----|-----|-----|-----|-----|-----|-----|-----|-----|-----|
| .0 | .0000 | .0040 | .0080 | .0120 | .0160 | .0199 | .0239 | .0279 | .0319 | .0359 |
| .1 | .0398 | .0438 | .0478 | .0517 | .0557 | .0596 | .0636 | .0675 | .0714 | .0753 |
| .2 | .0793 | .0832 | .0871 | .0910 | .0948 | .0987 | .1026 | .1064 | .1103 | .1141 |
| .3 | .1179 | .1217 | .1255 | .1293 | .1331 | .1368 | .1406 | .1443 | .1480 | .1517 |
| .4 | .1554 | .1591 | .1628 | .1664 | .1700 | .1736 | .1772 | .1808 | .1844 | .1879 |
| .5 | .1915 | .1950 | .1985 | .2019 | .2054 | .2088 | .2123 | .2157 | .2190 | .2224 |
| .6 | .2257 | .2291 | .2324 | .2357 | .2389 | .2422 | .2454 | .2486 | .2517 | .2549 |
| .7 | .2580 | .2611 | .2642 | .2673 | .2704 | .2734 | .2764 | .2794 | .2823 | .2852 |
| .8 | .2881 | .2910 | .2939 | .2967 | .2995 | .3023 | .3051 | .3078 | .3106 | .3133 |
| .9 | .3195 | .3186 | .3212 | .3238 | .3264 | .3289 | .3315 | .3340 | .3365 | .3389 |
| 1.0 | .3413 | .3438 | .3461 | .3485 | .3508 | .3531 | .3554 | .3577 | .3599 | .3621 |
| 1.1 | .3643 | .3665 | .3686 | .3708 | .3729 | .3749 | .3770 | .3790 | .3810 | .3830 |
| 1.2 | .3849 | .3869 | .3888 | .3907 | .3925 | .3944 | .3962 | .3980 | .3997 | .4015 |
| 1.3 | .4032 | .4049 | .4066 | .4082 | .4099 | .4115 | .4131 | .4147 | .4162 | .4177 |
| 1.4 | .4192 | .4207 | .4222 | .4236 | .4251 | .4265 | .4279 | .4292 | .4306 | .4319 |
| 1.5 | .4332 | .4345 | .4357 | .4370 | .4382 | .4394 | .4406 | .4418 | .4429 | .4441 |
| 1.6 | .4452 | .4463 | .4474 | .4484 | .4495 | .4505 | .4515 | .4525 | .4535 | .4545 |
| 1.7 | .4554 | .4564 | .4573 | .4582 | .4591 | .4599 | .4608 | .4616 | .4625 | .4633 |
| 1.8 | .4641 | .4649 | .4656 | .4664 | .4671 | .4678 | .4686 | .4693 | .4699 | .4706 |
| 1.9 | .4713 | .4719 | .4726 | .4732 | .4738 | .4744 | .4750 | .4756 | .4761 | .4767 |
| 2.0 | .4772 | .4778 | .4783 | .4788 | .4793 | .4798 | .4803 | .4808 | .4812 | .4817 |
| 2.1 | .4821 | .4826 | .4830 | .4834 | .4838 | .4842 | .4846 | .4850 | .4854 | .4857 |
| 2.2 | .4861 | .4864 | .4868 | .4871 | .4875 | .4878 | .4881 | .4884 | .4887 | .4890 |
| 2.3 | .4893 | .4896 | .4898 | .4901 | .4904 | .4906 | .4909 | .4911 | .4913 | .4916 |
| 2.4 | .4918 | .4920 | .4922 | .4925 | .4927 | .4929 | .4931 | .4932 | .4934 | .4936 |
| 2.5 | .4938 | .4940 | .4941 | .4943 | .4945 | .4946 | .4948 | .4949 | .4951 | .4952 |
| 2.6 | .4953 | .4955 | .4956 | .4957 | .4959 | .4960 | .4961 | .4962 | .4963 | .4964 |
| 2.7 | .4965 | .4966 | .4967 | .4968 | .4969 | .4970 | .4971 | .4972 | .4973 | .4974 |
| 2.8 | .4974 | .4975 | .4976 | .4977 | .4977 | .4978 | .4979 | .4979 | .4980 | .4981 |
| 2.9 | .4981 | .4982 | .4982 | .4983 | .4984 | .4984 | .4985 | .4985 | .4986 | .4986 |
| 3.0 | .4987 | .4987 | .4987 | .4988 | .4988 | .4989 | .4989 | .4989 | .4900 | .4990 |

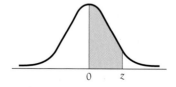

Standard score values are listed in the column headed "Z." To find the proportion of the total area occurring between the mean and any given $Z$ score, locate the entry indicated by the $Z$ score. For example, a $Z$ score of $+1.85$ is located by reading across to the column for .05 from the value of 1.8 in the "$Z$" column. The value in the table is .4678. Since the total area above the mean is equal to .5000, this means that only .0322 of the area is beyond the $Z$ score of $+1.85$.

# Critical Values of *r* for α = .05 and α = .01 (Two-Tailed Test)

| df* | α = .05 | α = .01 | df* | α = .05 | α = .01 |
|-----|---------|---------|-----|---------|---------|
| 1   | .99692  | .999877 | 17  | .456    | .575    |
| 2   | .9500   | .99000  | 18  | .444    | .561    |
| 3   | .878    | .9587   | 19  | .433    | .549    |
| 4   | .811    | .9172   | 20  | .423    | .537    |
| 5   | .754    | .875    | 25  | .381    | .487    |
| 6   | .707    | .834    | 30  | .349    | .449    |
| 7   | .666    | .798    | 35  | .325    | .418    |
| 8   | .632    | .765    | 40  | .304    | .393    |
| 9   | .602    | .735    | 45  | .288    | .372    |
| 10  | .576    | .708    | 50  | .273    | .354    |
| 11  | .553    | .684    | 60  | .250    | .325    |
| 12  | .532    | .661    | 70  | .232    | .302    |
| 13  | .514    | .641    | 80  | .217    | .283    |
| 14  | .497    | .623    | 90  | .205    | .267    |
| 15  | .482    | .606    | 100 | .195    | .254    |
| 16  | .468    | .590    |     |         |         |

*df* are equal to *N*–2, where *N* is the number of paired observations.

Reprinted with permission from Table IX-1. Percentage Points. Distribution of the Correlation Coefficient. When $p = 0$, *CRC Handbook of Tables for Probability and Statistics* (2nd ed.). Copyright 1968, CRC Press, Inc., Boca Raton, Florida.

# Appendix 3

# Critical Values of $t^*$

For any given $df$, the table shows the values of $t$ corresponding to various levels of probability. Obtained $t$ is significant at a given level if it is equal to or greater than the value shown in the table.

---

$^*$ Appendix 3 is taken from Table III of R. A. Fisher and R. Yates, 1967, *Statistical Tables for Biological, Agricultural and Medical Research* (6th ed.), New York: Hafner. With permission of the authors and publishers.

| | Level of significance for one-tailed test | | | | | |
|---|---|---|---|---|---|---|
| | .10 | .05 | .025 | .01 | .005 | .0005 |
| | Level of significance for two-tailed test | | | | | |
| df | .20 | .10 | .05 | .02 | .01 | .001 |
| 1 | 3.078 | 6.314 | 12.706 | 31.821 | 63.657 | 636.619 |
| 2 | 1.886 | 2.920 | 4.303 | 6.965 | 9.925 | 31.598 |
| 3 | 1.638 | 2.353 | 3.182 | 4.541 | 5.841 | 12.941 |
| 4 | 1.533 | 2.132 | 2.776 | 3.747 | 4.604 | 8.610 |
| 5 | 1.476 | 2.015 | 2.571 | 3.365 | 4.032 | 6.859 |
| 6 | 1.440 | 1.943 | 2.447 | 3.143 | 3.707 | 5.959 |
| 7 | 1.415 | 1.895 | 2.365 | 2.998 | 3.499 | 5.405 |
| 8 | 1.397 | 1.860 | 2.306 | 2.896 | 3.355 | 5.041 |
| 9 | 1.383 | 1.833 | 2.262 | 2.821 | 3.250 | 4.781 |
| 10 | 1.372 | 1.812 | 2.228 | 2.764 | 3.169 | 4.587 |
| 11 | 1.363 | 1.796 | 2.201 | 2.718 | 3.106 | 4.437 |
| 12 | 1.356 | 1.782 | 2.179 | 2.681 | 3.055 | 4.318 |
| 13 | 1.350 | 1.771 | 2.160 | 2.650 | 3.012 | 4.221 |
| 14 | 1.345 | 1.761 | 2.145 | 2.624 | 2.977 | 4.140 |
| 15 | 1.341 | 1.753 | 2.131 | 2.602 | 2.947 | 4.073 |
| 16 | 1.337 | 1.746 | 2.120 | 2.583 | 2.921 | 4.015 |
| 17 | 1.333 | 1.740 | 2.110 | 2.567 | 2.898 | 3.965 |
| 18 | 1.330 | 1.734 | 2.101 | 2.552 | 2.878 | 3.922 |
| 19 | 1.328 | 1.729 | 2.093 | 2.539 | 2.861 | 3.883 |
| 20 | 1.325 | 1.725 | 2.086 | 2.528 | 2.845 | 3.850 |
| 21 | 1.323 | 1.721 | 2.080 | 2.518 | 2.831 | 3.819 |
| 22 | 1.321 | 1.717 | 2.074 | 2.508 | 2.819 | 3.792 |
| 23 | 1.319 | 1.714 | 2.069 | 2.500 | 2.807 | 3.767 |
| 24 | 1.318 | 1.711 | 2.064 | 2.492 | 2.797 | 3.745 |
| 25 | 1.316 | 1.708 | 2.060 | 2.485 | 2.787 | 3.725 |
| 26 | 1.315 | 1.706 | 2.056 | 2.479 | 2.779 | 3.707 |
| 27 | 1.314 | 1.703 | 2.052 | 2.473 | 2.771 | 3.690 |
| 28 | 1.313 | 1.701 | 2.048 | 2.467 | 2.763 | 3.674 |
| 29 | 1.311 | 1.699 | 2.045 | 2.462 | 2.756 | 3.659 |
| 30 | 1.310 | 1.697 | 2.042 | 2.457 | 2.750 | 3.646 |
| 40 | 1.303 | 1.684 | 2.021 | 2.423 | 2.704 | 3.551 |
| 60 | 1.296 | 1.671 | 2.000 | 2.390 | 2.660 | 3.460 |
| 120 | 1.289 | 1.658 | 1.980 | 2.358 | 2.617 | 3.373 |
| ∞ | 1.282 | 1.645 | 1.960 | 2.326 | 2.576 | 3.291 |

# Appendix 4

# Code of Fair Testing Practices in Education
## Prepared by the Joint Committee on Testing Practices[1]

The Code of Fair Testing Practices in Education states the major obligations to test takers or professionals who develop or use educational tests. The Code is meant to apply broadly to the use of tests in education (admissions, educational assessment, educational diagnosis, and student placement). The Code is not designed to cover employment testing, licensure or certification testing, or other types of testing. Although the Code has relevance to many types of educational tests, it is directed primarily at professionally developed tests such as those sold by commercial test publishers or used in formally administered testing programs. The Code is not intended to cover tests made by individual teachers for use in their own classrooms.

The Code addresses the roles of test developers and test users separately. Test users are people who select tests, commission test development services, or make decisions on the basis of test scores. Test developers are people who actually construct tests as well as those who set policies for particular testing programs. The roles may, of course, overlap as when a state education agency commissions test development services, sets policies that control the test development process, and makes decisions on the basis of the test scores.

The Code presents standards for educational test developers and users in four areas:

**A.** Developing/Selecting Tests
**B.** Interpreting Scores
**C.** Striving for Fairness
**D.** Informing Test Takers

---

[1] The Code has been developed by the Joint Committee on Testing Practices, a cooperative effort of several professional organizations, that has as its aim the advancement, in the public interest, of the quality of testing practices. The Joint Committee was initiated by the American Educational Research Association, the American Psychological Association, and the National Council on Measurement in Education. In addition to these three groups, the American Association for Counseling and Development/Association for Measurement and Evaluation in Counseling and Development and the American Speech-Language-Hearing Association are now also sponsors of the Joint Committee.

This is not copyrighted material. Reproduction and dissemination are encouraged. Please cite this document as follows:

*Code of Fair Testing Practices in Education.* (1988) Washington, D.C. Joint Committee on Testing Practices. (Mailing Address: Joint Committee on Testing Practices, American Psychological Association, 1200 17th Street, NW, Washington, D.C. 20036.)

Organizations, institutions, and individual professionals who endorse the Code commit themselves to safeguarding the rights of test takers by following the principles listed. The Code is intended to be consistent with the relevant parts of the *Standards for Educational and Psychological Testing* (AERA, APA, NCME, 1985). However, the Code differs from the Standards in both audience and purpose. The Code is meant to be understood by the general public, it is limited to educational tests, and the primary focus is on those issues that affect the proper use of tests. The Code is not meant to add new principles over and above those in the Standards or to change the meaning of the Standards. The goal is rather to represent the spirit of a selected portion of the Standards in a way that is meaningful to test takers and/or their parents or guardians. It is the hope of the Joint Committee that the Code will also be judged to be consistent with existing codes of conduct and standards of other professional groups who use educational tests.

# Developing/Selecting Appropriate Tests[2]

*Test developers should provide the information that test users need to select appropriate tests.*

*Test users should select tests that meet the purpose for which they are to be used and that are appropriate for the intended test-taking populations.*

## Test Developers Should:

1. Define what each test measures and what the test should be used for. Describe the population (s) for which the test is appropriate.
2. Accurately represent the characteristics, usefulness, and limitations of tests for their intended purposes.
3. Explain relevant measurement concepts as necessary for clarity at the level of detail that is appropriate for the intended audience(s).
4. Describe the process of test development. Explain how the content and skills to be tested were selected.
5. Provide evidence that the test meets its intended purpose(s).
6. Provide either representative samples or complete copies of test questions, directions, answer sheets, manuals, and score reports to qualified users.

## Test Users Should:

1. First define the purpose for testing and the population to be tested. Then, select a test for that purpose and that population based on a thorough review of the available information.
2. Investigate potentially useful sources of information, in addition to test scores, to corroborate the information provided by tests.
3. Read the materials provided by test developers and avoid using tests for which unclear or incomplete information is provided.
4. Become familiar with how and when the test was developed and tried out.
5. Read independent evaluations of a test and of possible alternative measures. Look for evidence required to support the claims of test developers.
6. Examine specimen sets, disclosed tests or samples of questions, directions, answer sheets,

---

[2] Many of the statements in the Code refer to the selection of existing tests. However, in customized testing programs test developers are engaged to construct new tests. In those situations, the test development process should be designed to help ensure that the completed tests will be in compliance with the Code.

7. Indicate the nature of the evidence obtained concerning the appropriateness of each test for groups of different racial, ethnic, or linguistic backgrounds who are likely to be tested.
8. Identify and publish any specialized skills needed to administer each test and to interpret scores correctly.

manuals, and score reports before selecting a test.
7. Ascertain whether the test content and norms group(s) or comparison group(s) are appropriate for the intended test takers.
8. Select and use only those tests for which the skills needed to administer the test and interpret scores correctly are available.

# Interpreting Scores

*Test developers should help users interpret scores correctly.*

*Test users should interpret scores correctly.*

## Test Developers Should:

9. Provide timely and easily understood score reports that describe test performance clearly and accurately. Also explain the meaning and limitations of reported scores.
10. Describe the population(s) represented by any norms or comparison group(s), the dates the data were gathered, and the process used to select the samples of test takers.
11. Warn users to avoid specific, reasonably anticipated misuses of test scores.
12. Provide information that will help users follow reasonable procedures for setting passing scores when it is appropriate to use such scores with the test.
13. Provide information that will help users gather evidence to show that the test is meeting its intended purpose(s).

## Test Users Should:

9. Obtain information about the scale used for reporting scores, the characteristics of any norms or comparison group(s), and the limitations of the scores.
10. Interpret scores taking into account any major differences between the norms or comparison groups and the actual test takers. Also take into account any differences in test administration practices or familiarity with the specific questions in the test.
11. Avoid using tests for purposes not specifically recommended by the test developer unless evidence is obtained to support the intended use.
12. Explain how any passing scores were set and gather evidence to support the appropriateness of the scores.
13. Obtain evidence to help show that the test is meeting its intended purpose(s).

# Striving for Fairness

*Test developers should strive to make tests that are as fair as possible for test takers of different races, gender, ethnic backgrounds, or handicapping conditions.*

*Test users should select tests that have been developed in ways that attempt to make them as fair as possible for test takers of different races, gender, ethnic backgrounds, or handicapping conditions.*

## Test Developers Should:

14. Review and revise test questions and related materials to avoid potentially insensitive content or language.
15. Investigate the performance of test takers of different races, gender, and ethnic backgrounds when samples of sufficient size are available. Enact procedures that help to ensure that differences in performance are related primarily to the skills under assessment rather than to irrelevant factors.
16. When feasible, make appropriately modified forms of tests or administration procedures available for test takers with handicapping conditions. Warn test users of potential problems in using standard norms with modified tests or administration procedures that result in non comparable scores.

## Test Users Should:

14. Evaluate the procedures used by test developers to avoid potentially insensitive content or language.
15. Review the performance of test takers of different races, gender, and ethnic backgrounds when samples of sufficient size are available. Evaluate the extent to which performance differences may have been caused by inappropriate characteristics of the test.
16. When necessary and feasible, use appropriately modified forms of tests or administration procedures for test takers with handicapping conditions. Interpret standard norms with care in the light of the modifications that were made.

# Informing Test Takers

*Under some circumstances, test developers have direct communication with test takers. Under other circumstances, test users communicate directly with test takers. Whichever group communicates directly with test takers should provide the information described below.*

*Under some circumstances, test developers have direct control of tests and test scores. Under other circumstances, test users have such control. Whichever group has direct control of tests and test scores should take the steps described below.*

## Test Developers or Test Users Should:

17. When a test is optional, provide test takers or their parents/guardians with information to help them judge whether the test should be taken, or if an available alternative to the test should be used.
18. Provide test takers the information they need to be familiar with the coverage of the test, the types of question formats, the directions, and appropriate test-taking strategies. Strive to make such information equally available to all test takers.

## Test Developers or Test Users Should:

17. Provide test takers or their parents/guardians with information about rights test takers may have to obtain copies of tests and completed answer sheets, retake tests, have tests rescored, or cancel scores.
18. Tell test takers or their parents/guardians how long scores will be kept on file and indicate to whom and under what circumstances test scores will or will not be released.
19. Describe the procedures that test takers or their parents/guardians may use to register complaints and have problems resolved.

**Note:** The membership of the Working Group that developed the Code of Fair Testing Practices in Education and of the Joint Committee on Testing Practices that guided the Working Group was as follows:

Theodore P. Bartell
John R. Bergan
Esther E. Diamond
Richard P. Duran
Lorraine D. Eyde
Raymond D. Fowler
John J. Fremer
(Co-chair, JCTP and Chair,
    Code Working Group)

Edmund W. Gordon
Jo-Ida C. Hansen
James B. Lingwall
George F. Madaus
(Co-chair, JCTP)
Kevin L. Moreland
Jo-Ellen V. Perez
Robert J. Solomon
John T. Stewart

Carol Kehr Tittle
(Co-chair, JCTP)
Nicholas A. Vacc
Michael J. Zieky
Debra Boltas and Wayne
Camara of the American
    Psychological Association
    served as staff liaisons.

# Glossary

## A

**achievement** Previous learning.

**acquiescence** The tendency to agree or to endorse a test item as true.

**adverse impact** The effect of any test used for selection purposes if it systematically rejects substantially higher proportions of minority than majority job applicants.

**age differentiation** Discrimination based on the fact that older children have greater capabilities than do younger children.

**age scale** A test in which items are grouped according to age level. (The Binet scale, for example, grouped into one age level items that two-thirds to three-quarters of a representative group of children at a specific age could successfully pass.)

**anxiety** An unpleasant emotional state marked by worry, apprehension, and tension.

**aptitude** Potential for learning a specific skill (for example, musical aptitude).

**assessment** A procedure used to evaluate an individual so that one can describe the person in terms of current functioning and also so that one can predict future functioning. Tests are used in the assessment process.

## B

**basal** The level at which a minimum criterion number of correct responses is obtained.

**basal age** In the Stanford-Binet scale, the highest year level at which the subject successfully passes all tests.

**base rate** In decision analysis, the proportion of people expected to succeed on a criterion if they are chosen at random.

**biserial correlation** An index used to express the relationship between a continuous variable and an artificially dichotomous variable.

## C

**category format** A rating-scale format that often uses the categories 1 to 10.

**ceiling** The highest score possible on a test. When the test is too easy, many people may get the highest score and the test cannot discriminate between the top level performers and those at lower levels.

**class interval** The unit for the horizontal axis in a frequency distribution.

**closed-ended question** In interviewing, a question that can be answered specifically (for example, "yes" or "no"). Such questions generally require the interviewee to recall something.

**coefficient alpha** A generalized method for estimating reliability. Alpha is similar to the $KR_{20}$ formula, except that it allows items to take on values other than 0 and 1.

**coefficient of alienation** In correlation and regression analysis, the index of nonassociation between two variables.

**coefficient of determination** The correlation coefficient squared; gives an estimate of the percentage of variation in $Y$ that is known as a function of knowing $X$ (and vice versa).

**concurrent validity evidence** Evidence for criterion validity in which the test and the criterion are administered at the same point in time.

**confrontation** A statement that points out a discrepancy or inconsistency.

**construct validity evidence** A process used to establish the meaning of a test through a series of studies. To evaluate

evidence for construct validity, a researcher simultaneously defines some construct and develops the instrumentation to measure it. In the studies, observed correlations between the test and other measures provide evidence for the meaning of the test. See also *convergent evidence* and *discriminant evidence.*

**content validity evidence** The evidence that the content of a test represents the conceptual domain it is designed to cover.

**convergent evidence** Evidence obtained to demonstrate that a test measures the same attribute as do other measures that purport to measure the same thing. A form of construct validity evidence.

**correction for attenuation** Correction of the reduction, caused by low reliability, in the estimated correlation between a test and another measure. The correction for attenuation formula is used to estimate what the correlation would have been if the variables had been perfectly reliable.

**correlation coefficient** A mathematical index used to describe the direction and the magnitude of a relationship between two variables. The correlation coefficient ranges between $-1.0$ and 1.0.

**criterion-referenced test** A test that describes the specific types of skills, tasks, or knowledge of an individual relative to a well-defined mastery criterion. The content of criterion-referenced tests is limited to certain well-defined objectives.

**criterion validity evidence** The evidence that a test score corresponds to an accurate measure of interest. The measure of interest is called the *criterion.*

**cross validation** The process of evaluating a test or a regression equation for a sample other than the one used for the original studies.

# D

**deciles** Points that divide the frequency distribution into equal tenths.

**descriptive statistics** Methods used to provide a concise description of a collection of quantitative information.

**developmental quotient (DQ)** In the Gesell Developmental Schedules, a test score that is obtained by assessing the presence or absence of behaviors associated with maturation.

**dichotomous format** A test item format in which there are two alternatives for each item.

**differential validity** The extent to which a test has different meanings for different groups of people. For example, a test may be a valid predictor of college success for white but not for African American students.

**discriminability** In item analysis, how well an item performs in relation to some criterion. For example, items may be compared according to how well they separate groups who score high and low on the test. The index of discrimination would then be the association between performance on an item and performance on the whole test.

**discriminability analysis** See *discriminability.*

**discriminant analysis** A multivariate data analysis method for finding the linear combination of variables that best describes the classification of groups into discrete categories.

**discriminant evidence** Evidence obtained to demonstrate that a test measures something different from what other available tests measure. A form of construct validity evidence.

**distractors** Alternatives on a multiple-choice exam that are not correct or for which no credit is given.

**drift** The tendency for observers in behavioral studies to stray from the definitions they learned during training and to develop their own idiosyncratic definitions of behaviors.

**dyslexia** A specific reading disorder characterized by reading backwardness.

# E

**EEOC guidelines** A set of procedures created by the Equal Employment Opportunity Commission (EEOC) to ensure fairness in employment practices. The EEOC guidelines discuss the minimum requirements for the validity and reliability of the psychological tests used for employee selection.

**estimated learning potentials (ELPs)** In the SOMPA system, WISC-R scores adjusted for the socioeconomic background of the children. ELPs take the place of IQ scores.

**evaluative statement** A statement in interviewing that judges or evaluates.

# F

**face validity** The extent to which items on a test appear to be meaningful and relevant. Actually not evidence for validity because face validity is not a basis for inference.

**factor analysis** A set of multivariate data analysis methods for reducing large matrixes of correlations to fewer variables. The variables are linear combinations of the variables that were in the original correlation matrix.

**false negative** In test-decision theory, a case in which the test suggests a negative classification, yet the correct classification is positive.

**false positive** In test-decision analysis, a case in which the test suggests a positive classification, yet the correct classification is negative.

**frequency distribution** The systematic arrangement of scores on a measure to reflect how frequently each value on the measure occurred.

# G

**general cognitive index (GCI)** In the McCarthy Scales of Children's Abilities, a standard score with a mean of 100 and standard deviation of 16.

**group test** A test that a single test administrator can give to more than one person at a time.

# H

**hit rate** In test-decision analysis, the proportion of cases in which a test accurately predicts success or failure.

**hostile statement** In interviewing, a statement that reflects anger.

**human ability** Behaviors that reflect either what a person has learned or the person's capacity to emit a specific behavior; includes *achievement, aptitude,* and *intelligence.*

# I

**individual tests** Tests that can be given to only one person at a time.

**inferences** Logical deductions (from evidence) about something that one cannot observe directly.

**inferential statistics** Methods used to make inferences from a small group of observations, called a *sample.* These inferences are then applied to a larger group of individuals, known as a *population.* Typically, the researcher wants to make statements about the larger group but cannot make all of the necessary observations.

**intelligence** General potential independent of previous learning.

**intelligence quotient (IQ)** A unit for expressing the results of intelligence tests. The intelligence quotient is based on the ratio of the individual's mental age (MA) (as determined by the test) to actual or chronological age (CA): $IQ = MA/CA \times 100$.

**intercept** On a two-dimensional graph, the point on the $Y$ axis where $X$ equals 0. In regression, this is the point at which the regression line intersects the $Y$ axis.

**interquartile range** The interval of scores bounded by the 25th and the 75th percentiles.

**interval scale** A scale that one can use to rank order objects and on which the units reflect equivalent magnitudes of the property being measured.

**interview** A method of gathering information by talk, discussion, or direct questions.

**ipsative score** A test result presented in relative rather than absolute terms. Ipsative scores compare the individual against him- or herself. Each person thus provides his or her own frame of reference.

**isodensity curve** An ellipse on a scatterplot (or two-dimensional scatter diagram) that encircles a specified proportion of the cases constituting particular groups.

**item** A specific stimulus to which a person responds overtly and that can be scored or evaluated.

**item analysis** A set of methods used to evaluate test items. The most common techniques involve assessment of item difficulty and item discriminability.

**item characteristic curve** A graph prepared as part of the process of item analysis. One graph is prepared for each test item and shows the total test score on the $X$ axis and the proportion of test takers passing the item on the $Y$ axis.

**item difficulty** A form of item analysis used to assess how difficult items are. The most common index of difficulty is the percentage of test takers who respond with the correct choice.

**item discriminability** See *discriminability*.

### K

**Kuder-Richardson 20** A formula for estimating the internal consistency of a test. The $KR_{20}$ (or $KR_{20}$) method is equivalent to the average split-half correlation obtained from all possible splits of the items. For the $KR_{20}$ formula to be applied, all items must be scored either 0 or 1.

### L

**Likert format** A format for attitude scale items in which subjects indicate their degree of agreement to statements using these categories: strongly disagree, disagree, neither disagree nor agree, agree, strongly agree.

### M

**McCall's *T*** A standardized score system with a mean of 50 and a standard deviation of 10. McCall's $T$ can be obtained from a simple linear transformation of $Z$ scores ($T = 10Z + 50$).

**mean** The arithmetic average of a set of scores on a variable.

**measurement error** The component of an observed test score that is neither the true score nor the quality you wish to measure.

**median** The point on a frequency distribution marking the 50th percentile.

**mental age** A unit for expressing the results of intelligence tests. This unit is based on comparing the individual's performance on the test with the average performance of individuals in a specific chronological age group.

**multiple regression** A multivariate data analysis method that considers the relationship between a continuous outcome variable and the linear combination of two or more predictor variables.

**multivariate analysis** A set of methods for data analysis that considers the relationships between combinations of three or more variables.

### N

**nominal scales** Systems that arbitrarily assign numbers to objects. Mathematical manipulation of numbers from a nominal scale is not justified. For example, numbers on the backs of football players' uniforms are a nominal scale.

**normative sample** A comparison group consisting of individuals who have been administered a test under standard conditions—that is, with the instructions, format, and general procedures outlined in the test manual for administering the test (also called a *standardization sample*).

**norm-referenced test** A test that evaluates each individual relative to a normative group.

**norms** A summary of the performance of a group of individuals on which a test was standardized. The norms usually include the mean and the standard deviation for the reference group and information on how to translate a raw score into a percentile rank.

### O

**one-tailed test** A directional test of the null hypothesis. With a one-tailed test, the experimenter states the specific end of the null distribution that should be used for the region of rejection of the null hypothesis. For example, an experimenter studying weight loss may state that group B should lose more weight than group A. Thus, the null hypothesis would be rejected only if it was statistically improbable that the amount of weight group B lost was greater than group A. If group A lost more weight than group B, the null hypothesis would not be rejected.

**open-ended question** In interviewing, a question that usually cannot be answered specifically. Such questions require the interviewee to produce something spontaneously.

**ordinal scale** A scale that one can use to rank order objects or individuals.

### P

**parallel forms reliability** The method of reliability assessment used to evaluate the error associated with the use of a particular set of items. Equivalent forms of a test are developed by generating two forms using the same rules. The correlation between the two forms is the estimate of parallel forms reliability.

**Pearson product moment correlation** An index of correlation between two continuous variables.

**percentile band** The range of percentiles that are likely to represent a subject's true score. It is created by forming an interval one standard error of measurement above and below the obtained score and converting the resulting values to percentiles.

**percentile rank** The proportion of scores that fall below a particular score.

**performance scale** A test that consists of tasks that require a subject to do something rather than to answer questions.

**personality tests** Tests that measure overt and covert dispositions of individuals (the tendency that individuals will show a particular behavior or response in any given situation). Personality tests measure typical human behavior.

**point scale** A test in which points (0, 1, or 2, for example) are assigned to each item. In a point scale, all items with a particular content can be grouped together.

**polytomous format** A format for objective tests in which three or more alternative responses are given for each item. This format is popular for multiple-choice exams. Also called *polychotomous format*.

**predictive validity evidence** The evidence that a test forecasts scores on the criterion at some future time.

**probing statement** A statement in interviewing that demands more information than the interviewee has been willing to provide of his or her own accord.

**projective hypothesis** The proposal that when a person attempts to understand an ambiguous or vague stimulus, his or her interpretation reflects needs, feelings, experiences, prior conditioning, thought processes, and so forth.

**projective personality tests** Tests in which the stimulus or the required response or both are ambiguous. The general idea behind projective tests is that a person's interpretation of an ambiguous stimulus reflects his or her unique characteristics.

**prophecy formula** A formula developed by Spearman and Brown that one can use to correct for the loss of reliability that occurs when the split-half method is used and each half of the test is one-half as long as the whole test. The method can also be used to estimate how much the test length must be increased to bring the test to a desired level of reliability.

**psychological test** A device for measuring characteristics of human beings that pertain to overt (observable) and covert (intraindividual) behavior. A psychological test measures past, present, or future human behavior.

**psychological testing** The use of psychological tests. Psychological testing refers to all of the possible uses, applications, and underlying concepts of psychological tests.

## Q

**quartiles** Points that divide the frequency distribution into equal fourths.

## R

**randomly parallel tests** Tests created by successive random sampling of items from a domain or universe of items.

**ratio scale** An interval scale with an absolute zero, or point at which there is none of the property being measured.

**reactivity** The phenomenon that causes the reliability of a scale in behavior studies to be higher when an observer knows that his or her work is being monitored.

**reassuring statement** In interviewing, a statement intended to comfort or support.

**receptive vocabulary** In the Peabody Picture Vocabulary Test, a nonverbal estimate of verbal intelligence; in general, the ability to understand language.

**regression line** The best-fitting straight line through a set of points in a scatter diagram.

**reliability** The extent to which a score or measure is free of measurement error. Theoretically, reliability is the ratio of true score variance to observed score variance. This ratio can be estimated using a variety of correlational methods, including *coefficient alpha, Kuder-Richardson 20, test–retest*, and *parallel forms*.

**representative sample** A sample drawn in an unbiased or random fashion so that it is composed of individuals with characteristics similar to those for whom the test is to be used.

**residual** The difference between predicted and observed values from a regression equation.

**response style** The tendency to mark a test item in a certain way irrespective of content.

**restricted range** In correlation and regression, variability on one measure is used to forecast variability on a second measure. If the variability is restricted on either measure, the observed correlation is likely to be low. For example, the correlation between the GRE and performance among students in an elite graduate program is likely to be low because GRE scores among students admitted to the program might have very little variability. The true correlation considering all students at all universities may be higher.

## S

**scaled score** On the Wechsler tests, a standard score with a mean of 10 and a standard deviation of 3.

**scales** Tools that relate raw scores on test items to some defined theoretical or empirical distribution.

**scatter diagram** A picture of the relationship between two variables. For each individual, a pair of observations is obtained, and the values are plotted

in a two-dimensional space created by variables $X$ and $Y$.

**selection ratio** In test decision analysis, the proportion of applicants who are selected.

**self-report questionnaire** A questionnaire that provides a list of statements about an individual and requires him or her to respond in some way to each, such as "True" or "False."

**shrinkage** Many times a regression equation is created for one group and used to predict the performance of another group of subjects. This procedure tends to overestimate the magnitude of the relationship for the second group. The amount of decrease in the strength of the relationship from the original sample to the sample with which the equation is used is known as *shrinkage*.

**social ecology** A field of study that deals with the relationship between environments and behavior, the description of behavioral settings, and other related topics.

**social facilitation** Tendency of people to behave like the models around them.

**Spearman's rho** A method for finding the correlation between two sets of ranks.

**split-half reliability** A method for evaluating reliability in which a test is split into halves. The correlation between the halves of the test, corrected for the shortened length of the halves, is used as an estimate of reliability.

**standard administration** The procedures outlined in the test manual for administering a test.

**standard deviation** The square root of the average squared deviation around the mean (or the variance). It is used as a measure of variability in a distribution of scores.

**standard error of estimate** An index of the accuracy of a regression equation. It is equivalent to the standard deviation of the residuals from a regression analysis. Prediction is most accurate when the standard error of estimate is small.

**standard error of measurement** An index of the amount of error in a test or measure. The standard error of measurement is a standard deviation of a set of observations for the same test.

**standardization sample** A comparison group consisting of individuals who have been administered a test under standard conditions—that is, with the instructions, format, and general procedures outlined in the test manual for administering the test (also called a *normative sample*).

**standardized interview** An interview conducted under standard conditions that are well defined in a manual or procedure book.

**stanine system** A system for assigning the numbers 1 through 9 to a test score. The system was developed by the U.S. Air Force. The standardized stanine distribution has a mean of 5 and a standard deviation of approximately 2.

**state anxiety** An emotional reaction to a situation. State anxiety varies from one situation to the next.

**stress** A response to situations that pose demands, place constraints, or give opportunities.

**structured personality tests** Tests that provide a statement, usually of the self-report variety ("I like rock and roll music"), and require the subject to choose between two or more alternative responses ("True" or "False," for example). Sometimes called *objective personality tests*.

**subtest scatter** On the Wechsler tests, the degree of subtest variability.

## T

**Taylor-Russell tables** A series of tables one can use to evaluate the validity of a test in relation to the amount of information it contributes beyond what would be known by chance.

**test** A measurement device that quantifies behavior.

**test administration** The act of giving a test.

**test administrator** Person giving a test.

**test anxiety** Anxiety that occurs in test-taking situations.

**test battery** A collection of tests, the scores of which are used together in appraising an individual.

**test–retest reliability** A method for estimating how much measurement error is caused by time sampling, or administering the test at two different points in time. Test–retest reliability is usually estimated from the correlation between performances on two different administrations of the test.

**third variable** A variable that may account for the observed relationship between two other variables.

**tracking** The tendency to stay at about the same level of growth or performance relative to peers who are the same age.

**trait anxiety** A personality characteristic reflecting the differences among people in the intensity of their reaction to stressful situations.

**traits** Enduring or persistent characteristics of an individual that are independent of situations.

**T score** On the MMPI, a standard score with a mean of 50 and a standard deviation of 10. (See also *McCall's* T.)

**true score** The score that would be obtained on a test or measure if there were no measurement error. In practice, the true score can be estimated but not directly observed.

**two-tailed test** A nondirectional test of the null hypothesis. In contrast to a one-tailed test which states a specific direction, the two-tailed test is used to evaluate whether observations are significantly different from chance in either the upper or lower end of the sampling distribution.

## U

**understanding response** In interviewing, a statement that communicates understanding (also called an *empathy response*).

**unstructured interview** An interview conducted without any specific or particular questions or sequences of questions.

## V

**validity** The extent to which a test measures the quality it purports to measure. Types of validity evidence include *content validity, criterion validity*, and *construct validity evidence*.

**variance** The average squared deviation around the mean; the standard deviation squared.

# References

Aamodt, M. G. (2004). *Applied industrial/organizational psychology* (4th ed.). Belmont, CA: Wadsworth.

Abbott, R. D., Amtmann, D., & Munson, J. (2003). Exploratory and confirmatory methods in learning disabilities research. In H. L. Swanson & K. R. Harris (Eds.), *Handbook of learning disabilities* (pp. 471–482). New York: Guilford Press.

Abdelkhalek, A. M. (1994). Normative results on the Arabic Fear Survey Schedule 3. *Journal of Behavior Therapy and Experimental Psychiatry, 25*(1), 61–67.

Abel, J. S., & Russell, P. S. S. (2005). Communication and symbolic behaviour deficits in children with autism: Are they related to other autistic domains? *Autism, 9*(3), 333–334.

Abell, S. C., Horkheimer, R., & Nguyen, S. E. (1998). Intellectual evaluations of adolescents via human figure drawings: An empirical comparison of two methods. *Journal of Clinical Psychology, 54*, 811–815.

Abrams, D. M. (1999). Six decades of the Bellak Scoring System. In L. Gieser & M. I. Stein (Eds.), *Evocative images: The Thematic Apperception Test and the art of projection*. Washington: American Psychological Assocation.

Abramson, L. Y., Alloy, L. B., & Metalsky, G. I. (1995). Hopelessness depression: Explanatory style. In G. M. Buchanan & E. P. Seligman (Eds.), *Explanatory style* (pp. 113–134). Hillsdale, NJ: Erlbaum.

Abramson, T. (1969). The influence of examiner race on first-grade and kindergarten subjects' Peabody Picture Vocabulary Test scores. *Journal of Educational Measurement, 6*, 241–246.

Ackerman, M. J., & Pritzl, T. B. (2011). Child custody evaluation practices: A 20-year follow-up. *Family Court Review, 49*, 618–628. doi: 10.1111/j.1744-1617.2011.01397.x.

Acklin, M. W. (1995). Rorschach assessment of the borderline child. *Journal of Clinical Psychology, 51*(2), 294–302.

*Adarand Constructors, Inc. v. Pena, Secretary of Transportation et al.* (1995). 115 U. S. 2097.

Ægisdóttir, S., Spengler, P. M., & White, M. J. (2006). Should I pack my umbrella?: Clinical versus statistical prediction of mental health decisions. *Counseling Psychologist, 34*(3), 410–419.

Ægisdóttir, S., White, M. J., Spengler, P. M., Maugherman, A. S., Anderson, L. A., Cook, R. S., et al. (2006). The meta-analysis of clinical judgment project: Fifty-six years of accumulated research on clinical versus statistical prediction. *Counseling Psychologist, 34*(3), 341–382.

Affleck, G., Termen, H., Urrows, S., & Higgins, P. (1994). Person and contextual features of daily stress reactivity: Individual differences in relations of undesirable daily events with mood disturbance and chronic pain intensity. *Journal of Personality and Social Psychology, 66*(2), 329–340.

Aharonson, V., Halperin, I., & Korczyn, A. D. (2007). Computerized diagnosis of mild cognitive impairment. *Alzheimer's & Dementia, 3*(1), 23–27.

Ahern, S., & Beatty, J. (1979). Pupillary responses vary during information processing with scholastic aptitude test score. *Science, 205*, 1289–1292.

Aidman, E. V., & Shmelyov, A. G. (2002). Mimics: A symbolic conflict/cooperation simulation program, with embedded protocol recording and automatic psychometric assessment. *Behavior Research Methods, Instruments, and Computers, 34*(1), 83–89.

Aiken, L. R. (1987). *Assessment of intellectual functioning*. Newton, MA: Allyn & Bacon.

Aiken, L. S. (2008). Doctoral training in statistics, measurement, and methodology in psychology: Replication and extension of Aiken, West, Sechrest, and Reno's (1990) survey of PhD programs in North America. *American Psychologist, 63*(1), 32.

Akehurst, L., & Vrij, A. (1999). Creating suspects in police interviews. *Journal of Applied Social Psychology, 29*, 192–210.

Akutagawa, D. A. (1956). *A study in construct validity of the psychoanalytic concept of latent anxiety and a test of projection distance hypothesis*. Unpublished doctoral dissertation, University of Pittsburgh, PA.

Alain, C., Bernstein, L. J., He, Y., Cortese, F., & Zipursky, R. B. (2002). Visual feature conjunction in patients with schizophrenia: An event-related brain potential study. *Schizophrenia Research, 57*(1), 69–80.

*Albemarle Paper Company v. Moody.* (1975). 442 U.S. 405.

Alessandri, G., Vecchione, M., Caprara1, G., & Letzring, T.D. (2011). The Ego Resiliency Scale revised: A cross-cultural study in Italy, Spain, and the United States. *European Journal of Psychological Assessment* , 1–8. doi: 10.1027/1015-5759/a000102.

Alexander, G. E., Prohovnik, I., Stem, Y., & Mayeux, R. (1994). WAIS-R subtest profile and cortical perfusion in Alzheimer's disease. *Brain and Cognition, 24*(1), 24–43.

Alexopoulos, D., Haritos-Fatouros, M., Sakkas, D., Skaltsas, A., & Vlachos, O. (2000). Reliability and validity of the WISC-R for the age range 6 to 11 years in Greece. *Psychology: Journal of the Hellenic Psychological Society, 7*(1), 35–45.

Alfonso, V. C., & Flanagan, D. P. (1999). Assessment of cognitive functioning in preschoolers. In E. V. Nuttall, I. Romero, et al. (Eds.), *Assessing and screening preschoolers: Psychological and educational dimensions* (2nd ed.) (pp. 186–217). Boston: Allyn & Bacon.

Allalouf, A., & Ben-Shakhar, G. (1998). The effect of coaching on the predictive validity of scholastic aptitude tests. *Journal of Educational Measurement, 35*(1), 31–47.

Allard, G., & Faust, D. (2000). Errors in scoring objective personality tests. *Assessment, 7*(2), 119–129.

Allen, F. (1994). The diagnostic interview for genetic studies. *Archives of General Psychiatry, 51*(11), 863–864.

Allen, J. G., & Smith, W. H. (1993). Diagnosing dissociative disorders. *Bulletin of the Menninger Clinic, 57*(3), 328–343.

Allen, K. D., DeVellis, R. F., Renner, J. B., Kraus, V. B., & Jordan, J. M. (2007). Validity and factor structure of the AUSCAN Osteoarthritis Hand Index in a community-based sample. *Osteoarthritis Cartilage, 15*(7), 830–836.

Allen, M. J., & Yen, W. M. (1979). *Introduction to measurement theory.* Pacific Grove, CA: Brooks/Cole.

*Allen v. Alabama State Board of Education.* (1985). 612 F. Supp. 1046.

Allison, J., Blatt, S. J., & Zimet, C. N. (1968). *The interpretation of psychological tests.* New York: Harper & Row.

Allport, G. W., & Odbert, H. S. (1936). Trait-names, a psycholexical study. *Psychological Monographs, 47*(1).

Almkvist, O., Adveen, M., Henning, L., & Tallberg, I. M. (2007). Estimation of premorbid cognitive function based on word knowledge: The Swedish Lexical Decision Test (SLDT). *Scandinavian Journal of Psychology, 48*(3), 271–279.

Alpert, R., & Haber, R. N. (1960). Anxiety in academic achievement situations. *Journal of Abnormal and Social Psychology, 61*, 207–215.

Altmaier, E. M., McGuinnes, S. G., Wood, P., Ross, R. R., Bartley, J., & Smith, W. L. (1990). Defining successful performance among pediatric residents. *Pediatrics, 85*, 139–143.

Altmaier, E. M., Smith, W. L., O'Halloran, C. M., & Franken, E. A., Jr. (1992). The predictive utility of behavior-based interviewing compared with traditional interviewing in the selection of radiology residents. *Investigative Radiology, 27*(5), 385–389.

Alvarado, N. (1994). Empirical validity of the Thematic Apperception Test. *Journal of Personality Assessment, 63*(1), 59–79

American Educational Research Association (AERA), American Psychological Association (APA), & National Council on Measurement in Education (NCME) (1999). *Standards for educational and psychological testing.* Washington, DC: AERA.

American Psychiatric Association. (1980). *Diagnostic and statistical manual of mental disorders* (3rd ed.). Washington, DC: American Psychiatric Association.

American Psychiatric Association. (1995). *Diagnostic and statistical manual of mental disorders* (4th ed.). Washington, DC: American Psychiatric Association.

American Psychological Association (APA). (1954). *Psychology and its relations with other professions.* Washington, DC: American Psychological Association.

American Psychological Association (APA). (1974). *Standards for educational and psychological tests.* Washington, DC: American Psychological Association.

American Psychological Association (APA). (1992). *APA code of conduct.* Washington, DC: American Psychological Association.

American Psychological Association (2002). *The Ethical Principles of Psychologists and Code of Conduct.* Available at www.apa.org/ethics/code2002.html.

American Psychological Association (APA), American Educational Research Association (AERA), & National Council on Measurement in Education (NCME). (1999). *Standards for educational and psychological testing.* Washington, DC: AERA.

Ames, L. B., Metraux, R. W., & Walker, R. N. (1971). *Adolescent Rorschach responses.* New York: Brunner/Mazel.

*Ana Maria R. v. California Department of Education.* (1976). 96 U.S. 2040(c).

Anastasi, A. (1984). The K-ABC in historical and contemporary perspective. *Journal of Special Education, 78*(3), 357–366.

Anastasi, A. (1988). *Psychological testing* (6th ed.). New York: Macmillan.

Anastasi, A. (1993). A century of psychological testing: Origins, problems, and progress. In T. K. Fagan & G. R. VandenBos (Eds.), *Exploring applied psychology: Origins and critical analyses* (pp. 13–36). Washington, DC: American Psychological Association.

Anastasi, A. (1995). Psychology evolving: Linkages, hierarchies, and dimensions. In F. Kessel (Ed.), *Psychology, science, and human affairs: Essays in honor of William Bevan* (pp. 245–260). Boulder, CO: Westview.

Anastasi, A., & Urbina, S. (1997). *Psychological testing* (7th ed.). Upper Saddle River, NJ: Prentice-Hall.

Anderson, M. (2001). Conceptions of intelligence. *Journal of Child Psychology and Psychiatry and Allied Disciplines, 42*(2), 287–298.

Anderson, N. B., & McNeilly, M. (1991). Age, gender, and ethnicity as variables in psychophysiological assessment: Sociodemographics in context. *Psychological Assessment: A Journal of Consulting and Clinical Psychology, 3*, 376–384.

Anderson, N. H. (1991). *Contributions to information integration theory.* Hillsdale, NJ: Erlbaum.

Andersson, H. W. (1996). The Fagan Test of Infant Intelligence: Predictive validity in a random sample. *Psychological Reports, 78*, 1015–1026.

Andrews, J. J. W., Saklofske, D. H., & Janzen, H. L. (2001). *Handbook of psychoeducational assessment: Ability, achievement, and behavior in children.* San Diego: Academic Press.

Angoff, W. H. (1988). Promising areas for psychometric research. *Applied Measurement in Education, 1*(3), 203–206.

Angrilli, A., Sarlo, M., Palomba, D., & Schincaglia, M. (1997). Respiratory sinus arrhythmia in blood phobic subjects. *Perceptual and Motor Skills, 84*, 505–506.

Annalakshmi, N. (2006). TAT responses in relation to induced motivational set and reasoning ability. *Journal of the Indian Academy of Applied Psychology, 32*(3), 331–336.

Antony, M. M. (2001). Measures for specific phobia. In M. M. Antony & S. M. Orsillo (Eds.), *Practitioner's guide to empirically based measures of anxiety. AABT clinical assessment series* (pp. 133–158). New York: Klumer Academic/Plenum.

APA (2010). 2010 amendments to the 2002 "Ethical principles of psychologists and code of conduct." *American Psychologist, 65*(5), 493.

Arbisi, P. A., Ben-Porath, Y. S., & Mc-Nulty, J. (2002). A comparison of MMPI-2 validity in African American and Caucasian psychiatric inpatients. *Psychological Assessment, 14*(1), 3–15.

Archer, E. M., Hagan, L. D., Mason, J., Handel, R., & Archer, R. P. (2011, February 2). MMPI-2-RF characteristics of custody evaluation litigants. *Assessment.* Retrieved from http://asm.sagepub.com/content/early/2011/01/28/1073191110397469.abstract. doi: 10.1177/1073191110397469.

Archer, R. P., Maruish, M., Imhof, E. A., & Piotrowski, C. (1991). Psychological test usage with adolescent clients:

1990 survey. *Professional Psychology: Research and Practice, 22,* 247–252.

Arita, A. A., & Baer, R. A. (1998). Validity of selected MMPI-A content scales. *Psychological Assessment, 10,* 59–63.

Arkes, H. R. (1991). Costs and benefits from judgment errors: Implications for debiasing. *Psychological Bulletin, 110,* 486–489.

Aron, A., & Aron, E. (2003). *Statistics for psychology* (3rd ed.). Upper Saddle River, NJ: Prentice-Hall.

Aronow, E., Reznikoff, M., & Moreland, K. L. (1995). The Rorschach: Projective technique or psychometric test? *Journal of Personality Assessment, 64*(3), 213–228.

Aronson, J., Lustina, M. J., Good, C., Keough, K., Steele, C. M., & Brown, J. (1999). When white men can't do math: Necessary and sufficient factors in stereotype threat. *Journal of Experimental Social Psychology, 35*(1), 29–46.

Arrindell, W. A., van Nieuwenhuizen, C., & Lutejin, F. (2001). Chronic psychiatric status and satisfaction with life. *Personality and Individual Differences, 31*(2), 145–155.

Arthur, G. (1930). *Arthur point scale of performance tests.* Chicago: Stoelting.

Arvey, R. D., & Campion, J. E. (1982). The employment interview: A summary and review of recent research. *Personnel Psychology, 35,* 281–322.

Asher, J. J., & Sciarrino, J. A. (1974). Realistic work sample tests: A review. *Personnel Psychology, 27,* 519–533.

Ashton, M. C. (1998). Personality and job performance: The importance of narrow traits. *Journal of Organizational Behavior, 19,* 289–303.

*Association of Mexican-American Educators v. California.* (1996). 836 F. Supp. 1534.

Atkinson, J. W. (1981). Studying personality in the context of an advanced motivational psychology. *American Psychologist, 36,* 117–128.

Atkinson, L. (1990). Reliability and validity of ratio developmental quotients from the Cattell Infant Intelligence Scale. *American Journal of Mental Retardation, 95,* 215–219.

Atkinson, R. C. (2004, April 28). *College admissions and the SAT.* University of California Center for the Humanities Public Lecture.

Avolio, B. J., & Waidman, D. A. (1990). An examination of age and cognitive test performance across job complexity and occupational types. *Journal of Applied Psychology, 75,* 43–50.

Ax, A. F. (1953). The physiological differentiation between fear and anger in humans. *Psychosomatic Medicine, 15,* 433–442.

Aylward, G. P. (2011). Neuropsychological assessment of newborns, infants, and toddlers. In A. S. Davis (Ed.), *Handbook of pediatric neuropsychology,* Springer Publishing.

Azrin, N. H., Holz, W., Ulrich, R., & Goldiamond, I. (1961). The control of the content of conversation through reinforcement. *Journal of the Experimental Analysis of Behavior, 4,* 25–30.

Azrin, N. H., & Powell, J. (1968). Behavioral engineering: The reduction of smoking behavior by a conditioning apparatus and procedure. *Journal of Applied Behavior Analysis, 1,* 193–200.

Baburajan, P. K. (1998). Psychosocial factors associated with contraceptive initiation: A multivariate analysis. *Psychological Studies, 43,* 37–43.

Baddeley, A. D., Wilson, B. A., & Watts, F. N. (1995). *Handbook of memory disorders.* Chichester, England: Wiley.

Baehr, M. (1987). A review of employee evaluation procedures and a description of "high potential" executives and professionals. *Journal of Business and Psychology, 1,* 172–202.

Baer, R. A., & Sekirnjak, G. (1997). Detection of underreporting on the MMPI-2 in a clinical population: Effects of information about validity scales. *Journal of Personality Assessment, 69,* 555–567.

Bai, X., Wu, C., Zheng, R., & Ren, X. (2011). The psychometric evaluation of the Satisfaction with Life Scale using a nationally representative sample of China. *Journal of Happiness Studies, 12*(2), 183–197. doi: 10.1007/s10902-010-9186-x.

Baily, K. J. (2001). Social competence of children with autism classified as best-outcome following behavior analytic treatment. *Dissertation Abstracts International, 61,* 12B. (UMI No. 9997891).

Bajrić, E., Kobašlija1, S., & Hrvoje J. (2011). Children's Fear Survey Schedule (CFSS-DS) in children in Bosnia and Herzegovina. *Bosnian Journal of Basic Medical Science, 11*(4), 214–218.

Bakker, A. B., Demerouti, E., & ten Brummelhuis, L. L. (2011). Work engagement, performance, and active learning: The role of conscientiousness. *Journal of Vocational Behavior.* Retrieved from http://www.sciencedirect.com/science/article/pii/S0001879111001151.

Bandura, A. (1986a). The explanatory and predictive scope of self-efficacy theory. *Journal of Social & Clinical Psychology, 4,* 359–373.

Bandura, A. (1986b). *Social foundations of thought and action: A social cognitive theory.* Englewood Cliffs, NJ: Prentice-Hall.

Bandura, A. (1994). Regulative function of perceived self-efficacy. In M. G. Rumsey, C. B. Walker, & J. H. Harris (Eds.), *Personnel selection and classification* (pp. 261–271). Hillsdale, NJ: Erlbaum.

Banerji, M. (1992a). Factor structure of the Gessell-School Readiness Screening Test. *Journal of Psychoeducational Assessment, 10*(4), 342–354.

Banerji, M. (1992b). An integrated study of the predictive properties of the Gessell School Readiness Screening Test. *Journal of Psychoeducational Assessment, 10*(3), 240–256.

Banerji, M., & Ferron, J. (1998). Construct validity of scores on a developmental assessment with mathematical patterns tasks. *Educational and Psychological Measurement, 58,* 634–660.

Barak, A. (1999). Psychological applications on the Internet: A discipline on the threshold of a new millenium. *Applied and Preventive Psychology, 8,* 231–245.

Barak, A., & Cohen, L. (2002). Empirical examination of an online version of the Self-Directed Search. Thousand Oaks, CA: Sage.

Barber, T. X., & Silver, M. J. (1968). Fact, fiction, and the experimenter bias effect. *Psychological Bulletin Monograph Supplement, 70,* 1–29.

Bareak, B., & Lauter, D. (1991, November 5). 1991 rights bill a return to earlier path of bias redress. *Los Angeles Times,* pp. A1, A18.

Barenbaum, N. B., & Winter, D. G. (2003). Personality. In D. K. Freedheim (Ed.), *Handbook of psychology: History of psychology* (Vol. 1, pp. 177–203). New York: Wiley & Sons.

Barker, R. G. (1979). Settings of a professional lifetime. *Journal of Personality and Social Psychology, 37,* 2137–2157.

Barker, R. G., & Schoggen, P. (1973). *Qualities of community life.* San Francisco: Jossey-Bass.

Barlow, D. H. (2011). A prolegomenon to clinical psychology: Two 40-year odysseys. In D.H. Barlow (Ed.), *The Oxford handbook of clinical psychology* (pp. 3–). New York: Oxford Press

Barofsky, I. (2003). Cognitive approaches to summary measurement: Its application to the measurement of diversity in health-related quality of life assessments. *Quality of Life Research, 12*(3), 251–260.

Baron, I. S., & Fennell, E. B. (2000). Neuropsychological and intellectual assessment of children. In B. J. Sadock & V. A. Sadock (Eds.), *Comprehensive textbook of psychiatry* (7th ed.) (Vol. 1, pp. 722–732). Philadelphia: Lippincott, Williams & Wilkins.

Baron, R. A. (1986). Self-presentation in job interviews: When there can be "too much" of a good thing. *Journal of Applied Social Psychology, 16*, 16–28.

Barrett, G. V., & Dupinet, R. L. (1991). A reconsideration of testing for confidence rather than for intelligence. *American Psychologist, 46*, 1012–1024.

Barrick, M. R., & Mount, M. K. (1991). The Big Five Personality Dimen-sions and job performance: A meta-analysis. *Personnel Psychology, 44*, 1–26.

Barrick, M. R., Mount, M. K., & Judge, T. A. (2001). Personality and performance at the beginning of the new millennium: What do we know and where do we go next? *Personality and Performance, 9*(1–2), 9–30.

Bartell, S. S., & Solanto, M. V. (1995). Usefulness of the Rorschach Inkblot Test in assessment of attention deficit hyperactivity disorder. *Perceptual and Motor Skills, 80*(2), 531–541.

Bartholomew, D. J., & Knott, M. (1999). *Latent variable models and factor analysis.* New York: Oxford University Press.

Bartlett, C. J., & O'Leary, B. S. (1989). A differential prediction model to moderate the effects of heterogeneous groups in personnel selection and classification. *Personnel Psychology, 22*, 117.

Bartley, C. E., & Roesch, S. C. (2011). Coping with daily stress: The role of conscientiousness, *Personality and Individual Differences, 50*(1), 79–83. Retrieved from http://www.science-direct.com/science/article/pii/S0191886910004290.

Bartone, P. T. (1995). *A short hardiness scale.* Paper presented at the Annual Convention of the American Psychological Society, New York.

Bartone, P. T. (2007). Test–retest reliability of the dispositional resilience scale-15, a brief hardiness scale. *Psychological Reports, 101*(3), 943–944.

Bartone, P. T., Wright, K. M., Ingraham, L. H., & Ursano, R. J. (1989). The impact of a military air disaster on the health of assistance workers. *Journal of Nervous and Mental Disease, 177*, 317–328.

Basco, W. T., Jr., Way, D. P., Gilbert, G. E., & Hudson, A. (2002). Undergraduate institutional MCAT scores as predictors of USMLE step 1 performance. *Academy of Medicine, 77*(10 Suppl.), S13–16.

Basgul, S. S., Uneri, O. S., Akkaya, G. B., Etiler, N., & Coskun, A. (2011). Assessment of drawing age of children in early childhood and its correlates. *Psychology, 2*(4), 376–381. doi: 10.4236/psych.2011.24059.

Bates, T. C., & Shieles, A. (2003). Crystallized intelligence as product of speed and drive for experience: The relationship of inspection time and openness to g and Gc. *Intelligence, 31*(3), 275–287.

Baudin, N., Aluja, A., Rolland, J. P., & Blanch, A. (2011). The roll of personality in satisfaction with life and sport. *Behavioral Psychology/Psicología Conductual, 19*(2), 333–345.

Baxter, D. J., Barbaree, H. F., & Marshall, W. L. (1986). Sexual responses to consenting and forced sex in a large sample of rapists and nonrapists. *Behaviour Research and Therapy, 24*, 513–520.

Bay, M. (1998). An exploratory factor analysis of the Leiter-R. *Dissertation Abstracts International: Section B. The Physical Sciences and Engineering, 58*, 4513.

Bayles, K. A. (1990). Language and Parkinson disease. *Alzheimer's Disease and Associated Disorders, 4*, 171–180.

Bayley, N. (1969). *Manual: Bayley Scales of Infant Development.* New York: Psychological Corporation.

Beal, J. A. (1991). Methodological issues in conducting research on parent-infant attachment. *Journal of Pediatric Nursing, 6*, 11–15.

Beal-Alvarez, J. S., Lederberg, A. R., & Easterbrooks, S. R. (2011). Grapheme–phoneme acquisition of deaf preschoolers. *Journal of Deaf Studies and Deaf Education, 16*(4).

Beato, L., Cano, T. R., & Belmonte, A. (2003). Relationship of dissociative experiences to body shape concerns in eating disorders. *European Eating Disorders Review, 11*(1), 38–45.

Beck, A. T. (1967). *Depression: Clinical, experimental, and theoretical aspects.* New York: Harper & Row.

Beck, A. T. (1976). *Cognitive therapy and the emotional disorders.* New York: International Universities Press.

Beck, A. T., Brown, G., Steer, R. A., & Weissman, A. N. (1991). Factor analysis of the Dysfunctional Attitude Scale in a clinical population. *Psychological Assessment: Journal of Consulting and Clinical Psychology, 3*, 478–583.

Beck, A. T., & Rector, N. A. (2002). Delusions: A cognitive perspective. *Journal of Cognitive Psychotherapy, 16*(4), 455–468.

Beck, J. G., Carmin, C. H., & Henninger, N. J. (1998). The utility of the Fear Survey Schedule—III: An extended replication. *Journal of Anxiety Disorders, 12*, 177–182.

Beck, S. J. (1933). Configurational tendencies in Rorschach responses. *American Journal of Psychology, 45*, 433–443.

Beck, S. J. (1944). *Rorschach's test: Vol. 1. Basic processes.* New York: Grune & Stratton.

Beck, S. J. (1945). *Rorschach's test: Vol. 2. A variety of personality pictures.* New York: Grune & Stratton.

Beck, S. J. (1952). *Rorschach's test: Vol. 3. Advances in interpretation.* New York: Grune & Stratton.

Becker, B. J. (2003). Introduction to the Special Section on Metric in Meta-Analysis. *Psychological Methods, 8*(4), 403–405.

Beel-Bates, C. A. (2001). Visuospatial function in ambulatory aged women with probable Alzheimer's disease: A multiple case study. *Dissertation Abstracts International, 62*, 1B. (UMI No. 3000920).

Behrwind, S. D., Dafotakis, M., Halfter, S., Berthold-Losleben, M., Cieslik, E. C., & Eickhoff, S. B. (2011). Executive control in chronic schizophrenia: A perspective from manual stimulus-response compatibility task performance. *Behavioral Brain Research, 223*(1), 24–29.

Bell, N. L., Lassiter, K. S., Matthews, T. D., & Hutchinson, M. B. (2001). Comparison of the Peabody Picture Vocabulary Test–Third Edition and Wechsler Adult Intelligence Scale–Third Edition with university students. *Journal of Clinical Psychology, 57*(3), 417–422.

Bell, N. L., Matthews, T. D., Lassiter, K. S., & Leverett, J. (2002). Validity of the Wonderlic Personnel Test as a measure of fluid or crystallized intelligence: Implications for career assessment. *North American Journal of Psychology, 4*(1), 113–120.

Bell, T. K. (1990). Rapid sequential processing in dyslexic and ordinary readers. *Perceptual and Motor Skills*, *71*, 1155–1159.

Bellack, A. S. (Ed.). (1998). *Behavioral assessment: A practical handbook* (4th ed.). Needham Heights, MA: Allyn & Bacon.

Bellack, A. S., & Hersen, M. (1988). *Behavioral assessment: A practical handbook* (3rd ed.). New York: Pergamon Press.

Bellak, L. (1975). The *TAT, CAT, and SAT in clinical use* (3rd ed.). New York: Grune & Stratton.

Bellak, L. (1986). The *TAT, CAT, and SAT in clinical use* (4th ed.). New York: Grune & Stratton.

Bellak, L. (1996). The *TAT, CAT, and SAT in clinical use* (6th ed.). New York: Grune & Stratton.

Bellak, L. (1999). My perceptions of the Thematic Apperception Test in psychodiagnosis and psychotherapy. In L. G. Gieser & M. I. Stein (Eds.), *Evocative images: The Thematic Apperception Test and the art of projection*. Washington, DC: American Psychological Association.

Bellak, L., & Bellak, S. S. (1973). *Manual: Senior Apperception Technique*. Larchmont, NY: CPS.

Bem, D. J., & Allen, A. (1974). On predicting some of the people some of the time: The search for cross-situational consistencies in behavior. *Psychological Review*, *81*, 506–520.

Bem, D. J., & Funder, D. C. (1978). Predicting more of the people more of the time: Assessing the personality of situations. *Psychological Review*, *85*, 485–501.

Bender, L. (1962). *Bender-Gestalt Test*. Los Angeles, CA: Western Psychological Services.

Benejam, G. (2006). *Defining success factors for graduate students*. US: ProQuest Information & Learning.

Benjamin, G. A., & Gollan, J. K. (2003). Evidentiary standards and rules of evidence. In G. A. Benjamin & J. K. Gollan (Eds.), *Family evaluation in custody litigation: Reducing risks of ethical infractions and malpractice. Forensic practice guidebook* (pp. 17–28). Washington, DC: American Psychological Association.

Bennett, R. E. (2003). An electronic infrastructure for a future generation of tests. In H. F. O'Neil & R. S. Perez (Eds.), *Technology applications in education: A learning view* (pp. 267–281). Mahwah, NJ: Erlbaum.

Bennouna-Greene, M., Berna, F., Conway, M. A., Rathbone, C, J.,

Vidailhet, P., & Danion, J. M. (2011). Self-images and related autobiographical memories in schizophrenia. *Consciousness and Cognition*. Retrieved October 29, 2011 from http://www.sciencedirect.com/science/article/pii/S1053810011002662.

Ben-Porath, Y. S., & Butcher, J. N. (1989). The comparability of MMPI and MMPI-2 scales and profiles. *Psychological Assessment: Journal of Consulting and Clinical Psychology*, *1*, 1–3.

Ben-Porath, Y. S., & Butcher, J. N. (1991). The historical development of personality assessment. In C. E. Walker (Ed.), *Clinical psychology: Historical and research foundations*. New York: Plenum.

Bentler, P., & de Leeuw, J. (2011). Factor analysis via components analysis. *Psychometrika*, *76*(3), 461–470. doi:10.1007/s11336-011-9217-5.

Bentler, P. M. (1990). Comparative fit indexes in structural models. *Psychological Bulletin*, *107*(2), 238–246.

Bentler, P. M. (1991). Modeling of intervention effects. *Nida Research Monograph*, *107*, 159–182.

Bentler, P. M. (1994). On the quality of test statistics in covariance structure analysis: Caveat emptor. In C. R. Reynolds (Ed.), *Cognitive assessment: A multidisciplinary perspective. Perspectives on Individual differences* (pp. 237–260). New York: Plenum.

Benton, A. L., & Sivan, A. B. (2007). Clinical neuropsychology: A brief history. *Dis Mon*, *53*(3), 142–147.

Bereby-Meyer, Y., Meyer, J., & Flascher, O. M. (2002). *Prospect theory analysis of guessing in multiple choice tests*. New York: Wiley.

Berg, K, C., Peterson, C. B., Frazier, P., & Crow, S. J. (2011). Convergence of scores on the interview and questionnaire versions of the Eating Disorder Examination: A meta-analytic review. *Psychological Assessment*, *23*(3), 714–724. doi:10.1037/a0023246.

Bergan, A., McManis, D. L., & Melchert, P. A. (1971). Effects of social and token reinforcement on WISC block design performance. *Perceptual and Motor Skills*, *32*, 871–880.

Bergan, J. R., & Parra, E. B. (1979). Variations in IQ testing and instruction and the letter learning and achievement of Anglo and bilingual Mexican-American children. *Journal of Educational Psychology*, *71*, 819–826.

Berger, S. P., Hopkins, J., Bae, H., Hella, B., & Strickland, J. (2010). Infant assessment. In J. G. Bremner and

T. D. Wachs (Eds.), *Wiley-Blackwell handbook of infant development, volume 2* (2nd. ed.). Oxford, UK: Wiley-Blackwell. doi:10.1002/9781444327588.ch9.

Bergeron, R., & Floyd, R. G. (2006). Broad cognitive abilities of children with mental retardation: An analysis of group and individual profiles. *American Journal on Mental Retardation*, *111*(6), 417–432.

Bergner, M., Babbitt, R. A., Carter, W. B., & Gilson, B. S. (1981). The Sickness Impact Profile: Development and final revision of a health status measure. *Medical Care*, *19*, 787–788.

Bergstrom, B. A., & Lunz, M. E. (1999). CAT for certification and licensure. In E. Fritz Drasgow, E. Julie, B. Olson-Buchanan, et al. (Eds.), *Innovations in computerized assessment* (pp. 67–91). Mahwah, NJ: Erlbaum.

Bermant, G., Talwar, C., & Rozin, P. (2011.) To celebrate positive psychology and extend its horizons, In K. M. Sheldon, T. B. Kashdan, & M. F. Steger (Eds.), *Designing positive psychology: Taking stock and moving forward* (pp. 430–439). New York: Oxford University Press.

Bernheimer, L. P., & Keogh, B. K. (1988). Stability of cognitive performance of children with developmental delays. *American Journal of Mental Retardation*, *92*, 539–542.

Berry, L. M. (2003). *Employee selection*. Belmont, CA: Wadsworth.

Bersoff, D. N. (1979). Regarding psychologists testily: Legal regulation of psychological assessment in the public schools. In B. Sales & M. Novick (Eds.), *Perspectives in law and psychology: Testing and evaluation* (Vol. 3). New York: Plenum.

Bersoff, D. N. (1981). Testing and the law. *American Psychologist*, *36*, 1047–1057.

Betz, N. E. (2000). Contemporary issues in testing use. In E. C. Edward Watkins, Jr., E. Vicki, L. Campbell, et al. (Eds.), *Testing and assessment in counseling practice* (2nd ed.) (pp. 481–516). Mahwah, NJ: Erlbaum.

Beutler, L. E. & Berren, M. R. (Eds.). (1995). *Integrative assessment of adult personality*. New York: Guilford Press.

Bianchini, J. C. (1976, May). *Achievement tests and differentiated norms*. Paper presented at the U. S. Office of Education invitational conference on achievement testing of disadvantaged and minority students for educational program evaluation, Reston, VA.

Bickel, W. K., Christensen, D. R., & Marsch, L. A. (2011). A review of computer-based interventions used in the assessment, treatment, and research of drug addiction. *Substance Use & Misuse, 46*(1), 4–9.

Bigler, E. D. (2003). Neurobiology and neuropathology underlie the neuropsychological deficits associated with traumatic brain injury. *Archives of Clinical Neuropsychology, 18*(6), 595–621, 623–627.

Binet, A. (1890a). Perceptions d'enfants. *La Revue Philosophique, 30,* 582–611.

Binet, A. (1890b). Recherches sur les mouvements de quelques jeunes enfants. *La Revue Philosophique, 29,* 297–309.

Binet, A., & Henri, V. (1895). La psychologie individuelle. *L'Annee Psychologique, 2,* 411–463.

Binet, A., & Henri, V. (1896). La psychologie individuelle. *L'Annee Psychologique, 3,* 296–332.

Binet, A., & Simon, T. (1905). Methodes nouvelles pour le diagnostic du niveau intellectuel des anormaux. *L'Annee Psychologique, 11,* 191–244.

Birk, J. M. (1974). Interest inventories: A mixed blessing. *Vocational Guidance Quarterly, 22,* 280–286.

Biswas, P., Malhotra, S., Malhotra, A., & Gupta, N. (2006). Comparative study of neuropsychological correlates in schizophrenia with onset in childhood, adolescence, and adulthood. *European Child & Adolescent Psychiatry, 15*(6), 360–366.

Black, P., & Wiliam, D. (2007). Large-scale assessment systems: Design principles drawn from international comparisons. *Measurement: Interdisciplinary Research and Perspectives, 5*(1), 1–53.

Black, S. (2003). Distance learning. *Nursing Standards, 17*(19), 18–19.

Black, T. R. (1999). *Doing quantitative research in the social sciences: An integrated approach to research design, measurement and statistics.* London: Sage.

Black, W. C., Haggstrom, D. A., & Welch, H. G. (2002). All-cause mortality in randomized trials of cancer screening. *Journal of the National Cancer Institute, 94*(3), 167–173.

Black issues in higher education. (2001). *Black Issues in Higher Education, 17*(24), p. 14.

Blair, J. (2000). OCR issues revised guidance on high-stakes testing. *Education Week, 19*(17), 25.

Blais, M. A., Norman, D. K., Quintar, B., & Herzog, D. B. (1995). The effect of the administration method: A comparison of the Rapaport and Exner Rorschach systems. *Journal of Clinical Psychology, 51*(1), 119–121.

Blake, J. (1974). Developmental changes in visual information processing under backward masking. *Journal of Experimental Child Psychology, 17,* 133–146.

Blasczyk-Schiepa, S., Kazénb, M., Kuhlb, J., & Grygielskic, M. (2011). Appraisal of suicidal risk among adolescents and young adults through the Rorschach Test. *Journal of Personality Assessment, 93*(5), 518–526. doi: 10.1080/00223891.2011.594130.

Blatt, S. J. (1990). The Rorschach: A test of perception or an evaluation of representation? *Journal of Personality Assessment, 55,* 394–416.

Blazek, N. L., & Forbey, J. D. (2011). A comparison of validity rates between paper-and-pencil and computerized testing with the MMPI-2. *Assessment, 18*(1), 63–66.

Block, J. (1961). *The Q-sort method in personality assessment and psychiatric research.* Springfield, IL: Thomas.

Block, J., & Kremen, A. (1996). IQ and ego-resiliency: Conceptual and empirical connections and separateness. *Journal of Personality and Social Psychology, 70,* 349–361.

Blood, G. W. (1995). A behavioral-cognitive therapy program for adults who stutter: Computers and counseling. *Journal of Communication Disorders, 28*(2), 165–180.

Blumberg, T. A. (1995). A practitioner's view of the WISC-III. *Journal of School Psychology, 33*(1), 95–97.

*Board of Education v. Rowley.* (1982). 458 U.S. 176; 102 S. Ct. 3034; 73 L. Ed. 2d 690.

Board of Professional Affairs, American Psychological Association. (1998). Awards for distinguished professional contributions: John Exner. *American Psychologist, 53,* 391–392.

Bobic, J., Pavicevic, L., & Gomzi, M. (2000). Cognitive functional inefficiency in alcoholics. *Studia Psychologa, 42*(1–2), 105–110.

Bödecs, T., Horváth, B., Szilágyi, E., Gonda, X., Rihmer, Z., & Sándor, J. (2011). Effects of depression, anxiety, self-esteem, and health behaviour on neonatal outcomes in a population-based Hungarian sample. *European Journal of Obstetrics, Gynecology and Reproductive Biology, 154*(1), 45–50.

Boegels, S. M., van der Vleuten, C. P. M., Blok, G., & Kreutzkamp, R. (1996). Assessment and validation of diagnostic interviewing skills for mental health professionals. *Journal of Psychopathology and Behavioral Assessment, 17,* 217–230.

Boerum, L. J. (2000). Developing portfolios with disabled students. *Reading and Writing Quarterly, 16*(3), 211–238.

Bohil, C. J., Alicea, B., & Biocca, F. A. (2011). Virtual reality in neuroscience research and therapy. *Nature Reviews Neuroscience, 12,* 752–762. doi: 10.1038/nrn3122.

Bolen, L. M., Hewett, J. B., Hall, C. W., & Mitchell, C. C. (1992). Expanded Koppitz Scoring System of the Bender Gestalt Visual-Motor Test for adolescents: A pilot study. *Psychology in the Schools, 29*(2), 113–115.

Bolt, D. (2003). Essays on item response theory. *Psychometrika, 68*(1), 155–158.

Bolton, B. (1992). Review of the California Psychogical Inventory, Revised Edition. In J. J. Framer & J. C. Conely (Eds.), *Eleventh mental measurements yearbook* (pp. 558–562). Lincoln, NE: Buros Institute of Mental Measurements.

Bombardier, C., Ware, J., Russell, I. J., et al. (1986). Auranofin therapy in quality of life for patients with rheumatoid arthritis: Results of a multicenter trial. *American Journal of Medicine, 81,* 565–578.

Bondi, M. W., Houston, W. S., Salmon, D. P., Corey-Bloom, J., Katzman, R., Thal, L. J., et al. (2003). Neuropsychological deficits associated with Alzheimer's disease in the very old: Discrepancies in raw vs. standardized scores. *Journal of the International Neuropsychology Society, 9*(5), 783–795.

Bootzin, R. R., & McKnight, P. E. (2006). *Strengthening research methodology: Psychological measurement and evaluation* (1st ed.). Washington, DC: American Psychological Association.

Borman, W. C., & Hallman, G. L. (1991). Observational accuracy for assessors of work-sample performance: Consistency across task and individual differences correlate. *Journal of Applied Psychology, 76,* 11–18.

Bornstein, M. H., Hahn, C., Suwalsky, J. T. D., and Haynes, O. M. (2003). Socioeconomic status, parenting, and child development: The Hollingshead Four-Factor Index of Social Status and the Socioeconomic Index of Occupations. In M. H. Bornstein, & R. H. Bradley (Eds.), *Socioeconomic status, parenting, and child development:*

*Monographs in parenting series* (pp. 29–82). Mahwah, NJ: Erlbaum.

Bornstein, R. F., & Masling, J. M. (2005). *Scoring the Rorschach: Seven validated systems.* Mahwah, NJ: Lawrence Erlbaum Associates Publishers.

Borsboom, D., Mellenbergh, G. J., & van Heerden, J. (2002). Different kinds of DIF: A distinction between absolute and relative forms of measurement invariance and bias. Thousand Oaks, CA: Sage.

Bos, J. S. (1996). Factor structure of the field edition of the Leiter International Performance Scale—Revised. *Dissertation Abstracts International: Section B. The Physical Sciences and Engineering, 57,* 1494.

Bosshardt, M. J., Carter, G. W., Gialluca, K. A., Dunnette, M. D., et al. (1992). Predictive validation of an insurance agent support person selection battery [Special Issue: Test validity yearbook I]. *Journal of Business and Psychology, 7,* 213–224.

Botella, C., Villa, H., Banos, R., Perpina, C., & Garcia-Palacios, A. (1999). The treatment of claustrophobia with virtual reality: Changes in other phobic behaviors not specifically treated. *Cyberpsychology and Behavior, 2*(2), 135–141.

Botet, F., de Caceres, M. L., Rosales, S., & Costas, C. (1996). Behavior assessment of newborns from diabetic mothers. *Behavioral Neurology, 9*(1), 1–4.

Bottomley, A., Efficace, F., Thomas, R., Vanvoorden, V., & Ahmedzai, S. H. (2003). Health-related quality of life in non-small-cell lung cancer: Methodologic issues in randomized controlled trials. *Journal of Clinical Oncology, 21*(15), 2982–2992.

Boudreau, J. W., & Ramstad, P. M. (2003). Strategic industrial and organizational psychology and the role of utility analysis models. New York: Wiley.

Bourmenskaya, G. V. (2002). A study of individual differences by means of stage-by-stage formation of mental actions and notions. *Voprosky Psikhologii, 5,* 89–103.

Bowden, S. C., Saklofske, D. H., & Weiss, L. G. (2011). Invariance of the measurement model underlying the Wechsler Adult Intelligence Scale-IV in the United States and Canada. *Educational and Psychological Measurement, 71,* 186–199. doi: 10.1177/0013164410387382.

Bowers, K. S. (1973). Situationalism in psychology: An analysis and critique. *Psychological Review, 80,* 307–336.

Bowling, A. (2005). Mode of questionnaire administration can have seri-ous effects on data quality. *Journal of Public Health (Oxford), 27*(3), 281–291.

Bracken, B. A. (1985). A critical review of the Kaufman Assessment Battery for Children (K-ABC). *School Psychology Review, 14,* 21–35.

Bracken, B. A., & Walker, K. C. (1997). The utility of intelligence tests for preschool children. In D. P. Flanagan, J. L. Genshaft, et al. (Eds.), *Contemporary intellectual assessment: Theories, tests, and issues* (pp. 484–502). New York: Guilford.

Bradbury, T. N., & Fincham, F. D. (1990). Attributions in marriage: Review and critique. *Psychological Bulletin, 1070,* 333.

Bradley-Johnson, S. (2001). Cognitive assessment for the youngest children: A critical review of tests. *Journal of Psychoeducational Assessment, 19*(2), 19–44.

Brand, C. R. (1981). General intelligence and mental speed: Their relationship and development. In M. P. Friedman, J. P. Das, & N. O'Conner (Eds.), *Intelligence and teaming.* New York: Plenum.

Brandt, J. (2007). 2005 INS presidential address: Neuropsychological crimes and misdemeanors. *The Clinical Neuropsychologist, 21*(4), 553–568.

Bratko, D., & Marusic, I. (1997). Family study of the big five personality dimensions. *Personality and Individual Differences, 23,* 365–369.

Brawley, O. W., & Freeman, H. P. (1999). Race and outcomes: Is this the end of the beginning for minority health research? [editorial; comment]. *Journal of the National Cancer Institute, 91*(22), 1908–1909.

Bray, J. H. (2009). Vision for the future of psychology practice. *American Psychological Association Monitor, 40*(2), 5. Retrieved from http://www.apa.org/monitor/2009/02/pc.aspx.

Brayfield, A. H. (Ed.). (1965). Testing and public policy. *American Psychologist, 20,* 857–1005.

Brazelton, T. B. (1973). *Neonatal behavioral assessment scale.* Philadelphia: Lippincott.

Brazelton, T. B. (1984, November–December). *Neonatal behavioral assessment scale* (2nd ed.). Philadelphia: Lippincott.

Brazelton, T. B. (1993). Why children and parents must play while they eat: An interview with T. Berry Brazelton, MD [interview by Nancy I. Hahn].

*Journal of the American Dietetic Association, 93*(12), 1385–1387.

Bredemeier, M. (1991, November–December). IQ test ban for blacks called unconstitutional. *California Associations of School Psychologists Today,* pp. 22–23.

Breen, N., K., A. C., Meissner, H. I., Taplin, S. H., Tangka, F. K., Tiro, J. A., et al. (2007). Reported drop in mammography : Is this cause for concern? *Cancer, 109*(12), 2405–2409.

Breggin, P. R. (2002). Empathetic self-transformation in therapy. In P. R. Breggin, G. Breggin, & F. Bemak (Eds.), *Dimensions of empathetic therapy* (pp. 177–189). New York: Springer.

Breggin, R., Breggin, G., & Bemak, F. (Eds.). (2002). *Dimensions of empathetic therapy.* New York: Springer.

Breithaupt, K. J., Mills, C. N., & Melican, G. J. (2006). Facing the opportunities of the future. In D. Bartram, & R. K. Hambleton (Eds.), *Computer-based testing and the Internet: Issues and advances.* (pp. 219–251). New York: John Wiley & Sons, Inc.

Brennan, R. L. (1994). Variance components in generalizability theory. In C. R. Reynolds (Ed.), *Cognitive assessment: A multidisciplinary perspective* (pp. 175–207). New York: Plenum.

Bressani, R. V., & Downs, C. (2002). Youth independent living assessment: Testing the equivalence of web and paper/pencil versions of the Ansell-Casey Life Skills Assessment. *Computers in Human Behavior, 18*(4), 453–464.

Bridgeman, B., & A. Schmitt (1997). Fairness issues in test development and administration. In E. Warren, W. Willingham, E. Nancy, S. Cole, et al. (Eds.), *Gender and fair assessment* (pp. 185–226). Mahwah, NJ: Erlbaum.

Bridges, K. R. (2001). Using attributional style to predict academic performance: How does it compare to traditional methods? *Personality and Individual Differences, 31*(5), 723–730.

Bridges, K. R., & Harnish, R. J. (2010). Role of irrational beliefs in depression and anxiety: A review. *Health, 2*(8), 862–877. doi:10.4236/health.2010.28130.

Bridges, K. R., & Sanderman, R. (2002). The irrational beliefs inventory: Cross-cultural comparisons between American and Dutch samples. *Journal of Rational-Emotive and Cognitive Therapy, 20*(1), 65–71.

Brill, S. (1973). The secrecy behind the college boards. *New York Magazine*. (Reprinted by the NYG Corporation.)

Brillinger, D. R. (Ed.). (1994). *The collected works of John W. Tukey*. Belmont, CA: Wadsworth.

Britt, G. C., & Myers, B. J. (1994a). The effects of the Brazelton Intervention: A review. *Infant Mental Health Journal, 15*(3), 278–292.

Britt, G. C., & Myers, B. J. (1994b). Testing the effectiveness of BNAS intervention with a substance using population. *Infant Mental Health Journal, 15*, 293–304.

Britton, B. K., & Tidwell, P. (1995). Cognitive structure testing: A computer system for diagnosis of expert-novice differences. In P. D. Nichols, S. F. Chipman, & R. L. Brennan (Eds.), *Cognitively diagnostic assessment* (pp. 251–278). Hillsdale, NJ: Erlbaum.

Broaden, H. E. (1946). On the interpretation of the correlation coefficient as a measure of predictive efficiency. *Journal of Educational Psychology, 37*, 65–76.

Broaden, H. E. (1949). When tests pay off. *Personnel Psychology, 2*, 171–183.

Broks, P. (2003). *Into the silent land: Travels in neuropsychology*. New York: Atlantic Monthly Press.

*Brookhart v. Illinois State Board of Education*. (1983). 697 F. 2d. 179. 7th Cir.

Brooks, B. L., & Barlow, K. M. (2011). A methodology for assessing treatment response in Hashimoto's Encephalopathy: A case study demonstrating repeated computerized neuropsychological testing. *Journal of Child Neurology, 26*(6), 786–791. doi: 10.1177/0883073810391532.

Brosnan, M. J. (1998). The impact of computer anxiety and self-efficacy upon performance. *Journal of Computer Assisted Learning, 14*(3), 223–234.

Brown, D. C. (1994). Subgroup norming: Legitimate testing practice or reverse discrimination? *American Psychologist, 49*(11), 927–928.

Brown, F. G. (1979a). The algebra works—but what does it mean? *School Psychology Digest, 80*, 213–218.

Brown, F. G. (1979b). The SOMPA: A system of measuring potential abilities? *School Psychology Digest, 8*, 37–46.

Brown, J. S., & Burton, R. B. (1978). Diagnostic models for procedural bugs in basic mathematical skills. *Cognitive Science, 2*, 155–192.

Brown, M., Gordon, W. A., and Haddad, L. (2000). Models for predicting subjective quality of life in individuals with traumatic brain injury. *Brain Injury, 14*(1), 5–19.

*Brown v. Board of Education*. (1955). 347 U.S. 483 (1954), 349 U.S. 294.

Bryant, F. B. & Yarnold, P. R. (1995). Principal-components analysis and exploratory and confirmatory factor analysis. In L. G. Grimm & P. R. Yarnold (Eds.), *Reading and understanding multivariate statistics* (p. 9). Washington, DC: American Psychological Association.

Bryson, G., Greig, T., Lysaker, P., & Bell, M. (2003). Longitudinal Wisconsin Card Sorting performance in schizophrenia patients in rehabilitation. *Applied Neuropsychology, 9*(4), 203–209.

Buchanan, T., & Smith, J. L. (1999). Using the Internet for psychological research: Personality testing on the World Wide Web. *British Journal of Psychology, 90*(1), 125–144.

Buck, J. N. (1948). The H-T-P technique as a qualitative and quantitative scoring manual. *Journal of Clinical Psychology, 4*, 317–396.

Bureau-Chalot, F., Novella, J. L., Jolly, D., Ankri, J., Guillemin, F., & Blanchard, F. (2002). Feasibility, acceptability and internal consistency reliability of the nottingham health profile in dementia patients. *Gerontology, 48*(4), 220–225.

Burke, M. J., & Doran, L. I. (1989). A note on the economic utility of generalized validity coefficients. *Journal of Applied Psychology, 73*, 171–175.

Burnham, J. J. (2005). Fears of children in the United States: An examination of the American fear survey schedule with 20 new contemporary fear items. *Measurement and Evaluation in Counseling and Development, 38*(2), 78–91.

Burnham, J. J., & Giesen, J. (2005). The American fear survey schedule for children (FSCC-AM): A confirmatory factor analysis with elementary, middle, and high school students. *Research in the Schools, 12*(2), 89–95.

Burns, R. C., & Kaufman, S. H. (1970). *Kinetic Family Drawings (KF-D): An introduction to understanding through kinetic drawings*. New York: Brunner/Mazel.

Burns, R. C., & Kaufman, S. H. (1972). *Actions, styles, and symbols in Kinetic Family Drawings (K-F-D)*. New York: Brunner/Mazel.

Burnsa, G. N., & Christiansen, N. D. (2011). Methods of measuring faking behavior. *Human Performance, 24*(4), 358–372. doi:10.1080/08959285. 2011.597473.

Buros, O. K. (Ed.). (1970). *Personality tests and reviews*. Highland Park, NJ: Gryphon Press.

Buros, O. K. (Ed.). (1978). *The eighth mental measurements yearbook* (2 vols.). Highland Park, NJ: Gryphon Press.

Burton, D. B., Sepehri, A., Hecht, F., VandenBroek, A., Ryan, J. R., & Drabman, R. (2001). A confirmatory factor analysis of the WISC-III in a clinical sample with cross-validation in the standardized sample. *Child Neuropsychology, 7*(2), 104–116.

Burtona, D.L., Dutyb, K.J., & Leibowitzc, G.S. (2011). Differences between sexually victimized and nonsexually victimized male adolescent sexual abusers: Developmental antecedents and behavioral comparisons. *Journal of Child Sexual Abuse, 20*(1), 77–93. doi: 10.1080/10538712.2011.541010.

Burtt, H. E. (1926). *Principles of employment psychology*. Boston: Houghton Mifflin.

Bush, J. W. (1984). Relative preferences versus relative frequencies in health-related quality of life evaluations. In N. K. Wenger, M. E. Mattson, C. D. Furberg, & J. Elinson (Eds.), *Assessment of quality of life in clinical trials of cardiovascular therapies*. New York: LaJacq.

Butcher, H. L. (1972). Review of cooperative school and college ability tests: Series 2. In O. K. Buros (Ed.), *The seventh mental measurements yearbook* (Vol. 1). Highland Park, NJ: Gryphon Press.

Butcher, J. N. (1989). *MMPI-2 users' guide*. Minneapolis, MN: Natural Computer Systems.

Butcher, J. N. (1990). *MMPI-2 in psychological treatment*. New York: Oxford University Press.

Butcher, J. N. (2000). Dynamics of personality test responses: The empiricist's manifesto revisited. *Journal of Clinical Psychology, 56*(3), 375–386.

Butcher, J. N., Aidwin, C. M., Levenson, M. R., & Ben-Porath, Y. S. (1991). Personality and aging: A study of the MMPI-2 among older men. *Psychology and Aging, 6*, 361–370.

Butcher, J. N., Graham, J. R., Dahlstrom, W. G., Tellegen, A. M., & Kaernmer, B. (1989). *MMPI-2 manual for administrators and scoring*. Minneapolis: University of Minnesota Press.

Butcher, J. N., Graham, J. R., Williams, C. L., & Ben-Porath, Y. S. (1990). *Development and use of the MMPI-2 Content Scales*. Minneapolis: University of Minnesota Press.

Butcher, J. N., Perry, J. N., & Atlis, M. M. (2000). Validity and utility of computer-based test interpretation. *Psychological Assessments, 12*(1), 6–18.

Butters, N., Delis, D. C., & Lucas, J. A. (1995). Clinical assessment of memory disorders in amnesia and dementia. *Annual Review of Psychology, 46,* 493–523.

Byers, C. (2001). Interactive assessment: An approach to enhance teaching and learning. *Journal of Interactive Learning Research, 12*(4), 359–374.

Cacioppo, J. T., Berntson, G. G., & Anderson, B. L. (1991). Physiological approaches to the evaluation of psychotherapeutic process and outcome, 1991: Contributions from social psychophysiology. *Psychological Assessment: Journal of Consulting and Clinical Psychology, 3,* 321–336.

Cadenhead, K., Kumar, C., & Braff, D. (1996). Clinical and experimental characteristics of "hypothetically psychosis prone" college students. *Journal of Psychiatric Research, 30,* 331–340.

Cahan, S., & Noyman, A. (2001). The Kaufman Ability Battery for Children Mental Processing Scale: A valid measure of "pure" intelligence? *Educational and Psychological Measurement, 61*(5), 827–840.

Caldwell, M. B., & Knight, D. (1970). The effects of Negro and white examiners on Negro intelligence test performance. *Journal of Negro Education, 39,* 177–179.

Callahan, S., Roge, B., Cardenal, M., Cayrou, S., & Sztulman, H. (2001). Ego control and ego resiliency: French translation of a scale measuring these concepts and initial reliability and validity status. *Journal de Therapie Comportementale et Cognitive, 11*(4), 144–150.

Callender, J. C., & Dougherty, T. W. (1983). *Effects of interviewer training on interview information, interviewer behavior, and interview ratings: A field investigation.* Proceedings of the Southwest Division of the Academy of Management, Houston, TX.

Callinan, M., & Robertson, I. T. (2000). *Work sample testing.* London, United Kingdom: Blackwell.

Camaioni, L., Ercolani, A. P., Penge, R., Riccio, M., & Bernabei, P. (2001). Typical and atypical profiles of referential communication ability: A comparison of normal Ss and Ss with a specific learning disorder. *Psicologia Clinica Dello Sviluppo, 5*(1), 77–94.

Camara, W., & Echternacht, G. (2000). *The SAT-I and high school grades: Utility in predicting success in college.* (College Board Report No. RN-10). New York: College Entrance Examination Board.

Camara, W. J., & Schneider, D. L. (1994). Integrity tests: Facts and unresolved issues. *American Psychologist, 49*(2), 112–119.

Cameron, R., & Evers, S. E. (1990). Self-report issues in obesity and weight management: State of the art and future directions. *Behavioral Assessment, 12,* 91–106.

Camilli, G. (1999). Measurement error, multidimensionality, and scale shrinkage: A reply to Yen and Burket. *Journal of Educational Measurement, 36,* 73–78.

Camilli, G., Cizek, G. J., & Lugg, C. A. (2001). *Psychometric theory and the validation of performance standards: History and future perspectives.* Mahwah, NJ: Erlbaum.

Campbell, D. (2002). *The history and development of the Campbell Interest and Skill Survey.* Thousand Oaks, CA: Sage.

Campbell, D. P. (1974). *Manual for the SVIB-SCII Strong-Campbell Interest Inventory* (2nd ed.). Stanford, CA: Stanford University Press.

Campbell, D. P. (1977). *Manual for the Strong-Campbell Interest Inventory.* Stanford, CA: Stanford University Press.

Campbell, D. P. (1995, August). *The Campbell Interest and Skills Survey (SCII).* Paper presented at the annual meeting of the American Psychological Association, New York.

Campbell, D. P., Hyne, S. A., & Nilsen, D. (1992). *Manual for the Campbell Interest and Skill Survey.* Minneapolis, MN: National Computer Systems.

Campbell, D. T., & Fiske, D. W. (1959). Convergent and discriminant validation by the multitrait-multimethod matrix. *Psychological Bulletin, 56,* 81–105.

Campbell, J. M., Bell, S. K., & Keith, L. K. (2001). Concurrent validity of the Peabody Picture Vocabulary Test–Third Edition as an intelligence and achievement screener for low SES African American children. *Assessment, 8*(1), 85–94.

Campbell, K. A., Rohlman, D. S., Storzbach, D., & Binder, L. M. (1999). Test–retest reliability of psychological and neurobehavioral tests self-administered by computer. *Assessment, 6*(1), 21–32.

Campbell, S. L. (2011). Chaos theory and social work treatment. In F. J. Turner (Ed.), Social work treatment: Interlocking theoretical Approaches (5th ed.) (pp. 48–57). New York: Oxford University Press.

Campbell, T. W. (2003). Sex offenders and actuarial risk assessment: Ethical considerations. *Behavioral Science and the Law, 21*(2), 269–279.

Campbell, V. L. (2000). A framework for using tests in counseling. In E. C. Edward Watkins, Jr., E. Vicki, L. Campbell, et al. (Eds.), *Testing and assessment in counseling practice* (2nd ed.) (pp. 3–11). Mahwah, NJ: Erlbaum.

Campion, J. E. (1972). Work sampling for personnel selection. *Journal of Applied Psychology, 56,* 40–44.

Canals, J., Hernández-Martínez, C., Esparó, G., & Fernández-Ballart, J. (2011). Neonatal Behavioral Assessment Scale as a predictor of cognitive development and IQ in full-term infants: A 6-year longitudinal study. *Acta Paediatrica, 100,* 1331–1337. doi:10.1111/j.1651-2227.2011.02306.x.

Cane, D. B., Olinger, L. J., Gotlib, I. N., & Kuiper, N. A. (1986). Factor structure of the Dysfunctional Attitude Scale in a student population. *Journal of Clinical Psychology, 42,* 307–309.

Cannell, C. F., & Henson, R. (1974). Incentives, motives, and response bias. *Annals of Economic and Social Measurement, 3,* 307–317.

Caprara, G. V., Barbaranelli, C., & Comrey, A. L. (1995). Factor analysis of the NEO-PI Inventory and Comprey Personality Scales in an Italian sample. *Personality and Individual Differences, 18*(2), 193–200.

Carey, C. L., Woods, S. P., Damon, J., Halabi, C., Dean, D., Delis, D. C., et al. (2007). Discriminant validity and neuroanatomical correlates of rule monitoring in frontotemporal dementia and Alzheimer's disease. *Neuropsychologia, 46*(4), 1081–1087.

Carkhuff, R. R. (1969). *Helping and human relations: I. Selection and training; II. Practice and research.* New York: Holt, Rinehart & Winston.

Carkhuff, R. R., & Berenson, B. C. (1967). *Beyond counseling and therapy.* New York: Holt, Rinehart & Winston.

Carlbring, P., Björnstjerna, E., Bergström, A. F., Waara, J., & Andersson, G. (2007). Applied relaxation: An experimental analogue study of therapist vs.

computer administration. *Computers in Human Behavior, 23*(1), 2–10.

Carless, S. A. (1999). Career assessment: Holland's vocational interests, personality characteristics, and abili-ties. *Journal of Career Assessment, 7*(2), 125–144.

Carlin, J. B., & Rubin, D. B. (1991). Summarizing multiple-choice tests using three information statistics. *Psychological Bulletin, 110,* 338–349.

Carlozzi, N. E., Stout, J. C., Mills, J. A., Duff, K., Beglinger, L. J., & Aylward, E. H. (2011). Estimating premorbid IQ in the prodromal phase of a neurodegenerative disease. *The Clinical Neuropsychologist, 25*(5), 757–777. doi: 10.1080/13854046.2011.577811.

Carlson, R. E., Thayer, P. W., Mayfield, E. C., & Peterson, D. A. (1971). Improvements in the selection interview. *Personnel Journal, 50,* 268–275.

Carnoy, M. (2005). Have state accountability and high-stakes tests influenced student progression rates in high school? *Educational Measurement: Uses and Practice, 24*(4), 19–31.

Carper, M., McHugh, & R., Barlow, D. (2011). The dissemination of computer-based psychological treatment: A preliminary analysis of patient and clinician perceptions. *Administration and Policy in Mental Health and Mental Health Services Research,* 1–9. Retrieved from http://dx.doi.org/10.1007/s10488-011-0377-5.

Carr, A. C., Ancill, R. J., Ghosh, A., & Margo, A. (1981). Direct assessment of depression by microcomputer: A feasibility study. *Acta Psychiatrica Scandinavica, 64*(5), 415–422.

Carr, A. C., & Ghosh, A. (1983). Accuracy of behavioral assessment by computer. *British Journal of Psychiatry, 142,* 66–70.

Carr, M. A., Sweet, J. J., & Rossini, E. (1986). Diagnostic validity of the Luria-Nebraska Neuropsychological Battery—Children's revision. *Journal of Consulting and Clinical Psychology, 54,* 354–358.

Carro, I. L., Bernal, I. L., & Vea, H. B. (1998). Depression in Cuba: Validation of Beck Depression Inventory (BDI) and the Dysfunctional Attitudes Scale (DAS-A) with Cuban population. *Avances en Psicologia Clinica Latinoamericana, 16,* 111–120.

Carstairs, K. S. (2011). Rorschach assessment of parenting capacity: A case study. *Rorschachiana, 32*(1), 91–116. doi:10.1027/1192-5604/a000017.

Carvajal, H., Hardy, K., Harmon, K., Sellers, T. A., & Holmes, C. B. (1987). Relationships among scores on the Stanford-Binet IV, Peabody Picture Vocabulary Test–Revised, and Columbia Mental Maturity Scale. *Bulletin of the Psychonomic Society, 25*(4), 275–276.

Carvajal, H., Karr, S. K., Hardy, K. M., & Palmer, B. L. (1988). Relationships between scores on Stanford- Binet IV and scores on McCarthy Scales of Children's Abilities. *Bul-letin of the Psychonomic Society, 26*(4), 349.

Cascallar, A. S., & Dorans, N. J. (2005). Linking scores from tests of similar content given in different languages: An illustration involving methodological alternatives. *International Journal of Testing, 5*(4), 337–356.

Cascio, W. F. (1987). *Applied psychol-ogy in personnel management* (3rd ed.). Englewood Cliffs, NJ: Prentice-Hall.

Cascio, W. F. (1998). *Applied psychology in human resource management.* Englewood Cliffs, NJ: Prentice-Hall.

Cascio, W. F., & Ramos, R. A. (1986). Development and application of a new method for assessing job performance in behavioral economic terms. *Journal of Applied Psychology, 71,* 20–28.

Cash, T. F. (1985). The impact of grooming style on the evaluation of women in management. In M. Solomon (Ed.), *The psychology of fashion.* New York: Lexington Press.

Caspi, A., Roberts, B. W., & Shiner, R. L. (2005). Personality development: Stability and change. *Annual Review of Psychology, 56,* 453–484.

Castaneda, A., & Ramirez, M. (1974). *Cultural democracy, bicognitive development, and education.* New York: Academic Press.

Castellino, S., Tooze, J., Flowers, L., & Parsons, S. (2011). The Peabody Picture Vocabulary Test as a pre-screening tool for global cognitive functioning in childhood brain tumor survivors. *Journal of Neuro-Oncology, 104*(2), 559–563. doi:10.1007/s11060-010-0521-1.

Castenell, L. A., & Castenell, N. E. (1988). Norm-referenced testing in low-income blacks. *Journal of Counseling and Development, 67,* 205–206.

Cathers-Schiffman, T. A., & Thompson, M. S. (2007). Assessment of English- and Spanish-speaking students with the WISC-III and Leiter-R. *Journal of Psychoeducational Assessment, 25*(1), 41–52.

Cattell, J. M. (1890). Mental tests and measurements. *Mind, 15,* 373–380.

Cattell, R. B., Eber, H. W., & Tatsuoka, M. M. (1970). *Handbook for the Six-teen Personality Factor Questionnaire (16 PF).* Champaign, IL: Institute for Personality and Ability Testing.

Cattell, R. B., & Scheier, I. H. (1961). *The meaning and measurement of neuroticism and anxiety.* New York: Ronald Press.

Cautela, J. R., & Upper, D. (1976). The behavioral inventory battery: The use of self-report measures in behavioral analyses and therapy. In M. Hersen & A. S. Bellack (Eds.), *Behavioral assessment.* New York: Pergamon Press.

Cazassus, E. B. (2005). *The Wechsler Preschool and Primary Scales of Intelligence–third edition: Changes in language demands and the relationship between recent versions of the WPPSI and the PLS.* US: ProQuest Information & Learning.

Cesare, S. J. (1996). Subjective judgment and the selection interview: A methodological review. *Public Personnel Management, 25,* 291–306.

Chabanne, V., Peruch, P., & Thinus-Blanc, C. (2003). Virtual to real transfer of spatial learning in a complex environment: The role of path network and additional features. *Spatial Cognition and Computation, 31*(1), 43–59.

Chambers, L. W. (1996). The McMaster Health Index Questionnaire. In B. F. Spilker (Ed.), *Quality of life and Pharmcoeconomics in clinical trials* (2nd ed.) (pp. 267–279). New York: Raven.

Chamorro-Premuzic, T., Furnham, A., & Acherman, P. L. (2006). Ability and personality correlates of general knowledge. *Personality and Individual Differences, 41,* 419–429.

Champney, H., & Marshall, H. (1939). Optimal refinement of the rating scale. *Journal of Applied Psychology, 23,* 323–331.

Chan, D. (2009). So why ask me? Are self-report data really that bad? In C. E. Lance & R. J. Vandenberg (Eds.), *Statistical and methodological myths and urban legends: Doctrine, verity and fable in the organizational and social sciences* (p. 309). New York: Taylor & Francis Group.

Chan, G., Gelernter, J., Oslin, D., Farrer, L., & Kranzler, H. R. (2011). Empirically derived subtypes of opioid use and related behaviors. *Addiction, 106*(6), 1146–1154. doi:10.1111/j.1360-0443.2011.03390.x.

Chan, D. W. (2000). Identifying gifted and talented students in Hong Kong. *Roeper Review, 22*(2), 88–93.

Chan, K. -Y., Drasgow, F., & Sawin, L. L. (1999). What is the shelf life of a test? The effect of time on the psychometrics of a cognitive ability test battery. *Journal of Applied Psychology 84*(4), 610–619.

Chang, C. H., Ferris, D. L., Johnson, R. E., Rosen, C. C., & Tan, J. A. (2011, September 12). Core self-evaluations: A review and evaluation of the literature. *Journal of Management.* doi: 10.1177/0149206311419661. Retrieved from http://jom.sagepub.com/content/early/2011/09/09/0149206311419661.

Chang, H. Y., Yang, Y. L., Jensen, M. P., Lee, C.N., & Lai, Y. H. (2011). The experience of and coping with lumbopelvic pain among pregnant women in Taiwan. *Pain Medicine, 12*(6), 846–853. doi:10.1111/j.1526-4637.2011.01151.x

Chang, T. (2005). The validity and reliability of student ratings: Comparison between paper-pencil and online survey. *Chinese Journal of Psychology, 47*(2), 113–125.

Chapman, D. S., & Rowe, P. M. (2001). The impact of videoconference technology, interview structure, and interviewer gender on interviewer evaluations in the employment interview: A field experiment. *Journal of Occupational and Organizational Psychology, 74*(3), 279–298.

Chasnoff, I. J., Burns, K. A., & Burns, W. J. (1987). Cocaine use in pregnancy: Perinatal morbidity and mortality. *Neurotoxicology and Teratology, 9*, 291–293.

Chattin, S. H., & Bracken, B. A. (1989). School psychologists' evaluation of the K-ABC, McCarthy Scales, Stanford-Binet IV, and WISC-R. *Journal of Psychoeducational Assessment, 7*, 112–130.

Chen, E., Touyz, S. W., Beumont, P. J. V., Fairburn, C. G., Griffiths, R., Butow, P., Russell, J., Schotte, D. E., Gertler, R., & Basten, C. (2003). Comparison of group and individual cognitive-behavioral therapy for patients with bulimia nervosa. *International Journal of Eating Disorders, 33*(3), 241–254.

Chen, H., & Zhu, J. (2012). Measurement invariance of WISC-IV across normative and clinical samples. *Personality and Individual Differences, 52*(2) 161–166. Retrieved from http://www.sciencedirect.com/science/article/pii/S0191886911004521.

Chen, T. -Y. (2002). A Monte Carlo study of three new nonparametric tests for equivalence. *Dissertation Abstracts International: Section A. The Humanities and Social Sciences, 62*, 7A.

Chico-Libran, E. (2002). Dispositional optimism as a predictor of strategies coping. *Psicothema, 14*(3), 544–550.

Child, D. (2006). *The essentials of factor analysis* (3rd ed.). New York: Continuum International Publishing Group.

Choca, J. & Morris, J. (1992). Administering the Category Test by computer: Equivalence of results. *Clinical Neuropsychologist, 6*(1), 9–15.

Chong, B. H. (2000). Early childhood gifted education: Relationship of screening tests with measured intelligence. *Dissertation Abstracts International: Section A. The Humanities and Social Scienes, 61*, 5A.

Chun, K., & Campbell, J. B. (1974). Dimensionality of the Rotter Interpersonal Trust Scale. *Psychological Reports, 35*, 1059–1070.

Chung, C. Y., Liu, W. Y., Chang, C. J., Chen, C. L., Tang, S. F., & Wong, A. M. (2010). The relationship between parental concerns and final diagnosis in children with developmental delay. *Journal of Child Neurology, 26*, 413–419. doi: 10.1177/0883073810381922.

Cicchetti, D., Bronen, R., Spencer, S., Haut, S., Berg, A., Oliver, P., et al. (2006). Rating scales, scales of measurement, issues of reliability: Resolving some critical issues for clinicians and researchers. *Journal of Nervous and Mental Disease, 194*(8), 557–564.

Cicchetti, D. V. (1994). Guidelines, criteria, and rules of thumb for evaluating normed and standardized assessment instruments in psychology. *Psychological Assessment, 60*, 284–290.

Clapham, M. M. (1998). Structure of Figural Forms A and B of the Torrance Tests of Creative Thinking. *Educational and Psychological Measurement, 58*, 275–283.

Clarizio, H. F. (1979a). In defense of the IQ test. *School Psychology Digest, 8*(1), 79–88.

Clarizio, H. F. (1979b). SOMPA: A symposium continued: Commentaries. *School Psychology Digest, 8*(2), 207–209.

Clark, K. E. (1961). *The vocational interests of nonprofessional men.* Minneapolis: University of Minnesota Press.

Clark, K. E., & Campbell, D. P. (1965). *Manual for the Minnesota Vocational Interest Inventory.* New York: Psychological Corporation.

Clark, L. A., & Watson, D. (1998). Assessment. In E. Alan, E. Kazdin, et al. (Eds.), *Methodological issues and strategies in clinical research* (2nd ed.) (pp. 193–281). Washington, DC: American Psychological Association.

Clarke, R., Emberson, J. R., Parish, S., Palmer, A., Shipley, M., Linksted, P., et al. (2007). Cholesterol fractions and apolipoproteins as risk factors for heart disease mortality in older men. *Archives of Internal Medicine, 167*(13), 1373–1378.

Clauser, B. E. (2002). Advances in computerized scoring of complex item formats. *Applied Measurement in Education, 1*(4), 1–104.

Clay, E. J., Lankford, J. S., & Wilson, S. E. (1992). The effects of computerized versus paper-and-pencil administration on measures of negative affect. *Computers in Human Behavior, 8*(2–3), 203–209.

Cleary, T. A. (1968). Test bias: Prediction of grades of Negro and white students in integrated colleges. *Journal of Educational Measurement, 5*, 115–124.

Cleary, T. A., Humphreys, L. G., Kendrick, S. A., & Wesman, A. (1975). Educational uses of tests with disadvantaged populations. *American Psychologist, 30*, 15–41.

Cliff, N. (1987). *Analyzing multivariate data.* San Diego: Harcourt, Brace, Jovanovich.

Coakes, S. J., & Steed, L. G. (1999). *SPSS: Analysis without anguish. Versions 7.0, 7.5, 8.0 for Windows.* Brisbane, Australia: Wiley.

Cohen, A., Fiorello, C. A., & Farley, F. H. (2006). The cylindrical structure of the Wechsler Intelligence Scale for Children-IV: A retest of the Guttman model of intelligence. *Intelligence, 34*(6), 587–591.

Cohen, B. H., & Lea, R. B. (2004). *Essentials of statistics for the social and behavioral sciences.* Hoboken, NJ: Wiley.

Cohen, F., & Lazarus, R. S. (1994). Active coping processes, coping dispositions, and recovery from surgery. In A. Steptoe & J. Wardle (Eds.), *Psychosocial processes and health: A reader* (pp. 348–368). Cambridge, England: Cambridge University Press.

Cohen, J. (1960). A coefficient of agreement for nominal scales. *Educational and Psychological Measurement, 20*, 37–46.

Cohen, S., & Lichtenstein, E. (1990). Partner behaviors that support quitting smoking. *Journal of Consulting and Clinical Psychology, 58*, 304–309.

Cohen, T. R., Wolf, S. T., Panter, A. T., & Insko, C.A. (2011). Introducing the GASP scale: A new measure of guilt and shame proneness. *Journal of Personality and Social Psychology, 100*(5), 947–966. doi:10.1037/a0022641.

Coid, J., Yang, M., Roberts, A., Ullrich, S., Moran, P., Bebbing-ton, P., et al. (2006). Violence and psychiatric morbidity in the national household population of Britain: Public health implications. *British Journal of Psychiatry, 189*(1), 12–19.

Cole, N. S. (1973). Bias in selection. *Journal of Educational Measurement, 10*, 237–255.

Cole, N. S. (1981). Bias in testing. *American Psychologist, 36*, 1067–1077.

Coleman, J. C. (1973). Life stress and maladaptive behavior. *American Journal of Occupational Therapy, 27*, 169–180.

Coleman, M. R., Buysse, V., & Neitzel, J. (2006). Recognition and response: An early intervening system for young children at-risk for learning disabilities. Retrieved from http://www.ldonline.org.

Coles, C. D., Smith, I. E., & Falek, A. (1987). Prenatal alcohol exposure and infant behavior: Immediate effects and implications for later development. *Advances in Alcohol and Substance Abuse, 6*, 87–104.

College Board. (1999). *1999 collegebound seniors, national report.* Available at www.collegeboard.org/sat/cbsenior/yr1999/NAT/natbk499.html#income.

Collett, D. (2003). *Modeling binary data* (2nd ed.). Boca Raton, FL: Chapman & Hall/CRC.

Collins, R. L., Kashdan, T. B., & Gollnisch, G. (2003). The feasibility of using cellular phones to collect ecological momentary assessment data: Application to alcohol consumption. *Experimental Clinical Psychopharmacology, 11*(1), 73–78.

Colom, R., Flores-Mendoza, C., Quiroga, M. Á., & Privado, J. (2005). Working memory and general intelligence: The role of short-term storage. *Personality and Individual Differences, 39*(5), 1005–1014.

Colom, R., Flores-Mendoza, C., & Rebello, I. (2003). Working memory and intelligence. *Personality and Individual Differences, 34*(1), 33–39.

Colom, R., & Garcia-Lopez, O. (2002). Sex differences in fluid intelligence among high school graduates. *Personality and Individual Differences, 32*(3), 445–451.

Colvin, C. R., Block, J., & Funder, D. C. (1995). Overly positive self-evaluations and personality: Negative implications for mental health. *Journal of Personality and Social Psychology, 68*, 1152–1162.

Conklin, M. H., & Desselle, S. P. (2007). Development of a multidimensional scale to measure work satisfaction among pharmacy faculty members. *American Journal of Pharmaceutical Education, 71*(4), 61.

*Connecticut v. Teal.* (1982). 102 S. Ct. 2525.

Connolly, J. J., Kavanagh, E. J., & Viswesvaran, C. (2007). The convergent validity between self and observer ratings of personality: A meta-analytic review. *International Journal of Selection and Assessment, 15*(1), 110–117.

Constantine, M. G., & Watt, S. K. (2002). Cultural congruity, womanist identity attitudes, and life satisfaction among African American college women attending historically Black and predominately White institutions. *Journal of College Student Development, 43*(2), 184–194.

Constantino, G., & Malgady, R. G. (1999). The Tell-Me-A-Story Test: A multicultural offspring of the Thematic Apperception Test. In L. G. Gieser & M. I. Stein (Eds.). *Evocative images: The Thematic Apperception Test and the art of projection.* Washington, DC: American Psychological Association.

Constantino, G., Malgady, R. G., Colon-Malgady, G., & Bailey, J. (1992). Clinical utility of the TEMAS with nonminority children. *Journal of Personality Assessment, 59*(3), 433–438.

Cook, D. A., & Beckman, T. J. (2006). Current concepts in validity and reliability for psychometric instruments: Theory and application. *American Journal of Medicine, 119*(2), 166–167.

Cook, M. L., & Peterson, C. (1986). Depressive irrationality. *Cognitive Therapy and Research, 10*, 293–298.

Cooke, G., & Norris, D. M. (2011). Child custody and parental fitness. In E. Y. Drogin, F. M. Dattilio, R. L. Sadoff, & T. G. Gutheil (Eds.), Handbook of forensic assessment: Psychological and psychiatric perspectives. Hoboken, NJ: John Wiley & Sons. doi:10.1002/9781118093399.ch19.

Cooley, P. C., Rogers, S. M., Turner, C. F., Al-Tayyib, A. A., Willis, G., & Ganapathii, L. (2001). Using touch screen audio-CASI to obtain data on sensitive topics. *Computers in Human Behavior, 17*(3), 285–293.

Cooper, D. (1990). Factor structure of the Edwards Personal Preference Schedule in a vocational rehabilitation sample. *Journal of Clinical Psychology, 46*, 421–425.

Copple, C. E., & Succi, G. J. (1974). The comparative ease of processing standard English and black nonstandard English by lower-class black children. *Child Development, 45*, 1048–1053.

Corballis, M. C. (2011). A frontal approach to intelligence. *Brain: A Journal of Neurology, 134*(9), 2787–2790. doi:10.1093/brain/awr186.

Cordes, A. K. (1994). The reliability of observational data: I. Theories and methods for speech-language pathology. *Journal of Speech and Hearing Research, 37*(2), 264–278.

Corrigan, J. D., Bogner, J. A., Mysiw, W. J., Clinchot, D., & Fugate, L. (2001). Life satisfaction after traumatic brain injury. *Journal of Head Trauma Rehabilitation, 16*(6), 543–555.

Corrigan, P. W. (2007). How clinical diagnosis might exacerbate the stigma of mental illness. *Social Work, 52*(1), 31–39.

Cortadellas, Angel, M. (1995). Analysis of difficulties of the McCarthy Scale items for different ages and socioeconomic status [Spanish]. *Psicothema, 7*, 61–73.

Costa, P. T., Jr., & McCrae, R. R. (1985). *The NEO Personality Inventory: Manual.* New York: Psychological Assessment Resources.

Costa, P. T., & McCrae, R. R. (1992). *Revised NEO Personality Inventory (NEO-PI-R) and the NEO Five-Factor Inventory (NEO-FFI): Professional manual.* Odessa, FL: Psychological Assessment Resources.

Costa, P. T., Jr., & McCrae, R. R. (1995). Domains and facets: Hierarchical personality assessment using the revised NEO Personality Inventory. *Journal of Personality Assessment, 64*(1), 21–50.

Costa, P. T., McRae, R. R., & Jonsson, F. H. (2002). Validity and utility of the revised NEO personality inventory: Examples from Europe. In B. de Raad (Ed.), *Big five assessment* (2nd ed.) (pp. 61–72). Ashland, OH: Hogrefe & Huber.

Costa, P. T., McCrae, R. R., & Kay, G. G. (1995). Persons, places, and personality: Career assessment using the revised NEO Personality Inventory.

*Journal of Career Assessment, 76*(2), 123–139.

Costa R., Figueiredo B., Tendais I., Conde A., Pacheco A., & Teixeira C. (2010). Brazelton Neonatal Behavioral Assessment Scale: A psychometric study in a Portuguese sample. *Infant Behavior and Development, 33*(4), 510–517.

Costa, R. M. E., De Carvalho, L. A. V., Drummond, R., Wauke, A. P. T., & De Sa Guimaraes, M. (2002). The UFRJ-UERJ group: Interdisciplinary virtual reality experiments in neuropsychiatry. *Cyberpsychology and Behavior, 5*(5), 423–431.

Costantino, G., Dana, R. H., & Malgady, R. G. (2007). *TEMAS (tell-me-A-story) assessment in multicultural societies.* Mahwah, NJ: Lawrence Erlbaum Associates Publishers.

Costello, H., Moss, S., Prosser, H. & Hatton, C. (1997). Reliability of the ICD 10 version of the Psychiatric Assessment Schedule for adults with developmental disabilities (PAS-ADD). *Social Psychiatry and Psychiatric Epidemiology, 32,* 339–343.

Costello, J., & Dickie, J. (1970). Leiter and Stanford-Binet IQ's of preschool disadvantaged children. *Developmental Psychology, 2,* 314.

Cottraux, J. (2005). Recent developments in research and treatment for social phobia (social anxiety disorder). *Current Opinion in Psychiatry, 18*(1), 51–54.

Cox, D. R. (2006). *Principles of statistical inference.* Cambridge, New York: Cambridge University Press.

Craig, R. J. (2003). Assessing personality and psychopathology with interviews. In J. R. Graham & J. A. Naglieri (Eds.), *Handbook of psychology: Assessment psychology* (Vol. 10) (pp. 487–508). New York: Wiley.

Craig, R. J., & Olson, R. E. (1995). MCMI-II profiles and typologies for the patients seen in marital therapy. *Psychological Reports, 76*(1), 163–170.

Craig, R. J. & Olson, R. E. (2001). Adjective descriptions of personality disorders: A convergent validity study of the MCMI-III. *Journal of Personality Assessment, 77*(2), 259–271.

Cramer, P. (1999). Future directions for the Thematic Apperception Test. *Journal of Personality Assessment, 72,* 74–92.

Cramer, P., & Blatt, S. J. (1990). Use of the TAT to measure change in defense mechanisms following intensive psychotherapy. *Journal of Personality Assessment, 54,* 236–251.

*Crawford et al. v. Honig et al.* (1994). 37 F. 3d 485, 487.

Creamer, M., O'Donnell, M.L., Carboon,. I Lewis, V., Densley, K., McFarlane, A., Silove, D., Bryant, R.A. (2009). Evaluation of the Dispositional Hope Scale in injury survivors. *Journal of Research in Personality, 43*(4), 613–617.

Creed, P. A., Patton, W., Bartrum, D. (2002). Multidimensional properties of the LOT-R: Effects of optimism and pessimism on career and well-being related variables in adolescents. *Journal of Career Assessment, 10,* 42–61.

Crespin, T. R., & Austin, J. T. (2002). Computer technology applications in industrial and organizational psychology. *Cyber Psychology and Behavior, 5*(4), 279–303.

Crespo-Facorro, B., Barbadillo, L., Pelayo-Teran, J. M., & Rodriguez-Sanchez, J. M. (2007). Neuropsychological functioning and brain structure in schizophrenia. *International Review of Psychiatry, 19*(4), 325–336.

Cripe, L. I., Maxwell, J. K., & Hill, E. (1995). Multivariate discrimination function analysis of neurologic, pain, and psychiatric patients with the MMPI. *Journal of Clinical Psychology, 51*(2), 258–268.

Crisco, J. J., Dobbs, J. M., & Mulhern, R. K. (1988). Cognitive processing of children with Williams syndrome. *Developmental Medicine and Child Neurology, 30,* 650–656.

Crites, J. O. (1973). *Career Maturity Inventory: Theory and research handbook and administration and use manual.* Monterey, CA: CTB/McGraw-Hill.

Crites, J. O. (1974). The Career Maturity Inventory. In D. E. Super (Ed.), *Measuring vocational maturity for counseling and evaluation.* Washington, DC: National Vocational Guidance Association.

Crocker, L. M., & Algina, J. (1986). *Introduction to classical and modern test theory.* New York: Holt, Rinehart & Winston.

Crockett, D., Clark, C., & Klonoff, H. (1981). Introduction-overview of neuropsychology. In F. E. Filskov & T. J. Boll (Eds.), *Handbook of clinical neuropsychology.* New York: Wiley.

Crome, E., Baillie, A., Slade, T., & Ruscio, A. M. (2010). Social phobia: further evidence of dimensional structure. *Australian and New Zealand Journal of Psychiatry, 44*(11), 1012–1020.

Cronbach, L. J. (1951). Coefficient alpha and the internal structure of tests. *Psychometrika, 16,* 297–334.

Cronbach, L. J. (1975). Five decades of public controversy over mental testing. *American Psychologist, 30,* 1–14.

Cronbach, L. J. (1978). Black Intelligence Test of Cultural Homogeneity: A review. In O. K. Buros (Ed.), *The eighth mental measurements yearbook* (Vol. 1). Highland Park, NJ: Gryphon Press.

Cronbach, L. J. (1980). Validity on parole: How can we go straight? *New Directions for Testing and Measurement, 5,* 99–108.

Cronbach, L. J. (1989). Construct validation after thirty years. In R. Linn (Ed.), *Intelligence: Measurement, theory, and public policy.* Urbana: University of Illinois Press.

Cronbach, L. J. (1995). Giving method variance its due. In P. E. Shrout & S. T. Fiske (Eds.), *Personality research, methods, and theory: A festschrift honoring Donald W. Fiske* (pp. 145–157). Hillsdale, NJ: Erlbaum.

Cronbach, L. J., & Furby, L. (1970). How we should measure "change"—or should we? *Psychological Bulletin, 74,* 68–80.

Cronbach, L. J., & Gleser, G. C. (1965). *Psychological tests and personnel decisions.* Urbana: University of Illinois Press.

Cronbach, L. J., & Meehl, P. E. (1955). Construct validity in psychological tests. *Psychological Bulletin, 52,* 281–302.

Cronk, B. C. & West, J. L. (2002). Personality research on the Internet: A comparison of Web-based and traditional instruments in take-home and in-class settings. *Behavior Research Methods, Instruments, and Computers, 34*(2), 177–180.

Crosby, F. J., Iyer, A., Clayton, S., & Downing, R. A. (2003). Affirmative action. Psychological data and the policy debates. *American Psychologist, 58*(2), 93–115.

Crowe, S. F., Benedict, T., Enrico, J., Mancuso, N., Matthews, C., & Wallace, J. (1999). Cognitive determinants of performance on the Digit-Symbol-coding test, the Symbol Search Test of the WAIS-III, and the Symbol Digit Modalities Test: An analysis in a healthy sample. *Australian Psychologist, 34*(3), 204–210.

Crowe, T. V. (2003). Self-esteem scores among deaf college students: An examination of gender and parents' hearing status and signing ability. *Journal of Deaf Studies and Deaf Education, 8*(2), 199–206.

Cubelli, R., & Sala, S. D. (2007). What are neuropsychologists up to? *Cortex*, *43*(8), 1122–1124.

Cumella. E. J., & O'Connor, J. L. (2009). Assessing adolescents with the MMPI-A. In J. N. Butcher (Ed.), *Oxford handbook of clinical and personality assessment* (pp. 485–500). New York: Oxford University Press.

Cundick, B. P. (1985). Review of Incomplete Sentences Task. In J. V. Mitchell (Ed.), *Ninth mental measurements yearbook* (Vol. 1) (pp. 681–682). Highland Park, NJ: Gryphon Press.

Cureton, E. E., Cronbach, L. J., Meehl, P. E., Ebel, R. L., et al. (1996). *Validity*. Lanham, MD: University Press of America.

Cyranowski, J. M., Shear, M. K., Rucci, P., Fagiolini, A., Frank, E., Grochocinski, V. J., Kupfer, D. J., Banti, S., Armani, A., & Cassano, G. (2002). Adult separation anxiety: Psychometric properties of a new structure clinical interview. *Journal of Psychiatric Research*, *36*(2), 77–86.

Dahlstrom, W. G. (1969a). Invasion of privacy: How legitimate is the current concern over this issue? In J. N. Butcher (Ed.), *MMPI: Research developments and clinical applications*. New York: McGraw-Hill.

Dahlstrom, W. G. (1969b). Recurrent issues in the development of the MMPI. In J. N. Butcher (Ed.), *MMPI: Research developments and clinical applications*. New York: McGraw-Hill.

Dahlstrom, W. G., & Welsh, G. S. (1960). *An MMPI handbook. A guide to use in clinical practice and research*. Minneapolis: University of Minnesota Press.

Daini, S., & Bernardini, L. (2007). Emotional feelings in eating disorders: A Rorschach test quantitative analysis. *Journal of Projective Psychology & Mental Health*, *14*(1), 76–84.

Dale, B. A., McIntosh, D. E., Rothlisberg, B. A., Ward, K. E., & Bradley, M. (2011). Profile analysis of the Kaufman Assessment Battery for Children, Second Edition, with African American and Caucasian preschool children. *Psychology in the Schools*, *48*(5), 476–487.

D'Alessandro, D. U. (2005). *Development and validation of the child and adolescent dysfunctional attitudes scale: Tests of Beck's cognitive diathesis-stress theory of depression, of its causal mediation component, and of developmental effects*. US: ProQuest Information & Learning.

Dalessio, A. T., & Silverhart, T. A. (1994). Combining biodata test and interview

information: Predicting decisions and performance criteria. *Personnel Psychology*, *47*(2), 303–315.

Damarin, F. (1978b). Review of Cattell Infant Intelligence Scale. In O. K. Buros (Ed.), *The eighth mental measurements yearbook* (Vol. 1). Highland Park, NJ: Gryphon Press.

Dana, R. H. (2000). *Handbook of cross-cultural and multicultural personality assessment*. Mahwah, NJ: Erlbaum.

Dangel, H. L. (1970). *The biasing effect of pretest information on the MSC scores of mentally retarded children*. (Doctoral dissertation, Pennsylvania State University). (University Microfilms No. 7116,588).

Daniel, W. W. (1990). *Applied nonparametric statistics* (2nd ed.). Boston: PWS-Kent.

Dantzker, M. L. (2011). Psychological preemployment screening for police candidates: Seeking consistency if not standardization. *Professional Psychology: Research and Practice*, *42*(3), 276–283. doi:10.1037/a0023736.

Darlington, R. B. (1971). Another look at "cultural fairness." *Journal of Educational Measurement*, *8*, 71–82.

Darlington, R. B. (1978). Cultural test bias: Comment on Hunter and Schmidt. *Psychological Bulletin*, *85*, 673–674.

Darolia, C. R., & Joshi, H. L. (2004a). Psychometric evaluation of a short form of Holtzman inkblot technique. *Journal of Projective Psychology & Mental Health*, *11*(2), 124–132.

Darolia, C. R., & Joshi, H. L. (2004b). Standardization of Holtzman inkblot technique on Indian high school students. *Psychological Studies*, *49*(1), 52–58.

Das, J. P. (1973). Cultural deprivation and cognitive competence. In N. R. Ellis (Ed.), *International review of research in mental retardation* (Vol. 6). New York: Academic Press.

Das, J. P. (1987). Simultaneous and successive processes and K-ABC. *Journal of Special Education*, *18*, 229–238.

Datta, L. (1975). Foreword. In E. E. Diamond (Ed.), *Issues of sex bias and sex fairness in career interest measurement*. Washington, DC: National Institutes of Education.

Dattilo, J., Hoge, G., & Malley, S. M. (1996). Interviewing people with mental and physical complaints: The validity of the HY Scale and associated MMPI signs. *Journal of Clinical Psychology*, *42*, 754–760.

Daub, D., & Colarusso, R. P. (1996). The validity of the WJ-R, PIAT-R, and

DAB-2 reading subtests with students with learning disabilities. *Learning Disabilities Research and Practice*, *11*, 90–95.

Davidson, J. E., & Kemp, I. A. (2011). Contemporary models of intelligence. In R. Sternberg & S. Kaufman (Eds.), *The Cambridge handbook of intelligence* (pp. 58–85). New York: Cambridge University Press.

Davis, R. B. (1979). *Error analysis in high school mathematics, conceived as information processing pathology*. Paper presented at the annual meeting of the American Educational Research Association, San Francisco.

Davis, R. N. (1999). Web-based administration of a personality questionnaire: Comparison with traditional methods. *Behavior Research Methods, Instruments and Computers*, *31*(4), 572–577.

Dawes, R. M. (1999). Two methods for studying the incremental validity of a Rorschach variable. *Psychological Assessment*, *11*, 297–302.

Dawson, J. K., & Grant, I. (2000). Alcoholics' initial organization and problem-solving skills predict learning and memory performance on the Rey-Osterrieth complex figure. *Journal of the International Neuropsychological Society*, *6*(1), 12–19.

Day, D. V., & Sulsky, L. M. (1995). Effects of frame-of-reference training and information configuration on memory organization and rating accuracy. *Journal of Applied Psychology*, *80*, 158–167.

Dearborn, G. (1897). Blots of ink in experimental psychology. *Psychological Review*, *4*, 390–391.

*Debra P. v. Turlington*. (1979). 474 F. Supp. 244, 260 (M.D. Fla.).

De Corte, W., Lievens, F., & Sackett, P. R. (2007). Combining predictors to achieve optimal trade-offs between selection quality and adverse impact. *Journal of Applied Psychology*, *92*(5), 1380–1393.

Deffenbacher, J. L., Swerner, W. A., Whisman, M. A., Hill, R. A., & Sloan, R. D. (1986). Irrational beliefs and anxiety. *Cognitive Therapy and Research*, *10*, 281–292.

deGroot, A. M. (1988). Word associa-tion norms with reaction times. *Nederlands-Tiydschriftvoor-de-Psychologie-haar-Grensqebieden*, *43*, 280–296.

Dehn, M. J. (2008). *Working memory and academic learning: Assessment and intervention*. Hoboken, NJ: John Wiley & Sons.

Delery, J. E., & Kacmar, K. M. (1998). The influence of applicant and interviewer characteristics on use of impression management. *Journal of Applied Social Psychology, 28,* 1649–1669.

Delhees, K. H., & Cattell, R. B. (1971). *Manual for the Clinical Analysis Questionnaire (CAQ).* Champaign, IL: Institute for Personality and Ability Testing.

Delinsky, S. S., Thomas, J. J., Germain, S.A., Ellison C. K., Weigel, T. J., Levendusky, P. G., & Becker, A. E. (2011). Motivation to change among residential treatment patients with an eating disorder: Assessment of the multidimensionality of motivation and its relation to treatment outcome. *International Journal of Eating Disorders, 44*(4), 340–348. doi: 10.1002/eat.20809.

Delis, D. C., Filoteo, J. V., Massman, P. J., Kaplan, E., & Kramer, J. H. (1994). The clinical assessment of memory disorders. In E. Laird, S. Cermak, et al. (Eds.), *Neuropsychological explorations of memory and cognition: Essays in honor of Nelson Butters* (pp. 223–239). New York: Plenum.

Delis, D. C., Jacobson, M., et al. (2003). The myth of testing construct validity using factor analysis or correlations with normal or mixed clinical populations: Lessons from memory assessment. *Journal of the International Neuropsychological Society, 9*(6), 936–946.

Delis, D. C., Kramer, J. H., et al. (2004). Reliability and validity of the Delis-Kaplan Executive Function System: An update. *Journal of the International Neuropsychological Society, 10*(2), 301–303.

Delis, D. C., Kramer, J. H., Kaplan, E., & Ober, B. A. (1987). The *California Verbal Learning Test* (Research ed.). San Diego: Harcourt Brace Jovanovich.

Delis, D. C., Magsman, P. J., Butters, N., Salmon, D. P., Cermak, L. S., & Kramer, J. H. (1991). Profiles of demented and amnesic patients on the California Verbal Learning Test: Implications for the assessment of memory disorders. *Psychological Assessment: A Journal of Consulting and Clinical Psychology, 3,* 19–26.

Delis, D. C., & Wetter, S. R. (2007). Cogniform disorder and cogniform condition: Proposed diagnoses for excessive cognitive symptoms. *Archives of Clinical Neuropsychology, 22*(5), 589–604.

Demir, B., Batur, S., Mercan, S., & Ulug, B. (2002). Executive functions and personality profiles in early and late onset alcoholism. *Turk Psikoloju Dergisi, 17*(49), 63–76.

Deogun, J., & Spaulding, W. (2010). Conceptual development of mental health ontologies. In Z. Ras & L. Tsay (Eds.), *Advances in intelligent information systems* (pp. 265, 299–333). Berlin: Springer. doi: 10.1007/978-3-642-05183-8_13.

DeRosa, A., & Patalano, F. (1991). Effects of familiar proctor on fifth and sixth grade students' test anxiety. *Psychological Reports, 68,* 103–113.

DeRue, D. S., & Morgeson, F. P. (2007). Stability and change in person-team and person-role fit over time: The effects of growth satisfaction, performance, and general self-efficacy. *Journal of Applied Psychology, 92*(5), 1242.

*Detroit Edison Co. v. N. L. R. B.* (1979). 99 S. Ct. 1123.

Detwiler, F. R., & Ramanaiah, N. V. (1996). Structure of the Jackson Personality Inventory from the perspective of the five-factor model. *Psychological Reports, 79,* 411–416.

Devanand, D. P., Pelton, G. H., Marston, K., Camacho, Y., Roose, S. P., Stern, Y., & Sackheim, H. A. (2003). Sertraline treatment of elderly patients with depression and cognitive impairment. *International Journal of Geriatric Psychiatry, 18*(2), 123–130.

DeVellis, R. F. (1991). *Scale development: Theory and applications.* Newbury Park, CA: Sage.

DeVellis, R. F. (2003). *Scale development: Theory and applications* (2nd ed.). Thousand Oaks, CA: Sage.

DeVellis, R. F. (2006). Classical test theory. *Medical Care, 44*(11 Suppl 3), S50–59.

Devine, D., Parker, P. A., Fouladi, R. T., & Cohen, L. (2003). The association between social support, intrusive thoughts, avoidance, and adjustment following an experimental cancer treatment. *Psycho-Oncology, 12*(5), 453–462.

Devoe, E. R., & Faller, K. C. (2002). Question strategies in interviews with children who may have been sexually abused. *Child Welfare, 81*(1), 5–31.

DeWitt, M. B., Schreck, K. A., & Mulick, J. A. (1998). Use of Bayley Scales in individuals with profound mental retardation: Comparison of the first and second editions. *Journal of Developmental and Physical Disabilities, 10,* 307–313.

Diamond, E. E. (1979). Sex equality and measurement practices. *New Directions for Test and Measurement, 3,* 61–78.

Diamond, E. E., & Zytowski, D. G. (2000). The Kuder Occupational Interest Survey. In E. C. Edward Watkins, Jr., E. Vicki, L. Campbell, et al. (Eds.), *Testing and assessment in counseling practice* (2nd ed.) (pp. 263–294). Mahwah, NJ: Erlbaum.

*Diana v. State Board of Education.* (1970). C. A. No. C-70 37 RFP (N. D. Cal., filed Feb. 3, 1970).

Díaz, J. O., Abad, F. J., Ponsoda Gil, V., Aguado, D., & Díaz, J. (2011). Development, psychometric properties and new validity evidences of the web-based computerized adaptive test of English eCat. *Revista Electrónica de Metodología Aplicada, 16*(1), 50–65.

DiBello, L. V., Stout, W. F., & Roussos, L. A. (1995). Unified cognitive/ psychometric diagnostic assessment likelihood-based classification techniques. In P. D. Nichols, S. F. Chipman, & R. L. Brennan (Eds.), *Cognitively diagnostic assessment* (pp. 361–389). Hillsdale, NJ: Erlbaum.

di Blasi, F. D., Elia, F., Buono, S., Ramakers, G. J. A., & di Nuovo, S. F. (2007). Relationships between visual-motor and cognitive abilities in intellectual disabilities. *Perceptual and Motor Skills, 104*(3), 763–772.

DiCaccavo, A. (2010). All in the mind: cognitive behavioural therapy. *Psychology Review, 16*(2). ISSN 1750–3469.

Diener, E., Emmons, R. A., Larsen, R. J., & Griffin, S. (1985). The Satisfaction with Life Scale. *Journal of Personality Assessment, 49,* 71–75.

Diener, E., Sapyta, J. J., Suh, E. (1998). Subjective well-being is essential to well-being. *Psychological Inquiry, 9*(1), 33–37.

Diercke, K., Ollinger, I., Bermejo, J. L., Stucke, K., Lux, C. J. & Brunner, M. (2012). Dental fear in children and adolescents: A comparison of forms of anxiety management practised by general and paediatric dentists. *International Journal of Paediatric Dentistry, 22,* 60–67. doi:10.1111/j.1365-263X. 2011.01158.x.

Dierdorff, E. C., & Wilson, M. A. (2003). A meta-analysis of job analysis reliability. *Journal of Applied Psychology, 88*(4), 635–646.

Di Fabio, A., & Busoni, L. (2007). Fluid intelligence, personality traits and scholastic success: Empirical evidence in a sample of Italian high school students. *Personality and Individual Differences, 43*(8), 2095–2104.

Dige, N., & Wik, G. (2005). Adult attention deficit hyperactivity disorder identified by neuropsychological testing. *International Journal of Neuroscience, 115*(2), 169–183.

Dijkers, M. P. (2003). Individualization in quality of life measurement: instruments and approaches. *Archives of Physical Medicine and Rehabilitation, 84*(4 Suppl. 2), S3–S14.

Dikmen, S., & Machamer, J. E. (1995). Neurobehavioral outcomes and their determinants. *Journal of Head Trauma Rehabilitation, 10,* 74–78.

Dillard, J. P., & Marshall, L. J. (2003). Persuasion as a social skill. In J. O. Greene & B. R. Burleson, (Eds.), *Handbook of communication and social interaction skills,* (pp. 479–513). Mahwah, NJ: Erlbaum.

Dishion, T. J., Andrews, D. W., & Crosby, L. (1995). Antisocial boys and their friends in early adolescence: Relationship characteristics, quality, and interactional process. *Child Development, 66,* 139–151.

DiStefano, C., & Dombrowski, S. C. (2006). Investigating the theoretical structure of the Stanford-Binet, fifth edition. *Journal of Psychoeducational Assessment, 24*(2), 123–136.

Dixon, J. L. (1998). Concurrent validity of the Koppitz BenderGestalt Emotional Indicators among women with mental retardation. *Perceptual and Motor Skills, 86,* 195–197.

Dobko, P., & Kehoe, J. F. (1983). On the fair use of bias: A comment on Drasgow. *Psychological Bulletin, 93,* 604–608.

Doctor, R. (1972). Review of the Porteus Maze Test. In O. K. Buros (Ed.), *The seventh mental measurements yearbook* (Vol. 1). Highland Park, NJ: Gryphon Press.

Dodrill, C. B., & Warner, M. H. (1988). Further studies of the Wonderlic Personnel Test as a brief measure of intelligence. *Journal of Consulting and Clinical Psychology, 59,* 145–147.

Doerries, L. E., & Ridley, D. R. (1998). Time sensitivity and purpose in life: Contrasting theoretical perspectives of Myers-Briggs and Victor Frankl. *Psychological Reports, 83,* 67–71.

Doherty, E. M., & Nugent, E. (2011). Personality factors and medical training: A review of the literature. *Medical Education, 45*(2), 132–140. doi: 10.1111/j.1365-2923.2010.03760.x.

Dolezal, C., Marhefka, S., Santamaria, E., Leu, C. S., Brackis-Cott, E., & Mellins, C. (2011). A comparison of audio computer-assisted self-interviews to face-to-face interviews of sexual behavior among perinatally HIV-exposed youth. *Archives of Sexual Behavior,* 1–10. doi: 10.1007/s10508-011-9769-6.

Donahue, D., & Sattler, J. M. (1971). Personality variables affecting WAIS scores. *Journal of Consulting and Clinical Psychology, 36,* 441.

Donnay, D., Thompson, R., Morris, M., & Schaubhut, N. (2007). *Technical brief for the newly revised Strong Interest Inventory® assessment content, reliability, and validity.* Palo Alto, CA: Consulting Psychologist Press.

Dorans, N. J., & Drasgow, F. (1980). A note on cross-validating prediction equations. *Journal of Applied Psychology, 65,* 728–730.

Dougherty, T. W., Ebert, R. J., & Callender, J. C. (1986). Policy capturing in the employment interview. *Journal of Applied Psychology, 71,* 9–15.

Dougherty, T. W., Turban, D. B., & Callender, J. C. (1994). Confirming first impressions in the employment interview: A field study of interviewer behavior. *Journal of Applied Psychology, 79*(5), 659–665.

Douglas, J. (2002). Psychological treatment of food refusal in young children. *Child and Adolescent Mental Health, 7*(4), 173–180.

Dove, A. (1968). Taking the Chitling Test. *Newsweek, 72,* 51–52.

Downey, J., Elkin, E. J., Ehrhardt, A. A., Meyer-Bahlburg, H. F., Bell, J. J., & Morishima, A. (1991). Cognitive ability and everyday functioning in women with Turner Syndrome. *Journal of Learning Disabilities, 24,* 3239.

Drasgow, F. (1982). Biased test items and differential validity. *Psychological Bulletin, 92,* 526–531.

Drasgow, F., & Olson-Buchanan, J. (1999). *Innovations in computerized assessment.* Mahwah, NJ: Erlbaum.

Dreher, G. F., Ash, R. A., & Hancock, P. (1988). The role of the traditional research design in understanding the validity of the employment interview. *Personnel Psychology, 41,* 315–327.

Drigas, A., Koukianakis, L., & Papagerasimou, Y. (2011). Towards an ICT-based psychology: E-psychology. *Computers in Human Behavior, 27*(4), 1416–1423. doi:10.1016/j.chb.2010.07.045.

Drogin, E. Y., Dattilio, F. M., Sadoff, R. L., & Gutheil, T. G. (2011). Child

custody and parental fitness. In *Handbook of forensic assessment: Psychological and psychiatric perspectives* (pp. 443–458). Hoboken, NJ: John Wiley & Sons, Inc. doi:10.1002/9781118093399.

Dror, R., Malinger, Ben-Sira, L., Lev, D., Pick, C.G., & Lerman-Sagie, T. (2009). Developmental outcome of children with enlargement of the cisterna magna identified in utero. *Journal of Child Neurology, 24,* 1486–1492. doi:10.1177/0883073808331358.

Du, Y.B., Lee, C. T., Christinam, D., Belfer, M. L., Betancourt, T. S., O'Rourke, E. J., & Palfrey, J. S. (2011). The living environment and children's fears following the Indonesian tsunami. *Disasters,* doi:0.1111/j.1467-7717.2011.01271.x.

Duan, C., & Kivlighan, D. M., Jr. (2002). Relationship among therapist pre-session mood, therapist empathy, and session evaluation. *Psychotherapy Research, 21*(1), 23–37.

DuBois, P. H. (1966). A test-dominated society: China 115 B.C.–1905 A.D. In A. Anastasi (Ed.), *Testing problems in perspective.* Washington, DC: American Council on Education.

DuBois, P. H. (1970). *A history of psychological testing.* Boston: Allyn & Bacon.

DuBois, P. H. (1972). Increase in educational opportunity through measurement. *Proceedings of the 1971 Invitational Conference on Testing Problems.* Princeton, NJ: Educational Testing Service.

Dubowitz, H., Villodas, M. T., Litrownik, A. J., Pitts, S. C., Hussey, J. M., Thompson, R., Black, M. M., & Runyan, D. (2011). Psychometric properties of a youth self-report measure of neglectful behavior by parents. *Child Abuse & Neglect, 35*(6), 414–424.

Dunn, J. A. (1972). Review of the Goodenough-Harris Drawing Test. In O. K. Buros (Ed.), *The seventh mental measurements yearbook* (Vol. 1). Highland Park, NJ: Gryphon Press.

Dunn, L. M., & Dunn, D. M. (2007). *Peabody Picture Vocabulary Test, fourth edition (PPVT™-4).* Retrieved from http://www.pearsonassessments.com.

Dunn, L. M., & Dunn, I. M. (1981). *Peabody Picture Vocabulary Test– Revised.* Circle Pines, MN: American Guidance Service.

Dunnette, M. D. (1967). The assessment of managerial talent. In F. R. Wickert & D. E. McFarland (Eds.), *Measuring executive effectiveness.* New York: Appleton-Century-Crofts.

Dunnette, M. D. (1972). *Validity study results for jobs relevant to the petroleum refining industry.* Washington, DC: American Petroleum Institute.

Dunnette, M. D., & Borman, W. C. (1979). Personnel selection and classification systems. *Annual Review of Psychology, 30,* 477–525.

Dupue, R. A., & Monroe, S. M. (1986). Conceptualization and measurement of human disorder in life stress research: The problem of chronic disturbance. *Psychological Bulletin, 99,* 36–51.

Dush, D. M. (1985). Review of Incomplete Sentences Task. In J. V. Mitchell (Ed.), *The ninth mental measurements yearbook* (Vol. 1) (pp. 682–683). Highland Park, NJ: Gryphon Press.

Dvir, T., Eden, D., & Banjo, M. (1995). Self-fulfilling prophecy and gender: Can women be Pygmalion and Galatea? *Journal of Applied Psychology, 80,* 253–270.

Dwight, S. A., & Feigelson, M. E. (2000). A quantitative review of the effect of computerized testing on the measurement of social desirability. *Educational and Psychological Measurement, 60*(3), 340–360.

Eaton, N. K., Wing, H., & Mitchell, K. J. (1985). Alternative methods of estimating the dollar value of performance. *Personnel Psychology, 38,* 27–40.

Ebel, R. L. (1977). Comments on some problems of employment testing. *Personnel Psychology, 30,* 55–63.

Eby, M. D., Chin, J. L., Rollock, D., Schwartz, J. P., & Worrell, F. C. (2011). Professional psychology training in the era of a thousand flowers: Dilemmas and challenges for the future. *Training and Education in Professional Psychology, 5*(2), 57–68. doi:10.1037/a0023462.

Economides, A. A., & Roupas, C. (2007). Evaluation of computer adaptive testing systems. *International Journal of Web-Based Learning and Teaching Technologies, 2*(1), 70–87.

Edelstein, B. & Kalish, K. (1999). Clinical assessment of older adults. In E. John, C. Cavanaugh, E. Susan Krauss Whitbourne, et al. (Eds.), *Gerontology: An interdisciplinary perspective* (pp. 269–304). New York: Wiley.

Edelstein, K., D'Agostino, N., Bernstein, L. J., Nathan, P. C., Greenberg, M. L., Hodgson, D. C., Millar, B. A., Laperriere, N., & Spiegler, B. J. (2011). Long-term neurocognitive outcomes in young adult survivors of childhood acute lymphoblastic leukemia. *Journal of Pediatric Hematology/Oncology, 33*(6), 450–458. doi: 10.1097/MPH.0b013e31820d86f2.

Educational Testing Service. (1991). *Sex, race, ethnicity, and performance on the GRE General Test.* Princeton, NJ: Educational Testing Service.

Educational Testing Service. (2002). *GRE for educators: Interpreting scores on the GRE Analytical writing measure.* Princeton, NJ: Educational Testing Service.

Educational Testing Service. (2002). *GRE for test takers.* Princeton, NJ: Educational Testing Service.

Educational Testing Service (2007). *New verbal question type being added to computer-based general test in November 2007.* Princeton, NJ: Educational Testing Service.

Educational Testing Service (2011). About the GRE® revised General Test. Retrieved from http://www.ets.org/gre/revised_general/about.

Edwards, A. L. (1954). *Manual for the Edwards Personal Preference Sche-dule.* New York: Psychological Corporation.

Edwards, A. L. (1959). *Edwards Personal Preference Schedule.* New York: Psychological Corporation.

Edwards, A. W. F. (2003). Human genetic diversity: Lewontin's fallacy. *BioEssays, 25*(8), 798–801.

Edwards, O. W., & Oakland, T. D. (2006). Factorial invariance of Woodcock-Johnson III scores for African Americans and Caucasian Americans. *Journal of Psychoeducational Assessment, 24*(4), 358–366.

Egger, J. I., De May, H. R., Hubert, R. A., Dersen, J. J. L., van der Staak, C. P. F. (2003). Cross-cultural replication of the five-factor model and comparison of the NEO-PI-R and MMPI-2 PSY-5 scales in a Dutch psychiatric sample. *Psychological Assessment, 15*(1), 81–88.

Egger, J. I. M., Gringhuis, M., Breteler, M. A., De Mey, H. R. A., Wingbermühle, E., Derksen, J. J. L., et al. (2007). MMPI-2 clusters of alcohol-dependent patients and the relation to Cloninger's temperament-character inventory. *Acta Neuropsychiatrica, 19*(4), 238–243.

Eggly, S. (2002). Physician-patient coconstruction of illness narratives in the medical interview. *Health Communication, 14*(3), 339–360.

Ehrhart, K., & Makransky, G. (2007). Testing vocational interests and personality as predictors of person-vocation and person-job fit. *Journal of Career Assessment, 15*(2), 206–226.

Einarsdottir, S. (2002). Structural equivalence of vocational interests across culture and gender: Differential item functioning in the Strong Interest Inventory (Iceland). *Dissertation Abstracts International: Section B. The Physical Sciences and Engineering, 62,* 8B.

Eisenberger, R., & Cameron, J. (1998). Reward, intrinsic interest, and creativity: New findings. *American Psychologist, 53*(6), 676–679.

Ekman, P. (2003). *Emotions revealed: Recognizing faces and feelings to improve communication and emotional life.* New York: Times Books/Holt.

Ekman, P., Levenson, R. W., & Friesen, W. V. (1983). Autonomic nervous system activity distinguishes among emotions. *Science, 221,* 1208–1210.

Ekman, P., & O'Sullivan, M. (1991). Who can catch a liar? *American Psychologists, 46,* 913–920.

Ekren, U. W. (1962). *The effect of experimenter knowledge of subjects' scholastic standing on the performance of a task.* Unpublished master's thesis, Marquette University, WI.

El-Ansarey, B. M. (1997). The psychometric properties of NEO Five-Factor Inventory (NEO-FFI-S) based on the Kuwaiti society [Arabic]. *Derasat Nafseyah, 7,* 277–310.

Elashoff, J., & Snow, R. E. (Eds.). (1971). *Pygmalion revisited.* Worthington, OH: C. A. Jones.

El-Dib, M., Massaro, A. N., Glass, P., & Aly, H. (2011). Neurodevelopmental assessment of the newborn: An opportunity for prediction of outcome. *Brain and Development, 33*(2), 95–105. ISSN 0387-7604; doi: 10.1016/j.braindev.2010.04.004.

Elder, C., McNamara, T., & Congdon, P. (2003). Rasch techniques for detecting bias in performance assessments: an example comparing the performance of native and nonnative speakers on a test of academic English. *Journal of Applied Measurement, 4*(2), 181–197.

Elliott, C. D. (1990). *Differential ability scales.* San Antonio, TX: Psychological Corporation.

Elliot, R. (1988). Tests, abilities, race, and conflict. *Intelligence, 12,* 333–350.

Ellis, A. (1946). The validity of personality questionnaires. *Psychological Bulletin, 43,* 385–440.

Ellis, M. (2008). Race and medicine in nineteenth- and early twentieth-century America. *Social History of Medicine, 21*(1), 207.

Ellis, T. E. (1985). The hopelessness scale and social desirability: More data and a contribution from the Irrational Beliefs Test. *Journal of Clinical Psychology, 41,* 634–639.

Embretson, S. E., & Hershberger, S. L. (1999). *The new rules of measurement: What every psychologist and educator should know.* Mahwah, NJ: Erlbaum.

Emory, E. K., Tynan, W. D., & Dave, R. (1989). Neurobehavioral anomalies in neonates with seizures. *Journal of Clinical and Experimental Neuropsychology, 11,* 231–240.

Endler, N. S. (1973). The person versus the situation: A pseudo issue? A response to Alker. *Journal of Personality, 41,* 287–303.

Endler, N. S., & Hunt, J. McV. (1968). S-R inventories of hostility and comparisons of the proportions of variance from persons, responses, and situations for hostility and anxiousness. *Journal of Personality and Social Psychology, 9,* 309–315.

Endler, N. S., Kantor, L., & Parker, J. D. A. (1994). State-trait coping, state-trait anxiety and academic performance. *Personality and Individual Differences, 16*(5), 663–670.

Endler, N. S., & Magnusson, D. (1976). *Interactional psychology and personality.* Washington, DC: Hemisphere.

Endler, N. S., & Parker, J. D. A. (1990). *Coping Intervention for Stressful Situations.* Towanda, NY: Mulit-Health Systems Inc.

Endler, N. S., Parker, J. D. A., Bagby, R. M., & Cox, B. J. (1991). Multidimensionality of state and trait anxiety: Factor structure of the Endler multidimensional anxiety scales. *Journal of Personality and Social Psychology, 60,* 919–926.

Engel S. M., Wetmur, J., Chen, J., Zhu, C., Barr. D. B., et al. (2011). Prenatal exposure to organophosphates, paraoxonase 1, and cognitive development in childhood. *Environmental Health Perspectives, 119*(8). doi: 10.1289/ehp.1003183.

Epstein, J., & Klinkenberg, W. D. (2001). From Eliza to internet: a brief history of computerized assessment. *Computers in Human Behavior, 17*(3), 295–314.

Epstein, J., & Klinkenberg, W. D. (2002). Collecting data via the Internet: The development and deployment of a Web-based survey. *Journal of Technology in Human Services, 19*(2–3), 33–47.

Epstein, J., & Rotunda, R. J. (2000). The utility of computer versus clinician-authored assessments in aiding the prediction of patient symptomatolgy. *Computers in Human Behavior, 16*(5), 519–536.

Erard, R. E. (2005). What the Rorschach can contribute to child custody and parenting time evaluations. *Journal of Child Custody, 2*(1), 119–142.

Erdberg, S. P. (1969). *AIMPI differences associated with sex, race, and residence in a Southern sample.* Unpublished doctoral dissertation, University of Alabama, Birmingham.

Erdman, H. P., Klein, M. H., & Greist, J. H. (1985). Direct patient computer interviewing. *Journal of Consulting and Clinical Psychology, 53*(6), 760–773.

Erez, A., & Judge, T. A. (2001). Relationship of core self-evaluations to goal setting, motivation, and performance. *Journal of Applied Psychology, 86*(6), 1270–1279.

Ergene, T. (2003). Effective interventions on test anxiety reduction: A meta-analysis. *School Psychology International, 24*(3), 313–328.

Erickson, S. K., Lilienfeld, S. O., & Vitacco, M. J. (2007). Failing the burden of proof: The science and ethics of projective tests in custody evaluations. *Family Court Review, 45*(2), 185–192.

Erlanger, D., Feldman, D., Kutner, K., Kaushik, T., Kroger, H., & et al. (2003). Development and validation of a Web-based neuropsychological test protocol for sports-related return to play decision making. *Archives of Clinical Neuropsychology, 18*(3), 293–316.

Erlanger, D., Kaushik, T., Cantu, R., Barth, J. T., Broshek, D. K., Freeman, J. R., et al. (2003). Symptombased assessment of the severity of a concussion. *J Neurosurg, 98*(3), 477–484.

Esquivel, G. B., & Lopez, E. (1988). Correlations among measures of cognitive ability, creativity, and academic achievement for gifted minority children. *Perceptual and Motor Skills, 67,* 395–398.

ETAT: Expository text analysis tool. *Behavior Research Methods, Instruments, & Computers, 34*(1), 93–107.

Evans, D. C. (2003). A comparison of the other-directed stigmatization produced by legal and illegal forms of affirmative action. *Journal of Applied Psychology, 88*(1), 121–130.

Evans, J. H., Carlsen, R. N., & Mc-Grew, K. S. (1993). Classification of exceptional students with the Woodcock-Johnson PsychoEducational Battery–Revised. In B. A. Bracken & R. S. McCallum (Eds.), Woodcock-Johnson PsychoEducational Battery—Revised [Monograph]. *Journal of Psychoeducational Assessment,* pp. 6–19.

Evans, J. J., Floyd, R. G., McGrew, K. S., & Leforgee, M. H. (2003). The relations between measures of Cattell-Horn-Carroll (CHC) cognitive abilities and reading achievement during childhood and adolescence. *School Psychology Review, 31*(2), 246–262.

Everson, H. T., Millsap, R. E., & Rodriguez, C. M. (1991). Isolating gender differences in test anxiety: A confirmatory factor analysis of the test anxiety inventory. *Educational and Psychological Measurement, 51,* 243–251.

Ewart, C. K. (1991). Social action theory for a public health psychology. *American Psychologist, 46,* 931–946.

Ewing-Cobbs, L., Barnes, M., et al. (2004). Modeling of longitudinal academic achievement scores after pediatric traumatic brain injury. *Developments in Neuropsychology, 25*(1–2), 107–133.

Exner, J. E. (1976). Projective techniques. In I. B. Weiner (Ed.), *Clinical methods in psychology.* New York: Wiley.

Exner, J. E. (1993). *The Rorschach: A comprehensive system: Vol. 1. Basic foundation* (3rd ed.). New York: Wiley.

Exner, J. E. (1995). Narcissism in the comprehensive system for the Rorschach—Comment. *Clinical Psychology—Science and Practice, 2*(2), 200–206.

Exner, J. E. (1999). The Rorschach: Measurement concepts and issues of validity. In S. E. Embretson & S. L. Hershberger (Eds.), *The new rules of measurement.* Mahwah, NJ: Erlbaum.

Exner, J. E. (2003). *The Rorschach: A comprehensive system* (4th ed.). New York: Wiley.

Exner, J. E., Armbruster, G. L., & Viglione, D. (1978) The temporal stability of some Rorschach features. *Journal of Personality Assessment, 42,* 474–482.

Exner, J. E., & Farber, J. G. (1983). Peer nominations among female college students living in a dormitory setting. In *Workshops study 290* [unpublished]. Bayville, NY: Rorschach Workshops.

Exterkate, C. C., Bakker-Brehm, D. T., & de Jong, C. A. J. (2007). MMPI-2 profiles of women with eating disorders in a Dutch day treatment sample. *Journal of Personality Assessment, 88*(2), 178–186.

Eyde, L. D., Moreland, K. L., & Robertson, G. J. (with Primoff, E. S., & Most, R. B.). (1988, December). *Test user qualifications: A data-based approach to promoting good test use.* Washington, DC: American Psychological Association.

Eysenck, H. J. (1991). Raising IQ through vitamin and mineral supplementation: An introduction. *Personality and Individual Differences, 12,* 329–333.

Fagan, J. F. (1985). A new look at infant intelligence. In D. K. Detterman (Ed.), *Current topics in human intelligence: Research methodology* (Vol. 1) (pp. 223–246). Norwood, NJ: Ablex.

Fagundes, D. D., Haynes, W. O., Haak, N. J., and Moran, M. J. (1998). Task variability effects on the language test performance of Southern lower socioeconomic class African American and Caucasian five-year-olds. *Language, Speech, and Hearing Services in Schools, 29*(3), 148–157.

Fairburn, C. G., & Harrison, P. J. (2003). Eating disorders. *Lancet, 361*(9355), 407–416.

Fairtest (2007). Examining the GRE: Myths, misuses, and alternatives. The National Center for Fair and Open Testing. Retrieved from http://www.fairtest.org/facts/gre.htm.

Fan, X., Willson, V. T., & Reynolds, C. R. (1995). Assessing the similarity of the factor structure of the K-ABC for African-American and white children. *Journal of Psychoeducational Assessment, 13,* 120–131.

Farrell, A. D. (1989). The impact of computers on professional practice: A survey of current practices and attitudes. *Professional Psychology: Research and Practice, 20,* 172–178.

Farrell, A. D. (1991). Computers and behavioral assessment: Current applications, future possibilities, and obstacles to routine use. *Behavioral Assessment, 13,* 159–179.

Farrell, A. D. (1992). Behavioral assessment with adults. In R. T. Ammerman & M. Hersen (Eds.), *Handbook of behavior therapy with children and adults: A developmental and longitudinal perspective.* New York: Pergamon Press.

Farrell, M. M. (2001). A comparison between the UNIT and the Leiter-R with children having language impairment. *Dissertation Abstracts International 62,* 4A. (UMI No. 3010817).

Feifel, H., Strack, S., & Nagy, V. T. (1987). Degree of lifethreat and differential use of coping modes. *Journal of Psychosomatic Research, 31,* 91–99.

Feinstein, A. R., & Cicchetti, D. V. (1990). High agreement but low kappa: I. The problem of two paradoxes. *Journal of Clinical Epidemiology, 43,* 543–549.

Feldman, S. E., & Sullivan, D. S. (1960). Factors mediating the effects of enhanced rapport on children's performances. *Journal of Consulting and Clinical Psychology, 36,* 302.

Feldmann, G. M., Kelly, R. M., & Diehl, V. A. (2004). An interpretative analysis of five commonly used processing speed measures. *Journal of Psychoeducational Assessment, 22*(2), 151–163.

Felsten, G., & Wasserman, G. S. (1980). Visual masking: Mechanisms and theories. *Psychological Bulletin, 88,* 329–353.

Fenster A., Markus, K. A., Wiedemann, C. F., Brackett, M. A. & Fernandez, J. (2001). Selecting tomorrow's forensic psychologists: A fresh look at familiar predictors. *Educational and Psychological Measurement, 61*(2), 336–348.

Fenton, K. A., Mercer, C. H., McManus, S., Erens, B., Wellings, K., Macdowall, W., et al. (2005). Ethnic variations in sexual behaviour in Great Britain and risk of sexually-transmitted infections: A probability survey. *Lancet, 365*(9466), 1246–1255.

Ferrando, P. J. (1999). Likert scaling using continuous, censored, and graded response models: Effects on criterion-rated validity. *Applied Psychological Measurement, 23*(2), 161–175.

Ferrario, S. R., Zotti, A. M., Massara, G., & Nuvolone, G. (2003). A comparative assessment of psychological and psychosocial characteristics of cancer patients and their caregivers. *Psycho-Oncology, 12*(1), 1–7.

Ferro, J. M., & Madureira, S. (2002). Recovery from cognitive and behavioral deficits. In J. Bogousslavsky (Ed.), *Long-term effects of stroke* (pp. 149–181). New York: Marcel Dekker.

Feuer, M. J., National Research Council (U.S.) Committee on Equivalency and Linkage of Educational Tests, National Research Council (U.S.) Commission on Behavioral and Social Sciences and Education, & Board on Testing and Assessment. (1999). *Uncommon measures: Equivalence and linkage among educational tests.* Washington, DC: National Academy Press.

Fidler, L. J., Plante, E., & Vance, R. (2001). Identification of adults with developmental language impairments. *American Journal of Speech-Language Pathology, 20*(2). doi:10.1044/1058-0360(2010/09-0096.

Field, T., Diego, M., & Hernandez-Reif, M. (2010). Prenatal depression effects and interventions: A review. *Infant Behavior and Development, 33*(4), 409–418. ISSN 0163-6383; doi: 10.1016/j.infbeh.2010.04.005.

Field, T., Diego, M., Hernandez-Reif, M., Schanberg, S., & Kuhn, C. (2002). Relative right versus left frontal EEG in neonates. *Developmental Psychobiology, 41*(2), 147–155.

Field, T., Diego, M. A., Dieter, J., Hernandez-Reif, M., Schanberg, S., Kuhn, C., Yando, R., & Bendell, D. (2001). Depressed withdrawn and intrusive mothers' effects on their fetuses and neonates. *Infant Behavior and Development, 24*(1), 27–39.

Field, T. M. (1993). [Review of the book *Touch: The foundation of experience*]. *Contemporary Psychology, 38*(7), 735–736.

Fielding-Barnsley, R., & Purdie, N. (2003). Early intervention in the home for children at risk of reading failure. *Support for Learning, 18*(2), 77–82.

Finn, G. (2005). *Examining GRE validity with and without restricted sample range.* US: ProQuest Information & Learning.

Finn, S. E. (2011). Journeys through the valley of death: Multimethod psychological assessment and personality transformation in long-term psychotherapy. *Journal of Personality Assessment, 93*(2), 123–141.

Fish, D. D. (2001). The mechanisms of homogeneity: Individual and social structure influences on selection outcomes. *Dissertation Abstracts International, 61,* 9B.

Fish, J. M. (2002). *Race and Intelligence: Separating science from myth.* Mahwah, NJ: Erlbaum.

Fiske, D. W., & Baughman, E. E. (1953). Relationships between Rorschach scoring categories and the total number of responses. *Journal of Abnormal and Social Psychology, 48,* 25–32.

Fitts, W. H., & Warren, W. L. (1996). *Tennessee Self-Concept Scale* (2nd ed.). Los Angeles: Western Psychological Services.

Fitzgerald, C. (1997). The MBTI and leadership development: Personality and leadership reconsidered in changing times. In C. Fitzgerald, L. K. Kirby, et al. (Eds.), *Developing leaders: Research and applications in psychological type and leadership development: Integrating reality and vision, mind and heart* (pp. 33–59). Palo Alto, CA: Davies-Black.

Fitzgerald, S., Gray, N. S., & Snowden, R. J. (2007). A comparison of WAIS-R and WAIS-III in lower IQ range: Implications for learning disability diagnosis. *Journal of Applied Research in Intellectual Disabilities, 20*(4), 323–330.

Flanagan, D. P., & Alfonso, V. C. (1995). A critical review of the technical characteristics of new and recently revised intelligence tests for preschool children. *Journal of Psychoeducational Assessment, 13*, 66–90.

Flanagan, D. P., & McGrew, K. S. (1998). Interpreting intelligence tests from contemporary *Gf-Gc* theory: Joint confirmatory factor analysis of the WJ-R and KAIT in a non-white sample. *Journal of School Psychology, 36*, 151–182.

Flanagan, D. P., McGrew, K. S., & Ortiz, S. O. (2000). *The Wechsler Intelligence Scale and Gf-Gc theory: A contemporary approach to interpretation.* Needham Heights, MA: Allyn & Bacon.

Flanagan, J. C. (1954). The critical incident technique. *Psychological Bulletin, 51*, 327–358.

Flanagan, R. (1995). The utility of the Kaufman Assessment Battery for Children (K-ABC) and the Wechsler Intelligence Scales for Linguistically Different Children: Clinical considerations. *Psychology in the Schools, 32*(1), 5–11.

Flaugher, R. L. (1978). The many definitions of test bias. *American Psychologist, 33*, 671–679.

Flaugher, R. L., & Schrader, W. B. (1978). *Eliminating differentially difficult items as an approach to test bias* (RB-78-4). Princeton, NJ: Educational Testing Service.

Fleishman, E. A., & Quaintance, M. K. (1984). *Taxonomies of human performance: The description of human tasks.* Orlando, FL: Academic Press.

Fleiss, J. L. (1971). Measuring nominal scale agreement among many raters. *Psychological Bulletin, 76*, 378–382.

Fleiss, J. (1981). *Statistical methods for rates and proportions.* New York: Wiley.

Fletcher, J. M., Taylor, H. G., Levin, H., & Satz, P. (1995). Neuropsychological and intellectual assessment of children. In H. I. Kaplan & B. J. Saddock (Eds.), *Comprehensive textbook of psychiatry* (6th ed.) (pp. 581–601). Baltimore: Williams & Wilkens.

Fletcher, S. W. (1997). Whither scientific deliberation in health policy recommendations? Alice in the Wonderland of breast-cancer screening. *New England Journal of Medicine, 336*(16), 1180–1183.

Flett, G. L., & Blankstein, K. R. (1994). Worry as a component of test anxiety: A multidimensional analysis. In G. C. L. Davey & Frank Tallis (Eds.), *Worrying: Perspectives on theory, assessment and treatment* (pp. 219–239). Chichester, England: Wiley.

Flett, G. L., Endler, N. S., and Fairlie, P. (1999). The interaction model of anxiety and the threat of Quebec's separation from Canada. *Journal of Personality and Social Psychology, 76*(1), 143–150.

Florell, D. (2011). Using advancing technologies in the practice of school psychology, In T. M. Lionetti, E. P. Snyder, & R. W. Christner (Eds.), *A practical guide to building professional competencies in school psychology* (pp. 227–244). New York: Springer US. doi:10.1007/978-1-4419-6257-7_14.

Flores, G., & Tomany-Korman, S. C. (2008). Racial and ethnic disparities in medical and dental health, access to care, and use of services in US children. *Pediatrics, 121*(2), e286.

Floyd, R. G., Evans, J. J., & McGrew, K. S. (2003). Relations between measures of Cattell-Horn-Carroll (CHC) cognitive abilities and mathematics achievement across the school-age years. *Psychology in the Schools, 40*(2), 155–171.

Floyd, R. G., McCormack, A. C., Ingram, E. L., Davis, A. E., Bergeron, R., & Hamilton, G. (2006). Relations between the Woodcock-Johnson III clinical clusters and measures of executive functions from the Delis-Kaplan executive function system. *Journal of Psychoeducational Assessment, 24*(4), 303–317.

Flynn, D., Schaik, P., & van Wersch, A. (2004). A comparison of multi-item Likert and visual analogue scales for the assessment of transactionally defined coping function. *European Journal of Psychological Assessment, 20*(1), 49–58.

Flynn, J. R. (1999). Searching for justice: The discovery of IQ gains over time. *American Psychologist, 54*(1), 5–20.

Fogel, B. S., Schiffer, R. B., & Rao, S. M. (Eds.). (2000). *Synopsis of neuropsychiatry*: Philadelphia: Lippincott.

Foley, K. L., Reed, P. S., Mutran, E. J., & DeVellis, R. F. (2002). *Measurement adequacy of the CES-D among a sample of older African-Americans.* London, United Kingdom: Elsevier Science.

Folkman, S., & Lazarus, R. S. (1980). An analysis of coping in a middle aged community sample. *Journal of Health and Social Behavior, 21*, 219–239.

*Ford & Ford v. Long Beach Unified School Dist.*, 291 F.3d 1086 (9th Cir. 2002).

Forer, B. R. (1949). The fallacy of personal validation: A classroom demonstration of gullibility. *Journal of Abnormal and Social Psychology, 44*, 118–123.

Forrester, B. J., & Klaus, R. A. (1964). The effect of race of the examiner on intelligence test scores of Negro kindergarten children. *Peabody Papers in Human Development, 2*, 1–7.

Forsterling, F. (1988). *Attribution theory in clinical psychology.* New York: Wiley.

Forsyth, R. A. (1991). Do NAEP scales yield valid criterion-referenced interpretations? *Educational Measurement: Issues and Practice, 10*, 16.

Fowler, R. D. (1985). Landmarks in computer-assisted psychological assessment. *Journal of Consulting and Clinical Psychology, 53*, 748–759.

Fox, H. R. (1999). APA urges postponement of OCR resource guide on *High-stakes testing. Psychological Science Agenda, 12*, 13.

Franceschina, E., Dorz, S., & Bari, M. (2001). Computer and traditional administration of the Cognitive Behavioral Assessment 2.0. *Bollettino di Psicologia Applicata, 235*(48), 57–62.

Francis-Williams, J. (1974). *Children with specific learning disabilities* (2nd ed.). Oxford, England: Pergamon Press.

Frank, G. (1995). On the assessment of self representations and object representations from the Rorschach: A review of the research and commentary. *Psychological Reports, 76*(2), 659–671.

Frank, L. K. (1939). Projective methods for the study of personality. *Journal of Psychology, 8*, 343–389.

Franklin, R. D. (2003). *Prediction in forensic and neuropsychology: Sound statistical practices.* Mahwah, NJ: Erlbaum.

Frase, L. T., Almond, R. G., Burstein, J., Kukich, K., Sheehan, K. M., Steinberg, L. S., Mislevy, R. J., Singley, K., & Chodorow, M. (2003). Technology and assessment. In H. F. O'Neil & R. S. Perez (Eds.), *Technology applications in education: A learning view (213–244).* Mahwah, NJ: Erlbaum.

Frazer, R. A., & Wiersma, U. J. (2001). Prejudice versus discrimination in the employment interview: We may hire equally, but our memories harbor prejudice. *Human Relations, 54*(2), 173–191.

Frederiksen, C. (1969). Abilities transfer and information retrieval in verbal learning. *Multivariate Behavioral Research Monographs, 69,* 1–82.

Fredrickson, B. L. (2001). The role of positive emotions in positive psychology: The broaden-and-build theory of positive emotions. *American Psychologist, 56,* 218–226.

Fredrickson, B. L., & Joiner, T. (2002). Positive emotions trigger upward spirals toward emotional well-being. *Psychological Science, 13*(2), 172–175.

Fredrikson, M. (1991). Physiological responses to stressors: Implications for clinical assessment. *Psychological Assessment: A Journal of Consulting and Clinical Psychology, 3,* 350–355.

Freeman, F. S. (1955). *Theory and practice of psychological testing.* New York: Holt.

Freeman, H. P., & Payne, R. (2000). Racial injustice in health care. *New England Journal of Medicine, 342*(14), 1045–1047.

Freeman, L., & Miller, A. (2001). *Norm-referenced, criterion-referenced, and dynamic assessment: What exactly is the point?* United Kingdom: Pitman Publishing.

Freire, C., Ramos, R., Puertas, R., Lopez-Espinosa, M. J., Julvez, J., Aguilera, I., Cruz, F., Fernandez, M. F., Sunyer, J., & Olea, N. (2010). Association of traffic-related air pollution with cognitive development in children. *Journal of Epidemiology and Community Health, 64,* 223–228. doi:10.1136/jech.2008.084574.

Frey, B., Petersen, S., Edwards, L., Pedrotti, J., & Peyton, V. (2005). Item-writing rules: Collective wisdom. *Teaching and Teacher Education, 21*(4), 357–364.

Fried, Y., & Tiegs, R. B. (1995). Supervisors' role conflict and role ambiguity differential relations with performance ratings of subordinates and the moderating effect of screening ability. *Journal of Applied Psychology, 80,* 282–296.

Frisby, C. L. (1998). Culture and cultural differences. In E. Jonathan, H. Sandoval, E. Craig, L. Frisby, et al. (Eds.), *Test interpretation and diversity: Achieving equity in assessment* (pp. 51–73). Washington, DC: American Psychological Association.

Frumkin, R. M. (1997). Significant neglected sociocultural and physical factors affecting intelligence. *American Psychologist 52*(1), 76–77.

Fryback, D. G., Dunham, N. C., Palta, M., Hanmer, J., Buechner, J.,

Cherepanov, D., et al. (2007). US norms for six generic health-related quality-of-life indexes from the national health measurement study. *Medical Care, 45*(12), 1162–1170.

Fuchs, D., & Fuchs, L. S. (1986). Test procedure bias: A meta-analysis of examiner familiarity effects. *Review of Educational Research, 56,* 243–262.

Fuertes, J. N., & Sedlacek, W. E. (1994). Predicting the academic success of Hispanic college students using SAT scores. *College Student Journal, 28,* 350–352.

Fuller, G. B., & Vance, B. (1995). Interscorer reliability of the Modified Version of the Bender-Gestalt Test for Preschool and Primary School Children. *Psychology in the Schools, 32,* 264–266.

Funder, D. C. (1993). Judgments as data for personality and developmental psychology: Error versus accuracy. In D. C. Funder, R. D. Parke, C. Tomlinson-Keasey, & K. Widaman (Eds.), *Studying lives through time: Personality and development.* APA science volumes (pp. 121–146). Washington, DC: American Psychological Association.

Funder, D. C. (2001). Accuracy in personality judgment: Research and theory concerning an obvious question. Washington, DC: American Psychological Association.

Funder, D. C., Parke, R. D., Tomhnson-Keasey, C., & Widaman, K. (Eds.). (1993). *Studying lives through time: Personality and development.* Washington, DC: American Psychological Association.

Funder, D. C., & West, S. G. (1993). Consensus, self-other agreement, and accuracy in personality judgment: An introduction. *Journal of Personality, 61,* 457–476.

Furnham, A., & Petrides, K. V. (2003). Trait emotional intelligence and happiness. *Social Behavior and Personality, 31*(8), 815–824.

Furukawa, T., Sarason, I. G., & Sarason, B. R. (1998). Social support and adjustment to a novel social environment. *International Journal of Social Psychiatry, 44*(1), 56–70.

Gacano, C. B., & Meloy, J. R. (1994). *The Rorschach assessment of aggressive and psychopathic personalities.* Hillsdale, NJ: Erlbaum.

Gadermann, A., Guhn, M., & Zumbo, B. (2011). Investigating the substantive aspect of construct validity for the Satisfaction with Life Scale Adapted for Children: A focus on cognitive

processes. *Social Indicators Research, 100*(1), 37–60. doi:10.1007/s11205-010-9603-x.

Gaffner, D. C. & Hazler, R. J. (2002). Factors related to indecisiveness and career indecision in undecided college students. *Journal of College Student Development, 43*(3), 317–326.

Gallego, M. J., Emmelkamp, P. M. G., van der Kooij, M., & Mees, H. (2011). The effects of a Dutch version of an Internet-based treatment program for fear of public speaking: A controlled study. *International Journal of Clinical and Health Psychology, 11*(3), 459–472.

Galli, F., Pozzi, G., Frustaci, A., Allena, M., Anastasi, S., Chirumbolo, A., Ghiotto, N., Guidetti, V., Matarrese, A., Nappi, G., Pazzi, S., Quartesan, R., Sances, G., & Tassorelli, C. (2011). Differences in the personality profile of medication-overuse headache sufferers and drug addict patients: A comparative study using MMPI-2. *Headache: The Journal of Head and Face Pain, 51*(8), 1212–1227. Retrieved from http://dx.doi.org/10.1111/j.1526-4610.2011.01978.x. doi:10.1111/j.1526-4610.2011.01978.x.

Gallo, M., & Rinaldo, V. (2010). Intrinsic versus extrinsic motivation: A study of undergraduate student motivation in science. *Teaching and Learning, 6*(1).

Gallucci, N. T. (1997). Correlates of MMPI-A substance abuse scales. *Assessment, 4,* 87–94.

Galton, F. (1869). *Hereditary genius: An inquiry into its laws and consequences.* London: Collins.

Galton, F. (1879). Psychometric experiments. *Brain, 2,* 149–162.

Galton, F. (1883). *Inquiries into human faculty and its development.* London: Macmillan.

Gamble, K. R. (1972). The Holtzman Inkblot Technique: A review. *Psychological Bulletin, 77,* 172–194.

Garayzábal Heinze, E., Lens Villaverde, M., Moruno López, E., Conde Magro, T., Moura, L. F., Fernández, M., & Sampaio, A. (2011). General cognitive functioning and psycholinguistic abilities in children with Smith-Magenis Syndrome. *Psicothema, 23*(4), 725–731.

Garb, H. N., (1998). *Studying the clinician: Judgment research and psychological assessment.* Washington, DC: American Psychological Association.

Garb, H. N. (1999). Call for a moratorium on the use of the Rorschach Inkblot in clinical and forensic settings. *Assessment, 6,* 313–315.

Garb, H. N. (2007). Computer-administered interviews and rating scales. *Psychological Assessment, 19*(1), 4–13.

Garb, H. N., Florio, C. M., & Grove, W. M. (1998). The validity of the Rorschach and the Minnesota Multiphasic Personality Inventory: Results from meta-analyses. *Psychological Science, 9*, 402–404.

Garb, H. N., Wood, J. M., Lilienfeld, S. O., & Nezworski, M. T. (2005). Roots of the Rorschach controversy. *Clinical Psychology Review, 25*(1), 97–118.

Garb, H. N., Wood, J. M., Nezworski, M. T., Grove, W. M., & Stejskal, W. J. (2001). Towards a resolution of the Rorschach controversy. *Psychological Assessment, 13*, 433–448.

Garcia, H. A., Kelley, L. P., Rentz, T. O., & Lee, S. (2011). Pretreatment predictors of dropout from cognitive behavioral therapy for PTSD in Iraq and Afghanistan war veterans. *Psychological Services, 8*(1), 1–11.

Garcia, J. (1981). The logic and limits of mental aptitude testing. *American Psychologist, 36*, 1172–1180.

Garcia, N., & Fleming, J. (1998). Are standardized tests fair to African Americans? *Journal of Higher Education, 69*, 471.

Garcia, S. F., Cella, D., Clauser, S. B., Flynn, K. E., Lai, J. S., Reeve, B. B., et al. (2007). Standardizing patient-reported outcomes assessment in cancer clinical trials: A patient-reported outcomes measurement information system initiative. *Journal of Clinical Oncology, 25*(32), 5106–5112.

Garcia-Esteve, L., Ascaso, C., Ojuel, J., & Navarro, P. (2003). Validation of the Edinburgh Postnatal Depression Scale (EPDS) in Spanish mothers. *Journal of Affective Disorders, 75*(1), 71–76.

Garcia-Palacios, A., Hoffman, H., Carlin, A., Furness, T. A., & Botella, C. (2002). Virtual reality in the treatment of spider phobia: A controlled study. *Behavior & Research Therapy, 40*(9), 983–993.

Garcia-Palacios, A., Hoffman, H. G., See, S. K., Tsai, A., & Botella, C. (2001). Redefining therapeutic success with virtual reality exposure therapy. *Cyberpsychology and Behavior, 4*(3), 341–348.

Gardner, E. F., Rudman, H. C., Karlsen, B., & Merwin, J. C. (1982). *The Stanford Achievement Test: Seventh edition.* New York: Harcourt Brace Jovanovich.

Gardner, H. (1983). *Frames of mind: The theory of multiple intelligences.* New York: Basic Books.

Gardner, H. (1993). The relationship between early giftedness and later achievement. In *The origins and development of high ability* (pp. 175–186). Ciba Foundation Symposium: Vol. 178. Chichester, England: Wiley.

Gardner, H., Krechevsky, M., Sternberg, R. J., & Okagaki, L. (1994). Intelligence in context: Enhancing students' practical intelligence for school. In K. McGilly (Ed.), *Classroom lessons: Integrating cognitive theory and classroom practice* (pp. 105–127). Cambridge, MA: MIT Press.

Garfield, S. L. (2000). The Rorschach test in clinical diagnosis: A brief commentary. *Journal of Clinical Psychology, 56*, 431–434.

Garfield, S. L., & Sineps, J. (1959). An appraisal of Taulbee and Sisson's "Configurational analysis of MMPI profiles of psychiatric groups." *Journal of Consulting Psychology, 23*, 333–335.

Garlick, D. (2002). Understanding the nature of the general factor of intelligence: The role of individual differences in neural plasticity as an explanatory mechanism. *Psychological Review, 109*(1), 116–136.

Gass, C. S., & Curiel, R. E. (2011). Test anxiety in relation to measures of cognitive and intellectual functioning. *Archives of Clinical Neuropsychology, 26*(5), 396–404.

Gasser, C., Larson, L., & Borgen, F. (2007). Concurrent validity of the 2005 Strong Interest Inventory: An examination of gender and major field of study. *Journal of Career Assessment, 15*(1), 23–43.

Gasser, C. E., Larson, L. M., & Borgen, F. H. (2004). Contributions of personality and interests to explaining the educational aspirations of college students, *Journal of Career Assessment, 12*(4), 347–365. doi:10.1177/1069072704266644.

Gaston, L., Brunet, A., Koszychi, D., & Bradwejn, J. (1996). MMPI profiles of acute and chronic PTSD in a civilian sample. *Journal of Traumatic Stress, 9*, 817–832.

Gaston, M. F., Nelson, W. M., Hart, K. J., Quatman, G., & others. (1994). The equivalence of the MMPI and MMPI-2. *Assessment, 1*, 415–418.

Gati, I., & Tikotzki, Y. (1989). Strategies for collection and processing of occupational information in making career decisions. *Journal of Counseling Psychology, 36*, 430–439.

Gaudreau, P., Blondin, J. P., Lapierre, A. M. (2002). Athlete's coping during a competition: Relationship of coping strategies with positive affect, negative affect, and performance–goal discrepancy. *Psychology of Sport and Exercise, 3*(2), 125–150.

Gauvain, M. (1994). [Review of the book *The cultural context of infancy: Vol. 2: Multicultural and interdisciplinary approaches to parent–infant relations*]. *Merrill Palmer Quarterly Journal of Developmental Psychology, 40*(4), 568–572.

Gebauer, G. F., & Mackintosh, N. J. (2007). Psychometric intelligence dissociates implicit and explicit learning. *Journal of Experimental Psychology: Learning, Memory, and Cognition, 33*(1), 34–54.

Geer, J. H. (1965). The development of a scale to measure fear. *Behaviour Research and Therapy, 3*, 45–53.

Geiselman, R. E., Woodward, J. A., & Beatty, J. (1982). Individual differences in verbal memory performance: A test of alternative information-processing models. *Journal of Experimental Psychology: General, 111*, 109–134.

Geiser, S., & Studley, R. (2001). *UC and the SAT: Predictive validity and differential impact of the SAT I and SAT II at the University of California.* Available from www.ucop.edu/sas/research/researchandplanning/pdf/sat_study.pdf.

Geisinger, K. F. (1994). Crosscultural normative assessment: Translation and adaption issues influencing the normative interpretation of assessment instruments. *Psychological Assessment, 6*(4), 304–312.

Geisinger, K. F. (2003). Testing and assessment in cross-cultural psychology. In J. R. Graham & J. A. Naglieri (Eds.), *Handbook of psychology: Assessment psychology* (pp. 95–117). New York: Wiley.

Geisinger, K. F., Spies, R. A., Carlson, J. F., & Plake, B. S. (Eds.). (2007). *The seventeenth mental measurements yearbook.* Lincoln, NE: Buros Institute of Mental Measurements.

Gelman, A., & Hill, J. (2007). *Data analysis using regression and multilevel/hierarchical models.* Cambridge; New York: Cambridge University Press.

Gendreau, M., Hufford, M. R., & Stone, A. A. (2003). Measuring clinical pain in chronic widespread pain: Selected methodological issues. *Best Practices and Research in Clinical Rheumatology, 17*(4), 575–592.

Georgas, J., Weiss, L. G., van de Vijver, F. J., & Sakloske, D. H. (2003). *Culture and children's intelligence.* New York: Academic Press.

Gerken, K. C., Eliason, M. J., & Arthur, C. R. (1994). The assessment of at-risk infants and toddlers with the Mental Scale and the Batelle Developmental Inventory: Beyond the data. *Psychology in the Schools, 31*(3), 181–187.

Gesell, A. (1925). Monthly increments of development in infancy. *Journal of Genetic Psychology, 32*, 203–208.

Gesell, A., Halverson, H. M., Thompson, H., Ilg, F. L., Castner, B. M., Ames, L. B., & Amatruda, C. S. (1940). *The first five years of life: A guide to the study of the preschool child.* New York: Harper & Row.

Gibby, R. G., Miller, D. R., & Walker, E. L. (1953). The examiner's influence on the Rorschach protocol. *Journal of Consulting Psychology, 17*, 425–428.

*GI Forum et al. v. Texas Education Agency et al.* (1997). CA No. SA-97-CA1278EP.

Gilberstadt, H., & Duker, J. (1965). *A handbook for clinical and actuarial MMPI interpretation.* Philadelphia: Saunders.

Gilbert, G. E., Basco, W. T., Jr., Blue, A. V., & O'Sullivan, P. S. (2002). Predictive validity of the Medical College Admissions Test Writing Sample for the United States medical licensing examination steps 1 and 2. *Advances in Health Science Education Theory and Practices, 7*(3), 191–200.

Gillingham, W. H. (1970). An investigation of examiner influence on Wechsler Intelligence Scale for Children scores. *Dissertation Abstracts International, 31*, 2178. (University Microfilms No. 70-20, 458).

Gilpin, E. A., & Pierce, J. P. (2003). Concurrent use of tobacco products by California adolescents. *Preventive Medicine, 36*(5), 575–584.

Girotto, V., & Gonzalez, M. (2000). Strategies and models in statistical reasoning. In E. Walter Schaeken, E. Gino De Vooght, et al. (Eds.), *Deductive reasoning and strategies.* (pp. 267–285). Mahwah, NJ: Erlbaum.

Glaesmer, H., Grande, G., Braehler, E., & Roth, M. (2011). The German version of the Satisfaction with Life Scale (SWLS): Psychometric properties, validity, and population-based norms.

*European Journal of Psychological Assessment, 27*(2), 127–132. doi: 10.1027/1015-5759/a000058.

Glas, C. A. W., & Meijer, R. R. (2003). A Bayesian approach to person fit analysis in item response theory models. *Applied Psychological Measurement, 27*(3), 217–233.

Glaser, B. A., Calhoun, G. B., & Petrocelli, J. V. (2002). Personality characteristics of male juvenile offenders by adjudicated offenses as indicated by the MMPI-A. *Criminal Justice & Behavior, 29*(2), 183–201.

Gleaves, D. H., May, M. C., & Eberenz, K. P. (1996). Measuring and discriminating dissociative and borderline symptomatology among women with eating disorders. *Dissociation: Progress in the Dissociative Disorders, 9*, 110–117.

Glenn, D. M., Beckham, J. C., Sampson, W. S., Feldman, M. E., Hertzberg, M. A., & Moore, S. D. (2002). MMPI-2 profiles of Gulf and Vietnam combat veterans with chronic posttraumatic stress disorder. *Journal of Clinical Psychology, 58*(4), 371–381.

Glutting, J. J. (1989). Introduction to the structure and application of the Stanford-Binet Intelligence Scale–Fourth Edition. *Journal of School Psychology, 27*, 69–80.

Goldberg, A. L., & Pedulla, J. J. (2002). Performance differences according to test mode and computer familiarity on a practice Graduate Record Exam. *Educational and Psychological Measurement, 62*(6), 1053–1067.

Goldberg, L. R. (1974). Objective personality tests and measures. *Annual Review of Psychology, 25*, 343–366.

Golden, C. J. (1981). A standardized version of Luria's neuropsychological tests: Quantitative and qualitative approach in neuropsychological evaluation. In F. E. Filskov & T. J. Boll (Eds.), *Handbook of clinical neuropsychology.* New York: Wiley.

Golden, C. J., & Simmons, M. (2006). The relevance of the Rorschach inkblot test to modern assessment. *PsycCRITIQUES, 51*(17).

Goldman, B. A., & Osbourne, W. (1985). *Unpublished experimental mental measures* (Vol. 4). New York: Human Sciences Press.

Goldman, R. D. (1973). Hidden opportunities in the prediction of college grades for different subgroups. *Journal of Educational Measurement, 10*(3), 205–210.

Goldman, R. D., & Hartig, L. (1976). The WISC may not be a valid predictor of

school performance for primary-grade minority children. *American Journal of Mental Deficiency, 80*, 583–587.

Goldstein, D. J., Fogle, E. E., Wieber, J. L., & O'Shea, T. M. (1995). Comparison of the Bayley Scales of Infant Development–Second Edition and the Bayley Scales of Infant Development with premature infants. *Journal of Psychoeducational Assessment, 13*, 391–396.

Goldstein, G., Minshew, N. J., Allen, D. N., & Seaton, B. E. (2002). High-functioning autism and schizophrenia: A comparison of an early and late onset neurodevelopmental disorder. *Archives of Clinical Neuropsychology, 17*(5), 461–475.

Goldstein, L. H., Canavan, A. G., & Polkey, C. E. (1988). Verbal and abstract designs paired associate learning after unilateral temporal lobectomy. *Cortex, 24*, 41–52.

Golomb, B. A. (1998). Dietary fats and heart disease: Dogma challenged? *Journal of Clinical Epidemiology, 51*(6), 461–464.

Golomb, B. A., Stattin, H., & Mednick, S. (2000). *Low cholesterol and violent crime.* United Kingdom: Elsevier Science.

Gonzalez, K. (2002, June 28). *GRE general test to change format in October 2002.* Retrieved July, 28, 2003 from www.ets.org/textonly/news/ 01062801.html.

Goodman, J. (1977). The diagnostic fallacy: A critique of Jane Mercer's concept of mental retardation. *Journal of School Psychology, 15*, 197–206.

Goodman, J. (1979). "Ignorance" versus "stupidity"—the basic disagreement. *School Psychology Digest, 8*(2), 218–223.

Goodyear-Brown, P. (2011). Comprehensive and therapeutic assessment of child sexual abuse: A bridge to treatment. In P. Van Eys & A. Truss (Eds.), *Handbook of child sexual abuse* (pp. 143–170). John Wiley & Sons, Inc. doi:10.1002/9781118094822.ch7.

Gordon, B. (2004). Review of the Wechsler Preschool and Primary Scale of Intelligence, third edition (WPPSI-III). *Canadian Journal of School Psychology, 19*(1), 205–220.

Gordon, E. W., & Terrell, M. D. (1981). The changed social context of testing. *American Psychologist, 36*, 1167–1171.

Gorham, D. R., Moseley, E. C., & Holtzman, W. H. (1968). Norms for the computer-scored Holtzman Inkblot Technique. *Perceptual and Motor Skills, 26*(3), 1279–1305.

Gorman, J. (2011). Team coordination dynamics and the interactive approach: Emerging evidence and future work. In D. Schmorrow & C. Fidopiastis (Eds.), *Foundations of augmented cognition. Directing the future of adaptive systems* (pp. 298–307). Berlin: Springer. doi: 10.1007/978-3-642-21852-1_36.

Gotkin, T. D., & Reynolds, C. R. (1981). Factorial similarity of the WISC-R white and black children from the standardization sample. *Journal of Educational Psychology, 73*, 227–231.

Gottfredson, L. S. (1980). Construct validity of Holland's occupational typology in terms of prestige, census, Department of Labor, and other classification systems. *Journal of Applied Psychology, 65*, 697–714.

Gottfredson, L. S. (1994). The science and politics of race-norming. *American Psychologist, 49*, 955–963.

Gottlib, I. H., & Cine, D. B. (1989). Self report assessment of depression and anxiety. In P. C. Kendill & D. Watson (Eds.), *Anxiety and depression: Distinctive and overlapping features* (pp. 131–169). San Diego: Academic Press.

Gough, H. G. (1960). The adjective checklist as a personality assessment research technique. *Psychological Reports, 6*, 107–122.

Gough, H. G. (1987). *California Psychological Inventory, revised manual.* Palo Alto, CA: Consulting Psychologists Press.

Gough, H. G. (1995). Career assessment and the California Psychological Inventory. *Journal of Career Assessments, 30*, 101–122.

Gough, H. G. (1996). *California Psychological Inventory.* Retrieved February 2, 2003 from www.stevejudah.com/DescCalifornia.htm.

Gough, H. G., & Heilbrun, A. B., Jr. (1980). *The Adjective Checklist manual (revised).* Palo Alto, CA: Consulting Psychologists Press.

Gould, S. J. (1981). The *mismeasure of man.* New York: Norton.

Gould, S. J. (1996). The *mismeasure of man* (rev. ed.). New York: Norton.

Graham, F. K., & Kendall, B. S. (1960). Memory-for-Designs test: Revised general manual. *Perceptual Motor Skills, 11*, 147–190.

Grana-Gomez, J. L., Andreu, J. M., Rogers, H. L., & Arango-Lasprilla, J. C. (2003). Structural dimensions of the social representation of aggression. *Social Behavior & Personality, 31*(3), 223–236.

Grant, I., & Adams, K. M. (Eds.). (1996). *Neuropsychological assessment of neuropsychiatric disorders* (2nd ed.). New York: Oxford University Press.

Grant, I., & Heaton, R. K. (1990). Human immunodeficiency virustype I (HIV-1) and the brain. *Journal of Consulting and Clinical Psychology, 58*, 27–30.

Gray, J. R. (2003). Neural mechanisms of general fluid intelligence. *Nature Neuroscience, 6*, 316–322.

*GRE Guide.* (1990). Princeton, NJ: Educational Testing Service.

*GRE Guide.* (1991). Princeton, NJ: Educational Testing Service.

*GRE Guide.* (2003). Princeton, NJ: Educational Testing Service.

Greaud, V. A., & Green, B. F. (1986). Equivalence of conventional and computer presentation of speeded tests. *Applied Psychological Measurement, 10*, 23–34.

Green, B. F. (1978). In defense of measurement. *American Psychologist, 33*, 664–670.

Green, B. L., & Kenrick, D. T. (1994). The attractiveness of gender-typed traits at different relationship levels: Androgynous characteristics may be desirable after all. *Personality and Social Psychology Bulletin, 20*(3), 244–253.

Green, D. F., Jr., & Wing, H. (1988). *Analysis of job performance measurement data: Report of a workshop.* Washington, DC: National Academy Press.

Green, D. R., & Draper, J. F. (1972, September). *Exploratory studies of bias and achievement.* Paper presented at the meeting of the American Psychological Association, Honolulu, HI.

Green, K. E. (1983). Subjective judgment of multiple choice item characteristics. *Educational & Psychological Measurement, 43*, 563–570.

Green, P. (2003). Welcoming a paradigm shift in neuropsychology. *Archives of Clinical Neuropsychology, 18*(6), 625–627.

Greene, R. L. (2000). *The MMPI-2: An interpretive manual.* Boston: Allyn & Bacon.

Greenea, R. L. (2011). Some considerations for enhancing psychological assessment. *Journal of Personality Assessment, 93*(3), 198–203. doi: 10.1080/00223891.2011.558879.

Greenfield, P. M. (1998). The cultural evolution of IQ. In E. Ulric Neisser et al. (Eds.), *The rising curve: Longterm gains in IQ and related measures* (pp. 81–123). Washington, DC: American Psychological Association.

Gregory, R. J. (1999). *Foundations of intellectual assessment.* Boston: Allyn & Bacon.

Greisinger, K. F. (2003). Testing and assessment in cross-cultural psychology. In J. R. Graham & J. A. Naglieri (Eds.), *Handbook of psychology: Assessment psychology* (Vol. 10) (pp. 95–117). New York: Wiley.

Greist, J. H., Gustafson, D. H., Stauss, F. F., Rowse, G. L., Laughren, T. P., & Chiles, J. A. (1973). A computer interview for suicide-risk prediction. *American Journal of Psychiatry, 12*, 1327–1332.

Grenier, S., Schuurmans, J., Goldfarb, M., Préville, M., Boyer, R., O'Connor, K., Potvin, O., Hudon, C. & Scientific Committee of the ESA Study (2011). The epidemiology of specific phobia and subthreshold fear subtypes in a community-based sample of older adults. *Depression and Anxiety, 28*(6), 456–463. doi:10.1002/da.20812.

Gresham, F. M., McIntyre, L. L., Olson-Tinker, H., Dolstra, L., McLaughlin, V., & Van, M. (2004). Relevance of functional behavioral assessment research for schoolbased interventions and positive behavioral support. *Research in Developmental Disabilities, 25*(1), 19–37.

Greve, K. W., Bianchini, K. J., Mathias, C. W., & Houston, R. J. (2003). Detecting malingering performance on the Wechsler Adult Intelligence Scale. *Archives of Clinical Neuropsychology, 18*, 245–260.

*Griggs v. Duke Power Company.* (1971). 401 U.S. 424(a).

Grillis, A. E., & Ollendick, T. H. (2002). Issues in parent-child agreement: The case of structured diagnostic interviews. *Clinical Child & Family Psychology Review, 5*(1), 57–83.

Grim, L. G., & Yarnold, P. R. (Eds.). (1995). *Reading and understanding multivariate statistics.* Washington, DC: American Psychological Association.

Groenweg, G., Conway, D. G., & Stan, E. A. (1986). Performance of adults with developmental handicaps on alternate forms of the Peabody Picture Vocabulary Test. *Journal of Speech and Hearing Disorders, 51*, 259–263.

Groessl, E. J., Kaplan, R. M., & Cronan, T. A. (2003). Quality of wellbeing in older people with osteoarthritis. *Arthritis and Rheumatology, 49*(1), 23–28.

Groessl, E. J., Kaplan, R. M., Rejeski, W. J., Katula, J. A., King, A. C.,

Frierson, G., et al. (2007). Health-related quality of life in older adults at risk for disability. *American Journal of Preventive Medicine, 33*(3), 214–218.

Grossman, L. S., & Craig, R. J. (1995). Comparisons of the MCMI-II and 16 PF validity scales. *Journal of Personality Assessment, 64*(2), 384–389.

Groth-Marnat, G. (1999). *Handbook of psychological assessment* (3rd ed.). New York: Wiley.

Groth-Marnat, G. (2003). *Handbook of psychological assessment* (4th ed.). New York, NY: Wiley.

Groth-Marnat, G., & Shumaker, J. (1989). Computer-based psychological testing: Issues and guidelines. *American Journal of Orthopsychiatry, 59*, 257–263.

Guan, G., Tang, J., Xue, J., & Zhou, H. (2002). MMPI results of 105 patients with alcohol dependence. *Chinese Mental Health Journal, 16*(2), 116–120.

Guarnaccia, V., Dill, C. A., Sabatino, S., & Southwick, S. (2001). Scoring accuracy using the Comprehensive System for the Rorschach. *Journal of Personality Assessment, 77*, 464–474.

Gudjonsson, G. H., & Sigurdsson, J. F. (2003). The relationship of compliance with coping strategies and self-esteem. *European Journal of Psychological Assessment, 19*(2), 117–123.

Guedalia, J., Finkelstein, Y., Drukker, A., & Frishberg, Y. (2000). The use of Luria's method for the neurobehavioral assessment of encephalopathy in an adolescent: Application in a rehabilitation setting. *Archives of Clinical Neuropsychology, 15*(2), 177–184.

Guilford, J. P., & Zimmerman, W. S. (1956). Fourteen dimensions of temperament. *Psychological Monographs, 70*(10).

Guion, R. M., & Ironson, G. H. (1983). Latent trait theory for organizational research. *Organizational Behavior and Human Performance, 31*, 54–87.

Gullone, E., & King, N. J. (1992). Psychometric evaluation of a Revised Fear Survey Schedule for children and adolescents. *Journal of Child Psychology and Psychiatry and Allied Disciplines, 33*(6), 987–998.

Guthrie, R. V. (1976). *Even the rat was white: A historical view of psychology.* New York: Harper & Row.

Gutloff, K. (1999). Is high-stakes testing fair? *NEA Today, 17*, 6.

Gutman, A. (2011). Legal issues in hiring and promotion of police officers. In J. Kitaeff (Eds.), *Handbook of police psychology* (pp. 63–67). Hove, East Sussex: Taylor & Francis Group.

Guttman, L. (1950). Relation of scalogram analysis to other techniques. In S. A. Stouffer et al. (Eds.), *Measurement and prediction.* Princeton, NJ: Princeton University Press.

Guzzetta, F. (2009). Psychomotor development; the beginning of cognition, In F. Guzzetta & J. Libby (Eds.), *Neurology of the infant* (pp. 37–54). Montrouge, France: Eurotext.

Gyurke, J. S., Stone, B. J., & Beyer, M. (1990). A confirmatory factor analysis of the WPPSI-R. *Journal of Psychoeducational Assessment, 8*, 15–21.

Haberman, S. J. (2011). Use of e-rater® in Scoring of theTOEFL iBT® Writing Test. Research Report ETS RR–11-25, Educational Testing Service, Princeton, New Jersey. Retrieved from http://www.ets.org/Media/Research/pdf/RR-11-25.pdf.

Hagell, P., Whalley, D., McKenna, S. P., & Lindvall, O. (2003). Health status measurement in Parkinson's disease: Validity of the PDQ-39 and Nottingham Health Profile. *Movement Disorders, 18*(7), 773–783.

Hakel, M. D. (1986). Personnel selection and placement. *Annual Review of Psychology, 37*, 351–380.

Hale, J. B., Hoeppner, J. B., & Fiorello, C. A. (2002). Analyzing digit span components for assessment of attention processes. *Journal of Psychoeducational Assessment, 20*(2), 128–143.

Hall, V. C., Huppertz, J. W., & Levi, A. (1977). Attention and achievement exhibited by middle- and lower-class black and white elementary school boys. *Journal of Educational Psychology, 69*, 115–120.

Haller, N., & Exner, J. E. (1985). The reliability of Rorschach variables for inpatients presenting symptoms of depression and/or helplessness. *Journal of Personality Assessment, 49*, 516–521.

Hambleton, R. K. (1994). The rise and fall of criterion-referenced measurement? *Educational Measurement: Issues and Practice, 13*, 21–26.

Hambrick, D. Z., Rench, T. A., Poposki, E. M., Darowski, E. S., Roland, D., Bearden, R. M., Oswald, F. L., & Brou, R. (2011). The relationship between the ASVAB and multitasking in navy sailors: A process-specific approach. *Military Psychology, 23*(4), 365–380.

Hamel, M., Shaffer, T. W., & Erdberg, P. (2000). A study of nonpatient preadolescent Rorschach protocols. *Journal of Personality Assessments, 75*, 280–294.

Hammer, A. L., & Marting, M. S. (1985). *Manual for the Coping Resources Inventory.* Palo Alto, CA: Consulting Psychologists Press.

Hammond, S. (2006a). Multivariate data analysis. In G. Breakwell, S. Hammond, C. Fife-Schaw, & J. Smith (Eds.), *Research methods in psychology.* (pp. 414–443). Thousand Oaks, CA: Sage.

Hammond, S. (2006b). Using psychometric tests. In G. Breakwell, S. Hammond, C. Fife-Schaw, & J. Smith (Eds.), *Research methods in psychology* (3rd ed., pp. 182–209). Thousand Oaks, CA: Sage.

Hampson, E., & Kimura D. (1988). Reciprocal effects of hormonal fluctuations on human motor and perceptual-spatial skills. *Behavioral Neuroscience, 102*, 456–459.

Handel, R. W., Arnau, R. C., Archer, R. P., & Dandy, K. L. (2006). An evaluation of the MMPI-2 and MMPI-A true response inconsistency (TRIN) scales. *Assessment, 13*(1), 98–106.

Handel, R. W., Ben-Porath, Y. S., & Matt, M. (1999). Computerized adaptive assessment with the MMPI-2 in a clinical setting. *Psychological Assessment, 11*(3), 369–380.

Haney, W. (1981). Validity, vaudeville, and values: A short history of social concerns over standardized testing. *American Psychologist, 36*, 1021–1034.

Hanford, G. H. (1986). The SAT and statewide assessment: The distinction between measurement and evaluation. *Vital Speeches of the Day, 52*(24), 765–768.

Hanmer, J., Hays, R. D., & Fryback, D. G. (2007). Mode of administration is important in US national estimates of health-related quality of life. *Medical Care, 45*(12), 1171–1179.

Hansen, B. M., Dinesen, J., Hoff, B., & Greisen, G. (2002). Intelligence in preterm children at four years of age as a predictor of school function: A longitudinal controlled study. *Developmental Medicine and Child Neurology, 44*(8), 517–521.

Hansen, I., & Leuty, M. (2007). Evidence of validity for the Skill Scale scores of the Campbell Interest and Skill Survey. *Journal of Vocational Behavior, 71*(1), 23–44.

Hansen, J. –I. C. (2000). Interpretation of the Strong Interest Inventory. In E. C. Edward Watkins, Jr., E. Vicki, L. Campbell, et al. (Eds.), *Testing and assessment in counseling practice* (2nd ed.) (pp. 227–262). Mahwah, NJ: Erlbaum.

Hansen, J. C., & Campbell, D. P. (1985). *Manual for the SVIB-SCII* (4th ed.). Stanford, CA: Stanford University Press.

Hanson, M. A., Borman, W. C., Kubisiak, U. C., & Sager, C. E. (1999). Cross-domain analyses. In E. Norman, G. Peterson, E. Michael, D. Mumford, et al. (Eds.), *An occupational information system for the 21st century: The development of O*NET* (pp. 247–258). Washington, DC: American Psychological Association.

Hanson, M. A., Borman, W. C., Mogilka, H. J., Manning, C., & Hedge, J. W. (1999). Computerized assessment of skill for a highly technical job. In E. Fritz Drasgow, E. Julie, B. OlsonBuchanan, et al. (Eds.), *Innovations in computerized assessment* (pp. 197–220). Mahwah, NJ: Erlbaum.

Hanten, G., Dennis, M., et al. (2004). Childhood head injury and metacognitive processes in language and memory. *Developments in Neuropsychology, 25*(1–2), 85–106.

Hanton, S., Evans, L., & Neil, R. (2003). Hardiness and the competitive trait anxiety response. *Anxiety, Stress, & Coping, 16*(2), 167–184.

Harasym, P. H., Woloschuk, W., Mandin, H., & Brundin-Mather, R. (1996). Reliability and validity of interviewer's judgments of medical school candidates. *Academic Medicine, 71*, 540–542.

Harcourt Educational Measurement. (2002). *The Metropolitan Achievement Tests* (8th ed.). San Antonio, TX: Author.

Hardle, W., & Simar, L. (2007). *Applied multivariate statistical analysis*. New York: Springer.

Hardy, J. B., Welcher, D. W., Mellits, E. D., & Kagan, J. (1976). Pitfalls in the measurement of intelligence: Are standardized intelligence tests valid for measuring the intellectual potential of urban children? *Journal of Psychology, 94*, 43–51.

Haren, E. G. & Mitchell, C. W. (2003). Relationship between the Five-Factor Personality Model and coping styles. *Psychology and Education: An Interdisciplinary Journal, 40*(1), 38–49.

Harkness, A. R., McNulty, J. L., & Ben-Porath, Y. S. (1995). The personality psychopathology—5 (Psy5): Construct and MMPI-2 scales. *Psychological Assessment, 7*(1), 104–114.

Harlow, G., Boulmetis, J., Clark, P. G., Willis, G. H. (2003). Computer-assisted life stories. *Computers in Human Behavior, 19*(4), 391–406.

Harmon, L. W., Cole, N., Wysong, E., & Zytowski, D. G. (1973). AMEG commission report on sex bias in interest measurement. *Measurement and Evaluation in Guidance, 6*, 171–177.

Harrell, T. H., Honaker, L. M., Hetu, M., & Oberwager, J. (1987). Computerized versus traditional administration of the multidimensional aptitude battery-verbal scale: An examination of reliability and validity. *Computers in Human Behavior, 3*(2), 129–137.

Harris, D. B. (1963). *Children's drawings as measures of intellectual maturity: A revision and extension of the Goodenough Draw-a-Man Test*. New York: Harcourt, Brace, & World.

Harris, D. H. (2002). Human performance testing. In S. G. Charlton & T. G. O'Brien (Eds.), *Handbook of human factors testing and evaluation* (2nd ed.) (pp. 79–96). Mahwah, NJ: Erlbaum.

Harris, F. C., & Lahey, B. B. (1982). Subject reactivity in direct observational assessment: A review and critical analysis. *Clinical Psychology Review, 2*, 523–538.

Harris, L. M., Robinson, J., & Menzies, R. G. (2001). Predictors of panic symptoms during magnetic resonance imaging scans. *International Journal of Behavioral Medicine, 8*(1), 80–87.

Harris, M. M. (1989). Reconsidering the employment interview: A review of recent literature and suggestions for future research. *Personnel Psychology, 42*, 691–726.

Harris, W. G., Neider, D., Feldman, C., Fink, A., & Johnson, J. H. (1981). An online interpretive Rorschach approach: Using Exner's comprehensive system. *Behavior Research Methods and Instrumentation, 13*(4), 588–591.

Harrison, R. (1940a). Studies in the use and validity of the Thematic Apperception Test with mentally disordered patients: II. A quantitative validity study. *Character and Personality, 9*, 192–133.

Harrison, R. (1940b). Studies in the use and validity of the Thematic Apperception Test with mentally disordered patients: III. Validation by blind analysis. *Character and Personality, 9*, 134–138.

Hart, B., & Spearman, C. (1912). General ability, its existence and nature. *British Journal of Psychology, 5*, 51–84.

Hart, S. A., Petrill, S. A., Deckard, K. D., & Thompson, L. A. (2007). SES and CHAOS as environmental mediators of cognitive ability: A longitudinal genetic analysis. *Intelligence, 35*(3), 233–242.

Hartigan, J., & Wigdor, A. (1989). Fairness in employment testing. *Science, 245*, 14.

Hartlage, L. C., & Steele, C. T. (1977). WISC and WISC-R correlates of academic achievement. *Psychology in the Schools, 14*, 15–18.

Hartman, D. E. (1986). On the use of clinical psychology software: Practical, legal, and ethical concerns. *Professional Psychology: Research and Practice, 17*, 473–475.

Hartman, E. (2001). Rorschach administration: A comparison of the effect of two instructions. *Journal of Personality Assessment, 76*(3), 461–471.

Hartman, J. G., & Looney, M., Jr. (2003). *Norm-referenced and criterion-referenced reliability and validity of the Back-Saver Sit-and-Reach*. Mahwah, NJ: Erlbaum.

Hartung, P. J. (1999). Interest assessment using card sorts. In E. Mark, L. Savickas, E. Arnold, R. Spokane, et al. (Eds.), *Vocational interests: Meaning, measurement, and counseling use* (pp. 235–252). Palo Alto, CA: Consulting Psychologists Press.

Harty, H., Adkins, D. M., & Sherwood, R. D. (1984). Predictability of giftedness identification indices for two recognized approaches to elementary school gifted education. *Journal of Educational Research, 77*, 337–342.

Harwell, M. (1999). Evaluating the validity of educational rating data. *Educational and Psychological Measurement, 59*, 25–37.

Harwood, T. M., Beutler, L. E., & Groth-Marnat, G. (2011). *Integrative assessment of adult personality* (3rd ed.). New York: Guilford Press.

Hase, H. D., & Goldberg, L. R. (1967). Comparative validity of different strategies of constructing personality inventory scales. *Psychological Bulletin, 67*, 231–248.

Haskard, K. B., Williams, S. L., DiMatteo, M. R., Heritage, J., & Rosenthal, R. (2008). The provider's voice: Patient satisfaction and the content-filtered speech of nurses and physicians in primary medical care. *Journal of Nonverbal Behavior, 32*(1), 1–20.

Hathaway, S. R., & McKinley, J. C. (1943). *Manual for the Minnesota Multiphasic Personality Inventory*. New York: Psychological Corporation.

Hattie, J. (1980). Should creativity tests be administered under testlike conditions? An empirical study of three alternative conditions. *Journal of Educational Psychology, 72,* 87–98.

Hawkins-Gilligan, J., Dygdon, J. A., & Conger, A. J. (2011). Examining the nature of fear of flying. *Aviation, Space, and Environmental Medicine, 82*(10), 964–971.

Hawkley, L. C., Lavelle, L. A., Berntson, G. G. & Cacioppo, J. T. (2011). Mediators of the relationship between socioeconomic status and allostatic load in the Chicago Health, Aging, and Social Relations Study (CHASRS). *Psychophysiology, 48*(8), 1134–1145. doi:10.1111/j.1469-8986.2011.01185.x.

Hayes, F. B., & Martin, R. P. (1986). Effectiveness of the PPVT-R in the screening of young gifted children. *Journal of Psychoeducational Assessment, 4,* 27–33.

Hayes, J. S. (1997). Reliability and validity of the HOME preschool inventory in Jamaica. *Early Child Development and Care, 136,* 45–55.

Hayes, N., & Joseph, S. (2003). Big 5 correlates of three measures of subjective well-being. *Personality and Individual Differences, 34*(4), 723–727.

Hayes, R. D., Morales, L. S., & Reise, S. P. (2000). Item response theory and health outcomes measurement in the 21st century. *Med Care, 38* (9 Suppl), II28–42.

Haynes, S. N. (1990). Behavioral assessment of adults. In A. Goldstein & M. Hersen (Eds.), *Handbook of psychological assessment* (2nd ed.) (pp. 423–467). New York: Pergamon Press.

Haynes, S. N. (1991). Clinical application of psychophysiological assessment: An introduction. *Psychological Assessment: A Journal of Consulting and Clinical Psychology, 3,* 307–308.

Haynes, S. N. (1992). Behavioral assessment. In M. Hersen, A. Kazdin, & A. Bellack (Eds.), *The clinical psychology handbook* (2nd ed.) (pp. 430–446). New York: Pergamon Press.

Haynes, S. N. (1995). Introduction to the special section on chaos theory and psychological assessment. *Psychological Assessment, 7*(1), 3–4.

Haynes, S. N., Blaine, D., & Meyer, K. (1995). Dynamical models for psychological assessment: Phase space functions. *Psychological Assessment, 7*(1), 17–24.

Hays, M. (2004). Illustration clinique de l'observation selon la méthode de brazelton, dans une circonstance particulière d'accouchement: Processus de transformation des angoisses vitales en potentiel de lien vivant. *Neuropsychiatrie de l'enfance et de l'adolescence, 52*(3), 166–174.

Hays, P. A. (2001). Putting culture to the test: Considerations with standardized testing. In P. A. Hays (Ed.), *Addressing cultural complexities in practice: A framework for clinicians and counselors* (pp. 111–127). Washington, DC: American Psychological Association.

Hays, R. D., Brown, J., Brown, L. U., Spritzer, K. L., & Crall, J. J. (2006). Classical test theory and item response theory analyses of multi-item scales assessing parents' perceptions of their children's dental care. *Medical Care, 44* (11 Suppl 3), S60–68.

Hays, R. D., Liu, H., Spritzer, K., & Cella, D. (2007). Item response theory analyses of physical functioning items in the medical outcomes study. *Medical Care, 45*(5 Suppl 1), S32–38.

Healy, W., & Fernald, G. M. (1911). Tests for practical mental classification. *Psychological Monographs, 13*(2).

Hearst, E. (1979). One hundred years: Themes and perspectives. In E. Hearst (Ed.), *The first century of experimental psychology.* Hillsdale, NJ: Erlbaum.

Heatherton, T. F., & Wyland, C. L. (2003). Assessing self-esteem. In S. J. Lopez & C. R. Snyder (Eds.), *Positive psychological assessment: A handbook of models and measures* (pp. 219–233). Washington DC: American Psychological Association.

Heaton, R. K., & Pendleton, M. G. (1981). Use of neuropsychological tests to predict adult patients' everyday functioning. *Journal of Consulting and Clinical Psychology, 49,* 807–821.

Heiby, E. M. (1995a). Assessment of behavioral chaos with a focus on transitions in depression. *Psychological Assessment, 7*(1), 10–16.

Heiby, E. M. (1995b). Chaos theory, nonlinear dynamical models, and psychological assessment. *Psychological Assessment, 7*(1), 5–9.

Heider, F. (1944). Social perception and phenomenal causation. *Psychological Review, 51,* 358–374.

Heider, F. (1958). *The psychology of interpersonal relations.* New York: Wiley.

Heilbrun, A. B., Jr. (1972). Edwards Personal Preference Schedule. In O. K. Buros (Ed.), *The seventh mental measurements yearbook* (Vol. 1). Highland Park, NJ: Gryphon Press.

Heimberg, R. C., Keller, K. E., & Peca-Baker, T. (1986). Cognitive assessment of social-evaluative anxiety in the job interview: Job Interview Self-Statement Schedule. *Journal of Counseling Psychology, 33,* 190–195.

Heimberg, R. G. (2001). Current status of psychotherapeutic interventions for social phobia. *Journal of Clinical Psychiatry, 62*(1), 36–42.

Heimberg, R. G., & Coles, M. E. (1999). Reflections on innovations in cognitive behavioral treatments of anxiety disorders. *Cognitive and Behavioral Practice, 6*(3), 248–263.

Heinze, M. C., & Purisch, A. D. (2001). Beneath the mask: Use of psychological tests to detect and subtype malingering in criminal defendants. *Journal of Forensic Psychology, 1*(4), 23–52.

Heitzmann, C. A., & Kaplan, R. M. (1988). Assessment of measures for measuring social support. *Health Psychology, 7,* 75–109.

Heller, D., Judge, T. A., & Watson, D. (2002). The confounding role of personality and trait affectivity in the relationship between job and life satisfaction. *Journal of Organizational Behavior, 23*(7), 815–835.

Heller, K. (1971). Laboratory interview research as an analogue to treatment. In A. E. Bergin & S. L. Garfield (Eds.), *Handbook of psychotherapy and behavior change.* New York: Wiley.

Helmbold, N., & Rammsayer, T. (2006). Timing performance as a predictor of psychometric intelligence as measured by speed and power tests. *Journal of Individual Differences, 27*(1), 20–37.

Henderson, N. B., Fay, W. H., Lindemann, S. J., & Clarkson, Q. D. (1973). Will the IQ test ban decrease the effectiveness of reading prediction? *Journal of Educational Psychology, 65,* 345–355.

Henriksson, W. (1994). Meta-analysis as a method for integrating results of studies about effects of practice and coaching on test scores. *British Journal of Educational Psychology, 64,* 319–329.

Henry, P., & Bardo, H. R. (1990). Relationship between scores on developing cognitive abilities test and scores on medical college admissions test for nontraditional premedical students. *Psychological Reports, 67,* 55–63.

Henry, P., Bryson, S., & Henry, C. A. (1990). Black student attitudes toward standardized tests. *College Student Journal, 23,* 346–354.

Hensley, W. (1994). Height as a basis for physical attraction. *Adolescence, 29*(114), 469–474.

Herbert, W. (1982). Intelligence tests: Sizing up a newcomer. *Science News, 122,* 280–281.

Hermans, H., van der Pas, F. H., & Evenhuis, H. M. (2011). Instruments assessing anxiety in adults with intellectual disabilities: A systematic review. *Research in Developmental Disabilities, 32*(3), 861–870. doi:10.1016/j.ridd.2011.01.034.

Hernández-Martínez, C., Canals, J., Aranda, N., Ribot, B., Escribano, J., & Arija, V. (2011). Effects of iron deficiency on neonatal behavior at different stages of pregnancy. *Early Human Development, 87*(3), 165–169. ISSN 0378-3782; doi:10.1016/j.earlhumdev.2010.12.006. Retrieved from http://www.sciencedirect.com/science/article/pii/S0378378210007176.

Hernstein, R. J. (1981). Try again, Dr. Albee. *American Psychologist, 36,* 424–425.

Hernstein, R. J. (1982, August). IQ testing and the media. *Atlantic Monthly,* pp. 68–74.

Herrnstein, R. J., & Murray, C. A. (1994). *The bell curve: Intelligence and class structure in American life.* New York: Free Press.

Hersen, M., Kazdin, A. E., & Bellack, A. S. (1991). *The clinical psychology handbook* (2nd ed.). New York: Pergamon Press.

Hersh, J. B. (1971). Effects of referral information on testers. *Journal of Consulting and Clinical Psychology, 37,* 116–122.

Hershkowitz, I. (2002). The role of facilitative prompts in interviews of alleged sex and abuse victims. *Legal and Criminological Psychology, 7*(1), 63–71.

Hertz, M. R. (1937). Discussion on "Some recent Rorschach problems." *Rorschach Research Exchange, 2,* 53–65.

Hertz, M. R. (1938). Scoring the Rorschach Inkblot Test. *Journal of Genetic Psychology, 52,* 16–64.

Hertz, M. R. (1986). Rorschach bound: A 50-year memory. *Journal of Personality Assessment, 50,* 396–416.

Heubert, J. P., & Hauser, R. M. (1999). *High stakes: Testing for tracking, promotion and graduation.* Washington, DC: National Academy Press.

Heuchert, J. W. P., Parker, W. D., Stumpf, H., & Myburgh, C. P. H. (2000). The five-factor model of personality in South African college students. *American Behavioral Scientist, 44*(1), 112–125.

Hewitt, M. (2002). Attitudes toward interview mode and comparability of reporting sexual behavior by personal interview and audio computer-assisted self-interviewing: Analysis of the 1995 National Survey of Family Growth. *Sociological Methods and Research, 31*(1), 3–26.

Higgins, C. A. (2001). The effect of applicant influence tactics on recruiter perceptions of fit. *Dissertation Abstracts International 61,* 9A.

Higgins, E. T., & Bargh, J. A. (1987). Social cognition and social perception. *Annual Review of Psychology, 38,* 369–425.

Hill, E. F. (1972). *The Holtzman inkblot technique.* San Francisco: Jossey-Bass.

Hiller, J. B., Rosenthal, R., Bornstein, R. F., Berry, D. T. R., & Brunell-Neuleib, S. (1999). A comparative meta-analysis of Rorschach and MMPI validity. *Psychological Assessment, 11,* 278–296.

Hilsenroth, M. J., Fowler, J. C., & Padawer, J. R. (1998). The Rorschach Schizoprenia Index (SCZI): An examination of reliability, validity, and diagnostic efficiency. *Journal of Personality Assessment, 70,* 514–534.

Hinz, A., Klaiberg, A., Schumacher, J., & Brahler, E. (2003). The psychometric quality of the Nottingham Health Profile (NHP) in the general population. *Psychotherapy and Psychosomatic Medical Psychology, 53*(8), 353–358.

Hiscock, M., Inch, R., & Gleason, A. (2002). Raven's Progressive Matrices performance in adults with traumatic brain injury. *Applied Neuropsychology, 9*(3), 129–138.

Ho, D. (2005). Why affirmative action does not cause black students to fail the bar. *Yale Law Journal, 114,* 1–7.

*Hobson v. Hansen.* (1967). 269 F. Supp. 401 (D. D. C. 1967).

Hodapp, A. F., & Hass, J. K. (1997). Correlations between Wechsler Intelligence Scale for Children–III and Peabody Picture Vocabulary Test–Revised. *Psychological Reports, 80,* 491–495.

Hodges, K. (1994). Structured interviews for assessing children. *Journal of Child Psychology and Psychiatry and Allied Disciplines, 34*(1), 49–68.

Hoekstra, R. A., Bartels, M., Hudziak, J. J., Van Beijsterveldt, T. C., & Boomsma, D. I. (2007). Genetic and environmental covariation between autistic traits and behavioral problems. *Twin Research and Human Genetics, 10*(6), 853–860.

Hoekstra, R. A., Happé, F., Baron-Cohen, S. & Ronald, A. (2010). Limited genetic covariance between autistic traits and intelligence: Findings from a longitudinal twin study. *American Journal of Medical Genetics Part B: Neuropsychiatric Genetics, 153B,* 994–1007. doi:10.1002/ajmg.b.31066.

Hofer, J., & Chasiotis, A. (2011). Implicit motives across cultures. *Online readings in psychology and culture, unit 4.* Retrieved from http://scholarworks.gvsu.edu/orpc/vol4/iss1/5.

Hofer, J., & Holger B. (2011). Satisfying one's needs for competence and relatedness: Consequent domain-specific well-being depends on strength of implicit motives. *Personality and Social Psychology Bulletin, 37*(9), 1147–1158. doi:10.1177/0146167211408329.

Hofer, P. J., & Green, B. I. (1985). The challenge of competence and creativity in computerized psychological testing. *Journal of Consulting and Clinical Psychology, 53,* 826–838.

Hoff, K. (2010). Test review of the Wide Range Achievement Test 4. In R. A. Spies, J. F. Carlson, & K. F. Geisinger (Eds.), *The eighteenth mental measurements yearbook.* Retrieved from http://www.unl.edu/buros.

Hoffman, H., Loper, R. G., & Kammeier, M. L. (1974). Identifying future alcoholics with MMPI alcoholism scales. *Quarterly Journal of Studies on Alcohol, 35,* 490–498.

Hogan, J., & Quigley, A. M. (1986). Physical standards for employment and the courts. *American Psychologist, 41,* 1193–1217.

Hogarth, L., Dickinson, A., & Duka, T. (2005). Explicit knowledge of stimulus-outcome contingencies and stimulus control of selective attention and instrumental action in human smoking behaviour. *Psychopharmacology, 177*(4), 428–437.

Hogarth, L., Dickinson, A., Wright, A., Kouvaraki, M., & Duka, T. (2007). The role of drug expectancy in the control of human drug seeking. *Journal of Experimental Psychology: Animal Behavior Processes, 33*(4), 484–496.

Holaday, M., Smith, D. A., & Sherry, A. (2000). Sentence completion test: A review of the literature and results of a survey of members of the Society for Personality Assessment. *Jour-nal of Personality Assessment, 74,* 71–385.

Holahan, C. J. (1986). Environmental psychology. *Annual Review of Psychology, 37,* 381–407.

Holahan, C. J., & Moos, R. H. (1986). Personality, coping, and family support in stress resistance: A longitudinal analysis. *Journal of Personality and Social Psychology, 51,* 389–395.

Holden, C. (2003). Affirmative action. Careful use of race is OK, high court tells colleges. *Science, 300*(5628), 2012.

Holifield, J. E., Nelson, W. M., III, & Hart, K. J. (2002). MMPI profiles of sexually abused and nonabused outpatient adolescents. *Journal of Adolescent Research, 17*(2), 188–195.

Holland, J. L. (1975). *Manual for the Vocational Preference Inventory.* Palo Alto, CA: Consulting Psychologists Press.

Holland, J. L. (1985). The *Self-Directed Search: Professional manual.* Odessa, FL: Psychological Assessment Resources.

Holland, J. L. (1997). *Making vocational choices: A theory of vocational personalities and work environments* (3rd ed.). Odessa, FL: Psychological Assessment Resources.

Holland, J. L. (1999). Why interest inventories are also personality inventories. In E. Mark, L. Savickas, E. Arnold, R. Spokane, et al. (Eds.), *Vocational interests: Meaning, measurement, and counseling use.* (pp. 87–101). Palo Alto, CA: American Psychological Association.

Holland, J. L., & Gottfredson, G. D. (1976). Using a typology of persons and environments to explain careers: Some extensions and clarifications. *Counseling Psychologist, 6*, 20–29.

Holland, P. W., & Hoskens, M. (2003). *Classical test theory as a first-order item response theory: Application to true-score prediction from a possibly nonparallel test.* Washington, DC: Psychometric Society.

Holland, P. W., & Wainer, H. (1993). *Differential item functioning.* Hillsdale, NJ: Erlbaum.

Hollingworth, H. L. (1922). *Judging human character.* New York: Appleton-Century-Crofts.

Holmes, C. B., & Beishline, M. J. (1996). Correct classification, false positives, and false negatives in predicting completion of the Ph. D. from GRE scores. *Psychological Reports, 79*, 939–945.

Holt, R. R. (1967). Diagnostic testing: Present status and future prospects. *Journal of Nervous and Mental Disease, 141*, 444–464.

Holtzman, W. H., & Sells, S. B. (1954). Prediction of flying success by clinical analysis of test protocols. *Journal of Abnormal and Social Psychology, 49*, 485–490.

Holtzman, W. H., Thorpe, J. S., Swartz, J. D., & Herron, E. W. (1961). *Inkblot perception and personality.* Austin: University of Texas Press.

Hölzl, R., Kleinböhl, D., & Huse, E. (2005). Implicit operant learning of pain sensitization. *Pain, 115*(1), 12–20.

Honaker, L. M., Harrell, T. H., & Buffaloe, J. D. (1988). Equivalency of Microtest computer MMPI administration for standard and special scales. *Computers in Human Behavior, 4*(4), 323–337.

Hooper, S. R., Conner, R. E., & Umansky, W. (1986). The Cattell Infant Intelligence Scale: A review of the literature. *Developmental Review, 6*, 146–164.

Hooper, S. R., & March, J. S. (1995). Neuropsychology. In J. S. March (Ed.), *Anxiety disorders in children and adolescents* (pp. 35–60), New York: Guilford Press.

Hooper, V. S., & Mee Bell, S. (2006). Concurrent validity of the universal nonverbal intelligence test and the Leiter international performance scale-revised. *Psychology in the Schools, 43*(2), 143–148.

Hopko, D. R., Hunt, M. K., & Armento, M. E. A. (2005). Attentional task aptitude and performance anxiety. *International Journal of Stress Management, 12*(4), 389–408.

Horley, J. (2000). Measuring health: A review of "Quality of life measurement scales" (1997) (English) by A. Bowling. *Social Indicators Research, 49*(1), 115–120.

Horn, J., & Masunaga, H. (2006). In K. A. Ericsson, N. Charness, P. J. Feltovich, & R. R. Hoffman (Eds.), *A merging theory of expertise and intelligence.* New York: Cambridge University Press.

Horn, J. L. (1994). Theory of fluid and crystallized intelligence. In R. J. Sternberg (Ed.), *Encyclopedia of human intelligence* (pp. 443–451). New York: Macmillan.

Horn, J. L., & Blankson, N. (2005). In D. P. Flanagan, & P. L. Harrison (Eds.), *Foundations for better understanding of cognitive abilities.* New York: Guilford Press.

Horn, J. L., & Cattell, R. B. (1966). Refinement and test of the theory of fluid and crystallized intelligence. *Journal of Educational Psychology, 57*, 253–276.

Horn, J. L., & Noll, J. (1997). Human cognitive capabilities: *Gf-Gc* theory. In D. P. Flanagan, J. L. Genshaft, & P. L. Harrison (Eds.), *Contemporary intellectual assessment: Theories, tests, and issues.* (pp. 53–91). New York: Guilford Press.

Horney, D. J., Smith, H. E., McGurk, M., Weinman, J., Herold, J., Altman, K., & Llewellyn, C. D. (2011). Associations between quality of life, coping styles, optimism, and anxiety and depression in pretreatment patients with head and neck cancer. *Head & Neck, 33*(1), 65–71. doi:10.1002/hed.21407.

Horowitz, M. J., & Wilner, N. (1980). Life events, stress, and coping. In L. Poon (Ed.), *Aging in the eighties.* Washington, DC: American Psychological Association.

Hotelling, H. (1933). Analysis of a complex statistical variable into principal components. *Journal of Educational Psychology, 24*, 417–441, 498–520.

Houldin, A. D., & Forbes, E. J. (1990). Nursing students' personalities as measured by the California Psychological Inventory: Participants vs. nonparticipants in a program of research. *Psychological Reports, 67*, 1119–1122.

House, J. D. (1997). Predictive validity of Graduate Record Examination scores for outcomes of American Indian/Alaska Native students. *Psychological Reports, 81*, 337–338.

House, J. D. (1998). Age differences in prediction of student achievement from Graduate Record Examination scores. *Journal of Genetic Psychology, 159*, 379–382.

House, J. D. (1999). Predictive validity of the Graduate Record Examination for grades in graduate chemistry courses. *Psychological Reports, 85*(1), 41–44.

House, J. D., & Johnson, J. J. (1998). Predictive validity of the graduate record examination for grade performance in graduate psychology courses. *Psychological Reports, 82*, 1235–1238.

House, J. D., & Keeley, E. J. (1995). Gender bias in prediction of graduate grade performance from Miller Analogies Test scores. *Journal of Psychology, 129*, 353–355.

House, J. D., & Keeley, E. J. (1996). Differential prediction of adult student performance from Miller Analogies Test scores. *Journal of Genetic Psychology, 157*, 501–503.

Howard, J. L., & Ferris, G. R. (1996). The employment interview context: Social and situational influences on interviewer decisions. *Journal of Applied Social Psychology, 26*, 112–136.

Howell, D. (2008). *Fundamental statistics for the behavioral sciences* (6th ed.). Belmont, CA: Wadsworth.

Hsieh, F., Ferrer, E., Chen, S., Mauss, I. B., John, O., & Gross, J. J. (2011). A network approach for evaluating coherence in multivariate systems: An application to psychophysiological emotion data. *Psychometrika, 76*(1), 124–152, doi:10.1007/s11336-010-9194-0.

Hu, C., Cui, Z., Dai, X., Chen, X., Gao, B., Hou, Y., & Guan, Y. (2002). Coping style, mental health status, and personality of policemen. *Chinese Mental Health Journal, 16*(9), 642–643.

Huang, C., & Dong, N., (2011). Factor structures of the Rosenberg Self-Esteem Scale: A meta-analysis of pattern matrices. *European Journal of Psychological Assessment*, 1–7. http://www.psycontent.com/content/y7r153tg271h216n/?referencesMode=Show.

Huang, C. D., Church, A. T., & Katigbak, M. S. (1997). Identifying cultural differences in items and traits: Differential item functioning in the NEO Personality Inventory. *Journal of Cross-Cultural Psychology, 28*, 192–218.

Hubbs-Tait, L., Culp, A. M., Culp, R. E., & Miller, C. E. (2002). Relation of maternal cognitive stimulation, emotional support, and intrusive behavior during Head Start to children's kindergarten cognitive abilities. *Child Development, 73*(1), 110–131.

Huffcutt, A. I., Conway, J. M., Roth, P. L., & Stone, N. (2001). Identification and meta-analytic assessment of psychological constructs measured in employment interviews. *Journal of Applied Psychology, 86*(5), 897–913.

Huffcutt, A. I., & Roth, P. L. (1998). Racial group differences in employment interview evaluations. *Journal of Applied Psychology, 83*, 179–189.

Huffcutt, A. I., Roth, P. L., & McDaniel, M. A. (1996). A meta-analytic investigation of cognitive ability in employment interview evaluations: Moderating characteristics and implications for incremental validity. *Journal of Applied Psychology, 81*, 459–473.

Huffcutt, A., & Youngcourt, S. (2007). Employment interviews. In D. Whetzel, & G. Wheaton (Eds.), *Applied measurement: Industrial psychology in human resources management.* (pp. 181–200). Mahwah, NJ: Routledge.

Hugh, H. V. (1981). The interviewing computer: A technology for gathering comprehensive treatment information. *Behavior Research Methods and Instrumentation. 13*(4), 607–612.

Huibregtse, I., Admiraal, W., & Meara, P. (2002). *Scores on a yes-no vocabulary test: Correction for guessing and response style.* London, United Kingdom: Hodder Arnold.

Humphreys, K. L., Foley, K. M., Feinstein, B. A., Marx, B. P., Kaloupek, D. G., & Keane, T. M. (2011). The influence of externalizing comorbidity on psychophysiological reactivity among veterans with posttraumatic stress disorder. *Psychological Trauma: Theory, Research, Practice, and Policy.* Retrieved from http://psycnet.apa.org/psycinfo/2011-06225-001/. doi:10.1037/a0022644.

Hunsley, J., & Bailey, J. M. (1999). The clinical utility of the Rorschach: Unfulfilled promises and an uncertain future. *Psychological Assessment, 11*, 266–277.

Hunsley, J., & Bailey, J. M. (2001). Whither the Rorschach? An analysis of the evidence. *Psychological Assessment, 13*, 472–485.

Hunsley, J., & DiGiulio, G. (2001). Norms, norming, and clinical assessment. *Clinical Psychology: Science and Practice, 8*, 378–382.

Hunt, E. (1980). Intelligence as an information-processing concept. *British Journal of Psychology, 71*, 449–474.

Hunt, T. V. (1978). Review of McCarthy Scales of Children's Abilities. In O. K. Buros (Ed.), *The eighth mental measurements yearbook* (Vol. 1). Highland Park, NJ: Gryphon Press.

Hunter, J. E., & Schmidt, F. L. (1976). Critical analysis of statistical and ethical implications of various definitions of test bias. *Psychological Bulletin, 83*, 1053–1071.

Hunter, J. E., & Schmidt, F. L. (1978). Bias in defining test bias: Reply to Darlington. *Psychological Bulletin, 85*, 675–676.

Huprich, S. K. (2003). Evaluating the NEO Personality Inventory-Revised profiles in veterans with personality disorders. *Journal of Personality Disorders, 17*(1), 33–44.

Hurlburt, R. T. (2003). *Comprehending behavioral statistics* (3rd ed.). Belmont, CA: Wadsworth.

Hursh, D. (2005). The growth of high-stakes testing in the USA: Accountability, markets and the decline of educational quality. *British Educational Research Journal, 31*(5), 605–622.

Hurt, S. W., Reznikoff, M., & Clarkin, J. F. (1995). The Rorschach. In L. E. Beutler & M. R. Berren (Eds.), *Integrative assessment of adult personality* (pp. 187–205). New York: Guilford Press.

Iacoboni, M., & Mazziotta, J. C. (2007). Mirror neuron system: Basic findings and clinical applications. *Annals of Neurology, 62*(3), 213–218.

Iacono, W. G. (1991). Psychophysiological assessment of psychopathology. *Psychological Assessment: Journal of Consulting and Clinical Psychology, 3*, 309–320.

Imada, A. S., & Hakel, M. D. (1977). Influences of nonverbal communication and rater proximity on impressions and decisions in simulated employment interviews. *Journal of Applied Psychology, 62*, 295–300.

Impara, J. C., Plake, B. S., & Murphy, L. L. (1998). *The thirteenth mental measurements yearbook.* Lincoln, NE: Buros Institute of Mental Measurements.

Ingman, K. A., Ollendick, T. H., & Akande, A. (1999). Cross-cultural aspects of fears in African children and adolescents. *Behaviour Research and Therapy, 37*, 337–345.

Ingram, F., Caroselli, J., Robinson, H., Hetzel, R. D., Reed, K., & Masel, B. E. (1998). The PPVT-R: Validity as a quick screen of intelligence in a postacute rehabilitation setting for brain-injured adults. *Journal of Clinical Psychology, 54*, 877–884.

Ingram, R. E. (1980). *The GREs: Are we weighing them too heavily in graduate psychology admissions?* Unpublished manuscript, University of Kansas, Lawrence.

Institute for Applied Psychometrics. (2003). Current research projects. Retrieved July 31, 2003, from iapsych.com.

Insurance license exams will be revised. (1984, November 29). *Los Angeles Times*, Part 1, p. 5.

Ironson, G. H., & Sebkovial, N. J. (1979). A comparison of several methods for assessing item bias. *Journal of Educational Measurement, 16*, 209–225.

Iverson, G. L., Franzen, M. D., & Hammond, J. A. (1995). Examination of inmates' ability to malinger on the MMPI-2. *Psychological Assessment, 7*(1), 118–121.

Iwata, N., Mishima, N., Shimizu, T., Mizoue, T., Fukuhara, M., Hidano, T., & Spielberger, C. D. (1998). Positive and negative affect in the factor structure of the state-trait anxiety inventory for Japanese workers. *Psychological Reports, 82*(2), 651–656.

Jaccard, J., & Wan, C. K. (1995). Measurement error in the analysis of interaction effects between continuous predictors using multiple regression: Multiple indicator and structural equation approaches. *Psychological Bulletin, 117*(2), 348–357.

Jackson, D. N. (1967). *Personality Research Form Manual.* Goshen, NY: Research Psychologists Press.

Jackson, D. N. (1976a). *Jackson Personality Inventory.* Goshen, NY: Research Psychologists Press.

Jackson, D. N. (1976b). *Manual for the Jackson Personality Inventory.* Goshen, NY: Research Psychologists Press.

Jackson, D. N. (1997). *Jackson Personality Inventory–Revised.* London Ontario: Sigma Assessment Systems.

Jackson, D. N. (2002). *The constructs in people's heads.* Mahwah, NJ: Erlbaum.

Jackson, D. N., & Livesley, W. J. (1995). Possible contributions from personality assessment to the classification of personality disorders. In W. J. Livesley (Ed.), *The DSM-IV personality disorders: Diagnosis and treatment of mental disorders* (pp. 459–481). New York: Guilford Press.

Jackson, D. N., & Messick, S. (Eds.). (1967). *Problems in human assessment.* New York: McGraw-Hill.

Jackson, D. N., Paunonen, S. V., Fraboni, M., & Goffin, R. D. (1996). A five-factor versus six-factor model of personality structure. *Personality and Individual Differences, 20,* 33–45.

Jackson, E. W. (1980). Identification of gifted performance in young children. In W. C. Roedell, N. E. Jackson, & H. B. Robinson (Eds.), *Gifted young children.* New York: Teachers College Press.

Jacob, B. A. (2001). Getting tough, the impact of high school graduation exams. *Educational Evaluation, 23*(2), 99–121.

Jacobs, R. R., Conte, J. M., Day, D. V., Silva, J. M., et al. (1996). Selecting bus drivers: Multiple predictors, multiple perspectives on validity, and multiple estimates of utility. *Human Performance 9*(3), 199–217.

Jacobson, M. W., Bondi, M. W., & Salmon, D. P. (2002). Do neuropsychological tests detect preclinical Alzheimer's disease: Individual test versus cognitive discrepancy score analysis. *Neuropsychology, 16*(2).

Jacobson, M. W., Delis, D. C., & Bondi, M. W. (2002). Do neuropsychological tests detect preclinical Alzheimer's disease: Individual-test versus cognitive score analyses. *Neuropsychology, 16*(2), 132–139.

Jamieson, S. (2004). Likert scales: How to (ab)use them. *Medical Education, 38*(2), 1117–1118.

Janowsky, D. S., Morte, S., & Hong, L. (2002). Relationship of Myers-Briggs type indicator personality characteristics to suicidality in affective disorder patients. *Journal of Psychiatric Research, 36*(1), 33–39.

Janssen, A. J., Akkermans, R. P., Steiner, K., de Haes, O., Oostendorp, R., Kollée, L., & Nijhuis-van der Sanden, M. (2011). Unstable longitudinal motor performance in preterm infants from 6 to 24 months on the Bayley Scales of Infant Development—Second Edition. *Research in Developmental Disabilities, 32*(5)1902–1909. ISSN 0891-4222; doi:10.1016/j.ridd.2011.03.026.

Janssen, E. (2002). Psychophysiological measurement of sexual arousal. In M. W. Wiederman & B. E. Whitley, Jr. (Eds.), *Handbook for conducting research on human sexuality* (139–171). Mahwah, NJ: Erlbaum.

Janssen, E., Everaerd, W., Vanlunsen, R. H. W., & Oerlemans, S. (1994). Validation of a psychophysiological Waking Erectile Assessment (WEA) for the diagnosis of Male Erectile Disorder. *Urology, 43*(5), 686–695.

Jeanneret, P. R., Borman, W. C., Kubisiak, U. C., & Hanson, M. A. (1999). Generalized work activities. In E. Norman, G. Peterson, E. Michael, D. Mumford, et al. (Eds.), *An occupational information system for the 21st century: The development of O*NET* (pp. 105–125). Washington, DC: American Psychological Association.

Jennings, J. R. (1986). Bodily changes during attention. In M. G. H. Coles, E. Donchin, & S. W. Porges (Eds.), *Psychophysiology: Systems, processes, and applications.* New York: Guilford Press.

Jensen, A. R. (1969). How much can we boost IQ and scholastic achievement? *Harvard Educational Review, 39,* 1–23.

Jensen, A. R. (1972). *Genetics and education.* New York: Harper & Row.

Jensen, A. R. (1979). g—Outmoded theory or unconquered frontier? *Creative Science and Technology, 2,* 16–29.

Jensen, A. R. (1980). *Bias in mental testing.* New York: Free Press.

Jensen, A. R. (1982). Reaction time and psychometric "g." In H. J. Eysenck (Ed.), *A model for intelligence.* New York: Springer-Verlag.

Jensen, A. R. (1984). The black-white difference on the K-ABC: Implication for future tests. *Journal of Special Education, 18,* 377–408.

Jensen, A. R. (1985). The nature of black-white differences on various psychometric tests: Spearman's hypothesis. *Behavioral and Brain Sciences, 8,* 193–263.

Jensen, A. R. (1986). The "g" beyond factor analysis. In J. C. Conoley, J. A. Glover, & R. R. Ronnings (Eds.), *The influence of cognitive psychology on testing and measurement.* Hillsdale, NJ: Erlbaum.

Jensen, A. R., & Munro, E. (1979). Reaction time, movement time, and intelligence. *Intelligence, 3,* 121–126.

Jensen, C. L., Voigt, R. G., Llorente, A. M., Peters, S. U., Prager, T. C., Zou, Y. L., Rozelle, J. C., Turcich, M. R., Fraley, J. K., Anderson, R. E., & Heird, W. C. (2010). Effects of early maternal docosahexaenoic acid intake on neuropsychological status and visual acuity at five years of age of breast-fed term infants. *Journal of Pediatrics, 157*(6), 900–905. ISSN 0022-3476; doi:10.1016/j.jpeds.2010.06.006.

Jerusalem, M., & Schwarzer, R. (1992). *Self-efficacy: Thought control of action.* Washington, DC: Hemisphere.

Ji, C. C. (1998). Predictive validity of the Graduate Record Examination in education. *Psychological Reports, 82,* 899–904.

Jing, G., Deqing, T., & Longhui, L. (2001). Visual-motor deficits in children with learning disabilities. *Chinese Mental Health Journal, 15*(6), 388–390.

Johansson, C. B. (1976). *Manual for the Career Assessment Inventory.* Minneapolis, MN: National Computer Systems.

Johansson, C. B., & Johansson, J. C. (1978). *Manual supplement for the Career Assessment Inventory.* Minneapolis, MN: National Computer Systems.

Johansson, G., Johnson, J. V., & Hall, E. M. (1991). Smoking and sedentary behavior as related to work organization. *Social Science and Medicine, 32*(7), 837–846.

Johnson, J. H., Null, C., Butcher, J. N., & Johnson, K. N. (1984). Replicated items level factor analysis of the full MMPI. *Journal of Personality and Social Psychology, 47,* 105–114.

Johnson, J. L. (1994). The Thematic Apperception Test and Alzheimer's

Disease. *Journal of Personality Assessment, 62*(2), 314–319.

Johnson, M. R. (2003). Neonatal assessment. In T. H. Ollendick & C. S. Schroeder (Eds.), *Encyclopedia of clinical child and pediatric psychology* (pp. 400–402). New York: Plenum Publishers.

Johnson, N. E., Saccuzzo, D. P., Larson, G. E., Guertin, T. L., Christianson, L., & Longley, S. (1993). *The San Diego Test of Reasoning Ability (S. A. N. T. R. A.).* [Available from N. E. Johnson, Ph. D., & D. P. Saccuzzo, Ph. D., 6363 Alvarado Court, Suite 103; San Diego, CA 92120–4913]

Johnstone, B., Holland, D., & Larimore, C. (2000). Language and academic abilities. In G. Groth-Marnat (Ed.), *Neuropsychological assessment in clinical practice: A guide to test interpretation and integration* (pp. 335–354). New York: Wiley.

Jones, E. E., & Nisbett, R. E. (1971). *The actor and observer: Divergent perceptions of the causes of behavior.* Morristown, NJ: General Learning Press.

Jones, P. W., & Kaplan, R. M. (2003). Methodological issues in evaluating measures of health as outcomes for COPD. *European Respiration Journal Supplement, 41,* 13s–18s.

Jones, R. A. (1968). *A factored measure of Ellis' irrational belief system with personality and maladjustment correlates.* Unpublished doctoral dissertation, Texas Technological College, Lubbock.

Jones, R. N. (2003). Racial bias in the assessment of cognitive functioning of older adults. *Aging and Mental Health, 7*(2), 83–102.

Joy, S., Kaplan, E., & Fein, D. (2004). Speed and memory in the WAIS-III digit symbol–coding subtest across the adult lifespan. *Archives of Clinical Neuropsychology, 19*(6), 759–767.

Judge, T. A., & Bono, J. E. (2000). Five factor model of personality and transformational leadership. *Journal of Applied Psychology, 85*(5), 751–765.

Judge, T. A., & Bono, J. E. (2001). Relationship to core self-evaluations traits—Self-esteem, generalized self-efficacy, locus of control, and emotional stability—With job satisfaction and job performance: A meta-analysis. *Journal of Applied Psychology, 86*(1), 80–92.

Judge, T. A., Erez, A., Bono, J. E., & Thoresen, C. J. (2002). Are measures of self-esteem, neuroticism, locus of control, and generalized self-efficacy

indicators of a common core construct? *Journal of Personality and Social Psychology, 83*(3), 693–710.

Judge, T. A., & Larsen, R. J. (2001). Dispositional affect and job satisfaction: A review and theoretical extension. *Organizational Behavior and Human Decision Processes, 86*(1), 67–98.

Judge, T. A., Locke, E. A., Durham, C. C., & Kluger, A. N. (1998). Dispositional effects on job and life satisfaction: The role of core evaluations. *Journal of Applied Psychology, 83*(1), 17–34.

Judiesch, M. K., Schmidt, F. L., & Hunter, J. E. (1993). Has the problem of judgment in utility analysis been solved? *Journal of Applied Psychology, 78,* 903–911.

Jung, C. G. (1910). The association method. *American Journal of Psychology, 21,* 219–269.

Kagan, J., Moss, H. A., & Siegel, I. E. (1963). Psychological significance of styles of conceptualization. *Monographs of the Society for Research in Child Development, 28*(2, Serial No. 86), 73–124.

Kager, M. B. (2000). Factors that affect hiring: A study of age discrimination and hiring. *Dissertation Abstracts International, 60,* 11A.

Kahn, J. H., Hessling, R. M., & Russell, D. W. (2003). Social support, health, and well-being among the elderly: What is the role of negative affectivity? *Personality and Individual Differences, 35*(1), 5–17.

Kallingal, A. (1971). The prediction of grades for black and white students at Michigan State University. *Journal of Educational Measurement, 8,* 263–265.

Kamhi, A. G., Minor, J. S., & Mauer, D. (1990). Content analysis and intratest performance profiles on the Columbia and the TONI. *Journal of Speech and Hearing Research, 33,* 375–379.

Kamin, L. J. (1974). *The science and politics of IQ.* Hillsdale, NJ: Eribaum.

Kammeier, M. L., Hoffman, H., & Loper, R. G. (1973). Personality characteristics of alcoholics as college freshmen and at time of treatment. *Quarterly Journal of Studies on Alcohol, 34,* 390–399.

Kandel, E. C. (2006). *In search of memory: The emergence of a new science of mind.* New York: Norton & Company.

Kane, M. J., & Engle, R. W. (2002). *The role of prefrontal cortex in working-memory capacity, executive attention, and general fluid intelligence: An individual-differences perspective.* US:

Psychonomic Society, [URL: http://www.psychonomic.org].

Kane, R. L., Roebuck-Spencer, T., Short, P., Kabat, M., & Wilken, J. (2007). Identifying and monitoring cognitive deficits in clinical populations using automated neuropsychological assessment metrics (ANAM) tests. *Archives of Clinical Neuropsychology, 22 Suppl 1,* S115–126.

Kanfer, F. H., & Saslow, G. (1969). Behavioral diagnosis. In C. M. Franks (Ed.), *Behavior therapy: Appraisal and status.* New York: McGraw-Hill.

Kantrowitz, T., & Dawson, C., Fetzer, M. (2011). Computer adaptive testing (CAT): A faster, smarter, and more secure approach to pre-employment testing. *Journal of Business and Psychology, 26*(2), 227–232. doi:10.1007/s10869-011-9228-3.

Kaplan, C. (1993). Reliability and validity of test-session behavior observations: Putting the horse before the cart. *Journal of Psychoeducational Assessment, 11*(4), 314–322.

Kaplan, R. M. (1973). Components of trust: Note on use of Rotter's scale. *Psychological Reports, 33,* 13–14.

Kaplan, R. M. (1982). Nader's raid on the Educational Testing Service: Is it in the best interest of the consumer? *American Psychologist, 37,* 15–23.

Kaplan, R. M. (1985). The controversy related to the use of psychological tests. In B. B. Wolman (Ed.), *Handbook of Intelligence: Theories, measurements, and applications.* New York: Wiley.

Kaplan, R. M. (1987). Basic statistics for the behavioral sciences. Newton, MA: Allyn & Bacon.

Kaplan, R. M. (1990). Behavior as the central outcome in health care. *American Psychologist, 45,* 1211–1220.

Kaplan, R. M. (1993). *The hippocratic predicament.* San Diego, CA: Academic Press.

Kaplan, R. M. (1994a). Measures of health outcome in social support research. In S. A. Schumaker & S. M. Czajkowski (Eds.), *Social support and cardiovascular disease: Plenum series in behavioral psychophysiology and medicine* (pp. 65–94). New York: Plenum.

Kaplan, R. M. (1994b). Value judgment in the Oregon Medicaid experiment. *Medical Care, 32*(10), 975–988.

Kaplan, R. M. (1999). Health-related quality of life in mental health services evaluation. In E. Nancy, E. Miller, E. Kathryn, M. Magruder, et al. (Eds.), *Cost-effectiveness of psychotherapy: A guide for practitioners, researchers, and policymakers* (pp. 160–173). New York: Springer.

Kaplan, R. M. (2000). Two pathways to prevention. *American Psychologist*, 55(4), 382–396.

Kaplan, R. M. (2002). *Quality of life and chronic illness*. Malden, MA: Blackwell.

Kaplan, R. M. (2003). The significance of quality of life in health care. *Quality of Life Research*, 12(Suppl. 1), 3–16.

Kaplan, R. M. (2004). Achievements of the Veterans Health Study. *Journal of Ambulatory Care Management*, 27(1), 66–67.

Kaplan, R. M. (2008). *Disease, Drugs, and Dollars*. New York: Copernicus Press.

Kaplan, R. M., & Anderson, J. P. (1990). The general health policy model: An integrated approach. In B. Spilker (Ed.), *Quality of life assessments in clinical trials* (pp. 131–149). New York: Raven Press.

Kaplan, R. M., Anderson, J. P., Patterson, T. L., McCutchan, J. A., Weinrich, J. D., Heaton, R. K., Atkinson, J. H., Thal, L., Chandler, J., & Grant, I. (1995). Validity of the Quality of Well-Being Scale for persons with human immunodeficiency virus infection. HNRC Group. HIV Neurobehavioral Research Center. *Psychosomatic Medicine*, 57, 138–147.

Kaplan, R. M., Criqui, M. H., Denenberg, J. O., Bergan, J., & Fronek, A. (2003). Quality of life in patients with chronic venous disease: San Diego population study. *Journal of Vascular Surgery*, 37(5), 1047–1053.

Kaplan, R. M., & Ernst, J. (1983). Do category rating scales produce biased preference weights for a health index? *Medical Care*, 21, 193–207.

Kaplan, R. M., Feeny, D., and Revicki, D. A. (1999). Methods for assessing relative importance in preference based outcome measures. In E. C. R. B. Joyce, E. Hannah, M. McGee, et al. (Eds.), *Individual quality of life: Approaches to conceptualisation and assessment* (pp. 135–149). Amsterdam, Netherlands: Klewer.

Kaplan, R. M., Ganiats, T. G., Sieber, W. J., & Anderson, J. P. (1998). The Quality of Well-Being Scale: Critical similarities and differences with SF-36. *International Journal for Quality in Health Care*, 10(6), 509–520.

Kaplan, R. M., & Golomb, B. A. (2001). *Cost-effectiveness of statin medications*. Washington, DC: American Psychological Association.

Kaplan, R. M., & Grant, I. (2000). Statistics and experimental design.

In B. J. Sadcock & V. A. Sadock (Eds.), *Comprehensive Textbook of Psychiatry* (7th ed.). Baltimore: Williams & Wilkins.

Kaplan, R. M., & Groessl, E. J. (2002). Applications of costeffectiveness methodologies in behavioral medicine. *Journal of Consulting Clinical Psychology*, 70(3), 482–493.

Kaplan, R. M., Navarro, A. M., Castro, F. G., Elder, J. P., Mishra, S. I., Hubbell, A., Chrvala, C., Flores, E., Ramirez, A., Fernandezesquer, M. E., & Ruiz, E. (1996). Increased use of mammography among Hispanic women: Baseline results from the NCI cooperative group on cancer prevention in Hispanic communities. *American Journal of Preventive Medicine*, 12(6), 467–471.

Kaplan, R. M., & Ries, A. L. (1996), Cognitive-behavioral interventions and the quality of life of patients with chronic obstructive pulmonary disease. In J. Bach (Ed.), *Pulmonary rehabilitation: The obstructive and paralytic conditions* (pp. 133–144). Philadelphia: Hanley & Delfus.

Kaplan, R. M., & Ries, A. L. (2007). Quality of life: Concept and definition. *COPD: Journal of Chronic Obstructive Pulmonary Disease*, 4(3), 263–271.

Kaplan, R. M., Ries, A. L., Prewitt, L. M., & Eakin, E. (1994). Self-efficacy expectations predict survival for patients with chronic obstructive pulmonary disease. *Health Psychology*, 13, 366–368.

Kaplan, R. M., Sieber, W. J., and Ganiats, T. G. (1997). The Quality of Well-Being Scale: Comparison of the interviewer-administered version with a self-administered questionnaire. *Psychology and Health*, 12(6), 783–791.

Kaplan, R. M., & Toshima, M. T. (1992). Does a reduced fat diet cause retardation in child growth? *Preventive Medicine*, 21, 33–52.

Kaplan, S. L., & Alfonso, V. C. (1997). Confirmatory factor analysis of the Stanford-Binet Intelligence Scale: Fourth edition with preschoolers with developmental delays. *Journal of Psychoeducational Assessment*, 15, 226–236.

Kappelman, M. M. (1993). [Review of the book *Touchpoints: The essential reference: Your Child's Emotional and Behavioral Development*]. *Journal of Developmental and Behavioral Pediatrics*, 14(5), 350–351.

Kar, B. R., Rao, S. L., Chandramouli, B. A., & Thennarasu, K. (2011). Growth

patterns of neuropsychological functions in Indian children. *Frontiers in Psychology*, 2, 240. doi:10.3389/fpsyg.2011.00240.

Kar, B. R., Rao, S. L., Chandramouli, B. A., Thennarasu, K., & Satishchandra, P. (2010). Neuropsychological lateralization of brain dysfunction in children with mesial temporal sclerosis: A presurgical evaluation. *Journal of Child Neurology*, 25, 705–714.

Karageorgiou, E., Schulz, S., Gollub, R., Andreasen, N., Ho, B. C., Lauriello, J., Calhoun, V., Bockholt, H., Sponheim, S., & Georgopoulos, A. (2011). Neuropsychological testing and structural magnetic resonance imaging as diagnostic biomarkers early in the course of schizophrenia and related psychoses. *Neuroinformatics*, 9(4), 321–333. doi:10.1007/s12021-010-9094-6.

Kareken, D. A., Gur, R. C., & Saykin, A. J. (1995). Reading on the Wide-Range Achievement Test—Revised and parental education as predictors of IQ: Comparisons with the Barona formula. *Archives of Clinical Neuropsychology*, 10(2), 147–157.

Karim, J., Weisz, R., & Ur Rehman, S. (2011). International positive and negative affect schedule short-form (I-PANAS-SF): Testing for factorial invariance across cultures. *Procedia—Social and Behavioral Sciences*, 15, 2016–2022.

Karp, S. A. (Ed.). (1999). *Studies of objective/projective personality tests*. Brook/Andville, MD: Tests, Inc.

Kaszniak, A. W., & Christenson, G. (1994). Differential diagnosis of dementia and depression. In M. Storandt & G. R. VandenBos (Eds.), *Neuropsychological assessment of dementia and depression in older adults: A clinician's guide* (pp. 81–117). Washington, DC: American Psychological Association.

Kataoka, H. C., Latham, G. P., & Whyte, G. (1997). The relative resistance of the situational, patterned behavior, and conventional structured interviews to anchoring effects. *Human Performance*, 10(1), 47–63.

Katigbak, M. S., Church, A. T., Guanzon-Lapena, M. A., Carlota, A. J., & del Pilar, G. H. (2002). Are indigenous personality dimensions culture specific? Philipinne inventories and the five-factor model. *Journal of Personality & Social Psychology*, 82(1), 89–101.

Kaufman, A. S. (1978). Review of Columbia Mental Maturity Scale.

In O. K. Buros (Ed.), *The eighth mental measurements yearbook* (Vol. 1). Highland Park, NJ: Gryphon Press.

Kaufman, A. S. (1984). K-ABC and controversy. *Journal of Special Education, 18*(3), 409–444.

Kaufman, A. S. (1990). *Assessment of adolescent and adult intelligence.* Boston: Allyn & Bacon.

Kaufman, A. S., & Kaufman, N. L. (1983a). *K-ABC administration and scoring manual.* Circle Pines, MN: American Guidance Service.

Kaufman, A. S., & Kaufman, N. L. (1983b). *K-ABC interpretive manual.* Circle Pines, MN: American Guidance Service.

Kaufman, A. S., & Kaufman, N. L. (1993). *The Kaufman Adolescent and Adult Intelligence Test.* Circle Pines, MN: American Guidance Service.

Kaufman, A., & Kaufman, N. (2004a). *KABC-II manual.* Circle Pines, MN: American Guidance Service.

Kaufman, A., & Kaufman, N. (2004b). *KTEA-II comprehensive interpretation manual.* Circle Pines, MN: American Guidance Service.

Kaufman, A. S., Kaufman, R. W., & Kaufman, N. L. (1985). The Kaufman Assessment Battery for Children (K-ABC). In C. S. Newmark (Ed.), *Major psychological assessment instruments.* Newton, MA: Allyn & Bacon.

Kaufman, A. S., Lichtenberger, E. O., Fletcher-Janzen, E., & Kaufman, N. L. (2005). *Essentials of KABC-II assessment.* Hoboken, NJ: John Wiley & Sons, Inc.

Kaufman, J. C. (2009). Creativity, intelligence, and culture: Connections and possibilities. In P. Meusburger, J. Funke, E. Wunder, & P. Meusburger, (Eds.), *Milieus of Creativity* (pp. 155–168) Netherlands: Springer.

Kaufman, S. B., DeYoung, C. G., Reis, D. L., & Gray, J. R. (2011). General intelligence predicts reasoning ability even for evolutionarily familiar content. *Intelligence, 39*(5), 311–322.

Kazdin, A. E. (1977). Artifact, bias, and complexity of assessment: The ABC's of reliability. *Journal of Applied Behavior Analysis, 10*, 141–150.

Kazdin, A. E. (2004). *Research design in clinical psychology* (4th ed.). Needham Heights, MA: Allyn & Bacon.

Kefyalew, F. (1996). The reality of child participation in research: Experience from a capacity-building program. *Childhood, 3*, 203–213.

Keiser, R. E., & Prather, E. N. (1990). What is the TAT? A review of ten years of research. *Journal of Personality Assessment, 55*, 800–803.

Keith, T. Z., Fine, J. G., Taub, G. E., Reynolds, M. R., & Kranzler, J. H. (2006). Higher order, multisample, confirmatory factor analysis of the Wechsler Intelligence Scale for Children–fourth edition: What does it measure? *School Psychology Review, 35*(1), 108–127.

Kelemen, W. L., Winningham, R. G., & Weaver, C. A., III. (2007). Repeated testing sessions and scholastic aptitude in college students' metacognitive accuracy. *European Journal of Cognitive Psychology, 19*(4), 689–717.

Keller, S. D., Ware, J. E., Jr., Hatoum, H. T., & Kong, S. X. (1999). The SF-36 Arthritis-Specific Health Index (ASHI): II. Tests of validity in four clinical trials. *Medical Care, 37*(5 Suppl.), MS51–60.

Kellogg, R. T. (2003). *Cognitive psychology* (2nd ed.). Thousand Oaks, CA: Sage.

Kelly, H. H. (1967). Attribution theory in social psychology. In D. Levine (Ed.), *Nebraska Symposium on Motivation.* Lincoln: University of Nebraska Press.

Kendall, P. C., Williams, S., Pechacek, T. F., Graham, L. G., Shisslak, C. S., & Herzoff, N. (1979). Cognitive-behavioral and patient education interventions in cardiac catheterization procedures: The Palo Alto medical psychology project. *Journal of Consulting and Clinical Psychology, 47*, 49–58.

Kendler, K. S., Eaves, L. J., Loken, E. K., Pedersen, N. L., Middeldorp, C. M., Reynolds, C., Boomsma, D., Lichtenstein, P., Silberg, J., & Gardner, C. O. (2011). The impact of environmental experiences on symptoms of anxiety and depression across the life span. *Psychological Science, 22*, 1343–1352. doi:10.1177/0956797611417255.

Kennedy, R. B. (1994). The employment interview. *Journal of Employment Counseling, 31*, 110–114.

Kennedy, W. A., Van de Riet, V., & White, J. C., Jr. (1963). A normative sample of intelligence and achievement of Negro elementary school children in the Southeast United States. *Monographs of the Society for Research in Child Development, 28*(6, Serial No. 90).

Kent, G. H., & Rosanoff, A. J. (1910). A study of association in insanity. *American Journal of Insanity, 67*, 37–96, 317–390.

Kent, R. N., Kanowitz, J., O'Leary, K. D., & Cheiken, M. (1977). Observer reliability as a function of circumstances of assessment. *Journal of Applied Behavior Analysis, 10*, 317–324.

Kent, R. N., O'Leary, K. D., Diament, C., & Dietz, A. (1974). Expectation biases in observational evaluation of therapeutic change. *Journal of Consulting and Clinical Psychology, 42*, 774–780.

Kerlikowske, K., Grady, D., Rubin, S. M., Sandrock, C., & Ernster, V. L. (1995). Efficacy of screening mammography: A meta-analysis. *Journal of the American Medical Association, 273*(2), 149–154.

Kerner, D. N., Patterson, T. L., Grant, I., & Kaplan, R. M. (1998). Validity of the Quality of Well-Being Scale for patients with Alzheimer's disease. *Journal of Aging and Health, 10*(1), 44–61.

Kerner, J. (1857). Klexographien (Pt. VI). In R. Pissin (Ed.), *Kerners Werke.* Berlin, Germany: Bong.

Khanna, D., Ahmed, M., Furst, D. E., Ginsburg, S. S., Park, G. S., Hornung, R., et al. (2007). Health values of patients with systemic sclerosis. *Arthritis and Rheumatism, 57*(1), 86–93.

Khanna, M., Aschenbrand, S. G., & Kendall, P. C. (2007). New frontiers: Computer technology in the treatment of anxious youth. *The Behavior Therapist, 30*(1), 22–25.

Kido, D. K., Sheline, Y. I., & Reeve, A. (2000). Diagnostic testing. In E. Barry, S. Fogel, E. Randolph, B. Schiffer, et al. (Eds.), *Synopsis of neuropsychiatry* (pp. 27–52). Philadelphia: Lippincott.

Kiersh, E. (1979, January 15). Testing is the name, power is the game. *The Village Voice.*

Kim, B. H. (2011). Deception and applicant faking: Putting the pieces together. *International Review of Industrial and Organizational Psychology, 26*, 181–217. doi:10.1002/9781119992592.ch7.

Kim, K. H. (2006). Can we trust creativity tests? A review of the Torrance Tests of Creative Thinking (TTCT). *Creativity Research Journal, 18*(1), 3–14.

Kim, K. H. (2006). Is creativity unidimensional or multidimensional? Analyses of the Torrance Tests of Creative Thinking. *Creativity Research Journal, 18*(3), 251–259.

Kim, K. H., Cramond, B., & Bandalos, D. L. (2006). The latent structure and measurement invariance of scores on the Torrance Tests of Creative Thinking-figural. *Educational and*

*Psychological Measurement*, 66(3), 459–477.

Kimble, G. A., & Wertheimer, M. (Eds.). (2003). *Portraits of pioneers in psychology* (Vol. 5). Mahwah, NJ: Erlbaum.

Kimura, D. (1999). *Sex and cognition.* Cambridge, MA: MIT Press.

Kirkby, K. C. (1996). Computer-assisted treatment of phobias. *Psychiatric Services*, 47(2), 139–140.

Kirkpatrick, E. A. (1900). Individual tests of school children. *Psychological Review*, 7, 274–280.

Kirsch, I., Ed. (1999). *How expectancies shape experience.* Washington, DC: American Psychological Association.

Klausen, O., Moller, P., Holmeford, A., Reiseaeeter, S., & Asbjornsen, A. (2000). Lasting effects of orbitis media with effusion on language skills and listening performance. *Acta Oto-Laryngoloca*, 120(Suppl. 543), 73–76.

Kleberg, A., Westrup, B., Stjernqvist, K., & Lagercrantz, H. (2002). Indications of improved cognitive development at one year of age among infants born very prematurely who receive care based on the Newborn Individualized Developmental Care and Assessment Program (NIDCAP). *Early Human Development*, 68(2), 83–91.

Klein, B. P., & Mervis, C. B. (1999). Contrasting patterns of cognitive abilities of 9- and 10-year-olds with Williams syndrome or Down syndrome. *Developmental Neuropsychology*, 16(2), 177–196.

Klein, S. P. (2002). Law school admissions, LSATs, and the bar. *Academic Questions*, 15(1), 33–39.

Klieger, D. M., & Franklin, M. E. (1993). Validity of the Fear Survey Schedule in phobia research: A laboratory test. *Journal of Psychopathology and Behavioural Assessment*, 15(3), 207–217.

Klieger, D. M., & McCoy, M. L. (1994). Improving the concurrent validity of the Fear Survey Schedule—III. *Journal of Psychopathology and Behavioral Assessment*, 16(3), 201–220.

Klimstra, T. A., Crocetti, E., Hale, W. W. III, Fermani, A., & Meeus, W. H. J. (2011). Big five personality dimensions in Italian and Dutch adolescents: A cross-cultural comparison of mean-levels, sex differences, and associations with internalizing symptoms, *Journal of Research in Personality*, 45(3), 285–296. ISSN 0092-6566; doi:10.1016/j.jrp.2011.03.002. Retrieved from http://www.science-direct.com/science/article/pii/S0092656611000365.

Kline, P. (1994). *An easy guide to factor analysis.* London: Routledge.

Kline, R. B. (1989). Is the Fourth Edition Stanford-Binet a four-factor test? Confirmatory factor analyses of alternative methods for ages 2 through 23. *Journal of Psychoeducational Assessment*, 7, 4–13.

Klopfer, B., & Davidson, H. H. (1944). Form level rating: A preliminary proposal for appraising mode and level of thinking as expressed in Rorschach records. *Rorschach Research Exchange*, 8, 164–177.

Klopfer, B., & Davidson, H. H. (1962). *The Rorschach technique: An introductory manual.* Orlando: Harcourt Brace.

Klopfer, B., & Kelley, D. (1942). *The Rorschach technique.* Yonkers, NY: World Book.

Klopfer, B., & Kelly, D. M. (1946). *The Rorschach technique* (2nd ed.). Yonkers-on-Hudson, NY: World Book.

Knafl, K., Deatrick, J., Gallo, A., Holcombe, G., Bakitas, M., Dixon, J., & Grey, M. (2007). The analysis and interpretation of cognitive interviews for instrument development. *Research in Nursing & Health*, 30(2), 224–234.

Knapp-Lee, L. (2000). A complete career guidance program: The COP System. In E. C. Edward Watkins, Jr., E. Vicki, L. Campbell, et al. (Eds.), *Testing and assessment in counseling practice* (2nd ed.) (pp. 295–338). Mahwah, NJ: Erlbaum.

Knotek, P. C., Bayles, K. A., & Kaszniak, A. W. (1990). Response consistency on a semantic memory task in persons with dementia of the Alzheimer type. *Brain and Language*, 38, 465–475.

Knox, H. A. (1914). A scale based on the work at Ellis Island for estimating mental defect. *Journal of the American Medical Association*, 62, 741–747.

Kobasa, S. C. (1979). Stressful life events, personality and health: An inquiry into hardiness. *Journal of Personality and Social Psychology*, 37, 1–11.

Kocsis, R. N. (2011). The Structured Interview of Reported Symptoms 2nd Edition (SIRS-2): The new benchmark towards the assessment of malingering. *Journal of Forensic Psychology Practice*, 11(1), 73–81.

Koen, W. J., & Penland, A. L. (2002, April). *Special education: The effects of gender, ethnicity, and attractiveness on placement.* Poster session presented at the annual conference of the Western Psychological Association, Irvine, CA.

Kohli, M. A., Salyakina, D., Pfennig, A., Lucae, S., Horstmann, S., Menke, A.,

Kloiber, S., Hennings, J., Bradley, B. B., Ressler, K. J., Uhr, M., Müller-Myhsok, B., Holsboer, F., & Binder, E. B. (2010). Association of genetic variants in the neurotrophic receptor–encoding gene NTRK2 and a lifetime history of suicide attempts in depressed patients. *Archives of General Psychiatry*, 67(4), 348–359.

Kohnen, S., & Nickels, L. (2010). Teaching children with developmental spelling difficulties in a one-on-one context. *Australian Academic Press*, 34(1), 36–60. doi:10.1375/ajse. 34.1.36.

Kohs, S. C. (1923). *Intelligence measurement: A psychological and statistical study based upon the blockdesign tests.* New York: Macmillan.

Kok, F. (1992). Differential item functioning. In L. Verhoeven & J. H. A. L. De Jong (Eds.), The *construct of language proficiency: Applications of psychological models to language assessment* (pp. 115–124). Amsterdam, Netherlands: John Benjamins.

Koloski, N. A., Talley, N. J., & Boyce, P. M. (2000). The impact of functional gastrointestinal disorders on quality of life. *American Journal of Gastroenterology*, 95(1), 67–71.

Koltai, D. C., & Welsh-Bohmer, K. A. (2000). Geriatric neuropsycholog-ical assessment. In E. Rodney, D. Vanderploeg, et al. (Eds.), *Clinician's guide to neuropsychological assessment* (pp. 383–415). Mahwah, NJ: Erlbaum.

Konradt, U., Syperek, S., & Hertel, G. (2011). Testing on the Internet: Faking in a Web-based self-administered personality measure. *Journal of Business and Media Psychology*, 2(1), 1–10. www.journal-bmp.de.

Koopmans, P. C., Sanderman, R., Timmerman, I., & Emmelkamp, P. M. G. (1994) The Irrational Beliefs Inventory (IBI): Development and psychometric evaluation. *European Journal of Psychological Assessment*, 10(1), 15–27.

Koppitz, E. M. (1964). *The Bender Gestalt test for young children.* New York: Grune & Stratton.

Kosinski, M., Keller, S. D., Ware, J. E., Jr., Hatoum, H. T., & Kong, S. X. (1999). The SF-36 Health Survey as a generic outcome measure in clinical trials of patients with osteoarthritis and rheumatoid arthritis: Relative validity of scales in relation to clinical measures of arthritis severity. *Medical Care*, 37(5, Suppl.), MS23–39.

Kossowska, M. (2002). Relationship between cognitive strategies, intelligence, and personality. *Polish Psychological Bulletin, 33*(2), 47–54.

Kossowsky, J., Wilhelm, F. H., Roth, W. T., & Schneider, S. (2011). Separation anxiety disorder in children: Disorder-specific responses to experimental separation from the mother. *Journal of Child Psychology and Psychiatry.* doi:10.1111/j.1469-7610.2011.02465.x.

Kostman, S. S. (2005). An examination of the 'job suitability snapshot' on the personality assessment inventory and the California psychological inventory law enforcement, corrections, and public safety selection report, and its usefulness in predicting 'fitness for duty'. US: ProQuest Information & Learning.

Kounti, F., Tsolaki, M., & Kiosseoglou, G. (2006). Functional cognitive assessment scale (FUCAS): A new scale to assess executive cognitive function in daily life activities in patients with dementia and mild cognitive impairment. *Human Psychopharmacology: Clinical and Experimental, 21*(5), 305–311.

Kraepelin, E. (1912). *Lehrbuch der psychiatric.* Leipzig: Barth.

Kraiger, K., Hakel, M. D., & Cornelius, E. T., III. (1984). Exploring fantasies of TAT reliability. *Journal of Personality Assessments, 48*, 365–370.

Kranzler, G., & Moursund, J. (1999). *Statistics for the terrified* (2nd ed.). Upper Saddle River, NJ: Prentice- Hall.

Krasa, N. (2007). Is the Woodcock-Johnson III a test for all seasons?: Ceiling and item gradient considerations in its use with older students. *Journal of Psychoeducational Assessment, 25*(1), 3–16.

Kreiner, D. S., & Ryan, J. J. (2001). Memory and motor skill components of the WAIS-III Digit Symbol-Coding Subtest. *Clinical Neuropsychologist, 15*(1), 109–113.

Krikorian, R., & Bartok, J. A. (1998). Developmental data for the Porteus Maze Test. *Clinical Neuropsychologist, 12*, 305–310.

Krinsky, S. G. (1990). The feeling of knowing in deaf adolescents. *American Annals of the Deaf, 135*, 389–395.

Krishnamurthy, R., Archer, R. P., & Groth-Marnat, G. (2011). The Rorschach and performance-based assessment. In T. M. Harwood, L. E. Beutler, G. Groth-Marnat, & A. L. Austin (Eds.), *Integrative assessment of adult personality* (3rd ed.) (pp. 276–328, 280). New York: Guilford Press.

Kroese, J. M. (2003). Cognitive abilities and assessment of children with language impairment. In C. R. Reynold & R. W. Kamphaus (Eds.), *Handbook of psychological and educational assessment of children* (2nd ed.) (pp. 615–627). New York: Guilford Press.

Kröhne, U., & Martens, T. (2011). 11 computer-based competence tests in the national educational panel study: The challenge of mode effects. *Zeitschrift für Erziehungswissenschaft, 14*, 169–186. doi:10.1007/s11618-011-0185-4.

Krol, N. P. C. M., De Bruyn, E. E. J., van Aarle, E. J. M., & van den Bercken, J. H. L. (2001). Computerized screening for DSM classifications using CBCL/YSR extended checklists: A clinical try-out. *Computers in Human Behavior, 17*(3), 315–337.

Kuder, G. F. (1979). *Manual, Kuder Occupational Interest Survey, 1979 revision.* Chicago: Science Research Associates.

Kuder, G. F., & Richardson, M. W. (1937). The theory of the estimation of reliability. *Psychometrika, 2*, 151–160.

Kugler, L. M. (2007). *Methadone maintenance therapy and its effects on executive functioning.* US: ProQuest Information & Learning.

Kugu, N., Akyuez, G. Dogan, O., Ersan, E., & Izgic, F. (2002). Prevalence of eating disorders in a university population and the investigation of its relation with self-esteem, family functions, childhood abuse and neglect. *Psikiyatri Psikoloji Psikofarmakoloji Dergisi, 10*(3), 255–266.

Kuh, G. D., & Hu, S. (1999). Unraveling the complexity of the increase in college grades from the mid-1980s to the mid-1990s. *Educational Evaluation and Policy Analysis, 21*(3), 297–320.

Kulkarni, S. D., Sushil, K., Amin, R. A., Pathak, & N. R., Sharma, C. S. (2010). Correlation of muscular fitness with intelligence in school children. *Indian Journal of Applied-Basic Medical Sciences, 12b*(15), 23–28.

Kuncel, N. R., & Hezlett, S. A. (2007). Assessment: Standardized tests predict graduate students' success. *Science, 315* (5815), 1080–1081.

Kuncel, N. R., Hezlett, S. A., & Ones, D. S. (2001). A comprehensive meta-analysis of the predictive validity of the graduate record examination: Implications for graduate student selection and performance. *Psychological Bulletin, 127*(1), 162–181.

Kuncel, N. R., Wee, S., Serafin, L., & Hezlett, S. A. (2010). The validity of the Graduate Record Examination for master's and doctoral programs: A meta-analytic investigation. *Educational and Psychological Measurement, 70*(2), 340–352. doi:10.1177/0013164409344508.

Kush, J. C., Watkins, M. W., Ward, T. J., Ward, S. B., Canivez, G. L., & Worrell, F. C. (2001). Construct validity for white and black students from the WISC-III standardization sample and for black students referred for psychological evaluation. *School Psychology Review, 30*(1), 70–85.

Kwon, P. (2002). Comment on "Effects of acculturation on the MMPI-2 scores of Asian American students." *Journal of Personality Assessment, 78*(1), 187–189.

La Guardia, J. G. (2002). Interpersonal compartmentalization: An examination of self-concept variation, need satisfaction, and psychological vitality. *Dissertation Abstracts International, 62*, 8B.

Lahikainen, A. R., Kraav, I., Kirmanen, T., & Taimalu, M. (2006). Child-parent agreement in the assessment of young children's fears: A com-parative perspective. *Journal of Cross-Cultural Psychology, 37*(1), 100–119.

Lai, T. J., Guo, Y. I., Guo, N. W., & Hsu, C. C. (2001). Effects of prenatal exposure to polychlorinated biphenyls on cognitive development in children: A longitudinal study in Taiwan. *British Journal of Psychiatry, 178*(40), s49–s52.

Lakin, J. M., & Lai, E. R. (2011). Multigroup generalizability analysis of verbal, quantitative, and nonverbal ability tests for culturally and linguistically diverse students. *Educational and Psychological Measurement.* Retrieved from http://epm.sagepub.com/content/early/2011/07/19/0013164411408074.abstract?rss=1. doi:10.1177/0013164411408074.

Lally, M., & Nettelbeck, T. (1977). Intelligence, reaction time, and inspection time. *American Journal of Mental Deficiency, 82*, 273–281.

Lamp, R. E., & Krohn, E. J. (2001). A longitudinal predictive validity investigation of the SB: FE and KABC with at-risk children. *Journal of Psychoeducational Assessment, 19*(4), 334–349.

Lamp, R. E., & Traxler, A. J. (1973). The validity of the Slosson Intelligence Test for use with disadvantaged Head

Start and first grade children. *Journal of Community Psychology, 1*, 27–30.

Landis, C. (1936). Questionnaires and the study of personality. *Journal of Nervous and Mental Disease, 83*, 125–134.

Landis, C., Zubin, J., & Katz, S. E. (1935). Empirical evaluation of three personality adjustment inventories. *Journal of Educational Psychology, 26*, 321–330.

Landy, F., & Conte, J. (2006). *Work in the 21st century: An introduction to industrial and organizational psychology.* New York: Blackwell.

Landy, F. J. (1986). Stamp collecting versus science: Validation as hypothesis testing. *American Psychologist, 41*, 183–192.

Landy, F. J. (2003). *Validity generalization: Then and now.* Mahwah, NJ: Erlbaum.

Landy, F. J., Farr, J. L., & Jacobs, R. (1982). Utility concepts in performance measurement. *Organizational Behavior and Human Performance, 30*, 15–40.

Landy, F. J., & Shankster, L. J. (1994). Personnel selection and placement. *Annual Review of Psychology, 45*, 261–296.

Landy, F. J., Vance, R. J., Barnes-Farrell, J. L., & Steele, J. W. (1980). Statistical control of halo error in performance ratings. *Journal of Applied Psychology, 65*, 501–506.

Lane, B., & Gullone, E. (1999). Common fears: A comparison of adolescents' self-generated and fear survey schedule generated fears. *Journal of Genetic Psychology, 160*, 194–204.

Langdon, D. W., Rosenblatt, N., & Mellanby, J. H. (1998). Discrepantly poor verbal skills in poor readers: A failure of learning or ability? *British Journal of Psychology, 89*, 177–190.

Lange, R. T., & Chelune, G. J. (2006). Application of new WAIS-III/WMS-III discrepancy scores for evaluating memory functioning: Relationship between intellectual and memory ability. *Journal of Clinical and Experimental Neuropsychology, 28*(4), 592–604.

Lange, R. T., Schoenberg, M. R., Chelune, G. J., Scott, J. G., & Adams, R. L. (2005). Development of the WAIS-III general ability index estimate (GAI-E). *Clinical Neuro-psychologist, 19*(1), 73–86.

Langenbucher, J. W., Labouvie, E., Martin, C. S., Sanjuan, P. M., Bavly, L., Kirisci, L., et al. (2004). An application of item response theory analysis to alcohol, cannabis, and cocaine criteria in DSM-IV. *Journal of Abnormal Psychology, 113*(1), 72–80.

Langer, N., Pedroni, A., Gianotti, L. R., Hänggi, J., Knoch, D., & Jäncke, L. (2011). Functional brain network efficiency predicts intelligence. *Human Brain Mapping.* doi:10.1002/hbm.21297. Retrieved from http://onlinelibrary.wiley.com/doi/10.1002/hbm.21297/full.

Langhout, R. D., Rosselli, F., & Feinstein, J. (2007). Assessing classism in academic settings. *Review of Higher Education: Journal of the Association for the Study of Higher Education, 30*(2), 145–184.

Lanyon, B. P., & Lanyon, R. I. (1980). *Incomplete Sentences Task: Manual.* Chicago: Stoelting.

Larkin, J. E., & Pines, H. A. (1994). Affective consequences of self-monitoring style in a job interview setting. *Basic and Applied Social Psychology, 15*(3), 297–310.

LaRoque, S. D., & Obrzut, J. E. (2006). Pencil pressure and anxiety in drawings: A techno-projective approach. *Journal of Psychoeducational Assessment, 24*(4), 381–393.

Larrabee, L. L., & Kleinsaser, L. D. (1967). *The effect of experimenter bias on WISC performance.* Unpublished manuscript.

*Larry P. v. Wilson Riles,* 343 F. Supp. 1306 (N. D. Cal. 1972), affd 502 F. 2d 963 (9th Cir. 1979).

Larson, J. H., Parks, A. A., Harper, J. M., & Heath, V. A. (2001). A psychometric evaluation of the family rules from the past questionnaire. *Contemporary Family Therapy, 23*(1), 83–103.

Latham, G. P., & Whyte, G. (1994). The futility of utility analysis. *Personnel Psychology, 47*(1), 31–46.

Latham, V. M. (1987). Interviewee training: A review of some empirical literature. *Journal of Career Development, 14*, 96–107.

Laub, D. (2002). Testimonials in the treatment of genocidal trauma. *Journal of Applied Psychoanalytic Studies 4*(1), 63–87.

Laurent, J. (1997). Characteristics of the standard and supplemental batteries of the Woodcock-Johnson Tests of Cognitive Ability Revised with a college sample. *Journal of School Psychology, 35*, 403–416.

Lautenschlager, G. J., & Flaherty, V. L. (1990). Computer administration of questions: More desirable or more social desirability? *Journal of Applied Psychology, 75*, 310–314.

Law School Admissions Council. (2011). Diversity in law school: Racial/ethnic minority applicants. Retrieved from http://www.lsac.org/.

Lawlor, S., Richman, S., & Richman, C. L. (1997). The validity of using the SAT as a criterion for black and white students' admission to college. *College Student Journal, 31*, 507–515.

Lawrence, I., Rigol, G. W., Van Essen, T., & Jackson, C. A. (2002). *A historical perspective on the SAT: 1926–2001* (College Board Research Report No. 2002-7). New York: College Entrance Examination Board.

Law School Admissions Council (1994). *LSAT/LSDAS registration and information handbook, 1994–1995.* Newtown, Pennsylvania.

Lawshe, C. L. (1985). Inferences from personnel tests and their validities. *Journal of Applied Psychology, 70*, 237–238.

Lazarus, R. S. (1995). Psychosocial factors play a role in health, but we have to tackle them with more sophisticated research and thought. *Advances, 11*(2), 14–18.

Lazarus, R. S., & Folkman, S. (1984). *Stress, appraisal, and coping.* New York: Springer-Verlag.

Lazarus, R. S., Lazarus, B. N., & ebrary Inc. (2006). *Coping with aging.* From http://site.ebrary.com/lib/yale/Doc?id=10160516. Online book.

Leach, J. (2002). Personality profiles of prisoners of war and evaders. *Military Psychology, 14*(1), 73–81.

Leahy, R. L., & Dowd, E. T. (Eds.). (2002). *Clinical advances in cognitive psychotherapy: Theory and application.* New York: Springer.

Leavitt, W. M., Lombard, J. R., & Morris, J. C. (2011). Examining admission factors in an MPA program. *Journal of Public Affairs Education, 17*(3), 447–460.

Lee, J. A., Moreno, K. E., & Sympson, J. B. (1986). The effects of mode of test administration on test performance. *Educational and Psychological Measurement, 46*, 467–473.

Lee, J. M., Ku, J. H., Jang, D. P., Kim, D. H., Choi, Y. H., Kim, I. Y., & Kim, S. I. (2002). Virtual reality system for treatment of the fear of public speaking using image-based rendering and moving pictures. *Cyberpsychology and Behavior, 5*(3), 191–195.

Lee, K. J., Choi, Y. S., & Kim, J. E. (2011). Building an automated English sentence evaluation system for students learning English as a second language, *Computer Speech &*

*Language, 25*(2), 246–260. doi:10.1016/j.csl.2010.05.001.

Leekam, S. R., Libby, S. J., Wing, L., Gould, J., & Taylor, C. (2002). The Diagnostic Interview for Social and Communication Disorders: Algorithms for ICD-10 childhood autism and Wing and Gould autistic spectrum disorder. *Journal of Child Psychology and Psychiatry and Allied Disciplines, 43*(3), 327–342.

Leffard, S. A., Miller, J. A., Bernstein, J., DeMann, J. J., Mangis, II. A., & McCoy, E. L. B. (2006). Substantive validity of working memory measures in major cognitive functioning test batteries for children. *Applied Neuropsychology, 13*(4), 230–241.

Leichsenring, F. (1990). Discriminating borderline from neurotic patients: A study with the Holtzman Inkblot Technique. *Psychopathology, 23*, 21–26.

Leichsenring, F. (1991). Primary process thinking, primitive defensive operations and object relations in borderline and neurotic patients. *Psychopathology, 24*, 39–44.

Leman, N. (1995, September). The Great Sorting. *Atlantic Monthly*, pp. 84–100.

Lemke, S., & Moos, R. H. (1986). Quality of residential settings of elderly adults. *Journal of Gerontology, 41*, 268–276.

Leong, C., & Joshi, R. (1995). *Developmental and acquired dyslexia: Neuropsychological and neurolinguistic perspectives*. Dordrecht, Netherlands: Kluwer Academic Publishers.

Lerner, B. (1979). Tests and standards today: Attacks, counterattacks, and responses. *New Directions in Testing and Measurement, 1*(3), 15–31.

Leshem, R., & Glicksohn, J. (2007). The construct of impulsivity revisited. *Personality and Individual Differences, 43*(4), 681–691.

Leslie, L. K., Gordon, J. N., Ganger, W., & Gist, K. (2002). Developmental delay in young children in child welfare by initial placement type. *Infant Mental Health Journal, 23*(5), 496–516.

Lesser, G. S., Fifer, G., & Clark, D. H. (1965). Mental abilities of children from different social-class and cultural groups. *Monographs of the Society for Research in Child Development, 30*(4, Serial No. 102).

Lessler, J. T., Caspar, R. A., Penne, M. A., & Barker, P. R. (2000). Developing computer assisted interviewing (CAI) for the National Household Survey on Drug Abuse. *Journal of Drug Issues, 30*(1), 9–34.

Letendre, S., Marquie-Beck, J., Capparelli, E., Best, B., Clifford, D., Collier, A. C., et al. (2008). Validation of the CNS penetration-effectiveness rank for quantifying antiretroviral penetration into the central nervous system. *Archives of Neurology, 65*(1), 65–70.

Leung, S. F., French, P., Chui, C., & Arthur, D. (2007). Computerized mental health assessment in integrative health clinics: A cross-sectional study using structured interview. *International Journal of Mental Health Nursing, 16*(6), 441–446.

Levenson, H., Olkin, R., Herzoff, N., & DeLancy, M. (1986). MMPI evaluation of erectile dysfunction: Failure of organic vs. psychogenic decision rules. *Journal of Clinical Psychology, 42*, 752–754.

Leventhal, A. M., Gelernter, J., Oslin, D., Anton, R. F., Farrer, L. A., & Kranzler, H. R. (2011). Agitated depression in substance dependence. *Drug and Alcohol Dependence, 116*(1–3)163–169. doi:10.1016/j.drugalcdep.2010.12.012.

Levin, H. S., Song, J., Ewing-Cobbs, L., & Roberson, G. (2001). Porteus Maze performance following traumatic brain injury in children. *Neuropsychology, 15*(4), 557–567.

Levine, D. W., Lewis, M. A., Bowen, D. J., Kripke, D. F., Kaplan, R. M., Naughton, M. J., et al. (2003). *Reliability and validity of Women's Health Initiative Insomnia Rating Scale.* Washington, DC: American Psychological Association.

Levitas, A. S., Hurley, A. D., & Pary, R. (2002). The mental status examination in patients with mental retardation and developmental disabilities. *Mental Health Aspects of Developmental Disabilities (2–16), 4*(1).

Levy, S. (1979). E. T. S. and the "coaching" cover-up. *New Jersey Monthly, 3*(5), 4–7.

Lewandowski, D. G., & Saccuzzo, D. P. (1976). The decline of psychological testing: Have traditional procedures been fairly evaluated? *Professional Psychology, 7*, 177–184.

Lewin, T. (2009). A new look for graduate entrance test. *New York Times*. Retrieved from http://www.nytimes.com/2009/12/06/education/06gre.html.

Lewinsohn, P. N., & Teri, L. (1982). Selection of depressed and nondepressed subjects on the basis of self-report data. *Journal of Consulting and Clinical Psychology, 50*, 590–591.

Lewis, C. D., & Lorentz, S. (1994). Comparison of the Leiter International

Performance Scale and the Wechsler Intelligence Scales. *Psychological Reports, 74*(2), 521–522.

Lewis, L. E., & Drewett, R. F. (2006). Psychophysiological correlates of anxiety: A single-case study. *Journal of Anxiety Disorders, 20*(6), 829–835.

Lezak, M. D. (1983). *Neuropsychological assessment* (2nd ed.). New York: Oxford University Press.

Lezak, M. D. (1995). *Neuropsychological assessment* (3rd ed.). New York: Oxford University Press.

Li, C. R. (2002). Impaired detection of visual motion in schizophrenia patients. *Progress in Neuro-Psychopharmacology & Biological Psychiatry, 26*(5), 929–934.

Li, F., Wang, E., & Zhang, F. (2002). The multitrait-multirater approach to analyzing rating biases. *Acta Psychologica Sinica, 34*(1), 98–96.

Lichtenberg, P. A., & MacNeill, S. E. (2000). Neuropsychological assessment in geriatric facilities. In E. Victor Molinari et al. (Eds.), *Professional psychology in long term care: A comprehensive guide* (pp. 29–49). New York: Wiley.

Lichtenberger, E. (2005). General measures of cognition for the preschool child. *Mental Retardation and Developmental Disabilities Research Reviews, 11*(3), 197–208.

Lichtenberger, E. O., & Kaufman, A. S. (2003). *Essentials of WPSSI-III assessment*. New York: Wiley.

Liebert, R. M., & Morris, L. W. (1967). Cognitive and emotional components of test anxiety: A distinction and some initial data. *Psychological Reports, 20*, 975–978.

Lighthouse, A. G. (2006). *The relationship between SAT scores and grade point averages among post-secondary students with disabilities.* US: ProQuest Information & Learning.

Likert, R. (1932). A technique for the measurement of attitudes. *Archives of Psychology*, No. 40.

Lilienfeld, S. O., Alliger, G., & Mitchell, K. (1995). Why integrity testing remains controversial. *American Psychologist, 50*(6), 457–458.

Lilienfeld, S. O., Garb, H. N., & Wood, J. M. (2011). Unresolved questions concerning the effectiveness of psychological assessment as a therapeutic intervention: Comment on Poston and Hanson (2010). *Psychological Assessment, 23*(4), 1047–1055. doi:10.1037/a0025177.

Lilienfeld, S. O., Wood, J. M., & Garb, H. N. (2000). The scientific status of projective techniques. *Psychological Science in the Public Interest, 1,* 27–66.

Lincoln, R. K., Crosson, B., Bauer, R. M., & Cooper, P. V. (1994). Relationship between WAIS-R subtests and language measures after blunt head injury. *Clinical Neuropsychologist, 80,* 140–152.

Lindgren, T., Carlsson, A. M., & Lundbäck, E. (2007). No agreement between the Rorschach and self-assessed personality traits derived from the comprehensive system. *Scandinavian Journal of Psychology, 48*(5), 399–408.

Lindsey, M. L. (1998). Culturally competent assessment of African American clients. *Journal of Personality Assessment, 70*(1), 43–53.

Lindstrom, J. H., & Gregg, N. (2007). The role of extended time on the SAT® for students with learning disabilities and/or attention-deficit/hyperactivity disorder. *Learning Disabilities Research & Practice, 22*(2), 85–95.

Lindzey, G. (1952). The Thematic Apperception Test: Interpretive assumptions and related empirical evidence. *Psychological Bulletin, 49,* 1–25.

Linn, R. L. (1980). Test design and analysis for measurement of educational achievement. *New Directions for Testing and Measurement, 5,* 81–92.

Linn, R. L. (1994a). *Criterion-referenced measurement: A valuable perspective clouded by surplus meaning.* Annual Meeting of the American Educational Research Association: Crite-rion-referenced measurement: A 30-year retrospective (1993, Atlanta, Georgia). *Educational Measurement: Issues and Practice, 13,* 12–14.

Linn, R. L. (1994b). Fair test use: Research and policy. In M. G. Rumsey, C. B. Walker, & J. H. Harris (Eds.), *Personnel selection and classification* (pp. 363–375). Hillsdale, NJ: Erlbaum.

Linn, R. L., & Burton, E. (1994). Performance-based assessment: Implications of task specificity. *Educational Measurement: Issues and Practice, 13,* 15.

Lipsitz, J. D., Dworkin, R. H., & Erlenmeyer-Kimling, L. (1993). Wechsler comprehension and picture arrangement subtests and social adjustment. *Psychological Assessment, 5*(4), 430–437.

Lipsitz, S. (1969). *Effect of the race of the examiner on results of intelligence test performance of Negro and white children.* Unpublished master's thesis, Long Island University, NY.

Lis, A., Parolin, L., Calvo, V., Zennaro, A., & Meyer, G. (2007). The impact of administration and inquiry on Rorschach Comprehensive System protocols in a national reference sample. *Journal of Personality Assessment, 89*(1), 193–200.

Liss, P. H., & Haith, M. M. (1970). The speed of visual processing in children and adults: Effects of backward and forward masking. *Perception and Psychophysics, 8,* 396–398.

Litcher-Kelly, L., Martino, S. A., Broderick, J. E., & Stone, A. A. (2007). A systematic review of measures used to assess chronic musculoskeletal pain in clinical and randomized controlled clinical trials. *Journal of Pain, 8*(12), 906–913.

Little, K. B., & Schneidman, E. S. (1959). Congruencies among interpretations of psychological test and anamnestic data. *Psychological Monographs, 73*(6).

Liu, J., Cahn, M. F., & Dorans, N. J. (2006). An application of score equity assessment: Invariance of linkage of new SAT to old SAT across gender groups. *Journal of Educational Measurement, 43*(2), 113–129.

Liu, J., & Walker, M. E. (2007). In N. J. Dorans, M. Pommerich, & P. W. Holland (Eds.), *Score linking issues related to test content changes.* New York: Springer Science + Business Media.

Liu, K. K., Spicuzza, R., & Erickson, R. (1999). Focus-group research on Minnesota's implementation of graduation standards. *Journal of Educational Research, 92,* 312.

Llorente, A., Brouwers, P., Charurat, M., Magder, L., Malee, K., Mellins, C., Ware, J., Hittleman, J., Mofenson, L., Velez-Borras, J., & Adeniyi-Jones, S. (2003). Early neurodevelopmental markers predictive of mortality in infants infected with HIV-1. *Developmental Medicine and Child Neurology, 45*(2), 76–84.

LoBello, S. G., & Gulgoz, S. (1991). Factor analysis of the Wechsler Preschool and Primary Scale of Intelligence—Revised. *Psychological Assessment: A Journal of Consulting and Clinical Psychology, 3,* 130–132.

Lochman, J. E. (1995). Conduct Problems Prevention Research Group: Screening of child behavior problems for prevention programs at school entry [Special Section: Prediction and prevention of child and adolescent antisocial behavior]. *Journal of Consulting and Clinical Psychology, 63,* 549–559.

Locke, S., McGrew, K. S., & Ford, L. (2011). A multiple group confirmatory factor analysis of the structural invariance of the Cattell-Horn-Carroll theory of cognitive abilities across matched Canadian and U.S. samples. *WMF Press Bulletin, No. 1.* Retrieved from http://woodcock-munoz-foundation.org/press/pressbulletins.html.

Locke, S. D. & Gilbert, B. O. (1995). Method of psychological assessment, self-disclosure, and experiential differences: A study of computer, questionnaire, and interview assessment formats. *Journal of Social Behavior and Personality, 10,* 255–263.

Lockwood, C. A., Mansoor, Y., Homer-Smith, E., & Moses, J. A., Jr. (2011). Factor structure of the Benton Visual Retention Tests: Dimensionalization of the Benton Visual retention test, Benton Visual retention test— multiple choice, and the Visual Form Discrimination Test. *The Clinical Neuropsychologist, 25*(1), 90–107.

Loehlin, J. C. (1998). *Latent variable models: An introduction to factor, path, and structural analysis.* Mahwah, NJ: Erlbaum.

Loevinger, J. (1998). *Technical foundations for measuring ego development: The Washington University Sentence Completion Test.* Mahwah, NJ: Erlbaum.

Loffredo, D. A., & Opt, S. K. (1998). Relating the MBTI to communication apprehension, receiver apprehension, and argumentativeness. *Journal of Psychological Type, 47,* 21–27.

Lomax, C. L. & Lam, D. (2011). Investigation into activation of dysfunctional schemas in euthymic bipolar disorder following positive mood induction. *British Journal of Clinical Psychology, 50*(2), 115–126. doi:10.1348/014466510X497841.

Long, P. A., & Anthony, J. J. (1974). The measurement of retardation by a culture-specific test. *Psychology in the Schools, 11,* 310–312.

Longe, O., Maratos, F. A., Gilbert, P., Evans, G., Volker, F., Rockliff, H., & Rippon, G. (2010). Having a word with yourself: Neural correlates of self-criticism and self-reassurance. *NeuroImage, 49*(2), 1849–1856. doi:10.1016/j.neuroimage.2009.09.019.

Longford, N. T. (1997). Shrinkage estimation of linear combinations of true scores. *Psychometrika, 62,* 237–244.

Lopatovska, I., & Arapakis, I. (2011). Theories, methods and current research on emotions in library and information science, information retrieval and human–computer interaction. *Information Processing & Management, 47*(4), 575–592. doi:10.1016/j.ipm.2010.09.001.

Lord, E. (1950). Experimentally induced variations in Rorschach performance. *Psychological Monographs, 64*(10, Whole No. 316).

Lord, F. M. (1950). *Efficiency of prediction when a regression equation from one sample is used in a new sample* (Research Bulletin 50-40). Princeton, NJ: Educational Testing Service.

Lorenzo-Seva, U. (2003). A factor simplicity index. *Psychometrica, 68*(1), 49–60.

Lorian, C. N., Titov, N., & Grisham, J. R. (2011). Changes in risk-taking over the course of an Internet-delivered cognitive behavioral therapy treatment for generalized anxiety disorder. *Journal of Anxiety Disorders.* http://www.sciencedirect.com/science/article/pii/S0887618511001678.

Loughmiller, G. C., Ellison, R. L., Taylor, C. W., & Price, P. B. (1970). Predicting career performances of physicians using the biographical inventory approach. *Proceedings of the American Psychological Association, 5*, 153–154.

Löve, J., Moore, C., & Hensing, G. (2011). Validation of the Swedish translation of the general self-efficacy scale. *Quality of Life Research,* 1–5. doi:10.1007/s11136-011-0030-5. Retrieved from http://www.springerlink.com/content/e076624407873776/.

Lowman, R. L. (1991). *The clinical practice of career assessment.* Washington, DC: American Psychological Association.

Lowndes, C., Jayachandran, A., Banandur, P., Ramesh, B., Washington, R., Sangameshwar, B., Moses, S., Blanchard, J. & Alary, M. (2011). Polling booth surveys: A novel approach for reducing social desirability bias in HIV-related behavioural surveys in resource-poor settings. *AIDS and Behavior,* 1–9. doi:10.1007/s10461-011-0004-1.

Loy, D. L. (1959). The validity of the Taulbee-Sisson MMPI scale pairs in female psychiatric groups. *Journal of Clinical Psychology, 15*, 306–307.

Lubin, B., Larsen, R., & Matarazzo, J. (1984). Patterns of psychological test usage in the United States: 1935–1982. *American Psychologist, 39*, 451–454.

Lubin, B., & Sands, E. W. (1992). Bibliography of the psychometric properties of the Bender Visual-Motor Gestalt Test: 1970–1991. *Perceptual and Motor Skills, 75*(2), 385–386.

Lubin, B., Wallis, H. R., & Paine, C. (1971). Patterns of psychological test usage in the United States: 1935–1969. *Professional Psychology, 2*, 70–74.

Lucas, J. L., Wanberg, C. R., & Zytowski, D. G. (1997). Development of a career task self-efficacy scale: The Kuder Task Self-Efficacy Scale. *Journal of Vocational Behavior, 50*(3), 432–459.

Lucas, R. E., Diener, E., & Larsen, R. J. (2003). Measuring positive emotions. In S. J. Lopez & C. R. Snyder (Eds.), *Positive psychological assessment: A handbook of models and measures.* (pp. 201–218). Washington DC: American Psychological Association.

Ludgate, D. R. (2001). An examination of the relationship between personality variables and managerial behavior as measured by power and influence tactics in project planning. *Dissertation Abstracts International, 62*, 6A.

Lui, Z., Chen, X., Qin, S., Xue, J., Hao, W., Lu, X., Lui, B., Man, C., & Zhang, Z. (2002). Risk factors for female criminals. *Chinese Mental Health Journal, 16*(2), 106–108.

Lukin, M. E., Dowd, T., Plake, B. S., & Kraft, R. G. (1985). Comparing computerized versus traditional psychological assessment. *Computers in Human Behavior, 1*(1), 49–58.

Lundqvist, C., & Sabel, K. G. (2000). Brief report: The Brazelton Neonatal Assessment Scale detects differences among newborn infants of optimal health. *Journal of Pediatric Psychology, 25*(8), 577–582.

Lundqvist-Persson, C., Lau, G., Nordin, P., Bona, E. & Sabel, K. G. (2011, November 29). Preterm infants' early developmental status is associated with later developmental outcome. doi: 10.1111/j.1651-2227.2011.02526.x.

Lunemann, A. (1974). The correlational validity of I.Q. as a function of ethnicity and desegregation. *Journal of School Psychology, 12*, 263–268.

Lunneborg, C. (1978). Some information-processing correlates of measures of intelligence. *Multivariate Behavioral Research, 13*, 153–161.

Luo, D., Thompson, L. A., & Detterman, D. K. (2003). The causal factor underlying the correlation between psychometric *g* and scholastic performance. *Intelligence, 31*(1), 67–83.

Luo, D., Thompson, L. A., & Detterman, D. K. (2006). The criterion validity of tasks of basic cognitive processes. *Intelligence, 34*(1), 79–120.

Luria, A. R. (1966). *Higher cortical functions in man.* New York: Basic Books.

Luria, A. R. (1973). The *working brain.* New York: Basic Books.

Lurie, J. D., & Sox, H. C. (1999). Principles of medical decision making. *Spine, 24*(5), 493–498.

Lysaker, P. H., Clements, C. A., Wright, D. E., Evans, J., & Marks, K. A. (2001). Neurocognitive correlates of helplessness, hopelessness, and well-being in schizophrenia. *Journal of Nervous and Mental Disease, 189*(7), 457–462.

Mabon, H. (1998). Utility aspects of personality and performance. *Human Performance, 11*, 289–304.

Mabry, L. (1995). Review of the Wide Range Achievement Test–3. In *The 12th mental measurements yearbook* (pp. 1108–1110). Lincoln, NE: Buros Institute of Mental Measurements.

Machover, K. (1949). *Personality projection in the drawings of the human figure: A method of personality investigation.* Springfield, IL: Thomas.

Macias, M. M., Saylor, C. F., Greer, M. K., Charles, J. M., Bell, N., & Katikaneni, L. D. (1998). Infant screening: The usefulness of the Bayley Infant Neurodevelopment Screener and the Clinical Adaptive Test/Clinical Linguistic Auditory Milestone Scale. *Journal of Development and Behavioral Pediatrics, 19*, 155–161.

Mack, L. J., & Rybarczyk, B. D. (2011). Behavioral treatment of insomnia: A proposal for a stepped-care approach to promote public health. *Nature and Science of Sleep, 3*, 87–99. Retrieved from http://dx.doi.org/10.2147/NSS.S12975.

MacKinnon, R. A. (1980). Psychiatric interview. In H. I. Kaplan, A. M. Freedman, & B. J. Sadock (Eds.), *Comprehensive textbook for psychiatry* (Vol. 3). Baltimore: Williams & Wilkins.

Mackintosh, N. J. (1981). A new measure of intelligence. *Nature, 289*(5798), 529–530.

Magalette, P. R., & Oliver, J. M. (1999). The hope construct, will, and ways: Their relations with self-efficacy, optimism, and general well-being. *Journal of Clinical Psychology, 55*(5), 539–551.

Magnusson, D., & Endler, N. S. (1977). Interactional psychology: Present status and future prospects. In D. Magnusson & N. S. Endler (Eds.), *Personality at the crossroads: Current issues in interactional psychology.* Hillsdale, NJ: Erlbaum.

Maisto, S. A., McKay, J. R., & Connors, G. J. (1990). Self-report issues in substance abuse: State of the art and future directions. *Behavioral Assessment, 12*, 117–134.

Maj, M., Gaebel, W., Lopez-Ibor, J. J., & Sartorius, N. (Eds.). (2002). *Psychiatric diagnosis and classification.* New York: Wiley.

Majnemer, A., & Mazer, B. (1998). Neurologic evaluation of the newborn infant: Definition and psychometric properties. *Developmental Medicine and Child Neurology, 40*, 708–715.

Makkonen, I., Riikonen, R., Kuikka. J. T., Kokki, H., Bressler, J. P., Marshall, C., & Kaufmann, W. E. (2011). Brain derived neurotrophic factor and serotonin transporter binding as markers of clinical response to fluoxetine therapy in children with autism. *Journal of Pediatric Neurology, 9*(1), 1–8. doi:10.3233/JPN-2010-0446.

Malda, M., van de Vijver, F., Srinivasan, K., Transler, C., & Sukumaar, P. (2010). Traveling with cognitive tests: Testing the validity of a KABC-II adaptation in India. *Assessment, 17*, 107–115.

Malgady, R., Barcher, P. R., Davis, J., & Towner, G. (1980). Validity of the vocational adaptation rating scale: Prediction of mentally retarded workers' placement in sheltered workshops. *American Journal of Mental Deficiency, 84*, 633–640.

Malgady, R. G., Constantino, G., & Rogler, L. H. (1984). Development of a Thematic Apperception Test (TEMAS) for urban Hispanic children. *Journal of Consulting and Clinical Psychology, 52*(6), 986–996.

Malinchoc, M., Oxford, K. P., Colligan, R. C., & Morse, R. M. (1994). The Common Alcohol Logistic–Revised Scale (CAL-R): A revised alcoholism scale for the MMPI and MMPI-2. *Journal of Clinical Psychology, 50*(3), 436–445.

Mallinckrodt, C. H., Tamura, R. N., & Tanaka, Y. (2011). Recent developments in improving signal detection and reducing placebo response in psychiatric clinical trials. *Journal of Psychiatric Research, 45*(9), 1202–1207. doi:10.1016/j.jpsychires.2011.03.001.

Maloney, M. P., & Ward, M. P. (1976). *Psychological assessment: A conceptual approach.* New York: Oxford University Press.

Malreaux, J. (1999). A two-pronged attack on standardized tests is needed. *Black Issues in Higher Education, 73.*

Maltby, J., Wood, A. M., Day, L., Pinto, D. (2011) The position of authenticity within extant models of personality, *Personality and Individual Differences.* ISSN 0191-8869; doi:10.1016/j.paid.2011.10.014. Retrieved from http://www.sciencedirect.com/science/article/pii/S0191886911004697.

Maltby, N., Kirsch, I., Mayers, M., & Allen, G. J. (2002). Virtual reality exposure therapy for the treatment of fear of flying: A controlled investigation. *Journal of Consulting & Clinical Psychology, 70*(5), 1112–1118.

Mandes, E., & Gessner, T. (1988). Differential effects on verbal performance achievement levels on the WAIS-R as a function of progressive error rate on the Memory for Designs Test (MFD). *Journal of Clinical Psychology, 44*, 795–798.

Mandler, G., & Sarason, S. B. (1952). A study of anxiety and learning. *Journal of Abnormal and Social Psychology, 47*, 166–173.

Manners, J. & Derkin, K. (2001). A critical review of the validity of ego development theory and its measurement. *Journal of Personality Assessment, 77*, 541–567.

Mannheim, K. (1936). *Ideology and utopia.* London: Kegan, Paul, Trench, Trubner.

Mao, T. (2011). Study on word association knowledge and reading ability. *Applied Mechanics and Materials, 109*, 699–702. doi:10.4028/www.scientific.net/AMM.109.699.

Mapou, R. L., & Spector, J. (1995). *Clinical neuropsychological assessment: A cognitive approach.* New York: Plenum.

*Marchall et al. v. Georgia.* (1985). U.S. District Court for the Southern District of Georgia, CV482-233 (June 28, 1984), *aff'd,* 11th cir no 848771 (Oct. 29, 1985).

Marchand, Y., Lefebvre, C. D., & Connolly, J. F. (2006). Correlating digit span performance and event-related potentials to assess working memory. *International Journal of Psychophysiology, 62*(2), 280–289.

Marchman, V. A., Saccuman, C., & Wulfeck, B. (2004). Productive use of the English past tense in children with focal brain injury and specific language impairment. *Brain and Language, 88*, 202–214.

Marcus, S., Lopez, J. F., McDonough, S., MacKenzie, M. J., Flynn, H., Neal Jr., C. R., Gahagan, S., Volling, B., Kaciroti, N., Vazquez, D. M. (2011). Depressive symptoms during pregnancy: Impact on neuroendocrine and neonatal outcomes. *Infant Behavior and Development, 34*(1), 26–34. ISSN 0163-6383, 10.1016/j.infbeh.2010.07.002.

Mark, J. C. (1993). [Review of the book *The Thematic Apperception Test, the Children's Apperception Test, and the Senior Apperception Technique in clinical use,* 5th edition]. *Contemporary Psychology, 38*(9), 971–972.

Marlett, N. J., & Watson, D. (1968). Test anxiety and immediate or delayed feedback in a test-avoidance task. *Journal of Personality and Social Psychology, 8*, 200–203.

Marques, R. C., Dórea, J. G., Bernardi, J. V. E., Bastos, W. R., & Malm, O. (2009). Prenatal and postnatal mercury exposure, breastfeeding and neurodevelopment during the first 5 years. *Cognitive & Behavioral Neurology, 22*(2), 134–141. doi:10.1097/WNN.0b013e3181 a72248.

Marsh, H. W., & Bazeley, P. (1999). Multiple evaluations of grant proposals by independent assessors: Confirmatory factor analysis evaluations of reliability, validity, and structure. *Multivariate Behavioral Research 34*(1), 1–30.

Marsh, H. W., Hau, K., Artelt, C., Baumert, J., & Peschar, J. (2006). OECD's brief self-report measure of educational psychology's most useful affective constructs: Cross-cultural, psychometric comparisons across 25 countries. *International Journal of Testing, 6*(4), 311–360.

Marshalek, B., Lohman, D. F., & Snow, R. E. (1983). The complexity continuum in the Radex and hierarchical models of intelligence. *Journal of Intelligence, 7*, 107–127.

Martin, A., & Swinson, R. P. (2000). Cognitive strategies. In A. Martin & R. P. Swinson (Eds.), *Phobic disorders and panic in adults: A guide to assessment and treatment* (pp. 239–254). Washington, DC: American Psychological Association.

Martin, P., Johnson, M., Poon, L. W., Clayton, G. M., et al. (1994). Group or individual testing: Does it make a difference? *Educational Gerontology, 20*, 171–176.

Martin, R., Sawrie, S., Gilliam, F., Mackey, M., Faught, E., Knowlton, R., & Kuzniecky, R. (2002). Determining reliable cognitive change after epilepsy surgery: Development of reliable change indices and standardized regression-based change norms for the WMS-III and WASI-III. *Epilepsia, 43*(12), 1551–1558.

Martin, R. A., Berry, G. E., Dobranski, T., Horne, M., & others. (1996). Emotion perception threshold: Individual differences in emotional sensitivity. *Journal of Research in Personality, 30,* 290–305.

Masling, J. (2006). When Homer nods: An examination of some systematic errors in Rorschach scholarship. *Journal of Personality Assessment, 87*(1), 62–73.

Masling, J. M., & Bornstein, R. F. (2005). Scoring the Rorschach: Retrospect and prospect. In R. F. Bornstein, & J. M. Masling (Eds.), *Scoring the Rorschach: Seven validated systems.* (pp. 1–24). Mahwah, NJ: Lawrence Erlbaum Associates Publishers.

Massey, D., & Mooney, M. (2007). The effects of America's three affirmative action programs on academic performance. *Social Problems, 54*(1), 99–117.

Masters, B. N. (1988). Item discrimination: One more is worse. *Journal of Educational Measurement 25,* 15–29.

Masters, W., & Johnson, V. (1966). *Human sexual response.* Boston: Little, Brown.

Masuda, A., Twohig, M. P., Stormo, A. R., Feinstein, A. B., Chou, Y. Y., & Wendell, J. W. (2010). The effects of cognitive defusion and thought distraction on emotional discomfort and believability of negative self-referential thoughts. *Journal of Behavior Therapy and Experimental Psychiatry, 41*(1), 11–17. doi:10.1016/j.jbtep.2009.08.006.

Matarazzo, J. D. (1986). Computerized clinical psychological test interpretations: Unvalidated plus all mean and no sigma. *American Psychologist, 41,* 14–24.

Matarazzo, J. D. (1990). Psychological assessment versus psychological testing: Validation from Binet to the school, clinic, and court room. *American Psychologist, 45,* 999–1017.

Matheny, K. B., Curlette, W. L., Aysan, F., Herrington, A., Gfroerer, C. A., Thompson, D., & Hamarat, E. (2002). Coping resources, perceived stress and life satisfaction among Turkish and American university students. *International Journal of Stress Management, 9*(2), 81–97.

Mather, N., & Schrank, F. A. (2001). *Use of the WJ III discrepancy procedures for learning disabilities identification and diagnosis* (Assessment bulletin no. 3). Itasca, IL: Riverside.

Matias, R., & Turner, S. M. (1986). Concordance and discordance in speech anxiety assessment: The effects

of demand characteristics on the tri-partite assessment method. *Behavior Research and Therapy, 24,* 537–545.

Mattlar, C. (2004). The Rorschach comprehensive system is reliable, valid, and cost-effective. In A. Andronikof (Ed.), *Rorschachiana XXVI: Yearbook of the international Rorschach society.* (pp. 158–186). Ashland, OH: Hogrefe & Huber Publishers.

Mattson, D. C. (2011). Standardizing the formal elements art therapy scale (FEATS) rotation scale with computerized technology: A pilot study. *The Arts in Psychotherapy, 38*(2), 120–124. ISSN 0197-4556; doi:10.1016/j.aip.2011.02.003. Retrieved from http://www.sciencedirect.com/science/article/pii/S0197455611000207.

Mau, W., & Lynn, R. (2001). Gender differences on Scholastic Aptitude Test, the American College Test, and college grades. *Educational Psychology, 21*(2), 133–136.

Maurer, T. J., & Alexander, R. A. (1991). Contrast effects in behavioral measurement: An investigation of alternative process explanations. *Journal of Applied Psychology, 76,* 3–10.

Maurer, T. J., Solamon, J. M., Andrews, K. D., & Troxtel, D. D. (2001). Interviewee coaching, preparation strategies, and response strategies in relation to performance in situational employment interviews: An extension of Maurer, Solamon, and Troxtel (1998). *Journal of Applied Psychology, 86,* 709–717.

Mayer, D. M., & Hanges, P. J. (2003). Understanding the stereotype threat effect with "culture-free" tests: An examination of its mediators and measurement. *Human Performance, 16*(3), 207–230.

Mayfield, E. C. (1964). The selection interview: A re-evaluation of published research. *Personnel Psychology, 17,* 239–260.

Mazidi, M. (2005). Intensity and prevalence of current fears among Iranian university students. *Psychological Reports, 96*(1), 190–196.

McCabe, K. M., Yeh, M., Lau, A., Garland, A., & Hough, R. (2003). Racial/ethnic differences in caregiver strain and perceived social support among parents of youth with emotional and behavioral problems. *Mental Health Services Research, 5*(3), 137–147.

McCabe, S. E., Boyd, C. J., Couper, M. P., Crawford, S., & D'Arcy, H. (2002). Mode effects for collecting alcohol and other drug use data: Web

and U.S. mail. *Journal of Studies on Alcohol, 63*(6), 755–761.

McCall, R. B. (1994). *Fundamental statistics for behavioral sciences* (6th ed.). Fort Worth, TX: Harcourt Brace.

McCall, R. B. (2001). *Fundamental statistics for behavioral sciences* (8th ed.). Belmont, CA: Wadsworth.

McCall, W. A. (1939). *Measurement.* New York: Macmillan.

McCallum, R. S. (1990). Determining the factor structure of the Stanford-Binet: Fourth Edition—The right choice. *Journal of Psychoeducational Assessment, 8,* 436–442.

McCallum, R. S., Karnes, F. A. & Oehler-Stinnett, J. (1985). Construct validity of the K-ABC for gifted children. *Psychology in the Schools, 22,* 254–259.

McCarty, J. R., Noble, A. C., & Huntley, R. M. (1989). Effects of item wording on sex bias. *Journal of Educational Measurement, 26,* 285–293.

McCaulley, M. H., & Martin, C. R. (1995). Career assessment and the Myers-Briggs Type Indicator. *Journal of Career Assessment, 3,* 219–239.

McClelland, D. C. (1994). The knowledge-testing-educational complex strikes back. *American Psychologist, 490,* 66–69.

McClelland, D. C. (1999). How the test lives on: Extensions of the Thematic Apperception Test approach. In L. G. Gieser & M. I. Stein (Eds.). *Evocative images: The Thematic Apperception Test and the art of projection.* Washington, DC: American Psychological Association.

McCormick, E. J., & Ilgen, D. (1980). *Industrial psychology* (7th ed.). Englewood Cliffs, NJ: Prentice-Hall.

McCrae, R. R., & Costa, P. T. (2003). *Personality in adulthood: A five factor theory perspective* (2nd ed.). New York: Guilford Press.

McCrae, R. R., Costa, P. T., Del Pilar, G. H., Rolland, J. P., & Parker, W. D. (1998). Cross-cultural assessment of the five-factor model: The Revised NEO Personality Inventory. *Journal of Cross-Cultural Psychology, 29,* 171–188.

McCrowell, K. L., & Nagle, R. J. (1994). Comparability of the WPPSI-R and the S-B: IV among preschool children. *Journal of Psychoeducational Assessment, 12*(2), 126–134.

McDaniel, M. A. (1989). Biographical constructs for predicting employee suitability. *Journal of Applied Psychology, 74,* 964–970.

McDaniel, M. A., Whetzel, D. L., Schmidt, F. L., & Maurer, S. D.

(1994). The validity of employment interviews: A comprehensive review and meta-analysis. *Journal of Applied Psychology, 79*, 599–616.

McDonald, R. P. (1999). *Test theory: A unified treatment*. Mahwah, NJ: Erlbaum.

McDowell, I., & Newell, C. (1996). *Measuring health: A guide to rating scales and questionnaires* (2nd ed.). New York: Oxford University Press.

McEwen, J. (1992). The Nottingham Health Profile. In S. R. Walker & R. M. Rosser (Eds.), *Quality of life assessment: Key issues for the 1990s*. Dordreht, Netherlands: Kluwer Academic Publishers.

McFall, R. M., & McDonell, A. (1986). The continuous search for units of analysis in psychology: Beyond persons, situations, and their interactions. In R. O. Nelson & S. C. Hays (Eds.), *Conceptual foundations of behavioral assessment*. New York: Guilford Press.

McGhee, R. (1993). Fluid and crystallized intelligence: Confirmatory factor analyses of the Differential Abilities Scale, Detroit Tests of Learning Aptitude—3, and Woodcock-Johnson PsychoEducational Battery—Revised. In B. A. Bracken & R. S. McCallum (Eds.), *Woodcock-Johnson PsychoEducational Battery–Revised* [Monograph]. *Journal of Psychoeducational Assessment*, pp. 20–38.

McGill-Evans, J., & Harrison, M. J. (2001). Parent-child interactions, parenting stress, and developmental outcomes at 4 years. *Children's Health Care, 30*(2), 135–140.

McGivern, R. F., Berka, C., Langlais, M. L., & Chapman, S. (1991). Detection of deficits in temporal pattern discrimination using the Seashore Rhythm Test in young children with reading impairments. *Journal of Learning Disabilities, 24*, 58–62.

McGlone, M., & Pfiester, R. (2007). The generality and consequences of stereotype threat. *Sociology Compass, 1*(1), 174–190.

McGrath, R. E., Sweeney, M., O'Malley, W. B., & Carlton, T. K. (1998). Identifying psychological contributions to chronic pain complaints with the MMPI-2: The role of the K scale. *Journal of Personality Assessment, 70*, 448–459.

McGraw, K. O., Tew, M. D., & Williams, J. E. (2000). The integrity of web-delivered experiments: Can we trust the data? *Psychological Science, 11*(6), 502–506.

McGregor, C. M. (2001). Test review of the Neonatal Behavioral Assessment Scale (NBAS). In R. A. Spies, J. F. Carlson, & K. F. Geisinger (Eds.), *The fourteenth mental measurements yearbook*. Retrieved from http://www.unl.edu/buros.

McGrew, K. S. (1986). Investigation of the verbal/nonverbal structure of the Wookcock-Johnson: Implications for subtest interpretation and comparisons with the Wechsler scales. *Journal of Psychoeducational Assessment, 3*(1), 65–71.

McGrew, K. S., & Flanagan, D. P. (1998). *The intelligence test desk reference (ITDR)*. Boston: Allyn & Bacon.

McGrew, K. S., & Murphy, S. (1995). Uniqueness and general factor characteristics of the Woodcock-Johnson Tests of Cognitive Ability—Revised. *Journal of School Psychology, 33*, 235–245.

McGrew, K. S., & Woodcock, R. W. (2001). *Technical manual. Woodcock-Johnson III*. Itasca. IL: Riverside.

McGrew, S. (1993). The relationship between the Woodcock-Johnson Psycho-Educational Battery—Revised *Gf-Gc* cognitive clusters and reading achievement across the lifespan. In B. A. Bracken & R. S. McCallum (Eds.), *Woodcock-Johnson Psycho-Educational Battery—Revised* [Monograph]. *Journal of Psychoeducational Assessment*, pp. 39–53.

McHorney, C. A. (1999). Health status assessment methods for adults: past accomplishments and future challenges. *Annual Review of Public Health, 20*(3), 309–335.

McIntire, S. A., & Miller, L. A. (2000). *Foundations of psychological testing*. Boston: McGraw-Hill.

McKay, P. F., & Doverspike, D. (2001). African Americans' test-taking attitudes and their effect on cognitive ability test performance: Implications for public personnel management selection practice. *Public Personnel Management, 30*(1), 67–75.

McKenna, P., Clare, L., & Baddeley, A. D. (1995). Schizophrenia. In A. D. Baddeley, B. A. Wilson, & F. N. Watts (Eds.), *Handbook of memory disorders* (pp. 271–292). Chichester, England: Wiley.

McKown, C. (2007). Concurrent validity and clinical usefulness of several individually administered tests of children's social-emotional cognition. *Journal of Clinical Child and Adolescent Psychology, 36*(1), 29–41.

McLennan, N. A., & Arthur, N. (1999). Applying the Cognitive Information Processing approach to career problem solving and decision making to women's career development. *Journal of Employment Counseling, 36*(2), 82–96.

McMahon, R. C., Davidson, R. S., Gersh, D., & Flynn, P. (1991). A comparison of continuous and episodic drinkers using the MCMI, MMPI, and ALCEVAL-R. *Journal of Clinical Psychology, 47*, 148–159.

McMichael, A. J., Baghurst, P. A., Wigg, N. R., Vimpani, G. V., Robertson, E. F., & Roberts, R. J. (1988). Port Pirie Cohort Study: Environmental exposure to lead and children's abilities at the age of four years. *New England Journal of Medicine, 319*, 468–475.

McMinn, M. R., Bearse, J., Heyne, L. K. Smithberger, A., & Erb, A. L. (2011). Technology and independent practice: Survey findings and implications. *Professional Psychology: Research and Practice, 42*(2), 176–184. doi:10.1037/a0022719.

McNemar, O. W., & Landis, C. (1935). Childhood disease and emotional maturity in the psychopathic woman. *Journal of Abnormal and Social Psychology, 30*, 314–319.

McNemar, Q. (1969). *Psychological statistics* (4th ed.). New York: Wiley.

McRae, R. R. (2011.) Personality traits and the potential of positive psychology, In K. M. Sheldon, T. B. Kashdan, & M. F. Steger (Eds.), *Designing positive psychology: Taking stock and moving forward* (pp. 430–439). New York: Oxford University Press.

McReynolds, C. J., Ward, D. M., & Singer, O. (2002). Stigma, discrimination, and invisibility: Factors affecting successful integration of individuals diagnosed with schizophrenia. *Journal of Applied Rehabilitation Counseling, 33*(4), 32–39.

Medoff-Cooper, B., McGrath, J. M., & Bilker, W. (2000). Nutritive sucking and neurobehavioral development in preterm infants from 34 weeks PCA to term. *American Journal of Maternal Child Nursing, 25*(2), 64–70.

Meehl, P. E. (1951). *Research results for counselors*. St. Paul, MN: State Department of Education.

Meehl, P. E. (1954). Clin*ical versus statistical prediction: A theoretical analysis and a review of the evidence*. Minneapolis: University of Minnesota Press.

Meehl, P. E. (1956). Wanted—a good cookbook. *American Psychologist, 11*, 263–272.

Meehl, P. E. (1957). When shall we use our heads instead of the formula? *Journal of Counseling Psychology, 4,* 268–273.

Meehl, P. E. (1995). Utiles, hedons, and the mind-body problem, or, who's afraid of Vilfredo? In P. E. Shrout & S. T. Fiske (Eds.), *Personality research, methods, and theory: A festschrift honoring Donald W. Fiske* (pp. 45–66). Hillsdale, NJ: Erlbaum.

Meehl, P. E. (1997). Credentialed persons, credentialed knowledge. *Clinical Psychology: Science and Practice, 4,* 91–98.

Meehl, P. E., & Dahlstrom, W. G. (1960). Objective configural rules for discriminating psychotic from neurotic MMPI profiles. *Journal of Consulting Psychology, 24,* 375–387.

Meehl, P. E., & Rosen, A. (1955). Antecedent probability and the efficiency of psychometric signs, patterns or cutting scores. *Psychological Bulletin, 52,* 194–216.

Meersand, P. (2011). Psychological testing and the analytically trained child psychologist. *Psychoanalytical Psycholologist, 28,* 117–131.

Meesters, C., van Gastel, N., Ghys, A., & Merckelbach, H. (1998). Factor analyses of WISC-R and KABC in a Dutch sample of children referred for learning disabilities. *Journal of Clinical Psychology, 54,* 1053–1061.

Megargee, E. I. (1972). *The California Psychological Inventory Handbook.* San Francisco: Jossey-Bass.

Mehl, M. R., Pennebaker, J. W., Crow, D. M., Dabbs, J., & Price, J. H. (2001). The Electronically Activated Recorder (EAR) : A device for sampling naturalistic daily activities and conversations. *Behavior Research Methods, Instruments, and Computers, 33*(4), 517–523.

Mehrens, W. A. (2000). Defending a state graduation test: *GI Forum* v. *Texas Education Agency.* Measurement perspectives from an external evaluator. *Applied Measurement in Education, 13*(4), 387–401.

Meichenbaum, D. (1976). A cognitive-behavior modification approach to assessment. In M. Hersen & A. S. Bellack (Eds.), *Behavioral assessment.* New York: Pergamon Press.

Meichenbaum, D. (1999). Behandlung von Patienten mit posttraumatischen Belastungsstoerungen: Ein konstruktiv-narrativer Ansatz. [Treatment of patients with posttraumatic stress disorder: A constructive-narrative approach]. *Verhaltenstherapie, 9*(4), 186–189.

Meichenbaum, D. (2003). Cognitive behavior therapy: Folktales and the unexpurgated history. *Cognitive Therapy & Research, 27*(1), 125–129.

Meijer, R. R. (2003). Diagnosing item score patterns on a test using item response theory-based person fit statistics. Washington, DC: American Psychological Association.

Meikle, S., & Gerritse, R. (1970). NIMPI cookbook pattern frequencies in a psychiatric unit. *Journal of Clinical Psychology, 26,* 82–84.

Meinhardt, M., Hibbett, C., Koller, J., & Busch, R. (1993). Comparison of the Woodcock-Johnson PsychoEducational Battery—Revised and the Wechsler Intelligence Scale for Children—Revised with incarcerated adolescents. In B. A. Bracken & R. S. McCallum (Eds.), *Woodcock-Johnson PsychoEducational Battery—Revised* [Monograph]. *Journal of Psychoeducational Assessment,* pp. 64–70.

Melchert, T. P. (1998). Support for the validity of the Graduate Record Examination. *American Psychologist, 53,* 573–574.

Melei, J. P., & Hilgard, E. R. (1964). Attitudes toward hypnosis, self predictions, and hypnotic susceptibility. *International Journal of Clinical and Experimental Hypnosis, 12,* 99–108.

Mellenbergh, G. J. (1999). A note on simple gain precision. *Applied Psychological Measurement, 23*(1), 87–89

Meloy, J. R., & Singer, J. (1991). A psychoanalytic view of the Rorschach Comprehensive System "Special Scores." *Journal of Personality Assessment, 56,* 202–217.

Ment, L. R., Vohr, B., Allan, W., Katz, K. H., & Schneider, K. C., Westerveld, M., Duncan, C. C., & Makuch, R. W. (2003). Change in cognitive function over time in very low-birth-weight infants. *Journal of the American Medical Association, 289*(6), 705–711.

Mercer, J. R. (1971). Sociocultural factors in labeling mental retardates. *Peabody Journal of Education, 48,* 188–203.

Mercer, J. R. (1972, September). *Anticipated achievement: Computerizing the self-fulfilling prophecy.* Paper presented at the meeting of the American Psychological Association, Honolulu, HI.

Mercer, J. R. (1973). *Labeling the mentally retarded: Clinical and social system perspective on mental retardation.* Berkeley: University of California Press.

Mercer, J. R. (1979). In defense of racially and culturally nondiscriminatory assessment. *School Psychology Digest, 8*(1), 89–115.

Mercer, J. R. (1988). Ethnic differences in IQ scores: What do they mean? (A response to Lloyd Dunn) [Special Issue: Achievement testing: Science vs. ideology]. *Hispanic Journal of Behavioral Sciences, 10,* 199–218.

Merrell, K. W. (1999). *Behavioral, social, and emotional assessment of children and adolescents.* Mahwah NJ: Erlbaum.

Merrell, K. W. (2003). *Behavioral, social, and emotional assessment of children and adolescents* (2nd ed.). Mahwah, NJ: Erlbaum.

Merten, T. (1995). Factors influencing word-association responses: A reanalysis. *Creativity Research Journal, 8,* 249–263.

Mervis, C. B., & Robinson, B. F. (2003). Methodological issues in cross-group comparisons of language and cognitive development. In Y. Levy & J. Schaeffer (Eds.), *Language competence across populations: Toward a definition of special language impairment* (pp. 233–258). Mahwah, NJ: Erlbaum.

Messick, S. (1994). Foundations of validity: Meaning and consequences in psychological assessment. Second Conference of the European Association of Psychological Assessment Keynote Address (1993, Groningen, Netherlands). *European Journal of Psychological Assessment, 10*(1), 1–9.

Messick, S. J. (1998a). Alternative modes of assessment, uniform standards of validity. In Milton D. Hakel (Ed.), *Beyond multiple choice: Evaluating alternatives to traditional testing for selection* (pp. 59–74). Mahwah, NJ: Erlbaum.

Messick, S. (1998b). Test validity: A matter of consequence. *Social Indicators Research, 45*(1–3), 35–44.

Messick, S. J. (Ed.). (1999). *Assessment in higher education: Issues of access, quality, student development, and public policy.* Mahwah, NJ: Erlbaum.

Messick, S., & Jungeblut, A. (1981). Time and method in coaching for the SAT. *Psychological Bulletin, 89,* 191–216.

Meunier, C., & Rule, B. G. (1967). Anxiety, confidence, and conformity. *Journal of Personality, 35,* 498–504.

Meyer, G. J. (1992). Response frequency problems in the Rorschach: Clinical and research implications with suggestions for the future. *Journal of Personality Assessment, 58,* 231–244.

Meyer, G. J. (1999). Introduction to the special series on the utility of the Rorschach for clinical assessment. *Psychological Assessment, 11,* 235–239.

Meyer, G. J., Finn, S. E., Eyde, L. D., Kay, G. G., Moreland, K. L., Dies, R. R., Eisman, E. J., Kubiszyn, T. W., & Reed, G. M. (2003). Psychological testing and psychological assessment: A review of evidence and issues. In A. E. (Ed.), *Methodological issues and strategies in clinical research* (3rd ed.) (pp. 265–345). Washington, DC: American Psychological Association.

Meyer, R. G. (1993). *The clinician's handbook: Integrated diagnostics, assessment, and intervention in adult and adolescent psychopathology* (3rd ed.). Boston: Allyn & Bacon.

Miceli, N. S., Harvey, M., & Buckley, M. R. (2001). Potential discrimination in structured employment interviews. *Employee Responsibilities & Rights Journal, 12*(1), 15–38.

Michell, J. (1999). *Measurement in psychology: Critical history of a methodological concept.* New York: Cambridge University Press.

Middendorf, C. H., & Macan, T. H. (2002). Note-taking in the employment interview: Effects on recall and judgements. *Journal of Applied Psychology, 87*(2), 293–303.

Miele, F. (2002). *Intelligence, race, and genetics: Conversations with Arthur R. Jensen.* Boulder, CO: Westview Press.

Miettunen, J., Veijola, J., Isohanni, M., Paunio, T., Freimer, N., Jääskeläinen, E. Taanila, A., Ekelund, J., Järvelin, M., Peltonen, L., Joukamaa, M., & Lichtermann, D. (2011) Identifying schizophrenia and other psychoses with psychological scales in the general population. *Journal of Nervous & Mental Disease, 199*(4), 230–238. doi:10.1097/NMD. 0b013e3182125d2c.

Mikulay, S. M., & Goffin, R. D. (1998). Measuring and predicting counterproductivity in the laboratory using integrity and personality testing. *Educational and Psychological Measurement, 58*, 768–790.

Milgrom, P., Jie, Z., Yang, Z., & Tay, K. M. (1994). Cross-cultural validity of a Parent's Version of the Dental Fear Survey Schedule for Children in Chinese. *Behaviour Research and Therapy, 32*(1), 131–135.

Miller, A. B. (1991). Is routine mammography screening appropriate for women 40–49 years of age? *American Journal of Preventive Medicine, 91*, 55–62.

Miller, B., McCardle, P., & Hernandez, R. (2010). Advances and remaining challenges in adult literacy research. *Journal of Learning Disabilities, 43*, 101–107. doi:10.1177/ 0022219409359341.

Miller, E. T., Neal, D. J., Roberts, L. J., Baer, J. S., Cressler, S. O., Metrik, J., & Marlatt, G. A. (2002). Test-retest reliability of alcohol measures: Is there a difference between internet-based assessment and traditional methods? *Psychology of Addictive Behaviors, 16*(1), 56–63.

Miller, J. A. L., Scurfield, B. K., Drga, V., Galvin, S. J., & Whitmore, J. (2002). Nonparametric relationships between single-interval and two-interval forced-choice tasks in the theory of signal detectability. *Journal of Mathematical Psychology, 46*(4), 383–417.

Miller, J. G., & Kinsbourne, M. (2011). Culture and neuroscience in developmental psychology: Contributions and challenges. *Child development perspectives.* Retrieved from http://onlinelibrary.wiley.com/doi/10.1111/j.1750-8606.2011.00188.x/full. doi:10.1111/j.1750-8606.2011.00188.x.

Miller, J. M., Goodyear-Orwat, A., & Malott, R. W. (1996). The effects of intensive, extensive, structured study on GRE scores. *Journal of Behavioral Education, 6*(4), 369–379.

Miller, J. O., & Phillips, J. (1966). A preliminary evaluation of the Head Start and other metropolitan Nashville kindergartens. Unpublished manuscript, George Peabody College for Teachers, TN.

Miller-Loncar, C., Lester, B. M., Seifer, R., Lagasse, L. L., Bauer, C. R., Shankaran, S., et al. (2005). Predictors of motor development in children prenatally exposed to cocaine. *Neurotoxicology and Teratology, 27*(2), 213–220.

Millett, G. A., Ding, H., Marks, G., Jeffries, W., Bingham, T., Lauby, J., Murrill, C., Flores, S., & Stueve, A. (2011). Mistaken assumptions and missed opportunities: Correlates of undiagnosed hiv infection among black and latino men who have sex with men. *Journal of Acquired Immune Deficiency Syndromes, 58*(1), 64–71.

Millon, T. (1969). *Modern psychopathology: A biosocial approach to maladaptive learning and functioning.* Philadelphia: Saunders.

Millon, T. (1983). *Millon Clinical Multiaxial Inventory Manual* (2nd ed.). Minneapolis, MN: National Computer Systems.

Millon, T. (1985). The MCMI provides a good assessment of DSMI-II disorders: The MCMI-II will prove even better. *Journal of Personality Assessment, 49*, 379–391.

Millon T. (1987). *Millon Clinical Multiaxial Inventory—II (Manual).* Minneapolis, MN: National Computer Systems.

Mills, C. N., Potenza, M. T., Fremer, J. J., & Ward, W. C. (2002). *Computer based testing: Building the foundation for future assessments.* Mahwah, NJ: Erlbaum.

Min, K. H., Kim, J. H., Hwang, S. H. S., & Jahng, S. M. (1998). Variations in emotion response patterning across genders, generations, and personality types. *Korean Journal of Social & Personality Psychology, 12*(2), 119–140.

Minguez-Milio, J. A., Alcázar, J. L., Aubá, M., Ruiz-Zambrana, A., & Minguez, J. (2011). Perinatal outcome and long-term follow-up of extremely low birth weight infants depending on the mode of delivery. *Journal of Maternal-Fetal and Neonatal Medicine, 24*(10), 1235–1238.

Minton, B. A., & Pratt, S. (2006). Gifted and highly gifted students: How do they score on the SB5? *Roeper Review, 28*(4), 232–236.

Minton, H. L., & Schneider, F. W. (1980). *Differential psychology.* Pacific Grove, CA: Brooks/Cole.

Miranda, R., Gallagher, M., Bauchner, B., Vaysman, R. & Marroquín, B. (2011). Cognitive inflexibility as a prospective predictor of suicidal ideation among young adults with a suicide attempt history. *Depression and Anxiety.* doi:10.1002/da.20915.

Mirsky, A. F. (1989). The neuropsychology of attention: Elements of a complex behavior. In E. Ellen Perecman et al. (Eds.), *Integrating theory and practice in clinical neuropsychology* (pp. 75–91). Hillsdale, NJ: Erlbaum.

Mirsky, A. F. (1996). Disorders of attention: A neuropsychological perspective. In G. Reid Lyon, E. Norman, A. Krasnegor, et al. (Eds.), *Attention, memory, and executive function* (pp. 71–95). Baltimore: Williams & Wilkins.

Mirsky, A. F., Kugelmass, S., Ingraham, L. J., & Frenkel, E. (1995). Overview and summary: Twenty-five-year followup of high-risk children. *Schizophrenia Bulletin, 21*(2), 227–239.

Mischel, W. (1968). *Personality and assessment.* New York: Wiley.

Mischel, W. (1984). Convergences and challenges in the search for consistency. *American Psychologist, 39*, 351–364.

Mislevy, R. J. (2002). *Psychometric principles in student assessment*. Los Angeles, CA: Center for the Study of Evaluation National Center for Research on Evaluation Standards and Student Testing Graduate School of Education & Information Studies University of California Los Angeles.

Misri, S., Corral, M., Wardrop, A. A., & Kendrick, K. (2006). Quetiapine augmentation in lactation: A series of case reports. *Journal of Clinical Psychopharmacology, 26*(5), 508–511.

Mitchell, A. J., Smith, A. B., Al-salihy, Z., Rahim, T. A., Mahmud, M. Q., & Muhyaldin, A. S. (2011). Redefining diagnostic symptoms of depression using Rasch analysis: Testing an item bank suitable for DSM-V and computer adaptive testing. *Australian and New Zealand Journal of Psychiatry, 45*(10), 846–852.

Moe, V. (2002). Foster placed and adopted children exposed to in utero opiates and other substances: Prediction and outcome at four and a half years. *Journal of Developmental and Behavioral Pediatrics, 23*(5), 330–339.

Molfese, V. J., Modglin, A., Molfese, D. L. (2003). The role of environment in the development of readings skills: A longitudinal study of preschool and school-age measures. *Journal of Learning Disabilities, 36*(1), 59–67.

Monahan, J. (2003). Violence risk assessment. In A. M. Goldstein (Ed.), *Handbook of psychology: Forensic psychology* (Vol. 11) (pp. 527–540), New York: Wiley.

Moon, N. M., Mohay, H. A., & Gray, P. H. (2007). Developmental patterns from 1 to 4 years of extremely preterm infants who required home oxygen therapy. *Early Human Development, 83*(4), 209–216.

Moore, W. L., & Bell, J. M. (2011). Maneuvers of whiteness: 'Diversity' as a mechanism of retrenchment in the affirmative action discourse. *Critical Sociology, 37*(5), 597–613. doi:10.1177/0896920510380066.

Moos, R. H. (1973). Conceptualizations of human environment. *American Psychologist, 28*, 652–665.

Moos, R. H. (1986a). *Group Environment Scale* (2nd ed.). Palo Alto, CA: Consulting Psychologist Press.

Moos, R. H. (1986b). *Work Environment Scale* (2nd ed.). Palo Alto, CA: Consulting Psychologist Press.

Moos, R. H. (1987a). *Community-Oriented Programs Environment Scale manual* (2nd ed.). Palo Alto, CA: Consulting Psychologist Press.

Moos, R. H. (1987b). *Correctional Institutions Environment Scale manual* (2nd ed.). Palo Alto, CA: Consulting Psychologist Press.

Moos, R. H. (1987c). Person-environment congruence in work, school, and health care settings. *Journal of Vocational Behavior, 31*, 231–247.

Moos, R. H. (1987d). *University Residents Environment Scale* (2nd ed.). Palo Alto, CA: Consulting Psychologist Press.

Moos, R. H. (1987e). Ward *Atmosphere Scale Manual* (2nd ed.). Palo Alto, CA: Consulting Psychologist Press.

Moos, R. H. (2003). Social contexts: Transcending their power and their fragility. Netherlands: Kluwer Academic Publishers.

Moos, R. H., & Lemke, S. (1994). *Group residences for older adults: Physical features, policies, and social climate*. New York: Oxford University Press.

Moos, R. H., & Moos, B. (1986). *Family Environment Scale Manual* (2nd ed.). Palo Alto, CA: Consulting Psychologist Press.

Moos, R. H., & Truckett, E. (1986). *Classroom Environment Scale* (2nd ed.). Palo Alto, CA: Consulting Psychologist Press.

Morales, A. (1994). Validation of a psychophysiological Waking Erectile Assessment (WEA) for the diagnosis of Male Erectile Disorder: Comment. *Urology, 43*(5), 695–696.

Moreland, K. L. (1985). Validation of computer-based test interpretations: Problems and prospects. *Journal of Consulting and Clinical Psychology, 53*, 816–825.

Moreland, K. L., Reznikoff, M., & Aronow, E. (1995). Integrating Rorschach interpretation by carefully placing more of your eggs in the content basket. *Journal of Personality Assessment, 64*(2), 239–242.

Moreno, K. E., Segall, D. O., & Hetter, R. D. (1997). The use of computerized adaptive testing in the military. In R. F. Dillon et al. (Eds.), *Handbook on testing* (pp. 204–219). Westport, CT: Greenwood.

Morgan, M. J., Davies, G. M., & Willner, P. (1999). The questionnaire of smoking urges is sensitive to abstinence and exposure to smoking-related cues. *Behavioral Pharmacology, 10*(6–7), 619–626.

Morin, S. F., Steward, W. T., Charlebois, E. D., Remien, R. H., Pinkerton, S. D., Johnson, M. O., et al. (2005). Predicting HIV transmission risk among HIV-infected men who have sex with men: Findings from the healthy living project. *JAIDS Journal of Acquired Immune Deficiency Syndromes, 40*(2), 226–235.

Morrison, T., & Morrison, M. (1995). A meta-analytic assessment of the predictive validity of the quantitative and verbal components of the Graduate Record Examination with graduate grade point average representing the criterion of graduate success. *Educational and Psychological Measurement, 55*(2), 309–316.

Morrow, C. E., Bandstra, E. S., Emmalee, S., Anthony, J. C., Ofir, A. Y., Xue, L., & Reyes, M. L. (2001). Influence of prenatal cocaine exposure on full-term infant neurobehavioral functioning. *Neurotoxicology and Teratology, 23*(6), 533–544.

Moses, J. A., Pritchard, D. A., & Faustman, W. O. (1994). Modal profiles for the Luria-Nebraska Neuropsychological Battery. *Archives of Clinical Neuropsychology, 9*, 15–30.

Moshagen, M., Musch, J., & Erdfelder, E. (2011). A stochastic lie detector. *Behavior Research Methods, 1*–10. doi:10.3758/s13428-011-0144-2.

Motowidlo, S. J., Carter, G. W., Dunnette, M. D., Tippins, N., & others. (1992). Studies of the structured behavioral interview. *Journal of Applied Psychology, 77*, 571–587.

Moun, T. (1998). Mode of administration and interviewer effects in self-reported symptoms of anxiety and depression. *Social Indicators Research, 45*(1–3), 279–318.

Mühlberger, A., Bülthoff, H. H., Wiedemann, G., & Pauli, P. (2007). Virtual reality for the psychophysiological assessment of phobic fear: Responses during virtual tunnel driving. *Psychological Assessment, 19*(3), 340–346.

Mühlberger, A., Weik, A., Pauli, P., & Wiedemann, G. (2006). One-session virtual reality exposure treatment for fear of flying: 1-year follow-up and graduation flight accompaniment effects. *Psychotherapy Research, 16*(1), 26–40.

Muir, S. P., & Tracy, D. M. (1999). Collaborative essay testing. *College Teaching, 47*, 33.

Mulhollen, C. (2007). *The relationship between multiple intelligences and attitude toward independent learning in a high transactional distance environment*. US: ProQuest Information & Learning.

Mulsant, B. H., Kastango, K. B., Rosen, J., Stone, R. A., Mazumdar, S., & Pollock, B. G. (2002). *Inter-rater reliability in clinical trials of depressive disorders*. Washington, DC: American Psychiatric Association.

Munley, P. H., Bains, D. S., Bloem, W. D., & Busby, R. M. (1995). Post-traumatic stress disorder and the MMPI-2. *Journal of Traumatic Stress, 8*(1), 171–178.

Munoz-Eguileta, A. (2007) Irrational beliefs as predictors of emotional adjustment after divorce. *Journal of Rational-Emotive and Cognitive-Behavior Therapy, 25*(1), 1–16.

Munsinger, H. (1975). The adopted child's I.Q.: A critical review. *Psychological Bulletin, 82*, 623–659.

Mupinga, E. E., & Mupinga, D. M. (2005). Perceptions of international students toward GRE. *College Student Journal, 39*(2), 402–408.

Muris, P., & Field, A. P. (2011). The "normal" development of fear. In W. K. Silverman & A. P. Field (Eds.), *Anxiety disorders in children and adolescents* (2nd ed.) (pp. 76–89). New York: Cambridge University Press.

Muris, P., Merckelbach, H., Mayer, B., & Meesters, C. (1998). Common fears and their relationship to anxiety disorders symptomatology in normal children. *Personality and Individual Differences, 24*, 575–578.

Murisa, P., Huijdinga, J., Mayera, B., & de Vriesa, H. (2011). Does "yuck" mean "eek"? Fear responses in children after a disgust manipulation. *Journal of Behavior Therapy and Experimental Psychiatry, 43*(2), 765–769.

Murphy, K. R. (2003a). *The logic of validity generalization*. Mahwah, NJ: Erlbaum.

Murphy, K. R. (Ed.). (2003b). *Validity generalization: A critical review*. Mahwah, NJ: Erlbaum.

Murphy, K. R., & Dzieweczynski, J. L. (2005). Why don't measures of broad dimensions of personality perform better as predictors of job performance. *Human Performance, 18*(4), 343–357.

Murphy, L. L., Impara, J. C., Plake, B. S., & Buros Institute of Mental Measurements. (1999). *Tests in print V: An index to tests, test reviews, and the literature on specific tests*. Lincoln, NE: Buros Institute of Mental Measurements.

Murphy, R. (2010). Front matter, in dynamic assessment, intelligence and measurement. Chichester, UK: John Wiley & Sons, Ltd. doi:10.1002/9780470977484.fmatter.

Murray, H. A. (1938). *Explorations in personality*. New York: Oxford University Press.

Murray, H. A. (1943). *Thematic Appercep-tion Test*. Cambridge, MA: Harvard University Press.

Murstein, B. I. (1963). *Theory and research in projective techniques*. New York: Wiley.

Museum of Modern Art. (1955). *The family of man*. New York: Maco Magazine Corporation.

Musewicz, J., Marczyk, G., Knauss, L., & York D. (2009). Current assessment practice, personality measurement, and Rorschach usage by psychologists. *Journal of Personality Assessment, 91*(5), 453–461.

Naar-King, S., Ellis, D. A., & Frey, M. A. (2003). *Assessing children's well being: A handbook of measures*. Mahwah, NJ: Erlbaum.

Naglieri, J. A. (1985). Review of the Gesell Preschool Test. In J. V. Mitchell (Ed.), *The ninth mental measurements yearbook* (Vol. 1). Highland Park, NJ: Gryphon Press.

Naglieri, J. A., & Ford, D. Y. (2003). Addressing underrepresentation of gifted minority children using the Naglieri Nonverbal Ability Test (NNAT). *Gifted Child Quarterly, 47*(2), 155–160.

Nathanson, B. H., Higgins, T. L., Giglio, R. J., Munshi, I. A., & Steingrub, J. S. (2003). An exploratory study using data envelopment analysis to assess neurotrauma patients in the intensive care unit. *Health Care Management Science, 6*(1), 43–55.

National Cancer Institute. (1991, July). *Cancer Statistics Review: 1973–1988*. Bethesda, MD: Unpublished government report.

National Center for Education Statistics. (1995). *The condition of education 1995/ Indicator 21: Graduate Record Examination (GRE) scores*. Washington, DC: U.S. Department of Education.

National Center for Education Statistics. (2000). *Table 315, Scores on Graduate Record Examination (GRE) and subject matter tests: 1965–1999*. Washington, DC: U.S. Department of Education.

National Center for Education Statistics (2011). Average scores on General Record Examination (GRE) general subjects tests: 1965 through 2009. *Digest of Education Statistics*. Retrieved from http://nces.ed.gov/programs/digest/d10/tables/dt10_344.asp.

National Center for Health Statistics, Health Resources Administration, June 1976.

National Commission on Testing and Public Policy. (1990). From *gatekeeper to gateway: Transforming testing in America*. Chestnut Hill, MA: National Computer Systems, Boston College.

Naughton, M. J., & Shumaker, S. A. (2003). The case for domains of function in quality of life assessment. *Quality of Life Research, 12*(Suppl. 1), 73–80.

Neary, M. P., Cort, S., Bayliss, M. S., and Ware, J. E., Jr. (1999). Sustained virologic response is associated with improved health-related quality of life in relapsed chronic hepatitis C patients. *Seminars in Liver Disease, 19*(2 Suppl. 1), 77–85.

The neglected "R": The need for a writ-ing revolution. (2003). Report of the National Commission on Writing in America's Schools and Colleges. Retrieved May 10, 2003 from www.writingcommission.org/prod_downloads/writingcom/neglectedr.pdf

Neisser, U. (1998). *The rising curve: Long-term gains in IQ and related measures*. Washington, DC: American Psychological Association.

Neisser, U. A. (1967). *Cognitive psychology*. New York: Appleton-Century-Crofts.

Neisser, U., Boodoo, G., Bouchard, T. J., Jr., Boykin, A. W., Brody, N. Ceci, S. J., Halpern, D. F., Loehlin, J. C., Perloff, R., Sternberg, R. J., & Urbina, S. (1996). Intelligence: Knowns and unknowns. *American Psychologist, 51*, 77–101.

Nell, V. (2000). *Cross-cultural neuropsycho-logical assessment: Theory and practice*. Mahwah, NJ: Erlbaum.

Nellis, L., & Gridley, B. E. (1994). Review of the Bayley Scales of Infant Development, Second Edition. *Journal of School Psychology, 32*(2), 201–209.

Nelson, D. V., Novy, D. M., Averill, P. M., & Berry, L. A. (1996). Ethnic comparability of the MMPI in pain patients. *Journal of Clinical Psychology, 52*, 485–497.

Neto, F. (2002). Social adaptation difficulties of adolescents with immigrant backgrounds. *Social Behavior and Personality, 30*(4), 335–346.

Neto, F., Furnham, A., & Paz, R. (2007). Sex and culture differences in perceptions of estimated multiple intelligence for self and family: A Macanese-Portuguese comparison. *International Journal of Psychology, 42*(2), 124–133.

Nettelbeck, T. (1982). Inspection time: An index for intelligence? *Quarterly Journal of Experimental Psychology, 34A*, 299–312.

Nettelbeck, T., & Lally, M. (1976). Inspection time and measured intelligence. *British Journal of Psychology, 67,* 17–22.

Nevo, B., & Jager, R. S. (Eds.). (1993). *Educational and psychological testing: The test taker's outlook.* Gottingen, Germany: Huber.

Newman, C., Leahy, R. L., Beck, A. T., Reilly-Harrington, N. A., & Gyulia, L., (2003). Bipolar disorder: A cognitive therapy approach. *Behavioral & Cognitive Psychotherapy, 31*(1), 113–114.

Newman, J., Grobman, W. A., & Greenland, P. (2008). Combination polypharmacy for cardiovascular disease prevention in men: A decision analysis and cost-effectiveness model. *Preventive Cardiology, 11*(1), 36–41.

Newman, M. G. (1999). The clinical use of palmtop computers in the treatment of generalized anxiety disorder. *Cognitive & Behavioral Practice, 6*(3), 222–234.

Newman, M. G., Consoli, A., & Barr, T. C. (1997). Computers in assessment and cognitive behavioral treatment for clinical disorders: Anxiety as a case in point. *Behavior Therapy, 28*(2), 211–235.

Newman, M. G., Consoli, A., & Taylor, C. B. (1999). A palmtop computer program for the treatment of generalized anxiety disorder. *Behav Modif, 23*(4), 597–610.

Newman, M. G., Kenardy, J., Herman, S., & Taylor, C. B. (1997). Comparison of palm-top-computer-assisted brief cognitive-behavioral treatment to cognitive-behavioral treatment for panic disorder. *Journal of Consulting & Clinical Psychology, 65*(1), 178–183.

Newman, M. G., Szkodny, L. E., Llera, S. J., & Przeworski, A. (2011). A review of technology-assisted self-help and minimal contact therapies for drug and alcohol abuse and smoking addiction: Is human contact necessary for therapeutic efficacy? *Clinical Psychology Review, 31*(1), 178–186. doi:10.1016/j.cpr.2010.10.002.

Newton, R. L. (1954). The clinician as judge: Total Rorschachs and clinical case material. *Journal of Consulting Psychology, 18,* 248–250.

Nezworski, M. T., & Wood, J. M. (1995). Narcissism in the comprehensive system for the Rorschach. *Clinical Psychology—Science and Practice, 2,* 179–199.

Niccols, A., & Lachman, A. (2002). Stability of the Bayley Mental Scale of Infant Development with high risk infants. *British Journal of Developmental Disabilities, 48*(94, Pt. 1), 3–13.

Nichols, D. S., & Greene, R. L. (1997). Dimensions of deception in personality assessment: The example of the MMPI-2. *Journal of Personality Assessment, 68,* 251–266.

Nietfeld, J. L., Finney, S. J., Schraw, G., & McCrudden, M. T. (2007). A test of theoretical models that account for information processing demands. *Contemporary Educational Psychology, 32*(3), 499–515.

Nijenhuis, J., & van der Flier, H. (2007). The secular rise in IQs in the Netherlands: Is the Flynn effect on g? *Personality and Individual Differences, 43*(5), 1259–1265.

Nisbett, R. E. (2005). Heredity, environment, and race differences in IQ: A commentary on Rushton and Jensen (2005). *Psychology, Public Policy, and Law, 11*(2), 302–310.

Nittono, H. (1997). Personality needs and short-term memory. *Psychological Reports, 81,* 19–24.

Noftle, E. E., & Robins, R. W. (2007). Personality predictors of academic outcomes: Big five correlates of GPA and SAT scores. *Journal of Personality and Social Psychology, 93*(1), 116–130.

Norcross, J. C., & Beutler, I. E. (1997). Determining the therapeutic relationship of choice in brief psychotherapy. In J. N. Butcher (Ed.), *Personality assessment in managed care: A practitioner's guide.* New York: Oxford University Press.

Nordhov, S. M., Rønning, J. A., Dahl, L. B., Ulvund, S. E., Tunby, J., & Kaaresen, P. I. (2010). Early intervention improves cognitive outcomes for preterm infants: Randomized controlled trial. *Pediatrics, 126*(5), 1088–1094. doi:10.1542/peds.2010-0778.

Nordstrom, C. R., Huffaker, B. J., & Williams, K. B. (1998). When physical disabilities are not liabilities: The role of applicant and interviewer characteristics on employment interview outcomes. *Journal of Applied Social Psychology, 28,* 283–306.

Nores, M., & Barnett, W. S. (2010). Benefits of early childhood interventions across the world: (Under) investing in the very young. *Economics of Education Review, 29*(2), 271–282.

Norlin, J. W. (2003). *The special educator 2003 desk book.* Palm Beach Gardens, FL: LRP Publications.

Norman, G. (2003). Hi! How are you? Response shift, implicit theories and differing epistemologies. *Quality of Life Research, 12*(3), 239–249.

Norris, J. T., Pauli, R., & Bray, D. E. (2007). Mood change and computer anxiety: A comparison between computerised and paper measures of negative affect. *Computers in Human Behavior, 23*(6), 2875–2887.

North, M. M., North, S. M., & Coble, J. R. (1997). Virtual reality therapy: An effective treatment for psychological disorders. In G. Riva (Ed.), *Virtual reality in neuro-psychophysiology: Cognitive, clinical, and methodological issues in assessment and rehabilitation. Studies in Health Technology and Informatics, 58,* 112–119.

North, M. M., North, S. M., & Coble, J. R. (2002). Virtual reality therapy: An effective treatment for psychological disorders. In K. M. Stanney (Ed.), *Handbook of virtual environments: Design, implementation, and applications. Human factors and ergonomics* (1065–1078). Mahwah, NJ: Erlbaum.

Norton, E. H. (1978, July). *The Bakke decision and the future of affirmative action.* Statement of the Chair, U.S. Equal Employment Opportunity Commission, at the convention of the National Association for the Advancement of Colored People.

Novick, B. Z., & Arnold, M. M. (1995). *Why is my child having trouble at school? A parent's guide to learning disabilities.* New York: Putnam.

Novick, M. R. (1981). Federal guidelines and professional standards. *American Psychologist, 36,* 1035–1046.

Nugent, W. R. (2003). *A psychometric study of the Multi-Problem Screening Inventory depression subscale using item response and generalizability theories.* Thousand Oaks, CA: Sage.

Nunnally, J. C., & Bernstein, I. H. (1994). *Psychometric theory* (3rd ed.). New York: McGraw-Hill.

Nurius, P. S. (1990). A review of automated assessment. *Computers in human services, 6,* 265–281.

Nyborg, H., & Jensen, A. R. (2000). Black-white differences on various psychometric tests: Spearman's hypothesis tested on American armed services veterans. *Personality and Individual Differences, 28*(3), 593–599.

Nykodym, N., & Ruud, W. N. (1985). Intraview: Career development through business communication. *Journal of Employment Counseling, 22,* 161–165.

Nykodym, N., & Simonetti, J. L. (1981). *Communication: The key to business and organizational effectiveness.* Toledo, OH: Management Skills Books.

Nystul, M. S. (1999). *Introduction to counseling: An art and science perspective.* Boston, MA: Allyn & Bacon.

Oakland, T. (1979). Research on the ABIC and ELP: A revisit to an old topic. *School Psychology Digest, 8,* 209–213.

Oakland, T., & Feigenbaum, D. (1979). Multiple sources of test bias on the WISC-R and the Bender-Gestalt test. *Journal of Consulting and Clinical Psychology, 47,* 968–974.

Oakland, T., & Parmelee, R. (1985). Mental measurement of minoritygroup children. In B. B. Wolman (Ed.), *Handbook of intelligence: Theories, measurements, and applications.* New York: Wiley- Interscience.

Oberlander, T. F., Jacobson, S. W., Weinberg, J., Grunau, R. E., Molteno, C. D., & Jacobson, J. L. (2010). Prenatal alcohol exposure alters biobehavioral reactivity to pain in newborns. *Alcoholism: Clinical and Experimental Research, 34*(4), 575–749. doi:10.1111/j.1530-0277.2009.01137.x.

O'Connell, M. S., Hartman, N. S., McDaniel, M. A., Grubb, W. L., & Lawrence, A. (2007). Incremental validity of situational judgment tests for task and contextual job performance. *International Journal of Selection and Assessment, 15*(1), 19–29.

O'Donnell, J., Hawkins, J. D., & Abbott, R. D. (1995). Predicting serious delinquency and substance use among agressive boys [Special Section: Prediction and prevention of child and adolescent antisocial behavior]. *Journal of Consulting and Clinical Psychology, 63,* 529–537.

Oei, T. P. S., Evans, I., & Crook, G. M. (1990). Utility and validity of the STAI with anxiety disorder patients. *British Journal of Clinical Psychology, 29,* 429–432.

Ofiesh, N., Mather, N., & Russell, A. (2005). Using speeded cognitive, reading, and academic measures to determine the need for extended test time among university students with learning disabilities. *Journal of Psychoeducational Assessment, 23*(1), 35–52.

Ogloff, J. R. P. & Douglas, K. S. (2003). Psychological assessment in forensic settings. In J. R. Graham & J. A. Naglieri (Eds.), *Handbook of psychology: Assessment psychology* (Vol. 10) (pp. 345–363). New York: Wiley.

Okazaki, S., & Sue, S. (2003). *Methodological issues in assessment research with ethnic minorities.* Washington, DC: American Psychological Association.

O'Leary, K. D., & Kent, R. N. (1973). Behavior modification for social action: Research tactics and problems. In L. A. Hamerlynck, P. O. Davidson, & L. E. Acker (Eds.), *Critical issues in research and practice.* Champaign, IL: Research Press.

O'Leary, K. D., Kent, R. N., & Kanowitz, J. (1975). Shaping data collection congruent with experimental hypotheses. *Journal of Applied Behavior Analysis, 8,* 43–51.

Olmedo, E. L. (1981). Testing linguistic minorities. *American Psychologist, 36,* 1078–1085.

Ones, D. S., Chockalingam, V., & Schmidt, F. L. (1995). Integrity tests: Overlooked facts, resolved issues, and remaining questions. *American Psychologist, 50*(6), 456–457.

Oostdam, R., & Meijer, J. (2003). *Influence of test anxiety on measurement of intelligence.* Washington, DC: Psychological Reports.

Optale, G., Munari, A., Nasta, A., Pianon, C., Verde, J. B., & Viggiano, G. (1998). Virtual environments in the treatment of impotence and premature ejaculation. *Cyberpsychology & Behavior, 1*(3), 213–223.

Opton, E. (1977, April). From California, two views. *APA Monitor,* pp. 5–18.

Opton, E. (1979, December). A psychologist takes a closer look at the recent landmark *Larry P.* opinion. *APA Monitor,* pp. 1–4.

Oral, E., Güleç, M., Aydin, N., Ozan, E., & Kırpınar, I. (2011). Severe generalize cortical atrophy inconsistent with her age, and neurocognitive impairment in an untreated schizophrenia patient: A case report. *European Psychiatry, 26*(1), 1463. doi:10.1016/S0924-9338(11)73168-6.

Orfield, G., & Kornhaber, M. L. (2001). *Raising standards or raising barriers? Inequality and high-stakes testing in public education.* New York: Century Foundation Press.

Orlansky, J., Grafton, F., Martin, C. J., & Alley, W. (1990). *The current status of research and development on selection and classification of enlisted personnel.* Institute for Defense Analysis paper (IDA Document D-715, 72). Washington, DC: Institute for Defense Analysis.

Osberg, T. M., & Poland, D. L. (2002). Comparative accuracy of the MMPI-2 and the MMPI-A in the diagnosis of psychopathology in 18-year-olds. *Psychological Assessment, 14*(2), 164–169.

Osipow, S. H. (1983). *Theories of career development* (3rd ed.). Englewood Cliffs, NJ: Prentice-Hall.

Osipow, S. H. (1987). Counselling psychology: Theory, research, and practice in career counselling. *Annual Review of Psychology, 38,* 257–278.

Osipow, S. H. (1999). Assessing career indecision. *Journal of Vocational Behavior, 55*(1), 147–154.

Othmer, E. & Othmer, S. C. (2002). *The clinical interview using DSM-IVTR: Vol. 2. The difficult patient.* Washington, D.C.: American Psychiatric Publishing.

Ottem, E. (2002a). Confirmatory factor analysis of ITPA models with language-impaired children. *Scandinavian Journal of Psychology, 43*(4), 299–305.

Ottem, E. (2002b). The complementary nature of ITPA and WISC-R results for language-impaired children. *Scandinavian Journal of Educational Research, 46*(2), 145–160.

Overton, R. C., Harms, H. J., Taylor, L. R., & Zickar, M. J. (1997). Adapting to adaptive testing. *Personnel Psychology, 50*(1), 171–185.

Owen, D. (1985). *None of the above: Behind the myth of scholastic aptitude.* Boston: Houghton Mifflin.

Owen, P. R. (1998). Fears of Hispanic and Anglo children: Real-world fears in the 1990s. *Hispanic Journal of Behavioral Sciences, 20,* 483–491.

Pagano, R. R. (2004). *Understanding statistics in the behavioral sciences* (7th ed.). Belmont, CA: Wadsworth.

Palaniappan, A. K., & Torrance, E. P. (2001). Comparison between regular and streamlined versions of scoring of Torrance Tests of Creative Thinking. *Korean Journal of Thinking and Problem Solving, 11*(2), 5–7.

Palm, J. A. (2005). *Comprehensive system indices, constellations, and supplemental aggression ratings for the Rorschach inkblot method: Reliability and validity in a child and adolescent outpatient sample.* US: ProQuest Information & Learning.

Palmer, F. H. (1970). Socioeconomic status and intellectual performance among Negro preschool boys. *Developmental Psychology, 3,* 1–9.

Paolini, L., Yanez, A. P., & Kelly, W. E. (2006). An examination of worry and life satisfaction among college students. *Individual Differences Research, 4*(5), 331–339.

Parducci, A. (1968). The relativism of absolute judgments. *Scientific American, 219*(6), 84–90.

Parducci, A. (1995). *Happiness, pleasure, and judgment: The contextual theory and its applications.* Mahwah, NJ: Erlbaum.

*Parents in Action on Special Education v. Hannon.* (1980). USDC N111 (J. Grady pub. July 7, 1980).

Parisse, C., & Maillart, C. (2009). Specific language impairment as systemic developmental disorders. *Journal of Neurolinguistics, 22*(2), 109–122.

Park, C. L., Malone, M. R., Suresh, D. P., Bliss, D., & Rosen, R. I. (2008). Coping, meaning in life, and quality of life in congestive heart failure patients. *Quality of Life Research, 17*(1), 21–26.

Parker, J. D., Endler, N. S., & Bagby, R. M. (1993). If it changes, it might be unstable: Examining the factor structure of the Ways of Coping Questionnaire. *Psychological Assessment, 5*(3), 361–368.

Parker, K. (1983). A meta-analysis of the reliability and validity of the Rorschach. *Journal of Personality Assessment, 42,* 227–231.

Parks, K. M (2007). Intelligence redefined. *Observer, 20,* 37.

Parnell, B., Dunivan, G., Connolly, A., Jannelli, M.,Wells, E., & Geller, E. (2011). Validation of Web-based administration of the Pelvic Organ Prolapse/Urinary Incontinence Sexual Function Questionnaire (PISQ-12). *International Urogynecology Journal, 22*(3), 357–361. doi:10.1007/s00192-010-1297-8.

Parsons, O. A. (1970). Clinical neuropsychology. In C. D. Spielberger (Ed.), *Current topics in clinical and community psychology* (Vol. 2). New York: Academic Press.

Pasamanick, B. A., & Knobloch, H. (1955). Early language behavior in Negro children and the testing of intelligence. *Journal of Abnormal and Social Psychology, 50,* 401–402.

Pascanu, R., & Jaeger, H. (2011). A neurodynamical model for working memory. *Neural Networks, 24*(2), 199–207. ISSN 0893-6080; doi:10.1016/j.neunet.2010.10.003.

Pashley, P., Thornton, A., & Duffy, J. (2005). Access and diversity in law school admissions. In W. J. Camara, & E. W. Kimmel (Eds.), *Choosing students: Higher education admissions tools for the 21st century.* (pp. 231–249). Mahwah, NJ: Lawrence Erlbaum Associates Publishers.

Patrianakos-Hoobler, A. I., Msall, M. E., Huo, D., Marks, J. D., Plesha-Troyke, S. & Schreiber, M. D. (2010).

Predicting school readiness from neurodevelopmental assessments at age 2 years after respiratory distress syndrome in infants born preterm. *Developmental Medicine & Child Neurology, 52*(4), 379–385. doi:10.1111/j.1469-8749.2009.03343.x.

Patrick, D. L., Bushnell, D. M., & Rothman, M. (2004). Performance of two self-report measures for evaluating obesity and weight loss. *Obesity Research, 12*(1), 48–57.

Patrick, D. L., & Chiang, Y. P. (2002). Measurement of health outcomes in treatment effectiveness evaluations: conceptual and methodological challenges. *Med Care, 33* (9 Suppl), II14–25.

Patterson, M., Slate, J. R., Jones, C. H., & Steger, H. S. (1995). The effects of practice administrations in learning to administer and score the WAIS-R: A partial replication. *Educational and Psychological Measurement, 55*(1), 32–37.

Patterson, T. L., Kaplan, R. M., Grant, I., Semple, S. J., Moscona, S., Koch, W. L., et al. (1996). Quality of well-being in late-life psychosis. *Psychiatry Research, 63*(2–3), 169–181.

Patterson, T. L., Kaplan, R. M., & Jeste, D. V. (1999). Measuring the effect of treatment on quality of life in patients with schizophrenia: Focus on utility-based measures. *CNS Drugs, 12*(1), 49–64.

Pattishall, E. (1992). Smoking and body weight. *Health Psychology* (Suppl. 32), 3.

Paul, G. L., & Eriksen, C. W. (1964). Effects of test anxiety on "real life" examinations. *Journal of Personality, 32,* 480–494.

Paul, R., Cohen, R., Moser, D., Ott, B., Zawacki, T., & Gordon, N. (2001). Performance on the Hooper Visual Organizational Test in patients diagnosed with subcortical vascular dementia: Relation to naming performance. *Neuropsychiatry, Neuropsychology, and Behavioral Neurology, 14*(2), 93–97.

Paunonen, S. V., & Ashton, M. C. (1998). The structured assessment of personality across cultures. *Journal of Cross-Cultural Psychology, 29,* 150–170.

Pearson, K. (1901). *Mathematical contributions to the theory of evolution.* London: Dulau & Co.

Pedersen, N. L. (2002). Behavior genetics and the future of psychology. In C. von Hofsten & L. Baeckman (Eds.), *Psychology at the turn of the millennium. Vol. 2: Social, developmental, and clinical*

*perspectives* (pp. 3–16). Florence, KY: Taylor & Frances/Routledge.

Pedhazur, E. J. (1991). *Measurement, design, and analysis: An integrated approach.* Hillsdale, NJ: Erlbaum.

Pedhazur, E. J. (1997). *Multiple regression in behavioral research: Explanation and prediction* (3rd ed.). Fort Worth, TX: Harcourt Brace.

Pedulla et al. (2003). *Perceived effects of state-mandated testing programs on teaching and learning: Findings from a national survey of teachers.* Boston: Boston College, National Board on Educational Testing and Public Policy, Lynch School of Education.

Peluso, P. R., Liebovitch, L. S., Gottman, J. M., Norman, M. D., & Su, J. (2011). A mathematical model of psychotherapy: An investigation using dynamic non-linear equations to model the therapeutic relationship. *Psychotherapy Research.* Retrieved from http://www.tandfonline.com/doi/abs/10.1080/10503307.2011.622314.

Pena, L. M., Megargee, E. I., & Brody, E. (1996). MMPI-A patterns of male juvenile delinquents. *Psychological Assessment, 8,* 388–397.

Penfield, R. D. (2003a). IRT-Lab: Software for research and pedagogy in item response theory. *Applied Psychological Measurement, 27*(4), 301–302.

Penfield, R. D. (2003b). A score method of constructing asymmetric confidence intervals for the mean of a rating scale item. *Psychological Methods, 8*(2), 149–163.

Pennington, B. F., & Welsh, M. (1995). Neuropsychology and developmental psychopathology. In D. Cicchetti & D. J. Cohen (Eds.), *Developmental psychopathology* (Vol. 1) (pp. 254–290). New York: Wiley.

*People Who Care v. Rockford Board of Education School District No. 205.* (1997). 111 F. 3d 528 (7th Cir. 1997).

Peoples, V. Y. (1975). Measuring the vocational interest of women. In S. H. Osipow (Ed.), *Emerging women: Career analysis and outlooks.* Columbus, OH: Merrill.

Perkins, D. N., & Grotzer, T. A. (1997). Teaching intelligence. *American Psychologist, 52*(10), 1125–1133.

Perkins, E. L. (2002). Wise persons' personality temperaments: Differences and similarities found in the wise and compared with the general population. *Dissertation Abstracts International, 62,* 8B.

Perkos, S., Theodorakis, Y., & Chronni, S. (2002). Enhancing performance and skill acquisition in novice basketball players with instructional self-talk. *Sport Psychologist, 16*(4), 368–383.

Pernas, A., Iraurgi C. I., Bermejo, P., Basebe, N., Carou, M., Paez, D., & Cabarcos, A. (2001). Coping and affectivity in persona with HIV/AIDS. *Psiquis: Revista de Psiquiatria, Psicologia Medica y Psicosomatica, 22*(5), 30–35.

Perrez, M., Wilhelm, P., Schoebi, D., & Horner, M. (2001). Simultaneous computer-assisted assessment of causal attribution and social coping in families. In J. Fahrenberg & U. Freilberg (Eds.), *Progress in ambulatory assessment: Computer assisted psychological and psychophysiological methods in monitoring and field studies* (pp. 25–43). Kirkland, WA: Hogrefe & Huber.

Perry, W., Sprock, J., Schaible, D., & McDougall, A. (1995). Amphetamine on Rorschach measures in normal subjects. *Journal of Personality Assessment, 64*(3), 456–465.

Peterson, N. G., Mumford, M. D., Levin, K. Y., Green, J., & Waksberg, J. (1999). Research method: Development and field testing of the content model. In E. Norman, G. Peterson, E. Michael, D. Mumford, et al. (Eds.), *An occupational information system for the 21st century: The development of O\*NET* (pp. 31–47). Washington, DC: American Psychological Association.

Pettigrew, T. F. (1964). *A profile of the American Negro.* New York: Van Nostrand Reinhold.

Pettit, F. A. (1999). Exploring the use of the World Wide Web as a psychology data collection tool. *Computers in Human Behavior, 15*(1), 67–71.

Pettit, F. A. (2002). A comparison of world-wide web and paper-and-pencil personality questionnaires. *Behavior Research Methods, Instruments, & Computers, 34*(1), 6–18.

Pettit, J. W., Kline, J. P., Gencoz, T., Gencoz, F., & Joiner, T. E. (2002). Are happy people healthier? The specific role of positive affect in predicting self-reported health symptoms. *Journal of Research in Personality, 35*(4), 521–536.

Pfaffenberger, A. H., & Marko, P. W. (2011). Exceptional maturity of personality: An emerging field. In A. H. Pfaffenberger, P. W. Marko, & A. Combs (Eds.), *The postconventional personality: Assessing, researching, and theorizing higher development* (pp. 1–8). Albany: New York Press.

Pfeifer, C., & Sedlacek, W. (1971). The validity of academic predictors for black and white students at a predominantly white university. *Journal of Educational Measurement, 8,* 253–261.

Pfister, H. (1995). New technology for administering group tests. *Australian Psychologist, 30,* 24–26.

Phares, E. J., & Trull, T. J. (2000). *Clinical psychology* (6th ed.). Pacific Grove, CA: Brooks/Cole.

Phillips, S. E. (1994). High-stakes testing accommodations: Validity versus disabled rights. *Applied Measurement in Education, 7*(2), 93–120.

Phillips, S. E. (2002). Legal issues affecting special populations in large-scale testing programs. In G. Tindal & T. M. Haladyna (Eds.), *Large-scale assessment programs for all students: Validity, technical adequacy, and implementation* (pp. 109–148). Mahwah, NJ: Erlbaum.

Picard, R. W., & Klein, J. (2002). Computers that recognize and respond to user emotion: Theoretical and practical implications. *Interacting with Computer, 14*(2), 141–169.

Picone, L., Regine, A., & Ribaudo, F. (2001). Factorial validity of the McCarthy Scales of Children's Abilities by measuring cognitive ability in young children. *Bollettino di Psicologia Applicata, 234*(48), 21–31.

Piedmont, R. L. (1998). *The revised NEO Personality Inventory: Clinical and research applications: The Plenum series in social/clinical psychology.* New York: Plenum.

Pierce, J. P., Burns, D., Gilpen, E., Rosenberg, B., Johnson, M., & Bal, D. (1992). *California baseline tobacco survey.* Unpublished report. University of California, San Diego.

Piers, V. P., Harris, D. B., & Herzberg, D. S. (1999). *Piers Harris Children's Self-Concept Scale–second edition.* Los Angeles: Western Psychological Services.

Pinsoneault, T. B. (1999). Equivalency of computer assisted and paper-and-pencil administered versions of the Minnesota Multiphasic Personality Inventory-2. *Computers in Human Behavior, 12*(2), 291–300.

Pintor, L., & Bailles, E. (2005). Patients with psychogenic non-epileptic seizures: What happens to them? In T. A. Corales (Ed.), *Focus on post-traumatic stress disorder research.* (pp. 225–244). Hauppauge, NY: Nova Science Publishers.

Piotrowski, C. (1984). The status of projective techniques: Or, "wishing won't make it go away." *Journal of Clinical Psychology, 40,* 1495–1499.

Piotrowski, C. (1995). A review of the clinical and research use of the Bender-Gestalt Test. *Perceptual and Motor Skills, 81,* 1272–1274.

Piotrowski, C. (1997). Use of the Millon Clinical Multiaxial Inventory in clinical practice. *Perceptual and Motor Skills, 84,* 1185–1186.

Piotrowski, C., Sherry, D., & Keller, J. W. (1985). Psychodiagnostic test usage: Survey of the Society for Personality Assessment. *Journal of Personality Assessment, 49,* 115–119.

Piotrowski, Z. (1947). Rorschach compendium. *Psychiatric Quarterly, 21,* 79–101.

Piotrowski, Z. (1964). Digital computer interpretation of inkblot test data. *Psychiatric Quarterly, 38,* 1–26.

Piotrowski, Z. A. (1980). CPR: The psychological X-ray in mental disorders. In J. B. Sidowski, J. H. Johnson, & T. A. Williams (Eds.), *Technology in mental health care delivery systems* (pp. 85–108). Norwood, NJ: Ablex.

Pirelli, G., Gottdiener, W. H., & Zapf, P. A. (2011). A meta-analytic review of competency to stand trial research. *Psychology, Public Policy, and Law, 17*(1), 1–53. doi:10.1037/a0021713.

Plaisted, J. R., Gustavson, J. L., Wilkening, G. N., & Golden, C. J. (1983). The Luria-Nebraska Neuropsychological Battery Children's revision: Theory and current research findings. *Journal of Clinical Child Psychology, 12,* 13–21.

*Plessy v. Ferguson.* (1896). 163 U.S. 537.

Polansky, N., Freeman, W., Horowitz, M., Irwin, L., Papanis, N., Rapaport, D., & Whaley, F. (1949). Problems of interpersonal relations in research on groups. *Human Relations, 2,* 281–291.

Policy Analysis for California Education and Rennie Center for Education Research & Policy (PACE) (2011). *The road ahead for state assessments.* Cambridge, MA: Rennie Center for Education Research & Policy.

Pomaki, G., & Anagnostopoulou, T. (2003). A test and extension of the Demand/Control/Social support model: Prediction of wellness/health outcomes in Greek teachers. *Psychology and Health, 18*(4), 537–550.

Pomerlau, A., Leahey, L., & Malcuit, G. (1994). Evaluation of infant development during the first 12 months: Use of the Bayley Scales. *Canadian Journal of Behavioural Science—Revue Canadienne des sciences du Comportement, 26*(1), 85–103.

Pommerich, M. (2007). In N. J. Dorans, M. Pommerich, & P. W. Holland (Eds.), *Concordance: The good, the bad, and the ugly.* New York: Springer Science + Business Media.

Pomplun, M., & Custer, M. (2005). The construct validity of the Stanford-Binet 5 measures of working memory. *Assessment, 12*(3), 338–346.

Ponniah, K., Weissman, M. W., Bledsoe, S. E., Verdeli, H., Gameroff, M. J., Mufson, L., Fitterling, H., & Wickramaratne, P. (2011). Training in structured diagnostic assessment using DSM-IV criteria. *Research on Social Work Practice, 21*(4), 452–457. doi:10.1177/1049731511398151.

Pons, D., Atienza, F. L., Balaguer, I., & Garcia-Merita, M. (2002). Psychometric properties of Satisfaction with Life Scale in elderly. *Revista Iberoamericana de Diagnostico y Evaluacion Psicologica, 13*(1), 71–82.

Pons, L. (1989). Effects of age and sex upon availability of responses on a word-association test. *Perceptual and Motor Skills, 68*, 85–86.

Pope, K. S., Butcher, J. N., & Seelen, J. (2000). *The MMPI, MMPI-2, & MMPI-A in court: A practical guide for expert witnesses and attorneys* (2nd ed.). Washington, DC: American Psychological Association.

Popham, W. J. (1994). The instructional consequences of criterion-referenced clarity. *Educational Measurement: Issues and Practice, 13*(4), 15–18, 30.

Popper, S. E. (1997). Validity of using non-pilot subjects to represent pilots in a sustained acceleration environment. *Aviation Space and Environmental Medicine, 68*, 1081–1087.

Porter, S. C., Forbes, P., Manzi, S., & Kalish, L. A. (2010). Patients providing the answers: narrowing the gap in data quality for emergency care. *Quality and Safety in Health Care, 19*(5), 1–5. doi:10.1136/qshc.2009.032540.

Portoghese, C., Buttiglione, M., De Giacomo, A., Lafortezza, M., Lecce, P. A., Martinelli, D., Lozito,V., & Margari, L. (2010). Leiter-R versus developmental quotient for estimating cognitive function in preschoolers with pervasive developmental disorders. *Neuropsychiatric Disease and Treatment, 6*, 337–342.

Posthuma, R. A., Morgeson, F. P., & Campion, M. A. (2002). Beyond employment interview validity: A comprehensive narrative review of recent research and trends over time. *Personnel Psychology, 55*(1).

Potter, E. F. (1999). What should I put in my portfolio? Supporting young children's goals and evaluations. *Childhood Education, 75*, 210.

Powell, M. B., Wilson, J. C., & Hastya, M. K. (2002). Evaluation of the usefulness of 'Marvin'; a computerized assessment tool for investigative interviewers of children. *Computers in Human Behavior, 18*(5), 577–592.

Power, M. J., Katz, R., McGuffin, P., & Duggan, C. F. (1994). The Dysfunctional Attitude Scale (DAS): A comparison of Form A and Form B and proposals for a new subscaled version. *Journal of Research in Personality, 28*(3), 263–276.

Powers, D. E. (1999). *Coaching and the SAT I* (College Board Research Report No. RN-06, April 1999). New York: College Entrance Examination Board.

Powers, D. E. (2001). *Validity of GRE General test scores for admission to colleges of veterinary medicine* (No. GRE Board 98-09R). Princeton, NJ: Educational Testing Service.

Powers, D. E., Burstein, J. C., Chodorow, M., Fowles, M. E., & Kukich, K. (2000). *Comparing validity of automated and human essay scoring.* Princeton, NJ: Educational Testing Service.

Powers, D. E., Burstein, J. C., Chodorow, M., Fowles, M. E., & Kukich, K. (2002). Stumping Erater: Challenging the validity of automated essay scoring. *Computers in Human Behavior, 18*(2), 103–134.

Powers, D. E., & Rock, D. A. (1998). *Effects of coaching on SAT I: Reasoning scores* (College Board Research Report No. 98-6). New York: College Entrance Examination Board.

Preau, M., Protopopescu, C., Spire, B., Sobel, A., Dellamonica, P., Moatti, J. P., et al. (2007). Health related quality of life among both current and former injection drug users who are HIV-infected. *Drug and Alcohol Dependence, 86*(2–3), 175–182.

Prediger, D. J. (1999). Integrating interests and abilities for career exploration: General considerations. In M. L. Savickas & A. R. Spokane (Eds.), *Vocational interests: Meaning, measurement, and counseling use* (pp. 295–325). Palo Alto, CA: Davies-Black.

Prewett, P. N., & Farhney, M. R. (1994). The concurrent validity of the Matrix Analogies Test—Short Form with the Stanford Binet: Fourth Edition and KTEA-BF (academic achievement). *Psychology in the Schools, 31*(1), 20–25.

Prewett, P. N., & Matavich, M. A. (1994). A comparison of referred students' performance on the WISC-III and the Stanford Binet Intelligence Scale: Fourth Edition. *Journal of Psychoeducational Assessment, 12*(1), 42–48.

Price, K. H., & Garland, H. (1983). Compliance with a leader's suggestions as a function of perceived leader/member competence and potential reciprocity. *Journal of Applied Psychology, 66*, 329–336.

Price, L. R., Raju, N., Lurie, A., Wilkins, C., & Zhu, J. (2006). Conditional standard errors of measurement for composite scores on the Wechsler Preschool and Primary Scale of Intelligence-third edition. *Psychological Reports, 98*(1), 237–252.

Primi, R. (2002). Complexity of geometric inductive reasoning tasks: Contribution to the understanding of fluid intelligence. *Intelligence, 30*(1), 41–70.

Prince, R. J., & Guastello, S. J. (1990). The Barnum effect in a computerized Rorschach interpresentation system. *Journal of Psychology, 124*, 217–222.

Prinstein, M. J. (2004). The interview. In C. Williams-Nickelson (Ed.), *Internships in psychology: The APAGS workbook for writing successful appli-cations and finding the right match* (pp. 79–92). Washington, DC: American Psychological Association.

ProEd, ITPA-3: Illinois Test of Psycholinguistic Abilities–Third Edition. Retrieved November 29, 2011 from http://www.proedinc.com/customer/productView.aspx?ID=788.

Prout, H. T., & Sheldon, K. L. (1984). Classifying mental retardation in vocational rehabilitation: A study of diagnostic practices and their adherence to accepted guidelines. *Rehabilitation Counseling Bulletin, 28*, 125–128.

Pugh, R. C. (1968). Evidence for the validity of the behavioral dimensions of Teaching-Characteristics Schedule Scales. *Educational and Psychological Measurement, 28*(4), 1173–1179.

Pugliese, M. D., Lifshitz, F., Grad, G., Fort, P., & Marks-Katz, M. (1983). Fear of obesity: A cause of short stature and delayed puberty. *New England Journal of Medicine, 309*, 513–518.

Pull, C. B. (2005). Current status of virtual reality exposure therapy in anxiety disorders. *Current Opinion in Psychiatry, 18*(1), 7–14.

Pupo, M. C., Jorge, M. R., Schoedl, A. F., Bressan, R. A., Andreoli, S. B., Mello, M. F., & Mari, J. J. (2011). The accuracy of the Clinician-Administered PTSD Scale (CAPS) to identify PTSD cases in victims of urban violence. *Psychiatry Research*, 185(1–2), 157–160.

Pyne, J. M., Sieber, W. J., David, K., Kaplan, R. M., Hyman Rapaport, M., & Keith Williams, D. (2003). Use of the quality of well-being self-administered version (QWB-SA) in assessing health-related quality of life in depressed patients. *Journal of Affect Disord*, 76(1–3), 237–247.

Qi, C. H., Kaiser, A. P., Milan, S., & Hancock, T. (2006). Language performance of low-income African American and European American preschool children on the PPVT-III. *Language, Speech, and Hearing Services in Schools*, 37(1), 5–16.

Quay, L. C. (1971). Language dialect, reinforcement, and the intelligence-test performance of Negro children. *Child Development*, 42, 5–15.

Quenk, N. L. (2000). *Essentials of Myers-Briggs Type Indicator Assessment*. New York: Wiley.

Quinsey, V. L., Harris, G. T., Rice, M. E., & Cormier, C. A. (2006). Criticisms of actuarial risk assessment. In V. L. Quinsey, G. T. Harris, M. E. Rice, & C. A. Cormier (Eds.), *Violent offenders: Appraising and managing risk*, 2nd ed. (pp. 197–223). Washington, DC: American Psychological Association.

Raggio, D. J., Massingale, T. W., & Bass, J. D. (1994). Comparison of Vineland Adaptive Behavior Scales Survey Form age equivalent and standard score with the Bayley Mental Development Index. *Perceptual and Motor Skills*, 79(1), 203–206.

Raju, N. S., Burke, M. J., Normand, J., & Lezotte, D. V. (1993). What would be if what is wasn't? Rejoinder to Judiesch, Schmidt, and Hunter (1993). *Journal of Applied Psychology*, 78, 912–916.

Ralston, S. M. (1988). The effect of applicant race upon personnel selection decisions: A review with recommendations. *Employee Responsibilities and Rights Journal*, 1, 215–226.

Ramanaiah, N. V., Sharp, J. P., & Byravan, A. (1999). Hardiness and major personality factors. *Psychological Reports*, 84(2), 497–500.

Ramírez, J. M., & Andreu, J. M. (2006). Aggression, and some related psychological constructs (anger, hostility, and impulsivity): Some comments from a research project. *Neuroscience & Biobehavioral Reviews*, 30(3), 276–291.

Rammsayer, T. H., & Brandler, S. (2002). On the relationship between general fluid intelligence and psychophysical indicators of temporal resolution in the brain. *Journal of Research in Personality*, 36(5), 507–530.

Randolph, D. L., Smart, T. K., & Nelson, W. (1997). The Personality Research Form as a discriminator of attachment styles. *Journal of Social Behavior and Personality*, 12, 113–127.

Rao, S. M. (2000). Neuropsychological evaluation. In E. Barry, S. Fogel, E. Randolph, B. Schiffer, et al. (Eds.), *Synopsis of neuropsychiatry* (pp. 17–25). Philadelphia: Lippincott.

Rapaport, D., Gill, M. M., & Schafer, R. (1945–1946). *Diagnostic psychological testing* (2 vols.). Chicago: Yearbook Publishers.

Rapaport, D., Gill, M. M., & Schafer, R. (1968). *Diagnostic psychological testing* (Rev. ed., R. R. Holt, Ed.). New York: International Universities Press.

Rappaport, N. B., & McAnulty, D. P. (1985). The effect of accented speech on the scoring of ambiguous WISC-R responses by prejudiced and nonprejudiced raters. *Journal of Psychoeducational Assessment*, 3, 275–283.

Rasulis, R., Jr., Schuldberg, D., & Murtagh, M. (1996). Computer administered testing with the Rotter Incomplete Sentences Blank. *Computers in Human Behavior*, 12(4), 497–513.

Ratliff-Shaub, K., Hunt, C. E., Crowell, D., Golub, H., Smok-Pearsall, S., Palmer, P., Schafer, S., Bak, S., Cantey-Kiser, J., & O'Bell, R. (2001). Relationship between infant sleep position and motor development in preterm infants. *Journal of Developmental and Behavioral Pediatrics*, 22(5), 293–299.

Raven, J. (1986). *Manual for Raven's Progressive Matrices and Vocabulary Scales: Research supplement No. 3*. London: H. K. Lewis.

Raven, J. (1990). *Raven manual research supplement 3: American and international norms*. London: Oxford Psychologist Press.

Raven, J. (2000). The Raven's Progressive Matrices: Change and stability over culture and time. *Cognitive Psychology*, 41(1), 1–48.

Raven, J., Raven, J. C., & Court, J. H. (1998). *Standard progressive matrices, 1998 edition*. Oxford, England: Oxford University Press.

Ray, W. J. (2000). *Methods: Toward a science of behavior and experience* (6th ed.). Belmont, CA: Wadsworth.

Rayner, S., Roodenburg, J., & Roodenburg, E. (2012). Intellectual styles: Moving from models to measures and meaning, In R. J. Sternburg, L. F. Zhang, & S. Raynor (Eds.), *Handbook of intellectual styles: Preferences in cognition, learning, and thinking* (pp. 47–67). New York: Springer.

Reardon, R. C., & Lenz, J. G. (1999). Holland's theory and career assessment. *Journal of Vocational Behavior*, 55(1), 102–113.

Rebok, G., Brandt, J., & Folstein, M. (1990). Longitudinal cognitive decline in patients with Alzheimer's disease. *Journal of Geriatric Psychiatry and Neurology*, 3, 91–97.

Redden, S. C., Forness, S. R., Ramey, S. L., Ramey, C. T., Brezausek, C. M., & Kavale, K. A. (2001). Children at risk: Effects of a four-year head start transition program on special education identification. *Journal of Child and Family Studies*, 10(2), 255–270.

Redfield, J., & Paul, G. L. (1976). Bias in behavioral observation as a function of observer familiarity with subjects and typically of behavior. *Journal of Consulting and Clinical Psychology*, 44, 156.

Ree, M. J., & Carretta, T. R. (1994). Factor analysis of the ASVAB: Confirming a Vernon-like structure. *Educational and Psychological Measurement*, 54(2), 459–463.

Ree, M. J., & Carretta, T. R. (1995). Group differences in aptitude factor structure on the ASVAB. *Educational and Psychological Measurement*, 55(2), 268–277.

Reed, S. B. (2000). An investigation of the physical attractiveness stereotype. *Dissertation Abstracts International*, 60, 12B.

*Regents of the University of California v. Bakke*. (1978). 438 U.S. 265, 17 Fair Empl. Prac. Cas. (BNA) 1000.

Regenwetter, M. (2006). *Behavioral social choice: Probabilistic models, statistical inference, and applications*. Cambridge; New York: Cambridge University Press.

Reid, J. B. (1970). Reliability assessment of observation data: A possible methodological problem. *Child Development*, 41, 1143–1150.

Reid, J. B., & DeMaster, B. (1972). The efficacy of the spotcheck procedure in maintaining the reliability of data collected by observers in quasinatural settings: Two pilot studies. *Oregon Research Institute Research Bulletin*, 12.

Reise, S. P., & Waller, N. G. (2003). How many IRT parameters does it take to model psychopathology items? *Psychological Methods, 8*(2), 164–184.

Reisman, J. M. (1976). *A history of clinical psychology.* New York: Irvington.

Reitan, R. M. (1968). Theoretical and methodological bases of the Halstead-Reitan Neuropsychological Test Battery. In I. Grant & K. N. Adams (Eds.), *Neuropsychological assessment of neuropsychiatric disorders.* New York: Oxford University Press.

Reitan, R. M. (1976). Neuropsychology: The vulgarization that Luria always wanted. *Contemporary Psychology, 21,* 737–738.

Reitan, R. M., & Wolfson, D. (1997). Consistency of neuropsychological test scores of head-injured subjects involved in litigation compared with head-injured subjects not involved in litigation: Development of the Retest Consistency index. *Clinical Neuropsychologist, 11*(1), 69–76.

Reitan, R. M., & Wolfson, D. (1999). The two faces of mild head injury. *Archives of Clinical Neuropsychology, 14*(2), 191–202.

Reschly, D. J. (1981). Psychological testing in educational classification and placement. *American Psychologist, 36,* 1094–1102.

Reschly, D. J., Kicklighter, R., & McKee, P. (1988). Recent placement of litigation part III: Analysis of differences in Larry P., Marshal and S-1, and implications for future practices. *School Psychology Review, 17,* 39–50.

Reschly, D. J., & Sabers, D. L. (1979). Analysis of test bias in four groups with the regression definition. *Journal of Educational Measurement, 16,* 1–9.

Reschly, D. J., & Ward, S. M. (1991). Use of adaptive behavior measures and overrepresentation of black students in programs for students with mild mental retardation. *American Journal on Mental Retardation, 96,* 257–268.

Resnick, S. M., Trotman, K. M., Kawas, C., & Zonderman, A. B. (1995). Age-associated changes in specific errors on the Benton Visual Retention Test. *Journals of Gerontology Series B—Psychological Sciences and Social Sciences, 50B,* 171–178.

Retzlaff, P. D., and Gibertini, M. (2000). Neuropsychometric issues and problems. In E. Rodney, D. Vanderploeg, et al. (Eds.), *Clinician's guide to neuropsychological assessment* (pp. 277–299). Mahwah, NJ: Erlbaum.

Revicki, D. A., & Cella, D. F. (1997). Health status assessment for the twenty-first century: Item response theory, item banking, and computer adaptive testing. *Quality of life Research, 6*(6), 595–600.

Reynolds, C. R. (1980). An examination of bias in a pre-school battery across race and sex. *Journal of Educational Measurement, 17,* 137–146.

Reynolds, C. R. (1982). Determining statistically reliable strengths and weaknesses in the performance of single individuals on the Luria Nebraska Neuropsychological Battery. *Journal of Consulting and Clinical Psychology, 50,* 525–529.

Reynolds, C. R. (1986). Wide Range Achievement Test (WRAT-R), 1984 edition. *Journal of Counseling and Development, 64,* 540–541.

Reynolds, C. R., & Gutkin, J. R. (Eds.). (1999). *The handbook of school psychology* (3rd. ed.). New York: Wiley.

Reynolds, C. R., & Kamphaus, R. W. (1997). The Kaufman Assessment Battery for Children: Development, structure, and applications in neuropsychology. In A. M. Horton, D. Wedding, et al. (Eds.), *The neuropsychology handbook: Vol. 1. Foundations and assessment* (2nd ed.) (pp. 290–330). New York: Springer.

Reynolds, C. R., & Nigl, A. J. (1981). A regression analysis of differential validity: An intellectual assessment for black and white inner-city children. *Journal of Clinical and Child Psychology, 10,* 176–179.

Reynolds, C. R., & Ramsay, M. C. (2003). Bias in psychological assessment: An empirical review and recommendations. In J. R. Graham & J. A. Naglieri (Eds.), *Handbook of psychology: Assessment psychology* (Vol. 10) (pp. 67–93). New York: Wiley.

Reynolds, M. R., & Keith, T. Z. (2007). Spearman's law of diminishing returns in hierarchical models of intelligence for children and adolescents. *Intelligence, 35*(3), 267–281.

Richeson, N. & Thorson, J. A. (2002). The effect of autobiographical writing on the subjective well-being of older adults. *North American Journal of Psychology, 4*(3), 395–404.

Richman, W. L., Kiesler, S., Weisband, S., & Fritz, D. (1999). A meta-analytic study of social desirability distortion in computer-administered questionnaires, traditional questionnaires, and interviews. *Journal of Applied Psychology, 84*(5), 754–775.

Ridenour, T. A., Treloar, J. H., & Dean, R. S. (2003). Utility analysis for clinical decision-making in small treatment settings. *International Journal of Neurosciences, 113*(3), 417–430.

Ridge, S., Campbell, W., & Martin, D. (2002). Striving towards an understanding of Conscious Identification: Its definition and its effects. *Counseling Psychology Quarterly, 15*(1), 91–105.

Rieke, M. L., & Guastello, S. J. (1995). Unresolved issues in honesty and integrity testing. *American Psychologist, 50,* 458–459.

Riethmiller, R. J., & Handler, L. (1997). The great figure drawing controversy: The integration of research and clinical practice. *Journal of Personality Assessment, 69,* 488–496.

Riggio, R. E., Murphy, S. E., Pirozzolo, F. J. (Eds.) (2002). *Multiple intelligences and leadership.* Mahwah, NJ: Erlbaum.

Righetti-Veltema, M., Bousquet, A., & Manzano, J. (2003). Impact of postpartum depressive symptoms on mother and her 18-month-old infant. *European Child and Adolescent Psychiatry, 12*(2), 75–83.

Ritzler, B. A., & Alter, B. (1986). Rorschach teaching in APA-approved clinical graduate programs: Ten years later. *Journal of Personality Assessment, 50,* 44–49.

Ritzler, B. A., Sharkey, K. J., & Chudy, J. F. (1980). A comprehensive projective alternative to the TAT. *Journal of Personality Assessment, 44,* 358–362.

Rizza, M. G., McIntosh, D. E., & McCunn, A. (2001). Profile analysis of the Woodcock-Johnson III Tests of Cognitive Abilities with gifted students. *Psychology in the Schools, 38*(5), 447–455.

Roberts, B. W., Harms, P. D., Caspi, A., & Moffitt, T. E. (2007). Predicting the counterproductive employee in a child-to-adult prospective study. *Journal of Applied Psychology, 92*(5), 1427–1436.

Roberts, J. S., Laughlin, J. E., & Wendel, D. H. (1999). Validity issues in the Likert and Thurstone approaches to attitude measurement. *Educational and Psychological Measurement, 59*(2), 211–233.

Robins, R. W., Gosling, S. D., & Craik, K. H. (1999). An empirical analysis of trends in psychology. *American Psychologist, 54,* 117–128.

Robinson, P. L. (2007). *Predicting freshmen college success: The relationship between peer learning, help seeking, math self-efficacy, English self-efficacy and institutional integration.* US: ProQuest Information & Learning.

Roderiques, A. B. (2002). A comparison of ability-achievement discrepancy models for identifying learning disabilities. *Dissertation Abstracts International, 62*, 8A. (UMI No. 3022757).

Rodger, S. (1994). A survey of assessments used by paediatric occupational therapists. *Australian Occupational Therapy Journal, 41*, 137–142.

Rodger, S. C. (2002). Teacher clarity and student anxiety: An aptitude-treatment interaction experiment. *Dissertation Abstracts International: Section B. The Physical Sciences and Engineering, 63*, 4B.

Rodriguez, M. (2005). Three options are optimal for multiple-choice items: A meta-analysis of 80 years of research. *Educational Measurement: Issues and Practice, 24*(2), 3–13.

Roe, A., & Klos, D. (1969). Occupational classification. Coun*seling Psychologist, 1*, 84–92.

Roe, A., & Seigelman, M. (1964). The *origin of interests*. Washington, DC: American Personnel and Guidance Association.

Roeckelein, J. E. (2002). A demonstration of undergraduate students' first impression and their ratings of pathology. *Psychological Reports, 90*(2).

Rogers, C. R. (1959a). A tentative scale for the measurement of process in psychotherapy. In E. A. Rubinstein & M. B. Parloff (Eds.), *Research in psychotherapy*. Washington, DC: American Psychological Association.

Rogers, C. R. (1959b). A theory of therapy, personality, and interpersonal relationships, as developed in the client-centered framework. In S. Koch (Ed.), *Psychology: A study of science* (Vol. 3). New York: McGraw-Hill.

Rogers, C. R. (1961). *On becoming a person*. Boston: Houghton Mifflin.

Rogers, C. R. (1980). *A way of being*. Boston: Houghton Mifflin.

Rogers, R., Sewell, K. W., Harrison, K. S., & Jordan, M. J. (2006). The MMPI-2 restructured clinical scales: A paradigmatic shift in scale development. *Journal of Personality Assessment, 87*(2), 139–147.

Roid, G. H. (2003a). *Stanford Binet Intelligence Scales* (5th ed.) Itasca, IL: Riverside.

Roid, G. H. (2003b). *Stanford Binet Intelligence Scales* (5th ed.), Examiners Manual. Itasca, IL: Riverside.

Roid, G. H. (2003c). *Stanford Binet Intelligence Scales* (5th ed.), Technical Manual. Itasca, IL: Riverside.

Rolland, J. P., Parker, W. D., & Stumpf, H. (1998). A psychometric examination of the French translations of the NEO-PI-R and NEO-FFI. *Journal of Personality Assessment, 71*, 269–291.

Rollnick, J. D., Borsutsky, M., Huber, T. J., Mogk, H., Seifert, J., Emrich, H. M., & Schneider, U. (2002). Short-term cognitive improvement in schizophrenics treated with typical and atypical neuroleptics. *Neuropsychobiology, 45*(2), 74–80.

Roscoe, A. H. (1993). Heart rate as a psychophysiological measure for in-flight workload assessment. *Ergonomics, 36*(9), 1055–1062.

Rose, C. L., Murphy, L. B., Byard, L., & Nikzad, K. (2002). The role of Big Five personality factors in vigilance performance and workload. *European Journal of Personality, 16*(3), 185–200.

Rosenberg, M. (1965). *Society and the adolescent self-image*. Princeton, New Jersey: Princeton University Press.

Rosenfeld, P., Doherty, L. M., Vicino, S. M., Kantor, J., et al. (1989). Attitude assessment in organizations: Testing three microcomputer-based survey systems. *Journal of General Psychology, 116*, 145–154.

Rosenstein, R., & Glickman, A. S. (1994). Type size and performance of the elderly on the Wonderlic Personnel Test. *Journal of Applied Gerontology, 13*(2), 185–192.

Rosenthal, R. (1966). *Experimenter effects in behavioral research*. New York: Appleton-Century-Crofts.

Rosenthal, R. (2002a). *Experimenter and clinician effects in scientific inquiry and clinical practice*. Washington, DC: American Psychological Assocation.

Rosenthal, R. (2002b). *The Pygmalion effect and its mediating mechanisms*. San Diego, CA: Academic Press.

Rosenthal, R., & Fode, K. L. (1963). The effects of experimenter bias on the performance of the albino rat. *Behavioral Science, 8*, 183–189.

Rosenthal, R., & Jacobson, L. (1968). *Pygmalion in the classroom*. New York: Holt, Rinehart & Winston.

Rosenthal, R., & Rosnow, R. L. (1991). *Essentials of behavioral research: Method and data analysis* (2nd ed.). New York: McGraw-Hill.

Rosenthal, R., Rosnow, R. L., & Rubin, D. B. (2000). *Contrasts and effect sizes in behavioral research: A correlational approach*. New York: Cambridge University Press.

Rosner, J. (2003). On white preferences. *The Nation*, April 14, 2003.

Ross, G., & Lawson, K. (1997). Using the Bayley-II: Unresolved issues in assessing the development of prematurely born children. *Journal of Developmental and Behavioral Pediatrics, 18*, 109–111.

Roth, P. L., Huffcutt, A. I., & Bobko, P. (2003). Ethnic group differences in measures of job performance: A new meta-analysis. *Journal of Applied Psychology, 88*(4), 694–706.

Rothbaum, B. O., Anderson, P., Zimand, E., Hodges, L., Lang, D., & Wilson, J. (2006). Virtual reality exposure therapy and standard (in vivo) exposure therapy in the treatment of fear of flying. *Behavior Therapy, 37*(1), 80–90.

Rothstein, H. R. (2003). *Progress is our most important product: Contributions of validity generalization and meta-analysis to the development and communication of knowledge in I/O psychology*. Mahwah, NJ: Erlbaum.

Rotter, J. B. (1967). A new scale for the measurement of interpersonal trust. *Journal of Personality, 35*, 651–665.

Rotter, J. B., & Rafferty, J. E. (1950). *Manual: The Rotter Incomplete Sentences Blank*. San Antonio, TX: Psychological Corporation.

Rottinghaus, P., Coon, K., Gaffey, A., & Zytowski, D. (2007). Thirty-year stability and predictive validity of vocational interests. *Journal of Career Assessment, 15*(1), 5–22.

Roy, D. D., & Deb, N. C. (1999). Item-total-score correlations of state anxiety inventory across different months in Antarctic expedition. *Psychological Studies, 44*(1–2), 43–45.

Roznowski, M., & Reith, J. (1999). Examining the measurement quality of tests containing differentially functioning items: Do biased items result in poor measurement? *Educational and Psychological Measurement, 59*, 248–269.

Ruberto, G., Vassos, E., Lewis, C. M., Tatarelli, R., Girardi, P., et al. (2011). The Cognitive Impact of the ANK3 Risk Variant for Bipolar Disorder: Initial Evidence of Selectivity to Signal Detection during Sustained Attention. *Phase One, 6*(1), e16671. doi:10.1371/journal.pone.0016671.

Rubin, Z. (1970). Measurement of romantic love. *Journal of Personality and Social Psychology, 16*, 265–273.

Rubin, Z. (1973). *Liking and loving: An invitation to social psychology*. New York: Holt, Rinehart & Winston.

Rubin, Z. (1979, February 21). Los Angeles says it with love on a scale. *Los Angeles Times*.

Rubio, D. M., Berg-Weger, M., Tebb, S. S., Lee, E. S., & Rauch, S. (2003). Objectifying content validity: Conducting a content validity study in social work research. *Social Work Research, 27*(2), 94–104.

Rudner, L. & Gagne, P. (2001). *An overview of three approaches to scoring written essays by computer.* (Report No. EDO-TM-01-09) College Park, MD: ERIC Clearinghouse on Assessment and Evaluation (ERIC Document Reproduction Service No. ED458290).

Rudner, L. M. (1998). Online, interactive, computer adaptive testing tutorial. ERIC Clearinghouse on Assessment and Evaluation. Retrieved April 9, 2003 from http://ericae.net/scripts/cat.

Ruisel, I. (2001). Dichotomy in intelligence. *Studia Psychologica, 34*(4), 255–273.

Rush, A. J. (2003). Toward an understanding of bipolar disorder and its origin. *Journal of Clinical Psychiatry, 64*(16), 4–8.

Rushton, J. P. (1991). Do r-K strategies underlie human race differences? *Canadian Psychology, 32,* 29–42.

Rushton, J. P. & Irwing, P. (2011). The general factor of personality: Normal and abnormal. In T. Chamorro-Premuzic, S. von Stumm, & A. Furnham (Eds.), *The Wiley Blackwell handbook of individual differences* (pp. 132–162). West Sussex, UK: Blackwell Publishing.

Russell, E. W. (2000). The application of computerized scoring programs to neuropsychological assessment. In R. D. Vanderploeg (Ed.), *Clinician's guide to neuropsychological assessment* (pp. 483–515). Mahwah, NJ: Erlbaum.

Russell, L. B. (1986). *Is prevention better than cure?* Washington, DC: Brookings Institution.

Russo, A., & Warren, S. H. (1999). Collaborative test taking. *College Teaching, 47,* 18.

Rutter, M., Thorpe, K., Greenwood, R., Northstone, K., & Golding, J. (2003). Twins as a natural experiment to study the causes of mild language delay. *Journal of Child Psychology and Psychiatry and Allied Disciplines, 44*(3), 326–341.

Ryan, J. J., Paolo, A. M., & Van Fleet, J. N. (1994). Neurodiagnostic implications of abnormal verbal-performance IQ discrepancies on the WAIS-R: A comparison with the standardization sample. *Archives of Clinical Neuropsychology, 9*(3), 251–258.

Ryan, J. J., Sattler, J. M., & Lopez, S. J. (2000). Age effects in Wechsler Adult Intelligence Scale-III subtests. *Archives of Clinical Neuropsychology, 15*(4), 311–317.

Ryan, J. J., & Tree, H. A. (2007). Validity of WAIS-III performance scale subtests completed with the non-dominant hand. *Applied Neuropsychology, 14*(1), 52–55.

Ryan, J. M., & DeMark, S. (2002). Variation in achievement scores related to gender, item format, and content area tested. In G. Tindal & T. M. Haladyna (Eds.), *Large-scale assessment programs for all students: Validity, technical adequacy, and implementation* (pp. 67–88). Mahwah, NJ: Erlbaum.

Saccuzzo, D. P. (1975). Canonical correlation as a method of assessing the correlates of good and bad therapy hours. *Psychotherapy: Theory, Research and Practice, 12,* 253–256.

Saccuzzo, D. P. (1977). The practice of psychotherapy in America: Issues and trends. *Professional Psychology, 8,* 297–306.

Saccuzzo, D. P. (1981). Input capability and speed of processing in mental retardation: A reply to Stanovich and Purcell. *Journal of Abnormal Psychology, 90,* 172–174.

Saccuzzo, D. P. (1993). Measuring individual differences in cognition in schizophrenia and other disordered states: Backward masking paradigm. In D. K. Detterman (Ed.), *Individual differences and cognition: Current topics in human intelligence* (Vol. 3) (pp. 219–237). Norwood, NJ: Ablex.

Saccuzzo, D. P. (1994, August). *Coping with complexities of contemporary psychological testing: Negotiating shifting sands.* Invited presentation for the G. Stanley Hall Lecture Series, American Psychological Association 102nd Annual Meeting, Los Angeles.

Saccuzzo, D. P. (1999). Still crazy after all these years: California's persistent use of the MMPI as character evidence in criminal cases. *University of San Francisco Law Review, 33,* 379–400.

Saccuzzo, D. P., & Braff, D. L. (1981). Early information proces-sing deficits in schizophrenia: New findings using schizophrenic subgroups and manic controls. *Archives of General Psychiatry, 38,* 175–179.

Saccuzzo, D. P., & Braff, D. L. (1986). Information-processing abnormalities in schizophrenia and psychotic patients: Trait and state dependent components. *Schizophrenia Bulletin, 12,* 447–458.

Saccuzzo, D. P., Braff, D. L., Shine, A., & Lewandowski, D. G. (1981, April). A *differential WSC pattern in the retarded as a function of sex and race.* Paper presented at the meeting of the Western Psychological Association, Los Angeles.

Saccuzzo, D. P., Cadenhead, K., & Braff, D. L. (1996). Backward versus forward visual masking deficits in schizophrenia patients: Appear to be centrally not peripherally mediated. *American Journal of Psychiatry, 153,* 1564–1570.

Saccuzzo, D. P., Hirt, M., & Spencer, T. J. (1974). Backward masking as a measure of attention in schizophrenia. *Journal of Abnormal Psychology, 83,* 512–522.

Saccuzzo, D. P., & Johnson, N. E. (1995). Traditional psychometric test and proportionate representation: An intervention and program evaluation study. *Psychological Assessment, 7*(2), 183–194.

Saccuzzo, D. P., & Johnson, N. E. (2000). *The 5-minute IQ test: Item characteristics and reliability.* San Diego, CA: Applications of Psychology to Law.

Saccuzzo, D. P., Johnson, N. E., & Guertin, T. L. (1994). Information processing in gifted versus nongifted African-American, Latino, Filipino, and white children: Speeded versus nonspeeded paradigms. *Intelligence, 19,* 219–243.

Saccuzzo, D. P., Johnson, N. E., & Guertin, T. (1995). Traditional psychometric tests and proportionate representation: An intervention and program evaluation study. *Psychological Assessment, 7,* 183–194.

Saccuzzo, D. P., Johnson, N. E., & Russell, G. (1992). Verbal versus performance IQs for gifted African-American, Caucasian, Filipino, and Hispanic children. *Psychological Assessment, 4,* 239–244.

Saccuzzo, D. P., & Kaplan, R. M. (1984). *Clinical psychology.* Boston: Allyn & Bacon.

Saccuzzo, D. P., Kerr, M., Marcus, A., & Brown, R. (1979). Input capability and speed of information processing in mental retardation. *Journal of Abnormal Psychology, 88,* 312–317.

Saccuzzo, D., Kewley, & Johnson, N., et al. (2003). *An examination of positive affect measures.* (Naval Health Research Center Rep. No. TCN 02109/D. I. 0118).

Saccuzzo, D. P., & Larson, G. E. (1987, November). *Analysis of test-retest reliability for a battery of cognitive speed tests* (Technical Report 88-10). San Diego, CA: Navy Personnel Research and Development Center.

Saccuzzo, D. P., Larson, G. E., & Rimland, B. (1986). Visual, auditory and reaction time approaches to the measurement of speed of information-processing and individual differences in intelligence. *Personality and Individual Differences, 2,* 659–668.

Saccuzzo, D. P., & Lewandowski, D. G. (1976). The WISC as a diagnostic tool. *Journal of Clinical Psychology, 32,* 115–124.

Saccuzzo, D. P., & Marcus, A. (1983). *Speed of visual information-processing improves with practice in mental retardation.* Paper presented at the 91st Annual Convention of the American Psychological Association, Anaheim, CA.

Saccuzzo, D. P., & Michael, B. (1984). Speed of information processing and structural limitations in retarded and dual diagnosis retarded-schizophrenic persons. *American Journal of Mental Deficiency, 89,* 187–194.

Saccuzzo, D. P., & Miller, S. (1977). Critical interstimulus interval in delusional schizophrenics and normals. *Journal of Abnormal Psychology, 86,* 261–266.

Saccuzzo, D. P., & Schubert, D. (1981). Backward masking as a measure of slow processing in the schizophrenia spectrum of disorders. *Journal of Abnormal Psychology, 90,* 305–312.

Saccuzzo, D. P., & Schulte, R. (1978). The value of a master's degree for the Ph.D. pursuing student in psychology. *American Psychologist, 33,* 862–864.

Sackett, P. R. (1998). Performance assessment in education and professional certification: Lessons for personnel selection? In E. Milton, D. Hakel, et al. (Eds.), *Beyond multiple choice: Evaluating alternatives to traditional testing for selection* (pp. 113–129). Mahwah, NJ: Erlbaum.

Sackett, P. R. (2003). *The status of validity generalization research: Key issues in drawing inferences from cumulative research findings.* Mahwah, NJ: Erlbaum.

Sackett, P. R., Borneman, M. J., & Connelly, B. S. (2008). High-stakes testing in higher-education and employment: Appraising the evidence for validity and fairness. *American Psychologist, 63,* 215–227.

Sackett, P. R., & Lievens, F. (2008). Personnel selection. *Annual Review of Psychology, 59,* 1–32.

Sackett, P. R., Schmitt, N., Ellingson, J. E., & Kabin, M. B. (2001). High-stakes testing in employment, credentialing, and higher education. *American Psychologist, 56,* 302–318.

Sackett, P. R., & Wilk, S. L. (1994). Within-group norming and other forms of score adjustment in pre-employment testing. *American Psychologist, 49,* 929–954.

Safir, M., & Wallach, H. (2011). Current trends and future directions for virtual reality enhanced psychotherapy. In S. Brahnam & L. Jain (Eds.), *Advanced computational intelligence paradigms in healthcare: Virtual reality in psychotherapy, rehabilitation, and assessment, 3*(337), 32–45. Berlin: Springer. doi:10.1007/978-3-642-17824-5_3.

Saine, N. L., Lerkkanen, M.-K., Ahonen, T., Tolvanen, A. & Lyytinen, H. (2011). Computer-assisted remedial reading intervention for school beginners at risk for reading disability. *Child Development, 82*(3), 1013–1028. doi:10.1111/j.1467-8624.2011.01580.x.

Saklofske, D. H., Schwean, V. L., Yackulic, R. A., & Quinn, D. (1994). WISC-III and SV: FE performance of children with attention deficit hyperactivity disorder. *Canadian Journal of School Psychology, 10*(2), 167–171.

Sakuragi, A. (2006). *The applicability of Exner's comprehensive system of the Rorschach to a Japanese population.* US: ProQuest Information & Learning.

Salkind, N. J. (2007). *Encyclopedia of measurement and statistics.* Thousand Oaks, CA: Sage.

Saltzman, J., Strauss, E., Hunter, M., & Spellacy, F. (1998). Validity of the Wonderlic Personnel Test as a brief measure of intelligence in individuals referred for evaluation of head injury. *Archives of Clinical Neuropsychology, 13,* 611–616.

Salzinger, K. (2005). Clinical, statistical, and broken-leg predictions. *Behavior and Philosophy, 33,* 91–99.

Samuel, D. B., Hopwood, C. J., Ansell, E. B., Morey, L. C., Sanislow, C. A., Markowitz, J. C., Yen, S., Shea, M. T., Skodol, A. E., & Grilo, C. M. (2011). Comparing the temporal stability of self-report and interview assessed personality disorder. *Journal of Abnormal Psychology, 120*(3), 670–680. doi:10.1037/a0022647.

Sander, R. (2004). A systemic analysis of affirmative action in American law schools. *Stanford Law Review, 57,* 368–483.

Sanders, C. E. (1997). Assessment during the preschool years. In G. D. Phye et al. (Eds.), *Handbook of classroom assessment: Learning achievement and adjustment. Educational psychology series* (pp. 227–264). San Diego, CA: Academic Press.

Sands, W. A., Waters, B. K., & McBride, J. R. (1997). *Computerized adaptive testing: From inquiry to operation.* Washington, DC: American Psychological Association.

Sanford, K. (1998). Memories of feeling misunderstood, and a schema of partner empathic responding: New scales for marital research. *Journal of Social and Personal Relationships, 15,* 490–501.

Sangwan, S. (2001). Ecological factors as related to I.Q. of children. *Psycho-Lingua, 31*(2), 89–92.

Santosa, C. M., Strong, C. M., Nowakowska, C., Wang, P. W., Rennicke, C. M., & Ketter, T. A. (2007). Enhanced creativity in bipolar disorder patients: A controlled study. *Journal of Affective Disorders, 100*(1), 31–39.

Sapp, M. (1999). *Test anxiety: Applied research, assessment, and treatment interventions* (2nd ed.). Lanham, MD: University Press of America.

Sarason, B. R., & Sarason, I. G. (1994). Assessment of social support. In S. A. Shumaker & S. M. Czajkowski, (Eds.), *Social support and cardiovascular disease: Plenum series in behavioral psychophysiology and medicine* (pp. 41–63). New York: Plenum.

Sarason, I. G. (1958). Effects on verbal learning of anxiety, reassurance, and meaningfulness of material. *Journal of Experimental Psychology, 56,* 472–477.

Sarason, I. G. (1959). Intellectual and personality correlates of test anxiety. *Journal of Abnormal and Social Psychology, 59,* 272–275.

Sarason, I. G. (1961). The effects of anxiety and threat on solution of a difficult task. *Journal of Abnormal and Social Psychology, 62,* 165–168.

Sarason, I. G. (1975). Test anxiety, attention, and the general problem of anxiety. In C. D. Spielberger & I. G. Sarason (Eds.), *Stress and anxiety* (Vol. 1). New York: Halsted.

Sarason, I. G., Levine, H. M., Bashhnan, R. B., & Sarason, B. R. (1983). Assessing social support: The social support questionnaire. *Journal of Personality and Social Psychology, 44,* 127–139.

Sarason, I. G., & Palola, E. G. (1960). The relationship of test and general anxiety, difficulty of task, and experimental instructions to performance. *Journal of Experimental Psychology, 59,* 185–191.

Sarason, I. G., & Sarason, B. R. (1999). *Abnormal psychology: The problem of maladaptive behavior* (9th ed.). Upper Saddle River, NJ: Prentice-Hall.

Sarason, I. G., Sarason, B. R., & Pierce, G. R. (1990). *Social support: An interactional view.* New York: Wiley.

Sarason, I. G., Smith, R. E., & Diener, E. (1975). Personality research: Components of variance attributable to the person and the situation. *Journal of Personality and Social Psychology, 3,* 199–204.

Sarouphim, K. M. (2002). DISCOVER in high school. *Journal of Secondary Gifted Education, 14*(1), 30–38.

Satre, D. D., Chi, F. W., Eisendrath, S., & Weisner, C. (2011). Subdiagnostic alcohol use by depressed men and women seeking outpatient psychiatric services: Consumption patterns and motivation to reduce drinking. *Alcoholism: Clinical and Experimental Research, 35,* 695–702. doi:10.1111/j.1530-0277.2010.01387.x.

Sattler, J. M. (1970). Racial "experimenter effects" in experimentation, testing, interviewing, and psychotherapy. *Psychological Bulletin, 73,* 137–160.

Sattler, J. M. (1973a). Examiners' scoring style, accuracy, ability, and personality scores. *Journal of Clinical Psychology, 29,* 38–39.

Sattler, J. M. (1973b). Intelligence testing of ethnic minority-group and culturally disadvantaged children. In L. Mann & D. Sabatino (Eds.), *The first review of special education* (Vol. 2). Philadelphia: JSE Press.

Sattler, J. M. (1973c). Racial experimenter effects. In K. S. Miller & R. M. Dreger (Eds.), *Comparative studies of blacks and whites in the United States.* New York: Seminar Press.

Sattler, J. M. (1977). The effects of therapist-client racial similarity. In A. S. Gurman & A. M. Razin (Eds.), *Effective psychotherapy. A handbook of research* (pp. 252–290). Elmsford, NY: Pergamon Press.

Sattler, J. M. (1979a, April). *Intelligence tests on trial: Larry P. et al. v. Wilson Riles et al.* Paper presented at the meeting of the Western Psychological Association, San Diego, CA.

Sattler, J. M. (1979b). Standard intelligence tests are valid for measuring the intellectual potential of urban children:

Comments on pitfalls in the measurement of intelligence. *Journal of Psychology, 102,* 107–112.

Sattler, J. M. (1980, November). Intelligence tests on trial: An interview with Judges Robert F. Peckham and John F. Grady. *APA Monitor,* pp. 7–8.

Sattler, J. M. (1982). *Assessment of children's intelligence and special abilities.* Boston: Allyn & Bacon. Sattler, J. M. (1988). *Assessment of children* (3rd ed.). San Diego, CA: Sattler.

Sattler, J. M. (1992). *Assessment of children* (4th ed.). San Diego, CA: J. M. Sattler.

Sattler, J. M. (1998). *Clinical and forensic interviewing of children and families: Guidelines for the mental health, education, pediatric, and child maltreatment fields.* San Diego, CA: Author.

Sattler, J. M. (2002). *Assessment of children: Behavioral and clinical applications* (4th ed.). La Mesa, CA: Jerome M. Sattler.

Sattler, J. M. (2004). *Assessment of children: WISC-IV and WPPSI-III SUPPLEMENT.* La Mesa, CA: Jerome M. Sattler.

Sattler, J. M., & Gwynne, J. (1982). Ethnicity and Bender Visual Motor Test performance. *Journal of School Psychology, 20,* 69–71.

Sattler, J. M., Hillix, W. A., & Neher, L. A. (1970). Halo effect in examiner scoring of intelligence test responses. *Journal of Consulting and Clinical Psychology, 34,* 172–176.

Sattler, J. M., & Theye, F. (1967). Procedural, situational, and interpersonal variables in individual intelligence testing. *Psychological Bulletin, 68,* 347–360.

Sattler, J. M., & Winget, B. M. (1970). Intelligence testing procedures as affected by expectancy and IQ. *Journal of Clinical Psychology, 26,* 446–448.

Satz, P., & Fletcher, J. M. (1981). Emergent trends in neuropsychology: An overview. *Journal of Consulting and Clinical Psychology, 49,* 851–865.

Saunders, B. T., & Vitro, F. T. (1971). Examiner expectancy and bias as a function of the referral process in cognitive assessment. *Psychology in the Schools, 8,* 168–171.

Savickas, M. L. (1999). The psychology of interests. In E. Mark, L. Savickas, E. Arnold, R. Spokane et al. (Eds.), *Vocational interests: Meaning, measurement, and counseling use* (pp. 19–56). Palo Alto, CA: Davies-Black.

Savickas, M. L. (2000). Assessing career decision making. In E. C. Edward Watkins, Jr., E. Vicki, L. Campbell, et al. (Eds.), *Testing and assessment in*

*counseling practice* (2nd ed.) (pp. 429–477). Mahwah, NJ: Erlbaum.

Sawyer, J. (1966). Measurement and prediction, clinical and statistical. *Psychological Bulletin, 66,* 178–200.

Sawyer, M. G., Sarris, A., & Baghurst, P. (1992). The effect of computer-assisted interviewing on the clinical assessment of children. *Australian & New Zealand Journal of Psychiatry, 26*(2), 223–231.

Sawyer, M. G., Sarris, A., Quigley, R., & Baghurst, P. (1991). The attitude of parents to the use of computer-assisted interviewing in a child psychiatry service. *British Journal of Psychiatry, 157,* 675–678.

Sawyer, R. (2007). Indicators of usefulness of test scores. *Applied Measurement in Education, 20*(3), 255–271.

Schaefer, B. A., Koeter, M. W. J., Wouters, L., Emmelkamp, P. M. G., & Schene, A. H. (2003). What patient characteristics make clinicians recommend brief treatment? *Acta Psychiatrica Scandinavica, 107*(3), 188–196.

Schaefer, J. A., & Moos, R. H. (1996). Effects of work stressors and work climate on long-term care staff's job morale and functioning. *Research in Nursing and Health, 19*(1), 63–73.

Scheier, M. F., & Carver, C. S. (1985). Optimism, coping, and health: Assessment and implications of generalized outcome expectancies. *Health Psychology, 4,* 219–247.

Scheier, M. F., Carver, C. S., & Bridges, M. W. (1994). Distinguishing optimism from neuroticism (and trait anxiety, self-master, and self-esteem): A re-evaluation of the Life Orientation Test. *Journal of Personality and Social Psychology, 67,* 1063–1078.

Scheier, M. F., Weintraub, J. K., & Carver, C. S. (1986). Coping with stress: divergent strategies of optimists and pessimists. *J Pers Soc Psychol, 51*(6), 1257–1264.

Scheuneman, J. D. (1981). New look at bars and aptitude tests. *New Directions in Testing and Measurement, 12,* 5–25.

Scheuneman, J. D. (1987). An experimental, exploratory study of causes of bias in test items. *Journal of Educational Measurement, 24,* 97–118.

Schleicher, A. & Tamassia C. (2000). *Measuring student knowledge and skills: The PISA Assessment of Reading, Mathematical, and Scientific Literacy.* Retrieved April 16, 2003, from www.pisa.oecd.org/knowledge/home/intro.htm.

Schmidt, A. E. (2000). An approximation of a hierarchical logistic regression model used to establish the predictive validity of scores on a nursing licensure exam. *Educational & Psychological Measurement, 60*(3), 463–478.

Schmidt, F., & Hunter, J. (2003). *History, development, evolution, and impact of validity generalization and meta-analysis methods, 1975–2001.* Mahwah, NJ: Erlbaum.

Schmidt, F. L., & Hunter, J. E. (1983). Individual differences in productivity: An empirical test of estimates derived from studies of selection procedure utility. *Journal of Applied Psychology, 68,* 407–414.

Schmidt, F. L., Law, K., Hunter, J. E., Rothstein, H. R., et al. (1993). Refinements in validity generalization methods: Implications for the situational specificity hypothesis. *Journal of Applied Psychology, 78,* 3–12.

Schmidt, F. L., & Rothstein, H. R. (1994). Application of validity generalization to biodata scales in employment selection. In G. S. Stokes, M. D. Mumford, & W. A. Owens (Eds.), *Biodata handbook: Theory, research, and use of biographical information in selection and performance prediction* (pp. 237–260). Palo Alto, CA: CPP Books.

Schmidt, K. M., & Embretson, S. E. (2003). *Item response theory and measuring abilities.* New York: Wiley.

Schmitt, N. (1976). Social and situational determinants of interview decisions: Implications for the employment interview. *Personnel Psychology, 29,* 79–101.

Schmukle, S. C., Egloff, B., & Burns, L. R. (2002). The relationship between positive and negative affect in the Positive and Negative Affect Schedule. *Journal of Research in Personality, 36*(5), 463–475.

Schneider, L. M., & Briel, J. B. (1990). *Validity of the GRE: 1988–1989 Summary Report.* Princeton, NJ: Educational Testing Service.

Schneider, R. J., Goff, M., Anderson, S., & Borman, W. C. (2003). Computerized adaptive rating scales for measuring managerial performance. *International Journal of Selection & Assessment, 11* (2–3), 237–246.

Schoggen, P. (1979). Roger G. Barker and behavioral settings: A commentary. *Journal of Personality and Social Psychology, 37,* 2158–2160.

Scholz, U., Dona, B. G., Sud, S., & Schwarzer, R. (2002). Is general self-efficacy a universal construct? Psychometric findings from 25 countries.

*European Journal of Psychological Assessment, 18*(3), 242–251.

Schrank, F. A., Flanagan, D. P., Woodcock, R. W., & Mascolo, J. T. (2002). *Essentials of WJ III cognitive abilities assessment.* New York: Wiley.

Schrank, F. A., McGrew, K. S., & Woodcock, R. W. (2001). *Technical abstract (Assessment service bulletin no. 2).* Itasca, IL: Riverside.

Schroeder, H. E., & Kleinsaser, L. D. (1972). Examiner bias: A determinant of children's verbal behavior on the WISC. *Journal of Consulting and Clinical Psychology, 39,* 451–454.

Schuerger, J. M. (1995). Career assessment and the Sixteen Personality Factor Questionnaire. *Journal of Career Assessment, 3,* 157–175.

Schuerger, J. M., Tait, E., & Tavernelli, M. (1982). Temporal stability of personality by questionnaire. *Journal of Personality and Social Psychology, 43,* 176–182.

Schulenberg, S. E., & Yutrzenka, B. A. (1999). The equivalence of computerized and paper-and-pencil psychological instruments: Implications for measures of negative affect. *Behavior Research Methods, Instruments and Computers, 31*(2), 315–321.

Schuler, H. (1993). Is there a dilemma between validity and acceptance in the employment interview? In B. Nevo & R. S. Jager (Eds.), *Educational and psychological testing: The test taker's outlook* (pp. 239–250). Gottingen, Germany: Huber.

Schultz, C. B., & Sherman, R. H. (1976). Social class, development, and differences in reinforcer effectiveness. *Review of Educational Research, 46,* 25–59.

Schultz, D. S., & Loving, J. L. (2012). Challenges since Wikipedia: The availability of Rorschach information online and Internet users' reactions to online media coverage of the Rorschach–Wikipedia debate. *Journal of Personality Assessment, 94*(1), 73–81.

Schwab-Stone, M., Fallon, T., Briggs, M., & Crowther, B. (1994). Reliability of diagnostic reporting for children aged 6–11 years: A test-retest study of the Diagnostic Interview Schedule for Children–Revised. *American Journal of Psychiatry, 151*(7), 1048–1054.

Schwartz, R., & Gottman, J. (1976). Toward a task analysis of assertive behavior. *Journal of Consulting and Clinical Psychology, 44,* 910–920.

Schwarz, L. R., Gfeller, J. D., & Oliveri, M. V. (2006). Detecting feigned impairment with the digit span and

vocabulary subtests of the Wechsler Adult Intelligence Scale-third edition. *Clinical Neuropsychologist, 20*(4), 741–753.

Scott, L. H. (1981). Measuring intelligence with the Goodenough-Harris Drawing Test. *Psychological Bulletin, 89,* 483–505.

Scott, P., Burton, R. V., & Yarrow, M. (1967). Social reinforcement under natural conditions. *Child Development, 38,* 53–63.

Scott-Lennox, J. A., Wu, A. W., Boyer, J. G., & Ware, J. E., Jr. (1999). Reliability and validity of French, German, Italian, Dutch, and UK English translations of the Medical Outcomes Study HIV Health Survey. *Medical Care, 37*(9), 908–925.

Scurich, N., & John, R. (2011). A Bayesian approach to the group versus individual prediction controversy in actuarial risk assessment. *Law and Human Behavior,* 1–11. Retrieved from http://www.springerlink.com/content/l957226475617406/. doi:10.1007/s10979-011-9286-0.

Sechrest, L., Stickle, T. R., & Stewart, M. (1998). The role of assessment in clinical psychology. In A. Bellack, M. Hersen (Series Ed.), & C. R. Reynolds (Vol. Ed.), *Comprehensive clinical psychology* (Vol. 4, Chap. 1). New York: Pergamon Press.

Seewaldt, V. A. (2006). *Using the CCRT to interpret the TAT: Understanding the phenomenon of 'card pull'.* US: ProQuest Information & Learning.

Segal, D. L. (1997). Structured Interviewing and DSM classification. In S. M. Turner & M. Hersen (Eds.), *Adult psychopathology and diagnosis* (3rd ed.) (pp. 24–57). New York: Wiley.

Segal, H. G., Westen, D., Lohr, N. E., & Silk, K. R. (1993). Clinical assessment of object relations and social cognition using stories told to the Picture Arrangement subtest of the WAIS-R. *Journal of Personality Assessment, 61*(1), 58–80.

Segre, L. S., O'Hara, M. W., Arndt, S., & Stuart, S. (2007). The prevalence of postpartum depression: The relative significance of three social status indices. *Social Psychiatry and Psychiatric Epidemiology, 42*(4), 316–321.

Seguin, E. (1907). *Idiocy: Its treatment by the physiological method.* New York: Bureau of Publications, Teachers College, Columbia University. (Original work published 1866).

Seidman, L. J., Buka, S. L., Goldstein, J. M., & Tsuang, M. T. (2006).

Intellectual decline in schizo-phrenia: Evidence from a prospec-tive birth cohort 28-year follow-up study. *Journal of Clinical and Experimental Neuropsychology, 28*(2), 225–242.

Self, P. A., & Horowitz, F. D. (1979). The behavioral assessment of the neonate: An overview. In J. D. Osofsky (Ed.), *Handbook of infant development*. New York: Wiley.

Seligmann, J., Coppola, V., Howard, L., & Lee, E. D. (1979, May 28). A really final exam. *Newsweek*, pp. 97–98.

Sena, J. D., Lowe, P. A., & Lee, S. W. (2007). Significant predictors of test anxiety among students with and without learning disabilities. *Journal of Learning Disabilities, 40*(4), 360–376.

Senior, C., Phillips, M. L., Barns, J., & David, A. S. (1999). An investigation into the perception of dominance from schematic faces: A study using the World-Wide Web. *Behavior Research Methods, Instruments and Computers, 31*(2), 341–346.

Sethuraman, R., Kerin, R. A., & Cron, W. L. (2005). A field study comparing online and offline data collection methods for identifying product attributes preferences using conjoint analysis. *Journal of Business Research, 58*(5), 602–610.

Sexton, M., Fox, N. L., & Hebel, J. R. (1990). Prenatal exposure to tobacco: II. Effects on cognitive functioning at age three. *International Journal of Epidemiology, 19*, 72–77.

Shaffer, D. (1994). Structured interviews for assessing children. *Journal of Child Psychology and Psychiatry and Allied Disciplines, 35*(4), 783–784.

Shaffer, L. (1953). Of whose reality I cannot doubt. *American Psychologist, 8*, 608–623.

Shaffer, T. W., & Erdberg, P. (1996, July). *Cooperative movement in the Rorschach response: A qualitative approach*. Paper presented at the 15th International Congress of Rorschach and Projective Methods, Boston, MA.

Shaffer, T. W., Erdberg, P., & Horaian, J. (1999). Current nonpatient data for the Rorschach, WAIS-R, and MMPI-2. *Journal of Personality Assessment, 73*, 305–316.

Shakow, D., Hilgard, E. R., Kelly, E. L., Sanford, R. N., & Shaffer, L. F. (1947). Recommended graduate training in clinical psychology. *American Psychologist, 2*, 539–558.

Shalit, P., True, A., & Thommes, J. A. (2007). Quality of life and tolerability after administration of enfuvirtide with a thin-walled needle: QUALITE study. *HIV Clinical Trials, 8*(1), 24–35.

Shapiro, S. K., & Simpson, R. G. (1994). Patterns and predictors of performance on the Bender-Gestalt and the Developmental Test of Visual Motor Integration in a sample of behaviorally and emotionally disturbed adolescents. *Journal of Psychoeducational Assessment, 12*(3), 254–263.

Sharkey, K. J., & Ritzler, B. A. (1985). Comparing diagnostic validity of the TAT and a new Picture Projective Test. *Journal of Personality Assessment, 49*, 406–412.

Shattuck, D. W., Mirza, M., Adisetiyo, V., Hojatkashani, C., Salamon, G., Narr, K. L., et al. (2008). Construction of a 3d probabilistic atlas of human cortical structures. *Neuroimage, 39*(3), 1064–1080.

Shavelson, R. J., & Ruiz-Primo, M. A. (2000). On the psychometrics of assessing science understanding. In E. Joel, J. Mintzes, E. James, H. Wandersee, et al. (Eds.), *Assessing science understanding: A human constructivist view* (pp. 303–341). San Diego, CA: Academic Press.

Shaywitz, B. A., Fletcher, J. M., & Shaywitz, S. E. (1995). Defining and classifying learning disabilities and attention-deficit/hyperactivity disorder. *Journal of Child Neurology, 10*, S50–S57.

Sheldon, B. (2011). *Cognitive-behavioural therapy*. New York: Routledge.

Shermis, M. D., & Lombard, D. (1998). Effects of computer-based test administrations on test anxiety and performance. *Computers in Human Behavior, 14*(1), 111–123.

Shermis, M. D., Mzumara, H. R., & Bublitz, S. T. (2001). On test and computer anxiety: Test performance under CAT and SAT conditions. *Journal of Educational Computing Research, 24*(1), 57–75.

Sherrer, M. V. (2011). The role of cognitive appraisal in adaptation to traumatic stress in adults with serious mental illness: A critical review. *Trauma Violence & Abuse, 12*(3), 151–167. doi:10.1177/1524838011404254.

Sherry, A., Henson, R. K., & Lewis, J. G. (2003). Evaluating the appropriateness of college-age norms for use with adolescents on the NEO Personality Inventory-Revised. *Assessment, 10*(1), 71–78.

Shibata, S. (2002). A Macintosh and Windows program for assessing body-image disturbance using adjustable image distortion. *Behavior Research Methods, Instruments, and Computers, 34*(1), 90–92.

Shibre, T., Kebede, D., Alem, A., Negash, A., Deyassa, N., Fekada, A., Fekada, D., Jacobsson, L., & Kullgren, G. (2003). Schizophrenia: Illness impact on family members in a traditional society—Rural Ethiopia. *Social Psychiatry & Psychiatric Epidemiology, 38*(1), 27–34.

Shiffman, S., Fischer, L. A., Paty, J. A., Gnys, M., et al. (1995). Drinking and smoking: A field study of their association. *Annals of Behavioral Medicine, 16*(3), 203–209.

Shimmel, J., & Langer, P. (2001). Raising the graduation bar for the schools: Expectations vs outcomes. *Psychological Reports, 89*(2), 317–325.

Shore, G. N., & Rapport, M. D. (1998). The Fear Survey Schedule for Children—Revised (FSSC-HI): Ethnocultural variations in children's fearfulness. *Journal of Anxiety Disorder, 12*, 437–461.

Shores, E. A., & Carstairs, J. R. (1998). Accuracy of the MMPI-2 computerized Minnesota Report in identifying fake-good and fake-bad response sets. *Clinical Neuropsychologist, 12*, 101–106.

Short, P., Cernich, A., Wilken, J. A., & Kane, R. L. (2007). Initial construct validation of frequently employed ANAM measures through structural equation modeling. *Archives of Clinical Neuropsychology, 22 Suppl 1*, S63–77.

Shrout, P. E., Spitzer, R. L., & Fleiss, J. L. (1987). Quantification of agreement in psychiatric diagnosis revisited. *Archives of General Psychiatry, 44*(2), 172–177.

Shull-Senn, S., Weatherly, M., Morgan, S. K., & Bradley-Johnson, S. (1995). Stability reliability for elementary-age students on the Woodcock-Johnson Psychoeducational Battery—Revised (Achievement section) and the Kaufman Test of Educational Achievement. *Psychology in the Schools, 32*, 86–92.

Shultz, M. M., & Zedeck, S. (2011). Predicting lawyer effectiveness: Broadening the basis for law school admission decisions. *Law & Social Inquiry, 36*(3), 620–661. doi:10.1111/j.1747-4469.2011.01245.x.

Shumaker, S. A., & Berzon, R. (1995). *The international assessment of health-related quality of life: Theory, translation, measurement and analysis*. New York: Oxford University Press.

Sidick, J. T., Barrett, G. V., & Doverspike, D. (1994). Three alternative multiple choice tests: An attractive option. *Personnel Psychology, 47,* 829–835.

Signer, B. R. (1991). CAI and at-risk minority urban high school students. *Psychology & Marketing, 8*(4), 243–258.

Sijtsma, K., & Verweij, A. C. (1999). Knowledge of solution strategies and IRT modeling of items for transitive reasoning. *Applied Psychological Measurement, 23*(1), 55–68.

Silva, J. M., & Jacobs, R. R. (1993). Performance as a function of increased minority hiring. *Journal of Applied Psychology, 78,* 591–601.

Silver, H., & Shlomo, N. (2001). Perception of facial emotions in chronic schizophrenia does not correlate with negative symptoms but correlates with cognitive and motor dysfunction. *Schizophrenia Research, 52*(3), 265–273.

Silver, N. C., & Dunlap, W. P. (1987). Averaging correlation coefficients: Should Fisher's Z transformation be used? *Journal of Applied Psychology, 72,* 146–148.

Sim, J., & Wright, C. C. (2005). The kappa statistic in reliability studies: Use, interpretation, and sample size requirements. *Physical Therapy, 85*(3), 257–268.

*Simmons v. Hooks.* (1994). 843 F. Supp. 1296 (E. D. Ark. 1994).

Simms, L. J., Goldberg, L. R., Roberts, J. E., Watson, D., Welte, J., & Rotterman, J. H. (2011). Computerized adaptive assessment of personality disorder: Introducing the CAT–PD project. *Journal of Personality Assessment, 93*(4), 380–389. doi:10.1080/00223891.2011.577475.

Sines, J. O. (1970). Actuarial versus clinical prediction in psychopathology. *British Journal of Psychiatry, 116,* 129–144.

Sines, L. K. (1959). The relative contribution of four kinds of data to accuracy in personality assessment. *Journal of Counseling Psychology, 23,* 483–492.

Singh, L. (1986). Standardization of n-power measuring instrument (T. A. T.). *Journal of Psychological Researches, 28,* 14–20.

Sinha, D. K. (1986). Relationships of graduation requirements and course offerings to Scholastic Aptitude Test performance of seniors in high schools. *Journal of Educational Research, 80,* 5–9.

Sireci, S. G. (1998). The construct of content validity. *Social Indicators Research, 45*(1–3), 83–117.

Sivas, F., Ercin, O., Tanyolac, O., Barca, N., Aydog, S., & Ozoran, K. (2003). The Nottingham health profile in rheumatoid arthritis: correlation with other health status measurements and clinical variables. *Rheumatol Int.*

Slack, W. V. & Slack, C. W. (1977). Talking to a computer about emotional problems: A comparative study. *Psychotherapy: Theory, Research & Practice, 14*(2), 156–164.

Slaney, K. L., Storey, J. E., & Barnes, J. (2011). Is my test valid? Guidelines for the practicing psychologist for evaluating the psychometric properties of measures. *International Journal of Forensic Mental Health, 10*(4).

Slatkoff, J. (2007). *Validity of the MMPI–A structural summary in a forensic sample: Effects of ethnicity, gender, and age.* US: ProQuest Information & Learning.

Sletten, I. W., Ulett, G., Altman, H., & Sundland, D. (1970). The Missouri Standard System of Psychiatry (SSOP): Computer generated diagnosis. *Archives of General Psychiatry, 23*(1), 73–79.

Slotnick, R. (2007). A review of: "Career advising: an academic advisor's guide." In Virginia Gordon (Ed.), *Community College Journal of Research and Practice, 31*(2), 163–165.

Smith, A. E., & Knight-Jones, E. B. (1990). The abilities of very low-birthweight children and their classroom controls. *Developmental Medicine and Child Neurology, 32,* 590–601.

Smith, B., & Sechrest, L. (1991). Treatment of aptitude X treatment interactions. *Journal of Consulting and Clinical Psychology, 59,* 233–244.

Smith, E. V., Jr., Wakely, M. B., De Kruif, R. E. L., & Swartz, C. W. (2003). *Optimizing rating scales for self-efficacy (and other) research.* Thousand Oaks, CA: Sage.

Smith, G. A., & Stanley, G. (1983). Clocking "g": Relating intelligence and measures of timed performance. *Intelligence, 7,* 353–358.

Smith, M., & George, D. (1994). Selection methods. In E. Cary, L. Cooper, E. Ivan, T. Robertson, et al. (Eds.), *Key reviews in managerial psychology: Concepts and research for practice* (pp. 54–96). New York: Wiley.

Smith, R. (2005). *Mental functioning of children with HIV infection: The preschool and early school-age years.* US: ProQuest Information & Learning.

Smith, T. W., Pope, M. K., Rhodewalt, F., & Poulton, J. L. (1989). Optimism, neuroticism, coping, and symptom reports: An alternative interpretation of the life orientation test. *Journal of Personality and Social Psychology, 56,* 640–648.

Smith, T. W., & Zurawski, R. M. (1983). Assessment of irrational beliefs: The question of discriminant validity. *Journal of Clinical Psychology, 39,* 976–979.

Snelbaker, A. J., Wilkinson, G. S., Robertson, G. J., & Glutting, J. J. (2001). Wide Range Achievement Test 3 (WRAT-3). In W. I. Dorfman & M. Hersen (Eds.), *Understanding psychological assessment. Perspective on individual differences* (pp. 259–274). New York: Kluwer Academic/Plenum.

Snow, J. H. (1998). Clinical use of the Benton Visual Retention Test for children and adolescents with learning disabilities. *Archives of Clinical Neuropsychology, 13,* 629–636.

Snow, R. E. (1969). Review of *Pygmalion in the Classroom* by R. Rosenthal and L. Jacobson. *Contemporary Psychology, 14,* 197–199.

Snow, R. E. (1991). Aptitude treatment interaction as a framework for research on individual differences in psychotherapy. *Journal of Consulting and Clinical Psychology, 59,* 205–216.

Snyder, C. R., Harris, C., Anderson, J. R., Holleran, S. A., Irving, L. M., Sigman, S. T., et al. (1991). The will and the ways: Development and validation of an individual differences measure of hope. *Journal of Personality and Social Psychology, 60*(4), 570–585.

Snyder, C. R., Shorey, H. S., Cheavens, J., Pulvers, K. M., Adams, V. G., & Wiklund, C. (2002). Hope and academic success in college. *Journal of Educational Psychology, 94*(4), 820–826.

Snyder, C. R., Sympson, S. C., Michael, S. T., & Cheavens, J. (2001). Optimism and hope constructs: Variants on a positive expectancy theme. In E. C. Chang (Ed.), *Optimism & pessimism: Implications for theory, research, and practice,* p. 101–125. 395p.

Snyderman, M., & Rothman, S. (1987). Survey of expert opinion in intelligence and aptitude testing. *American Psychologist, 42,* 137–144.

Sohn, W. J. (2002). Using differential item functioning (DIF) procedures for investigating the cross-cultural equivalence of personality test. *Dissertation Abstracts International, 62,* 8B.

Sostek, A. M. (1978). Review of the Brazelton Neonatal Assessment Scale. In O. K. Buros (Ed.), *The eighth mental measurements yearbook* (Vol. 1). Highland Park, NJ: Gryphon Press.

Sousa, D. A. (2001). *How the brain learns: A classroom teacher's guide* (2nd ed.). Thousand Oaks, CA: Corwin Press.

South, M., Larson, M. J., White, S. E., Dana, J. & Crowley, M. J. (2011). Better fear conditioning is associated with reduced symptom severity in autism spectrum disorders. *Autism Research*, 4(6), 412–421. doi:10.1002/aur.221.

Space, L. G. (1981). The computer as psychometrician. *Behavior Research Methods and Instrumentation*, 13(4), 595–606.

Spangler, W. D. (1992). Validity of questionnaire and TAT measures of need for achievement: Two meta-analyses. *Psychological Bulletin*, 112, 140–154.

Spear, J. H. (2007) Prominent schools or other active specialties? A fresh look at some trends in psychology. *Review of General Psychology*, 11, 363–380.

Spearman, C. E. (1904). General intelligence objectively determined and measured. *American Journal of Psychology*, 15, 201–293.

Spearman, C. E. (1923). The *nature of intelligence and the principles of cognition*. London: Macmillan.

Spearman, C. E. (1927). *The abilities of man*. New York: Macmillan.

Sperry, R. W. (1968). Hemisphere deconnection and unity in conscious awareness. *American Psychologist*, 23, 723–733.

Spielberger, C. D., Anton, W. B., & Bedell, J. (1976). The nature and treatment of test anxiety. In M. Zuckerman & C. D. Spielberger (Eds.), *Emotions and anxiety: New concepts, methods and applications*. Hillsdale, NJ: Erlbaum.

Spielberger, C. D., Auerbach, S. M., Wadsworth, A. P., Dun, T. M., & Taulbee, E. S. (1975). Emotional reactions to surgery. *Journal of Consulting and Clinical Psychology*, 40, 33–38.

Spielberger, C. D., Foreyt, J. P., Reheiser, E. C., & Poston, W. S. C. (1998). Motivational, emotional, and personality characteristics of smokeless tobacco users compared with cigarette smokers. *Personality and Individual Differences*, 25(5), 821–832.

Spielberger, C. D., Gorsuch, R. L., & Lushene, R. E. (1970). *Manual for the State-Trait Anxiety Inventory*. Palo Alto, CA: Consulting Psychologists Press.

Spielberger, C. D., & Sydeman, S. J. (1994). State-Trait Anxiety Inventory and State-Trait Anger Expression Inventory. In M. E. Maruish (Ed.), *The use of psychological testing for treatment planning and outcome assessment* (pp. 292–321). Hillsdale, NJ: Erlbaum.

Spiers, P. A. (1982). The Luria Nebraska Neuropsychological Battery revisited: A theory in practice or just practicing? *Journal of Consulting and Clinical Psychology*, 50, 301–306.

Spilker, B. (1990). *Quality of life assessment in clinical trials*. New York: Raven Press.

Spilker, B. (Ed.). (1996). *Quality of life and pharmacoeconomics in clinical trials* (2nd ed.). New York: Raven Press.

Spirrison, C. L., & Choi, S. (1998). Psychometric properties of a Korean version of the revised NeoPersonality Inventory. *Psychological Reports*, 83, 263–274.

Spitzer, R. L., & Wakefield, J. C. (1999). DSM-IV diagnostic criterion for clinical significance: Does it help solve the false positives problem? *American Journal of Psychiatry*, 156(12), 1856–1864.

Spitzer, R. L., Williams, J. B. W., Gibbon, M., & First, M. B. (1990a). *Structured clinical interview for DSM-III-R—patient edition* (SCIDP, 9/l/89 version). Washington DC: American Psychiatric Press.

Spitzer, R. L., Williams, J. B. W., Gibbon, M., & First, M. B. (1990b). *Structured clinical interview for DSM-III-R—personality disorders* (SCID-II, 9/1/89 version). Washington, DC: American Psychiatric Press.

Spitzer, R. L., Williams, J. B. W., Gibbon, M., & First, M. B. (1992). The structured clinical interview for DSM-III-R (SCID). I: History, rationale, and description. *Arch Gen Psychiatry*, 49(8), 624–629.

Spokane, A. R., & Catalano, M. (2000). The Self-Directed Search: A theory-driven array of self-guiding career interventions. In E. C. Edward Watkins, Jr., E. Vicki, L. Campbell, et al. (Eds.), *Testing and assessment in counseling practice* (2nd ed.) (pp. 339–370). Mahwah, NJ: Erlbaum.

Squire, L. R., & Butters, N. (1984). *The neurosychology of memory*. New York: Guilford Press.

Srsic, C. S., Stimac, A. P., & Walsh, W. B. (2001). Self-Directed Search. Dordrecht, Netherlands: Kluwer Academic Publishers.

Stallones, R. A., (1983). Ischemic heart disease and lipids in blood and diet. *Annual Review of Nutrition*, 3, 155–185.

Stankov, L. (2003). Complexity in human intelligence. In Sternberg, R. J., Lautrey, J., (Eds.), *Models of intelligence: International perspectives*. (27-42).

Washington, DC: American Psychological Association.

Stanley, J. C. (1971). Reliability. In R. L. Thorndike (Ed.), *Educational measurement*. Washington, DC: American Council on Education.

Stannard, L., Wolfgang, C. H., Jones, I., & Phelps, P. (2001). A longitudinal study of the predictive relations among construction play and mathematical achievement. *Early Child Development and Care*, 167, 115–125.

Statistical Package for the Social Sciences. (1995). *Statistical Package for the Social Sciences reference guide*. Chicago: Author.

Steadman, H. J., Mulvey, E. P., Monahan, J., Robbins, P. C., Appelbaum, P. S., Grisso, T., Roth, L. H., & Silver, E. (1998). Violence by people discharged from acute psychiatric inpatient facilities and by others in the same neighborhoods. *Archives of General Psychiatry*, 55(5), 393–401.

Steele, C. M. (1997). A threat in the air: How stereotypes shape intellectual identity and performance. *American Psychologist*, 52(6), 613–629.

Steele, C. M., & Aronson, J. (1995). Stereotype threat and the intellectual test performance of African Americans. *Journal of Personality and Social Psychology*, 69(5), 797–811.

Steele, C. M., & Aronson, J. (1998). Stereotype threat and the test performance of academically successful African Americans. In E. C. Jencks, E. M. Phillips, et al. (Eds.), *The black-white test score gap* (pp. 401–427). Washington, DC: American Psychological Association.

Steele, C. M., & Aronson, J. A. (2004). Stereotype threat does not live by Steele and Aronson (1995) alone. *American Psychologist*, 59(1), 47–48.

Steele, C. M., & Davies, P. G. (2003). Stereotype threat and employment testing: A commentary. *Human Performance*, 16(3), 311–326.

Stein, D. J., Hollander, E., & ebrary Inc. (2002). *Anxiety disorders co-morbid with depression social anxiety disorder, post-traumatic stress disorder, generalized anxiety disorder, and obsessive-compulsive disorder*. Florence, KY: Taylor & Francis.

Steinberg, L., & Thissen, D. (1995). Item response theory in personal-ity research. In P. E. Shrout & S. T. Fiske (Eds.), *Personality research, methods, and theory: A festschrift honoring Donald W. Fiske*. Hillsdale, NJ: Erlbaum.

Steinberg, M. L., Krejci, J. A., Collett, K., Brandon, T. H., Ziedonis, D. M., & Chen, K. (2007). Relationship between self-reported task persistence and history of quitting smoking, plans for quitting smoking, and current smoking status in adolescents. *Addictive Behaviors, 32*(7), 1451–1460.

*Stell v. Savannah-Chatham County Board of Education.* (1964). 210 F. Supp. 667, 668 (S.D. Ga. 1963), rev'd 333 F.2d 55 (5th Cir. 1964), cert denied, 379 U.S. 933 (1964).

Stephenson, W. (1953). *The study of behavior.* Chicago: University of Chicago Press.

Steptoe, A., & Johnston, D. (1991). Clinical applications of cardiovascular assessment. *Psychological Assessment: A Journal of Consulting and Clinical Psychology, 3,* 337–349.

Stern, D. N. (2010). A new look at parent–infant interaction. In B. M. Lester and J. D. Sparrow (Eds.), *Nurturing children and families: Building on the legacy of T. Berry Brazelton* (pp. 73–82). Oxford, UK: Wiley-Blackwell. doi:10.1002/9781444324617.ch7.

Stern, W. (1912). *Die psychologische Methoden der Intelligenzprufung.* Leipzig, Germany: Barth.

Sternberg, R. J. (1984). The Kaufman Assessment Battery for Children: An information processing analysis and critique. *Journal of Special Education, 180,* 269–279.

Sternberg, R. J. (1985). *Beyond IQ: A triarchic theory of human intelligence.* New York: Cambridge University Press.

Sternberg, R. J. (1986). *Intelligence applied: Understanding and increasing your intellectual skills.* San Diego, CA: Harcourt Brace Jovanovich.

Sternberg, R. J. (1988). *The triarchic mind: A theory of human intelligence.* New York: Viking.

Sternberg, R. J. (1991). Death, taxes, and bad intelligence tests. *Intelligence, 15,* 257–269.

Sternberg, R. J. (2001). Successful intelligence: Understanding what Spearmann had rather than what he studied. In J. M. Collis & S. Messick (Eds.), *Intelligence and personality: Bridging the gap in theory and measurement* (pp. 347–373). Mahwah, NJ: Erlbaum.

Sternberg, R. J., & Gardner, M. K. (1982). A componential interpretation of the general factor in human intelligence. In H. J. Eysenck (Ed.), *A model for intelligence.* New York: Springer-Verlag.

Sternberg, R. J., & Williams, W. M. (1997). Does the Graduate Record Examination predict meaningful success in the graduate training of psychologists? *American Psychologist, 52,* 630–641.

Stevens, K. B., & Price, J. R. (1999). Adult reading assessment: Are we doing the best with what we have? *Applied Neuropsychology, 6*(2), 68–78.

Stevens, M. C., Kaplan, R. F., & Hesselbrock, V. M. (2003). Executive-cognitive functioning in the development of antisocial personality disorder. *Addictive Behaviors, 28*(2), 285–300.

Stevens, S. S. (1966). A metric for the social consensus. *Science, 151,* 530–541.

Stevenson, J. D. (1986). Alternate form reliability and concurrent validity of the PPVT-R for referred rehabilitation agency adults. *Journal of Clinical Psychology, 42,* 650–653.

Steverink, N., Veenstra, R., Oldehinkel, A., Gans, R., & Rosmalen, J. (2011). Is social stress in the first half of life detrimental to later physical and mental health in both men and women? *European Journal of Ageing, 8*(1), 21–30. Retrieved from http://dx.doi.org/10.1007/s10433-011-0178-4. doi:10.1007/s10433-011-0178-4.

Steward, R. J., Gimenez, M. M., & Jackson, J. D. (1995). A study of personal preferences of successful university students as related to race/ethnicity, and sex: Implications and recommendations for training, practice, and future research. *Journal of College Student Development, 36,* 123–131.

Stewart, A. L., & Ware, J. E. (Eds.). (1992). *Measuring functioning and well-being: The medical outcomes study approach.* Durham, NC: Duke University Press.

Stewart, J. L. (2007). *External correlates of the MMPI-2 restructured clinical scales in an American Indian outpatient sample.* US: ProQuest Information & Learning.

Stinchfield, R. (2003). *Reliability, validity, and classification accuracy of a measure of DSM-IV diagnostic criteria for pathological gambling.* Washington, DC: American Psychiatric Association.

Stirling, J., White, C., Lewis, S., Hopkins, R., Tantam, D., Huddy, A., et al. (2003). Neurocognitive function and outcome in first-episode schizophrenia: A 10-year follow-up of an epidemiological cohort. *Schizophrenia Research, 65*(2), 75–86.

Stoeber, J., & Kersting, M. (2007). Perfectionism and aptitude test performance: Testees who strive for perfection achieve better test results. *Personality and Individual Differences, 42*(6), 1093–1103.

Stoelhorst, G. M. S. J., Rijken, M., Martens, S. E., van Zwieten, P. H. T., Feenstra, J., Zwinderman, A. H., Wit, J.-M., & Veen, S. (2003). Developmental outcome at 18 and 24 months of age in very preterm children: A cohort study from 1996-1997. *Early Human Development, 72*(2), 83–95.

Stokols, D. (1978). Environmental psychology. *Annual Review of Psychology, 29,* 253–295.

Stokols, D. (1992). Establishing and maintaining healthy environments: Toward a social ecology of health promotion. *American Psychologist, 47*(l), 6–22.

Stokols, D. (2000). *Theory development in environmental psychology: A pro-spective view.* Dordrecht, Netherlands: Kluwer Academic Publishers.

Stokols, D., Clitheroe, C., & Zmuidzinas, M. (2002). *Qualities of work environments that promote perceived support for creativity.* Mahwah, NJ: Erlbaum.

Stone, A. A. (1995). Measurement of affective response. In S. Cohen, R. C. Kessler, & L. U. Gordon (Eds.), *Measuring stress: A guide for health and social scientists* (pp. 148–171). New York: Oxford University Press.

Stone, A. A., & Broderick, J. E. (2007). Real-time data collection for pain: Appraisal and current status. *Pain Medicine, 8 Suppl 3,* S85–93.

Stone, A. A., Broderick, J. E., et al. (2004). Understanding recall of weekly pain from a momentary assessment perspective: Absolute agreement, between- and within-person consistency, and judged change in weekly pain. *Pain, 107*(1–2), 61–69.

Stone, A. A., Broderick, J. E., Schwartz, J. E., Shiffman, S., Litcher-Kelly, L., & Calvanese, P. (2003). Intensive momentary reporting of pain with an electronic diary: Reactivity, compliance, and patient satisfaction. *Pain, 104*(1–2), 343–351.

Stone, A. A., Kennedy-Moore, E., & Neale, J. M. (1995). Association between daily coping and end-of-day mood. *Health Psychology, 14*(4), 341–349.

Stone, A. A., & Shiffman, S. (1994). Ecological momentary assessment (EMA) in behavioral medicine. *Annals of Behavioral Medicine, 16*(3), 199–202.

Stone, A. A., Shiffman, S. S., & DeVries, M. W. (1999). Ecological momentary assessment. In E. D. Kahneman,

E. E. Diener, et al. (Eds.), *Well-being: The foundations of hedonic psychology* (pp. 26– 39). New York: Russell Sage Foundation.

Stone, A. A., Shiffman, S., Schwartz, J. E., Broderick, J. E., & Hufford, M. R. (2003). Patient compliance with paper and electronic diaries. *Controlled Clinical Trials, 24*(2), 182–199.

Stone, E., & Davey, T. (2011). *Computer-adaptive testing for students with disabilities: A review of the literature.* Educational Testing Service: Research Report ETS RR–11-32. Retrieved from http://www.ets.org/Media/Research/pdf/RR-11-32.pdf.

Stone, V. E., Catania, J. A., & Binson, D. (1999). Measuring change in sexual behavior: Concordance between survey measures. *Journal of Sex Research, 36*(1), 102.

Stout, W. (2002). Psychometrics: From practice to theory and back: 15 years of nonparametric multidimensional IRT, DIF/test equity, and skills diagnostic assessment. *Psychometrika, 67*(4), 485–518.

Strack, S., Choca, J. P., & Gurtman, M. B. (2001). Circular structure of the MCMI-III personality disorder scales. *Journal of Personality Disorders, 15*(3), 263–274.

Strassberg, D. S. (1997). A crossnational validity study of four MMPI-2 content scales. *Journal of Personality Assessment, 69*, 596–606.

Strassberg, D. S., Ross, S., & Todt, E. H. (1995). MMPI performance among women with bulimia: A cluster-analytic study. *Addictive Behaviors, 20*(1), 137–140.

Strauss, M. E., & Brandt, J. (1990). Are there neuropsychologic manifestations of the gene for Huntington's disease in asymptomatic, at-risk individuals? *Archives of Neurology, 47*, 905–908.

Strauss, M., Lessen-Firestone, J., Starr, R., Jr., & Ostrea, E., Jr. (1975). Behavior of narcotics-addicted newborns. *Child Development, 46*, 887–893.

Strauss, S. G., Miles, J. A., & Levesque, L. L. (2001). The effects of video-conference, telephone, and face-to-face media on interviewer and applicant judgements in employment interviews. *Journal of Management, 27*(3), 363–381.

Stricker, L. J., Rock, D. A., Pollack, J. M., & Wenglinsky, H. H. (2002). *Measuring educational disadvantage of SAT candidates.* (College Board Research Report No. 2002-1). College Entrance Examination Board, New York.

Strong, C. H., Donders, J., & Van Dyke, S. (2005). Validity of demographically corrected norms for the WAIS-III. *Journal of Clinical and Experimental Neuropsychology, 27*(6), 746–758.

Strong, E. K., Jr., & Campbell, D. P. (1966). *Manual for Strong Vocational Interest Blank.* Stanford, CA: Stanford University Press.

Stumpf, H., & Stanley, J. C. (2002). Group data on high school grade point average and scores on academic aptitude tests as predictors of institutional graduation rates. *Educational and Psychological Measurement, 62*(6), 1042–1052.

Sue, S. (1999). Science, ethnicity, and bias. *American Psychologist, 54*(12), 1070–1077.

Sue, S. (2003). *Science, ethnicity, and bias: Where have we gone wrong?* Washington, DC: American Psychological Association.

Suinn, R. M. (1969). The STABS, a measure of test anxiety for behavior therapy: Normative data. *Behaviour Research and Therapy, 7*, 335–339.

Sullivan, J., Beech, A. R., Leam A. C., & Gannon T. A. (2011). Comparing intra-familial and extra-familial child sexual abusers with professionals who have sexually abused children with whom they work. *International Journal of Offender Therapy and Comparative Criminology, 55*, 56–74, doi:10.1177/0306624X09359194.

Summerfeldt, L. J., & Antony, M. M. (2002). Structured and semistructured diagnostic interviews. In M. M. Antony & D. H. Barlow (Eds.), *Handbook of assessment and treatment planning for psychological disorders* (pp. 3–37). New York: Guilford Press.

Sumner, A. W. (2005). *Latent classes of the GRE-Q.* US: ProQuest Information & Learning.

Sun, Q., Chen, Y. L., Z. B., Han, S. P., Dong, X. Y., Qiu, Y. F., Sha, L., & Guo, X. R. (2011, February 4). Long-term consequences of the early treatment of children with congenital hypothyroidism detected by neonatal screening in Nanjing, China: A 12-year follow-up study. *Journal of Tropical Pediatrics.* http://tropej.oxford-journals.org/content/early/2011/02/03/tropej.fmr010.abstract. doi:10.1093/tropej/fmr010.

Sun, Q., Pan, J., & Tong, R. (2004). Sexual behavior of neurotic patients. *Chinese Mental Health Journal, 18*(11), 791–793.

Sunderman, G. (2008). *Holding NCLB accountable: Achieving accountability,*

*equity, and school reform.* New York: Corwin Press.

Super, D. E. (1953). A theory of vocational development. *American Psychologist, 8*, 185–190.

Super, D. E., & Hall, D. T. (1978). Career development: Exploitation and planning. *Annual Review of Psychology, 29*, 333–372.

Sutherland, S. (1992). *Irrationality: Why we don't think straight!* New Brunswick, NJ: Rutgers University Press.

Sutin, A. R., & Costa, P. T. (2011). The five factor model of personality traits, In S. J. Lopez (Ed.), *The encyclopedia of positive psychology, volume 1.* Hoboken, NJ: Wiley-Blackwell.

Suzuki, L. A., & Valencia, R. R. (1997). Race-ethnicity and measured intelligence: Educational implications. *American Psychologist, 52*, 1103–1114.

Svensson, L., & Oest, L. G. (1999). Fears in Swedish children: A normative study of the Fear Survey Schedule for Children–Revised. *Scandinavian Journal of Behaviour Therapy, 28*, 23–36.

Swallen, K. C. (2003). Race and genomics. *N Engl J Med, 348*(25), 2581–2582.

Swami, V., Papanicolaou, A. & Furnham, A. (2011). Examining mental health literacy and its correlates using the overclaiming technique. *British Journal of Psychology, 102*(3), 662–675. doi:10.1111/j.2044-8295.2011.02036.x.

Swanda, R. M., Haaland, K. Y., & LaRue, A. (2000). Clinical neuropsychology and intellectual assessment of adults. In B. J. Sadock & V. A. Sadock (Eds.), *Comprehensive Textbook of Psychiatry* (Vol. 1) (pp. 689–702). Philadelphia: Lippincott Williams & Wilkins.

Sweet, J. J., Wolfe, P., Sattlberger, E., Numan, B., Rosenfeld, J. P., Clinger-man, S., & Nies, K. J. (2000). Further investigation of traumatic brain injury versus insufficient effort with the California Verbal Learning Test. *Archives of Clinical Neuropsychology, 15*(2), 105–113.

Sweet, R. C. (1970). Variations in the intelligence test performance of lower-class children as a function of feedback or monetary reinforcement. *Dissertation Abstracts International, 31*(2A), 648–649. (University Microfilms No. 70-37,21).

Sweet, S. A. (1999). *Data analysis with SPSS.* Boston: Allyn & Bacon.

Swindell, J. S., Coverdale, J. H., Crisp-Han, H., & McCullough, L. B. (2010). Focus on patient management: Responsibly managing psychiatric inpatient refusal of medical or surgical diagnostic work-up. *Psychiatric Services*, *61*(9), 868–870.

Symonds, P. M. (1924). On the loss of reliability in ratings due to coarseness of the scale. *Journal of Experimental Psychology*, *7*, 456–461.

Szasz, T. S. (1961). *The myth of mental illness*. New York: Harper & Row.

Tabachnick, B. G., & Fidell, L. S. (1989). *Using multivariate statistics* (2nd ed.). New York: Harper & Row.

Tabachnick, B. G., & Fidell, L. S. (1996). *Using multivariate statistics* (3rd ed.). New York: Harper-Collins.

Taghavi, M. R., Goodarzi, M. A., Kazemi, H., & Ghorbani, M. A. (2006). Irrational beliefs in major depression and generalized anxiety disorders in an Iranian sample: A preliminary study. *Perceptual and Motor Skills*, *102*(1), 187–196.

Tallent, N. (1987). Computer-generated psychological reports: A look at the modern psychometrics machine. *Journal of Personality Assessment*, *51*(1), 95–108.

Tan, U., & Tan, M. (1998). Curvelinear correlations between total testosterone levels and fluid intelligence in men and women. *International Journal of Neuroscience*, *95*, 77–83.

Taplin, P. S., & Reid, J. B. (1973). Effects of instructional set and experimenter influence on observer reliability. *Child Development*, *44*, 547–554.

Tarafder, S., Mukhopadhyay, P., & Basu, S. (2004). Personality profile of siblings of children with autism: A comparative study. *Journal of Projective Psychology & Mental Health*, *11*(1), 52–58.

Tatsuoka, K. K., & Tatsuoka, M. M. (1997). Computerized cognitive diagnostic adaptive testing: Effect on remedial instruction. *Journal of Educational Measurement*, *34*(1), 3–21.

Taylor, C. W., Price, P. B., Richards, J. M., Jr., & Jacobsen, T. L. (1965). An investigation of the criterion problem for a group of medical general practitioners. *Journal of Applied Psychology*, *49*, 399–406.

Taylor, H. C., & Russell, J. T. (1939). The relationship of validity coefficients to the practical effectiveness of tests in selection: Discussion and tables. *Journal of Applied Psychology*, *23*, 565–578.

Taylor, J., & Deane, F. P. (2002). *Development of a short form of the Test Anxiety Inventory (TAI)*. Washington, DC: Heldref.

Taylor, M., Pietrobon, R., Taverniers, J., Leon, M., Fern, B. (2011).

Relationships of hardiness to physical and mental health status in military men: A test of mediated effects. *Journal of Behavioral Medicine*, 1–9. Retrieved from http://www.springerlink.com/content/ d5767251073t3447/. doi:10.1007/s10865-011-9387-8.

Taylor, R. L., Sternberg, L., & Partenio, I. (1986). Performance of urban and rural children on the SOMPA: Preliminary investigation. *Perceptual and Motor Skills*, *63*, 1219–1223.

Taylor, T. R. (1994). A review of three approaches to cognitive assessment, and a proposed integrated approach based on a unifying theoretical framework. *South African Journal of Psychology*, *24*, 183–193.

Tazaki, M., & Landlaw, K. (2006). Behavioural mechanisms and cognitive-behavioural interventions of somatoform disorders. *International Review of Psychiatry*, *18*(1), 67–73.

Te'eni, D. R. (1998). Nomothetics and idiographics as antonyms: Two mutually exclusive purposes for using the Rorschach. *Journal of Personality Assessment*, *70*, 232–247.

Tellegen, A. (2003). *Introducing the new MMPI-2 Restructured Clinical (RC) Scales—The first variant version of the clinical scales*. Minneapolis: University of Minnesota Press Test Division.

Temp, G. (1971). Test bias: Validity of the SAT for blacks and whites in thirteen integrated institutions. *Journal of Educational Measurement*, *8*, 245–251.

Templer, D. I., Schmitz, S. P., & Corgiat, M. D. (1985). Comparison of the Stanford-Binet with the Wechsler Adult Intelligence Scale—Revised: Preliminary report. *Psychological Reports*, *57*, 335–336.

Ten Berge, M., & Veerkamp, J. S. J. (2005). The impact of behavioural and emotional problems in children's dental fear development. In P. L. Gower (Ed.), *New research on the psychology of fear*. (pp. 141–151). Hauppauge, NY: Nova Science Publishers.

Teng, E. L., Wimer, C., Roberts, E., Darnasio, A. R., Eslinger, P. J., Folstein, M. F., Tune, L. E., Whitehouse, P. J., Bardolph, E. L., & Chui, H. C. (1989). Alzheimer's dementia: Performance on parallel forms of the dementia assessment battery. *Journal of Clinical and Experimental Neuropsychology*, *11*, 899–912.

Tennen, H., Affleck, G., & Tennen, R. (2002). Clipped feathers: The theory and measurement of hope. *Psychological Inquiry*, *13*(4), 311–317.

Tenopyr, M. L. (1993). Construct validation needs in vocational behavior theories. *Journal of Vocational Behavior*, *43*(1), 84–89.

Tenopyr, M. L. (1998). Measure me not: The test taker's new bill of rights. In M. D. Hakel (Ed.), *Beyond multiple choice: Evaluating alternatives to traditional testing for selection* (pp. 17–22). Mahwah, NJ: Erlbaum.

Teplin, L. A., & Schwartz, J. (1989). Screening for severe mental disorder in jails: The development of the Referral Decision Scale. *Law and Human Behavior*, *13*, 118.

Terman, L. M. (1916). *The measurement of intelligence*. Boston: Houghton Mifflin.

Terraciano, A., McCrae, R. R., & Costa, P. T. (2003). Factorial and construct validity of the Italian Positive and Negative Affect Schedule (PANAS). *European Journal of Psychological Assessment*, *19*(2), 131–141.

Terrell, F., Taylor, J., & Terrell, S. L. (1978). Effects of type of social reinforcement on the intelligence test performance of lower-class black children. *Journal of Consulting and Clinical Psychology*, *46*, 1538–1539.

Terrill, D. R., Friedman, D. G., Gottschalk, L. A., & Haaga, D. A. F. (2002). Construct validity of the Life Orientation Test. *Journal of Personality Assessment*, *79*(3), 550–563.

Tett, R. P., Fox, K. E., & Wang, A. (2005). Development and validation of a self-report measure of emotional intelligence as a multidimensional trait domain. *Personality and Social Psychology Bulletin*, *31*(7), 859–888.

Thalmayer, A. G., Saucier, G., & Eigenhuis, A. (2011). Comparative validity of brief to medium-length big five and big six personality questionnaires. *Psychological Assessment*, *23*(4), 995–1009. doi:10.1037/a0024165.

Thayer, P. W. (1992). Construct validation: Do we understand our criteria? *Human Performance*, *5*, 97–108.

Thayer, P. W., & Kalat, J. W. (1998). Questionable criteria. *American Psychologist*, *53*, 566.

The Gesell Institute (2010). *Gesell Institute 2009-2010 annual report*, 7. http://www.gesellinstitute.org/pdf/Gesell-l0910AR.pdf.

The Gesell Institute (2011). *Gesell developmental observation*. http://www.gesellinstitute.org/pdf/GDOR_Overview_2011_11-08-11.pdf.

The Psychological Corporation (2001). *Wechsler Individual Achievement*

*Test®—Second Edition.* Retrieved July 28, 2003 from: http://www.harcourt.com/bu_info/tpc.html.

The Psychological Corporation (2003). *Technical Reports.* Retrieved July 28, 2003 from: http://www.harcourt.com/bu_info/tpc.html.

The Status of the Teaching Profession 2003. Research Findings and Policy. Available online at www.cftl.org.

Thoits, P. A. (2011). Resisting the stigma of mental illness. *Social Psychology Quarterly, 74*(1), 6–28. doi:10.1177/0190272511398019.

Thomas, J., & Altareb, B. (2011). Cognitive vulnerability to depression: An exploration of dysfunctional attitudes and ruminative response styles in the United Arab Emirates. *Psychology and Psychotherapy: Theory, Research and Practice.* doi:10.1111/j.2044-8341.2011.02015.x.

Thomas, J. C. & Selthon, L. (2003). Planning data collection and performing analysis. In J. C. Thomas & M. Hersen (Eds.), *Understanding research in clinical and counseling psychology.* (pp. 319–339). Mahwah, NJ: Erlbaum.

Thompson, B. (2006). *Foundations of behavioral statistics: An insight-based approach.* New York: Guilford Press.

Thompson, D. E., & Thompson, T. A. (1982). Court standards for job analysis in test validation. *Personnel Psychology, 35,* 865–874.

Thompson, S. B., & Chinnery, H. (2011). Normative values for 18–30 age group of Benton Visual Retention Test scores and pre-morbid intelligence quotients: New data comparisons for diagnosing memory and visual spatial deficits in Alzheimer's disease and stroke. *Brain, 2*(5).

Thompson, S. B. N., Ennis, E., Coffin, T., & Farman, S. (2007). Design and evaluation of a computerised version of the Benton visual retention test. *Computers in Human Behavior, 23*(5), 2383–2393.

Thorndike, E. L. (1904). *An introduction to the theory of mental and social measurements.* New York: Science Press.

Thorndike, E. L. (1920). A constant error in psychological rating. *Journal of Applied Psychology, 4,* 25–29.

Thorndike, E. L. (1921). Intelligence and its measurement: A symposium. *Journal of Educational Psychology, 12,* 123–147, 195–216.

Thorndike, R. L. (1968). Review of *Pygmalion in the Classroom* by R. Rosenthal and L. Jacobson. *American Educational Research Journal, 5,* 708–711.

Thorndike, R. L. (1971). Concepts of culture-fairness. *Journal of Educational Measurement, 8,* 63–70.

Thorndike, R. L. (1973). *Stanford- Binet Intelligence Scale, Form L-M, 1972 norms tables.* Boston: Houghton Mifflin.

Thorndike, R. L., Hagen, E. P., & Sattler, J. M. (1986). *Technical manual: Stanford-Binet Intelligence Scale: Fourth Edition.* Chicago: Riverside.

Thorndike, R. M. (1990a). Origins of intelligence and its measurement. *Journal of Psychoeducational Assessment, 8,* 223–230.

Thorndike, R. M. (1990b). Would the real factors of the Stanford-Binet Fourth Edition please come forward? *Journal of Psychoeducational Assessment, 8,* 412–435.

Thorson, J. A., & Powell, F. C. (1996). Women, aging, and sense of humor. *Humor: International Journal of Humor Research, 9,* 169–186.

Thurstone, L. L. (1938). Primary mental abilities. *Psychometric Monographs, 1.*

Timbrook, R. E., & Graham, J. R. (1994). Ethnic differences on the MMPI-2? *Psychological Assessment, 6*(3), 212–217.

Timmerman, M. E., & Kiers, H. A. L. (2003). Four simultaneous component models for the analysis of multivariate time series from more than one subject to model intraindividual and interindividual differences. *Psychometrica, 68*(1), 105–121.

Tittle, C. K. (1983). Studies of the effects of career interest inventories: Expanding outcome criteria to include women's experience. *Journal of Vocational Behavior, 22,* 148–158.

Todd, M., H. Tennen, et al. (2004). Do we know how we cope? Relating daily coping reports to global and time-limited retrospective assessments. *Journal of Personal and Social Psychology, 86*(2), 310–319.

Tomes, Y. I. (2011). Building competency in cross-cultural school psychology. In Lionetti, T. M., Snyder, E. P., Christner, R. W. (Eds.), *A practical guide to building professional competencies in school psychology* (pp. 35–49). U.S.: Springer.

Tong, F., & Zhu, L. (2006). An investigation of the relationship between psycholinguistic abilities and intelligence structure in children with learning disabilities. *Chinese Journal of Clinical Psychology, 14*(6), 578–579.

Tong, S., Baghurst, P., Vimpani, G., & McMichael, A. (2007). Socioeconomic position, maternal IQ, home environment, and cognitive development. *Journal of Pediatrics, 151*(3), 284–288, 288 e281.

Torrance, E. P. (1970). Broadening concepts of giftedness in the 70's. *Gifted Child Quarterly, 14,* 199–208.

Torrance, E. P. (1977). *Discovery and nurturance of giftedness in the culturally different.* Reston, VA: Council for Exceptional Children.

Torre, E., Zeppegno, P., Usai, C., Torre, E. M., Artioli, P., Guaiana, G. & Olgiati, P. (2001). Burn-out: Quantitative aspects and personality styles: A study. *Minerva Psichiatrica, 42*(2), 83–89.

Tourangeau, R., Couper, M. P., & Steiger, D. M. (2003). Humanizing self-administration surveys: Experiments on social presence in Web and IVR surveys. *Computers in Human Behavior, 19*(1), 1–24.

Towne, R. L. (2003). Test review of the Illinois Test of Psycholoinguistic Abilities, Third Edition. In B. S. Plake, J. C. Impara, & R. A. Spies (Eds.), *The fifteenth edition mental measurements yearbook.* Retrieved from http://www.unl.edu/buros.

Treisman, G. J., & Clark, M. R. (2011).Chronic pain and addiction: A behaviorist perspective. *Advances in Psychosomatic Medicine, 30,* 8–21. doi:10.1159/000324063.

Triandis, H. C., Dunnette, M. D., & Hough, L. M. (1994). *Handbook of industrial and organizational psychology* (Vol. 4, 2nd ed.). Palo Alto, CA: Consulting Psychologists Press.

Tronick, E. Z. (1987). The neonatal behavioral assessment scale as a biomarker of the effects of environmental agents on the newborn. *Environmental Health Perspectives, 74,* 185–189.

Tronick, E., & Brazelton, T. B. (1975). Clinical uses of the Brazelton Neonatal Behavioral Assessment. In B. Friedlander, G. Sterritt, & G. Kirk (Eds.), *Exceptional infant* (Vol. 3). New York: Brunner/Mazel.

Trotter, M. A., & Endler, N. S. (1999). An empirical test of the interaction model of anxiety in a competitive equestrian setting. *Personality and Individual Differences, 27*(5), 861–875.

Truax, C. B., & Carkhuff, R. R. (1967). *Toward effective counseling and psychotherapy: Training and practice.* Chicago: Aldine Atherton.

Truax, C. B., & Mitchell, K. M. (1971). Research on certain therapist interpersonal skills in relation to process and outcome. In A. E. Bergin & S. L. Garfield (Eds.), *Handbook of psychotherapy and behavior change*. New York: Wiley.

Truxillo, D. M., Seitz, R., & Bauer, T. N. (2008). The role of cognitive ability in self-efficacy and self-assessed test performance 1. *Journal of Applied Social Psychology, 38*(4), 903–918.

Tryon, W. W. (1991). *Activity measurement in psychology and medicine*. New York: Plenum.

Tryon, W. W., & Bernstein, D. (2003). Understanding measurement. In J. C. Thomas & M. Hersen (Eds.), *Understanding research in clinical and counseling psychology*. (pp. 27–68). Mahwah, NJ: Erlbaum.

Tsatsanis, K. D., Dartnall, N., Cicchetti, D., Sparrow, S. S., Klin, A., & Volkmar, F. R. (2003). Concurrent validity and classification accuracy of the Leiter and Leiter-R in low-functioning children with autism. *Journal of Autism and Developmental Disorders, 33*(1), 23–30.

Tseng H. M., Tiplady, B., Macleod, H. A., & Wright, P. (1998). Computer anxiety: A comparison of pen-based personal digital assistants, conventional computer and paper assessments of mood and performance. *British Journal of Psychological Society, 89*(4), 599–610.

Tucker, C. L., Slifer, K. J., & Dahlquist, L. M. (2001). Reliability and validity of the Brief Behavioral Distress Scale: A measure of children's distress during invasive medical procedures. *Journal of Pediatric Psychology, 26*(8), 513–523.

Tuel, B. D., & Betz, N. E. (1998). Relationships of career self-efficacy expectations to the Myers-Briggs Type Indicator and the Personal Styles Scales. *Measurement and Evaluation in Counseling and Development, 31*, 150–163.

Tukey, J. W. (1977). *Exploratory data analysis*. Reading, MA: Addison-Wesley.

Tulsky, D. S., & Rosenthal, M. (2003). Measurement of quality of life in rehabilitation medicine: Emerging issues. *Archives of Physical and Medical Rehabilitation, 84*(4 Suppl. 2), S1–2.

Tulsky, D., Zhu, J., & Ledbetter, M. (1997). *WAIS-III WMS-III technical manual*. San Antonio, TX: Psychological Corporation.

Turgeon, L., & Chartrand, E. (2003). Psychometric properties of the French Canadian version of the State-Trait Anxiety Inventory for Children. Thousand Oaks, CA: Sage.

Turkheimer, E. (1991). Individual and group differences in adoption studies of IQ. *Psychological Bulletin, 110*, 392–405.

Turner, C. F., Ku, L., Rogers, S. M., Lindberg, L. D., & Pleck, J. H. (1998). Adolescent sexual behavior, drug use, and violence: Increased reporting with computer survey technology. *Science, 280*, 867–873.

Turner, D. R. (1966). Predictive efficiency as a function of amount of information and level of professional experience. *Journal of Projective Techniques and Personality Assessment, 30*, 4–11.

Turner, J. A., Herron, L., & Weiner, P. (1986). Utility of the MMPI Pain Assessment Index in predicting outcomes after lumbar surgery. *Journal of Clinical Psychology, 42*, 764–769.

Turner, R. J. (1981). Social support as a contingency in psychological well-being. *Journal of Health and Social Behavior, 22*, 357–367.

Turpin, G. (1991). The psychophysiological assessment of anxiety disorders: Three-systems measurement and beyond. *Psychological Assessment: A Journal of Consulting and Clinical Psychology, 3*, 366–375.

Tyler, L. E. (1969). *The work of the counselor* (3rd ed.). New York: Appleton-Century-Crofts.

Tyler, L. E., & Walsh, W. B. (1979). *Tests and measurements* (3rd ed.). Englewood Cliffs, NJ: Prentice-Hall.

Uber, J. W. (2005). *An example of ethical errors in assessment: Differentiating psychiatric diagnoses with a modified Bender Visual Motor Gestalt Test*. US: ProQuest Information & Learning.

Ulrich, L., & Trumbo, D. (1965). The selection interview since 1949. *Psychological Bulletin, 63*, 100–116.

*United States v. City of Buffalo.* (1985). 37 U.S. 628 (W.D. N.Y. 1985).

Unruh, M., Miskulin, D., et al. (2004). Racial differences in health-related quality of life among hemodialysis patients. *Kidney International, 65*(4), 1482–1491.

Uutela, T., Hakala, M., & Kautiainen, H. (2003). Validity of the Nottingham Health Profile in a Finnish out-patient population with rheumatoid arthritis. *Rheumatology* (Oxford), *42*(7), 841–845.

Vale, C. D., Keller, L. S., & Bentz, V. J. (1986). Development and validation of a computerized interpretation system for personnel tests. *Personnel Psychology, 39*(3), 525–542.

Valencia, R. R. (1988). The McCarthy Scales and Hispanic children: A review

of psychometric research. *Hispanic Journal of Behavioral Sciences, 10*, 81–104.

Valencia, R. R., & Lopez, R. (1992). Assessment of racial and ethnic minority students: Problems and prospects. In M. Zeidner & R. Most (Eds.), *Psychological testing: An inside view*. Palo Alto, CA: Consulting Psychologists Press.

Valencia, R. R., Rankin, R. J., & Livingston, R. (1995). K-ABC content bias: Comparisons between Mexican American and white children. *Psychology in the Schools, 32*, 153–169.

van Baar, A. (1990). Development of infants of drug dependent mothers. *Journal of Child Psychology and Psychiatry and Allied Disciplines, 31*, 911–920.

Vandenburg, S. G., & Vogler, G. P. (1985). Genetic determinants of intelligence. In B. B. Wolman (Ed.), *Handbook of intelligence*. New York: Wiley.

van der Linden, D., te Nijenhuis, J., & Bakker, A. B. (2010). The general factor of personality: A meta-analysis of big five intercorrelations and a criterion-related validity study. *Journal of Research in Personality, 44*, 315–327.

van der Linden, W. J., Scrams, D. J., & Schnipke, D. L. (1999). Using response-time constraints to control for differential speededness in computerized adaptive testing. *Applied Psychological Measurement, 23*(3), 195–210.

Vandevijer, F. J. R., & Harsveld, M. (1994). The incomplete equivalence of the paper-and-pencil and computerized versions of the General Aptitude Test Battery. *Journal of Applied Psychology, 79*(6), 852–859.

van Leeuwen, M., van den Berg, S., & Boomsma, D. (2008). A twin-family study of general IQ. *Learning and Individual Differences, in press*.

Van Scotter, J., Motowidlo, S. J., & Cross, T. C. (2000). *Effects of task performance and contextual performance on systemic rewards*. Washington, DC: American Psychological Association.

Vansickle, T. R., Kimmel, C., & Kapes, J. T. (1989). Test equivalency of the computer-based paper-pencil versions of the Strong-Campbell Interest Inventory. *Measurement and Evaluation in Counseling and Development, 22*(2), 89–93.

Vassend, O., Quale, A. J., Røise, O., & Schanke, A. K. (2011). Predicting the long-term impact of acquired severe injuries on functional health status: the role of optimism, emotional distress and pain. *Spinal Cord, 49,* 1193–1197. doi:10.1038/sc.2011.70.

Vecchione, M., Alessandri, G., & Barbaranelli, C. (2011). Paper-and-pencil and Web-based testing: The measurement invariance of the big five personality tests in applied settings. *Assessment, 18*(4). doi:10.1177/1073191111419091.

Velox, A. J. (2005). *Use of the Rorschach as personality assessment tool with African American students.* US: ProQuest Information & Learning.

Verdon, B. (2011). The case of thematic tests adapted to older adults: On the importance of differentiating latent and manifest contents in projective tests. *Rorschachiana, 32*(1), 46–71. doi:10.1027/1192-5604/a000015.

Vernon, S. W., Tiro, J. A., Vojvodic, R. W., Coan, S., Diamond, P. M., Greisinger, A., et al. (2008). Reliability and validity of a questionnaire to measure colorectal cancer screening behaviors: Does mode of survey administration matter? *Cancer Epidemiology Biomarkers and Prevention, 17*(4), 758–767.

Verschuren, W. M., Jacobs, D. R., Bloemberg, B. P., Kromhout, D., Menotti, A., Aravanis, C., Blackburn, H., Buzina, R., Dontas, A. S., Fidanza, F., & others. (1995). Serum total cholesterol and long-term coronary heart disease mortality in different cultures: Twenty-five-year follow-up of the seven countries study. *Journal of the American Medical Association, 274*(2), 131–136.

Vicario, C. M., Martino, D., Spata, F., Defazio, G., Giacchè, R., Martino, V., Rappo, G., Pepi, A. M., Silvestri, P. R., & Cardona, F. (2010). Time processing in children with Tourette's syndrome. *Brain and Cognition, 73*(1), 28–34. ISSN 0278-2626; doi:10.1016/j.bandc.2010.01.008.

Vickers, D., Nettelbeck, T., & Wilson, R. J. (1972). Perceptual indices of performance: The measurement of "inspection time" and "noise" in the visual system. *Perception, 1,* 263–295.

A victory for affirmative action (2003). Lancet, 352(9377), 1.

Vidal-Abarca, E., Reyes, H., Gilabert, R., Calpe, J., Soria, E., Graesser, A. C. (2002). ETAT: Expository test analysis tool. *Behavior Research Methods, Instruments, & Computers, 34*(1), 93–107.

Viera, A. J., & Garrett, J. M. (2005). Understanding interobserver agreement: The kappa statistic. *Family Medicine, 37*(5), 360–363.

Viet, C. T., & Ware, J. E. (1989). An improved test of the disaggregation hypothesis of job and life satisfaction. *Journal of Occupational Psychology, 62,* 33–39.

Vigil-Colet, A., & Codorniu-Raga, M. J. (2002). How inspection time and paper and pencil measures of processing speed are related to intelligence. *Personality & Individual Differences, 33*(7), 1149–1161.

Viglione, D. (1999). A review of recent research addressing the utility of the Rorschach. *Psychological Assessment, 11,* 251–265.

Viglione, D. J., & Hilsenroth, M. K. (2001). The Rorschach: Facts, fictions, and future. *Psychological Assessment, 13*(4), 452–471.

Vincelli, F., & Riva, G. (2000). Immersive virtual reality in clinical psychology and psychotherapy. *Rivista di Psichiatria, 35*(4), 153–162.

Vispoel, W. P., Rocklin, T. R., & Tianyou, W. (1994). Individual differences and test administration procedures: A comparison of fixed-item, computer-adaptive, and self-adaptive testing. *Applied Measurement in Education, 7*(1), 53–80.

Vlaeyen, J. W. S., de Jong, J. R., Onghena, P., Kerckhoffs-Hanssen, M., & Kole-Snijders, A. M. J. (2002). Can pain-related fear be reduced? The application of cognitive-behavioural exposure in vivo. *Pain Research and Management, 7,* 144–153.

von Stumm, S., Chamorro-Premuzic, T., & Ackerman, P. L. (2011) Re-visiting intelligence–personality associations. In T. Chamorro-Premuzic, S. von Stumm, & A. Furnham (Eds.), *The Wiley-Blackwell handbook of individual differences.* Oxford, UK: Wiley-Blackwell. doi:10.1002/9781405184359.ch8.

Vorstenboscha, V., Antonya, M. M., Koernera, N., & Boivinb, B. K. (2012). Assessing dog fear: Evaluating the psychometric properties of the Dog Phobia Questionnaire. *Journal of Behavior Therapy and Experimental Psychiatry, 43*(2), 780–786.

Vraniak, D. (1997). Mapping contexts for supporting American Indian families of youth with disabilities. *Families, Systems and Health, 15*(3), 283–302.

Wagner, E. E., Alexander, R. A., Roos, G., & Adair, H. (1986). Optimum split-half reliabilities for the

Rorschach: Projective techniques are more reliable than we think. *Journal of Personality Assessment, 50,* 107–112.

Wagner, E. E., & Flamos, O. (1988). Optimized split-half reliability for the Bender Visual Motor Gestalt Test: Further evidence for the use of the maximization procedure. *Journal of Personality Assessment, 52,* 454–458.

Wagner, P. A. (1994). Adaptations for administering the Peabody Picture Vocabulary Test—Revised to individuals with severe communications and motor dysfunctions. *Mental Retardation, 32*(2), 107–112.

Wagner, R. (1949). The employment interview: A critical review. *Personnel Psychology, 2,* 17–46.

Wagner, R. K. (1997). Intelligence, training, and employment. *American Psychologist, 52*(10), 1059–1069.

Wainer, H. (2000). *Computerized adaptive testing: A primer* (2nd ed.). Mahwah, NJ: Erlbaum.

Wainwright, D., & Calnan, M. (2002). *Work stress: The making of a modern epidemic.* Philadelphia: Open University Press.

Wald, J. & Taylor, S. (2000). Efficacy of virtual reality exposure therapy to treat driving phobia: A case report. *Journal of Behavior Therapy and Experimental Psychology, 31*(3–4), 249–257.

Waldman, I. D., Weinberg, R. A., & Scarr, S. (1994). Racial-group differences in IQ in the Minnesota Transracial Adoption Study: A reply to Levin and Lynn. *Intelligence, 19,* 29–44.

Walker, A. M., Rablen, R. A., & Rogers, C. R. (1960). Development of a scale to measure process changes in psychotherapy. *Journal of Clinical Psychology, 16,* 79–85.

Walker, M. T. (2001). Practical applications of the Rogerian perspective in post-modern psychotherapy. *Journal of Systematic Therapies, 20*(2), 41–57.

Walker, S., & Rosser, R. (1992). *Quality of life assessment: Key issues for the 1990s.* Dordrect, Netherlands: Kluwer Press.

Waller, N. G. (1999). Searching for structure in the MMPI. In S. E. Embretson & S. L. Hershberger (Eds.), *The new rules of measurement.* Mahwah, NJ: Erlbaum.

Walsh, W. (2007). Introduction: Special section on vocational interest. *Journal of Career Assessment, 15*(1), 3–4.

Walsh, W. B. (2003). *Counseling psychology and optimal human functioning.* Mahwah, N. J.: Erlbaum.

Wang, C., Chang, H.-H., & Huebner, A. (2011). Restrictive Stochastic item selection methods in cognitive diagnostic computerized adaptive testing. *Journal of Educational Measurement, 48*(3), 255–273. doi:10.1111/j.1745-3984.2011.00145.x.

Wang, S., Jiao, H., Young, M., Brooks, T., & Olson, J. (2008). Comparability of computer-based and paper-and-pencil testing in K–12 reading assessments: A meta-analysis of testing mode effects. *Educational and Psychological Measurement, 68*(5).

Wang, Z., & Thompson, B. (2007). Is the Pearson $r^2$ Biased, and if So, What Is the Best Correction Formula? *Journal of Experimental Education, 72*(2), 109–125.

Ward, L. C. (1995). Correspondence of the MMPI-2 and MCMI-II male substance abusers. *Journal of Personality Assessment, 64*(2), 390–393.

Ward, L. C., & Perry, M. S. (1998). Measurement of social introversion by the MMPI-2. *Journal of Personality Assessment, 70*, 171–182.

Ward, T. J., et al. (1989). The effect of computerized tests on the performance and attitudes of college students. *Journal of Educational Computing Research, 5*, 327–333.

*Wards Cove Packing Company v. Antonio.* (1989). 490, U.S. 642.

Ware, J. E., Jr. (2000). SF-36 health survey update. *Spine, 25*(24), 3130–3139.

Ware, J. E., Jr. (2003). Conceptualization and measurement of health-related quality of life: Comments on an evolving field. *Archives of Physical and Medical Rehabilitation, 84*(4 Suppl. 2), S43–51.

Ware, J. E., Jr., Bayliss, M. S., Mannocchia, M., & Davis, G. L. (1999). Health-related quality of life in chronic hepatitis C: Impact of disease and treatment response. *Hepatology, 30*(2), 550–555.

Ware, J. E., Jr., & Gandek, B. (1998). Overview of the SF-36 Health Survey and the International Quality of Life Assessment (IQOLA) Project. *Journal of Clinical Epidemiology, 51*(11), 903–912.

Ware, J. E., & Kosinski, M. (2001). Interpreting SF-36 summary health measures: A response. *Quality of Life Research, 10*(5), 405–413, 415–420.

Ware, J. E., Jr., Kosinski, M., Bayliss, M. S., McHorney, C. A., Rogers, W. H., & Raczek, A. (1995). Comparison of methods for the scoring and statistical analysis of SF-36 health profile and summary measures: Summary of results from the Medical

Outcomes Study. *Medical Care, 33*, AS264–AS279.

Warner-Benson, D. M. (2001). The effect of a modified test administration procedure on the performance of male and female African American inner-city school children on a group administered intelligence test. *Dissertation Abstracts International Section A. The Humanities and Social Sciences, 61*, 10A.

Warren, J. (2011). School counselor consultation: Teachers' experiences with rational emotive behavior therapy. *Journal of Rational-Emotive & Cognitive-Behavior Therapy*, 1–15. doi:10.1007/s10942-011-0139-z.

Warzecha, G. (1991). The challenge to psychological assessment from modern computer technology. *European Review of Applied Psychology, 41*(3), 213–220.

Washington, J. A., & Craig, H. K. (1999). Performance of at-risk African American Preschoolers on the Peabody Picture Vocabulary Test-III. *Language, Speech, and Hearing Services in Schools, 30*(1), 75–82.

*Washington v. Davis.* (1976). 96 U.S. 2040(c).

Wasik, B. H., Ramey, C. T., Bryant, D. M., & Sparling, J. J. (1990). A longitudinal study of two early intervention strategies: Project CARE. *Child Development, 61*, 1682–1696.

Watkins, C. E., Jr., & Campbell, V. L. (Eds.). (2000). *Testing and assessment in counseling practice* (2nd ed.). Mahwah, NJ: Erlbaum.

Watkins, C. E., Jr., Campbell, V. L., Nieberding, R., & Hallmark, R. (1995). Contemporary practice of psychological assessment by clinical psychologists. *Professional Psychology: Research and Practice, 26*, 54–60.

Watkins, M. W., Glutting, J. J., & Lei, P. (2007). Validity of the full-scale IQ when there is significant variability among WISC-III and WISC-IV factor scores. *Applied Neuropsychology, 14*(1), 13–20.

Watson, C. W., & Klett, W. G. (1975). The Henmon-Nelson, Cardall-Miles, Slosson, and Quick Tests as predictors of NAIS IQ. *Journal of Clinical Psychology, 31*, 310–313.

Watson, D. (1988). The vicissitudes of mood measurement: Effects of varying descriptors, time frames, and response formats on measures of positive and negative affect. *Journal of Personality and Social Psychology, 55*, 128–141.

Watson, D., Clark, L. A., & Tellegen, A. (1988). Development and validation of brief measures of positive and negative

affect: The PANAS scales. *Journal of Personality and Social Psychology, 54*, 1063–1070.

*Watson v. Fort Worth Bank and Trust.* (1988). 487 U.S. 977.

Weber, B., Schneider, B., Fritze, J., Gille, B., Hornung, S., Kuhner, T., & Maurer, K. (2003). Acceptance of computerized compared to paper-and-pencil assessment in psychiatric inpatients. *Computers in Human Behavior, 19*(1), 81–93.

Weber, C. P. (2001). The relationship of mental status and estrogen use on visual-motor and visual-spatial abilities. *Dissertation Abstracts International, 61*, 9B. (UMI No. 9986387)

Webster, E. C. (1964). *Decision making in the employment interview.* Montreal: Industrial Relations Center, McGill University.

Webster, J. S., & Dostrow, V. (1982). Efficacy of a decision-tree approach to the Luria-Nebraska Neuropsychological Battery. *Journal of Consulting and Clinical Psychology, 50*, 313–315.

Wechsler, D. (1939). *The measurement of adult intelligence.* Baltimore: Williams & Wilkins.

Wechsler, D. (1955). *Manual: Wechsler Adult Intelligence Scale.* New York: Psychological Corporation. Wechsler, D. (1958). *The measurement and appraisal of adult intelligence* (4th ed.). Baltimore: Williams & Wilkins.

Wechsler, D. (1981). *Wechsler Adult Intelligence Scale—Revised.* New York: Psychological Corporation.

Wechsler, D. (1989). *Wechsler Preschool and Primary Scale of Intelligence–Revised (WPPSI-R).* San Antonio, TX: Psychological Corporation.

Wechsler, D. (1991a). *WISC-III manual.* San Antonio, TX: The Psychological Corporation.

Wechsler, D. (1991b). *Wechsler Intelligence Scales for Children–Third Edition.* San Antonio, TX: Psychological Corporation.

Wechsler, D. (2002). *WPPSI-III administration and scoring manual.* San Antonio: The Psychological Corporation.

Wechsler, D. (2003). *WISC-IV administration and scoring manual.* San Antonio: The Psychological Corporation.

Wechsler, D., Coalson, D. L., & Engi Raiford, S. (2008). *WAIS-IV: Technical and interpretive manual.* San Antonio, TX: The Psychological Corporation.

Weeks, J. R., Morison, S. J., Millson, W. A., & Fettig, D. M. (1995). A comparison of Native, Metis, and

Caucasian offender profiles on the MCMI. *Canadian Journal of Behavioural Science—Revue Canadienne des Sciences du Comportement, 27*(2), 187–198.

Weigel, R. G. (1999). One size does not fit all. *Consulting Psychology Journal: Practice and Research, 51*(1), 47–56.

Weiner, B. (1991). Metaphors in motivation and attribution. *American Psychologist, 46*, 921–930.

Weiner, B. (1994). Ability versus effort revisited: The moral determinants of achievement evaluation and achievement as a moral system. *Educational Psychologist, 29*(3), 163–172.

Weiner, B., Graham, S., Peter, O., & Zmuidinas, M. (1991). Public confession and forgiveness. *Journal of Personality, 59*, 281–312.

Weiner, I. B. (2003). *Principles of Rorschach interpretation* (2nd ed.) Mahwah, NJ: Erlbaum.

Weiner, I. B., & Craighead, W. E. (2010). *The Corsini encyclopedia of psychology, volume 4* (pp. 1776–1777). Hoboken, NJ: John Wiley & Sons.

Weinstein, C. E., & Way, P. J. (2003). Educational psychology. In D. K. Freedheim (Ed.), *Handbook of psychology: History of psychology* (Vol. 1). New York: Wiley.

Weiss, D. J. (Ed.). (1983). *New horizons in testing.* New York: Academic Press.

Weiss, D. J. (1985). Adaptive testing by computer. *Journal of Consulting and Clinical Psychology, 53*, 774–789.

Weiss, D. J., & Yoes, M. E. (1991). Item response theory. In R. K. Hambleton & J. N. Zaal (Eds.), *Advances in educational and psychological testing: Theory and applications. Evaluation in education and human services series* (pp. 69–95). Boston, MA: Kluwer Academic Publishers.

Weiss, L. G., Oakland, T., & Aylward, G. (2010). *Bayley-III clinical use and interpretation.* Burlington, MA: Elsevier.

Weiss, L. G., Saklofske, D. H., Coalson, D., & Engi-Raiford, S. (2010). Wechsler's theory of intelligence: Past and present. In D. Coalson, S. Engi Raiford, D. Saklofske, & L. Weiss (Eds.), *WAIS-IV: Advances in the assessment of intelligence* (pp. 3–24). London: Elsevier, Inc.

Weissman, A. N. (1979). The Dysfunctional Attitude Scale: A validation study. *Dissertation Abstracts International, 40*, 1389A–1390B. (University Microfilms No. 7919,533).

Weissman, A. N., & Beck, A. T. (1978, November). *Development and*

validation of the Dysfunctional Attitude Scale: A preliminary investigation.* Paper presented at the meeting of the Association for the Advancement of Behavior Therapy, Chicago.

Weissman, M. M., Sholomskas, D., Pottenger, M., Prusoff, B. A., & Locke, B. Z. (1977). Assessing depressive symptoms in five psychiatric populations: A validation study. *American Journal of Epidemiology, 106*, 203–214.

Welch, H. G. (2004). *Should I be tested for cancer?* Berkeley: University of California Press.

Welsh, G. S. (1948). An extension of Hathaway's MMPI profile coding system. *Journal of Consulting Psychology, 12*, 343–344.

Welsh, K., Butters, N., Hughes, J., Mobs, R., & Hayman, A. (1991). Detection of abnormal memory decline in mad cases of Alzheimer's disease using CERAD Neuropsychological Measures. *Archives of Neurology, 48*, 278–281.

Wermiel, S., & Trost, C. (1986, June 20). Justices say hostile job environment due to sex harrassment violates rights. *Wall Street Journal*, p. 2.

Werner, H. (1937). Process and achievement: The basic problem of education and developmental psychology. *Hayward Educational Review, 7*, 353–368.

Wertz, F. J., Charmaz, K., McMullen, L. M., Josselson, R., Anderson, R., & McSpadden, E. (2011). Contemporary movement, methodological pluralism, and challenges. *In five ways of doing qualitative analysis: Phenomenological psychology* (pp. 75–110). New York: Guilford Press.

Wesman, A. G. (1971). Writing the test item. In R. L. Thorndike (Ed.), *Educational measurement* (2nd ed.). Washington, DC: American Council on Education.

Westenberg, P. M., Gullone, E., Bokhorst, C. L., Heyne, D. A., & King, N. J. (2007). Social evaluation fear in childhood and adolescence: Normative developmental course and continuity of individual differences. *British Journal of Developmental Psychology, 25*(3), 471–483.

Wetherell, M. (2011). The winds of change: Some challenges in reconfiguring social psychology for the future. *British Journal of Social Psychology, 50*(3), 399–404. doi:10.1111/j. 2044-8309.2011.02038.x.

Wheeler, L., & Reitan, R. M. (1962). A presence and alaterality of brain damage predicted from response to a

short aphasia screening test. *Perceptual and Motor Skills, 15*, 783–799.

Whetzel, D., & Wheaton, G. (2007). *Applied measurement: Industrial psychology in human resources management.* Mahwah, NJ: Routledge.

Whipple, C. M. (1910). *Manual of mental and physical tests.* Baltimore: Warwick & York.

Whisman, M. A., Johnson, D. P., & Smolen, A. (2011). Dysfunctional attitudes and the serotonin transporter promoter polymorphism (5-HTTLPR). *Behavior Therapy, 42*(2), 300–305. doi:10.1016/j. beth.2010.08.007.

Whitaker, H. A. (2006). Reducing personality structures to brain mechanisms. *PsycCRITIQUES, 51*(46).

Whiteside-Mansell, L., & Corwyn, R. F. (2003). Mean and covariance structures analysis: An examination of the Rosenberg Self-Esteem Scale among adolescents and adults. *Educational and Psychological Measurement, 63*(1), 163–173.

Whittington, D. (2004, April 5). The achievement gap: Should we rely on SAT scores to tell us anything about it? *Education Policy Analysis Archives, 12*(12).

Whyte, G., & Latham, G. (1997). The futility of utility analysis revisited: When even an expert fails. *Personnel Psychology, 50*(3), 601–610.

Wiberg, M. (2003). An optimal design approach to criterion-referenced computerized testing. *Journal of Educational and Behavioral Statistics, 28*(2), 97–110.

Wichers, M., Lothmann, C., Simons, C. J. P., Nicolson, N. A., & Peeters, F. (2011). The dynamic interplay between negative and positive emotions in daily life predicts response to treatment in depression: A momentary assessment study. *British Journal of Clinical Psychology.* doi:10.1111/ j.2044-8260.2011.02021.x.

Wicker, A. W. (1979). Ecological psychology: Some recent and prospective developments. *American Psychologist, 34*, 755–765.

Wicker, A. W., & Kirmeyer, S. L. (1976). From church to laboratory to national park. In S. Wapner, S. B. Conen, & B. Kaplan (Eds.), *Experiencing the environment.* New York: Plenum.

Wickham, T. (1978). *WISC patterns in acting-out delinquents, poor readers, and normal controls.* Unpublished doctoral dissertation, United States International University, San Diego.

Wiederhold, B. K., Gervirtz, R. N., & Spira, J. L. (2001). Virtual reality exposure therapy vs. imagery desensitization therapy in the treatment of flying phobia. In G. Riva & C. Galimberti (Eds.), *Towards cyberpsychology: Mind, cognition and society in the internet age* (pp. 253–273). Washington, DC: IOS.

Wiederhold, B. K., Jang, D. P., Kim, S. I., Wiederhold, M. D. (2002). Physiological monitoring as an objective tool in virtual reality therapy. *Cyberpsychology and Behavior, 5*(1), 77–82.

Wiesner, W. H., & Cronshaw, S. F. (1988). A meta-analytic investigation of the impact of interview format and degree of structure on the validity of the employment interview. *Journal of Occupational Psychology, 61*, 275–290.

Wiggan, G. (2007). Race, school achievement, and educational inequality: Toward a student-based inquiry perspective. *Review of Educational Research, 77*(3), 310.

Wiggins, J. G. (1994). Would you want your child to be a psychologist? *American Psychologist, 49*(6), 485–492.

Wiggins, J. S. (1973). *Personality and prediction: Principles of personality assessment.* Reading, MA: Addison-Wesley.

Wild, C. L., McPeek, W. M., Koffler, S. L., Braun, H. I., & Cowell, W. (1989). Concurrent validity of verbal item types for ethnic and gender subgroups. *GRE Publication Report 84–10p.* Princeton, NJ: Educational Testing Service.

Wilder, J. (1950). The law of initial values. *Psychosomatic Medicine, 12*, 392–401.

Wilkinson, G. S., & Robertson, G. J. (2006). Wide Range Achievement Test 4 (WRAT4) professional manual. *Psychological Assessment Resources, Inc.* Retrieved from http://portal.wpspublish.com/portal/page?_pageid=53, 118660&_dad=portal&_schema= PORTAL.

Wilkinson, L. (1999). Statistical methods in psychology journals: Guidelines and explanations. *American Psychologist, 54*(8), 594–604.

Williams, J. E. (1994). Anxiety measurement: Construct validity and test performance. *Measurement and Evaluation in Counseling and Development, 27*, 302–307.

Williams, J. M., Voelker, S., & Ricciardi, P. W. (1995). Predictive validity of the K-ABC for exceptional preschoolers. *Psychology in the Schools, 32*, 178–185.

Williams, M. L., Freeman, R. C., Bowen, A. M., & Saunders, L. (1998). The acceptability of a computer HIV/AIDS risk assessment to not-in-treatment drug users. *AIDS Care, 10*(6), 701–711.

Williams, R. L. (1974). Scientific racism and I.Q.: The silent mugging of the black community. *Psychology Today, 7*, 32–41.

Williams, T. O. J., Fall, A., Eaves, R. C., Darch, C., & Woods-Groves, S. (2007). Factor analysis of the KeyMath-revised normative update form A. *Assessment for Effective Intervention, 32*(2), 113–120.

Williams, W. M., & Ceci, S. J. (1997). Are Americans becoming more or less alike? Trends in race, class, and ability differences in intelligence. *American Psychologist, 52*, 1226–1235.

Williamson, L. G., Campion, J. E., Malos, S. B., Roehling, M. V., & Campion, M. (1997). Employment interview on trial: Linking interview structure with litigation outcomes. *Journal of Applied Psychology, 82*, 900–912.

Williamson, W. D., Wilson, G. S., Lifschitz, M. H., & Thurbers, S. A. (1990). Nonhandicapped very-low-birth-weight infants at one year of age developmental profile. *Pediatrics, 85*, 405–410.

Willingham, W. W., Pollack, J. M., & Lewis, C. (2000). *Grades and test scores: Accounting for observed differences* (ETS Research Report 00-15). Princeton, NJ: Educational Testing Service.

Wilson, M., De Boeck, P., Moss, P., & Draney, K. (2003). Measurement: Interdisciplinary research and perspectives. 1(1).

Wilson, M., Smith, N. C., Chattington, M., Ford, M., & Marple-Horvat, D. E. (2006). The role of effort in moderating the anxiety-performance relationship: Testing the prediction of processing efficiency theory in simulated rally driving. *Journal of Sports Sciences, 24*(11), 1223–1233.

Wing, K. R. (1976). *The law and the public's health.* St. Louis, MO: Mosby.

Winkler, A. (2002, November). Highstakes testing: Division in the ranks—Standardized testing draws lines between new and veteran teachers. *Phi Delta Kappan.* Winkler, M. H., Weyers, P., Mucha, R. F., Stippekohl, B., Stark, R., & Pauli, P. (2011). Conditioned cues for smoking elicit preparatory responses in healthy smokers. *Psychopharmacology, 213*(4), 781–789. doi:10.1007/s00213-010-2033-2.

Winter, D. G., & Stewart, A. J. (1977). Power motive reliability, as a function of retest instructions. *Journal of Consulting and Clinical Psychology, 42*, 436–440.

Wise, S. L., Finney, S. J., Enders, C. K., Freeman, S. A., & Severance, D. D. (1999). Examinee judgments of changes in item difficulty: Implications for item review in computerized adaptive testing. *Applied Measurement in Education, 12*(2), 185–199.

Wissler, C. (1901). The correlation of mental and physical tests. *Psychological Review, 3* (Monograph Supp. 16).

Witherspoon, D. J., Wooding, S., Rogers, A. R., Marchani, E. E., Watkins, W. S., Batzer, M. A., et al. (2007). Genetic similarities within and between human populations. *Genetics, 176*(1), 351.

Witmer, J. M., Bernstein, A. V., & Dunham, R. M. (1971). The effects of verbal approval and disapproval upon the performance of third and fourth grade children of four subtests of the Wechsler Intelligence Scale for Children. *Journal of School Psychology, 9*, 347–356.

Witt, J. C., & Gresham, F. M. (1985). Review of the Wechsler Intelligence Scale for Children—Revised. In J. V. Mitchell (Ed.), *The ninth mental measurements yearbook* (Vol. 1). Highland Park, NJ: Gryphon Press.

Wittenborn, J. R., & Sarason, S. B. (1949). Exceptions to certain Rorschach criteria of pathology. *Journal of Consulting Psychology, 13*, 21–27.

Wolach, A. H., & McHale, M. A. (2002). Computer program to generate operant schedules. *Behavior Research Methods, Instruments, and Computers, 34*(2), 245–249.

Wolber, G. J., Reynolds, B., Ehrmantraut, J. E., & Nelson, A. J. (1997). In search of a measure of intellectual functioning for an inpatient psychiatric population with low cognitive ability. *Psychiatric Rehabilitation Journal, 21*, 59–63.

Wolk, R. L., & Wolk, R. B. (1971). *Manual: Gerontological Apperception Test.* New York: Behavioral Publications.

Wolpe, J., & Lang, P. J. (1964). A fear survey schedule for use in behavior therapy. *Behaviour Research and Therapy, 2*, 27–30.

Wong, K. F. E., & Kwong, J. Y. Y. (2007). Effects of rater goals on rating patterns: Evidence from an experimental field study. *Journal of Applied Psychology, 92*(2), 577.

Wong, P. S., Jamadi, M. (2010). Projective tests. In C. S. Clauss-Ehlers (Eds.), *Encyclopedia of cross-cultural school psychology* (pp. 763–766). Springer, US. doi:10.1007/978-0-387-71799-9_335.

Wood, D. P., Murphy, J., Center, K., McLay, R., Reeves, D., Pyne, J., et al. (2007). Combat-related posttraumatic stress disorder: A case report using virtual reality exposure therapy with physiological monitoring. *CyberPsychology & Behavior, 10*(2), 309–315.

Wood, J. M., & Lilienfeld, S. O. (1999). The Rorschach Inkblot Test: A case of overstatement? *Assessment, 6*, 341–349.

Wood, J. M., Lilienfeld, S. O., Garb, H. N., & Nezworski, M. T. (2000). Limitations of the Rorschach as a diagnostic tool: A reply to Garfield (2000), Lerner (2000), and Weiner (2000). *Journal of Clinical Psychology, 56*(3), 441–448.

Wood, J. M., Lilienfeld, S. O., Nezworski, M. T., & Garb, H. N. (2001). Coming to grips with negative evidence for the comprehensive system for the Rorschach: A comment on Gacono, Loving, and Bodholdt; Ganellen; and Bornstein. *Journal of Personality Assessment. 77*(1), 48–70.

Wood, J. M., Lilienfeld, S. O., Nezworski, M. T., Garb, H. N., Allen, K. H., & Wildermuth, J. L. (2010). Validity of Rorschach Inkblot scores for discriminating psychopaths from nonpsychopaths in forensic populations: A meta-analysis. *Psychological Assessment, 22*(2), 336–349. doi:10.1037/a0018998.

Wood, J. M., Nezworski, M. T., Garb, H. N., & Lilienfeld, S. O. (2001). The misperception of psychopathology: Problems with the norms of the Comprehensive System for the Rorschach. *Clinical Psychology: Science and Practice, 8*, 350–373.

Wood, J. M., Nezworski, M. T., Lilienfeld, S. O., & Garb, H. N. (2003). *What's wrong with the Rorschach? Science confronts the controversial inkblot test.* San Francisco: Jossey-Bass.

Wood, J. M., Nezworski, T., Lilienfeld, S. O., & Garb, H. N. (2011). *What's wrong with the Rorschach: Science confronts the controversial inkblot test.* Hoboken, NJ: John Wiley & Sons.

Wood, J. M., Nezworski, T., & Stejskal, W. J. (1996). The comprehensive system for the Rorschach: A critical examination. *Psychological Science, 7*, 3–10.

Wood, P. S., Smith, W. L., Altmaier, E. M., Tarico, V. S., & Franken, E. A. (1990). A prospective study of cognitive and non-cognitive selection criteria as predictors of resident performance. *Investigative Radiology, 25*, 855–859.

Woodcock, R. W., & Johnson, M. (1989). *Woodcock-Johnson Psycho-Educational Battery—Revised.* Chicago: Riverside.

Woodcock, R. W., McGrew, K. S., & Mather, N. (2001). *Woodcock-Johnson III battery.* Itasca, IL: Riverside.

Woods, S. P., Iudicello, J. E., Moran, L. M., Carey, C. L., Dawson, M. S., & Grant, I. (2008). HIV-associated prospective memory impairment increases risk of dependence in everyday functioning. *Neuropsychology, 22*(1), 110–117.

Woodworth, R. S. (1920). *Personal data sheet.* Chicago: Stoelting.

Woolfson, L. M., Taylor, R. J., & Mooney, L. (2011). Parental attributions of controllability as a moderator of the relationship between developmental disability and behaviour problems. *Child: Care, Health and Development, 37*, 184–194. doi:10.1111/j.1365-2214.2010.01103.x.

World Health Organization (WHO). (1948). *Constitution of the World Health Organization.* Geneva, Switzerland: WHO Basic Documents.

Worling, J. A. (2001). Personality-based typology of adolescent male sexual offenders: Differences in recidivism rates, victim-selection characteristics, and personal victimization histories. *Sexual Abuse: Journal of Research and Treatment, 13*(3), 149–166.

Wright, O. R., Jr. (1969). Summary of research on the selection interview since 1964. *Personnel Psychology, 22*, 391–413.

Wright, T. L., & Tedeschi, R. G. (1975). Factor analysis of the interpersonal trust scale. *Journal of Consulting and Clinical Psychology, 43*, 470–477.

Wrightman, L. F. (1988). An examination of sex differences in WAT scores from the perspective of sound consequences. *Applied Measurement in Education, 11*, 255–277.

Wrightsman, L. F. (1998). *Psychology and the legal system* (4th ed.). Belmont, CA: Wadsworth.

Wuyek, L. A., Antony, M. M., & McCabe, R. E. (2011). Psychometric properties of the panic disorder severity scale: Clinician-administered and self-report versions. *Clinical Psychology & Psychotherapy, 18*(3), 234–243. doi:10.1002/cpp.703.

Wyman, P. (1998). Integrating the MBTI and the Enneagram in psychotherapy: The core self and the defense system. *Journal of Psychological Type, 46*, 28–40.

Wyse, A. E. & Reckase, M. D. (2011). Examining rounding rules in Angoff-type standard-setting methods. *Educational and Psychological Measurement.* Retrieved from http://epm.sagepub.com/citmgr?gca=spepm;0013164411413572v1. doi:10.1177/0013164411413572.

Xu, F., Fu, G., & Zhang, T. (1996). A use of the Bender-Gestalt Test (BGT) in mentally retarded children [Chinese]. *Chinese Mental Health Journal, 10*, 208–209.

Yan, L., Yang, X., & Wang, H. (2001). Effects of gingo bilboa on cognition of patients at the early stage of Alzheimer's disease. *Chinese Mental Health Journal, 15*(1), 31–32.

Yanai, H. (2003). *New developments in psychometrics: Proceedings of the International Meeting of the Psychometric Society* (Tokyo). New York: Springer.

Yang, Y., Bringsjord, S., & Bello, P. (2006). The mental possible worlds mechanism and the lobster problem: An analysis of a complex GRE logical reasoning task. *Journal of Experimental & Theoretical Artificial Intelligence, 18*(2), 157–168.

Yarcheski, T. J., Mahon, N. E., & Yarcheski, A. (2003). Social support, self-esteem, and positive health practices of early adolescents. *Psychological Reports, 92*(1), 99–103.

Yerkes, R. M. (Ed.). (1921). Psychological examining in the United States Army. *Memoirs of the National Academy of Sciences, 15.*

Yoon, K., Schmidt, F., & Ilies, R. (2002). Cross-cultural construct validity of the five-factor model of personality among Korean employees. *Journal of Cross-Cultural Psychology, 33*(3), 217–235.

Yu, C. K. (2011). The mechanisms of defense and dreaming. *Dreaming, 21*(1), 51–69. doi:10.1037/a0022867.

Yurong, H., Dun, X., & Xiurong, X. (2001). Clinical analysis of 95 children with autistic disorder. *Chinese Mental Health Journal, 15*(6), 396–397.

Zautra, A. J. (2003). *Emotions, stress, and health.* London: Oxford University Press.

Zedeck, S., & Blood, M. R. (1974). *Foundations of behavioral science research in organizations.* Pacific Grove, CA: Brooks/Cole.

Zedeck, S., & Cascio, W. F. (1984). Psychological issues in personnel decisions. *Annual Review of Psychology, 35*, 461–518.

Zedeck, S., Tziner, A., & Middlestadt, S. E. (1983). Interviewer validity and reliability: An individual analysis approach. *Personnel Psychology, 36,* 355–370.

Zeidner, M. (1987). Test of the cultural bias hypothesis: Some Israeli findings. *Journal of Applied Psychology, 72,* 38–48.

Zeidner, M. (1990). Does test anxiety bias scholastic aptitude performance by gender and sociocultural group? *Journal of Personality Assessment, 55,* 145–160.

Zeidner, M., & Hammer, A. (1990). Life events and coping resources as predictors of stress symptoms in adolescents. *Personality and Individual Differences, 11,* 693–703.

Zimmerman, B. J., Greenberg, D., & Weinstein, C. E. (1994). Self-regulating academic study time: A strategy approach. In D. H. Schunk & B. J. Zimmerman (Eds.), *Self-regulation of learning and performance: Issues and educational applications* (pp. 181–199). Hillsdale, NJ: Erlbaum.

Zimmerman, M., & Coryell, W. (1987). The Inventory to Diagnose Depression (IDD): A self-report scale to diagnose major depressive disorders. *Journal of Consulting and Clinical Psychology, 55,* 55–59.

Ziskin, J. (1995). *Coping with psychiatric and psychological testimony* (5th ed.). Los Angeles: Law and Psychology Press.

Zores, L. S., & Williams, P. B. (1980). A look at the content bias in IQ tests. *Journal of Educational Measurement, 17,* 313–322.

Zubin, J. (1954). Failures of the Rorschach technique. *Journal of Projective Techniques, 18,* 303–315.

Zubin, J. (1972). Discussion of symposium on newer approaches to personality assessment. *Journal of Personality Assessment, 36,* 427–434.

Zuckerman, M. (1960). The development of an affect adjective check list measure of anxiety. *Journal of Consulting Psychology, 24,* 457–462.

Zuckerman, M. (1971). Physiological measures of sexual arousal in the human. *Psychological Bulletin, 75,* 297–329.

Zuckerman, M. (1990). Some dubious premises in research and theory on racial differences. *American Psychologist, 45,* 1297–1303.

Zumbo, B. D. (1998). Opening remarks to the special issue on validity theory and the methods used in validation: Perspectives from the social and behavioral sciences. *Social Indicators Research, 45*(1), 1–3.

Zwick, R., & Green, J. G. (2007). New perspectives on the correlation of SAT scores, high school grades, and socioeconomic factors. *Journal of Educational Measurement, 44*(1), 23–45.

Zyphur, M. J., Islam, G., & Landis, R. S. (2007). Testing 1, 2, 3, . . . 4? the personality of repeat SAT test takers and their testing outcomes. *Journal of Research in Personality, 41*(3), 715–722.

Zytowski, D. G. (1976). Predictive validity of the Kuder Occupational Interest Survey: A 12–19 year follow-up. *Journal of Counseling Psychology, 23,* 921–233.

Zytowski, D. G. (1977). The effects of being interest inventoried. *Journal of Vocational Behavior, 11,* 153–158.

Zytowski, D. G. (1985). *Kuder Occupational Interest Survey Form DD manual supplement.* Chicago: Science Research Associates.

Zytowski, D. G. (1992). Three generations: The continuing evolution of Frederic Kuder's interest inventories. *Journal of Counseling and Development, 71,* 245–248.

Zytowski, D. G. (1996). Three decades of interest inventory results: A case study. *Career Development Quarterly, 45*(2), 141–148.

# Subject Index